The definitive guide from the makers

CW01667011

GMAT Official Guide 2018

Book + Online

The ONLY source of real GMAT® questions from past exams

This edition includes
130 never-before-seen questions

Graduate Management Admission Council®

mba.com

GMAT® OFFICIAL GUIDE 2018

Copyright © 2017 by the Graduate Management Admission Council®. All rights reserved.

Published by John Wiley & Sons, Inc., Hoboken, New Jersey.

No part of this publication may be reproduced, stored in a retrieval system or transmitted in any form or by any means, electronic, mechanical, photocopying, recording, scanning or otherwise, except as permitted under Sections 107 or 108 of the 1976 United States Copyright Act, without either the prior written permission of the Publisher, or authorization through payment of the appropriate per-copy fee to the Copyright Clearance Center, 222 Rosewood Drive, Danvers, MA 01923, (978) 750-8400, fax (978) 646-8600, or on the web at www.copyright.com. Requests to the Publisher for permission should be addressed to the Permissions Department, John Wiley & Sons, Inc., 111 River Street, Hoboken, NJ 07030, (201) 748-6011, fax (201) 748-6008, or online at http://www.wiley.com/go/permissions.

The publisher and the author make no representations or warranties with respect to the accuracy or completeness of the contents of this work and specifically disclaim all warranties, including without limitation warranties of fitness for a particular purpose. No warranty may be created or extended by sales or promotional materials. The advice and strategies contained herein may not be suitable for every situation. This work is sold with the understanding that the publisher is not engaged in rendering legal, accounting, or other professional services. If professional assistance is required, the services of a competent professional person should be sought. Neither the publisher nor the author shall be liable for damages arising here from. The fact that an organization or Website is referred to in this work as a citation and/or a potential source of further information does not mean that the author or the publisher endorses the information the organization or Website may provide or recommendations it may make. Further, readers should be aware that Internet Websites listed in this work may have changed or disappeared between when this work was written and when it is read.

Trademarks: Wiley, the Wiley logo, and related trademarks are trademarks or registered trademarks of John Wiley & Sons, Inc. and/or its affiliates. The GMAC and GMAT logos, GMAC®, GMASS®, GMAT®, GMAT CAT®, Graduate Management Admission Council®, and Graduate Management Admission Test® are registered trademarks of the Graduate Management Admission Council® (GMAC) in the United States and other countries. All other trademarks are the property of their respective owners. John Wiley & Sons, Inc., is not associated with any product or vendor mentioned in this book.

For general information on our other products and services or to obtain technical support please contact our Customer Care Department within the U.S. at (877) 762-2974, outside the U.S. at (317) 572-3993 or fax (317) 572-4002.

John Wiley & Sons, Inc., also publishes its books in a variety of electronic formats and by print-on-demand. Not all content that is available in standard print versions of this book may appear or be packaged in all book formats. If you have purchased a version of this book that did not include media that is referenced by or accompanies a standard print version, you may request this media by visiting http://booksupport.wiley.com. For more information about Wiley products, visit us at www.wiley.com.

ISBN: 978-81-265-6704-1

Printed by: Sanat Printers.

10 9 8 7 6 5 4 3 2 1

Table of Contents

	Letter from the President and CEO, GMAC®	**v**
1.0	**What Is the GMAT® Exam?**	**2**
1.0	What Is the GMAT® Exam?	3
1.1	Why Take the GMAT® Exam?	3
1.2	GMAT® Exam Format	4
1.3	What Is the Content of the Test Like?	5
1.4	Integrated Reasoning Section	6
1.5	Quantitative Section	6
1.6	Verbal Section	6
1.7	Analytical Writing Assessment	7
1.8	What Computer Skills Will I Need?	7
1.9	What Are the Test Centers Like?	7
1.10	How Are Scores Calculated?	7
1.11	Test Development Process	8
2.0	**How to Prepare**	**10**
2.0	How to Prepare	11
2.1	How Should I Prepare to Take the Test?	11
2.2	What About Practice Tests?	11
2.3	How Should I Use the Diagnostic Test?	12
2.4	Where Can I Get Additional Practice?	12
2.5	General Test-Taking Suggestions	12
3.0	**Diagnostic Test**	**14**
3.0	Diagnostic Test	15
3.1	Quantitative Questions	16
3.2	Verbal Questions	23
3.3	Quantitative and Verbal Answer Keys	40
3.4	Interpretive Guide	40
3.5	Quantitative Answer Explanations	41
3.6	Verbal Answer Explanations	60
4.0	**Math Review**	**100**
4.0	Math Review	101
4.1	Arithmetic	102
4.2	Algebra	114
4.3	Geometry	122
4.4	Word Problems	134
5.0	**Problem Solving**	**142**
5.0	Problem Solving	143
5.1	Test-Taking Strategies	144
5.2	The Directions	144
5.3	Practice Questions	146
5.4	Answer Key	181
5.5	Answer Explanations	183
6.0	**Data Sufficiency**	**264**
6.0	Data Sufficiency	265
6.1	Test-Taking Strategies	266
6.2	The Directions	268
6.3	Practice Questions	270
6.4	Answer Key	288
6.5	Answer Explanations	289

7.0	**Reading Comprehension**	**356**
7.0	Reading Comprehension	**357**
7.1	What Is Measured	**358**
7.2	Test-Taking Strategies	**360**
7.3	The Directions	**361**
7.4	Practice Questions	**362**
7.5	Answer Key	**423**
7.6	Answer Explanations	**424**
8.0	**Critical Reasoning**	**504**
8.0	Critical Reasoning	**505**
8.1	What Is Measured	**506**
8.2	Test-Taking Strategies	**506**
8.3	The Directions	**507**
8.4	Practice Questions	**508**
8.5	Answer Key	**546**
8.6	Answer Explanations	**547**
9.0	**Sentence Correction**	**672**
9.0	Sentence Correction	**673**
9.1	Basic English Grammar Rules	**673**
9.2	Study Suggestions	**678**
9.3	What Is Measured	**678**
9.4	Test-Taking Strategies	**678**
9.5	The Directions	**679**
9.6	Practice Questions	**680**
9.7	Answer Key	**709**
9.8	Answer Explanations	**710**
10.0	**Integrated Reasoning**	**788**
10.0	Integrated Reasoning	**789**
10.1	What Is Measured	**789**
10.2	The Question Types	**790**
10.3	Test-Taking Strategies	**797**
10.4	The Directions	**799**
11.0	**Analytical Writing Assessment**	**800**
11.0	Analytical Writing Assessment	**801**
11.1	What Is Measured	**801**
11.2	Test-Taking Strategies	**802**
11.3	The Directions	**802**
11.4	GMAT® Scoring Guide: Analysis of an Argument	**803**
11.5	Sample: Analysis of an Argument	**805**
11.6	Analysis of an Argument Sample Topics	**809**
Appendix A	**Answer Sheets**	**841**
	Diagnostic Answer Sheet—Quantitative	**841**
	Diagnostic Answer Sheet—Verbal	**841**
	Problem Solving Answer Sheet	**842**
	Data Sufficiency Answer Sheet	**843**
	Reading Comprehension Answer Sheet	**844**
	Critical Reasoning Answer Sheet	**845**
	Sentence Correction Answer Sheet	**846**

Dear GMAT Test-Taker,

Thank you for your interest in graduate management education. Taking the GMAT® exam lets schools know that you're serious about your graduate business education. By using the *Official Guide* to prepare for the GMAT, you're taking a very important step toward achieving your goals and pursuing admission to a high-quality business school or master's program.

This book, *GMAT® Official Guide 2018,* is designed to help you prepare for and build confidence to do your best on the GMAT exam. It's the only guide of its kind on the market that includes real GMAT exam questions published by the Graduate Management Admission Council (GMAC), the makers of the exam.

GMAC was founded by the world's leading business schools in 1953. The GMAT exam was developed to help people who aspire to careers in management demonstrate their command of the skills needed for success in the classroom. Schools use and trust the GMAT exam as part of their admissions process because it's an excellent predictor of classroom success and your ability to excel in your chosen program.

Today more than 6,500 graduate programs around the world use the GMAT exam to establish their MBA, graduate-level management degrees and specialized programs as hallmarks of excellence. Nine out of 10 new MBA enrollments at Top 50 US full-time MBA programs are made using a GMAT score.

These facts make us proud and drive us to keep improving the GMAT as well as play a role in helping you find and gain admission to the best school or program for you. We're committed to ensuring that no talent goes undiscovered, and that more people around the world can pursue opportunities in graduate management education.

I applaud your commitment to educational success, and I know that this book and the other Official GMAT preparation materials available at mba.com will give you the confidence to achieve your personal best on the GMAT exam and launch or reinvigorate a rewarding career.

I wish you the best success on all your educational and professional endeavors in the future.

Sincerely,

Sangeet Chowfla
CEO of the Graduate Management Admission Council

GMAT® Official Guide 2018

1.0 What Is the GMAT® Exam?

1.0 What Is the GMAT® Exam?

The Graduate Management Admission Test® (GMAT®) exam is a standardized exam used in admissions decisions by more than 6,500 graduate management programs worldwide. It helps you gauge, and demonstrate to schools, your academic potential for success in graduate-level management studies.

The four-part exam measures your Analytical Writing, Verbal, Quantitative, and Integrated Reasoning skills—higher-order reasoning skills that management faculty worldwide have identified as important for incoming students to have. "Higher-order" reasoning skills involve complex judgments, and include critical thinking, analysis, and problem solving. Unlike undergraduate grades and curricula, which vary in their meaning across regions and institutions, your GMAT scores provide a standardized, statistically valid and reliable measure of how you are likely to perform academically in the core curriculum of a graduate management program. The GMAT exam's validity, fairness, and value in admissions have been well-established through numerous academic studies.

The GMAT exam is delivered entirely in English and solely on a computer. It is not a test of business knowledge, subject matter mastery, English vocabulary, or advanced computational skills. The GMAT exam also does not measure other factors related to success in graduate management study, such as job experience, leadership ability, motivation, and interpersonal skills. Your GMAT score is intended to be used as one admissions criterion among other, more subjective, criteria, such as admissions essays and interviews.

1.1 Why Take the GMAT® Exam?

Launched in 1954 by a group of nine business schools to provide a uniform measure of the academic skills needed to succeed in their programs, the GMAT exam is now used by more than 6,500 graduate management programs at approximately 2,100 institutions worldwide.

Taking the GMAT exam helps you stand out in the admissions process and demonstrate your readiness and commitment to pursuing graduate management education. Schools use GMAT scores to help them select the most qualified applicants—because they know that candidates who take the GMAT exam are serious about earning a graduate business degree, and it's a proven predictor of a student's ability to succeed in his or her chosen program. When you consider which programs to apply to, you can look at a school's use of the GMAT exam as one indicator of quality. Schools that use the GMAT exam typically list score ranges or average scores in their class profiles, so you may also find these profiles helpful in gauging the academic competitiveness of a program you are considering and how well your performance on the exam compares with that of the students enrolled in the program.

Myth -vs- FACT

M **– If I don't achieve a high score on the GMAT, I won't get into my top choice schools.**

F – There are great schools available for candidates at any GMAT score range.

Fewer than 50 of the more than 250,000 people taking the GMAT exam each year get a perfect score of 800; and many more get into top business school programs around the world each year. Admissions Officers use GMAT scores as one component in their admissions decisions, in conjunction with undergraduate records, application essays, interviews, letters of recommendation, and other information when deciding whom to accept into their programs. Visit School Finder on mba.com to learn about schools that are the best fit for you.

No matter how you perform on the GMAT exam, you should contact the schools that interest you to learn more and to ask how they use GMAT scores and other criteria (such as your undergraduate grades, essays, and letters of recommendation) in their admissions processes. School admissions offices, web sites, and materials published by schools are the key sources of information when you are doing research about where you might want to go to business school.

For more information on the GMAT, test preparation materials, registration, how to use and send your GMAT scores to schools, and applying to business school, please visit mba.com.

1.2 GMAT® Exam Format

The GMAT exam consists of four separately timed sections (see the table on the next page). For the Analytical Writing Assessment (AWA) essay prompt, you will have 30 minutes to type your essay on a computer keyboard. The 30-minute Integrated Reasoning section features 12 question prompts in four different formats. There are two 75-minute, multiple-choice sections: the Quantitative section, with 37 questions, and the Verbal section, with 41 questions.

The Verbal and Quantitative sections of the GMAT exam are computer adaptive, which means that the test draws from a large bank of questions to tailor itself to your ability level, and you won't get many questions that are too hard or too easy for you. The first question will be of medium difficulty. As you answer each question, the computer scores your answer and uses it—as well as your responses to all preceding questions—to select the next question.

Computer-adaptive tests become more difficult the more questions you answer correctly, but if you get a question that seems easier than the last one, it does not necessarily mean you answered the last question incorrectly. The test has to cover a range of content, both in the type of question asked and the subject matter presented.

Myth -vs- FACT

M – **Getting an easier question means I answered the last one wrong.**

F – **You should not become distracted by the difficulty level of a question.**

Most people are not skilled at estimating question difficulty, so don't worry when taking the test or waste valuable time trying to determine the difficulty of the question you are answering.

To ensure that everyone receives the same content, the test selects a specific number of questions of each type. The test may call for your next problem to be a relatively hard data sufficiency question involving arithmetic operations. But, if there are no more relatively difficult data sufficiency questions involving arithmetic, you might be given an easier question.

Because the computer uses your answers to select your next questions, you may not skip questions or go back and change your answer to a previous question. If you don't know the answer to a question, try to eliminate as many choices as possible, then select the answer you think is best.

Though the individual questions are different, the mix of question types is the same for every GMAT exam. Your score is determined by the difficulty and statistical characteristics of the questions you answer as well as the number of questions you answer correctly. By adapting to each test-taker, the GMAT exam is able to accurately and efficiently gauge skill levels over a full range of abilities, from very high to very low.

The test includes the types of questions found in this book and in the online Integrated Reasoning component, but the format and presentation of the questions are different on the computer. When you take the test:

- Only one question or question prompt at a time is presented on the computer screen.
- The answer choices for the multiple-choice questions will be preceded by circles, rather than by letters.

- Different question types appear in random order in the multiple-choice and Integrated Reasoning sections.
- You must select your answer using the computer.
- You must choose an answer and confirm your choice before moving on to the next question.
- You may not go back to previous screens to change answers to previous questions.

Format of the GMAT® Exam

	Questions	Timing
Analytical Writing Analysis of an Argument	1	30 min.
Integrated Reasoning Multi-Source Reasoning Table Analysis Graphics Interpretation Two-Part Analysis	12	30 min.
Optional break		up to 8 min.
Quantitative Problem Solving Data Sufficiency	37	75 min.
Optional break		up to 8 min.
Verbal Reading Comprehension Critical Reasoning Sentence Correction	41	75 min.
	Total Time:	210 min.

1.3 What Is the Content of the Test Like?

The GMAT exam measures higher-order analytical skills encompassing several types of reasoning. The Analytical Writing Assessment asks you to analyze the reasoning behind an argument and respond in writing; the Integrated Reasoning section asks you to interpret and synthesize information from multiple sources and in different formats to make reasoned conclusions; the Quantitative section asks you to reason quantitatively using basic arithmetic, algebra, and geometry; and the Verbal section asks you to read and comprehend written material and to reason and evaluate arguments.

Test questions may address a variety of subjects, but all of the information you need to answer the questions will be included on the exam, with no outside knowledge of the subject matter necessary. The GMAT exam is not a test of business knowledge, English vocabulary, or advanced computational skills. You will need to read and write in English and have basic math and English skills to perform well on the test, but its difficulty comes from the English analytical and critical thinking abilities.

The questions in this book are organized by question type and from easiest to most difficult, but keep in mind that when you take the test, you may see different types of questions in any order within each section.

1.4 Integrated Reasoning Section

The Integrated Reasoning section highlights the relevant skills that business managers in today's data-driven world need in order to analyze sophisticated streams of data and solve complex problems. It measures your ability to understand and evaluate multiple sources and types of information—graphic, numeric, and verbal—as they relate to one another; use both quantitative and verbal reasoning to solve complex problems; and solve multiple problems in relation to one another.

Four types of questions are used in the Integrated Reasoning section:

- Multi-Source Reasoning
- Table Analysis
- Graphics Interpretation
- Two-Part Analysis

Integrated Reasoning questions may be quantitative, verbal, or a combination of both. You will have to interpret graphics and sort tables to extract meaning from data, but advanced statistical knowledge and spreadsheet manipulation skills are not necessary. You will have access to an on-screen calculator with basic functions for the Integrated Reasoning section, but note that the calculator is *not* available on the Quantitative section.

To review the Integrated Reasoning question types and test-taking tips, see chapter 10. For practice questions of each format, with full answer explanations, visit the Integrated Reasoning online component using your unique access code found in the inside front cover of the book.

1.5 Quantitative Section

The GMAT Quantitative section measures your ability to reason quantitatively, solve quantitative problems, and interpret graphic data.

Two types of multiple-choice questions are used in the Quantitative section:

- Problem Solving
- Data Sufficiency

Both are intermingled throughout the Quantitative section, and require basic knowledge of arithmetic, elementary algebra, and commonly known concepts of geometry.

To review the basic mathematical concepts that you will need to answer Quantitative questions, see the math review in chapter 4. For test-taking tips specific to the question types in the Quantitative section, practice questions, and answer explanations, see chapters 5 and 6.

1.6 Verbal Section

The GMAT Verbal section measures your ability to read and comprehend written material and to reason and evaluate arguments. The Verbal section includes reading sections from several different content areas. Although you may be generally familiar with some of the material, neither the reading passages nor the questions assume detailed knowledge of the topics discussed.

Three types of multiple-choice questions are intermingled throughout the Verbal section:

- Reading Comprehension
- Critical Reasoning
- Sentence Correction

All three require basic knowledge of the English language, but the Verbal section is not a test of advanced vocabulary.

For test-taking tips specific to each question type in the Verbal section, practice questions, and answer explanations, see chapters 7 through 9.

1.7 Analytical Writing Assessment

The Analytical Writing Assessment (AWA) consists of one 30-minute writing task: Analysis of an Argument. The AWA measures your ability to think critically, communicate your ideas, and formulate an appropriate and constructive critique. You will type your essay on a computer keyboard.

For test-taking tips, sample essay responses, answer explanations, and sample Analysis of an Argument topics, see chapter 11.

1.8 What Computer Skills Will I Need?

The GMAT exam requires only computer skills. You will type your AWA essay on the computer keyboard using standard word-processing keystrokes. In the Integrated Reasoning and multiple-choice sections, you will select your responses using either your computer mouse or the keyboard. The Integrated Reasoning section includes basic computer navigation and functions, such as clicking on tabs and using drop-down menus to sort tables and select answers.

1.9 What Are the Test Centers Like?

The GMAT exam is administered under standardized conditions at test centers worldwide. Each test center has a proctored testing room with individual computer workstations that allow you to sit for the exam under quiet conditions and with some privacy. You will be able to take two optional 8-minute breaks during the course of the exam. You may not take notes or scratch paper with you into the testing room, but an erasable notepad and marker will be provided for you to use during the test.

1.10 How Are Scores Calculated?

Verbal and Quantitative sections are scored on a scale of 0 to 60, with scores below 6 or above 51 extremely rare. The Total GMAT score ranges from 200 to 800 and is based on your performance in these two sections. Your score is determined by:

- The number of questions you answer
- The number of questions you answer correctly or incorrectly
- The level of difficulty and other statistical characteristics of each question

Your Verbal, Quantitative, and Total GMAT scores are determined by a complex mathematical procedure that takes into account the difficulty of the questions that were presented to you and how you answered them. When you answer the easier questions correctly, you get a chance to answer harder questions, making it possible to earn a higher score. After you have completed all the questions on the test, or when your time is expired, the computer will calculate your scores. Your scores on the Verbal and Quantitative sections are combined to produce your Total score which ranges from 200 to 800 in 10 point increments.

The Analytical Writing Assessment consists of one writing task, Analysis of an Argument, and your essay will be scored two times independently. Essays are evaluated by college and university faculty members from a variety of disciplines, including management education, who rate the overall quality of your critical thinking and writing. (For details on how readers are qualified, visit mba.com.) In addition, your response may be scored by an automated scoring program designed to reflect the judgment of expert readers.

Your essay is scored on a scale of 0 to 6, in half point increments, with 6 being the highest score and 0 the lowest. A score of zero is given for responses that are off topic, are in a foreign language, merely attempt to copy the topic, consist only of keystroke characters, or are blank. Your AWA score is typically the average of two independent ratings. If the independent scores vary by more than a point, a third reader adjudicates, but because of ongoing training and monitoring, discrepancies are rare.

Your Integrated Reasoning section is scored on a scale of 1 to 8, in one-point increments. You must answer all parts of a single question correctly in order to receive credit. No partial credit is given. Like your AWA score, your Integrated Reasoning score will not count toward your Total score.

Your Analytical Writing Assessment and Integrated Reasoning scores are computed and reported separately from the other sections of the test and have no effect on your Verbal, Quantitative, or Total scores. The schools that you have designated to receive your scores may receive a copy of your Analytical Writing Assessment essay with your score report. Your own copy of your score report will not include your essay.

Your GMAT score includes a percentile ranking that compares your skill level with other test-takers from the past three years. The percentile rank of your score shows the percentage of tests taken with scores lower than your score. Every July, percentile ranking tables are updated. Visit mba.com to view the most recent percentile rankings tables.

1.11 Test Development Process

The GMAT exam is developed by experts who use standardized procedures to ensure high-quality, widely-appropriate test material. All questions are subjected to independent reviews and are revised or discarded as necessary. Multiple-choice questions are tested during GMAT exam administrations. Analytical Writing Assessment tasks are tested on mba.com registrants and then assessed for their fairness and reliability. For more information on test development, visit mba.com.

To register for the GMAT exam, go to www.mba.com

2.0 How to Prepare

2.0 How to Prepare

2.1 How Should I Prepare to Take the Test?

The GMAT® exam is designed specifically to measure reasoning skills needed for management education, and the test contains several question formats unique to the GMAT exam. At a minimum, you should be familiar with the test format and the question formats before you sit for the test. Because the GMAT exam is a timed exam, you should practice answering test questions, not only to better understand the question formats and the skills they require, but also to help you learn to pace yourself so you can finish each section when you sit for the exam.

Because the exam measures reasoning rather than subject matter knowledge, you most likely will not find it helpful to memorize facts. You do not need to study advanced mathematical concepts, but you should be sure your grasp of basic arithmetic, algebra, and geometry is sound enough that you can use these skills in quantitative problem solving. Likewise, you do not need to study advanced vocabulary words, but you should have a firm understanding of basic English vocabulary and grammar for reading, writing, and reasoning.

> ***Myth* -vs- FACT**
>
> *M* – **You need very advanced math skills to get a high GMAT score.**
>
> F – **The GMAT measures your reasoning and critical thinking abilities, rather than your advanced math skills.**
>
> The GMAT exam only requires basic quantitative skills. You should review the math skills (algebra, geometry, basic arithmetic) presented in this guide (chapter 4) and the *GMAT® Official Guide Quantitative Review 2018*. The difficulty of GMAT Quantitative questions stems from the logic and analysis used to solve the problems and not the underlying math skills.

This book and other study materials released by the Graduate Management Admission Council (GMAC) are the ONLY source of questions that have been retired from the GMAT exam. All questions that appear or have appeared on the GMAT exam are copyrighted and owned by GMAC, which does not license them to be reprinted elsewhere. Accessing live Integrated Reasoning, Quantitative, or Verbal test questions in advance or sharing test content during or after you take the test is a serious violation, which could cause your scores to be canceled and schools to be notified. In cases of a serious violation, you may be banned from future testing and other legal remedies may be pursued.

2.2 What About Practice Tests?

The Quantitative and Verbal sections of the GMAT exam are computer adaptive, and the Integrated Reasoning section includes questions that require you to use the computer to sort tables and navigate to different sources of information. Our official practice materials will help you get comfortable with the format of the test and better prepare for exam day. Two full-length GMAT practice exams are available at no charge for those who have created an account on mba.com. The practice exams include computer-adaptive Quantitative and Verbal sections, plus additional practice questions, information about the test, and tutorials to help you become familiar with how the GMAT exam will appear on the computer screen at the test center.

To maximize your studying efforts with the free practice exams, you should leverage official practice materials as you start to prepare for the test. Take one practice test to make yourself familiar with the exam and to get a baseline score. After you have studied using this book and other study materials, take the second practice test to determine whether you need to shift your focus to other areas you need to strengthen. Note that the free practice tests may include questions that are also published in this book. As your test day approaches, consider taking more official practice tests to help measure your progress and give you a better idea of how you might score on exam day.

2.3 How Should I Use the Diagnostic Test?

This book contains a Diagnostic Test to help you determine the types of Quantitative and Verbal questions that you need to practice most. You should take the Diagnostic Test around the same time that you take the first GMAT practice test. The Diagnostic Test will give you a rating—*below average, average, above average, or excellent*—of your skills in each type of GMAT test question. These ratings will help you identify areas to focus on as you prepare for the GMAT exam.

The Diagnostic Test does not include Integrated Reasoning or Analytical Writing Assessment questions.

Use the results of the Diagnostic Test to help you select the right chapter of this book to start with. Next, read the introductory material carefully, and answer the practice questions in that chapter. Remember, the questions in the chapters are organized by difficulty, from easiest to most difficult. Make sure you follow the directions for each type of question and try to work as quickly and as efficiently as possible. Then review the explanations for the correct answers, spending as much time as necessary to familiarize yourself with the range of questions or problems presented.

2.4 Where Can I Get Additional Practice?

If you would like additional practice, *GMAT® Official Guide 2018 Quantitative Review* and *GMAT® Official Guide 2018 Verbal Review* each offer 300 additional questions that are not published in this guide. You can also find more Quantitative, Verbal, and Integrated Reasoning practice questions, full-length, computer-adaptive practice exams, Analytical Writing Assessment practice prompts, and other helpful study materials at mba.com.

2.5 General Test-Taking Suggestions

Specific test-taking strategies for individual question types are presented later in this book. The following are general suggestions to help you perform your best on the test.

1. **Use your time wisely.**
   Although the GMAT exam stresses accuracy more than speed, it is important to use your time wisely. On average, you will have about 1¾ minutes for each Verbal question, about 2 minutes for each Quantitative question, and about 2½ minutes for each Integrated Reasoning question, some of which have multiple questions. Once you start the test, an onscreen clock will show the time you have left. You can hide this display if you want, but it is a good idea to check the clock periodically to monitor your progress. The clock will automatically alert you when 5 minutes remain for the section you are working on.

2. **Answer practice questions ahead of time.**
   After you become generally familiar with all question types, use the practice questions in this book and the online Integrated Reasoning component to prepare for the actual test. It may be useful to time yourself as you answer the practice questions to get an idea of how long you will have for each question when you sit for the actual test, as well as to determine whether you are answering quickly enough to finish the test in the allotted time.

3. **Read all test directions carefully.**
The directions explain exactly what is required to answer each question type. If you read hastily, you may miss important instructions and impact your ability to answer correctly. To review directions during the test, click on the Help icon. But be aware that the time you spend reviewing directions will count against your time allotment for that section of the test.

4. **Read each question carefully and thoroughly.**
Before you answer a question, determine exactly what is being asked and then select the best choice. Never skim a question or the possible answers; skimming may cause you to miss important information or nuances.

5. **Do not spend too much time on any one question.**
If you do not know the correct answer, or if the question is too time consuming, try to eliminate choices you know are wrong, select the best of the remaining answer choices, and move on to the next question. Not completing sections and randomly guessing answers to questions at the end of each test section can significantly lower your score. As long as you have worked on each section, you will receive a score even if you do not finish one or more sections in the allotted time. You will not earn points for questions you never get to see.

6. **Confirm your answers ONLY when you are ready to move on.**
On the Quantitative and Verbal sections, once you have selected your answer to a multiple-choice question, you will be asked to confirm it. Once you confirm your response, you cannot go back and change it. You may not skip questions. In the Integrated Reasoning section, there may be several questions based on information provided in the same question prompt. When there is more than one response on a single screen, you can change your response to any of the questions on the screen before moving on to the next screen. However, you may not navigate back to a previous screen to change any responses.

7. **Plan your essay answer before you begin to write.**
The best way to approach the Analysis of an Argument section is to read the directions carefully, take a few minutes to think about the question, and plan a response before you begin writing. Take time to organize your ideas and develop them fully, but leave time to reread your response and make any revisions that you think would improve it.

Myth -vs- FACT

M – **It is more important to respond correctly to the test questions than it is to finish the test.**

F – **There is a significant penalty for not completing the GMAT exam.**

Pacing is important. If you are stumped by a question, give it your best guess and move on. If you guess incorrectly, the computer program will likely give you an easier question, which you are likely to answer correctly, and the computer will rapidly return to giving you questions matched to your ability. If you don't finish the test, your score will be reduced. Failing to answer five verbal questions, for example, could reduce your score from the 91st percentile to the 77th percentile.

Myth -vs- FACT

M – **The first 10 questions are critical and you should invest the most time on those.**

F – **All questions count.**

The computer-adaptive testing algorithm uses each answered question to obtain an *initial* estimate. However, as you continue to answer questions, the algorithm self-corrects by computing an updated estimate on the basis of all the questions you have answered, and then administers items that are closely matched to this new estimate of your ability. Your final score is based on all your responses and considers the difficulty of all the questions you answered. Taking additional time on the first 10 questions will not game the system and can hurt your ability to finish the test.

3.0 Diagnostic Test

3.0 Diagnostic Test

Like the practice sections later in the book, the Diagnostic Test uses questions from real GMAT® exams. The purpose of the Diagnostic Test is to help you determine how skilled you are in answering each of the five types of questions on the GMAT exam: problem solving, data sufficiency, reading comprehension, critical reasoning, and sentence correction.

Scores on the Diagnostic Test are designed to help you answer the question, "If all the questions on the GMAT exam were like the questions in this section, how well would I do?" Your scores are classified as being *excellent, above average, average,* or *below average,* relative to the scores of other test-takers. You can use this information to focus your test-preparation activities.

Instructions

1. Take your time answering these questions. The Diagnostic Test is not timed.
2. If you are stumped by a question, you should guess and move on, just like you should do on the real GMAT exam.
3. You can take one segment at a time, if you want. It is better to finish an entire section (Quantitative or Verbal) in one sitting, but this is not a requirement.
4. You can go back and change your answers in the Diagnostic Test.
5. After you take the test, check your answers using the answer key that follows the test. The number of correct answers is your raw score.
6. Convert your raw score, using the table provided.

Note: The Diagnostic Test is designed to give you guidance on how to prepare for the GMAT exam; however, a strong score on one type of question does not guarantee that you will perform as well on the real GMAT exam. The statistical reliability of scores on the Diagnostic Test ranges from 0.75 to 0.89, and the subscale classification is about 85%–90% accurate, meaning that your scores on the Diagnostic Test are a good, but not perfect, measure of how you are likely to perform on the real test. Use the tests on the free online software to obtain a good estimate of your expected GMAT Verbal, Quantitative, and Total scores.

You should not compare the number of questions you got right in each section. Instead, you should compare how your responses are rated in each section.

3.1 Quantitative Questions

Problem Solving

Solve the problem and indicate the best of the answer choices given.

Numbers: All numbers used are real numbers.

Figures: All figures accompanying problem solving questions are intended to provide information useful in solving the problems. Figures are drawn as accurately as possible. Exceptions will be clearly noted. Lines shown as straight are straight, and lines that appear jagged are also straight. The positions of points, angles, regions, etc., exist in the order shown, and angle measures are greater than zero. All figures lie in a plane unless otherwise indicated.

1. Last month a certain music club offered a discount to preferred customers. After the first compact disc purchased, preferred customers paid $3.99 for each additional compact disc purchased. If a preferred customer purchased a total of 6 compact discs and paid $15.95 for the first compact disc, then the dollar amount that the customer paid for the 6 compact discs is equivalent to which of the following?

(A) 5(4.00) + 15.90
(B) 5(4.00) + 15.95
(C) 5(4.00) + 16.00
(D) 5(4.00 – 0.01) + 15.90
(E) 5(4.00 – 0.05) + 15.95

2. The average (arithmetic mean) of the integers from 200 to 400, inclusive, is how much greater than the average of the integers from 50 to 100, inclusive?

(A) 150
(B) 175
(C) 200
(D) 225
(E) 300

3. The sequence $a_1, a_2, a_3, \cdots, a_n, \cdots$ is such that $a_n = \frac{a_{n-1} + a_{n-2}}{2}$ for all $n \geq 3$. If $a_3 = 4$ and $a_5 = 20$ what is the value of a_6 ?

(A) 12
(B) 16
(C) 20
(D) 24
(E) 28

4. Among a group of 2,500 people, 35 percent invest in municipal bonds, 18 percent invest in oil stocks, and 7 percent invest in both municipal bonds and oil stocks. If 1 person is to be randomly selected from the 2,500 people, what is the probability that the person selected will be one who invests in municipal bonds but NOT in oil stocks?

(A) $\frac{9}{50}$
(B) $\frac{7}{25}$
(C) $\frac{7}{20}$
(D) $\frac{21}{50}$
(E) $\frac{27}{50}$

5. A closed cylindrical tank contains 36π cubic feet of water and is filled to half its capacity. When the tank is placed upright on its circular base on level ground, the height of the water in the tank is 4 feet. When the tank is placed on its side on level ground, what is the height, in feet, of the surface of the water above the ground?

(A) 2
(B) 3
(C) 4
(D) 6
(E) 9

6. A marketing firm determined that, of 200 households surveyed, 80 used neither Brand A nor Brand B soap, 60 used only Brand A soap, and for every household that used both brands of soap, 3 used only Brand B soap. How many of the 200 households surveyed used both brands of soap?

(A) 15
(B) 20
(C) 30
(D) 40
(E) 45

7. A certain club has 10 members, including Harry. One of the 10 members is to be chosen at random to be the president, one of the remaining 9 members is to be chosen at random to be the secretary, and one of the remaining 8 members is to be chosen at random to be the treasurer. What is the probability that Harry will be either the member chosen to be the secretary or the member chosen to be the treasurer?

(A) $\frac{1}{720}$
(B) $\frac{1}{80}$
(C) $\frac{1}{10}$
(D) $\frac{1}{9}$
(E) $\frac{1}{5}$

8. If a certain toy store's revenue in November was $\frac{2}{5}$ of its revenue in December and its revenue in January was $\frac{1}{4}$ of its revenue in November, then the store's revenue in December was how many times the average (arithmetic mean) of its revenues in November and January?

(A) $\frac{1}{4}$
(B) $\frac{1}{2}$
(C) $\frac{2}{3}$
(D) 2
(E) 4

9. A researcher computed the mean, the median, and the standard deviation for a set of performance scores. If 5 were to be added to each score, which of these three statistics would change?

(A) The mean only
(B) The median only
(C) The standard deviation only
(D) The mean and the median
(E) The mean and the standard deviation

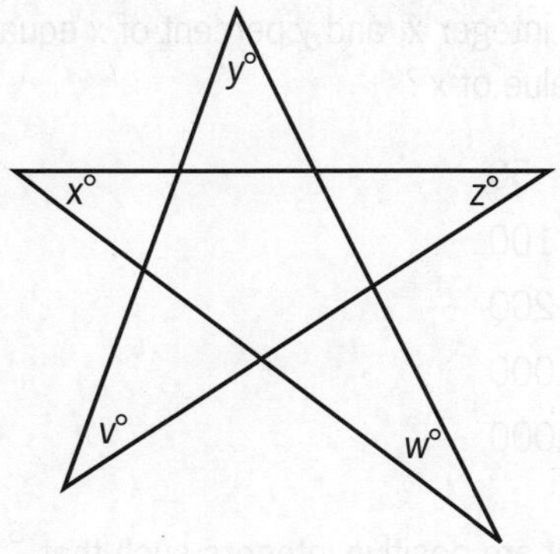

10. In the figure shown, what is the value of $v + x + y + z + w$?

(A) 45
(B) 90
(C) 180
(D) 270
(E) 360

11. Of the three-digit integers greater than 700, how many have two digits that are equal to each other and the remaining digit different from the other two?

(A) 90
(B) 82
(C) 80
(D) 45
(E) 36

12. Positive integer y is 50 percent of 50 percent of positive integer x, and y percent of x equals 100. What is the value of x ?

(A) 50
(B) 100
(C) 200
(D) 1,000
(E) 2,000

13. If s and t are positive integers such that $\frac{s}{t} = 64.12$, which of the following could be the remainder when s is divided by t ?

(A) 2
(B) 4
(C) 8
(D) 20
(E) 45

14. Of the 84 parents who attended a meeting at a school, 35 volunteered to supervise children during the school picnic and 11 volunteered both to supervise children during the picnic and to bring refreshments to the picnic. If the number of parents who volunteered to bring refreshments was 1.5 times the number of parents who neither volunteered to supervise children during the picnic nor volunteered to bring refreshments, how many of the parents volunteered to bring refreshments?

(A) 25
(B) 36
(C) 38
(D) 42
(E) 45

15. The product of all the prime numbers less than 20 is closest to which of the following powers of 10 ?

(A) 10^9
(B) 10^8
(C) 10^7
(D) 10^6
(E) 10^5

16. If $\sqrt{3-2x} = \sqrt{2x} + 1$, then $4x^2 =$

(A) 1
(B) 4
(C) $2 - 2x$
(D) $4x - 2$
(E) $6x - 1$

17. If $n = \sqrt{\frac{16}{81}}$, what is the value of $\sqrt{n}$?

(A) $\frac{1}{9}$
(B) $\frac{1}{4}$
(C) $\frac{4}{9}$
(D) $\frac{2}{3}$
(E) $\frac{9}{2}$

18. If n is the product of the integers from 1 to 8, inclusive, how many different prime factors greater than 1 does n have?

(A) Four
(B) Five
(C) Six
(D) Seven
(E) Eight

19. If k is an integer and $2 < k < 7$, for how many different values of k is there a triangle with sides of lengths 2, 7, and k ?

(A) One
(B) Two
(C) Three
(D) Four
(E) Five

20. A right circular cone is inscribed in a hemisphere so that the base of the cone coincides with the base of the hemisphere. What is the ratio of the height of the cone to the radius of the hemisphere?

(A) $\sqrt{3}:1$
(B) 1:1
(C) $\frac{1}{2}:1$
(D) $\sqrt{2}:1$
(E) 2:1

21. John deposited \$10,000 to open a new savings account that earned 4 percent annual interest, compounded quarterly. If there were no other transactions in the account, what was the amount of money in John's account 6 months after the account was opened?

(A) \$10,100
(B) \$10,101
(C) \$10,200
(D) \$10,201
(E) \$10,400

22. A container in the shape of a right circular cylinder is $\frac{1}{2}$ full of water. If the volume of water in the container is 36 cubic inches and the height of the container is 9 inches, what is the diameter of the base of the cylinder, in inches?

(A) $\frac{16}{9\pi}$
(B) $\frac{4}{\sqrt{\pi}}$
(C) $\frac{12}{\sqrt{\pi}}$
(D) $\sqrt{\frac{2}{\pi}}$
(E) $4\sqrt{\frac{2}{\pi}}$

23. If the positive integer *x* is a multiple of 4 and the positive integer *y* is a multiple of 6, then *xy* must be a multiple of which of the following?

I. 8
II. 12
III. 18

(A) II only
(B) I and II only
(C) I and III only
(D) II and III only
(E) I, II, and III

24. Aaron will jog from home at *x* miles per hour and then walk back home by the same route at *y* miles per hour. How many miles from home can Aaron jog so that he spends a total of *t* hours jogging and walking?

(A) $\frac{xt}{y}$
(B) $\frac{x+t}{xy}$
(C) $\frac{xyt}{x+y}$
(D) $\frac{x+y+t}{xy}$
(E) $\frac{y+t}{x}-\frac{t}{y}$

Data Sufficiency

Each data sufficiency problem consists of a question and two statements, labeled (1) and (2), which contain certain data. Using these data and your knowledge of mathematics and everyday facts (such as the number of days in July or the meaning of the word *counterclockwise*), decide whether the data given are sufficient for answering the question and then indicate one of the following answer choices:

A **Statement (1) ALONE is sufficient, but statement (2) alone is not sufficient.**
B **Statement (2) ALONE is sufficient, but statement (1) alone is not sufficient.**
C **BOTH statements TOGETHER are sufficient, but NEITHER statement ALONE is sufficient.**
D **EACH statement ALONE is sufficient.**
E **Statements (1) and (2) TOGETHER are NOT sufficient.**

Note: In data sufficiency problems that ask for the value of a quantity, the data given in the statements are sufficient only when it is possible to determine exactly one numerical value for the quantity.

Example:

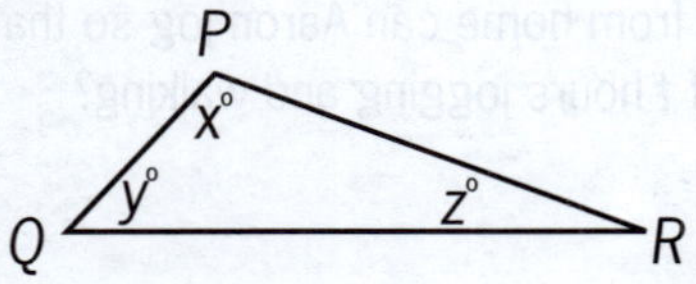

In $\triangle PQR$, what is the value of x?

(1) $PQ = PR$

(2) $y = 40$

Explanation: According to statement (1) $PQ = PR$; therefore, $\triangle PQR$ is isosceles and $y = z$. Since $x + y + z = 180$, it follows that $x + 2y = 180$. Since statement (1) does not give a value for y, you cannot answer the question using statement (1) alone. According to statement (2), $y = 40$; therefore, $x + z = 140$. Since statement (2) does not give a value for z, you cannot answer the question using statement (2) alone. Using both statements together, since $x + 2y = 180$ and the value of y is given, you can find the value of x. Therefore, BOTH statements (1) and (2) TOGETHER are sufficient to answer the question, but NEITHER statement ALONE is sufficient.

Numbers: All numbers used are real numbers.

Figures:

- **Figures conform to the information given in the question, but will not necessarily conform to the additional information given in statements (1) and (2).**
- **Lines shown as straight are straight, and lines that appear jagged are also straight.**
- **The positions of points, angles, regions, etc., exist in the order shown, and angle measures are greater than zero.**
- **All figures lie in a plane unless otherwise indicated.**

25. If the units digit of integer n is greater than 2, what is the units digit of n?

 (1) The units digit of n is the same as the units digit of n^2.

 (2) The units digit of n is the same as the units digit of n^3.

26. What is the value of the integer p?

 (1) Each of the integers 2, 3, and 5 is a factor of p.

 (2) Each of the integers 2, 5, and 7 is a factor of p.

27. If the length of Wanda's telephone call was rounded up to the nearest whole minute by her telephone company, then Wanda was charged for how many minutes for her telephone call?

 (1) The total charge for Wanda's telephone call was $6.50.

 (2) Wanda was charged $0.50 more for the first minute of the telephone call than for each minute after the first.

28. What is the perimeter of isosceles triangle MNP?

 (1) $MN = 16$

 (2) $NP = 20$

29. In a survey of retailers, what percent had purchased computers for business purposes?

 (1) 85 percent of the retailers surveyed who owned their own store had purchased computers for business purposes.

 (2) 40 percent of the retailers surveyed owned their own store.

30. The only gift certificates that a certain store sold yesterday were worth either $100 each or $10 each. If the store sold a total of 20 gift certificates yesterday, how many gift certificates worth $10 each did the store sell yesterday?

 (1) The gift certificates sold by the store yesterday were worth a total of between $1,650 and $1,800.

 (2) Yesterday the store sold more than 15 gift certificates worth $100 each.

31. Is the standard deviation of the set of measurements $x_1, x_2, x_3, x_4, \ldots, x_{20}$ less than 3?

 (1) The variance for the set of measurements is 4.

 (2) For each measurement, the difference between the mean and that measurement is 2.

32. Is the range of the integers 6, 3, y, 4, 5, and x greater than 9?

 (1) $y > 3x$

 (2) $y > x > 3$

33. Is $\frac{5^{x+2}}{25} < 1$?

 (1) $5^x < 1$

 (2) $x < 0$

34. Of the companies surveyed about the skills they required in prospective employees, 20 percent required both computer skills and writing skills. What percent of the companies surveyed required neither computer skills nor writing skills?

 (1) Of those companies surveyed that required computer skills, half required writing skills.

 (2) 45 percent of the companies surveyed required writing skills but not computer skills.

35. What is the value of $w + q$?

 (1) $3w = 3 - 3q$

 (2) $5w + 5q = 5$

36. If X and Y are points in a plane and X lies inside the circle C with center O and radius 2, does Y lie inside circle C?

 (1) The length of line segment XY is 3.

 (2) The length of line segment OY is 1.5.

37. Is $x > y$?

 (1) $x = y + 2$

 (2) $\frac{x}{2} = y - 1$

38. If Paula drove the distance from her home to her college at an average speed that was greater than 70 kilometers per hour, did it take her less than 3 hours to drive this distance?

(1) The distance that Paula drove from her home to her college was greater than 200 kilometers.

(2) The distance that Paula drove from her home to her college was less than 205 kilometers.

39. In the *xy*-plane, if line *k* has negative slope and passes through the point $(-5, r)$, is the *x*-intercept of line *k* positive?

(1) The slope of line *k* is -5.

(2) $r > 0$

40. If \$5,000 invested for one year at *p* percent simple annual interest yields \$500, what amount must be invested at *k* percent simple annual interest for one year to yield the same number of dollars?

(1) $k = 0.8p$

(2) $k = 8$

41. If $\frac{x+y}{z} > 0$, is $x < 0$?

(1) $x < y$

(2) $z < 0$

42. Does the integer *k* have at least three different positive prime factors?

(1) $\frac{k}{15}$ is an integer.

(2) $\frac{k}{10}$ is an integer.

43. In City X last April, was the average (arithmetic mean) daily high temperature greater than the median daily high temperature?

(1) In City X last April, the sum of the 30 daily high temperatures was 2,160°.

(2) In City X last April, 60 percent of the daily high temperatures were less than the average daily high temperature.

44. If *m* and *n* are positive integers, is $(\sqrt{m})^n$ an integer?

(1) $(\sqrt{m})$ is an integer.

(2) $(\sqrt{n})$ is an integer.

45. Of the 66 people in a certain auditorium, at most 6 people have their birthdays in any one given month. Does at least one person in the auditorium have a birthday in January?

(1) More of the people in the auditorium have their birthday in February than in March.

(2) Five of the people in the auditorium have their birthday in March.

46. Last year the average (arithmetic mean) salary of the 10 employees of Company X was \$42,800. What is the average salary of the same 10 employees this year?

(1) For 8 of the 10 employees, this year's salary is 15 percent greater than last year's salary.

(2) For 2 of the 10 employees, this year's salary is the same as last year's salary.

47. In a certain classroom, there are 80 books, of which 24 are fiction and 23 are written in Spanish. How many of the fiction books are written in Spanish?

(1) Of the fiction books, there are 6 more that are not written in Spanish than are written in Spanish.

(2) Of the books written in Spanish, there are 5 more nonfiction books than fiction books.

48. If *p* is the perimeter of rectangle *Q*, what is the value of *p*?

(1) Each diagonal of rectangle *Q* has length 10.

(2) The area of rectangle *Q* is 48.

3.2 Verbal Questions

Reading Comprehension

Each of the reading comprehension questions is based on the content of a passage. After reading the passage, answer all questions pertaining to it on the basis of what is stated or implied in the passage. For each question, select the best answer of the choices given.

According to economic signaling theory, consumers may perceive the frequency with which an unfamiliar brand is advertised as a cue that the brand is of high quality. The notion that highly advertised brands are associated with high-quality products does have some empirical support. Marquardt and McGann found that heavily advertised products did indeed rank high on certain measures of product quality. **Because large advertising expenditures represent a significant investment on the part of a manufacturer, only companies that expect to recoup these costs in the long run, through consumers' repeat purchases of the product, can afford to spend such amounts.**

However, two studies by Kirmani have found that although consumers initially perceive expensive advertising as a signal of high brand quality, at some level of spending the manufacturer's advertising effort may be perceived as unreasonably high, implying low manufacturer confidence in product quality. If consumers perceive excessive advertising effort as a sign of a manufacturer's desperation, the result may be less favorable brand perceptions. In addition, a third study by Kirmani, of print advertisements, found that the use of color affected consumer perception of brand quality. Because consumers recognize that color advertisements are more expensive than black and white, the point at which repetition of an advertisement is perceived as excessive comes sooner for a color advertisement than for a black-and-white advertisement.

49. Which of the following best describes the purpose of the sentence in lines 10–15 ?

(A) To show that economic signaling theory fails to explain a finding

(B) To introduce a distinction not accounted for by economic signaling theory

(C) To account for an exception to a generalization suggested by Marquardt and McGann

(D) To explain why Marquardt and McGann's research was conducted

(E) To offer an explanation for an observation reported by Marquardt and McGann

50. The primary purpose of the passage is to

(A) present findings that contradict one explanation for the effects of a particular advertising practice

(B) argue that theoretical explanations about the effects of a particular advertising practice are of limited value without empirical evidence

(C) discuss how and why particular advertising practices may affect consumers' perceptions

(D) contrast the research methods used in two different studies of a particular advertising practice

(E) explain why a finding about consumer responses to a particular advertising practice was unexpected

51. Kirmani's research, as described in the passage, suggests which of the following regarding consumers' expectations about the quality of advertised products?

(A) Those expectations are likely to be highest if a manufacturer runs both black-and-white and color advertisements for the same product.

(B) Those expectations can be shaped by the presence of color in an advertisement as well as by the frequency with which an advertisement appears.

(C) Those expectations are usually high for frequently advertised new brands but not for frequently advertised familiar brands.

(D) Those expectations are likely to be higher for products whose black-and-white advertisements are often repeated than for those whose color advertisements are less often repeated.

(E) Those expectations are less definitively shaped by the manufacturer's advertisements than by information that consumers gather from other sources.

52. Kirmani's third study, as described in the passage, suggests which of the following conclusions about a black-and-white advertisement?

(A) It can be repeated more frequently than a comparable color advertisement could before consumers begin to suspect low manufacturer confidence in the quality of the advertised product.

(B) It will have the greatest impact on consumers' perceptions of the quality of the advertised product if it appears during periods when a color version of the same advertisement is also being used.

(C) It will attract more attention from readers of the print publication in which it appears if it is used only a few times.

(D) It may be perceived by some consumers as more expensive than a comparable color advertisement.

(E) It is likely to be perceived by consumers as a sign of higher manufacturer confidence in the quality of the advertised product than a comparable color advertisement would be.

53. The passage suggests that Kirmani would be most likely to agree with which of the following statements about consumers' perceptions of the relationship between the frequency with which a product is advertised and the product's quality?

(A) Consumers' perceptions about the frequency with which an advertisement appears are their primary consideration when evaluating an advertisement's claims about product quality.

(B) Because most consumers do not notice the frequency of advertisement, it has little impact on most consumers' expectations regarding product quality.

(C) Consumers perceive frequency of advertisement as a signal about product quality only when the advertisement is for a product that is newly on the market.

(D) The frequency of advertisement is not always perceived by consumers to indicate that manufacturers are highly confident about their products' quality.

(E) Consumers who try a new product that has been frequently advertised are likely to perceive the advertisement's frequency as having been an accurate indicator of the product's quality.

The idea of the brain as an information processor—a machine manipulating blips of energy according to fathomable rules—has come to dominate neuroscience. However, one enemy of the brain-as-computer metaphor is John R. Searle, a philosopher who argues that since computers simply follow algorithms, they cannot deal with important aspects of human thought such as meaning and content. Computers are syntactic, rather than semantic, creatures. People, on the other hand, understand meaning because they have something Searle obscurely calls the causal powers of the brain.

Yet how would a brain work if not by reducing what it learns about the world to information—some kind of code that can be transmitted from neuron to neuron? What else could meaning and content be? If the code can be cracked, a computer should be able to simulate it, at least in principle. But even if a computer could simulate the workings of the mind, Searle would claim that the machine would not really be thinking; it would just be acting as if it were. His argument proceeds thus: if a computer were used to simulate a stomach, with the stomach's churnings faithfully reproduced on a video screen, the machine would not be digesting real food. It would just be blindly manipulating the symbols that generate the visual display.

Suppose, though, that a stomach were simulated using plastic tubes, a motor to do the churning, a supply of digestive juices, and a timing mechanism. If food went in one end of the device, what came out the other end would surely be digested food. Brains, unlike stomachs, are information processors, and if one information processor were made to simulate another information processor, it is hard to see how one and not the other could be said to think. Simulated thoughts and real thoughts are made of the same element: information. The representations of the world that humans carry around in their heads are already simulations. To accept Searle's argument, one would have to deny the most fundamental notion in psychology and neuroscience: that brains work by processing information.

54. The main purpose of the passage is to

(A) propose an experiment

(B) analyze a function

(C) refute an argument

(D) explain a contradiction

(E) simulate a process

55. Which of the following is most consistent with Searle's reasoning as presented in the passage?

(A) Meaning and content cannot be reduced to algorithms.

(B) The process of digestion can be simulated mechanically, but not on a computer.

(C) Simulated thoughts and real thoughts are essentially similar because they are composed primarily of information.

(D) A computer can use "causal powers" similar to those of the human brain when processing information.

(E) Computer simulations of the world can achieve the complexity of the brain's representations of the world.

56. The author of the passage would be most likely to agree with which of the following statements about the simulation of organ functions?

(A) An artificial device that achieves the functions of the stomach could be considered a valid model of the stomach.

(B) Computer simulations of the brain are best used to crack the brain's codes of meaning and content.

(C) Computer simulations of the brain challenge ideas that are fundamental to psychology and neuroscience.

(D) Because the brain and the stomach both act as processors, they can best be simulated by mechanical devices.

(E) The computer's limitations in simulating digestion suggest equal limitations in computer-simulated thinking.

57. It can be inferred that the author of the passage believes that Searle's argument is flawed by its failure to

(A) distinguish between syntactic and semantic operations

(B) explain adequately how people, unlike computers, are able to understand meaning

(C) provide concrete examples illustrating its claims about thinking

(D) understand how computers use algorithms to process information

(E) decipher the code that is transmitted from neuron to neuron in the brain

58. From the passage, it can be inferred that the author would agree with Searle on which of the following points?

(A) Computers operate by following algorithms.

(B) The human brain can never fully understand its own functions.

(C) The comparison of the brain to a machine is overly simplistic.

(D) The most accurate models of physical processes are computer simulations.

(E) Human thought and computer-simulated thought involve similar processes of representation.

59. Which of the following most accurately represents Searle's criticism of the brain-as-computer metaphor, as that criticism is described in the passage?

(A) The metaphor is not experimentally verifiable.

(B) The metaphor does not take into account the unique powers of the brain.

(C) The metaphor suggests that a brain's functions can be simulated as easily as those of a stomach.

(D) The metaphor suggests that a computer can simulate the workings of the mind by using the codes of neural transmission.

(E) The metaphor is unhelpful because both the brain and the computer process information.

Women's grassroots activism and their vision of a new civic consciousness lay at the heart of social reform in the United States throughout the Progressive Era, the period between the depression of 1893 and America's entry into the Second World War. Though largely disenfranchised except for school elections, white middle-class women reformers won a variety of victories, notably in the improvement of working conditions, especially for women and children. Ironically, though, child labor legislation pitted women of different classes against one another. To the reformers, child labor and industrial home work were equally inhumane practices that should be outlawed, but, as a number of women historians have recently observed, working-class mothers did not always share this view. Given the precarious finances of working-class families and the necessity of pooling the wages of as many family members as possible, working-class families viewed the passage and enforcement of stringent child labor statutes as a personal economic disaster and made strenuous efforts to circumvent child labor laws. Yet reformers rarely understood this resistance in terms of the desperate economic situation of working-class families, interpreting it instead as evidence of poor parenting. This is not to dispute women reformers' perception of child labor as a terribly exploitative practice, but their understanding of child labor and their legislative solutions for ending it failed to take account of the economic needs of working-class families.

60. The primary purpose of the passage is to

(A) explain why women reformers of the Progressive Era failed to achieve their goals

(B) discuss the origins of child labor laws in the late nineteenth and early twentieth centuries

(C) compare the living conditions of working-class and middle-class women in the Progressive Era

(D) discuss an oversight on the part of women reformers of the Progressive Era

(E) revise a traditional view of the role played by women reformers in enacting Progressive Era reforms

61. The view mentioned in line 17 of the passage refers to which of the following?

(A) Some working-class mothers' resistance to the enforcement of child labor laws

(B) Reformers' belief that child labor and industrial home work should be abolished

(C) Reformers' opinions about how working-class families raised their children

(D) Certain women historians' observation that there was a lack of consensus between women of different classes on the issue of child labor and industrial home work

(E) Working-class families' fears about the adverse consequences that child labor laws would have on their ability to earn an adequate living

62. The author of the passage mentions the observations of women historians (lines 15–17) most probably in order to

(A) provide support for an assertion made in the preceding sentence (lines 10–12)

(B) raise a question that is answered in the last sentence of the passage (lines 27–32)

(C) introduce an opinion that challenges a statement made in the first sentence of the passage

(D) offer an alternative view to the one attributed in the passage to working-class mothers

(E) point out a contradiction inherent in the traditional view of child labor reform as it is presented in the passage

63. The passage suggests that which of the following was a reason for the difference of opinion between working-class mothers and women reformers on the issue of child labor?

(A) Reformers' belief that industrial home work was preferable to child labor outside the home
(B) Reformers' belief that child labor laws should pertain to working conditions but not to pay
(C) Working-class mothers' resentment at reformers' attempts to interfere with their parenting
(D) Working-class mothers' belief that child labor was an inhumane practice
(E) Working-class families' need for every employable member of their families to earn money

64. The author of the passage asserts which of the following about women reformers who tried to abolish child labor?

(A) They alienated working-class mothers by attempting to enlist them in agitating for progressive causes.
(B) They underestimated the prevalence of child labor among the working classes.
(C) They were correct in their conviction that child labor was deplorable but shortsighted about the impact of child labor legislation on working-class families.
(D) They were aggressive in their attempts to enforce child labor legislation, but were unable to prevent working-class families from circumventing them.
(E) They were prevented by their nearly total disenfranchisement from making significant progress in child labor reform.

65. According to the passage, one of the most striking achievements of white middle-class women reformers during the Progressive Era was

(A) gaining the right to vote in school elections
(B) mobilizing working-class women in the fight against child labor
(C) uniting women of different classes in grassroots activism
(D) improving the economic conditions of working-class families
(E) improving women's and children's working conditions

Critical Reasoning

Each of the critical reasoning questions is based on a short argument, a set of statements, or a plan of action. For each question, select the best answer of the choices given.

66. Vasquez-Morrell Assurance specializes in insuring manufacturers. Whenever a policyholder makes a claim, a claims adjuster determines the amount that Vasquez-Morrell is obligated to pay. Vasquez-Morrell is cutting its staff of claims adjusters by 15 percent. To ensure that the company's ability to handle claims promptly is affected as little as possible by the staff cuts, consultants recommend that Vasquez-Morrell lay off those adjusters who now take longest, on average, to complete work on claims assigned to them.

Which of the following, if true, most seriously calls into question the consultants' criterion for selecting the staff to be laid off?

(A) If the time that Vasquez-Morrell takes to settle claims increases significantly, it could lose business to other insurers.
(B) Supervisors at Vasquez-Morrell tend to assign the most complex claims to the most capable adjusters.
(C) At Vasquez-Morrell, no insurance payments are made until a claims adjuster has reached a final determination on the claim.
(D) There are no positions at Vasquez-Morrell to which staff currently employed as claims adjusters could be reassigned.
(E) The premiums that Vasquez-Morrell currently charges are no higher than those charged for similar coverage by competitors.

67. Prolonged spells of hot, dry weather at the end of the grape-growing season typically reduce a vineyard's yield, because the grapes stay relatively small. In years with such weather, wine producers can make only a relatively small quantity of wine from a given area of vineyards. Nonetheless, in regions where wine producers generally grow their own grapes, analysts typically expect a long, hot, dry spell late in the growing season to result in increased revenues for local wine producers.

Which of the following, if true, does most to justify the analysts' expectation?

(A) The lower a vineyard's yield, the less labor is required to harvest the grapes.
(B) Long, hot, dry spells at the beginning of the grape-growing season are rare, but they can have a devastating effect on a vineyard's yield.
(C) Grapes grown for wine production are typically made into wine at or near the vineyard in which they were grown.
(D) When hot, dry spells are followed by heavy rains, the rains frequently destroy grape crops.
(E) Grapes that have matured in hot, dry weather make significantly better wine than ordinary grapes.

68. In the past, most children who went sledding in the winter snow in Verland used wooden sleds with runners and steering bars. Ten years ago, smooth plastic sleds became popular; they go faster than wooden sleds but are harder to steer and slow. The concern that plastic sleds are more dangerous is clearly borne out by the fact that the number of children injured while sledding was much higher last winter than it was 10 years ago.

Which of the following, if true in Verland, most seriously undermines the force of the evidence cited?

(A) A few children still use traditional wooden sleds.

(B) Very few children wear any kind of protective gear, such as helmets, while sledding.

(C) Plastic sleds can be used in a much wider variety of snow conditions than wooden sleds can.

(D) Most sledding injuries occur when a sled collides with a tree, a rock, or another sled.

(E) Because the traditional wooden sleds can carry more than one rider, an accident involving a wooden sled can result in several children being injured.

69. Metal rings recently excavated from seventh-century settlements in the western part of Mexico were made using the same metallurgical techniques as those used by Ecuadorian artisans before and during that period. These techniques are sufficiently complex to make their independent development in both areas unlikely. Since the people of these two areas were in cultural contact, archaeologists hypothesize that the metallurgical techniques used to make the rings found in Mexico were learned by Mexican artisans from Ecuadorian counterparts.

Which of the following would it be most useful to establish in order to evaluate the archaeologists' hypothesis?

(A) Whether metal objects were traded from Ecuador to western Mexico during the seventh century

(B) Whether travel between western Mexico and Ecuador in the seventh century would have been primarily by land or by sea

(C) Whether artisans from western Mexico could have learned complex metallurgical techniques from their Ecuadorian counterparts without actually leaving western Mexico

(D) Whether metal tools were used in the seventh-century settlements in western Mexico

(E) Whether any of the techniques used in the manufacture of the metal rings found in western Mexico are still practiced among artisans in Ecuador today

70. Following several years of declining advertising sales, the *Greenville Times* reorganized its advertising sales force. Before reorganization, the sales force was organized geographically, with some sales representatives concentrating on city-center businesses and others concentrating on different outlying regions. The reorganization attempted to increase the sales representatives' knowledge of clients' businesses by having each sales representative deal with only one type of industry or of retailing. After the reorganization, revenue from advertising sales increased.

In assessing whether the improvement in advertising sales can properly be attributed to the reorganization, it would be most helpful to find out which of the following?

(A) What proportion of the total revenue of the *Greenville Times* is generated by advertising sales?

(B) Has the circulation of the *Greenville Times* increased substantially in the last two years?

(C) Among all the types of industry and retailing that use the *Greenville Times* as an advertising vehicle, which type accounts for the largest proportion of the newspaper's advertising sales?

(D) Do any clients of the sales representatives of the *Greenville Times* have a standing order with the *Times* for a fixed amount of advertising per month?

(E) Among the advertisers in the *Greenville Times*, are there more types of retail business or more types of industrial business?

71. Motorists in a certain country frequently complain that traffic congestion is much worse now than it was 20 years ago. No real measure of how much traffic congestion there was 20 years ago exists, but the motorists' complaints are almost certainly unwarranted. The country's highway capacity has tripled in the last twenty years, thanks to a vigorous highway construction program, whereas the number of automobiles registered in the country has increased by only 75 percent.

Which of the following, if true, most seriously weakens the argument?

(A) Most automobile travel is local, and the networks of roads and streets in the country's settled areas have changed little over the last 20 years.

(B) Gasoline prices are high, and miles traveled per car per year have not changed much over the last 20 years.

(C) The country's urban centers have well-developed public transit systems that carry most of the people who commute into those centers.

(D) The average age of automobiles registered in the country is lower now than it was 20 years ago.

(E) Radio stations have long been broadcasting regular traffic reports that inform motorists about traffic congestion.

72. The percentage of households with an annual income of more than $40,000 is higher in Merton County than in any other county. However, the percentage of households with an annual income of $60,000 or more is higher in Sommer County.

If the statements above are true, which of the following must also be true?

(A) The percentage of households with an annual income of $80,000 is higher in Sommer County than in Merton County.

(B) Merton County has the second highest percentage of households with an annual income of $60,000 or more.

(C) Some households in Merton County have an annual income between $40,000 and $60,000.

(D) The number of households with an annual income of more than $40,000 is greater in Merton County than in Sommer County.

(E) Average annual household income is higher in Sommer County than in Merton County.

73. Tiger beetles are such fast runners that they can capture virtually any nonflying insect. However, when running toward an insect, a tiger beetle will intermittently stop and then, a moment later, resume its attack. Perhaps the beetles cannot maintain their pace and must pause for a moment's rest; but an alternative hypothesis is that while running, tiger beetles are unable to adequately process the resulting rapidly changing visual information and so quickly go blind and stop.

Which of the following, if discovered in experiments using artificially moved prey insects, would support one of the two hypotheses and undermine the other?

(A) When a prey insect is moved directly toward a beetle that has been chasing it, the beetle immediately stops and runs away without its usual intermittent stopping.

(B) In pursuing a swerving insect, a beetle alters its course while running and its pauses become more frequent as the chase progresses.

(C) In pursuing a moving insect, a beetle usually responds immediately to changes in the insect's direction, and it pauses equally frequently whether the chase is up or down an incline.

(D) If, when a beetle pauses, it has not gained on the insect it is pursuing, the beetle generally ends its pursuit.

(E) The faster a beetle pursues an insect fleeing directly away from it, the more frequently the beetle stops.

74. Guillemots are birds of Arctic regions. They feed on fish that gather beneath thin sheets of floating ice, and they nest on nearby land. Guillemots need 80 consecutive snow-free days in a year to raise their chicks, so until average temperatures in the Arctic began to rise recently, the guillemots' range was limited to the southernmost Arctic coast. Therefore, if the warming continues, the guillemots' range will probably be enlarged by being extended northward along the coast.

    Which of the following, if true, most seriously weakens the argument?

    (A) Even if the warming trend continues, there will still be years in which guillemot chicks are killed by an unusually early snow.
    (B) If the Arctic warming continues, guillemots' current predators are likely to succeed in extending their own range farther north.
    (C) Guillemots nest in coastal areas, where temperatures are generally higher than in inland areas.
    (D) If the Arctic warming continues, much of the thin ice in the southern Arctic will disappear.
    (E) The fish that guillemots eat are currently preyed on by a wider variety of predators in the southernmost Arctic regions than they are farther north.

75. Some batches of polio vaccine used around 1960 were contaminated with SV40, a virus that in monkeys causes various cancers. Some researchers now claim that this contamination caused some cases of a certain cancer in humans, mesothelioma. This claim is not undercut by the fact that a very careful survey made in the 1960s of people who had received the contaminated vaccine found no elevated incidence of any cancer, since __________.

    (A) most cases of mesothelioma are caused by exposure to asbestos
    (B) in some countries, there was no contamination of the vaccine
    (C) SV40 is widely used in laboratories to produce cancers in animals
    (D) mesotheliomas take several decades to develop
    (E) mesothelioma was somewhat less common in 1960 than it is now

76. Gortland has long been narrowly self-sufficient in both grain and meat. However, as per capita income in Gortland has risen toward the world average, per capita consumption of meat has also risen toward the world average, and it takes several pounds of grain to produce one pound of meat. Therefore, since per capita income continues to rise, whereas domestic grain production will not increase, Gortland will soon have to import either grain or meat or both.

    Which of the following is an assumption on which the argument depends?

    (A) The total acreage devoted to grain production in Gortland will soon decrease.
    (B) Importing either grain or meat will not result in a significantly higher percentage of Gortlanders' incomes being spent on food than is currently the case.
    (C) The per capita consumption of meat in Gortland is increasing at roughly the same rate across all income levels.
    (D) The per capita income of meat producers in Gortland is rising faster than the per capita income of grain producers.
    (E) People in Gortland who increase their consumption of meat will not radically decrease their consumption of grain.

77. The Hazelton coal-processing plant is a major employer in the Hazelton area, but national environmental regulations will force it to close if it continues to use old, polluting processing methods. However, to update the plant to use newer, cleaner methods would be so expensive that the plant will close unless it receives the tax break it has requested. In order to prevent a major increase in local unemployment, the Hazelton government is considering granting the plant's request.

Which of the following would be most important for the Hazelton government to determine before deciding whether to grant the plant's request?

(A) Whether the company that owns the plant would open a new plant in another area if the present plant were closed

(B) Whether the plant would employ far fewer workers when updated than it does now

(C) Whether the level of pollutants presently being emitted by the plant is high enough to constitute a health hazard for local residents

(D) Whether the majority of the coal processed by the plant is sold outside the Hazelton area

(E) Whether the plant would be able to process more coal when updated than it does now

78. A physically active lifestyle has been shown to help increase longevity. In the Wistar region of Bellaria, the average age at death is considerably higher than in any other part of the country. Wistar is the only mountainous part of Bellaria. A mountainous terrain makes even such basic activities as walking relatively strenuous; it essentially imposes a physically active lifestyle on people. Clearly, this circumstance explains the long lives of people in Wistar.

Which of the following, if true, most seriously weakens the argument?

(A) In Bellaria all medical expenses are paid by the government, so that personal income does not affect the quality of health care a person receives.

(B) The Wistar region is one of Bellaria's least populated regions.

(C) Many people who live in the Wistar region have moved there in middle age or upon retirement.

(D) The many opportunities for hiking, skiing, and other outdoor activities that Wistar's mountains offer make it a favorite destination for vacationing Bellarians.

(E) Per capita spending on recreational activities is no higher in Wistar than it is in other regions of Bellaria.

79. Cheever College offers several online courses via remote computer connection, in addition to traditional classroom-based courses. A study of student performance at Cheever found that, overall, the average student grade for online courses matched that for classroom-based courses. In this calculation of the average grade, course withdrawals were weighted as equivalent to a course failure, and the rate of withdrawal was much lower for students enrolled in classroom-based courses than for students enrolled in online courses.

If the statements above are true, which of the following must also be true of Cheever College?

(A) Among students who did not withdraw, students enrolled in online courses got higher grades, on average, than students enrolled in classroom-based courses.

(B) The number of students enrolled per course at the start of the school term is much higher, on average, for the online courses than for the classroom-based courses.

(C) There are no students who take both an online and a classroom-based course in the same school term.

(D) Among Cheever College students with the best grades, a significant majority take online, rather than classroom-based, courses.

(E) Courses offered online tend to deal with subject matter that is less challenging than that of classroom-based courses.

80. For years the beautiful Renaissance buildings in Palitito have been damaged by exhaust from the many tour buses that come to the city. There has been little parking space, so most buses have idled at the curb during each stop on their tour, and idling produces as much exhaust as driving. The city has now provided parking that accommodates a third of the tour buses, so damage to Palitito's buildings from the buses' exhaust will diminish significantly.

Which of the following, if true, most strongly supports the argument?

(A) The exhaust from Palitito's few automobiles is not a significant threat to Palitito's buildings.
(B) Palitito's Renaissance buildings are not threatened by pollution other than engine exhaust.
(C) Tour buses typically spend less than one-quarter of the time they are in Palitito transporting passengers from one site to another.
(D) More tourists come to Palitito by tour bus than by any other single means of transportation.
(E) Some of the tour buses that are unable to find parking drive around Palitito while their passengers are visiting a site.

81. During the 1980s and 1990s, the annual number of people who visited the Sordellian Mountains increased continually, and many new ski resorts were built. Over the same period, however, the number of visitors to ski resorts who were caught in avalanches decreased, even though there was no reduction in the annual number of avalanches in the Sordellian Mountains.

Which of the following, if true in the Sordellian Mountains during the 1980s and 1990s, most helps to explain the decrease?

(A) Avalanches were most likely to happen when a large new snowfall covered an older layer of snow.
(B) Avalanches destroyed at least some buildings in the Sordellian Mountains in every year.
(C) People planning new ski slopes and other resort facilities used increasingly accurate information about which locations are likely to be in the path of avalanches.
(D) The average length of stay for people visiting the Sordellian Mountains increased slightly.
(E) Construction of new ski resorts often led to the clearing of wooded areas that had helped to prevent avalanches.

82. A year ago, Dietz Foods launched a yearlong advertising campaign for its canned tuna. Last year Dietz sold 12 million cans of tuna compared to the 10 million sold during the previous year, an increase directly attributable to new customers brought in by the campaign. Profits from the additional sales, however, were substantially less than the cost of the advertising campaign. Clearly, therefore, the campaign did nothing to further Dietz's economic interests.

Which of the following, if true, most seriously weakens the argument?

(A) Sales of canned tuna account for a relatively small percentage of Dietz Foods' profits.
(B) Most of the people who bought Dietz's canned tuna for the first time as a result of the campaign were already loyal customers of other Dietz products.
(C) A less expensive advertising campaign would have brought in significantly fewer new customers for Dietz's canned tuna than did the campaign Dietz Foods launched last year.
(D) Dietz made money on sales of canned tuna last year.
(E) In each of the past five years, there was a steep, industry-wide decline in sales of canned tuna.

Sentence Correction

Each of the sentence correction questions presents a sentence, part or all of which is underlined. Beneath the sentence you will find five ways of phrasing the underlined part. The first of these repeats the original; the other four are different. Follow the requirements of standard written English to choose your answer, paying attention to grammar, word choice, and sentence construction. Select the answer that produces the most effective sentence; your answer should make the sentence clear, exact, and free of grammatical error. It should also minimize awkwardness, ambiguity, and redundancy.

83. Unlike the buildings in Mesopotamian cities, which were arranged haphazardly, the same basic plan was followed for all cities of the Indus Valley: with houses laid out on a north-south, east-west grid, and houses and walls were built of standard-size bricks.

(A) the buildings in Mesopotamian cities, which were arranged haphazardly, the same basic plan was followed for all cities of the Indus Valley: with houses

(B) the buildings in Mesopotamian cities, which were haphazard in arrangement, the same basic plan was used in all cities of the Indus Valley: houses were

(C) the arrangement of buildings in Mesopotamian cities, which were haphazard, the cities of the Indus Valley all followed the same basic plan: houses

(D) Mesopotamian cities, in which buildings were arranged haphazardly, the cities of the Indus Valley all followed the same basic plan: houses were

(E) Mesopotamian cities, which had buildings that were arranged haphazardly, the same basic plan was used for all cities in the Indus Valley: houses that were

84. New data from United States Forest Service ecologists show that for every dollar spent on controlled small-scale burning, forest thinning, and the training of fire-management personnel, it saves seven dollars that would not be spent on having to extinguish big fires.

(A) that for every dollar spent on controlled small-scale burning, forest thinning, and the training of fire-management personnel, it saves seven dollars that would not be spent on having to extinguish

(B) that for every dollar spent on controlled small-scale burning, forest thinning, and the training of fire-management personnel, seven dollars are saved that would have been spent on extinguishing

(C) that for every dollar spent on controlled small-scale burning, forest thinning, and the training of fire-management personnel saves seven dollars on not having to extinguish

(D) for every dollar spent on controlled small-scale burning, forest thinning, and the training of fire-management personnel, that it saves seven dollars on not having to extinguish

(E) for every dollar spent on controlled small-scale burning, forest thinning, and the training of fire-management personnel, that seven dollars are saved that would not have been spent on extinguishing

85. Like the grassy fields and old pastures that the upland sandpiper needs for feeding and nesting when it returns in May after wintering in the Argentine Pampas, the sandpipers vanishing in the northeastern United States is a result of residential and industrial development and of changes in farming practices.

(A) the sandpipers vanishing in the northeastern United States is a result of residential and industrial development and of changes in

(B) the bird itself is vanishing in the northeastern United States as a result of residential and industrial development and of changes in

(C) that the birds themselves are vanishing in the northeastern United States is due to residential and industrial development and changes to

(D) in the northeastern United States, sandpipers' vanishing due to residential and industrial development and to changes in

(E) in the northeastern United States, the sandpipers' vanishing, a result of residential and industrial development and changing

86. The results of two recent unrelated studies support the idea that dolphins may share certain cognitive abilities with humans and great apes; the studies indicate dolphins as capable of recognizing themselves in mirrors—an ability that is often considered a sign of self-awareness—and to grasp spontaneously the mood or intention of humans.

(A) dolphins as capable of recognizing themselves in mirrors—an ability that is often considered a sign of self-awareness—and to grasp spontaneously

(B) dolphins' ability to recognize themselves in mirrors—an ability that is often considered as a sign of self-awareness—and of spontaneously grasping

(C) dolphins to be capable of recognizing themselves in mirrors—an ability that is often considered a sign of self-awareness—and to grasp spontaneously

(D) that dolphins have the ability of recognizing themselves in mirrors—an ability that is often considered as a sign of self-awareness—and spontaneously grasping

(E) that dolphins are capable of recognizing themselves in mirrors—an ability that is often considered a sign of self-awareness—and of spontaneously grasping

87. According to scholars, the earliest writing was probably not a direct rendering of speech, but was more likely to begin as a separate and distinct symbolic system of communication, and only later merged with spoken language.

(A) was more likely to begin as

(B) more than likely began as

(C) more than likely beginning from

(D) it was more than likely begun from

(E) it was more likely that it began

88. In 1995 Richard Stallman, a well-known critic of the patent system, testified in Patent Office hearings that, to test the system, a colleague of his had managed to win a patent for one of Kirchhoff's laws, an observation about electric current first made in 1845 and now included in virtually every textbook of elementary physics.

(A) laws, an observation about electric current first made in 1845 and

(B) laws, which was an observation about electric current first made in 1845 and it is

(C) laws, namely, it was an observation about electric current first made in 1845 and

(D) laws, an observation about electric current first made in 1845, it is

(E) laws that was an observation about electric current, first made in 1845, and is

89. Excavators at the Indus Valley site of Harappa in eastern Pakistan say the discovery of inscribed shards dating to circa 2800–2600 B.C. indicate their development of a Harappan writing system, the use of inscribed seals impressed into clay for marking ownership, and the standardization of weights for trade or taxation occurred many decades, if not centuries, earlier than was previously believed.

(A) indicate their development of a Harappan writing system, the use of

(B) indicate that the development of a Harappan writing system, using

(C) indicates that their development of a Harappan writing system, using

(D) indicates the development of a Harappan writing system, their use of

(E) indicates that the development of a Harappan writing system, the use of

90. The Supreme Court has ruled that public universities can collect student activity fees even with students' objections to particular activities, so long as the groups they give money to will be chosen without regard to their views.

(A) with students' objections to particular activities, so long as the groups they give money to will be
(B) if they have objections to particular activities and the groups that are given the money are
(C) if they object to particular activities, but the groups that the money is given to have to be
(D) from students who object to particular activities, so long as the groups given money are
(E) though students have an objection to particular activities, but the groups that are given the money be

91. Despite the increasing number of women graduating from law school and passing bar examinations, the proportion of judges and partners at major law firms who are women have not risen to a comparable extent.

(A) the proportion of judges and partners at major law firms who are women have not risen to a comparable extent
(B) the proportion of women judges and partners at major law firms have not risen comparably
(C) the proportion of judges and partners at major law firms who are women has not risen comparably
(D) yet the proportion of women judges and partners at major law firms has not risen to a comparable extent
(E) yet the proportion of judges and partners at major law firms who are women has not risen comparably

92. Seldom more than 40 feet wide and 12 feet deep, but it ran 363 miles across the rugged wilderness of upstate New York, the Erie Canal connected the Hudson River at Albany to the Great Lakes at Buffalo, providing the port of New York City with a direct water link to the heartland of the North American continent.

(A) Seldom more than 40 feet wide and 12 feet deep, but it ran 363 miles across the rugged wilderness of upstate New York, the Erie Canal connected
(B) Seldom more than 40 feet wide or 12 feet deep but running 363 miles across the rugged wilderness of upstate New York, the Erie Canal connected
(C) It was seldom more than 40 feet wide and 12 feet deep, and ran 363 miles across the rugged wilderness of upstate New York, but the Erie Canal, connecting
(D) The Erie Canal was seldom more than 40 feet wide or 12 feet deep and it ran 363 miles across the rugged wilderness of upstate New York, which connected
(E) The Erie Canal, seldom more than 40 feet wide and 12 feet deep, but running 363 miles across the rugged wilderness of upstate New York, connecting

93. In 1923, the Supreme Court declared a minimum wage for women and children in the District of Columbia as unconstitutional, and ruling that it was a form of price-fixing and, as such, an abridgment of the right of contract.

(A) the Supreme Court declared a minimum wage for women and children in the District of Columbia as unconstitutional, and
(B) the Supreme Court declared as unconstitutional a minimum wage for women and children in the District of Columbia, and
(C) the Supreme Court declared unconstitutional a minimum wage for women and children in the District of Columbia,
(D) a minimum wage for women and children in the District of Columbia was declared unconstitutional by the Supreme Court,
(E) when the Supreme Court declared a minimum wage for women and children in the District of Columbia as unconstitutional,

94. Researchers have found that individuals who have been blind from birth, and who thus have never seen anyone gesture, nevertheless make hand motions when speaking just as frequently and in virtually the same way as sighted people do, and that they will gesture even when conversing with another blind person.

(A) who thus have never seen anyone gesture, nevertheless make hand motions when speaking just as frequently and in virtually the same way as sighted people do, and that they will gesture

(B) who thus never saw anyone gesturing, nevertheless make hand motions when speaking just as frequent and in virtually the same way as sighted people did, and that they will gesture

(C) who thus have never seen anyone gesture, nevertheless made hand motions when speaking just as frequently and in virtually the same way as sighted people do, as well as gesturing

(D) thus never having seen anyone gesture, nevertheless made hand motions when speaking just as frequent and in virtually the same way as sighted people did, as well as gesturing

(E) thus never having seen anyone gesture, nevertheless to make hand motions when speaking just as frequently and in virtually the same way as sighted people do, and to gesture

95. Like embryonic germ cells, which are cells that develop early in the formation of the fetus and that later generate eggs or sperm, embryonic stem cells have the ability of developing themselves into different kinds of body tissue.

(A) embryonic stem cells have the ability of developing themselves into different kinds of body tissue

(B) embryonic stem cells have the ability to develop into different kinds of body tissue

(C) in embryonic stem cells there is the ability to develop into different kinds of body tissue

(D) the ability to develop themselves into different kinds of body tissue characterizes embryonic stem cells

(E) the ability of developing into different kinds of body tissue characterizes embryonic stem cells

96. Critics contend that the new missile is a weapon whose importance is largely symbolic, more a tool for manipulating people's perceptions than to fulfill a real military need.

(A) for manipulating people's perceptions than to fulfill

(B) for manipulating people's perceptions than for fulfilling

(C) to manipulate people's perceptions rather than that it fulfills

(D) to manipulate people's perceptions rather than fulfilling

(E) to manipulate people's perceptions than for fulfilling

97. As an actress and, more importantly, as a teacher of acting, Stella Adler was one of the most influential artists in the American theater, who trained several generations of actors including Marlon Brando and Robert De Niro.

(A) Stella Adler was one of the most influential artists in the American theater, who trained several generations of actors including

(B) Stella Adler, one of the most influential artists in the American theater, trained several generations of actors who include

(C) Stella Adler was one of the most influential artists in the American theater, training several generations of actors whose ranks included

(D) one of the most influential artists in the American theater was Stella Adler, who trained several generations of actors including

(E) one of the most influential artists in the American theater, Stella Adler, trained several generations of actors whose ranks included

98. By developing the Secure Digital Music Initiative, the recording industry associations of North America, Japan, and Europe hope to create a standardized way of distributing songs and full-length recordings on the Internet that will protect copyright holders and foil the many audio pirates who copy and distribute digital music illegally.

(A) of distributing songs and full-length recordings on the Internet that will protect copyright holders and foil the many audio pirates who copy and distribute

(B) of distributing songs and full-length recordings on the Internet and to protect copyright holders and foiling the many audio pirates copying and distributing

(C) for distributing songs and full-length recordings on the Internet while it protects copyright holders and foils the many audio pirates who copy and distribute

(D) to distribute songs and full-length recordings on the Internet while they will protect copyright holders and foil the many audio pirates copying and distributing

(E) to distribute songs and full-length recordings on the Internet and it will protect copyright holders and foiling the many audio pirates who copy and distribute

99. Whereas a ramjet generally cannot achieve high speeds without the initial assistance of a rocket, high speeds can be attained by scramjets, or supersonic combustion ramjets, in that they reduce airflow compression at the entrance of the engine and letting air pass through at supersonic speeds.

(A) high speeds can be attained by scramjets, or supersonic combustion ramjets, in that they reduce

(B) that high speeds can be attained by scramjets, or supersonic combustion ramjets, is a result of their reducing

(C) the ability of scramjets, or supersonic combustion ramjets, to achieve high speeds is because they reduce

(D) scramjets, or supersonic combustion ramjets, have the ability of attaining high speeds when reducing

(E) scramjets, or supersonic combustion ramjets, can attain high speeds by reducing

100. It will not be possible to implicate melting sea ice in the coastal flooding that many global warming models have projected: just like a glass of water that will not overflow due to melting ice cubes, so melting sea ice does not increase oceanic volume.

(A) like a glass of water that will not overflow due to melting ice cubes,

(B) like melting ice cubes that do not cause a glass of water to overflow,

(C) a glass of water will not overflow because of melting ice cubes,

(D) as melting ice cubes that do not cause a glass of water to overflow,

(E) as melting ice cubes do not cause a glass of water to overflow,

3.3 Quantitative and Verbal Answer Keys

Quantitative

1. A	17. D	33. D
2. D	18. A	34. C
3. E	19. A	35. D
4. B	20. B	36. B
5. B	21. D	37. A
6. A	22. E	38. B
7. E	23. B	39. E
8. E	24. C	40. D
9. D	25. E	41. C
10. C	26. E	42. C
11. C	27. E	43. B
12. C	28. E	44. A
13. E	29. E	45. D
14. B	30. A	46. E
15. C	31. D	47. D
16. E	32. C	48. C

Verbal

49. E	67. E	85. B
50. C	68. C	86. E
51. B	69. A	87. B
52. A	70. B	88. A
53. D	71. A	89. E
54. C	72. C	90. D
55. A	73. B	91. C
56. A	74. D	92. B
57. B	75. D	93. C
58. A	76. E	94. A
59. B	77. B	95. B
60. D	78. C	96. B
61. B	79. A	97. C
62. A	80. C	98. A
63. E	81. C	99. E
64. C	82. E	100. E
65. E	83. D	
66. B	84. B	

3.4 Interpretive Guide

The following table provides a guide for interpreting your score, on the basis of the number of questions you got right.

Interpretive Guide

	Excellent	Above Average	Average	Below Average
Problem Solving	19–24	16–18	10–15	0–9
Data Sufficiency	19–24	16–18	10–15	0–9
Reading Comprehension	16–17	14–15	9–13	0–8
Critical Reasoning	14–17	9–13	6–8	0–5
Sentence Correction	16–18	11–15	8–10	0–7

Remember, you should not compare the number of questions you got right in each section. Instead, you should compare how your response rated in each section.

3.5 Quantitative Answer Explanations

Problem Solving

The following discussion is intended to familiarize you with the most efficient and effective approaches to the kinds of problems common to problem solving questions. The particular questions in this chapter are generally representative of the kinds of quantitative questions you will encounter on the GMAT exam. Remember that it is the problem solving strategy that is important, not the specific details of a particular question.

1. Last month a certain music club offered a discount to preferred customers. After the first compact disc purchased, preferred customers paid $3.99 for each additional compact disc purchased. If a preferred customer purchased a total of 6 compact discs and paid $15.95 for the first compact disc, then the dollar amount that the customer paid for the 6 compact discs is equivalent to which of the following?

(A) 5(4.00) + 15.90

(B) 5(4.00) + 15.95

(C) 5(4.00) + 16.00

(D) 5(4.00 – 0.01) + 15.90

(E) 5(4.00 – 0.05) + 15.95

Arithmetic Operations on rational numbers

The cost of the 6 compact discs, with $15.95 for the first one and $3.99 for the other 5 discs, can be expressed as 5(3.99) + 15.95. It is clear from looking at the answer choices that some regrouping of the values is needed because none of the answer choices uses $3.99 in the calculation.

If $4.00 is used instead of $3.99, each one of the 5 additional compact discs is calculated at $0.01 too much, and the total cost is 5(0.01) = $0.05 too high. There is an overage of $0.05 that must be subtracted from the $15.95, or thus $15.95 – $0.05 = $15.90. Therefore, the cost can be expressed as 5(4.00) + 15.90.

The correct answer is A.

2. The average (arithmetic mean) of the integers from 200 to 400, inclusive, is how much greater than the average of the integers from 50 to 100, inclusive?

(A) 150

(B) 175

(C) 200

(D) 225

(E) 300

Arithmetic Statistics

In the list of integers from 200 to 400 inclusive, the middle value is 300. For every integer above 300, there exists an integer below 300 that is the same distance away from 300; thus the average of the integers from 200 to 400, inclusive, will be kept at 300. In the same manner, the average of the integers from 50 to 100, inclusive, is 75.

The difference is 300 – 75 = 225.

The correct answer is D.

3. The sequence $a_1, a_2, a_3, \ldots, a_n, \ldots$ is such that $a_n = \frac{a_{n-1} + a_{n-2}}{2}$ for all $n \geq 3$. If $a_3 = 4$ and $a_5 = 20$, what is the value of a_6?

(A) 12

(B) 16

(C) 20

(D) 24

(E) 28

Algebra Applied problems

According to this formula, it is necessary to know the two prior terms in the sequence to determine the value of a term; that is, it is necessary to know both a_{n-1} and a_{n-2} to find a_n. Therefore, to find a_6, the values of a_5 and a_4 must be determined. To find a_4, let $a_n = a_5$, which makes $a_{n-1} = a_4$ and $a_{n-2} = a_3$. Then, by substituting the given values into the formula

$$a_n = \frac{a_{n-1} + a_{n-2}}{2}$$

$$a_5 = \frac{a_4 + a_3}{2}$$

$$20 = \frac{a_4 + 4}{2} \qquad \text{substitute known values}$$

$$40 = a_4 + 4 \qquad \text{multiply both sides}$$

$$36 = a_4 \qquad \text{subtract 4 from both sides}$$

Then, letting $a_n = a_6$, substitute the known values:

$$a_6 = \frac{a_5 + a_4}{2}$$

$$a_6 = \frac{20 + 36}{2} \qquad \text{substitute known values}$$

$$a_6 = \frac{56}{2} \qquad \text{simplify}$$

$$a_6 = 28$$

The correct answer is E.

4. Among a group of 2,500 people, 35 percent invest in municipal bonds, 18 percent invest in oil stocks, and 7 percent invest in both municipal bonds and oil stocks. If 1 person is to be randomly selected from the 2,500 people, what is the probability that the person selected will be one who invests in municipal bonds but NOT in oil stocks?

(A) $\frac{9}{50}$

(B) $\frac{7}{25}$

(C) $\frac{7}{20}$

(D) $\frac{21}{50}$

(E) $\frac{27}{50}$

Arithmetic Probability

Since there are 2,500 people, 2,500(0.35) = 875 people invest in municipal bonds, and 2,500(0.07) = 175 of those people invest in both municipal bonds and oil stocks. Therefore, there are 875 − 175 = 700 people who invest in municipal bonds but not in oil stocks. Probability of an event =

$$\frac{\text{Number of desired outcomes}}{\text{Total number of outcomes that can occur}}.$$

Probability of investing in municipal bonds but not in oil stocks $= \frac{700}{2{,}500} = \frac{7}{25}$

The correct answer is B.

5. A closed cylindrical tank contains 36π cubic feet of water and is filled to half its capacity. When the tank is placed upright on its circular base on level ground, the height of the water in the tank is 4 feet. When the tank is placed on its side on level ground, what is the height, in feet, of the surface of the water above the ground?

(A) 2

(B) 3

(C) 4

(D) 6

(E) 9

Geometry Volume

Since the cylinder is half full, it will be filled to half its height, whether it is upright or on its side. When the cylinder is on its side, half its height is equal to its radius.

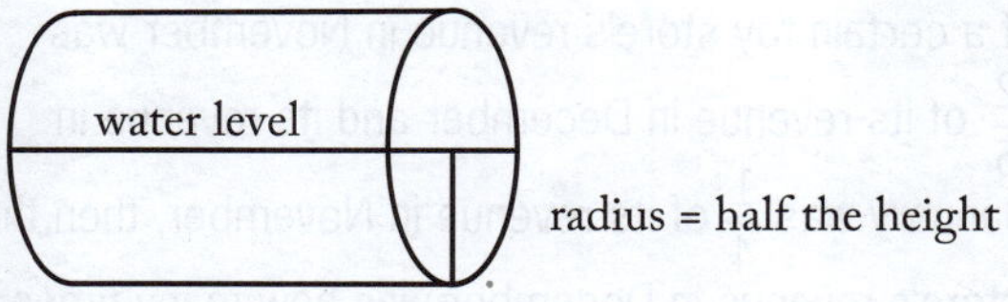

Using the information about the volume of water in the upright cylinder, solve for this radius to determine the height of the water when the cylinder is on its side.

$V = \pi r^2 h$	volume = (π)(radius^2)(height)
$36\pi = \pi r^2 h$	known volume of water is 36π
$36 = r^2(4)$	substitute 4 for h; divide both sides by π
$9 = r^2$	solve for r
$3 = r$	radius = height of the water in the cylinder on its side

The correct answer is B.

6. A marketing firm determined that, of 200 households surveyed, 80 used neither Brand A nor Brand B soap, 60 used only Brand A soap, and for every household that used both brands of soap, 3 used only Brand B soap. How many of the 200 households surveyed used both brands of soap?

(A) 15
(B) 20
(C) 30
(D) 40
(E) 45

Arithmetic Operations on rational numbers

Since it is given that 80 households use neither Brand A nor Brand B, then 200 – 80 = 120 must use Brand A, Brand B, or both. It is also given that 60 households use only Brand A and that three times as many households use Brand B exclusively as use both brands. If x is the number of households that use both Brand A and Brand B, then $3x$ use Brand B alone. A Venn diagram can be helpful for visualizing the logic of the given information for this item:

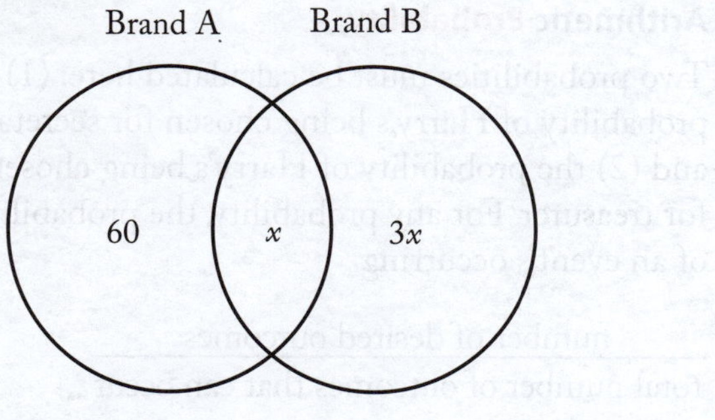

All the sections in the circles can be added up and set equal to 120, and then the equation can be solved for x:

$60 + x + 3x = 120$	
$60 + 4x = 120$	combine like terms
$4x = 60$	subtract 60 from both sides
$x = 15$	divide both sides by 4

The correct answer is A.

7. A certain club has 10 members, including Harry. One of the 10 members is to be chosen at random to be the president, one of the remaining 9 members is to be chosen at random to be the secretary, and one of the remaining 8 members is to be chosen at random to be the treasurer. What is the probability that Harry will be either the member chosen to be the secretary or the member chosen to be the treasurer?

(A) $\frac{1}{720}$
(B) $\frac{1}{80}$
(C) $\frac{1}{10}$
(D) $\frac{1}{9}$
(E) $\frac{1}{5}$

Arithmetic Probability

Two probabilities must be calculated here: (1) the probability of Harry's being chosen for secretary and (2) the probability of Harry's being chosen for treasurer. For any probability, the probability of an event's occurring

$$\frac{\text{number of desired outcomes}}{\text{total number of outcomes that can occur}}.$$

(1) If Harry is to be secretary, he first CANNOT have been chosen for president, and then he must be chosen for secretary. The probability that he will be chosen for president is $\frac{1}{10}$, so the probability of his NOT being chosen for president is $1-\frac{1}{10}=\frac{9}{10}$. Then, the probability of his being chosen for secretary is $\frac{1}{9}$.

Once he is chosen, the probability that he will be selected for treasurer is 0, so the probability that he will NOT be selected for treasurer is $1-0=1$. Thus, the probability that Harry will be chosen for secretary is $\left(\frac{9}{10}\right)\left(\frac{1}{9}\right)(1)=\frac{1}{10}$.

(2) If Harry is to be treasurer, he needs to be NOT chosen for president, then NOT chosen for secretary, and then finally chosen for treasurer.

The probability that he will NOT be chosen for president is again $1-\frac{1}{10}=\frac{9}{10}$. The probability of his NOT being chosen for secretary is $1-\frac{1}{9}=\frac{8}{9}$. The probability of his being chosen for treasurer is $\frac{1}{8}$, so the probability that Harry will be chosen for treasurer is $\left(\frac{9}{10}\right)\left(\frac{8}{9}\right)\left(\frac{1}{8}\right)=\frac{1}{10}$.

(3) So, finally, the probability of Harry's being chosen as either secretary or treasurer is thus $\frac{1}{10}+\frac{1}{10}=\frac{2}{10}=\frac{1}{5}$.

The correct answer is E.

8. If a certain toy store's revenue in November was $\frac{2}{5}$ of its revenue in December and its revenue in January was $\frac{1}{4}$ of its revenue in November, then the store's revenue in December was how many times the average (arithmetic mean) of its revenues in November and January?

(A) $\frac{1}{4}$

(B) $\frac{1}{2}$

(C) $\frac{2}{3}$

(D) 2

(E) 4

Arithmetic Statistics

Let n be the store's revenue in November, d be the store's revenue in December, and j be the store's revenue in January. The information from the problem can be expressed as $n=\frac{2}{5}d$ and $j=\frac{1}{4}n$. Substituting $\frac{2}{5}d$ for n in the second equation gives $j=\frac{1}{4}\left(\frac{2}{5}d\right)=\frac{1}{10}d$. Then, the average of the revenues in November and January can be found by using these values in the formula

$$\text{average}=\frac{\text{sum of values}}{\text{number of values}},$$ as follows:

$$\text{average}=\frac{\frac{2}{5}d+\frac{1}{10}d}{2}=\frac{\frac{4}{10}d+\frac{1}{10}d}{2}=\frac{\frac{5}{10}d}{2}=\frac{1}{2}d\left(\frac{1}{2}\right)=\frac{1}{4}d$$

Solve for the store's revenue in December by multiplying both sides of this equation by 4:

$$\text{average}=\frac{1}{4}d$$

$$4(\text{average})=d$$

Thus, the store's revenue in December was 4 times its average revenue in November and January.

The correct answer is E.

9. A researcher computed the mean, the median, and the standard deviation for a set of performance scores. If 5 were to be added to each score, which of these three statistics would change?

(A) The mean only
(B) The median only
(C) The standard deviation only
(D) The mean and the median
(E) The mean and the standard deviation

Arithmetic Statistics

If 5 were added to each score, the mean would go up by 5, as would the median. However, the spread of the values would remain the same, simply centered around a new value. So, the standard deviation would **NOT** change.

The correct answer is D.

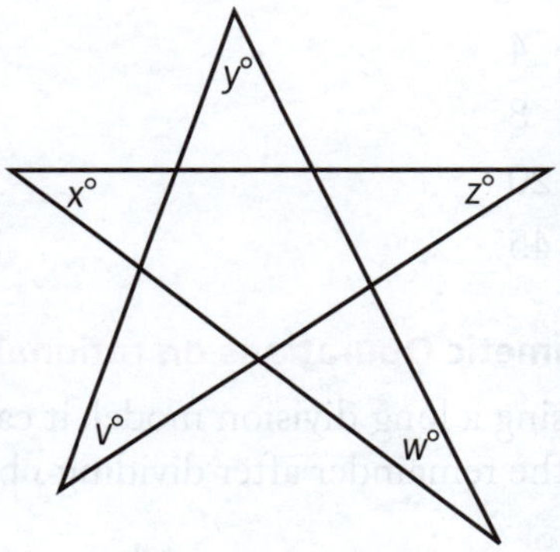

10. In the figure shown, what is the value of $v + x + y + z + w$?

(A) 45
(B) 90
(C) 180
(D) 270
(E) 360

Geometry Angles and their measure

In the following figure, the center section of the star is a pentagon.

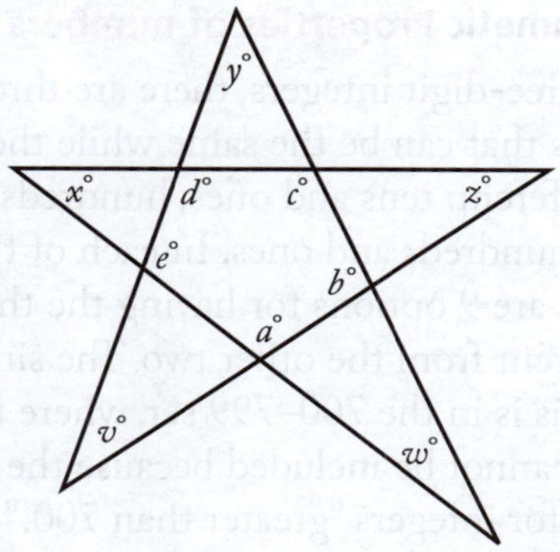

The sum of the interior angles of any polygon is $180(n - 2)$, where n is the number of sides. Thus, $a + b + c + d + e = 180(5 - 2) = 180(3) = 540$.

Each of the interior angles of the pentagon defines a triangle with two of the angles at the points of the star. This gives the following five equations:

$$a + x + z = 180$$
$$b + v + y = 180$$
$$c + x + w = 180$$
$$d + v + z = 180$$
$$e + y + w = 180$$

Summing these 5 equations gives:

$$a + b + c + d + e + 2v + 2x + 2y + 2z + 2w = 900.$$

Substituting 540 for $a + b + c + d + e$ gives:

$$540 + 2v + 2x + 2y + 2w = 900.$$

From this:

$2v + 2x + 2y + 2z + 2w = 360$	subtract 540 from both sides
$2(v + x + y + z + w) = 360$	factor out 2 on the left side
$v + x + y + z + w = 180$	divide both sides by 2

The correct answer is C.

11. Of the three-digit integers greater than 700, how many have two digits that are equal to each other and the remaining digit different from the other two?

(A) 90
(B) 82
(C) 80
(D) 45
(E) 36

Arithmetic Properties of numbers

In three-digit integers, there are three pairs of digits that can be the same while the other digit is different: tens and ones, hundreds and tens, and hundreds and ones. In each of these pairs, there are 9 options for having the third digit be different from the other two. The single exception to this is in the 700–799 set, where the number 700 cannot be included because the problem calls for integers "greater than 700." So, in the 700–799 set, there are only 8 options for when the tens and ones are the same. This is shown in the table below.

Number of digits available for the third digit when two given digits are the same

Same	701–799	800–899	900–999
tens and ones	8	9	9
hundreds and tens	9	9	9
hundreds and ones	9	9	9

Thus, of the three-digit integers greater than 700, there are 9(9) – 1 = 80 numbers that have two digits that are equal to each other when the remaining digit is different from these two.

The correct answer is C.

12. Positive integer y is 50 percent of 50 percent of positive integer x, and y percent of x equals 100. What is the value of x?

(A) 50
(B) 100
(C) 200
(D) 1,000
(E) 2,000

Arithmetic; Algebra Percents Simultaneous equations

Because y is a positive integer, y percent is notated as $\frac{y}{100}$. According to the problem,

$y = 0.50(0.50x)$ and $\left(\frac{y}{100}\right)x = 100$.

The first equation simplifies to $y = 0.25x$, and multiplying the second equation by 100 gives $xy = 10{,}000$.

Substituting the simplified first equation into this second equation gives:

$x(0.25x) = 10{,}000$

$0.25x^2 = 10{,}000$ simplify left side

$x^2 = 40{,}000$ divide both sides by 0.25

$x = 200$ solve for the value of x

The correct answer is C.

13. If s and t are positive integers such that $\frac{s}{t} = 64.12$, which of the following could be the remainder when s is divided by t?

(A) 2
(B) 4
(C) 8
(D) 20
(E) 45

Arithmetic Operations on rational numbers

By using a long division model, it can be seen that the remainder after dividing s by t is $s - 64t$:

$$\begin{array}{r} 64 \\ t\overline{)\ \ \ s} \\ \underline{-64t} \\ s-64t \end{array}$$

Then, the given equation can be written as $64.12t = s$. By splitting portions of t into its integer multiple and its decimal multiple, this becomes $64t + 0.12t = s$, or $0.12t = s - 64t$, which is the remainder. So, $0.12t$ = remainder. Test the answer choices to find the situation in which t is an integer.

A	$0.12t = 2$ or $t = 16.67$	NOT an integer
B	$0.12t = 4$ or $t = 33.33$	NOT an integer
C	$0.12t = 8$ or $t = 66.67$	NOT an integer
D	$0.12t = 20$ or $t = 166.67$	NOT an integer
E	$0.12t = 45$ or $t = 375$	INTEGER

The correct answer is E.

14. Of the 84 parents who attended a meeting at a school, 35 volunteered to supervise children during the school picnic and 11 volunteered both to supervise children during the picnic and to bring refreshments to the picnic. If the number of parents who volunteered to bring refreshments was 1.5 times the number of parents who neither volunteered to supervise children during the picnic nor volunteered to bring refreshments, how many of the parents volunteered to bring refreshments?

(A) 25
(B) 36
(C) 38
(D) 42
(E) 45

Arithmetic Operations on rational numbers

Out of the 35 parents who agreed to supervise children during the school picnic, 11 parents are also bringing refreshments, so $35 - 11 = 24$ parents are only supervising children. Let x be the number of parents who volunteered to bring refreshments, and let y be the number of parents who declined to supervise or to bring refreshments. The fact that the number of parents who volunteered to bring refreshments is 1.5 times the number who did not volunteer at all can then be expressed as $x = 1.5y$. A Venn diagram, such as the one below, can be helpful in answering problems of this kind.

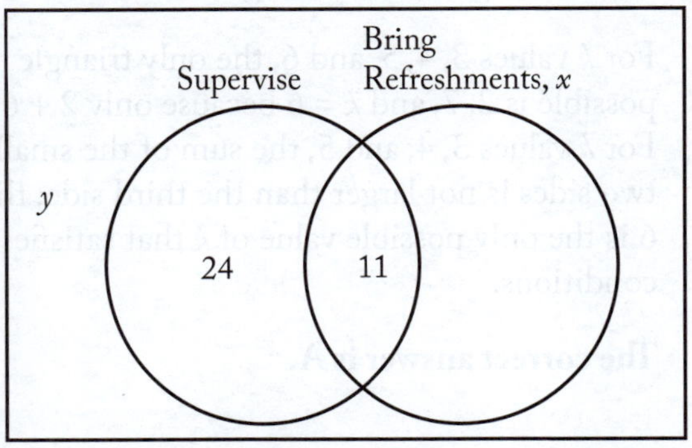

Then, the sum of the sections can be set equal to the total number of parents at the picnic, and the equation can be solved for y:

$y + 24 + x = 84$	sum of sections = total parents at picnic
$y + x = 60$	subtract 24 from each side
$y = 60 - x$	subtract x from each side

Then, substituting the value $60 - x$ for y in the equation $x = 1.5y$ gives the following:

$x = 1.5(60 - x)$	
$x = 90 - 1.5x$	distribute the 1.5
$2.5x = 90$	add $1.5x$ to both sides
$x = 36$	divide both sides by 2.5

The correct answer is B.

15. The product of all the prime numbers less than 20 is closest to which of the following powers of 10 ?

(A) 10^9
(B) 10^8
(C) 10^7
(D) 10^6
(E) 10^5

Arithmetic Properties of numbers

The prime numbers less than 20 are 2, 3, 5, 7, 11, 13, 17, and 19. Their product is 9,699,690 (arrived at as follows: $2 \times 3 \times 5 \times 7 \times 11 \times 13 \times 17 \times 19 = 9{,}699{,}690$). This is closest to $10{,}000{,}000 = 10^7$ ($10 \times 10 \times 10 \times 10 \times 10 \times 10 \times 10 = 10{,}000{,}000$).

The correct answer is C.

16. If $\sqrt{3-2x} = \sqrt{2x} + 1$ then, $4x^2 =$

(A) 1
(B) 4
(C) $2 - 2x$
(D) $4x - 2$
(E) $6x - 1$

Algebra Second-degree equations

Work with the equation to create $4x^2$ on one side.

$\sqrt{3-2x} = \sqrt{2x}+1$	
$\left(\sqrt{3-2x}\right)^2 = \left(\sqrt{2x}+1\right)^2$	square both sides
$3-2x = 2x+2\sqrt{2x}+1$	
$2-4x = 2\sqrt{2x}$	move all non-square-root terms to one side (i.e., subtract $2x$ and 1)
$1-2x = \sqrt{2x}$	divide both sides by 2
$(1-2x)^2 = \left(\sqrt{2x}\right)^2$	square both sides
$1-4x+4x^2 = 2x$	
$4x^2 = 6x-1$	isolate the $4x^2$ (add $4x$ and subtract 1 from both sides)

The correct answer is E.

17. If $n = \sqrt{\frac{16}{81}}$, what is the value of $\sqrt{n}$?

(A) $\frac{1}{9}$

(B) $\frac{1}{4}$

(C) $\frac{4}{9}$

(D) $\frac{2}{3}$

(E) $\frac{9}{2}$

Arithmetic Operations on radical expressions

Work the problem.

Since $n = \sqrt{\frac{16}{81}} = \frac{4}{9}$, then $\sqrt{n} = \sqrt{\frac{4}{9}} = \frac{2}{3}$.

The correct answer is D.

18. If n is the product of the integers from 1 to 8, inclusive, how many different prime factors greater than 1 does n have?

(A) Four

(B) Five

(C) Six

(D) Seven

(E) Eight

Arithmetic Properties of numbers

If n is the product of the integers from 1 to 8, then its prime factors will be the prime numbers from 1 to 8. There are four prime numbers between 1 and 8: 2, 3, 5, and 7.

The correct answer is A.

19. If k is an integer and $2 < k < 7$, for how many different values of k is there a triangle with sides of lengths 2, 7, and k?

(A) One

(B) Two

(C) Three

(D) Four

(E) Five

Geometry Triangles

In a triangle, the sum of the smaller two sides must be larger than the largest side.

For k values 3, 4, 5, and 6, the only triangle possible is 2, 7, and $k = 6$ because only $2 + 6 > 7$. For k values 3, 4, and 5, the sum of the smaller two sides is not larger than the third side; thus, 6 is the only possible value of k that satisfies the conditions.

The correct answer is A.

20. A right circular cone is inscribed in a hemisphere so that the base of the cone coincides with the base of the hemisphere. What is the ratio of the height of the cone to the radius of the hemisphere?

(A) $\sqrt{3}:1$
(B) 1:1
(C) $\frac{1}{2}:1$
(D) $\sqrt{2}:1$
(E) 2:1

Geometry Volume

As the diagram below shows, the height of the cone will be the radius of the hemisphere, so the ratio is 1:1.

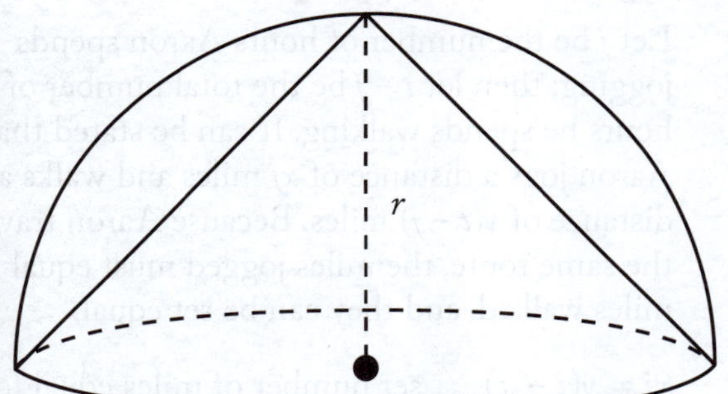

The correct answer is B.

21. John deposited $10,000 to open a new savings account that earned 4 percent annual interest, compounded quarterly. If there were no other transactions in the account, what was the amount of money in John's account 6 months after the account was opened?

(A) $10,100
(B) $10,101
(C) $10,200
(D) $10,201
(E) $10,400

Arithmetic Operations on rational numbers

Since John's account is compounded quarterly, he receives $\frac{1}{4}$ of his annual interest, or 1%, every 3 months. This is added to the amount already in the account to accrue interest for the next quarter. After 6 months, this process will have occurred twice, so the amount in John's account will then be ($10,000)(1.01)(1.01) = $10,000(1.01)^2 = $10,201.

The correct answer is D.

22. A container in the shape of a right circular cylinder is $\frac{1}{2}$ full of water. If the volume of water in the container is 36 cubic inches and the height of the container is 9 inches, what is the diameter of the base of the cylinder, in inches?

(A) $\frac{16}{9\pi}$
(B) $\frac{4}{\sqrt{\pi}}$
(C) $\frac{12}{\sqrt{\pi}}$
(D) $\sqrt{\frac{2}{\pi}}$
(E) $4\sqrt{\frac{2}{\pi}}$

Geometry Volume

For a right cylinder, volume = π(radius)^2(height). Since the volume of water is 36 cubic inches and since this represents $\frac{1}{2}$ the container, the water is occupying $\frac{1}{2}$ the container's height, or $9\left(\frac{1}{2}\right) = 4.5$ inches. Let r be the radius of the cylinder.

$36 = \pi r^2(4.5)$

$8 = \pi r^2$ divide both sides by 4.5

$\frac{8}{\pi} = r^2$ divide both sides by π

$\sqrt{\frac{8}{\pi}} = r$ take the square root of both sides

$\frac{2\sqrt{2}}{\sqrt{\pi}} = r$ simplify the $\sqrt{8}$ to get the radius

Then, since the diameter is twice the length of the radius, the diameter equals

$$2\left(\frac{2\sqrt{2}}{\sqrt{\pi}}\right)=4\frac{\sqrt{2}}{\sqrt{\pi}}=4\sqrt{\frac{2}{\pi}}.$$

The correct answer is E.

23. If the positive integer x is a multiple of 4 and the positive integer y is a multiple of 6, then xy must be a multiple of which of the following?

I. 8
II. 12
III. 18

(A) II only
(B) I and II only
(C) I and III only
(D) II and III only
(E) I, II, and III

Arithmetic **Properties of numbers**

The product xy must be a multiple of $4(6) = 24$ and any of its factors. Test each alternative.

I.	$\frac{24}{8}=3$	8 is a factor of 24 MUST be a multiple of 8
II.	$\frac{24}{12}=2$	12 is a factor of 24 MUST be a multiple of 12
III.	$\frac{24}{18}=1\frac{1}{3}$	18 is NOT a factor of 24 NEED NOT be a multiple of 18

The correct answer is B.

24. Aaron will jog from home at x miles per hour and then walk back home by the same route at y miles per hour. How many miles from home can Aaron jog so that he spends a total of t hours jogging and walking?

(A) $\frac{xt}{y}$

(B) $\frac{x+t}{xy}$

(C) $\frac{xyt}{x+y}$

(D) $\frac{x+y+t}{xy}$

(E) $\frac{y+t}{x}-\frac{t}{y}$

Algebra **Simplifying algebraic expressions**

Let j be the number of hours Aaron spends jogging; then let $t-j$ be the total number of hours he spends walking. It can be stated that Aaron jogs a distance of xj miles and walks a distance of $y(t-j)$ miles. Because Aaron travels the same route, the miles jogged must equal the miles walked, and they can be set equal.

$xj = y(t-j)$	set number of miles equal to each other
$xj = yt - jy$	distribute the y
$xj + jy = yt$	add jy to both sides to get all terms with j to one side
$j(x+y) = yt$	factor out the j
$j=\frac{yt}{x+y}.$	divide both sides by $x+y$

So, the number of hours Aaron spends jogging is $j=\frac{yt}{x+y}$.

The number of miles he can jog is xj or, by substitution of this value of j, $x\left(\frac{yt}{x+y}\right)=\frac{xyt}{x+y}$.

The correct answer is C.

Data Sufficiency

The following section on data sufficiency is intended to familiarize you with the most efficient and effective approaches to the kinds of problems common to data sufficiency. The particular questions in this chapter are generally representative of the kinds of data sufficiency questions you will encounter on the GMAT exam. Remember that it is the problem solving strategy that is important, not the specific details of a particular question.

25. If the units digit of integer n is greater than 2, what is the units digit of n?

    (1) The units digit of n is the same as the units digit of n^2.

    (2) The units digit of n is the same as the units digit of n^3.

Arithmetic Arithmetic operations

If the units digit of n is greater than 2, then it can only be the digits 3, 4, 5, 6, 7, 8, or 9.

(1) To solve this problem, it is necessary to find a digit that is the same as the units digit of its square. For example, both 43 squared (1,849) and 303 squared (91,809) have a units digit of 9, which is different from the units digit of 43 and 303. However, 25 squared (625) and 385 squared (148,225) both have a units digit of 5, and 16 and 226 both have a units digit of 6 and their squares (256 and 51,076, respectively) do, too. However, there is no further information to choose between 5 or 6; NOT sufficient.

(2) Once again, 5 and 6 are the only numbers which, when cubed, will both have a 5 or 6 respectively in their units digits. However, the information given does not distinguish between them; NOT sufficient.

Since (1) and (2) together yield the same information but with no direction as to which to choose, there is not enough information to determine the answer.

The correct answer is E;
both statements together are still not sufficient.

26. What is the value of the integer p?

    (1) Each of the integers 2, 3, and 5 is a factor of p.

    (2) Each of the integers 2, 5, and 7 is a factor of p.

Arithmetic Properties of numbers

(1) These are factors of p, but it is not clear that they are the only factors of p; NOT sufficient.

(2) These are factors of p, but it is not clear that they are the only factors of p; NOT sufficient.

Taken together, (1) and (2) overlap, but again there is no clear indication that these are the only factors of p.

The correct answer is E;
both statements together are still not sufficient.

27. If the length of Wanda's telephone call was rounded up to the nearest whole minute by her telephone company, then Wanda was charged for how many minutes for her telephone call?

    (1) The total charge for Wanda's telephone call was \$6.50.

    (2) Wanda was charged \$0.50 more for the first minute of the telephone call than for each minute after the first.

Arithmetic Arithmetic operations

(1) This does not give any information as to the call's cost per minute; NOT sufficient.

(2) From this, it can be determined only that the call was longer than one minute and that the charge for the first minute was \$0.50 more than the charge for each succeeding minute; NOT sufficient.

Taking (1) and (2) together, the number of minutes cannot be determined as long as the cost of each minute after the first is unknown. For example, if the cost of each minute after the first minute were \$0.40, then the cost of the first minute would be \$0.90. Then the total cost of the other minutes would be \$6.50 – \$0.90 = \$5.60, and \$5.60 ÷ \$0.40 would yield 14. In this case, the time of the call would be 1 + 14 = 15 minutes. If, however, the cost of each minute after the first minute were \$0.15, then the cost of the first minute would be \$0.65. Then \$6.50 – \$0.65 would be \$5.85, and this in turn, when divided by \$0.15, would yield 39 minutes, for a total call length of 40 minutes. More information on the cost of each minute after the first minute is still needed.

The correct answer is E;
both statements together are still not sufficient.

28. What is the perimeter of isosceles triangle *MNP* ?

(1) $MN = 16$
(2) $NP = 20$

Geometry Triangles

The perimeter of a triangle is the sum of all three sides. In the case of an isosceles triangle, two of the sides are equal. To determine the perimeter of this triangle, it is necessary to know both the length of an equal side and the length of the base of the triangle.

(1) Only gives the length of one side; NOT sufficient.

(2) Only gives the length of one side; NOT sufficient.

Since it is unclear whether *MN* or *NP* is one of the equal sides, it is not possible to determine the length of the third side or the perimeter of the triangle. The perimeter could be either $((2)(16)) + 20 = 52$ or $((2)(20)) + 16 = 56$.

The correct answer is E;
both statements together are still not sufficient.

29. In a survey of retailers, what percent had purchased computers for business purposes?

(1) 85 percent of the retailers surveyed who owned their own store had purchased computers for business purposes.

(2) 40 percent of the retailers surveyed owned their own store.

Arithmetic Percents

(1) With only this, it cannot be known what percent of the retailers not owning their own store had purchased computers, and so it cannot be known how many retailers purchased computers overall; NOT sufficient.

(2) While this permits the percent of owners and nonowners in the survey to be deduced, the overall percent of retailers who had purchased computers cannot be determined; NOT sufficient.

Using the information from both (1) and (2), the percent of surveyed owner-retailers who had purchased computers can be deduced, and the percent of nonowner-retailers can also be deduced. However, the information that would permit a determination of either the percent of nonowner-retailers who had purchased computers or the overall percent of all retailers (both owners and nonowners) who had purchased computers is still not provided.

The correct answer is E;
both statements together are still not sufficient.

30. The only gift certificates that a certain store sold yesterday were worth either \$100 each or \$10 each. If the store sold a total of 20 gift certificates yesterday, how many gift certificates worth \$10 each did the store sell yesterday?

(1) The gift certificates sold by the store yesterday were worth a total of between \$1,650 and \$1,800.

(2) Yesterday the store sold more than 15 gift certificates worth \$100 each.

Algebra Applied problems; Simultaneous equations; Inequalities

Let x represent the number of \$100 certificates sold, and let y represent the number of \$10 certificates sold. Then the given information can be expressed as $x + y = 20$ or thus $y = 20 - x$. The value of the \$100 certificates sold is $100x$, and the value of the \$10 certificates sold is $10y$.

(1) From this, it is known that $100x + 10y > 1{,}650$. Since $y = 20 - x$, this value can be substituted for y, and the inequality can be solved for x:

$100x + 10y > 1{,}650$	
$100x + 10(20 - x) > 1{,}650$	substitute for y
$100x + 200 - 10x > 1{,}650$	distribute
$90x + 200 > 1{,}650$	simplify
$90x > 1{,}450$	subtract 200 from both sides
$x > 16.1$	

Thus, more than 16 of the \$100 certificates were sold. If 17 \$100 certificates were sold, then it must be that 3 \$10 certificates were also sold for a total of \$1,730, which satisfies the condition of being between \$1,650 and \$1,800. If, however, 18 \$100 certificates were sold, then it must be that 2 \$10 certificates were sold, and this totals \$1,820, which is more than \$1,800 and fails to satisfy the condition. Therefore, 3 of the \$10 certificates were sold; SUFFICIENT.

(2) From this it can be known only that the number of \$10 certificates sold was 4 or fewer; NOT sufficient.

The correct answer is A;
statement 1 alone is sufficient.

31. Is the standard deviation of the set of measurements $x_1, x_2, x_3, x_4, \ldots, x_{20}$ less than 3 ?

(1) The variance for the set of measurements is 4.
(2) For each measurement, the difference between the mean and that measurement is 2.

Arithmetic Statistics

In determining the standard deviation, the difference between each measurement and the mean is squared, and then the squared differences are added and divided by the number of measurements. The quotient is the variance and the positive square root of the variance is the standard deviation.

(1) If the variance is 4, then the standard deviation $= \sqrt{4} = 2$, which is less than 3; SUFFICIENT.

(2) For each measurement, the difference between the mean and that measurement is 2. Therefore, the square of each difference is 4, and the sum of all the squares is $4 \times 20 = 80$. The standard deviation is $\sqrt{\frac{80}{20}} = \sqrt{4} = 2$, which is less than 3; SUFFICIENT.

The correct answer is D;
each statement alone is sufficient.

32. Is the range of the integers 6, 3, y, 4, 5, and x greater than 9 ?

(1) $y > 3x$
(2) $y > x > 3$

Arithmetic Statistics

The range of a set of integers is equal to the difference between the largest integer and the smallest integer. The range of the set of integers 3, 4, 5, and 6 is 3, which is derived from 6 – 3.

(1) Although it is known that $y > 3x$, the value of x is unknown. If, for example, $x = 1$, then the value of y would be greater than 3. However, if $x = 2$, then the value of y would be greater than 6, and, since 6 would no longer be the largest integer, the range would be affected. Because the actual values of x and y are unknown, the value of the range is also unknown; NOT sufficient.

(2) If $x > 3$ and $y > x$, then x could be 4 and y could be 5. Then the range of the 6 integers would still be 6 – 3 or 3. However, if x were 4 and y were 15, then the range of the 6 integers would be 15 – 3, or 12. There is no means to establish the values of x and y, beyond the fact that they both are greater than 3; NOT sufficient.

Taking (1) and (2) together, it is known that $x > 3$ and that $y > 3x$. Since the smallest integer that x could be is thus 4, then $y > 3(4)$ or $y > 12$. Therefore, the integer y must be 13 or larger. When y is equal to 13, the range of the 6 integers is $13 - 3 = 10$, which is larger than 9. As y increases in value, the value of the range will also increase.

The correct answer is C;
both statements together are sufficient.

33. Is $\frac{5^{x+2}}{25} < 1$?

(1) $5^x < 1$

(2) $x < 0$

Algebra Inequalities

Note that $x^{r+s} = (x^r)(x^s)$

(1) If $5^x < 1$, then $\frac{5^{x+2}}{25} < 1$ since $\frac{5^{x+2}}{25} = \frac{5^x \cdot 5^2}{25} = 5^x$; SUFFICIENT.

(2) If $x < 0$, then

$x + 2 < 2$ add 2 to both sides

$5^{x+2} < 5^2$ because $a < b$ implies $5^a < 5^b$

$\frac{5^{x+2}}{25} < 1$ divide both sides by $5^2 = 25$;

SUFFICIENT.

The correct answer is D;
each statement alone is sufficient.

34. Of the companies surveyed about the skills they required in prospective employees, 20 percent required both computer skills and writing skills. What percent of the companies surveyed required neither computer skills nor writing skills?

(1) Of those companies surveyed that required computer skills, half required writing skills.

(2) 45 percent of the companies surveyed required writing skills but not computer skills.

Arithmetic Percents

The surveyed companies could be placed into one of the following four categories:

1. Requiring computer skills and requiring writing skills
2. Requiring computer skills but not requiring writing skills
3. Not requiring computer skills but requiring writing skills
4. Not requiring either computer skills or writing skills

It is given that 20 percent of the surveyed companies fell into category 1. It is necessary to determine what percent of the surveyed companies fell into category 4.

(1) This helps identify the percentage in category 2. Since $\frac{1}{2}$ the companies that required computer skills also required writing skills (i.e., those in category 1), then the other $\frac{1}{2}$ of the companies that required computer skills did not require writing skills (thus category 2 = category 1). However, this information only establishes that 20 percent required computer skills, but not writing skills; NOT sufficient.

(2) While this establishes category 3, that is, that 45 percent required writing skills but not computer skills, no further information is available; NOT sufficient.

Taking (1) and (2) together, the first three categories add up to 85 percent (20 + 20 + 45). Therefore, category 4 would be equal to 100 – 85 = 15 percent of the surveyed companies required neither computer skills nor writing skills.

The correct answer is C;
both statements together are sufficient.

35. What is the value of $w + q$?

(1) $3w = 3 - 3q$

(2) $5w + 5q = 5$

Algebra First- and second-degree equations

(1) If $3q$ is added to both sides of this equation, it can be rewritten as $3w + 3q = 3$. When each term is then divided by 3, it yields $w + q = 1$; SUFFICIENT.

(2) When each term in this equation is divided by 5, it becomes $w + q = 1$; SUFFICIENT.

The correct answer is D;
each statement alone is sufficient.

36. If X and Y are points in a plane and X lies inside the circle C with center O and radius 2, does Y lie inside circle C?

(1) The length of line segment XY is 3.

(2) The length of line segment OY is 1.5.

Geometry Circles

(1) The maximum distance between two points that lie on a circle is equal to the diameter, or 2 times the radius. Since the radius of circle C is 2, the diameter in this case is 4. It cannot be assumed, however, that X and Y are points on the diameter; X can lie anywhere within the circle. When the distance between X and Y is 3, it is still possible either that Y is within the circle or that Y is outside the circle; NOT sufficient.

(2) If the length of the line segment OY is 1.5 and the circle has a radius of 2, then the distance from the center O to point Y is less than the radius, and point Y must therefore lie within the circle; SUFFICIENT.

The correct answer is B; statement 2 alone is sufficient.

37. Is $x > y$?

(1) $x = y + 2$

(2) $\frac{x}{2} = y - 1$

Algebra First- and second-degree equations

(1) Since 2 has to be added to y in order to make it equal to x, it can be reasoned that $x > y$; SUFFICIENT.

(2) Multiplying both sides of this equation by 2 results in $x = 2(y - 1)$ or $x = 2y - 2$. If y were 0, then x would be -2, and y would be greater than x. If y were a negative number like -2, then $x = 2(-2) - 2 = 6$, and again y would be greater than x. However, if y were a positive number such as 4, then $x = 2(4) - 2 = 6$, and $x > y$. Since there is no other information concerning the value of y, it cannot be determined if $x > y$; NOT sufficient.

The correct answer is A; statement 1 alone is sufficient.

38. If Paula drove the distance from her home to her college at an average speed that was greater than 70 kilometers per hour, did it take her less than 3 hours to drive this distance?

(1) The distance that Paula drove from her home to her college was greater than 200 kilometers.

(2) The distance that Paula drove from her home to her college was less than 205 kilometers.

Arithmetic Distance problem

A distance problem uses the formula distance = rate × time. To find the time, the formula would be rearranged as time = $\frac{\text{distance}}{\text{rate}}$. To solve this problem, it is necessary to know the rate (given here as 70 kilometers per hour) and the distance.

(1) If D is the distance Paula drove then $D > 200$ and $\frac{D}{70} > \frac{200}{70} = 2\frac{6}{7}$ so $t > 2\frac{6}{7}$ and t may or may not be less than 3; NOT sufficient.

(2) If D is the distance Paula drove then $D < 205$ and $\frac{D}{70} < \frac{205}{70} = 2\frac{13}{14}$ so $t < 2\frac{13}{14} < 3$; SUFFICIENT.

The correct answer is B; statement 2 alone is sufficient.

39. In the xy-plane, if line k has negative slope and passes through the point $(-5,r)$, is the x-intercept of line k positive?

(1) The slope of line k is -5.

(2) $r > 0$

Geometry Coordinate geometry

The x-intercept is the x-coordinate of the point in which the line k crosses the x-axis and would have the coordinates $(x,0)$.

(1) Knowing the slope of the line does not help in determining the x-intercept, since from point $(-5,r)$ the line k extends in both directions. Without knowing the value of r, the x-intercept could be -5 if r were 0, or it could be other numbers, both positive and negative, depending on the value of r; NOT sufficient.

(2) Knowing that $r > 0$ suggests that the x-intercept is not -5; the point $(-5,r)$, where r is a positive number, does lie in quadrant II. It could, however, be any point with an x-coordinate of -5 in that quadrant and line k could have any negative slope, and so the line k would vary with the value of r. Therefore, the x-intercept of line k cannot be determined; NOT sufficient.

Using (1) and (2) together does not help in the determination of the x-intercept, since the point $(-5,r)$ could have any positive y-coordinate and thus line k could cross the x-axis at many different places.

The correct answer is E;
both statements together are still not sufficient.

40. If \$5,000 invested for one year at p percent simple annual interest yields \$500, what amount must be invested at k percent simple annual interest for one year to yield the same number of dollars?

(1) $k = 0.8p$

(2) $k = 8$

Arithmetic Interest problem

With simple annual interest, the formula to use is interest = principal × rate × time. It is given that $\$500 = \$5{,}000 \times \frac{p}{100} \times 1$ (year), so $p = 10$ percent interest.

(1) If p is 10 percent, then $k = 0.8\,p$ is 0.08. Using the same formula, the time is again 1 year; the interest is the same amount; and the rate is 0.08, or 8 percent. Thus, $\$500 = \text{principal} \times 0.08 \times 1$, or principal \$6,250; SUFFICIENT.

(2) If $k = 8$, then the rate is 8 percent, and the same formula and procedure as above are employed again; SUFFICIENT.

The correct answer is D;
each statement alone is sufficient.

41. If $\frac{x+y}{z} > 0$, is $x < 0$?

(1) $x < y$

(2) $z < 0$

Algebra Inequalities

If $\frac{x+y}{z} > 0$, then either one of two cases holds true. Either $(x+y) > 0$ **and** $z > 0$, or $(x+y) < 0$ **and** $z < 0$. In other words, in order for the term to be greater than zero, it must be true that either 1) both the numerator and denominator are greater than 0 or 2) both the numerator and denominator are less than 0.

(1) Regardless of whether $(x+y)$ is positive or negative, the positive or negative value of z must be in agreement with the sign of $(x+y)$ in order for $\frac{x+y}{z} > 0$. However, there is no information about z here; NOT sufficient.

(2) If $z < 0$, then $(x+y)$ must be less than 0. However, this statement gives no information about $(x+y)$; NOT sufficient.

This can be solved using (1) and (2) together. From (2), it is known that $z < 0$, and, going back to the original analysis, for the term to be greater than zero, $(x+y)$ must also be less than 0. If $x + y < 0$ then $x < -y$. But $x < y$ from (1) so

$$x + x < -y + y$$
$$2x < 0$$
$$x < 0.$$

The correct answer is C;
both statements together are sufficient.

42. Does the integer k have at least three different positive prime factors?

(1) $\frac{k}{15}$ is an integer.

(2) $\frac{k}{10}$ is an integer.

Arithmetic Properties of numbers

(1) The prime factors of 15 are 3 and 5. So in this case, k has at least 2 different positive prime factors, but it is unknown if there are more positive prime factors; NOT sufficient.

(2) The prime factors of 10 are 2 and 5, showing that k has at least these 2 different positive prime factors, but k might or might not have more; NOT sufficient.

Taking (1) and (2) together, since k is divisible by both 10 and 15, it must be divisible by their different positive prime factors of 2, 3, and 5. Thus k has at least 3 different positive prime factors.

The correct answer is C;
both statements together are sufficient.

43. In City X last April, was the average (arithmetic mean) daily high temperature greater than the median daily high temperature?

(1) In City X last April, the sum of the 30 daily high temperatures was 2,160°.

(2) In City X last April, 60 percent of the daily high temperatures were less than the average daily high temperature.

Arithmetic Statistics

The formula for calculating the arithmetic mean, or the average, is as follows:

$$\text{Average} = \frac{\text{sum of } v \text{ values}}{v}$$

(1) These data will produce an average of $\frac{2160}{30} = 72°$ for last April in City X. However, there is no information regarding the median for comparison; NOT sufficient.

(2) The median is the middle temperature of the data. As such, 50 percent of the daily high temperatures will be at or above the median, and 50 percent will be at or below the median. If 60 percent of the daily high temperatures were less than the average daily high temperature, then the average of the daily highs must be greater than the median; SUFFICIENT.

The correct answer is B;
statement 2 alone is sufficient.

44. If m and n are positive integers, is $\left(\sqrt{m}\right)^n$ an integer?

(1) $\left(\sqrt{m}\right)$ is an integer.

(2) $\left(\sqrt{n}\right)$ is an integer.

Arithmetic Properties of numbers

(1) If $\left(\sqrt{m}\right)$ is an integer and n is a positive integer, then $\left(\sqrt{m}\right)^n$ is an integer because an integer raised to a positive integer is an integer; SUFFICIENT.

(2) The information that $\left(\sqrt{n}\right)$ is an integer is not helpful in answering the question. For example, if $m = 2$ and $n = 9$, $\sqrt{9} = 3$, which is an integer, but $\left(\sqrt{2}\right)^9 = \left(16\sqrt{2}\right)$, which is not an integer. But if $m = 4$ and $n = 9$, then $\sqrt{9} = 3$, which is an integer, and $\left(\sqrt{4}\right)^9 = 2^9 = 512$ is an integer; NOT sufficient.

The correct answer is A;
statement 1 alone is sufficient.

45. Of the 66 people in a certain auditorium, at most 6 people have birthdays in any one given month. Does at least one person in the auditorium have a birthday in January?

(1) More of the people in the auditorium have birthdays in February than in March.

(2) Five of the people in the auditorium have birthdays in March.

Algebra Sets and functions

Because it is given that 6 is the greatest number of individuals who can have birthdays in any particular month, these 66 people could be evenly distributed across 11 of the 12 months of the year. That is to say, it could be possible for the distribution to be $11 \times 6 = 66$, and thus any given month, such as January, would not have a person with a birthday. Assume that January has no people with birthdays, and see if this assumption is disproved.

(1) The information that more people have February birthdays than March birthdays indicates that the distribution is not even. Therefore, March is underrepresented and must thus have fewer than 6 birthdays. Since no month can have more than 6 people with birthdays, and every month but January already has as many people with birthdays as it can have, January has to have at least 1 person with a birthday; SUFFICIENT.

(2) Again, March is underrepresented with only 5 birthdays, and none of the other months can have more than 6 birthdays. Therefore, the extra birthday (from March) must occur in January; SUFFICIENT.

The correct answer is D;
each statement alone is sufficient.

46. Last year the average (arithmetic mean) salary of the 10 employees of Company X was $42,800. What is the average salary of the same 10 employees this year?

(1) For 8 of the 10 employees, this year's salary is 15 percent greater than last year's salary.

(2) For 2 of the 10 employees, this year's salary is the same as last year's salary.

Arithmetic Statistics

(1) Since all 10 employees did not receive the same 15 percent increase, it cannot be assumed that the mean this year is 15 percent higher than last year. It remains unknown whether these 8 salaries were the top 8 salaries, the bottom 8 salaries, or somewhere in-between. Without this type of information from last year, the mean for this year cannot be determined; NOT sufficient.

(2) If 2 salaries remained the same as last year, then 8 salaries changed. Without further information about the changes, the mean for this year cannot be determined; NOT sufficient.

Even taking (1) and (2) together, it remains impossible to tell the mean salary for this year without additional data.

The correct answer is E;
both statements together are still not sufficient.

47. In a certain classroom, there are 80 books, of which 24 are fiction and 23 are written in Spanish. How many of the fiction books are written in Spanish?

(1) Of the fiction books, there are 6 more that are not written in Spanish than are written in Spanish.

(2) Of the books written in Spanish, there are 5 more nonfiction books than fiction books.

Algebra Sets and functions

Let x represent the fiction books that are written in Spanish. A table could be set up like the one below, filling in the information that is known or able to be known:

	Spanish	Non-Spanish	Total
Fiction	x		24
Nonfiction			56
Total	23	57	80

(1) If x represents the fiction books written in Spanish, then $x + 6$ can now be used to represent the fiction books that are not written in Spanish. From the table above, it can be seen then that $x + x + 6 = 24$, or $2x = 18$. Therefore, x, or the number of fiction books written in Spanish, is 9; SUFFICIENT.

(2) If x represents the fiction books written in Spanish, then $x + 5$ can now be used to represent the nonfiction books written in Spanish. From the table, it can be said that $x + x + 5 = 23$, or $2x = 18$. Therefore, x, or the number of fiction books written in Spanish, is 9; SUFFICIENT.

The correct answer is D;
each statement alone is sufficient.

48. If p is the perimeter of rectangle Q, what is the value of p?

(1) Each diagonal of rectangle Q has length 10.

(2) The area of rectangle Q is 48.

Geometry Rectangles; Perimeter; Area

The perimeter of a rectangle is equal to 2 times the rectangle's length plus 2 times the rectangle's width, or $p = 2l + 2w$. The diagonals of a rectangle are equal. In a rectangle, because a diagonal forms a right triangle, the length of a diagonal is equal to the square root of the length squared plus the width squared, or $d = \sqrt{l^2 + w^2}$.

(1) If a diagonal = 10, then $10 = \sqrt{l^2 + w^2}$, or, by squaring both sides, $100 = l^2 + w^2$. Without knowing the value or the relationship between the other two sides of the right triangle, it is impossible to solve for l or w, and thus for the perimeter of the rectangle; NOT sufficient.

(2) If the area of the rectangle is 48, then it can be stated that $lw = 48$. However, without further information, the perimeter cannot be determined. For example, l could be 6 and w could be 8, and the perimeter would then be $12 + 16 = 28$. However, it could also be that l is 4 and w is 12, and in that case the perimeter would be $8 + 24 = 32$; NOT sufficient.

Using (1) and (2) together, it is possible to solve this problem. Since from (2) $lw = 48$, then $w = \frac{48}{l}$. Substituting this into $100 = l^2 + w^2$ from (1) the equation can be solved as follows:

$100 = l^2 + \left(\frac{48}{l}\right)^2$	substitution
$100l^2 = l^4 + 2{,}304$	multiply both sides by l^2
$l^4 - 100l^2 + 2{,}304 = 0$	move all terms to one side
$(l^2 - 64)(l^2 - 36) = 0$	factor like a quadratic
$l^2 = 64,\ l^2 = 36$	solve for l^2

Since l is a length, it must be positive, so l is either 8 or 6. When $l = 8, w = \frac{48}{8} = 6$, and when $l = 6, w = \frac{48}{6} = 8$, both of which give the same perimeter.

The correct answer is C;
both statements together are sufficient.

3.6 Verbal Answer Explanations

Reading Comprehension

The following discussion is intended to familiarize you with the most efficient and effective approaches to the kinds of problems common to reading comprehension. The particular questions in this chapter are generally representative of the kinds of reading comprehension questions you will encounter on the GMAT exam. Remember that it is the problem solving strategy that is important, not the specific details of a particular question.

Questions 1–5 refer to the passage on page 23.

49. Which of the following best describes the purpose of the sentence in lines 10–15 ?

(A) To show that economic signaling theory fails to explain a finding

(B) To introduce a distinction not accounted for by economic signaling theory

(C) To account for an exception to a generalization suggested by Marquardt and McGann

(D) To explain why Marquardt and McGann's research was conducted

(E) To offer an explanation for an observation reported by Marquardt and McGann

Logical structure

Marquardt and McGann found a correlation between highly advertised products and high-quality products. The connection can be explained by understanding that companies may invest heavily in such advertising, anticipating that recurring purchases of high-quality products will eventually recover these advertising costs. The consumers will continue to buy these products over time because of loyalty to their high quality. The statement in bold provides this explanation for the correlation noted by Marquardt and McGann.

A The sentence does not explain a failure of the economic signaling theory.

B Economic signaling theory is about perceptions of quality, but this explanation is about actual quality and its correlation with advertising.

C No exception is mentioned in Marquardt and McGann's work.

D The sentence does not examine why or how the research was undertaken.

E **Correct.** This statement provides an explanation of why highly advertised products *did indeed rank high on certain measures of product quality.*

The correct answer is E.

50. The primary purpose of the passage is to

(A) present findings that contradict one explanation for the effects of a particular advertising practice

(B) argue that theoretical explanations about the effects of a particular advertising practice are of limited value without empirical evidence

(C) discuss how and why particular advertising practices may affect consumers' perceptions

(D) contrast the research methods used in two different studies of a particular advertising practice

(E) explain why a finding about consumer responses to a particular advertising practice was unexpected

Main idea

The primary purpose can be determined only by evaluating the whole passage. The first paragraph discusses consumers' perceptions of quality based on frequency of advertising. The second paragraph discusses three studies that show how consumers base their evaluations of products on the kinds of advertising they see. Therefore, the purpose of the whole passage is to show how consumers' perceptions of products are shaped by certain advertising practices.

A The passage shows that expensive advertising works to a certain point, but not after it; this method examines a continuum, not a contradiction.

B Most of the passage is devoted to empirical evidence.

C **Correct.** The passage shows how the frequency and the kind of advertising influence consumers' perceptions about the quality of the products advertised.

D The passage reports the findings of four studies but does not mention research methods.

E The passage does not indicate that any of the findings were unexpected.

The correct answer is C.

51. Kirmani's research, as described in the passage, suggests which of the following regarding consumers' expectations about the quality of advertised products?

(A) Those expectations are likely to be highest if a manufacturer runs both black-and-white and color advertisements for the same product.

(B) Those expectations can be shaped by the presence of color in an advertisement as well as by the frequency with which an advertisement appears.

(C) Those expectations are usually high for frequently advertised new brands but not for frequently advertised familiar brands.

(D) Those expectations are likely to be higher for products whose black-and-white advertisements are often repeated than for those whose color advertisements are less often repeated.

(E) Those expectations are less definitively shaped by the manufacturer's advertisements than by information that consumers gather from other sources.

Inference

The question's use of the word *suggests* means that the answer depends on making an inference. This research is discussed in the second paragraph. Kirmani found that too much advertising tended to make the consumers believe that manufacturers were desperate. The use of color was also found to affect consumers' perceptions of brand quality. Realizing that color advertising is more expensive than black-and-white, consumers react more quickly to what they perceive to be its overuse than they do to a repetition of black-and-white advertisements.

A This situation is not discussed in the research, at least as it is reported in this passage.

B **Correct.** It can be inferred that consumers' perceptions of product quality are influenced by the use of color in an advertisement and by the frequency of the advertisement's appearance.

C The research does not make a distinction between new and familiar brands.

D The research indicates only that consumers can tolerate black-and-white advertisements for a longer time than color advertisements before dismissing them as excessive.

E There is no discussion of what consumers learn from other sources.

The correct answer is B.

52. Kirmani's third study, as described in the passage, suggests which of the following conclusions about a black-and-white advertisement?

(A) It can be repeated more frequently than a comparable color advertisement could before consumers begin to suspect low manufacturer confidence in the quality of the advertised product.

(B) It will have the greatest impact on consumers' perceptions of the quality of the advertised product if it appears during periods when a color version of the same advertisement is also being used.

(C) It will attract more attention from readers of the print publication in which it appears if it is used only a few times.

(D) It may be perceived by some consumers as more expensive than a comparable color advertisement.

(E) It is likely to be perceived by consumers as a sign of higher manufacturer confidence in the quality of the advertised product than a comparable color advertisement would be.

Inference

Kirmani's third study is discussed in the final two sentences. Consumers suspect expensive advertising results from a manufacturer's lack of confidence in the quality of the product. Consumers reach the point at which they find advertising *excessive* more quickly with color advertising than with black-and-white advertising because they understand that the addition of color increases advertising expenses. It is reasonable to infer that the reverse is also true and thus that consumers will tolerate lengthier repetitions of black-and-white advertising without becoming suspicious of product quality.

A **Correct.** Consumers find color advertising excessive more quickly and thus can be expected to find black-and-white advertising excessive less quickly.

B The study does not discuss concurrent appearances of color and black-and-white advertisements for the same product.

C The sole conclusion about frequency is that consumers can tolerate a greater frequency of black-and-white advertisements than color advertisements.

D It is stated that consumers understand that color advertisements are more expensive.

E The research certainly does not report this finding.

The correct answer is A.

53. The passage suggests that Kirmani would be most likely to agree with which of the following statements about consumers' perceptions of the relationship between the frequency with which a product is advertised and the product's quality?

(A) Consumers' perceptions about the frequency with which an advertisement appears are their primary consideration when evaluating an advertisement's claims about product quality.

(B) Because most consumers do not notice the frequency of advertisement, it has little impact on most consumers' expectations regarding product quality.

(C) Consumers perceive frequency of advertisement as a signal about product quality only when the advertisement is for a product that is newly on the market.

(D) The frequency of advertisement is not always perceived by consumers to indicate that manufacturers are highly confident about their products' quality.

(E) Consumers who try a new product that has been frequently advertised are likely to perceive the advertisement's frequency as having been an accurate indicator of the product's quality.

Inference

The first sentence of the second paragraph provides the answer to this question: *at some level of spending the manufacturer's advertising effort may be perceived as unreasonably high, implying low manufacturer confidence in product quality*. Thus, it is logical to assume that if a product is advertised too frequently, consumers may believe that the manufacturer is spending excessive amounts on advertising because that manufacturer is not confident of the product's quality.

A Kirmani's research, as reported here, does not support this claim.

B Kirmani's research examines how consumers respond to the frequency of advertising; the research does not indicate that consumers do not notice frequency.

C The research does not distinguish between new and familiar products.

D **Correct**. Excessive advertising may lead consumers to believe that the manufacturer lacks confidence in the quality of the product.

E Kirmani's research does not specifically address new products.

The correct answer is D.

Questions 6–11 refer to the passage on page 25.

54. The main purpose of the passage is to

(A) propose an experiment

(B) analyze a function

(C) refute an argument

(D) explain a contradiction

(E) simulate a process

Main idea

Determining the main purpose comes from considering the passage as a whole. The first paragraph begins by noting that *the idea of the brain as an information processor* is generally accepted by neuroscientists. The author then presents Searle as an *enemy* of this position and explains Searle's belief that human thought is more than information processing. The second paragraph questions Searle's position, and the third asserts that the brain is an information processor, refuting Searle's argument.

A The author uses the idea of a mechanical simulation of a stomach as a metaphor for a computer's simulation of thought; this is not a proposal for an experiment.

B The author analyzes Searle's position, but no function is analyzed.

C **Correct**. The author explains Searle's argument in order to refute it.

D The author points out a weakness in Searle's thinking, but not a contradiction.

E The simulation of a process is included as a metaphor, but it is not essential to the passage.

The correct answer is C.

55. Which of the following is most consistent with Searle's reasoning as presented in the passage?

(A) Meaning and content cannot be reduced to algorithms.

(B) The process of digestion can be simulated mechanically, but not on a computer.

(C) Simulated thoughts and real thoughts are essentially similar because they are composed primarily of information.

(D) A computer can use "causal powers" similar to those of the human brain when processing information.

(E) Computer simulations of the world can achieve the complexity of the brain's representations of the world.

Evaluation

Searle's position is stated in the first paragraph: because computers merely follow algorithms, *they cannot deal with important aspects of human thought such as meaning and content*. Thus, Searle believes that meaning and content cannot be reduced to algorithms.

A **Correct**. Searle believes that meaning and content cannot be reduced to algorithms.

B The author argues for the mechanical simulation, but offers no evidence that Searle would agree.

C This statement reflects the author's position, but it is the opposite of Searle's.

D Searle asserts that only people, not computers, have *the causal powers of the brain*.

E The passage does not discuss computer simulations of the world.

The correct answer is A.

56. The author of the passage would be most likely to agree with which of the following statements about the simulation of organ functions?

(A) An artificial device that achieves the functions of the stomach could be considered a valid model of the stomach.

(B) Computer simulations of the brain are best used to crack the brain's codes of meaning and content.

(C) Computer simulations of the brain challenge ideas that are fundamental to psychology and neuroscience.

(D) Because the brain and the stomach both act as processors, they can best be simulated by mechanical devices.

(E) The computer's limitations in simulating digestion suggest equal limitations in computer-simulated thinking.

Application

To answer this question, think about how the author would respond to each statement. Anticipating the author's response depends on understanding the author's point of view. In this passage, the author is arguing against Searle's view of the brain and in favor of the brain as information processor. The author believes that the computer can be a model of the brain and uses the example of the mechanical stomach to support his position on simulations.

A **Correct**. The first two sentences of the third paragraph imply that a mechanical device is a valid model.

B The author believes a computer can simulate the brain but does not comment on how these simulations should be used. There is no way to predict the author's reaction to this statement.

C The author would reject this statement since neuroscience and psychology do in fact see the brain as an information processor.

D The author agrees that both the brain and the stomach act as processors; believes that the computer, a nonmechanical device, can simulate the brain; and offers a way that a mechanical device could simulate the stomach. The author does not suggest that mechanical devices are the best way to simulate both their processes.

E This statement reflects Searle's viewpoint, which the author rejects.

The correct answer is A.

57. It can be inferred that the author of the passage believes that Searle's argument is flawed by its failure to

(A) distinguish between syntactic and semantic operations

(B) explain adequately how people, unlike computers, are able to understand meaning

(C) provide concrete examples illustrating its claims about thinking

(D) understand how computers use algorithms to process information

(E) decipher the code that is transmitted from neuron to neuron in the brain

Inference

The author's attitude toward Searle's argument is apparent in the first paragraph, which ends with the author's summary of what Searle is saying. Computers understand structures, Searle argues, but only people understand meaning. How do people understand meaning? The author notes that Searle is not able to answer this question and is able only to assert that people have *causal powers of the brain*.

A The author makes it clear in the first paragraph that Searle does distinguish between the two. In Searle's view computers are syntactic, interpreting structure or arrangement, rather than semantic, understanding meaning.

B **Correct.** The first paragraph ends with the contrast between people and computers: *People, on the other hand, understand meaning because they have something Searle obscurely calls the causal powers of the brain*. By calling Searle's explanation obscure, the author implies that Searle has not adequately clarified how people understand meaning.

C Nothing in the passage criticizes Searle for not providing concrete examples. Indeed, in the second paragraph, the author anticipates how Searle would react to one concrete example, the computer simulation of the stomach.

D In the first paragraph, the author says that Searle argues that *computers simply follow algorithms*; whether or not Searle understands how they use algorithms is irrelevant.

E Since, as the author suggests in the first paragraph, Searle does not believe information could be a code transmitted from neuron to neuron, he cannot be expected to decipher that code.

The correct answer is B.

58. From the passage, it can be inferred that the author would agree with Searle on which of the following points?

(A) Computers operate by following algorithms.
(B) The human brain can never fully understand its own functions.
(C) The comparison of the brain to a machine is overly simplistic.
(D) The most accurate models of physical processes are computer simulations.
(E) Human thought and computer-simulated thought involve similar processes of representation.

Inference

An inference requires going beyond the material explicitly stated in the passage to the author's ideas that underlie that material. The author and Searle take opposite points of view on the brain as information processor. Their area of agreement is narrow. However, they do both agree that computers work by following algorithms.

A **Correct**. The first paragraph explains that Searle dismisses computers because they *simply follow algorithms*; while the author disagrees with Searle on virtually every other point, no disagreement is voiced here.

B The first paragraph shows this to be Searle's position, but not the author's.

C The first paragraph shows this to be Searle's position, but not the author's.

D The second paragraph explains Searle's rejection of this position.

E The final paragraph establishes this as the author's position, but not Searle's.

The correct answer is A.

59. Which of the following most accurately represents Searle's criticism of the brain-as-computer metaphor, as that criticism is described in the passage?

(A) The metaphor is not experimentally verifiable.
(B) The metaphor does not take into account the unique powers of the brain.
(C) The metaphor suggests that a brain's functions can be simulated as easily as those of a stomach.
(D) The metaphor suggests that a computer can simulate the workings of the mind by using the codes of neural transmission.
(E) The metaphor is unhelpful because both the brain and the computer process information.

Inference

Searle's criticism of the brain-as-computer metaphor is discussed in the first paragraph. Computers are merely machines; only people are endowed with *causal powers of the brain* that allow them to understand meaning and content.

A Searle does not believe in the value of the metaphor, so its verification is beside the point.

B **Correct**. Searle believes that people have something computers do not, *causal powers of the brain* for understanding *important aspects of human thought*.

C Comparing the brain to a computer, the metaphor does not make this suggestion.

D In the second paragraph, the author says, *but even if a computer could simulate the workings of the mind,* making it clear that presently it cannot; this statement does not reflect why Searle rejects the metaphor.

E This is not the basis of Searle's objection since he does not accept the premise that the brain is an information processor.

The correct answer is B.

Questions 12–17 refer to the passage on page 27.

60. The primary purpose of the passage is to

(A) explain why women reformers of the Progressive Era failed to achieve their goals
(B) discuss the origins of child labor laws in the late nineteenth and early twentieth centuries
(C) compare the living conditions of working-class and middle-class women in the Progressive Era
(D) discuss an oversight on the part of women reformers of the Progressive Era
(E) revise a traditional view of the role played by women reformers in enacting Progressive Era reforms

Main idea

Understanding the author's purpose comes only from reflecting on the passage as a whole. The beginning of the passage notes the success of middle-class women reformers in improving working conditions for women and children. The middle discusses the position of working-class mothers, who were more concerned with the economic survival of their families than with labor reform and consequently tried to circumvent the laws. The close of the passage observes that, although middle-class reformers were right to point out exploitation of children, they failed to understand the economic plight of working-class families, who needed the income earned by every possible member. The purpose of this passage is to show the failure of middle-class reformers to understand the economic position of working-class families.

A Lines 6–10 emphasize the victories of the reformers.

B The passage discusses the effects, rather than the origins, of child labor laws.

C Living conditions of middle-class and working-class women are not compared.

D **Correct.** As is made clear, especially in the final sentence of the passage, women reformers failed to understand the economic needs of working-class families.

E A traditional view is not compared with a newer, revised view of the reformers.

The correct answer is D.

61. The *view* mentioned in line 17 of the passage refers to which of the following?

(A) Some working-class mothers' resistance to the enforcement of child labor laws
(B) Reformers' belief that child labor and industrial home work should be abolished
(C) Reformers' opinions about how working-class families raised their children
(D) Certain women historians' observation that there was a lack of consensus between women of different classes on the issue of child labor and industrial home work
(E) Working-class families' fears about the adverse consequences that child labor laws would have on their ability to earn an adequate living

Inference

To find what this appearance of *view* refers to, it is necessary to look back to the beginning of the sentence. *This view*, not shared by working-class mothers, refers to the reformers' conviction that *child labor and industrial home work were equally inhumane practices that should be outlawed.*

A *This view* must refer back to a point already stated; resistance to child labor laws is not discussed until the following sentence.

B **Correct.** *This view* refers to the position of reformers stated earlier in the same sentence: that *child labor and industrial home work...should be outlawed.*

C *This view* must refer back to a point already stated; the reformers' belief that resistance to child labor laws was due to poor parenting is discussed later in the passage.

D A number of women historians have said that working-class mothers did not always share the *view* of middle-class women reformers about child labor.

E *This view* must refer back to a point already stated; the fears of working-class families are examined in the following sentence.

The correct answer is B.

62. The author of the passage mentions the observations of women historians (lines 15–17) most probably in order to

(A) provide support for an assertion made in the preceding sentence (lines 10–12)
(B) raise a question that is answered in the last sentence of the passage (lines 27–32)
(C) introduce an opinion that challenges a statement made in the first sentence of the passage
(D) offer an alternative view to the one attributed in the passage to working-class mothers
(E) point out a contradiction inherent in the traditional view of child labor reform as it is presented in the passage

Evaluation

In lines 10–12, the author asserts that child labor laws *pitted women of different classes against one another*. The view of the middle-class women reformers is stated, and then, to show that working-class mothers did not hold the same opinion, the author turns to the recent work of women historians to support this statement.

A **Correct.** The author uses the recent work of women historians to support the statement that women of different social classes were pitted against one another.

B The women historians *have recently observed*; the verb *observed* introduces a statement rather than a question.

C The reference to women historians has to do with working-class mothers; it does not challenge women's activism and role in social reform.

D The passage supports what the women historians say about working-class mothers.

E The author does not define or present the *traditional* view of child labor reform, nor is any inherent contradiction pointed out.

The correct answer is A.

63. The passage suggests that which of the following was a reason for the difference of opinion between working-class mothers and women reformers on the issue of child labor?

(A) Reformers' belief that industrial home work was preferable to child labor outside the home
(B) Reformers' belief that child labor laws should pertain to working conditions but not to pay
(C) Working-class mothers' resentment at reformers' attempts to interfere with their parenting
(D) Working-class mothers' belief that child labor was an inhumane practice
(E) Working-class families' need for every employable member of their families to earn money

Inference

The question's use of the word *suggests* means that the answer depends on making an inference. Lines 12–23 examine the different views of middle-class reformers and working-class mothers on child labor laws. While the reformers saw child labor as an *inhumane* practice that should be *outlawed*, working class mothers understood *the necessity of pooling the wages of as many family members as possible* and viewed child labor legislation as *a personal economic disaster.*

A Lines 12–14 show that reformers regarded both kinds of work as *equally inhumane practices that should be outlawed.*

B Pay is not specifically discussed in the passage.

C Lines 24–27 indicate that the reformers believed working-class resistance to child labor laws was a sign of poor parenting, but nothing is said about the working-class response to this view.

D Lines 12–17 say that the reformers held this position, but *working class mothers did not always share this view.*

E Correct. Lines 17–23 explain that working-class families needed *the wages of as many family members as possible.*

The correct answer is E.

64. The author of the passage asserts which of the following about women reformers who tried to abolish child labor?

(A) They alienated working-class mothers by attempting to enlist them in agitating for progressive causes.

(B) They underestimated the prevalence of child labor among the working classes.

(C) They were correct in their conviction that child labor was deplorable but shortsighted about the impact of child labor legislation on working-class families.

(D) They were aggressive in their attempts to enforce child labor legislation, but were unable to prevent working-class families from circumventing them.

(E) They were prevented by their nearly total disenfranchisement from making significant progress in child labor reform.

Supporting ideas

This question is based on information explicitly stated in the final sentence of the passage. Women reformers viewed *child labor as a terribly exploitative practice* but they *failed to take account of the economic needs of working-class families.*

A The passage does not say that reformers tried to enlist working-class mothers in progressive causes.

B No evidence is offered to support such a statement.

C Correct. The final sentence makes clear that the reformers recognized child labor as *exploitative* but did not understand *the economic needs of working-class families.*

D The reformers' activities involved promoting legislation; there is no evidence in the passage that the reformers themselves attempted to enforce these laws.

E. Lines 6–10 show that the reformers improved working conditions for women and children, despite their disenfranchisement.

The correct answer is C.

65. According to the passage, one of the most striking achievements of white middle-class women reformers during the Progressive Era was

(A) gaining the right to vote in school elections
(B) mobilizing working-class women in the fight against child labor
(C) uniting women of different classes in grassroots activism
(D) improving the economic conditions of working-class families
(E) improving women's and children's working conditions

Supporting ideas

The question's use of the phrase *according to the passage* indicates that the answer can be found through careful reading of the passage. This question is based on information explicitly stated in lines 7–10, which state that *white middle-class women reformers won a variety of victories, notably in the improvement of working conditions, especially for women and children*.

A Lines 6–7 show that women already had the right to vote in school elections.

B Lines 20–24 show that working-class families tried to *circumvent child labor laws*.

C Lines 11–12 say that one product of grassroots activism, child labor legislation, *pitted women of different classes against one another*.

D Lines 31–32 say that the reformers *failed to take account of the economic needs of working-class families*.

E **Correct**. The passage states that reformers improved the working conditions of women and children.

The correct answer is E.

Critical Reasoning

The following discussion is intended to familiarize you with the most efficient and effective approaches to critical reasoning questions. The particular questions in this chapter are generally representative of the kinds of critical reasoning questions you will encounter on the GMAT exam. Remember that it is the problem solving strategy that is important, not the specific details of a particular question.

66. Vasquez-Morrell Assurance specializes in insuring manufacturers. Whenever a policyholder makes a claim, a claims adjuster determines the amount that Vasquez-Morrell is obligated to pay. Vasquez-Morrell is cutting its staff of claims adjusters by 15 percent. To ensure that the company's ability to handle claims promptly is affected as little as possible by the staff cuts, consultants recommend that Vasquez-Morrell lay off those adjusters who now take longest, on average, to complete work on claims assigned to them.

Which of the following, if true, most seriously calls into question the consultants' criterion for selecting the staff to be laid off?

(A) If the time that Vasquez-Morrell takes to settle claims increases significantly, it could lose business to other insurers.
(B) Supervisors at Vasquez-Morrell tend to assign the most complex claims to the most capable adjusters.
(C) At Vasquez-Morrell, no insurance payments are made until a claims adjuster has reached a final determination on the claim.
(D) There are no positions at Vasquez-Morrell to which staff currently employed as claims adjusters could be reassigned.
(E) The premiums that Vasquez-Morrell currently charges are no higher than those charged for similar coverage by competitors.

Evaluation of a Plan

Situation An insurance company must reduce its staff of claims adjusters. To ensure continuing promptness in handling claims, consultants advise the company to lay off those adjusters who take the longest to complete claims.

Reasoning *What problem could there be with the criterion?* The consultants' criterion is the time an adjuster takes to settle a claim. However, some claims are naturally more complicated and require more time. If it is true that the company now assigns these time-consuming cases to its most capable adjusters, then these adjusters would be likely to be the ones who take longest to complete their cases. Laying off the adjusters who take the longest would thus mean laying off the company's most capable staff, which could very well decrease its ability to handle claims promptly.

A The consultants' advice makes sense if increased time to handle claims causes the company to lose business.

B **Correct.** This statement properly identifies the problem with the consultants' criterion.

C This statement merely describes the process of handling a claim; it does not provide any information about the criterion for layoffs.

D The consultants make no recommendations for reassigning staff, so indicating that there are no positions available does not call their advice into question.

E The consultants do not recommend a change in premiums; noting that they are similar to competitors' premiums does not undermine the plan that the consultants recommend.

The correct answer is B.

67. Prolonged spells of hot, dry weather at the end of the grape-growing season typically reduce a vineyard's yield, because the grapes stay relatively small. In years with such weather, wine producers can make only a relatively small quantity of wine from a given area of vineyards. Nonetheless, in regions where wine producers generally grow their own grapes, analysts typically expect a long, hot, dry spell late in the growing season to result in increased revenues for local wine producers.

Which of the following, if true, does most to justify the analysts' expectation?

(A) The lower a vineyard's yield, the less labor is required to harvest the grapes.

(B) Long, hot, dry spells at the beginning of the grape-growing season are rare, but they can have a devastating effect on a vineyard's yield.

(C) Grapes grown for wine production are typically made into wine at or near the vineyard in which they were grown.

(D) When hot, dry spells are followed by heavy rains, the rains frequently destroy grape crops.

(E) Grapes that have matured in hot, dry weather make significantly better wine than ordinary grapes.

Argument Construction

Situation Hot, dry weather at the end of the grape-growing season reduces yield, so winemakers can only produce a small quantity of wine. However, analysts expect that this weather will increase winemakers' revenues.

Reasoning *What additional piece of information explains the analysts' expectations?* The same conditions that lead to low quantity also lead to something that increases revenues. What could this be? If these weather conditions lead to higher-quality wine that will sell for higher prices, the analysts' expectations for increased revenues are justified.

A Lower labor costs mean less expenditure for the winemakers; this does not explain how revenues would increase.

B This statement about low yields does not explain an increase in revenues.

C The proximity of production to the vineyard is irrelevant to the question of how hot, dry weather can be responsible for decreased yield and increased revenues.

D This statement gives another example of weather's effect on grape crops, but it does not explain how revenues are increased.

E **Correct**. This statement properly provides the explanation that the weather conditions will lead to better wines. With better wines typically commanding higher prices, the winemakers will gain the increased revenues that the analysts anticipate.

The correct answer is E.

68. In the past, most children who went sledding in the winter snow in Verland used wooden sleds with runners and steering bars. Ten years ago, smooth plastic sleds became popular; they go faster than wooden sleds but are harder to steer and slow. The concern that plastic sleds are more dangerous is clearly borne out by the fact that the number of children injured while sledding was much higher last winter than it was 10 years ago.

Which of the following, if true in Verland, most seriously undermines the force of the evidence cited?

(A) A few children still use traditional wooden sleds.

(B) Very few children wear any kind of protective gear, such as helmets, while sledding.

(C) Plastic sleds can be used in a much wider variety of snow conditions than wooden sleds can.

(D) Most sledding injuries occur when a sled collides with a tree, a rock, or another sled.

(E) Because the traditional wooden sleds can carry more than one rider, an accident involving a wooden sled can result in several children being injured.

Argument Evaluation

Situation Ten years ago, wooden sleds began to be replaced by plastic sleds that go faster but are harder to control. Plastic sleds are more dangerous than wooden sleds because more children suffered injuries last year than they did 10 years ago.

Reasoning *What weakens this argument?* This argument depends on a comparison of two kinds of sleds. Any evidence that would either strengthen or weaken the argument must indicate a comparison. Evidence that applies only to one kind of sled or to both kinds of sleds equally cannot weaken this argument. Consider the implications of the evidence presented in the answer choices. If plastic sleds can be used in a wider variety of conditions than wooden sleds can, then plastic sleds can be used more frequently. It is possible that more frequent use, rather than the sleds themselves, has led to more accidents.

A The limited use of some wooden sleds does not weaken the argument.

B The absence of protective gear would affect accidents with both kinds of sleds.

C **Correct**. This statement weakens the argument by providing an alternate explanation for the increased accidents.

D This statement is true of accidents with both kinds of sleds.

E This explains why wooden sleds may be dangerous but does not weaken the argument that plastic sleds are even more dangerous.

The correct answer is C.

69. Metal rings recently excavated from seventh-century settlements in the western part of Mexico were made using the same metallurgical techniques as those used by Ecuadorian artisans before and during that period. These techniques are sufficiently complex to make their independent development in both areas unlikely. Since the people of these two areas were in cultural contact, archaeologists hypothesize that the metallurgical techniques used to make the rings found in Mexico were learned by Mexican artisans from Ecuadorian counterparts.

Which of the following would it be most useful to establish in order to evaluate the archaeologists' hypothesis?

(A) Whether metal objects were traded from Ecuador to western Mexico during the seventh century

(B) Whether travel between western Mexico and Ecuador in the seventh century would have been primarily by land or by sea

(C) Whether artisans from western Mexico could have learned complex metallurgical techniques from their Ecuadorian counterparts without actually leaving western Mexico

(D) Whether metal tools were used in the seventh-century settlements in western Mexico

(E) Whether any of the techniques used in the manufacture of the metal rings found in western Mexico are still practiced among artisans in Ecuador today

Argument Evaluation

Situation Metal rings excavated from seventh-century settlements in western Mexico were made with the same complex techniques used in Ecuador before and during a period when the two cultures were known to be in contact. Mexican artisans are thought to have learned the techniques from Ecuadorian artisans.

Reasoning *What point could best be applied in evaluating this hypothesis?* Consider what specific information would help to assess the archaeologists' theory. It is given that the two areas had some cultural contact. If it were determined that metal objects were traded from one culture to the other, it could be possible that the metalworking techniques were passed along as well. Such evidence would be relevant to the hypothesis that Mexican artisans saw the work of their Ecuadorian counterparts and, from this exchange, learned the techniques to make the metal rings.

A **Correct.** This statement properly identifies information that would be useful in the evaluation of the archaeologists' hypothesis.

B The means of travel is irrelevant to the hypothesis about the source of the techniques.

C The hypothesis is not about where Mexican artisans learned the techniques, but whether they learned them from the Ecuadorians.

D The existence of metal tools provides no helpful information in establishing whether the Ecuadorians were the source of the metallurgical techniques.

E The comparison to the present day is irrelevant to the hypothesis.

The correct answer is A.

70. Following several years of declining advertising sales, the *Greenville Times* reorganized its advertising sales force. Before reorganization, the sales force was organized geographically, with some sales representatives concentrating on city-center businesses and others concentrating on different outlying regions. The reorganization attempted to increase the sales representatives' knowledge of clients' businesses by having each sales representative deal with only one type of industry or of retailing. After the reorganization, revenue from advertising sales increased.

In assessing whether the improvement in advertising sales can properly be attributed to the reorganization, it would be most helpful to find out which of the following?

(A) What proportion of the total revenue of the *Greenville Times* is generated by advertising sales?

(B) Has the circulation of the *Greenville Times* increased substantially in the last two years?

(C) Among all the types of industry and retailing that use the *Greenville Times* as an advertising vehicle, which type accounts for the largest proportion of the newspaper's advertising sales?

(D) Do any clients of the sales representatives of the *Greenville Times* have a standing order with the *Times* for a fixed amount of advertising per month?

(E) Among the advertisers in the *Greenville Times*, are there more types of retail business or more types of industrial business?

Evaluation of a Plan

Situation In the face of declining advertising sales, a newspaper reorganizes its sales force so that sales representatives have a better understanding of businesses. Revenue from advertising sales increased after the reorganization.

Reasoning *What additional evidence would help determine the source of the increased revenue?* In order to attribute the increased revenue to the reorganization of the sales force, other possible causes must be eliminated. Newspaper advertising rates are linked to circulation; when circulation increases, higher rates can be charged and revenues will increase. An alternate explanation might be a significant rise in circulation, so it would be particularly helpful to know if circulation had increased.

A The question concerns only increased revenue from advertising sales; the proportion of advertising revenue to total revenue is outside the scope of the question.

B **Correct.** This statement provides another possible explanation for increased revenue of advertising sales, and so the answer to this question would help to clarify the reason for the increased revenue.

C Knowing how the advertising sales break down by type of business might be useful for other purposes, but it does not help to show the cause of the increase.

D A fixed amount of advertising would not explain increased revenue, so the answer to this question would be irrelevant.

E Distinguishing between the types of businesses will not contribute to determining whether the reorganization was responsible for the increased revenue.

The correct answer is B.

71. Motorists in a certain country frequently complain that traffic congestion is much worse now than it was 20 years ago. No real measure of how much traffic congestion there was 20 years ago exists, but the motorists' complaints are almost certainly unwarranted. The country's highway capacity has tripled in the last twenty years, thanks to a vigorous highway construction program, whereas the number of automobiles registered in the country has increased by only 75 percent.

Which of the following, if true, most seriously weakens the argument?

(A) Most automobile travel is local, and the networks of roads and streets in the country's settled areas have changed little over the last twenty years.

(B) Gasoline prices are high, and miles traveled per car per year have not changed much over the last 20 years.

(C) The country's urban centers have well-developed public transit systems that carry most of the people who commute into those centers.

(D) The average age of automobiles registered in the country is lower now than it was 20 years ago.

(E) Radio stations have long been broadcasting regular traffic reports that inform motorists about traffic congestion.

Argument Evaluation

Situation Motorists complain that traffic congestion in their country is much worse than it was twenty years ago. But these complaints have no basis since the highway capacity in this country has tripled in the same period, whereas the number of cars registered has risen by only 75 percent.

Reasoning *Which point most undermines the argument that the complaints are unwarranted?* Consider that the response to the generalized complaints about congestion discusses only the topic of highway capacity. What if the congestion that motorists are complaining about is not on highways but on local roads? Discovering that travel tends to be local in this country and that the local roads have not been improved in the last twenty years would seriously weaken the argument.

A **Correct.** This statement properly identifies a weakness in the argument: the response to the broad complaint addresses a different subject, highway capacity, not the issue of traffic congestion encountered by most motorists.

B If high gas prices actually prevented motorists from driving, and if motorists' driving habits were the same as they were twenty years ago, then these points should strengthen the argument that there is no basis for their complaints.

C The number of commuters who use public transit does not affect the argument that the motorists' complaints have no basis.

D The age of registered cars is irrelevant to the argument.

E The radio broadcasts attest to the existence of traffic, but not to its increase, so they do not affect the argument.

The correct answer is A.

72. The percentage of households with an annual income of more than \$40,000 is higher in Merton County than in any other county. However, the percentage of households with an annual income of \$60,000 or more is higher in Sommer County.

If the statements above are true, which of the following must also be true?

(A) The percentage of households with an annual income of \$80,000 is higher in Sommer County than in Merton County.
(B) Merton County has the second highest percentage of households with an annual income of \$60,000 or more.
(C) Some households in Merton County have an annual income between \$40,000 and \$60,000.
(D) The number of households with an annual income of more than \$40,000 is greater in Merton County than in Sommer County.
(E) Average annual household income is higher in Sommer County than in Merton County.

Argument Construction

Situation The percentage of households with annual incomes of more than \$40,000 is higher in Merton County than in any other county; the percentage of households with annual incomes of \$60,000 or more is higher in Sommer County.

Reasoning *On the basis of this information, what point must be true?* The given information makes clear that Merton County has some households that exceed \$40,000 in annual income. Sommer County has a higher percentage of households with annual incomes at or above \$60,000. A higher percentage of the Merton County households must in turn have annual incomes of \$60,000 or less. Thus, the annual income of some households in Merton County is between \$40,000 and \$60,000.

A Since it is possible that there are no households with an annual income of \$80,000 in Sommer County, this statement does not follow from the situation.

B It is not possible to make this determination on the basis of the available evidence; Merton County may have no households at all with an income of more than \$60,000.

C **Correct.** This statement properly identifies a conclusion that can be drawn from the given information: in order for the percentage of \$40,000-plus incomes to be higher in Merton county than any other county while Sommer has the highest percentage of \$60,000-plus incomes, there must be some households in Merton County that bring in between \$40,000 and \$60,000 annually.

D On the basis of information about the *percentages* of households, it is not possible to arrive at this conclusion about the *number* of households.

E From the given information, it is not possible to determine where the average income is greater. It is entirely possible that the number of \$60,000-plus incomes in Sommer County is quite small and that the number of \$40,000-plus incomes in Merton County is substantial.

The correct answer is C.

73. Tiger beetles are such fast runners that they can capture virtually any nonflying insect. However, when running toward an insect, a tiger beetle will intermittently stop and then, a moment later, resume its attack. Perhaps the beetles cannot maintain their pace and must pause for a moment's rest; but an alternative hypothesis is that while running, tiger beetles are unable to adequately process the resulting rapidly changing visual information and so quickly go blind and stop.

Which of the following, if discovered in experiments using artificially moved prey insects, would support one of the two hypotheses and undermine the other?

(A) When a prey insect is moved directly toward a beetle that has been chasing it, the beetle immediately stops and runs away without its usual intermittent stopping.

(B) In pursuing a swerving insect, a beetle alters its course while running and its pauses become more frequent as the chase progresses.

(C) In pursuing a moving insect, a beetle usually responds immediately to changes in the insect's direction, and it pauses equally frequently whether the chase is up or down an incline.

(D) If, when a beetle pauses, it has not gained on the insect it is pursuing, the beetle generally ends its pursuit.

(E) The faster a beetle pursues an insect fleeing directly away from it, the more frequently the beetle stops.

Argument Evaluation

Situation Two hypotheses are offered to explain the sudden stop that tiger beetles make while pursuing their prey: (1) they cannot maintain the rapid pace and must rest, and (2) they run too quickly to process visual information and so temporarily go blind.

Reasoning *What point would strengthen one of the two hypotheses and weaken the other?* Consider the information provided in each answer choice, remembering that information that supports one hypothesis must necessarily detract from the other. Any information that is not about pursuit or that affects the two hypotheses equally may be dismissed from consideration. If the frequency of stopping increases when the beetle follows a swerving insect and must constantly change its course, then the second hypothesis is strengthened; the beetle's pauses increase as the variety of visual information that it needs to deal with increases.

A The hypotheses concern ongoing pursuit; since this information is not about the beetle's continuing pursuit of prey, it neither strengthens nor weakens either hypothesis.

B **Correct.** This statement provides information that strengthens the second hypothesis: the swerving pursuit and the resulting continual course adjustments appear to be forcing the beetle to stop with increasing frequency to sort out the erratic visual information.

C In this experiment, since neither vision nor tiredness appears to be problematic, the beetle could be stopping for either reason; this information neither strengthens nor weakens either hypothesis.

D This information is irrelevant since both the hypotheses are about mid-pursuit behaviors.

E The correlation of frequency of stops with speed affects both hypotheses equally; the pauses could be equally due to an inability to maintain the pace or due to a need to process the visual information.

The correct answer is B.

74. Guillemots are birds of Arctic regions. They feed on fish that gather beneath thin sheets of floating ice, and they nest on nearby land. Guillemots need 80 consecutive snow-free days in a year to raise their chicks, so until average temperatures in the Arctic began to rise recently, the guillemots' range was limited to the southernmost Arctic coast. Therefore, if the warming continues, the guillemots' range will probably be enlarged by being extended northward along the coast.

Which of the following, if true, most seriously weakens the argument?

(A) Even if the warming trend continues, there will still be years in which guillemot chicks are killed by an unusually early snow.

(B) If the Arctic warming continues, guillemots' current predators are likely to succeed in extending their own range farther north.

(C) Guillemots nest in coastal areas, where temperatures are generally higher than in inland areas.

(D) If the Arctic warming continues, much of the thin ice in the southern Arctic will disappear.

(E) The fish that guillemots eat are currently preyed on by a wider variety of predators in the southernmost Arctic regions than they are farther north.

Argument Evaluation

Situation In the southern Arctic, guillemots find their prey beneath thin sheets of ice, nest nearby, and require 80 snow-free days to raise their young. A warming trend means that their range may be enlarged by extending northward along the coast.

Reasoning *Which point weakens the argument about the enlargement of the guillemots' range?* How could the birds move northward and simultaneously not enlarge their range? Consider the assumption implied by the idea of *enlargement*. If the guillemots lost their southern habitat, then their northward move would be a displacement rather than an enlargement. If their source of food was no longer available to them in the southern Arctic, then they would abandon that area as part of their range.

A An exceptional year is not an argument against an enlarged range because *an unusually early snow* could happen in the southern Arctic as well.

B If their current predators also migrate northward, then the guillemots' situation has not changed, so this is not an argument against their enlarged range.

C The argument suggests that they will move not inland, but *northward along the coast*.

D **Correct**. This statement properly identifies a factor that weakens the argument: the guillemots' move northward would not enlarge their range if they lost their food source, fish found under thin ice, in the southern Arctic.

E The possibility that they may find prey more easily in the north does not mean that they would abandon the southern Arctic, and so this point does not weaken the argument.

The correct answer is D.

75. Some batches of polio vaccine used around 1960 were contaminated with SV40, a virus that in monkeys causes various cancers. Some researchers now claim that this contamination caused some cases of a certain cancer in humans, mesothelioma. This claim is not undercut by the fact that a very careful survey made in the 1960s of people who had received the contaminated vaccine found no elevated incidence of any cancer, since ______.

(A) most cases of mesothelioma are caused by exposure to asbestos
(B) in some countries, there was no contamination of the vaccine
(C) SV40 is widely used in laboratories to produce cancers in animals
(D) mesotheliomas take several decades to develop
(E) mesothelioma was somewhat less common in 1960 than it is now

Argument Construction

Situation Researchers claim that contaminated polio vaccine administered in 1960 caused some cases of mesothelioma, a type of cancer. Their claim is not undermined by the results of a 1960s survey showing that those who received the contaminated vaccine had no elevated incidence of cancer.

Reasoning *Why did the survey results not challenge the researchers' claim?* The survey did not reveal a higher incidence of mesothelioma. This question then requires completing a sentence that establishes cause. What could be the reason that the people surveyed in the 1960s showed no signs of the disease? If the disease takes decades to develop, then those people surveyed would not yet have shown any signs of it; less than a decade had passed between their exposure to the vaccine and the survey.

A The contaminated vaccine is said to have caused *some* cases, not *most*; the question remains why the survey results pose no obstacle to the researchers' claim.

B The claim is only about contaminated vaccine, not uncontaminated vaccine.

C That the virus can cause cancers in laboratory animals had already been provided as a given; this additional information is irrelevant to the survey of people who received contaminated vaccine.

D **Correct.** This statement properly identifies the reason that the survey does not call into question the researchers' claim: the people surveyed in the 1960s showed no signs of disease because the cancer takes decades to develop.

E The frequency of mesothelioma in the general population is not related to the claim that contaminated vaccine caused the disease in a specific population.

The correct answer is D.

76. Gortland has long been narrowly self-sufficient in both grain and meat. However, as per capita income in Gortland has risen toward the world average, per capita consumption of meat has also risen toward the world average, and it takes several pounds of grain to produce one pound of meat. Therefore, since per capita income continues to rise, whereas domestic grain production will not increase, Gortland will soon have to import either grain or meat or both.

Which of the following is an assumption on which the argument depends?

(A) The total acreage devoted to grain production in Gortland will soon decrease.

(B) Importing either grain or meat will not result in a significantly higher percentage of Gortlanders' incomes being spent on food than is currently the case.

(C) The per capita consumption of meat in Gortland is increasing at roughly the same rate across all income levels.

(D) The per capita income of meat producers in Gortland is rising faster than the per capita income of grain producers.

(E) People in Gortland who increase their consumption of meat will not radically decrease their consumption of grain.

Argument Construction

Situation A country previously self-sufficient in grain and meat will soon have to import one or the other or both. Consumption of meat has risen as per capita income has risen, and it takes several pounds of grain to produce one pound of meat.

Reasoning *What conditions must be true for the conclusion to be true?* Meat consumption is rising. What about grain consumption? A sharp reduction in the amount of grain consumed could compensate for increased meat consumption, making the conclusion false. If people did radically decrease their grain consumption, it might not be necessary to import grain or meat or both. Since the argument concludes that the imports are necessary, it assumes grain consumption will not plunge.

A The argument makes no assumptions about the acreage devoted to grain; it assumes only that the demand for grain will rise.

B The argument does not discuss the percentage of their income that Gortlanders spend on food, so an assumption about this topic is not needed.

C The argument involves only meat consumption in general, not its distribution by income level.

D Since the argument does not refer to the incomes of meat producers and grain producers, it cannot depend on an assumption about them.

E **Correct**. This statement properly identifies the assumption that there will be no great decrease in grain consumption.

The correct answer is E.

77. The Hazelton coal-processing plant is a major employer in the Hazelton area, but national environmental regulations will force it to close if it continues to use old, polluting processing methods. However, to update the plant to use newer, cleaner methods would be so expensive that the plant will close unless it receives the tax break it has requested. In order to prevent a major increase in local unemployment, the Hazelton government is considering granting the plant's request.

Which of the following would be most important for the Hazelton government to determine before deciding whether to grant the plant's request?

(A) Whether the company that owns the plant would open a new plant in another area if the present plant were closed

(B) Whether the plant would employ far fewer workers when updated than it does now

(C) Whether the level of pollutants presently being emitted by the plant is high enough to constitute a health hazard for local residents

(D) Whether the majority of the coal processed by the plant is sold outside the Hazelton area

(E) Whether the plant would be able to process more coal when updated than it does now

Evaluation of a Plan

Situation Because of the expenses of mandatory updating, a plant that is a major employer in the local area will close unless it receives the tax break it has requested from the local government.

Reasoning *What point is most critical to the evaluation of the request?* Consider the information provided in the answer choices. The plant is important to the local government primarily because it is a major employer of local residents. What if updating the plant significantly reduced the number of employees needed? It is crucial for the local government to determine whether the plant will continue to employ the same number of people once it has updated.

A The local government is concerned only with the local area, so a new site outside that area is irrelevant.

B **Correct**. This statement properly identifies a factor that is critical to the plant's argument and the local government's decision.

C Updating is mandatory under national environmental regulations, whether the local residents are affected by the plant's pollutants or not.

D At issue is the plant's role as a major employer; where its product is sold is irrelevant.

E The amount of coal processed by the updated plant is irrelevant to the critical issue of the number of people employed to process that coal.

The correct answer is B.

78. A physically active lifestyle has been shown to help increase longevity. In the Wistar region of Bellaria, the average age at death is considerably higher than in any other part of the country. Wistar is the only mountainous part of Bellaria. A mountainous terrain makes even such basic activities as walking relatively strenuous; it essentially imposes a physically active lifestyle on people. Clearly, this circumstance explains the long lives of people in Wistar.

Which of the following, if true, most seriously weakens the argument?

(A) In Bellaria all medical expenses are paid by the government, so that personal income does not affect the quality of health care a person receives.

(B) The Wistar region is one of Bellaria's least populated regions.

(C) Many people who live in the Wistar region have moved there in middle age or upon retirement.

(D) The many opportunities for hiking, skiing, and other outdoor activities that Wistar's mountains offer make it a favorite destination for vacationing Bellarians.

(E) Per capita spending on recreational activities is no higher in Wistar than it is in other regions of Bellaria.

Argument Evaluation

Situation People in one region of a country live longer than people in other areas. The higher average age at time of death is attributed to the healthy lifestyle of the people in this region, where the mountainous terrain demands a physically active life.

Reasoning *What point weakens the argument?* Consider what assumption underlies the argument that the physically active lifestyle required of living in Wistar is responsible for its residents' relative longevity. The mountainous environment necessitates lifelong levels of rigorous physical activity that build a more robust population. What if a significant portion of the population has not been conditioned since childhood to the demands of the terrain? It is assumed here that the healthy lifestyle imposed by the terrain has shaped residents from birth and accounts for their longer life span. If many residents only moved there later in life, the argument is weakened.

A The argument is not about the quality of health care throughout the country, but the length of the residents' lives in a particular region.

B The rate of population density does not affect the argument.

C **Correct**. This statement properly identifies a point that weakens the argument.

D The area's popularity as a vacation destination does not affect the longevity of the local residents.

E The argument establishes that merely living in the region is strenuous; the spending on recreational activities is irrelevant.

The correct answer is C.

79. Cheever College offers several online courses via remote computer connection, in addition to traditional classroom-based courses. A study of student performance at Cheever found that, overall, the average student grade for online courses matched that for classroom-based courses. In this calculation of the average grade, course withdrawals were weighted as equivalent to a course failure, and the rate of withdrawal was much lower for students enrolled in classroom-based courses than for students enrolled in online courses.

If the statements above are true, which of the following must also be true of Cheever College?

(A) Among students who did not withdraw, students enrolled in online courses got higher grades, on average, than students enrolled in classroom-based courses.

(B) The number of students enrolled per course at the start of the school term is much higher, on average, for the online courses than for the classroom-based courses.

(C) There are no students who take both an online and a classroom-based course in the same school term.

(D) Among Cheever College students with the best grades, a significant majority take online, rather than classroom-based, courses.

(E) Courses offered online tend to deal with subject matter that is less challenging than that of classroom-based courses.

Argument Construction

Situation A comparison of online and classroom courses showed similar average grades. In determining average grades, a course withdrawal was weighted as a course failure. The rate of withdrawal was higher from online than from classroom courses.

Reasoning *What conclusion about the courses can be derived from this comparison?* Consider the ramifications of the methodology used to calculate the grade averages for the two types of courses. Because of course withdrawals, the online courses experienced a higher rate of failure, but the average grade for these courses still matched the average grade for classroom courses. From this it is logical to conclude that, for the two averages to match, the students who remained in the online courses must have had higher initial average grades than those in classroom courses.

A **Correct.** This statement properly identifies the logical conclusion that the higher percentage of withdrawals from online classes requires higher grades, on average, to compensate for the higher rate of failure.

B A number of students cannot be derived from a discussion of average grades and rates of withdrawal.

C This conclusion cannot be determined on the basis of the information provided.

D The information is about average grades; the argument does not provide any basis for a conclusion about best grades.

E It is impossible to determine the difficulty of subject matter from this information.

The correct answer is A.

80. For years the beautiful Renaissance buildings in Palitito have been damaged by exhaust from the many tour buses that come to the city. There has been little parking space, so most buses have idled at the curb during each stop on their tour, and idling produces as much exhaust as driving. The city has now provided parking that accommodates a third of the tour buses, so damage to Palitito's buildings from the buses' exhaust will diminish significantly.

Which of the following, if true, most strongly supports the argument?

(A) The exhaust from Palitito's few automobiles is not a significant threat to Palitito's buildings.

(B) Palitito's Renaissance buildings are not threatened by pollution other than engine exhaust.

(C) Tour buses typically spend less than one-quarter of the time they are in Palitito transporting passengers from one site to another.

(D) More tourists come to Palitito by tour bus than by any other single means of transportation.

(E) Some of the tour buses that are unable to find parking drive around Palitito while their passengers are visiting a site.

Argument Evaluation

Situation Tour buses have damaged Renaissance buildings with their exhaust fumes because lack of parking has kept the buses idling at curbs. Providing new parking for a third of the buses should significantly reduce the damage caused by the exhaust.

Reasoning *What point strengthens the argument?* The argument for reduced damage relies on the reduction of the vehicles' exhaust fumes. Any additional evidence regarding the extent to which the vehicular emissions are likely to be reduced also supports the argument for the benefits of the new parking spaces. Learning that tour buses spend not just a few minutes but most of their time idling at the curb strengthens the argument. The new parking spaces will allow a third of the tour buses to spend 75 percent of their time with their engines off, causing no damage at all.

A If automobile exhaust is not a threat, the argument is not affected.

B This statement does not address the question of whether the new parking will reduce the damage caused by engine exhaust from the buses.

C **Correct.** This statement properly cites a factor that supports the argument: since most of the buses' time has been spent producing damaging exhaust, the new parking should reduce the damage significantly.

D This statement about tourists' chosen means of transportation is irrelevant to the issue of what the buses do while in the city.

E It is given that the new parking will only provide space for a third of the buses, and thus some buses will continue to idle and some to drive around, continuing to contribute equally to the building damage. This statement does not strengthen the argument.

The correct answer is C.

81. During the 1980s and 1990s, the annual number of people who visited the Sordellian Mountains increased continually, and many new ski resorts were built. Over the same period, however, the number of visitors to ski resorts who were caught in avalanches decreased, even though there was no reduction in the annual number of avalanches in the Sordellian Mountains.

Which of the following, if true in the Sordellian Mountains during the 1980s and 1990s, most helps to explain the decrease?

(A) Avalanches were most likely to happen when a large new snowfall covered an older layer of snow.

(B) Avalanches destroyed at least some buildings in the Sordellian Mountains in every year.

(C) People planning new ski slopes and other resort facilities used increasingly accurate information about which locations are likely to be in the path of avalanches.

(D) The average length of stay for people visiting the Sordellian Mountains increased slightly.

(E) Construction of new ski resorts often led to the clearing of wooded areas that had helped prevent avalanches.

Argument Construction

Situation Over a certain period, new ski resorts accommodated an increasing number of visitors at the same time that fewer visitors were caught in avalanches. Yet there were no fewer avalanches than usual during this period.

Reasoning *What explains the apparent contradiction of increased visitors but fewer visitors caught in avalanches?* More resort visitors would imply more avalanche-related accidents, but the average has shifted so that fewer visitors are being caught in the avalanches. It must be that fewer visitors are exposed to this danger; consider the answer choices to identify a logical reason for this improvement in their exposure. If the likely paths of avalanches had become better understood, that information would have been applied to identify safer locations for new ski slopes and ski resorts. The facilities would thus have been built well out of the way of avalanches, resulting in fewer visitors trapped in avalanches.

A This likelihood would remain true from year to year; it does not explain the decrease.

B This point does not explain why fewer visitors were caught in these avalanches.

C **Correct.** This statement properly identifies a factor that explains the decreased number of accidents.

D The greater length of stay would seem to expose visitors to greater danger.

E This information points to an expected increase, rather than decrease, in visitors who might be caught by avalanches.

The correct answer is C.

82. A year ago, Dietz Foods launched a yearlong advertising campaign for its canned tuna. Last year Dietz sold 12 million cans of tuna compared to the 10 million sold during the previous year, an increase directly attributable to new customers brought in by the campaign. Profits from the additional sales, however, were substantially less than the cost of the advertising campaign. Clearly, therefore, the campaign did nothing to further Dietz's economic interests.

Which of the following, if true, most seriously weakens the argument?

(A) Sales of canned tuna account for a relatively small percentage of Dietz Foods' profits.

(B) Most of the people who bought Dietz's canned tuna for the first time as a result of the campaign were already loyal customers of other Dietz products.

(C) A less expensive advertising campaign would have brought in significantly fewer new customers for Dietz's canned tuna than did the campaign Dietz Foods launched last year.

(D) Dietz made money on sales of canned tuna last year.

(E) In each of the past five years, there was a steep, industry-wide decline in sales of canned tuna.

Argument Evaluation

Situation An advertising campaign was responsible for increased sales of canned tuna. Since the profits from the increased sales were less than the costs of the campaign, the campaign did not contribute to the company's economic interests.

Reasoning *Which point weakens the argument?* Consider the basis of the argument: if profits are lower than costs, the campaign made no contribution to the company's financial well-being. In what case might this be untrue? What if the advertising campaign reversed an industry-wide trend of declining sales? If Dietz experienced increasing sales, while other companies experienced decreased sales, then the campaign did contribute to the economic interests of the company, and the argument is considerably weakened.

A The issue is not the percentage of profits that canned tuna contributes, but the success of the advertising campaign.

B If the customers bought the tuna because of the campaign, it is irrelevant to the argument that they also bought other Dietz products.

C This information neither strengthens nor weakens the argument.

D The argument is not about profits only, but about whether the advertising campaign contributed to the economic interests of the company.

E **Correct.** This statement properly identifies a factor that weakens the argument: the campaign secured the benefits of increased sales at a time when the entire industry was experiencing a decline in sales.

The correct answer is E.

Sentence Correction

The following discussion is intended to familiarize you with the most efficient and effective approaches to sentence correction questions. The particular questions in this chapter are generally representative of the kinds of sentence correction questions you will encounter on the GMAT exam. Remember that it is the problem solving strategy that is important, not the specific details of a particular question.

83. Unlike the buildings in Mesopotamian cities, which were arranged haphazardly, the same basic plan was followed for all cities of the Indus Valley: with houses laid out on a north-south, east-west grid, and houses and walls were built of standard-size bricks.

(A) the buildings in Mesopotamian cities, which were arranged haphazardly, the same basic plan was followed for all cities of the Indus Valley: with houses

(B) the buildings in Mesopotamian cities, which were haphazard in arrangement, the same basic plan was used in all cities of the Indus Valley: houses were

(C) the arrangement of buildings in Mesopotamian cities, which were haphazard, the cities of the Indus Valley all followed the same basic plan: houses

(D) Mesopotamian cities, in which buildings were arranged haphazardly, the cities of the Indus Valley all followed the same basic plan: houses were

(E) Mesopotamian cities, which had buildings that were arranged haphazardly, the same basic plan was used for all cities in the Indus Valley: houses that were

Comparison-contrast; Modifying clause

The contrast introduced by *unlike* must be logical and clear. Contrasting *the buildings in Mesopotamian cities* with *the same basic plan* does not make sense; *Mesopotamian cities* should be contrasted with *the cities of the Indus Valley*. Also, it needs to be clear that it was the *buildings* in the cities that were *arranged haphazardly* rather than the *cities*. The second half of the sentence needs *houses were laid out* to be parallel in structure to *and houses and walls were built*.

A Illogically contrasts *the buildings in Mesopotamian cities* with *the same basic plan*; not clear whether *which were arranged haphazardly* modifies *cities or buildings; with houses* lacks parallelism and is confusing.

B Illogically contrasts *the buildings in Mesopotamian cities* with *the same basic plan*; does not clarify what *which were haphazard in arrangement* modifies.

C Illogically contrasts *the arrangement of buildings* with *the cities of the Indus Valley*; not clear whether *which were haphazard* modifies *buildings* or *cities; houses* not followed by a verb.

D **Correct.** In this sentence, *Mesopotamian cities* are properly contrasted with *the cities of the Indus Valley; in which buildings were arranged haphazardly* expresses the idea clearly; and *houses* is followed by *were* as required.

E Illogically contrasts *Mesopotamian cities* with *the same basic plan; houses that were* lacks parallelism and is confusing.

The correct answer is D.

84. New data from United States Forest Service ecologists show that for every dollar spent on controlled small-scale burning, forest thinning, and the training of fire-management personnel, it saves seven dollars that would not be spent on having to extinguish big fires.

(A) that for every dollar spent on controlled small-scale burning, forest thinning, and the training of fire-management personnel, it saves seven dollars that would not be spent on having to extinguish

(B) that for every dollar spent on controlled small-scale burning, forest thinning, and the training of fire-management personnel, seven dollars are saved that would have been spent on extinguishing

(C) that for every dollar spent on controlled small-scale burning, forest thinning, and the training of fire-management personnel saves seven dollars on not having to extinguish

(D) for every dollar spent on controlled small-scale burning, forest thinning, and the training of fire-management personnel, that it saves seven dollars on not having to extinguish

(E) for every dollar spent on controlled small-scale burning, forest thinning, and the training of fire-management personnel, that seven dollars are saved that would not have been spent on extinguishing

Logical predication; Rhetorical construction

The pronoun *it* (*it saves seven dollars*) has no referent. Making *seven dollars* the subject of the clause eliminates this problem, and it also fulfills a reader's expectation that after the phrase beginning *for every dollar* another specific amount will be given to balance it. This change in structure also allows the awkward and wordy clause *that would not be spent on having to extinguish* to be rewritten so that *spent* balances *saved: seven dollars are saved that would have been spent on extinguishing*, and the unnecessary *having to* is omitted.

A *It* has no referent; *not be spent* is awkward; *on having to extinguish* is wordy.

B **Correct**. This sentence properly uses *seven dollars* as the subject of the clause to balance *every dollar* in the introductory phrase; the phrasing is concise and parallel.

C *Saves* does not have a subject; construction is not a complete sentence; *not having to extinguish* is wordy and awkward.

D *That* introduces a subordinate rather than main clause, making a sentence fragment; *it* has no referent; *not having to extinguish* is wordy and awkward.

E Introductory *that* makes a sentence fragment; *that would not have been spent on extinguishing* is awkward and illogical.

The correct answer is B.

85. Like the grassy fields and old pastures that the upland sandpiper needs for feeding and nesting when it returns in May after wintering in the Argentine Pampas, the sandpipers vanishing in the northeastern United States is a result of residential and industrial development and of changes in farming practices.

(A) the sandpipers vanishing in the northeastern United States is a result of residential and industrial development and of changes in

(B) the bird itself is vanishing in the northeastern United States as a result of residential and industrial development and of changes in

(C) that the birds themselves are vanishing in the northeastern United States is due to residential and industrial development and changes to

(D) in the northeastern United States, sandpipers' vanishing due to residential and industrial development and to changes in

(E) in the northeastern United States, the sandpipers' vanishing, a result of residential and industrial development and changing

Comparison; Sentence structure

The comparison introduced by *like* must be logical and clear; the point of this comparison is that both the habitat and the bird are disappearing for similar reasons. The comparison must use comparable grammatical components; *the bird itself* is a noun phrase and matches the noun phrases *grassy fields* and *old pastures*.

A Illogically compares *the sandpipers vanishing* to *grassy fields and old pastures*; omits apostrophe in *sandpipers' vanishing*; wordy.

B Correct. This sentence properly compares *the bird itself* to *grassy fields and old pastures; is vanishing* as the verb strengthens the sentence by making the comparison clearer.

C Does not finish the comparison begun with *like* but instead substitutes a clause (*that the birds themselves are vanishing*).

D Illogically compares *the sandpipers' vanishing* to *grassy fields and old pastures*; creates a sentence fragment.

E Illogically compares *the sandpipers' vanishing* to *grassy fields and old pastures*; creates a sentence fragment.

The correct answer is B.

86. The results of two recent unrelated studies support the idea that dolphins may share certain cognitive abilities with humans and great apes; the studies indicate <u>dolphins as capable of recognizing themselves in mirrors—an ability that is often considered a sign of self-awareness—and to grasp spontaneously</u> the mood or intention of humans.

(A) dolphins as capable of recognizing themselves in mirrors—an ability that is often considered a sign of self-awareness—and to grasp spontaneously

(B) dolphins' ability to recognize themselves in mirrors—an ability that is often considered as a sign of self-awareness—and of spontaneously grasping

(C) dolphins to be capable of recognizing themselves in mirrors—an ability that is often considered a sign of self-awareness—and to grasp spontaneously

(D) that dolphins have the ability of recognizing themselves in mirrors—an ability that is often considered as a sign of self-awareness—and spontaneously grasping

(E) that dolphins are capable of recognizing themselves in mirrors—an ability that is often considered a sign of self-awareness—and of spontaneously grasping

Grammatical construction; Parallelism

In the context of this sentence, *the studies indicate* must introduce a clause; the clause must begin with *that* and have a subject, *dolphins*, and a verb, *are* (the complete verb phrase would be *are capable of*). The two capabilities should be parallel: *capable of recognizing…and of spontaneously grasping*.

A Context requires a clause, but this construction is not a clause; *capable of recognizing* is not parallel to *to grasp spontaneously.*

B Construction is not a clause, and a clause is required; *dolphins' ability to recognize* is not parallel to *of spontaneously grasping.*

C A clause is required following *the studies indicate; to be capable of recognizing* is not parallel to *to grasp spontaneously.*

D *Have the ability of* is wordy and unidiomatic; *of recognizing* and *spontaneously grasping* are not parallel.

E **Correct.** *That* introduces the subordinate clause necessary to complete this sentence properly; *of recognizing* and *of spontaneously grasping* are parallel.

The correct answer is E.

87. According to scholars, the earliest writing was probably not a direct rendering of speech, but was more likely to begin as a separate and distinct symbolic system of communication, and only later merged with spoken language.

(A) was more likely to begin as

(B) more than likely began as

(C) more than likely beginning from

(D) it was more than likely begun from

(E) it was more likely that it began

Idiom; Verb form

This sentence is a comparison in which *probably not x* is balanced by *but more than likely y.* When *more* is used in the comparative form of an adjective (*more difficult*) or adverb (*more likely*), it is followed by *than.* The words used to show the comparison between *x* and *y, but more than likely*, must also introduce the correct verb form, allowing *y* to fit grammatically into the rest of the sentence. The subject of the sentence has three verbs, all of which should be parallel: *the earliest writing was…began…merged. Was…to begin* is not parallel and results in a construction that is not grammatically correct.

A In this context, *more likely* is not a complete idiomatic expression; *was…to begin* is not parallel to *was* and *merged.*

B **Correct.** In this sentence, *more than likely* is the correct comparative construction; the simple past tense *began*, parallel to *was* and *merged*, fits grammatically into the sentence.

C Subject should be followed by three verbs; *beginning from* is not a verb.

D Use of the pronoun *it* makes this construction a main clause, in which case the comma after *communication* must be omitted and *began* must be used to be parallel to *merged; was…begun* is not the correct tense.

E In this awkward, unclear, and wordy construction, the first *it* must be followed by *is*, not *was*, because the theory is current; the second *it* acts as the subject of the subordinate clause, and this usage requires the omission of the comma after *communication.*

The correct answer is B.

88. In 1995 Richard Stallman, a well-known critic of the patent system, testified in Patent Office hearings that, to test the system, a colleague of his had managed to win a patent for one of Kirchhoff's laws, an observation about electric current first made in 1845 and now included in virtually every textbook of elementary physics.

(A) laws, an observation about electric current first made in 1845 and

(B) laws, which was an observation about electric current first made in 1845 and it is

(C) laws, namely, it was an observation about electric current first made in 1845 and

(D) laws, an observation about electric current first made in 1845, it is

(E) laws that was an observation about electric current, first made in 1845, and is

Logical predication; Parallelism

The function of the entire long phrase (*observation...physics*) that follows *one of Kirchhoff's laws* is to describe that law. It is a noun phrase in apposition, which means that it has the same syntactic relation to all the other parts of the sentence that the noun phrase *one of Kirchhoff's laws* does. Within the long modifying phrase, parallelism is maintained by balancing *an observation...first made* with *and now included.*

A **Correct**. In this sentence, the noun phrase in apposition properly identifies and explains the law, using parallel structure and concise expression.

B *Which* is ambiguous because it could refer to *one* or to *laws; it is* violates the parallelism of *first made* and *now included.*

C *It* is ambiguous; the introduction of *it was* does not allow this construction to fit grammatically into the sentence.

D The referent of *it* is unclear; *it is* creates a run-on sentence and violates the parallelism of *first made* and *now included.*

E *That* appears to refer to *laws* rather than *one*, but the verb is singular; setting off the phrase *first made in 1845* in commas distorts meaning; *is* violates parallelism.

The correct answer is A.

89. Excavators at the Indus Valley site of Harappa in eastern Pakistan say the discovery of inscribed shards dating to circa 2800–2600 B.C. indicate their development of a Harappan writing system, the use of inscribed seals impressed into clay for marking ownership, and the standardization of weights for trade or taxation occurred many decades, if not centuries, earlier than was previously believed.

(A) indicate their development of a Harappan writing system, the use of

(B) indicate that the development of a Harappan writing system, using

(C) indicates that their development of a Harappan writing system, using

(D) indicates the development of a Harappan writing system, their use of

(E) indicates that the development of a Harappan writing system, the use of

Agreement; Idiom; Parallelism

In long sentences such as this one, the relationship between parts of the sentence may be difficult to see. Here, the main clause of the sentence is *excavators...say* and the logical sequence that follows is *the discovery...indicates that.* The subject of this first subordinate clause is the singular noun *discovery*, which should be followed by the singular verb *indicates* rather than by the plural *indicate*, as is done in the original sentence. *Their*, used with either *development* or *use*, has no clear or logical referent in any of the alternatives. The subject of the following subordinate (*that*) clause, which has *occurred* as its verb, is a series of three phrases, which must be parallel, especially in a sentence of this length and complexity: *the development of..., the use of..., and the standardization of....*

A *Indicate* does not agree with *discovery*; the pronoun *their* has no logical referent, and *their development* is not parallel to *the use* and *the standardization.*

B *Indicate* does not agree with *discovery; using* is not parallel to *the development* and *the standardization.*

C *Their* has no logical referent; the series of three elements should be parallel, but here all are different.

D The pronoun *their* has no logical referent, and *their use* is not parallel to *the development* and *the standardization*; the preferred sentence structure would have *indicates* followed by *that* when introducing a clause.

E **Correct**. In this sentence, *indicates* agrees with *discovery* and is followed by *that* to introduce a clause; the three parallel phrases begin with an article (*the*), a noun, and the preposition *of.*

The correct answer is E.

90. The Supreme Court has ruled that public universities can collect student activity fees even with students' objections to particular activities, so long as the groups they give money to will be chosen without regard to their views.

(A) with students' objections to particular activities, so long as the groups they give money to will be
(B) if they have objections to particular activities and the groups that are given the money are
(C) if they object to particular activities, but the groups that the money is given to have to be
(D) from students who object to particular activities, so long as the groups given money are
(E) though students have an objection to particular activities, but the groups that are given the money be

Logical predication; Rhetorical construction

The underlined portion of the sentence fails to establish a clear relationship among *universities*, *students*, and *groups*. To which of these three does *they* refer? It would appear that the *universities* must give the money, but *they* does not have a referent. Furthermore, *they* is followed by *their views*, and in this case *their* must refer to *groups*. Wordy and awkward phrasing as well as an unnecessary shift in verb tense (*will be chosen*) compound the difficulty of understanding this sentence in its original form.

A *With students' objections*...is awkward and dense; *they* does not have a referent; the future *will be* is incorrect since the Supreme Court *has* already *ruled*.

B Referent for *they* is *student activity fees*, which cannot possibly *have objections*...; the use of *and* is illogical.

C *They* refers to student *activity fees* rather than *students*; *but* does not have the requisite sense of *with the provision that*; *have to be* is wordy.

D **Correct**. In this sentence, *from students who object* is clear and idiomatic; *so long as* is used appropriately; *groups given money* eliminates the problem of a pronoun without a referent; *are* is the proper tense.

E *Have an objection* is an unnecessarily wordy way to say *object*; the verb *be* does not complete the latter part of the sentence.

The correct answer is D.

91. Despite the increasing number of women graduating from law school and passing bar examinations, the proportion of judges and partners at major law firms who are women have not risen to a comparable extent.

(A) the proportion of judges and partners at major law firms who are women have not risen to a comparable extent
(B) the proportion of women judges and partners at major law firms have not risen comparably
(C) the proportion of judges and partners at major law firms who are women has not risen comparably
(D) yet the proportion of women judges and partners at major law firms has not risen to a comparable extent
(E) yet the proportion of judges and partners at major law firms who are women has not risen comparably

Agreement; Rhetorical construction

When a number of plural nouns appear in phrases between a singular subject and the verb, it can be easy to overlook the true subject of the verb. Here, *judges, partners, firms*, and *women* all occur between the singular subject, *proportion*, and the verb, which should also be singular, *has risen*. Concise expression is particularly important in a long construction; *to a comparable extent* may be more concisely expressed as *comparably*.

A Plural verb, *have risen*, does not agree with the singular subject, *proportion*.

B *Have risen* does not agree with *proportion*; here, *women* applies only to *judges*, not to *partners at major law firms*.

C **Correct**. In this sentence, *has risen* agrees with *proportion*, and *comparably* is more concise than *to a comparable extent*. The modifying clause *who are women* follows (1) *judges* and (2) *partners at major law firms* as closely as is possible given the content of the sentence; this positioning has the virtue of being clear in its meaning.

D The contrast has already been introduced by *despite*, so the addition of *yet* is illogical and ungrammatical; *to a comparable extent* is wordy.

E *Despite* introduces the contrast; adding *yet* is illogical and results in an ungrammatical construction.

The correct answer is C.

92. Seldom more than 40 feet wide and 12 feet deep, but it ran 363 miles across the rugged wilderness of upstate New York, the Erie Canal connected the Hudson River at Albany to the Great Lakes at Buffalo, providing the port of New York City with a direct water link to the heartland of the North American continent.

(A) Seldom more than 40 feet wide and 12 feet deep, but it ran 363 miles across the rugged wilderness of upstate New York, the Erie Canal connected

(B) Seldom more than 40 feet wide or 12 feet deep but running 363 miles across the rugged wilderness of upstate New York, the Erie Canal connected

(C) It was seldom more than 40 feet wide and 12 feet deep, and ran 363 miles across the rugged wilderness of upstate New York, but the Erie Canal, connecting

(D) The Erie Canal was seldom more than 40 feet wide or 12 feet deep and it ran 363 miles across the rugged wilderness of upstate New York, which connected

(E) The Erie Canal, seldom more than 40 feet wide and 12 feet deep, but running 363 miles across the rugged wilderness of upstate New York, connecting

Logical predication; Grammatical construction

The phrase *seldom...deep* is the first half of a modifier that describes *the Erie Canal.* However, because a comma incorrectly follows *deep*, this phrase appears to be the entire modifier, which must agree with the noun or pronoun that immediately follows it. This phrase cannot modify the conjunction *but*, and *it* has no referent; *but it ran* is not a logical or grammatical construction following the modifying phrase. Substituting *running* for *it ran* creates an adjective phrase parallel to the first adjective phrase (*seldom... deep*). To contrast the small size reported in the first phrase with the great distance reported in the second, the two phrases may be joined with *but*; together they create a single modifier correctly modifying *the Erie Canal. The Erie Canal* is then the subject of the sentence and requires the verb *connected* to provide a logical statement.

A *But it ran* cannot logically or grammatically follow the modifying phrase.

B **Correct**. This sentence properly has the single modifier consisting of two contrasting parts.

C Neither *and* nor *but* acts as a logical connector; the use of *connecting* results in a sentence fragment.

D The paired concepts of width and depth should be joined by *and*, not *or*; this construction calls for two main clauses to be separated by a comma after *deep*; *which* is ambiguous.

E The two halves of the modifier should not be separated by a comma after *deep*; the subject is awkwardly and confusingly placed at a great distance from the predicate; the use of *connecting* rather than *connected* creates a sentence fragment.

The correct answer is B.

93. In 1923, the Supreme Court declared a minimum wage for women and children in the District of Columbia as unconstitutional, and ruling that it was a form of price-fixing and, as such, an abridgment of the right of contract.

(A) the Supreme Court declared a minimum wage for women and children in the District of Columbia as unconstitutional, and

(B) the Supreme Court declared as unconstitutional a minimum wage for women and children in the District of Columbia, and

(C) the Supreme Court declared unconstitutional a minimum wage for women and children in the District of Columbia,

(D) a minimum wage for women and children in the District of Columbia was declared unconstitutional by the Supreme Court,

(E) when the Supreme Court declared a minimum wage for women and children in the District of Columbia as unconstitutional,

Idiom; Grammatical construction

This sentence depends on the correct use of an idiom: *the court declares x unconstitutional*. The inverted form should be used here because of the long phrases involved: *the court declares unconstitutional x*. *The Supreme Court* is the subject of the sentence; *declared* is the verb. *Ruling... contract* acts as a modifier describing the action of the main clause; because the modifier is subordinate to the main clause, the conjunction *and* must be omitted. *And* is used to join two independent clauses, not a clause and its modifier.

A *Declared...as unconstitutional* is not the correct idiom; the use of *and* creates an ungrammatical construction.

B *Declared as unconstitutional* is not the correct idiom; the use of *and* creates an ungrammatical construction.

C **Correct**. In this sentence, the correct idiom is used, and the modifier is grammatically and logically attached to the main clause.

D Passive voice construction is weak and wordy; its use causes the modifier to be misplaced and ambiguous.

E *Declared...as unconstitutional* is not the correct idiom; *when* transforms the main clause into a subordinate clause, resulting in a sentence fragment.

The correct answer is C.

94. Researchers have found that individuals who have been blind from birth, and <u>who thus have never seen anyone gesture, nevertheless make hand motions when speaking just as frequently and in virtually the same way as sighted people do, and that they will gesture</u> even when conversing with another blind person.

(A) who thus have never seen anyone gesture, nevertheless make hand motions when speaking just as frequently and in virtually the same way as sighted people do, and that they will gesture

(B) who thus never saw anyone gesturing, nevertheless make hand motions when speaking just as frequent and in virtually the same way as sighted people did, and that they will gesture

(C) who thus have never seen anyone gesture, nevertheless made hand motions when speaking just as frequently and in virtually the same way as sighted people do, as well as gesturing

(D) thus never having seen anyone gesture, nevertheless made hand motions when speaking just as frequent and in virtually the same way as sighted people did, as well as gesturing

(E) thus never having seen anyone gesture, nevertheless to make hand motions when speaking just as frequently and in virtually the same way as sighted people do, and to gesture

Parallelism; Verb form; Diction

The researchers have found (1) *that individuals... make hand motions...as sighted people do* and (2) *that they will gesture...with another blind person*. In the original sentence, the two findings are reported in two parallel subordinate clauses introduced by *that*. The verb tenses are logical and parallel: *who have been blind* and *who have never seen* indicate a condition that began in the past and continues in the present; *make* and *do* refer to present actions. The verb *make* (*hand motions*) is correctly modified by the adverb *frequently* to show how the action of the verb is carried out. The emphatic future *will gesture* is properly used here with *even* to emphasize the extreme or the unexpected.

A **Correct**. Although the original sentence is complicated, the parallelism of its structure and phrasing allows its meaning to be clear and its expression effective.

B Verbs *saw* and *did* indicate action completed in the past; the simple past tense is not appropriate in either case; the adjective *frequent* cannot modify the verb; awkward and muddy.

C *Made* indicates past action, but the present tense is logically required; *as well as gesturing* violates the parallelism of the two subordinate (*that*) clauses; choppy and unclear.

D *Having seen* is not parallel to *have been; made* and *did* do not show ongoing action; *frequent* incorrectly modifies the verb; *as well as gesturing* destroys the parallelism of the two subordinate (*that*) clauses; awkward and unclear.

E Replacing the verb *make* with the infinitive *to make* results in an ungrammatical construction that fails to complete the sentence.

The correct answer is A.

95. Like embryonic germ cells, which are cells that develop early in the formation of the fetus and that later generate eggs or sperm, <u>embryonic stem cells have the ability of developing themselves into different kinds of body tissue</u>.

(A) embryonic stem cells have the ability of developing themselves into different kinds of body tissue

(B) embryonic stem cells have the ability to develop into different kinds of body tissue

(C) in embryonic stem cells there is the ability to develop into different kinds of body tissue

(D) the ability to develop themselves into different kinds of body tissue characterizes embryonic stem cells

(E) the ability of developing into different kinds of body tissue characterizes embryonic stem cells

Idiom; Grammatical construction

Two constructions create problems in the original sentence. The first is the unidiomatic construction *have the ability of developing; ability* must be followed by an infinitive, *to develop*, not a phrase. The second problematic construction is *to develop themselves into*. In this biological context, the verb *develop* means to progress from an earlier to a later stage; it is used intransitively, which means that it cannot take an object. The pronoun *themselves* acts as an object, creating a construction that is not grammatical or logical. Omitting the pronoun removes the problem.

A *Ability* is incorrectly followed by *of developing*; a pronoun cannot follow *develop*, when it is used, as it is here, in its intransitive sense.

B **Correct**. *Ability* is properly followed by the infinitive in this sentence, and the pronoun *themselves* is omitted.

C This awkward and wordy construction violates the parallelism of *like embryonic germ cells…embryonic stem cells…*.

D The two parts of the comparison must be parallel; *like embryonic germ cells* must be followed by *embryonic stem cells*, not *the ability to develop*.

E *Ability* is followed by the unidiomatic *of developing* rather than *to develop*; the main clause must begin with *embryonic stem cells* to balance and complete *like embryonic germ cells*.

The correct answer is B.

96. Critics contend that the new missile is a weapon whose importance is largely symbolic, more a tool <u>for manipulating people's perceptions than to fulfill</u> a real military need.

(A) for manipulating people's perceptions than to fulfill

(B) for manipulating people's perceptions than for fulfilling

(C) to manipulate people's perceptions rather than that it fulfills

(D) to manipulate people's perceptions rather than fulfilling

(E) to manipulate people's perceptions than for fulfilling

Parallelism

This sentence uses the comparative construction *more x than y* where *x* and *y* must be parallel. Here, *x* is *a tool for manipulating people's perceptions*, and *y* is *to fulfill a real military need. A tool* does not need to be repeated in the second half of the comparison because it is understood, but the wording of the two phrases does need to match. There are two acceptable solutions: (1) *for manipulating* can be followed by *for fulfilling* or (2) *to manipulate* can be followed by *to fulfill.*

A *For manipulating* is not parallel to *to fulfill.*

B **Correct**. *For manipulating* and *for fulfilling* are parallel in this sentence.

C *To manipulate* is not parallel to *that it fulfills.*

D *To manipulate* is not parallel to *fulfilling.*

E *To manipulate* is not parallel to *for fulfilling.*

The correct answer is B.

97. As an actress and, more importantly, as a teacher of acting, Stella Adler was one of the most influential artists in the American theater, who trained several generations of actors including Marlon Brando and Robert De Niro.

(A) Stella Adler was one of the most influential artists in the American theater, who trained several generations of actors including

(B) Stella Adler, one of the most influential artists in the American theater, trained several generations of actors who include

(C) Stella Adler was one of the most influential artists in the American theater, training several generations of actors whose ranks included

(D) one of the most influential artists in the American theater was Stella Adler, who trained several generations of actors including

(E) one of the most influential artists in the American theater, Stella Adler, trained several generations of actors whose ranks included

Logical predication

The original sentence contains a number of modifiers, but not all of them are correctly expressed. The clause *who trained...* describes *Stella Adler*, yet a relative clause such as this one must be placed immediately after the noun or pronoun it modifies, and this clause follows *theater* rather than *Adler*. Replacing *who trained* with *training* corrects the error because the phrase *training...* modifies the whole preceding clause rather than the single preceding noun. *Several generations of actors including* shows the same error in reverse; *including* modifies the whole phrase, but the two actors named are not *generations of actors*. The more limiting clause *whose ranks included* (referring to *actors*) is appropriate here.

A Relative (*who*) clause follows *theater* rather than *Adler*; *including* refers to *generations of actors*, when the reference should be to *actors* only.

B This construction, in which the subject is both preceded and followed by modifiers, is awkward; the verbs should be consistently in the past tense, but *include* is present tense.

C **Correct**. In this sentence, substituting *training* for *who trained* and *whose ranks included* for *including* eliminates the modification errors.

D Introductory modifier must be immediately followed by *Stella Adler*, not *one...*; *including* refers to *generations of actors* rather than to *actors* only.

E Introductory modifier must be immediately followed by *Stella Adler*, not one.

The correct answer is C.

98. By developing the Secure Digital Music Initiative, the recording industry associations of North America, Japan, and Europe hope to create a standardized way of distributing songs and full-length recordings on the Internet that will protect copyright holders and foil the many audio pirates who copy and distribute digital music illegally.

(A) of distributing songs and full-length recordings on the Internet that will protect copyright holders and foil the many audio pirates who copy and distribute

(B) of distributing songs and full-length recordings on the Internet and to protect copyright holders and foiling the many audio pirates copying and distributing

(C) for distributing songs and full-length recordings on the Internet while it protects copyright holders and foils the many audio pirates who copy and distribute

(D) to distribute songs and full-length recordings on the Internet while they will protect copyright holders and foil the many audio pirates copying and distributing

(E) to distribute songs and full-length recordings on the Internet and it will protect copyright holders and foiling the many audio pirates who copy and distribute

Parallelism

The original sentence depends on the parallelism of its verbs to make its point clearly and effectively. *A standardized way...will protect* and (*will* understood) *foil; pirates...copy and distribute.* In the first pair of parallel verbs, *will* does not need to be repeated because it is understood.

A **Correct**. The verbs *will protect* and (*will*) *foil* are parallel in this sentence, as are the verbs *copy* and *distribute.*

B *And to protect* distorts meaning, suggesting that protection comes in addition to *the standardized way; foiling* is not parallel to *to protect.*

C *Way for* should instead be *way of;* the pronoun reference in *while it protects* is ambiguous; construction suggests that protection comes from something other than the *standardized way.*

D Pronoun *they* has no referent; use of *while* suggests that protection comes from something other than the *standardized way* of distribution.

E *And it will protect* distorts meaning, suggesting that protection comes in addition to *the standardized way; will protect* and *foiling* are not parallel.

The correct answer is A.

99. Whereas a ramjet generally cannot achieve high speeds without the initial assistance of a rocket, high speeds can be attained by scramjets, or supersonic combustion ramjets, in that they reduce airflow compression at the entrance of the engine and letting air pass through at supersonic speeds.

(A) high speeds can be attained by scramjets, or supersonic combustion ramjets, in that they reduce

(B) that high speeds can be attained by scramjets, or supersonic combustion ramjets, is a result of their reducing

(C) the ability of scramjets, or supersonic combustion ramjets, to achieve high speeds is because they reduce

(D) scramjets, or supersonic combustion ramjets, have the ability of attaining high speeds when reducing

(E) scramjets, or supersonic combustion ramjets, can attain high speeds by reducing

Rhetorical construction

The underlined portion of the original sentence is wordy and ineffective. Transforming it from passive (*high speeds can be attained by scramjets*) to active voice (*scramjets can attain high speeds*) eliminates much of the problem. As the subject of the main clause, *scramjets* correctly parallels *a ramjet*, the subject of the subordinate clause; the contrast is thus clearly and effectively drawn. *In that they reduce* is wordy and awkward; it can be replaced by the more concise phrase *by reducing*.

A Passive voice contributes to a wordy, awkward, and ineffective construction; *in that they reduce* is also wordy and awkward.

B Passive voice and subordinate (*that*) clause constructions are wordy, awkward, and ineffective.

C *The ability...is because* is not a grammatical construction; *scramjets*, not *the ability*, should be parallel to *a ramjet*.

D *Have the ability of attaining* is wordy; *when* does not indicate the cause-and-effect relationship.

E **Correct**. *Scramjets* parallels *a ramjet* for an effective contrast in this sentence; the active voice is clear and concise; *by reducing* shows how scramjets attain high speeds.

The correct answer is E.

100. It will not be possible to implicate melting sea ice in the coastal flooding that many global warming models have projected: just like a glass of water that will not overflow due to melting ice cubes, so melting sea ice does not increase oceanic volume.

(A) like a glass of water that will not overflow due to melting ice cubes,

(B) like melting ice cubes that do not cause a glass of water to overflow,

(C) a glass of water will not overflow because of melting ice cubes,

(D) as melting ice cubes that do not cause a glass of water to overflow,

(E) as melting ice cubes do not cause a glass of water to overflow,

Diction; Parallelism

The preposition *like* introduces nouns and noun phrases; the conjunction *as* introduces verbs or clauses, so *as* is required here. The comparative construction used here is *just as x so y; x* and *y* must be parallel. The *y* clause is written in effective subject-verb-object order: *melting sea ice does not increase oceanic volume*. The original wordy, awkward *x* clause is not parallel. To make it parallel, *melting ice cubes* should be the subject of the clause, *do not cause...to overflow* the verb phrase, and a *glass of water* the object.

A *Like* is used in place of *as*; the two elements of comparison are not parallel.

B *Like* is used in place of *as; that* violates parallelism.

C *As* or *just as* is needed to introduce the clause; the two clauses are not parallel.

D *That* violates the parallelism of the two clauses and creates an ungrammatical construction.

E **Correct**. This sentence has *just as* properly introducing the first clause, and the two clauses are parallel.

The correct answer is E.

4.0 Math Review

4.0 Math Review

Although this chapter provides a review of some of the mathematical concepts of arithmetic, algebra, and geometry, it is not intended to be a textbook. You should use this chapter to familiarize yourself with the kinds of topics that may be tested in the GMAT® exam. You may wish to consult an arithmetic, algebra, or geometry book for a more detailed discussion of some of the topics.

Section 4.1, "Arithmetic," includes the following topics:

1. Properties of Integers
2. Fractions
3. Decimals
4. Real Numbers
5. Ratio and Proportion
6. Percents
7. Powers and Roots of Numbers
8. Descriptive Statistics
9. Sets
10. Counting Methods
11. Discrete Probability

Section 4.2, "Algebra," does not extend beyond what is usually covered in a first-year high school algebra course. The topics included are as follows:

1. Simplifying Algebraic Expressions
2. Equations
3. Solving Linear Equations with One Unknown
4. Solving Two Linear Equations with Two Unknowns
5. Solving Equations by Factoring
6. Solving Quadratic Equations
7. Exponents
8. Inequalities
9. Absolute Value
10. Functions

Section 4.3, "Geometry," is limited primarily to measurement and intuitive geometry or spatial visualization. Extensive knowledge of theorems and the ability to construct proofs, skills that are usually developed in a formal geometry course, are not tested. The topics included in this section are the following:

1. Lines
2. Intersecting Lines and Angles
3. Perpendicular Lines
4. Parallel Lines
5. Polygons (Convex)
6. Triangles
7. Quadrilaterals
8. Circles
9. Rectangular Solids and Cylinders
10. Coordinate Geometry

Section 4.4, "Word Problems," presents examples of and solutions to the following types of word problems:

1. Rate Problems
2. Work Problems
3. Mixture Problems
4. Interest Problems
5. Discount
6. Profit
7. Sets
8. Geometry Problems
9. Measurement Problems
10. Data Interpretation

4.1 Arithmetic

1. Properties of Integers

An *integer* is any number in the set $\{\ldots -3, -2, -1, 0, 1, 2, 3, \ldots\}$. If x and y are integers and $x \neq 0$, then x is a *divisor* (*factor*) of y provided that $y = xn$ for some integer n. In this case, y is also said to be *divisible* by x or to be a *multiple* of x. For example, 7 is a divisor or factor of 28 since $28 = (7)(4)$, but 8 is not a divisor of 28 since there is no integer n such that $28 = 8n$.

If x and y are positive integers, there exist unique integers q and r, called the *quotient* and *remainder*, respectively, such that $y = xq + r$ and $0 \leq r < x$. For example, when 28 is divided by 8, the quotient is 3 and the remainder is 4 since $28 = (8)(3) + 4$. Note that y is divisible by x if and only if the remainder r is 0; for example, 32 has a remainder of 0 when divided by 8 because 32 is divisible by 8. Also, note that when a smaller integer is divided by a larger integer, the quotient is 0 and the remainder is the smaller integer. For example, 5 divided by 7 has the quotient 0 and the remainder 5 since $5 = (7)(0) + 5$.

Any integer that is divisible by 2 is an *even integer*; the set of even integers is $\{\ldots -4, -2, 0, 2, 4, 6, 8, \ldots\}$. Integers that are not divisible by 2 are *odd integers*; $\{\ldots -3, -1, 1, 3, 5, \ldots\}$ is the set of odd integers.

If at least one factor of a product of integers is even, then the product is even; otherwise the product is odd. If two integers are both even or both odd, then their sum and their difference are even. Otherwise, their sum and their difference are odd.

A *prime* number is a positive integer that has exactly two different positive divisors, 1 and itself. For example, 2, 3, 5, 7, 11, and 13 are prime numbers, but 15 is not, since 15 has four different positive divisors, 1, 3, 5, and 15. The number 1 is not a prime number since it has only one positive divisor. Every integer greater than 1 either is prime or can be uniquely expressed as a product of prime factors. For example, $14 = (2)(7)$, $81 = (3)(3)(3)(3)$, and $484 = (2)(2)(11)(11)$.

The numbers $-2, -1, 0, 1, 2, 3, 4, 5$ are *consecutive integers*. Consecutive integers can be represented by $n, n + 1, n + 2, n + 3, \ldots$, where n is an integer. The numbers 0, 2, 4, 6, 8 are *consecutive even integers*, and 1, 3, 5, 7, 9 are *consecutive odd integers*. Consecutive even integers can be represented by $2n, 2n + 2, 2n + 4, \ldots$, and consecutive odd integers can be represented by $2n + 1, 2n + 3, 2n + 5, \ldots$, where n is an integer.

Properties of the integer 1. If n is any number, then $1 \cdot n = n$, and for any number $n \neq 0$, $n \cdot \frac{1}{n} = 1$.

The number 1 can be expressed in many ways; for example, $\frac{n}{n} = 1$ for any number $n \neq 0$.

Multiplying or dividing an expression by 1, in any form, does not change the value of that expression.

Properties of the integer 0. The integer 0 is neither positive nor negative. If n is any number, then $n + 0 = n$ and $n \cdot 0 = 0$. Division by 0 is not defined.

2. Fractions

In a fraction $\frac{n}{d}$, n is the *numerator* and d is the *denominator*. The denominator of a fraction can never be 0, because division by 0 is not defined.

Two fractions are said to be *equivalent* if they represent the same number. For example, $\frac{8}{36}$ and $\frac{14}{63}$ are equivalent since they both represent the number $\frac{2}{9}$. In each case, the fraction is reduced to lowest terms by dividing both numerator and denominator by their *greatest common divisor* (gcd). The gcd of 8 and 36 is 4 and the gcd of 14 and 63 is 7.

Addition and subtraction of fractions.

Two fractions with the same denominator can be added or subtracted by performing the required operation with the numerators, leaving the denominators the same. For example, $\frac{3}{5}+\frac{4}{5}=\frac{3+4}{5}=\frac{7}{5}$ and $\frac{5}{7}-\frac{2}{7}=\frac{5-2}{7}=\frac{3}{7}$. If two fractions do not have the same denominator, express them as equivalent fractions with the same denominator. For example, to add $\frac{3}{5}$ and $\frac{4}{7}$, multiply the numerator and denominator of the first fraction by 7 and the numerator and denominator of the second fraction by 5, obtaining $\frac{21}{35}$ and $\frac{20}{35}$, respectively; $\frac{21}{35}+\frac{20}{35}=\frac{41}{35}$.

For the new denominator, choosing the *least common multiple* (lcm) of the denominators usually lessens the work. For $\frac{2}{3}+\frac{1}{6}$, the lcm of 3 and 6 is 6 (not 3 × 6 = 18), so $\frac{2}{3}+\frac{1}{6}=\frac{2}{3}\times\frac{2}{2}+\frac{1}{6}=\frac{4}{6}+\frac{1}{6}=\frac{5}{6}$.

Multiplication and division of fractions.

To multiply two fractions, simply multiply the two numerators and multiply the two denominators.

For example, $\frac{2}{3}\times\frac{4}{7}=\frac{2\times4}{3\times7}=\frac{8}{21}$.

To divide by a fraction, invert the divisor (that is, find its *reciprocal*) and multiply. For example, $\frac{2}{3}\div\frac{4}{7}=\frac{2}{3}\times\frac{7}{4}=\frac{14}{12}=\frac{7}{6}$.

In the problem above, the reciprocal of $\frac{4}{7}$ is $\frac{7}{4}$. In general, the reciprocal of a fraction $\frac{n}{d}$ is $\frac{d}{n}$, where n and d are not zero.

Mixed numbers.

A number that consists of a whole number and a fraction, for example, $7\frac{2}{3}$, is a mixed number: $7\frac{2}{3}$ means $7+\frac{2}{3}$.

To change a mixed number into a fraction, multiply the whole number by the denominator of the fraction and add this number to the numerator of the fraction; then put the result over the denominator of the fraction. For example, $7\frac{2}{3}=\frac{(3\times7)+2}{3}=\frac{23}{3}$.

3. Decimals

In the decimal system, the position of the period or *decimal point* determines the place value of the digits. For example, the digits in the number 7,654.321 have the following place values:

Thousands		Hundreds	Tens	Ones or units		Tenths	Hundredths	Thousandths
7	,	6	5	4	.	3	2	1

Some examples of decimals follow.

$$0.321 = \frac{3}{10} + \frac{2}{100} + \frac{1}{1{,}000} = \frac{321}{1{,}000}$$

$$0.0321 = \frac{0}{10} + \frac{3}{100} + \frac{2}{1{,}000} + \frac{1}{10{,}000} = \frac{321}{10{,}000}$$

$$1.56 = 1 + \frac{5}{10} + \frac{6}{100} = \frac{156}{100}$$

Sometimes decimals are expressed as the product of a number with only one digit to the left of the decimal point and a power of 10. This is called *scientific notation.* For example, 231 can be written as 2.31×10^2 and 0.0231 can be written as 2.31×10^{-2}. When a number is expressed in scientific notation, the exponent of the 10 indicates the number of places that the decimal point is to be moved in the number that is to be multiplied by a power of 10 in order to obtain the product. The decimal point is moved to the right if the exponent is positive and to the left if the exponent is negative. For example, 2.013×10^4 is equal to 20,130 and 1.91×10^{-4} is equal to 0.000191.

Addition and subtraction of decimals.

To add or subtract two decimals, the decimal points of both numbers should be lined up. If one of the numbers has fewer digits to the right of the decimal point than the other, zeros may be inserted to the right of the last digit. For example, to add 17.6512 and 653.27, set up the numbers in a column and add:

$$\begin{array}{r} 17.6512 \\ +\,653.2700 \\ \hline 670.9212 \end{array}$$

Likewise for 653.27 minus 17.6512:

$$\begin{array}{r} 653.2700 \\ -17.6512 \\ \hline 635.6188 \end{array}$$

Multiplication of decimals.

To multiply decimals, multiply the numbers as if they were whole numbers and then insert the decimal point in the product so that the number of digits to the right of the decimal point is equal to the sum of the numbers of digits to the right of the decimal points in the numbers being multiplied. For example:

$$\begin{array}{rl} 2.09 & \text{(2 digits to the right)} \\ \times 1.3 & \text{(1 digit to the right)} \\ \hline 627 & \\ 2090 & \\ \hline 2.717 & (2+1=3 \text{ digits to the right}) \end{array}$$

Division of decimals.

To divide a number (the dividend) by a decimal (the divisor), move the decimal point of the divisor to the right until the divisor is a whole number. Then move the decimal point of the dividend the same number of places to the right, and divide as you would by a whole number. The decimal point in the quotient will be directly above the decimal point in the new dividend. For example, to divide 698.12 by 12.4:

$$12.4\overline{)698.12}$$

will be replaced by:

$$124\overline{)6981.2}$$

and the division would proceed as follows:

$$\begin{array}{r} 56.3 \\ 124\overline{)6981.2} \\ \underline{620} \\ 781 \\ \underline{744} \\ 372 \\ \underline{372} \\ 0 \end{array}$$

4. Real Numbers

All *real* numbers correspond to points on the number line and all points on the number line correspond to real numbers. All real numbers except zero are either positive or negative.

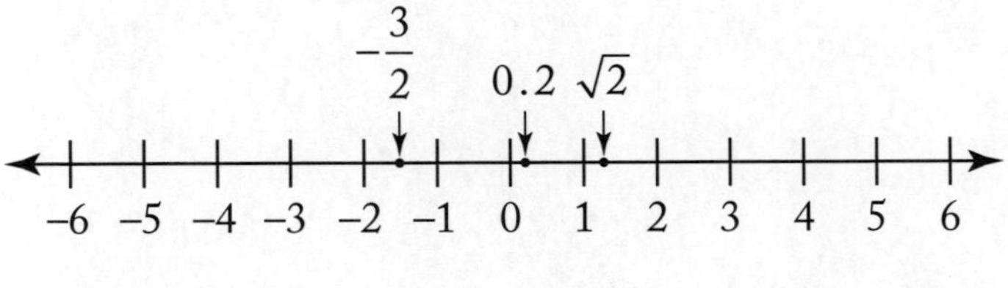

On a number line, numbers corresponding to points to the left of zero are negative and numbers corresponding to points to the right of zero are positive. For any two numbers on the number line, the number to the left is less than the number to the right; for example, $-4 < -3 < -\frac{3}{2} < -1$, and $1 < \sqrt{2} < 2$.

To say that the number n is between 1 and 4 on the number line means that $n > 1$ and $n < 4$, that is, $1 < n < 4$. If n is "between 1 and 4, inclusive," then $1 \le n \le 4$.

The distance between a number and zero on the number line is called the *absolute value* of the number. Thus 3 and −3 have the same absolute value, 3, since they are both three units from zero. The absolute value of 3 is denoted $|3|$. Examples of absolute values of numbers are

$$|-5| = |5| = 5, \left|-\frac{7}{2}\right| = \frac{7}{2}, \text{ and } |0| = 0.$$

Note that the absolute value of any nonzero number is positive.

Here are some properties of real numbers that are used frequently. If x, y, and z are real numbers, then

(1) $x + y = y + x$ and $xy = yx$.
For example, $8 + 3 = 3 + 8 = 11$, and $(17)(5) = (5)(17) = 85$.

(2) $(x + y) + z = x + (y + z)$ and $(xy)z = x(yz)$.
For example, $(7 + 5) + 2 = 7 + (5 + 2) = 7 + (7) = 14$, and $\left(5\sqrt{3}\right)\left(\sqrt{3}\right) = (5)\left(\sqrt{3}\sqrt{3}\right) = (5)(3) = 15$.

(3) $xy + xz = x(y + z)$.
For example, $718(36) + 718(64) = 718(36 + 64) = 718(100) = 71{,}800$.

(4) If x and y are both positive, then $x + y$ and xy are positive.

(5) If x and y are both negative, then $x + y$ is negative and xy is positive.

(6) If x is positive and y is negative, then xy is negative.

(7) If $xy = 0$, then $x = 0$ or $y = 0$. For example, $3y = 0$ implies $y = 0$.

(8) $|x + y| \le |x| + |y|$. For example, if $x = 10$ and $y = 2$, then $|x + y| = |12| = 12 = |x| + |y|$; and if $x = 10$ and $y = -2$, then $|x + y| = |8| = 8 < 12 = |x| + |y|$.

5. Ratio and Proportion

The *ratio* of the number a to the number b ($b \ne 0$) is $\frac{a}{b}$.

A ratio may be expressed or represented in several ways. For example, the ratio of 2 to 3 can be written as 2 to 3, 2:3, or $\frac{2}{3}$. The order of the terms of a ratio is important. For example, the ratio of the number of months with exactly 30 days to the number with exactly 31 days is $\frac{4}{7}$, not $\frac{7}{4}$.

A *proportion* is a statement that two ratios are equal; for example, $\frac{2}{3} = \frac{8}{12}$ is a proportion. One way to solve a proportion involving an unknown is to cross multiply, obtaining a new equality. For example, to solve for n in the proportion $\frac{2}{3} = \frac{n}{12}$, cross multiply, obtaining $24 = 3n$; then divide both sides by 3, to get $n = 8$.

6. Percents

Percent means *per hundred* or *number out of 100*. A percent can be represented as a fraction with a denominator of 100, or as a decimal. For example:

$$37\% = \frac{37}{100} = 0.37.$$

To find a certain percent of a number, multiply the number by the percent expressed as a decimal or fraction. For example:

$$20\% \text{ of } 90 = 0.2 \times 90 = 18$$

or

$$20\% \text{ of } 90 = \frac{20}{100} \times 90 = \frac{1}{5} \times 90 = 18.$$

Percents greater than 100%.

Percents greater than 100% are represented by numbers greater than 1. For example:

$$300\% = \frac{300}{100} = 3$$
$$250\% \text{ of } 80 = 2.5 \times 80 = 200.$$

Percents less than 1%.

The percent 0.5% means $\frac{1}{2}$ of 1 percent. For example, 0.5% of 12 is equal to $0.005 \times 12 = 0.06$.

Percent change.

Often a problem will ask for the percent increase or decrease from one quantity to another quantity. For example, "If the price of an item increases from \$24 to \$30, what is the percent increase in price?" To find the percent increase, first find the amount of the increase; then divide this increase by the original amount, and express this quotient as a percent. In the example above, the percent increase would be found in the following way: the amount of the increase is $(30 - 24) = 6$. Therefore, the percent increase is $\frac{6}{24} = 0.25 = 25\%$.

Likewise, to find the percent decrease (for example, the price of an item is reduced from \$30 to \$24), first find the amount of the decrease; then divide this decrease by the original amount, and express this quotient as a percent. In the example above, the amount of decrease is $(30 - 24) = 6$.

Therefore, the percent decrease is $\frac{6}{30} = 0.20 = 20\%$.

Note that the percent increase from 24 to 30 is not the same as the percent decrease from 30 to 24.

In the following example, the increase is greater than 100 percent: If the cost of a certain house in 1983 was 300 percent of its cost in 1970, by what percent did the cost increase?

If n is the cost in 1970, then the percent increase is equal to $\frac{3n-n}{n}=\frac{2n}{n}=2$, or 200%.

7. Powers and Roots of Numbers

When a number k is to be used n times as a factor in a product, it can be expressed as k^n, which means the nth power of k. For example, $2^2=2\times2=4$ and $2^3=2\times2\times2=8$ are powers of 2.

Squaring a number that is greater than 1, or raising it to a higher power, results in a larger number; squaring a number between 0 and 1 results in a smaller number. For example:

$$3^2=9 \quad (9>3)$$
$$\left(\frac{1}{3}\right)^2=\frac{1}{9} \quad \left(\frac{1}{9}<\frac{1}{3}\right)$$
$$(0.1)^2=0.01 \quad (0.01<0.1)$$

A *square root* of a number n is a number that, when squared, is equal to n. The square root of a negative number is not a real number. Every positive number n has two square roots, one positive and the other negative, but $\sqrt{n}$ denotes the positive number whose square is n. For example, $\sqrt{9}$ denotes 3. The two square roots of 9 are $\sqrt{9}=3$ and $-\sqrt{9}=-3$.

Every real number r has exactly one real *cube root,* which is the number s such that $s^3=r$. The real cube root of r is denoted by $\sqrt[3]{r}$. Since $2^3=8$, $\sqrt[3]{8}=2$. Similarly, $\sqrt[3]{-8}=-2$, because $(-2)^3=-8$.

8. Descriptive Statistics

A list of numbers, or numerical data, can be described by various statistical measures. One of the most common of these measures is the *average,* or *(arithmetic) mean,* which locates a type of "center" for the data. The average of n numbers is defined as the sum of the n numbers divided by n. For example, the average of 6, 4, 7, 10, and 4 is $\frac{6+4+7+10+4}{5}=\frac{31}{5}=6.2$.

The *median* is another type of center for a list of numbers. To calculate the median of n numbers, first order the numbers from least to greatest; if n is odd, the median is defined as the middle number, whereas if n is even, the median is defined as the average of the two middle numbers. In the example above, the numbers, in order, are 4, 4, 6, 7, 10, and the median is 6, the middle number.

For the numbers 4, 6, 6, 8, 9, 12, the median is $\frac{6+8}{2}=7$. Note that the mean of these numbers is 7.5.

The median of a set of data can be less than, equal to, or greater than the mean. Note that for a large set of data (for example, the salaries of 800 company employees), it is often true that about half of the data is less than the median and about half of the data is greater than the median; but this is not always the case, as the following data show.

3, 5, 7, 7, 7, 7, 7, 7, 8, 9, 9, 9, 9, 10, 10

Here the median is 7, but only $\frac{2}{15}$ of the data is less than the median.

The *mode* of a list of numbers is the number that occurs most frequently in the list. For example, the mode of 1, 3, 6, 4, 3, 5 is 3. A list of numbers may have more than one mode. For example, the list 1, 2, 3, 3, 3, 5, 7, 10, 10, 10, 20 has two modes, 3 and 10.

The degree to which numerical data are spread out or dispersed can be measured in many ways. The simplest measure of dispersion is the *range,* which is defined as the greatest value in the numerical data minus the least value. For example, the range of 11, 10, 5, 13, 21 is 21 – 5 = 16. Note how the range depends on only two values in the data.

One of the most common measures of dispersion is the *standard deviation.* Generally speaking, the more the data are spread away from the mean, the greater the standard deviation. The standard deviation of n numbers can be calculated as follows: (1) find the arithmetic mean, (2) find the differences between the mean and each of the n numbers, (3) square each of the differences, (4) find the average of the squared differences, and (5) take the nonnegative square root of this average. Shown below is this calculation for the data 0, 7, 8, 10, 10, which have arithmetic mean 7.

x	$x-7$	$(x-7)^2$
0	–7	49
7	0	0
8	1	1
10	3	9
10	3	9
	Total	68

Standard deviation $\sqrt{\dfrac{68}{5}} \approx 3.7$

Notice that the standard deviation depends on every data value, although it depends most on values that are farthest from the mean. This is why a distribution with data grouped closely around the mean will have a smaller standard deviation than will data spread far from the mean. To illustrate this, compare the data 6, 6, 6.5, 7.5, 9, which also have mean 7. Note that the numbers in the second set of data seem to be grouped more closely around the mean of 7 than the numbers in the first set. This is reflected in the standard deviation, which is less for the second set (approximately 1.1) than for the first set (approximately 3.7).

There are many ways to display numerical data that show how the data are distributed. One simple way is with a *frequency distribution,* which is useful for data that have values occurring with varying frequencies. For example, the 20 numbers

–4	0	0	–3	–2	–1	–1	0	–1	–4
–1	–5	0	–2	0	–5	–2	0	0	–1

are displayed on the next page in a frequency distribution by listing each different value x and the frequency f with which x occurs.

Data Value x	Frequency f
–5	2
–4	2
–3	1
–2	3
–1	5
0	7
Total	20

From the frequency distribution, one can readily compute descriptive statistics:

Mean: $= \frac{(-5)(2)+(-4)(2)+(-3)(1)+(-2)(3)+(-1)(5)+(0)(7)}{20} = -1.6$

Median: –1 (the average of the 10th and 11th numbers)

Mode: 0 (the number that occurs most frequently)

Range: $0 - (-5) = 5$

Standard deviation: $\sqrt{\frac{(-5+1.6)^2(2)+(-4+1.6)^2(2)+\ldots+(0+1.6)^2(7)}{20}} \approx 1.7$

9. Sets

In mathematics a *set* is a collection of numbers or other objects. The objects are called the *elements* of the set. If S is a set having a finite number of elements, then the number of elements is denoted by $|S|$. Such a set is often defined by listing its elements; for example, $S = \{-5, 0, 1\}$ is a set with $|S| = 3$. The order in which the elements are listed in a set does not matter; thus $\{-5, 0, 1\} = \{0, 1, -5\}$. If all the elements of a set S are also elements of a set T, then S is a *subset* of T; for example, $S = \{-5, 0, 1\}$ is a subset of $T = \{-5, 0, 1, 4, 10\}$.

For any two sets A and B, the *union* of A and B is the set of all elements that are in A *or* in B *or* in both. The *intersection* of A and B is the set of all elements that are both in A *and* in B. The union is denoted by $A \cup B$ and the intersection is denoted by $A \cap B$. As an example, if $A = \{3, 4\}$ and $B = \{4, 5, 6\}$, then $A \cup B = \{3, 4, 5, 6\}$ and $A \cap B = \{4\}$. Two sets that have no elements in common are said to be *disjoint* or *mutually exclusive*.

The relationship between sets is often illustrated with a *Venn diagram* in which sets are represented by regions in a plane. For two sets S and T that are not disjoint and neither is a subset of the other, the intersection $S \cap T$ is represented by the shaded region of the diagram below.

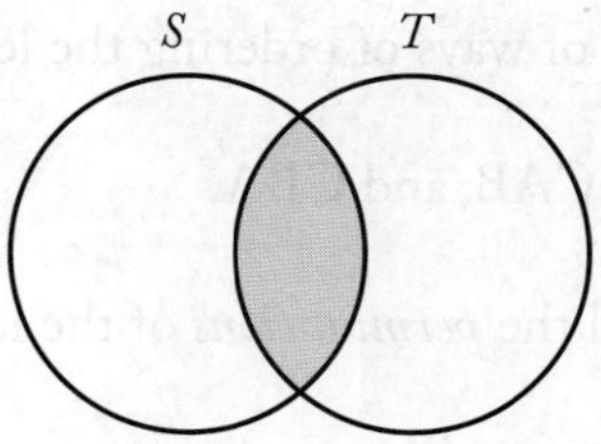

This diagram illustrates a fact about any two finite sets S and T: the number of elements in their union equals the sum of their individual numbers of elements minus the number of elements in their intersection (because the latter are counted twice in the sum); more concisely,

$$|S \cup T| = |S| + |T| - |S \cap T|.$$

This counting method is called the general addition rule for two sets. As a special case, if S and T are disjoint, then

$$|S \cup T| = |S| + |T|$$

since $|S \cap T| = 0$.

10. Counting Methods

There are some useful methods for counting objects and sets of objects without actually listing the elements to be counted. The following principle of multiplication is fundamental to these methods.

If an object is to be chosen from a set of m objects and a second object is to be chosen from a different set of n objects, then there are mn ways of choosing both objects simultaneously.

As an example, suppose the objects are items on a menu. If a meal consists of one entree and one dessert and there are 5 entrees and 3 desserts on the menu, then there are $5 \times 3 = 15$ different meals that can be ordered from the menu. As another example, each time a coin is flipped, there are two possible outcomes, heads and tails. If an experiment consists of 8 consecutive coin flips, then the experiment has 2^8 possible outcomes, where each of these outcomes is a list of heads and tails in some order.

A symbol that is often used with the multiplication principle is the *factorial.* If n is an integer greater than 1, then n factorial, denoted by the symbol $n!$, is defined as the product of all the integers from 1 to n. Therefore,

$$2! = (1)(2) = 2,$$
$$3! = (1)(2)(3) = 6,$$
$$4! = (1)(2)(3)(4) = 24, \text{ etc.}$$

Also, by definition, $0! = 1! = 1$.

The factorial is useful for counting the number of ways that a set of objects can be ordered. If a set of n objects is to be ordered from 1st to nth, then there are n choices for the 1st object, $n - 1$ choices for the 2nd object, $n - 2$ choices for the 3rd object, and so on, until there is only 1 choice for the nth object.

Thus, by the multiplication principle, the number of ways of ordering the n objects is

$$n(n-1)(n-2)\cdots(3)(2)(1) = n!.$$

For example, the number of ways of ordering the letters A, B, and C is 3!, or 6:

ABC, ACB, BAC, BCA, CAB, and CBA.

These orderings are called the *permutations* of the letters A, B, and C.

A permutation can be thought of as a selection process in which objects are selected one by one in a certain order. If the order of selection is not relevant and only k objects are to be selected from a larger set of n objects, a different counting method is employed.

Specifically, consider a set of n objects from which a complete selection of k objects is to be made without regard to order, where $0 \le k \le n$. Then the number of possible complete selections of k objects is called the number of *combinations* of n objects taken k at a time and is denoted by $\binom{n}{k}$.

The value of $\binom{n}{k}$ is given by $\binom{n}{k} = \frac{n!}{k!(n-k)!}$.

Note that $\binom{n}{k}$ is the number of k-element subsets of a set with n elements. For example, if $S = \{A, B, C, D, E\}$, then the number of 2-element subsets of S, or the number of combinations of 5 letters taken 2 at a time, is $\binom{5}{2} = \frac{5!}{2!3!} = \frac{120}{(2)(6)} = 10$.

The subsets are {A, B}, {A, C}, {A, D}, {A, E}, {B, C}, {B, D}, {B, E}, {C, D}, {C, E}, and {D, E}. Note that $\binom{5}{2} = 10 = \binom{5}{3}$ because every 2-element subset chosen from a set of 5 elements corresponds to a unique 3-element subset consisting of the elements *not* chosen.

In general, $\binom{n}{k} = \binom{n}{n-k}$.

11. Discrete Probability

Many of the ideas discussed in the preceding three topics are important to the study of discrete probability. Discrete probability is concerned with *experiments* that have a finite number of *outcomes*. Given such an experiment, an *event* is a particular set of outcomes. For example, rolling a number cube with faces numbered 1 to 6 (similar to a 6-sided die) is an experiment with 6 possible outcomes: 1, 2, 3, 4, 5, or 6. One event in this experiment is that the outcome is 4, denoted {4}; another event is that the outcome is an odd number: {1, 3, 5}.

The probability that an event E occurs, denoted by $P(E)$, is a number between 0 and 1, inclusive. If E has no outcomes, then E is *impossible* and $P(E) = 0$; if E is the set of all possible outcomes of the experiment, then E is *certain* to occur and $P(E) = 1$. Otherwise, E is possible but uncertain, and $0 < P(E) < 1$. If F is a subset of E, then $P(F) \le P(E)$. In the example above, if the probability of each of the 6 outcomes is the same, then the probability of each outcome is $\frac{1}{6}$, and the outcomes are said to be *equally likely.* For experiments in which all the individual outcomes are equally likely, the probability of an event E is

$$P(E)=\frac{\text{The number of outcomes in } E}{\text{The total number of possible outcomes}}.$$

In the example, the probability that the outcome is an odd number is

$$P(\{1,3,5\})=\frac{|\{1,3,5\}|}{6}=\frac{3}{6}=\frac{1}{2}.$$

Given an experiment with events E and F, the following events are defined:
"*not* E" is the set of outcomes that are not outcomes in E;
"E *or* F" is the set of outcomes in E or F or both, that is, $E \cup F$;
"E *and* F" is the set of outcomes in both E and F, that is, $E \cap F$.

The probability that E does not occur is $P(\text{not } E) = 1 - P(E)$. The probability that "$E$ or F" occurs is $P(E \text{ or } F) = P(E) + P(F) - P(E \text{ and } F)$, using the general addition rule at the end of section 4.1.9 ("Sets"). For the number cube, if E is the event that the outcome is an odd number, $\{1, 3, 5\}$, and F is the event that the outcome is a prime number, $\{2, 3, 5\}$, then $P(E \text{ and } F)=P(\{3,5\})=\frac{2}{6}=\frac{1}{3}$ and so $P(E \text{ or } F)=P(E)+P(F)-P(E \text{ and } F)=\frac{3}{6}+\frac{3}{6}-\frac{2}{6}=\frac{4}{6}=\frac{2}{3}$.

Note that the event "E or F" is $E \cup F=\{1, 2, 3, 5\}$, and hence $P(E \text{ or } F)=\frac{|\{1,2,3,5\}|}{6}=\frac{4}{6}=\frac{2}{3}$.

If the event "E and F" is impossible (that is, $E \cap F$ has no outcomes), then E and F are said to be *mutually exclusive* events, and $P(E \text{ and } F) = 0$. Then the general addition rule is reduced to $P(E \text{ or } F) = P(E) + P(F)$.

This is the special addition rule for the probability of two mutually exclusive events.

Two events A and B are said to be *independent* if the occurrence of either event does not alter the probability that the other event occurs. For one roll of the number cube, let $A = \{2, 4, 6\}$ and let $B = \{5, 6\}$. Then the probability that A occurs is $P(A)=\frac{|A|}{6}=\frac{3}{6}=\frac{1}{2}$, while, *presuming B occurs,* the probability that A occurs is

$$\frac{|A\cap B|}{|B|}=\frac{|\{6\}|}{|\{5,6\}|}=\frac{1}{2}.$$

Similarly, the probability that B occurs is $P(B)=\frac{|B|}{6}=\frac{2}{6}=\frac{1}{3}$, while, *presuming A occurs,* the probability that B occurs is

$$\frac{|B\cap A|}{|A|}=\frac{|\{6\}|}{|\{2,4,6\}|}=\frac{1}{3}.$$

Thus, the occurrence of either event does not affect the probability that the other event occurs. Therefore, A and B are independent.

The following multiplication rule holds for any independent events E and F: $P(E \text{ and } F) = P(E)P(F)$.

For the independent events A and B above, $P(A \text{ and } B) = P(A)P(B) = \left(\frac{1}{2}\right)\left(\frac{1}{3}\right) = \left(\frac{1}{6}\right)$.

Note that the event "A and B" is $A \cap B = \{6\}$, and hence $P(A \text{ and } B) = P(\{6\}) = \frac{1}{6}$. It follows from the general addition rule and the multiplication rule above that if E and F are independent, then

$$P(E \text{ or } F) = P(E) + P(F) - P(E)P(F).$$

For a final example of some of these rules, consider an experiment with events A, B, and C for which $P(A) = 0.23$, $P(B) = 0.40$, and $P(C) = 0.85$. Also, suppose that events A and B are mutually exclusive and events B and C are independent. Then

$$\begin{aligned} P(A \text{ or } B) &= P(A) + P(B) \text{ (since } A \text{ or } B \text{ are mutually exclusive)} \\ &= 0.23 + 0.40 \\ &= 0.63 \\ P(B \text{ or } C) &= P(B) + P(C) - P(B)P(C) \text{ (by independence)} \\ &= 0.40 + 0.85 - (0.40)(0.85) \\ &= 0.91 \end{aligned}$$

Note that $P(A \text{ or } C)$ and $P(A \text{ and } C)$ cannot be determined using the information given. But it can be determined that A and C are *not* mutually exclusive since $P(A) + P(C) = 1.08$, which is greater than 1, and therefore cannot equal $P(A \text{ or } C)$; from this it follows that $P(A \text{ and } C) \geq 0.08$. One can also deduce that $P(A \text{ and } C) \leq P(A) = 0.23$, since $A \cap C$ is a subset of A, and that $P(A \text{ or } C) \geq P(C) = 0.85$ since C is a subset of $A \cup C$. Thus, one can conclude that $0.85 \leq P(A \text{ or } C) \leq 1$ and $0.08 \leq P(A \text{ and } C) \leq 0.23$.

4.2 Algebra

Algebra is based on the operations of arithmetic and on the concept of an *unknown quantity,* or *variable.* Letters such as x or n are used to represent unknown quantities. For example, suppose Pam has 5 more pencils than Fred. If F represents the number of pencils that Fred has, then the number of pencils that Pam has is $F + 5$. As another example, if Jim's present salary S is increased by 7%, then his new salary is $1.07S$. A combination of letters and arithmetic operations, such as $F + 5, \frac{3x^2}{2x-5}$, and $19x^2 - 6x + 3$, is called an *algebraic expression.*

The expression $19x^2 - 6x + 3$ consists of the *terms* $19x^2, -6x$, and 3, where 19 is the *coefficient* of x^2, -6 is the coefficient of x^1, and 3 is a *constant term* (or coefficient of $x^0 = 1$). Such an expression is called a *second degree* (or *quadratic*) *polynomial in x* since the highest power of x is 2. The expression $F + 5$ is a *first degree* (or *linear*) *polynomial in F* since the highest power of F is 1. The expression $\frac{3x^2}{2x-5}$ is not a polynomial because it is not a sum of terms that are each powers of x multiplied by coefficients.

1. Simplifying Algebraic Expressions

Often when working with algebraic expressions, it is necessary to simplify them by factoring or combining *like* terms. For example, the expression $6x + 5x$ is equivalent to $(6 + 5)x$, or $11x$. In the expression $9x - 3y$, 3 is a factor common to both terms: $9x - 3y = 3(3x - y)$. In the expression $5x^2 + 6y$, there are no like terms and no common factors.

If there are common factors in the numerator and denominator of an expression, they can be divided out, provided that they are not equal to zero.

For example, if $x \neq 3$, then $\frac{x-3}{x-3}$ is equal to 1; therefore,

$$\begin{aligned}\frac{3xy-9y}{x-3} &= \frac{3y(x-3)}{x-3}\\ &= (3y)(1)\\ &= 3y\end{aligned}$$

To multiply two algebraic expressions, each term of one expression is multiplied by each term of the other expression. For example:

$$\begin{aligned}(3x-4)(9y+x) &= 3x(9y+x)-4(9y+x)\\ &= (3x)(9y)+(3x)(x)+(-4)(9y)+(-4)(x)\\ &= 27xy+3x^2-36y-4x\end{aligned}$$

An algebraic expression can be evaluated by substituting values of the unknowns in the expression. For example, if $x = 3$ and $y = -2$, then $3xy - x^2 + y$ can be evaluated as

$$3(3)(-2)-(3)^2+(-2) = -18-9-2 = -29$$

2. Equations

A major focus of algebra is to solve equations involving algebraic expressions. Some examples of such equations are

$5x - 2 = 9 - x$ (a linear equation with one unknown)

$3x + 1 = y - 2$ (a linear equation with two unknowns)

$5x^2 + 3x - 2 = 7x$ (a quadratic equation with one unknown)

$\frac{x(x-3)(x^2+5)}{x-4} = 0$ (an equation that is factored on one side with 0 on the other)

The *solutions* of an equation with one or more unknowns are those values that make the equation true, or "satisfy the equation," when they are substituted for the unknowns of the equation. An equation may have no solution or one or more solutions. If two or more equations are to be solved together, the solutions must satisfy all the equations simultaneously.

Two equations having the same solution(s) are *equivalent equations.* For example, the equations

$$2+x=3$$

$$4+2x=6$$

each have the unique solution $x = 1$. Note that the second equation is the first equation multiplied by 2. Similarly, the equations

$$3x-y=6$$

$$6x-2y=12$$

have the same solutions, although in this case each equation has infinitely many solutions. If any value is assigned to x, then $3x - 6$ is a corresponding value for y that will satisfy both equations; for example, $x = 2$ and $y = 0$ is a solution to both equations, as is $x = 5$ and $y = 9$.

3. Solving Linear Equations with One Unknown

To solve a linear equation with one unknown (that is, to find the value of the unknown that satisfies the equation), the unknown should be isolated on one side of the equation. This can be done by performing the same mathematical operations on both sides of the equation. Remember that if the same number is added to or subtracted from both sides of the equation, this does not change the equality; likewise, multiplying or dividing both sides by the same nonzero number does not change the equality. For example, to solve the equation $\frac{5x-6}{3}=4$ for x, the variable x can be isolated using the following steps:

$$5x-6=12 \quad \text{(multiplying by 3)}$$

$$5x=18 \quad \text{(adding 6)}$$

$$x=\frac{18}{5} \quad \text{(dividing by 5)}$$

The solution, $\frac{18}{5}$, can be checked by substituting it for x in the original equation to determine whether it satisfies that equation:

$$\frac{5\left(\frac{18}{5}\right)-6}{3}=\frac{18-6}{3}=\frac{12}{3}=4$$

Therefore, $x=\frac{18}{5}$ is the solution.

4. Solving Two Linear Equations with Two Unknowns

For two linear equations with two unknowns, if the equations are equivalent, then there are infinitely many solutions to the equations, as illustrated at the end of section 4.2.2 ("Equations"). If the equations are not equivalent, then they have either one unique solution or no solution. The latter case is illustrated by the two equations:

$$3x+4y=17$$

$$6x+8y=35$$

Note that $3x + 4y = 17$ implies $6x + 8y = 34$, which contradicts the second equation. Thus, no values of x and y can simultaneously satisfy both equations.

There are several methods of solving two linear equations with two unknowns. With any method, if a contradiction is reached, then the equations have no solution; if a trivial equation such as $0 = 0$ is reached, then the equations are equivalent and have infinitely many solutions. Otherwise, a unique solution can be found.

One way to solve for the two unknowns is to express one of the unknowns in terms of the other using one of the equations, and then substitute the expression into the remaining equation to obtain an equation with one unknown. This equation can be solved and the value of the unknown substituted into either of the original equations to find the value of the other unknown. For example, the following two equations can be solved for x and y.

$$(1)\quad 3x + 2y = 11$$
$$(2)\quad x - y = 2$$

In equation (2), $x = 2 + y$. Substitute $2 + y$ in equation (1) for x:

$$3(2 + y) + 2y = 11$$
$$6 + 3y + 2y = 11$$
$$6 + 5y = 11$$
$$5y = 5$$
$$y = 1$$

If $y = 1$, then $x - 1 = 2$ and $x = 2 + 1 = 3$.

There is another way to solve for x and y by eliminating one of the unknowns. This can be done by making the coefficients of one of the unknowns the same (disregarding the sign) in both equations and either adding the equations or subtracting one equation from the other. For example, to solve the equations

$$(1)\quad 6x + 5y = 29$$
$$(2)\quad 4x - 3y = -6$$

by this method, multiply equation (1) by 3 and equation (2) by 5 to get

$$18x + 15y = 87$$
$$20x - 15y = -30$$

Adding the two equations eliminates y, yielding $38x = 57$, or $x = \frac{3}{2}$. Finally, substituting $\frac{3}{2}$ for x in one of the equations gives $y = 4$. These answers can be checked by substituting both values into both of the original equations.

5. Solving Equations by Factoring

Some equations can be solved by factoring. To do this, first add or subtract expressions to bring all the expressions to one side of the equation, with 0 on the other side. Then try to factor the nonzero side into a product of expressions. If this is possible, then using property (7) in section 4.1.4 ("Real Numbers") each of the factors can be set equal to 0, yielding several simpler equations that possibly can be solved. The solutions of the simpler equations will be solutions of the factored equation. As an example, consider the equation $x^3 - 2x^2 + x = -5(x-1)^2$:

$$x^3 - 2x^2 + x + 5(x-1)^2 = 0$$

$$x\left(x^2 - 2x + 1\right) + 5(x-1)^2 = 0$$

$$x(x-1)^2 + 5(x-1)^2 = 0$$

$$(x+5)(x-1)^2 = 0$$

$$x + 5 = 0 \text{ or } (x-1)^2 = 0$$

$$x = -5 \text{ or } x = 1.$$

For another example, consider $\dfrac{x(x-3)\left(x^2+5\right)}{x-4} = 0$. A fraction equals 0 if and only if its numerator equals 0. Thus, $x(x-3)(x^2+5) = 0$:

$$x = 0 \text{ or } x - 3 = 0 \text{ or } x^2 + 5 = 0$$

$$x = 0 \text{ or } x = 3 \text{ or } x^2 + 5 = 0.$$

But $x^2 + 5 = 0$ has no real solution because $x^2 + 5 > 0$ for every real number. Thus, the solutions are 0 and 3.

The solutions of an equation are also called the *roots* of the equation. These roots can be checked by substituting them into the original equation to determine whether they satisfy the equation.

6. Solving Quadratic Equations

The standard form for a *quadratic equation* is

$$ax^2 + bx + c = 0,$$

where a, b, and c are real numbers and $a \neq 0$; for example:

$$x^2 + 6x + 5 = 0$$

$$3x^2 - 2x = 0, \text{ and}$$

$$x^2 + 4 = 0$$

Some quadratic equations can easily be solved by factoring. For example:

(1) $$x^2 + 6x + 5 = 0$$

$$(x+5)(x+1) = 0$$

$$x + 5 = 0 \text{ or } x + 1 = 0$$

$$x = -5 \text{ or } x = -1$$

$$\text{(2)} \qquad 3x^2 - 3 = 8x$$
$$3x^2 - 8x - 3 = 0$$
$$(3x+1)(x-3) = 0$$
$$3x+1 = 0 \text{ or } x-3 = 0$$
$$x = -\frac{1}{3} \text{ or } x = 3$$

A quadratic equation has at most two real roots and may have just one or even no real root. For example, the equation $x^2 - 6x + 9 = 0$ can be expressed as $(x - 3)^2 = 0$, or $(x - 3)(x - 3) = 0$; thus the only root is 3. The equation $x^2 + 4 = 0$ has no real root; since the square of any real number is greater than or equal to zero, $x^2 + 4$ must be greater than zero.

An expression of the form $a^2 - b^2$ can be factored as $(a - b)(a + b)$.

For example, the quadratic equation $9x^2 - 25 = 0$ can be solved as follows.

$$(3x-5)(3x+5) = 0$$
$$3x-5 = 0 \text{ or } 3x+5 = 0$$
$$x = \frac{5}{3} \text{ or } x = -\frac{5}{3}$$

If a quadratic expression is not easily factored, then its roots can always be found using the *quadratic formula:* If $ax^2 + bx + c = 0$ $(a \neq 0)$, then the roots are

$$x = \frac{-b+\sqrt{b^2\ 4ac}}{2a} \text{ and } x = \frac{-b\ \sqrt{b^2\ 4ac}}{2a}$$

These are two distinct real numbers unless $b^2 - 4ac \leq 0$. If $b^2 - 4ac = 0$, then these two expressions for x are equal to $-\frac{b}{2a}$, and the equation has only one root. If $b^2 - 4ac < 0$, then $\sqrt{b^2 - 4ac}$ is not a real number and the equation has no real roots.

7. Exponents

A positive integer exponent of a number or a variable indicates a product, and the positive integer is the number of times that the number or variable is a factor in the product. For example, x^5 means $(x)(x)(x)(x)(x)$; that is, x is a factor in the product 5 times.

Some rules about exponents follow.

Let x and y be any positive numbers, and let r and s be any positive integers.

(1) $(x^r)(x^s) = x^{(r+s)}$; for example, $(2^2)(2^3) = 2^{(2+3)} = 2^5 = 32$.

(2) $\frac{x^r}{x^s} = x^{(r-s)}$; for example, $\frac{4^5}{4^2} = 4^{5-2} = 4^3 = 64$.

(3) $(x^r)(y^r) = (xy)^r$; for example, $(3^3)(4^3) = 12^3 = 1{,}728$.

(4) $\left(\frac{x}{y}\right)^r = \frac{x^r}{y^r}$; for example, $\left(\frac{2}{3}\right)^3 = \frac{2^3}{3^3} = \frac{8}{27}$.

(5) $(x^r)^s = x^{rs} = (x^s)^r$; for example, $(x^3)^4 = x^{12} = (x^4)^3$.

(6) $x^{-r} = \frac{1}{x^r}$; for example, $3^{-2} = \frac{1}{3^2} = \frac{1}{9}$.

(7) $x^0 = 1$; for example, $6^0 = 1$.

(8) $x^{\frac{r}{s}} = \left(x^{\frac{1}{s}}\right)^r = \left(x^r\right)^{\frac{1}{s}} = \sqrt[s]{x^r}$; for example, $8^{\frac{2}{3}} = \left(8^{\frac{1}{3}}\right)^2 = \left(8^2\right)^{\frac{1}{3}} = \sqrt[3]{8^2} = \sqrt[3]{64} = 4$ and $9^{\frac{1}{2}} = \sqrt{9} = 3$.

It can be shown that rules 1 – 6 also apply when r and s are not integers and are not positive, that is, when r and s are any real numbers.

8. Inequalities

An *inequality* is a statement that uses one of the following symbols:

$\neq$ not equal to

$>$ greater than

$\geq$ greater than or equal to

$<$ less than

$\leq$ less than or equal to

Some examples of inequalities are $5x - 3 < 9$, $6x \geq y$, and $\frac{1}{2} < \frac{3}{4}$. Solving a linear inequality with one unknown is similar to solving an equation; the unknown is isolated on one side of the inequality. As in solving an equation, the same number can be added to or subtracted from both sides of the inequality, or both sides of an inequality can be multiplied or divided by a positive number without changing the truth of the inequality. However, multiplying or dividing an inequality by a negative number reverses the order of the inequality. For example, $6 > 2$, but $(-1)(6) < (-1)(2)$.

To solve the inequality $3x - 2 > 5$ for x, isolate x by using the following steps:

$$3x - 2 > 5$$

$$3x > 7 \quad \text{(adding 2 to both sides)}$$

$$x > \frac{7}{3} \quad \text{(dividing both sides by 3)}$$

To solve the inequality $\frac{5x-1}{-2} < 3$ for x, isolate x by using the following steps:

$$\frac{5x-1}{-2} < 3$$

$$5x - 1 > -6 \quad \text{(multiplying both sides by } -2\text{)}$$

$$5x > -5 \quad \text{(adding 1 to both sides)}$$

$$x > -1 \quad \text{(dividing both sides by 5)}$$

9. Absolute Value

The absolute value of x, denoted $|x|$, is defined to be x if $x \geq 0$ and $-x$ if $x < 0$. Note that $\sqrt{x^2}$ denotes the nonnegative square root of x^2, and so $\sqrt{x^2} = |x|$.

10. Functions

An algebraic expression in one variable can be used to define a *function* of that variable. A function is denoted by a letter such as f or g along with the variable in the expression. For example, the expression $x^3 - 5x^2 + 2$ defines a function f that can be denoted by

$$f(x) = x^3 - 5x^2 + 2.$$

The expression $\frac{2z+7}{\sqrt{z+1}}$ defines a function g that can be denoted by

$$g(z) = \frac{2z+7}{\sqrt{z+1}}.$$

The symbols "$f(x)$" or "$g(z)$" do not represent products; each is merely the symbol for an expression, and is read "f of x" or "g of z."

Function notation provides a short way of writing the result of substituting a value for a variable. If $x = 1$ is substituted in the first expression, the result can be written $f(1) = -2$, and $f(1)$ is called the "value of f at $x = 1$." Similarly, if $z = 0$ is substituted in the second expression, then the value of g at $z = 0$ is $g(0) = 7$.

Once a function $f(x)$ is defined, it is useful to think of the variable x as an input and $f(x)$ as the corresponding output. In any function there can be no more than one output for any given input. However, more than one input can give the same output; for example, if $h(x) = |x + 3|$, then $h(-4) = 1 = h(-2)$.

The set of all allowable inputs for a function is called the *domain* of the function. For f and g defined above, the domain of f is the set of all real numbers and the domain of g is the set of all numbers greater than -1. The domain of any function can be arbitrarily specified, as in the function defined by "$h(x) = 9x - 5$ for $0 \leq x \leq 10$." Without such a restriction, the domain is assumed to be all values of x that result in a real number when substituted into the function.

The domain of a function can consist of only the positive integers and possibly 0. For example, $a(n) = n^2 + \frac{n}{5}$ for $n = 0, 1, 2, 3, \ldots$.

Such a function is called a *sequence* and $a(n)$ is denoted by a_n. The value of the sequence a_n at $n = 3$ is $a_3 = 3^2 + \frac{3}{5} = 9.60$. As another example, consider the sequence defined by $b_n = (-1)^n (n!)$ for $n = 1, 2, 3, \ldots$ A sequence like this is often indicated by listing its values in the order $b_1, b_2, b_3, \ldots, b_n, \ldots$ as follows:

$-1, 2, -6, \ldots, (-1)^n(n!), \ldots$, and $(-1)^n(n!)$ is called the nth term of the sequence.

4.3 Geometry

1. Lines

In geometry, the word "line" refers to a straight line that extends without end in both directions.

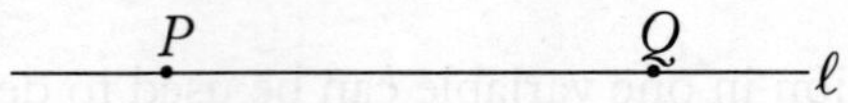

The line above can be referred to as line PQ or line ℓ. The part of the line from P to Q is called a *line segment*. P and Q are the *endpoints* of the segment. The notation $\overline{PQ}$ is used to denote line segment PQ and PQ is used to denote the length of the segment.

2. Intersecting Lines and Angles

If two lines intersect, the opposite angles are called *vertical angles* and have the same measure. In the figure

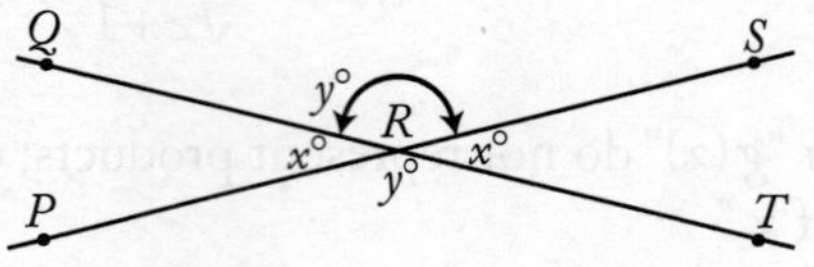

$\angle PRQ$ and $\angle SRT$ are vertical angles and $\angle QRS$ and $\angle PRT$ are vertical angles. Also, $x + y = 180°$ since PRS is a straight line.

3. Perpendicular Lines

An angle that has a measure of 90° is a *right angle.* If two lines intersect at right angles, the lines are *perpendicular.* For example:

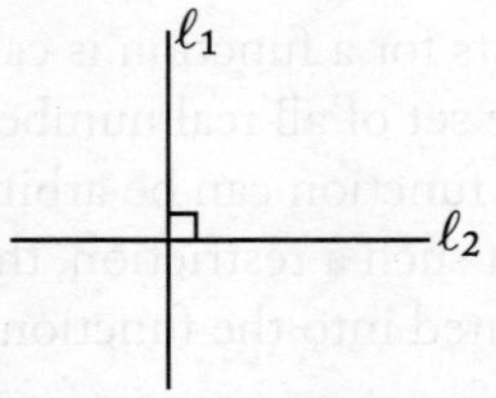

ℓ_1 and ℓ_2 above are perpendicular, denoted by $\ell_1 \perp \ell_2$. A right angle symbol in an angle of intersection indicates that the lines are perpendicular.

4. Parallel Lines

If two lines that are in the same plane do not intersect, the two lines are *parallel.* In the figure

lines ℓ_1 and ℓ_2 are parallel, denoted by $\ell_1 \parallel \ell_2$. If two parallel lines are intersected by a third line, as shown below, then the angle measures are related as indicated, where $x + y = 180°$.

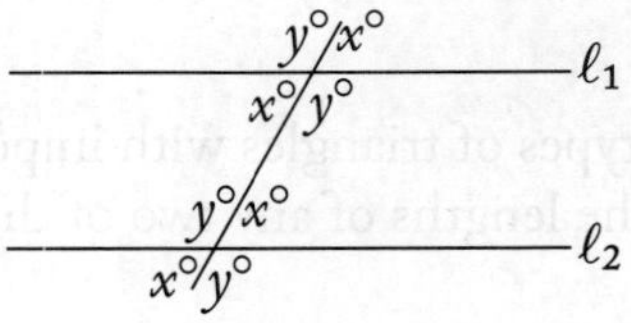

5. Polygons (Convex)

A *polygon* is a closed plane figure formed by three or more line segments, called the *sides* of the polygon. Each side intersects exactly two other sides at their endpoints. The points of intersection of the sides are *vertices.* The term "polygon" will be used to mean a convex polygon, that is, a polygon in which each interior angle has a measure of less than 180°.

The following figures are polygons:

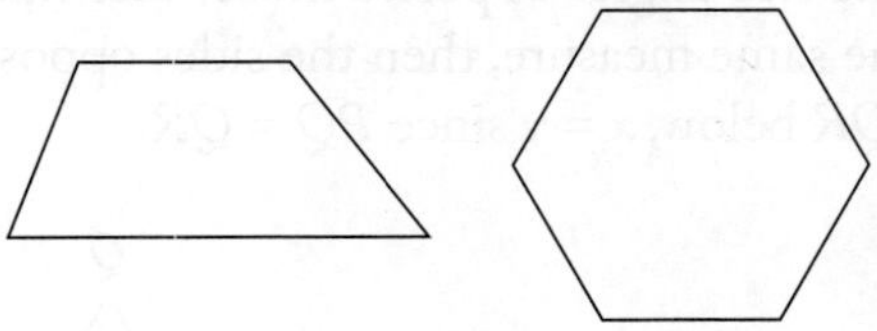

The following figures are not polygons:

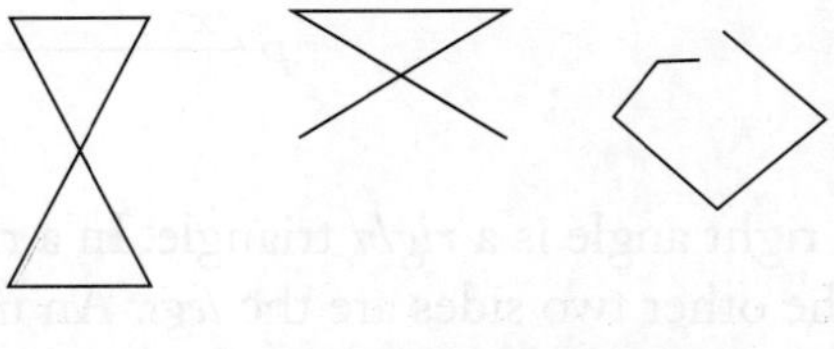

A polygon with three sides is a *triangle*; with four sides, a *quadrilateral*; with five sides, a *pentagon*; and with six sides, a *hexagon.*

The sum of the interior angle measures of a triangle is 180°. In general, the sum of the interior angle measures of a polygon with n sides is equal to $(n - 2)180°$. For example, this sum for a pentagon is $(5 - 2)180° = (3)180° = 540°$.

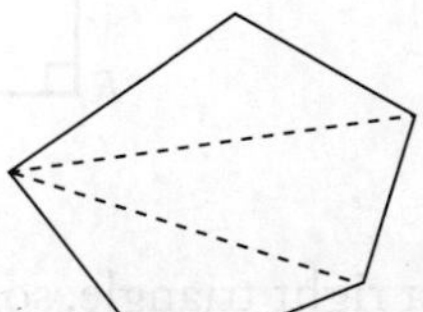

Note that a pentagon can be partitioned into three triangles and therefore the sum of the angle measures can be found by adding the sum of the angle measures of three triangles.

The *perimeter* of a polygon is the sum of the lengths of its sides.

The commonly used phrase "area of a triangle" (or any other plane figure) is used to mean the area of the region enclosed by that figure.

6. Triangles

There are several special types of triangles with important properties. But one property that all triangles share is that the sum of the lengths of any two of the sides is greater than the length of the third side, as illustrated below.

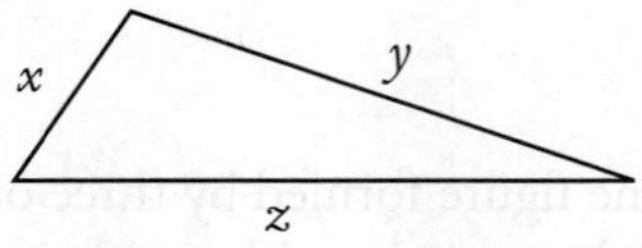

$x + y > z$, $x + z > y$, and $y + z > x$

An *equilateral* triangle has all sides of equal length. All angles of an equilateral triangle have equal measure. An *isosceles* triangle has at least two sides of the same length. If two sides of a triangle have the same length, then the two angles opposite those sides have the same measure. Conversely, if two angles of a triangle have the same measure, then the sides opposite those angles have the same length. In isosceles triangle PQR below, $x = y$ since $PQ = QR$.

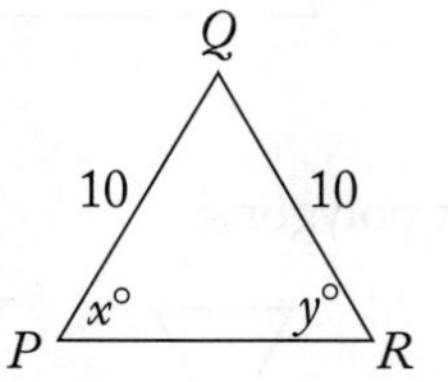

A triangle that has a right angle is a *right* triangle. In a right triangle, the side opposite the right angle is the *hypotenuse,* and the other two sides are the *legs.* An important theorem concerning right triangles is the *Pythagorean theorem,* which states: In a right triangle, the square of the length of the hypotenuse is equal to the sum of the squares of the lengths of the legs.

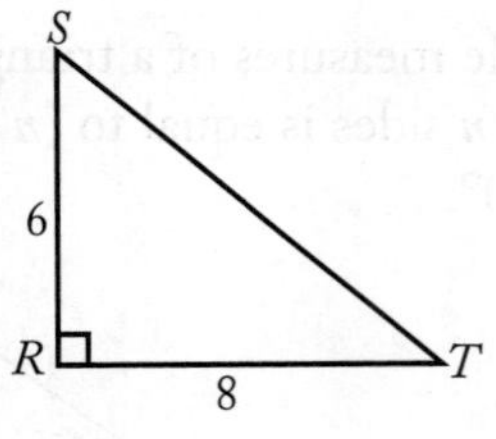

In the figure above, ΔRST is a right triangle, so $(RS)^2 + (RT)^2 = (ST)^2$. Here, $RS = 6$ and $RT = 8$, so $ST = 10$, since $6^2 + 8^2 = 36 + 64 = 100 = (ST)^2$ and $ST = \sqrt{100}$. Any triangle in which the lengths of the sides are in the ratio 3:4:5 is a right triangle. In general, if a, b, and c are the lengths of the sides of a triangle and $a^2 + b^2 = c^2$, then the triangle is a right triangle.

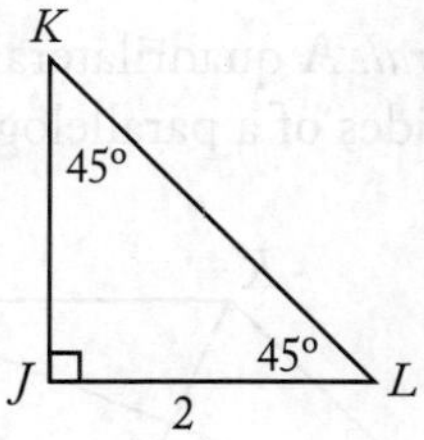

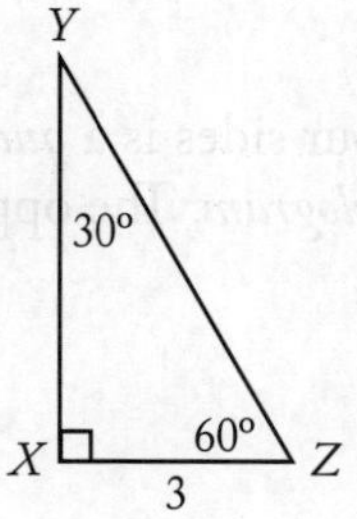

In 45°– 45°– 90° triangles, the lengths of the sides are in the ratio $1{:}1{:}\sqrt{2}$. For example, in ΔJKL, if $JL = 2$, then $JK = 2$ and $KL = 2\sqrt{2}$. In 30°– 60°– 90° triangles, the lengths of the sides are in the ratio $1{:}\sqrt{3}{:}2$. For example, in ΔXYZ, if $XZ = 3$, then $XY = 3\sqrt{3}$ and $YZ = 6$.

The *altitude* of a triangle is the segment drawn from a vertex perpendicular to the side opposite that vertex. Relative to that vertex and altitude, the opposite side is called the *base.*

The area of a triangle is equal to:

$$\frac{(\text{the length of the altitude}) \times (\text{the length of the base})}{2}$$

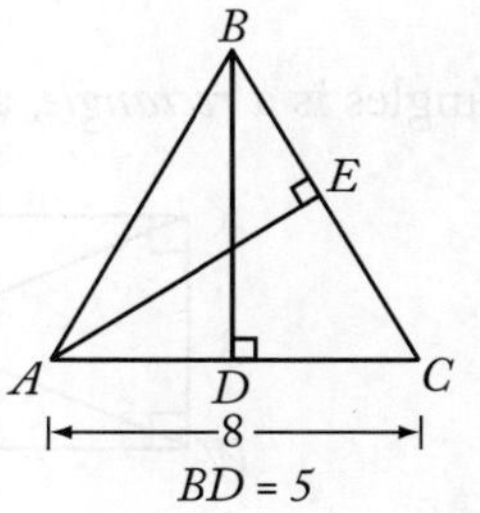

In ΔABC, $\overline{BD}$ is the altitude to base $\overline{AC}$ and $\overline{AE}$ is the altitude to base $\overline{BC}$. The area of ΔABC is equal to

$$\frac{BD \times AC}{2} = \frac{5 \times 8}{2} = 20.$$

The area is also equal to $\frac{AE \times BC}{2}$. If ΔABC above is isosceles and $AB = BC$, then altitude $\overline{BD}$ bisects the base; that is, $AD = DC = 4$. Similarly, any altitude of an equilateral triangle bisects the side to which it is drawn.

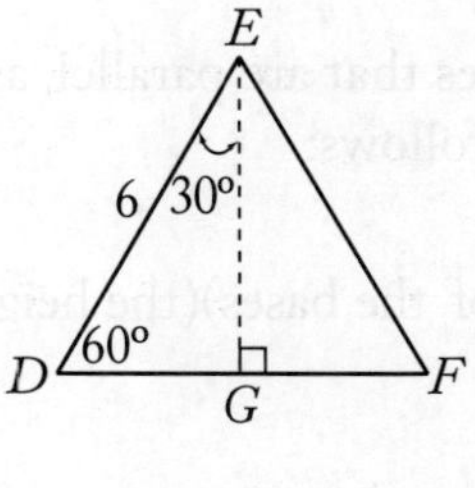

In equilateral triangle DEF, if $DE = 6$, then $DG = 3$ and $EG = 3\sqrt{3}$. The area of ΔDEF is equal to $\frac{3\sqrt{3} \times 6}{2} = 9\sqrt{3}$.

7. Quadrilaterals

A polygon with four sides is a *quadrilateral.* A quadrilateral in which both pairs of opposite sides are parallel is a *parallelogram.* The opposite sides of a parallelogram also have equal length.

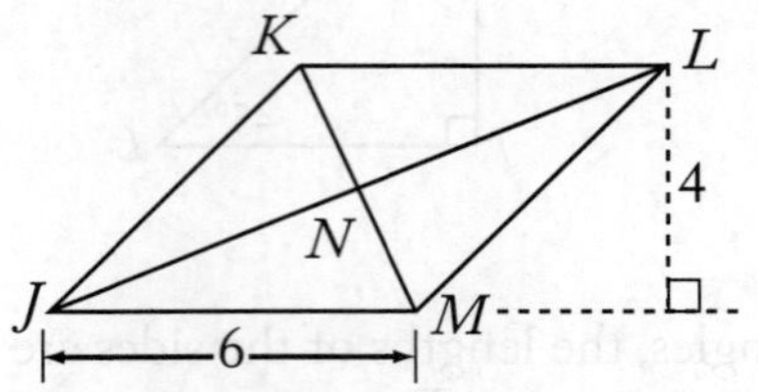

In parallelogram $JKLM$, $\overline{JK} \parallel \overline{LM}$ and $JK = LM$; $\overline{KL} \parallel \overline{JM}$ and $KL = JM$.

The diagonals of a parallelogram bisect each other (that is, $KN = NM$ and $JN = NL$).

The area of a parallelogram is equal to

(the length of the altitude) × (the length of the base).

The area of $JKLM$ is equal to $4 \times 6 = 24$.

A parallelogram with right angles is a *rectangle,* and a rectangle with all sides of equal length is a *square.*

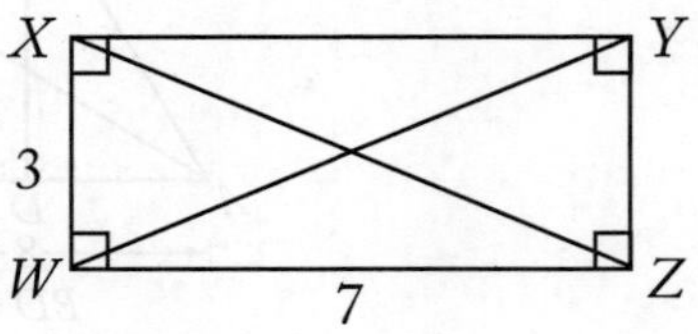

The perimeter of $WXYZ = 2(3) + 2(7) = 20$ and the area of $WXYZ$ is equal to $3 \times 7 = 21$. The diagonals of a rectangle are equal; therefore $WY = XZ = \sqrt{9+49} = \sqrt{58}$.

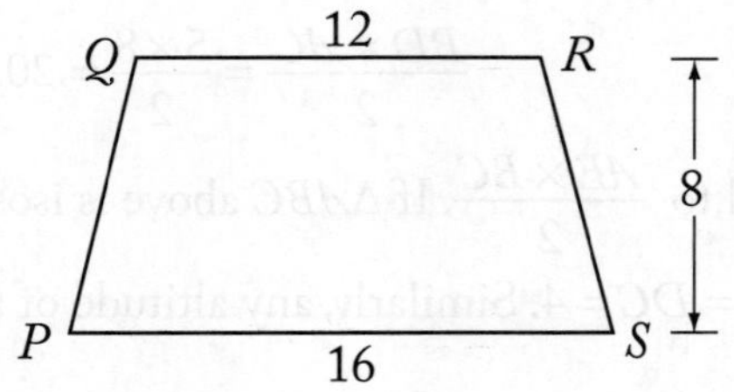

A quadrilateral with two sides that are parallel, as shown above, is a *trapezoid.* The area of trapezoid $PQRS$ may be calculated as follows:

$$\frac{1}{2}(\text{the sum of the lengths of the bases})(\text{the height}) = \frac{1}{2}(QR + PS)(8) = \frac{1}{2}(28 \times 8) = 112.$$

8. Circles

A *circle* is a set of points in a plane that are all located the same distance from a fixed point (the *center* of the circle).

A *chord* of a circle is a line segment that has its endpoints on the circle. A chord that passes through the center of the circle is a *diameter* of the circle. A *radius* of a circle is a segment from the center of the circle to a point on the circle. The words "diameter" and "radius" are also used to refer to the lengths of these segments.

The *circumference* of a circle is the distance around the circle. If r is the radius of the circle, then the circumference is equal to $2\pi r$, where π is approximately $\frac{22}{7}$ or 3.14. The *area* of a circle of radius r is equal to πr^2.

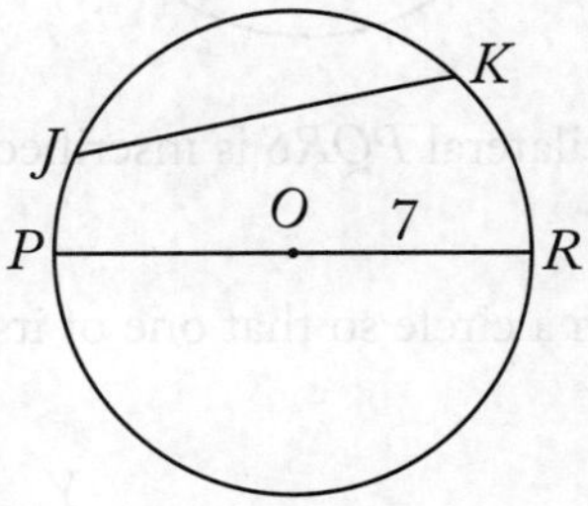

In the circle above, O is the center of the circle and $\overline{JK}$ and $\overline{PR}$ are chords. $\overline{PR}$ is a diameter and $\overline{OR}$ is a radius. If $OR = 7$, then the circumference of the circle is $2\pi(7) = 14\pi$ and the area of the circle is $\pi(7)^2 = 49\pi$.

The number of degrees of arc in a circle (or the number of degrees in a complete revolution) is 360.

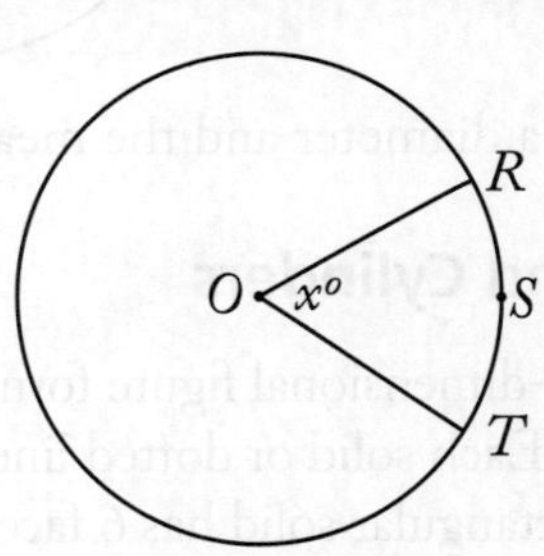

In the circle with center O above, the length of arc RST is $\frac{x}{360}$ of the circumference of the circle; for example, if $x = 60$, then arc RST has length $\frac{1}{6}$ of the circumference of the circle.

A line that has exactly one point in common with a circle is said to be *tangent* to the circle, and that common point is called the *point of tangency.* A radius or diameter with an endpoint at the point of tangency is perpendicular to the tangent line, and, conversely, a line that is perpendicular to a radius or diameter at one of its endpoints is tangent to the circle at that endpoint.

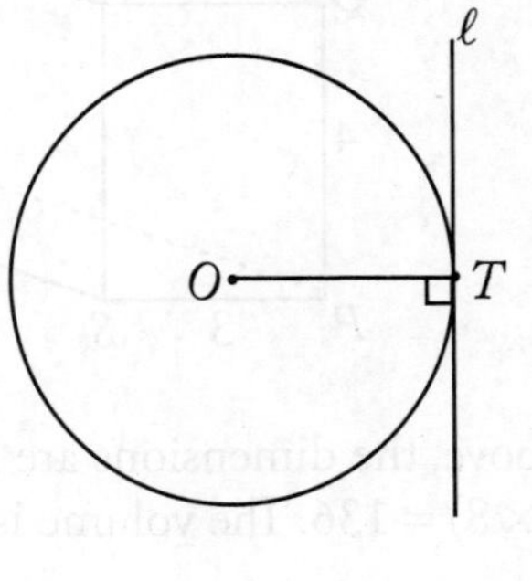

The line ℓ above is tangent to the circle and radius $\overline{OT}$ is perpendicular to ℓ.

If each vertex of a polygon lies on a circle, then the polygon is *inscribed* in the circle and the circle is *circumscribed* about the polygon. If each side of a polygon is tangent to a circle, then the polygon is *circumscribed* about the circle and the circle is *inscribed* in the polygon.

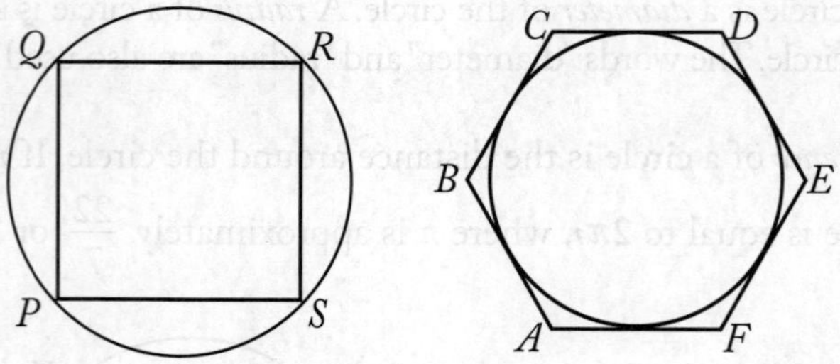

In the figure above, quadrilateral *PQRS* is inscribed in a circle and hexagon *ABCDEF* is circumscribed about a circle.

If a triangle is inscribed in a circle so that one of its sides is a diameter of the circle, then the triangle is a right triangle.

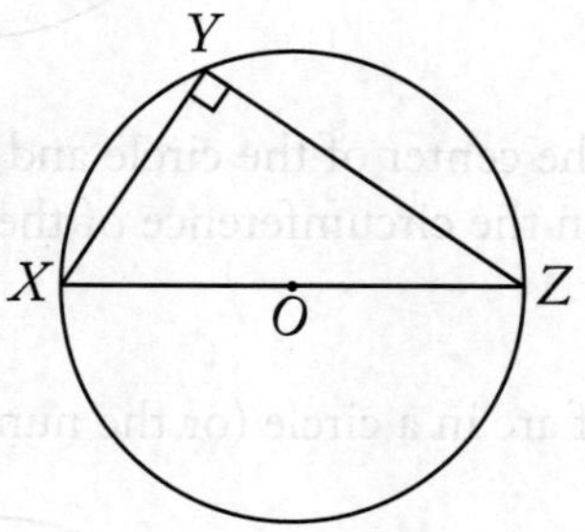

In the circle above, $\overline{XZ}$ is a diameter and the measure of $\angle XYZ$ is 90°.

9. Rectangular Solids and Cylinders

A *rectangular solid* is a three-dimensional figure formed by 6 rectangular surfaces, as shown below. Each rectangular surface is a *face*. Each solid or dotted line segment is an *edge*, and each point at which the edges meet is a *vertex*. A rectangular solid has 6 faces, 12 edges, and 8 vertices. Opposite faces are parallel rectangles that have the same dimensions. A rectangular solid in which all edges are of equal length is a *cube*.

The *surface area* of a rectangular solid is equal to the sum of the areas of all the faces. The *volume* is equal to

$$(\text{length}) \times (\text{width}) \times (\text{height});$$

$$\text{in other words, } (\text{area of base}) \times (\text{height}).$$

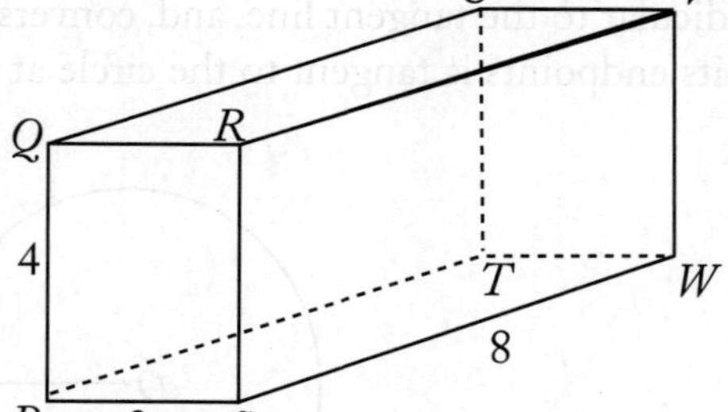

In the rectangular solid above, the dimensions are 3, 4, and 8. The surface area is equal to $2(3 \times 4) + 2(3 \times 8) + 2(4 \times 8) = 136$. The volume is equal to $3 \times 4 \times 8 = 96$.

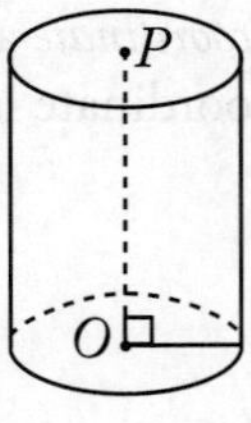

The figure above is a right circular *cylinder.* The two bases are circles of the same size with centers O and P, respectively, and altitude (height) $\overline{OP}$ is perpendicular to the bases. The surface area of a right circular cylinder with a base of radius r and height h is equal to $2(\pi r^2) + 2\pi rh$ (the sum of the areas of the two bases plus the area of the curved surface).

The volume of a cylinder is equal to $\pi r^2 h$, that is,

$$(\text{area of base}) \times (\text{height}).$$

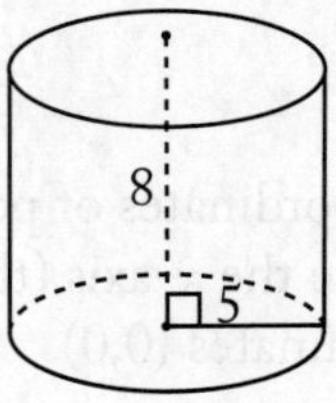

In the cylinder above, the surface area is equal to

$$2(25\pi) + 2\pi(5)(8) = 130\pi,$$

and the volume is equal to

$$25\pi(8) = 200\pi.$$

10. Coordinate Geometry

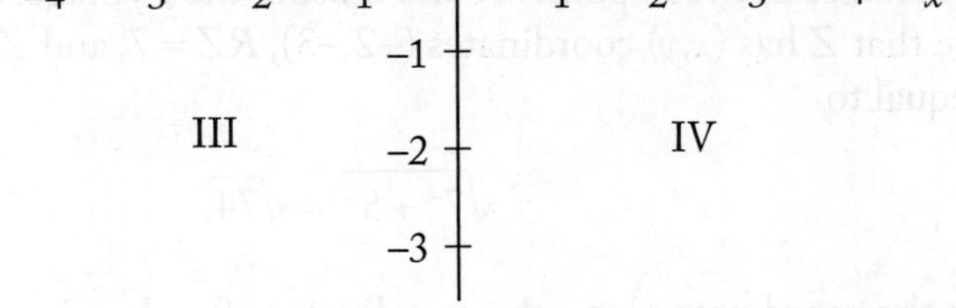

The figure above shows the (rectangular) *coordinate plane.* The horizontal line is called the *x-axis* and the perpendicular vertical line is called the *y-axis.* The point at which these two axes intersect, designated O, is called the *origin.* The axes divide the plane into four quadrants, I, II, III, and IV, as shown.

Each point in the plane has an *x-coordinate* and a *y-coordinate.* A point is identified by an ordered pair (x,y) of numbers in which the x-coordinate is the first number and the y-coordinate is the second number.

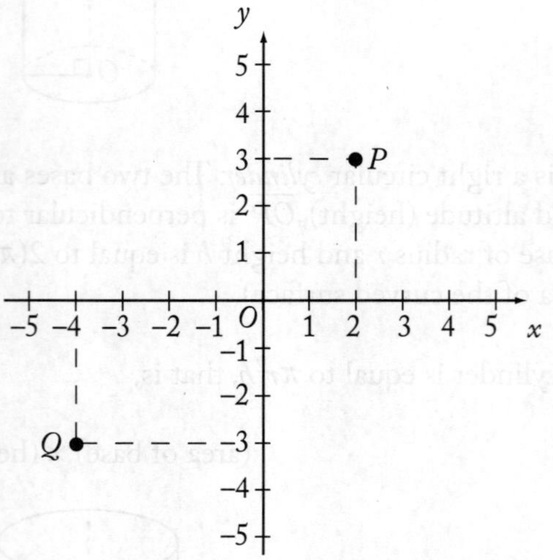

In the graph above, the (x,y) coordinates of point P are (2,3) since P is 2 units to the right of the y-axis (that is, $x = 2$) and 3 units above the x-axis (that is, $y = 3$). Similarly, the (x,y) coordinates of point Q are (−4,−3). The origin O has coordinates (0,0).

One way to find the distance between two points in the coordinate plane is to use the Pythagorean theorem.

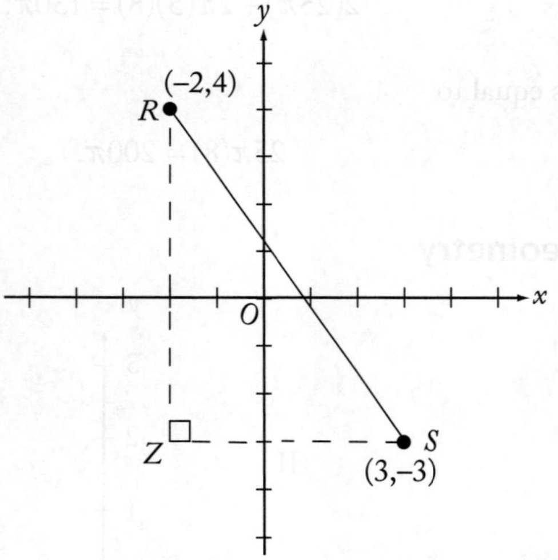

To find the distance between points R and S using the Pythagorean theorem, draw the triangle as shown. Note that Z has (x,y) coordinates (−2,−3), $RZ = 7$, and $ZS = 5$. Therefore, the distance between R and S is equal to

$$\sqrt{7^2 + 5^2} = \sqrt{74}.$$

For a line in the coordinate plane, the coordinates of each point on the line satisfy a linear equation of the form $y = mx + b$ (or the form $x = a$ if the line is vertical). For example, each point on the line on the next page satisfies the equation $y = -\frac{1}{2}x + 1$. One can verify this for the points (−2,2), (2,0), and (0,1) by substituting the respective coordinates for x and y in the equation.

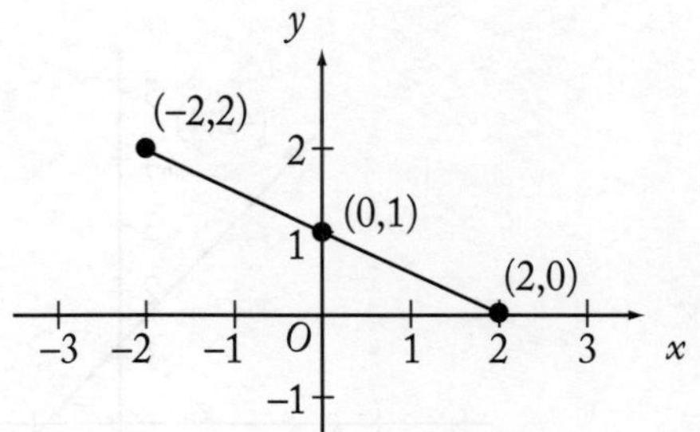

In the equation $y = mx + b$ of a line, the coefficient m is the *slope* of the line and the constant term b is the *y-intercept* of the line. For any two points on the line, the slope is defined to be the ratio of the difference in the y-coordinates to the difference in the x-coordinates. Using $(-2, 2)$ and $(2, 0)$ above, the slope is

$$\frac{\text{The difference in the } y\text{-coordinates}}{\text{The difference in the } x\text{-coordinates}} = \frac{0-2}{2-(-2)} = \frac{-2}{4} = -\frac{1}{2}.$$

The y-intercept is the y-coordinate of the point at which the line intersects the y-axis. For the line above, the y-intercept is 1, and this is the resulting value of y when x is set equal to 0 in the equation $y = -\frac{1}{2}x + 1$. The *x-intercept* is the x-coordinate of the point at which the line intersects the x-axis. The x-intercept can be found by setting $y = 0$ and solving for x. For the line $y = -\frac{1}{2}x + 1$, this gives

$$-\frac{1}{2}x + 1 = 0$$

$$-\frac{1}{2}x = -1$$

$$x = 2.$$

Thus, the x-intercept is 2.

Given any two points (x_1, y_1) and (x_2, y_2) with $x_1 \neq x_2$, the equation of the line passing through these points can be found by applying the definition of slope. Since the slope is $m = \frac{y_2 - y_1}{x_2 - x_1}$, then using a point known to be on the line, say (x_1, y_1), any point (x, y) on the line must satisfy $\frac{y - y_1}{x - x_1} = m$, or $y - y_1 = m(x - x_1)$. (Using (x_2, y_2) as the known point would yield an equivalent equation.) For example, consider the points $(-2, 4)$ and $(3, -3)$ on the line below.

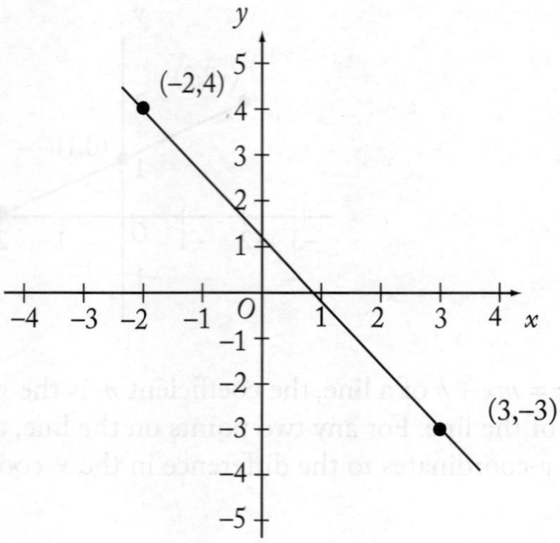

The slope of this line is $\frac{-3-4}{3-(-2)}=\frac{-7}{5}$, so an equation of this line can be found using the point (3,–3) as follows:

$$y-(-3)=-\frac{7}{5}(x-3)$$

$$y+3=-\frac{7}{5}x+\frac{21}{5}$$

$$y=-\frac{7}{5}x+\frac{6}{5}$$

The y-intercept is $\frac{6}{5}$. The *x-intercept* can be found as follows:

$$0=-\frac{7}{5}x+\frac{6}{5}$$

$$\frac{7}{5}x=\frac{6}{5}$$

$$x=\frac{6}{7}$$

Both of these intercepts can be seen on the graph.

If the slope of a line is negative, the line slants downward from left to right; if the slope is positive, the line slants upward. If the slope is 0, the line is horizontal; the equation of such a line is of the form $y = b$ since $m = 0$. For a vertical line, slope is not defined, and the equation is of the form $x = a$, where a is the x-intercept.

There is a connection between graphs of lines in the coordinate plane and solutions of two linear equations with two unknowns. If two linear equations with unknowns x and y have a unique solution, then the graphs of the equations are two lines that intersect in one point, which is the solution. If the equations are equivalent, then they represent the same line with infinitely many points or solutions. If the equations have no solution, then they represent parallel lines, which do not intersect.

There is also a connection between functions (see section 4.2.10) and the coordinate plane. If a function is graphed in the coordinate plane, the function can be understood in different and useful ways. Consider the function defined by

$$f(x) = -\frac{7}{5}x + \frac{6}{5}.$$

If the value of the function, $f(x)$, is equated with the variable y, then the graph of the function in the xy-coordinate plane is simply the graph of the equation

$$y = -\frac{7}{5}x + \frac{6}{5}$$

shown above. Similarly, any function $f(x)$ can be graphed by equating y with the value of the function:

$$y = f(x).$$

So for any x in the domain of the function f, the point with coordinates $(x, f(x))$ is on the graph of f, and the graph consists entirely of these points.

As another example, consider a quadratic polynomial function defined by $f(x) = x^2 - 1$. One can plot several points $(x, f(x))$ on the graph to understand the connection between a function and its graph:

x	$f(x)$
−2	3
−1	0
0	−1
1	0
2	3

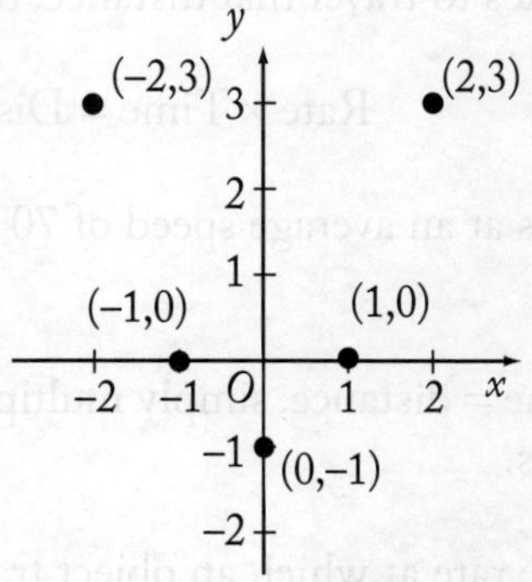

If all the points were graphed for $-2 \le x \le 2$, then the graph would appear as follows.

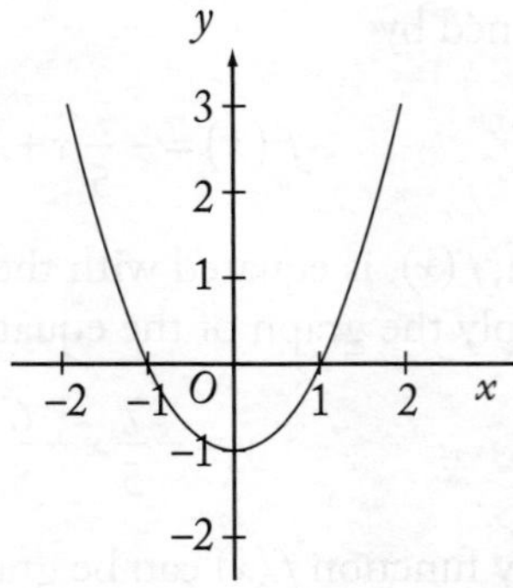

The graph of a quadratic function is called a *parabola* and always has the shape of the curve above, although it may be upside down or have a greater or lesser width. Note that the roots of the equation $f(x) = x^2 - 1 = 0$ are $x = 1$ and $x = -1$; these coincide with the x-intercepts since x-intercepts are found by setting $y = 0$ and solving for x. Also, the y-intercept is $f(0) = -1$ because this is the value of y corresponding to $x = 0$. For any function f, the x-intercepts are the solutions of the equation $f(x) = 0$ and the y-intercept is the value $f(0)$.

4.4 Word Problems

Many of the principles discussed in this chapter are used to solve word problems. The following discussion of word problems illustrates some of the techniques and concepts used in solving such problems.

1. Rate Problems

The distance that an object travels is equal to the product of the average speed at which it travels and the amount of time it takes to travel that distance, that is,

$$\text{Rate} \times \text{Time} = \text{Distance.}$$

Example 1: If a car travels at an average speed of 70 kilometers per hour for 4 hours, how many kilometers does it travel?

Solution: Since rate × time = distance, simply multiply 70 km/hour × 4 hours. Thus, the car travels 280 kilometers in 4 hours.

To determine the average rate at which an object travels, divide the total distance traveled by the total amount of traveling time.

Example 2: On a 400-mile trip, Car X traveled half the distance at 40 miles per hour (mph) and the other half at 50 mph. What was the average speed of Car X ?

Solution: First it is necessary to determine the amount of traveling time. During the first 200 miles, the car traveled at 40 mph; therefore, it took $\frac{200}{40} = 5$ hours to travel the first 200 miles.

During the second 200 miles, the car traveled at 50 mph; therefore, it took $\frac{200}{50} = 4$ hours to travel the second 200 miles. Thus, the average speed of Car X was $\frac{400}{9} = 44\frac{4}{9}$ mph. Note that the average speed is *not* $\frac{40+50}{2} = 45$.

Some rate problems can be solved by using ratios.

Example 3: If 5 shirts cost $44, then, at this rate, what is the cost of 8 shirts?

Solution: If c is the cost of the 8 shirts, then $\frac{5}{44} = \frac{8}{c}$. Cross multiplication results in the equation

$$5c = 8 \times 44 = 352$$

$$c = \frac{352}{5} = 70.40$$

The 8 shirts cost $70.40.

2. Work Problems

In a work problem, the rates at which certain persons or machines work alone are usually given, and it is necessary to compute the rate at which they work together (or vice versa).

The basic formula for solving work problems is $\frac{1}{r} + \frac{1}{s} = \frac{1}{h}$, where r and s are, for example, the number of hours it takes Rae and Sam, respectively, to complete a job when working alone, and h is the number of hours it takes Rae and Sam to do the job when working together. The reasoning is that in 1 hour Rae does $\frac{1}{r}$ of the job, Sam does $\frac{1}{s}$ of the job, and Rae and Sam together do $\frac{1}{h}$ of the job.

Example 1: If Machine X can produce 1,000 bolts in 4 hours and Machine Y can produce 1,000 bolts in 5 hours, in how many hours can Machines X and Y, working together at these constant rates, produce 1,000 bolts?

Solution:

$$\frac{1}{4} + \frac{1}{5} = \frac{1}{h}$$

$$\frac{5}{20} + \frac{4}{20} = \frac{1}{h}$$

$$\frac{9}{20} = \frac{1}{h}$$

$$9h = 20$$

$$h = \frac{20}{9} = 2\frac{2}{9}$$

Working together, Machines X and Y can produce 1,000 bolts in $2\frac{2}{9}$ hours.

Example 2: If Art and Rita can do a job in 4 hours when working together at their respective constant rates and Art can do the job alone in 6 hours, in how many hours can Rita do the job alone?

Solution:

$$\frac{1}{6}+\frac{1}{R}=\frac{1}{4}$$
$$\frac{R+6}{6R}=\frac{1}{4}$$
$$4R+24=6R$$
$$24=2R$$
$$12=R$$

Working alone, Rita can do the job in 12 hours.

3. Mixture Problems

In mixture problems, substances with different characteristics are combined, and it is necessary to determine the characteristics of the resulting mixture.

Example 1: If 6 pounds of nuts that cost \$1.20 per pound are mixed with 2 pounds of nuts that cost \$1.60 per pound, what is the cost per pound of the mixture?

Solution: The total cost of the 8 pounds of nuts is

$$6(\$1.20)+2(\$1.60)=\$10.40.$$

The cost per pound is $\frac{\$10.40}{8}=\$1.30.$

Example 2: How many liters of a solution that is 15 percent salt must be added to 5 liters of a solution that is 8 percent salt so that the resulting solution is 10 percent salt?

Solution: Let n represent the number of liters of the 15% solution. The amount of salt in the 15% solution $[0.15n]$ plus the amount of salt in the 8% solution $[(0.08)(5)]$ must be equal to the amount of salt in the 10% mixture $[0.10(n+5)]$. Therefore,

$$0.15n+0.08(5)=0.10(n+5)$$
$$15n+40=10n+50$$
$$5n=10$$
$$n=2 \text{ liters}$$

Two liters of the 15% salt solution must be added to the 8% solution to obtain the 10% solution.

4. Interest Problems

Interest can be computed in two basic ways. With simple annual interest, the interest is computed on the principal only and is equal to (principal) × (interest rate) × (time). If interest is compounded, then interest is computed on the principal as well as on any interest already earned.

Example 1: If \$8,000 is invested at 6 percent simple annual interest, how much interest is earned after 3 months?

Solution: Since the annual interest rate is 6%, the interest for 1 year is

$$(0.06)(\$8,000) = \$480.$$

The interest earned in 3 months is $\frac{3}{12}(\$480) = \$120.$

Example 2: If \$10,000 is invested at 10 percent annual interest, compounded semiannually, what is the balance after 1 year?

Solution: The balance after the first 6 months would be

$$10,000 + (10,000)(0.05) = \$10,500.$$

The balance after one year would be $10,500 + (10,500)(0.05) = \$11,025.$

Note that the interest rate for each 6-month period is 5%, which is half of the 10% annual rate. The balance after one year can also be expressed as

$$10,000\left(1 + \frac{0.10}{2}\right)^2 \text{ dollars.}$$

5. Discount

If a price is discounted by n percent, then the price becomes $(100 - n)$ percent of the original price.

Example 1: A certain customer paid \$24 for a dress. If that price represented a 25 percent discount on the original price of the dress, what was the original price of the dress?

Solution: If p is the original price of the dress, then $0.75p$ is the discounted price and $0.75p = \$24$, or $p = \$32$. The original price of the dress was \$32.

Example 2: The price of an item is discounted by 20 percent and then this reduced price is discounted by an additional 30 percent. These two discounts are equal to an overall discount of what percent?

Solution: If p is the original price of the item, then $0.8p$ is the price after the first discount. The price after the second discount is $(0.7)(0.8)p = 0.56p$. This represents an overall discount of 44 percent (100% – 56%).

6. Profit

Gross profit is equal to revenues minus expenses, or selling price minus cost.

Example: A certain appliance costs a merchant \$30. At what price should the merchant sell the appliance in order to make a gross profit of 50 percent of the cost of the appliance?

Solution: If s is the selling price of the appliance, then $s - 30 = (0.5)(30)$, or $s = \$45$. The merchant should sell the appliance for \$45.

7. Sets

If S is the set of numbers 1, 2, 3, and 4, you can write $S = \{1, 2, 3, 4\}$. Sets can also be represented by Venn diagrams. That is, the relationship among the members of sets can be represented by circles.

Example 1: Each of 25 people is enrolled in history, mathematics, or both. If 20 are enrolled in history and 18 are enrolled in mathematics, how many are enrolled in both history and mathematics?

Solution: The 25 people can be divided into three sets: those who study history only, those who study mathematics only, and those who study history and mathematics. Thus a Venn diagram may be drawn as follows, where n is the number of people enrolled in both courses, $20 - n$ is the number enrolled in history only, and $18 - n$ is the number enrolled in mathematics only.

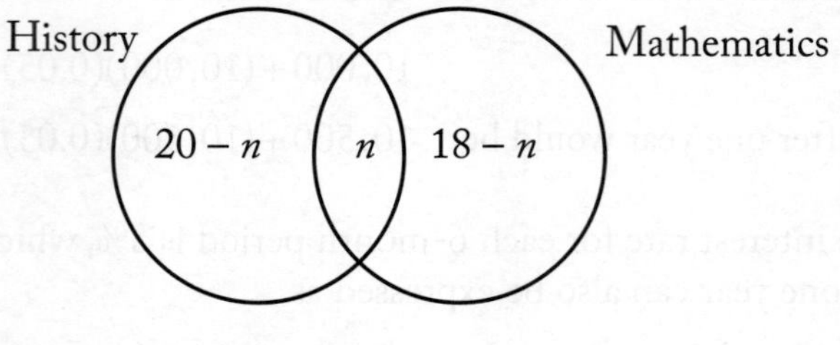

Since there is a total of 25 people, $(20 - n) + n + (18 - n) = 25$, or $n = 13$. Thirteen people are enrolled in both history and mathematics. Note that $20 + 18 - 13 = 25$, which is the general addition rule for two sets (see section 4.1.9).

Example 2: In a certain production lot, 40 percent of the toys are red and the remaining toys are green. Half of the toys are small and half are large. If 10 percent of the toys are red and small, and 40 toys are green and large, how many of the toys are red and large?

Solution: For this kind of problem, it is helpful to organize the information in a table:

	Red	Green	Total
Small	10%		50%
Large			50%
Total	40%	60%	100%

The numbers in the table are the percentages given. The following percentages can be computed on the basis of what is given:

	Red	Green	Total
Small	10%	40%	50%
Large	30%	20%	50%
Total	40%	60%	100%

Since 20% of the number of toys (n) are green and large, $0.20n = 40$ (40 toys are green and large), or $n = 200$. Therefore, 30% of the 200 toys, or $(0.3)(200) = 60$, are red and large.

8. Geometry Problems

The following is an example of a word problem involving geometry.

Example:

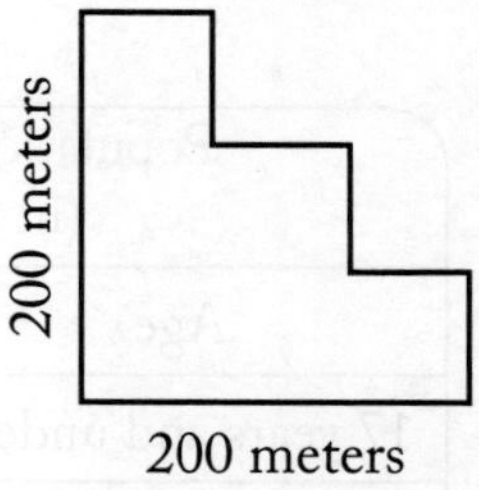

The figure above shows an aerial view of a piece of land. If all angles shown are right angles, what is the perimeter of the piece of land?

Solution: For reference, label the figure as

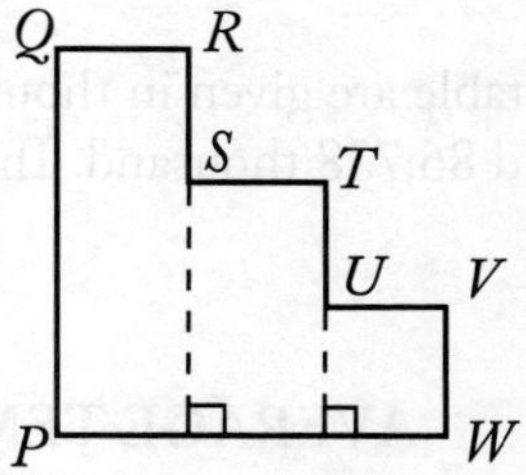

If all the angles are right angles, then $QR + ST + UV = PW$, and $RS + TU + VW = PQ$. Hence, the perimeter of the land is $2PW + 2PQ = 2 \times 200 + 2 \times 200 = 800$ meters.

9. Measurement Problems

Some questions on the GMAT involve metric units of measure, whereas others involve English units of measure. However, except for units of time, if a question requires conversion from one unit of measure to another, the relationship between those units will be given.

Example: A train travels at a constant rate of 25 meters per second. How many kilometers does it travel in 5 minutes? (1 kilometer = 1,000 meters)

Solution: In 1 minute the train travels (25)(60) = 1,500 meters, so in 5 minutes it travels 7,500 meters. Since 1 kilometer = 1,000 meters, it follows that 7,500 meters equals $\frac{7,500}{1,000}$, or 7.5 kilometers.

10. Data Interpretation

Occasionally a question or set of questions will be based on data provided in a table or graph. Some examples of tables and graphs are given below.

Example 1:

Population by Age Group (in thousands)	
Age	Population
17 years and under	63,376
18–44 years	86,738
45–64 years	43,845
65 years and over	24,054

How many people are 44 years old or younger?

Solution: The figures in the table are given in thousands. The answer in thousands can be obtained by adding 63,376 thousand and 86,738 thousand. The result is 150,114 thousand, which is 150,114,000.

Example 2:

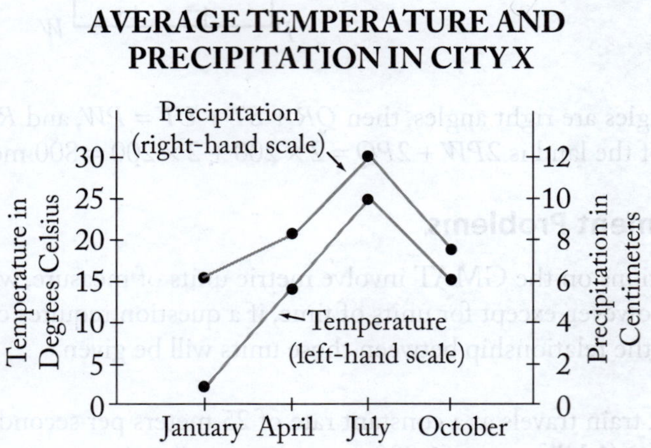

What are the average temperature and precipitation in City X during April?

Solution: Note that the scale on the left applies to the temperature line graph and the one on the right applies to the precipitation line graph. According to the graph, during April the average temperature is approximately 14° Celsius and the average precipitation is approximately 8 centimeters.

Example 3:

DISTRIBUTION OF AL'S WEEKLY NET SALARY

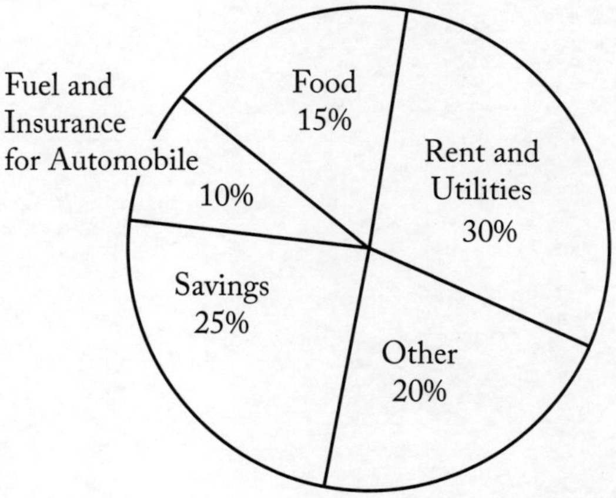

Al's weekly net salary is \$350. To how many of the categories listed was at least \$80 of Al's weekly net salary allocated?

Solution: In the circle graph, the relative sizes of the sectors are proportional to their corresponding values and the sum of the percents given is 100%. Note that $\frac{80}{350}$ is approximately 23%, so at least \$80 was allocated to each of 2 categories—Rent and Utilities, and Savings—since their allocations are each greater than 23%.

5.0 Problem Solving

5.0 Problem Solving

The Quantitative section of the GMAT® exam uses problem solving and data sufficiency questions to gauge your skill level. This chapter focuses on problem solving questions. Remember that quantitative questions require knowledge of the following:

- Arithmetic
- Elementary algebra
- Commonly known concepts of geometry

Problem solving questions are designed to test your basic mathematical skills and understanding of elementary mathematical concepts, as well as your ability to reason quantitatively, solve quantitative problems, and interpret graphic data. The mathematics knowledge required to answer the questions is no more advanced than what is generally taught in secondary school (or high school) mathematics classes.

In these questions, you are asked to solve each problem and select the best of the five answer choices given. Begin by reading the question thoroughly to determine exactly what information is given and to make sure you understand what is being asked. Scan the answer choices to understand your options. If the problem seems simple, take a few moments to see whether you can determine the answer. Then, check your answer against the choices provided.

If you do not see your answer among the choices, or if the problem is complicated, take a closer look at the answer choices and think again about what the problem is asking. See whether you can eliminate some of the answer choices and narrow down your options. If you are still unable to narrow the answer down to a single choice, reread the question. Keep in mind that the answer will be based solely on the information provided in the question—don't allow your own experience and assumptions to interfere with your ability to find the correct answer to the question.

If you find yourself stuck on a question or unable to select the single correct answer, keep in mind that you have about two minutes to answer each quantitative question. You may run out of time if you take too long to answer any one question; you may simply need to pick the answer that seems to make the most sense. Although guessing is generally not the best way to achieve a high GMAT score, making an educated guess is a good strategy for answering questions you are unsure of. Even if your answer to a particular question is incorrect, your answers to other questions will allow the test to accurately gauge your ability level.

The following pages include test-taking strategies, directions that will apply to questions of this type, sample questions, an answer key, and explanations for all the problems. These explanations present problem solving strategies that could be helpful in answering the questions.

5.1 Test-Taking Strategies

1. **Pace yourself.**

   Consult the on-screen timer periodically. Work as carefully as possible, but do not spend valuable time checking answers or pondering problems that you find difficult.

2. **Use the erasable notepad provided at the test center.**

   Working a problem out may help you avoid errors in solving the problem. If diagrams or figures are not presented, it may help to draw your own.

3. **Read each question carefully to determine what is being asked.**

   For word problems, take one step at a time, reading each sentence carefully and translating the information into equations or other useful mathematical representations.

4. **Scan the answer choices before attempting to answer a question.**

   Scanning the answers can prevent you from putting answers in a form that is not given (e.g., finding the answer in decimal form, such as 0.25, when the choices are given in fractional form, such as $\frac{1}{4}$). Also, if the question requires approximations, a shortcut could serve well (e.g., you may be able to approximate 48 percent of a number by using half).

5. **Don't waste time trying to solve a problem that is too difficult for you.**

   Make your best guess and then move on to the next question.

5.2 The Directions

These directions are very similar to those you will see for problem solving questions when you take the GMAT exam. If you read them carefully and understand them clearly before sitting for the GMAT exam, you will not need to spend too much time reviewing them once the test begins.

Solve the problem and indicate the best of the answer choices given.

Numbers: All numbers used are real numbers.

Figures: A figure accompanying a problem solving question is intended to provide information useful in solving the problem. Figures are drawn as accurately as possible. Exceptions will be clearly noted. Lines shown as straight are straight, and lines that appear jagged are also straight. The positions of points, angles, regions, etc., exist in the order shown, and angle measures are greater than zero. All figures lie in a plane unless otherwise indicated.

5.3 Practice Questions

Solve the problem and indicate the best of the answer choices given.
Numbers: **All numbers used are real numbers.**
Figures: **A figure accompanying a problem solving question is intended to provide information useful in solving the problem. Figures are drawn as accurately as possible. Exceptions will be clearly noted. Lines shown as straight are straight, and lines that appear jagged are also straight. The positions of points, angles, regions, etc., exist in the order shown, and angle measures are greater than zero. All figures lie in a plane unless otherwise indicated.**

1. The price of a coat in a certain store is $500. If the price of the coat is to be reduced by $150, by what percent is the price to be reduced?

(A) 10%
(B) 15%
(C) 20%
(D) 25%
(E) 30%

2. On a vacation, Rose exchanged $500.00 for euros at an exchange rate of 0.80 euro per dollar and spent $\frac{3}{4}$ of the euros she received. If she exchanged the remaining euros for dollars at an exchange rate of $1.20 per euro, what was the dollar amount she received?

(A) $60.00
(B) $80.00
(C) $100.00
(D) $120.00
(E) $140.00

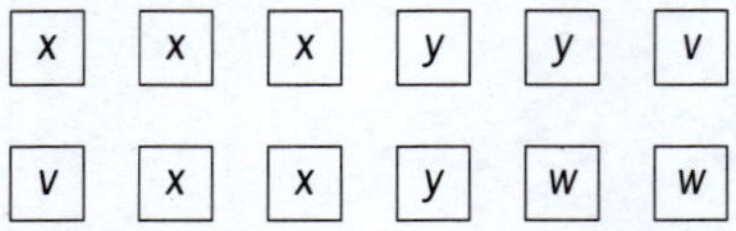

3. Each of the 12 squares shown is labeled *x*, *y*, *v*, or *w*. What is the ratio of the number of these squares labeled *x* or *y* to the number of these squares labeled *v* or *w*?

(A) 1:2
(B) 2:3
(C) 4:3
(D) 3:2
(E) 2:1

4. $\frac{1}{3}+\frac{1}{2}-\frac{5}{6}+\frac{1}{5}+\frac{1}{4}-\frac{9}{20}=$

(A) 0
(B) $\frac{2}{15}$
(C) $\frac{2}{5}$
(D) $\frac{9}{20}$
(E) $\frac{5}{6}$

5. Bouquets are to be made using white tulips and red tulips, and the ratio of the number of white tulips to the number of red tulips is to be the same in each bouquet. If there are 15 white tulips and 85 red tulips available for the bouquets, what is the greatest number of bouquets that can be made using all the tulips available?

(A) 3
(B) 5
(C) 8
(D) 10
(E) 13

6. 125% of 5 =

(A) 5.125
(B) 5.25
(C) 6
(D) 6.125
(E) 6.25

7. Today Rebecca, who is 34 years old, and her daughter, who is 8 years old, celebrate their birthdays. How many years will pass before Rebecca's age is twice her daughter's age?

(A) 10
(B) 14
(C) 18
(D) 22
(E) 26

8. When traveling at a constant speed of 32 miles per hour, a certain motorboat consumes 24 gallons of fuel per hour. What is the fuel consumption of this boat at this speed measured in miles traveled per gallon of fuel?

(A) $\frac{2}{3}$
(B) $\frac{3}{4}$
(C) $\frac{4}{5}$
(D) $\frac{4}{3}$
(E) $\frac{3}{2}$

9. A case contains c cartons. Each carton contains b boxes, and each box contains 100 paper clips. How many paper clips are contained in 2 cases?

(A) $100bc$
(B) $\frac{100b}{c}$
(C) $200bc$
(D) $\frac{200b}{c}$
(E) $\frac{200}{bc}$

10. A technician makes a round-trip to and from a certain service center by the same route. If the technician completes the drive to the center and then completes 10 percent of the drive from the center, what percent of the round-trip has the technician completed?

(A) 5%
(B) 10%
(C) 25%
(D) 40%
(E) 55%

11. Raffle tickets numbered consecutively from 101 through 350 are placed in a box. What is the probability that a ticket selected at random will have a number with a hundreds digit of 2 ?

(A) $\frac{2}{5}$
(B) $\frac{2}{7}$
(C) $\frac{33}{88}$
(D) $\frac{99}{250}$
(E) $\frac{100}{249}$

12. When Leo imported a certain item, he paid a 7 percent import tax on the portion of the total value of the item in excess of $1,000. If the amount of the import tax that Leo paid was $87.50, what was the total value of the item?

(A) $1,600
(B) $1,850
(C) $2,250
(D) $2,400
(E) $2,750

13. A collection of 16 coins, each with a face value of either 10 cents or 25 cents, has a total face value of $2.35. How many of the coins have a face value of 25 cents?

(A) 3
(B) 5
(C) 7
(D) 9
(E) 11

14. The number of cars sold at a certain dealership on six of the last seven business days were 4, 7, 2, 8, 3, and 6, respectively. If the number of cars sold on the seventh business day was either 2, 4, or 5, for which of the three values does the average (arithmetic mean) number of cars sold per business day for the seven business days equal the median number of cars sold per day for the seven days?

I. 2

II. 4

III. 5

(A) II only
(B) III only
(C) I and II only
(D) II and III only
(E) I, II, and III

15. If it is assumed that 60 percent of those who receive a questionnaire by mail will respond and 300 responses are needed, what is the minimum number of questionnaires that should be mailed?

(A) 400
(B) 420
(C) 480
(D) 500
(E) 600

16. If $1 < x < y < z$, which of the following has the greatest value?

(A) $z(x + 1)$
(B) $z(y + 1)$
(C) $x(y + z)$
(D) $y(x + z)$
(E) $z(x + y)$

17. A rectangular garden is to be twice as long as it is wide. If 360 yards of fencing, including the gate, will completely enclose the garden, what will be the length of the garden, in yards?

(A) 120
(B) 140
(C) 160
(D) 180
(E) 200

18. A rectangular floor that measures 8 meters by 10 meters is to be covered with carpet squares that each measure 2 meters by 2 meters. If the carpet squares cost $12 apiece, what is the total cost for the number of carpet squares needed to cover the floor?

(A) $200
(B) $240
(C) $480
(D) $960
(E) $1,920

19. If $893 \times 78 = p$, which of the following is equal to 893×79?

(A) $p + 1$
(B) $p + 78$
(C) $p + 79$
(D) $p + 893$
(E) $p + 894$

20. Thabo owns exactly 140 books, and each book is either paperback fiction, paperback nonfiction, or hardcover nonfiction. If he owns 20 more paperback nonfiction books than hardcover nonfiction books, and twice as many paperback fiction books as paperback nonfiction books, how many hardcover nonfiction books does Thabo own?

(A) 10
(B) 20
(C) 30
(D) 40
(E) 50

21. If the average (arithmetic mean) of the four numbers 3, 15, 32, and $(N + 1)$ is 18, then $N =$

(A) 19
(B) 20
(C) 21
(D) 22
(E) 29

22. Abdul, Barb, and Carlos all live on the same straight road, on which their school is also located. The school is halfway between Abdul's house and Barb's house. Barb's house is halfway between the school and Carlos's house. If the school is 4 miles from Carlos's house, how many miles is Abdul's house from Carlos's house?

(A) $1\frac{1}{3}$
(B) 2
(C) 4
(D) 6
(E) 8

23. During a certain time period, Car X traveled north along a straight road at a constant rate of 1 mile per minute and used fuel at a constant rate of 5 gallons every 2 hours. During this time period, if Car X used exactly 3.75 gallons of fuel, how many miles did Car X travel?

(A) 36
(B) 37.5
(C) 40
(D) 80
(E) 90

24. Cheryl purchased 5 identical hollow pine doors and 6 identical solid oak doors for the house she is building. The regular price of each solid oak door was twice the regular price of each hollow pine door. However, Cheryl was given a discount of 25% off the regular price of each solid oak door. If the regular price of each hollow pine door was \$40, what was the total price of all 11 doors?

(A) \$320
(B) \$540
(C) \$560
(D) \$620
(E) \$680

25. If $\left|y - \frac{1}{2}\right| < \frac{11}{2}$, which of the following could be a value of y?

(A) -11
(B) $-\frac{11}{2}$
(C) $\frac{11}{2}$
(D) 11
(E) 22

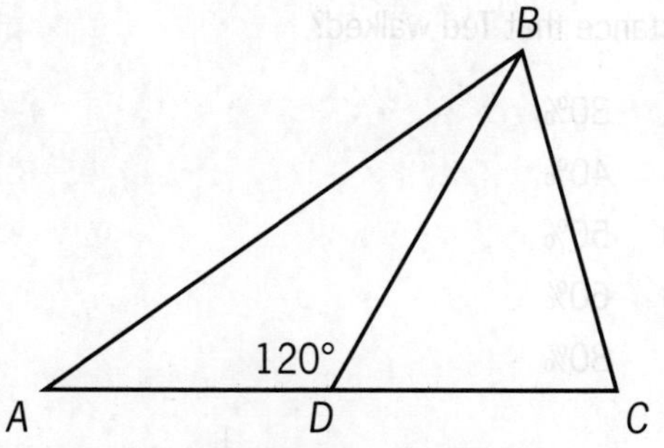

Note: Not drawn to scale.

26. In the figure shown, $AC = 2$ and $BD = DC = 1$. What is the measure of angle ABD?

(A) 15°
(B) 20°
(C) 30°
(D) 40°
(E) 45°

27. If $k^2 = m^2$, which of the following must be true?

(A) $k = m$
(B) $k = -m$
(C) $k = |m|$
(D) $k = -|m|$
(E) $|k| = |m|$

28. Makoto, Nishi, and Ozuro were paid a total of \$780 for waxing the floors at their school. Each was paid in proportion to the number of hours he or she worked. If Makoto worked 15 hours, Nishi worked 20 hours, and Ozuro worked 30 hours, how much was Makoto paid?

(A) \$52
(B) \$117
(C) \$130
(D) \$180
(E) \$234

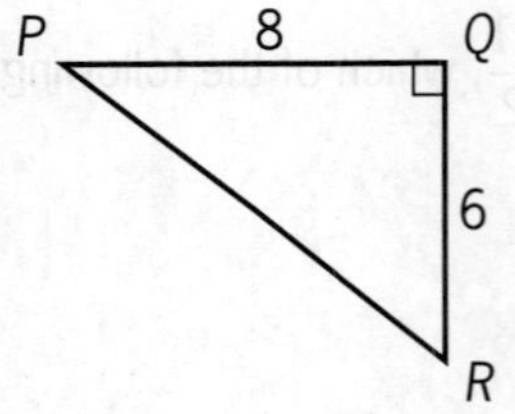

29. The figure above shows a path around a triangular piece of land. Mary walked the distance of 8 miles from P to Q and then walked the distance of 6 miles from Q to R. If Ted walked directly from P to R, by what percent did the distance that Mary walked exceed the distance that Ted walked?

(A) 30%
(B) 40%
(C) 50%
(D) 60%
(E) 80%

30. At a supermarket, John spent $\frac{1}{2}$ of his money on fresh fruits and vegetables, $\frac{1}{3}$ on meat products, and $\frac{1}{10}$ on bakery products. If he spent the remaining \$6 on candy, how much did John spend at the supermarket?

(A) \$60
(B) \$80
(C) \$90
(D) \$120
(E) \$180

31. If $(1 - 1.25)N = 1$, then $N =$

(A) −400
(B) −140
(C) −4
(D) 4
(E) 400

32. A carpenter constructed a rectangular sandbox with a capacity of 10 cubic feet. If the carpenter were to make a similar sandbox twice as long, twice as wide, and twice as high as the first sandbox, what would be the capacity, in cubic feet, of the second sandbox?

(A) 20
(B) 40
(C) 60
(D) 80
(E) 100

33. The quotient when a certain number is divided by $\frac{2}{3}$ is $\frac{9}{2}$. What is the number?

(A) $\frac{4}{27}$
(B) $\frac{1}{3}$
(C) 3
(D) 6
(E) $\frac{27}{4}$

34. If a sphere with radius r is inscribed in a cube with edges of length e, which of the following expresses the relationship between r and e ?

(A) $r = \frac{1}{2}e$
(B) $r = e$
(C) $r = 2e$
(D) $r = \sqrt{e}$
(E) $r = \frac{1}{4}e^2$

35. If $2x + y = 7$ and $x + 2y = 5$, then $\frac{x+y}{3} =$

(A) 1
(B) $\frac{4}{3}$
(C) $\frac{17}{5}$
(D) $\frac{18}{5}$
(E) 4

36. City X has a population 4 times as great as the population of City Y, which has a population twice as great as the population of City Z. What is the ratio of the population of City X to the population of City Z ?

(A) 1:8
(B) 1:4
(C) 2:1
(D) 4:1
(E) 8:1

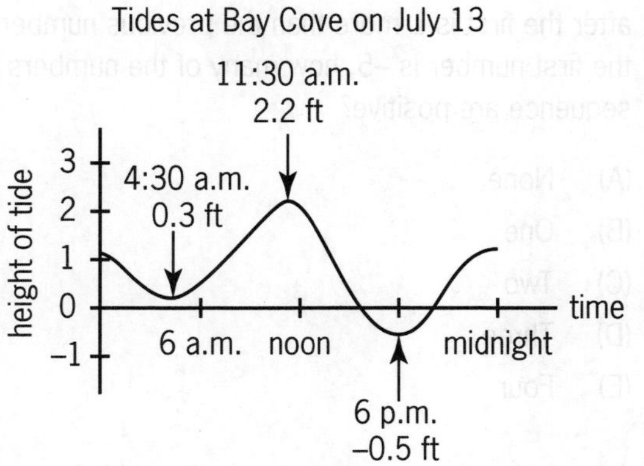

37. The graph above shows the height of the tide, in feet, above or below a baseline. Which of the following is closest to the difference, in feet, between the heights of the highest and lowest tides on July 13 at Bay Cove?

(A) 1.7
(B) 1.9
(C) 2.2
(D) 2.5
(E) 2.7

38. A manufacturer of a certain product can expect that between 0.3 percent and 0.5 percent of the units manufactured will be defective. If the retail price is $2,500 per unit and the manufacturer offers a full refund for defective units, how much money can the manufacturer expect to need to cover the refunds on 20,000 units?

(A) Between $15,000 and $25,000
(B) Between $30,000 and $50,000
(C) Between $60,000 and $100,000
(D) Between $150,000 and $250,000
(E) Between $300,000 and $500,000

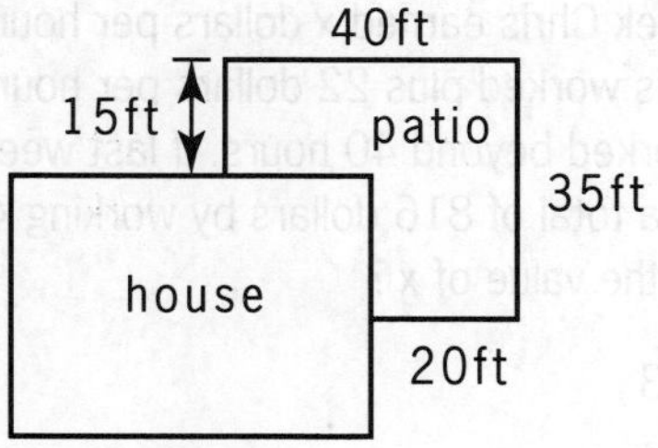

39. A flat patio was built alongside a house as shown in the figure above. If all angles are right angles, what is the area of the patio in square feet?

(A) 800
(B) 875
(C) 1,000
(D) 1,100
(E) 1,125

40. The sum of the weekly salaries of 5 employees is $3,250. If each of the 5 salaries is to increase by 10 percent, then the average (arithmetic mean) weekly salary per employee will increase by

(A) $52.50
(B) $55.00
(C) $57.50
(D) $62.50
(E) $65.00

41. A student's average (arithmetic mean) test score on 4 tests is 78. What must be the student's score on a 5th test for the student's average score on the 5 tests to be 80 ?

(A) 80
(B) 82
(C) 84
(D) 86
(E) 88

42. Last week Chris earned x dollars per hour for the first 40 hours worked plus 22 dollars per hour for each hour worked beyond 40 hours. If last week Chris earned a total of 816 dollars by working 48 hours, what is the value of x ?

(A) 13
(B) 14
(C) 15
(D) 16
(E) 17

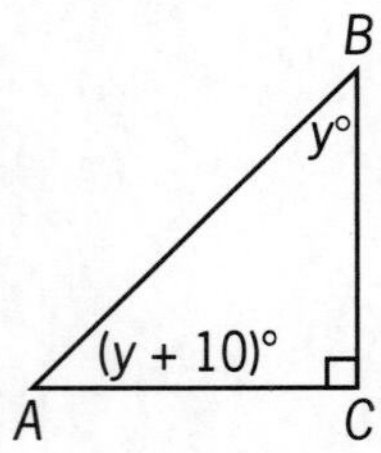

43. In the figure above, what is the ratio of the measure of angle B to the measure of angle A ?

(A) 2 to 3
(B) 3 to 4
(C) 3 to 5
(D) 4 to 5
(E) 5 to 6

44. If n is a prime number greater than 3, what is the remainder when n^2 is divided by 12 ?

(A) 0
(B) 1
(C) 2
(D) 3
(E) 5

45. $\dfrac{1}{1+\frac{1}{3}} - \dfrac{1}{1+\frac{1}{2}} =$

(A) $-\frac{1}{3}$
(B) $-\frac{1}{6}$
(C) $-\frac{1}{12}$
(D) $\frac{1}{12}$
(E) $\frac{1}{3}$

46. The positive two-digit integers x and y have the same digits, but in reverse order. Which of the following must be a factor of $x + y$?

(A) 6
(B) 9
(C) 10
(D) 11
(E) 14

47. In a certain sequence of 8 numbers, each number after the first is 1 more than the previous number. If the first number is –5, how many of the numbers in the sequence are positive?

(A) None
(B) One
(C) Two
(D) Three
(E) Four

48. A total of s oranges are to be packaged in boxes that will hold r oranges each, with no oranges left over. When n of these boxes have been completely filled, what is the number of boxes that remain to be filled?

(A) $s - nr$
(B) $s - \frac{n}{r}$
(C) $rs - n$
(D) $\frac{s}{n} - r$
(E) $\frac{s}{r} - n$

49. If $0 < a < b < c$, which of the following statements must be true?

I. $2a > b + c$
II. $c - a > b - a$
III. $\frac{c}{a} < \frac{b}{a}$

(A) I only
(B) II only
(C) III only
(D) I and II
(E) II and III

50. In the xy-plane, the origin O is the midpoint of line segment PQ. If the coordinates of P are (r,s), what are the coordinates of Q?

(A) (r,s)

(B) $(s,-r)$

(C) $(-s,-r)$

(D) $(-r,s)$

(E) $(-r,-s)$

51. Which of the following equations is NOT equivalent to $10y^2 = (x + 2)(x - 2)$?

(A) $30y^2 = 3x^2 - 12$

(B) $20y^2 = (2x - 4)(x + 2)$

(C) $10y^2 + 4 = x^2$

(D) $5y^2 = x^2 - 2$

(E) $y^2 = \dfrac{x^2 - 4}{10}$

	Monday	Tuesday	Wednesday	Thursday
Company *A*	45	55	50	50
Company *B*	10	30	30	10
Company *C*	34	28	28	30
Company *D*	39	42	41	38
Company *E*	50	60	60	70

52. The table shows the numbers of packages shipped daily by each of five companies during a 4-day period. The standard deviation of the numbers of packages shipped daily during the period was greatest for which of the five companies?

(A) *A*

(B) *B*

(C) *C*

(D) *D*

(E) *E*

53. Company Q plans to make a new product next year and sell each unit of this new product at a selling price of \$2. The variable costs per unit in each production run are estimated to be 40% of the selling price, and the fixed costs for each production run are estimated to be \$5,040. Based on these estimated costs, how many units of the new product will Company Q need to make and sell in order for their revenue to equal their total costs for each production run?

(A) 4,200

(B) 3,150

(C) 2,520

(D) 2,100

(E) 1,800

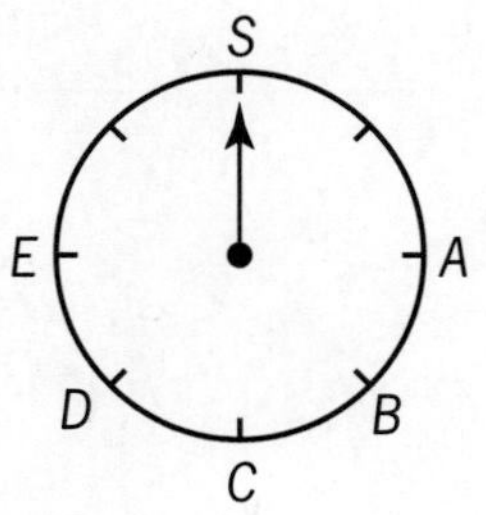

54. The dial shown above is divided into equal-sized intervals. At which of the following letters will the pointer stop if it is rotated clockwise from S through 1,174 intervals?

(A) *A*

(B) *B*

(C) *C*

(D) *D*

(E) *E*

Estimated Number of Home-Schooled Students by State, January 2001

State	Number (in thousands)
A	181
B	125
C	103
D	79
E	72

55. According to the table shown, the estimated number of home-schooled students in State A is approximately what percent greater than the number in State D ?

(A) 25%
(B) 55%
(C) 100%
(D) 125%
(E) 155%

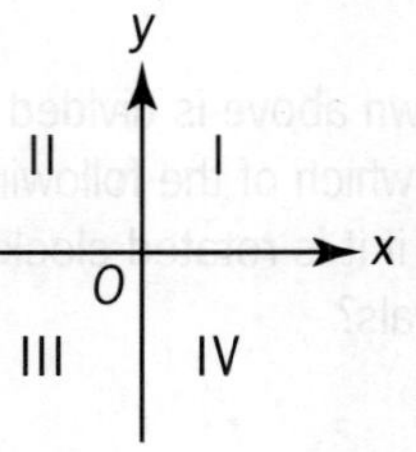

56. The graph of the equation $xy = k$, where $k < 0$, lies in which two of the quadrants shown above?

(A) I and II
(B) I and III
(C) II and III
(D) II and IV
(E) III and IV

57. When n liters of fuel were added to a tank that was already $\frac{1}{3}$ full, the tank was filled to $\frac{7}{9}$ of its capacity. In terms of n, what is the capacity of the tank, in liters?

(A) $\frac{10}{9}n$
(B) $\frac{4}{3}n$
(C) $\frac{3}{2}n$
(D) $\frac{9}{4}n$
(E) $\frac{7}{3}n$

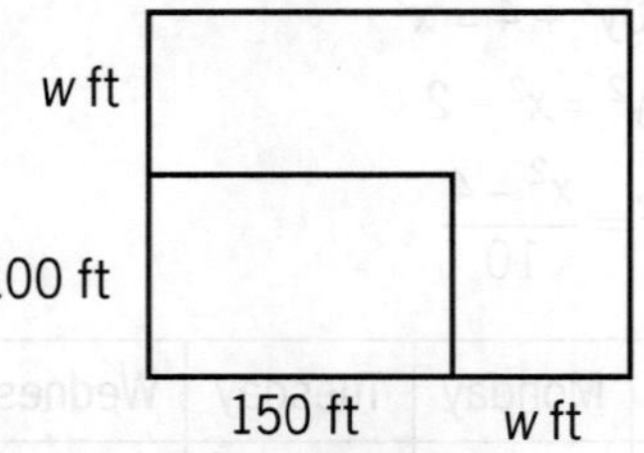

Note: Not drawn to scale.

58. The smaller rectangle in the figure above represents the original size of a parking lot before its length and width were each extended by w feet to make the larger rectangular lot shown. If the area of the enlarged lot is twice the area of the original lot, what is the value of w ?

(A) 25
(B) 50
(C) 75
(D) 100
(E) 200

59. $\frac{1}{0.75-1} =$

(A) –4
(B) –0.25
(C) 0.25
(D) 0.75
(E) 4

60. Kevin invested \$8,000 for one year at a simple annual interest rate of 6 percent and invested \$10,000 for one year at an annual interest rate of 8 percent compounded semiannually. What is the total amount of interest that Kevin earned on the two investments?

(A) \$880
(B) \$1,088
(C) \$1,253
(D) \$1,280
(E) \$1,296

61. The harvest yield from a certain apple orchard was 350 bushels of apples. If x of the trees in the orchard each yielded 10 bushels of apples, what fraction of the harvest yield was from these x trees?

(A) $\frac{x}{35}$
(B) $1-\frac{x}{35}$
(C) 10x
(D) 35 – x
(E) 350 – 10x

62. If n is an integer, which of the following must be even?

(A) $n+1$
(B) $n+2$
(C) $2n$
(D) $2n+1$
(E) n^2

63. The sum $\frac{7}{8}+\frac{1}{9}$ is between

(A) $\frac{1}{2}$ and $\frac{3}{4}$
(B) $\frac{3}{4}$ and 1
(C) 1 and $1\frac{1}{4}$
(D) $1\frac{1}{4}$ and $1\frac{1}{2}$
(E) $1\frac{1}{2}$ and 2

64. Car X averages 25.0 miles per gallon of gasoline and Car Y averages 11.9 miles per gallon. If each car is driven 12,000 miles, approximately how many more gallons of gasoline will Car Y use than Car X ?

(A) 320
(B) 480
(C) 520
(D) 730
(E) 920

65. If y is an integer, then the least possible value of $|23-5y|$ is

(A) 1
(B) 2
(C) 3
(D) 4
(E) 5

66. $\sqrt{80}+\sqrt{125}=$

(A) $9\sqrt{5}$
(B) $20\sqrt{5}$
(C) $41\sqrt{5}$
(D) $\sqrt{205}$
(E) 100

$$y = kx + 3$$

67. In the equation above, k is a constant. If $y = 17$ when $x = 2$, what is the value of y when $x = 4$?

(A) 34
(B) 31
(C) 14
(D) 11
(E) 7

68. Which of the following is greatest?

(A) $10\sqrt{3}$
(B) $9\sqrt{4}$
(C) $8\sqrt{5}$
(D) $7\sqrt{6}$
(E) $6\sqrt{7}$

69. Al and Ben are drivers for SD Trucking Company. One snowy day, Ben left SD at 8:00 a.m. heading east and Al left SD at 11:00 a.m. heading west. At a particular time later that day, the dispatcher retrieved data from SD's vehicle tracking system. The data showed that, up to that time, Al had averaged 40 miles per hour and Ben had averaged 20 miles per hour. It also showed that Al and Ben had driven a combined total of 240 miles. At what time did the dispatcher retrieve data from the vehicle tracking system?

(A) 1:00 p.m.
(B) 2:00 p.m.
(C) 3:00 p.m.
(D) 5:00 p.m.
(E) 6:00 p.m.

70. Of the land owned by a farmer, 90 percent was cleared for planting. Of the cleared land, 40 percent was planted with soybeans and 50 percent of the cleared land was planted with wheat. If the remaining 720 acres of cleared land was planted with corn, how many acres did the farmer own?

(A) 5,832
(B) 6,480
(C) 7,200
(D) 8,000
(E) 8,889

71. At the start of an experiment, a certain population consisted of 3 animals. At the end of each month after the start of the experiment, the population size was double its size at the beginning of that month. Which of the following represents the population size at the end of 10 months?

(A) 2^3
(B) 3^2
(C) $2(3^{10})$
(D) $3(2^{10})$
(E) $3(10^2)$

72. If $\left(\frac{1}{3}+\frac{1}{4}+\frac{1}{5}+\frac{1}{6}\right)=r\left(\frac{1}{9}+\frac{1}{12}+\frac{1}{15}+\frac{1}{18}\right)$, then $r=$

(A) $\frac{1}{3}$
(B) $\frac{4}{3}$
(C) 3
(D) 4
(E) 12

73. If x and y are positive integers such that y is a multiple of 5 and $3x + 4y = 200$, then x must be a multiple of which of the following?

(A) 3
(B) 6
(C) 7
(D) 8
(E) 10

74. Which of the following expressions can be written as an integer?

I. $\left(\sqrt{82}+\sqrt{82}\right)^2$

II. $(82)\left(\sqrt{82}\right)$

III. $\frac{\left(\sqrt{82}\right)\left(\sqrt{82}\right)}{82}$

(A) None
(B) I only
(C) III only
(D) I and II
(E) I and III

75. Four staff members at a certain company worked on a project. The amounts of time that the four staff members worked on the project were in the ratio 2 to 3 to 5 to 6. If one of the four staff members worked on the project for 30 hours, which of the following CANNOT be the total number of hours that the four staff members worked on the project?

(A) 80
(B) 96
(C) 160
(D) 192
(E) 240

76. Pumping alone at their respective constant rates, one inlet pipe fills an empty tank to $\frac{1}{2}$ of capacity in 3 hours and a second inlet pipe fills the same empty tank to $\frac{2}{3}$ of capacity in 6 hours. How many hours will it take both pipes, pumping simultaneously at their respective constant rates, to fill the empty tank to capacity?

(A) 3.25
(B) 3.6
(C) 4.2
(D) 4.4
(E) 5.5

77. In the *xy*-coordinate plane, which of the following points must lie on the line $kx + 3y = 6$ for every possible value of k?

(A) (1,1)
(B) (0,2)
(C) (2,0)
(D) (3,6)
(E) (6,3)

78. If $x^2 - 2 < 0$, which of the following specifies all the possible values of x?

(A) $0 < x < 2$
(B) $0 < x < \sqrt{2}$
(C) $-\sqrt{2} < x < \sqrt{2}$
(D) $-2 < x < 0$
(E) $-2 < x < 2$

Book number	Pages in book	Total pages read
1	253	253
2	110	363
3	117	480
4	170	650
5	155	805
6	50	855
7	205	1,060
8	70	1,130
9	165	1,295
10	105	1,400
11	143	1,543
12	207	1,750

79. Shawana made a schedule for reading books during 4 weeks (28 days) of her summer vacation. She has checked out 12 books from the library. The number of pages in each book and the order in which she plans to read the books are shown in the table above. She will read exactly 50 pages each day. The only exception will be that she will never begin the next book on the same day that she finishes the previous one, and therefore on some days she may read fewer than 50 pages. At the end of the 28th day, how many books will Shawana have finished?

(A) 7
(B) 8
(C) 9
(D) 10
(E) 11

80. In Western Europe, x bicycles were sold in each of the years 1990 and 1993. The bicycle producers of Western Europe had a 42 percent share of this market in 1990 and a 33 percent share in 1993. Which of the following represents the decrease in the annual number of bicycles produced and sold in Western Europe from 1990 to 1993 ?

(A) 9% of $\frac{x}{100}$

(B) 14% of $\frac{x}{100}$

(C) 75% of $\frac{x}{100}$

(D) 9% of x

(E) 14% of x

81. If k is a positive integer, what is the remainder when $(k + 2)(k^3 - k)$ is divided by 6 ?

(A) 0
(B) 1
(C) 2
(D) 3
(E) 4

82. Which of the following fractions is closest to $\frac{1}{2}$?

(A) $\frac{4}{7}$

(B) $\frac{5}{9}$

(C) $\frac{6}{11}$

(D) $\frac{7}{13}$

(E) $\frac{9}{16}$

83. If $p \neq 0$ and $p - \frac{1-p^2}{p} = \frac{r}{p}$, then $r =$

(A) $p + 1$
(B) $2p - 1$
(C) $p^2 + 1$
(D) $2p^2 - 1$
(E) $p^2 + p - 1$

84. If the range of the six numbers 4, 3, 14, 7, 10, and x is 12, what is the difference between the greatest possible value of x and the least possible value of x ?

(A) 0
(B) 2
(C) 12
(D) 13
(E) 15

85. What number is 108 more than two-thirds of itself?

(A) 72
(B) 144
(C) 162
(D) 216
(E) 324

86. A doctor prescribed 18 cubic centimeters of a certain drug to a patient whose body weight was 120 pounds. If the typical dosage is 2 cubic centimeters per 15 pounds of body weight, by what percent was the prescribed dosage greater than the typical dosage?

(A) 8%
(B) 9%
(C) 11%
(D) 12.5%
(E) 14.8%

87. Company P had 15 percent more employees in December than it had in January. If Company P had 460 employees in December, how many employees did it have in January?

(A) 391
(B) 400
(C) 410
(D) 423
(E) 445

88. The function f is defined by $f(x) = \sqrt{x} - 10$ for all positive numbers x. if $u = f(t)$ for some positive numbers t and u, what is t in terms of u?

(A) $\sqrt{\sqrt{u}+10}$
(B) $\left(\sqrt{u}+10\right)^2$
(C) $\sqrt{u^2+10}$
(D) $(u+10)^2$
(E) $(u^2+10)^2$

89. A glass was filled with 10 ounces of water, and 0.01 ounce of the water evaporated each day during a 20-day period. What percent of the original amount of water evaporated during this period?

(A) 0.002%
(B) 0.02%
(C) 0.2%
(D) 2%
(E) 20%

90. If m and p are positive integers and $m^2 + p^2 < 100$, what is the greatest possible value of mp?

(A) 36
(B) 42
(C) 48
(D) 49
(E) 51

91. If $\frac{x}{y} = \frac{c}{d}$ and $\frac{d}{c} = \frac{b}{a}$, which of the following must be true?

I. $\frac{y}{x} = \frac{b}{a}$

II. $\frac{x}{a} = \frac{y}{b}$

III. $\frac{y}{a} = \frac{x}{b}$

(A) I only
(B) II only
(C) I and II only
(D) I and III only
(E) I, II, and III

92. If k is an integer and $(0.0025)(0.025)(0.00025) \times 10^k$ is an integer, what is the least possible value of k?

(A) −12
(B) −6
(C) 0
(D) 6
(E) 12

93. If $a(a + 2) = 24$ and $b(b + 2) = 24$, where $a \neq b$, then $a + b =$

(A) −48
(B) −2
(C) 2
(D) 46
(E) 48

94. In a recent election, Ms. Robbins received 8,000 votes cast by independent voters, that is, voters not registered with a specific political party. She also received 10 percent of the votes cast by those voters registered with a political party. If N is the total number of votes cast in the election and 40 percent of the votes cast were cast by independent voters, which of the following represents the number of votes that Ms. Robbins received?

(A) $0.06N + 3{,}200$
(B) $0.1N + 7{,}200$
(C) $0.4N + 7{,}200$
(D) $0.1N + 8{,}000$
(E) $0.06N + 8{,}000$

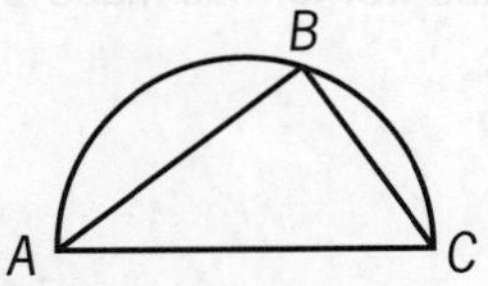

95. In the figure shown, the triangle is inscribed in the semicircle. If the length of line segment AB is 8 and the length of line segment BC is 6, what is the length of arc ABC?

(A) 15π
(B) 12π
(C) 10π
(D) 7π
(E) 5π

96. A manufacturer makes and sells 2 products, P and Q. The revenue from the sale of each unit of P is \$20.00 and the revenue from the sale of each unit of Q is \$17.00. Last year the manufacturer sold twice as many units of Q as P. What was the manufacturer's average (arithmetic mean) revenue per unit sold of these 2 products last year?

(A) \$28.50
(B) \$27.00
(C) \$19.00
(D) \$18.50
(E) \$18.00

97. On a certain day, orangeade was made by mixing a certain amount of orange juice with an equal amount of water. On the next day, orangeade was made by mixing the same amount of orange juice with twice the amount of water. On both days, all the orangeade that was made was sold. If the revenue from selling the orangeade was the same for both days and if the orangeade was sold at \$0.60 per glass on the first day, what was the price per glass on the second day?

(A) \$0.15
(B) \$0.20
(C) \$0.30
(D) \$0.40
(E) \$0.45

98. A worker carries jugs of liquid soap from a production line to a packing area, carrying 4 jugs per trip. If the jugs are packed into cartons that hold 7 jugs each, how many jugs are needed to fill the last partially filled carton after the worker has made 17 trips?

(A) 1
(B) 2
(C) 4
(D) 5
(E) 6

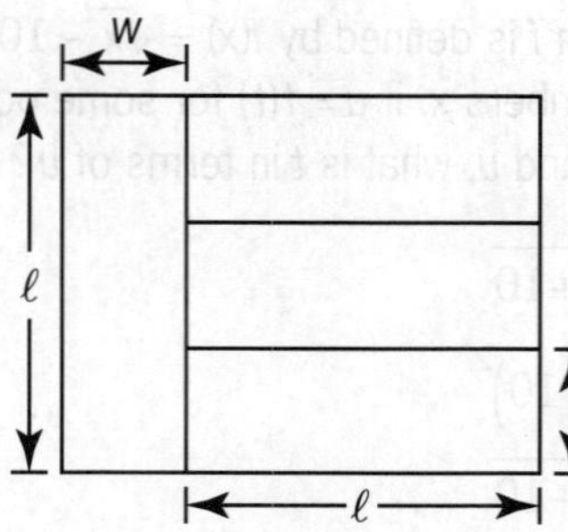

99. The figure shown above represents a modern painting that consists of four differently colored rectangles, each of which has length ℓ and width w. If the area of the painting is 4,800 square inches, what is the width, in inches, of each of the four rectangles?

(A) 15
(B) 20
(C) 25
(D) 30
(E) 40

100. A certain fruit stand sold apples for \$0.70 each and bananas for \$0.50 each. If a customer purchased both apples and bananas from the stand for a total of \$6.30, what total number of apples and bananas did the customer purchase?

(A) 10
(B) 11
(C) 12
(D) 13
(E) 14

101. In the xy-plane, what is the slope of the line with equation $3x + 7y = 9$?

(A) $-\frac{7}{3}$
(B) $-\frac{3}{7}$
(C) $\frac{3}{7}$
(D) 3
(E) 7

102. Working simultaneously and independently at an identical constant rate, four machines of a certain type can produce a total of x units of product P in 6 days. How many of these machines, working simultaneously and independently at this constant rate, can produce a total of 3x units of product P in 4 days?

(A) 24
(B) 18
(C) 16
(D) 12
(E) 8

103. At a certain school, the ratio of the number of second graders to the number of fourth graders is 8 to 5, and the ratio of the number of first graders to the number of second graders is 3 to 4. If the ratio of the number of third graders to the number of fourth graders is 3 to 2, what is the ratio of the number of first graders to the number of third graders?

(A) 16 to 15
(B) 9 to 5
(C) 5 to 16
(D) 5 to 4
(E) 4 to 5

104. The symbol Δ denotes one of the four arithmetic operations: addition, subtraction, multiplication, or division. If $6 \Delta 3 \le 3$, which of the following must be true?

I. $2 \Delta 2 = 0$
II. $2 \Delta 2 = 1$
III. $4 \Delta 2 = 2$

(A) I only
(B) II only
(C) III only
(D) I and II only
(E) I, II, and III

105. The average distance between the Sun and a certain planet is approximately 2.3×10^{14} inches. Which of the following is closest to the average distance between the Sun and the planet, in kilometers? (1 kilometer is approximately 3.9×10^4 inches.)

(A) 7.1×10^8
(B) 5.9×10^9
(C) 1.6×10^{10}
(D) 1.6×10^{11}
(E) 5.9×10^{11}

106. If $mn \neq 0$ and 25 percent of n equals $37\frac{1}{2}$ percent of m, what is the value of $\frac{12n}{m}$?

(A) 18
(B) $\frac{32}{3}$
(C) 8
(D) 3
(E) $\frac{9}{8}$

107. In the coordinate plane, a circle has center (2,–3) and passes through the point (5,0). What is the area of the circle?

(A) 3π
(B) $3\sqrt{2}\pi$
(C) $3\sqrt{3}\pi$
(D) 9π
(E) 18π

108. Last year Joe grew 1 inch and Sally grew 200 percent more than Joe grew. How many inches did Sally grow last year?

(A) 0
(B) 1
(C) 2
(D) 3
(E) 4

109. The cost C, in dollars, to remove p percent of a certain pollutant from a pond is estimated by using the formula $C = \frac{100{,}000P}{100 - P}$. According to this estimate, how much more would it cost to remove 90 percent of the pollutant from the pond than it would cost to remove 80 percent of the pollutant?

(A) \$500,000
(B) \$100,000
(C) \$50,000
(D) \$10,000
(E) \$5,000

110. If $xy \neq 0$ and $x^2y^2 - xy = 6$, which of the following could be y in terms of x?

I. $\frac{1}{2x}$
II. $-\frac{2}{x}$
III. $\frac{3}{x}$

(A) I only
(B) II only
(C) I and II
(D) I and III
(E) II and III

111. At a certain instant in time, the number of cars, N, traveling on a portion of a certain highway can be estimated by the formula

$$N = \frac{20Ld}{600 + s^2}$$

where L is the number of lanes in the same direction, d is the length of the portion of the highway, in feet, and s is the average speed of the cars, in miles per hour. Based on the formula, what is the estimated number of cars traveling on a $\frac{1}{2}$-mile portion of the highway if the highway has 2 lanes in the same direction and the average speed of the cars is 40 miles per hour? (5,280 feet = 1 mile)

(A) 155
(B) 96
(C) 80
(D) 48
(E) 24

112. $\sqrt{4.8 \times 10^9}$ is closest in value to

(A) 2,200
(B) 70,000
(C) 220,000
(D) 7,000,000
(E) 22,000,000

113. Three printing presses, R, S, and T, working together at their respective constant rates, can do a certain printing job in 4 hours. S and T, working together at their respective constant rates, can do the same job in 5 hours. How many hours would it take R, working alone at its constant rate, to do the same job?

(A) 8
(B) 10
(C) 12
(D) 15
(E) 20

114. For a party, three solid cheese balls with diameters of 2 inches, 4 inches, and 6 inches, respectively, were combined to form a single cheese ball. What was the approximate diameter, in inches, of the new cheese ball? (The volume of a sphere is $\frac{4}{3}\pi r^3$, where r is the radius.)

(A) 12
(B) 16
(C) $\sqrt[3]{16}$
(D) $3\sqrt[3]{8}$
(E) $2\sqrt[3]{36}$

115. The sum of all the integers k such that $-26 < k < 24$ is

(A) 0
(B) −2
(C) −25
(D) −49
(E) −51

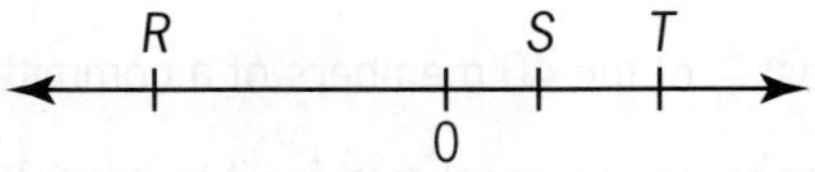

116. The number line shown contains three points *R*, *S*, and *T*, whose coordinates have absolute values *r*, *s*, and *t*, respectively. Which of the following equals the average (arithmetic mean) of the coordinates of the points *R*, *S*, and *T*?

(A) s

(B) $s+t-r$

(C) $\frac{r-s-t}{3}$

(D) $\frac{r+s+t}{3}$

(E) $\frac{s+t-r}{3}$

117. Mark and Ann together were allocated *n* boxes of cookies to sell for a club project. Mark sold 10 boxes less than *n* and Ann sold 2 boxes less than *n*. If Mark and Ann have each sold at least one box of cookies, but together they have sold less than *n* boxes, what is the value of *n*?

(A) 11
(B) 12
(C) 13
(D) 14
(E) 15

118. A certain high school has 5,000 students. Of these students, *x* are taking music, *y* are taking art, and *z* are taking both music and art. How many students are taking neither music nor art?

(A) $5{,}000 - z$
(B) $5{,}000 - x - y$
(C) $5{,}000 - x + z$
(D) $5{,}000 - x - y - z$
(E) $5{,}000 - x - y + z$

119. Yesterday's closing prices of 2,420 different stocks listed on a certain stock exchange were all different from today's closing prices. The number of stocks that closed at a higher price today than yesterday was 20 percent greater than the number that closed at a lower price. How many of the stocks closed at a higher price today than yesterday?

(A) 484
(B) 726
(C) 1,100
(D) 1,320
(E) 1,694

120. Each person who attended a company meeting was either a stockholder in the company, an employee of the company, or both. If 62 percent of those who attended the meeting were stockholders and 47 percent were employees, what percent were stockholders who were <u>not</u> employees?

(A) 34%
(B) 38%
(C) 45%
(D) 53%
(E) 62%

121. A gym class can be divided into 8 teams with an equal number of players on each team or into 12 teams with an equal number of players on each team. What is the lowest possible number of students in the class?

(A) 20
(B) 24
(C) 36
(D) 48
(E) 96

Accounts	Amount Budgeted	Amount Spent
Payroll	$110,000	$117,000
Taxes	40,000	42,000
Insurance	2,500	2,340

122. The table shows the amount budgeted and the amount spent for each of three accounts in a certain company. For which of these accounts did the amount spent differ from the amount budgeted by more than 6 percent of the amount budgeted?

(A) Payroll only
(B) Taxes only
(C) Insurance only
(D) Payroll and Insurance
(E) Taxes and Insurance

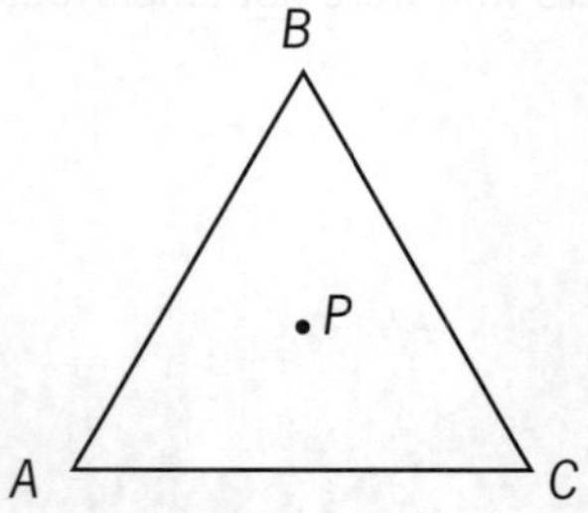

123. In the figure above, triangle *ABC* is equilateral, and point *P* is equidistant from vertices *A*, *B*, and *C*. If triangle *ABC* is rotated clockwise about point *P*, what is the minimum number of degrees the triangle must be rotated so that point *B* will be in the position where point *A* is now?

(A) 60
(B) 120
(C) 180
(D) 240
(E) 270

124. At least $\frac{2}{3}$ of the 40 members of a committee must vote in favor of a resolution for it to pass. What is the greatest number of members who could vote against the resolution and still have it pass?

(A) 19
(B) 17
(C) 16
(D) 14
(E) 13

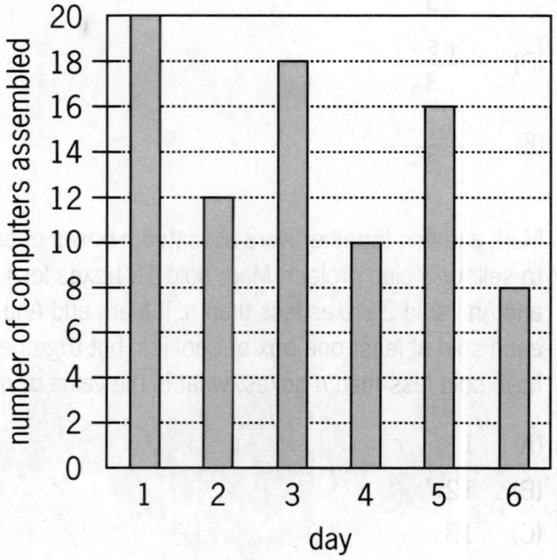

125. The graph shows the number of computers assembled during each of 6 consecutive days. From what day to the next day was the percent change in the number of computers assembled the greatest in magnitude?

(A) From Day 1 to Day 2
(B) From Day 2 to Day 3
(C) From Day 3 to Day 4
(D) From Day 4 to Day 5
(E) From Day 5 to Day 6

126. If $n = 20! + 17$, then n is divisible by which of the following?

I. 15
II. 17
III. 19

(A) None
(B) I only
(C) II only
(D) I and II
(E) II and III

127. The product of two negative numbers is 160. If the lesser of the two numbers is 4 less than twice the greater, what is the greater number?

(A) −20
(B) −16
(C) −10
(D) −8
(E) −4

128. According to a certain estimate, the depth $N(t)$, in centimeters, of the water in a certain tank at t hours past 2:00 in the morning is given by $N(t) = -20(t-5)^2 + 500$ for $0 \le t \le 10$. According to this estimate, at what time in the morning does the depth of the water in the tank reach its maximum?

(A) 5:30
(B) 7:00
(C) 7:30
(D) 8:00
(E) 9:00

129. After driving to a riverfront parking lot, Bob plans to run south along the river, turn around, and return to the parking lot, running north along the same path. After running 3.25 miles south, he decides to run for only 50 minutes more. If Bob runs at a constant rate of 8 minutes per mile, how many miles farther south can he run and still be able to return to the parking lot in 50 minutes?

(A) 1.5
(B) 2.25
(C) 3.0
(D) 3.25
(E) 4.75

130. Alex deposited x dollars into a new account that earned 8 percent annual interest, compounded annually. One year later Alex deposited an additional x dollars into the account. If there were no other transactions and if the account contained w dollars at the end of two years, which of the following expresses x in terms of w?

(A) $\frac{w}{1+1.08}$

(B) $\frac{w}{1.08+1.16}$

(C) $\frac{w}{1.16+1.24}$

(D) $\frac{w}{1.08+(1.08)^2}$

(E) $\frac{w}{(1.08)^2+(1.08)^3}$

131. M is the sum of the reciprocals of the consecutive integers from 201 to 300, inclusive. Which of the following is true?

(A) $\frac{1}{3} < M < \frac{1}{2}$

(B) $\frac{1}{5} < M < \frac{1}{3}$

(C) $\frac{1}{7} < M < \frac{1}{5}$

(D) $\frac{1}{9} < M < \frac{1}{7}$

(E) $\frac{1}{12} < M < \frac{1}{9}$

132. Working simultaneously at their respective constant rates, Machines A and B produce 800 nails in x hours. Working alone at its constant rate, Machine A produces 800 nails in y hours. In terms of x and y, how many hours does it take Machine B, working alone at its constant rate, to produce 800 nails?

(A) $\frac{x}{x+y}$

(B) $\frac{y}{x+y}$

(C) $\frac{xy}{x+y}$

(D) $\frac{xy}{x-y}$

(E) $\frac{xy}{y-x}$

133. In the Johnsons' monthly budget, the dollar amounts allocated to household expenses, food, and miscellaneous items are in the ratio 5:2:1, respectively. If the total amount allocated to these three categories is \$1,800, what is the amount allocated to food?

(A) \$900
(B) \$720
(C) \$675
(D) \$450
(E) \$225

	Number of Marbles in Each of Three Bags	Percent of Marbles in Each Bag That Are Blue (to the nearest tenth)
Bag *P*	37	10.8%
Bag *Q*	x	66.7%
Bag *R*	32	50.0%

134. If $\frac{1}{3}$ of the total number of marbles in the three bags listed in the table above are blue, how many marbles are there in bag *Q* ?

(A) 5
(B) 9
(C) 12
(D) 23
(E) 46

135. $\frac{(0.0036)(2.8)}{(0.04)(0.1)(0.003)} =$

(A) 840.0
(B) 84.0
(C) 8.4
(D) 0.84
(E) 0.084

136. If *n* is an integer greater than 6, which of the following must be divisible by 3 ?

(A) $n(n + 1)(n - 4)$
(B) $n(n + 2)(n - 1)$
(C) $n(n + 3)(n - 5)$
(D) $n(n + 4)(n - 2)$
(E) $n(n + 5)(n - 6)$

Age Category (in years)	Number of Employees
Less than 20	29
20–29	58
30–39	36
40–49	21
50–59	10
60–69	5
70 and over	2

137. The table above gives the age categories of the 161 employees at Company X and the number of employees in each category. According to the table, if *m* is the median age, in years, of the employees at Company X, then *m* must satisfy which of the following?

(A) $20 \le m \le 29$
(B) $25 \le m \le 34$
(C) $30 \le m \le 39$
(D) $35 \le m \le 44$
(E) $40 \le m \le 49$

138. If *x* and *y* are positive numbers such that $x + y = 1$, which of the following could be the value of $100x + 200y$?

I. 80
II. 140
III. 199

(A) II only
(B) III only
(C) I and II
(D) I and III
(E) II and III

139. If X is the hundredths digit in the decimal $0.1X$ and if Y is the thousandths digit in the decimal $0.02Y$, where X and Y are nonzero digits, which of the following is closest to the greatest possible value of $\frac{0.1X}{0.02Y}$?

(A) 4
(B) 5
(C) 6
(D) 9
(E) 10

140. Clarissa will create her summer reading list by randomly choosing 4 books from the 10 books approved for summer reading. She will list the books in the order in which they are chosen. How many different lists are possible?

(A) 6
(B) 40
(C) 210
(D) 5,040
(E) 151,200

141. If n is a positive integer and the product of all the integers from 1 to n, inclusive, is divisible by 990, what is the least possible value of n?

(A) 8
(B) 9
(C) 10
(D) 11
(E) 12

142. The probability that event M will <u>not</u> occur is 0.8 and the probability that event R will <u>not</u> occur is 0.6. If events M and R cannot both occur, which of the following is the probability that either event M or event R will occur?

(A) $\frac{1}{5}$
(B) $\frac{2}{5}$
(C) $\frac{3}{5}$
(D) $\frac{4}{5}$
(E) $\frac{12}{25}$

143. The total cost for Company X to produce a batch of tools is \$10,000 plus \$3 per tool. Each tool sells for \$8. The gross profit earned from producing and selling these tools is the total income from sales minus the total production cost. If a batch of 20,000 tools is produced and sold, then Company X's gross profit per tool is

(A) \$3.00
(B) \$3.75
(C) \$4.50
(D) \$5.00
(E) \$5.50

144. If Q is an odd number and the median of Q consecutive integers is 120, what is the largest of these integers?

(A) $\frac{Q-1}{2}+120$
(B) $\frac{Q}{2}+119$
(C) $\frac{Q}{2}+120$
(D) $\frac{Q+119}{2}$
(E) $\frac{Q+120}{2}$

145. A ladder of a fire truck is elevated to an angle of 60° and extended to a length of 70 feet. If the base of the ladder is 7 feet above the ground, how many feet above the ground does the ladder reach?

(A) 35
(B) 42
(C) $35\sqrt{3}$
(D) $7+35\sqrt{3}$
(E) $7+42\sqrt{3}$

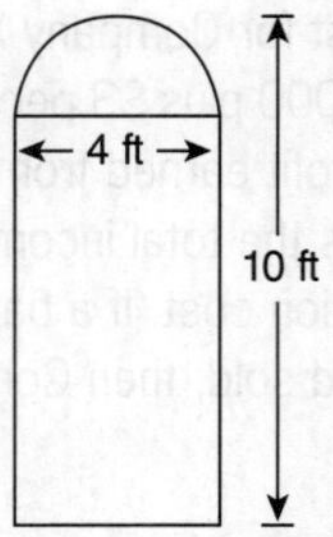

146. The window in the figure above consists of a rectangle and a semicircle with dimensions as shown. What is the area, in square feet, of the window?

(A) $40 + 8\pi$
(B) $40 + 2\pi$
(C) $32 + 8\pi$
(D) $32 + 4\pi$
(E) $32 + 2\pi$

147. If there are fewer than 8 zeros between the decimal point and the first nonzero digit in the decimal expansion of $\left(\frac{t}{1{,}000}\right)^4$, which of the following numbers could be the value of t?

I. 3
II. 5
III. 9

(A) None
(B) I only
(C) II only
(D) III only
(E) II and III

148. A three-digit code for certain locks uses the digits 0, 1, 2, 3, 4, 5, 6, 7, 8, 9 according to the following constraints. The first digit cannot be 0 or 1, the second digit must be 0 or 1, and the second and third digits cannot both be 0 in the same code. How many different codes are possible?

(A) 144
(B) 152
(C) 160
(D) 168
(E) 176

149. Jackie has two solutions that are 2 percent sulfuric acid and 12 percent sulfuric acid by volume, respectively. If these solutions are mixed in appropriate quantities to produce 60 liters of a solution that is 5 percent sulfuric acid, approximately how many liters of the 2 percent solution will be required?

(A) 18
(B) 20
(C) 24
(D) 36
(E) 42

150. If Jake loses 8 pounds, he will weigh twice as much as his sister. Together they now weigh 278 pounds. What is Jake's present weight, in pounds?

(A) 131
(B) 135
(C) 139
(D) 147
(E) 188

151. For each student in a certain class, a teacher adjusted the student's test score using the formula $y = 0.8x + 20$, where x is the student's original test score and y is the student's adjusted test score. If the standard deviation of the original test scores of the students in the class was 20, what was the standard deviation of the adjusted test scores of the students in the class?

(A) 12
(B) 16
(C) 28
(D) 36
(E) 40

152. Last year 26 members of a certain club traveled to England, 26 members traveled to France, and 32 members traveled to Italy. Last year no members of the club traveled to both England and France, 6 members traveled to both England and Italy, and 11 members traveled to both France and Italy. How many members of the club traveled to at least one of these three countries last year?

(A) 52
(B) 67
(C) 71
(D) 73
(E) 79

153. A store reported total sales of \$385 million for February of this year. If the total sales for the same month last year was \$320 million, approximately what was the percent increase in sales?

(A) 2%
(B) 17%
(C) 20%
(D) 65%
(E) 83%

154. When positive integer x is divided by positive integer y, the remainder is 9. If $\frac{x}{y} = 96.12$, what is the value of y?

(A) 96
(B) 75
(C) 48
(D) 25
(E) 12

155. If $x(2x + 1) = 0$ and $\left(x + \frac{1}{2}\right)(2x - 3) = 0$, then $x =$

(A) -3
(B) $-\frac{1}{2}$
(C) 0
(D) $\frac{1}{2}$
(E) $\frac{3}{2}$

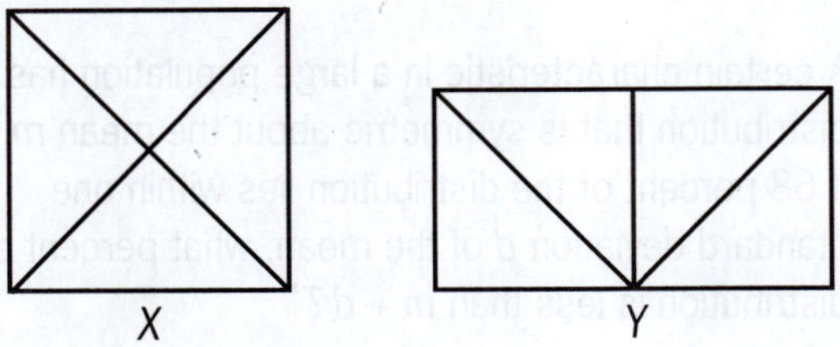

156. Figures X and Y above show how eight identical triangular pieces of cardboard were used to form a square and a rectangle, respectively. What is the ratio of the perimeter of X to the perimeter of Y?

(A) $2:3$
(B) $\sqrt{2}:2$
(C) $2\sqrt{2}:3$
(D) $1:1$
(E) $\sqrt{2}:1$

157. A certain experimental mathematics program was tried out in 2 classes in each of 32 elementary schools and involved 37 teachers. Each of the classes had 1 teacher and each of the teachers taught at least 1, but not more than 3, of the classes. If the number of teachers who taught 3 classes is n, then the least and greatest possible values of n, respectively, are

(A) 0 and 13
(B) 0 and 14
(C) 1 and 10
(D) 1 and 9
(E) 2 and 8

158. For the positive numbers, n, $n + 1$, $n + 2$, $n + 4$, and $n + 8$, the mean is how much greater than the median?

(A) 0
(B) 1
(C) $n + 1$
(D) $n + 2$
(E) $n + 3$

159. The interior of a rectangular carton is designed by a certain manufacturer to have a volume of x cubic feet and a ratio of length to width to height of 3:2:2. In terms of x, which of the following equals the height of the carton, in feet?

(A) $\sqrt[3]{x}$
(B) $\sqrt[3]{\frac{2x}{3}}$
(C) $\sqrt[3]{\frac{3x}{2}}$
(D) $\frac{2}{3}\sqrt[3]{x}$
(E) $\frac{3}{2}\sqrt[3]{x}$

160. The present ratio of students to teachers at a certain school is 30 to 1. If the student enrollment were to increase by 50 students and the number of teachers were to increase by 5, the ratio of students to teachers would then be 25 to 1. What is the present number of teachers?

(A) 5
(B) 8
(C) 10
(D) 12
(E) 15

161. What is the smallest integer n for which $25^n > 5^{12}$?

(A) 6
(B) 7
(C) 8
(D) 9
(E) 10

162. Sixty percent of the members of a study group are women, and 45 percent of those women are lawyers. If one member of the study group is to be selected at random, what is the probability that the member selected is a woman lawyer?

(A) 0.10
(B) 0.15
(C) 0.27
(D) 0.33
(E) 0.45

163. Each year for 4 years, a farmer increased the number of trees in a certain orchard by $\frac{1}{4}$ of the number of trees in the orchard the preceding year. If all of the trees thrived and there were 6,250 trees in the orchard at the end of the 4-year period, how many trees were in the orchard at the beginning of the 4-year period?

(A) 1,250
(B) 1,563
(C) 2,250
(D) 2,560
(E) 2,752

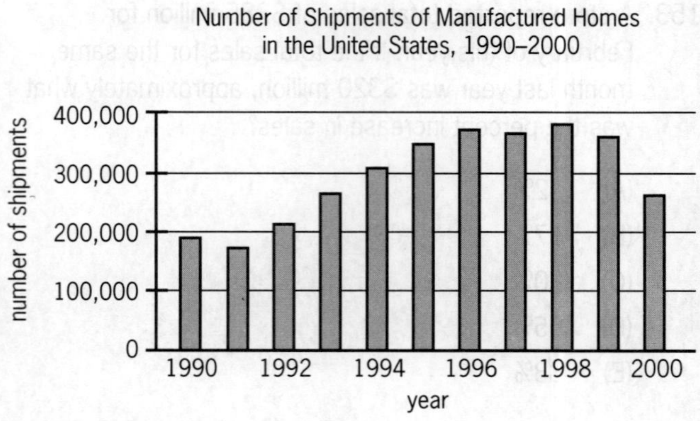

164. According to the chart shown, which of the following is closest to the median annual number of shipments of manufactured homes in the United States for the years from 1990 to 2000, inclusive?

(A) 250,000
(B) 280,000
(C) 310,000
(D) 325,000
(E) 340,000

165. For the positive integers a, b, and k, $a^k \| b$ means that a^k is a divisor of b, but a^{k+1} is not a divisor of b. If k is a positive integer and $2^k \| 72$, then k is equal to

(A) 2
(B) 3
(C) 4
(D) 8
(E) 18

166. A certain characteristic in a large population has a distribution that is symmetric about the mean m. If 68 percent of the distribution lies within one standard deviation d of the mean, what percent of the distribution is less than $m + d$?

(A) 16%
(B) 32%
(C) 48%
(D) 84%
(E) 92%

167. Four extra-large sandwiches of exactly the same size were ordered for m students, where $m > 4$. Three of the sandwiches were evenly divided among the students. Since 4 students did not want any of the fourth sandwich, it was evenly divided among the remaining students. If Carol ate one piece from each of the four sandwiches, the amount of sandwich that she ate would be what fraction of a whole extra-large sandwich?

(A) $\frac{m+4}{m(m-4)}$

(B) $\frac{2m-4}{m(m-4)}$

(C) $\frac{4m-4}{m(m-4)}$

(D) $\frac{4m-8}{m(m-4)}$

(E) $\frac{4m-12}{m(m-4)}$

168. Which of the following equations has $1 + \sqrt{2}$ as one of its roots?

(A) $x^2 + 2x - 1 = 0$

(B) $x^2 - 2x + 1 = 0$

(C) $x^2 + 2x + 1 = 0$

(D) $x^2 - 2x - 1 = 0$

(E) $x^2 - x - 1 = 0$

169. In Country C, the unemployment rate among construction workers dropped from 16 percent on September 1, 1992, to 9 percent on September 1, 1996. If the number of construction workers was 20 percent greater on September 1, 1996, than on September 1, 1992, what was the approximate percent change in the number of unemployed construction workers over this period?

(A) 50% decrease

(B) 30% decrease

(C) 15% decrease

(D) 30% increase

(E) 55% increase

170. In a box of 12 pens, a total of 3 are defective. If a customer buys 2 pens selected at random from the box, what is the probability that neither pen will be defective?

(A) $\frac{1}{6}$

(B) $\frac{2}{9}$

(C) $\frac{6}{11}$

(D) $\frac{9}{16}$

(E) $\frac{3}{4}$

171. At a certain fruit stand, the price of each apple is 40 cents and the price of each orange is 60 cents. Mary selects a total of 10 apples and oranges from the fruit stand, and the average (arithmetic mean) price of the 10 pieces of fruit is 56 cents. How many oranges must Mary put back so that the average price of the pieces of fruit that she keeps is 52 cents?

(A) 1

(B) 2

(C) 3

(D) 4

(E) 5

172. A pharmaceutical company received \$3 million in royalties on the first \$20 million in sales of the generic equivalent of one of its products and then \$9 million in royalties on the next \$108 million in sales. By approximately what percent did the ratio of royalties to sales decrease from the first \$20 million in sales to the next \$108 million in sales?

(A) 8%

(B) 15%

(C) 45%

(D) 52%

(E) 56%

Times at Which the Door
Opened from 8:00 to 10:00

8:00	8:06	8:30	9:05
8:03	8:10	8:31	9:11
8:04	8:18	8:54	9:29
8:04	8:19	8:57	9:31

173. The light in a restroom operates with a 15-minute timer that is reset every time the door opens as a person goes in or out of the room. Thus, after someone enters or exits the room, the light remains on for only 15 minutes unless the door opens again and resets the timer for another 15 minutes. If the times listed above are the times at which the door opened from 8:00 to 10:00, approximately how many minutes during this two-hour period was the light off?

(A) 10
(B) 25
(C) 35
(D) 40
(E) 70

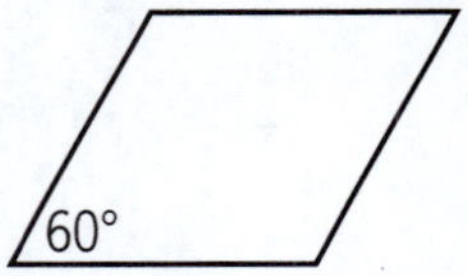

174. The parallelogram shown has four sides of equal length. What is the ratio of the length of the shorter diagonal to the length of the longer diagonal?

(A) $\frac{1}{2}$
(B) $\frac{1}{\sqrt{2}}$
(C) $\frac{1}{2\sqrt{2}}$
(D) $\frac{1}{\sqrt{3}}$
(E) $\frac{1}{2\sqrt{3}}$

175. If p is the product of the integers from 1 to 30, inclusive, what is the greatest integer k for which 3^k is a factor of p?

(A) 10
(B) 12
(C) 14
(D) 16
(E) 18

176. If $n = 3^8 - 2^8$, which of the following is NOT a factor of n?

(A) 97
(B) 65
(C) 35
(D) 13
(E) 5

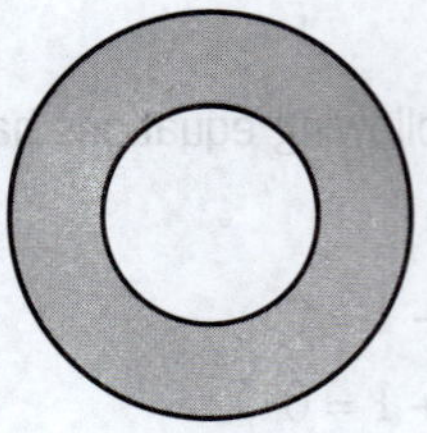

177. In the figure shown, if the area of the shaded region is 3 times the area of the smaller circular region, then the circumference of the larger circle is how many times the circumference of the smaller circle?

(A) 4
(B) 3
(C) 2
(D) $\sqrt{3}$
(E) $\sqrt{2}$

178. Club X has more than 10 but fewer than 40 members. Sometimes the members sit at tables with 3 members at one table and 4 members at each of the other tables, and sometimes they sit at tables with 3 members at one table and 5 members at each of the other tables. If they sit at tables with 6 members at each table except one and fewer than 6 members at that one table, how many members will be at the table that has fewer than 6 members?

(A) 1
(B) 2
(C) 3
(D) 4
(E) 5

179. In order to complete a reading assignment on time, Terry planned to read 90 pages per day. However, she read only 75 pages per day at first, leaving 690 pages to be read during the last 6 days before the assignment was to be completed. How many days in all did Terry have to complete the assignment on time?

(A) 15
(B) 16
(C) 25
(D) 40
(E) 46

180. If $s > 0$ and $\sqrt{\frac{r}{s}} = s$, what is r in terms of s?

(A) $\frac{1}{s}$
(B) $\sqrt{s}$
(C) $s\sqrt{s}$
(D) s^3
(E) $s^2 - s$

181. If $3 < x < 100$, for how many values of x is $\frac{x}{3}$ the square of a prime number?

(A) Two
(B) Three
(C) Four
(D) Five
(E) Nine

182. A researcher plans to identify each participant in a certain medical experiment with a code consisting of either a single letter or a pair of distinct letters written in alphabetical order. What is the least number of letters that can be used if there are 12 participants, and each participant is to receive a different code?

(A) 4
(B) 5
(C) 6
(D) 7
(E) 8

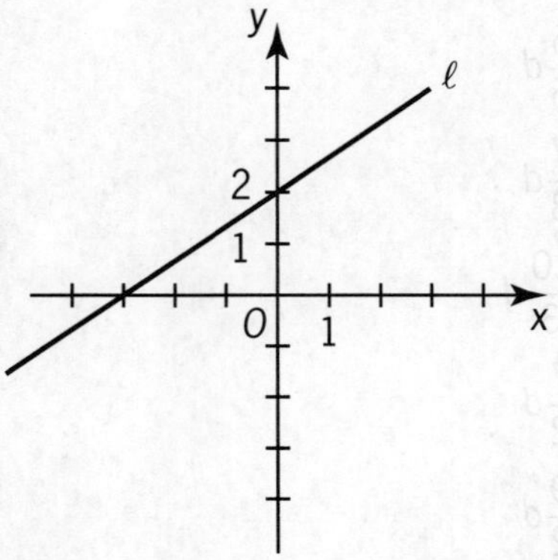

183. The graph of which of the following equations is a straight line that is parallel to line ℓ in the figure above?

(A) $3y - 2x = 0$
(B) $3y + 2x = 0$
(C) $3y + 2x = 6$
(D) $2y - 3x = 6$
(E) $2y + 3x = -6$

184. An object thrown directly upward is at a height of h feet after t seconds, where $h = -16(t - 3)^2 + 150$. At what height, in feet, is the object 2 seconds after it reaches its maximum height?

(A) 6
(B) 86
(C) 134
(D) 150
(E) 166

185. Which of the following is equivalent to the pair of inequalities $x + 6 > 10$ and $x - 3 \leq 5$?

(A) $2 \leq x < 16$
(B) $2 \leq x < 4$
(C) $2 < x \leq 8$
(D) $4 < x \leq 8$
(E) $4 \leq x < 16$

186. David has d books, which is 3 times as many as Jeff and $\frac{1}{2}$ as many as Paula. How many books do the three of them have altogether, in terms of d ?

(A) $\frac{5}{6}d$
(B) $\frac{7}{3}d$
(C) $\frac{10}{3}d$
(D) $\frac{7}{2}d$
(E) $\frac{9}{2}d$

187. There are 8 teams in a certain league and each team plays each of the other teams exactly once. If each game is played by 2 teams, what is the total number of games played?

(A) 15
(B) 16
(C) 28
(D) 56
(E) 64

188. At his regular hourly rate, Don had estimated the labor cost of a repair job as $336 and he was paid that amount. However, the job took 4 hours longer than he had estimated and, consequently, he earned $2 per hour less than his regular hourly rate. What was the time Don had estimated for the job, in hours?

(A) 28
(B) 24
(C) 16
(D) 14
(E) 12

189. If $\frac{p}{q} < 1$, and p and q are positive integers, which of the following must be greater than 1 ?

(A) $\sqrt{\frac{p}{q}}$
(B) $\frac{p}{q^2}$
(C) $\frac{p}{2q}$
(D) $\frac{q}{p^2}$
(E) $\frac{q}{p}$

190. To mail a package, the rate is x cents for the first pound and y cents for each additional pound, where $x > y$. Two packages weighing 3 pounds and 5 pounds, respectively, can be mailed separately or combined as one package. Which method is cheaper, and how much money is saved?

(A) Combined, with a savings of $x - y$ cents
(B) Combined, with a savings of $y - x$ cents
(C) Combined, with a savings of x cents
(D) Separately, with a savings of $x - y$ cents
(E) Separately, with a savings of y cents

191. If money is invested at r percent interest, compounded annually, the amount of the investment will double in approximately $\frac{70}{r}$ years. If Pat's parents invested $5,000 in a long-term bond that pays 8 percent interest, compounded annually, what will be the approximate total amount of the investment 18 years later, when Pat is ready for college?

(A) $20,000
(B) $15,000
(C) $12,000
(D) $10,000
(E) $9,000

192. On a recent trip, Cindy drove her car 290 miles, rounded to the nearest 10 miles, and used 12 gallons of gasoline, rounded to the nearest gallon. The actual number of miles per gallon that Cindy's car got on this trip must have been between

(A) $\frac{290}{12.5}$ and $\frac{290}{11.5}$

(B) $\frac{295}{12}$ and $\frac{285}{11.5}$

(C) $\frac{285}{12}$ and $\frac{295}{12}$

(D) $\frac{285}{12.5}$ and $\frac{295}{11.5}$

(E) $\frac{295}{12.5}$ and $\frac{285}{11.5}$

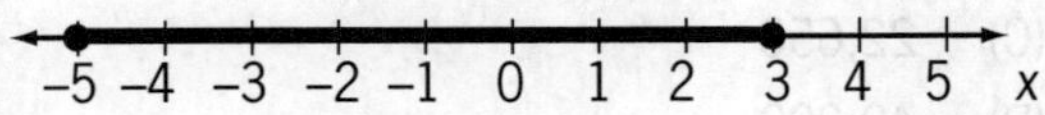

193. Which of the following inequalities is an algebraic expression for the shaded part of the number line above?

(A) $|x| \le 3$

(B) $|x| \le 5$

(C) $|x-2| \le 3$

(D) $|x-1| \le 4$

(E) $|x+1| \le 4$

194. In a small snack shop, the average (arithmetic mean) revenue was \$400 per day over a 10-day period. During this period, if the average daily revenue was \$360 for the first 6 days, what was the average daily revenue for the last 4 days?

(A) \$420

(B) \$440

(C) \$450

(D) \$460

(E) \$480

195. If *y* is the smallest positive integer such that 3,150 multiplied by *y* is the square of an integer, then *y* must be

(A) 2

(B) 5

(C) 6

(D) 7

(E) 14

196. If [x] is the greatest integer less than or equal to x, what is the value of [−1.6] + [3.4] + [2.7] ?

(A) 3

(B) 4

(C) 5

(D) 6

(E) 7

197. In the first week of the year, Nancy saved \$1. In each of the next 51 weeks, she saved \$1 more than she had saved in the previous week. What was the total amount that Nancy saved during the 52 weeks?

(A) \$1,326

(B) \$1,352

(C) \$1,378

(D) \$2,652

(E) \$2,756

198. In a certain sequence, the term x_n is given by the formula $x_n = 2x_{n-1} - \frac{1}{2}(x_{n-2})$ for all $n \ge 2$. If $x_0 = 3$ and $x_1 = 2$, what is the value of x_3 ?

(A) 2.5

(B) 3.125

(C) 4

(D) 5

(E) 6.75

199. During a trip, Francine traveled x percent of the total distance at an average speed of 40 miles per hour and the rest of the distance at an average speed of 60 miles per hour. In terms of x, what was Francine's average speed for the entire trip?

(A) $\frac{180-x}{2}$

(B) $\frac{x+60}{4}$

(C) $\frac{300-x}{5}$

(D) $\frac{600}{115-x}$

(E) $\frac{12{,}000}{x+200}$

200. If $n = (33)^{43} + (43)^{33}$, what is the units digit of n?

(A) 0

(B) 2

(C) 4

(D) 6

(E) 8

201. Team A and Team B are competing against each other in a game of tug-of-war. Team A, consisting of 3 males and 3 females, decides to line up male, female, male, female, male, female. The lineup that Team A chooses will be one of how many different possible lineups?

(A) 9

(B) 12

(C) 15

(D) 36

(E) 720

202. A border of uniform width is placed around a rectangular photograph that measures 8 inches by 10 inches. If the area of the border is 144 square inches, what is the width of the border, in inches?

(A) 3

(B) 4

(C) 6

(D) 8

(E) 9

203. If $d = \frac{1}{2^3 \times 5^7}$ is expressed as a terminating decimal, how many nonzero digits will d have?

(A) One

(B) Two

(C) Three

(D) Seven

(E) Ten

204. For any positive integer n, the sum of the first n positive integers equals $\frac{n(n+1)}{2}$. What is the sum of all the even integers between 99 and 301?

(A) 10,100

(B) 20,200

(C) 22,650

(D) 40,200

(E) 45,150

205. How many prime numbers between 1 and 100 are factors of 7,150?

(A) One

(B) Two

(C) Three

(D) Four

(E) Five

206. A sequence of numbers $a_1, a_2, a_3, \ldots$ is defined as follows: $a_1 = 3$, $a_2 = 5$, and every term in the sequence after a_2 is the product of all terms in the sequence preceding it, e.g., $a_3 = (a_1)(a_2)$ and $a_4 = (a_1)(a_2)(a_3)$. If $a_n = t$ and $n > 2$, what is the value of a_{n+2} in terms of t?

(A) $4t$

(B) t^2

(C) t^3

(D) t^4

(E) t^8

207. Last year the price per share of Stock X increased by k percent and the earnings per share of Stock X increased by m percent, where k is greater than m. By what percent did the ratio of price per share to earnings per share increase, in terms of k and m?

(A) $\frac{k}{m}\%$

(B) $(k - m)\%$

(C) $\frac{100(k-m)}{100+k}\%$

(D) $\frac{100(k-m)}{100+m}\%$

(E) $\frac{100(k-m)}{100+k+m}\%$

208. Of the 300 subjects who participated in an experiment using virtual-reality therapy to reduce their fear of heights, 40 percent experienced sweaty palms, 30 percent experienced vomiting, and 75 percent experienced dizziness. If all of the subjects experienced at least one of these effects and 35 percent of the subjects experienced exactly two of these effects, how many of the subjects experienced only one of these effects?

(A) 105
(B) 125
(C) 130
(D) 180
(E) 195

209. If $m^{-1} = -\frac{1}{3}$, then m^{-2} is equal to

(A) -9
(B) -3
(C) $-\frac{1}{9}$
(D) $\frac{1}{9}$
(E) 9

210. A photography dealer ordered 60 Model X cameras to be sold for \$250 each, which represents a 20 percent markup over the dealer's initial cost for each camera. Of the cameras ordered, 6 were never sold and were returned to the manufacturer for a refund of 50 percent of the dealer's initial cost. What was the dealer's approximate profit or loss as a percent of the dealer's initial cost for the 60 cameras?

(A) 7% loss
(B) 13% loss
(C) 7% profit
(D) 13% profit
(E) 15% profit

211. Seven pieces of rope have an average (arithmetic mean) length of 68 centimeters and a median length of 84 centimeters. If the length of the longest piece of rope is 14 centimeters more than 4 times the length of the shortest piece of rope, what is the maximum possible length, in centimeters, of the longest piece of rope?

(A) 82
(B) 118
(C) 120
(D) 134
(E) 152

212. What is the difference between the sixth and the fifth terms of the sequence 2, 4, 7, ... whose nth term is $n+2^{n-1}$?

(A) 2
(B) 3
(C) 6
(D) 16
(E) 17

213. From the consecutive integers −10 to 10, inclusive, 20 integers are randomly chosen with repetitions allowed. What is the least possible value of the product of the 20 integers?

(A) $(-10)^{20}$
(B) $(-10)^{10}$
(C) 0
(D) $-(10)^{19}$
(E) $-(10)^{20}$

214. The letters D, G, I, I, and T can be used to form 5-letter strings such as DIGIT or DGIIT. Using these letters, how many 5-letter strings can be formed in which the two occurrences of the letter I are separated by at least one other letter?

(A) 12

(B) 18

(C) 24

(D) 36

(E) 48

215. Last Sunday a certain store sold copies of Newspaper A for \$1.00 each and copies of Newspaper B for \$1.25 each, and the store sold no other newspapers that day. If *r* percent of the store's revenue from newspaper sales was from Newspaper A and if *p* percent of the newspapers that the store sold were copies of Newspaper A, which of the following expresses *r* in terms of *p* ?

(A) $\frac{100p}{125-p}$

(B) $\frac{150p}{250-p}$

(C) $\frac{300p}{375-p}$

(D) $\frac{400p}{500-p}$

(E) $\frac{500p}{625-p}$

216. $\frac{0.99999999}{1.0001}-\frac{0.99999991}{1.0003}=$

(A) 10^{-8}

(B) $3(10^{-8})$

(C) $3(10^{-4})$

(D) $2(10^{-4})$

(E) 10^{-4}

217. For the past *n* days, the average (arithmetic mean) daily production at a company was 50 units. If today's production of 90 units raises the average to 55 units per day, what is the value of *n* ?

(A) 30

(B) 18

(C) 10

(D) 9

(E) 7

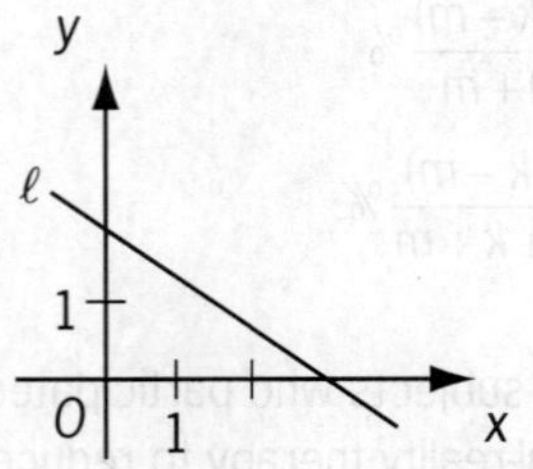

218. In the coordinate system above, which of the following is the equation of line ℓ ?

(A) $2x-3y=6$

(B) $2x+3y=6$

(C) $3x+2y=6$

(D) $2x-3y=-6$

(E) $3x-2y=-6$

219. If a two-digit positive integer has its digits reversed, the resulting integer differs from the original by 27. By how much do the two digits differ?

(A) 3

(B) 4

(C) 5

(D) 6

(E) 7

220. In an electric circuit, two resistors with resistances x and y are connected in parallel. In this case, if r is the combined resistance of these two resistors, then the reciprocal of r is equal to the sum of the reciprocals of x and y. What is r in terms of x and y?

(A) xy

(B) $x+y$

(C) $\frac{1}{x+y}$

(D) $\frac{xy}{x+y}$

(E) $\frac{x+y}{xy}$

221. Xavier, Yvonne, and Zelda each try independently to solve a problem. If their individual probabilities for success are $\frac{1}{4}$, $\frac{1}{2}$, and $\frac{5}{8}$, respectively, what is the probability that Xavier and Yvonne, but not Zelda, will solve the problem?

(A) $\frac{11}{8}$

(B) $\frac{7}{8}$

(C) $\frac{9}{64}$

(D) $\frac{5}{64}$

(E) $\frac{3}{64}$

222. If $\frac{1}{x}-\frac{1}{x+1}=\frac{1}{x+4}$, then x could be

(A) 0

(B) −1

(C) −2

(D) −3

(E) −4

223. $\left(\frac{1}{2}\right)^{-3}\left(\frac{1}{4}\right)^{-2}\left(\frac{1}{16}\right)^{-1}=$

(A) $\left(\frac{1}{2}\right)^{-48}$

(B) $\left(\frac{1}{2}\right)^{-11}$

(C) $\left(\frac{1}{2}\right)^{-6}$

(D) $\left(\frac{1}{8}\right)^{-11}$

(E) $\left(\frac{1}{8}\right)^{-6}$

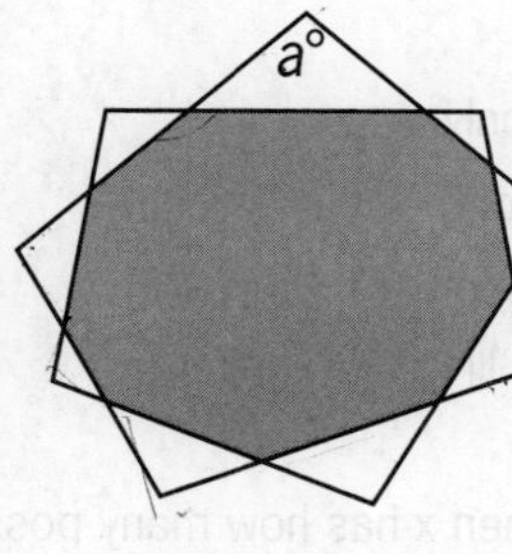

224. The figure shown above consists of a shaded 9-sided polygon and 9 unshaded isosceles triangles. For each isosceles triangle, the longest side is a side of the shaded polygon and the two sides of equal length are extensions of the two adjacent sides of the shaded polygon. What is the value of a?

(A) 100

(B) 105

(C) 110

(D) 115

(E) 120

225. List T consists of 30 positive decimals, none of which is an integer, and the sum of the 30 decimals is S. The estimated sum of the 30 decimals, E, is defined as follows. Each decimal in T whose tenths digit is even is rounded up to the nearest integer, and each decimal in T whose tenths digit is odd is rounded down to the nearest integer; E is the sum of the resulting integers. If $\frac{1}{3}$ of the decimals in T have a tenths digit that is even, which of the following is a possible value of $E - S$?

I. −16
II. 6
III. 10

(A) I only
(B) I and II only
(C) I and III only
(D) II and III only
(E) I, II, and III

226. If $5 - \frac{6}{x} = x$, then x has how many possible values?

(A) None
(B) One
(C) Two
(D) A finite number greater than two
(E) An infinite number

227. Seed mixture X is 40 percent ryegrass and 60 percent bluegrass by weight; seed mixture Y is 25 percent ryegrass and 75 percent fescue. If a mixture of X and Y contains 30 percent ryegrass, what percent of the weight of the mixture is X?

(A) 10%
(B) $33\frac{1}{3}\%$
(C) 40%
(D) 50%
(E) $66\frac{2}{3}\%$

228. How many of the integers that satisfy the inequality $\frac{(x+2)(x+3)}{x-2} \geq 0$ are less than 5?

(A) 1
(B) 2
(C) 3
(D) 4
(E) 5

229. Of the 150 houses in a certain development, 60 percent have air-conditioning, 50 percent have a sunporch, and 30 percent have a swimming pool. If 5 of the houses have all three of these amenities and 5 have none of them, how many of the houses have exactly two of these amenities?

(A) 10
(B) 45
(C) 50
(D) 55
(E) 65

230. The value of $\frac{2^{-14} + 2^{-15} + 2^{-16} + 2^{-17}}{5}$ is how many times the value of 2^{-17}?

(A) $\frac{3}{2}$
(B) $\frac{5}{2}$
(C) 3
(D) 4
(E) 5

5.4 Answer Key

1. E	31. C	61. A	91. C
2. D	32. D	62. C	92. E
3. E	33. C	63. B	93. B
4. A	34. A	64. C	94. E
5. B	35. B	65. B	95. E
6. E	36. E	66. A	96. E
7. C	37. E	67. B	97. D
8. D	38. D	68. B	98. B
9. C	39. C	69. B	99. B
10. E	40. E	70. D	100. B
11. A	41. E	71. D	101. B
12. C	42. D	72. C	102. B
13. B	43. D	73. E	103. E
14. B	44. B	74. E	104. C
15. D	45. D	75. D	105. B
16. E	46. D	76. B	106. A
17. A	47. C	77. B	107. E
18. B	48. E	78. C	108. D
19. D	49. B	79. B	109. A
20. B	50. E	80. D	110. E
21. C	51. D	81. A	111. D
22. D	52. B	82. D	112. B
23. E	53. A	83. D	113. E
24. C	54. E	84. D	114. E
25. C	55. D	85. E	115. D
26. C	56. D	86. D	116. E
27. E	57. D	87. B	117. A
28. D	58. B	88. D	118. E
29. B	59. A	89. D	119. D
30. C	60. E	90. D	120. D

121.	B
122.	D
123.	D
124.	E
125.	D
126.	C
127.	D
128.	B
129.	A
130.	D
131.	A
132.	E
133.	D
134.	B
135.	A
136.	A
137.	A
138.	E
139.	D
140.	D
141.	D
142.	C
143.	C
144.	A
145.	D
146.	E
147.	A
148.	B
149.	E
150.	E
151.	B
152.	B
153.	C
154.	B
155.	B
156.	C
157.	A
158.	B
159.	B
160.	E
161.	B
162.	C
163.	D
164.	C
165.	B
166.	D
167.	E
168.	D
169.	B
170.	C
171.	E
172.	C
173.	B
174.	D
175.	C
176.	C
177.	C
178.	E
179.	B
180.	D
181.	B
182.	B
183.	A
184.	B
185.	D
186.	C
187.	C
188.	B
189.	E
190.	A
191.	A
192.	D
193.	E
194.	D
195.	E
196.	A
197.	C
198.	C
199.	E
200.	A
201.	D
202.	A
203.	B
204.	B
205.	D
206.	D
207.	D
208.	D
209.	D
210.	D
211.	D
212.	E
213.	E
214.	D
215.	D
216.	D
217.	E
218.	B
219.	A
220.	D
221.	E
222.	C
223.	B
224.	A
225.	B
226.	C
227.	B
228.	D
229.	D
230.	C

5.5 Answer Explanations

The following discussion is intended to familiarize you with the most efficient and effective approaches to the kinds of problems common to problem solving questions. The particular questions in this chapter are generally representative of the kinds of problem solving questions you will encounter on the GMAT exam. Remember that it is the problem solving strategy that is important, not the specific details of a particular question.

1. The price of a coat in a certain store is $500. If the price of the coat is to be reduced by $150, by what percent is the price to be reduced?

(A) 10%
(B) 15%
(C) 20%
(D) 25%
(E) 30%

Arithmetic Percents

A reduction of $150 from $500 represents a percent decrease of $\left(\frac{150}{500}\times 100\right)\% = 30\%$. Therefore, the price of the coat was reduced by 30%.

The correct answer is E.

2. On a vacation, Rose exchanged $500.00 for euros at an exchange rate of 0.80 euro per dollar and spent $\frac{3}{4}$ of the euros she received. If she exchanged the remaining euros for dollars at an exchange rate of $1.20 per euro, what was the dollar amount she received?

(A) $60.00
(B) $80.00
(C) $100.00
(D) $120.00
(E) $140.00

Arithmetic Operations with rational numbers

At the exchange rate of 0.80 euro per dollar, Rose exchanged $500.00 for (0.80)(500) = 400 euros. She spent $\frac{3}{4}(400) = 300$ euros, had 400 − 300 = 100 euros left, and exchanged them for dollars at the exchange rate of $1.20 per euro. Therefore, the dollar amount she received was (1.20)(100) = $120.00.

The correct answer is D.

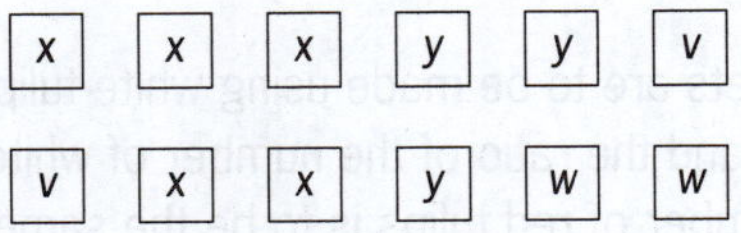

3. Each of the 12 squares shown is labeled x, y, v, or w. What is the ratio of the number of these squares labeled x or y to the number of these squares labeled v or w?

(A) 1:2
(B) 2:3
(C) 4:3
(D) 3:2
(E) 2:1

Arithmetic Ratio and proportion

By a direct count, there are 8 squares labeled x or y (5 labeled x, 3 labeled y) and there are 4 squares labeled v or w (2 labeled v, 2 labeled w). Therefore, the ratio of the number of squares labeled x or y to the number of squares labeled v or w is 8:4, which reduces to 2:1.

The correct answer is E.

4. $\frac{1}{3}+\frac{1}{2}-\frac{5}{6}+\frac{1}{5}+\frac{1}{4}-\frac{9}{20}=$

(A) 0

(B) $\frac{2}{15}$

(C) $\frac{2}{5}$

(D) $\frac{9}{20}$

(E) $\frac{5}{6}$

Arithmetic Operations with rational numbers

A number that is divisible by each of the denominators is 60. Therefore, 60 can be used as a common denominator, which gives the following:

$$\frac{20}{60}+\frac{30}{60}-\frac{50}{60}+\frac{12}{60}+\frac{15}{60}-\frac{27}{60}=$$
$$\frac{20+30-50+12+15-27}{60}=\frac{0}{60}=0.$$

The correct answer is A.

5. Bouquets are to be made using white tulips and red tulips, and the ratio of the number of white tulips to the number of red tulips is to be the same in each bouquet. If there are 15 white tulips and 85 red tulips available for the bouquets, what is the greatest number of bouquets that can be made using all the tulips available?

(A) 3
(B) 5
(C) 8
(D) 10
(E) 13

Arithmetic Applied problems; Properties of numbers

Because all the tulips are to be used and the same number of white tulips will be in each bouquet, the number of white tulips in each bouquet times the number of bouquets must equal the total number of white tulips, or 15. Thus, the number of bouquets must be a factor of 15, and so the number must be 1, 3, 5, or 15. Also, the number of red tulips in each bouquet times the number of bouquets must equal the total number of red tulips, or 85. Thus, the number of bouquets must be a factor of 85, and so the number must be 1, 5, 17, or 85. Since the number of bouquets must be 1, 3, 5, or 15, and the number of bouquets must be 1, 5, 17, or 85, it follows that the number of bouquets must be 1 or 5, and thus the greatest number of bouquets that can be made is 5. Note that each of the 5 bouquets will have 3 white tulips, because (5)(3) = 15, and each of the 5 bouquets will have 17 red tulips, because (5)(17) = 85.

The correct answer is B.

6. 125% of 5 =

(A) 5.125
(B) 5.25
(C) 6
(D) 6.125
(E) 6.25

Arithmetic Percents

125% of 5 represents $\frac{125}{100}\times 5$, or $1.25\times 5=6.25$.

The correct answer is E.

7. Today Rebecca, who is 34 years old, and her daughter, who is 8 years old, celebrate their birthdays. How many years will pass before Rebecca's age is twice her daughter's age?

(A) 10
(B) 14
(C) 18
(D) 22
(E) 26

Algebra Applied problems

Let x be the desired number of years. In x years, Rebecca will be $34 + x$ years old and her daughter will be $8 + x$ years old. From the given information, it follows that $34 + x = 2(8 + x)$. The last equation is equivalent to $34 + x = 16 + 2x$, which has solution $x = 18$.

The correct answer is C.

8. When traveling at a constant speed of 32 miles per hour, a certain motorboat consumes 24 gallons of fuel per hour. What is the fuel consumption of this boat at this speed measured in miles traveled per gallon of fuel?

(A) $\frac{2}{3}$

(B) $\frac{3}{4}$

(C) $\frac{4}{5}$

(D) $\frac{4}{3}$

(E) $\frac{3}{2}$

Arithmetic Operations with rational numbers

If the motorboat consumes 24 gallons of fuel in 1 hour, then it consumes 1 gallon of fuel in $\frac{1}{24}$ hour. If the motorboat travels 32 miles in 1 hour, then it travels $\frac{32}{24}=\frac{4}{3}$ miles in $\frac{1}{24}$ hour, which is the length of time it takes to consume 1 gallon of fuel. Thus, the motorboat travels $\frac{4}{3}$ miles per gallon of fuel.

The correct answer is D.

9. A case contains *c* cartons. Each carton contains *b* boxes, and each box contains 100 paper clips. How many paper clips are contained in 2 cases?

(A) $100bc$

(B) $\frac{100b}{c}$

(C) $200bc$

(D) $\frac{200b}{c}$

(E) $\frac{200}{bc}$

Algebra Simplifying algebraic expressions

Each case has bc boxes, each of which has 100 paper clips. The total number of paper clips in 2 cases is thus $2(bc)(100) = 200bc$.

The correct answer is C.

10. A technician makes a round-trip to and from a certain service center by the same route. If the technician completes the drive to the center and then completes 10 percent of the drive from the center, what percent of the round-trip has the technician completed?

(A) 5%

(B) 10%

(C) 25%

(D) 40%

(E) 55%

Arithmetic Percents

In completing the drive to the service center, the technician has completed 50% of the round-trip. The drive from the center is the other 50% of the round-trip. In completing 10% of the drive from the center, the technician has completed an additional 10% of 50%, or 5% of the round-trip. Thus, the technician has completed 50% + 5% = 55% of the round-trip.

The correct answer is E.

11. Raffle tickets numbered consecutively from 101 through 350 are placed in a box. What is the probability that a ticket selected at random will have a number with a hundreds digit of 2 ?

(A) $\frac{2}{5}$

(B) $\frac{2}{7}$

(C) $\frac{33}{88}$

(D) $\frac{99}{250}$

(E) $\frac{100}{249}$

Arithmetic Probability

There are 250 integers from 101 to 350 inclusive, 100 of which (that is, 200 through 299) have a hundreds digit of 2. Therefore, the probability that a ticket selected from the box at random will have a hundreds digit of 2 can be expressed as $\frac{100}{250}=\frac{2}{5}$.

The correct answer is A.

12. When Leo imported a certain item, he paid a 7 percent import tax on the portion of the total value of the item in excess of $1,000. If the amount of the import tax that Leo paid was $87.50, what was the total value of the item?

(A) $1,600
(B) $1,850
(C) $2,250
(D) $2,400
(E) $2,750

Algebra **First-degree equations**

Letting x represent the total value of the item, convert the words to symbols and solve the equation.

$$\begin{aligned} 7\% \text{ of value in excess of } \$1{,}000 &= 87.50 \\ 0.07(x-1{,}000) &= 87.50 \\ x-1{,}000 &= 1{,}250 \\ x &= 2{,}250 \end{aligned}$$

The correct answer is C.

13. A collection of 16 coins, each with a face value of either 10 cents or 25 cents, has a total face value of $2.35. How many of the coins have a face value of 25 cents?

(A) 3
(B) 5
(C) 7
(D) 9
(E) 11

Algebra **First-degree equations**

Let x represent the number of coins each with a face value of 25 cents. Then, since there are 16 coins in all, $16 - x$ represents the number of coins each with a face value of 10 cents. The total face value of the coins is $2.35 or 235 cents so,

$$\begin{aligned} 25x + 10(16 - x) &= 235 && \text{given} \\ 25x + 160 - 10x &= 235 && \text{distributive property} \\ 15x + 160 &= 235 && \text{combine like terms} \\ 15x &= 75 && \text{subtract 160 from both sides} \\ x &= 5 && \text{divide both sides by 15} \end{aligned}$$

Therefore, 5 of the coins have a face value of 25 cents.

The correct answer is B.

14. The numbers of cars sold at a certain dealership on six of the last seven business days were 4, 7, 2, 8, 3, and 6, respectively. If the number of cars sold on the seventh business day was either 2, 4, or 5, for which of the three values does the average (arithmetic mean) number of cars sold per business day for the seven business days equal the median number of cars sold per day for the seven days?

I. 2
II. 4
III. 5

(A) II only
(B) III only
(C) I and II only
(D) II and III only
(E) I, II, and III

Arithmetic **Statistics**

Listed in numerical order, the given numbers are 2, 3, 4, 6, 7, and 8. If the seventh number were 2 or 4, then the numbers in numerical order would be 2, 2, 3, 4, 6, 7, and 8 or 2, 3, 4, 4, 6, 7, and 8. In either case the median would be 4 and the average would be $\frac{2+2+3+4+6+7+8}{7} = \frac{32}{7}$ or $\frac{2+3+4+4+6+7+8}{7} = \frac{34}{7}$, neither of which equals 4. So, for neither of the values in I or II does the average equal the median. If the seventh number were 5, then the numbers in numerical order would be 2, 3, 4, 5, 6, 7, and 8. The median would be 5 and the average would be $\frac{2+3+4+5+6+7+8}{7} = \frac{35}{7} = 5$. Thus, for the value in III, the average equals the median.

The correct answer is B.

15. If it is assumed that 60 percent of those who receive a questionnaire by mail will respond and 300 responses are needed, what is the minimum number of questionnaires that should be mailed?

(A) 400
(B) 420
(C) 480
(D) 500
(E) 600

Arithmetic Percents

From the given information, 60% of the minimum number of questionnaires is equal to 300. This has the form "60% of what number equals 300," and the number can be determined by dividing 300 by 60%. Performing the calculation gives $300 \div \frac{60}{100} = 300 \times \frac{100}{60} = 500$.

The correct answer is D.

16. If $1 < x < y < z$, which of the following has the greatest value?

(A) $z(x + 1)$

(B) $z(y + 1)$

(C) $x(y + z)$

(D) $y(x + z)$

(E) $z(x + y)$

Algebra Inequalities

This problem can be solved by calculating each of the options for a fixed and appropriate choice of values for each of the variables. For example, if $x = 2, y = 3$, and $z = 4$, then $1 < x < y < z$ and the values of the options are as follows:

A $z(x + 1) = 4(2 + 1) = 12$

B $z(y + 1) = 4(3 + 1) = 16$

C $x(y + z) = 2(3 + 4) = 14$

D $y(x + z) = 3(2 + 4) = 18$

E $z(x + y) = 4(2 + 3) = 20$

This problem can also be solved by the use of algebraic ordering principles in a way that does not assume the same answer option is true for each choice of values of x, y, and z such that $1 < x < y < z$. First, note that neither the value of the expression in A nor the value of the expression in B can ever have the greatest value, since the value of the expression in E is greater than the value of the expression in A (because $y > 1$) and the value of the expression in E is greater than the value of the expression in B (because $x > 1$). Also, the value of the expression in D is greater than the value of the expression in C, since $y > x$ implies $yz > xz$, which implies $xy + yz > xy + xz$, which implies $y(x + z) > x(y + z)$, and so the value of the expression in C cannot be the greatest. Finally, the value of the expression in E is greater than the value of the expression in D, since $z > y$ implies $xz > xy$, which implies $xz + yz > xy + yz$, which implies $z(x + y) > y(x + z)$, and so the value of the expression in D cannot be the greatest. Since none of the values of the expressions in A, B, C, or D can be the greatest, it follows that the value of the expression in E is the greatest.

The correct answer is E.

17. A rectangular garden is to be twice as long as it is wide. If 360 yards of fencing, including the gate, will completely enclose the garden, what will be the length of the garden, in yards?

(A) 120

(B) 140

(C) 160

(D) 180

(E) 200

Geometry Quadrilaterals; Perimeter

Let the width of the rectangle be x. Then the length is $2x$. Since the perimeter of a rectangle is twice the sum of the length and width, it follows that

$360 = 2(x + 2x)$

$360 = 6x$

$120 = 2x$

So, the length is 120.

The correct answer is A.

18. A rectangular floor that measures 8 meters by 10 meters is to be covered with carpet squares that each measure 2 meters by 2 meters. If the carpet squares cost $12 apiece, what is the total cost for the number of carpet squares needed to cover the floor?

(A) $200

(B) $240

(C) $480

(D) $960

(E) $1,920

Geometry Area (Rectangles)

The area of the floor is (10 m)(8 m) = 80 m^2 and the area of each carpet square is (2 m)(2 m) = 4 m^2. Therefore, the number of carpet squares needed to cover the floor is $\frac{80}{4} = 20$, and these 20 carpet squares have a total cost of (20)($12) = $240.

The correct answer is B.

19. If $893 \times 78 = p$, which of the following is equal to 893×79 ?

(A) $p + 1$

(B) $p + 78$

(C) $p + 79$

(D) $p + 893$

(E) $p + 894$

Arithmetic Properties of numbers

$893 \times 79 = 893 \times (78 + 1)$	since $79 = 78 + 1$
$= (893 \times 78) + 893$	distributive property
$= p + 893$	since $p = 893 \times 78$

The correct answer is D.

20. Thabo owns exactly 140 books, and each book is either paperback fiction, paperback nonfiction, or hardcover nonfiction. If he owns 20 more paperback nonfiction books than hardcover nonfiction books, and twice as many paperback fiction books as paperback nonfiction books, how many hardcover nonfiction books does Thabo own?

(A) 10

(B) 20

(C) 30

(D) 40

(E) 50

Algebra Simultaneous first-degree equations

Let F represent the number of paperback fiction books that Thabo owns; N_p, the number of paperback nonfiction books; and N_h, the number of hardcover nonfiction books. It is given that $F + N_p + N_h = 140$, $N_p = N_h + 20$, and $F = 2N_p = 2(N_h + 20)$. It follows that

$F + N_p + N_h$	$= 140$	given
$2(N_h + 20) + (N_h + 20) + N_h$	$= 140$	by substitution
$4N_h + 60$	$= 140$	combine like terms
$4N_h$	$=$ 80	subtract 60 from both sides
N_h	$=$ 20	divide both sides by 4

The correct answer is B.

21. If the average (arithmetic mean) of the four numbers 3, 15, 32, and $(N + 1)$ is 18, then $N =$

(A) 19

(B) 20

(C) 21

(D) 22

(E) 29

Arithmetic Statistics

From the given information and the definition of average, it follows that $\frac{3+15+32+(N+1)}{4} = 18$, or $\frac{51+N}{4} = 18$. Multiplying both sides of the last equation by 4 gives $51 + N = 72$. Therefore, $N = 72 - 51 = 21$.

The correct answer is C.

22. Abdul, Barb, and Carlos all live on the same straight road, on which their school is also located. The school is halfway between Abdul's house and Barb's house. Barb's house is halfway between the school and Carlos's house. If the school is 4 miles from Carlos's house, how many miles is Abdul's house from Carlos's house?

(A) $1\frac{1}{3}$

(B) 2

(C) 4

(D) 6

(E) 8

Geometry Applied problems

In the diagram, A represents the location of Abdul's house, S represents the location of the school, B represents the location of Barb's house, and C represents the location of Carlos's house. Because the school is halfway between Abdul's house and Barb's house, S is the midpoint of $\overline{AB}$, and because Barb's house is halfway between the school and Carlos's house, B is the midpoint of $\overline{SC}$. Therefore, $AS = SB = BC$. Finally, since $SC = 4$, it follows that $AS = SB = BC = 2$ and hence $AC = 2 + 2 + 2 = 6$.

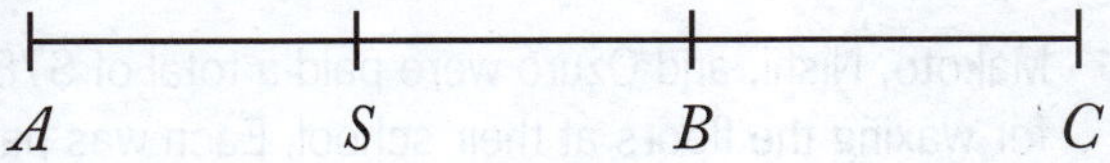

The correct answer is D.

23. During a certain time period, Car X traveled north along a straight road at a constant rate of 1 mile per minute and used fuel at a constant rate of 5 gallons every 2 hours. During this time period, if Car X used exactly 3.75 gallons of fuel, how many miles did Car X travel?

(A) 36
(B) 37.5
(C) 40
(D) 80
(E) 90

Arithmetic Applied problems

The car traveled at a rate of $1\frac{\text{mi}}{\text{min}} = \left(1\frac{\text{mi}}{\cancel{\text{min}}}\right)\left(60\frac{\cancel{\text{min}}}{\text{hr}}\right) = 60\frac{\text{mi}}{\text{hr}}$ using fuel at a rate of 5 gallons every 2 hours, or $\frac{5\text{ gal}}{2\text{ hr}}$. If the usage rate in miles per gallon was known, then that usage rate times 3.75 gallons would give the number of miles.

One approach to finding this usage rate is to consider whether multiplying or dividing the known rates $60\frac{\text{mi}}{\text{hr}}$ and $\frac{5\text{ gal}}{2\text{ hr}}$ will lead to unit cancellations that result in miles per gallon. The following calculation shows that dividing these two known rates leads to the appropriate unit cancellations:

$$60\frac{\text{mi}}{\text{hr}} \div \frac{5\text{ gal}}{2\text{ hr}} = 60\frac{\text{mi}}{\cancel{\text{hr}}} \times \frac{2\cancel{\text{ hr}}}{5\text{ gal}} = 24\frac{\text{mi}}{\text{gal}}.$$

Therefore, after using 3.75 gal of fuel, the car has traveled $24\frac{\text{mi}}{\text{gal}} \times 3.75\text{ gal} = 90$ miles.

The correct answer is E.

24. Cheryl purchased 5 identical hollow pine doors and 6 identical solid oak doors for the house she is building. The regular price of each solid oak door was twice the regular price of each hollow pine door. However, Cheryl was given a discount of 25% off the regular price of each solid oak door. If the regular price of each hollow pine door was \$40, what was the total price of all 11 doors?

(A) \$320
(B) \$540
(C) \$560
(D) \$620
(E) \$680

Algebra Applied problems; Percents

The price of each pine door is \$40, so the price of 5 pine doors is 5(\$40) = \$200. The price of each oak door is twice that of a pine door, and thus \$80, which becomes (0.75)(\$80) = \$60 when the 25% discount is applied. Therefore, the price of 6 oak doors at the 25% discount is 6(\$60) = \$360, and hence the total price of all 11 doors is \$200 + \$360 = \$560.

The correct answer is C.

25. If $\left|y - \frac{1}{2}\right| < \frac{11}{2}$, which of the following could be a value of y?

(A) -11
(B) $-\frac{11}{2}$
(C) $\frac{11}{2}$
(D) 11
(E) 22

Algebra Inequalities; Absolute value

Since $\left|y-\frac{1}{2}\right|<\frac{11}{2}$ is equivalent to $-\frac{11}{2}<y-\frac{1}{2}<\frac{11}{2}$, or $-\frac{10}{2}<y<\frac{12}{2}$, select the value that lies between $-\frac{10}{2}=-5$ and $\frac{12}{2}=6$. That value is $\frac{11}{2}$.

The correct answer is C.

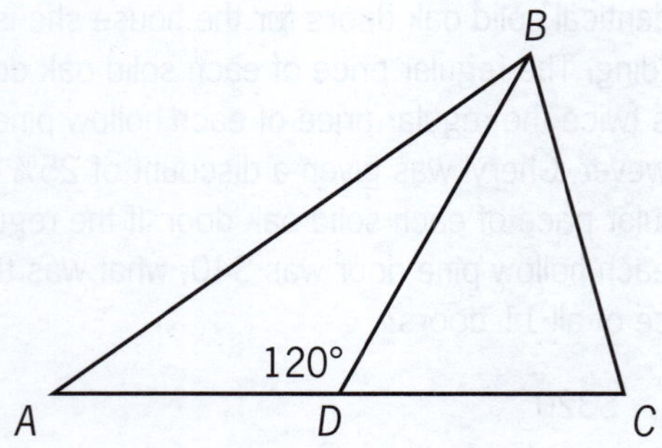

26. In the figure shown, $AC = 2$ and $BD = DC = 1$. What is the measure of angle ABD?

(A) 15°
(B) 20°
(C) 30°
(D) 40°
(E) 45°

Geometry Triangles

Since $AC = AD + DC$, and it is given that $AC = 2$ and $DC = 1$, it follows that $AD = 1$. Therefore, $AD = BD = 1$ and ΔABD is an isosceles triangle where the measure of $\angle ABD$ is equal to the measure of $\angle BAD$. Letting $x°$ be the common degree measure of these two angles, it follows that $x° + x° + 120° = 180°$, or $2x° = 60°$, or $x° = 30°$.

The correct answer is C.

27. If $k^2 = m^2$, which of the following must be true?

(A) $k = m$
(B) $k = -m$
(C) $k = |m|$
(D) $k = -|m|$
(E) $|k| = |m|$

Algebra Simplifying algebraic expressions

One method of solving this is to first take the nonnegative square root of both sides of the equation $k^2 = m^2$ and then make use of the fact that $\sqrt{u^2} = |u|$. Doing this gives $|k| = |m|$. Alternatively, if (k, m) is equal to either of the pairs (1,1) or (–1,1), then $k^2 = m^2$ is true. However, each of the answer choices except $|k| = |m|$ is false for at least one of these two pairs.

The correct answer is E.

28. Makoto, Nishi, and Ozuro were paid a total of \$780 for waxing the floors at their school. Each was paid in proportion to the number of hours he or she worked. If Makoto worked 15 hours, Nishi worked 20 hours, and Ozuro worked 30 hours, how much was Makoto paid?

(A) \$52
(B) \$117
(C) \$130
(D) \$180
(E) \$234

Arithmetic Ratio and proportion

Makoto, Nishi, and Ozuro worked a total of $15 + 20 + 30 = 65$ hours and were paid a total of \$780. Each was paid in proportion to the number of hours he or she worked. Therefore, Makoto was paid $\frac{15}{65}(\$780) = \$180$.

The correct answer is D.

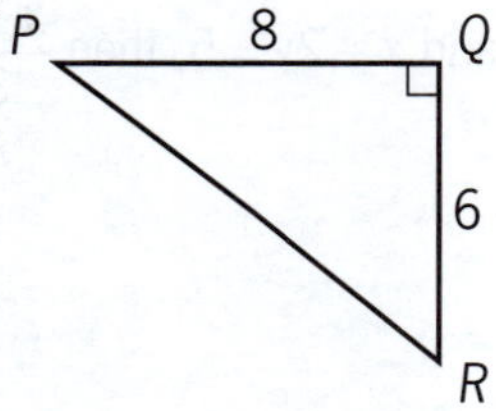

29. The figure above shows a path around a triangular piece of land. Mary walked the distance of 8 miles from P to Q and then walked the distance of 6 miles from Q to R. If Ted walked directly from P to R, by what percent did the distance that Mary walked exceed the distance that Ted walked?

(A) 30%

(B) 40%

(C) 50%

(D) 60%

(E) 80%

Geometry Pythagorean theorem

Mary walked a distance of $6 + 8 = 14$ miles. The distance that Ted walked, PR, can be found by using the Pythagorean theorem $6^2 + 8^2 = (PR)^2$, or $(PR)^2 = 100$. Taking square roots, it follows that Ted walked 10 miles. Therefore, the distance Mary walked exceeded the distance Ted walked by $14 - 10 = 4$ miles and 4 is 40% of 10.

The correct answer is B.

30. At a supermarket, John spent $\frac{1}{2}$ of his money on fresh fruits and vegetables, $\frac{1}{3}$ on meat products, and $\frac{1}{10}$ on bakery products. If he spent the remaining \$6 on candy, how much did John spend at the supermarket?

(A) \$60

(B) \$80

(C) \$90

(D) \$120

(E) \$180

Arithmetic Fractions

The amount spent was

$$\frac{1}{2}+\frac{1}{3}+\frac{1}{10}=\frac{15}{30}+\frac{10}{30}+\frac{3}{30}=\frac{28}{30}=\frac{14}{15} \text{ of the total}$$

so the \$6 left was $\frac{1}{15}$ of the total. It follows that the total is $(15)(\$6) = \$90$.

The correct answer is C.

31. If $(1 - 1.25)N = 1$, then $N =$

(A) −400

(B) −140

(C) −4

(D) 4

(E) 400

Algebra Operations with rational numbers

Since $(1 - 1.25)N = -0.25N = -\frac{1}{4}N$, the equation becomes $-\frac{1}{4}N = 1$, which has solution $N = -4$.

The correct answer is C.

32. A carpenter constructed a rectangular sandbox with a capacity of 10 cubic feet. If the carpenter were to make a similar sandbox twice as long, twice as wide, and twice as high as the first sandbox, what would be the capacity, in cubic feet, of the second sandbox?

(A) 20

(B) 40

(C) 60

(D) 80

(E) 100

Geometry Volume

When all the dimensions of a three-dimensional object are changed by a factor of 2, the capacity, or volume, changes by a factor of $(2)(2)(2) = 2^3 = 8$. Thus the capacity of the second sandbox is $10(8) = 80$ cubic feet.

The correct answer is D.

33. The quotient when a certain number is divided by $\frac{2}{3}$ is $\frac{9}{2}$. What is the number?

(A) $\frac{4}{27}$

(B) $\frac{1}{3}$

(C) 3

(D) 6

(E) $\frac{27}{4}$

Arithmetic Operations with rational numbers

Recall the definition of division: $a \div b = c$ means $a = bc$. For example, if a certain number divided by 2 equals 3, then the number is $2 \times 3 = 6$. For this problem, a certain number divided by $\frac{2}{3}$ equals $\frac{9}{2}$, so the number is $\frac{2}{3} \times \frac{9}{2} = 3$.

This problem can also be solved by algebra. Let N be the number. Then $\frac{N}{\frac{2}{3}} = \frac{9}{2}$, or $N = \frac{2}{3} \times \frac{9}{2} = 3$.

The correct answer is C.

34. If a sphere with radius *r* is inscribed in a cube with edges of length *e*, which of the following expresses the relationship between *r* and *e* ?

(A) $r = \frac{1}{2}e$

(B) $r = e$

(C) $r = 2e$

(D) $r = \sqrt{e}$

(E) $r = \frac{1}{4}e^2$

Geometry Volume

A sphere inscribed in a cube touches, but does not extend beyond, each of the 6 sides of the cube, and thus the diameter of the sphere is equal to the distance between a pair of opposite sides of the cube, which is equal to the edge length of the cube. Therefore, the radius of the sphere is equal to half the edge length of the cube, or $r = \frac{1}{2}e$.

The correct answer is A.

35. If $2x + y = 7$ and $x + 2y = 5$, then $\frac{x+y}{3} =$

(A) 1

(B) $\frac{4}{3}$

(C) $\frac{17}{5}$

(D) $\frac{18}{5}$

(E) 4

Algebra Simultaneous equations

Adding the equations $2x + y = 7$ and $x + 2y = 5$ gives $3x + 3y = 12$, or $x + y = 4$. Dividing both sides of the last equation by 3 gives $\frac{x+y}{3} = \frac{4}{3}$.

The correct answer is B.

36. City X has a population 4 times as great as the population of City Y, which has a population twice as great as the population of City Z. What is the ratio of the population of City X to the population of City Z ?

(A) 1:8

(B) 1:4

(C) 2:1

(D) 4:1

(E) 8:1

Arithmetic Ratio and Proportion

Let X, Y, and Z be the populations of Cities X, Y, and Z, respectively. It is given that $X = 4Y$, and $Y = 2Z$ or $Z = \frac{Y}{2}$. Then, $\frac{X}{Z} = \frac{4Y}{\frac{Y}{2}} = (4Y)\left(\frac{2}{Y}\right) = \frac{8}{1}$.

The correct answer is E.

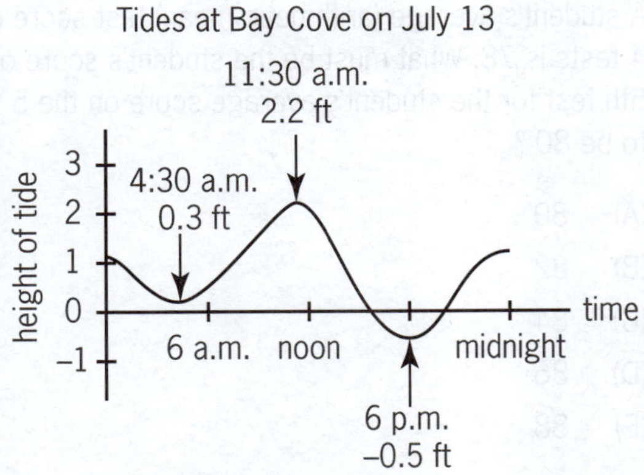

37. The graph above shows the height of the tide, in feet, above or below a baseline. Which of the following is closest to the difference, in feet, between the heights of the highest and lowest tides on July 13 at Bay Cove?

(A) 1.7
(B) 1.9
(C) 2.2
(D) 2.5
(E) 2.7

Arithmetic Interpretation of graphs and tables

From the graph, the highest tide is 2.2 ft above the baseline and the lowest tide is 0.5 ft below the baseline. Therefore, the difference between the heights of the highest tide and the lowest tide is $[2.2 - (-0.5)]$ ft = $(2.2 + 0.5)$ ft = 2.7 ft.

The correct answer is E.

38. A manufacturer of a certain product can expect that between 0.3 percent and 0.5 percent of the units manufactured will be defective. If the retail price is $2,500 per unit and the manufacturer offers a full refund for defective units, how much money can the manufacturer expect to need to cover the refunds on 20,000 units?

(A) Between $15,000 and $25,000
(B) Between $30,000 and $50,000
(C) Between $60,000 and $100,000
(D) Between $150,000 and $250,000
(E) Between $300,000 and $500,000

Arithmetic Applied problems

The expected number of defective units is between 0.3% and 0.5% of 20,000, or between $(0.003)(20{,}000) = 60$ and $(0.005)(20{,}000) = 100$. Since each unit has a retail price of $2,500, the amount of money needed to cover the refunds for the expected number of defective units is between 60($2,500) and 100($2,500), or between $150,000 and $250,000.

The correct answer is D.

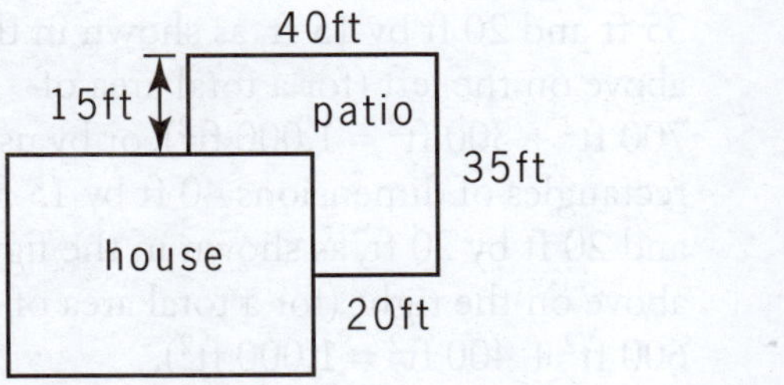

39. A flat patio was built alongside a house as shown in the figure above. If all angles shown are right angles, what is the area of the patio in square feet?

(A) 800
(B) 875
(C) 1,000
(D) 1,100
(E) 1,125

Geometry Area

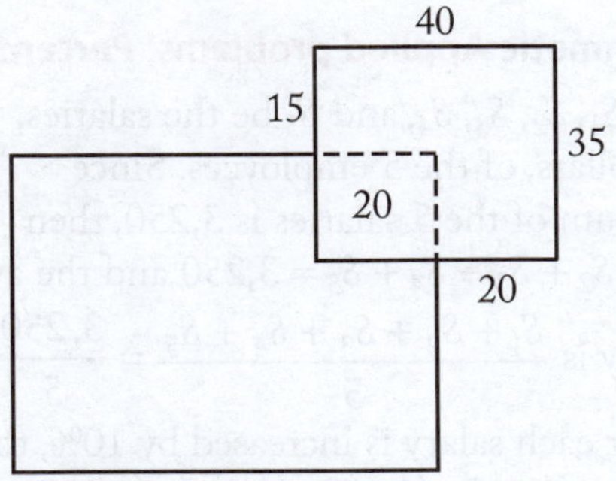

The area of the patio can be calculated by imagining the patio to be a rectangle of dimensions 40 ft by 35 ft that has a lower-left square corner of dimensions 20 ft by 20 ft covered up, as shown in the figure above. The area of the patio will be the area of the uncovered part of the rectangle, and therefore the area of the patio, in square feet, is $(40)(35) - (20)(20) = 1{,}400 - 400 = 1{,}000$.

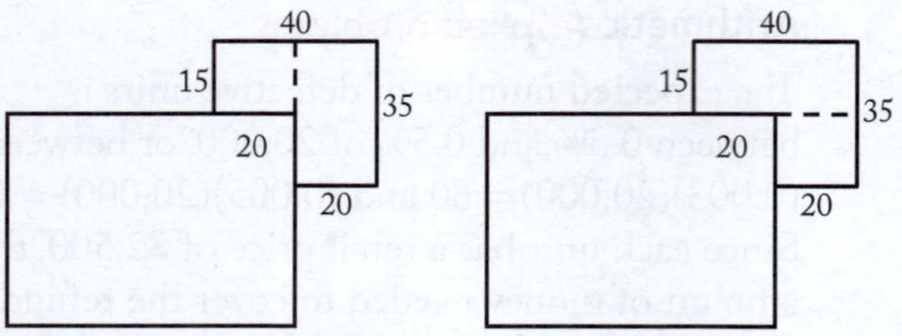

Alternatively, the area of the patio can be calculated by dividing the patio into two rectangles and adding the areas of the two rectangles. This can be done in two ways: by using rectangles of dimensions 20 ft by 35 ft and 20 ft by 15 ft, as shown in the figure above on the left (for a total area of 700 ft^2 + 300 ft^2 = 1,000 ft^2), or by using rectangles of dimensions 40 ft by 15 ft and 20 ft by 20 ft, as shown in the figure above on the right (for a total area of 600 ft^2 + 400 ft^2 = 1,000 ft^2).

The correct answer is C.

40. The sum of the weekly salaries of 5 employees is \$3,250. If each of the 5 salaries is to increase by 10 percent, then the average (arithmetic mean) weekly salary per employee will increase by

(A) \$52.50
(B) \$55.00
(C) \$57.50
(D) \$62.50
(E) \$65.00

Arithmetic Applied problems; Percents

Let S_1, S_2, S_3, S_4, and S_5 be the salaries, in dollars, of the 5 employees. Since the sum of the 5 salaries is 3,250, then $S_1 + S_2 + S_3 + S_4 + S_5 = 3{,}250$ and the average salary is $\frac{S_1 + S_2 + S_3 + S_4 + S_5}{5} = \frac{3{,}250}{5} = 650$. After each salary is increased by 10%, the salaries will be $(1.1)S_1$, $(1.1)S_2$, $(1.1)S_3$, $(1.1)S_4$, and $(1.1)S_5$ and the average salary, in dollars, will be $\frac{(1.1)S_1 + (1.1)S_2 + (1.1)S_3 + (1.1)S_4 + (1.1)S_5}{5} = 1.1 \times \left(\frac{S_1 + S_2 + S_3 + S_4 + S_5}{5}\right) = 1.1 \times 650 = 715$. Therefore, the increase in the average salary is \$715 − \$650 = \$65.

The correct answer is E.

41. A student's average (arithmetic mean) test score on 4 tests is 78. What must be the student's score on a 5th test for the student's average score on the 5 tests to be 80 ?

(A) 80
(B) 82
(C) 84
(D) 86
(E) 88

Arithmetic Statistics

The average of the student's first 4 test scores is 78, so the sum of the first 4 test scores is $4(78) = 312$. If x represents the fifth test score, then the sum of all 5 test scores is $312 + x$ and the average of all 5 test scores is $\frac{312 + x}{5}$. But the average of all 5 test scores is 80 so

$$\frac{312 + x}{5} = 80$$

$$312 + x = 400$$

$$x = 88$$

The correct answer is E.

42. Last week Chris earned x dollars per hour for the first 40 hours worked plus 22 dollars per hour for each hour worked beyond 40 hours. If last week Chris earned a total of 816 dollars by working 48 hours, what is the value of x ?

(A) 13
(B) 14
(C) 15
(D) 16
(E) 17

Algebra Applied problems

Chris worked 40 hours at a rate of \$$x$ per hour, 48 − 40 = 8 hours at a rate of \$22 per hour, and earned a total of \$816.

$40x + 8(22) = 816$	given information
$40x + 176 = 816$	multiply 8 and 22
$40x = 640$	subtract 176 from both sides
$x = 16$	divide both sides by 40

The correct answer is D.

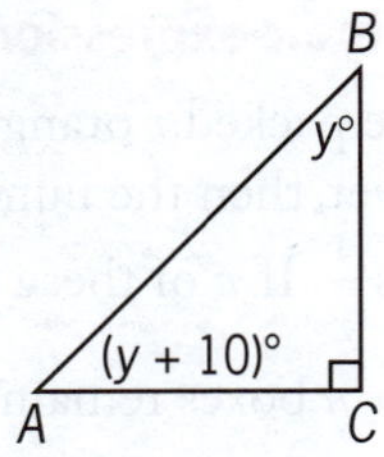

43. In the figure above, what is the ratio of the measure of angle *B* to the measure of angle *A* ?

(A) 2 to 3
(B) 3 to 4
(C) 3 to 5
(D) 4 to 5
(E) 5 to 6

Geometry Angles

Because the sum of the degree measures of the three interior angles of a triangle is 180, it follows that $y + (y + 10) + 90 = 180$. Therefore, $2y = 80$, and hence $y = 40$. The ratio of the measure of angle *B* to the measure of angle *A* can now be determined: $\frac{y}{y+10} = \frac{40}{50} = \frac{4}{5}$.

The correct answer is D.

44. If *n* is a prime number greater than 3, what is the remainder when n^2 is divided by 12 ?

(A) 0
(B) 1
(C) 2
(D) 3
(E) 5

Arithmetic Properties of numbers

The simplest way to solve this problem is to choose a prime number greater than 3 and divide its square by 12 to see what the remainder is. For example, if $n = 5$, then $n^2 = 25$, and the remainder is 1 when 25 is divided by 12. A second prime number can be used to check the result. For example, if $n = 7$, then $n^2 = 49$, and the remainder is 1 when 49 is divided by 12. Because only one of the answer choices can be correct, the remainder must be 1.

For the more mathematically inclined, consider the remainder when each prime number *n* greater than 3 is divided by 6. The remainder cannot be 0 because that would imply that *n* is divisible by 6, which is impossible since *n* is a prime number. The remainder cannot be 2 or 4 because that would imply that *n* is even, which is impossible since *n* is a prime number greater than 3. The remainder cannot be 3 because that would imply that *n* is divisible by 3, which is impossible since *n* is a prime number greater than 3. Therefore, the only possible remainders when a prime number *n* greater than 3 is divided by 6 are 1 and 5. Thus, *n* has the form $6q + 1$ or $6q + 5$, where *q* is an integer, and, therefore, n^2 has the form $36q^2 + 12q + 1 = 12(3q^2 + q) + 1$ or $36q^2 + 60q + 25 = 12(3q^2 + 5q + 2) + 1$. In either case, n^2 has a remainder of 1 when divided by 12.

The correct answer is B.

45. $\frac{1}{1+\frac{1}{3}} - \frac{1}{1+\frac{1}{2}} =$

(A) $-\frac{1}{3}$
(B) $-\frac{1}{6}$
(C) $-\frac{1}{12}$
(D) $\frac{1}{12}$
(E) $\frac{1}{3}$

Arithmetic Operations with rational numbers

Perform the arithmetic calculations as follows:

$$\begin{aligned}\frac{1}{1+\frac{1}{3}} - \frac{1}{1+\frac{1}{2}} &= \frac{1}{\frac{4}{3}} - \frac{1}{\frac{3}{2}}\\ &= \frac{3}{4} - \frac{2}{3}\\ &= \frac{9}{12} - \frac{8}{12}\\ &= \frac{9-8}{12}\\ &= \frac{1}{12}\end{aligned}$$

The correct answer is D.

46. The positive two-digit integers x and y have the same digits, but in reverse order. Which of the following must be a factor of x + y ?

(A) 6
(B) 9
(C) 10
(D) 11
(E) 14

Arithmetic Properties of numbers

Let m and n be digits. If $x = 10m + n$, then $y = 10n + m$. Adding x and y gives $x + y = (10m + n) + (10n + m) = 11m + 11n = 11(m + n)$, and therefore 11 is a factor of $x + y$.

The correct answer is D.

47. In a certain sequence of 8 numbers, each number after the first is 1 more than the previous number. If the first number is –5, how many of the numbers in the sequence are positive?

(A) None
(B) One
(C) Two
(D) Three
(E) Four

Arithmetic Sequences

The sequence consists of eight consecutive integers beginning with –5:

$-5, -4, -3, -2, -1, 0, 1, 2$

In this sequence exactly two of the numbers are positive.

The correct answer is C.

48. A total of s oranges are to be packaged in boxes that will hold r oranges each, with no oranges left over. When n of these boxes have been completely filled, what is the number of boxes that remain to be filled?

(A) $s - nr$
(B) $s - \frac{n}{r}$
(C) $rs - n$
(D) $\frac{s}{n} - r$
(E) $\frac{s}{r} - n$

Algebra Algebraic expressions

If s oranges are packed r oranges to a box with no oranges left over, then the number of boxes that will be filled is $\frac{s}{r}$. If n of these boxes are already filled, then $\frac{s}{r} - n$ boxes remain to be filled.

The correct answer is E.

49. If $0 < a < b < c$, which of the following statements must be true?

I. $2a > b + c$
II. $c - a > b - a$
III. $\frac{c}{a} < \frac{b}{a}$

(A) I only
(B) II only
(C) III only
(D) I and II
(E) II and III

Algebra Inequalities

Given $0 < a < b < c$, Statement I is not necessarily true. If, for example, $a = 1$, $b = 2$, and $c = 3$, then $0 < a < b < c$, but $2a = 2(1) < 2 + 3 = b + c$.

Given $0 < a < b < c$, then $c > b$, and subtracting a from both sides gives $c - a > b - a$. Therefore, Statement II is true.

Given $0 < a < b < c$, Statement III is not necessarily true. If, for example, $a = 1$, $b = 2$, and $c = 3$, then $0 < a < b < c$, but $\frac{c}{a} = \frac{3}{1} > \frac{2}{1} = \frac{b}{a}$.

The correct answer is B.

50. In the xy-plane, the origin O is the midpoint of line segment PQ. If the coordinates of P are (r,s), what are the coordinates of Q ?

(A) (r,s)
(B) (s,–r)
(C) (–s,–r)
(D) (–r,s)
(E) (–r,–s)

Algebra Coordinate geometry

Let (x,y) be the coordinates of Q. The midpoint of (r,s) and (x,y) is $\left(\frac{r+x}{2},\frac{s+y}{2}\right)$. Since the midpoint is (0,0), it follows that $\frac{r+x}{2}=0$ and $\frac{s+y}{2}=0$. Therefore, $r+x=0$ and $s+y=0$, or $x=-r$ and $y=-s$, or $(x,y)=(-r,-s)$.

This problem can also be solved by observing that Q is the reflection of P about the origin, and so $Q=(-r,-s)$ (i.e., change the sign of each of the coordinates of P to obtain the coordinates of Q).

The correct answer is E.

51. Which of the following equations is NOT equivalent to $10y^2=(x+2)(x-2)$?

(A) $30y^2=3x^2-12$

(B) $20y^2=(2x-4)(x+2)$

(C) $10y^2+4=x^2$

(D) $5y^2=x^2-2$

(E) $y^2=\frac{x^2-4}{10}$

Algebra Simplifying algebraic expressions

When $x=2$ or $x=-2$, the equation becomes $10y^2=0$, or $y=0$. Since, in the equation given in (D), y does not become 0 when $x=2$, it follows that the equation given in (D) is not equivalent to the given equation. Alternatively, when each of the equations given in (A) through (E) is solved for $10y^2$ in terms of x, only the resulting equation in (D) fails to give an expression in terms of x that is equivalent to $(x+2)(x-2)=x^2-4$.

The correct answer is D.

	Monday	Tuesday	Wednesday	Thursday
Company A	45	55	50	50
Company B	10	30	30	10
Company C	34	28	28	30
Company D	39	42	41	38
Company E	50	60	60	70

52. The table shows the numbers of packages shipped daily by each of five companies during a 4-day period. The standard deviation of the numbers of packages shipped daily during the period was greatest for which of the five companies?

(A) A

(B) B

(C) C

(D) D

(E) E

Arithmetic Statistics

Since the standard deviation of a data set is a measure of how widely the data are scattered about their mean, find the mean number of packages shipped by each company and then determine the company for which the data is most widely scattered about its mean.

For Company A, the mean number of packages shipped is $\frac{45+55+2(50)}{4}=50$. Two of the data points are each 50 and the other two each differ from 50 by 5.

For Company B, the mean number of packages shipped is $\frac{2(10)+2(30)}{4}=20$. Each of the data points differs from 20 by 10. Thus, the data for Company B is more widely scattered about its mean of 20 than the data for Company A is about its mean of 50.

For Company C, the mean number of packages shipped is $\frac{34+2(28)+30}{4}=30$. One data point is 30, two others each differ from 30 by only 2, and the fourth data point differs from 30 by only 4. Therefore, the data for Company C is not as widely scattered about its mean of 30 as the data for Company B is about its mean of 20.

For Company D, the mean number of packages shipped is $\frac{39 + 42 + 41 + 38}{4} = 40$. Two of the data points each differ from 40 by only 1 and the other two each differ from 40 by only 2. Therefore, the data for Company D is not as widely scattered about its mean of 40 as the data for Company B is about its mean of 20.

For Company E, the mean number of packages shipped is $\frac{50 + 2(60) + 70}{4} = 60$. Two of the data points are each 60 and the other two each differ from 60 by 10. Therefore, the data for Company E is not as widely scattered about its mean of 60 as the data for Company B is about its mean of 20.

Thus, the data for Company B is most widely scattered about its mean and, therefore, the standard deviation of the number of packages shipped daily by the five companies is greatest for Company B.

For those interested, the standard deviations for the five companies can be calculated as follows:

For A: $\sqrt{\frac{(45-50)^2+(55-50)^2+2(50-50)^2}{4}}$

$= \sqrt{\frac{2(25)}{4}} = \sqrt{\frac{25}{2}} = \sqrt{12.5}$.

For B: $\sqrt{\frac{2(10-20)^2+2(30-20)^2}{4}} = \sqrt{\frac{4(100)}{4}}$

$= \sqrt{100}$.

For C: $\sqrt{\frac{(34-30)^2+2(28-30)^2+(30-30)^2}{4}}$

$= \sqrt{\frac{24}{4}} = \sqrt{6}$.

For D:

$\sqrt{\frac{(39-40)^2+(42-40)^2+(41-40)^2+(38-40)^2}{4}}$

$= \sqrt{\frac{10}{4}} = \sqrt{2.5}$.

For E: $\sqrt{\frac{(50-60)^2+2(60-60)^2+(70-60)^2}{4}}$

$= \sqrt{\frac{200}{4}} = \sqrt{50}$.

The correct answer is B.

53. Company Q plans to make a new product next year and sell each unit of this new product at a selling price of $2. The variable costs per unit in each production run are estimated to be 40% of the selling price, and the fixed costs for each production run are estimated to be $5,040. Based on these estimated costs, how many units of the new product will Company Q need to make and sell in order for their revenue to equal their total costs for each production run?

(A) 4,200
(B) 3,150
(C) 2,520
(D) 2,100
(E) 1,800

Algebra Applied problems

Let x be the desired number of units to be sold at a price of $2 each. Then the revenue for selling these units is 2x$, and the total cost for selling these units is (40%)($2.00)$x$ = 0.80x$ plus a fixed cost of $5,040.

revenue = total cost	given requirement
$2x = 0.8x + 5{,}040$	given information
$1.2x = 5{,}040$	subtract $0.8x$ from both sides
$x = 4{,}200$	divide both sides by 1.2

The correct answer is A.

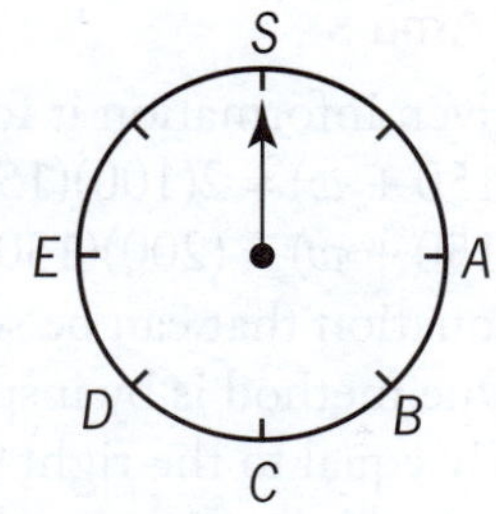

54. The dial shown above is divided into equal-sized intervals. At which of the following letters will the pointer stop if it is rotated clockwise from *S* through 1,174 intervals?

(A) *A*
(B) *B*
(C) *C*
(D) *D*
(E) *E*

Arithmetic Properties of numbers

There are 8 intervals in each complete revolution. Dividing 8 into 1,174 gives 146 with remainder 6. Therefore, 1,174 intervals is equivalent to 146 complete revolutions followed by an additional 6 intervals measured clockwise from *S*, which places the pointer at *E*.

The correct answer is E.

Estimated Number of Home-Schooled Students by State, January 2001

State	Number (in thousands)
A	181
B	125
C	103
D	79
E	72

55. According to the table shown, the estimated number of home-schooled students in State A is approximately what percent greater than the number in State D ?

(A) 25%
(B) 55%
(C) 100%
(D) 125%
(E) 155%

Arithmetic Percents

The percent increase from the number in State D to the number in State A is

$$= \left(\frac{181{,}000 - 79{,}000}{79{,}000} \times 100\right)\% \quad \text{expression for percent increase}$$

$$= \left(\frac{181 - 79}{79} \times 100\right)\% \quad \text{reduce fraction}$$

$$= \left(\frac{102}{79} \times 100\right)\% \quad \text{subtract}$$

$$\approx \left(\frac{100}{80} \times 100\right)\% \quad \text{approximate}$$

$$= (1.25 \times 100)\% \quad \text{divide}$$

$$= 125\% \quad \text{multiply}$$

The correct answer is D.

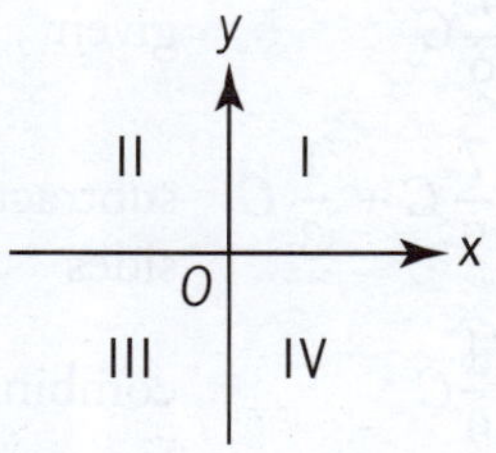

56. The graph of the equation $xy = k$, where $k < 0$, lies in which two of the quadrants shown above?

(A) I and II
(B) I and III
(C) II and III
(D) II and IV
(E) III and IV

Algebra Coordinate geometry

If a point lies on the graph of $xy = k$, then the product of the point's *x*- and *y*-coordinates is *k*. Since *k* is negative, it follows that for any such point, the product of the point's *x*- and *y*-coordinates is negative. Therefore, for any such point, the point's *x*- and *y*-coordinates have opposite signs, and hence the point must be in quadrant II or in quadrant IV.

The correct answer is D.

57. When n liters of fuel were added to a tank that was already $\frac{1}{3}$ full, the tank was filled to $\frac{7}{9}$ of its capacity. In terms of n, what is the capacity of the tank, in liters?

(A) $\frac{10}{9}n$

(B) $\frac{4}{3}n$

(C) $\frac{3}{2}n$

(D) $\frac{9}{4}n$

(E) $\frac{7}{3}n$

Algebra Applied problems

Let C represent the capacity of the tank, in liters. It follows that

$\frac{1}{3}C + n = \frac{7}{9}C$	given
$n = \frac{7}{9}C - \frac{1}{3}C$	subtract $\frac{1}{3}C$ from both sides
$n = \frac{4}{9}C$	combine like terms
$\frac{9}{4}n = C$	divide both sides by $\frac{4}{9}$

The correct answer is D.

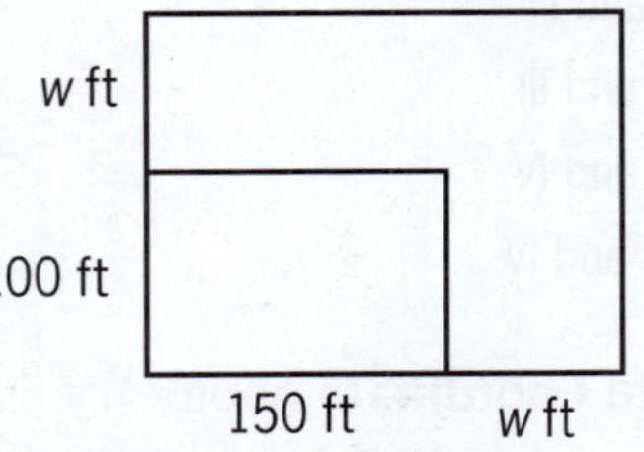

Note: Not drawn to scale.

58. The smaller rectangle in the figure above represents the original size of a parking lot before its length and width were each extended by w feet to make the larger rectangular lot shown. If the area of the enlarged lot is twice the area of the original lot, what is the value of w?

(A) 25

(B) 50

(C) 75

(D) 100

(E) 200

Geometry Area

From the given information it follows that $(100 + w)(150 + w) = 2(100)(150)$, or $(100 + w)(150 + w) = (200)(150)$. This is a quadratic equation that can be solved by several methods. One method is by inspection. The left side is clearly equal to the right side when $w = 50$. Another method is by factoring. Expanding the left side gives $(100)(150) + 250w + w^2 = (200)(150)$, or $w^2 + 250w - (100)(150) = 0$. Factoring the left side gives $(w - 50)(w + 300) = 0$, which has $w = 50$ as its only positive solution.

The correct answer is B.

59. $\frac{1}{0.75-1} =$

(A) −4

(B) −0.25

(C) 0.25

(D) 0.75

(E) 4

Arithmetic Operations with rational numbers

Perform the arithmetic calculations as follows:

$$\frac{1}{0.75-1} = \frac{1}{\frac{3}{4}-1} = \frac{1}{-\frac{1}{4}} = -4$$

The correct answer is A.

60. Kevin invested \$8,000 for one year at a simple annual interest rate of 6 percent and invested \$10,000 for one year at an annual interest rate of 8 percent compounded semiannually. What is the total amount of interest that Kevin earned on the two investments?

(A) \$880

(B) \$1,088

(C) \$1,253

(D) \$1,280

(E) \$1,296

Arithmetic Applied problems

The amount of interest after one year is the total value of the investment after one year minus the total initial value of the investment. The total value of the investment after one year is $\$8{,}000(1.06) + \$10{,}000(1.04)^2 = \$8{,}480 + \$10{,}816$, so the amount of interest is $(\$8{,}480 + \$10{,}816) - (\$8{,}000 + \$10{,}000) = \$480 + \$816 = \$1{,}296$.

The correct answer is E.

61. The harvest yield from a certain apple orchard was 350 bushels of apples. If x of the trees in the orchard each yielded 10 bushels of apples, what fraction of the harvest yield was from these x trees?

(A) $\frac{x}{35}$

(B) $1-\frac{x}{35}$

(C) $10x$

(D) $35 - x$

(E) $350 - 10x$

Algebra Algebraic expressions

Since each of the x trees yielded 10 bushels, the total number of bushels yielded by these trees was $10x$. Since the yield of the entire orchard was 350 bushels, $\frac{10x}{350} = \frac{x}{35}$ was the fraction of the total yield from these x trees.

The correct answer is A.

62. If n is an integer, which of the following must be even?

(A) $n + 1$

(B) $n + 2$

(C) $2n$

(D) $2n + 1$

(E) n^2

Arithmetic Properties of integers

A quick look at the answer choices reveals the expression $2n$ in answer choice C. $2n$ is a multiple of 2 and hence must be even.

Since only one answer choice can be correct, the other answer choices need not be checked. However, for completeness:

A $n + 1$ is odd if n is even and even if n is odd. Therefore, it is not true that $n + 1$ must be even.

B $n + 2$ is even if n is even and odd if n is odd. Therefore, it is not true that $n + 2$ must be even.

D $2n + 1$ is odd whether n is even or odd. Therefore, it is not true that $2n + 1$ must be even.

E n^2 is even if n is even and odd if n is odd. Therefore, it is not true that n^2 must be even.

The correct answer is C.

63. The sum $\frac{7}{8}+\frac{1}{9}$ is between

(A) $\frac{1}{2}$ and $\frac{3}{4}$

(B) $\frac{3}{4}$ and 1

(C) 1 and $1\frac{1}{4}$

(D) $1\frac{1}{4}$ and $1\frac{1}{2}$

(E) $1\frac{1}{2}$ and 2

Arithmetic Operations with rational numbers

Since $\frac{1}{9}<\frac{1}{8}$, $\frac{7}{8}+\frac{1}{9}<\frac{7}{8}+\frac{1}{8}=1$, and answer choices C, D, and E can be eliminated. Since $\frac{7}{8}>\frac{6}{8}=\frac{3}{4}$, $\frac{7}{8}+\frac{1}{9}>\frac{3}{4}$, and answer choice A can be eliminated. Thus, $\frac{3}{4}<\frac{7}{8}+\frac{1}{9}<1$.

The correct answer is B.

64. Car X averages 25.0 miles per gallon of gasoline and Car Y averages 11.9 miles per gallon. If each car is driven 12,000 miles, approximately how many more gallons of gasoline will Car Y use than Car X ?

(A) 320
(B) 480
(C) 520
(D) 730
(E) 920

Arithmetic Applied problems

Car X uses 1 gallon of gasoline for every 25 miles it is driven, so Car X uses $\frac{1}{25}$ of a gallon for every 1 mile it is driven. Therefore Car X will use $(12{,}000)\left(\frac{1}{25}\right) = 480$ gallons of gasoline when it is driven 12,000 miles. Car Y uses 1 gallon of gasoline for every 11.9 or $\frac{119}{10}$ miles it is driven, so Car Y uses $\frac{10}{119}$ of a gallon for every 1 mile it is driven. Therefore Car Y will use $(12{,}000)\left(\frac{10}{119}\right) \approx (12{,}000)\left(\frac{10}{120}\right) = 1{,}000$ gallons of gasoline when it is driven 12,000 miles. Thus, Car Y will use approximately 1,000 – 480 = 520 more gallons of gasoline than Car X.

The correct answer is C.

65. If y is an integer, then the least possible value of $|23 - 5y|$ is

(A) 1
(B) 2
(C) 3
(D) 4
(E) 5

Arithmetic Absolute value; Operations with integers

Since y is an integer, $23 - 5y$ is also an integer. The task is to find the integer y for which $|23 - 5y|$ is the least. If $y \geq 0, -5y \leq 0$, and $23 - 5y \leq 23$. On the other hand, if $y \leq 0, -5y \geq 0$, and $23 - 5y \geq 23$. Therefore, the least possible value of $|23 - 5y|$ occurs at a nonnegative value of y. From the chart below, it is clear that the least possible integer value of $|23 - 5y|$ is 2, which occurs when $y = 5$.

y	$\|23 - 5y\|$
0	23
1	18
2	13
3	8
4	3
5	2
6	7
7	12

Alternatively, since $|23 - 5y| \geq 0$, the minimum possible real value of $|23 - 5y|$ is 0. The integer value of y for which $|23 - 5y|$ is least is the integer closest to the solution of the equation $23 - 5y = 0$. The solution is $y = \frac{23}{5} = 4.6$ and the integer closest to 4.6 is 5.

The correct answer is B.

66. $\sqrt{80} + \sqrt{125} =$

(A) $9\sqrt{5}$
(B) $20\sqrt{5}$
(C) $41\sqrt{5}$
(D) $\sqrt{205}$
(E) 100

Arithmetic Operations with radical expressions

Rewrite each radical in the form $a\sqrt{b}$, where a and b are positive integers and b is as small as possible, and then add.

$$\begin{aligned}\sqrt{80} + \sqrt{125} &= \sqrt{16(5)} + \sqrt{25(5)} \\ &= \left(\sqrt{16}\right)\left(\sqrt{5}\right) + \left(\sqrt{25}\right)\left(\sqrt{5}\right) \\ &= 4\sqrt{5} + 5\sqrt{5} \\ &= 9\sqrt{5}\end{aligned}$$

The correct answer is A.

$$y = kx + 3$$

67. In the equation above, k is a constant. If $y = 17$ when $x = 2$, what is the value of y when $x = 4$?

(A) 34
(B) 31
(C) 14
(D) 11
(E) 7

Algebra First-degree equations

If $y = kx + 3$ and $y = 17$ when $x = 2$, then

$17 = 2k + 3$

$14 = 2k$

$7 = k$

Therefore, $y = 7x + 3$. When $x = 4$, $y = 7(4) + 3 = 31$.

The correct answer is B.

68. Which of the following is greatest?

(A) $10\sqrt{3}$
(B) $9\sqrt{4}$
(C) $8\sqrt{5}$
(D) $7\sqrt{6}$
(E) $6\sqrt{7}$

Arithmetic Operations on radical expressions

Since all the expressions represent positive numbers, the expression that has the greatest squared value will be the expression that has the greatest value.

$\left(10\sqrt{3}\right)^2 = 100 \times 3 = 300$ (not greatest)

$\left(9\sqrt{4}\right)^2 = 81 \times 4 = 324$ (greatest)

$\left(8\sqrt{5}\right)^2 = 64 \times 5 = 320$ (not greatest)

$\left(7\sqrt{6}\right)^2 = 49 \times 6 = 294$ (not greatest)

$\left(6\sqrt{7}\right)^2 = 36 \times 7 = 252$ (not greatest)

The correct answer is B.

69. Al and Ben are drivers for SD Trucking Company. One snowy day, Ben left SD at 8:00 a.m. heading east and Al left SD at 11:00 a.m. heading west. At a particular time later that day, the dispatcher retrieved data from SD's vehicle tracking system. The data showed that, up to that time, Al had averaged 40 miles per hour and Ben had averaged 20 miles per hour. It also showed that Al and Ben had driven a combined total of 240 miles. At what time did the dispatcher retrieve data from the vehicle tracking system?

(A) 1:00 p.m.
(B) 2:00 p.m.
(C) 3:00 p.m.
(D) 5:00 p.m.
(E) 6:00 p.m.

Algebra Applied problems

Let t be the number of hours after 8:00 a.m. that Ben drove. Then, in t hours, Ben drove $20t$ miles and Al, who began driving 3 hours after Ben began driving, drove $40(t - 3)$ miles. Therefore, their combined total distance at that time can be expressed as $(20t + 40t - 120)$ miles $= (60t - 120)$ miles. It follows that $60t - 120 = 240$, or $60t = 360$, or $t = 6$, which corresponds to 6 hours after 8:00 a.m. or 2:00 p.m.

The correct answer is B.

70. Of the land owned by a farmer, 90 percent was cleared for planting. Of the cleared land, 40 percent was planted with soybeans and 50 percent of the cleared land was planted with wheat. If the remaining 720 acres of cleared land was planted with corn, how many acres did the farmer own?

(A) 5,832
(B) 6,480
(C) 7,200
(D) 8,000
(E) 8,889

Arithmetic Applied problems; Percents

Corn was planted on 100% – (40% + 50%) = 10% of the cleared land, and the cleared land represents 90% of the farmer's land. Therefore, corn was planted on 10% of 90%, or (0.10)(0.90) = 0.09 = 9%, of the farmer's land. It is given that corn was planted on 720 acres, so if x is the number of acres the farmer owns, then $0.09x = 720$ and $x = \frac{720}{0.09} = 8{,}000$.

The correct answer is D.

71. At the start of an experiment, a certain population consisted of 3 animals. At the end of each month after the start of the experiment, the population size was double its size at the beginning of that month. Which of the following represents the population size at the end of 10 months?

(A) 2^3

(B) 3^2

(C) $2(3^{10})$

(D) $3(2^{10})$

(E) $3(10^2)$

Arithmetic Applied problems; Sequences

The population doubles each month, so multiply the previous month's population by 2 to get the next month's population. Thus, at the end of the 1st month the population will be (3)(2), at the end of the 2nd month the population will be (3)(2)(2), at the end of the 3rd month the population will be (3)(2)(2)(2), and so on. Therefore, at the end of the 10th month the population will be the product of 3 and ten factors of 2, which equals $3(2^{10})$.

The correct answer is D.

72. If $\left(\frac{1}{3}+\frac{1}{4}+\frac{1}{5}+\frac{1}{6}\right) = r\left(\frac{1}{9}+\frac{1}{12}+\frac{1}{15}+\frac{1}{18}\right)$, then $r =$

(A) $\frac{1}{3}$

(B) $\frac{4}{3}$

(C) 3

(D) 4

(E) 12

Arithmetic Operations with rational numbers

$$\left(\frac{1}{3}+\frac{1}{4}+\frac{1}{5}+\frac{1}{6}\right) = r\left(\frac{1}{9}+\frac{1}{12}+\frac{1}{15}+\frac{1}{18}\right)$$

$$\left(\frac{1}{3}+\frac{1}{4}+\frac{1}{5}+\frac{1}{6}\right) = r\left(\frac{1}{3}\right)\left(\frac{1}{3}+\frac{1}{4}+\frac{1}{5}+\frac{1}{6}\right)$$

$$1 = r\left(\frac{1}{3}\right)$$

$$3 = r$$

Alternatively,

$$\left(\frac{1}{3}+\frac{1}{4}+\frac{1}{5}+\frac{1}{6}\right) = r\left(\frac{1}{9}+\frac{1}{12}+\frac{1}{15}+\frac{1}{18}\right)$$

$$\left(\frac{20}{60}+\frac{15}{60}+\frac{12}{60}+\frac{10}{60}\right) = r\left(\frac{20}{180}+\frac{15}{180}+\frac{12}{180}+\frac{10}{180}\right)$$

$$\left(\frac{20+15+12+10}{60}\right) = r\left(\frac{20+15+12+10}{180}\right)$$

$$\left(\frac{20+15+12+10}{60}\right)\left(\frac{180}{20+15+12+10}\right) = r$$

$$\frac{180}{60} = r$$

$$3 = r$$

The correct answer is C.

73. If x and y are positive integers such that y is a multiple of 5 and $3x + 4y = 200$, then x must be a multiple of which of the following?

(A) 3

(B) 6

(C) 7

(D) 8

(E) 10

Arithmetic Properties of numbers

Since it is given that y is a multiple of 5, let $y = 5q$, where q is a positive integer. It is given that $3x + 4y = 200$, so $3x + 4(5q) = 200$ or $3x + 20q = 200$. It follows that $3x = 200 - 20q = 20(10 - q)$. Since 3 is prime and is not a factor of 20, then 3 must be a factor of $10 - q$, which means the only possible values of q are 1, 4, and 7. This is summarized in the following table.

q	$10 - q$	$20(10 - q)$	$3x$	x
1	9	180	180	60
4	6	120	120	40
7	3	60	60	20

In each case, the value of x is a multiple of 10.

Alternatively, since $3x = 20(10 - q)$, the factors of the product of 3 and x must correspond to the factors of the product of 20 and $(10 - q)$. Since the factors of 20 include 10, then x must have a factor of 10, which means that x is a multiple of 10.

The correct answer is E.

74. Which of the following expressions can be written as an integer?

I. $\left(\sqrt{82}+\sqrt{82}\right)^2$

II. $(82)\left(\sqrt{82}\right)$

III. $\dfrac{\left(\sqrt{82}\right)\left(\sqrt{82}\right)}{82}$

(A) None
(B) I only
(C) III only
(D) I and II
(E) I and III

Arithmetic Operations with radical expressions

Expression I represents an integer because $\left(\sqrt{82}+\sqrt{82}\right)^2=\left(2\sqrt{82}\right)^2=(4)(82)$.
Expression II does not represent an integer because $(82)\sqrt{82}=\sqrt{82^3}$ and $82^3 = 2^3 \times 41^3$ is not a perfect square. Regarding this last assertion, note that the square of any integer has the property that each of its distinct prime factors is repeated an even number of times. For example, $24^2 = (2^3 \times 3)^2 = 2^6 \times 3^2$ has the prime factor 2 repeated 6 times and the prime factor 3 repeated twice. Expression III represents an integer, because $\dfrac{\left(\sqrt{82}\right)\left(\sqrt{82}\right)}{82}=\dfrac{82}{82}=1$.

The correct answer is E.

75. Four staff members at a certain company worked on a project. The amounts of time that the four staff members worked on the project were in the ratio 2 to 3 to 5 to 6. If one of the four staff members worked on the project for 30 hours, which of the following CANNOT be the total number of hours that the four staff members worked on the project?

(A) 80
(B) 96
(C) 160
(D) 192
(E) 240

Arithmetic Ratio and proportion

For a certain value of x, the numbers of hours worked on the project by the four staff members are $2x$, $3x$, $5x$, and $6x$, for a total of $16x$. It is given that one of these four numbers is equal to 30. If $2x = 30$, then $x = 15$ and $16x = 16(15) = 240$, which is (E). If $3x = 30$, then $x = 10$ and $16x = 16(10) = 160$, which is (C). If $5x = 30$, then $x = 6$ and $16x = 16(6) = 96$, which is (B). If $6x = 30$, then $x = 5$ and $16x = 16(5) = 80$, which is (A).

The correct answer is D.

76. Pumping alone at their respective constant rates, one inlet pipe fills an empty tank to $\frac{1}{2}$ of capacity in 3 hours and a second inlet pipe fills the same empty tank to $\frac{2}{3}$ of capacity in 6 hours. How many hours will it take both pipes, pumping simultaneously at their respective constant rates, to fill the empty tank to capacity?

(A) 3.25
(B) 3.6
(C) 4.2
(D) 4.4
(E) 5.5

Arithmetic Applied problems

The first pipe can fill $\frac{1}{2}$ of the tank in 3 hours, which is equivalent to the rate of filling $\frac{1}{2} \div 3 = \frac{1}{6}$ of the tank per hour. The second pipe can fill $\frac{2}{3}$ of the tank in 6 hours, which is equivalent to the rate of filling $\frac{2}{3} \div 6 = \frac{1}{9}$ of the tank per hour. Together, they can fill the tank at a rate of $\frac{1}{6} + \frac{1}{9} = \frac{5}{18}$ of the tank per hour. Thus, when both pipes are used at the same time, they will fill the tank in $\frac{18}{5} = 3.6$ hours.

The correct answer is B.

77. In the *xy*-coordinate plane, which of the following points must lie on the line $kx + 3y = 6$ for every possible value of k?

(A) (1,1)

(B) (0,2)

(C) (2,0)

(D) (3,6)

(E) (6,3)

Algebra Coordinate geometry

Substituting the various answer choices for (x,y) into $kx + 3y = 6$ gives the following equations:

A $k + 3 = 6$

B $0 + 3(2) = 6$

C $2k + 3(0) = 6$

D $3k + 3(6) = 6$

E $6k + 3(3) = 6$

Each of these, except for the equation in B, holds for only one value of k. The equation in B does not include k and therefore holds for every value of k.

The correct answer is B.

78. If $x^2 - 2 < 0$, which of the following specifies all the possible values of x?

(A) $0 < x < 2$

(B) $0 < x < \sqrt{2}$

(C) $-\sqrt{2} < x < \sqrt{2}$

(D) $-2 < x < 0$

(E) $-2 < x < 2$

Algebra Inequalities

The corresponding equality $x^2 - 2 = 0$ has two solutions, $x = \sqrt{2}$ and $x = -\sqrt{2}$, and thus there are three intervals to test for inclusion in the solution of the inequality: $x < -\sqrt{2}$, $-\sqrt{2} < x < \sqrt{2}$, and $x > \sqrt{2}$. Choose $x = -2$, $x = 0$, and $x = 2$ from these intervals, respectively, to test whether the inequality holds. Then for these choices, the inequality becomes $(-2)^2 - 2 < 0$ (False), $(0)^2 - 2 < 0$ (True), and $(2)^2 - 2 < 0$ (False). Therefore, the solution consists of only the interval $-\sqrt{2} < x < -\sqrt{2}$. Alternatively, the graph of $y = x^2 - 2$ is easily seen to be a parabola that opens upward with vertex at $(0, -2)$ and x-intercepts at $x = \sqrt{2}$ and $x = -\sqrt{2}$. The solution to the inequality is the set of the x-coordinates of the portion of this parabola that lies below the x-axis, which is $-\sqrt{2} < x < \sqrt{2}$.

The correct answer is C.

Book number	Pages in book	Total pages read
1	253	253
2	110	363
3	117	480
4	170	650
5	155	805
6	50	855
7	205	1,060
8	70	1,130
9	165	1,295
10	105	1,400
11	143	1,543
12	207	1,750

79. Shawana made a schedule for reading books during 4 weeks (28 days) of her summer vacation. She has checked out 12 books from the library. The number of pages in each book and the order in which she plans to read the books are shown in the table above. She will read exactly 50 pages each day. The only exception will be that she will never begin the next book on the same day that she finishes the previous one, and therefore on some days she may read fewer than 50 pages. At the end of the 28th day, how many books will Shawana have finished?

(A) 7
(B) 8
(C) 9
(D) 10
(E) 11

Arithmetic Operations with integers

Book 1: 6 days—50 pages on each of Days 1–5, 3 pages on Day 6 [5(50) + 3 = 253]

Book 2: 3 days—50 pages on each of Days 7 and 8, 10 pages on Day 9 [2(50) + 10 = 110]

Book 3: 3 days—50 pages on each of Days 10 and 11, 17 pages on Day 12 [2(50) + 17 = 117]

Book 4: 4 days—50 pages on each of Days 13–15, 20 pages on Day 16 [3(50) + 20 = 170]

Book 5: 4 days—50 pages on each of Days 17–19, 5 pages on Day 20 [3(50) + 5 = 155]

Book 6: 1 day—50 pages on Day 21 [1(50) = 50]

Book 7: 5 days—50 pages on each of Days 22–25, 5 pages on Day 26 [4(50) + 5 = 205]

Book 8: 2 days—50 pages on Day 27, 20 pages on Day 28 [50 + 20 = 70]

At this point, Shawana has read on a total of 28 days and has finished 8 books.

The correct answer is B.

80. In Western Europe, x bicycles were sold in each of the years 1990 and 1993. The bicycle producers of Western Europe had a 42 percent share of this market in 1990 and a 33 percent share in 1993. Which of the following represents the decrease in the annual number of bicycles produced and sold in Western Europe from 1990 to 1993?

(A) 9% of $\frac{x}{100}$
(B) 14% of $\frac{x}{100}$
(C) 75% of $\frac{x}{100}$
(D) 9% of x
(E) 14% of x

Arithmetic Percents

Of the x bicycles sold in Western Europe in 1990, 42% of them were produced in Western Europe. It follows that the number of bicycles produced and sold in Western Europe in 1990 was $0.42x$. Similarly, of the x bicycles sold in Western Europe in 1993, 33% were produced in Western Europe. It follows that the number of bicycles produced and sold in Western Europe in 1993 was $0.33x$. Therefore, the decrease in the annual number of bicycles produced and sold in Western Europe from 1990 to 1993 was $0.42x - 0.33x = 0.09x$, which is 9% of x.

The correct answer is D.

81. If k is a positive integer, what is the remainder when $(k + 2)(k^3 - k)$ is divided by 6 ?

(A) 0
(B) 1
(C) 2
(D) 3
(E) 4

Algebra Properties of numbers

Since k can be any positive integer, the remainder must be the same regardless of the value of k. If $k = 2$, for example, then $(k + 2)(k^3 - k) = (2 + 2)(2^3 - 2) = (4)(6)$, which is a multiple of 6, and therefore, the remainder when divided by 6 is 0.

Alternatively, factor the given expression:

$$(k+2)(k^3-k) = (k+2)(k)(k^2-1)$$
$$= (k+2)(k)(k+1)(k-1)$$

Now, rearrange the factors in ascending order $(k-1)(k)(k+1)(k+2)$, and observe that for any positive integer k, the factors are 4 consecutive integers, two of which are even and one of which is divisible by 3. Therefore, $(k+2)(k^3-k)$ is divisible by both 2 and 3. Thus, $(k+2)(k^3-k)$ is divisible by 6 with 0 remainder.

The correct answer is A.

82. Which of the following fractions is closest to $\frac{1}{2}$?

(A) $\frac{4}{7}$
(B) $\frac{5}{9}$
(C) $\frac{6}{11}$
(D) $\frac{7}{13}$
(E) $\frac{9}{16}$

Arithmetic Fractions

Find the distance between each fraction and $\frac{1}{2}$:

$$\left|\frac{4}{7}-\frac{1}{2}\right| = \left|\frac{8}{14}-\frac{7}{14}\right| = \frac{1}{14}$$

$$\left|\frac{5}{9}-\frac{1}{2}\right| = \left|\frac{10}{18}-\frac{9}{18}\right| = \frac{1}{18}$$

$$\left|\frac{6}{11}-\frac{1}{2}\right| = \left|\frac{12}{22}-\frac{11}{22}\right| = \frac{1}{22}$$

$$\left|\frac{7}{13}-\frac{1}{2}\right| = \left|\frac{14}{26}-\frac{13}{26}\right| = \frac{1}{26}$$

$$\left|\frac{9}{16}-\frac{1}{2}\right| = \left|\frac{9}{16}-\frac{8}{16}\right| = \frac{1}{16}$$

Each distance is the reciprocal of a positive integer, the greatest of which is 26. Therefore, $\frac{1}{26}$ is the least of the distances and $\frac{7}{13}$ is the fraction closest to $\frac{1}{2}$.

Alternatively, asking which fraction is closest to $\frac{1}{2}$ is equivalent to asking which of the fractions, when doubled, is closest to 1. The fractions after doubling are $\frac{8}{7}, \frac{10}{9}, \frac{12}{11}, \frac{14}{13}$, and $\frac{18}{16} = \frac{9}{8}$. Each of these fractions can be expressed as $\frac{n+1}{n} = 1 + \frac{1}{n}$ for some integer n. Of these fractions, the one closest to 1 is the one for which $\frac{1}{n}$ is least, or in other words, the one for which n is greatest. That fraction is $\frac{14}{13}$, and therefore the closest of the original fractions to $\frac{1}{2}$ is $\left(\frac{1}{2}\right)\left(\frac{14}{13}\right) = \frac{7}{13}$.

The correct answer is D.

83. If $p \neq 0$ and $p - \frac{1-p^2}{p} = \frac{r}{p}$, then $r =$

(A) $p + 1$
(B) $2p - 1$
(C) $p^2 + 1$
(D) $2p^2 - 1$
(E) $p^2 + p - 1$

Algebra Simplifying algebraic expressions

$p - \frac{1-p^2}{p} = \frac{r}{p}$ given

$p^2 - (1-p^2) = r$ multiply both sides by p

$2p^2 - 1 = r$ combine like terms

The correct answer is D.

84. If the range of the six numbers 4, 3, 14, 7, 10, and x is 12, what is the difference between the greatest possible value of x and the least possible value of x ?

(A) 0
(B) 2
(C) 12
(D) 13
(E) 15

Arithmetic Statistics

The range of the six numbers 3, 4, 7, 10, 14, and x is 12. If x were neither the greatest nor the least of the six numbers, then the greatest and least of the six numbers would be 14 and 3. But, this cannot be possible because the range of the six numbers would be $14 - 3 = 11$ and not 12 as stated. Therefore, x must be either the greatest or the least of the six numbers. If x is the greatest of the six numbers, then 3 is the least, and $x - 3 = 12$. It follows that $x = 15$. On the other hand, if x is the least of the six numbers, then 14 is the greatest, and $14 - x = 12$. It follows that $x = 2$. Thus, there are only two possible values of x, namely 15 and 2, and so the difference between the greatest and least possible values of x is $15 - 2 = 13$.

The correct answer is D.

85. What number is 108 more than two-thirds of itself?

(A) 72
(B) 144
(C) 162
(D) 216
(E) 324

Algebra First-degree equations

Let x be the number that is 108 more than two-thirds of itself. Then, $108 + \frac{2}{3}x = x$. Solve for x as follows:

$$108 + \frac{2}{3}x = x$$

$$108 = \frac{1}{3}x$$

$$324 = x$$

The correct answer is E.

86. A doctor prescribed 18 cubic centimeters of a certain drug to a patient whose body weight was 120 pounds. If the typical dosage is 2 cubic centimeters per 15 pounds of body weight, by what percent was the prescribed dosage greater than the typical dosage?

(A) 8%
(B) 9%
(C) 11%
(D) 12.5%
(E) 14.8%

Arithmetic Percents

If the typical dosage is 2 cubic centimeters per 15 pounds of body weight, then the typical dosage for a person who weighs 120 pounds is $2\left(\frac{120}{15}\right) = 2(8) = 16$ cubic centimeters. The prescribed dosage of 18 cubic centimeters is, therefore, $\left(\left(\frac{18-16}{16}\right) \times 100\right)\%$ or 12.5% greater than the typical dosage.

The correct answer is D.

87. Company P had 15 percent more employees in December than it had in January. If Company P had 460 employees in December, how many employees did it have in January?

(A) 391
(B) 400
(C) 410
(D) 423
(E) 445

Arithmetic Percents

It is given that 460 is 115% of the number of employees in January. Therefore, the number of employees in January was

$$\frac{460}{1.15} = \frac{460}{1.15}\left(\frac{100}{100}\right) = \left(\frac{460}{115}\right)(100) = (4)(100) = 400.$$

The correct answer is B.

88. The function f is defined by $f(x) = \sqrt{x} - 10$ for all positive numbers x. If $u = f(t)$ for some positive numbers t and u, what is t in terms of u ?

(A) $\sqrt{\sqrt{u}+10}$
(B) $\left(\sqrt{u}+10\right)^2$
(C) $\sqrt{u^2+10}$
(D) $(u + 10)^2$
(E) $(u^2 + 10)^2$

Algebra Functions

The question can be answered by solving $u = \sqrt{t} - 10$ for t in terms of u. Adding 10 to both sides of this equation gives $u + 10 = \sqrt{t}$. Squaring both sides of the last equation gives $(u + 10)^2 = t$, which gives t in terms of u.

The correct answer is D.

89. A glass was filled with 10 ounces of water, and 0.01 ounce of the water evaporated each day during a 20-day period. What percent of the original amount of water evaporated during this period?

(A) 0.002%
(B) 0.02%
(C) 0.2%
(D) 2%
(E) 20%

Arithmetic Percents

Since 0.01 ounce of water evaporated each day for 20 days, a total of 20(0.01) = 0.2 ounce evaporated. Then, to find the percent of the original amount of water that evaporated, divide the amount that evaporated by the original amount and multiply by 100 to convert the decimal to a percent. Thus, $\frac{0.2}{10} \times 100 = 0.02 \times 100$ or 2%.

The correct answer is D.

90. If m and p are positive integers and $m^2 + p^2 < 100$, what is the greatest possible value of mp ?

(A) 36
(B) 42
(C) 48
(D) 49
(E) 51

Arithmetic Operations with integers

Trying various integer values for m and corresponding values of p that satisfy $m^2 + p^2 < 100$ might be the quickest way to solve this problem. First, $m < 10$ and $p < 10$; otherwise, $m^2 + p^2 < 100$ is not true.

If $m = 9$, then for $m^2 + p^2 < 100$ to be true, $p < \sqrt{100-81} = \sqrt{19}$, so $p \le 4$, and the greatest possible value for mp is (9)(4) = 36.

Similarly, if $m = 8$, then $p < \sqrt{100-64} = \sqrt{36}$, so $p \le 5$, and the greatest possible value for mp is (8)(5) = 40.

If $m = 7$, then $p < \sqrt{100-49} = \sqrt{51}$, so $p \le 7$, and the greatest possible value for mp is (7)(7) = 49.

If $m = 6$, then $p < \sqrt{100-36} = \sqrt{64}$, so $p \le 7$, and the greatest possible value for mp is (6)(7) = 42.

If $m \le 5$ and $p \le 9$, it follows that $mp \le 45$.

Thus, the greatest possible value for mp is 49.

The correct answer is D.

91. If $= \frac{x}{y} = \frac{c}{d}$ and $\frac{d}{c} = \frac{b}{a}$, which of the following must be true?

I. $\frac{y}{x} = \frac{b}{a}$

II. $\frac{x}{a} = \frac{y}{b}$

III. $\frac{y}{a} = \frac{x}{b}$

(A) I only
(B) II only
(C) I and II only
(D) I and III only
(E) I, II, and III

Algebra Ratio and proportion

Equation I is true:

$\frac{x}{y} = \frac{c}{d}$ given

$\frac{y}{x} = \frac{d}{c}$ take reciprocals

$\frac{d}{c} = \frac{b}{a}$ given

$\frac{y}{x} = \frac{b}{a}$ use last two equations

Equation II is true:

$\frac{y}{x} = \frac{b}{a}$ Equation I (shown true)

$y = \frac{bx}{a}$ multiply both sides by x

$\frac{y}{b} = \frac{x}{a}$ divide both sides by b

Equation III is false, since otherwise it would follow that:

$y = \frac{bx}{a}$ from above

$\frac{y}{a} = \frac{bx}{a^2}$ divide both sides by a

$\frac{x}{b} = \frac{bx}{a^2}$ use Equation III (assumed true)

$x = \frac{b^2x}{a^2}$ multiply both sides by b

From this it follows that Equation III will hold only if $\frac{b^2}{a^2} = 1$, which can be false. For example, if $x = a = c = 1$ and $y = b = d = 2$ (a choice of values for which $\frac{x}{y} = \frac{c}{d}$ and $\frac{d}{c} = \frac{b}{a}$ are true), then $\frac{b^2}{a^2} \neq 1$ and Equation III is $\frac{2}{1} = \frac{1}{2}$, which is false.

The correct answer is C.

92. If k is an integer and $(0.0025)(0.025)(0.00025) \times 10^k$ is an integer, what is the least possible value of k ?

(A) –12
(B) –6
(C) 0
(D) 6
(E) 12

Arithmetic Properties of numbers

Let $N = (0.0025)(0.025)(0.00025) \times 10^k$. Rewriting each of the decimals as an integer times a power of 10 gives $N = (25 \times 10^{-4})(25 \times 10^{-3})(25 \times 10^{-5}) \times 10^k = (25)^3 \times 10^{k-12}$. Since the units digit of $(25)^3$ is 5, it follows that if $k = 11$, then the tenths digit of N would be 5, and thus N would not be an integer; and if $k = 12$, then N would be $(25)^3 \times 10^0 = (25)^3$, which is an integer. Therefore, the least value of k such that N is an integer is 12.

The correct answer is E.

93. If $a(a + 2) = 24$ and $b(b + 2) = 24$, where $a \neq b$, then $a + b =$

(A) –48
(B) –2
(C) 2
(D) 46
(E) 48

Algebra Second-degree equations

$a(a + 2) = 24$ given

$a^2 + 2a = 24$ use distributive property

$a^2 + 2a - 24 = 0$ subtract 24 from both sides

$(a + 6)(a - 4) = 0$ factor

So, $a + 6 = 0$, which means that $a = -6$, or $a - 4 = 0$, which means $a = 4$. The equation with the variable b has the same solutions, and so $b = -6$ or $b = 4$.

Since $a \neq b$, then $a = -6$ and $b = 4$, which means $a + b = -6 + 4 = -2$, or $a = 4$ and $b = -6$, which means that $a + b = 4 + (-6) = -2$

The correct answer is B.

94. In a recent election, Ms. Robbins received 8,000 votes cast by independent voters, that is, voters not registered with a specific political party. She also received 10 percent of the votes cast by those voters registered with a political party. If N is the total number of votes cast in the election and 40 percent of the votes cast were cast by independent voters, which of the following represents the number of votes that Ms. Robbins received?

(A) $0.06N + 3{,}200$
(B) $0.1N + 7{,}200$
(C) $0.4N + 7{,}200$
(D) $0.1N + 8{,}000$
(E) $0.06N + 8{,}000$

Algebra Percents

If N represents the total number of votes cast and 40% of the votes cast were cast by independent voters, then 60% of the votes cast, or $0.6N$ votes, were cast by voters registered with a political party. Ms. Robbins received 10% of these, and so Ms. Robbins received $(0.10)(0.6N) = 0.06N$ votes cast by voters registered with a political party. Thus, Ms. Robbins received $0.06N$ votes cast by voters registered with a political party and 8,000 votes cast by independent voters, so she received $0.06N + 8{,}000$ votes in all.

The correct answer is E.

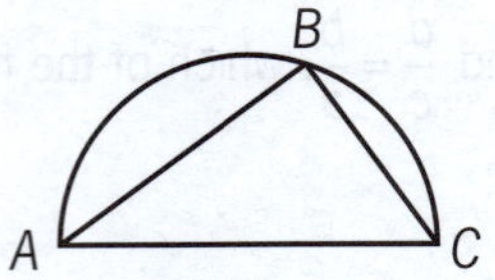

95. In the figure shown, the triangle is inscribed in the semicircle. If the length of line segment AB is 8 and the length of line segment BC is 6, what is the length of arc ABC ?

(A) 15π
(B) 12π
(C) 10π
(D) 7π
(E) 5π

Geometry Circles, triangles

Because ΔABC is inscribed in a semicircle, $\angle ABC$ is a right angle. Applying the Pythagorean theorem gives $(AB)^2 + (BC)^2 = (AC)^2$. Then substituting the given lengths, $8^2 + 6^2 = (AC)^2$, and so $(AC)^2 = 100$ and $AC = 10$. Thus, the diameter of the circle is 10, the circumference of the entire circle is 10π, and the length of arc ABC is half the circumference of the circle, or 5π.

The correct answer is E.

96. A manufacturer makes and sells 2 products, P and Q. The revenue from the sale of each unit of P is \$20.00 and the revenue from the sale of each unit of Q is \$17.00. Last year the manufacturer sold twice as many units of Q as P. What was the manufacturer's average (arithmetic mean) revenue per unit sold of these 2 products last year?

(A) \$28.50
(B) \$27.00
(C) \$19.00
(D) \$18.50
(E) \$18.00

Arithmetic Statistics

Let x represent the number of units of Product P the manufacturer sold last year. Then $2x$ represents the number of units of Product Q the manufacturer sold last year, and $x + 2x = 3x$ represents the total number of units of Products P and Q the manufacturer sold last year. The total revenue from the sale of Products P and Q was $\$(20x) + \$(17(2x)) = \$(54x)$, so the average revenue per unit sold was $\frac{\$(54x)}{3x} = \$18$.

The correct answer is E.

97. On a certain day, orangeade was made by mixing a certain amount of orange juice with an equal amount of water. On the next day, orangeade was made by mixing the same amount of orange juice with twice the amount of water. On both days, all the orangeade that was made was sold. If the revenue from selling the orangeade was the same for both days and if the orangeade was sold at \$0.60 per glass on the first day, what was the price per glass on the second day?

(A) \$0.15
(B) \$0.20
(C) \$0.30
(D) \$0.40
(E) \$0.45

Arithmetic Applied problems

The ratio of the amount of orangeade made and sold on the first day to amount of orangeade made and sold on the second day is 2:3, because the orangeade on the first day was 1 part orange juice and 1 part water, while on the second day it was 1 part orange juice and 2 parts water. Thus, the ratio of the number of glasses of orangeade made and sold on the first day to the number of glasses of orangeade made and sold on the second day is 2:3. Since the revenues for each day were equal and 2 glasses were sold on the first day for every 3 glasses that were sold on the second day, $2(\$0.60) = 3p$, where p represents the price per glass at which the orangeade was sold on the second day. Therefore, $p = \left(\frac{2}{3}\right)(\$0.60) = \$0.40$.

The correct answer is D.

98. A worker carries jugs of liquid soap from a production line to a packing area, carrying 4 jugs per trip. If the jugs are packed into cartons that hold 7 jugs each, how many jugs are needed to fill the last partially filled carton after the worker has made 17 trips?

(A) 1
(B) 2
(C) 4
(D) 5
(E) 6

Arithmetic Remainders

Carrying 4 jugs per trip, the worker carries a total of $4(17) = 68$ jugs in 17 trips. At 7 jugs per carton, these jugs will completely fill 9 cartons with 5 jugs left over since $(9)(7) + 5 = 68$. To fill the 10th carton, $7 - 5 = 2$ jugs are needed.

The correct answer is B.

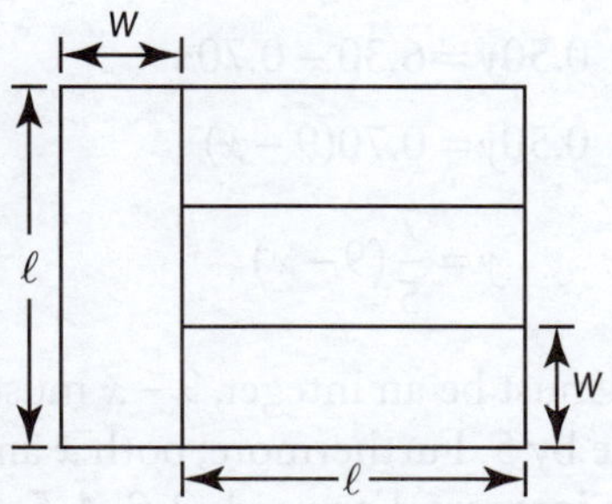

99. The figure shown above represents a modern painting that consists of four differently colored rectangles, each of which has length ℓ and width w. If the area of the painting is 4,800 square inches, what is the width, in inches, of each of the four rectangles?

(A) 15
(B) 20
(C) 25
(D) 30
(E) 40

Geometry Area

From the figure, $\ell = 3w$, and the area of the painting is $\ell(w + \ell)$. Substituting $3w$ for ℓ gives $3w(w + 3w) = 3w(4w) = 12w^2$. It is given that the area is 4,800 square inches, so $12w^2 = 4{,}800$, $w^2 = 400$, and $w = 20$.

The correct answer is B.

100. A certain fruit stand sold apples for \$0.70 each and bananas for \$0.50 each. If a customer purchased both apples and bananas from the stand for a total of \$6.30, what total number of apples and bananas did the customer purchase?

(A) 10
(B) 11
(C) 12
(D) 13
(E) 14

Algebra First-degree equations; Operations with integers

If each apple sold for \$0.70, each banana sold for \$0.50, and the total purchase price was \$6.30, then $0.70x + 0.50y = 6.30$, where x and y are positive integers representing the number of apples and bananas, respectively, the customer purchased.

$$0.70x + 0.50y = 6.30$$
$$0.50y = 6.30 - 0.70x$$
$$0.50y = 0.70(9 - x)$$
$$y = \frac{7}{5}(9 - x)$$

Since y must be an integer, $9 - x$ must be divisible by 5. Furthermore, both x and y must be positive integers. For $x = 1, 2, 3, 4, 5, 6, 7, 8$, the corresponding values of $9 - x$ are 8, 7, 6, 5, 4, 3, 2, and 1. Only one of these, 5, is divisible by 5.

Therefore, $x = 4$ and $y = \frac{7}{5}(9-4) = 7$ and the total number of apples and bananas the customer purchased is $4 + 7 = 11$.

The correct answer is B.

101. In the xy-plane, what is the slope of the line with equation $3x + 7y = 9$?

(A) $-\frac{7}{3}$
(B) $-\frac{3}{7}$
(C) $\frac{3}{7}$
(D) 3
(E) 7

Algebra Coordinate geometry

Since the given equation of the line is equivalent to $7y = -3x + 9$, or $y = -\frac{3}{7}x + \frac{9}{7}$, the slope of the line is $-\frac{3}{7}$. Alternatively, choose 2 points lying on the line and then use the slope formula for these 2 points. For example, substitute $x = 0$ in $7y = -3x + 9$ and solve for y to get $\left(0, \frac{9}{7}\right)$, substitute $y = 0$ in $7y = -3x + 9$ and solve for x to get (3,0), then use the slope formula to get $\frac{\frac{9}{7} - 0}{0 - 3} = \frac{\frac{9}{7}}{-3} = -\frac{3}{7}$.

The correct answer is B.

102. Working simultaneously and independently at an identical constant rate, 4 machines of a certain type can produce a total of x units of product P in 6 days. How many of these machines, working simultaneously and independently at this constant rate, can produce a total of 3x units of product P in 4 days?

(A) 24
(B) 18
(C) 16
(D) 12
(E) 8

Algebra Applied problems

Define a *machine day* as 1 machine working for 1 day. Then, 4 machines each working 6 days is equivalent to $(4)(6) = 24$ machine days. Thus, x units of product P were produced in 24 machine days, and $3x$ units of product P will require $(3)(24) = 72$ machine days, which is equivalent to $\frac{72}{4} = 18$ machines working independently and simultaneously for 4 days.

The correct answer is B.

103. At a certain school, the ratio of the number of second graders to the number of fourth graders is 8 to 5, and the ratio of the number of first graders to the number of second graders is 3 to 4. If the ratio of the number of third graders to the number of fourth graders is 3 to 2, what is the ratio of the number of first graders to the number of third graders?

(A) 16 to 15

(B) 9 to 5

(C) 5 to 16

(D) 5 to 4

(E) 4 to 5

Arithmetic Ratio and proportion

If F, S, T, and R represent the number of first, second, third, and fourth graders, respectively, then the given ratios are: (i) $\frac{S}{R} = \frac{8}{5}$, (ii) $\frac{F}{S} = \frac{3}{4}$, and (iii) $\frac{T}{R} = \frac{3}{2}$. The desired ratio is $\frac{F}{T}$. From (i), $S = \frac{8}{5}R$, and from (ii), $F = \frac{3}{4}S$. Combining these results, $F = \frac{3}{4}S = \frac{3}{4}\left(\frac{8}{5}R\right) = \frac{6}{5}R$. From (iii), $T = \frac{3}{2}R$. Then $\frac{F}{T} = \frac{\frac{6}{5}R}{\frac{3}{2}R} = \frac{6}{5} \cdot \frac{2}{3} = \frac{4}{5}$. So, the ratio of the number of first graders to the number of third graders is 4 to 5.

The correct answer is E.

104. The symbol Δ denotes one of the four arithmetic operations: addition, subtraction, multiplication, or division. If $6 \,\Delta\, 3 \le 3$, which of the following must be true?

I. $2 \,\Delta\, 2 = 0$

II. $2 \,\Delta\, 2 = 1$

III. $4 \,\Delta\, 2 = 2$

(A) I only

(B) II only

(C) III only

(D) I and II only

(E) I, II, and III

Arithmetic Operations with integers

If Δ represents addition, subtraction, multiplication, or division, then $6 \,\Delta\, 3$ is equal to either $6 + 3 = 9$, or $6 - 3 = 3$, or $6 \times 3 = 18$, or $6 \div 3 = 2$. Since it is given that $6 \,\Delta\, 3 \le 3$, Δ represents either subtraction or division.

Statement I is true for subtraction since $2 - 2 = 0$ but not true for division since $2 \div 2 = 1$.

Statement II is not true for subtraction since $2 - 2 = 0$ but is true for division since $2 \div 2 = 1$.

Statement III is true for subtraction since $4 - 2 = 2$ and is true for division since $4 \div 2 = 2$. Therefore, only Statement III must be true.

The correct answer is C.

105. The average distance between the Sun and a certain planet is approximately 2.3×10^{14} inches. Which of the following is closest to the average distance between the Sun and the planet, in kilometers? (1 kilometer is approximately 3.9×10^4 inches.)

(A) 7.1×10^8

(B) 5.9×10^9

(C) 1.6×10^{10}

(D) 1.6×10^{11}

(E) 5.9×10^{11}

Arithmetic Measurement conversion

Convert to kilometers and then estimate.

$$\left(2.3\times10^{14}\text{ in}\right)\left(\frac{1\text{ km}}{3.9\times10^{4}\text{ in}}\right) = \frac{2.3\times10^{14}}{3.9\times10^{4}}\text{km}$$

$$= \frac{2.3}{3.9}\times10^{14-4}\text{km}$$

$$\approx \frac{2}{4}\times10^{10}$$

$$= 0.5\times10^{10}$$

$$= 5\times10^{9}$$

The correct answer is B.

106. If $mn \neq 0$ and 25 percent of n equals $37\frac{1}{2}$ percent of m, what is the value of $\frac{12n}{m}$?

(A) 18
(B) $\frac{32}{3}$
(C) 8
(D) 3
(E) $\frac{9}{8}$

Algebra Percents; First-degree equations

It is given that $(25\%)n = (37.5\%)m$, or $0.25n = 0.375m$. The value of $\frac{12n}{m}$ can be found by first finding the value of $\frac{n}{m}$ and then multiplying the result by 12. Doing this gives $\frac{12n}{m} = \left(\frac{0.375}{0.25}\right)(12) = 18$. Alternatively, the numbers involved allow for a series of simple equation transformations to be carried out, such as the following:

$0.25n = 0.375m$	given
$25n = 37.5m$	multiply both sides by 100
$50n = 75m$	multiply both sides by 2
$2n = 3m$	divide both sides by 25
$12n = 18m$	multiply both sides by 6
$\frac{12n}{m} = 18$	divide both sides by m

The correct answer is A.

107. In the coordinate plane, a circle has center (2,−3) and passes through the point (5,0). What is the area of the circle?

(A) 3π
(B) $3\sqrt{2}\pi$
(C) $3\sqrt{3}\pi$
(D) 9π
(E) 18π

Geometry Coordinate geometry; Circles; Area

The area of a circle is given by πr^2, where r is the radius of the circle. The value of r^2 is the square of the distance from the center to a point of the circle. Using the distance formula, $r^2 = (2-5)^2 + (-3-0)^2 = 9 + 9 = 18$. Therefore, the area of the circle is 18π.

The correct answer is E.

108. Last year Joe grew 1 inch and Sally grew 200 percent more than Joe grew. How many inches did Sally grow last year?

(A) 0
(B) 1
(C) 2
(D) 3
(E) 4

Arithmetic Percents

Joe grew 1 inch last year and Sally grew 200 percent more than Joe grew, so Sally grew 1 inch plus 200 percent of 1 inch or $1 + 2(1) = 3$ inches.

The correct answer is D.

109. The cost C, in dollars, to remove p percent of a certain pollutant from a pond is estimated by using the formula $C = \frac{100{,}000p}{100-p}$. According to this estimate, how much more would it cost to remove 90 percent of the pollutant from the pond than it would cost to remove 80 percent of the pollutant?

(A) \$500,000
(B) \$100,000
(C) \$50,000
(D) \$10,000
(E) \$5,000

Algebra; Arithmetic Simplifying algebraic expressions; Operations on rational numbers

Removing 90% of the pollutant from the pond would cost $\frac{(100{,}000)(90)}{100-90} = \frac{9{,}000{,}000}{10} =$ 900,000 dollars, and removing 80% of the pollutant would cost $\frac{(100{,}000)(80)}{100-80} = \frac{8{,}000{,}000}{20} = 400{,}000$ dollars. The difference is, then, \$900,000 − \$400,000 = \$500,000.

The correct answer is A.

110. If $xy \neq 0$ and $x^2y^2 - xy = 6$, which of the following could be y in terms of x?

I. $\frac{1}{2x}$

II. $-\frac{2}{x}$

III. $\frac{3}{x}$

(A) I only
(B) II only
(C) I and II
(D) I and III
(E) II and III

Algebra Second-degree equations

$x^2y^2 - xy = 6$ given

$x^2y^2 - xy - 6 = 0$ subtract 6 from both sides

$(xy + 2)(xy - 3) = 0$ factor

So, $xy + 2 = 0$, which means $xy = -2$ and $y = -\frac{2}{x}$, or $xy - 3 = 0$, which means that $xy = 3$ and $y = \frac{3}{x}$. Thus, y in terms of x could be given by the expressions in II or III.

The correct answer is E.

111. At a certain instant in time, the number of cars, N, traveling on a portion of a certain highway can be estimated by the formula

$$N = \frac{20Ld}{600 + s^2}$$

where L is the number of lanes in the same direction, d is the length of the portion of the highway, in feet, and s is the average speed of the cars, in miles per hour. Based on the formula, what is the estimated number of cars traveling on a $\frac{1}{2}$- mile portion of the highway if the highway has 2 lanes in the same direction and the average speed of the cars is 40 miles per hour? (5,280 feet = 1 mile)

(A) 155
(B) 96
(C) 80
(D) 48
(E) 24

Algebra Simplifying algebraic expressions

Substitute $L = 2$, $d = \frac{1}{2}(5{,}280)$, $s = 40$ into the given formula and calculate the value for N.

$$N = \frac{20(2)\left(\frac{1}{2}\right)(5{,}280)}{600 + 40^2}$$

$$= \frac{20(5{,}280)}{600 + 1{,}600}$$

$$= \frac{20(5{,}280)}{2{,}200}$$

$$= \frac{2(528)}{22}$$

$$= \frac{528}{11}$$

$$= 48$$

The correct answer is D.

112. $\sqrt{4.8 \times 10^9}$ is closest in value to

(A) 2,200
(B) 70,000
(C) 220,000
(D) 7,000,000
(E) 22,000,000

Arithmetic Operations on radical expressions

$\sqrt{4.8 \times \sqrt{10^9}} = \sqrt{48 \times 10^8}$ substitute 48×10^8 for 4.8×10^9

$= \sqrt{48} \times \sqrt{10^8}$ $\sqrt{ab} = \sqrt{a} \times \sqrt{b}$

$\approx \sqrt{49} \times \sqrt{10^8}$ $49 \approx 48$

and then

$\sqrt{49} \times \sqrt{10^8} = 7 \times 10^4$ $\sqrt{49} = 7$, $\sqrt{10^8} = \sqrt{(10^4)^2} = 10^4$

$= 70{,}000$

The correct answer is B.

113. Three printing presses, R, S, and T, working together at their respective constant rates, can do a certain printing job in 4 hours. S and T, working together at their respective constant rates, can do the same job in 5 hours. How many hours would it take R, working alone at its constant rate, to do the same job?

(A) 8
(B) 10
(C) 12
(D) 15
(E) 20

Algebra Applied problems

Let r be the portion of the job that printing press R, working alone, completes in 1 hour; and let s and t be the corresponding portions, respectively, for printing press S and printing press T. From the given information, it follows that $r + s + t = \frac{1}{4}$ and $s + t = \frac{1}{5}$. Subtracting these two equations gives $r = \frac{1}{4} - \frac{1}{5} = \frac{1}{20}$. It follows that printing press R, working alone, will complete $\frac{1}{20}$ of the job in 1 hour, and therefore printing press R, working alone, will complete the job in 20 hours.

The correct answer is E.

114. For a party, three solid cheese balls with diameters of 2 inches, 4 inches, and 6 inches, respectively, were combined to form a single cheese ball. What was the approximate diameter, in inches, of the new cheese ball? (The volume of a sphere is $\frac{4}{3}\pi r^3$, where r is the radius.)

(A) 12
(B) 16
(C) $\sqrt[3]{16}$
(D) $3\sqrt[3]{8}$
(E) $2\sqrt[3]{36}$

Geometry Volume

Since the diameters of the cheese balls are given as 2 inches, 4 inches, and 6 inches, the radii of the cheese balls are 1 inch, 2 inches, and 3 inches, respectively. Using $V = \frac{4}{3}\pi r^3$, the combined volume of the 3 cheese balls is $\frac{4}{3}\pi\left(1^3 + 2^3 + 3^3\right)$ or $\frac{4}{3}\pi(36)$ cubic inches.

Thus, if R represents the radius of the new cheese ball, then the volume of the new cheese ball is $\frac{4}{3}\pi R^3 = \frac{4}{3}\pi(36)$ and $R^3 = 36$, from which it follows that $R = \sqrt[3]{36}$ inches. Therefore, the diameter of the new cheese ball is $2R = 2\sqrt[3]{36}$ inches.

The correct answer is E.

115. The sum of all the integers k such that $-26 < k < 24$ is

(A) 0
(B) −2
(C) −25
(D) −49
(E) −51

Arithmetic Operations on integers

In the sum of all integers k such that $-26 < k < 24$, the positive integers from 1 through 23 can be paired with the negative integers from −1 through −23. The sum of these pairs is 0 because $a + (-a) = 0$ for all integers a. Therefore, the sum of all integers k such that $-26 < k < 24$ is $-25 + (-24) + (23)(0) = -49$.

The correct answer is D.

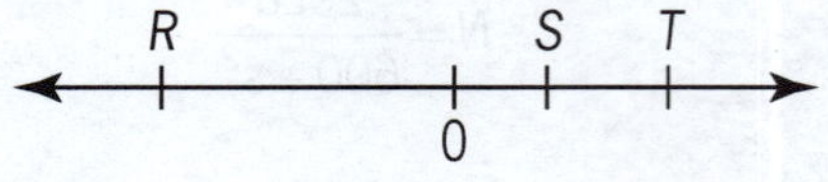

116. The number line shown contains three points R, S, and T, whose coordinates have absolute values r, s, and t, respectively. Which of the following equals the average (arithmetic mean) of the coordinates of the points R, S, and T?

(A) s
(B) $s + t - r$
(C) $\frac{r - s - t}{3}$
(D) $\frac{r + s + t}{3}$
(E) $\frac{s + t - r}{3}$

Arithmetic Absolute value; Number line

Because point R is to the left of 0 on the number line, the coordinate of R is negative. It is given that r is the absolute value of the coordinate of R and so the coordinate of R is $-r$. Because points S and T are to the right of 0 on the number line, their coordinates are positive. It is given that s and t are the absolute values of the coordinates of S and T, and so the coordinates of S and T are s and t. The arithmetic mean of the coordinates of R, S, and T is $\dfrac{s+t-r}{3}$.

The correct answer is E.

117. Mark and Ann together were allocated n boxes of cookies to sell for a club project. Mark sold 10 boxes less than n and Ann sold 2 boxes less than n. If Mark and Ann have each sold at least one box of cookies, but together they have sold less than n boxes, what is the value of n ?

(A) 11
(B) 12
(C) 13
(D) 14
(E) 15

Algebra Inequalities

Mark sold $n-10$ boxes and Ann sold $n-2$ boxes. Because each person sold at least one box, it follows that $n-10 \geq 1$ and $n-2 \geq 1$, which implies that $n \geq 11$. On the other hand, together they sold less than n boxes, so $(n-10)+(n-2) < n$, which implies that $n < 12$. Therefore, n is an integer such that $n \geq 11$ and $n < 12$, which implies that $n = 11$.

The correct answer is A.

118. A certain high school has 5,000 students. Of these students, x are taking music, y are taking art, and z are taking both music and art. How many students are taking neither music nor art?

(A) $5{,}000 - z$
(B) $5{,}000 - x - y$
(C) $5{,}000 - x + z$
(D) $5{,}000 - x - y - z$
(E) $5{,}000 - x - y + z$

Algebra Sets

Since x students are taking music, y students are taking art, and z students are taking both music and art, the number of students taking only music is $x - z$, and the number of students taking only art is $y - z$, as illustrated by the following Venn diagram.

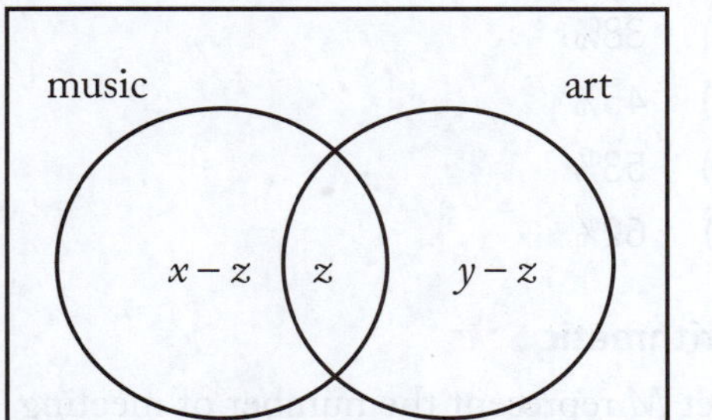

Therefore, the number of students taking neither music nor art is $5{,}000 - [(x-z)+z+(y-z)] = 5{,}000 - x - y + z$.

The correct answer is E.

119. Yesterday's closing prices of 2,420 different stocks listed on a certain stock exchange were all different from today's closing prices. The number of stocks that closed at a higher price today than yesterday was 20 percent greater than the number that closed at a lower price. How many of the stocks closed at a higher price today than yesterday?

(A) 484
(B) 726
(C) 1,100
(D) 1,320
(E) 1,694

Arithmetic Percents

Let n be the number of stocks that closed at a lower price today than yesterday. Then $1.2n$ is the number of stocks that closed at a higher price today than yesterday, and $1.2n$ is the value asked for. Because the total number of stocks is 2,420, it follows that $n + 1.2n = 2{,}420$, or $2.2n = 2{,}420$.

Therefore, $n = \dfrac{2{,}420}{2.2} = 1{,}100$, and hence

$1.2n = (1.2)(1{,}100) = 1{,}320$.

The correct answer is D.

120. Each person who attended a company meeting was either a stockholder in the company, an employee of the company, or both. If 62 percent of those who attended the meeting were stockholders and 47 percent were employees, what percent were stockholders who were not employees?

(A) 34%

(B) 38%

(C) 45%

(D) 53%

(E) 62%

Arithmetic Sets

Let M represent the number of meeting attendees. Then, since 62% of M or $0.62M$ were stockholders and 47% of M or $0.47M$ were employees, it follows that $0.62M + 0.47M = 1.09M$ were either stockholders, employees, or both. Since $1.09M$ exceeds M, the excess $1.09M - M = 0.09M$ must be the number of attendees who were both stockholders and employees, leaving the rest $0.62M - 0.09M = 0.53M$, or 53%, of the meeting attendees to be stockholders but not employees.

The correct answer is D.

121. A gym class can be divided into 8 teams with an equal number of players on each team or into 12 teams with an equal number of players on each team. What is the lowest possible number of students in the class?

(A) 20

(B) 24

(C) 36

(D) 48

(E) 96

Arithmetic Properties of numbers

The lowest value that can be divided evenly by 8 and 12 is their least common multiple (LCM). Since $8 = 2^3$ and $12 = 2^2(3)$, the LCM is $2^3(3) = 24$.

The correct answer is B.

Accounts	Amount Budgeted	Amount Spent
Payroll	$110,000	$117,000
Taxes	40,000	42,000
Insurance	2,500	2,340

122. The table shows the amount budgeted and the amount spent for each of three accounts in a certain company. For which of these accounts did the amount spent differ from the amount budgeted by more than 6 percent of the amount budgeted?

(A) Payroll only

(B) Taxes only

(C) Insurance only

(D) Payroll and Insurance

(E) Taxes and Insurance

Arithmetic Percents

For Payroll, 6% of the budgeted amount is (0.06)($110,000) = $6,600. Since $117,000 – $110,000 = $7,000 > $6,600, the amount spent differed from the amount budgeted by more than 6%.

For Taxes, 6% of the budgeted amount is (0.06)($40,000) = $2,400. Since $42,000 – $40,000 = $2,000 < $2,400, the amount spent did not differ from the amount budgeted by more than 6%.

For Insurance, 6% of the budgeted amount is (0.06)($2,500) = $150. Since $2,500 – $2,340 = $160 > $150, the amount spent differed from the amount budgeted by more than 6%.

Thus, the amount spent differed from the amount budgeted by more than 6% for Payroll and Insurance.

The correct answer is D.

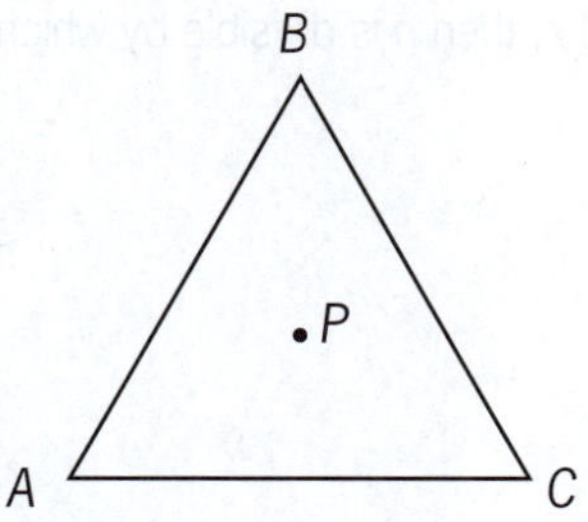

123. In the figure above, triangle *ABC* is equilateral, and point *P* is equidistant from vertices *A*, *B*, and *C*. If triangle *ABC* is rotated clockwise about point *P*, what is the minimum number of degrees the triangle must be rotated so that point *B* will be in the position where point *A* is now?

(A) 60
(B) 120
(C) 180
(D) 240
(E) 270

Geometry Angles

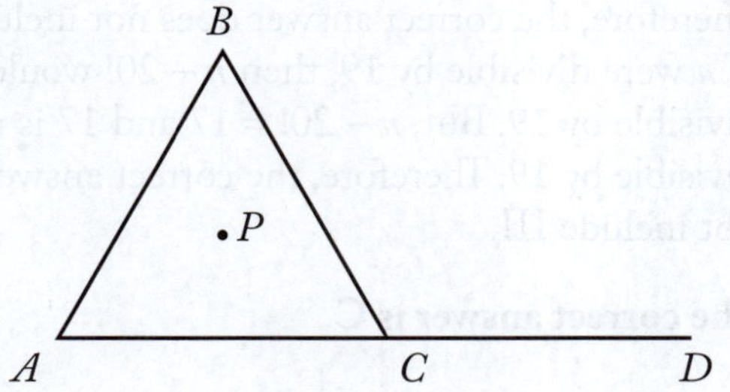

Since ΔABC is equilateral, the measure of $\angle ACB$ is 60°. Therefore, the measure of $\angle BCD$ is $180° - 60° = 120°$. Rotating the figure clockwise about point *P* through an angle of 120° will produce the figure shown below.

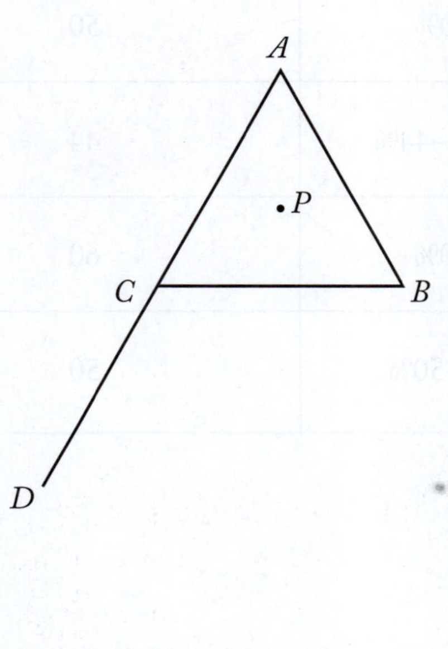

Then rotating this figure clockwise about point *P* through an angle of 120° will produce the figure shown below.

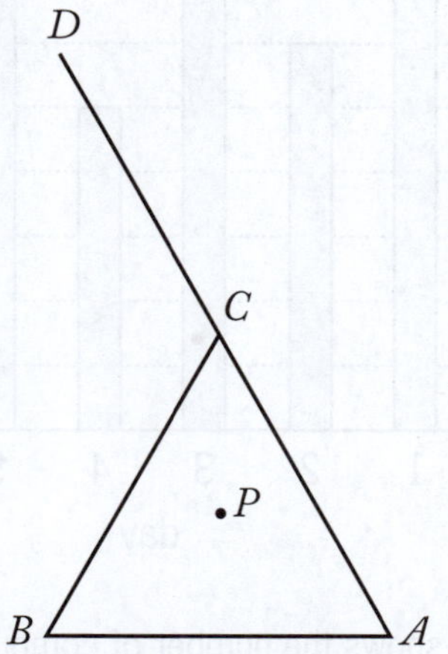

In this figure, point *B* is in the position where point *A* was in the original figure. The triangle was rotated clockwise about point *P* through $120° + 120° = 240°$.

The correct answer is D.

124. At least $\frac{2}{3}$ of the 40 members of a committee must vote in favor of a resolution for it to pass. What is the greatest number of members who could vote against the resolution and still have it pass?

(A) 19
(B) 17
(C) 16
(D) 14
(E) 13

Arithmetic Operations on rational numbers

If at least $\frac{2}{3}$ of the members must vote in favor of a resolution, then no more than $\frac{1}{3}$ of the members can be voting against it. On this 40-member committee, $\frac{1}{3}(40) = 13\frac{1}{3}$, which means that no more than 13 members can vote against the resolution and still have it pass.

The correct answer is E.

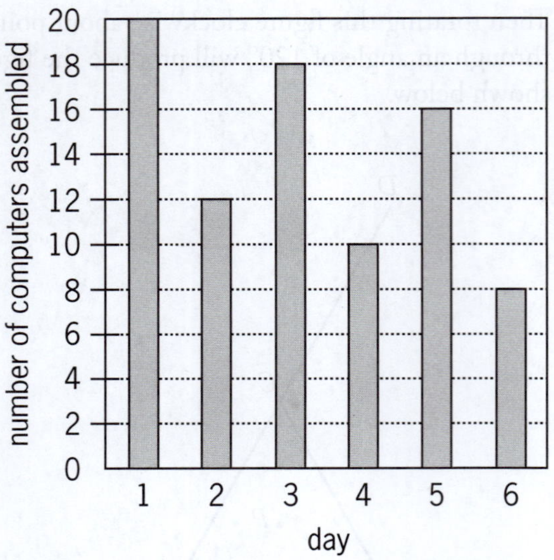

125. The graph shows the number of computers assembled during each of 6 consecutive days. From what day to the next day was the percent change in the number of computers assembled the greatest in magnitude?

(A) From Day 1 to Day 2
(B) From Day 2 to Day 3
(C) From Day 3 to Day 4
(D) From Day 4 to Day 5
(E) From Day 5 to Day 6

Arithmetic Percents

The following table shows the percent change from each day to the next and the magnitude of the percent change.

Time period	Percent change	Magnitude of percent change
From Day 1 to Day 2	$\left(\frac{12-20}{20}\times 100\right)\% = \left(-\frac{8}{20}\times 100\right)\% = -40\%$	40
From Day 2 to Day 3	$\left(\frac{18-12}{12}\times 100\right)\% = \left(\frac{6}{12}\times 100\right)\% = 50\%$	50
From Day 3 to Day 4	$\left(\frac{10-18}{18}\times 100\right)\% = \left(-\frac{8}{18}\times 100\right)\% \approx -44\%$	44
From Day 4 to Day 5	$\left(\frac{16-10}{10}\times 100\right)\% = \left(\frac{6}{10}\times 100\right)\% = 60\%$	60
From Day 5 to Day 6	$\left(\frac{8-16}{16}\times 100\right)\% = \left(-\frac{8}{16}\times 100\right)\% = -50\%$	50

The correct answer is D.

126. If $n = 20! + 17$, then n is divisible by which of the following?

I. 15
II. 17
III. 19

(A) None
(B) I only
(C) II only
(D) I and II
(E) II and III

Arithmetic Properties of numbers

Because 20! is the product of all integers from 1 through 20, it follows that 20! is divisible by each integer from 1 through 20. In particular, 20! is divisible by each of the integers 15, 17, and 19. Since 20! and 17 are both divisible by 17, their sum is divisible by 17, and hence the correct answer will include II. If n were divisible by 15, then $n - 20!$ would be divisible by 15. But, $n - 20! = 17$ and 17 is not divisible by 15. Therefore, the correct answer does not include I. If n were divisible by 19, then $n - 20!$ would be divisible by 19. But, $n - 20! = 17$ and 17 is not divisible by 19. Therefore, the correct answer does not include III.

The correct answer is C.

127. The product of two negative numbers is 160. If the lesser of the two numbers is 4 less than twice the greater, what is the greater number?

(A) −20

(B) −16

(C) −10

(D) −8

(E) −4

Algebra Second-degree equations

Let x and y be the two numbers, where x is the lesser of the two numbers and y is the number desired. From the given information it follows that $xy = 160$ and $x = 2y - 4$, from which it follows that $(2y - 4)y = 160$. Dividing both sides of the last equation by 2 gives $(y - 2)y = 80$. Thus, 80 is to be written as a product of two negative numbers, one that is 2 less than the other. Trying simple factorizations of 80 quickly leads to the value of y: $(-40)(-2) = 80$, $(-20)(-4) = 80$, $(-10)(-8) = 80$. Therefore, $y = -8$. Note that because −8 is one of the answer choices, it is not necessary to ensure there are no other negative solutions to the equation $(y - 2)y = 80$.

Alternatively, $(y - 2)y = 80$ can be written as $y^2 - 2y - 80 = 0$. Factoring the left side gives $(y + 8)(y - 10) = 0$, and $y = -8$ is the only negative solution.

The correct answer is D.

128. According to a certain estimate, the depth $N(t)$, in centimeters, of the water in a certain tank at t hours past 2:00 in the morning is given by $N(t) = -20(t - 5)^2 + 500$ for $0 \le t \le 10$. According to this estimate, at what time in the morning does the depth of the water in the tank reach its maximum?

(A) 5:30

(B) 7:00

(C) 7:30

(D) 8:00

(E) 9:00

Algebra Functions

When $t = 5$, the value of $-20(t - 5)^2 + 500$ is 500. For all values of t between 0 and 10, inclusive, except $t = 5$, the value of $-20(t - 5)^2$ is negative and $-20(t - 5)^2 + 500 < 500$. Therefore, the tank reaches its maximum depth 5 hours after 2:00 in the morning, which is 7:00 in the morning.

The correct answer is B.

129. After driving to a riverfront parking lot, Bob plans to run south along the river, turn around, and return to the parking lot, running north along the same path. After running 3.25 miles south, he decides to run for only 50 minutes more. If Bob runs at a constant rate of 8 minutes per mile, how many miles farther south can he run and still be able to return to the parking lot in 50 minutes?

(A) 1.5

(B) 2.25

(C) 3.0

(D) 3.25

(E) 4.75

Algebra Applied problems

After running 3.25 miles south, Bob has been running for $(3.25\text{ miles})\left(8\dfrac{\text{minutes}}{\text{mile}}\right) = 26$ minutes. Thus, if t is the number of additional minutes that Bob can run south before turning around, then the number of minutes that Bob will run north, after turning around, will be $t + 26$. Since Bob will be running a total of 50 minutes after the initial 26 minutes of running, it follows that $t + (t + 26) = 50$, or $t = 12$. Therefore, Bob can run south an additional $\dfrac{12\text{ minutes}}{8\dfrac{\text{minutes}}{\text{mile}}} = 1.5$ miles before turning around.

The correct answer is A.

130. Alex deposited x dollars into a new account that earned 8 percent annual interest, compounded annually. One year later Alex deposited an additional x dollars into the account. If there were no other transactions and if the account contained w dollars at the end of two years, which of the following expresses x in terms of w?

(A) $\frac{w}{1+1.08}$

(B) $\frac{w}{1.08+1.16}$

(C) $\frac{w}{1.16+1.24}$

(D) $\frac{w}{1.08+(1.08)^2}$

(E) $\frac{w}{(1.08)^2+(1.08)^3}$

Algebra Applied problems

At the end of the first year, the value of Alex's initial investment was $x(1.08)$ dollars, and after he deposited an additional x dollars into the account, its value was $[x(1.08) + x]$ dollars. At the end of the second year, the value was w dollars, where $w = [x(1.08) + x](1.08) = x(1.08)^2 + x(1.08) = x[(1.08)^2 + 1.08]$. Thus, $x = \frac{w}{1.08+(1.08)^2}$.

The correct answer is D.

131. M is the sum of the reciprocals of the consecutive integers from 201 to 300, inclusive. Which of the following is true?

(A) $\frac{1}{3}<M<\frac{1}{2}$

(B) $\frac{1}{5}<M<\frac{1}{3}$

(C) $\frac{1}{7}<M<\frac{1}{5}$

(D) $\frac{1}{9}<M<\frac{1}{7}$

(E) $\frac{1}{12}<M<\frac{1}{9}$

Arithmetic Estimation

Because $\frac{1}{300}$ is less than each of the 99 numbers $\frac{1}{201}, \frac{1}{202}, \ldots, \frac{1}{299}$, it follows that $\frac{1}{300}+\frac{1}{300}+\cdots+\frac{1}{300}$ (the sum of 99 identical values) is less than $\frac{1}{201}+\frac{1}{202}+\cdots+\frac{1}{299}$. Therefore, adding $\frac{1}{300}$ to both sides of this last inequality, it follows that $\frac{1}{300}+\frac{1}{300}+\cdots+\frac{1}{300}$ (the sum of 100 identical values) is less than $\frac{1}{201}+\frac{1}{202}+\cdots+\frac{1}{299}+\frac{1}{300}=M$. Hence, $(100)\left(\frac{1}{300}\right)<M$ or $\frac{1}{3}<M$. Also, because $\frac{1}{200}$ is greater than each of the 100 numbers $\frac{1}{201}, \frac{1}{202}, \ldots, \frac{1}{300}$, it follows that $\frac{1}{200}+\frac{1}{200}+\cdots+\frac{1}{200}$ (the sum of 100 identical values) is greater than $\frac{1}{201}+\frac{1}{202}+\cdots+\frac{1}{300}$. Hence, $(100)\left(\frac{1}{200}\right)>M$ or $\frac{1}{2}>M$. From $\frac{1}{3}<M$ and $\frac{1}{2}>M$, it follows that $\frac{1}{3}<M<\frac{1}{2}$.

The correct answer is A.

132. Working simultaneously at their respective constant rates, Machines A and B produce 800 nails in x hours. Working alone at its constant rate, Machine A produces 800 nails in y hours. In terms of x and y, how many hours does it take Machine B, working alone at its constant rate, to produce 800 nails?

(A) $\frac{x}{x+y}$

(B) $\frac{y}{x+y}$

(C) $\frac{xy}{x+y}$

(D) $\frac{xy}{x-y}$

(E) $\frac{xy}{y-x}$

Algebra Applied problems

Let R_A and R_B be the constant rates, in nails per hour, at which Machines A and B work, respectively. Then it follows from the given information that $R_A + R_B = \frac{800}{x}$ and $R_A = \frac{800}{y}$. Hence, $\frac{800}{y} + R_B = \frac{800}{x}$, or

$$R_B = \frac{800}{x} - \frac{800}{y} = 800\left(\frac{1}{x} - \frac{1}{y}\right) = 800\left(\frac{y-x}{xy}\right).$$

Therefore, the time, in hours, it would take Machine B to produce 800 nails is given by

$$\frac{800}{800\left(\frac{y-x}{xy}\right)} = \frac{xy}{y-x}.$$

The correct answer is E.

133. In the Johnsons' monthly budget, the dollar amounts allocated to household expenses, food, and miscellaneous items are in the ratio 5:2:1, respectively. If the total amount allocated to these three categories is $1,800, what is the amount allocated to food?

(A) $900
(B) $720
(C) $675
(D) $450
(E) $225

Algebra Applied problems

Since the ratio is 5:2:1, let $5x$ be the money allocated to household expenses, $2x$ be the money allocated to food, and $1x$ be the money allocated to miscellaneous items. The given information can then be expressed in the following equation and solved for x.

$$5x + 2x + 1x = \$1,800$$
$$8x = \$1,800 \quad \text{combine like terms}$$
$$x = \$225 \quad \text{divide both sides by 8}$$

The money allocated to food is $2x = 2(\$225) = \$450$.

The correct answer is D.

	Number of Marbles in Each of Three Bags	Percent of Marbles in Each Bag That Are Blue (to the nearest tenth)
Bag P	37	10.8%
Bag Q	x	66.7%
Bag R	32	50.0%

134. If $\frac{1}{3}$ of the total number of marbles in the three bags listed in the table above are blue, how many marbles are there in bag Q?

(A) 5
(B) 9
(C) 12
(D) 23
(E) 46

Algebra Percents

What is the value of x, the number of marbles in bag Q? From the given information and rounded to the nearest integer, bag P has $(37)(0.108) = 4$ blue marbles, bag Q has $(x)(0.667) = \frac{2}{3}x$ blue marbles, and bag R has $(32)(0.5) = 16$ blue marbles. Therefore, the total number of blue marbles is equal to $4 + \frac{2}{3}x + 16 = 20 + \frac{2}{3}x$. It is given that $\frac{1}{3}$ of the total number of marbles are blue, so the total number of blue marbles is also equal to $\frac{1}{3}(37 + x + 32) = \frac{1}{3}x + 23$. It follows that

$$20 + \frac{2}{3}x = \frac{1}{3}x + 23, \text{ or } \frac{1}{3}x = 3, \text{ or } x = 9.$$

The correct answer is B.

135. $\dfrac{(0.0036)(2.8)}{(0.04)(0.1)(0.003)} =$

(A) 840.0
(B) 84.0
(C) 8.4
(D) 0.84
(E) 0.084

Arithmetic Operations with rational numbers

To make the calculations less tedious, convert the decimals to whole numbers times powers of 10 as follows:

$$\frac{(0.0036)(2.8)}{(0.04)(0.1)(0.003)}$$
$$=\frac{(36\times10^{-4})(28\times10^{-1})}{(4\times10^{-2})(1\times10^{-1})(3\times10^{-3})}$$
$$=\frac{(36)(28)}{(4)(1)(3)}\times10^{(-4-1)-(-2-1-3)}$$
$$=\frac{(36)(28)}{(4)(1)(3)}\times10^{-5-(-6)}$$
$$=\frac{(36)(28)}{(4)(1)(3)}\times10^{-5+6}$$
$$=\left(\frac{36}{3}\right)\left(\frac{28}{4}\right)\times10^{-5+6}$$
$$=(12)(7)\times10^{1}$$
$$=84\times10$$
$$=840$$

The correct answer is A.

136. If n is an integer greater than 6, which of the following must be divisible by 3 ?

(A) $n(n+1)(n-4)$
(B) $n(n+2)(n-1)$
(C) $n(n+3)(n-5)$
(D) $n(n+4)(n-2)$
(E) $n(n+5)(n-6)$

Arithmetic Properties of numbers

The easiest and quickest way to do this problem is to choose an integer greater than 6, such as 7, and eliminate answer choices in which the value of the expression is not divisible by 3:

A $7(7+1)(7-4)=(7)(8)(3)$, which is divisible by 3, so A cannot be eliminated.

B $7(7+2)(7-1)=(7)(9)(6)$, which is divisible by 3, so B cannot be eliminated.

C $7(7+3)(7-5)=(7)(10)(2)$, which is not divisible by 3, so C can be eliminated.

D $7(7+4)(7-2)=(7)(11)(5)$, which is not divisible by 3, so D can be eliminated.

E $7(7+5)(7-6)=(7)(12)(1)$, which is divisible by 3, so E cannot be eliminated.

Choose another integer greater than 6, such as 8, and test the remaining answer choices:

A $8(8+1)(8-4)=(8)(9)(4)$, which is divisible by 3, so A cannot be eliminated.

B $8(8+2)(8-1)=(8)(10)(7)$, which is not divisible by 3, so B can be eliminated.

E $8(8+5)(8-6)=(8)(13)(2)$, which is not divisible by 3, so E can be eliminated.

Thus, A is the only answer choice that has not been eliminated.

For the more mathematically inclined, if n is divisible by 3, then the expression in each answer choice is divisible by 3. Assume, then, that n is not divisible by 3. If the remainder when n is divided by 3 is 1, then $n = 3q + 1$ for some integer q. All of the expressions $n - 4$, $n - 1$, $n + 2$, and $n + 5$ are divisible by 3 [i.e., $n - 4 = 3q - 3 = 3(q - 1)$, $n - 1 = 3q$, $n + 2 = 3q + 3 = 3(q + 1)$, $n + 5 = 3q + 6 = 3(q + 2)$], and none of the expressions $n - 6$, $n - 5$, $n - 2$, $n + 1$, $n + 3$, and $n + 4$ is divisible by 3. Therefore, if the remainder when n is divided by 3 is 1, only the expressions in answer choices A, B, and E are divisible by 3. On the other hand, if the remainder when n is divided by 3 is 2, then $n = 3q + 2$ for some integer q. All of the expressions $n - 5$, $n - 2$, $n + 1$, and $n + 4$ are divisible by 3 [i.e., $n - 5 = 3q - 3 = 3(q - 1)$, $n - 2 = 3q$, $n + 1 = 3q + 3 = 3(q + 1)$, $n + 4 = 3q + 6 = 3(q + 2)$], and none of the expressions $n - 6$, $n - 4$, $n - 1$, $n + 2$, $n + 3$, and $n + 5$ is divisible by 3. Therefore, if the remainder when n is divided by 3 is 2, only the expressions in answer choices A, C, and D are divisible by 3. Only the expression in answer choice A is divisible by 3 regardless of whether n is divisible by 3, has a remainder of 1 when divided by 3, or has a remainder of 2 when divided by 3.

The correct answer is A.

Age Category (in years)	Number of Employees
Less than 20	29
20–29	58
30–39	36
40–49	21
50–59	10
60–69	5
70 and over	2

137. The table above gives the age categories of the 161 employees at Company X and the number of employees in each category. According to the table, if *m* is the median age, in years, of the employees at Company X, then *m* must satisfy which of the following?

(A) $20 \le m \le 29$
(B) $25 \le m \le 34$
(C) $30 \le m \le 39$
(D) $35 \le m \le 44$
(E) $40 \le m \le 49$

Arithmetic Statistics

The median of 161 ages is the 81st age when the ages are listed in order. Since 29 of the ages are less than 20, the median age must be greater than or equal to 20. Since 58 of the ages are between 20 and 29, a total of $29 + 58 = 87$ of the ages are less than or equal to 29, and thus the median age is less than or equal to 29. Therefore, the median age is greater than or equal to 20 and less than or equal to 29.

The correct answer is A.

138. If *x* and *y* are positive numbers such that $x + y = 1$, which of the following could be the value of $100x + 200y$?

I. 80
II. 140
III. 199

(A) II only
(B) III only
(C) I and II
(D) I and III
(E) II and III

Algebra Simultaneous equations; Inequalities

Since $x + y = 1$, then $y = 1 - x$ and $100x + 200y$ can be expressed as $100x + 200(1 - x) = 200 - 100x$. Test each value.

I. If $200 - 100x = 80$, then $x = \frac{200-80}{100} = 1.2$ and $y = 1 - 1.2 = -0.2$. Since *y* must be positive, 80 cannot be a value of $100x + 200y$.

II. If $200 - 100x = 140$, then $x = \frac{200-140}{100} = 0.6$ and $y = 1 - 0.6 = 0.4$, so 140 can be a value of $100x + 200y$.

III. If $200 - 100x = 199$, then $x = \frac{200-199}{100} = 0.01$ and $y = 1 - 0.01 = 0.99$, so 199 can be a value of $100x + 200y$.

The correct answer is E.

139. If *X* is the hundredths digit in the decimal 0.1*X* and if *Y* is the thousandths digit in the decimal 0.02*Y*, where *X* and *Y* are nonzero digits, which of the following is closest to the greatest possible value of $\frac{0.1X}{0.02Y}$?

(A) 4
(B) 5
(C) 6
(D) 9
(E) 10

Arithmetic Operations with decimals; Place value

The greatest possible value of $\frac{0.1X}{0.02Y}$ will occur when 0.1*X* has the greatest possible value and 0.02*Y* has the least possible value. Since *X* and *Y* are nonzero digits, this means than *X* must be 9 and *Y* must be 1. The greatest possible value of $\frac{0.1X}{0.02Y}$ is then $\frac{0.19}{0.021} \approx 9.05$, which is closest to 9.

The correct answer is D.

140. Clarissa will create her summer reading list by randomly choosing 4 books from the 10 books approved for summer reading. She will list the books in the order in which they are chosen. How many different lists are possible?

(A) 6
(B) 40
(C) 210
(D) 5,040
(E) 151,200

Arithmetic Elementary combinatorics

Any of the 10 books can be listed first. Any of the 9 books remaining after the first book is listed can be listed second. Any of the 8 books remaining after the first and second books are listed can be listed third. Any of the 7 books remaining after the first, second, and third books are listed can be listed fourth. By the multiplication principle, there are $(10)(9)(8)(7) = 5{,}040$ different lists possible.

The correct answer is D.

141. If n is a positive integer and the product of all the integers from 1 to n, inclusive, is divisible by 990, what is the least possible value of n?

(A) 8
(B) 9
(C) 10
(D) 11
(E) 12

Arithmetic Properties of numbers

For convenience, let N represent the product of all integers from 1 through n. Then, since N is divisible by 990, every prime factor of 990 must also be a factor of N. The prime factorization of 990 is $2 \times 3^2 \times 5 \times 11$, and therefore, 11 must be a factor of N. Then, the least possible value of N with factors of $2, 5, 3^2$, and 11 is $1 \times 2 \times 3 \times \cdots \times 11$, and the least possible value of n is 11.

The correct answer is D.

142. The probability that event M will <u>not</u> occur is 0.8 and the probability that event R will <u>not</u> occur is 0.6. If events M and R cannot both occur, which of the following is the probability that either event M or event R will occur?

(A) $\frac{1}{5}$
(B) $\frac{2}{5}$
(C) $\frac{3}{5}$
(D) $\frac{4}{5}$
(E) $\frac{12}{25}$

Arithmetic Probability

Let $P(M)$ be the probability that event M will occur, let $P(R)$ be the probability that event R will occur, and let $P(M \text{ and } R)$ be the probability that events M and R both occur. Then the probability that either event M or event R will occur is $P(M) + P(R) - P(M \text{ and } R)$. From the given information, it follows that $P(M) = 1.0 - 0.8 = 0.2$, $P(R) = 1.0 - 0.6 = 0.4$, and $P(M \text{ and } R) = 0$. Therefore, the probability that either event M or event R will occur is $0.2 + 0.4 - 0 = 0.6 = \frac{3}{5}$.

The correct answer is C.

143. The total cost for Company X to produce a batch of tools is \$10,000 plus \$3 per tool. Each tool sells for \$8. The gross profit earned from producing and selling these tools is the total income from sales minus the total production cost. If a batch of 20,000 tools is produced and sold, then Company X's gross profit per tool is

(A) \$3.00
(B) \$3.75
(C) \$4.50
(D) \$5.00
(E) \$5.50

Arithmetic Applied problems

The total cost to produce 20,000 tools is \$10,000 + \$3(20,000) = \$70,000. The revenue resulting from the sale of 20,000 tools is \$8(20,000) = \$160,000. The gross profit is

$160,000 − $70,000 = $90,000, and the gross profit per tool is $\frac{\$90,000}{20,000} = \$4.50$.

The correct answer is C.

144. If Q is an odd number and the median of Q consecutive integers is 120, what is the largest of these integers?

(A) $\frac{Q-1}{2} + 120$

(B) $\frac{Q}{2} + 119$

(C) $\frac{Q}{2} + 120$

(D) $\frac{Q+119}{2}$

(E) $\frac{Q+120}{2}$

Arithmetic Statistics

For an odd number of data values, the median is the middle number. Thus, 120 is the middle number, and so half of the $Q - 1$ remaining values are at most 120 and the other half of the $Q - 1$ remaining values are at least 120. In particular, $\frac{Q-1}{2}$ data values lie to the right of 120 when the data values are listed in increasing order from left to right, and so the largest data value is $120 + \frac{Q-1}{2}$. Alternatively, it is evident that (B), (C), or (E) cannot be correct since these expressions do not have an integer value when Q is odd. For the list consisting of the single number 120 (i.e., if $Q = 1$), (D) fails because $\frac{Q+119}{2} = \frac{1+119}{2} = 60 \neq 120$ and (A) does not fail because $\frac{Q-1}{2} + 120 = \frac{1-1}{2} + 120 = 120$.

The correct answer is A.

145. A ladder of a fire truck is elevated to an angle of 60° and extended to a length of 70 feet. If the base of the ladder is 7 feet above the ground, how many feet above the ground does the ladder reach?

(A) 35

(B) 42

(C) $35\sqrt{3}$

(D) $7+35\sqrt{3}$

(E) $7+42\sqrt{3}$

Geometry Triangles

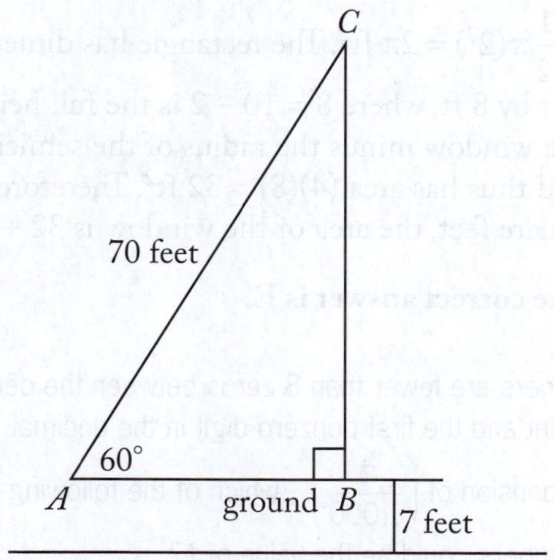

Given the figure above, determine BC. Then add 7 to determine how far above the ground the ladder reaches.

Triangle ΔABC is a 30°–60°–90° triangle with hypotenuse $\overline{AC}$ of length 70 feet. Since the lengths of the sides of a 30°–60°–90° triangle are in the ratio $1:2:\sqrt{3}$, $\frac{AB}{AC} = \frac{1}{2}$ and so $AB = \frac{1}{2}AC = 35$, and $\frac{AB}{BC} = \frac{1}{\sqrt{3}}$ and so $BC = AB\sqrt{3} = 35\sqrt{3}$.

Therefore, the ladder reaches $7 + 35\sqrt{3}$ feet above the ground.

The correct answer is D.

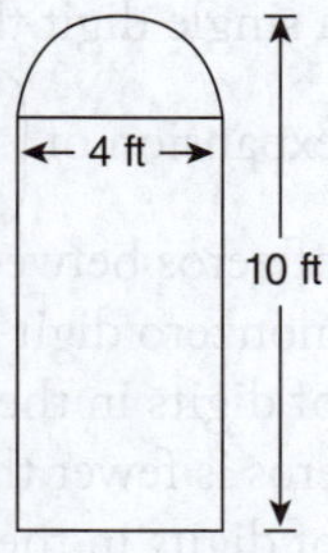

146. The window in the figure above consists of a rectangle and a semicircle with dimensions as shown. What is the area, in square feet, of the window?

(A) 40 + 8π

(B) 40 + 2π

(C) 32 + 8π

(D) 32 + 4π

(E) 32 + 2π

Geometry Area

The semicircle has a radius of 2 ft, and thus its area is $\frac{1}{2}\pi(2^2) = 2\pi$ ft^2. The rectangle has dimensions 4 ft by 8 ft, where $8 = 10 - 2$ is the full height of the window minus the radius of the semicircle, and thus has area $(4)(8) = 32$ ft^2. Therefore, in square feet, the area of the window is $32 + 2\pi$.

The correct answer is E.

147. If there are fewer than 8 zeros between the decimal point and the first nonzero digit in the decimal expansion of $\left(\frac{t}{1{,}000}\right)^4$, which of the following numbers could be the value of t?

I. 3
II. 5
III. 9

(A) None
(B) I only
(C) II only
(D) III only
(E) II and III

Arithmetic Properties of numbers; Decimals

The decimal expansion of $\left(\frac{1}{1{,}000}\right)^4 = 10^{-12}$ has 11 zeros to the right of the decimal point followed by a single digit that is 1. Therefore, in the decimal expansion of $\left(\frac{t}{1{,}000}\right)^4 = t^4 \times 10^{-12}$, the number of zeros between the decimal point and the first nonzero digit is equal to 12 minus the number of digits in the integer t^4. Since this number of zeros is fewer than 8, it follows that the number of digits in the integer t^4 is greater than 4. The integer t cannot be 3, because the number of digits in $3^4 = 81$ is not greater than 4. The integer t cannot be 5, because the number of digits in $5^4 = 625$ is not greater than 4. The integer t cannot be 9, because the number of digits in $9^4 = 6{,}561$ is not greater than 4. Therefore, none of 3, 5, or 9 could be the value of t.

The correct answer is A.

148. A three-digit code for certain locks uses the digits 0, 1, 2, 3, 4, 5, 6, 7, 8, 9 according to the following constraints. The first digit cannot be 0 or 1, the second digit must be 0 or 1, and the second and third digits cannot both be 0 in the same code. How many different codes are possible?

(A) 144
(B) 152
(C) 160
(D) 168
(E) 176

Arithmetic Elementary combinatorics

Since the first digit cannot be 0 or 1, there are 8 digits possible for the first digit. Since the second digit must be 0 or 1, there are 2 digits possible for the second digit. If there were no other restrictions, all 10 digits would be possible for the third digit, making the total number of possible codes $8 \times 2 \times 10 = 160$. But, the additional restriction that the second and third digits cannot both be 0 in the same code eliminates the 8 codes 2-0-0, 3-0-0, 4-0-0, 5-0-0, 6-0-0, 7-0-0, 8-0-0, and 9-0-0. Therefore, there are $160 - 8 = 152$ possible codes.

The correct answer is B.

149. Jackie has two solutions that are 2 percent sulfuric acid and 12 percent sulfuric acid by volume, respectively. If these solutions are mixed in appropriate quantities to produce 60 liters of a solution that is 5 percent sulfuric acid, approximately how many liters of the 2 percent solution will be required?

(A) 18
(B) 20
(C) 24
(D) 36
(E) 42

Algebra Simultaneous equations

Let x represent the quantity of the 2% sulfuric acid solution in the mixture, from which it follows that the 2% sulfuric acid solution contributes $0.02x$ liters of sulfuric acid to the mixture. Let y represent the quantity of the 12% sulfuric acid solution in the mixture, from which it follows that the 12% sulfuric acid solution contributes $0.12y$ liters of sulfuric acid to the mixture. Since there are 60 liters of the mixture, $x + y = 60$. The quantity of sulfuric acid in the mixture, which is 5% sulfuric acid, is then $(0.05)(60) = 3$ liters. Therefore, $0.02x + 0.12y = 3$. Substituting $60 - x$ for y gives $0.02x + 0.12(60 - x) = 3$. Then,

$0.02x + 0.12(60 - x) = 3$	given
$0.02x + 7.2 - 0.12x = 3$	use distributive property
$7.2 - 0.1x = 3$	combine like terms
$-0.1x = -4.2$	subtract 7.2 from both sides
$x = 42$	divide both sides by −0.1

The correct answer is E.

150. If Jake loses 8 pounds, he will weigh twice as much as his sister. Together they now weigh 278 pounds. What is Jake's present weight, in pounds?

(A) 131
(B) 135
(C) 139
(D) 147
(E) 188

Algebra Systems of equations

Let J represent Jake's weight and S represent his sister's weight. Then $J - 8 = 2S$ and $J + S = 278$. Solve the second equation for S and get $S = 278 - J$. Substituting the expression for S into the first equation gives

$$J - 8 = 2(278 - J)$$
$$J - 8 = 556 - 2J$$
$$J + 2J = 556 + 8$$
$$3J = 564$$
$$J = 188$$

The correct answer is E.

151. For each student in a certain class, a teacher adjusted the student's test score using the formula $y = 0.8x + 20$, where x is the student's original test score and y is the student's adjusted test score. If the standard deviation of the original test scores of the students in the class was 20, what was the standard deviation of the adjusted test scores of the students in the class?

(A) 12
(B) 16
(C) 28
(D) 36
(E) 40

Arithmetic Statistics

Let n be the number of students in the class, let $\mu = \frac{\sum x}{n}$ be the mean of the students' unadjusted scores. It follows that the standard deviation of the unadjusted scores is $20 = \sqrt{\frac{\sum(x-\mu)^2}{n}}$.

To find the standard deviation of the adjusted scores, first find their mean: $\frac{\sum(0.8x + 20)}{n} = \frac{0.8\sum x}{n} + \frac{20n}{n} = 0.8\mu + 20$. Then, subtract the adjusted mean from each adjusted score: $(0.8x + 20) - (0.8\mu + 20) = 0.8(x - \mu)$. Next, square each difference: $(0.8(x - \mu))^2 = 0.64(x - \mu)^2$. Next, find the average of the squared differences: $\frac{\sum 0.64(x-\mu)^2}{n} = \frac{0.64\sum(x-\mu)^2}{n}$.

Finally, take the nonnegative square root:

$$\sqrt{\frac{0.64\sum(x-\mu)^2}{n}} = 0.8\sqrt{\frac{\sum(x-\mu)^2}{n}} = 0.8(20) = 16.$$

The correct answer is B.

152. Last year 26 members of a certain club traveled to England, 26 members traveled to France, and 32 members traveled to Italy. Last year no members of the club traveled to both England and France, 6 members traveled to both England and Italy, and 11 members traveled to both France and Italy. How many members of the club traveled to at least one of these three countries last year?

(A) 52
(B) 67
(C) 71
(D) 73
(E) 79

Arithmetic Applied problems

The numbers in the following diagram represent the numbers of members of the club who traveled to the indicated countries, and these numbers can be determined as follows. Since no members traveled to both England and France, both regions that form the overlap of England and France are labeled with 0. It follows that none of the 6 members who traveled to both England and Italy traveled to France, and so the region corresponding to England and Italy only is labeled with 6. It also follows that none of the 11 members who traveled to both France and Italy traveled to England, and so the region corresponding to France and Italy only is labeled with 11. At this point it can be determined that $26 - 6 = 20$ members traveled to England only, $26 - 11 = 15$ members traveled to France only, and $32 - (6 + 11) = 15$ members traveled to Italy only.

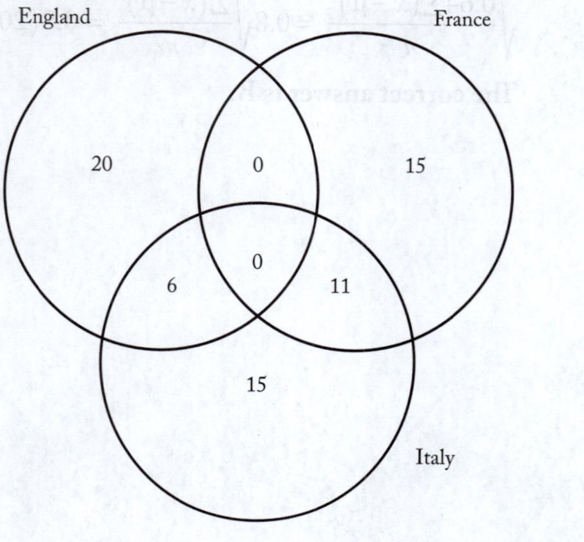

From the diagram it follows that $20 + 15 + 6 + 11 + 15 = 67$ members traveled to at least one of these three countries.

The correct answer is B.

153. A store reported total sales of \$385 million for February of this year. If the total sales for the same month last year was \$320 million, approximately what was the percent increase in sales?

(A) 2%
(B) 17%
(C) 20%
(D) 65%
(E) 83%

Arithmetic Percents

The percent increase in sales from last year to this year is 100 times the quotient of the difference in sales for the two years divided by the sales last year. Thus, the percent increase is

$$\frac{385-320}{320}\times 100 = \frac{65}{320}\times 100$$
$$= \frac{13}{64}\times 100$$
$$\approx \frac{13}{65}\times 100$$
$$= \frac{1}{5}\times 100$$
$$= 20\%$$

The correct answer is C.

154. When positive integer x is divided by positive integer y, the remainder is 9. If $\frac{x}{y} = 96.12$, what is the value of y?

(A) 96
(B) 75
(C) 48
(D) 25
(E) 12

Arithmetic Properties of numbers

The remainder is 9 when x is divided by y, so $x = yq + 9$ for some positive integer q. Dividing both sides by y gives $\frac{x}{y} = q + \frac{9}{y}$.

But, $\frac{x}{y} = 96.12 = 96 + 0.12$. Equating the two expressions for $\frac{x}{y}$ gives $q + \frac{9}{y} = 96 + 0.12$.

Thus, $q = 96$ and $\frac{9}{y} = 0.12$.

$$9 = 0.12y$$
$$y = \frac{9}{0.12}$$
$$y = 75$$

The correct answer is B.

155. If $x(2x + 1) = 0$ and $\left(x + \frac{1}{2}\right)(2x - 3) = 0$, then $x =$

(A) -3

(B) $-\frac{1}{2}$

(C) 0

(D) $\frac{1}{2}$

(E) $\frac{3}{2}$

Algebra Second-degree equations; Simultaneous equations

Setting each factor equal to 0, it can be seen that the solution set to the first equation is $\left\{0, -\frac{1}{2}\right\}$ and the solution set to the second equation is $\left\{-\frac{1}{2}, \frac{3}{2}\right\}$. Therefore, $-\frac{1}{2}$ is the solution to both equations.

The correct answer is B.

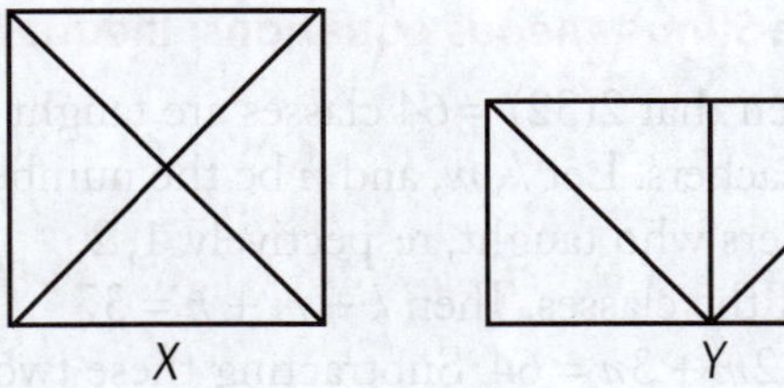

156. Figures X and Y above show how eight identical triangular pieces of cardboard were used to form a square and a rectangle, respectively. What is the ratio of the perimeter of X to the perimeter of Y?

(A) 2:3

(B) $\sqrt{2}:2$

(C) $2\sqrt{2}:3$

(D) 1:1

(E) $\sqrt{2}:1$

Geometry Perimeter

Because Figure X is a square and the diagonals of a square are the same length, are perpendicular, and bisect each other, it follows that each triangular piece is a 45°–45°–90° triangle. Thus, the length of each side of the square is $a\sqrt{2}$, and the perimeter is $4a\sqrt{2}$. The perimeter of the rectangle is $2(a + 2a) = 6a$. It follows that the ratio of the perimeter of the square to the perimeter of the rectangle is $\frac{4a\sqrt{2}}{6a} = \frac{2\sqrt{2}}{3}$, or $2\sqrt{2} : 3$.

The correct answer is C.

157. A certain experimental mathematics program was tried out in 2 classes in each of 32 elementary schools and involved 37 teachers. Each of the classes had 1 teacher and each of the teachers taught at least 1, but not more than 3, of the classes. If the number of teachers who taught 3 classes is n, then the least and greatest possible values of n, respectively, are

(A) 0 and 13

(B) 0 and 14

(C) 1 and 10

(D) 1 and 9

(E) 2 and 8

Algebra **Simultaneous equations; Inequalities**

It is given that $2(32) = 64$ classes are taught by 37 teachers. Let k, m, and n be the number of teachers who taught, respectively, 1, 2, and 3 of the classes. Then $k + m + n = 37$ and $k + 2m + 3n = 64$. Subtracting these two equations gives $m + 2n = 64 - 37 = 27$, or $2n = 27 - m$, and therefore $2n \leq 27$. Because n is an integer, it follows that $n \leq 13$ and B cannot be the answer. Since $n = 0$ is possible, which can be seen by using $m = 27$ and $k = 10$ (obtained by solving $2n = 27 - m$ with $n = 0$, then by solving $k + m + n = 37$ with $n = 0$ and $m = 27$), the answer must be A.

It is not necessary to ensure that $n = 13$ is possible to answer the question. However, it is not difficult to see that $k = 23$, $m = 1$, and $n = 13$ satisfy the given conditions.

The correct answer is A.

158. For the positive numbers, n, $n + 1$, $n + 2$, $n + 4$, and $n + 8$, the mean is how much greater than the median?

(A) 0

(B) 1

(C) $n + 1$

(D) $n + 2$

(E) $n + 3$

Algebra **Statistics**

Since the five positive numbers n, $n + 1$, $n + 2$, $n + 4$, and $n + 8$ are in ascending order, the median is the third number, which is $n + 2$. The mean of the five numbers is

$$\frac{n + (n + 1) + (n + 2) + (n + 4) + (n + 8)}{5}$$

$$= \frac{5n + 15}{5}$$

$$= n + 3$$

Since $(n + 3) - (n + 2) = 1$, the mean is 1 greater than the median.

The correct answer is B.

159. The interior of a rectangular carton is designed by a certain manufacturer to have a volume of x cubic feet and a ratio of length to width to height of 3:2:2. In terms of x, which of the following equals the height of the carton, in feet?

(A) $\sqrt[3]{x}$

(B) $\sqrt[3]{\frac{2x}{3}}$

(C) $\sqrt[3]{\frac{3x}{2}}$

(D) $\frac{2}{3}\sqrt[3]{x}$

(E) $\frac{3}{2}\sqrt[3]{x}$

Geometry; Arithmetic **Volume; Ratio and proportion**

Letting c represent the constant of proportionality, the length, width, and height, in feet, of the carton can be expressed as $3c$, $2c$, and $2c$, respectively. The volume of the carton is then $(3c)(2c)(2c) = 12c^3$ cubic feet. But, the volume is x cubic feet, and so $12c^3 = x$. Then, $c^3 = \frac{x}{12}$ and $c = \sqrt[3]{\frac{x}{12}}$. The height of the carton is $2c$ and in terms of x, $2c = 2\sqrt[3]{\frac{x}{12}}$. Since $2 = \sqrt[3]{8}$ and $\left(\sqrt[3]{a}\right)\left(\sqrt[3]{b}\right) = \sqrt[3]{ab}$, the height of the carton can be expressed as $2\sqrt[3]{\frac{x}{12}} = \sqrt[3]{8\left(\frac{x}{12}\right)} = \sqrt[3]{\frac{2x}{3}}$.

The correct answer is B.

160. The present ratio of students to teachers at a certain school is 30 to 1. If the student enrollment were to increase by 50 students and the number of teachers were to increase by 5, the ratio of students to teachers would then be 25 to 1. What is the present number of teachers?

(A) 5

(B) 8

(C) 10

(D) 12

(E) 15

Algebra Applied problems

Let s be the present number of students, and let t be the present number of teachers. According to the problem, the following two equations apply:

$$\frac{30}{1} = \frac{s}{t} \quad \text{Current student to teacher ratio}$$

$$\frac{s+50}{t+5} = \frac{25}{1} \quad \text{Future student to teacher ratio}$$

Solving the first equation for s gives $s = 30t$. Substitute this value of s into the second equation, and solve for t.

$$\frac{30t+50}{t+5} = \frac{25}{1}$$

$$30t + 50 = 25t + 125 \quad \text{multiply both sides by } t+5$$

$$5t = 75 \quad \text{simplify by subtraction}$$

$$t = 15$$

The correct answer is E.

161. What is the smallest integer n for which $25^n > 5^{12}$?

(A) 6

(B) 7

(C) 8

(D) 9

(E) 10

Arithmetic Operations with rational numbers

Because $5^2 = 25$, a common base is 5. Rewrite the left side with 5 as a base: $25^n = (5^2)^n = 5^{2n}$. It follows that the desired integer is the least integer n for which $5^{2n} > 5^{12}$. This will be the least integer n for which $2n > 12$, or the least integer n for which $n > 6$, which is 7.

The correct answer is B.

162. Sixty percent of the members of a study group are women, and 45 percent of those women are lawyers. If one member of the study group is to be selected at random, what is the probability that the member selected is a woman lawyer?

(A) 0.10

(B) 0.15

(C) 0.27

(D) 0.33

(E) 0.45

Arithmetic Probability

For simplicity, suppose there are 100 members in the study group. Since 60 percent of the members are women, there are 60 women in the group. Also, 45 percent of the women are lawyers so there are $0.45(60) = 27$ women lawyers in the study group. Therefore the probability of selecting a woman lawyer is $\frac{27}{100} = 0.27$.

The correct answer is C.

163. Each year for 4 years, a farmer increased the number of trees in a certain orchard by $\frac{1}{4}$ of the number of trees in the orchard the preceding year. If all of the trees thrived and there were 6,250 trees in the orchard at the end of the 4-year period, how many trees were in the orchard at the beginning of the 4-year period?

(A) 1,250

(B) 1,563

(C) 2,250

(D) 2,560

(E) 2,752

Arithmetic Operations on rational numbers

Increasing the number of trees each year by $\frac{1}{4}$ of the number of trees in the orchard the preceding year is equivalent to making the number of trees increase 25% per year, compounded yearly. If there were n trees at the beginning of the 4-year period, then there will be $1.25n$ trees at the end of the first year, $1.25(1.25n) = (1.25)^2n$ trees at the end of the second year, $1.25[(1.25)^2n] = (1.25)^3n$ trees at the end of the third year, and $1.25[(1.25)^3n] = (1.25)^4n$ trees at the end of the fourth year. Hence, $6{,}250 = (1.25)^4n$ and $n = \frac{6{,}250}{(1.25)^4}$. The arithmetic can be greatly simplified by rewriting $(1.25)^4$ as $\left(\frac{5}{4}\right)^4 = \frac{5^4}{4^4}$ and 6,250 as $(625)(10) = (5^4)(10)$. Then $\frac{6{,}250}{(1.25)^4} = (5^4)(10)\left(\frac{4^4}{5^4}\right) = (10)(4^4) = 2{,}560$.

The correct answer is D.

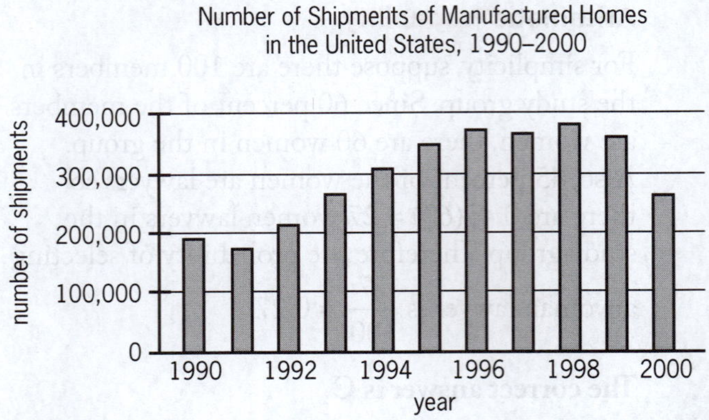

164. According to the chart shown, which of the following is closest to the median annual number of shipments of manufactured homes in the United States for the years from 1990 to 2000, inclusive?

(A) 250,000
(B) 280,000
(C) 310,000
(D) 325,000
(E) 340,000

Arithmetic Interpretation of graphs and tables; Statistics

From the chart, the approximate numbers of shipments are as follows:

Year	Number of shipments
1990	190,000
1991	180,000
1992	210,000
1993	270,000
1994	310,000
1995	350,000
1996	380,000
1997	370,000
1998	390,000
1999	360,000
2000	270,000

Since there are 11 entries in the table and 11 is an odd number, the median of the numbers of shipments is the 6th entry when the numbers of shipments are arranged in order from least to greatest. In order, from least to greatest, the first 6 entries are:

Number of shipments
180,000
190,000
210,000
270,000
270,000
310,000

The 6th entry is 310,000.

The correct answer is C.

165. For the positive integers a, b, and k, $a^k \| b$ means that a^k is a divisor of b, but a^{k+1} is not a divisor of b. If k is a positive integer and $2^k \| 72$, then k is equal to

(A) 2
(B) 3
(C) 4
(D) 8
(E) 18

Arithmetic Property of numbers

Since $72 = (2^3)(3^2)$, it follows that 2^3 is a divisor of 72 and 2^4 is not a divisor of 72. Therefore, $2^3 \| 72$, and hence $k = 3$.

The correct answer is B.

166. A certain characteristic in a large population has a distribution that is symmetric about the mean m. If 68 percent of the distribution lies within one standard deviation d of the mean, what percent of the distribution is less than $m + d$?

(A) 16%
(B) 32%
(C) 48%
(D) 84%
(E) 92%

Arithmetic Statistics

Since 68% lies between $m - d$ and $m + d$, a total of $(100 - 68)\% = 32\%$ lies to the left of $m - d$ and to the right of $m + d$. Because the distribution is symmetric about m, half of the 32% lies to the right of $m + d$. Therefore, 16% lies to the right of $m + d$, and hence $(100 - 16)\% = 84\%$ lies to the left of $m + d$.

The correct answer is D.

167. Four extra-large sandwiches of exactly the same size were ordered for m students, where $m > 4$. Three of the sandwiches were evenly divided among the students. Since 4 students did not want any of the fourth sandwich, it was evenly divided among the remaining students. If Carol ate one piece from each of the four sandwiches, the amount of sandwich that she ate would be what fraction of a whole extra-large sandwich?

(A) $\frac{m+4}{m(m-4)}$

(B) $\frac{2m-4}{m(m-4)}$

(C) $\frac{4m-4}{m(m-4)}$

(D) $\frac{4m-8}{m(m-4)}$

(E) $\frac{4m-12}{m(m-4)}$

Algebra Applied problems

Since each of 3 of the sandwiches was evenly divided among m students, each piece was $\frac{1}{m}$ of a sandwich. Since the fourth sandwich was evenly divided among $m - 4$ students, each piece was $\frac{1}{m-4}$ of the fourth sandwich. Carol ate 1 piece from each of the four sandwiches, so she ate a total of

$$(3)\frac{1}{m}+\frac{1}{m-4}=\frac{3(m-4)+m}{m(m-4)}=\frac{4m-12}{m(m-4)}$$

The correct answer is E.

168. Which of the following equations has $1 + \sqrt{2}$ as one of its roots?

(A) $x^2 + 2x - 1 = 0$

(B) $x^2 - 2x + 1 = 0$

(C) $x^2 + 2x + 1 = 0$

(D) $x^2 - 2x - 1 = 0$

(E) $x^2 - x - 1 = 0$

Algebra Second-degree equations

This problem can be solved by working backwards to construct a quadratic equation with $1 + \sqrt{2}$ as a root that does not involve radicals.

$x = 1 + \sqrt{2}$	set x to the desired value
$x - 1 = \sqrt{2}$	subtract 1 from both sides
$(x - 1)^2 = 2$	square both sides
$x^2 - 2x + 1 = 2$	expand the left side
$x^2 - 2x - 1 = 0$	subtract 2 from both sides

The correct answer is D.

169. In Country C, the unemployment rate among construction workers dropped from 16 percent on September 1, 1992, to 9 percent on September 1, 1996. If the number of construction workers was 20 percent greater on September 1, 1996, than on September 1, 1992, what was the approximate percent change in the number of unemployed construction workers over this period?

(A) 50% decrease

(B) 30% decrease

(C) 15% decrease

(D) 30% increase

(E) 55% increase

Arithmetic Percents

Let U_1 and U_2 be the numbers of unemployed construction workers on September 1, 1992, and September 1, 1996, respectively, and let N be the number of construction workers on September 1, 1992. Then, from the given information, $1.2N$ is the number of construction workers on September 1, 1996, $U_1 = 0.16N$, and $U_2 = 0.09(1.2N)$. Therefore, the percent change from September 1, 1992, to September 1, 1996, of unemployed construction workers is given by

$$\left(\frac{U_2 - U_1}{U_1} \times 100\right)\%$$
$$= \left(\frac{0.09(1.2N) - 0.16N}{0.16N} \times 100\right)\%$$
$$= \left(\frac{0.108 - 0.16}{0.16} \times 100\right)\%$$
$$= \left(\frac{108 - 160}{160} \times 100\right)\%$$
$$= \left(-\frac{13}{40} \times 100\right)\%$$
$$\approx \left(-\frac{13}{39} \times 100\right)\%$$
$$\approx \left(-\frac{1}{3} \times 100\right)\%$$
$$\approx -30\%$$

The correct answer is B.

170. In a box of 12 pens, a total of 3 are defective. If a customer buys 2 pens selected at random from the box, what is the probability that neither pen will be defective?

(A) $\frac{1}{6}$

(B) $\frac{2}{9}$

(C) $\frac{6}{11}$

(D) $\frac{9}{16}$

(E) $\frac{3}{4}$

Arithmetic Probability

Let A represent the event that the first pen purchased is not defective and let B represent the event that the second pen purchased is not defective, where A and B are dependent events. Since there are 3 defective pens in the box of 12 pens, there are 9 pens in the box that are not defective. Using standard probability notation, $P(A) = \frac{9}{12}$ and $P(B$, given that A has occurred$) = \frac{8}{11}$. (Event A has occurred so there are 11 pens left in the box and 8 of them are not defective.) Then, using the multiplication rule for dependent events, P(neither pen is defective) $= P(A \text{ and } B) = P(A) \times P(B$, given that A has occurred$) = \frac{9}{12} \times \frac{8}{11} = \frac{6}{11}$.

Alternately, the probability of selecting 2 pens, neither of which is defective, from a box containing 12 pens, 3 of which are defective, and therefore, 9 of which are non-defective is the number of ways to select 2 non-defective pens from 9 non-defective pens over the number of ways to select 2 pens from 12 pens

$$= \frac{\binom{9}{2}}{\binom{12}{2}} = \frac{\frac{9 \times 8}{2}}{\frac{12 \times 11}{2}} = \frac{6}{11}.$$

The correct answer is C.

171. At a certain fruit stand, the price of each apple is 40 cents and the price of each orange is 60 cents. Mary selects a total of 10 apples and oranges from the fruit stand, and the average (arithmetic mean) price of the 10 pieces of fruit is 56 cents. How many oranges must Mary put back so that the average price of the pieces of fruit that she keeps is 52 cents?

(A) 1

(B) 2

(C) 3

(D) 4

(E) 5

Algebra Statistics

If Mary selected x apples, then she selected $(10 - x)$ oranges. The average price of the 10 pieces of fruit is $\frac{40x+60(10-x)}{10} = 56$. From this,

$\frac{40x+60(10-x)}{10} = 56$	given
$40x+60(10-x) = 560$	multiply both sides by 10
$40x+600-60x = 560$	distribution property
$600-20x = 560$	combine like terms
$-20x = -40$	subtract 600 from both sides
$x = 2$	divide both sides by -20

Thus, Mary selected 2 apples and 8 oranges. Next, let y be the number of oranges Mary needs to put back, so that the average price of the $[2 + (8 - y)]$ pieces of fruit Mary keeps is 52 cents. Then,

$\frac{(40)(2)+(60)(8-y)}{2+(8-y)} = 52$	given
$\frac{80+480-60y}{10-y} = 52$	distributive property
$80+480-60y = 52(10-y)$	multiply both sides by $10-y$
$560-60y = 520-52y$	distributive property
$8y = 40$	subtract $520-60y$ from both sides
$y = 5$	divide both sides by 8

Therefore, Mary must put back 5 oranges, so that the average price of the fruit she keeps (that is, the average price of 2 apples and 3 oranges) is 52 cents.

The correct answer is E.

172. A pharmaceutical company received \$3 million in royalties on the first \$20 million in sales of the generic equivalent of one of its products and then \$9 million in royalties on the next \$108 million in sales. By approximately what percent did the ratio of royalties to sales decrease from the first \$20 million in sales to the next \$108 million in sales?

(A) 8%
(B) 15%
(C) 45%
(D) 52%
(E) 56%

Arithmetic Percents

The ratio of royalties to sales for the first \$20 million in sales is $\frac{3}{20}$, and the ratio of royalties to sales for the next \$108 million in sales is $\frac{9}{108} = \frac{1}{12}$. The percent decrease in the royalties to sales ratios is 100 times the quotient of the difference in the ratios divided by the ratio of royalties to sales for the first \$20 million in sales or

$$\frac{\frac{1}{12}-\frac{3}{20}}{\frac{3}{20}} \times 100 = \left(\frac{1}{12}-\frac{3}{20}\right) \times \frac{20}{3} \times 100$$

$$= \left(\frac{1}{12} \times \frac{20}{3} - 1\right) \times 100$$

$$= \left(\frac{5}{9} - 1\right) \times 100$$

$$= -\frac{4}{9} \times 100$$

$$\approx -0.44 \times 100$$

$$\approx 45\% \text{ decrease}$$

The correct answer is C.

Times at Which the Door
Opened from 8:00 to 10:00

8:00	8:06	8:30	9:05
8:03	8:10	8:31	9:11
8:04	8:18	8:54	9:29
8:04	8:19	8:57	9:31

173. The light in a restroom operates with a 15-minute timer that is reset every time the door opens as a person goes in or out of the room. Thus, after someone enters or exits the room, the light remains on for only 15 minutes unless the door opens again and resets the timer for another 15 minutes. If the times listed above are the times at which the door opened from 8:00 to 10:00, approximately how many minutes during this two-hour period was the light off?

(A) 10
(B) 25
(C) 35
(D) 40
(E) 70

Arithmetic **Operations with integers**

Look for two consecutive times that are more than 15 minutes apart

8:03 – 8:00 = 3 minutes

8:04 – 8:03 = 1 minute

8:04 – 8:04 = 0 minutes

8:06 – 8:04 = 2 minutes

8:10 – 8:06 = 4 minutes

8:18 – 8:10 = 8 minutes

8:19 – 8:18 = 1 minute

8:30 – 8:19 = 11 minutes

8:31 – 8:30 = 1 minute

8:54 – 8:31 = 23 minutes, so the light is off for 23 – 15 = 8 minutes

8:57 – 8:54 = 3 minutes

9:05 – 8:57 = 8 minutes

9:11 – 9:05 = 6 minutes

9:29 – 9:11 = 18 minutes, so the light is off for 18 – 15 = 3 minutes

9:31 – 9:29 = 2 minutes

10:00 – 9:31 = 29 minutes, so the light is off for 29 – 15 = 14 minutes

Thus, the light is off for a total of 8 + 3 + 14 = 25 minutes during the two-hour period.

Alternatively, the light comes on at 8:00 when the door is opened and is scheduled to go off at 8:15. So, when the door is opened at 8:03, twice at 8:04, at 8:06, and 8:10, the light is still on, but by the door being opened at these times, the timer has been reset to turn the light off at 8:18, 8:19, 8:21, and 8:25, respectively. Therefore, the light is still on when the door is opened at 8:18, 8:19, 8:30, and 8:31, but the timer has been reset to turn the light off at 8:33, 8:34, 8:45, and 8:46, respectively. The light is therefore off from 8:46 until the door is opened again at 8:54, which is an interval of 8 minutes. The light is still on when the door is opened at 8:57, 9:05, and 9:11, but the timer has been reset to turn the light off at 9:12, 9:20, and 9:26, respectively. The light is off from 9:26 until the door is opened again at 9:29, which is an interval of 3 minutes. The light is still on when the door is opened again at 9:31, and the timer has been reset to turn the light off at 9:46. Since, according to the chart, the door is not opened again before 10:00, the light remains off from 9:46 until 10:00, which is an interval of 14 minutes. Thus, the light is off a total of 8 + 3 + 14 = 25 minutes during the two-hour period.

The correct answer is B.

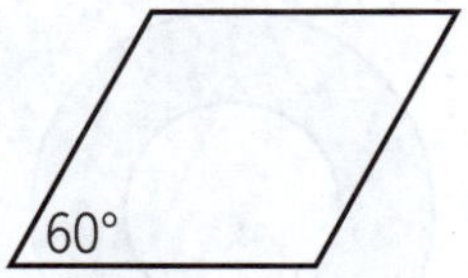

174. The parallelogram shown has four sides of equal length. What is the ratio of the length of the shorter diagonal to the length of the longer diagonal?

(A) $\frac{1}{2}$

(B) $\frac{1}{\sqrt{2}}$

(C) $\frac{1}{2\sqrt{2}}$

(D) $\frac{1}{\sqrt{3}}$

(E) $\frac{1}{2\sqrt{3}}$

Geometry Quadrilaterals; Triangles

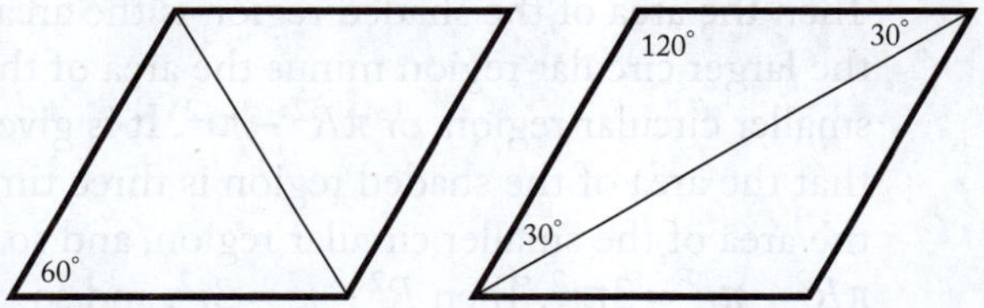

First, opposite angles of a parallelogram have equal measure, and the sum of the measures of adjacent angles is 180°. This means that each of the angles adjacent to the angle labeled 60° has measure 120°.

Since all four sides of the parallelogram have equal length, say x units, the shorter diagonal divides the parallelogram into two isosceles triangles. An isosceles triangle with one angle measuring 60° is equilateral, and so the shorter diagonal has length x units.

The longer diagonal divides the parallelogram into two isosceles triangles with one angle measuring 120° and each of the other angles measuring $\frac{180-120}{2} = 30°$, as shown in the figure above on the right.

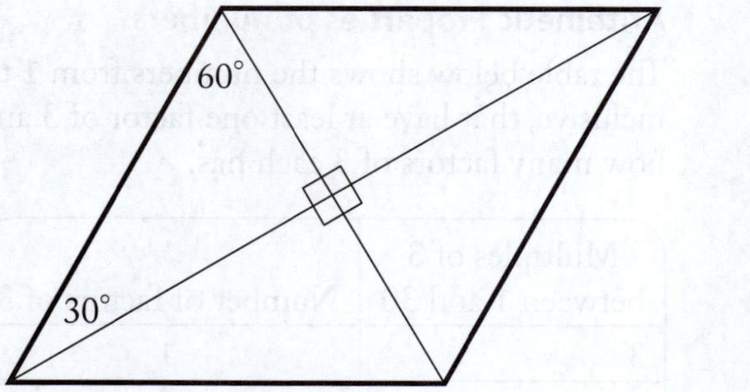

Then, because the diagonals of a parallelogram are perpendicular and bisect each other, the two diagonals divide the parallelogram into four 30°-60°-90° triangles, each with hypotenuse x units long. The sides of a 30°-60°-90° triangle are in the ratio of $1 : \sqrt{3} : 2$ and so, if y represents the length of the side opposite the 60° angle, then $\frac{x}{2} = \frac{y}{\sqrt{3}}$ and $y = \frac{x\sqrt{3}}{2}$. But, y is half the length of the longer diagonal, so the longer diagonal has length $x\sqrt{3}$ units. Therefore, the ratio of the length of the shorter diagonal to the length of the longer diagonal is $\frac{x}{x\sqrt{3}} = \frac{1}{\sqrt{3}}$.

The correct answer is D.

175. If p is the product of the integers from 1 to 30, inclusive, what is the greatest integer k for which 3^k is a factor of p ?

(A) 10

(B) 12

(C) 14

(D) 16

(E) 18

Arithmetic Properties of numbers

The table below shows the numbers from 1 to 30, inclusive, that have at least one factor of 3 and how many factors of 3 each has.

Multiples of 3 between 1 and 30	Number of factors of 3
3	1
$6 = 2 \times 3$	1
$9 = 3 \times 3$	2
$12 = 2 \times 2 \times 3$	1
$15 = 3 \times 5$	1
$18 = 2 \times 3 \times 3$	2
$21 = 3 \times 7$	1
$24 = 2 \times 2 \times 2 \times 3$	1
$27 = 3 \times 3 \times 3$	3
$30 = 2 \times 3 \times 5$	1

The sum of the numbers in the right column is 14. Therefore, 3^{14} is the greatest power of 3 that is a factor of the product of the first 30 positive integers.

The correct answer is C.

176. If $n = 3^8 - 2^8$, which of the following is NOT a factor of n?

(A) 97
(B) 65
(C) 35
(D) 13
(E) 5

Arithmetic Properties of numbers

Since $3^8 - 2^8$ is the difference of the perfect squares $(3^4)^2$ and $(2^4)^2$, then $3^8 - 2^8 = (3^4 + 2^4)(3^4 - 2^4)$. But $3^4 - 2^4$ is also the difference of the perfect squares $(3^2)^2$ and $(2^2)^2$ so $3^4 - 2^4 = (3^2 + 2^2)(3^2 - 2^2)$ and therefore $3^8 - 2^8 = (3^4 + 2^4)(3^2 + 2^2)(3^2 - 2^2)$. It follows that $3^8 - 2^8$ can be factored as $(81 + 16)(9 + 4)(9 - 4) = (97)(13)(5)$. Therefore, 7 is not a factor of $3^8 - 2^8$, and hence $35 = 5 \times 7$ is not a factor of $3^8 - 2^8$. It is easy to see that each of 97, 13, and 5 is a factor of $3^8 - 2^8$, and so is 65, since $65 = 5 \times 13$, although this additional analysis is not needed to arrive at the correct answer.

The correct answer is C.

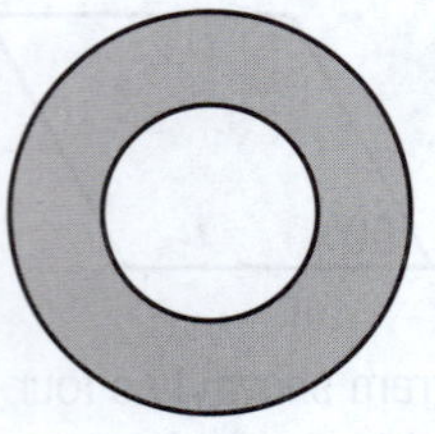

177. In the figure shown, if the area of the shaded region is 3 times the area of the smaller circular region, then the circumference of the larger circle is how many times the circumference of the smaller circle?

(A) 4
(B) 3
(C) 2
(D) $\sqrt{3}$
(E) $\sqrt{2}$

Geometry Circles

Let R represent the radius of the larger circle and r represent the radius of the smaller circle. Then the area of the shaded region is the area of the larger circular region minus the area of the smaller circular region, or $\pi R^2 - \pi r^2$. It is given that the area of the shaded region is three times the area of the smaller circular region, and so $\pi R^2 - \pi r^2 = 3\pi r^2$. Then $R^2 - r^2 = 3r^2$, and so $R^2 = 4r^2$ and $R = 2r$. The circumference of the larger circle is $2\pi R = 2\pi(2r) = 2(2\pi r)$, which is 2 times the circumference of the smaller circle.

The correct answer is C.

178. Club X has more than 10 but fewer than 40 members. Sometimes the members sit at tables with 3 members at one table and 4 members at each of the other tables, and sometimes they sit at tables with 3 members at one table and 5 members at each of the other tables. If they sit at tables with 6 members at each table except one and fewer than 6 members at that one table, how many members will be at the table that has fewer than 6 members?

(A) 1
(B) 2
(C) 3
(D) 4
(E) 5

Arithmetic Properties of numbers

Let n be the number of members that Club X has. Since the members can be equally divided into groups of 4 each with 3 left over, and the members can be equally divided into groups of 5 each with 3 left over, it follows that $n - 3$ is divisible by both 4 and 5. Therefore, $n - 3$ must be a multiple of $(4)(5) = 20$. Also, because the only multiple of 20 that is greater than 10 and less than 40 is 20, it follows that $n - 3 = 20$, or $n = 23$. Finally, when these 23 members are divided into the greatest number of groups of 6 each, there will be 5 members left over, since $23 = (3)(6) + 5$.

The correct answer is E.

179. In order to complete a reading assignment on time, Terry planned to read 90 pages per day. However, she read only 75 pages per day at first, leaving 690 pages to be read during the last 6 days before the assignment was to be completed. How many days in all did Terry have to complete the assignment on time?

(A) 15
(B) 16
(C) 25
(D) 40
(E) 46

Algebra Applied problems

Let n be the number of days that Terry read at the slower rate of 75 pages per day. Then $75n$ is the number of pages Terry read at this slower rate, and $75n + 690$ is the total number of pages Terry needs to read. Also, $n + 6$ is the total number of days that Terry will spend on the reading assignment. The requirement that Terry average 90 pages per day is equivalent to $\frac{75n+690}{n+6} = 90$.

Then

$$\frac{75n+690}{n+6} = 90$$
$$75n+690 = 90n+540$$
$$150 = 15n$$
$$10 = n$$

Therefore, the total number of days that Terry has to complete the assignment on time is $n + 6 = 10 + 6 = 16$.

The correct answer is B.

180. If $s > 0$ and $\sqrt{\frac{r}{s}} = s$, what is r in terms of s?

(A) $\frac{1}{s}$
(B) $\sqrt{s}$
(C) $s\sqrt{s}$
(D) s^3
(E) $s^3 - s$

Algebra Equations

Solve the equation for r as follows:

$$\sqrt{\frac{r}{s}} = s$$

$\frac{r}{s} = s^2$ square both sides of the equation

$r = s^3$ multiply both sides by s

The correct answer is D.

181. If $3 < x < 100$, for how many values of x is $\frac{x}{3}$ the square of a prime number?

(A) Two
(B) Three
(C) Four
(D) Five
(E) Nine

Arithmetic Properties of numbers

If $\frac{x}{3}$ is the square of a prime, then possible values of $\frac{x}{3}$ are $2^2, 3^2, 5^2, 7^2, \ldots$. Therefore, possible values of x are $3 \times 2^2 = 12$, $3 \times 3^2 = 27$, $3 \times 5^2 = 75$, $3 \times 7^2 = 147, \ldots$. Since only three of these values, namely 12, 27, and 75, are between 3 and 100, there are three values of x such that $\frac{x}{3}$ is the square of a prime number.

The correct answer is B.

182. A researcher plans to identify each participant in a certain medical experiment with a code consisting of either a single letter or a pair of distinct letters written in alphabetical order. What is the least number of letters that can be used if there are 12 participants, and each participant is to receive a different code?

(A) 4

(B) 5

(C) 6

(D) 7

(E) 8

Arithmetic Elementary combinatorics

None of the essential aspects of the problem is affected if the letters are restricted to be the first *n* letters of the alphabet, for various positive integers *n*. With the 3 letters *a*, *b*, and *c*, there are 6 codes: *a*, *b*, *c*, *ab*, *ac*, and *bc*. With the 4 letters *a*, *b*, *c*, and *d*, there are 10 codes: *a*, *b*, *c*, *d*, *ab*, *ac*, *ad*, *bc*, *bd*, and *cd*. Clearly, more than 12 codes are possible with 5 or more letters, so the least number of letters that can be used is 5.

The correct answer is B.

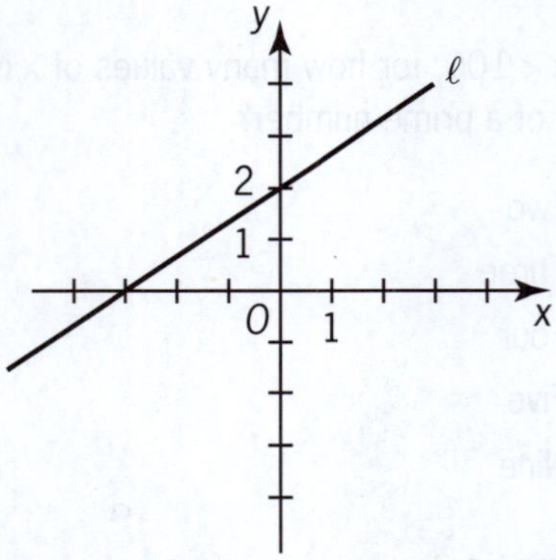

183. The graph of which of the following equations is a straight line that is parallel to line ℓ in the figure above?

(A) $3y - 2x = 0$

(B) $3y + 2x = 0$

(C) $3y + 2x = 6$

(D) $2y - 3x = 6$

(E) $2y + 3x = -6$

Algebra Coordinate geometry

From the graph, line ℓ contains points (–3,0) and (0,2), so the slope of line ℓ is $\frac{0-2}{-3-0} = \frac{2}{3}$. Any line parallel to line ℓ has slope $\frac{2}{3}$. Rewrite each of the equations given in the answer choices in slope-intercept form $y = mx + b$, where m is the slope and b is the y-intercept, to find the equation whose graph is a line with slope $\frac{2}{3}$. For answer choice A, $3y - 2x = 0$ so $3y = 2x$ and $y = \frac{2}{3}x$. The graph of this equation is a line with slope $\frac{2}{3}$.

The correct answer is A.

184. An object thrown directly upward is at a height of h feet after t seconds, where $h = -16(t-3)^2 + 150$. At what height, in feet, is the object 2 seconds after it reaches its maximum height?

(A) 6

(B) 86

(C) 134

(D) 150

(E) 166

Algebra Applied problems

Since $(t-3)^2$ is positive when $t \neq 3$ and zero when $t = 3$, it follows that the *minimum* value of $(t-3)^2$ occurs when $t = 3$. Therefore, the *maximum* value of $-16(t-3)^2$, and also the maximum value of $-16(t-3)^2 + 150$, occurs when $t = 3$. Hence, the height 2 seconds after the maximum height is the value of h when $t = 5$, or $-16(5-3)^2 + 150 = 86$.

The correct answer is B.

185. Which of the following is equivalent to the pair of inequalities $x + 6 > 10$ and $x - 3 \le 5$?

(A) $2 \le x < 16$

(B) $2 \le x < 4$

(C) $2 < x \le 8$

(D) $4 < x \le 8$

(E) $4 \le x < 16$

Algebra Inequalities

Solve the inequalities separately and combine the results.

$$x + 6 > 10$$
$$x > 4$$
$$x - 3 \le 5$$
$$x \le 8$$

Since $x > 4$, then $4 < x$. Combining $4 < x$ and $x \le 8$ gives $4 < x \le 8$.

The correct answer is D.

186. David has d books, which is 3 times as many as Jeff and $\frac{1}{2}$ as many as Paula. How many books do the three of them have altogether, in terms of d?

(A) $\frac{5}{6}d$

(B) $\frac{7}{3}d$

(C) $\frac{10}{3}d$

(D) $\frac{7}{2}d$

(E) $\frac{9}{2}d$

Algebra Applied problems; Simultaneous equations

Let J be the number of books that Jeff has, and let P be the number of books Paula has. Then, the given information about David's books can be expressed as $d = 3J$ and $d = \frac{1}{2}P$. Solving these two equations for J and P gives $\frac{d}{3} = J$ and $2d = P$. Thus, $d + J + P = d + \frac{d}{3} + 2d = 3\frac{1}{3}d = \frac{10}{3}d$.

The correct answer is C.

187. There are 8 teams in a certain league and each team plays each of the other teams exactly once. If each game is played by 2 teams, what is the total number of games played?

(A) 15

(B) 16

(C) 28

(D) 56

(E) 64

Arithmetic Operations on rational numbers

Since no team needs to play itself, each team needs to play 7 other teams. In addition, each game needs to be counted only once, rather than once for each team that plays that game. Since two teams play each game, $\frac{8 \times 7}{2} = 28$ games are needed.

The correct answer is C.

188. At his regular hourly rate, Don had estimated the labor cost of a repair job as $336 and he was paid that amount. However, the job took 4 hours longer than he had estimated and, consequently, he earned $2 per hour less than his regular hourly rate. What was the time Don had estimated for the job, in hours?

(A) 28

(B) 24

(C) 16

(D) 14

(E) 12

Algebra Second-degree equations

Let r be Don's regular hourly rate and t be the number of hours he estimated the repair job to take. Then $rt = 336$ is Don's estimated labor cost. Since Don was paid $336 for doing $t + 4$ hours of work at an hourly rate of $r - 2$, it also follows that $(r - 2)(t + 4) = 336$. Then

$$(r-2)(t+4) = 336$$
$$rt - 2t + 4r - 8 = 336$$
$$-2t + 4r - 8 = 0 \quad \text{since } rt = 336 \text{ from above}$$
$$-2t^2 + 4rt - 8t = 0 \quad \text{multiply both sides by } t$$
$$-2t^2 + 4(336) - 8t = 0 \quad \text{since } rt = 336$$
$$t^2 + 4t - 672 = 0 \quad \text{divide both sides by } -2$$
$$(t-24)(t+28) = 0 \quad \text{factor}$$

Alternatively, from the third line above,

$$-2t+4r-8=0$$

$$-2t+4\left(\frac{336}{t}\right)-8=0 \quad \text{since } rt=336 \text{ from above gives } r=\frac{336}{t}$$

$$-2t^2+4(336)-8t=0 \quad \text{multiply both sides by } t$$

$$t^2+4t-672=0 \quad \text{divide both sides by } -2$$

$$(t-24)(t+28)=0 \quad \text{factor}$$

So, $t-24=0$, which means $t=24$, or $t+28=0$, which means $t=-28$. Since an estimated time cannot be negative, $t=24$.

The correct answer is B.

189. If $\frac{p}{q}<1$, and p and q are positive integers, which of the following must be greater than 1 ?

(A) $\sqrt{\frac{p}{q}}$

(B) $\frac{p}{q^2}$

(C) $\frac{p}{2q}$

(D) $\frac{q}{p^2}$

(E) $\frac{q}{p}$

Arithmetic Properties of numbers

Since p and q are positive integers, $0<\frac{p}{q}<1$.

A Since $\frac{p}{q}<1$, then $q>p$. Taking the square root of both sides of the inequality gives $\sqrt{q}>\sqrt{p}$. Then, $\sqrt{\frac{p}{q}}=\frac{\sqrt{p}}{\sqrt{q}}$, so here the denominator will still be larger than the numerator. CANNOT be greater than 1.

B Squaring the denominator increases the denominator, which decreases the value of the fraction. CANNOT be greater than 1.

C Multiplying the denominator by 2 increases the denominator, which decreases the value of the fraction. CANNOT be greater than 1.

D Since $\frac{p}{q}<1$, then $q>p$. When $p^2<q$, this expression will be greater than 1, but p^2 need not be less than q. For example, if $p=2$ and $q=100$, $\frac{p}{q}=\frac{2}{100}$ and $\frac{q}{p^2}=\frac{100}{2^2}=\frac{100}{4}=25>1$.

However, if $p=3$ and $q=4$, then $\frac{p}{q}=\frac{3}{4}$ and $\frac{q}{p^2}=\frac{4}{3^2}=\frac{4}{9}<1$. NEED NOT be greater than 1.

E Again, since $\frac{p}{q}<1$, then $q>p$. Thus, the reciprocal, $\frac{q}{p}$, always has a value greater than 1 because the numerator will always be a larger positive integer than the denominator. MUST be greater than 1.

The correct answer is E.

190. To mail a package, the rate is x cents for the first pound and y cents for each additional pound, where $x>y$. Two packages weighing 3 pounds and 5 pounds, respectively, can be mailed separately or combined as one package. Which method is cheaper, and how much money is saved?

(A) Combined, with a savings of $x-y$ cents
(B) Combined, with a savings of $y-x$ cents
(C) Combined, with a savings of x cents
(D) Separately, with a savings of $x-y$ cents
(E) Separately, with a savings of y cents

Algebra Applied problems

Shipping the two packages separately would cost $1x+2y$ for the 3-pound package and $1x+4y$ for the 5-pound package. Shipping them together (as a single 8-pound package) would cost $1x+7y$. By calculating the sum of the costs for shipping the two packages separately minus the cost for shipping the one combined package, it is possible to determine the difference in cost, as shown.

$((1x+2y)+(1x+4y))-(1x+7y)$ (cost for 3 lb. + cost for 5 lb.) – cost for 8 lb.

$=(2x+6y)-(1x+7y)$ combine like terms

$=2x+6y-1x-7y$ distribute the negative

$=x-y$ combine like terms

Since $x > y$, this value is positive, which means it costs more to ship two packages separately. Thus it is cheaper to mail one combined package at a cost savings of $x - y$ cents.

The correct answer is A.

191. If money is invested at r percent interest, compounded annually, the amount of the investment will double in approximately $\frac{70}{r}$ years. If Pat's parents invested \$5,000 in a long-term bond that pays 8 percent interest, compounded annually, what will be the approximate total amount of the investment 18 years later, when Pat is ready for college?

(A) \$20,000
(B) \$15,000
(C) \$12,000
(D) \$10,000
(E) \$9,000

Algebra Applied problems

Since the investment will double in $\frac{70}{r}=\frac{70}{8}=8.75\approx 9$ years, the value of the investment over 18 years can be approximated by doubling its initial value twice. Therefore, the approximate value will be $(\$5,000)(2)(2)=\$20,000$.

The correct answer is A.

192. On a recent trip, Cindy drove her car 290 miles, rounded to the nearest 10 miles, and used 12 gallons of gasoline, rounded to the nearest gallon. The actual number of miles per gallon that Cindy's car got on this trip must have been between

(A) $\frac{290}{12.5}$ and $\frac{290}{11.5}$
(B) $\frac{295}{12}$ and $\frac{285}{11.5}$
(C) $\frac{285}{12}$ and $\frac{295}{12}$
(D) $\frac{285}{12.5}$ and $\frac{295}{11.5}$
(E) $\frac{295}{12.5}$ and $\frac{285}{11.5}$

Arithmetic Estimation

The lowest number of miles per gallon can be calculated using the lowest possible miles and the highest amount of gasoline. Also, the highest number of miles per gallon can be calculated using the highest possible miles and the lowest amount of gasoline.

Since the miles are rounded to the nearest 10 miles, the number of miles is between 285 and 295. Since the gallons are rounded to the nearest gallon, the number of gallons is between 11.5 and 12.5. Therefore, the lowest number of miles per gallon is $\frac{\text{lowest miles}}{\text{highest gallons}}=\frac{285}{12.5}$ and the highest number of miles per gallon is $\frac{\text{highest miles}}{\text{lowest gallons}}=\frac{295}{11.5}$

The correct answer is D.

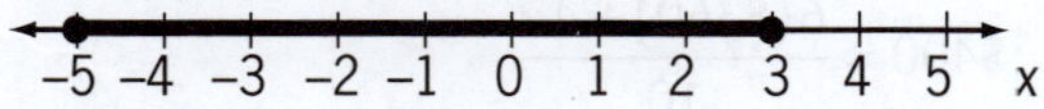

193. Which of the following inequalities is an algebraic expression for the shaded part of the number line above?

(A) $|x| \le 3$
(B) $|x| \le 5$
(C) $|x-2| \le 3$
(D) $|x-1| \le 4$
(E) $|x+1| \le 4$

Algebra Inequalities

The number line above shows $-5 \le x \le 3$. To turn this into absolute value notation, as all the choices are written, the numbers need to be opposite signs of the same value.

Since the distance between –5 and 3 is 8 ($3 - (-5) = 8$), that distance needs to be split in half with –4 to one side and 4 to the other. Each of these two values is 1 more than the values in the inequality above, so adding 1 to all terms in the inequality gives $-4 \le x + 1 \le 4$, which is the same as $|x + 1| \le 4$.

The correct answer is E.

194. In a small snack shop, the average (arithmetic mean) revenue was $400 per day over a 10-day period. During this period, if the average daily revenue was $360 for the first 6 days, what was the average daily revenue for the last 4 days?

(A) $420
(B) $440
(C) $450
(D) $460
(E) $480

Arithmetic; Algebra Statistics; Applied problems

Let x be the average daily revenue for the last 4 days. Using the formula $\text{average} = \dfrac{\text{sum of values}}{\text{number of values}}$, the information regarding the average revenues for the 10-day and 6-day periods can be expressed as follows and solved for x:

$$\$400 = \frac{6(\$360) + 4x}{10}$$

$\$4{,}000 = \$2{,}160 + 4x$	multiply both sides by 10
$\$1{,}840 = 4x$	subtract $2,160 from both sides
$\$460 = x$	divide both sides by 4

The correct answer is D.

195. If y is the smallest positive integer such that 3,150 multiplied by y is the square of an integer, then y must be

(A) 2
(B) 5
(C) 6
(D) 7
(E) 14

Arithmetic Properties of numbers

To find the smallest positive integer y such that $3{,}150y$ is the square of an integer, first find the prime factorization of 3,150 by a method similar to the following:

$$\begin{aligned}3{,}150 &= 10 \times 315\\ &= (2 \times 5) \times (3 \times 105)\\ &= 2 \times 5 \times 3 \times (5 \times 21)\\ &= 2 \times 5 \times 3 \times 5 \times (3 \times 7)\\ &= 2 \times 3^2 \times 5^2 \times 7\end{aligned}$$

To be a perfect square, $3{,}150y$ must have an even number of each of its prime factors. At a minimum, y must have one factor of 2 and one factor of 7 so that $3{,}150y$ has two factors of each of the primes 2, 3, 5, and 7. The smallest positive integer value of y is then $(2)(7) = 14$.

The correct answer is E.

196. If $[x]$ is the greatest integer less than or equal to x, what is the value of $[-1.6] + [3.4] + [2.7]$?

(A) 3
(B) 4
(C) 5
(D) 6
(E) 7

Arithmetic Computation with integers

The greatest integer that is less than or equal to –1.6 is –2. It cannot be –1 because –1 is greater than –1.6. The greatest integer that is less than or equal to 3.4 is 3. It cannot be 4 because 4 is greater than 3.4. The greatest integer that is less than or equal to 2.7 is 2. It cannot be 3 because 3 is greater than 2.7. Therefore, $[-1.6] + [3.4] + [2.7] = -2 + 3 + 2 = 3$.

The correct answer is A.

197. In the first week of the year, Nancy saved \$1. In each of the next 51 weeks, she saved \$1 more than she had saved in the previous week. What was the total amount that Nancy saved during the 52 weeks?

(A) \$1,326
(B) \$1,352
(C) \$1,378
(D) \$2,652
(E) \$2,756

Arithmetic Operations on rational numbers

In dollars, the total amount saved is the sum of 1, (1 + 1), (1 + 1 + 1), and so on, up to and including the amount saved in the 52nd week, which was \$52. Therefore, the total amount saved in dollars was 1 + 2 + 3 + … + 50 + 51 + 52. This sum can be easily evaluated by grouping the terms as (1 + 52) + (2 + 51) + (3 + 50) + … + (26 + 27), which results in the number 53 added to itself 26 times. Therefore, the sum is (26)(53) = 1,378.

Alternatively, the formula for the sum of the first n positive integers is $\frac{n(n+1)}{2}$. Therefore, the sum of the first 52 positive integers is $\frac{52(53)}{2} = 26(53) = 1{,}378$.

The correct answer is C.

198. In a certain sequence, the term x_n is given by the formula $x_n = 2x_{n-1} - \frac{1}{2}(x_{n-2})$ for all $n \geq 2$. If $x_0 = 3$ and $x_1 = 2$, what is the value of x_3?

(A) 2.5
(B) 3.125
(C) 4
(D) 5
(E) 6.75

Algebra Simplifying algebraic expressions

Given the formula $x_n = 2x_{n-1} - \frac{1}{2}(x_{n-2})$ with $x_0 = 3$ and $x_1 = 2$, then

$$\begin{aligned} x_2 &= 2x_1 - \frac{1}{2}x_0 \\ &= 2(2) - \frac{1}{2}(3) \\ &= \frac{5}{2} \\ x_3 &= 2x_2 - \frac{1}{2}x_1 \\ &= 2\left(\frac{5}{2}\right) - \frac{1}{2}(2) \\ &= 5 - 1 \\ &= 4 \end{aligned}$$

The correct answer is C.

199. During a trip, Francine traveled x percent of the total distance at an average speed of 40 miles per hour and the rest of the distance at an average speed of 60 miles per hour. In terms of x, what was Francine's average speed for the entire trip?

(A) $\frac{180-x}{2}$
(B) $\frac{x+60}{4}$
(C) $\frac{300-x}{5}$
(D) $\frac{600}{115-x}$
(E) $\frac{12{,}000}{x+200}$

Algebra Applied problems

Assume for simplicity that the total distance of Francine's trip is 100 miles. Then the table below gives all of the pertinent information.

Distance	Rate	Time $= \frac{\text{Distance}}{\text{Rate}}$
x	40	$\frac{x}{40}$
$100 - x$	60	$\frac{100-x}{60}$

The total time for Francine's trip is

$$\frac{x}{40}+\frac{100-x}{60}=\frac{3x}{120}+\frac{2(100-x)}{120}$$
$$=\frac{3x+2(100-x)}{120}$$
$$=\frac{3x+200-2x}{120}$$
$$=\frac{x+200}{120}$$

Francine's average speed over the entire trip is

$$\frac{\text{total distance}}{\text{total time}}=\frac{100}{\frac{x+200}{120}}=\frac{12,000}{x+200}.$$

The correct answer is E.

200. If $n = (33)^{43} + (43)^{33}$, what is the units digit of n?

(A) 0
(B) 2
(C) 4
(D) 6
(E) 8

Arithmetic Properties of numbers

If the units digit of an integer n is 3, then the units digits of $n^1, n^2, n^3, n^4, n^5, n^6, n^7$, and n^8 are, respectively, 3, 9, 7, 1, 3, 9, 7, and 1. Thus, the units digit of the powers of n form the sequence in which the digits 3, 9, 7, and 1 repeat indefinitely in that order. Since $43 = (10)(4) + 3$, the 43rd number in the sequence is 7, and therefore the units digit of $(33)^{43}$ is 7. Since $33 = (8)(4) + 1$, the 33rd number of this sequence is 3, and therefore, the units digit of $(43)^{33}$ is 3. Thus, the units digit of $(33)^{43} + (43)^{33}$ is the units digit of $7 + 3$, which is 0.

The correct answer is A.

201. Team A and Team B are competing against each other in a game of tug-of-war. Team A, consisting of 3 males and 3 females, decides to line up male, female, male, female, male, female. The lineup that Team A chooses will be one of how many different possible lineups?

(A) 9
(B) 12
(C) 15
(D) 36
(E) 720

Arithmetic Elementary combinatorics

Any of the 3 males can be first in the line, and any of the 3 females can be second. Either of the 2 remaining males can be next, followed by either of the 2 remaining females. The last 2 places in the line are filled with the only male left followed by the only female left. By the multiplication principle, there are $3 \times 3 \times 2 \times 2 \times 1 \times 1 = 36$ different lineups possible.

The correct answer is D.

202. A border of uniform width is placed around a rectangular photograph that measures 8 inches by 10 inches. If the area of the border is 144 square inches, what is the width of the border, in inches?

(A) 3
(B) 4
(C) 6
(D) 8
(E) 9

Algebra Second-degree equations

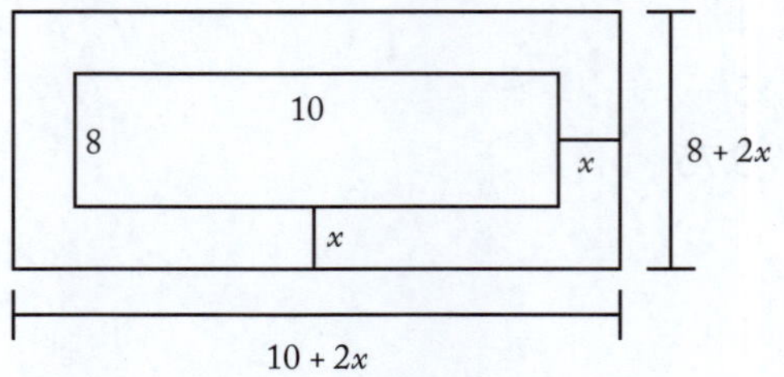

Note: Figure not drawn to scale.

Let x be the width, in inches, of the border. The photograph with the border has dimensions $(10 + 2x)$ inches and $(8 + 2x)$ inches with an area of $(10 + 2x)(8 + 2x) = (80 + 36x + 4x^2)$ square inches. The photograph without the border has dimensions 10 inches and 8 inches with an area of (10)(8) = 80 square inches. The area of the border is then the difference between the areas of the photograph with and without the border or $(80 + 36x + 4x^2) - 80 = 36x + 4x^2$ square inches. It is given that the area of the border is 144 square inches so,

$$36x + 4x^2 = 144$$
$$4x^2 + 36x - 144 = 0$$
$$x^2 + 9x - 36 = 0$$
$$(x - 3)(x + 12) = 0$$

So, $x - 3 = 0$, which means $x = 3$, or $x + 12 = 0$, which means $x = -12$.

Thus, after discarding $x = -12$ since the width of the border must be positive, $x = 3$.

The correct answer is A.

203. If $d = \frac{1}{2^3 \times 5^7}$ is expressed as a terminating decimal, how many nonzero digits will d have?

(A) One
(B) Two
(C) Three
(D) Seven
(E) Ten

Arithmetic Operations on rational numbers

It will be helpful to use the fact that a factor that is an integer power of 10 has no effect on the number of nonzero digits a terminating decimal has.

$$\frac{1}{2^3 \times 5^7} = \frac{1}{2^3 \times 5^3} \times \frac{1}{5^4}$$
$$= \left(\frac{1}{2 \times 5}\right)^3 \times \left(\frac{1}{5}\right)^4$$
$$= \left(\frac{1}{10}\right)^3 \times \left(\frac{1}{5}\right)^4$$
$$= 10^{-3} \times (0.2)^4$$
$$= 10^{-3} \times (0.0016)$$
$$= 0.0000016$$

The correct answer is B.

204. For any positive integer n, the sum of the first n positive integers equals $\frac{n(n+1)}{2}$. What is the sum of all the even integers between 99 and 301 ?

(A) 10,100
(B) 20,200
(C) 22,650
(D) 40,200
(E) 45,150

Algebra Simplifying expressions; Arithmetic Computation with integers

The given formula translates into $1 + 2 + ... + n = \sum_{k=1}^{n} k = \frac{n(n+1)}{2}$. The sum of the even integers between 99 and 301 is the sum of the even integers from 100 through 300, or the sum of the 50th even integer through the 150th even integer. To get this sum, find the sum of the first 150 even integers and subtract the sum of the first 49 even integers. In symbols,

$$\sum_{k=1}^{150} 2k - \sum_{k=1}^{49} 2k = 2\sum_{k=1}^{150} k - 2\sum_{k=1}^{49} k$$
$$= 2\left(\frac{150(150+1)}{2}\right) - 2\left(\frac{49(49+1)}{2}\right)$$
$$= 150(151) - 49(50)$$
$$= 50[3(151) - 49]$$
$$= 50(453 - 49)$$
$$= 50(404)$$
$$= 20,200$$

The correct answer is B.

205. How many prime numbers between 1 and 100 are factors of 7,150 ?

(A) One
(B) Two
(C) Three
(D) Four
(E) Five

Arithmetic Properties of numbers

To find the number of prime numbers between 1 and 100 that are factors of 7,150, find the prime factorization of 7,150 using a method similar to the following:

$$\begin{aligned}7{,}150 &= 10 \times 715\\ &= (2 \times 5) \times (5 \times 143)\\ &= 2 \times 5 \times 5 \times (11 \times 13)\end{aligned}$$

Thus, 7,150 has four prime factors: 2, 5, 11, and 13.

The correct answer is D.

206. A sequence of numbers a_1, a_2, a_3, . . . is defined as follows: $a_1 = 3$, $a_2 = 5$, and every term in the sequence after a_2 is the product of all terms in the sequence preceding it, e.g., $a_3 = (a_1)(a_2)$ and $a_4 = (a_1)(a_2)(a_3)$. If $a_n = t$ and $n > 2$, what is the value of a_{n+2} in terms of t?

(A) $4t$

(B) t^2

(C) t^3

(D) t^4

(E) t^8

Algebra Sequences

It is given that $a_n = (a_1)(a_2) \ldots (a_{n-1})$ and $a_n = t$. Therefore, $a_{n+1} = (a_1)(a_2) \ldots (a_{n-1})(a_n) = (a_n)(a_n) = t^2$ and $a_{n+2} = (a_1)(a_2) \ldots (a_n)(a_{n+1}) = (a_{n+1})(a_{n+1}) = (t^2)(t^2) = t^4$.

The correct answer is D.

207. Last year the price per share of Stock X increased by k percent and the earnings per share of Stock X increased by m percent, where k is greater than m. By what percent did the ratio of price per share to earnings per share increase, in terms of k and m?

(A) $\frac{k}{m}\%$

(B) $(k-m)\%$

(C) $\frac{100(k-m)}{100+k}\%$

(D) $\frac{100(k-m)}{100+m}\%$

(E) $\frac{100(k-m)}{100+k+m}\%$

Algebra Percents

If P and E are the price and earnings per share before the increase, then $\left(1+\frac{k}{100}\right)P$ and $\left(1+\frac{m}{100}\right)E$ are the price and earnings per share after the increase. Therefore, the percent increase in the ratio of price per share to earnings per share can be expressed as follows:

$$\left(\frac{(\text{ratio after increases})-(\text{ratio before increases})}{(\text{ratio before increases})}\times 100\right)\%$$

$$=\left[\left(\frac{(\text{ratio after increases})}{(\text{ratio before increases})}-1\right)\times 100\right]\%$$

$$=\left[\left(\frac{\frac{\left(1+\frac{k}{100}\right)P}{\left(1+\frac{m}{100}\right)E}}{\frac{P}{E}}-1\right)\times 100\right]\%$$

$$=\left[\left(\frac{\frac{\left(1+\frac{k}{100}\right)}{\left(1+\frac{m}{100}\right)}\cdot\frac{P}{E}}{\frac{P}{E}}-1\right)\times 100\right]\%$$

$$=\left[\left(\frac{\frac{\left(1+\frac{k}{100}\right)}{\left(1+\frac{m}{100}\right)}}{1}-1\right)\times 100\right]\%$$

$$=\left[\left(\frac{1+\frac{k}{100}}{1+\frac{m}{100}}-1\right)\times 100\right]\%$$

$$= \left[\left(\frac{1+\frac{k}{100}}{1+\frac{m}{100}} \cdot \frac{100}{100} - 1\right) \times 100\right]\%$$

$$= \left[\left(\frac{100+k}{100+m} - 1\right) \times 100\right]\%$$

$$= \left(\frac{(100+k)-(100+m)}{100+m} \times 100\right)\%$$

$$= \left(\frac{k-m}{100+m} \times 100\right)\%$$

$$= \frac{100(k-m)}{100+m}\%$$

The correct answer is D.

208. Of the 300 subjects who participated in an experiment using virtual-reality therapy to reduce their fear of heights, 40 percent experienced sweaty palms, 30 percent experienced vomiting, and 75 percent experienced dizziness. If all of the subjects experienced at least one of these effects and 35 percent of the subjects experienced exactly two of these effects, how many of the subjects experienced only one of these effects?

(A) 105
(B) 125
(C) 130
(D) 180
(E) 195

Arithmetic Applied problems

Let a be the number who experienced only one of the effects, b be the number who experienced exactly two of the effects, and c be the number who experienced all three of the effects. Then $a + b + c = 300$, since each of the 300 participants experienced at least one of the effects. From the given information, $b = 105$ (35% of 300), which gives $a + 105 + c = 300$, or $a + c = 195$ (Eq. 1). Also, if the number who experienced sweaty palms (40% of 300, or 120) is added to the number who experienced vomiting (30% of 300, or 90), and this sum is added to the number who experienced dizziness (75% of 300, or 225), then each participant who experienced only one of the effects is counted exactly once, each participant who experienced exactly two of the effects is counted exactly twice, and each participant who experienced all three of the effects is counted exactly 3 times. Therefore, $a + 2b + 3c = 120 + 90 + 225 = 435$. Using $b = 105$, it follows that $a + 2(105) + 3c = 435$, or $a + 3c = 225$ (Eq. 2). Then solving the system defined by Eq. 1 and Eq. 2,

$$\begin{cases} a + c = 195 \\ a + 3c = 225 \end{cases} \quad \text{multiply 1st equation by } -3$$

$$\begin{cases} -3a - 3c = -585 \\ a + 3c = 225 \end{cases} \quad \text{add equations}$$

$$-2a = -360, \text{ or } a = 180$$

The correct answer is D.

209. If $m^{-1} = -\frac{1}{3}$, then m^{-2} is equal to

(A) -9
(B) -3
(C) $-\frac{1}{9}$
(D) $\frac{1}{9}$
(E) 9

Arithmetic Negative exponents

Using rules of exponents, $m^{-2} = m^{-1 \cdot 2} = \left(m^{-1}\right)^2$, and since $m^{-1} = -\frac{1}{3}$, $m^{-2} = \left(-\frac{1}{3}\right)^2 = \frac{1}{9}$.

The correct answer is D.

210. A photography dealer ordered 60 Model X cameras to be sold for \$250 each, which represents a 20 percent markup over the dealer's initial cost for each camera. Of the cameras ordered, 6 were never sold and were returned to the manufacturer for a refund of 50 percent of the dealer's initial cost. What was the dealer's approximate profit or loss as a percent of the dealer's initial cost for the 60 cameras?

(A) 7% loss
(B) 13% loss
(C) 7% profit
(D) 13% profit
(E) 15% profit

Arithmetic Percents

Given that \$250 is 20% greater than a camera's initial cost, it follows that the initial cost for each camera was $\left(\$\frac{250}{1.2}\right)$. Therefore, the initial cost for the 60 cameras was $60\left(\$\frac{250}{1.2}\right)$. The total revenue is the sum of the amount obtained from selling 60 – 6 = 54 cameras for \$250 each and the $\left(\frac{1}{2}\right)\left(\$\frac{250}{1.2}\right)$ refund for each of 6 cameras, or $(54)(\$250)+(6)\left(\frac{1}{2}\right)\left(\$\frac{250}{1.2}\right)$. The total profit, as a percent of the total initial cost, is $\left(\frac{(\text{total revenue})-(\text{total initial cost})}{(\text{total initial cost})}\times 100\right)\% = \left(\left(\frac{(\text{total revenue})}{(\text{total initial cost})}-1\right)\times 100\right)\%$. Using the numerical expressions obtained above, $\frac{(\text{total revenue})}{(\text{total initial cost})}-1$

$$=\frac{(54)(250)+6\left(\frac{1}{2}\right)\left(\frac{250}{1.2}\right)}{(60)\left(\frac{250}{1.2}\right)}-1 \quad \text{by substitution}$$

$$=\frac{54+3\left(\frac{1}{1.2}\right)}{(60)\left(\frac{1}{1.2}\right)}-1 \quad \text{by canceling 250s}$$

$$=\frac{54(1.2)+3}{60}-1 \quad \text{by multiplying top and bottom by 1.2 and then canceling 1.2}$$

$$=\frac{67.8}{60}-1$$

$$=1.13-1$$

$$=0.13$$

Finally, (0.13 × 100)% = 13%, which represents a profit since it is positive.

The correct answer is D.

211. Seven pieces of rope have an average (arithmetic mean) length of 68 centimeters and a median length of 84 centimeters. If the length of the longest piece of rope is 14 centimeters more than 4 times the length of the shortest piece of rope, what is the maximum possible length, in centimeters, of the longest piece of rope?

(A) 82
(B) 118
(C) 120
(D) 134
(E) 152

Algebra Statistics

Let a, b, c, d, e, f, and g be the lengths, in centimeters, of the pieces of rope, listed from least to greatest. From the given information it follows that $d = 84$ and $g = 4a + 14$. Therefore, listed from least to greatest, the lengths are a, b, c, 84, e, f, and $4a + 14$. The maximum value of $4a + 14$ will occur when the maximum value of a is used, and this will be the case only if the shortest 3 pieces all have the same length. Therefore, listed from least to greatest, the lengths are a, a, a, 84, e, f, and $4a + 14$. The maximum value for $4a + 14$ will occur when e and f are as small as possible. Since e and f are to the right of the median, they must be at least 84 and so 84 is the least possible value for each of e and f. Therefore, listed from least to greatest, the lengths are a, a, a, 84, 84, 84, and $4a + 14$. Since the average length is 68, it follows that $\frac{a+a+a+84+84+84+(4a+14)}{7}=68$, or $a = 30$. Hence, the maximum length of the longest piece is $(4a + 14) = [4(30) + 14] = 134$ centimeters.

The correct answer is D.

212. What is the difference between the sixth and the fifth terms of the sequence 2, 4, 7, … whose nth term is $n+2^{n-1}$?

(A) 2
(B) 3
(C) 6
(D) 16
(E) 17

Algebra Simplifying algebraic expressions

According to the given formula, the sixth term of the sequence is $6 + 2^{6-1} = 6 + 2^5$ and the fifth term is $5 + 2^{5-1} = 5 + 2^4$. Then,

$$\begin{aligned}(6+2^5)-(5+2^4) &= (6-5)+(2^5-2^4)\\ &= 1+2^4(2-1)\\ &= 1+2^4\\ &= 1+16\\ &= 17\end{aligned}$$

The correct answer is E.

213. From the consecutive integers –10 to 10, inclusive, 20 integers are randomly chosen with repetitions allowed. What is the least possible value of the product of the 20 integers?

(A) $(-10)^{20}$
(B) $(-10)^{10}$
(C) 0
(D) $-(10)^{19}$
(E) $-(10)^{20}$

Arithmetic Properties of numbers

If –10 is chosen an odd number of times and 10 is chosen the remaining number of times (for example, choose –10 once and choose 10 nineteen times, or choose –10 three times and choose 10 seventeen times), then the product of the 20 chosen numbers will be $-(10)^{20}$. Note that $-(10)^{20}$ is less than $-(10)^{19}$, the only other negative value among the answer choices.

The correct answer is E.

214. The letters D, G, I, I, and T can be used to form 5-letter strings such as DIGIT or DGIIT. Using these letters, how many 5-letter strings can be formed in which the two occurrences of the letter I are separated by at least one other letter?

(A) 12
(B) 18
(C) 24
(D) 36
(E) 48

Arithmetic Elementary combinatorics

There are 6 ways to select the locations of the 2 occurrences of the letter I, and this number can be determined by listing all such ways as shown below, where the symbol * is used in place of the letters D, G, and T:

I*I**, I**I*, I***I, *I*I*, *I**I, **I*I

Alternatively, the number of ways to select the locations of the 2 occurrences of the letter I can be determined by using $\binom{5}{2} - 4 = \frac{5!}{(2!)(3!)} - 4 = 10 - 4 = 6$, which is the number of ways to select 2 of the 5 locations minus the 4 ways in which the 2 selected locations are adjacent.

For each of these 6 ways to select the locations of the 2 occurrences of the letter I, there are 6 ways to select the locations of the letters D, G, and T, which can be determined by using $3! = 6$ or by listing all such ways:

DGT, DTG, GDT, GTD, TDG, TGD

It follows that the number of ways to select the locations of the 5 letters to form 5-letter strings is $(6)(6) = 36$.

The correct answer is D.

215. Last Sunday a certain store sold copies of Newspaper A for \$1.00 each and copies of Newspaper B for \$1.25 each, and the store sold no other newspapers that day. If *r* percent of the store's revenue from newspaper sales was from Newspaper A and if *p* percent of the newspapers that the store sold were copies of Newspaper A, which of the following expresses *r* in terms of *p* ?

(A) $\frac{100p}{125-p}$

(B) $\frac{150p}{250-p}$

(C) $\frac{300p}{375-p}$

(D) $\frac{400p}{500-p}$

(E) $\frac{500p}{625-p}$

Algebra Simultaneous equations

Let N be the total number of newspapers that the store sold. Then, the number of copies of Newspaper A the store sold was $p\%$ of $N=\left(\frac{p}{100}\right)N$ and the revenue from those copies of Newspaper A, in dollars, was $(1.00)\left(\frac{p}{100}\right)N=\left(\frac{p}{100}\right)N$. The number of copies of Newspaper B the store sold was $(100-p)\%$ of $N=\left(\frac{100-p}{100}\right)N$ and the revenue from those copies of Newspaper B, in dollars, was $(1.25)\left(\frac{100-p}{100}\right)N=\left(\frac{5}{4}\right)\left(\frac{100-p}{100}\right)N$.

The store's total revenue from newspaper sales, in dollars, was $\left(\frac{p}{100}\right)N+\left(\frac{5}{4}\right)\left(\frac{100-p}{100}\right)N$, and the fraction of that revenue from the sale of Newspaper A was

$$\frac{\frac{p}{100}N}{\frac{p}{100}N+\left(\frac{5}{4}\right)\left(\frac{100-p}{100}\right)N}=\frac{\frac{p}{100}}{\frac{4p}{400}+\left(\frac{500-5p}{400}\right)}$$

$$=\frac{\frac{p}{100}}{\frac{4p+500-5p}{400}}$$

$$=\frac{\frac{p}{100}}{\frac{500-p}{400}}$$

$$=\left(\frac{p}{100}\right)\left(\frac{400}{500-p}\right)$$

$$=\frac{4p}{500-p}$$

Since r percent of the store's newspaper sales revenue was from Newspaper A, $\frac{r}{100}=\frac{4p}{500-p}$, and so $r=\frac{400p}{500-p}$.

The correct answer is D.

216. $\frac{0.99999999}{1.0001}-\frac{0.99999991}{1.0003}=$

(A) 10^{-8}

(B) $3(10^{-8})$

(C) $3(10^{-4})$

(D) $2(10^{-4})$

(E) 10^{-4}

Arithmetic Operations on rational numbers

Calculations with lengthy decimals can be avoided by writing 0.99999999 as $1-10^{-8}$, 0.99999991 as $1-9(10^{-8})$, 1.0001 as $1+10^{-4}$, and 1.0003 as $1+3(10^{-4})$. Doing this gives

$$\frac{1-10^{-8}}{1+10^{-4}}-\frac{1-9(10^{-8})}{1+3(10^{-4})}$$

$$=\frac{[1+10^{-4}][1-10^{-4}]}{1+10^{-4}}-\frac{1-9(10^{-8})}{1+3(10^{-4})}$$

$$=\frac{1-10^{-4}}{1}-\frac{1-9(10^{-8})}{1+3(10^{-4})}$$

$$=\frac{[1-10^{-4}][1+3(10^{-4})]-[1-9(10^{-8})]}{1+3(10^{-4})}$$

$$=\frac{1+3(10^{-4})-10^{-4}-3(10^{-8})-1+9(10^{-8})}{1+3(10^{-4})}$$

$$=\frac{2(10^{-4})+6(10^{-8})}{1+3(10^{-4})}$$

$$=\frac{[2(10^{-4})][1+3(10^{-4})]}{1+3(10^{-4})}$$

$$=2(10^{-4})$$

The correct answer is D.

217. For the past n days, the average (arithmetic mean) daily production at a company was 50 units. If today's production of 90 units raises the average to 55 units per day, what is the value of n ?

(A) 30

(B) 18

(C) 10

(D) 9

(E) 7

Arithmetic; Algebra Statistics; Applied problems; Simultaneous equations

Let x be the total production of the past n days.

Using the formula average $= \frac{\text{sum of values}}{\text{number of values}}$, the information in the problem can be expressed in the following two equations

$50 = \frac{x}{n}$ daily average of 50 units over the past n days

$55 = \frac{x+90}{n+1}$ increased daily average when including today's 90 units

Solving the first equation for x gives $x = 50n$. Then substituting $50n$ for x in the second equation gives the following that can be solved for n:

$$55 = \frac{50n+90}{n+1}$$

$55(n+1) = 50n + 90$ multiply both sides by $(n+1)$

$55n + 55 = 50n + 90$ distribute the 55

$5n = 35$ subtract $50n$ and 55 from both sides

$n = 7$ divide both sides by 5

The correct answer is E.

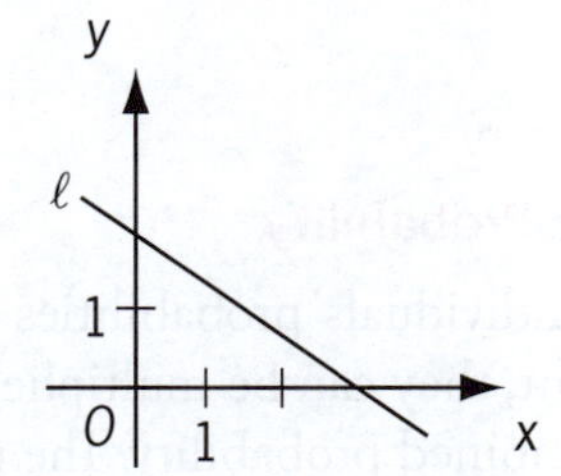

218. In the coordinate system above, which of the following is the equation of line ℓ?

(A) $2x - 3y = 6$
(B) $2x + 3y = 6$
(C) $3x + 2y = 6$
(D) $2x - 3y = -6$
(E) $3x - 2y = -6$

Geometry Simple coordinate geometry

The line is shown going through the points (0,2) and (3,0). The slope of the line can be found with the formula slope $= \frac{\text{change in } y}{\text{change in } x} = \frac{y_2 - y_1}{x_2 - x_1}$ for two points (x_1,y_1) and (x_2,y_2). Thus, the slope of this line equals $\frac{0-2}{3-0} = -\frac{2}{3}$. Using the formula for a line of $y = mx + b$, where m is the slope and b is the y-intercept (in this case, 2), an equation for this line is $y = -\frac{2}{3}x + 2$. Since this equation must be compared to the available answer choices, the following further steps should be taken:

$y = -\frac{2}{3}x + 2$

$3y = -2x + 6$ multiply both sides by 3

$2x + 3y = 6$ add $2x$ to both sides

This problem can also be solved as follows. From the graph, when $x = 0$, y is positive; when $y = 0$, x is positive. This eliminates all but B and C. Of these, B is the only line containing (0,2). Still another way is to use (0,2) to eliminate A, C, and E, and then use (3,0) to eliminate D.

The correct answer is B.

219. If a two-digit positive integer has its digits reversed, the resulting integer differs from the original by 27. By how much do the two digits differ?

(A) 3
(B) 4
(C) 5
(D) 6
(E) 7

Algebra Applied problems

Let the one two-digit integer be represented by $10t + s$, where s and t are digits, and let the other integer with the reversed digits be represented by $10s + t$. The information that the difference between the integers is 27 can be expressed in the following equation, which can be solved for the answer.

$(10s + t) - (10t + s) = 27$

$10s + t - 10t - s = 27$ distribute the negative

$9s - 9t = 27$ combine like terms

$s - t = 3$ divide both sides by 9

Thus, it is seen that the two digits s and t differ by 3.

The correct answer is A.

220. In an electric circuit, two resistors with resistances x and y are connected in parallel. In this case, if r is the combined resistance of these two resistors, then the reciprocal of r is equal to the sum of the reciprocals of x and y. What is r in terms of x and y?

(A) xy

(B) $x + y$

(C) $\frac{1}{x+y}$

(D) $\frac{xy}{x+y}$

(E) $\frac{x+y}{xy}$

Algebra Applied problems

Note that two numbers are reciprocals of each other if and only if their product is 1. Thus the reciprocals of r, x, and y are $\frac{1}{r}$, $\frac{1}{x}$, and $\frac{1}{y}$, respectively. So, according to the problem, $\frac{1}{r} = \frac{1}{x} + \frac{1}{y}$. To solve this equation for r, begin by creating a common denominator on the right side by multiplying the first fraction by $\frac{y}{y}$ and the second fraction by $\frac{x}{x}$:

$$\frac{1}{r} = \frac{1}{x} + \frac{1}{y}$$

$$\frac{1}{r} = \frac{y}{xy} + \frac{x}{xy}$$

$$\frac{1}{r} = \frac{x+y}{xy} \quad \text{combine the fractions on the right side}$$

$$r = \frac{xy}{x+y} \quad \text{invert the fractions on both sides}$$

The correct answer is D.

221. Xavier, Yvonne, and Zelda each try independently to solve a problem. If their individual probabilities for success are $\frac{1}{4}$, $\frac{1}{2}$, and $\frac{5}{8}$, respectively, what is the probability that Xavier and Yvonne, but not Zelda, will solve the problem?

(A) $\frac{11}{8}$

(B) $\frac{7}{8}$

(C) $\frac{9}{64}$

(D) $\frac{5}{64}$

(E) $\frac{3}{64}$

Arithmetic Probability

Since the individuals' probabilities are independent, they can be multiplied to figure out the combined probability. The probability of Xavier's success is given as $\frac{1}{4}$, and the probability of Yvonne's success is given as $\frac{1}{2}$. Since the probability of Zelda's success is given as $\frac{5}{8}$, then the probability of her NOT solving the problem is $1 - \frac{5}{8} = \frac{3}{8}$.

Thus, the combined probability is $\left(\frac{1}{4}\right)\left(\frac{1}{2}\right)\left(\frac{3}{8}\right) = \frac{3}{64}$.

The correct answer is E.

222. If $\frac{1}{x}-\frac{1}{x+1}=\frac{1}{x+4}$, then x could be

(A) 0
(B) –1
(C) –2
(D) –3
(E) –4

Algebra Second-degree equations

Solve the equation for x. Begin by multiplying all the terms by $x(x+1)(x+4)$ to eliminate the denominators.

$$\frac{1}{x}-\frac{1}{x+1}=\frac{1}{x+4}$$

$$(x+1)(x+4)-x(x+4)=x(x+1)$$

$(x+4)(x+1-x)=x(x+1)$ factor the $(x+4)$ out front on the left side

$(x+4)(1)=x(x+1)$ simplify

$(x+4)=x^2+x$ distribute the x on the right side

$4=x^2$ subtract x from both sides

$\pm 2=x$ take the square root of both sides

Both – 2 and 2 are square roots of 4 since $(-2^2)=4$ and $(2^2)=4$. Thus, x could be – 2.

This problem can also be solved as follows. Rewrite the left side as, $\frac{(x+1)-x}{x(x+1)}=\frac{1}{x(x+1)}$, then set equal to the right side to get $\frac{1}{x(x+1)}=\frac{1}{x+4}$. Next, cross multiply: $(1)(x+4)=x(x+1)(1)$. Therefore, $x+4=x^2+x$, or $x^2=4$, so $x=\pm 2$.

The correct answer is C.

223. $\left(\frac{1}{2}\right)^{-3}\left(\frac{1}{4}\right)^{-2}\left(\frac{1}{16}\right)^{-1}=$

(A) $\left(\frac{1}{2}\right)^{-48}$
(B) $\left(\frac{1}{2}\right)^{-11}$
(C) $\left(\frac{1}{2}\right)^{-6}$
(D) $\left(\frac{1}{8}\right)^{-11}$
(E) $\left(\frac{1}{8}\right)^{-6}$

Arithmetic Operations on rational numbers

It is clear from the answer choices that all three factors need to be written with a common denominator, and they thus become

$$\left(\frac{1}{2}\right)^{-3}=\left(\frac{1}{2}\right)^{-3}$$

$$\left(\frac{1}{4}\right)^{-2}=\left(\left(\frac{1}{2}\right)^{2}\right)^{-2}=\left(\frac{1}{2}\right)^{-4}$$

$$\left(\frac{1}{16}\right)^{-1}=\left(\left(\frac{1}{2}\right)^{4}\right)^{-1}=\left(\frac{1}{2}\right)^{-4}$$

So, $\left(\frac{1}{2}\right)^{-3}\left(\frac{1}{4}\right)^{-2}\left(\frac{1}{16}\right)^{-1}=$

$$\left(\frac{1}{2}\right)^{-3}\left(\frac{1}{2}\right)^{-4}\left(\frac{1}{2}\right)^{-4}=\left(\frac{1}{2}\right)^{-3-4-4}=\left(\frac{1}{2}\right)^{-11}.$$

The correct answer is B.

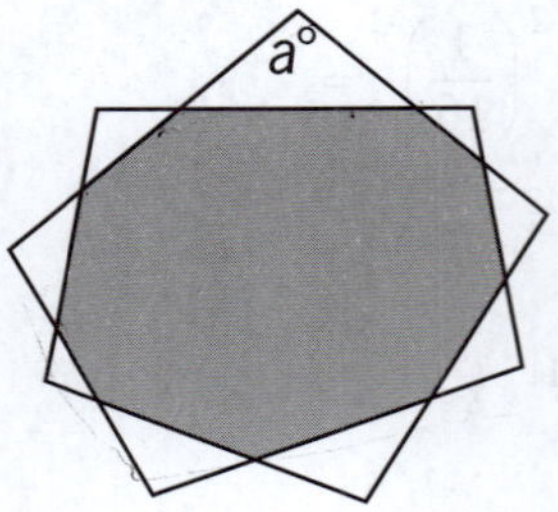

224. The figure shown above consists of a shaded 9-sided polygon and 9 unshaded isosceles triangles. For each isosceles triangle, the longest side is a side of the shaded polygon and the two sides of equal length are extensions of the two adjacent sides of the shaded polygon. What is the value of *a* ?

(A) 100
(B) 105
(C) 110
(D) 115
(E) 120

Geometry Polygons

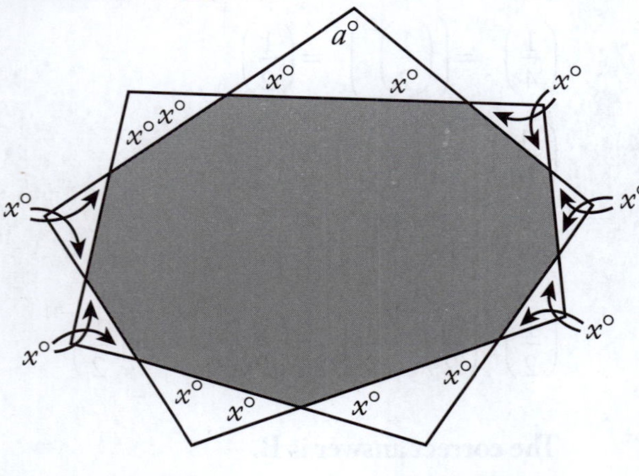

Let $x°$ represent the measure of each base angle of the triangle with vertex angle labeled $a°$. Each base angle of this triangle and one base angle of a triangle with which it shares a vertex are vertical angles and have the same measure. Thus, the base angles of these triangles also have measure $x°$. This pattern continues for the base angles of each pair of triangles that share a vertex, so each base angle of each of the 9 triangles has measure $x°$, as shown above. Also, the vertex angle of each of the 9 triangles has measure $a° = 180° - 2x°$.

Each interior angle of the shaded polygon has measure $(180 - x)°$ since each forms a straight angle with an angle that has measure $x°$, and the sum of the measures is $(9)(180 - x)°$. But the sum of the interior angles of a polygon with n sides is $(n - 2)(180°)$, so the sum of the interior angles of a 9-sided polygon is $(7)(180°) = 1{,}260°$. Therefore, $(9)(180 - x)° = 1{,}260°$ and $x = 40$. Finally, $a = 180 - 2x = 180 - 2(40) = 100$.

The correct answer is A.

225. List *T* consists of 30 positive decimals, none of which is an integer, and the sum of the 30 decimals is *S*. The estimated sum of the 30 decimals, *E*, is defined as follows. Each decimal in *T* whose tenths digit is even is rounded up to the nearest integer, and each decimal in *T* whose tenths digit is odd is rounded down to the nearest integer; *E* is the sum of the resulting integers. If $\frac{1}{3}$ of the decimals in *T* have a tenths digit that is even, which of the following is a possible value of $E - S$?

I. -16
II. 6
III. 10

(A) I only
(B) I and II only
(C) I and III only
(D) II and III only
(E) I, II, and III

Arithmetic Operations on rational numbers

Since $\frac{1}{3}$ of the 30 decimals in T have an even tenths digit, it follows that $\frac{1}{3}(30) = 10$ decimals in T have an even tenths digit. Let T_E represent the list of these 10 decimals, let S_E represent the sum of all 10 decimals in T_E, and let E_E represent the estimated sum of all 10 decimals in T_E after rounding. The remaining 20 decimals in T have an odd tenths digit. Let T_O represent the list of these 20 remaining decimals, let S_O represent the sum of all 20 decimals in T_O, and let E_O represent the estimated sum of all 20 decimals in T_O after rounding. Note that $E = E_E + E_O$ and $S = S_E + S_O$ and hence $E - S = (E_E + E_O) - (S_E + S_O) = (E_E - S_E) + (E_O - S_O)$.

The least values of $E_E - S_E$ occur at the extreme where each decimal in T_E has tenths digit 8. Here, the difference between the rounded integer and the original decimal is greater than 0.1. (For example, the difference between the integer 15 and 14.899 that has been rounded to 15 is 0.101.) Hence, $E_E - S_E > 10(0.1) = 1$. The greatest values of $E_E - S_E$ occur at the other extreme, where each decimal in T_E has tenths digit 0. Here, the difference between the rounded integer and the original decimal is less than 1. (For example, the difference between the integer 15 and 14.001 that has been rounded to 15 is 0.999.) Hence, $E_E - S_E < 10(1) = 10$. Thus, $1 < E_E - S_E < 10$.

Similarly, the least values of $E_O - S_O$ occur at the extreme where each decimal in T_O has tenths digit 9. Here, the difference between the rounded integer and the original decimal is greater than -1. (For example, the difference between the integer 14 and 14.999 that has been rounded to 14 is -0.999.) Hence $E_O - S_O > 20(-1) = -20$. The greatest values of $E_O - S_O$ occur at the other extreme where each decimal in T_O has tenths digit 1. Here, the difference between the rounded integer and the original decimal is less than or equal to -0.1. (For example, the difference between the integer 14 and 14.1 that has been rounded to 14 is -0.1.) Hence, $E_O - S_O \leq 20(-0.1) = -2$. Thus, $-20 < E_O - S_O \leq -2$.

Adding the inequalities $1 < E_E - S_E < 10$ and $-20 < E_O - S_O \leq -2$ gives $-19 < (E_E - S_E) + (E_O - S_O) < 8$. Therefore, $-19 < (E_E + E_O) - (S_E + S_O) < 8$ and $-19 < E - S < 8$. Thus, of the values -16, 6, and 10 for $E - S$, only -16 and 6 are possible.

Note that if T contains 10 repetitions of the decimal 1.8 and 20 repetitions of the decimal 1.9, $S = 10(1.8) + 20(1.9) = 18 + 38 = 56$, $E = 10(2) + 20(1) = 40$, and $E - S = 40 - 56 = -16$. Also, if T contains 10 repetitions of the decimal 1.2 and 20 repetitions of the decimal 1.1, $S = 10(1.2) + 20(1.1) = 12 + 22 = 34$, $E = 10(2) + 20(1) = 40$, and $E - S = 40 - 34 = 6$.

The correct answer is B.

226. If $5 - \frac{6}{x} = x$, then x has how many possible values?

(A) None
(B) One
(C) Two
(D) A finite number greater than two
(E) An infinite number

Algebra Second-degree equations

Solve the equation to determine how many values are possible for x.

$$5 - \frac{6}{x} = x$$
$$5x - 6 = x^2$$
$$0 = x^2 - 5x + 6$$
$$0 = (x-3)(x-2)$$
$$x = 3 \text{ or } 2$$

The correct answer is C.

227. Seed mixture X is 40 percent ryegrass and 60 percent bluegrass by weight; seed mixture Y is 25 percent ryegrass and 75 percent fescue. If a mixture of X and Y contains 30 percent ryegrass, what percent of the weight of the mixture is X ?

(A) 10%
(B) $33\frac{1}{3}$%
(C) 40%
(D) 50%
(E) $66\frac{2}{3}$%

Algebra Applied problems

Let X be the amount of seed mixture X in the final mixture, and let Y be the amount of seed mixture Y in the final mixture. The final mixture of X and Y needs to contain 30 percent ryegrass seed, so any other kinds of grass seed are irrelevant to the solution to this problem. The information about the ryegrass percentages for X, Y, and the final mixture can be expressed in the following equation and solved for X.

$$0.40X + 0.25Y = 0.30(X + Y)$$

$0.40X + 0.25Y = 0.30X + 0.30Y$ — distribute the 0.30 on the right side

$0.10X = 0.05Y$ — subtract $0.30X$ and $0.25Y$ from both sides

$X = 0.5Y$ — divide both sides by 0.10

Using this, the percent of the weight of the combined mixture $(X+Y)$ that is X is

$$\frac{X}{X+Y}=\frac{0.5Y}{0.5Y+Y}=\frac{0.5Y}{1.5Y}=\frac{0.5}{1.5}=0.33\overline{3}=33\frac{1}{3}\%$$

The correct answer is B.

228. How many of the integers that satisfy the inequality $\frac{(x+2)(x+3)}{x-2}\geq 0$ are less than 5 ?

(A) 1

(B) 2

(C) 3

(D) 4

(E) 5

Algebra Inequalities

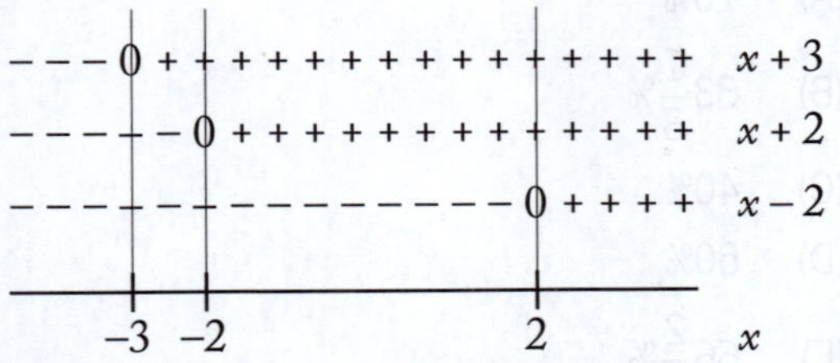

Pictorially, the number line above shows the algebraic signs of the expressions $(x+3)$, $(x+2)$, and $(x-2)$. For example, $x+3$ is 0 when $x=-3$, $x+3$ is negative when $x<-3$, and $x+3$ is positive when $x>-3$. The expression $\frac{(x+2)(x+3)}{x-2}$ will be positive in the intervals of the number line where the number of minus signs is even. Therefore $\frac{(x+2)(x+3)}{x-2}$ is positive for values of x such that $-3<x<-2$ and for values of x such that $x>2$. The only integer values of x in these intervals that are also less than 5 are 3 and 4. Also, $\frac{(x+2)(x+3)}{x-2}$ will be zero if and only if $(x+2)(x+3)=0$, which has two integer solutions less than 5, namely, $x=-2$ and $x=-3$.

Therefore, there are four integers less than 5 that satisfy $\frac{(x+2)(x+3)}{x-2}\geq 0$ and those integers are -3, -2, 3, and 4.

Alternatively, $\frac{(x+2)(x+3)}{x-2}$ will be zero if and only if $(x+2)(x+3)=0$, which has two integer solutions less than 5, namely, $x=-2$ and $x=-3$. Also, $\frac{(x+2)(x+3)}{x-2}$ will be positive if $(x+2)(x+3)$ and $x-2$ are both positive or both negative, and for no other values of x. On the one hand, $(x+2)(x+3)$ will be positive when $x+2$ and $x+3$ are both positive, which will be the case when $x>-2$ and $x>-3$ and thus when $x>-2$. On the other hand, $(x+2)(x+3)$ will be positive when $x+2$ and $x+3$ are both negative, which will be the case when $x<-2$ and $x<-3$ and thus when $x<-3$. So, $(x+2)(x+3)$ will be positive when $x<-3$ or $x>-2$. (This result can also be deduced from the fact that the graph of $y=(x+2)(x+3)$ is a parabola with x-intercepts $(-2,0)$ and $(-3,0)$ that opens upward.) Since $x-2$ will be positive when $x>2$, it follows that $(x+2)(x+3)$ and $x-2$ are both positive when $x>2$, which includes exactly two integer values less than 5, namely, $x=3$ and $x=4$. There are no integer values of x such that $(x+2)(x+3)$ and $x-2$ are both negative, since $(x+2)(x+3)$ is negative if and only if x lies between -3 and -2 and there are no integers between -3 and -2. Therefore, there are exactly 4 integer values of x less than 5 such that $\frac{(x+2)(x+3)}{x-2}\geq 0$.

Two of the values, $x=-2$ and $x=-3$, arise from solutions to $\frac{(x+2)(x+3)}{x-2}=0$, and two of the values, $x=3$ and $x=4$, arise from solutions to $\frac{(x+2)(x+3)}{x-2}>0$.

The correct answer is D.

229. Of the 150 houses in a certain development, 60 percent have air-conditioning, 50 percent have a sunporch, and 30 percent have a swimming pool. If 5 of the houses have all three of these amenities and 5 have none of them, how many of the houses have exactly two of these amenities?

(A) 10
(B) 45
(C) 50
(D) 55
(E) 65

Arithmetic Sets

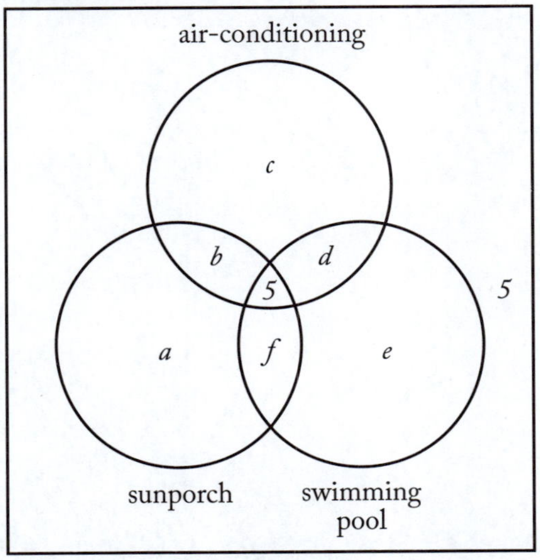

Since 60% of the 150 houses have air-conditioning, $b + c + d + 5 = 0.6(150) = 90$, so $b + c + d = 85$ (i). Similarly, since 50% have a sunporch, $a + b + f + 5 = 0.5(150) = 75$, so $a + b + f = 70$ (ii). Likewise, since 30% have a swimming pool, $d + e + f + 5 = 0.3(150) = 45$, so $d + e + f = 40$ (iii). Adding equations (i), (ii), and (iii) gives $(b + c + d) + (a + b + f) + (d + e + f) = 195$, or $a + 2b + c + 2d + e + 2f = 195$ (iv). But $a + b + c + d + e + f + 5 + 5 = 150$, or $a + b + c + d + e + f = 140$ (v). Subtracting equation (v) from equation (iv) gives $b + d + f = 55$, so 55 houses have exactly two of the amenities.

The correct answer is D.

230. The value of $\frac{2^{-14}+2^{-15}+2^{-16}+2^{-17}}{5}$ is how many times the value of 2^{-17}?

(A) $\frac{3}{2}$
(B) $\frac{5}{2}$
(C) 3
(D) 4
(E) 5

Arithmetic Negative exponents

If the value of $\frac{2^{-14}+2^{-15}+2^{-16}+2^{-17}}{5}$ is x times the value of 2^{-17}, then

$$x\left(2^{-17}\right)=\frac{2^{-14}+2^{-15}+2^{-16}+2^{-17}}{5}$$

$$x=\frac{\frac{2^{-14}+2^{-15}+2^{-16}+2^{-17}}{5}}{2^{-17}}$$

$$=\frac{2^{-14}+2^{-15}+2^{-16}+2^{-17}}{5}\times 2^{17}$$

$$=\frac{\left(2^{-14}+2^{-15}+2^{-16}+2^{-17}\right)\times 2^{17}}{5}$$

$$=\frac{2^{-14+17}+2^{-15+17}+2^{-16+17}+2^{-17+17}}{5}$$

$$=\frac{2^{3}+2^{2}+2^{1}+2^{0}}{5}$$

$$=\frac{8+4+2+1}{5}$$

$$=3$$

The correct answer is C.

6.0 Data Sufficiency

6.0 Data Sufficiency

Data sufficiency questions appear in the Quantitative section of the GMAT® exam. Multiple-choice data sufficiency questions are intermingled with problem solving questions throughout the section. You will have 75 minutes to complete the Quantitative section of the GMAT exam, or about 2 minutes to answer each question. These questions require knowledge of the following topics:

- Arithmetic
- Elementary algebra
- Commonly known concepts of geometry

Data sufficiency questions are designed to measure your ability to analyze a quantitative problem, recognize which given information is relevant, and determine at what point there is sufficient information to solve a problem. In these questions, you are to classify each problem according to the five fixed answer choices, rather than find a solution to the problem.

Each data sufficiency question consists of a question, often accompanied by some initial information, and two statements, labeled (1) and (2), which contain additional information. You must decide whether the information in each statement is sufficient to answer the question or—if neither statement provides enough information—whether the information in the two statements together is sufficient. It is also possible that the statements, in combination, do not give enough information to answer the question.

Begin by reading the initial information and the question carefully. Next, consider the first statement. Does the information provided by the first statement enable you to answer the question? Go on to the second statement. Try to ignore the information given in the first statement when you consider whether the second statement provides information that, by itself, allows you to answer the question. Now you should be able to say, for each statement, whether it is sufficient to determine the answer.

Next, consider the two statements in tandem. Do they, together, enable you to answer the question?

Look again at your answer choices. Select the one that most accurately reflects whether the statements provide the information required to answer the question.

6.1 Test-Taking Strategies

1. Do not waste valuable time solving a problem.

You only need to determine whether sufficient information is given to solve it.

2. Consider each statement separately.

First, decide whether each statement alone gives sufficient information to solve the problem. Be sure to disregard the information given in statement (1) when you evaluate the information given in statement (2). If either, or both, of the statements give(s) sufficient information to solve the problem, select the answer corresponding to the description of which statement(s) give(s) sufficient information to solve the problem.

3. Judge the statements in tandem if neither statement is sufficient by itself.

It is possible that the two statements together do not provide sufficient information. Once you decide, select the answer corresponding to the description of whether the statements together give sufficient information to solve the problem.

4. Answer the question asked.

For example, if the question asks, "What is the value of y?" for an answer statement to be sufficient, you must be able to find one and only one value for y. Being able to determine minimum or maximum values for an answer (e.g., $y = x + 2$) is not sufficient, because such answers constitute a range of values rather than the specific value of y.

5. Be very careful not to make unwarranted assumptions based on the images represented.

Figures are not necessarily drawn to scale; they are generalized figures showing little more than intersecting line segments and the relationships of points, angles, and regions. For example, if a figure described as a rectangle looks like a square, do *not* conclude that it is actually a square just by looking at the figure.

If statement 1 is sufficient, then the answer must be **A or D.**

If statement 2 is not sufficient, then the answer must be **A.**

If statement 2 is sufficient, then the answer must be **D.**

If statement 1 is not sufficient, then the answer must be **B, C, or E.**

If statement 2 is sufficient, then the answer must be **B.**

If statement 2 is not sufficient, then the answer must be **C or E.**

If both statements together are sufficient, then the answer must be **C.**

If both statements together are still not sufficient, then the answer must be **E.**

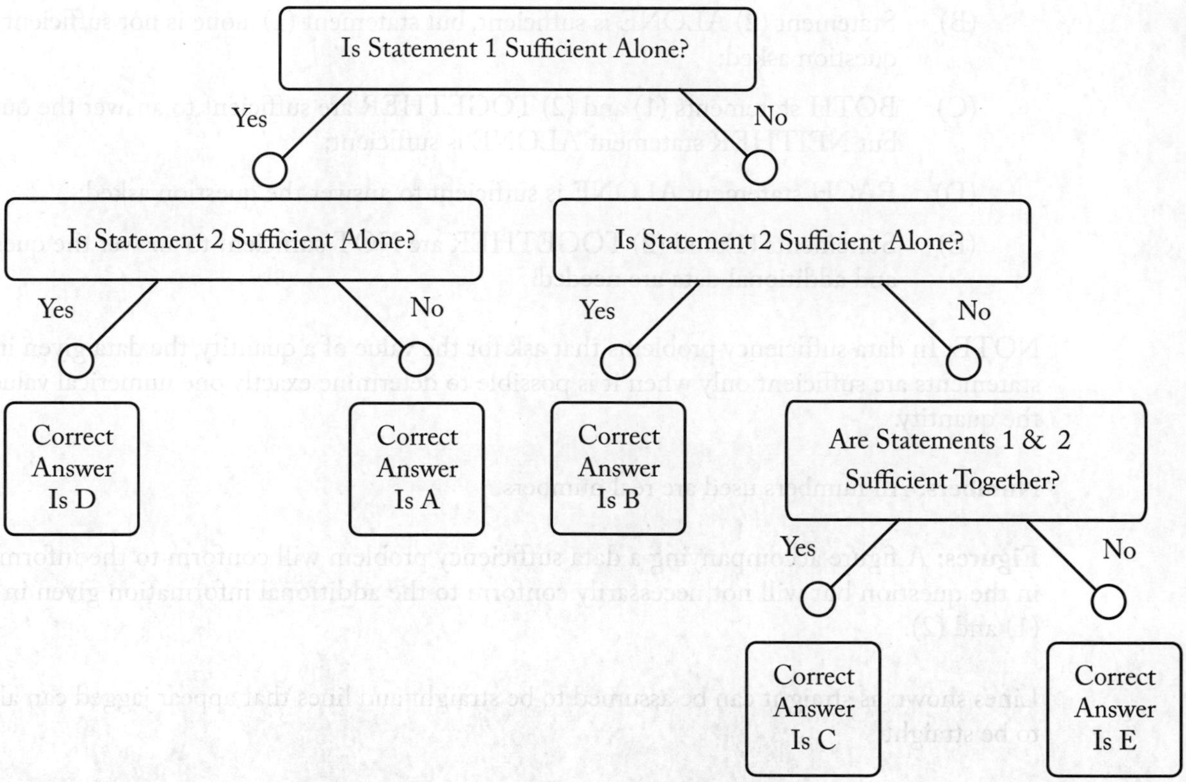

6.2 The Directions

These directions are similar to those you will see for data sufficiency questions when you take the GMAT exam. If you read the directions carefully and understand them clearly before going to sit for the test, you will not need to spend much time reviewing them when you take the GMAT exam.

Each data sufficiency problem consists of a question and two statements, labeled (1) and (2), that give data. You have to decide whether the data given in the statements are *sufficient* for answering the question. Using the data given in the statements *plus* your knowledge of mathematics and everyday facts (such as the number of days in July or the meaning of *counterclockwise*), you must indicate whether the data given in the statements are sufficient for answering the questions and then indicate one of the following answer choices:

(A) Statement (1) ALONE is sufficient, but statement (2) alone is not sufficient to answer the question asked;

(B) Statement (2) ALONE is sufficient, but statement (1) alone is not sufficient to answer the question asked;

(C) BOTH statements (1) and (2) TOGETHER are sufficient to answer the question asked, but NEITHER statement ALONE is sufficient;

(D) EACH statement ALONE is sufficient to answer the question asked;

(E) Statements (1) and (2) TOGETHER are NOT sufficient to answer the question asked, and additional data are needed.

NOTE: In data sufficiency problems that ask for the value of a quantity, the data given in the statements are sufficient only when it is possible to determine exactly one numerical value for the quantity.

Numbers: All numbers used are real numbers.

Figures: A figure accompanying a data sufficiency problem will conform to the information given in the question but will not necessarily conform to the additional information given in statements (1) and (2).

Lines shown as straight can be assumed to be straight and lines that appear jagged can also be assumed to be straight.

You may assume that the positions of points, angles, regions, and so forth exist in the order shown and that angle measures are greater than zero degrees.

All figures lie in a plane unless otherwise indicated.

To register for the GMAT exam go to www.mba.com

6.3 Practice Questions

Each data sufficiency problem consists of a question and two statements, labeled (1) and (2), which contain certain data. Using these data and your knowledge of mathematics and everyday facts (such as the number of days in July or the meaning of the word *counterclockwise*), decide whether the data given are sufficient for answering the question and then indicate one of the following answer choices:

A Statement (1) ALONE is sufficient, but statement (2) alone is not sufficient.
B Statement (2) ALONE is sufficient, but statement (1) alone is not sufficient.
C BOTH statements TOGETHER are sufficient, but NEITHER statement ALONE is sufficient.
D EACH statement ALONE is sufficient.
E Statements (1) and (2) TOGETHER are NOT sufficient.

Note: In data sufficiency problems that ask for the value of a quantity, the data given in the statements are sufficient only when it is possible to determine exactly one numerical value for the quantity.

Example:

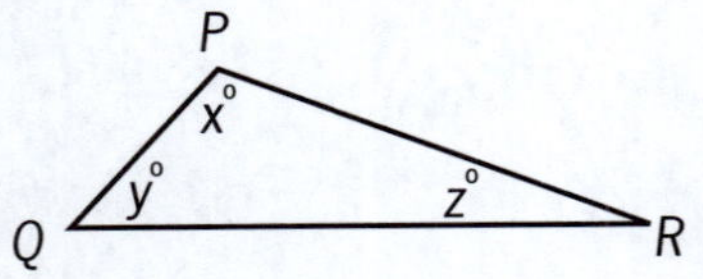

In, ΔPQR what is the value of x?

(1) $PQ = PR$

(2) $y = 40$

Explanation: According to statement (1) $PQ = PR$; therefore, ΔPQR is isosceles and $y = z$. Since $x + y + z = 180$, it follows that $x + 2y = 180$. Since statement (1) does not give a value for y, you cannot answer the question using statement (1) alone. According to statement (2), $y = 40$; therefore, $x + z = 140$. Since statement (2) does not give a value for z, you cannot answer the question using statement (2) alone. Using both statements together, since $x + 2y = 180$ and the value of y is given, you can find the value of x. Therefore, BOTH statements (1) and (2) TOGETHER are sufficient to answer the questions, but NEITHER statement ALONE is sufficient.

Numbers: All numbers used are real numbers.

Figures:

- Figures conform to the information given in the question, but will not necessarily conform to the additional information given in statements (1) and (2).
- Lines shown as straight are straight, and lines that appear jagged are also straight.
- The positions of points, angles, regions, etc., exist in the order shown, and angle measures are greater than zero.
- All figures lie in a plane unless otherwise indicated.

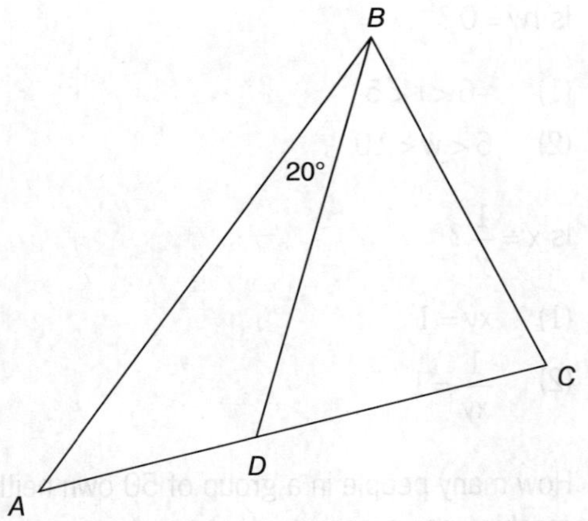

231. In the figure above, point D is on $\overline{AC}$. What is the degree measure of $\angle BAC$?

(1) The measure of $\angle BDC$ is 60°.

(2) The degree measure of $\angle BAC$ is less than the degree measure of $\angle BCD$.

232. A citrus fruit grower receives \$15 for each crate of oranges shipped and \$18 for each crate of grapefruit shipped. How many crates of oranges did the grower ship last week?

(1) Last week the number of crates of oranges that the grower shipped was 20 more than twice the number of crates of grapefruit shipped.

(2) Last week the grower received a total of \$38,700 from the crates of oranges and grapefruit shipped.

233. A certain mixture of paint requires blue, yellow, and red paints in ratios of 2:3:1, respectively, and no other ingredients. If there are ample quantities of the blue and red paints available, is there enough of the yellow paint available to make the desired amount of the mixture?

(1) Exactly 20 quarts of the mixture are needed.

(2) Exactly 10 quarts of the yellow paint are available.

234. If Pat saved \$600 of his earnings last month, how much did Pat earn last month?

(1) Pat spent $\frac{1}{2}$ of his earnings last month for living expenses and saved $\frac{1}{3}$ of the remainder.

(2) Of his earnings last month, Pat paid twice as much in taxes as he saved.

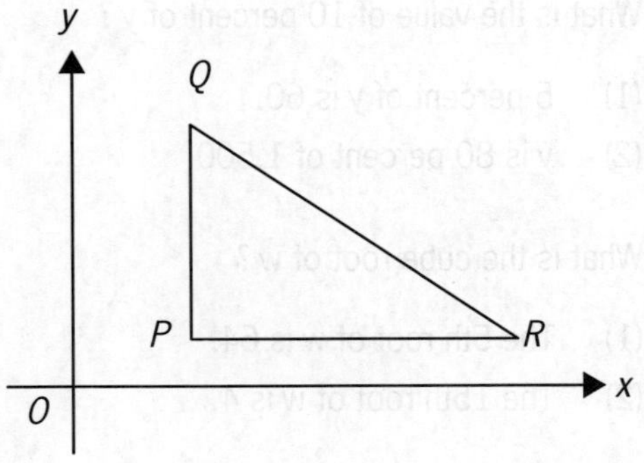

235. In the xy-plane above, is angle QPR a right angle?

(1) Points P and Q have the same x-coordinate.

(2) Points P and R have the same y-coordinate.

236. Each of the marbles in a jar is either red or white or blue. If one marble is to be selected at random from the jar, what is the probability that the marble will be blue?

(1) There are a total of 24 marbles in the jar, 8 of which are red.

(2) The probability that the marble selected will be white is $\frac{1}{2}$.

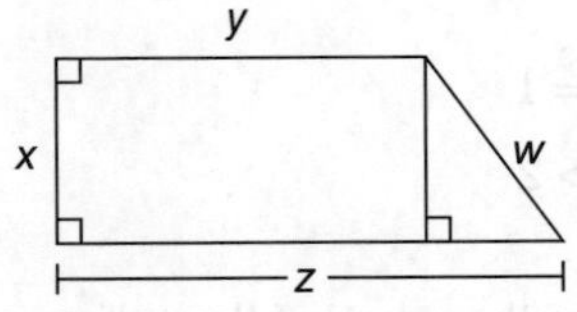

237. In the figure above, what is the value of z?

(1) $x = y = 1$

(2) $w = 2$

238. Water is pumped into a partially filled tank at a constant rate through an inlet pipe. At the same time, water is pumped out of the tank at a constant rate through an outlet pipe. At what rate, in gallons per minute, is the amount of water in the tank increasing?

(1) The amount of water initially in the tank is 200 gallons.

(2) Water is pumped into the tank at a rate of 10 gallons per minute and out of the tank at a rate of 10 gallons every $2\frac{1}{2}$ minutes.

239. What is the value of 10 percent of y?

(1) 5 percent of y is 60.

(2) y is 80 percent of 1,500.

240. What is the cube root of w?

(1) The 5th root of w is 64.

(2) The 15th root of w is 4.

241. If sequence S has 120 terms, what is the 105th term of S?

(1) The first term of S is −8.

(2) Each term of S after the first term is 10 more than the preceding term.

242. The number of seats in the first row of an auditorium is 18 and the number of seats in each row thereafter is 2 more than in the previous row. What is the total number of seats in the rows of the auditorium?

(1) The number of rows of seats in the auditorium is 27.

(2) The number of seats in the last row is 70.

243. If $u > 0$ and $v > 0$, which is greater, u^v or v^u?

(1) $u = 1$

(2) $v > 2$

244. What was the range of the selling prices of the 30 wallets sold by a certain store yesterday?

(1) $\frac{1}{3}$ of the wallets had a selling price of $24 each.

(2) The lowest selling price of the wallets was $\frac{1}{3}$ the highest selling price of the wallets.

245. Three houses are being sold through a real estate agent. What is the asking price for the house with the second-largest asking price?

(1) The difference between the greatest and the least asking price is $130,000.

(2) The difference between the two greater asking prices is $85,000.

246. Is $rw = 0$?

(1) $-6 < r < 5$

(2) $6 < w < 10$

247. Is $x = \frac{1}{y}$?

(1) $xy = 1$

(2) $\frac{1}{xy} = 1$

248. How many people in a group of 50 own neither a fax machine nor a laser printer?

(1) The total number of people in the group who own a fax machine or a laser printer or both is less than 50.

(2) The total number of people in the group who own both a fax machine and a laser printer is 15.

249. What is the value of w^{-2}?

(1) $w^{-1} = \frac{1}{2}$

(2) $w^3 = 8$

250. A certain investment earned a fixed rate of 4 percent interest per year, compounded annually, for five years. The interest earned for the third year of the investment was how many dollars greater than that for the first year?

(1) The amount of the investment at the beginning of the second year was $4,160.00.

(2) The amount of the investment at the beginning of the third year was $4,326.40.

251. On a recent trip, Mary drove 50 miles. What was the average speed at which she drove the 50 miles?

(1) She drove 30 miles at an average speed of 60 miles per hour and then drove the remaining 20 miles at an average speed of 50 miles per hour.

(2) She drove a total of 54 minutes.

252. What is the value of t?

(1) $s + t = 6 + s$

(2) $t^3 = 216$

253. For a certain car repair, the total charge consisted of a charge for parts, a charge for labor, and a 6 percent sales tax on both the charge for parts and the charge for labor. If the charge for parts, excluding sales tax, was \$50.00, what was the total charge for the repair?

(1) The sales tax on the charge for labor was \$9.60.

(2) The total sales tax was \$12.60.

254. George has a total of *B* books in his library, 25 of which are hardcover fiction books. What is the value of *B* ?

(1) 40 of the *B* books are fiction and the rest are nonfiction.

(2) 60 of the *B* books are hardcovers and the rest are paperbacks.

255. Is $w + h^4$ positive?

(1) *h* is positive.

(2) *w* is positive.

256. In Mr. Smith's class, what is the ratio of the number of boys to the number of girls?

(1) There are 3 times as many girls as boys in Mr. Smith's class.

(2) The number of boys is $\frac{1}{4}$ of the total number of boys and girls in Mr. Smith's class.

257. If the sequence *S* has 300 terms, what is the 293rd term of *S* ?

(1) The 298th term of *S* is –616, and each term of *S* after the first is 2 less than the preceding term.

(2) The first term of *S* is –22.

258. If *a* is a 3-digit integer and *b* is a 3-digit integer, is the units digit of the product of *a* and *b* greater than 5 ?

(1) The units digit of *a* is 4.

(2) The units digit of *b* is 7.

259. In each of the last five years, Company K donated *p* percent of its annual profits to a certain scholarship fund. Did Company K donate more than \$10,000 to the scholarship fund last year?

(1) Two years ago, Company K had annual profits of \$3 million and donated \$15,000 to the scholarship fund.

(2) Last year, Company K had annual profits of \$2.5 million.

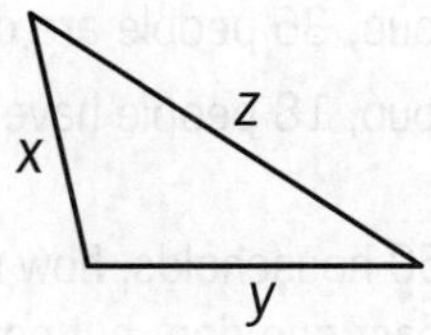

260. Is the area of the triangular region above less than 20 ?

(1) $x^2 + y^2 \neq z^2$

(2) $x + y < 13$

261. *A*, *B*, *C*, and *D* are points on a line. If *C* is the midpoint of line segment *AB* and if *D* is the midpoint of line segment *CB*, is the length of line segment *DB* greater than 5 ?

(1) The length of line segment *AC* is greater than 8.

(2) The length of line segment *CD* is greater than 6.

262. The people in a line waiting to buy tickets to a show are standing one behind the other. Adam and Beth are among the people in the line, and Beth is standing behind Adam with a number of people between them. If the number of people in front of Adam plus the number of people behind Beth is 18, how many people in the line are behind Beth?

(1) There are a total of 32 people in the line.

(2) 23 people in the line are behind Adam.

263. Square *ABCD* is inscribed in circle *O*. What is the area of square region *ABCD* ?

(1) The area of circular region *O* is 64π.

(2) The circumference of circle *O* is 16π.

264. Lines *k* and *m* are parallel to each other. Is the slope of line *k* positive?

(1) Line *k* passes through the point (3,2).

(2) Line *m* passes through the point (–3,2).

265. In cross section, a tunnel that carries one lane of one-way traffic is a semicircle with radius 4.2 m. Is the tunnel large enough to accommodate the truck that is approaching the entrance to the tunnel?

(1) The maximum width of the truck is 2.4 m.

(2) The maximum height of the truck is 4 m.

266. In a certain group of 50 people, how many are doctors who have a law degree?

(1) In the group, 36 people are doctors.

(2) In the group, 18 people have a law degree.

267. Of a group of 50 households, how many have at least one cat or at least one dog, but not both?

(1) The number of households that have at least one cat and at least one dog is 4.

(2) The number of households that have no cats and no dogs is 14.

268. On a certain date, Hannah invested $5,000 at *x* percent simple annual interest and a different amount at *y* percent simple annual interest. What amount did Hannah invest at *y* percent simple annual interest?

(1) The total amount of interest earned by Hannah's two investments in one year was $900.

(2) Hannah invested the $5,000 at 6 percent simple annual interest.

269. Do at least 60 percent of the students in Pat's class walk to school?

(1) At least 60 percent of the female students in Pat's class walk to school.

(2) The number of students in Pat's class who walk to school is twice the number of students who do not walk to school.

270. The profit from the sale of a certain appliance increases, though not proportionally, with the number of units sold. Did the profit exceed $4 million on sales of 380,000 units?

(1) The profit exceeded $2 million on sales of 200,000 units.

(2) The profit exceeded $5 million on sales of 350,000 units.

271. If *n* is an integer, is *n* even?

(1) $n^2 - 1$ is an odd integer.

(2) $3n + 4$ is an even integer.

272. Carmen currently works 30 hours per week at her part-time job. If her gross hourly wage were to increase by $1.50, how many fewer hours could she work per week and still earn the same gross weekly pay as before the increase?

(1) Her gross weekly pay is currently $225.00.

(2) An increase of $1.50 would represent an increase of 20 percent of her current gross hourly wage.

273. A certain plumber charges $92 for each job completed in 4 hours or less and $23 per hour for each job completed in more than 4 hours. If it took the plumber a total of 7 hours to complete two separate jobs, what was the total amount charged by the plumber for the two jobs?

(1) The plumber charged $92 for one of the two jobs.

(2) The plumber charged $138 for one of the two jobs.

274. If *x* and *y* are positive numbers, is $\frac{x+1}{y+1} > \frac{x}{y}$?

(1) $x > 1$

(2) $x < y$

275. If *a* and *b* are positive integers, is $\frac{a}{b} < \frac{9}{11}$?

(1) $\frac{a}{b} < 0.818$

(2) $\frac{b}{a} > 1.223$

276. Every object in a box is either a sphere or a cube, and every object in the box is either red or green. How many objects are in the box?

(1) There are six cubes and five green objects in the box.

(2) There are two red spheres in the box.

277. If x and y are positive integers, is xy even?

(1) $x^2 + y^2 - 1$ is divisible by 4.

(2) $x + y$ is odd.

278. If a and b are integers, is $a + b + 3$ an odd integer?

(1) ab is an odd integer.

(2) $a - b$ is an even integer.

279. If x and y are positive integers, what is the value of $\sqrt{x} + \sqrt{y}$?

(1) $x + y = 15$

(2) $\sqrt{xy} = 6$

280. A certain truck uses $\frac{1}{12} + kv^2$ gallons of fuel per mile when its speed is v miles per hour, where k is a constant. At what speed should the truck travel so that it uses $\frac{5}{12}$ gallon of fuel per mile?

(1) The value of k is $\frac{1}{10,800}$.

(2) When the truck travels at 30 miles per hour, it uses $\frac{1}{6}$ gallon of fuel per mile.

281. If $x = 2t$ and $y = \frac{t}{3}$, what is the value of $x^2 - y^2$?

(1) $t^2 - 3 = 6$

(2) $t^3 = -27$

282. Last school year, each of the 200 students at a certain high school attended the school for the entire year. If there were 8 cultural performances at the school during the last school year, what was the average (arithmetic mean) number of students attending each cultural performance?

(1) Last school year, each student attended at least one cultural performance.

(2) Last school year, the average number of cultural performances attended per student was 4.

283. A clothing manufacturer makes jackets that are wool or cotton or a combination of wool and cotton. The manufacturer has 3,000 pounds of wool and 2,000 pounds of cotton on hand. Is this enough wool and cotton to make at least 1,000 jackets?

(1) Each wool jacket requires 4 pounds of wool, and no cotton.

(2) Each cotton jacket requires 6 pounds of cotton, and no wool.

284. Each month, Jim receives a base salary plus a 10 percent commission on the price of each car he sells that month. If Jim sold 15 cars last month, what was the total amount of base salary and commissions that Jim received that month?

(1) Last month, Jim's base salary was $3,000.

(2) Last month, Jim sold 3 cars whose prices totaled $60,000 and 5 cars whose prices totaled $120,000.

285. If x is a positive integer greater than 1, what is the value of x ?

(1) 2x is a common factor of 18 and 24.

(2) x is a factor of 6.

286. By what percentage was the price of a certain television set discounted for a sale?

(1) The price of the television set before it was discounted for the sale was 25 percent greater than the discounted price.

(2) The price of the television set was discounted by $60 for the sale.

287. Jack wants to use a circular rug on his rectangular office floor to cover two small circular stains, each less than $\frac{\pi}{100}$ square feet in area and each more than 3 feet from the nearest wall. Can the rug be placed to cover both stains?

(1) Jack's rug covers an area of 9π square feet.

(2) The centers of the stains are less than 4 feet apart.

×	*a*	*b*	*c*
a	*d*	*e*	*f*
b	*e*	*g*	*h*
c	*f*	*h*	*j*

288. In the multiplication table above, each letter represents an integer. What is the value of c ?

(1) $c = f$

(2) $h \neq 0$

289. If n is an integer, is $(0.1)^n$ greater than $(10)^n$?

(1) $n > -10$

(2) $n < 10$

290. For a basic monthly fee of F yen (¥F), Naoko's first cell phone plan allowed him to use a maximum of 420 minutes on calls during the month. Then, for each of x additional minutes he used on calls, he was charged ¥M, making his total charge for the month ¥T, where $T = F + xM$. What is the value of F ?

(1) Naoko used 450 minutes on calls the first month and the total charge for the month was ¥13,755.

(2) Naoko used 400 minutes on calls the second month and the total charge for the month was ¥13,125.

291. The weights of all dishes of type X are exactly the same, and the weights of all dishes of type Y are exactly the same. Is the weight of 1 dish of type X less than the weight of 1 dish of type Y ?

(1) The total weight of 3 dishes of type X and 2 dishes of type Y is less than the total weight of 2 dishes of type X and 4 dishes of type Y.

(2) The total weight of 4 dishes of type X and 3 dishes of type Y is less than the total weight of 3 dishes of type X and 4 dishes of type Y.

292. If r and t are three-digit positive integers, is r greater than t ?

(1) The tens digit of r is greater than each of the three digits of t.

(2) The tens digit of r is less than either of the other two digits of r.

293. Is the product of two positive integers x and y divisible by the sum of x and y ?

(1) $x = y$

(2) $x = 2$

294. A certain high school with a total enrollment of 900 students held a science fair for three days last week. How many of the students enrolled in the high school attended the science fair on all three days?

(1) Of the students enrolled in the school, 30 percent attended the science fair on two or more days.

(2) Of the students enrolled in the school, 10 percent of those that attended the science fair on at least one day attended on all three days.

295. The average (arithmetic mean) price of the 3 items that Kate purchased from a clothing store was \$50. If there was no sales tax on any item that had a price of less than \$80 and 6 percent sales tax on all other items, what was the total sales tax on the 3 items that Kate purchased?

(1) The price of the most expensive item that Kate purchased from the store was \$100.

(2) The price of the least expensive item that Kate purchased from the store was \$10.

296. A company makes and sells two products, P and Q. The costs per unit of making and selling P and Q are \$8.00 and \$9.50, respectively, and the selling prices per unit of P and Q are \$10.00 and \$13.00, respectively. In one month the company sold a total of 834 units of these products. Was the total profit on these items more than \$2,000.00 ?

(1) During the month, more units of P than units of Q were sold.

(2) During the month, at least 100 units of Q were sold.

297. Jill has applied for a job with each of two different companies. What is the probability that she will get job offers from both companies?

 (1) The probability that she will get a job offer from neither company is 0.3.

 (2) The probability that she will get a job offer from exactly one of the two companies is 0.5.

298. A scientist recorded the number of eggs in each of 10 birds' nests. What was the standard deviation of the numbers of eggs in the 10 nests?

 (1) The average (arithmetic mean) number of eggs for the 10 nests was 4.

 (2) Each of the 10 nests contained the same number of eggs.

299. A conveyor belt moves bottles at a constant speed of 120 centimeters per second. If the conveyor belt moves a bottle from a loading dock to an unloading dock, is the distance that the conveyor belt moves the bottle less than 90 meters? (1 meter = 100 centimeters)

 (1) It takes the conveyor belt less than 1.2 minutes to move the bottle from the loading dock to the unloading dock.

 (2) It takes the conveyor belt more than 1.1 minutes to move the bottle from the loading dock to the unloading dock.

300. If x, y, and z are positive numbers, what is the value of the average (arithmetic mean) of x and z?

 (1) $x - y = y - z$

 (2) $x^2 - y^2 = z$

301. The rectangular rug shown in the figure above has an accent border. What is the area of the portion of the rug that excludes the border?

 (1) The perimeter of the rug is 44 feet.

 (2) The width of the border on all sides is 1 foot.

302. Terry holds 12 cards, each of which is red, white, green, or blue. If a person is to select a card randomly from the cards Terry is holding, is the probability less than $\frac{1}{2}$ that the card selected will be either red or white?

 (1) The probability that the person will select a blue card is $\frac{1}{3}$.

 (2) The probability that the person will select a red card is $\frac{1}{6}$.

303. If $y \neq 2xz$, what is the value of $\frac{2xz + yz}{2xz - y}$?

 (1) $2x + y = 3$

 (2) $z = 2$

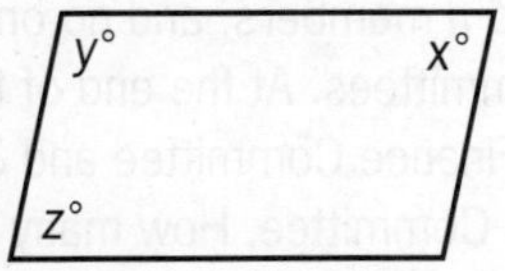

304. In the parallelogram shown, what is the value of x?

 (1) $y = 2x$

 (2) $x + z = 120$

305. In a product test of a common cold remedy, x percent of the patients tested experienced side effects from the use of the drug and y percent experienced relief of cold symptoms. What percent of the patients tested experienced both side effects and relief of cold symptoms?

 (1) Of the 1,000 patients tested, 15 percent experienced neither side effects nor relief of cold symptoms.

 (2) Of the patients tested, 30 percent experienced relief of cold symptoms without side effects.

306. Is $x < 5$?

 (1) $x^2 > 5$

 (2) $x^2 + x < 5$

307. Is $4^{x+y} = 8^{10}$?

 (1) $x - y = 9$

 (2) $\frac{y}{x} = \frac{1}{4}$

308. Is zp negative?

(1) $pz^4 < 0$

(2) $p + z^4 = 14$

309. In each game of a certain tournament, a contestant either loses 3 points or gains 2 points. If Pat had 100 points at the beginning of the tournament, how many games did Pat play in the tournament?

(1) At the end of the tournament, Pat had 104 points.

(2) Pat played fewer than 10 games.

310. At the beginning of the year, the Finance Committee and the Planning Committee of a certain company each had n members, and no one was a member of both committees. At the end of the year, 5 members left the Finance Committee and 3 members left the Planning Committee. How many members did the Finance Committee have at the beginning of the year?

(1) The ratio of the total number of members who left at the end of the year to the total number of members at the beginning of the year was 1:6.

(2) At the end of the year, 21 members remained on the Planning Committee.

311. Can a certain rectangular sheet of glass be positioned on a rectangular tabletop so that it covers the entire tabletop and its edges are parallel to the edges of the tabletop?

(1) The tabletop is 36 inches wide by 60 inches long.

(2) The area of one side of the sheet of glass is 2,400 square inches.

312. In a random sample of 80 adults, how many are college graduates?

(1) In the sample, the number of adults who are <u>not</u> college graduates is 3 times the number who are college graduates.

(2) In the sample, the number of adults who are <u>not</u> college graduates is 40 more than the number who are college graduates.

313. Max purchased a guitar for a total of $624, which consisted of the price of the guitar and the sales tax. Was the sales tax rate greater than 3 percent?

(1) The price of the guitar that Max purchased was less than $602.

(2) The sales tax for the guitar that Max purchased was less than $30.

314. What is the sum of a certain pair of consecutive odd integers?

(1) At least one of the integers is negative.

(2) At least one of the integers is positive.

315. If $a < x < b$ and $c < y < d$, is $x < y$?

(1) $a < c$

(2) $b < c$

316. How many people are directors of both Company K and Company R?

(1) There were 17 directors present at a joint meeting of the directors of Company K and Company R, and no directors were absent.

(2) Company K has 12 directors and Company R has 8 directors.

317. The sum of 4 different odd integers is 64. What is the value of the greatest of these integers?

(1) The integers are consecutive odd numbers.

(2) Of these integers, the greatest is 6 more than the least.

318. Was the number of books sold at Bookstore X last week greater than the number of books sold at Bookstore Y last week?

(1) Last week, more than 1,000 books were sold at Bookstore X on Saturday and fewer than 1,000 books were sold at Bookstore Y on Saturday.

(2) Last week, less than 20 percent of the books sold at Bookstore X were sold on Saturday and more than 20 percent of the books sold at Bookstore Y were sold on Saturday.

319. From May 1 to May 30 in the same year, the balance in a checking account increased. What was the balance in the checking account on May 30 ?

(1) If, during this period of time, the increase in the balance in the checking account had been 12 percent, then the balance in the account on May 30 would have been \$504.

(2) During this period of time, the increase in the balance in the checking account was 8 percent.

320. If x and y are positive, is $x < 10 < y$?

(1) $x < y$ and $xy = 100$

(2) $x^2 < 100 < y^2$

321. A merchant discounted the sale price of a coat and the sale price of a sweater. Which of the two articles of clothing was discounted by the greater dollar amount?

(1) The percent discount on the coat was 2 percentage points greater than the percent discount on the sweater.

(2) Before the discounts, the sale price of the coat was \$10 less than the sale price of the sweater.

322. A taxi company charges f cents for the first mile of the taxi ride and m cents for each additional mile. How much does the company charge for a 10-mile taxi ride?

(1) The company charges \$0.90 for a 2-mile ride.

(2) The company charges \$1.20 for a 4-mile ride.

323. If the positive integer n is added to each of the integers 69, 94, and 121, what is the value of n?

(1) $69 + n$ and $94 + n$ are the squares of two consecutive integers.

(2) $94 + n$ and $121 + n$ are the squares of two consecutive integers.

324. Guy's net income equals his gross income minus his deductions. By what percent did Guy's net income change on January 1, 1989, when both his gross income and his deductions increased?

(1) Guy's gross income increased by 4 percent on January 1, 1989.

(2) Guy's deductions increased by 15 percent on January 1, 1989.

325. If the ratio of the number of teachers to the number of students is the same in School District M and School District P, what is the ratio of the number of students in School District M to the number of students in School District P ?

(1) There are 10,000 more students in School District M than there are in School District P.

(2) The ratio of the number of teachers to the number of students in School District M is 1 to 20.

326. For a certain city's library, the average cost of purchasing each new book is \$28. The library receives \$15,000 from the city each year; the library also receives a bonus of \$2,000 if the total number of items checked out over the course of the year exceeds 5,000. Did the library receive the bonus last year?

(1) The library purchased an average of 50 new books each month last year and received enough money from the city to cover this cost.

(2) The lowest number of items checked out in one month was 459.

327. Each gift certificate sold yesterday by a certain bookstore cost either \$10 or \$50. If yesterday the bookstore sold more than 5 gift certificates that cost \$50 each, what was the total number of gift certificates sold yesterday by the bookstore?

(1) Yesterday the bookstore sold fewer than 10 gift certificates that cost \$10 each.

(2) The total cost of gift certificates sold yesterday by the bookstore was \$460.

328. What is the tens digit of positive integer x?

(1) x divided by 100 has a remainder of 30.

(2) x divided by 110 has a remainder of 30.

329. Three dice, each of which has its 6 sides numbered 1 through 6, are tossed. The sum of the 3 numbers that are facing up is 12. Is at least 1 of these numbers 5 ?

(1) None of the 3 numbers that are facing up is divisible by 3.

(2) Of the numbers that are facing up, 2, but not all 3, are equal.

330. On the number line, point *R* has coordinate *r* and point *T* has coordinate *t*. Is $t < 0$?

(1) $-1 < r < 0$

(2) The distance between *R* and *T* is equal to r^2.

331. *S* is a set of points in the plane. How many distinct triangles can be drawn that have three of the points in *S* as vertices?

(1) The number of distinct points in *S* is 5.

(2) No three of the points in *S* are collinear.

332. Stores L and M each sell a certain product at a different regular price. If both stores discount their regular price of the product, is the discount price at Store M less than the discount price at Store L ?

(1) At Store L the discount price is 10 percent less than the regular price; at Store M the discount price is 15 percent less than the regular price.

(2) At Store L the discount price is \$5 less than the regular store price; at Store M the discount price is \$6 less than the regular price.

333. If *d* denotes a decimal, is $d \geq 0.5$?

(1) When *d* is rounded to the nearest tenth, the result is 0.5.

(2) When *d* is rounded to the nearest integer, the result is 1.

334. In the two-digit integers 3■ and 2▲, the symbols ■ and ▲ represent different digits, and the product (3■)(2▲) is equal to 864. What digit does ■ represent?

(1) The sum of ■ and ▲ is 10.

(2) The product of ■ and ▲ is 24.

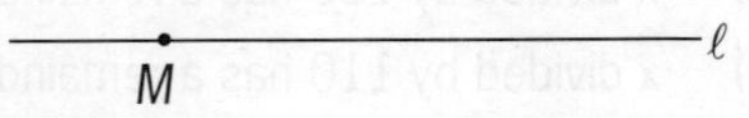

335. Two points, *N* and *Q* (not shown), lie to the right of point *M* on line ℓ. What is the ratio of the length of *QN* to the length of *MQ* ?

(1) Twice the length of *MN* is 3 times the length of *MQ*.

(2) Point *Q* is between points *M* and *N*.

336. Did the sum of the prices of three shirts exceed \$60 ?

(1) The price of the most expensive of the shirts exceeded \$30.

(2) The price of the least expensive of the shirts exceeded \$20.

337. What is the total number of coins that Bert and Claire have?

(1) Bert has 50 percent more coins than Claire.

(2) The total number of coins that Bert and Claire have is between 21 and 28.

338. A telephone station has *x* processors, each of which can process a maximum of *y* calls at any particular time, where *x* and *y* are positive integers. If 500 calls are sent to the station at a particular time, can the station process all of the calls?

(1) $x = 600$

(2) $100 < y < 200$

	Price per Flower
Roses	\$1.00
Daisies	\$0.50

339. Kim and Sue each bought some roses and some daisies at the prices shown above. If Kim bought the same total number of roses and daisies as Sue, was the price of Kim's purchase of roses and daisies higher than the price of Sue's purchase of roses and daisies?

(1) Kim bought twice as many daisies as roses.

(2) Kim bought 4 more roses than Sue bought.

340. Jazz and blues recordings accounted for 6 percent of the \$840 million revenue from the sales of recordings in Country Y in 2000. What was the revenue from the sales of jazz and blues recordings in Country Y in 1998 ?

(1) Jazz and blues recordings accounted for 5 percent of the revenue from the sales of recordings in Country Y in 1998.

(2) The revenue from the sales of jazz and blues recordings in Country Y increased by 40 percent from 1998 to 2000.

341. On a certain nonstop trip, Marta averaged x miles per hour for 2 hours and y miles per hour for the remaining 3 hours. What was her average speed, in miles per hour, for the entire trip?

(1) $2x + 3y = 280$

(2) $y = x + 10$

342. If x is a positive integer, what is the value of $\sqrt{x+24} - \sqrt{x}$?

(1) $\sqrt{x}$ is an integer.

(2) $\sqrt{x+24}$ is an integer.

343. A tank is filled with gasoline to a depth of exactly 2 feet. The tank is a cylinder resting horizontally on its side, with its circular ends oriented vertically. The inside of the tank is exactly 6 feet long. What is the volume of the gasoline in the tank?

(1) The inside of the tank is exactly 4 feet in diameter.

(2) The top surface of the gasoline forms a rectangle that has an area of 24 square feet.

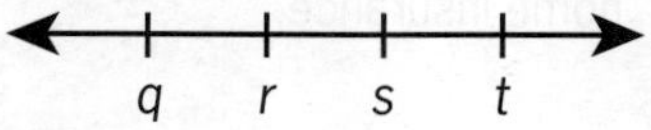

344. Of the four numbers represented on the number line above, is r closest to zero?

(1) $q = -s$

(2) $-t < q$

345. A group consisting of several families visited an amusement park where the regular admission fees were ¥5,500 for each adult and ¥4,800 for each child. Because there were at least 10 people in the group, each paid an admission fee that was 10% less than the regular admission fee. How many children were in the group?

(1) The total of the admission fees paid for the adults in the group was ¥29,700.

(2) The total of the admission fees paid for the children in the group was ¥4,860 more than the total of the admission fees paid for the adults in the group.

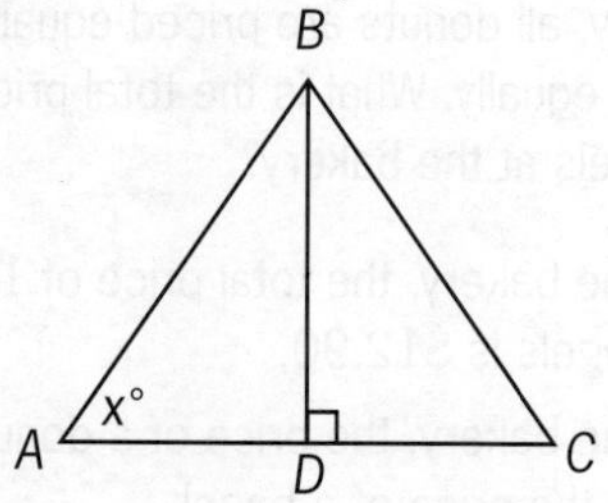

346. What is the area of triangular region ABC above?

(1) The product of BD and AC is 20.

(2) $x = 45$

347. In the xy-coordinate plane, is point R equidistant from points (–3,–3) and (1,–3) ?

(1) The x-coordinate of point R is –1.

(2) Point R lies on the line $y = -3$.

348. What is the ratio of the average (arithmetic mean) height of students in class X to the average height of students in class Y ?

(1) The average height of the students in class X is 120 centimeters.

(2) The average height of the students in class X and class Y combined is 126 centimeters.

349. Is the positive two-digit integer N less than 40 ?

(1) The units digit of N is 6 more than the tens digit.

(2) N is 4 less than 4 times the units digit.

350. If $2^{x+y} = 4^8$, what is the value of y ?

(1) $x^2 = 81$

(2) $x - y = 2$

351. Each week a certain salesman is paid a fixed amount equal to $300, plus a commission equal to 5 percent of the amount of his sales that week over $1,000. What is the total amount the salesman was paid last week?

(1) The total amount the salesman was paid last week is equal to 10 percent of the amount of his sales last week.

(2) The salesman's sales last week totaled $5,000.

352. At a bakery, all donuts are priced equally and all bagels are priced equally. What is the total price of 5 donuts and 3 bagels at the bakery?

(1) At the bakery, the total price of 10 donuts and 6 bagels is \$12.90.

(2) At the bakery, the price of a donut is \$0.15 less than the price of a bagel.

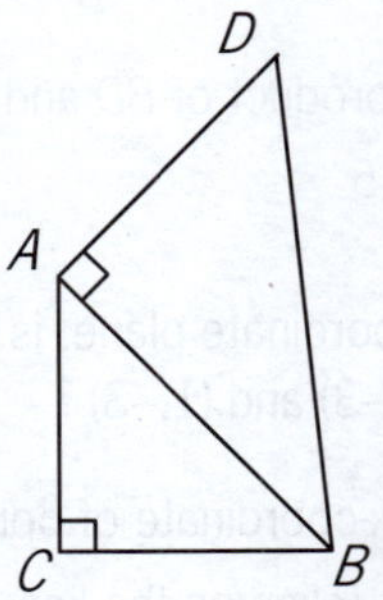

353. In the figure above, is the area of triangular region ABC equal to the area of triangular region DBA?

(1) $(AC)^2 = 2(AD)^2$

(2) ΔABC is isosceles.

354. If r and s are positive integers, can the fraction $\frac{r}{s}$ be expressed as a decimal with only a finite number of nonzero digits?

(1) s is a factor of 100.

(2) r is a factor of 100.

355. If $r > 0$ and $s > 0$, is $\frac{r}{s} < \frac{s}{r}$?

(1) $\frac{r}{3s} = \frac{1}{4}$

(2) $s = r + 4$

356. If k is an integer such that $56 < k < 66$, what is the value of k?

(1) If k were divided by 2, the remainder would be 1.

(2) If $k + 1$ were divided by 3, the remainder would be 0.

357. If x is a positive integer, then is x prime?

(1) $3x + 1$ is prime.

(2) $5x + 1$ is prime.

$k, n, 12, 6, 17$

358. What is the value of n in the list above?

(1) $k < n$

(2) The median of the numbers in the list is 10.

359. If x and y are integers, what is the value of $x + y$?

(1) $3 < \frac{x+y}{2} < 4$

(2) $2 < x < y < 5$

360. Last year, if Arturo spent a total of \$12,000 on his mortgage payments, real estate taxes, and home insurance, how much did he spend on his real estate taxes?

(1) Last year, the total amount that Arturo spent on his real estate taxes and home insurance was $33\frac{1}{3}$ percent of the amount that he spent on his mortgage payments.

(2) Last year, the amount that Arturo spent on his real estate taxes was 20 percent of the total amount he spent on his mortgage payments and home insurance.

361. If a, b, c, and d are positive numbers, is $\frac{a}{b} < \frac{c}{d}$?

(1) $0 < \frac{c-a}{d-b}$

(2) $\left(\frac{ad}{bc}\right)^2 < \frac{ad}{bc}$

362. Is the number of members of Club X greater than the number of members of Club Y?

(1) Of the members of Club X, 20 percent are also members of Club Y.

(2) Of the members of Club Y, 30 percent are also members of Club X.

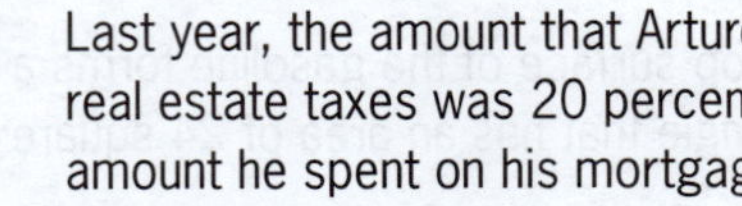

363. On the number line above, p, q, r, s, and t are five consecutive even integers in increasing order. What is the average (arithmetic mean) of these five integers?

(1) $q + s = 24$

(2) The average (arithmetic mean) of q and r is 11.

364. If $\lceil x \rceil$ denotes the least integer greater than or equal to x, is $\lceil x \rceil = 0$?

(1) $-1 < x < 1$

(2) $x < 0$

365. If x and y are integers, is $x > y$?

(1) $x + y > 0$

(2) $y^x < 0$

366. If r and s are the roots of the equation $x^2 + bx + c = 0$, where b and c are constants, is $rs < 0$?

(1) $b < 0$

(2) $c < 0$

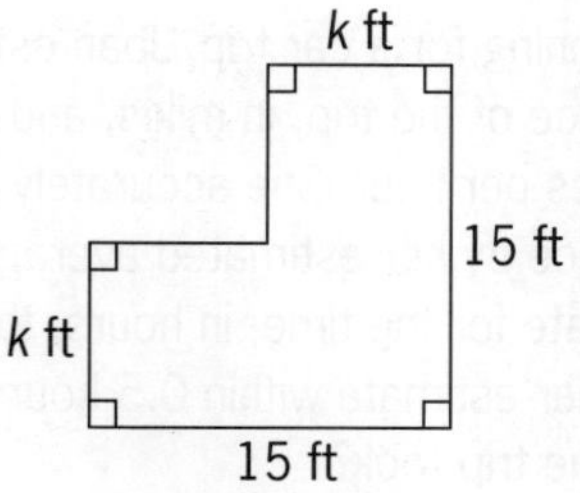

367. The figure above represents an L-shaped garden. What is the value of k ?

(1) The area of the garden is 189 square feet.

(2) The perimeter of the garden is 60 feet.

368. The only articles of clothing in a certain closet are shirts, dresses, and jackets. The ratio of the number of shirts to the number of dresses to the number of jackets in the closet is 9:4:5, respectively. If there are more than 7 dresses in the closet, what is the total number of articles of clothing in the closet?

(1) The total number of shirts and jackets in the closet is less than 30.

(2) The total number of shirts and dresses in the closet is 26.

TOTAL EXPENSES FOR THE
FIVE DIVISIONS OF COMPANY H

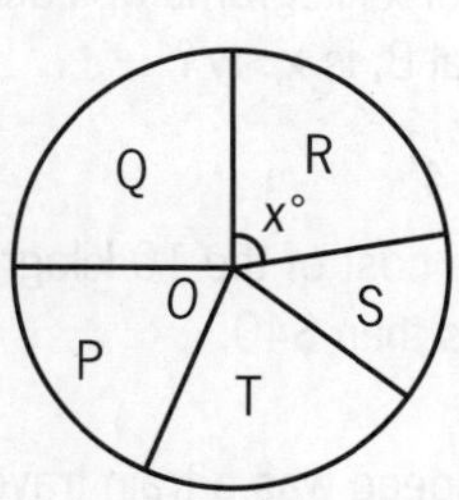

369. The figure above represents a circle graph of Company H's total expenses broken down by the expenses for each of its five divisions. If O is the center of the circle and if Company H's total expenses are $5,400,000, what are the expenses for Division R ?

(1) $x = 94$

(2) The total expenses for Divisions S and T are twice as much as the expenses for Division R.

370. If x is negative, is $x < -3$?

(1) $x^2 > 9$

(2) $x^3 < -9$

371. What is the number of cans that can be packed in a certain carton?

(1) The interior volume of this carton is 2,304 cubic inches.

(2) The exterior of each can is 6 inches high and has a diameter of 4 inches.

r	s	t
u	v	w
x	y	z

372. Each of the letters in the table above represents one of the numbers 1, 2, or 3, and each of these numbers occurs exactly once in each row and exactly once in each column. What is the value of r ?

(1) $v + z = 6$

(2) $s + t + u + x = 6$

373. Material A costs \$3 per kilogram, and Material B costs \$5 per kilogram. If 10 kilograms of Material K consists of x kilograms of Material A and y kilograms of Material B, is $x > y$?

(1) $y > 4$

(2) The cost of the 10 kilograms of Material K is less than \$40.

374. At what speed was a train traveling on a trip when it had completed half of the total distance of the trip?

(1) The trip was 460 miles long and took 4 hours to complete.

(2) The train traveled at an average rate of 115 miles per hour on the trip.

375. Tom, Jane, and Sue each purchased a new house. The average (arithmetic mean) price of the three houses was \$120,000. What was the median price of the three houses?

(1) The price of Tom's house was \$110,000.

(2) The price of Jane's house was \$120,000.

376. What is the value of x if $x^3 < x^2$?

(1) $-2 < x < 2$

(2) x is an integer greater than -2.

377. For any integers x and y, min(x, y) and max(x, y) denote the minimum and the maximum of x and y, respectively. For example, min(5, 2) = 2 and max(5, 2) = 5. For the integer w, what is the value of min(10, w)?

(1) w = max(20, z) for some integer z

(2) w = max(10, w)

378. A certain bookcase has 2 shelves of books. On the upper shelf, the book with the greatest number of pages has 400 pages. On the lower shelf, the book with the least number of pages has 475 pages. What is the median number of pages for all of the books on the 2 shelves?

(1) There are 25 books on the upper shelf.

(2) There are 24 books on the lower shelf.

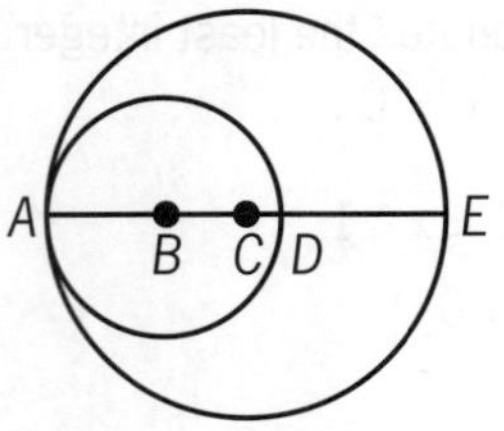

379. In the figure above, points A, B, C, D, and E lie on a line. A is on both circles, B is the center of the smaller circle, C is the center of the larger circle, D is on the smaller circle, and E is on the larger circle. What is the area of the region inside the larger circle and outside the smaller circle?

(1) $AB = 3$ and $BC = 2$

(2) $CD = 1$ and $DE = 4$

380. In planning for a car trip, Joan estimated both the distance of the trip, in miles, and her average speed, in miles per hour. She accurately divided her estimated distance by her estimated average speed to obtain an estimate for the time, in hours, that the trip would take. Was her estimate within 0.5 hour of the actual time that the trip took?

(1) Joan's estimate for the distance was within 5 miles of the actual distance.

(2) Joan's estimate for her average speed was within 10 miles per hour of her actual average speed.

381. A certain list consists of 3 different numbers. Does the median of the 3 numbers equal the average (arithmetic mean) of the 3 numbers?

(1) The range of the 3 numbers is equal to twice the difference between the greatest number and the median.

(2) The sum of the 3 numbers is equal to 3 times one of the numbers.

382. Line ℓ lies in the xy-plane and does not pass through the origin. What is the slope of line ℓ?

(1) The x-intercept of line ℓ is twice the y-intercept of line ℓ.

(2) The x- and y-intercepts of line ℓ are both positive.

$$y = ax - 5$$
$$y = x + 6$$
$$y = 3x + b$$

383. In the *xy*-plane, the straight-line graphs of the three equations above each contain the point (p,r). If a and b are constants, what is the value of b?

(1) $a = 2$

(2) $r = 17$

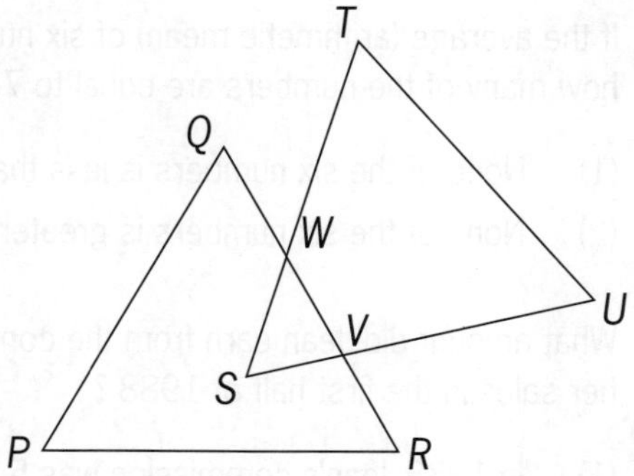

384. In the figure above, *PQR* and *STU* are identical equilateral triangles, and $PQ = 6$. What is the perimeter of polygon *PQWTUVR*?

(1) Triangle *SWV* has perimeter 9.

(2) *VW* has length 3.5.

385. The range of the numbers in set *S* is *x*, and the range of the numbers in set *T* is *y*. If all of the numbers in set *T* are also in set *S*, is *x* greater than *y*?

(1) Set *S* consists of 7 numbers.

(2) Set *T* consists of 6 numbers.

386. The hypotenuse of a right triangle is 10 cm. What is the perimeter, in centimeters, of the triangle?

(1) The area of the triangle is 25 square centimeters.

(2) The 2 legs of the triangle are of equal length.

Shipment	**S1**	**S2**	**S3**	**S4**	**S5**	**S6**
Fraction of the Total Value of the Six Shipments	$\frac{1}{4}$	$\frac{1}{5}$	$\frac{1}{6}$	$\frac{3}{20}$	$\frac{2}{15}$	$\frac{1}{10}$

387. Six shipments of machine parts were shipped from a factory on two trucks, with each shipment entirely on one of the trucks. Each shipment was labeled either S1, S2, S3, S4, S5, or S6. The table shows the value of each shipment as a fraction of the total value of the six shipments. If the shipments on the first truck had a value greater than $\frac{1}{2}$ of the total value of the six shipments, was S3 shipped on the first truck?

(1) S2 and S4 were shipped on the first truck.

(2) S1 and S6 were shipped on the second truck.

388. If *x*, *y*, and *z* are three-digit positive integers and if $x = y + z$, is the hundreds digit of *x* equal to the sum of the hundreds digits of *y* and *z*?

(1) The tens digit of *x* is equal to the sum of the tens digits of *y* and *z*.

(2) The units digit of *x* is equal to the sum of the units digits of *y* and *z*.

	Favorable	**Unfavorable**	**Not Sure**
Candidate M	40	20	40
Candidate N	30	35	35

389. The table above shows the results of a survey of 100 voters who each responded "Favorable" or "Unfavorable" or "Not Sure" when asked about their impressions of Candidate M and of Candidate N. What was the number of voters who responded "Favorable" for both candidates?

(1) The number of voters who did not respond "Favorable" for either candidate was 40.

(2) The number of voters who responded "Unfavorable" for both candidates was 10.

390. A school administrator will assign each student in a group of n students to one of m classrooms. If $3 < m < 13 < n$, is it possible to assign each of the n students to one of the m classrooms so that each classroom has the same number of students assigned to it?

(1) It is possible to assign each of $3n$ students to one of m classrooms so that each classroom has the same number of students assigned to it.
(2) It is possible to assign each of $13n$ students to one of m classrooms so that each classroom has the same number of students assigned to it.

391. If q, s, and t are all different numbers, is $q < s < t$?

(1) $t - q = |t - s| + |s - q|$
(2) $t > q$

392. What is the median number of employees assigned per project for the projects at Company Z ?

(1) 25 percent of the projects at Company Z have 4 or more employees assigned to each project.
(2) 35 percent of the projects at Company Z have 2 or fewer employees assigned to each project.

393. Last year, a certain company began manufacturing product X and sold every unit of product X that it produced. Last year the company's total expenses for manufacturing product X were equal to \$100,000 plus 5 percent of the company's total revenue from all units of product X sold. If the company made a profit on product X last year, did the company sell more than 21,000 units of product X last year?

(1) The company's total revenue from the sale of product X last year was greater than \$110,000.
(2) For each unit of product X sold last year, the company's revenue was \$5.

394. Beginning in January of last year, Carl made deposits of \$120 into his account on the 15th of each month for several consecutive months and then made withdrawals of \$50 from the account on the 15th of each of the remaining months of last year. There were no other transactions in the account last year. If the closing balance of Carl's account for May of last year was \$2,600, what was the range of the monthly closing balances of Carl's account last year?

(1) Last year the closing balance of Carl's account for April was less than \$2,625.
(2) Last year the closing balance of Carl's account for June was less than \$2,675.

395. Are all of the numbers in a certain list of 15 numbers equal?

(1) The sum of all the numbers in the list is 60.
(2) The sum of any 3 numbers in the list is 12.

396. If the average (arithmetic mean) of six numbers is 75, how many of the numbers are equal to 75 ?

(1) None of the six numbers is less than 75.
(2) None of the six numbers is greater than 75.

397. What amount did Jean earn from the commission on her sales in the first half of 1988 ?

(1) In 1988 Jean's commission was 5 percent of the total amount of her sales.
(2) The amount of Jean's sales in the second half of 1988 averaged \$10,000 per month more than in the first half.

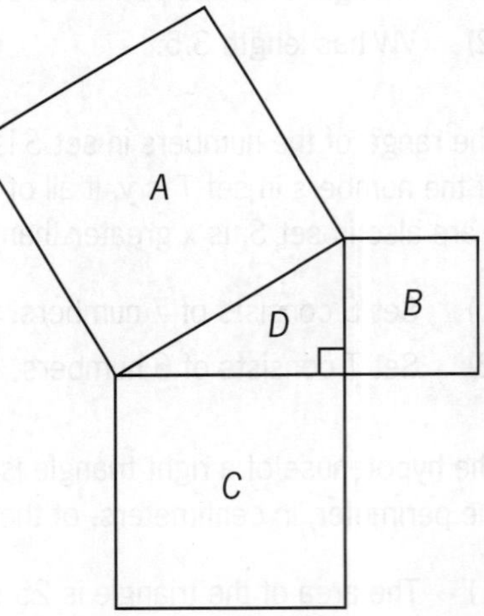

398. In the figure above, if the area of triangular region D is 4, what is the length of a side of square region A ?

(1) The area of square region B is 9.
(2) The area of square region C is $\frac{64}{9}$.

399. If n is a positive integer and $k = 5.1 \times 10^n$, what is the value of k?

(1) $6{,}000 < k < 500{,}000$

(2) $k^2 = 2.601 \times 10^9$

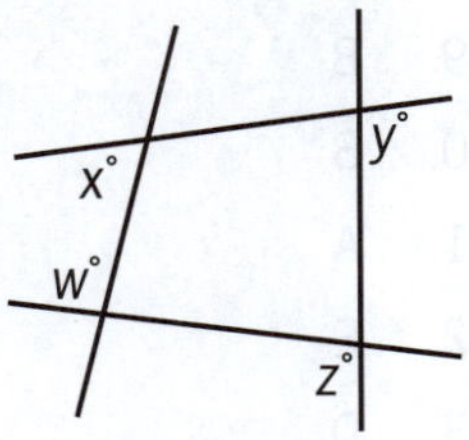

400. What is the value of $x + y$ in the figure above?

(1) $w = 95$

(2) $z = 125$

401. If n and k are positive integers, is $\sqrt{n+k} > 2\sqrt{n}$?

(1) $k > 3n$

(2) $n + k > 3n$

402. In a certain business, production index p is directly proportional to efficiency index e, which is in turn directly proportional to investment index i. What is p if $i = 70$?

(1) $e = 0.5$ whenever $i = 60$.

(2) $p = 2.0$ whenever $i = 50$.

403. If n is a positive integer, what is the tens digit of n?

(1) The hundreds digit of $10n$ is 6.

(2) The tens digit of $n + 1$ is 7.

404. What is the value of $\frac{2t + t - x}{t - x}$?

(1) $\frac{2t}{t - x} = 3$

(2) $t - x = 5$

6.4 Answer Key

231. A
232. C
233. C
234. A
235. C
236. C
237. C
238. B
239. D
240. D
241. C
242. D
243. C
244. E
245. E
246. E
247. D
248. E
249. D
250. D
251. D
252. D
253. D
254. E
255. B
256. D
257. A
258. C
259. C
260. E
261. B
262. C
263. D
264. E
265. C
266. E
267. C
268. E
269. B
270. B
271. D
272. D
273. B
274. B
275. D
276. E
277. D
278. D
279. C
280. D
281. D
282. B
283. C
284. E
285. A
286. A
287. C
288. E
289. E
290. B
291. B
292. C
293. C
294. E
295. A
296. E
297. C
298. B
299. A
300. E
301. E
302. E
303. E
304. D
305. E
306. B
307. C
308. E
309. E
310. D
311. E
312. D
313. A
314. C
315. B
316. C
317. D
318. C
319. C
320. D
321. E
322. C
323. D
324. E
325. E
326. D
327. E
328. A
329. C
330. C
331. C
332. C
333. B
334. D
335. A
336. B
337. C
338. A
339. B
340. B
341. A
342. E
343. D
344. A
345. C
346. A
347. A
348. E
349. D
350. B
351. D
352. A
353. C
354. A
355. D
356. E
357. E
358. C
359. D
360. B
361. B
362. C
363. D
364. C
365. C
366. B
367. A
368. D
369. A
370. A
371. E
372. D
373. B
374. E
375. B
376. B
377. D
378. C
379. D
380. E
381. D
382. A
383. D
384. A
385. E
386. D
387. B
388. A
389. A
390. B
391. A
392. C
393. B
394. C
395. B
396. D
397. E
398. D
399. D
400. C
401. A
402. B
403. A
404. A

6.5 Answer Explanations

The following discussion of data sufficiency is intended to familiarize you with the most efficient and effective approaches to the kinds of problems common to data sufficiency. The particular questions in this chapter are generally representative of the kinds of data sufficiency questions you will encounter on the GMAT exam. Remember that it is the problem solving strategy that is important, not the specific details of a particular question.

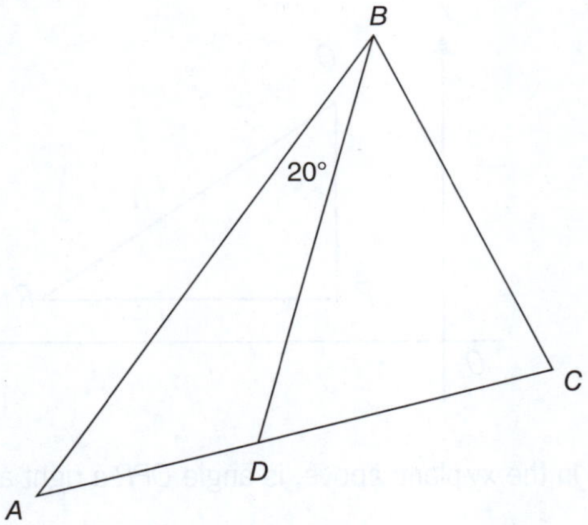

231. In the figure above, point D is on $\overline{AC}$. What is the degree measure of $\angle BAC$?

(1) The measure of $\angle BDC$ is 60°.

(2) The degree measure of $\angle BAC$ is less than the degree measure of $\angle BCD$.

Geometry Angles

(1) Given that the measure of $\angle BDC$ is 60°, it follows that the measure of $\angle BDA$ is $180° - 60° = 120°$. Therefore, since the measures of the angles in a triangle add to 180°, the measure of $\angle BAC$ is $180 - (20° + 120°) = 40°$; SUFFICIENT.

(2) Given that the degree measure of $\angle BAC$ is less than the degree measure of $\angle BCD$, when the line segment $\overline{AC}$ rotates a few degrees counterclockwise about point A and point D stays on $\overline{AC}$, then the degree measure of $\angle BAC$ decreases (and the degree measure of $\angle BCD$ increases, and the degree measure of $\angle ABD$ remains 20°). Therefore, the degree measure of $\angle BAC$ can vary; NOT sufficient.

The correct answer is A; statement 1 alone is sufficient.

232. A citrus fruit grower receives \$15 for each crate of oranges shipped and \$18 for each crate of grapefruit shipped. How many crates of oranges did the grower ship last week?

(1) Last week the number of crates of oranges that the grower shipped was 20 more than twice the number of crates of grapefruit shipped.

(2) Last week the grower received a total of \$38,700 from the crates of oranges and grapefruit shipped.

Algebra Simultaneous equations

If x represents the number of crates of oranges and y represents the number of crates of grapefruit, find a unique value for x.

(1) Translating from words into symbols gives $x = 2y + 20$, but there is no information about y and no way to find a unique value for x from this equation. For example, if $y = 10$, then $x = 40$, but if $y = 100$, then $x = 220$; NOT sufficient.

(2) Translating from words to symbols gives $15x + 18y = 38{,}700$, but there is no way to find a unique value for x from this equation. For example, if $y = 2{,}150$, then $x = 0$ and if $y = 0$, then $x = 2{,}580$; NOT sufficient.

Taking (1) and (2) together gives a system of two equations in two unknowns. Substituting the equation from (1) into the equation from (2) gives a single equation in the variable y. This equation can be solved for a unique value of y from which a unique value of x can be determined.

The correct answer is C; both statements together are sufficient.

233. A certain mixture of paint requires blue, yellow, and red paints in ratios of 2:3:1, respectively, and no other ingredients. If there are ample quantities of the blue and red paints available, is there enough of the yellow paint available to make the desired amount of the mixture?

(1) Exactly 20 quarts of the mixture are needed.

(2) Exactly 10 quarts of the yellow paint are available.

Arithmetic Ratios

Given that the mixture requires blue paint, yellow paint, and red paint in the ratios 2:3:1, it follows that $\frac{3}{2+3+1} = \frac{1}{2}$ of the mixture will be yellow paint. Determining whether there is enough yellow paint available depends on how much of the mixture is needed and how much yellow paint is available.

(1) This indicates that exactly 20 quarts of the paint mixture are needed, so $\frac{1}{2}(20) = 10$ quarts of yellow paint are needed. However, there is no information about how much yellow paint is available; NOT sufficient.

(2) This indicates that exactly 10 quarts of yellow paint are available, but there is no information about how much of the mixture or how much yellow paint is needed; NOT sufficient.

Taking (1) and (2) together, 10 quarts of yellow paint are needed and 10 quarts are available.

The correct answer is C;
both statements together are sufficient.

234. If Pat saved $600 of his earnings last month, how much did Pat earn last month?

(1) Pat spent $\frac{1}{2}$ of his earnings last month for living expenses and saved $\frac{1}{3}$ of the remainder.

(2) Of his earnings last month, Pat paid twice as much in taxes as he saved.

Arithmetic Operations with rational numbers

Let E be Pat's earnings last month. Find a unique value for E.

(1) Pat spent $\frac{1}{2}E$ for living expenses and so $E - \frac{1}{2}E = \frac{1}{2}E$ remained. Pat saved $\frac{1}{3}$ of what remained, so Pat saved $\frac{1}{3}\left(\frac{1}{2}E\right) = \frac{1}{6}E$.

But Pat saved $600, so $600 = \frac{1}{6}E$ and this gives a unique value for E; SUFFICIENT.

(2) Pat saved $600 last month and paid 2($600) in taxes, but there is no way to determine Pat's earnings last month; NOT sufficient.

The correct answer is A;
statement 1 alone is sufficient.

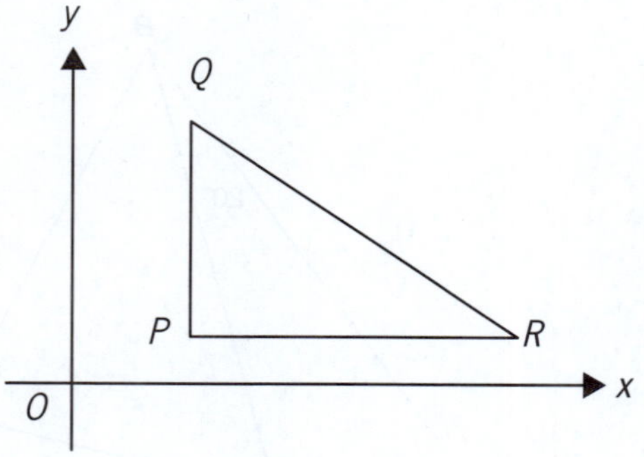

235. In the xy-plane above, is angle QPR a right angle?

(1) Points P and Q have the same x-coordinate.

(2) Points P and R have the same y-coordinate.

Geometry Simple coordinate geometry

(1) Because points P and Q have the same x-coordinate, it follows that side $\overline{PQ}$ is vertical (i.e., parallel to the y-axis). Therefore, angle QPR will be a right angle if and only if side $\overline{PR}$ is horizontal (i.e., parallel to the x-axis). However, depending on the location of point R in relation to point P, side $\overline{PR}$ may or may not be horizontal; NOT sufficient.

(2) Because points P and R have the same y-coordinate, it follows that side $\overline{PR}$ is horizontal. Therefore, angle QPR will be a right angle if and only if side $\overline{PQ}$ is vertical. However, depending on the location of point Q in relation to point P, side $\overline{PQ}$ may or may not be vertical; NOT sufficient.

Given (1) and (2), it follows that $\overline{PQ}$ is vertical and $\overline{PR}$ is horizontal. Therefore, angle QPR is a right angle.

The correct answer is C;
both statements together are sufficient.

236. Each of the marbles in a jar is either red or white or blue. If one marble is to be selected at random from the jar, what is the probability that the marble will be blue?

(1) There are a total of 24 marbles in the jar, 8 of which are red.

(2) The probability that the marble selected will be white is $\frac{1}{2}$.

Arithmetic Probability

This problem can be solved by determining the number of marbles in the jar and the number that are blue.

(1) This indicates that there are 24 marbles in the jar and 8 of them are red. The number of marbles that are blue is not known; NOT sufficient.

(2) This indicates neither the number of marbles in the jar nor the number that are blue; NOT sufficient.

Taking (1) and (2) together, there are 24 marbles in the jar, 8 of which are red and $\frac{1}{2}(24) = 12$ of which are white. Then, the number of blue marbles is $24 - 8 - 12 = 4$, and the probability that one marble selected at random will be blue is $\frac{4}{24} = \frac{1}{6}$.

The correct answer is C;
both statements together are sufficient.

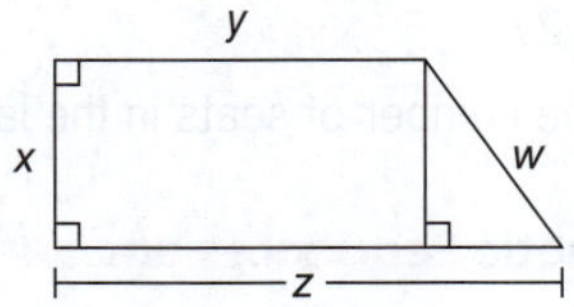

237. In the figure above, what is the value of z?

(1) $x = y = 1$

(2) $w = 2$

Geometry Triangles; Pythagorean theorem

(1) Given that $x = y = 1$, the length of the base of the triangle to the right, which equals $z - y = z - 1$, can vary, and thus the value of z can vary; NOT sufficient.

(2) Given that $w = 2$, all dimensions of the rectangle to the left can vary, and thus the value of z can vary; NOT sufficient.

Taking (1) and (2) together, then $z = y + (z - y) = 1 + (z - 1)$, and the value of z 1 can be determined by applying the Pythagorean theorem to the triangle that has hypotenuse of length $w = 2$ and sides of lengths $x = 1$ and $z - 1$. Specifically, the Pythagorean theorem gives $1^2 + (z - 1)^2 = 2^2$, or $1 + (z - 1)^2 = 4$, and solving this equation gives $(z - 1)^2 = 3$, or $z - 1 = \sqrt{3}$, or $z = 1 + \sqrt{3}$.

The correct answer is C;
both statements together are sufficient.

238. Water is pumped into a partially filled tank at a constant rate through an inlet pipe. At the same time, water is pumped out of the tank at a constant rate through an outlet pipe. At what rate, in gallons per minute, is the amount of water in the tank increasing?

(1) The amount of water initially in the tank is 200 gallons.

(2) Water is pumped into the tank at a rate of 10 gallons per minute and out of the tank at a rate of 10 gallons every $2\frac{1}{2}$ minutes.

Arithmetic Work Problem

If both the rate of the water being pumped into the tank and the rate of the water being pumped out of the tank are known, then the rate at which the total amount of water in the tank is changing can be determined, but not if only one of these quantities is known.

(1) This only gives the amount of water in the tank initially; NOT sufficient.

(2) This information provides both the needed rates. Since the water is being pumped out of the tank at the rate of 10 gallons every $2\frac{1}{2}$ minutes, that is, 4 gallons every minute, and since 10 gallons are pumped into the tank every minute, the rate at which the water is increasing in the tank is $10 - 4 = 6$ gallons per minute; SUFFICIENT.

The correct answer is B;
statement 2 alone is sufficient.

239. What is the value of 10 percent of y?

(1) 5 percent of y is 60.

(2) y is 80 percent of 1,500.

Arithmetic Percents

This problem can be solved by determining the value of y.

(1) If 5 percent of y is 60, then $0.05y = 60$ and $y = \frac{60}{0.05} = 1,200$; SUFFICIENT.

(2) If y is 80 percent of 1,500, then $y = (0.80)(1,500) = 1,200$; SUFFICIENT.

The correct answer is D; each statement alone is sufficient.

240. What is the cube root of w?

(1) The 5th root of w is 64.

(2) The 15th root of w is 4.

Arithmetic Operations with radical expressions

Determine the cube root of w, or determine the value of $w^{\frac{1}{3}}$.

(1) Given the 5th root of w is 64,

then $w^{\frac{1}{5}} = 64$ and $\left(w^{\frac{1}{5}}\right)^{\frac{5}{3}} = 64^{\frac{5}{3}}$.

Since $\left(w^{\frac{1}{5}}\right)^{\frac{5}{3}} = w^{\left(\frac{1}{5}\right)\left(\frac{5}{3}\right)} = w^{\frac{1}{3}}$

then $w^{\frac{1}{3}} = \left(64^{\frac{5}{3}}\right) = \left(64^{\frac{1}{3}}\right)^5 = 4^5$;

SUFFICIENT.

(2) Given the 15th root of w is 4, then $w^{\frac{1}{15}} = 4$ and $\left(w^{\frac{1}{15}}\right)^5 = 4^5$. Since $\left(w^{\frac{1}{15}}\right)^5 = w^{\frac{5}{15}} = w^{\frac{1}{3}}$,

then $w^{\frac{1}{3}} = 4^5$; SUFFICIENT.

The correct answer is D; each statement alone is sufficient.

241. If sequence S has 120 terms, what is the 105th term of S?

(1) The first term of S is –8.

(2) Each term of S after the first term is 10 more than the preceding term.

Arithmetic Sequences

This problem can be solved by determining at least one term of the sequence and how each term is derived from the preceding term(s).

(1) This indicates that the first term of the sequence is –8, but does not indicate how subsequent terms are derived; NOT sufficient.

(2) This indicates how each term is derived from the preceding term, but does not indicate at least one term of the sequence; NOT sufficient.

Taking (1) and (2) together, the first term is –8 and each subsequent term is 10 more than the preceding term from which the 105th term can be determined.

The correct answer is C; both statements together are sufficient.

242. The number of seats in the first row of an auditorium is 18 and the number of seats in each row thereafter is 2 more than in the previous row. What is the total number of seats in the rows of the auditorium?

(1) The number of rows of seats in the auditorium is 27.

(2) The number of seats in the last row is 70.

Arithmetic Sequences and series

Determine the number of seats in the auditorium.

It is given that the first row has 18 seats, and since each row after the first row has 2 more seats than the previous row, the second row has 20 seats, the third row has 22 seats, and so on. The total number of seats in the auditorium can be determined if and only if the number of rows in the auditorium can be determined.

(1) The number of rows is given to be 27, so the total number of seats can be determined; SUFFICIENT.

(2) The last row has 70 seats. Let n be the number of rows in the auditorium. Since the first row has 18 seats, the second row has $18 + 2 = 20$ seats, and the third row has $20 + 2 = 18 + 2(2) = 22$ seats, it follows that the nth row has $18 + (n - 1)(2)$ seats. Then

$$18+(n-1)(2)=70$$
$$18+2n-2=70$$
$$2n=54$$
$$n=27$$

Thus the number of rows can be determined; SUFFICIENT.

The correct answer is D; each statement alone is sufficient.

243. If $u > 0$ and $v > 0$, which is greater, u^v or v^u?

(1) $u = 1$

(2) $v > 2$

Arithmetic Exponents

(1) Given that $u = 1$, then $u^v = 1^v = 1$ and $v^u = v^1 = v$. If $v = 2$, then $u^v = 1$ is less than $v^u = 2$. However, if $v = 0.5$, then $u^v = 1$ is greater than $v^u = 0.5$; NOT sufficient.

(2) Given that $v > 2$, it is possible that u^v is less than v^u (for example, if $u = 1$ and $v = 4$, then $u^v = 1^4 = 1$ and $v^u = 4^1$ 4), and it is possible that u^v is greater than v^u (for example, if $u = 3$ and $v = 4$, then $u^v = 3^4 = 81$ and $v^u = 4^3 = 64$); NOT sufficient.

Taking (1) and (2) together, it follows from (1) that $u^v = 1$ and $v^u = v$, and it follows from (2) that $v > 2$. Therefore, $u^v = 1 < 2 < v = v^u$, and so v^u is greater than u^v.

The correct answer is C; both statements together are sufficient.

244. What was the range of the selling prices of the 30 wallets sold by a certain store yesterday?

(1) $\frac{1}{3}$ of the wallets had a selling price of \$24 each.

(2) The lowest selling price of the wallets was $\frac{1}{3}$ the highest selling price of the wallets.

Arithmetic Statistics

Since the range of a data set is the greatest value in the data set minus the least value in the data set, this problem can be solved if the least selling price and the greatest selling price of the wallets sold by the store yesterday can be determined.

(1) This indicates that 10 of the wallets had a selling price of \$24 each, but does not indicate the least selling price or the greatest selling price of the wallets sold by the store yesterday; NOT sufficient.

(2) This indicates that $L = \frac{1}{3}G$, where L represents the least selling price and G represents the greatest selling price, but does not give enough information to determine $G - L$; NOT sufficient.

Taking (1) and (2) together, the least and greatest selling prices of the wallets sold by the store yesterday could be \$10 and \$30 for a range of \$30 – \$10 = \$20, or the least and greatest selling prices of the wallets sold by the store yesterday could be \$20 and \$60 for a range of \$60 – \$20 = \$40.

The correct answer is E; both statements together are still not sufficient.

245. Three houses are being sold through a real estate agent. What is the asking price for the house with the second-largest asking price?

(1) The difference between the greatest and the least asking price is \$130,000.

(2) The difference between the two greater asking prices is \$85,000.

Algebra Simultaneous equations

Let x, y, and z, where $x \leq y \leq z$, be the asking prices of the three houses. This problem can be solved by determining the value of y.

(1) This indicates that $z - x = \$130{,}000$, but does not give the value of y; NOT sufficient.

(2) This indicates that $z - y = \$85{,}000$, but does not give the value of y; NOT sufficient.

Taking (1) and (2) together, x, y, and z could be \$100,000, \$145,000, and \$230,000, respectively, in which case the second highest selling price is \$145,000, or they could be \$200,000, \$245,000, and \$330,000, respectively, in which case the second highest selling price is \$245,000.

The correct answer is E;
both statements together are still not sufficient.

246. Is $rw = 0$?

(1) $-6 < r < 5$

(2) $6 < w < 10$

Algebra Inequalities

This problem can be solved if it can be determined that either or both of r and w is zero or that neither r nor w is zero.

(1) This indicates that r can be, but does not have to be, zero and gives no indication of the value of w; NOT sufficient.

(2) This indicates that w cannot be zero, but gives no indication of the value of r; NOT sufficient.

Taking (1) and (2) together, r could be zero, in which case $rw = 0$ **or** r could be nonzero, in which case $rw \neq 0$.

The correct answer is E;
both statements together are still not sufficient.

247. Is $x = \frac{1}{y}$?

(1) $xy = 1$

(2) $\frac{1}{xy} = 1$

Algebra Equations

(1) This indicates that neither x nor y can be zero because if $x = 0$ or $y = 0$, then $xy = 0$. Since $xy = 1$ and $y \neq 0$, then dividing both sides by y gives $x = \frac{1}{y}$; SUFFICIENT.

(2) This indicates that neither x nor y can be zero because if $x = 0$ or $y = 0$, then $xy = 0$, and division by zero is undefined. Multiplying both sides of the equation $\frac{1}{xy} = 1$ by x gives $\frac{1}{y} = x$; SUFFICIENT.

The correct answer is D;
each statement alone is sufficient.

248. How many people in a group of 50 own neither a fax machine nor a laser printer?

(1) The total number of people in the group who own a fax machine or a laser printer or both is less than 50.

(2) The total number of people in the group who own both a fax machine and a laser printer is 15.

Algebra Sets

(1) This indicates that the total number who own either a fax machine or a laser printer or both is less than 50, but does not indicate how much less than 50 the total number is. Thus, the number of people in the group who own neither a fax machine nor a laser printer cannot be determined; NOT sufficient.

(2) This indicates that, of the 50 people, 15 own both a fax machine and a laser printer, but does not indicate how many own one or the other. Thus, the number of people in the group who own neither a fax machine nor a laser printer cannot be determined; NOT sufficient.

Taking (1) and (2) together, it is known that 15 people own both a fax machine and a laser printer and that the total number who own either a fax machine or a laser printer or both is less than 50, but the exact number who own neither still cannot be determined. For example, if 20 people own only a fax machine and 10 people own only a laser printer, then both (1) and (2) are true and the number of people who own neither a fax machine nor a laser printer is $50 - 20 - 10 - 15 = 5$. However, if 10 people own only a fax machine and 10 people own only a laser printer, then both (1) and (2) are true and the number of people who own neither a fax machine nor a laser printer is $50 - 10 - 10 - 15 = 15$.

The correct answer is E;
both statements together are still not sufficient.

249. What is the value of w^{-2}?

(1) $w^{-1} = \frac{1}{2}$

(2) $w^3 = 8$

Algebra Exponents

(1) Since $w^{-1} = \frac{1}{2}$, then $(w^{-1})^2 = \left(\frac{1}{2}\right)^2 = \frac{1}{4}$ or $w^{-2} = \frac{1}{4}$; SUFFICIENT.

(2) Since $w^3 = 8$, then $w = \sqrt[3]{8} = 2$ and $w^{-2} = 2^{-2} = \frac{1}{4}$; SUFFICIENT.

The correct answer is D; each statement alone is sufficient.

250. A certain investment earned a fixed rate of 4 percent interest per year, compounded annually, for five years. The interest earned for the third year of the investment was how many dollars greater than that for the first year?

(1) The amount of the investment at the beginning of the second year was $4,160.00.

(2) The amount of the investment at the beginning of the third year was $4,326.40.

Arithmetic Applied problems; Percents

This problem can be solved by determining the dollar amount of the interest earned for the third year minus the dollar amount of interest earned in the first year, or, in symbols, $[A(1.04)^3 - A(1.04)^2] - [A(1.04)^1 - A]$, where A represents the dollar amount of the investment. This can be determined if the value of A can be determined.

(1) This indicates that $A(1.04)^1 = \$4,160.00$, since the amount of the investment at the beginning of the second year is the same as the amount of the investment at the end of the first year. Thus, the value of A can be determined by dividing 4,160.00 by 1.04; SUFFICIENT.

(2) This indicates that $A(1.04)^2 = \$4,326.40$, since the amount of the investment at the beginning of the third year is the same as the amount of the investment at the end of the second year. Thus, the value of A can be determined by dividing 4,326.40 by $(1.04)^2$; SUFFICIENT.

The correct answer is D; each statement alone is sufficient.

251. On a recent trip, Mary drove 50 miles. What was the average speed at which she drove the 50 miles?

(1) She drove 30 miles at an average speed of 60 miles per hour and then drove the remaining 20 miles at an average speed of 50 miles per hour.

(2) She drove a total of 54 minutes.

Arithmetic Rate problem

Mary drove 50 miles. Determine the average speed at which she drove the 50 miles.

If the time it took Mary to drive the 50 miles can be determined, then her average speed can be determined: distance = speed × time, or $\frac{\text{distance}}{\text{speed}} = \text{time}$.

(1) It is given that she drove the first 30 miles at an average speed of 60 miles per hour, so she drove the first 30 miles in $\frac{30}{60} = \frac{1}{2}$ hour. It is also given that she drove the remaining 20 miles at an average speed of 50 miles per hour, so she drove the remaining 20 miles in $\frac{20}{50} = \frac{2}{5}$ hours. Thus, she drove the 50 miles in a total of $\frac{1}{2} + \frac{2}{5} = \frac{9}{10}$ hours, and thus her average speed for the 50 miles can be determined; SUFFICIENT.

(2) It is given that she drove a total of 54 minutes, and thus her average speed for the 50 miles can be determined; SUFFICIENT.

The correct answer is D; each statement alone is sufficient.

252. What is the value of t?

(1) $s + t = 6 + s$

(2) $t^3 = 216$

Algebra Equations

(1) Given that $s + t = 6 + s$, subtracting s from both sides gives $t = 6$; SUFFICIENT.

(2) Given that $t^3 = 216$, taking the cube root of both sides gives $t = 6$; SUFFICIENT.

The correct answer is D; each statement alone is sufficient.

253. For a certain car repair, the total charge consisted of a charge for parts, a charge for labor, and a 6 percent sales tax on both the charge for parts and the charge for labor. If the charge for parts, excluding sales tax, was \$50.00, what was the total charge for the repair?

(1) The sales tax on the charge for labor was \$9.60.

(2) The total sales tax was \$12.60.

Arithmetic Applied problems; Percents

To find the total charge, T, for the repair, requires determining the value, in dollars, of $T = (1.06)(50 + L) = 53 + 1.06L$, where L represents the charge, in dollars, for labor. This value can be determined if the value of L can be determined.

(1) This indicates that $0.06L = 9.60$, from which L can be determined by dividing 9.60 by 0.06; SUFFICIENT.

(2) This indicates that $(0.06)(50 + L) = 12.60$. So, $3.00 + 0.06L = 12.60$ or $0.06L = 9.60$, which is the same as the equation in (1); SUFFICIENT.

The correct answer is D;
each statement alone is sufficient.

254. George has a total of *B* books in his library, 25 of which are hardcover fiction books. What is the value of *B* ?

(1) 40 of the *B* books are fiction and the rest are nonfiction.

(2) 60 of the *B* books are hardcovers and the rest are paperbacks.

Arithmetic Applied problems

The diagram below incorporates the given information that George has a total of B books, of which 25 are both fiction and hardcover. In the diagram, x represents the number of books that are fiction and not hardcover, and y represents the number of books that are hardcover and not fiction.

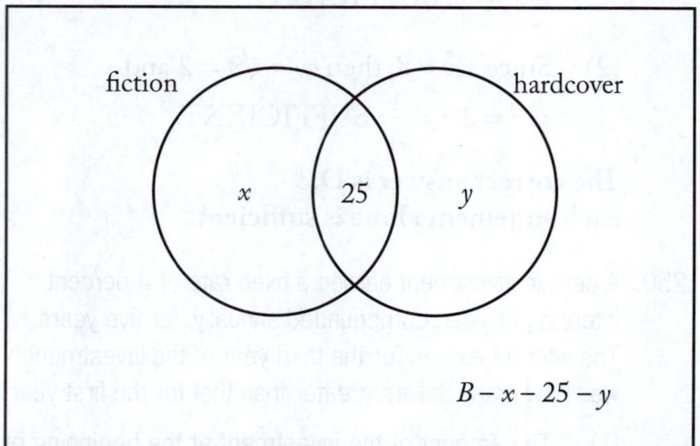

(1) Given that 40 of the books are fiction, it follows that $x + 25 = 40$, or $x = 15$. Using this additional information, the diagram (shown below) clearly shows that the value of B cannot be determined. For example, $y = 35$ and $B = 80$ is possible (note that $B - 40 - y = 5$), and $y = 35$ and $B = 100$ is possible (note that $B - 40 - y = 25$); NOT sufficient.

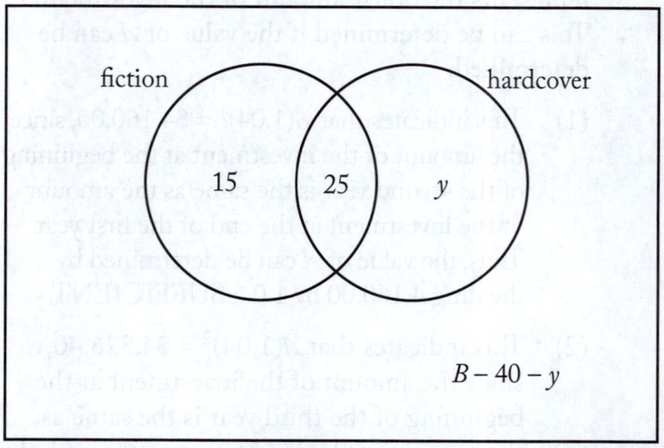

(2) Given that 60 of the books are hardcover, it follows that $25 + y = 60$, or $y = 35$. Using this additional information, the diagram (shown below) clearly shows that the value of B cannot be determined. For example, $x = 15$ and $B = 80$ is possible (note that $B - x - 60 = 5$), and $x = 15$ and $B = 100$ is possible (note that $B - x - 60 = 25$); NOT sufficient.

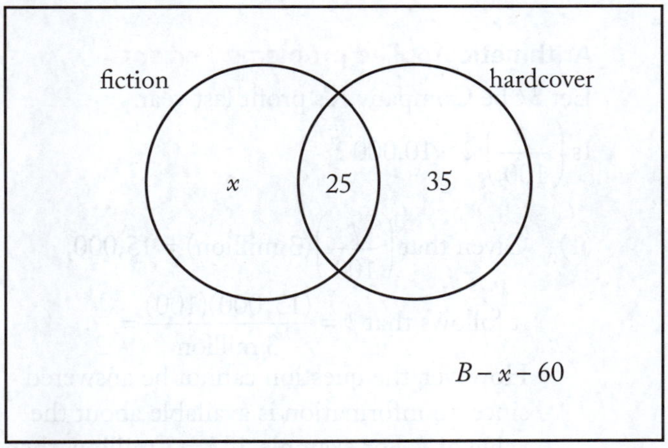

Taking (1) and (2) together, there is still not enough information to determine the value of B, since in the diagram below $B = 80$ is possible and $B = 100$ is possible.

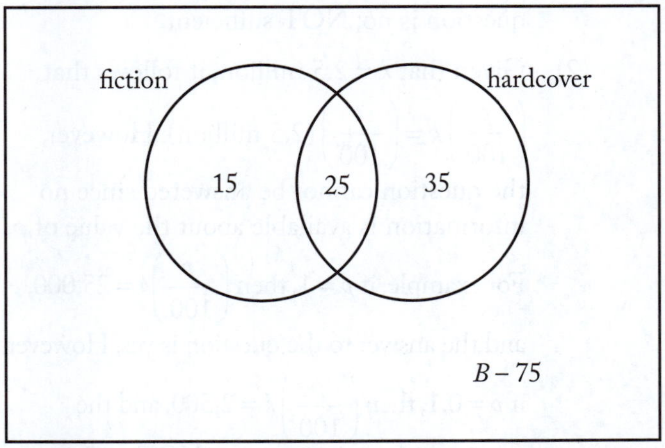

The correct answer is E;
both statements together are still not sufficient.

255. Is $w + h^4$ positive?

(1) h is positive.

(2) w is positive.

Arithmetic Properties of numbers

(1) Given that h is positive, then $w + h^4$ can be positive (for example, when $w = 1$ and $h = 1$) and $w + h^4$ can be negative (for example, when $w = -2$ and $h = 1$); NOT sufficient.

(2) Given that w is positive, then because $h^4 \geq 0$, it follows that $w + h^4 \geq w + 0 = w$ and thus $w + h^4 > 0$ since $w > 0$; SUFFICIENT.

The correct answer is B;
statement 2 alone is sufficient.

256. In Mr. Smith's class, what is the ratio of the number of boys to the number of girls?

(1) There are 3 times as many girls as boys in Mr. Smith's class.

(2) The number of boys is $\frac{1}{4}$ of the total number of boys and girls in Mr. Smith's class.

Algebra Ratio and proportion

Letting B be the number of boys and G be the number of girls, determine the value of $\frac{B}{G}$.

(1) It is given that $G = 3B$, so $\frac{1}{3} = \frac{B}{G}$; SUFFICIENT.

(2) It is given that $B = \frac{1}{4}(B + G)$. Therefore, $4B = B + G$, or $3B = G$, or $\frac{B}{G} = \frac{1}{3}$; SUFFICIENT.

The correct answer is D;
each statement alone is sufficient.

257. If the sequence S has 300 terms, what is the 293rd term of S?

(1) The 298th term of S is –616, and each term of S after the first is 2 less than the preceding term.

(2) The first term of S is –22.

Arithmetic Sequences and series

Determine the 293rd term of the sequence S, or S_{293}.

(1) It is given that the 298th term of S is -616, and each term of S after the first term is 2 less than the preceding term. Therefore, $S_{298} = -616 = S_{297} - 2$, and so $S_{297} = -616 + 2 = -614$. Similarly, S_{296}, S_{295}, S_{294}, and S_{293} can be determined, each from the term preceding it; SUFFICIENT.

(2) It is given that $S_1 = -22$, but there is no information on how subsequent terms are related to S_1 and therefore no way to determine S_{293}; NOT sufficient.

The correct answer is A;
statement 1 alone is sufficient.

258. If a is a 3-digit integer and b is a 3-digit integer, is the units digit of the product of a and b greater than 5 ?

(1) The units digit of a is 4.

(2) The units digit of b is 7.

Arithmetic Operations with integers

Determine whether the units digit of the product of the two 3-digit integers a and b is greater than 5.

(1) It is given that the units digit of a is 4. If the units digit of b is 0 or 1, then the units digit of ab is not greater than 5. However, if the units digit of b is 2, then the units digit of ab is greater than 5; NOT sufficient.

(2) It is given that the units digit of b is 7. If the units digit of a is 0, then the units digit of ab is not greater than 5. However, if the units digit of a is 1, then the units digit of ab is greater than 5; NOT sufficient.

Taking (1) and (2) together, the units digit of a is 4 and the units digit of b is 7. Therefore, the units digit of ab is 8, which is greater than 5.

The correct answer is C;
both statements together are sufficient.

259. In each of the last five years, Company K donated p percent of its annual profits to a certain scholarship fund. Did Company K donate more than \$10,000 to the scholarship fund last year?

(1) Two years ago, Company K had annual profits of \$3 million and donated \$15,000 to the scholarship fund.

(2) Last year, Company K had annual profits of \$2.5 million.

Arithmetic Applied problems; Percents

Let $\$k$ be Company K's profit last year.

Is $\left(\frac{p}{100}\right)k > 10{,}000$?

(1) Given that $\left(\frac{p}{100}\right)(3 \text{ million}) = 15{,}000$, it follows that $p = \frac{(15{,}000)(100)}{3 \text{ million}} = \frac{1}{2}$. However, the question cannot be answered since no information is available about the value of k. For example, if $k = 3$ million, then $\left(\frac{p}{100}\right)k = 15{,}000$, and the answer to the question is yes. However, if $k = 1$ million, then $\left(\frac{p}{100}\right)k = 5{,}000$, and the answer to the question is no; NOT sufficient.

(2) Given that $k = 2.5$ million, it follows that $\left(\frac{p}{100}\right)k = \left(\frac{p}{100}\right)(2.5 \text{ million})$. However, the question cannot be answered since no information is available about the value of p. For example, if $p = 1$, then $\left(\frac{p}{100}\right)k = 25{,}000$, and the answer to the question is yes. However, if $p = 0.1$, then $\left(\frac{p}{100}\right)k = 2{,}500$, and the answer to the question is no; NOT sufficient.

Taking (1) and (2) together, the values of both p and k can be determined. Therefore, the value of $\left(\frac{p}{100}\right)k$ can be determined, and thus the answer to the question can be determined.

The correct answer is C;
both statements together are sufficient.

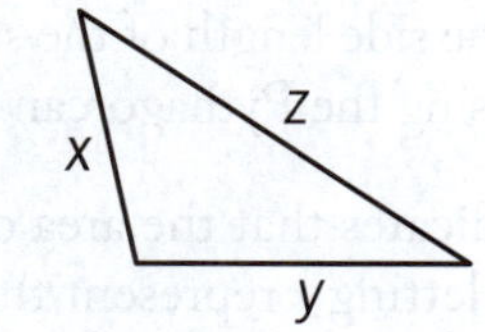

260. Is the area of the triangular region above less than 20 ?

(1) $x^2 + y^2 \neq z^2$
(2) $x + y < 13$

Geometry Triangles; Area

Determine whether the area of the given triangle is less than 20.

(1) This indicates the triangle is not a right triangle but gives no information about the base and height or how to determine them in order to find the area; NOT sufficient.

(2) This indicates that two sides of the triangle have lengths x and y such that $x + y < 13$. If, for example, the triangle is a right triangle with $x = 3$ and $y = 4$, then $x + y = 3 + 4 = 7 < 13$ and the area of the triangle is $\frac{1}{2}(3)(4) = 6$, which is less than 20. But if the triangle is a right triangle with $x = y = \sqrt{42}$, then $x + y = \sqrt{42} + \sqrt{42} = 2\sqrt{42} = \sqrt{168} < \sqrt{169} = 13$ and the area is $\frac{1}{2}(\sqrt{42})(\sqrt{42}) = 21$, which is greater than 20; NOT sufficient.

Taking (1) and (2) together, since the triangle is not a right triangle from (1), the diagrams show two other possibilities: an obtuse triangle and an acute triangle.

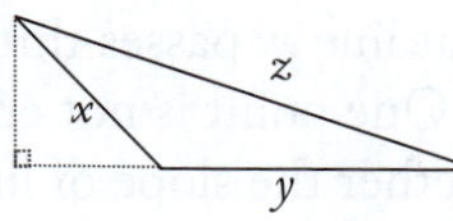

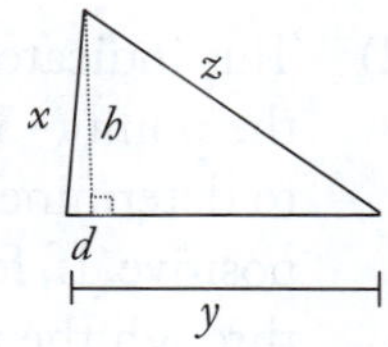

For the obtuse triangle, $h < x$ since because h is a leg of a right triangle with hypotenuse x. The area A is given by $A = \frac{1}{2}yh < \frac{1}{2}xy$. If $x = y = 6$, then $x + y = 6 + 6 = 12 < 13$ and $A < \frac{1}{2}(6^2) = 18$. The area of the triangular region is less than 20 for the obtuse triangle. For the acute triangle, if $x = y = \sqrt{42}$, then $x + y = \sqrt{42} + \sqrt{42} = 2\sqrt{42} = \sqrt{168} < \sqrt{169} = 13$. Let $d = 1$. Then, $h^2 = (\sqrt{42})^2 - 1 = 42 - 1 = 41$ and $h = \sqrt{41}$. Thus, for the acute triangle, the area of the triangular region is $\frac{1}{2}yh = \frac{1}{2}(\sqrt{42})(\sqrt{41})$ and $\frac{1}{2}(\sqrt{42})(\sqrt{41}) > \frac{1}{2}(\sqrt{40})(\sqrt{40})$ or $\frac{1}{2}(\sqrt{42})(\sqrt{41}) > 20$. Therefore, it is possible that the area of the triangular region can be less than 20 (in the case of the obtuse triangle) and it is possible that the area of the triangular region can be greater than 20 (in the case of the acute triangle).

The correct answer is E;
both statements together are still not sufficient.

261. A, B, C, and D are points on a line. If C is the midpoint of line segment AB and if D is the midpoint of line segment CB, is the length of line segment DB greater than 5 ?

(1) The length of line segment AC is greater than 8.
(2) The length of line segment CD is greater than 6.

Geometry Lines and segments

It is given that C is the midpoint of $\overline{AB}$, so $AC = CB = \frac{1}{2}(AB)$. It is given that D is the midpoint of $\overline{CB}$, so $CD = DB = \frac{1}{2}(CB)$. Determine if $DB > 5$.

(1) Given that $AC > 8$, it follows that $CB > 8$ since $AC = CB$, and so $DB = \frac{1}{2}(CB) > \frac{1}{2}(8)$ or $DB > 4$. However, this means that DB could be 6 and $6 > 5$ or DB could be 4.1 and $4.1 < 5$; NOT sufficient.

(2) Given that $CD > 6$, it follows that $DB > 6$ since $CD = DB$; SUFFICIENT.

The correct answer is B;
statement 2 alone is sufficient.

262. The people in a line waiting to buy tickets to a show are standing one behind the other. Adam and Beth are among the people in the line, and Beth is standing behind Adam with a number of people between them. If the number of people in front of Adam plus the number of people behind Beth is 18, how many people in the line are behind Beth?

(1) There are a total of 32 people in the line.
(2) 23 people in the line are behind Adam.

Arithmetic Order

Beth is standing in line behind Adam with a number of people between them. Let x be the number of people ahead of Adam, let y be the number of people between Adam and Beth, and let z be the number of people behind Beth. It is given that $x + z = 18$. Determine z.

(1) This indicates that there are 32 people in the line. Two of these people are Adam and Beth, so there are 30 other people in line besides Adam and Beth. Therefore, $x + y + z = 30$ and $x + z = 18$. From this, $y = 12$, but z cannot be determined uniquely. For example, if $x = 5$, then $z = 13$, but if $x = 10$, then $z = 8$; NOT sufficient.

(2) This indicates that $y + 1 + z = 23$ because the people behind Adam consist of the people between Adam and Beth, Beth herself, and the people behind Beth. If, for example, $y = 4$, then $z = 18$, but if $y = 9$, then $z = 13$; NOT sufficient.

Taking (1) and (2) together, $y = 12$ from (1) and $y + z = 22$ from (2). Therefore, $z = 10$, and there are 10 people in line behind Beth.

The correct answer is C;
both statements together are sufficient.

263. Square $ABCD$ is inscribed in circle O. What is the area of square region $ABCD$?

(1) The area of circular region O is 64π.
(2) The circumference of circle O is 16π.

Geometry Circles; Area

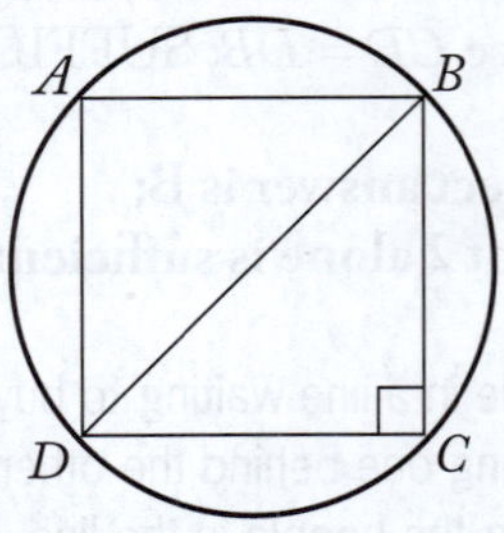

Since the area of square $ABCD$ is the square of its side length, to solve this problem it is necessary to determine the side length of $ABCD$. From the figure, a diameter of the circle coincides with a diagonal of the square. If the length of a diameter of the circle can be determined, then the length of a diagonal of the square can be determined, from which the side length of the square can be determined using the Pythagorean theorem.

(1) This indicates that the area of the circle is 64π, so letting r represent the radius of the circle, $\pi r^2 = 64\pi$. Thus, $r^2 = 64$, $r = 8$, and $d = 2(8) = 16$, where d represents the length of the diameter of the circle and also the diagonal of the square; SUFFICIENT.

(2) This indicates that the circumference of the circle is 16π, so letting d represent the length of the diameter of the circle as well as the diagonal of the square, $\pi d = 16\pi$. Thus, $d = 16$; SUFFICIENT.

The correct answer is D;
each statement alone is sufficient.

264. Lines k and m are parallel to each other. Is the slope of line k positive?

(1) Line k passes through the point (3,2).
(2) Line m passes through the point (–3,2).

Geometry Coordinate geometry

(1) This indicates that line k passes through the point (3,2). One point is not enough to determine whether the slope of line k is positive. If, for example, line k also passes through the point (0,0), then the slope of line k is $\frac{2-0}{3-0} = \frac{2}{3}$, which is positive. But if line k also passes through the point (5,0), then the slope of line k is $\frac{2-0}{3-5} = \frac{2}{-2}$, which is negative; NOT sufficient.

(2) This indicates that line m passes through the point (–3,2). One point is not enough to determine whether the slope of line m is positive. If, for example, line m also passes through the point (0,0), then the slope of line m is $\frac{2-0}{-3-0} = \frac{2}{-3}$, which is negative. In this case, the slope of line k is also negative since parallel lines k and m have the same slope. But if line m also passes through the point (0,5), then the slope of line m is $\frac{2-5}{-3-0} = \frac{-3}{-3}$, which is positive. In this case, the slope of line k is also positive since parallel lines k and m have the same slope; NOT sufficient.

Taking (1) and (2) together gives no more information than (1) or (2) alone and so whether the slope of line k is positive cannot be determined.

The correct answer is E; both statements together are still not sufficient.

265. In cross section, a tunnel that carries one lane of one-way traffic is a semicircle with radius 4.2 m. Is the tunnel large enough to accommodate the truck that is approaching the entrance to the tunnel?

(1) The maximum width of the truck is 2.4 m.

(2) The maximum height of the truck is 4 m.

Geometry Circles; Pythagorean theorem

(1) Given that the maximum width of the truck is 2.4 m, it is possible that the tunnel is large enough (for example, if the maximum height of the truck is sufficiently small) and it is possible that the tunnel is not large enough (for example, if the maximum height of the truck is sufficiently large); NOT sufficient.

(2) Given that the maximum height of the truck is 4 m, it is possible that the tunnel is large enough (for example, if the maximum width is sufficiently small) and it is possible that the tunnel is not large enough (for example, if the maximum width of the truck is sufficiently large); NOT sufficient.

Taking (1) and (2) together, it is possible for the truck to pass through the tunnel, because even if the truck were rectangular with width 2.4 m and height 4 m, the truck could pass through the tunnel if it were centered in the tunnel as shown in the diagram. In this position, it follows from the Pythagorean theorem that every point on the truck is located at most a distance of $\sqrt{(1.2)^2 + 4^2}$ meters from the center axis of the tunnel, and this distance is less than 4.2 meters, the radius of the tunnel, since $(1.2)^2 + 4^2 = 17.44$ is less than $(4.2)^2 = 17.64$.

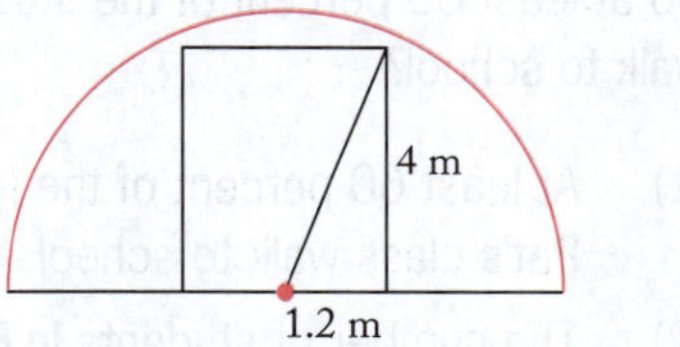

The correct answer is C; both statements together are sufficient.

266. In a certain group of 50 people, how many are doctors who have a law degree?

(1) In the group, 36 people are doctors.

(2) In the group, 18 people have a law degree.

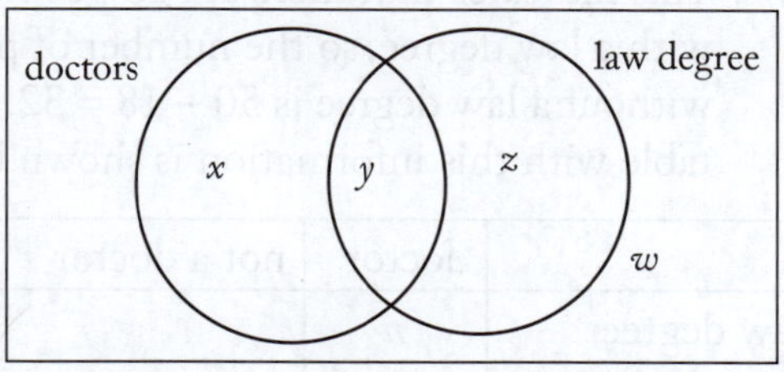

Arithmetic Sets

Using the labels in the Venn diagram, $w + x + y + z = 50$. Determine the value of y.

(1) This indicates that $x + y = 36$ but does not give a unique value for y. For example, if $x = 18$, then $y = 18$; but if $x = 10$, then $y = 26$; NOT sufficient.

(2) This indicates that $y + z = 18$ but does not give a unique value for y. For example, if $z = 8$, then $y = 10$; but if $z = 10$, then $y = 8$; NOT sufficient.

Taking (1) and (2) together, if $w = 6$, $x = 26$, $y = 10$, and $z = 8$, then $w + x + y + z = 50$, $x + y = 36$, and $y + z = 18$. In this case, $y = 10$. However, if $w = 2$, $x = 30$, $y = 6$, and $z = 12$, then $w + x + y + z = 50$, $x + y = 36$, and $y + z = 18$. In this case, $y = 6$.

Alternatively, this problem can be solved by means of a contingency table. Letting n represent the number of doctors with a law degree, the table with the given information is shown below.

	doctor	not a doctor	total
law degree	n		
no law degree			
total			50

(1) This indicates that there are 36 doctors, so the number of people who are not doctors is 50 – 36 = 14. The table with this information is shown below.

	doctor	not a doctor	total
law degree	n		
no law degree			
total	36	14	50

It is obvious from the table that there is not enough information to determine the value of n, the number of doctors with a law degree; NOT sufficient.

(2) This indicates that there are 18 people with a law degree, so the number of people without a law degree is $50 - 18 = 32$. The table with this information is shown below.

	doctor	not a doctor	total
law degree	n		18
no law degree			32
total			50

It is obvious from the table that there is not enough information to determine the value of n, the number of doctors with a law degree; NOT sufficient.

The table with the information from both (1) and (2) is shown below.

	doctor	not a doctor	total
law degree	n		18
no law degree			32
total	36	14	50

It is obvious from the table that there is still not enough information to determine the value of n, the number of doctors with a law degree.

The correct answer is E;
both statements together are still not sufficient.

267. Of a group of 50 households, how many have at least one cat or at least one dog, but not both?

(1) The number of households that have at least one cat and at least one dog is 4.

(2) The number of households that have no cats and no dogs is 14.

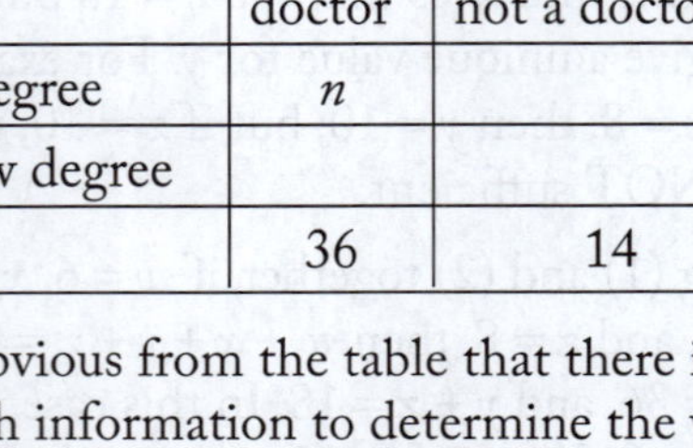

Arithmetic Sets

Using the labels on the Venn diagram, $w + x + y + z = 50$. Determine the value of $x + z$.

(1) This indicates that $y = 4$, so $w + x + z = 46$, but the value of $x + z$ cannot be uniquely determined; NOT sufficient.

(2) This indicates that $w = 14$, so $x + y + z = 36$, but the value of $x + z$ cannot be uniquely determined; NOT sufficient.

Taking (1) and (2) together, $14 + x + 4 + z = 50$, so $x + z = 50 - 14 - 4 = 32$.

The correct answer is C;
both statements together are sufficient.

268. On a certain date, Hannah invested \$5,000 at x percent simple annual interest and a different amount at y percent simple annual interest. What amount did Hannah invest at y percent simple annual interest?

(1) The total amount of interest earned by Hannah's two investments in one year was \$900.

(2) Hannah invested the \$5,000 at 6 percent simple annual interest.

Algebra Applied problems

Let \$$A$ be the amount that Hannah invested at y percent. Determine the value of A.

(1) Given that the sum of $\frac{x}{100}(\$5{,}000)$ and $\frac{y}{100}(\$A)$ is \$900, or $50x + \frac{Ay}{100} = 900$, it is clear that more than one value of A is possible; NOT sufficient.

(2) Given that $x = 6$, it is clear that more than one value of A is possible; NOT sufficient.

(1) and (2) together are not sufficient because more than one value of A is possible such that $50(6) + \frac{Ay}{100} = 900$, or $Ay = 60{,}000$. For example, $A = 10{,}000$ and $y = 6$ is possible, and $A = 20{,}000$ and $y = 3$ is also possible.

The correct answer is E;
both statements together are still not sufficient.

269. Do at least 60 percent of the students in Pat's class walk to school?

(1) At least 60 percent of the female students in Pat's class walk to school.

(2) The number of students in Pat's class who walk to school is twice the number of students who do not walk to school.

Arithmetic Percents

This problem can be solved by determining the total number of students in Pat's class and the number who walk to school.

(1) This indicates that at least 60% of the female students in Pat's class walk to school. However, it does not give any information about the other students in Pat's class; NOT sufficient.

(2) Letting x represent the number of students in Pat's class who do not walk to school, this indicates that $2x$ students in Pat's class walk to school and that the total number of students in Pat's class is $x + 2x = 3x$. From this, the percent of students in Pat's class who walk to school is $\left[\frac{2x}{3x}100\right]\% = \left[\frac{2}{3}(100)\right]\%$; SUFFICIENT.

The correct answer is B; statement 2 alone is sufficient.

270. The profit from the sale of a certain appliance increases, though not proportionally, with the number of units sold. Did the profit exceed $4 million on sales of 380,000 units?

(1) The profit exceeded $2 million on sales of 200,000 units.

(2) The profit exceeded $5 million on sales of 350,000 units.

Arithmetic Arithmetic operations; Proportions

(1) If the profits did increase proportionally, it might be reasonable to expect a profit of $4 million on sales of 400,000 units. However, it is given that the profits do not increase proportionally. Without knowing how the profits increase, it is impossible to tell the profits on sales of 380,000 units; NOT sufficient.

(2) It is given that the profits do increase with the number of units sold. Therefore, since the profit on sales of just 350,000 units well exceeded $4 million, then sales of 350,000 + 30,000 = 380,000 units would also have a profit exceeding $4 million; SUFFICIENT.

The correct answer is B; statement 2 alone is sufficient.

271. If n is an integer, is n even?

(1) $n^2 - 1$ is an odd integer.

(2) $3n + 4$ is an even integer.

Arithmetic Properties of numbers

Determine if the integer n is even.

(1) Since $n^2 - 1$ is odd, n^2 is even and so n is even; SUFFICIENT.

(2) Since $3n + 4$ is even, $3n$ is even and so n is even; SUFFICIENT.

The correct answer is D; each statement alone is sufficient.

272. Carmen currently works 30 hours per week at her part-time job. If her gross hourly wage were to increase by $1.50, how many fewer hours could she work per week and still earn the same gross weekly pay as before the increase?

(1) Her gross weekly pay is currently $225.00.

(2) An increase of $1.50 would represent an increase of 20 percent of her current gross hourly wage.

Arithmetic Operations with rational numbers

Let w be Carmen's gross hourly wage and let n be the number of hours fewer Carmen will need to work. Find a unique value for n such that $30w = (30 - n)(w + 1.50)$.

(1) Since Carmen's gross weekly pay is currently $225.00, then $30w = 225$ and $w = 7.50$. Substituting 7.50 for w gives $30(7.50) = (30 - n)(7.50 + 1.50)$, which can be solved for a unique value of n; SUFFICIENT.

(2) Since 1.50 is 20 percent of Carmen's current gross hourly pay, $1.50 = 0.20w$ and $w = 7.50$. This is the same information that was gained from statement (1) and will lead to the same result; SUFFICIENT.

The correct answer is D; each statement alone is sufficient.

273. A certain plumber charges \$92 for each job completed in 4 hours or less and \$23 per hour for each job completed in more than 4 hours. If it took the plumber a total of 7 hours to complete two separate jobs, what was the total amount charged by the plumber for the two jobs?

(1) The plumber charged \$92 for one of the two jobs.

(2) The plumber charged \$138 for one of the two jobs.

Arithmetic Applied problems

Find the total amount charged for two jobs lasting a total of 7 hours if the plumber charges \$92 for a job lasting 4 hours or less and \$23 per hour for a job lasting more than 4 hours.

(1) This indicates that one of the two jobs lasted 4 hours or less. If that job lasted 2 hours, then the other job lasted 5 hours, and the charge for that job would be (\$23)(5) = \$115, making the total for the two jobs \$92 + \$115 = \$207. However, if the jobs lasted 1 hour and 6 hours, respectively, then the total charge for the two jobs would be \$92 + (6)(\$23) = \$92 + \$138 = \$230; NOT sufficient.

(2) This indicates that one job lasted $\frac{\$138}{\$23} = 6$ hours. Therefore, the other job lasted for 1 hour and the charge for that job was \$92, making the total charge for the two jobs \$92 + \$138 = \$230; SUFFICIENT.

The correct answer is B; statement 2 alone is sufficient.

274. If x and y are positive numbers, is $\frac{x+1}{y+1} > \frac{x}{y}$?

(1) $x > 1$

(2) $x < y$

Algebra Inequalities

Since y is positive, multiplying both sides of the inequality $\frac{x+1}{y+1} > \frac{x}{y}$ by $y(y+1)$ gives $y(x+1) > x(y+1)$ or $xy + y > xy + x$, which is equivalent to $y > x$. So, determining whether the inequality $\frac{x+1}{y+1} > \frac{x}{y}$ is true is equivalent to determining whether the inequality $y > x$ is true.

(1) This indicates that $x > 1$. If, for example, $x = 3$ and $y = 4$, then $y > x$ is true. However, if $x = 4$ and $y = 3$, then $y > x$ is not true; NOT sufficient.

(2) This indicates that $x < y$, so $y > x$ is true; SUFFICIENT.

The correct answer is B; statement 2 alone is sufficient.

275. If a and b are positive integers, is $\frac{a}{b} < \frac{9}{11}$?

(1) $\frac{a}{b} < 0.818$

(2) $\frac{b}{a} > 1.223$.

Arithmetic Inequalities

If $11a < 9b$ and b is positive, then $\frac{11a}{b} < 9$ and $\frac{a}{b} < \frac{9}{11}$. Therefore, this problem can be solved by determining if $11a < 9b$.

(1) From this,

$\frac{a}{b} < 0.818$ given

$a < 0.818b$ multiply both sides by b, which is positive

$11a < 8.998b$ multiply both sides by 11

Then, since $8.998b < 9b$, it follows that $11a < 9b$; SUFFICIENT.

(2) From this,

$\frac{b}{a} > 1.223$ given

$b > 1.223a$ multiply both sides by a, which is positive

$9b > 11.007a$ multiply both sides by 9

Then, since $11.007a > 11a$, it follows that $9b > 11a$; SUFFICIENT.

The correct answer is D; each statement alone is sufficient.

276. Every object in a box is either a sphere or a cube, and every object in the box is either red or green. How many objects are in the box?

(1) There are six cubes and five green objects in the box.

(2) There are two red spheres in the box.

Arithmetic Sets

This problem can be solved using a contingency table set up as shown below, where T represents the number to be determined.

	cube	sphere	total
red			
green			
total			T

(1) The following table displays the information that there are 6 cubes and 5 green objects:

	cube	sphere	total
red			
green			5
total	6		T

It is obvious that there is not enough information to determine a unique value for T; NOT sufficient.

(2) The following table displays the information that there are 2 red spheres:

	cube	sphere	total
red		2	
green			
total			T

It is obvious that there is not enough information to determine a unique value for T; NOT sufficient.

The following table displays the information from (1) and (2) taken together:

	cube	sphere	total
red		2	
green			5
total	6		T

It is obvious that there is still not enough information to determine a unique value for T.

The correct answer is E;
both statements together are still not sufficient.

277. If x and y are positive integers, is xy even?

(1) $x^2 + y^2 - 1$ is divisible by 4.

(2) $x + y$ is odd.

Arithmetic Properties of numbers

Determine whether the product of two positive integers, x and y, is even.

(1) This indicates that $x^2 + y^2 - 1$ is divisible by 4, so $x^2 + y^2 - 1 = 4q$ for some integer q. Then $x^2 + y^2 = 4q + 1$, which means $x^2 + y^2$ is odd. Both x^2 and y^2 cannot be even because, in that case, their sum would be even, and both cannot be odd because, in that case, their sum would also be even. Therefore, one of x^2 and y^2 is even, and the other is odd. It follows that one of x or y is even and the other is odd, so xy is even; SUFFICIENT.

(2) If $x + y$ is odd, then one of x and y is even and the other is odd because if both were even or both were odd, the sum would be even. It follows that xy is even; SUFFICIENT.

The correct answer is D;
each statement alone is sufficient.

278. If a and b are integers, is $a + b + 3$ an odd integer?

(1) ab is an odd integer.

(2) $a - b$ is an even integer.

Arithmetic Properties of numbers

Determine whether $a + b + 3$ is odd for integers a and b.

(1) This indicates that, since ab is odd, both a and b are odd because if one of a or b is even or both a and b are even, then ab is even. Therefore, $a + b$ is even and $a + b + 3$ is odd; SUFFICIENT.

(2) This indicates that, since $a - b$ is even, both a and b are even or both are odd because if one of them is even and the other is odd, then $a - b$ is odd. Therefore, $a + b$ is even, and $a + b + 3$ is odd; SUFFICIENT.

The correct answer is D;
each statement alone is sufficient.

279. If x and y are positive integers, what is the value of $\sqrt{x}+\sqrt{y}$?

(1) $x+y=15$

(2) $\sqrt{xy}=6$

Algebra Operations with radicals

(1) From this, if $x = 1$ and $y = 14$, then $x+y=15$ and $\sqrt{x}+\sqrt{y}=\sqrt{1}+\sqrt{14}=1+\sqrt{14}$. But $\sqrt{14}<\sqrt{16}=4$, so $1+\sqrt{14}<1+4=5$. However, if $x = 9$ and $y = 6$, then $x + y = 15$ and $\sqrt{x}+\sqrt{y}=\sqrt{9}+\sqrt{6}=3+\sqrt{6}$. But $\sqrt{6}>\sqrt{4}=2$ so, $3+\sqrt{6}>3+2=5$; NOT sufficient.

(2) From this, if $x = 1$ and $y = 36$, then $\sqrt{xy}=6$ and $\sqrt{x}+\sqrt{y}=\sqrt{1}+\sqrt{36}=1+6=7$. However, if $x = 4$ and $y = 9$, then $\sqrt{xy}=6$ and $\sqrt{x}+\sqrt{y}=\sqrt{4}+\sqrt{9}=2+3=5$; NOT sufficient.

Taking (1) and (2) together, $x + y = 15$ and $\sqrt{xy}=6$, so

$$\begin{aligned}\sqrt{x(15-x)} &= 6 && \text{substitute } 15-x \text{ for } y\\ x(15-x) &= 36 && \text{square both sides}\\ 15x-x^2 &= 36 && \text{use distributive property}\\ x^2-15x+36 &= 0 && \text{collect like terms}\\ (x-12)(x-3) &= 0 && \text{factor}\end{aligned}$$

Thus, $x = 12$ or $x = 3$. If $x = 12$, then $y = 3$ and $\sqrt{x}+\sqrt{y}=\sqrt{12}+\sqrt{3}$. If $x = 3$, then $y = 12$ and $\sqrt{x}+\sqrt{y}=\sqrt{3}+\sqrt{12}$.

Algebraically, if the value of $\left(\sqrt{x}+\sqrt{y}\right)^2=\left(\sqrt{x}\right)^2+2\sqrt{xy}+\left(\sqrt{y}\right)^2=x+y+2\sqrt{xy}$ can be determined, then the value of $\sqrt{x}+\sqrt{y}$ can be determined, and conversely.

(1) From this, $\left(\sqrt{x}+\sqrt{y}\right)^2=x+y+2\sqrt{xy}=15+2\sqrt{x(15-x)}$, but the value of x is unknown, and the value of $\left(\sqrt{x}+\sqrt{y}\right)^2$ cannot be determined; NOT sufficient.

(2) From this, $\left(\sqrt{x}+\sqrt{y}\right)^2=x+y+2\sqrt{xy}=x+\frac{36}{x}+2(6)$, but the value of x is unknown, and the value of $\left(\sqrt{x}+\sqrt{y}\right)^2$ cannot be determined; NOT sufficient.

Taking (1) and (2) together, $\left(\sqrt{x}+\sqrt{y}\right)^2=x+y+2\sqrt{xy}=15+(2)(6)=27$ and so $\sqrt{x}+\sqrt{y}=\sqrt{27}=3\sqrt{3}$. Note that in the nonalgebraic solution $\sqrt{x}+\sqrt{y}=\sqrt{3}+\sqrt{12}$ and $\sqrt{3}+\sqrt{12}=\sqrt{3}+2\sqrt{3}=3\sqrt{3}$.

The correct answer is C;
both statements together are sufficient.

280. A certain truck uses $\frac{1}{12}+kv^2$ gallons of fuel per mile when its speed is v miles per hour, where k is a constant. At what speed should the truck travel so that it uses $\frac{5}{12}$ gallon of fuel per mile?

(1) The value of k is $\frac{1}{10{,}800}$.

(2) When the truck travels at 30 miles per hour, it uses $\frac{1}{6}$ gallon of fuel per mile.

Algebra Applied problems

This problem can be solved by determining the positive value of v so that $\frac{1}{12}+kv^2=\frac{5}{12}$.

(1) This indicates the value of k and so the value of v can be determined by solving $\frac{1}{12}+\frac{1}{10{,}800}v^2=\frac{5}{12}$ for v; SUFFICIENT.

(2) This indicates that $\frac{1}{12}+k(30)^2=\frac{1}{6}$. The value of k can be determined by solving this equation for k. Then that value of k can be substituted into $\frac{1}{12}+kv^2=\frac{5}{12}$, which can then be solved for the value of v; SUFFICIENT.

The correct answer is D;
each statement alone is sufficient.

281. If $x = 2t$ and $y = \frac{t}{3}$, what is the value of $x^2 - y^2$?

(1) $t^2 - 3 = 6$

(2) $t^3 = -27$

Algebra Simplifying algebraic expressions

This problem can be solved by determining the value of $x^2 - y^2 = (2t)^2 - \left(\frac{t}{3}\right)^2 = 4t^2 - \frac{t^2}{9}$, and this can be determined if the value of t^2 or the value of t can be determined.

(1) This indicates that $t^2 - 3 = 6$ and so $t^2 = 6 + 3 = 9$; SUFFICIENT.

(2) This indicates that $t^3 = -27$ and so $t = -3$; SUFFICIENT.

The correct answer is D; each statement alone is sufficient.

282. Last school year, each of the 200 students at a certain high school attended the school for the entire year. If there were 8 cultural performances at the school during the last school year, what was the average (arithmetic mean) number of students attending each cultural performance?

(1) Last school year, each student attended at least one cultural performance.

(2) Last school year, the average number of cultural performances attended per student was 4.

Arithmetic Statistics

Determine the average number of students attending each of 8 cultural performances at a school that has 200 students.

(1) This indicates that each student attended at least one cultural performance, but the average number of students attending each performance cannot be uniquely determined. It could be as low as $\frac{200}{8} = 25$ students if each student attended exactly one performance, or it could be as high as $\frac{200}{1} = 200$ if each student attended every performance; NOT sufficient.

(2) This indicates that, since the average number of performances attended per student was 4, $\frac{\text{total attendance at performances}}{\text{total number of students}} = 4$, so the total attendance at the performances is $(4)(200) = 800$ students. It follows that the average number of students attending each performance is $\frac{800}{8} = 100$; SUFFICIENT.

The correct answer is B; statement 2 alone is sufficient.

283. A clothing manufacturer makes jackets that are wool or cotton or a combination of wool and cotton. The manufacturer has 3,000 pounds of wool and 2,000 pounds of cotton on hand. Is this enough wool and cotton to make at least 1,000 jackets?

(1) Each wool jacket requires 4 pounds of wool, and no cotton.

(2) Each cotton jacket requires 6 pounds of cotton, and no wool.

Arithmetic Applied problems

(1) Given that each wool jacket requires 4 pounds of wool and no cotton, then at most a total of 750 wool jackets can be made (because $\frac{3{,}000}{4} = 750$), and possibly no other jackets. Therefore, it is possible that there is enough wool and cotton to make at least 1,000 jackets (for example, if there is enough cotton to make 250 cotton jackets) and it is possible that there is not enough wool and cotton to make at least 1,000 jackets (for example, if there is less than the amount of cotton needed to make 250 cotton jackets); NOT sufficient.

(2) Given that each cotton jacket requires 6 pounds of cotton and no wool, then at most a total of 333 cotton jackets can be made (because rounding $\frac{2{,}000}{6}$ down to the nearest integer gives 333), and possibly no other jackets. Therefore, it is possible that there is enough wool and cotton to make at least 1,000 jackets (for example, if there is enough wool to make 667 wool jackets), and it is possible that there is not enough wool

and cotton to make at least 1,000 jackets (for example, if there is less than the amount of wool needed to make 667 wool jackets); NOT sufficient.

Taking (1) and (2) together, there is enough wool and cotton to make 750 wool jackets and 333 cotton jackets for a total of 1,083 jackets.

The correct answer is C;
both statements together are sufficient.

284. Each month, Jim receives a base salary plus a 10 percent commission on the price of each car he sells that month. If Jim sold 15 cars last month, what was the total amount of base salary and commissions that Jim received that month?

(1) Last month, Jim's base salary was $3,000.

(2) Last month, Jim sold 3 cars whose prices totaled $60,000 and 5 cars whose prices totaled $120,000.

Arithmetic Applied problems

Determine the total of Jim's base salary plus a 10% commission on the price of each of the 15 cars he sold last month.

(1) This indicates that Jim's base salary was $3,000 but gives no information about the prices of the 15 cars he sold last month; NOT sufficient.

(2) This indicates that Jim's commission on 8 cars that he sold last month can be determined but gives no information about his base salary or about the prices of the other 7 cars he sold last month; NOT sufficient.

Taking (1) and (2) together gives Jim's base salary and information about the prices of 8 of the 15 cars he sold last month, but does not provide information about the selling prices of the other 7 cars he sold.

The correct answer is E;
both statements together are still not sufficient.

285. If x is a positive integer greater than 1, what is the value of x ?

(1) 2x is a common factor of 18 and 24.

(2) x is a factor of 6.

Arithmetic Properties of numbers

(1) Given that $2x$, where x is an integer greater than 1, is a common factor of 18 and 24, then $2x$ is an even integer greater than or equal to 4 that is a factor of 18 and 24. The factors of 18 are 1, 2, 3, 6, 9, and 18. The factors of 24 are 1, 2, 3, 4, 6, 8, 12, and 24. Since the only even integer greater than or equal to 4 that belongs to both lists is 6, it follows that $2x = 6$, or $x = 3$; SUFFICIENT.

(2) Given that x, an integer greater than 1, is a factor of 6, then x could be 2, 3, or 6; NOT sufficient.

The correct answer is A;
statement 1 alone is sufficient.

286. By what percent was the price of a certain television set discounted for a sale?

(1) The price of the television set before it was discounted for the sale was 25 percent greater than the discounted price.

(2) The price of the television set was discounted by $60 for the sale.

Arithmetic Percents

Let B represent the price, in dollars, for the television before the sale and let D represent the discounted price, in dollars. The percent by which B was discounted to obtain D can be determined if the value of $\frac{B-D}{B}$ can be determined.

(1) This indicates that B is 25% greater than D or that $B = 1.25D$. Then, $\frac{B-D}{B} = \frac{1.25D - D}{1.25D} = \frac{0.25}{1.25} = 0.2$ or 20%; SUFFICIENT.

(2) This indicates that $D = B - 60$, but B is unknown. For example, B could be 100 and the value of $\frac{B-D}{B}$ would be $\frac{60}{100}$, or B could be 500 and the value of $\frac{B-D}{B}$ would be $\frac{60}{500}$; NOT sufficient.

The correct answer is A;
statement 1 alone is sufficient.

287. Jack wants to use a circular rug on his rectangular office floor to cover two small circular stains, each less than $\frac{\pi}{100}$ square feet in area and each more than 3 feet from the nearest wall. Can the rug be placed to cover both stains?

(1) Jack's rug covers an area of 9π square feet.

(2) The centers of the stains are less than 4 feet apart.

Geometry Applied problems; Circles

If a circle with radius r has area less than $\frac{\pi}{100}$, then $\pi r^2 < \frac{\pi}{100}$, or $r^2 < \frac{1}{100}$. Hence, $r < \frac{1}{10}$, so the circle's radius is less than $\frac{1}{10}$ ft.

(1) Given that the circular rug has area 9π ft^2, the radius of the rug, R ft, satisfies the equation $\pi R^2 = 9\pi$, and so $R^2 = 9$, or $R = 3$. If the centers of the circular stains are 4 ft apart, then the midpoint of the centers will be a distance of at most $\left(\frac{1}{10}+2+\frac{1}{10}\right)$ ft = 2.2 ft from any point on the stains.

Thus, if the circular rug (which has radius 3 ft) were placed so that its center lies on that midpoint, then the rug would cover both stains. However, if the centers of the circular stains are 7 ft apart, then the circular rug (which has diameter 6 ft) cannot be placed to cover both stains; NOT sufficient.

(2) Given that the centers of the circular stains are less than 4 ft apart, it is not possible to determine whether the circular rug can be placed to cover both stains since nothing is given about the size of the circular rug; NOT sufficient.

Taking (1) and (2) together, the centers of the circular stains are less than 4 ft apart and it follows from the discussion in (1) that the circular rug can be placed to cover both stains.

The correct answer is C;
both statements together are sufficient.

×	a	b	c
a	d	e	f
b	e	g	h
c	f	h	j

288. In the multiplication table above, each letter represents an integer. What is the value of c?

(1) $c = f$

(2) $h \neq 0$

Arithmetic Properties of numbers

(1) Given that $c = f$, the examples below, in which $a = b = 1$, show that the value of c could be 1 and the value of c could be 2; NOT sufficient.

×	1	1	1
1	1	1	1
1	1	1	1
1	1	1	1

×	1	1	2
1	1	1	2
1	1	1	2
2	2	2	4

(2) Given that $h \neq 0$, the examples in (1) show that the value of c could be 1 and the value of c could be 2; NOT sufficient.

Taking (1) and (2) together is of no more help than either (1) or (2) taken separately because the same examples used to show that (1) is not sufficient also show that (2) is not sufficient.

The correct answer is E;
both statements together are still not sufficient.

289. If n is an integer, is $(0.1)^n$ greater than $(10)^n$?

(1) $n > -10$

(2) $n < 10$

Arithmetic Exponents

$(0.1)^n = \frac{1}{10^n}$ will be greater than 10^n if 1 is greater than 10^{2n}, and this will be the case if and only if $n < 0$. Determine if $n < 0$.

(1) This indicates that n is greater than –10. This includes nonnegative values of n as well as negative values of n; NOT sufficient.

(2) This indicates that n is less than 10, but this includes negative values of n as well as nonnegative values of n; NOT sufficient.

Taking (1) and (2) together, n can have any value between –10 and 10 and can therefore be negative or nonnegative.

The correct answer is E; both statements together are still not sufficient.

290. For a basic monthly fee of F yen (¥F), Naoko's first cell phone plan allowed him to use a maximum of 420 minutes on calls during the month. Then, for each of x additional minutes he used on calls, he was charged ¥M, making his total charge for the month ¥T, where $T = F + xM$. What is the value of F?

(1) Naoko used 450 minutes on calls the first month and the total charge for the month was ¥13,755.

(2) Naoko used 400 minutes on calls the second month and the total charge for the month was ¥13,125.

Algebra Simultaneous equations

(1) Given that Naoko used 450 minutes and was charged ¥13,125, it follows that $F + (450 - 420)M = 13{,}755$, or $F + 30M = 13{,}755$. However, the value of F cannot be determined. For example, $F = 13{,}005$ and $M = 25$ is possible, and $F = 13{,}035$ and $M = 24$ is possible; NOT sufficient.

(2) Given that Naoko used 400 minutes and was charged ¥13,125, it follows that $F = 13{,}125$, since Naoko did not use more than 420 minutes; SUFFICIENT.

The correct answer is B; statement 2 alone is sufficient.

291. The weights of all dishes of type X are exactly the same, and the weights of all dishes of type Y are exactly the same. Is the weight of 1 dish of type X less than the weight of 1 dish of type Y?

(1) The total weight of 3 dishes of type X and 2 dishes of type Y is less than the total weight of 2 dishes of type X and 4 dishes of type Y.

(2) The total weight of 4 dishes of type X and 3 dishes of type Y is less than the total weight of 3 dishes of type X and 4 dishes of type Y.

Algebra Inequalities

Let x be the weight of a type X dish and let y be the weight of a type Y dish. Determine whether $x < y$.

(1) Given that $3x + 2y < 2x + 4y$, or $x < 2y$, it is possible that $x < y$ is true (for example, if $x = 2$ and $y = 3$) and it is possible that $x < y$ is false (for example, if $x = 3$ and $y = 2$); NOT sufficient.

(2) Given that $4x + 3y < 3x + 4y$, it follows that $x < y$; SUFFICIENT.

The correct answer is B; statement 2 alone is sufficient.

292. If r and t are three-digit positive integers, is r greater than t?

(1) The tens digit of r is greater than each of the three digits of t.

(2) The tens digit of r is less than either of the other two digits of r.

Arithmetic Properties of numbers

Let r_3, r_2, and r_1 be the hundreds, tens, and units digits, respectively, of the 3-digit integer r, and let t_3, t_2, and t_1 be the hundreds, tens, and units digits, respectively, of the 3-digit integer t.

(1) Given that r_2 is greater than each of t_3, t_2, and t_1, then r could be greater than t (for example, if $r = 242$ and $t = 222$) and r could be less than t (for example, if $r = 242$ and $t = 333$); NOT sufficient.

(2) Given that r_2 is less than either of r_1 or r_3, then r could be greater than t (for example, if $r = 212$ and $t = 111$) and r could be less than t (for example, if $r = 212$ and $t = 222$); NOT sufficient.

Taking (1) and (2) together, $r_3 > r_2$ follows from (2) and $r_2 > t_3$ follows from (1). Therefore, $r_3 > t_3$ and hence r is greater than t.

The correct answer is C; both statements together are sufficient.

293. Is the product of two positive integers x and y divisible by the sum of x and y?

(1) x = y

(2) x = 2

Arithmetic Properties of numbers

(1) Given that $x = y$, then xy could be divisible by $x + y$ (for example, if $x = y = 2$, then $xy = 4$ is divisible by $x + y = 4$) and xy could fail to be divisible by $x + y$ (for example, if $x = y = 3$, then $xy = 9$ is not divisible by $x + y = 6$); NOT sufficient.

(2) Given that $x = 2$, then xy could be divisible by $x + y$ (for example, if $x = y = 2$, then $xy = 4$ is divisible by $x + y = 4$) and xy could fail to be divisible by $x + y$ (for example, if $x = 2$ and $y = 3$, then $xy = 6$ is not divisible by $x + y = 5$); NOT sufficient.

Taking (1) and (2) together, it follows that $x = y = 2$, and so $xy = 4$ is divisible by $x + y = 4$.

The correct answer is C; both statements together are sufficient.

294. A certain high school with a total enrollment of 900 students held a science fair for three days last week. How many of the students enrolled in the high school attended the science fair on all three days?

(1) Of the students enrolled in the school, 30 percent attended the science fair on two or more days.

(2) Of the students enrolled in the school, 10 percent of those that attended the science fair on at least one day attended on all three days.

Algebra Simultaneous equations

Let a, b, and c be the numbers of students who attended on exactly one day, exactly two days, and exactly three days, respectively, and let n be the number of students who did not attend on any of the three days. Given that $a + b + c + n = 900$, determine the value of c.

(1) Given that $(30\%)(900) = b + c$, or $b + c = 270$, more than one positive integer value for c is possible; NOT sufficient.

(2) Given that $(10\%)(a + b + c) = c$, or $a + b + c = 10c$, or $a + b = 9c$, more than one positive integer value for c is possible; NOT sufficient.

(1) and (2) together are not sufficient because more than one positive integer value for c is possible. Although there are 4 variables and only 3 linear equations involving these 4 variables, which implies there exist infinitely many *real number* solutions, the variables in the present problem are further restricted to be *positive integers*. However, specific values of c can be obtained using the equations:

I. $a + b + c + n = 900$ (from the information in the question)

II. $b + c = 270$ (from statement (1))

III. $a + b = 9c$ (from statement (2))

IV. $10c + n = 900$ (from combining I and III)

For example, if $n = 600$, then $c = 30$ from IV, $b = 240$ from II, and $a = 30$ from III. On the other hand, if $n = 500$, then $c = 40$ from IV, $b = 230$ from II, and $a = 130$ from III.

The correct answer is E; both statements together are still not sufficient.

295. The average (arithmetic mean) price of the 3 items that Kate purchased from a clothing store was \$50. If there was no sales tax on any item that had a price of less than \$80 and 6 percent sales tax on all other items, what was the total sales tax on the 3 items that Kate purchased?

(1) The price of the most expensive item that Kate purchased from the store was \$100.

(2) The price of the least expensive item that Kate purchased from the store was \$10.

Arithmetic Applied problems; Percents

Kate purchased 3 items, the average price of which was \$50, and paid 6% sales tax on each item priced over \$80. Determine the total tax that Kate paid.

Given that the average of the 3 prices is \$50, it follows that the sum of the 3 prices is (3)(\$50) = \$150.

(1) One of the prices is \$100. Therefore, the sum of the 2 remaining prices is \$150 − \$100 = \$50. Hence, each of the remaining items has a price that is less than \$80 and thus is not taxed. It follows that the total sales tax on the 3 items is the sales tax on the \$100 item, which equals (6%)(\$100) = \$6; SUFFICIENT.

(2) One of the prices is \$10. Therefore, the sum of the 2 remaining prices is \$150 − \$10 = \$140. If the 2 remaining prices are \$70 and \$70, then none of the items has a price greater than \$80, and hence the total sales tax on the 3 items is \$0. If the 2 remaining prices are \$40 and \$100, then the total sales tax on the 3 items is (6%)(\$100) = \$6; NOT sufficient.

This solution assumes tax is not included in the quoted prices. If tax were included in the quoted prices, then some minor adjustments in the numerical examples would be needed. However, the sufficiency of (1) and insufficiency of (2) would not be affected.

The correct answer is A;
statement 1 alone is sufficient.

296. A company makes and sells two products, P and Q. The costs per unit of making and selling P and Q are \$8.00 and \$9.50, respectively, and the selling prices per unit of P and Q are \$10.00 and \$13.00, respectively. In one month the company sold a total of 834 units of these products. Was the total profit on these items more than \$2,000.00 ?

(1) During the month, more units of P than units of Q were sold.

(2) During the month, at least 100 units of Q were sold.

Arithmetic **Applied problems**

It is given that the profit on each unit of P is \$10.00 − \$8.00 = \$2.00, and the profit on each unit of Q is \$13.00 − \$9.50 = \$3.50. Also if p and q represent the number of units of Products P and Q made and sold, then it is given that $p + q = 834$. Determining if the total profit on these items was more than \$2,000 requires determining how many units of at least one of the products were sold.

(1) This indicates that $p > q$, but does not give a specific value for p or q; NOT sufficient.

(2) This indicates that $q \geq 100$, but does not give a specific value for q; NOT sufficient.

Taking (1) and (2) together, $p > q$ and $q \geq 100$, so $p > 100$, but a specific value for p or q cannot be determined.

The correct answer is E;
both statements together are still not sufficient.

297. Jill has applied for a job with each of two different companies. What is the probability that she will get job offers from both companies?

(1) The probability that she will get a job offer from neither company is 0.3.

(2) The probability that she will get a job offer from exactly one of the two companies is 0.5.

Arithmetic **Probability**

Let $P(2)$ be the probability that she will get a job offer from both companies, $P(1)$ be the probability that she will get a job offer from exactly one of the companies, and $P(0)$ be the probability that she will get a job offer from neither company. Then $P(2) + P(1) + P(0) = 1$. What is the value of $P(2)$?

(1) Given that $P(0) = 0.3$, it follows that $P(2) + P(1) + 0.3 = 1$, or $P(2) + P(1) = 0.7$. However, the value of $P(2)$ cannot be determined, since nothing is known about the value of $P(1)$ other than $0 \leq P(1) \leq 0.7$; NOT sufficient.

(2) (2) Given that $P(1) = 0.5$, it follows that $P(2) + 0.5 + P(0) = 1$, or $P(2) + P(0) = 0.5$. However, the value of $P(2)$ cannot be determined, since nothing is known about the value of $P(0)$ other than $0 \leq P(1) \leq 0.5$; NOT sufficient.

Taking (1) and (2) together, it follows that $P(2) + 0.5 + 0.3 = 1$, or $P(2) = 0.2$.

The correct answer is C;
both statements together are sufficient.

298. A scientist recorded the number of eggs in each of 10 birds' nests. What was the standard deviation of the numbers of eggs in the 10 nests?

(1) The average (arithmetic mean) number of eggs for the 10 nests was 4.
(2) Each of the 10 nests contained the same number of eggs.

Arithmetic Statistics

Note that if all of the values of a data set are equal to the same number, say x, the difference between each data value and the average is $x - x = 0$, the sum of the squares of these differences is 0, and so the standard deviation is 0. On the other hand, if the values in a data set are not all equal, then the standard deviation will be positive.

(1) If each of the 10 nests had 4 eggs, then the average would be 4 and the standard deviation would be 0. If 8 nests had 4 eggs, 1 nest had 3 eggs, and 1 nest had 5 eggs, then the average would be 4 and the standard deviation would be positive; NOT sufficient.

(2) Since all of the data values are equal to the same number, the standard deviation is 0; SUFFICIENT.

The correct answer is B; statement 2 alone is sufficient.

299. A conveyor belt moves bottles at a constant speed of 120 centimeters per second. If the conveyor belt moves a bottle from a loading dock to an unloading dock, is the distance that the conveyor belt moves the bottle less than 90 meters? (1 meter = 100 centimeters)

(1) It takes the conveyor belt less than 1.2 minutes to move the bottle from the loading dock to the unloading dock.
(2) It takes the conveyor belt more than 1.1 minutes to move the bottle from the loading dock to the unloading dock.

Arithmetic Applied problems

Since the rate at which the conveyor belt moves is given as 120 centimeters per second, which is equivalent to $\frac{120}{100} = 1.2$ meters per second, the conveyor will move less than 90 meters if it moves for less than $\frac{90}{1.2} = 75$ seconds.

(1) This indicates that the length of time the conveyor belt moves is less than 1.2 minutes, which is equivalent to $(1.2)(60) = 72$ seconds and $72 < 75$; SUFFICIENT.

(2) This indicates that the length of time the conveyor belt moves is more than 1.1 minutes, which is equivalent to $(1.1)(60) = 66$ seconds, but does not indicate how much more than 66 seconds the conveyor moves. If the conveyor moves for 70 seconds $(70 > 66)$, for example, it moves less than 90 meters since $70 < 75$. However, if the conveyor belt moves for 80 seconds $(80 > 66)$, then it moves more than 90 meters since $80 > 75$; NOT sufficient.

The correct answer is A; statement 1 alone is sufficient.

300. If x, y, and z are positive numbers, what is the value of the average (arithmetic mean) of x and z?

(1) $x - y = y - z$
(2) $x^2 - y^2 = z$

Algebra Statistics; Simplifying algebraic expressions

(1) Given that $x - y = y - z$, it follows that $x + z = 2y$, or $y = \frac{x+z}{2}$. Therefore, y is the average of x and z. However, it is not possible to determine the value of y. For example, $x = y = z = 3$ gives three positive numbers that satisfy $x - y = y - z$, and $x = y = z = 4$ gives three positive numbers that satisfy $x - y = y - z$; NOT sufficient.

(2) Given that $x^2 - y^2 = z$, it is not possible to determine the value of $\frac{x+z}{2}$, the average of the x and z. For example, if $x = 3$, $y = 2$, and $z = 5$, then $x^2 - y^2 = z$ is true (because $3^2 - 2^2 = 9 - 4 = 5$) and $\frac{x+z}{2} = \frac{3+5}{2} = 4$. However, if $x = 5$, $y = 4$, and $z = 9$, then $x^2 - y^2 = z$ is true (because

$5^2 - 4^2 = 25 - 16 = 9$) and $\frac{x + z}{2} = \frac{5 + 9}{2} = 7$; NOT sufficient.

Taking (1) and (2) together, it follows that $x + z = 2y$ and $x^2 - y^2 = z$, so $x + (x^2 - y^2) = 2y$, or $x + x^2 = y^2 + 2y$. Adding 1 to both sides of this last equation gives $x + x^2 + 1 = y^2 + 2y + 1 = (y + 1)^2$, which simplifies the task of finding positive numbers x, y, and z that satisfy both (1) and (2) and for which the values of $\frac{x + z}{2} = y$ can be different. For one example, letting $x = 1$ gives $x + x^2 + 1 = 3$, and thus $(y + 1)^2 = 3$. Solving for a positive value of y gives $y + 1 = \sqrt{3}$, or $y = \sqrt{3} - 1$, and by using $x + z = 2y$, the corresponding value of z is $2y - x = 2(\sqrt{3} - 1) - 1 = 2\sqrt{3} - 3$. Note that $2\sqrt{3} - 3$ is positive because $(2\sqrt{3})^2 = 4(3) = 12$ is greater than $3^2 = 9$. The values $x = 1$, $y = \sqrt{3} - 1$, and $z = 2\sqrt{3} - 3$ satisfy both (1) and (2), and for this choice of values of x, y, and z, the value of $\frac{x + z}{2} = y$ is $\sqrt{3} - 1$. For another example, letting $x = 2$ gives $x + x^2 + 1 = 7$, and thus $(y + 1)^2 = 7$. Solving for a positive value of y gives $y + 1 = \sqrt{7}$, or $y = \sqrt{7} - 1$, and by using $x + z = 2y$, the corresponding value of z is $2y - x = 2(\sqrt{7} - 1) - 2 = 2\sqrt{7} - 4$. Note that $2\sqrt{7} - 4$ is positive because $(2\sqrt{7})^2 = 4(7) = 28$ is greater than $4^2 = 16$. The values $x = 2$, $y = \sqrt{7} - 1$, and $z = 2\sqrt{7} - 4$ satisfy both (1) and (2), and for this choice of values of x, y, and z, the value of $\frac{x + z}{2} = y$ is $\sqrt{7} - 1$; NOT sufficient.

The correct answer is E;
both statements together are still not sufficient.

301. The rectangular rug shown in the figure above has an accent border. What is the area of the portion of the rug that excludes the border?

(1) The perimeter of the rug is 44 feet.

(2) The width of the border on all sides is 1 foot.

Geometry Rectangles; Perimeter

(1) Given that the perimeter of the rug is 44 ft, then the rectangular rug could have area 121 ft^2 (length = 11 ft and width = 11 ft) and the rectangular rug could have area 96 ft^2 (length = 16 ft and width = 6 ft). Moreover, no information is given about the width of the accent border, so even if the area of the rectangular rug could be determined, it would still not be possible to determine the area of the portion of the rug that excludes the border; NOT sufficient.

(2) Given that the width of the border is 1 ft, the area of the portion of the rug that excludes the border is $(L - 2)(W - 2)$ ft^2, where L ft and W ft are the length and width, respectively, of the rug. If $L = W = 11$, then $(L - 2)(W - 2) = 81$. However, if $L = 16$ and $W = 6$, then $(L - 2)(W - 2) = 56$; NOT sufficient.

Taking (1) and (2) together, the area could be 81 ft^2 or 56 ft^2 as shown by the examples in (1) and (2).

The correct answer is E;
both statements together are still not sufficient.

302. Terry holds 12 cards, each of which is red, white, green, or blue. If a person is to select a card randomly from the cards Terry is holding, is the probability less than $\frac{1}{2}$ that the card selected will be either red or white?

(1) The probability that the person will select a blue card is $\frac{1}{3}$.

(2) The probability that the person will select a red card is $\frac{1}{6}$.

Arithmetic Probability

Determine if the probability is less than $\frac{1}{2}$ that a card selected at random from 12 cards, each of which is red, white, green, or blue, will be either red or white. That is, determine whether the number of cards that are red or white is less than $\frac{1}{2}(12) = 6$.

(1) It is given that the probability is $\frac{1}{3}$ that the selected card will be blue. This means that $\frac{1}{3}(12) = 4$ of the cards are blue. However, there is no information about how many of the 8 remaining cards are red, how many are white, or how many are green. If, for example, there are 2 red cards, 2 white cards, and 4 green cards, then the number of cards that are red or white is $2 + 2 = 4$, which is less than 6. On the other hand, if there are 3 red cards, 4 white cards, and 1 green card, then the number of cards that are red or white is $3 + 4 = 7$, which is not less than 6; NOT sufficient.

(2) It is given that the probability is $\frac{1}{6}$ that the selected card will be red. This means that $\frac{1}{6}(12) = 2$ of the cards are red. However, there is no information about how many of the 10 remaining cards are white, how many are blue, or how many are green. If, for example, there are 3 white cards, 5 blue cards, and 2 green cards, then the number of cards that are red or white is $2 + 3 = 5$, which is less than 6. On the other hand, if there are 7 white cards, 1 blue card, and 2 green cards, then the number of cards that are red or white is $2 + 7 = 9$, which is not less than 6; NOT sufficient.

Taking (1) and (2) together, there are 4 blue cards and 2 red cards. However, there is no information about how many of the 6 remaining cards are white or how many are green. If, for example, there are 3 white cards and 3 green cards, then the number of cards that are red or white is $2 + 3 = 5$, which is less than 6. On the other hand, if there are 5 white cards and 1 green card, then the number of cards that are red or white is $2 + 5 = 7$, which is not less than 6.

The correct answer is E;
both statements together are still not sufficient.

303. If $y \neq 2xz$, what is the value of $\frac{2xz + yz}{2xz - y}$?

(1) $2x + y = 3$

(2) $z = 2$

Algebra Simplifying algebraic expressions

The task is to determine the value of $\frac{2xz + yz}{2xz - y} = \frac{z(2x + y)}{2xz - y}$

(1) This indicates $2x + y = 3$, and so $\frac{2xz + yz}{2xz - y} = \frac{3z}{2xz - y}$. However, this is not enough to determine the value of $\frac{2xz + yz}{2xz - y}$. For example, if $x = 1$, $y = 1$, and $z = 2$, then $2x + y = 3$ and $\frac{2xz + yz}{2xz - y} = 2$, but if $x = 0$, $y = 3$, and $z = 2$, then $2x + y = 3$ and $\frac{2xz + yz}{2xz - y} = -2$; NOT sufficient.

(2) This indicates that $z = 2$, and so $\frac{2xz + yz}{2xz - y} = \frac{4x + 2y}{4x - y}$. However, this is not enough to determine the value of $\frac{2xz + yz}{2xz - y}$. For example, if $x = 1$, $y = 1$, and $z = 2$, then $\frac{2xz + yz}{2xz - y} = 2$, but if $x = 0$, $y = 3$, and $z = 2$, then $\frac{2xz + yz}{2xz - y} = -2$; NOT sufficient.

Taking (1) and (2) together is not enough to determine the value of $\frac{2xz + yz}{2xz - y}$ because the same examples used to show that (1) is not sufficient were also used to show that (2) is not sufficient.

The correct answer is E;
both statements together are still not sufficient.

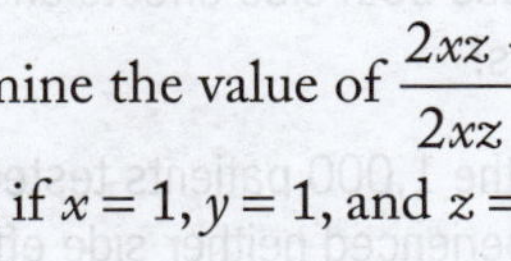

304. In the parallelogram shown, what is the value of x ?

(1) $y = 2x$

(2) $x + z = 120$

Geometry Angles

(1) Given that $y = 2x$ and the fact that adjacent angles of a parallelogram are supplementary, it follows that $180 = x + y = x + 2x = 3x$, or $180 = 3x$. Solving this equation gives $x = 60$; SUFFICIENT.

(2) Given that $x + z = 120$ and the fact that opposite angles of a parallelogram have the same measure, it follows that $120 = x + z = x + x$, or $120 = 2x$. Solving this equation gives $x = 60$; SUFFICIENT.

The correct answer is D;
each statement alone is sufficient.

305. In a product test of a common cold remedy, x percent of the patients tested experienced side effects from the use of the drug and y percent experienced relief of cold symptoms. What percent of the patients tested experienced both side effects and relief of cold symptoms?

(1) Of the 1,000 patients tested, 15 percent experienced neither side effects nor relief of cold symptoms.

(2) Of the patients tested, 30 percent experienced relief of cold symptoms without side effects.

Algebra Sets

One way to solve problems about sets is by using a contingency table. For the information given in this problem with T representing the total number of people tested, the table might be as follows:

	side effects	no side effects	totals
relief of symptoms			$\left(\frac{y}{100}\right)T$
no relief of symptoms			
totals	$\left(\frac{x}{100}\right)T$		T

(1) Using the information in (1) gives the following table, where 15% of 1,000 is 150.

	side effects	no side effects	totals
relief of symptoms			$\left(\frac{y}{100}\right)(1{,}000)$
no relief of symptoms		150	
totals	$\left(\frac{x}{100}\right)(1{,}000)$		1,000

If $x = 55$ and $y = 55$, then the table becomes

	side effects	no side effects	totals
relief of symptoms	250	300	550
no relief of symptoms	300	150	450
totals	550	450	1,000

and this gives $\frac{250}{1{,}000} = 25\%$ as the percent of patients tested who experienced both side effects and relief of cold symptoms.

However, if $x = 55$ and $y = 50$, then the table becomes

	side effects	no side effects	totals
relief of symptoms	200	300	500
no relief of symptoms	350	150	500
totals	550	450	1,000

and this gives $\frac{200}{1{,}000} = 20\%$ as the percent of patients tested who experienced both side effects and relief of cold symptoms; NOT sufficient.

(2) This indicates that 30% of the patients tested experienced relief of cold symptoms without side effects. The same examples that were used for (1) can be used here, also, to show that different values can be obtained

for the percent of patients tested who experienced both side effects and relief of cold symptoms; NOT sufficient.

Since the examples satisfy both (1) and (2), these statements taken together are not sufficient to determine the percent of patients tested who experienced both side effects and relief of cold symptoms.

The correct answer is E;
both statements together are still not sufficient.

306. Is $x < 5$?

(1) $x^2 > 5$

(2) $x^2 + x < 5$

Algebra Inequalities

(1) Given that $x^2 > 5$, then $x < 5$ can be true (for example, if $x = -3$) and $x < 5$ can be false (for example, if $x = 6$); NOT sufficient.

(2) Given that $x^2 + x < 5$, then $x < 5 - x^2$. Also, since $x^2 \geq 0$ is true for any real number x, it follows that $-x^2 \leq 0$, or after adding 5 to both sides, $5 - x^2 \leq 5$. From $x < 5 - x^2$ and $5 - x^2 \leq 5$, it follows that $x < 5$; SUFFICIENT.

The correct answer is B;
statement 2 alone is sufficient.

307. Is $4^{x+y} = 8^{10}$?

(1) $x - y = 9$

(2) $\frac{y}{x} = \frac{1}{4}$

Algebra Properties of numbers

The question is equivalent to determining whether $(2^2)^{x+y} = (2^3)^{10}$, which in turn is equivalent to determining whether $2^{2(x+y)} = 2^{30}$, which in turn is equivalent to determining whether $2(x + y) = 30$, or $x + y = 15$.

(1) Given that $x - y = 9$, it is possible that $x + y = 15$ (for example, $x = 12$ and $y = 3$) and it is possible that $x + y \neq 15$ (for example, $x = 10$ and $y = 1$); NOT sufficient.

(2) Given that $\frac{y}{x} = \frac{1}{4}$, or $x = 4y$, it is possible that $x + y = 15$ (for example, $x = 12$ and $y = 3$) and it is possible that $x + y \neq 15$ (for example, $x = 4$ and $y = 1$); NOT sufficient.

Given (1) and (2) together, $x - y = 9$ and $x = 4y$, it follows that $4y - y = 9$, or $y = 3$, and $x = 4y = 4(3) = 12$. Therefore, $x + y = 12 + 3 = 15$.

The correct answer is C;
both statements together are sufficient.

308. Is zp negative?

(1) $pz^4 < 0$

(2) $p + z^4 = 14$

Arithmetic Properties of numbers

(1) Given that $pz^4 < 0$, zp can be negative (choose $p = -2$ and $z = 2$) and zp can be nonnegative (choose $p = -2$ and $z = -2$); NOT sufficient.

(2) Given that $p + z^4 = 14$, the same examples used to show that (1) is not sufficient can be used for (2); NOT sufficient.

Taking (1) and (2) together is of no more help than either (1) or (2) taken separately because the same examples used to show that (1) is not sufficient also show that (2) is not sufficient.

The correct answer is E;
both statements together are still not sufficient.

309. In each game of a certain tournament, a contestant either loses 3 points or gains 2 points. If Pat had 100 points at the beginning of the tournament, how many games did Pat play in the tournament?

(1) At the end of the tournament, Pat had 104 points.

(2) Pat played fewer than 10 games.

Arithmetic Computation with integers

Pat either lost 3 points or gained 2 points in each game she played. Therefore, since she had 100 points at the beginning of the tournament, her score at the end of the tournament was $100 - 3x + 2y$, where x and y represent, respectively, the number of games in which she lost 3 points and the number of games in which she gained 2 points. Determine the value of $x + y$.

(1) This indicates that $100 - 3x + 2y = 104$, but no information is given about the values of x or y. For example, the values of x and y could be 0 and 2, respectively, so that $x + y = 2$ or the values of x and y could be 2 and 5, respectively, so that $x + y = 7$; NOT sufficient.

(2) This indicates that Pat played fewer than 10 games, but in each of the examples above, Pat played fewer than 10 games; NOT sufficient.

Since the examples given satisfy both (1) and (2), taking (1) and (2) together does not give enough information to determine the value of $x + y$.

The correct answer is E;
both statements together are still not sufficient.

310. At the beginning of the year, the Finance Committee and the Planning Committee of a certain company each had n members, and no one was a member of both committees. At the end of the year, 5 members left the Finance Committee and 3 members left the Planning Committee. How many members did the Finance Committee have at the beginning of the year?

(1) The ratio of the total number of members who left at the end of the year to the total number of members at the beginning of the year was 1:6.

(2) At the end of the year, 21 members remained on the Planning Committee.

Algebra Applied problems

(1) It is given that $\frac{8}{2n} = \frac{1}{6}$, since a total of $3 + 5 = 8$ members left at the end of the year and there were a total of $n + n = 2n$ members at the beginning of the year. It follows that $(8)(6) = (2n)(1)$, or $n = 24$; SUFFICIENT.

(2) It is given that $n - 3 = 21$, since 3 members from the original n members left the Planning Committee at the end of the year. It follows that $n = 21 + 3 = 24$; SUFFICIENT.

The correct answer is D;
each statement alone is sufficient.

311. Can a certain rectangular sheet of glass be positioned on a rectangular tabletop so that it covers the entire tabletop and its edges are parallel to the edges of the tabletop?

(1) The tabletop is 36 inches wide by 60 inches long.

(2) The area of one side of the sheet of glass is 2,400 square inches.

Geometry Area

Determine whether the length and width of the sheet of glass are greater than or equal to the length and width of the tabletop.

(1) The length and width of the tabletop are given, but nothing can be determined about the dimensions of the sheet of glass; NOT sufficient.

(2) The area of the sheet of glass is given, but nothing can be determined about the dimensions of the tabletop; NOT sufficient.

(1) and (2) together are not sufficient because the information given does not specify the length and width of the sheet of glass. For example, the length and width of the sheet of glass could be 40 inches and 60 inches and, since $40 \geq 36$ and $60 \geq 60$, the answer to the question would be "Yes." On the other hand, the length and width of the sheet of glass could be 100 inches and 24 inches, and in this case the answer to the question would be "No" because 24 is not greater than or equal to 36 or 60.

The correct answer is E;
both statements together are still not sufficient.

312. In a random sample of 80 adults, how many are college graduates?

(1) In the sample, the number of adults who are not college graduates is 3 times the number who are college graduates.

(2) In the sample, the number of adults who are not college graduates is 40 more than the number who are college graduates.

Algebra First-degree equations

Let C be the number of college graduates and let N be the number who are not college graduates. Then, $C + N = 80$. Find the value of C.

(1) Since the number who are not college graduates is 3 times the number who are, $N = 3C$. Then $C + 3C = 80$, $4C = 80$, and $C = 20$; SUFFICIENT.

(2) Since the number who are not college graduates is 40 more than the number who are college graduates, $N = C + 40$. Then $C + (C + 40) = 80$, $2C + 40 = 80$, $2C = 40$, and $C = 20$; SUFFICIENT.

The correct answer is D;
each statement alone is sufficient.

313. Max purchased a guitar for a total of \$624, which consisted of the price of the guitar and the sales tax. Was the sales tax rate greater than 3 percent?

(1) The price of the guitar that Max purchased was less than \$602.

(2) The sales tax for the guitar that Max purchased was less than \$30.

Arithmetic Applied problems; Percents

Letting P be the price, in dollars, of the guitar and r% be the sales tax rate, it is given that $P\left(1+\frac{r}{100}\right) = 624$. Determine if $r > 3$.

(1) Given that $P < 602$, then $624 = P\left(1+\frac{r}{100}\right) < 602\left(1+\frac{r}{100}\right)$, and so $1+\frac{r}{100} > \frac{624}{602}$. Therefore, $\frac{r}{100} > \frac{624}{602} - 1 = \frac{22}{602} = \frac{11}{301} > \frac{3}{100}$, because $(11)(100) > (3)(301)$, and so $r > 100\left(\frac{3}{100}\right) = 3$; SUFFICIENT.

(2) Given that the sales tax was less than \$30, it is not possible to determine whether the sales tax rate was greater than 3%. Since $(0.03)(\$624) = \$18.72$, a 3% sales tax rate on the price corresponds to a sales tax that is less than \$18.72, since the price is less than \$624. Therefore, it is possible that the sales tax is less than \$30 and the sales tax rate is less than 3%, since any sales tax rate less than 3% would give a sales tax that is less than \$18.72 (and hence less than \$30). However, it is also possible that the sales tax is less than \$30 and the sales tax rate is 4% (which is greater than 3%), since a 4% sales tax rate implies $P\left(1+\frac{4}{100}\right) = 624$, or $P = \frac{62,400}{104} = 600$, and thus the sales tax would be $0.04(\$600) = \$24 < \$30$; NOT sufficient.

The correct answer is A;
statement 1 alone is sufficient.

314. What is the sum of a certain pair of consecutive odd integers?

(1) At least one of the integers is negative.

(2) At least one of the integers is positive.

Arithmetic Properties of numbers

(1) Given that at least one of the integers is negative, the sum could be -4 (if the integers were -3 and -1) and the sum could be 0 (if the integers were -1 and 1); NOT sufficient.

(2) Given that at least one of the integers is positive, the sum could be 0 (if the integers were -1 and 1) and the sum could be 4 (if the integers were 1 and 3); NOT sufficient.

Taking (1) and (2) together, the smaller of the two numbers cannot be less than -1 (otherwise (2) would not be true) and the larger of the two numbers cannot be greater than 1 (otherwise (1) would not be true). Therefore, the integers must be -1 and 1, and the sum must be 0.

The correct answer is C;
both statements together are sufficient.

315. If $a < x < b$ and $c < y < d$, is $x < y$?

(1) $a < c$

(2) $b < c$

Algebra Inequalities

Given $a < x < b$ and $c < y < d$, determine if $x < y$.

(1) Even though $a < c$, there is no information on the relative size of x and c. For example, if $a = 3$, $x = 10$, $b = 12$, $c = 4$, $y = 6$, and $d = 7$, $a < c$ because $3 < 4$ and $x > y$, since $10 > 6$. If, on the other hand, $a = 3$, $x = 4$, $b = 12$, $c = 4$, $y = 6$, and $d = 7$, $a < c$, because $3 < 4$ and $x < y$, since $4 < 6$; NOT sufficient.

(2) If $b < c$, then $a < x < b < c < y < d$ and so $x < y$; SUFFICIENT.

The correct answer is B;
statement 2 alone is sufficient.

316. How many people are directors of both Company K and Company R ?

(1) There were 17 directors present at a joint meeting of the directors of Company K and Company R, and no directors were absent.

(2) Company K has 12 directors and Company R has 8 directors.

Algebra Sets

(1) This clarifies that Company K and Company R together have 17 individuals serving as directors. However, there is no information as to the distribution of the Company K directors, the Company R directors, and the joint directors; NOT sufficient.

(2) This gives the number of directors in each company but no information as to the number of joint directors; NOT sufficient.

Taking (1) and (2) together, it is known from (2) that there are 20 directorships in all. If at a joint meeting, there are only 17 people present, then $20 - 17 = 3$ people must be joint directors.

The correct answer is C;
both statements together are sufficient.

317. The sum of 4 different odd integers is 64. What is the value of the greatest of these integers?

(1) The integers are consecutive odd numbers.

(2) Of these integers, the greatest is 6 more than the least.

Arithmetic Properties of numbers

Determine the greatest of four odd integers whose sum is 64.

(1) This indicates that the integers are consecutive odd integers. Letting z represent the greatest of the four integers, it follows that $(z - 6) + (z - 4) + (z - 2) + z = 64$, from which a unique value of z can be determined; SUFFICIENT.

(2) Letting w, x, y, and z represent four different odd integers, where $w < x < y < z$, this indicates that $z - w = 6$ or $w = z - 6$. This means that $x = z - 4$ and $y = z - 2$ since w, x, y, and z must be different odd integers and it must be true that $w < x < y < z$. From $w + x + y + z = 64$, it follows that $(z - 6) + (z - 4) + (z - 2) + z = 64$ from which a unique value of z can be determined; SUFFICIENT.

The correct answer is D;
each statement alone is sufficient.

318. Was the number of books sold at Bookstore X last week greater than the number of books sold at Bookstore Y last week?

(1) Last week, more than 1,000 books were sold at Bookstore X on Saturday and fewer than 1,000 books were sold at Bookstore Y on Saturday.

(2) Last week, less than 20 percent of the books sold at Bookstore X were sold on Saturday and more than 20 percent of the books sold at Bookstore Y were sold on Saturday.

Arithmetic Inequalities

Determine if Bookstore X sold more books last week than Bookstore Y.

(1) This indicates that Bookstore X sold more books on Saturday than Bookstore Y, but it gives no information about the numbers of books sold by the two bookstores on the other days of last week; NOT sufficient.

(2) This gives information about the percents of the books sold last week that were sold on Saturday, but it gives no information about the actual numbers of books sold at

the two bookstores last week. Therefore, a comparison of the numbers of books sold last week by Bookstore X and Bookstore Y is not possible; NOT sufficient.

Taking (1) and (2) together, if x represents the number of books that Bookstore X sold on Saturday and T_X represents the total number of books that Bookstore X sold last week, then $x > 1{,}000$ and $x < 0.2T_X$. It follows that $1{,}000 < 0.2T_X$ and so $T_X > 5{,}000$. Similarly, if y represents the number of books that Bookstore Y sold on Saturday and T_Y represents the total number of books that Bookstore Y sold last week, then $y < 1{,}000$ and $y > 0.2T_Y$. It follows that $0.2T_Y < 1{,}000$, and so $T_Y < 5{,}000$. Combining the inequalities gives $T_Y < 5{,}000 < T_X$, and so $T_Y < T_X$, which means that Bookstore X sold more books last week than Bookstore Y.

The correct answer is C;
both statements together are sufficient.

319. From May 1 to May 30 in the same year, the balance in a checking account increased. What was the balance in the checking account on May 30 ?

(1) If, during this period of time, the increase in the balance in the checking account had been 12 percent, then the balance in the account on May 30 would have been \$504.

(2) During this period of time, the increase in the balance in the checking account was 8 percent.

Arithmetic Applied problems; Percents

(1) Given that the amount on May 30 would have been \$504 if the increase had been 12%, it follows that the amount on May 1 was $\$\frac{504}{1.12} = \$450$. However, the balance on May 30 cannot be determined because the (actual) percent increase is not given. For example, if the increase had been 10%, then the balance on May 30 would have been (1.1)(\$450) = \$495, which is different from \$504; NOT sufficient.

(2) Given that the increase was 8%, the amount on May 30 could be \$108 (if the amount on May 1 was \$100) and the amount on May 30 could be \$216 (if the amount on May 1 was \$200); NOT sufficient.

Taking (1) and (2) together, it follows that the amount on May 30 was (\$450)(1.08) = \$486.

The correct answer is C;
both statements together are sufficient.

320. If x and y are positive, is $x < 10 < y$?

(1) $x < y$ and $xy = 100$

(2) $x^2 < 100 < y^2$

Algebra Inequalities

(1) Given that $x < y$, multiply both sides by x, which is positive, to get $x^2 < xy$. Then, since $xy = 100$, it follows that $x^2 < 100$. Similarly, multiply both sides of $x < y$ by y, which is positive, to get $xy < y^2$. Again, since $xy = 100$, it follows that $100 < y^2$. Combining $x^2 < 100$ and $100 < y^2$ gives $x^2 < 100 < y^2$, from which it follows that $\sqrt{x^2} < \sqrt{100} < \sqrt{y^2}$ and, therefore, $x < 10 < y$, since x and y are both positive; SUFFICIENT.

(2) Given that $x^2 < 100 < y^2$, it follows that $x < 10 < y$ as shown in (1) above; SUFFICIENT.

The correct answer is D;
each statement alone is sufficient.

321. A merchant discounted the sale price of a coat and the sale price of a sweater. Which of the two articles of clothing was discounted by the greater dollar amount?

(1) The percent discount on the coat was 2 percentage points greater than the percent discount on the sweater.

(2) Before the discounts, the sale price of the coat was \$10 less than the sale price of the sweater.

Arithmetic Applied problems; Percents

(1) Given that the discount on the coat was 2 percentage points greater than the discount on the sweater, the sweater could have been discounted by the greater dollar amount (\$30 sweater with 10% discount is a discount of \$3; \$20 coat with 12% discount is a discount of \$2.40) and the coat could have been discounted by the greater dollar amount (\$110 sweater with 10% discount is a

discount of \$11; \$100 coat with 12% discount is a discount of \$12); NOT sufficient.

(2) Given that the coat's sale price was \$10 less than the sweater's sale price, the same examples used to show that (1) is not sufficient can be used for (2); NOT sufficient.

Taking (1) and (2) together is of no more help than either (1) or (2) taken separately because the same examples used to show that (1) is not sufficient also show that (2) is not sufficient.

The correct answer is E;
both statements together are still not sufficient.

322. A taxi company charges *f* cents for the first mile of the taxi ride and *m* cents for each additional mile. How much does the company charge for a 10-mile taxi ride?

(1) The company charges \$0.90 for a 2-mile ride.

(2) The company charges \$1.20 for a 4-mile ride.

Arithmetic Applied problems

If a taxi company charges f cents for the first mile and m cents for each additional mile, determine the charge for a 10-mile taxi ride, which can be expressed as $f + 9m$

(1) Since the charge for a 2-mile ride is \$0.90, $f + m = 0.90$, and so $f + 9m = 0.90 + 8m$, but the value of m is unknown; NOT sufficient.

(2) Since the charge for a 4-mile ride is \$1.20, $f + 3m = 1.20$, and so $f + 9m = 1.20 + 6m$, but the value of m is unknown; NOT sufficient.

Taking (1) and (2) together and subtracting the equation in (1) from the equation in (2) gives $2m = 0.30$ from which $m = 0.15$. Then from (1), $f + 0.15 = 0.90$ and $f = 0.75$. Therefore, the charge for a 10-mile taxi ride is \$0.75 + 9(\$0.15) = \$2.10.

Alternatively, the graphs of $f + m = 0.90$ and $f + 3m = 1.20$ in the (f,m) coordinate plane are lines that intersect at exactly one point, and therefore values of f and m can be determined, from which $f + 9m$ can then be determined.

The correct answer is C;
both statements together are sufficient.

323. If the positive integer *n* is added to each of the integers 69, 94, and 121, what is the value of *n* ?

(1) 69 + *n* and 94 + *n* are the squares of two consecutive integers.

(2) 94 + *n* and 121 + *n* are the squares of two consecutive integers.

Algebra Computation with integers

Determine the value of the positive integer n.

(1) This indicates that $69 + n$ and $94 + n$ are the squares of two consecutive integers. Letting x and $(x + 1)$ represent the consecutive integers, it follows that $(x + 1)^2 - x^2 = x^2 + 2x + 1 - x^2 = 2x + 1$. Therefore, $(94 + n) - (69 + n) = 2x + 1$ or $25 = 2x + 1$, from which $x = 12$. Then $12^2 = 69 + n$ and $n = 144 - 69 = 75$ or $(12 + 1)^2 = 94 + n$ and $n = 169 - 94 = 75$; SUFFICIENT.

(2) This indicates that $94 + n$ and $121 + n$ are the squares of two consecutive integers. Letting x and $(x + 1)$ represent the consecutive integers, it follows that $(x + 1)^2 - x^2 = x^2 + 2x + 1 - x^2 = 2x + 1$. Therefore, $(121 + n) - (94 + n) = 2x + 1$ or $27 = 2x + 1$, from which $x = 13$. Then $13^2 = 94 + n$ and $n = 169 - 94 = 75$ or $(13 + 1)^2 = 121 + n$ and $n = 196 - 121 = 75$; SUFFICIENT.

The correct answer is D;
each statement alone is sufficient.

324. Guy's net income equals his gross income minus his deductions. By what percent did Guy's net income change on January 1, 1989, when both his gross income and his deductions increased?

(1) Guy's gross income increased by 4 percent on January 1, 1989.

(2) Guy's deductions increased by 15 percent on January 1, 1989.

Arithmetic Percents

Let g_b represent Guy's gross income and d_b Guy's deductions before January 1, 1989. Let g_a represent Guy's gross income and d_a Guy's deductions after January 1, 1989. Determine by what percent Guy's net income (gross income minus deductions) changed on January 1, 1989, when both his gross income and his deductions increased, or find $\frac{(g_a - d_a)-(g_b - d_b)}{g_b - d_b}$ as a percent.

(1) Guy's gross income increased by 4 percent on January 1, 1989, so $g_a = 1.04\,g_b$. Then, $\frac{(g_a - d_a)-(g_b - d_b)}{g_b - d_b} = \frac{(1.04g_b - d_a)-(g_b - d_b)}{g_b - d_b}$, However, no information is given about the values of g_b, d_a, or d_b, and so $\frac{(g_a - d_a)-(g_b - d_b)}{g_b - d_b}$ cannot be determined; NOT sufficient.

(2) Guy's deductions increased by 15 percent on January 1, 1989, so $d_a = 1.15d_b$. Then, $\frac{(g_a - d_a)-(g_b - d_b)}{g_b - d_b} = \frac{(g_a - 1.15d_b)-(g_b - d_b)}{g_b - d_b}$. However, no information is given about the values of g_a, g_b, or d_b, and so $\frac{(g_a - d_a)-(g_b - d_b)}{g_b - d_b}$ cannot be determined; NOT sufficient.

Taking (1) and (2) together gives $\frac{(1.04g_b - 1.15d_b)-(g_b - d_b)}{g_b - d_b} = \frac{0.04g_b - 0.15d_b}{g_b - d_b}$, which cannot be determined since the values of g_b and d_b are unknown.

The correct answer is E; both statements together are still not sufficient.

325. If the ratio of the number of teachers to the number of students is the same in School District M and School District P, what is the ratio of the number of students in School District M to the number of students in School District P ?

(1) There are 10,000 more students in School District M than there are in School District P.

(2) The ratio of the number of teachers to the number of students in School District M is 1 to 20.

Algebra Ratios

Given that $\frac{T_M}{S_M} = \frac{T_P}{S_P}$, where T_M and S_M are the numbers of teachers and students, respectively, in District M, and T_P and S_P are the numbers of teachers and students, respectively, in District P, find the value of $\frac{S_M}{S_P}$.

(1) Given that $S_M = S_P + 10{,}000$, then $\frac{S_M}{S_P} = \frac{S_P + 10{,}000}{S_P}$, but the value of S_P is unknown; NOT sufficient.

(2) Given that $\frac{T_M}{S_M} = \frac{1}{20}$ and $\frac{T_M}{S_M} = \frac{T_P}{S_P}$, then $\frac{T_P}{S_P} = \frac{1}{20}$. Therefore, $S_P = 20T_P$ and $S_M = 20T_M$. It follows that $\frac{S_M}{S_P} = \frac{20T_M}{20T_P}$, but the values of T_M and T_P are unknown; NOT sufficient.

Taking (1) and (2) together, if $S_P = 1{,}000$, $S_M = 1{,}000 + 10{,}000 = 11{,}000$, $T_P = \frac{1{,}000}{20} = 50$, and $T_M = \frac{11{,}000}{20} = 550$, then $\frac{S_M}{S_P} = \frac{11}{1}$. However, if $S_P = 5{,}000$, $S_M = 5{,}000 + 10{,}000 = 15{,}000$, $T_P = \frac{5{,}000}{20} = 250$, and $T_M = \frac{15{,}000}{20} = 750$, then $\frac{S_M}{S_P} = \frac{3}{1}$. Therefore, the value of $\frac{S_M}{S_P}$ cannot be determined.

The correct answer is E; both statements together are still not sufficient.

326. For a certain city's library, the average cost of purchasing each new book is \$28. The library receives \$15,000 from the city each year; the library also receives a bonus of \$2,000 if the total number of items checked out over the course of the year exceeds 5,000. Did the library receive the bonus last year?

(1) The library purchased an average of 50 new books each month last year and received enough money from the city to cover this cost.

(2) The lowest number of items checked out in one month was 459.

Arithmetic Applied problems

(1) Given that the library purchased an average of 50 new books each month, for the entire year the library purchased a total of (50)(12) = 600 books for a total cost of (600)($28) = $16,800. Excluding any possible bonus, the library received $15,000 from the city. Since this amount received from the city is not enough to cover the cost of the books, and the information provided in (1) says that the total amount received from the city was enough to cover the cost of the books, it follows that the library received a bonus; SUFFICIENT.

(2) Given that the least number of books checked out in one month was 459, it follows that the total number of books checked out for the year was at least (12)(459) = 5,508. Since this is greater than 5,000, it follows that the total number of books checked out for the year was greater than 5,000 and the library received a bonus; SUFFICIENT.

The correct answer is D;
each statement alone is sufficient.

327. Each gift certificate sold yesterday by a certain bookstore cost either $10 or $50. If yesterday the bookstore sold more than 5 gift certificates that cost $50 each, what was the total number of gift certificates sold yesterday by the bookstore?

(1) Yesterday the bookstore sold fewer than 10 gift certificates that cost $10 each.

(2) The total cost of gift certificates sold yesterday by the bookstore was $460.

Arithmetic Computation with integers

Let x be the number of $10 gift certificates sold yesterday and let y be the number of $50 gift certificates sold yesterday. It is given that $y > 5$. Determine the value of $x + y$.

(1) It is given that $x < 10$, so x could be 0, 1, 2, 3, . . ., 9. Since $y > 5$, y could be 6, 7, 8, . . ., and then $x + y$ could be, for example, $0 + 6 = 6$ or $2 + 8 = 10$; NOT sufficient.

(2) It is given that $10x + 50y = 460$. Several values of x and y with $y > 5$ will satisfy this equation and give different values for $x + y$, as shown below; NOT sufficient.

x	y	$10x + 50y$	$x + y$
16	6	460	22
11	7	460	18
6	8	460	14
1	9	460	10

Taking (1) and (2) together, it can be seen from the table that all the requirements are satisfied by $x = 6$ and $y = 8$ and also by $x = 1$ and $y = 9$, but the value of $x + y$ is not uniquely determined; NOT sufficient.

The correct answer is E;
both statements together are still not sufficient.

328. What is the tens digit of positive integer x ?

(1) x divided by 100 has a remainder of 30.

(2) x divided by 110 has a remainder of 30.

Arithmetic Properties of numbers

(1) Having a remainder of 30 when x is divided by 100 can only happen if x has a tens digit of 3 and a ones digit of 0, as in 130, 230, 630, and so forth; SUFFICIENT.

(2) When 140 is divided by 110, the quotient is 1 R30. However, 250 divided by 110 yields a quotient of 2 R30, and 360 divided by 110 gives a quotient of 3 R30. Since there is no consistency in the tens digit, more information is needed; NOT sufficient.

The correct answer is A;
statement 1 alone is sufficient.

329. Three dice, each of which has its 6 sides numbered 1 through 6, are tossed. The sum of the 3 numbers that are facing up is 12. Is at least 1 of these numbers 5 ?

(1) None of the 3 numbers that are facing up is divisible by 3.

(2) Of the numbers that are facing up, 2, but not all 3, are equal.

Arithmetic Properties of integers

When three dice, each with its 6 faces numbered 1 through 6, are tossed and the sum of the three integers facing up is 12, the possible outcomes are {1, 5, 6}, {2, 4, 6}, {2, 5, 5}, {3, 3, 6}, {3, 4, 5}, and {4, 4, 4}. Determine if, in the outcome described, at least one of the numbers is 5.

(1) This indicates that none of the numbers is divisible by three. The outcome could be {4, 4, 4}. In this case, none of the three numbers is 5. On the other hand, the outcome could be {2, 5, 5}. In this case, at least one of the numbers is 5; NOT sufficient.

(2) This indicates that two of the numbers, but not all three, are equal. The outcome could be {3, 3, 6}. In this case, none of the three numbers is 5. On the other hand, the outcome could be {2, 5, 5}. In this case, at least one of the numbers is 5; NOT sufficient.

Taking (1) and (2) together, of the possible outcomes {1, 5, 6}, {2, 4, 6}, {3, 3, 6}, and {3, 4, 5} are eliminated because they do not satisfy (1), and {4, 4, 4} is eliminated because it does not satisfy (2). This leaves only {2, 5, 5}, and at least one number is 5.

The correct answer is C;
both statements together are sufficient.

330. On the number line, point *R* has coordinate *r* and point *T* has coordinate *t*. Is $t < 0$?

(1) $-1 < r < 0$

(2) The distance between *R* and *T* is equal to r^2.

Arithmetic Number line

Determine if *t*, the coordinate of point *T* on the number line, is negative.

(1) This indicates that *r*, the coordinate of point *R* on the number line, lies between –1 and 0, but gives no information about the location of *T* in relation to either point *R* or 0; NOT sufficient.

(2) This indicates that the distance between *R* and *T*, which can be expressed as $|r - t|$, is r^2. If $r = 2$, for example, then $|2 - t| = 4$ so $2 - t = 4$ or $2 - t = -4$. If $2 - t = 4$, then $t = -2$, which is negative. If $2 - t = -4$, then $t = 6$, which is not negative; NOT sufficient.

Taking (1) and (2) together, if $r - t \geq 0$, then $r - t = r^2$ and $t = r - r^2 = r(1 - r)$. Since $-1 < r < 0$, it follows that $1 < 1 - r < 2$, and so *t* is the product of a negative number (*r*) and a positive number $(1 - r)$ and is therefore negative. Similarly, if $r - t < 0$, then $|r - t| = -(r - t) = t - r = r^2$ and $t = r^2 + r = r(r + 1)$. Since $-1 < r < 0$, it follows that $0 < r + 1 < 1$, and so *t* is the product of a negative number (*r*) and the positive number $(r + 1)$ and is therefore negative.

The correct answer is C;
both statements together are sufficient.

331. *S* is a set of points in the plane. How many distinct triangles can be drawn that have three of the points in *S* as vertices?

(1) The number of distinct points in *S* is 5.

(2) No three of the points in *S* are collinear.

Arithmetic Elementary combinatorics

(1) Given that the number of points in *S* is 5, the number of triangles can be 0 (if the points are collinear) and the number of triangles can be greater than 0 (if the points are not all collinear); NOT sufficient.

(2) Given that no three points of *S* are collinear, the number of triangles can be 1 (if *S* consists of 3 points) and the number of triangles can be 4 (if *S* consists of 4 points); NOT sufficient.

Taking (1) and (2) together, the number of distinct triangles must be $\binom{5}{3} = \frac{5!}{3!(5-3)!} = 10$, which is the number of combinations of 5 points taken 3 at a time.

The correct answer is C;
both statements together are sufficient.

332. Stores L and M each sell a certain product at a different regular price. If both stores discount their regular price of the product, is the discount price at Store M less than the discount price at Store L ?

(1) At Store L the discount price is 10 percent less than the regular price; at Store M the discount price is 15 percent less than the regular price.

(2) At Store L the discount price is $5 less than the regular store price; at Store M the discount price is $6 less than the regular price.

Arithmetic Percents

Let L_r and L_d be the regular and discounted prices, respectively, at Store L, and let M_r and M_d be the regular and discounted prices, respectively, at Store M. Determine if $M_d < L_d$.

(1) Knowing that $L_d = (1 - 0.10)L_r = 0.90L_r$ and that $M_d = (1 - 0.15)M_r = 0.85M_r$ gives no information for comparing M_d and L_d; NOT sufficient.

(2) Knowing that $L_d = L_r - 5$ and that $M_d = M_r - 6$ gives no information for comparing M_d and L_d; NOT sufficient.

Taking (1) and (2) together gives $0.90L_r = L_r - 5$ and $0.85\ M_r = M_r - 6$, from which it follows that $0.10L_r = 5$ or $L_r = 50$ and $0.15M_r = 6$ or $M_r = 40$. Then $L_d = 50 - 5 = 45$ and $M_d = 40 - 6 = 34$. Therefore, $M_d < L_d$.

The correct answer is C;
both statements together are sufficient.

333. If d denotes a decimal, is $d \geq 0.5$?

(1) When d is rounded to the nearest tenth, the result is 0.5.

(2) When d is rounded to the nearest integer, the result is 1.

Arithmetic Rounding; Estimating

(1) In this case, for example, the value of d could range from the decimal 0.45 to 0.54. Some of these, such as 0.51 or 0.52, are greater than or equal to 0.5, and others, such as 0.47 or 0.48, are less than 0.5; NOT sufficient.

(2) When the result of rounding d to the nearest integer is 1, d could range in value from the decimal 0.50 to 1.49, which are greater than or equal to 0.5; SUFFICIENT.

The correct answer is B;
statement 2 alone is sufficient.

334. In the two-digit integers 3■ and 2▲, the symbols ■ and ▲ represent different digits, and the product (3■)(2▲) is equal to 864. What digit does ■ represent?

(1) The sum of ■ and ▲ is 10.

(2) The product of ■ and ▲ is 24.

Arithmetic Properties of numbers

(1) Given that ■ + ▲ = 10, then the possible products ■▲ are (1)(9) = (9)(1) = 9, (2)(8) = (8)(2) = 16, (3)(7) = (7)(3) = 21, (4)(6) = (6)(4) = 24, and (5)(5) = 25. Since (3■)(2▲) = 864 has units digit 4, it follows that ■▲ must also have units digit 4. Since only two of the possible products of ■▲ has units digit 4, it follows that ■ = 4 and ▲ = 6, or ■ = 6 and ▲ = 4. If ■ = 4 and ▲ = 6, then (3■)(2▲) = (34) (26) = 884 ≠ 864, and if ■ = 6 and ▲ = 4, then (3■)(2▲) = (36)(24) = 864. Therefore, ■ = 6; SUFFICIENT.

(2) Given that ■▲ = 24, and that both ■ and ▲ are digits, there are four possibilities for the values of ■ and ▲.
(a) ■ = 3 and ▲ = 8, which gives (3■)(2▲) = (33)(28) = 924 ≠ 864;
(b) ■ = 4 and ▲ = 6, which gives (3■)(2▲) = (34)(26) = 884 ≠ 864;
(c) ■ = 6 and ▲ = 4, which gives (3■)(2▲) = (36)(24) = 864;
(d) ■ = 8 and ▲ = 3, which gives (3■)(2▲) = (38)(23) = 874 ≠ 864.
Therefore, ■ = 6; SUFFICIENT.

The correct answer is D;
each statement alone is sufficient.

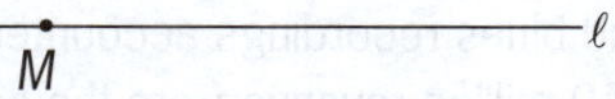

335. Two points, *N* and *Q* (not shown), lie to the right of point *M* on line ℓ. What is the ratio of the length of *QN* to the length of *MQ* ?

(1) Twice the length of *MN* is 3 times the length of *MQ*.

(2) Point *Q* is between points *M* and *N*.

Algebra Order

(1) Given that twice the length of *MN* is 3 times the length of *MQ*, it follows that the points are ordered from left to right as *M*, *Q*, and *N*. Thus, letting $MQ = x$ and $QN = y$, it is given that $2(x + y) = 3x$ and the value of $\frac{y}{x}$ is to be determined. The given equation can be rewritten as $2x + 2y = 3x$, or $2y = x$, or $\frac{y}{x} = \frac{1}{2}$; SUFFICIENT.

(2) Given that *Q* is between *M* and *N*, the ratio of *QN* to *MQ* can be close to zero (if *Q* and *N* are close together and both far from *M*) and the ratio of *QN* to *MQ* can be large (if *M* and *Q* are close together and both far from *N*); NOT sufficient.

The correct answer is A;
statement 1 alone is sufficient.

336. Did the sum of the prices of three shirts exceed \$60 ?

(1) The price of the most expensive of the shirts exceeded \$30.

(2) The price of the least expensive of the shirts exceeded \$20.

Arithmetic Applied problems

(1) Given that the price of the most expensive shirt exceeded \$30, the sum of the prices of the shirts can be under \$60 (if the prices were \$10, \$10, and \$35) and the sum of the prices of the shirts can be over \$60 (if the prices were \$10, \$10, and \$50); NOT sufficient.

(2) Given that the price of the least expensive shirt exceeded \$20, it follows that the sum of the prices of the shirts exceeds 3(\$20) = \$60; SUFFICIENT.

The correct answer is B;
statement 2 alone is sufficient.

337. What is the total number of coins that Bert and Claire have?

(1) Bert has 50 percent more coins than Claire.

(2) The total number of coins that Bert and Claire have is between 21 and 28.

Arithmetic Computation with integers

Determine the total number of coins Bert and Claire have. If *B* represents the number of coins that Bert has and *C* represents the number of coins that Claire has, determine $B + C$.

(1) Bert has 50% more coins than Claire, so $B = 1.5C$, and $B + C = 1.5C + C = 2.5C$, but the value of *C* can vary; NOT sufficient.

(2) The total number of coins Bert and Claire have is between 21 and 28, so $21 < B + C < 28$ and, therefore, $B + C$ could be 22, 23, 24, 25, 26, or 27; NOT sufficient.

Taking (1) and (2) together, $21 < 2.5C < 28$ and then $\frac{21}{2.5} < C < \frac{28}{2.5}$ or $8.4 < C < 11.2$.
If $C = 9$, then $B = (1.5)(9) = 13.5$; if $C = 10$, then $B = (1.5)(10) = 15$; and if $C = 11$, then $B = (1.5)(11) = 16.5$. Since *B* represents a number of coins, *B* is an integer. Therefore, $B = 15$, $C = 10$, and $B + C = 25$.

The correct answer is C;
both statements together are sufficient.

338. A telephone station has x processors, each of which can process a maximum of y calls at any particular time, where x and y are positive integers. If 500 calls are sent to the station at a particular time, can the station process all of the calls?

(1) $x = 600$

(2) $100 < y < 200$

Algebra Applied problems

At a particular time, the telephone station can process a maximum of *xy* calls, where *x* and *y* are positive integers. Determine whether $xy \geq 500$.

(1) Given that $x = 600$, it follows that $xy \geq 600$ since $y \geq 1$ (y is a positive integer); SUFFICIENT.

(2) Given that $100 < y < 200$, $xy < 500$ is possible (if $x = 3$ and $y = 150$) and $xy \geq 500$ is possible (if $x = 10$ and $y = 150$); NOT sufficient.

The correct answer is A; statement 1 alone is sufficient.

	Price per Flower
Roses	\$1.00
Daisies	\$0.50

339. Kim and Sue each bought some roses and some daisies at the prices shown above. If Kim bought the same total number of roses and daisies as Sue, was the price of Kim's purchase of roses and daisies higher than the price of Sue's purchase of roses and daisies?

(1) Kim bought twice as many daisies as roses.

(2) Kim bought 4 more roses than Sue bought.

Algebra Applied problems

Let R_K be the number of roses that Kim bought, let R_S be the number of roses that Sue bought, and let T be the total number of roses and daisies each bought. Then Kim bought $(T - R_K)$ daisies and Sue bought $(T - R_S)$ daisies.

For the roses and daisies, Kim paid a total of $\$[R_K + \frac{1}{2}(T - R_K)] = \$\frac{1}{2}(R_K + T)$ and Sue paid a total of $\$[R_S + \frac{1}{2}(T - R_S)] = \$\frac{1}{2}(R_S + T)$. Determine whether $\frac{1}{2}(R_K + T) > \frac{1}{2}(R_S + T)$, or equivalently, determine whether $R_K > R_S$.

(1) Given that $T - R_K = 2R_K$, or $T = 3R_K$, it is not possible to determine whether $R_K > R_S$ because no information is provided about the value of R_S; NOT sufficient.

(2) Given that $R_K = R_S + 4$, it follows that $R_K > R_S$; SUFFICIENT.

The correct answer is B; statement 2 alone is sufficient.

340. Jazz and blues recordings accounted for 6 percent of the \$840 million revenue from the sales of recordings in Country Y in 2000. What was the revenue from the sales of jazz and blues recordings in Country Y in 1998 ?

(1) Jazz and blues recordings accounted for 5 percent of the revenue from the sales of recordings in Country Y in 1998.

(2) The revenue from the sales of jazz and blues recordings in Country Y increased by 40 percent from 1998 to 2000.

Arithmetic Percents

It is given that jazz and blues recordings accounted for 6% of the \$840 million revenue of recordings in Country Y in 2000. Determine the revenue from the sales of jazz and blues recordings in 1998.

(1) This indicates that jazz and blues recordings accounted for 5% of the revenue from the sales of recordings in Country Y in 1998. However, no information is given to indicate what the revenue from the sales of recordings was in 1998. Therefore, the revenue from sales of jazz and blues recordings in 1998 cannot be determined; NOT sufficient.

(2) This indicates that the revenue from the sales of jazz and blues recordings in Country Y increased by 40% from 1998 to 2000. Letting R_{1998} and R_{2000} represent the revenue from the sales of jazz and blues recordings in 1998 and 2000, respectively, then $R_{2000} = 1.4R_{1998}$, and so $(0.06)(\$840 \text{ million}) = 1.4R_{1998}$, from which R_{1998} can be determined; SUFFICIENT.

The correct answer is B; statement 2 alone is sufficient.

341. On a certain nonstop trip, Marta averaged x miles per hour for 2 hours and y miles per hour for the remaining 3 hours. What was her average speed, in miles per hour, for the entire trip?

(1) $2x + 3y = 280$

(2) $y = x + 10$

Algebra Rate problems

Marta traveled a total of $(2x + 3y)$ miles in $2 + 3 = 5$ hours for an average speed of $\left(\frac{2x+3y}{5}\right)$ miles per hour. Determine the value of $\frac{2x+3y}{5}$.

(1) Given that $2x + 3y = 280$, it follows that $\frac{2x+3y}{5} = \frac{280}{5}$; SUFFICIENT.

(2) Given that $y = x + 10$, it follows that $\frac{2x+3y}{5} = \frac{2x+3(x+10)}{5} = x + 6$. Therefore, the value of $\frac{2x+3y}{5}$ can be 56 (if $x = 50$ and $y = 60$) and the value of $\frac{2x+3y}{5}$ can be 61 (if $x = 55$ and $y = 65$); NOT sufficient.

The correct answer is A; statement 1 alone is sufficient.

342. If x is a positive integer, what is the value of $\sqrt{x+24} - \sqrt{x}$?

(1) $\sqrt{x}$ is an integer.

(2) $\sqrt{x+24}$ is an integer.

Arithmetic Operations with radicals

Determine the value of $\sqrt{x+24} - \sqrt{x}$.

(1) This indicates that x is a perfect square. If $x = 1$, then $\sqrt{x+24} - \sqrt{x} = \sqrt{1+24} - \sqrt{1} = 5 - 1 = 4$. However, if $x = 25$, then $\sqrt{x+24} - \sqrt{x} = \sqrt{25+24} - \sqrt{25} = 7 - 5 = 2$; NOT sufficient.

(2) This indicates that $\sqrt{x+24}$ is an integer. In each of the examples above, $\sqrt{x+24}$ is an integer; NOT sufficient.

Because the same examples were used to establish that neither (1) nor (2) is sufficient, it is not possible to determine the value of $\sqrt{x+24} - \sqrt{x}$ from the given information.

The correct answer is E; both statements together are still not sufficient.

343. A tank is filled with gasoline to a depth of exactly 2 feet. The tank is a cylinder resting horizontally on its side, with its circular ends oriented vertically. The inside of the tank is exactly 6 feet long. What is the volume of the gasoline in the tank?

(1) The inside of the tank is exactly 4 feet in diameter.

(2) The top surface of the gasoline forms a rectangle that has an area of 24 square feet.

Geometry Cylinders; Volume

(1) Given that the diameter of the cylindrical tank is 4 ft, it follows that its radius is 2 ft. Therefore, the radius and height of the cylindrical tank are known, and hence the volume of the gasoline is half the volume of the cylinder, or $\frac{1}{2}\pi r^2 h = \frac{1}{2}\pi\,(2\text{ ft})^2(6\text{ ft}) = 12\pi\text{ ft}^3$; SUFFICIENT.

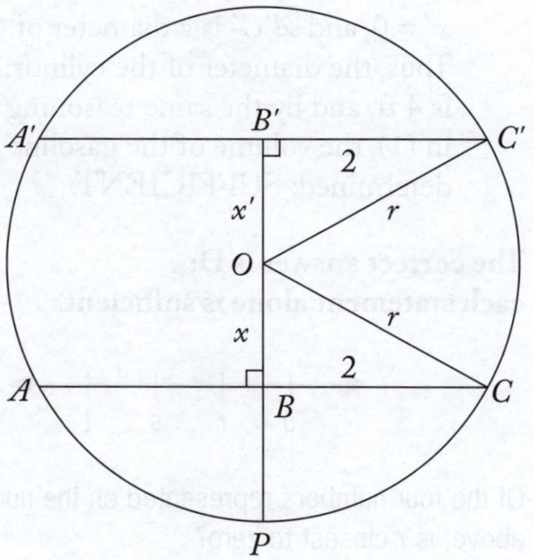

(2) Given that the rectangular surface of the gasoline forms a rectangle with area 24 ft^2 and length 6 ft, the width of the rectangular surface is 4 ft. Let r ft be the radius of the cylinder. The figure shows a vertical cross-section of the cylindrical tank—a circle with center O—with the two possibilities for the location of the top surface of the gasoline: the depth of the gasoline is less than or equal to r ft ($\overline{AC}$ marks the location of the top surface of the gasoline and $BP = 2$ ft is the depth of the gasoline) or the depth of the gasoline is greater than or equal to r ft ($\overline{A'C'}$ marks the location of the top surface of the gasoline and $B'P = 2$ ft

is the depth of the gasoline). For the first possibility, ΔOBC is a right triangle with hypotenuse $\overline{OC}$ of length r ft, so letting $OB = x$ ft, it follows from the Pythagorean theorem that $r^2 = x^2 + 2^2 = x^2 + 4$. However, because $r = OB + BP = x + 2$, it follows that $r^2 = (x + 2)^2 = x^2 + 4x + 4$. Therefore, $x^2 + 4 = x^2 + 4x + 4$, so $4x = 0$, $x = 0$, and $\overline{AC}$ is a diameter of the circle. Thus, the diameter of the cylindrical tank is 4 ft, and by the same reasoning used in (1), the volume of the gasoline can be determined. For the second possibility, $\Delta OB'C'$ is a right triangle with hypotenuse $\overline{OC'}$ of length r ft, so letting $B'O = x'$ ft, it follows from the Pythagorean theorem that $r^2 = (x')^2 + 2^2 = (x')^2 + 4$. However, because $r = B'P - B'O = 2 - x'$, it follows that $r^2 = (2 - x')^2 = 4 - 4x' + (x')^2$. Therefore, $(x')^2 + 4 = 4 - 4x' + (x')^2$, so $0 = -4x'$, $x' = 0$, and $\overline{A'C'}$ is a diameter of the circle. Thus, the diameter of the cylindrical tank is 4 ft, and by the same reasoning used in (1), the volume of the gasoline can be determined; SUFFICIENT.

The correct answer is D;
each statement alone is sufficient.

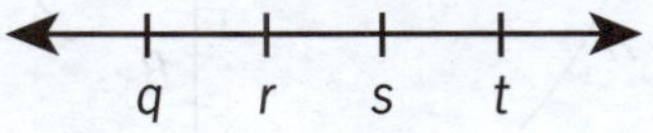

344. Of the four numbers represented on the number line above, is r closest to zero?

(1) $q = -s$
(2) $-t < q$

Algebra Order

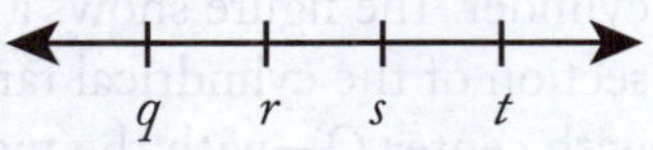

Referring to the figure above, in which it may be assumed that q, r, s, and t are different numbers, determine if r is closest to 0.

(1) Since $q = -s$, one of q and s is positive and the other is negative. Since s is to the right of q, then s is positive and q is negative. Also, 0 is halfway between q and s, so q and s are the same distance from 0. If $r = 0$, then, of q, r, s, and t, r is closest to 0 because it IS 0. If $r \neq 0$ then either (i) $q < 0 < r < s < t$ or (ii) $q < r < 0 < s < t$.

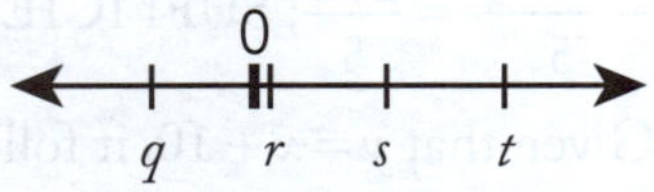

(i) If $q < 0 < r < s < t$, as shown above, r is closer to 0 than s is because r is between 0 and s, and r is clearly closer to 0 than t is because t is farther away from 0 than s is. Also, since q and s are the same distance from 0 and r is closer to 0 than s is, then r is closer to 0 than q is. Therefore, r is closest to 0.

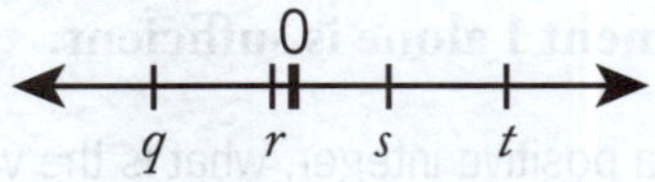

(ii) If $q < r < 0 < s < t$, as shown above, r is closer to 0 than q is because r is between 0 and q. Also, r is closer to 0 than s is because r is closer to 0 than q is and q and s are the same distance from 0. Moreover, r is closer to 0 than t is because t is farther away from 0 than s is. Therefore, r is closest to 0.

In each case, r is closest to 0; SUFFICIENT.

(2) If $-t < q$, then $-t$ is to the left of q. If $t = 5$, $s = 4$, $r = 3$, and $q = -2$, then $-5 < -2$, so (2) is satisfied. In this case, q is closest to 0. On the other hand, if $t = 5$, $s = 4$, $r = -1$, and $q = -2$, then $-5 < -2$, so (2) is satisfied, but r is closest to 0; NOT sufficient.

The correct answer is A;
statement 1 alone is sufficient.

345. A group consisting of several families visited an amusement park where the regular admission fees were ¥5,500 for each adult and ¥4,800 for each child. Because there were at least 10 people in the group, each paid an admission fee that was 10% less than the regular admission fee. How many children were in the group?

(1) The total of the admission fees paid for the adults in the group was ¥29,700.

(2) The total of the admission fees paid for the children in the group was ¥4,860 more than the total of the admission fees paid for the adults in the group.

Arithmetic Simultaneous equations

Determine the number of children in a group of at least 10 people who visited an amusement park.

(1) This indicates that $(0.9)(5{,}500)A = 29{,}700$, where A represents the number of adults in the group. From this, the number of adults can be determined. However, the number of children in the group cannot be determined without additional information about the exact number of people in the group; NOT sufficient.

(2) If C and A represent the numbers of children and adults, respectively, in the group, this indicates that $(0.9)(4{,}800)C = (0.9)(5{,}500)A + 4{,}860$, or $48C = 55A + 54$, or $48C - 55A = 54$, which is a single equation with two variables from which unique values of C and A cannot be determined, even under the assumptions that C and A are integers such that $C + A \geq 10$. For example, the values of C and A could be 8 and 6, respectively, since $(48)(8) - (55)(6) = 54$, or the values of C and A could be 63 and 54, respectively, since $(48)(63) - (55)(54) = 54$; NOT sufficient.

Taking (1) and (2) together, it follows that

$$A = \frac{29{,}700}{(0.9)(5{,}500)} = 6 \text{ and}$$

$$C = \frac{(0.9)(5{,}500)(6) + 4{,}860}{(0.9)(4{,}800)} = 8.$$

The correct answer is C;
both statements together are sufficient.

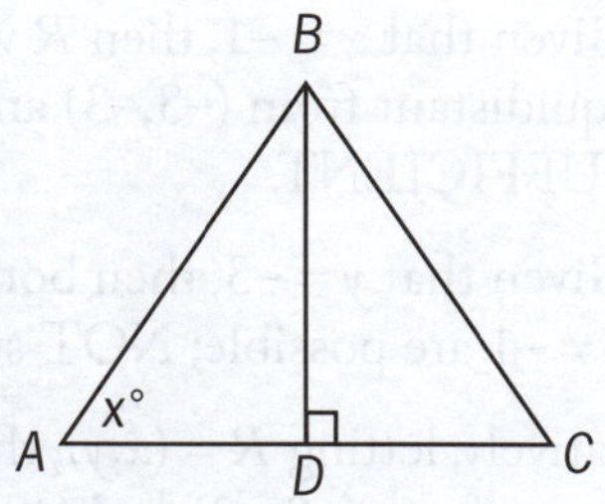

346. What is the area of triangular region ABC above?

(1) The product of BD and AC is 20.

(2) $x = 45$

Geometry Triangles; Area

The area of $\Delta ABC = \frac{BD \times AC}{2}$.

(1) The product of BD and AC is given as 20, so the area of ΔABC is $\frac{20}{2}$ or 10; SUFFICIENT.

(2) With the measurement of x being 45, it is concluded that ΔABD is a 45–45–90 right triangle, where the length of side BD is equal to the length of side AD. However, with no lengths of any side known, there is not enough information to calculate the area; NOT sufficient.

The correct answer is A;
statement 1 alone is sufficient.

347. In the xy-coordinate plane, is point R equidistant from points (–3,–3) and (1,–3)?

(1) The x-coordinate of point R is –1.

(2) Point R lies on the line $y = -3$.

Algebra Coordinate geometry

Determine if point R is equidistant from (–3,–3) and (1,–3). Letting $R = (x,y)$, then R will be equidistant from (–3,–3) and (1,–3) if and only if R lies on the perpendicular bisector of the line segment with endpoints (–3,–3) and (1,–3), or equivalently, if and only if R lies on the vertical line that consists of all points with x-coordinate equal to $\frac{-3+1}{2} = -1$. Therefore, determine if $x = -1$.

(1) Given that $x = -1$, then R will be equidistant from (–3,–3) and (1,–3); SUFFICIENT.

(2) Given that $y = -3$, then both $x = -1$ and $x \neq -1$ are possible; NOT sufficient.

Alternatively, letting $R = (x,y)$, then R will be equidistant from (–3,–3) and (1,–3) if and only if the distance between (x,y) and (–3,–3) is the same as the distance between (x,y) and (1,–3), or if and only if $\sqrt{(x+3)^2+(y+3)^2} = \sqrt{(x-1)^2+(y+3)^2}$ or if and only if $(x + 3)^2 + (y + 3)^2 = (x - 1)^2 + (y + 3)^2$, or if and only if $(x + 3)^2 = (x - 1)^2$.

(1) Given that $x = -1$, then $(-1 + 3)^2 = 4$ and $(-1 - 1)^2 = 4$; SUFFICIENT.

(2) Given that $y = -3$, then it is impossible to determine if $(x + 3)^2 = (x - 1)^2$; NOT sufficient.

The correct answer is A;
statement 1 alone is sufficient.

348. What is the ratio of the average (arithmetic mean) height of students in class X to the average height of students in class Y ?

(1) The average height of the students in class X is 120 centimeters.

(2) The average height of the students in class X and class Y combined is 126 centimeters.

Arithmetic Statistics

(1) Given that the average height of the students in class X is 120 cm, but given no information about the average height of the students in class Y, the desired ratio cannot be determined; NOT sufficient.

(2) Given that the average height of the students in class X and class Y combined is 126 cm, the ratio of the averages of the individual classes cannot be determined. For example, if class X consists of 10 students, each of whom has height 120 cm, and class Y consists of 10 students, each of whom has height 132 cm, then the average height of the students in class X and class Y combined is $\frac{10(120)+10(132)}{20} = 126$ cm and the ratio of the averages of the individual classes is $\frac{120}{132}$. However, if class X consists of 10 students, each of whom has height 120 cm and class Y consists of 20 students, each of whom has height 129 cm, then the average height of the students in class X and class Y combined is $\frac{10(120) + 20(129)}{30} = 126$ cm and the ratio of the averages of the individual classes is $\frac{120}{129}$; NOT sufficient.

Taking (1) and (2) together is of no more help than either (1) or (2) taken separately because the same examples used to show that (2) is not sufficient include the information from (1).

The correct answer is E;
both statements together are still not sufficient.

349. Is the positive two-digit integer N less than 40 ?

(1) The units digit of N is 6 more than the tens digit.

(2) N is 4 less than 4 times the units digit.

Arithmetic Place value

Determine if the two-digit integer N is less than 40. Letting the tens digit be t and the units digit be u, then $N = 10t + u$. Determine if $10t + u < 40$.

(1) Given that $u = t + 6$, then $N = 10t + (t + 6) = 11t + 6$. Since u is a digit, $u = t + 6 \leq 9$, so $t \leq 3$. Therefore, $N = 11t + 6 \leq 11(3) + 6 = 39$; SUFFICIENT.

(2) Given that $N = 4u - 4$, then since u is a digit and $u \leq 9$, it follows that $N = 4u - 4 \leq 4(9) - 4 = 32$; SUFFICIENT.

The correct answer is D;
each statement alone is sufficient.

350. If $2^{x+y} = 4^8$, what is the value of y ?

(1) $x^2 = 81$

(2) $x - y = 2$

Algebra Exponents

Since $4^8 = (2^2)^8 = 2^{16}$, the equation $2^{x+y} = 4^8$ becomes $2^{x+y} = 2^{16}$, which is equivalent to $x + y = 16$.

(1) Given that $x^2 = 81$, then both $x = 9$ and $x = -9$ are possible. Therefore, $y = 7$ is possible (choose $x = 9$) and $y = 25$ is possible (choose $x = -9$); NOT sufficient.

(2) Given that $x - y = 2$, it follows that $-x + y = -2$. Adding the last equation to $x + y = 16$ gives $2y = 14$, or $y = 7$; SUFFICIENT.

The correct answer is B;
statement 2 alone is sufficient.

351. Each week a certain salesman is paid a fixed amount equal to $300, plus a commission equal to 5 percent of the amount of his sales that week over $1,000. What is the total amount the salesman was paid last week?

(1) The total amount the salesman was paid last week is equal to 10 percent of the amount of his sales last week.

(2) The salesman's sales last week totaled $5,000.

Algebra Applied problems

Let P be the salesman's pay for last week and let S be the amount of his sales last week. Then $P = 300 + 0.05(S - 1{,}000)$. Determine the value of P.

(1) Given $P = 0.10S$, then $0.10S = 300 + 0.05(S - 1{,}000)$. This equation can be solved for a unique value of S, from which the value of P can be determined; SUFFICIENT.

(2) Given $S = 5{,}000$, then $P = 300 + 0.05(5{,}000 - 1{,}000)$; SUFFICIENT.

The correct answer is D;
each statement alone is sufficient.

352. At a bakery, all donuts are priced equally and all bagels are priced equally. What is the total price of 5 donuts and 3 bagels at the bakery?

(1) At the bakery, the total price of 10 donuts and 6 bagels is $12.90.

(2) At the bakery, the price of a donut is $0.15 less than the price of a bagel.

Algebra Simultaneous equations

Let x be the price, in dollars, of each donut and let y be the price, in dollars, of each bagel. Find the value of $5x + 3y$.

(1) Given that $10x + 6y = 12.90$, since $5x + 3y = \frac{1}{2}(10x + 6y)$, it follows that $5x + 3y = \frac{1}{2}(12.90)$; SUFFICIENT.

(2) Given that $x = y - 0.15$, then $5x + 3y = 5(y - 0.15) + 3y = 8y - 0.75$, which varies as y varies; NOT sufficient.

The correct answer is A;
statement 1 alone is sufficient.

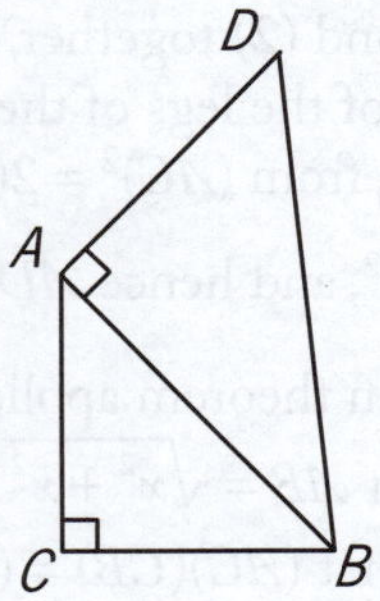

353. In the figure above, is the area of triangular region ABC equal to the area of triangular region DBA ?

(1) $(AC)^2 = 2(AD)^2$

(2) ΔABC is isosceles.

Geometry Triangles; Area

Determine whether $\frac{1}{2}(AC)(CB) = \frac{1}{2}(AD)(AB)$ or, equivalently, whether $(AC)(CB) = (AD)(AB)$.

(1) Given that $(AC)^2 = 2(AD)^2$, then $\sqrt{2}$ and 1 could be the values of AC and AD, respectively. If, for example, $CB = \sqrt{2}$, then

$AB = \sqrt{(\sqrt{2})^2 + (\sqrt{2})^2} = 2$ by the Pythagorean theorem applied to ΔABC.

Hence, $(AC)(CB) = (\sqrt{2})(\sqrt{2})$ and $(AD)(AB) = (1)(2)$, from which it follows that $(AC)(CB) = (AD)(AB)$. On the other hand, if $CB = 1$, then $AB = \sqrt{(\sqrt{2})^2 + 1^2} = \sqrt{3}$ by the Pythagorean theorem applied to ΔABC. Hence, $(AC)(CB) = (\sqrt{2})(1)$ and $(AD)(AB) = (1)(\sqrt{3})$, from which it follows that $(AC)(CB) \neq (AD)(AB)$; NOT sufficient.

(2) Given that ΔABC is isosceles then, by varying the value of AD, the area of ΔABC may or may not be equal to the area of ΔDBA. For example, if $AC = CB = 1$, then $(AC)(CB) = (1)(1) = 1$ and $AB = \sqrt{2}$ by the Pythagorean theorem applied to ΔABC. If $AD = \frac{1}{\sqrt{2}}$, then $(AD)(AB) = \left(\frac{1}{\sqrt{2}}\right)(\sqrt{2}) = 1$, and $(AC)(CB) = (AD)(AB)$. On the other hand, if $AD = 1$, $(AD)(AB) = (1)(\sqrt{2}) = \sqrt{2}$ and $(AC)(CB) \neq (AD)(AB)$; NOT sufficient.

Given (1) and (2) together, let $AC = CB = x$ be the length of the legs of the isosceles triangle ABC. Then, from $(AC)^2 = 2(AD)^2$, it follows that $x^2 = 2(AD)^2$, and hence $AD = \frac{x}{\sqrt{2}}$. Also, by the Pythagorean theorem applied to ΔABC, it follows that $AB = \sqrt{x^2 + x^2} = x\sqrt{2}$. Therefore, it follows that $(AC)(CB) = (x)(x) = x^2$ and $(AD)(AB) = \left(\frac{x}{\sqrt{2}}\right)(x\sqrt{2}) = x^2$, and so $(AC)(CB) = (AD)(AB)$.

The correct answer is C;
both statements together are sufficient.

354. If r and s are positive integers, can the fraction $\frac{r}{s}$ be expressed as a decimal with only a finite number of nonzero digits?

(1) s is a factor of 100.
(2) r is a factor of 100.

Arithmetic **Properties of numbers**

Determine if $\frac{r}{s}$, where r and s are positive integers, can be expressed as a decimal with a finite number of nonzero decimal digits.

(1) It is given that s is a factor of 100 and so $s = 1, 2, 4, 5, 10, 20, 25, 50,$ or 100. This means that $\frac{r}{s}$ must be one of the quotients $\frac{r}{1}, \frac{r}{2}, \frac{r}{4}, \frac{r}{5}, \frac{r}{10}, \frac{r}{20}, \frac{r}{25}, \frac{r}{50}$ or $\frac{r}{100}$. Thus, $\frac{r}{s}$ must be one of the products $r(1)$, $r(0.5), r(0.25), r(0.20), r(0.1), r(0.05)\ r(0.04)$, $r(0.02)$, or $r(0.01)$. In each case, $\frac{r}{s}$ is the product of an integer and a decimal with a finite number of nonzero digits, and hence, $\frac{r}{s}$ can be expressed as a decimal with a finite number of nonzero digits. In fact, it suffices to note this is true for $\frac{r}{100}$, since each of the other possibilities is a positive integer times $\frac{r}{100}$ (for example, $\frac{r}{20}$ is 5 times $\frac{r}{100}$); SUFFICIENT.

(2) It is given that r is a factor of 100. If $r = 4$ and $s = 5$, then $\frac{r}{s} = 0.8$, which is a decimal with a finite number of nonzero digits. On the other hand, if $r = 4$ and $s = 7$, then $\frac{r}{s} = 0.\overline{571428}$, which is not a decimal with a finite number of nonzero digits; NOT sufficient.

The correct answer is A;
statement 1 alone is sufficient.

355. If $r > 0$ and $s > 0$, is $\frac{r}{s} < \frac{s}{r}$?

(1) $\frac{r}{3s} = \frac{1}{4}$
(2) $s = r + 4$

Algebra **Ratios**

Given positive numbers r and s, determine if $\frac{r}{s} < \frac{s}{r}$.

(1) If $\frac{r}{3s} = \frac{1}{4}$, then $\frac{r}{s} = \frac{3}{4}$, $\frac{s}{r} = \frac{4}{3}$, and so $\frac{r}{s} < \frac{s}{r}$, since $\frac{3}{4} < \frac{4}{3}$; SUFFICIENT.

(2) If $s = r + 4$, then $\frac{r}{s} = \frac{r}{r+4}$ and $\frac{s}{r} = \frac{r+4}{r}$. Since $r + 4 > r$, $\frac{r}{r+4} < 1$ and $\frac{r+4}{r} > 1$, so $\frac{r}{s} < \frac{s}{r}$; SUFFICIENT.

The correct answer is D; each statement alone is sufficient.

356. If k is an integer such that $56 < k < 66$, what is the value of k?

(1) If k were divided by 2, the remainder would be 1.

(2) If $k + 1$ were divided by 3, the remainder would be 0.

Arithmetic Properties of integers

Determine the value of the integer k, where $56 < k < 66$.

(1) It is given that the remainder is 1 when k is divided by 2, which implies that k is odd. Therefore, the value of k can be 57, 59, 61, 63, or 65; NOT sufficient.

(2) It is given that the remainder is 0 when $k + 1$ is divided by 3, which implies that $k + 1$ is divisible by 3. Since $56 < k < 66$ (equivalently, $57 < k + 1 < 67$), the value of $k + 1$ can be 60, 63, or 66 so the value of k can be 59, 62, or 65; NOT sufficient.

Taking (1) and (2) together, 59 and 65 appear in both lists of possible values for k; NOT sufficient.

The correct answer is E; both statements together are still not sufficient.

357. If x is a positive integer, then is x prime?

(1) $3x + 1$ is prime.

(2) $5x + 1$ is prime.

Arithmetic Properties of numbers

Determine if the positive integer x is prime.

(1) This indicates that $3x + 1$ is prime. If $x = 2$, then $3x + 1 = 7$ is prime and so is x. However, if $x = 6$, then $3x + 1 = 19$ is prime, but 6 is not prime; NOT sufficient.

(2) This indicates that $5x + 1$ is prime. If $x = 2$, then $5x + 1 = 11$ is prime and so is x. However, if $x = 6$, then $5x + 1 = 31$ is prime, but 6 is not prime; NOT sufficient.

Because the same examples were used to establish that neither (1) nor (2) is sufficient, it is not possible to determine whether x is prime from the given information.

The correct answer is E; both statements together are still not sufficient.

$k, n, 12, 6, 17$

358. What is the value of n in the list above?

(1) $k < n$

(2) The median of the numbers in the list is 10.

Arithmetic Statistics

Given the list $k, n, 12, 6, 17$, determine the value of n.

(1) Although $k < n$, no information is given about the value of k or n; NOT sufficient.

(2) Since the median of the numbers in the list is 10 and there are 5 numbers in the list, 10 is one of those 5 numbers. Therefore, $n = 10$ or $k = 10$. If $n = 10$, then the value of n has been determined. However, if $k = 10$, then n can be any number that is 10 or less, so the value of n cannot be determined; NOT sufficient.

Taking (1) and (2) together, if $k < n$ and the median of the list is 10, then 12 and 17 are to the right of the median and the list in ascending order is either $6, k, n, 12, 17$ or $k, 6, n, 12, 17$. In either case, n is the middle number, and since the median is 10, $n = 10$.

The correct answer is C; both statements together are sufficient.

359. If x and y are integers, what is the value of x + y?

(1) $3 < \frac{x+y}{2} < 4$

(2) $2 < x < y < 5$

Arithmetic Computation with integers

Determine the value of $x + y$ for integers x and y.

(1) Given that $3 < \frac{x+y}{2} < 4$, then $6 < x + y < 8$. Since $x + y$ is an integer and 7 is the only integer greater than 6 and less than 8, it follows that the value of $x + y$ is 7; SUFFICIENT.

(2) Given that $2 < x < y < 5$, then $2 < x < 5$, and hence $x = 3$ or $x = 4$. Likewise, $2 < y < 5$, and hence $y = 3$ or $y = 4$. With the additional restriction that $x < y$, it follows that $x = 3$ and $y = 4$, and thus $x + y = 7$; SUFFICIENT.

The correct answer is D; each statement alone is sufficient.

360. Last year, if Arturo spent a total of $12,000 on his mortgage payments, real estate taxes, and home insurance, how much did he spend on his real estate taxes?

(1) Last year, the total amount that Arturo spent on his real estate taxes and home insurance was $33\frac{1}{3}$ percent of the amount that he spent on his mortgage payments.

(2) Last year, the amount that Arturo spent on his real estate taxes was 20 percent of the total amount he spent on his mortgage payments and home insurance.

Arithmetic Applied problems

Let M, R, and H be the amounts that Arturo spent last year on mortgage payments, real estate taxes, and home insurance, respectively. Given that $M + R + H = 12{,}000$, determine the value of R.

(1) Given that $R + H = \frac{1}{3}M$ and $M + R + H = 12{,}000$, then $M + \frac{1}{3}M = 12{,}000$, or $M = 9{,}000$. However, the value of R cannot be determined, since it is possible that $R = 2{,}000$ (use $M = 9{,}000$ and $H = 1{,}000$) and it is possible that $R = 1{,}000$ (use $M = 9{,}000$ and $H = 2{,}000$); NOT sufficient.

(2) Given that $R = \frac{1}{5}(M + H)$, or $5R = M + H$ and $M + R + H = 12{,}000$, which can be rewritten as $(M + H) + R = 12{,}000$, then $5R + R = 12{,}000$, or $R = 2{,}000$; SUFFICIENT.

The correct answer is B; statement 2 alone is sufficient.

361. If a, b, c, and d are positive numbers, is $\frac{a}{b} < \frac{c}{d}$?

(1) $0 < \frac{c-a}{d-b}$

(2) $\left(\frac{ad}{bc}\right)^2 < \frac{ad}{bc}$

Algebra Inequalities

Determine whether $\frac{a}{b} < \frac{c}{d}$, where a, b, c, and d are positive numbers.

(1) Given that $0 < \frac{c-a}{d-b}$, then $a = 2$, $b = 3$, $c = 6$, and $d = 8$ are possible values for a, b, c, and d because $\frac{c-a}{d-b} = \frac{6-2}{8-3} = \frac{4}{5}$ and $\frac{4}{5} > 0$. For these values, $\frac{a}{b} < \frac{c}{d}$ is true because $\frac{2}{3} < \frac{6}{8}$. On the other hand, $a = 4$, $b = 6$, $c = 2$, and $d = 3$ are also possible values of a, b, c, and d because $\frac{c-a}{d-b} = \frac{2-4}{3-6} = \frac{2}{3}$ and $\frac{2}{3} > 0$. For these values, $\frac{a}{b} < \frac{c}{d}$ is false because $\frac{4}{6} = \frac{2}{3}$; NOT sufficient.

(2) Given that $\left(\frac{ad}{bc}\right)^2 < \frac{ad}{bc}$, then

$\frac{ad}{bc} < 1$	dividing both sides by the positive number $\frac{ad}{bc}$
$\frac{ad}{b} < c$	multiplying both sides by the positive number c
$\frac{a}{b} < \frac{c}{d}$	dividing both sides by the positive number d; SUFFICIENT

The correct answer is B; statement 2 alone is sufficient.

362. Is the number of members of Club X greater than the number of members of Club Y ?

(1) Of the members of Club X, 20 percent are also members of Club Y.

(2) Of the members of Club Y, 30 percent are also members of Club X.

Arithmetic Sets

Let a be the number of members in Club X that do not belong to Club Y, let b be the number of members in Club Y that do not belong to Club X, and let c be the number of members that belong to both Club X and to Club Y. Determine whether $a + c > b + c$, or equivalently, whether $a > b$.

(1) If $a = 80$, $b = 79$, and $c = 20$, then 20 percent of the members of Club X are also members of Club Y (because $c = 20$ is 20 percent of $a + c = 100$) and $a > b$ is true. However, if $a = 80$, $b = 80$, and $c = 20$, then 20 percent of the members of Club X are also members of Club Y (because $c = 20$ is 20 percent of $a + c = 100$) and $a > b$ is false. Therefore, it cannot be determined whether $a > b$; NOT sufficient.

(2) If $a = 71$, $b = 70$, and $c = 30$, then 30 percent of the members of Club Y are also members of Club X (because $c = 30$ is 30 percent of $b + c = 100$) and $a > b$ is true. However, if $a = 70$, $b = 70$, and $c = 30$, then 30 percent of the members of Club Y are also members of Club X (because $c = 30$ is 30 percent of $b + c = 100$) and $a > b$ is false. Therefore, it cannot be determined whether $a > b$; NOT sufficient.

Now assume both (1) and (2). From (1) it follows that $\frac{c}{a+c} = 0.20 = \frac{1}{5}$, or $5c = a + c$, and so $a = 4c$. From (2) it follows that $\frac{c}{b+c} = 0.30 = \frac{3}{10}$, or $10c = 3b + 3c$, and so $7c = 3b$ and $b = \frac{7}{3}c$. Since $4c > \frac{7}{3}c$ (from the statements it can be deduced that $c > 0$), it follows that $a > b$. Therefore, (1) and (2) together are sufficient.

The correct answer is C;
both statements together are sufficient.

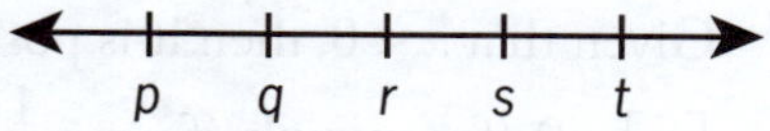

363. On the number line above, p, q, r, s, and t are five consecutive even integers in increasing order. What is the average (arithmetic mean) of these five integers?

(1) $q + s = 24$

(2) The average (arithmetic mean) of q and r is 11.

Arithmetic Properties of numbers

Since p, q, r, s, and t are consecutive even integers listed in numerical order, the 5 integers can also be given as p, $p + 2$, $p + 4$, $p + 6$, and $p + 8$. Determine the average of these 5 integers, which is the value of $\frac{p+(p+2)+(p+4)+(p+6)+(p+8)}{5} = \frac{5p+20}{5} = p + 4$

(1) Given that $q + s = 24$, then $(p + 2) + (p + 6) = 24$. Therefore, $2p + 8 = 24$, or $p = 8$, and hence $p + 4 = 12$; SUFFICIENT.

(2) Given that $\frac{q+r}{2} = 11$, then $q + r = (2)(11) = 22$, or $(p + 2) + (p + 4) = 22$. Therefore, $2p + 6 = 22$, or $p = 8$, and hence $p + 4 = 12$; SUFFICIENT.

The correct answer is D;
each statement alone is sufficient.

364. If $\lceil x \rceil$ denotes the least integer greater than or equal to x, is $\lceil x \rceil = 0$?

(1) $-1 < x < 1$

(2) $x < 0$

Algebra Functions

Determine if $\lceil x \rceil$, the least integer greater than or equal to x, is equal to 0, which is the same as determining if x satisfies $-1 < x \leq 0$.

(1) Given that $-1 < x < 1$, then it is possible that $\lceil x \rceil = 0$ (for example, if $x = 0$, then $\lceil x \rceil = 0$) and it is possible that $\lceil x \rceil \neq 0$ (for example, if $x = \frac{1}{2}$, then $\lceil x \rceil = 1 \neq 0$); NOT sufficient.

(2) Given that $x < 0$, then it is possible that $\lceil x \rceil = 0$ (for example, if $x = -\frac{1}{2}$, then $\lceil x \rceil = 0$) and it is possible that $\lceil x \rceil \neq 0$ (for example, if $x = -5$, then $\lceil x \rceil = -5 \neq 0$); NOT sufficient.

Taking (1) and (2) together gives $-1 < x < 0$, which implies that $\lceil x \rceil = 0$.

The correct answer is C; both statements together are sufficient.

365. If x and y are integers, is $x > y$?

(1) $x + y > 0$

(2) $y^x < 0$

Arithmetic Properties of integers

Determine if the integer x is greater than the integer y.

(1) It is given that $x + y > 0$, and so $-x < y$. If, for example, $x = -3$ and $y = 4$, then $x + y = -3 + 4 = 1 > 0$ and $x < y$. On the other hand, if $x = 4$ and $y = -3$, then $x + y = 4 - 3 = 1 > 0$ and $x > y$; NOT sufficient.

(2) It is given that $y^x < 0$, so $y < 0$. If, for example, $x = 3$ and $y = -2$, then $(-2)^3 = -8 < 0$ and $x > y$. On the other hand, if $x = -3$ and $y = -2$, then $(-2)^{-3} = -\frac{1}{8} < 0$ and $x < y$; NOT sufficient.

Taking (1) and (2) together, from (2) y is negative and from (1) $-x$ is less than y. Therefore, $-x$ is negative, and hence x is positive. Since x is positive and y is negative, it follows that $x > y$.

The correct answer is C; both statements together are sufficient.

366. If r and s are the roots of the equation $x^2 + bx + c = 0$, where b and c are constants, is $rs < 0$?

(1) $b < 0$

(2) $c < 0$

Algebra Second-degree equations

Determine whether the product of the roots to $x^2 + bx + c = 0$, where b and c are constants, is negative.

If r and s are the roots of the given equation, then $(x - r)(x - s) = x^2 + bx + c$. This implies that $x^2 - (r + s)x + rs = x^2 + bx + c$, and so $rs = c$. Therefore, rs is negative if and only if c is negative.

(1) Given that $b < 0$, then c could be negative or positive. For example, if $b = -1$ and $c = -6$, then the given equation would be $x^2 - x - 6 = (x - 3)(x + 2) = 0$, and the product of its roots would be $(3)(-2)$, which is negative. On the other hand, if $b = -6$ and $c = 5$, then the given equation would be $x^2 - 6x + 5 = (x - 5)(x - 1) = 0$, and the product of its roots would be $(5)(1)$, which is positive; NOT sufficient.

(2) Given that $c < 0$, it follows from the explanation above that $rs < 0$; SUFFICIENT.

The correct answer is B; statement 2 alone is sufficient.

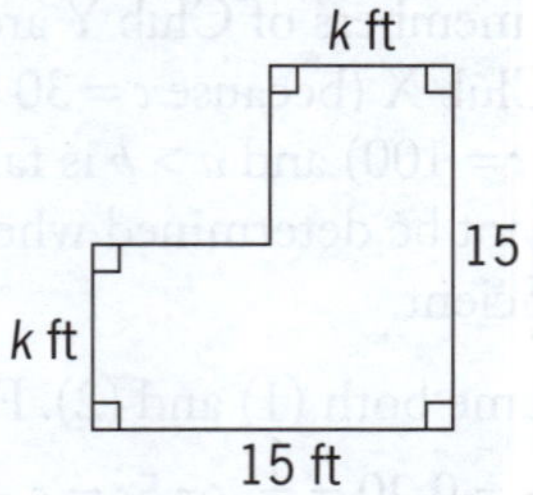

367. The figure above represents an L-shaped garden. What is the value of k?

(1) The area of the garden is 189 square feet.

(2) The perimeter of the garden is 60 feet.

Geometry Polygons

(1) Given that the area of the garden is 189 ft^2, and observing that area of the garden can be calculated by imagining the garden as a square with dimensions 15 ft by 15 ft from which its upper-right square corner

with dimensions $(15 - k)$ ft by $(15 - k)$ ft is removed, it follows that $189 = (15)^2 - (15 - k)^2$. Therefore, $(15 - k)^2 = 225 - 189 = 36$, so $15 - k = 6$ or $15 - k = -6$. The figure implies $15 - k > 0$, so it follows that $15 - k = 6$, or $k = 9$; SUFFICIENT.

(2) Given that the perimeter of the garden is 60 ft, and because $15 + 15 + k + (15 - k) + (15 - k) + k = 60$, any value of k between 0 and 15 is possible, since for any such value of k the sum of the lengths of all the sides would be 60 ft; NOT sufficient.

The correct answer is A; statement 1 alone is sufficient.

368. The only articles of clothing in a certain closet are shirts, dresses, and jackets. The ratio of the number of shirts to the number of dresses to the number of jackets in the closet is 9:4:5, respectively. If there are more than 7 dresses in the closet, what is the total number of articles of clothing in the closet?

(1) The total number of shirts and jackets in the closet is less than 30.

(2) The total number of shirts and dresses in the closet is 26.

Arithmetic Ratio and proportion

Letting s, d, and j represent, respectively, the numbers of shirts, dresses, and jackets in the closet, then $s = 9x$, $d = 4x$, and $j = 5x$, where x is a positive integer. It is given that $4x > 7$, and so $4x \geq 8$ or $x \geq 2$ since x is an integer. Determine the value of $9x + 4x + 5x = 18x$.

(1) This indicates that $9x + 5x < 30$, and so $14x \leq 28$ or $x \leq 2$ since x is an integer. It follows from $x \geq 2$ and $x \leq 2$ that $x = 2$ and $18x = 36$; SUFFICIENT.

(2) This indicates that $9x + 4x = 26$ or $13x = 26$, or $x = 2$. It follows that $18x = 36$; SUFFICIENT.

The correct answer is D; each statement alone is sufficient.

TOTAL EXPENSES FOR THE FIVE DIVISIONS OF COMPANY H

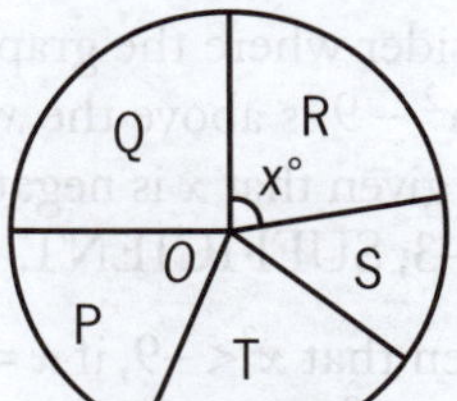

369. The figure above represents a circle graph of Company H's total expenses broken down by the expenses for each of its five divisions. If O is the center of the circle and if Company H's total expenses are \$5,400,000, what are the expenses for Division R ?

(1) $x = 94$

(2) The total expenses for Divisions S and T are twice as much as the expenses for Division R.

Geometry Circles

In this circle graph, the expenses of Division R are equal to the value of $\frac{x}{360}$ multiplied by \$5,400,000, or \$15,000x. Therefore, it is necessary to know the value of x in order to determine the expenses for Division R.

(1) The value of x is given as 94, so the expenses of Division R can be determined; SUFFICIENT.

(2) This gives a comparison among the expenses of some of the divisions of Company H, but no information is given about the value of x; NOT sufficient.

The correct answer is A; statement 1 alone is sufficient.

370. If x is negative, is $x < -3$?

(1) $x^2 > 9$

(2) $x^3 < -9$

Algebra Properties of numbers

(1) Given that $x^2 > 9$, it follows that $x < -3$ or $x > 3$, a result that can be obtained in a variety of ways. For example, consider the equivalent inequality $(|x|)^2 > 9$ that reduces

to $|x| > 3$, or consider when the two factors of $x^2 - 9$ are both positive and when the two factors of $x^2 - 9$ are both negative, or consider where the graph of the parabola $y = x^2 - 9$ is above the x-axis, etc. Since it is also given that x is negative, it follows that $x < -3$; SUFFICIENT.

(2) Given that $x^3 < -9$, if $x = -4$, then $x^3 = -64$, and so $x^3 < -9$ and it is true that $x < -3$. However, if $x = -3$, then $x^3 = -27$, and so $x^3 < -9$, but it is not true that $x < -3$; NOT sufficient.

The correct answer is A;
statement 1 alone is sufficient.

371. What is the number of cans that can be packed in a certain carton?

(1) The interior volume of this carton is 2,304 cubic inches.

(2) The exterior of each can is 6 inches high and has a diameter of 4 inches.

Geometry Rectangular solids and cylinders

(1) No information about the size of the cans is given; NOT sufficient.

(2) No information about the size of the carton is given; NOT sufficient.

Taking (1) and (2) together, there is still not enough information to answer the question. If the carton is a rectangular solid that is 1 inch by 1 inch by 2,304 inches and the cans are cylindrical with the given dimensions, then 0 cans can be packed into the carton. However, if the carton is a rectangular solid that is 16 inches by 12 inches by 12 inches and the cans are cylindrical with the given dimensions, then 1 or more cans can be packed into the carton.

The correct answer is E;
both statements together are still not sufficient.

r	s	t
u	v	w
x	y	z

372. Each of the letters in the table above represents one of the numbers 1, 2, or 3, and each of these numbers occurs exactly once in each row and exactly once in each column. What is the value of r?

(1) $v + z = 6$

(2) $s + t + u + x = 6$

Arithmetic Properties of numbers

In the following discussion, "row/column convention" means that each of the numbers 1, 2, and 3 appears exactly once in any given row and exactly once in any given column.

(1) Given that $v + z = 6$, then both v and z are equal to 3, since no other sum of the possible values is equal to 6. Applying the row/column convention to row 2, and then to row 3, it follows that neither u nor x can be 3. Since neither u nor x can be 3, the row/column convention applied to column 1 forces r to be 3; SUFFICIENT.

(2) If $u = 3$, then $s + t + x = 3$. Hence, $s = t = x = 1$, since the values these variables can have does not permit another possibility. However, this assignment of values would violate the row/column convention for row 1, and thus u cannot be 3. If $x = 3$, then $s + t + u = 3$. Hence, $s = t = u = 1$, since the values these variables can have does not permit another possibility. However, this assignment of values would violate the row/column convention for row 1, and thus x cannot be 3. Since neither u nor x can be 3, the row/column convention applied to column 1 forces r to be 3; SUFFICIENT.

The correct answer is D;
each statement alone is sufficient.

373. Material A costs \$3 per kilogram, and Material B costs \$5 per kilogram. If 10 kilograms of Material K consists of x kilograms of Material A and y kilograms of Material B, is $x > y$?

(1) $y > 4$

(2) The cost of the 10 kilograms of Material K is less than \$40.

Algebra Inequalities

Since $x + y = 10$, the relation $x > y$ is equivalent to $x > 10 - x$, or $x > 5$.

(1) The given information is consistent with $x = 5.5$ and $y = 4.5$, and the given information is also consistent with $x = y = 5$. Therefore, it is possible for $x > y$ to be true and it is possible for $x > y$ to be false; NOT sufficient.

(2) Given that $3x + 5y < 40$, or $3x + 5(10 - x) < 40$, then $3x - 5x < 40 - 50$. It follows that $-2x < -10$, or $x > 5$; SUFFICIENT.

The correct answer is B;
statement 2 alone is sufficient.

374. At what speed was a train traveling on a trip when it had completed half of the total distance of the trip?

(1) The trip was 460 miles long and took 4 hours to complete.

(2) The train traveled at an average rate of 115 miles per hour on the trip.

Arithmetic Applied problems

Determine the speed of the train when it had completed half the total distance of the trip.

(1) Given that the train traveled 460 miles in 4 hours, the train could have traveled at the constant rate of 115 miles per hour for 4 hours, and thus it could have been traveling 115 miles per hour when it had completed half the total distance of the trip. However, the train could have traveled 150 miles per hour for the first 2 hours (a distance of 300 miles) and 80 miles per hour for the last 2 hours (a distance of 160 miles), and thus it could have been traveling 150 miles per hour when it had completed half the total distance of the trip; NOT sufficient.

(2) Given that the train traveled at an average rate of 115 miles per hour, each of the possibilities given in the explanation for (1) could occur, since 460 miles in 4 hours gives an average speed of $\frac{460}{4} = 115$ miles per hour; NOT sufficient.

Assuming (1) and (2), each of the possibilities given in the explanation for (1) could occur. Therefore, (1) and (2) together are not sufficient.

The correct answer is E;
both statements together are still not sufficient.

375. Tom, Jane, and Sue each purchased a new house. The average (arithmetic mean) price of the three houses was \$120,000. What was the median price of the three houses?

(1) The price of Tom's house was \$110,000.

(2) The price of Jane's house was \$120,000.

Arithmetic Statistics

Let T, J, and S be the purchase prices for Tom's, Jane's, and Sue's new houses. Given that the average purchase price is 120,000, or $T + J + S = 3(120{,}000)$, determine the median purchase price.

(1) Given $T = 110{,}000$, the median could be 120,000 (if $J = 120{,}000$ and $S = 130{,}000$) or 125,000 (if $J = 125{,}000$ and $S = 125{,}000$); NOT sufficient.

(2) Given $J = 120{,}000$, the following two cases include every possibility consistent with $T + J + S = (3)(120{,}000)$, or $T + S = (2)(120{,}000)$.

(i) $T = S = 120{,}000$

(ii) One of T or S is less than 120,000 and the other is greater than 120,000.

In each case, the median is clearly 120,000; SUFFICIENT.

The correct answer is B;
statement 2 alone is sufficient.

376. What is the value of x if $x^3 < x^2$?

(1) $-2 < x < 2$

(2) x is an integer greater than −2.

Algebra **Inequalities**

The inequality $x^3 < x^2$ is equivalent to $x^3 - x^2 < 0$, or $x^2(x-1) < 0$. Since this inequality is false for $x = 0$, it follows that $x \neq 0$, and hence $x^2 > 0$. Therefore, $x^2(x-1) < 0$ can only hold if $x - 1 < 0$, or if $x < 1$. Thus, the problem is equivalent to determining the value of x given that $x \neq 0$ and $x < 1$.

(1) Given that $-2 < x < 2$, it is not possible to determine the value of x. For example, the value of x could be −1 (note that $-1 < 1$) and the value of x could be 0.5 (note that $0.5 < 1$); NOT sufficient.

(2) Given that the value of x is an integer greater than −2, then the value of x must be among the integers −1, 0, 1, 2, 3, ... However, from the discussion above, $x \neq 0$ and $x < 1$, so the value of x can only be −1; SUFFICIENT.

The correct answer is B;
statement 2 alone is sufficient.

377. For any integers x and y, min(x, y) and max(x, y) denote the minimum and the maximum of x and y, respectively. For example, min(5, 2) = 2 and max(5, 2) = 5. For the integer w, what is the value of min(10, w) ?

(1) w = max(20, z) for some integer z.

(2) w = max(10, w)

Arithmetic **Properties of numbers**

If $w \geq 10$, then $(10, w) = 10$, and if $w < 10$, then $(10, w) = w$. Therefore, the value of min$(10, w)$ can be determined if the value of w can be determined.

(1) Given that $w = \max(20, z)$ then $w \geq 20$. Hence, $w \geq 10$, and so min$(10, w) = 10$; SUFFICIENT.

(2) Given that $w = \max(10, w)$, then $w \geq 10$, and so min$(10, w) = 10$; SUFFICIENT.

The correct answer is D;
each statement alone is sufficient.

378. A certain bookcase has 2 shelves of books. On the upper shelf, the book with the greatest number of pages has 400 pages. On the lower shelf, the book with the least number of pages has 475 pages. What is the median number of pages for all of the books on the 2 shelves?

(1) There are 25 books on the upper shelf.

(2) There are 24 books on the lower shelf.

Arithmetic **Statistics**

(1) The information given says nothing about the number of books on the lower shelf. If there are fewer than 25 books on the lower shelf, then the median number of pages will be the number of pages in one of the books on the upper shelf or the average number of pages in two books on the upper shelf. Hence, the median will be at most 400. If there are more than 25 books on the lower shelf, then the median number of pages will be the number of pages in one of the books on the lower shelf or the average number of pages in two books on the lower shelf. Hence, the median will be at least 475; NOT sufficient.

(2) An analysis very similar to that used in (1) shows the information given is not sufficient to determine the median; NOT sufficient.

Given both (1) and (2), it follows that there is a total of 49 books. Therefore, the median will be the 25th book when the books are ordered by number of pages. Since the 25th book in this ordering is the book on the upper shelf with the greatest number of pages, the median is 400. Therefore, (1) and (2) together are sufficient.

The correct answer is C;
both statements together are sufficient.

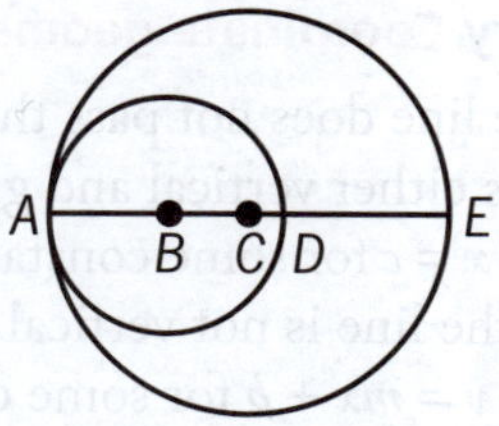

379. In the figure above, points A, B, C, D, and E lie on a line. A is on both circles, B is the center of the smaller circle, C is the center of the larger circle, D is on the smaller circle, and E is on the larger circle. What is the area of the region inside the larger circle and outside the smaller circle?

(1) $AB = 3$ and $BC = 2$

(2) $CD = 1$ and $DE = 4$

Geometry Circles

If R is the radius of the larger circle and r is the radius of the smaller circle, then the desired area is $\pi R^2 - \pi r^2$. Thus, if both the values of R and r can be determined, then the desired area can be determined.

(1) Given that $AB = r = 3$ and $BC = 2$, then $AB + BC = R = 3 + 2 = 5$; SUFFICIENT.

(2) Given that $CD = 1$ and $DE = 4$, then $CD + DE = R = 1 + 4 = 5$. Since $\overline{AE}$ is a diameter of the larger circle, then $AD + DE = 2R$. Also, since $\overline{AD}$ is a diameter of the smaller circle, then $AD = 2r$. Thus, $2r + DE = 2R$ or $2r + 4 = 10$, and so $r = 3$; SUFFICIENT.

The correct answer is D;
each statement alone is sufficient.

380. In planning for a trip, Joan estimated both the distance of the trip, in miles, and her average speed, in miles per hour. She accurately divided her estimated distance by her estimated average speed to obtain an estimate for the time, in hours, that the trip would take. Was her estimate within 0.5 hour of the actual time that the trip took?

(1) Joan's estimate for the distance was within 5 miles of the actual distance.

(2) Joan's estimate for her average speed was within 10 miles per hour of her actual average speed.

Arithmetic Applied problems; Estimating

(1) Given that Joan's estimate for the distance was within 5 miles of the actual distance, it is not possible to determine whether her estimate for the time was within 0.5 hour without information about her estimated average speed. For example, if her estimated distance was 20 miles and was within 5 miles of the actual distance, then the actual distance would be between 15 and 25 miles. If her estimated speed was 20 miles per hour (mph) and was within, say, 10 mph of her actual speed, then her actual speed would be between 10 and 30 mph. Her estimated time would then be $\frac{20}{20} = 1.0$ hour and the actual time would be between $\frac{15}{30} = 0.5$ hour (least distance over greatest speed) and $\frac{25}{10} = 2.5$ hours (greatest distance over least speed). Since 1.0 hour is between 0.5 hour and 2.5 hours, her estimate for the time could equal the actual time, and thus it is possible that her estimate of the time is within 0.5 hour of the actual time. However, her estimate for the time could be as much as $2.5 - 1.0 = 1.5$ hours over the actual time, and thus it is possible that her estimate of the time is not within 0.5 hour; NOT sufficient.

(2) Given that Joan's estimate for her average speed was within 10 miles per hour of her actual average speed, the same examples used in (1) can be used to show that it cannot be determined whether her estimate for the time would be within 0.5 hour of the actual time; NOT sufficient.

Taking (1) and (2) together is of no more help than either (1) or (2) taken separately because the same examples used to show that (1) is not sufficient also show that (2) is not sufficient.

The correct answer is E;
both statements together are still not sufficient.

381. A certain list consists of 3 different numbers. Does the median of the 3 numbers equal the average (arithmetic mean) of the 3 numbers?

(1) The range of the 3 numbers is equal to twice the difference between the greatest number and the median.

(2) The sum of the 3 numbers is equal to 3 times one of the numbers.

Arithmetic Statistics

Let the numbers be x, y, and z so that $x < y < z$. Determine whether $y = \frac{x+y+z}{3}$, or equivalently, whether $3y = x + y + z$, or equivalently, whether $2y = x + z$.

(1) Given that the range is equal to twice the difference between the greatest number and the median, it follows that $z - x = 2(z - y)$, or $z - x = 2z - 2y$, or $2y = x + z$; SUFFICIENT.

(2) Given that the sum of the 3 numbers equals 3 times one of the numbers, it follows that $x + y + z = 3x$ or $x + y + z = 3y$ or $x + y + z = 3z$. If $x + y + z = 3x$, then $y + z = 2x$, or $(y - x) + (z - x) = 0$. Also, if $x + y + z = 3z$, then $x + y = 2z$, or $0 = (z - x) + (z - y)$. In each of these cases, the sum of two positive numbers is zero, which is impossible. Therefore, it must be true that $x + y + z = 3y$, from which it follows that $x + z = 2y$, and hence by the initial comments, the median of the 3 numbers equals the average of the 3 numbers; SUFFICIENT.

The correct answer is D;
each statement alone is sufficient.

382. Line ℓ lies in the *xy*-plane and does not pass through the origin. What is the slope of line ℓ ?

(1) The *x*-intercept of line ℓ is twice the *y*-intercept of line ℓ.

(2) The *x*- and *y*-intercepts of line ℓ are both positive.

Geometry Coordinate geometry

Since the line does not pass through the origin, the line is either vertical and given by the equation $x = c$ for some constant c such that $c \neq 0$, or the line is not vertical and given by the equation $y = mx + b$ for some constants m and b such that $b \neq 0$. Determine whether the line is not vertical, and if so, determine the slope of the line, which is the value of m.

(1) Given that the *x*-intercept of the line is twice the *y*-intercept of the line, it follows that the line is not vertical, since a vertical line that does not pass through the origin will not have a *y*-intercept. Thus, the line is given by the equation $y = mx + b$. The *x*-intercept of the line is the solution to $0 = mx + b$, or $mx = -b$, which has solution $x = -\frac{b}{m}$, and the *y*-intercept of the line is b. Therefore, $-\frac{b}{m} = 2b$. Since $b \neq 0$, both sides of the last equation can be divided by b to get $-\frac{1}{m} = 2$, or $m = -2$; SUFFICIENT.

(2) Given that the *x*- and *y*-intercepts of the line are both positive, it is not possible to determine the slope of the line. For example, if the line is given by $y = -x + 1$, then the *x*-intercept is 1 (solve $-x + 1 = 0$), the *y*-intercept is 1 ($b = 1$), and the slope is -1. However, if the line is given by $y = -2x + 2$, then the *x*-intercept is 1 (solve $-2x + 2 = 0$), the *y*-intercept is 2 ($b = 2$), and the slope is -2; NOT sufficient.

The correct answer is A;
statement 1 alone is sufficient.

$$y = ax - 5$$
$$y = x + 6$$
$$y = 3x + b$$

383. In the *xy*-plane, the straight-line graphs of the three equations above each contain the point (p,r). If a and b are constants, what is the value of b ?

(1) $a = 2$

(2) $r = 17$

Algebra Coordinate geometry

Since (p,r) is on each of the lines, each of the following three equations is true:

(i) $r = ap - 5$

(ii) $r = p + 6$

(iii) $r = 3p + b$

Determine the value of b.

(1) Given that $a = 2$, Equations (i) and (ii) become $r = 2p - 5$ and $r = p + 6$. Subtracting equations gives $0 = p - 11$, or $p = 11$. Now using $r = p + 6$, it follows that $r = 11 + 6 = 17$. Finally, using $p = 11$ and $r = 17$ in Equation (iii) gives $17 = 3(11) + b$, or $b = 17 - 33 = -16$; SUFFICIENT.

(2) Given that $r = 17$, Equation (ii) becomes $17 = p + 6$, and so $p = 17 - 6 = 11$. Using $r = 17$ and $p = 11$, Equation (iii) becomes $17 = 3(11) + b$, or $b = 17 - 33 = -16$; SUFFICIENT.

The correct answer is D;
each statement alone is sufficient.

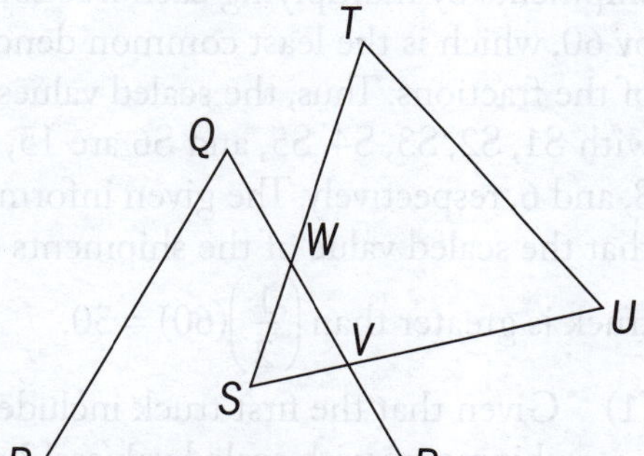

384. In the figure above, *PQR* and *STU* are identical equilateral triangles, and $PQ = 6$. What is the perimeter of polygon *PQWTUVR* ?

(1) Triangle *SWV* has perimeter 9.

(2) *VW* has length 3.5.

Geometry Triangles; Perimeter

(1) Given that triangle *SWV* has perimeter 9, the perimeter of polygon *PQWTUVR* can be determined, since the perimeter of polygon *PQWTUVR* equals the sum of the perimeters of the two equilateral triangles, which is $3(6) + 3(6) = 36$, minus the perimeter of triangle *SWV*; SUFFICIENT.

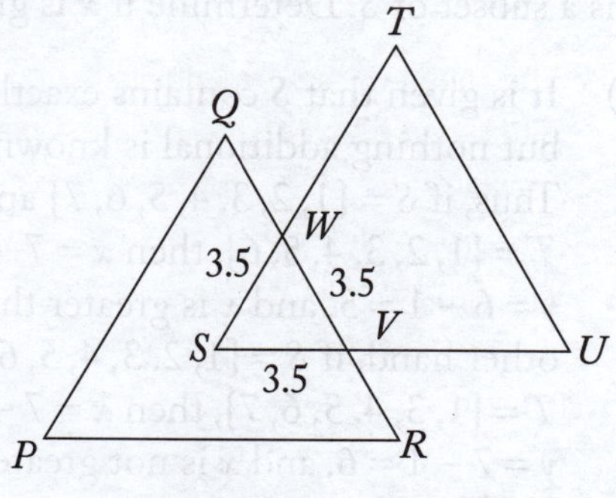

Figure 1

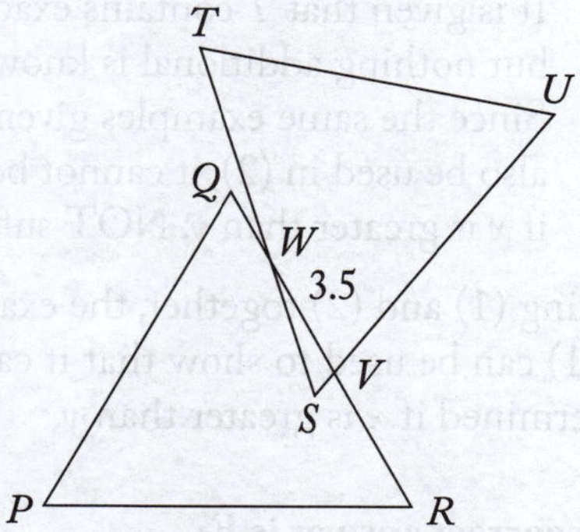

Figure 2

(2) Given that $VW = 3.5$, and using the fact that the perimeter of polygon *PQWTUVR* equals the sum of the perimeters of the two equilateral triangles, which is $3(6) + 3(6) = 36$, minus the perimeter of triangle *SWV*, it is not possible to determine the perimeter of polygon *PQWTUVR*. For example, the perimeter of polygon *PQWTUVR* could be $36 - 3(3.5) = 25.5$ (arrange triangles *PQR* and *STU* so that $VW = WS = SV = 3.5$, as shown in Figure 1), and the perimeter of polygon *PQWTUVR* could be greater than 25.5 (arrange triangles *PQR* and *STU* so that $VW = 3.5$, *WS* is slightly greater than 3.5, and *SV* is close to 0, as shown in Figure 2); NOT sufficient.

The correct answer is A;
statement 1 alone is sufficient.

385. The range of the numbers in set *S* is *x*, and the range of the numbers in set *T* is *y*. If all of the numbers in set *T* are also in set *S*, is *x* greater than *y* ?

(1) Set *S* consists of 7 numbers.

(2) Set *T* consists of 6 numbers.

Arithmetic Statistics

Set S has a range of x, set T has a range of y, and T is a subset of S. Determine if x is greater than y.

(1) It is given that S contains exactly 7 numbers, but nothing additional is known about T. Thus, if $S = \{1, 2, 3, 4, 5, 6, 7\}$ and $T = \{1, 2, 3, 4, 5, 6\}$, then $x = 7 - 1 = 6$, $y = 6 - 1 = 5$, and x is greater than y. On the other hand, if $S = \{1, 2, 3, 4, 5, 6, 7\}$ and $T = \{1, 3, 4, 5, 6, 7\}$, then $x = 7 - 1 = 6$, $y = 7 - 1 = 6$, and x is not greater than y; NOT sufficient.

(2) It is given that T contains exactly 6 numbers, but nothing additional is known about T. Since the same examples given in (1) can also be used in (2), it cannot be determined if x is greater than y; NOT sufficient.

Taking (1) and (2) together, the examples used in (1) can be used to show that it cannot be determined if x is greater than y.

The correct answer is E;
both statements together are still not sufficient.

386. The hypotenuse of a right triangle is 10 cm. What is the perimeter, in centimeters, of the triangle?

(1) The area of the triangle is 25 square centimeters.

(2) The 2 legs of the triangle are of equal length.

Geometry Triangles

If x and y are the lengths of the legs of the triangle, then it is given that $x^2 + y^2 = 100$. Determining the value of $x + y + 10$, the perimeter of the triangle, is equivalent to determining the value of $x + y$.

(1) Given that the area is 25, then $\frac{1}{2}xy = 25$, or $xy = 50$. Since $(x + y)^2 = x^2 + y^2 + 2xy$, it follows that $(x + y)^2 = 100 + 2(50)$, or $x + y = \sqrt{200}$; SUFFICIENT.

(2) Given that $x = y$, since $x^2 + y^2 = 100$, it follows that $2x^2 = 100$, or $x = \sqrt{50}$. Hence, $x + y = x + x = 2x = 2\sqrt{50}$; SUFFICIENT.

The correct answer is D;
each statement alone is sufficient.

Shipment	S1	S2	S3	S4	S5	S6
Fraction of the Total Value of the Six Shipments	$\frac{1}{4}$	$\frac{1}{5}$	$\frac{1}{6}$	$\frac{3}{20}$	$\frac{2}{15}$	$\frac{1}{10}$

387. Six shipments of machine parts were shipped from a factory on two trucks, with each shipment entirely on one of the trucks. Each shipment was labeled either S1, S2, S3, S4, S5, or S6. The table shows the value of each shipment as a fraction of the total value of the six shipments. If the shipments on the first truck had a value greater than $\frac{1}{2}$ of the total value of the six shipments, was S3 shipped on the first truck?

(1) S2 and S4 were shipped on the first truck.

(2) S1 and S6 were shipped on the second truck.

Arithmetic Operations on rational numbers

Given that the shipments on the first truck had a value greater than $\frac{1}{2}$ of the total value of the 6 shipments, determine if S3 was shipped on the first truck.

To avoid dealing with fractions, it will be convenient to create scaled values of the shipments by multiplying each fractional value by 60, which is the least common denominator of the fractions. Thus, the scaled values associated with S1, S2, S3, S4, S5, and S6 are 15, 12, 10, 9, 8, and 6, respectively. The given information is that the scaled value of the shipments on the first truck is greater than $\left(\frac{1}{2}\right)(60) = 30$.

(1) Given that the first truck includes shipments with scaled values 12 and 9, it may or may not be the case that S3 (the shipment with scaled value 10) is on the first truck. For example, the first truck could contain only S2, S3, and S4, for a total scaled value $12 + 10 + 9 = 31 > 30$. Or, the first truck could contain only S1, S2, and S4, for a total scaled value $15 + 12 + 9 = 36 > 30$; NOT sufficient.

(2) Given that the second truck includes shipments with scaled values 15 and 6, the second truck cannot contain S3. Otherwise, the second truck would contain shipments with scaled values 15, 6, and 10, for a total

scaled value $15 + 6 + 10 = 31$, leaving at most a total scaled value 29 (which is not greater than 30) for the first truck; SUFFICIENT.

The correct answer is B; statement 2 alone is sufficient.

388. If x, y, and z are three-digit positive integers and if $x = y + z$, is the hundreds digit of x equal to the sum of the hundreds digits of y and z?

(1) The tens digit of x is equal to the sum of the tens digits of y and z.

(2) The units digit of x is equal to the sum of the units digits of y and z.

Arithmetic Place value

Letting $x = 100a + 10b + c$, $y = 100p + 10q + r$, and $z = 100t + 10u + v$, where a, b, c, p, q, r, t, u, and v are digits, determine if $a = p + t$.

(1) It is given that $b = q + u$ (which implies that $c + v \le 9$ because if $c + v > 9$, then in the addition process a ten would need to be carried over to the tens column and b would be $q + u + 1$). Since b is a digit, $0 \le b \le 9$. Hence, $0 \le q + u \le 9$, and so $0 \le 10(q + u) \le 90$. Therefore, in the addition process, there are no hundreds to carry over from the tens column to the hundreds column, so $a = p + t$; SUFFICIENT.

(2) It is given that $c = r + v$. If $x = 687$, $y = 231$, and $z = 456$, then, $y + z = 231 + 456 = 687 = x$, $r + v = 1 + 6 = 7 = c$, and $p + t = 2 + 4 = 6 = a$. On the other hand, if $x = 637$, $y = 392$, and $z = 245$, then $y + z = 392 + 245 = 637 = x$, $r + v = 2 + 5 = 7 = c$, and $p + t = 3 + 2 = 5 \ne 6 = a$; NOT sufficient.

The correct answer is A; statement 1 alone is sufficient.

	Favorable	Unfavorable	Not Sure
Candidate M	40	20	40
Candidate N	30	35	35

389. The table above shows the results of a survey of 100 voters who each responded "Favorable" or "Unfavorable" or "Not Sure" when asked about their impressions of Candidate M and of Candidate N. What was the number of voters who responded "Favorable" for both candidates?

(1) The number of voters who did not respond "Favorable" for either candidate was 40.

(2) The number of voters who responded "Unfavorable" for both candidates was 10.

Arithmetic Sets

If x is the number of voters who responded "Favorable" for both candidates, then it follows from the table that the number of voters who responded "Favorable" to at least one candidate is $40 + 30 - x = 70 - x$. This is because $40 + 30$ represents the number of voters who responded "Favorable" for Candidate M added to the number of voters who responded "Favorable" for Candidate N, a calculation that counts twice each of the x voters who responded "Favorable" for both candidates.

(1) Given that there were 40 voters who did not respond "Favorable" for either candidate and there were 100 voters surveyed, the number of voters who responded "Favorable" to at least one candidate is $100 - 40 = 60$. Therefore, from the comments above, it follows that $70 - x = 60$, and hence $x = 10$; SUFFICIENT.

(2) The information given affects only the numbers of voters in the categories "Unfavorable" for Candidate M only, "Unfavorable" for Candidate N only, and "Unfavorable" for both candidates. Thus, the numbers of voters in the categories "Favorable" for Candidate M only, "Favorable" for Candidate N only, and "Favorable" for both candidates are not affected. Since these latter categories are only constrained to have certain integer values that have a total sum of $70 - x$, more

than one possibility exists for the value of x. For example, the numbers of voters in the categories "Favorable" for Candidate M only, "Favorable" for Candidate N only, and "Favorable" for both candidates could be 25, 15, and 15, respectively, which gives $70 - x = 25 + 15 + 15$, or $x = 15$. However, the numbers of voters in the categories "Favorable" for Candidate M only, "Favorable" for Candidate N only, and "Favorable" for both candidates could be 30, 20, and 10, respectively, which gives $70 - x = 30 + 20 + 10$, or $x = 10$; NOT sufficient.

The correct answer is A; statement 1 alone is sufficient.

390. A school administrator will assign each student in a group of n students to one of m classrooms. If $3 < m < 13 < n$, is it possible to assign each of the n students to one of the m classrooms so that each classroom has the same number of students assigned to it?

(1) It is possible to assign each of $3n$ students to one of m classrooms so that each classroom has the same number of students assigned to it.

(2) It is possible to assign each of $13n$ students to one of m classrooms so that each classroom has the same number of students assigned to it.

Arithmetic Properties of numbers

Determine if n is divisible by m.

(1) Given that $3n$ is divisible by m, then n is divisible by m if $m = 9$ and $n = 27$ (note that $3 < m < 13 < n$, $3n = 81$, and $m = 9$, so $3n$ is divisible by m) and n is not divisible by m if $m = 9$ and $n = 30$ (note that $3 < m < 13 < n$, $3n = 90$, and $m = 9$, so $3n$ is divisible by m); NOT sufficient.

(2) Given that $13n$ is divisible by m, then $13n = qm$, or $\frac{n}{m} = \frac{q}{13}$, for some integer q.

Since 13 is a prime number that divides qm (because $13n = qm$) and 13 does not divide m (because $m < 13$), it follows that 13 divides q.

Therefore, $\frac{q}{13}$ is an integer, and since $\frac{n}{m} = \frac{q}{13}$, then $\frac{n}{m}$ is an integer. Thus, n is divisible by m; SUFFICIENT.

The correct answer is B; statement 2 alone is sufficient.

391. If q, s, and t are all different numbers, is $q < s < t$?

(1) $t - q = |t - s| + |s - q|$

(2) $t > q$

Algebra Absolute value

(1) It is given that $t - q = |t - s| + |s - q|$, which can be rewritten without absolute values in four mutually exclusive and collectively exhaustive cases by making use of the algebraic definition of absolute value. Recall that $|x| = x$ if $x > 0$, and $|x| = -x$ if $x < 0$. Thus, for example, if $t - s < 0$, then $|t - s| = -(t - s)$.

Case 1: $t > s$ and $s > q$. In this case, $t - s > 0$ and $s - q > 0$, and so $t - q = |t - s| + |s - q|$ is equivalent to $t - q = (t - s) + (s - q)$, which is an identity. Therefore, the case for which $t > s$ and $s > q$ is consistent with the given information and the assumption $t - q = |t - s| + |s - q|$.

Case 2: $t > s$ and $s < q$. In this case, $t - s > 0$ and $s - q < 0$, and so $t - q = |t - s| + |s - q|$ is equivalent to $t - q = (t - s) - (s - q)$, or $s = q$, which is not consistent with the assumption that q, s, and t are all different numbers. Therefore, the case for which $t > s$ and $s < q$ is not consistent with the given information and the assumption $t - q = |t - s| + |s - q|$.

Case 3: $t < s$ and $s > q$. In this case, $t - s < 0$ and $s - q > 0$, and so $t - q = |t - s| + |s - q|$ is equivalent to $t - q = -(t - s) + (s - q)$, or $t = s$, which is not consistent with the assumption that q, s, and t are all different numbers. Therefore, the case for which $t < s$ and $s > q$ is not consistent with the given information and the assumption $t - q = |t - s| + |s - q|$.

Case 4: $t < s$ and $s < q$. In this case, $t - s < 0$ and $s - q < 0$, and so $t - q = |t - s| + |s - q|$ is equivalent to $t - q = -(t - s) - (s - q)$, or $t = q$, which is not consistent with the assumption that q, s, and t are all different numbers. Therefore, the case for which $t < s$ and $s < q$ is not consistent with the given information and the assumption $t - q = |t - s| + |s - q|$. The only case that is consistent with the given information and the assumption $t - q = |t - s| + |s - q|$ is Case 1. Therefore, it follows that $t > s$ and $s > q$, and this implies $q < s < t$; SUFFICIENT.

(2) Given that $t > q$, it is possible that $q < s < t$ is true (for example, when s is between t and q) and it is possible that $q < s < t$ is false (for example, when s is greater than t); NOT sufficient.

The correct answer is A; statement 1 alone is sufficient.

392. What is the median number of employees assigned per project for the projects at Company Z ?

(1) 25 percent of the projects at Company Z have 4 or more employees assigned to each project.

(2) 35 percent of the projects at Company Z have 2 or fewer employees assigned to each project.

Arithmetic Statistics

(1) Although 25 percent of the projects have 4 or more employees, there is essentially no information about the middle values of the numbers of employees per project. For example, if there were a total of 100 projects, then the median could be 2 (75 projects that have exactly 2 employees each and 25 projects that have exactly 4 employees each) or the median could be 3 (75 projects that have exactly 3 employees each and 25 projects that have exactly 4 employees each); NOT sufficient.

(2) Although 35 percent of the projects have 2 or fewer employees, there is essentially no information about the middle values of the numbers of employees per project. For example, if there were a total of 100 projects, then the median could be 3 (35 projects that have exactly 2 employees each and 65 projects that have exactly 3 employees each) or the median could be 4 (35 projects that have exactly 2 employees each and 65 projects that have exactly 4 employees each); NOT sufficient.

Given both (1) and (2), 100 – (25 + 35) percent = 40 percent of the projects have exactly 3 employees. Therefore, when the numbers of employees per project are listed from least to greatest, 35 percent of the numbers are 2 or less and (35 + 40) percent = 75 percent are 3 or less, and hence the median is 3.

The correct answer is C; both statements together are sufficient.

393. Last year, a certain company began manufacturing product X and sold every unit of product X that it produced. Last year the company's total expenses for manufacturing product X were equal to \$100,000 plus 5 percent of the company's total revenue from all units of product X sold. If the company made a profit on product X last year, did the company sell more than 21,000 units of product X last year?

(1) The company's total revenue from the sale of product X last year was greater than \$110,000.

(2) For each unit of product X sold last year, the company's revenue was \$5.

Algebra Applied problems

For a company that made a profit last year from selling product X and had total expenses for product X of $\$100{,}000 + 0.05R$, where R is the total revenue for selling product X, determine whether the company sold more than 21,000 units of product X last year.

Note that since the company made a profit, revenue – cost, which is given by $R - (\$100{,}000 + 0.05R) = 0.95R - \$100{,}000$, must be positive.

(1) It is given that $R > \$110{,}000$. It is possible to vary the unit price and the number of units sold so that $R > \$110{,}000$ and *more than* 21,000 units were sold, and also so that $R > \$110{,}000$ and *less than* 21,000 units were sold. For example, if 25,000 units were sold for \$10 per unit, then

$R = 25{,}000(\$10) = \$250{,}000 > \$110{,}000$ and $25{,}000 > 21{,}000$. On the other hand, if 20,000 units were sold for \$10 per unit, then $R = 20{,}000(\$10) = \$200{,}000 > \$110{,}000$ and $20{,}000 < 21{,}000$; NOT sufficient.

(2) It is given that the company's revenue for each unit of product X was \$5. If the company manufactured and sold x units of product X, then its revenue was $\$5x$. Because the company made a profit, $0.95(\$5x) - \$100{,}000 > 0$, and so

$$0.95(\$5x) - \$100{,}000 > 0$$
$$\$4.75x - \$100{,}000 > 0$$
$$\$4.75x > \$100{,}000$$
$$x > 21{,}052; \text{ SUFFICIENT.}$$

To avoid long division in the last step, note that $4.75(21{,}000) = 99{,}750$, and thus from $4.75x > 100{,}000$, it follows that $x > 21{,}000$.

The correct answer is B;
statement 2 alone is sufficient.

394. Beginning in January of last year, Carl made deposits of \$120 into his account on the 15th of each month for several consecutive months and then made withdrawals of \$50 from the account on the 15th of each of the remaining months of last year. There were no other transactions in the account last year. If the closing balance of Carl's account for May of last year was \$2,600, what was the range of the monthly closing balances of Carl's account last year?

(1) Last year the closing balance of Carl's account for April was less than \$2,625.

(2) Last year the closing balance of Carl's account for June was less than \$2,675.

Arithmetic Statistics

(1) If Carl began making \$50 withdrawals on or before May 15, his account balance on April 16 would be at least \$50 greater than it was on the last day of May. Thus, his account balance on April 16 would be at least \$2,600 + \$50 = \$2,650, which is contrary to the information given in (1). Therefore, Carl did not begin making \$50 withdrawals until June 15 or later. These observations can be used to give at least two possible ranges. Carl could have had an account balance of \$2,000 on January 1, made \$120 deposits in each of the first 11 months of the year, and then made a \$50 withdrawal on December 15, which gives a range of monthly closing balances of (120)(10). Also, Carl could have had an account balance of \$2,000 on January 1, made \$120 deposits in each of the first 10 months of the year, and then made \$50 withdrawals on November 15 and on December 15, which gives a range of monthly closing balances of (120)(9); NOT sufficient.

(2) On June 1, Carl's account balance was the same as its closing balance was for May, namely \$2,600. Depending on whether Carl made a \$120 deposit or a \$50 withdrawal on June 15, Carl's account balance on June 16 was either \$2,720 or \$2,550. It follows from the information given in (2) that Carl's balance on June 16 was \$2,550. Therefore, Carl began making \$50 withdrawals on or before June 15. These observations can be used to give at least two possible ranges. Carl could have had an account balance of \$2,680 on January 1, made one \$120 deposit on January 15, and then made a \$50 withdrawal in each of the remaining 11 months of the year (this gives a closing balance of \$2,600 for May), which gives a range of monthly closing balances of (50)(11). Also, Carl could have had an account balance of \$2,510 on January 1, made \$120 deposits on January 15 and on February 15, and then made a \$50 withdrawal in each of the remaining 10 months of the year (this gives a closing balance of \$2,600 for May), which gives a range of monthly closing balances of (50)(10); NOT sufficient.

Given both (1) and (2), it follows from the remarks above that Carl began making \$50 withdrawals on June 15. Therefore, the changes to Carl's account balance for each month of last year are known. Since the closing balance for May is given, it follows that the closing balances for each month of last year are known, and hence the range of these 12 known values can be determined.

The correct answer is C;
both statements together are sufficient.

395. Are all of the numbers in a certain list of 15 numbers equal?

(1) The sum of all the numbers in the list is 60.

(2) The sum of any 3 numbers in the list is 12.

Arithmetic Properties of numbers

(1) If there are 15 occurrences of the number 4 in the list, then the sum of the numbers in the list is 60 and all the numbers in the list are equal. If there are 13 occurrences of the number 4 in the list, 1 occurrence of the number 3 in the list, and 1 occurrence of the number 5 in the list, then the sum of the numbers in the list is 60 and not all the numbers in the list are equal; NOT sufficient.

(2) Given that the sum of any 3 numbers in the list is 12, arrange the numbers in the list in numerical order, from least to greatest: $a_1 \le a_2 \le a_3 \le \ldots \le a_{15}$.

If $a_1 < 4$, then $a_1 + a_2 + a_3 < 4 + a_2 + a_3$. Therefore, from (2), $12 < 4 + a_2 + a_3$, or $8 < a_2 + a_3$, and so at least one of the values a_2 and a_3 must be greater than 4. Because $a_2 \le a_3$, it follows that $a_3 > 4$. Since the numbers are arranged from least to greatest, it follows that $a_4 > 4$ and $a_5 > 4$. But then, $a_3 + a_4 + a_5 > 4 + 4 + 4 = 12$, contrary to (2), and so $a_1 < 4$ is not true. Therefore, $a_1 \ge 4$. Since a_1 is the least of the 15 numbers, $a_n \ge 4$ for $n = 1, 2, 3, \ldots, 15$.

If $a_{15} > 4$, then $a_{13} + a_{14} + a_{15} > a_{13} + a_{14} + 4$. Therefore, from (2), $12 > a_{13} + a_{14} + 4$, or $8 > a_{13} + a_{14}$, and so at least one of the values a_{13} and a_{14} must be less than 4. Because $a_{13} \le a_{14}$, it follows that $a_{13} < 4$. Since the numbers are arranged from least to greatest, it follows that $a_{11} < 4$ and $a_{12} < 4$. But then $a_{11} + a_{12} + a_{13} < 4 + 4 + 4 = 12$, contrary to (2). Therefore, $a_{15} \le 4$. Since a_{15} is the greatest of the 15 numbers, $a_n \le 4$ for $n = 1, 2, 3, \ldots, 15$.

It has been shown that, for $n = 1, 2, 3, \ldots, 15$, each of $a_n \ge 4$ and $a_n \le 4$ is true. Therefore, $a_n = 4$ for $n = 1, 2, 3, \ldots, 15$; SUFFICIENT.

The correct answer is B;
statement 2 alone is sufficient.

396. If the average (arithmetic mean) of six numbers is 75, how many of the numbers are equal to 75 ?

(1) None of the six numbers is less than 75.

(2) None of the six numbers is greater than 75.

Arithmetic Statistics

If the average of six numbers is 75, then $\frac{1}{6}$ of the sum of the numbers is 75. Therefore, the sum of the numbers is (6)(75).

(1) If one of the numbers is greater than 75, then we can write that number as $75 + x$ for some positive number x. Consequently, the sum of the 6 numbers must be at least $(5)(75) + (75 + x) = (6)(75) + x$, which is greater than (6)(75), contrary to the fact that the sum is equal to (6)(75). Hence, none of the numbers can be greater than 75. Since none of the numbers can be less than 75 (given information) and none of the numbers can be greater than 75, it follows that each of the numbers is equal to 75; SUFFICIENT.

(2) If one of the numbers is less than 75, then we can write that number as $75 - x$ for some positive number x. Consequently, the sum of the 6 numbers must be at most $(5)(75) + (75 - x) = (6)(75) - x$, which is less than (6)(75), contrary to the fact that the sum is equal to (6)(75). Hence, none of the numbers can be less than 75. Since none of the numbers can be less than 75 and none of the numbers can be greater than 75 (given information), it follows that each of the numbers is equal to 75; SUFFICIENT.

The correct answer is D;
each statement alone is sufficient.

397. What amount did Jean earn from the commission on her sales in the first half of 1988 ?

(1) In 1988 Jean's commission was 5 percent of the total amount of her sales.

(2) The amount of Jean's sales in the second half of 1988 averaged \$10,000 per month more than in the first half.

Arithmetic Applied problems

Let A be the amount of Jean's sales in the first half of 1988. Determine the value of A.

(1) If the amount of Jean's sales in the first half of 1988 was \$10,000, then her commission in the first half of 1988 would have been (5%)(\$10,000) = \$500. On the other hand, if the amount of Jean's sales in the first half of 1988 was \$100,000, then her commission in the first half of 1988 would have been (5%)(\$100,000) = \$5,000; NOT sufficient.

(2) No information is given that relates the amount of Jean's sales to the amount of Jean's commission; NOT sufficient.

Given (1) and (2), from (1) the amount of Jean's commission in the first half of 1988 is (5%)A. From (2) the amount of Jean's sales in the second half of 1988 is A + \$60,000. Both statements together do not give information to determine the value of A.

The correct answer is E;
both statements together are still not sufficient.

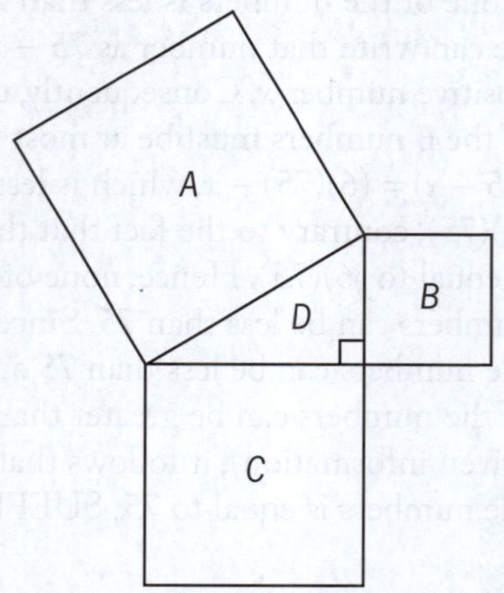

398. In the figure above, if the area of triangular region D is 4, what is the length of a side of square region A?

(1) The area of square region B is 9.

(2) The area of square region C is $\frac{64}{9}$.

Geometry Area

The area of the triangular region D can be represented by $\frac{1}{2}bh$, where b is the base of the triangle (and is equal to the length of a side of the square region C) and h is the height of the triangle (and is equal to the length of a side of the square region B). The area of any square is equal to the length of a side squared. The Pythagorean theorem is used to find the length of a side of a right triangle, when the length of the other 2 sides of the triangle are known and is represented by $a^2 + b^2 = c^2$, where a and b are the lengths of the 2 perpendicular sides of the triangle and c is the length of the hypotenuse.

Although completed calculations are provided in what follows, keep in mind that completed calculations are not needed to solve this problem.

(1) If the area of B is 9, then the length of each side is 3. Therefore, $h = 3$. Then, b can be determined, since the area of the triangle is, by substitution, $4 = \frac{1}{2}(3b)$ or $8 = 3b$ or $\frac{8}{3} = b$. Once b is known, the Pythagorean theorem can be used: $\left(\frac{8}{3}\right)^2 + 3^2 = c^2$ or $\frac{64}{9} + 9 = c^2$ or $\frac{145}{9} = c^2$. The length of a side of A is thus $\sqrt{\frac{145}{9}}$; SUFFICIENT.

(2) If the area of C is $\frac{64}{9}$, then the length of each side is $\frac{8}{3}$. Therefore, $b = \frac{8}{3}$. The area of a triangle is $A = \frac{1}{2}bh$ so $4 = \frac{1}{2}\left(\frac{8}{3}h\right)$, $8 = \frac{8}{3}h$, and $3 = h$. Once h is known, the Pythagorean theorem can be used as above; SUFFICIENT.

The correct answer is D;
each statement alone is sufficient.

399. If n is a positive integer and $k = 5.1 \times 10^n$, what is the value of k?

(1) $6{,}000 < k < 500{,}000$

(2) $k^2 = 2.601 \times 10^9$

Arithmetic Properties of numbers

Given that $k = 5.1 \times 10^n$, where n is a positive integer, then the value of k must follow the pattern shown in the following table:

n	k
1	51
2	510
3	5,100
4	51,000
5	510,000
6	5,100,000
.	.
.	.
.	.

(1) Given that $6{,}000 < k < 500{,}000$, then k must have the value 51,000, and so $n = 4$; SUFFICIENT.

(2) Given that $k^2 = 2.601 \times 10^9$, then $k = \sqrt{2.601 \times 10^9} = \sqrt{2{,}601 \times 10^6} = \sqrt{2{,}601} \times \sqrt{10^6}$ $= 51 \times 10^3 = 51{,}000$, and so $n = 4$; SUFFICIENT.

The correct answer is D; each statement alone is sufficient.

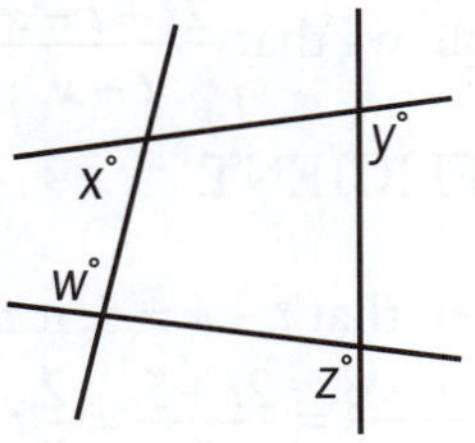

400. What is the value of $x + y$ in the figure above?

(1) $w = 95$

(2) $z = 125$

Geometry Angles

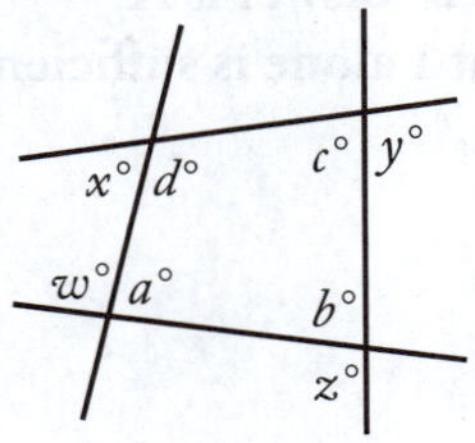

In the figure above, a, b, c, and d are the degree measures of the interior angles of the quadrilateral formed by the four lines and $a + b + c + d = 360$. Then

$w + x + y + z$

$= (180 - a) + (180 - d) + (180 - c) + (180 - b)$

$= 720 - (a + b + c + d)$

$= 720 - 360$

$= 360.$

Determine the value of $x + y$.

(1) Given that $w = 95$, then $95 + x + y + z = 360$ and $x + y + z = 265$. If $z = 65$, for example, then $x + y = 200$. On the other hand, if $z = 100$, then $x + y = 165$; NOT sufficient.

(2) Given that $z = 125$, then $w + x + y + 125 = 360$ and $w + x + y = 235$. If $w = 35$, for example, then $x + y = 200$. On the other hand, if $w = 100$, then $x + y = 135$; NOT sufficient.

Taking (1) and (2) together, $95 + x + y + 125 = 360$, and so $x + y = 140$.

The correct answer is C; both statements together are sufficient.

401. If n and k are positive integers, is $\sqrt{n+k} > 2\sqrt{n}$?

(1) $k > 3n$

(2) $n + k > 3n$

Algebra Inequalities

Determine if $\sqrt{n+k} > 2\sqrt{n}$. Since each side is positive, squaring each side preserves the inequality, so $\sqrt{n+k} > 2\sqrt{n}$ is equivalent to $(\sqrt{n+k})(\sqrt{n+k}) > (2\sqrt{n})(2\sqrt{n})$, which in turn is equivalent to $n + k > 4n$, or to $k > 3n$.

(1) Given that $k > 3n$, then $\sqrt{n+k} > 2\sqrt{n}$; SUFFICIENT.

(2) Given that $n + k > 3n$, then $k > 2n$. However, it is possible for $k > 2n$ to be true and $k > 3n$ to be false (for example, $k = 3$ and $n = 1$) and it is possible for $k > 2n$ to be true and $k > 3n$ to be true (for example, $k = 4$ and $n = 1$); NOT sufficient.

The correct answer is A; statement 1 alone is sufficient.

402. In a certain business, production index p is directly proportional to efficiency index e, which is in turn directly proportional to investment index i. What is p if $i = 70$?

(1) $e = 0.5$ whenever $i = 60$.

(2) $p = 2.0$ whenever $i = 50$.

Arithmetic Proportions

(1) This gives only values for e and i, and, while p is directly proportional to e, the nature of this proportion is unknown. Therefore, p cannot be determined; NOT sufficient.

(2) Since p is directly proportional to e, which is directly proportional to i, then p is directly proportional to i. Therefore, the following proportion can be set up: $\frac{p}{i} = \frac{2.0}{50}$. If $i = 70$, then $\frac{p}{70} = \frac{2.0}{50}$. Through cross multiplying, this equation yields $50p = 140$, or $p = 2.8$; SUFFICIENT.

The preceding approach is one method that can be used. Another approach is as follows: It is given that $p = Ke = K(Li) = (KL)i$, where K and L are the proportionality constants, and the value of $70KL$ is to be determined. Statement (1) allows us to determine the value of L, but gives nothing about K, and thus (1) is not sufficient. Statement (2) allows us to determine the value of KL, and thus (2) is sufficient.

The correct answer is B;
statement 2 alone is sufficient.

403. If n is a positive integer, what is the tens digit of n?

(1) The hundreds digit of $10n$ is 6.

(2) The tens digit of $n + 1$ is 7.

Arithmetic Properties of numbers

(1) Given that the hundreds digit of $10n$ is 6, the tens digit of n is 6, since the hundreds digit of $10n$ is always equal to the tens digit of n; SUFFICIENT.

(2) Given that the tens digit of $n + 1$ is 7, it is possible that the tens digit of n is 7 (for example, $n = 70$) and it is possible that the tens digit of n is 6 (for example, $n = 69$); NOT sufficient.

The correct answer is A;
statement 1 alone is sufficient.

404. What is the value of $\frac{2t + t - x}{t - x}$?

(1) $\frac{2t}{t - x} = 3$

(2) $t - x = 5$

Algebra Simplifying algebraic expressions

Determine the value of $\frac{2t + t - x}{t - x}$.

(1) Since $\frac{2t}{t - x} = 3$ and $\frac{2t + t - x}{t - x} = \frac{2t}{t - x} + \frac{t - x}{t - x} = \frac{2t}{t - x} + 1$, it follows that $\frac{2t + t - x}{t - x} = 3 + 1$; SUFFICIENT.

(2) Given that $t - x = 5$, it follows that $\frac{2t + t - x}{t - x} = \frac{2t + 5}{5} = \frac{2}{5}t + 1$, which can vary when the value of t varies. For example, $\frac{2}{5}t + 1 = 3$ if $t = 5$ (choose $x = 0$ to have $t - x = 5$) and $\frac{2}{5}t + 1 = 5$ if $t = 10$ (choose $x = 5$ to have $t - x = 5$); NOT sufficient.

The correct answer is A;
statement 1 alone is sufficient.

To register for the GMAT exam go to www.mba.com

7.0 Reading Comprehension

7.0 Reading Comprehension

Reading comprehension questions appear in the Verbal section of the GMAT® exam. The Verbal section uses multiple-choice questions to measure your ability to read and comprehend written material, to reason and evaluate arguments, and to correct written material to conform to standard written English. Because the Verbal section includes content from a variety of topics, you may be generally familiar with some of the material; however, neither the passages nor the questions assume knowledge of the topics discussed. Reading comprehension questions are intermingled with critical reasoning and sentence correction questions throughout the Verbal section of the test.

You will have 75 minutes to complete the Verbal section, or an average of about 1¾ minutes to answer each question. Keep in mind you will need time to read the written passages—and that time is not factored into the 1¾ minute average. Therefore, you should plan to proceed more quickly through the reading comprehension questions in order to give yourself enough time to read the passages thoroughly.

Reading comprehension questions begin with written passages up to 350 words long. The passages discuss topics from the social sciences, humanities, the physical or biological sciences, and such business-related fields as marketing, economics, and human resource management. The passages are accompanied by questions that will ask you to interpret the passage, apply the information you gather from the reading, and make inferences (or informed assumptions) based on the reading. For these questions, you will see a split computer screen. The written passage will remain visible on the left side as each question associated with that passage appears, in turn, on the right side. You will see only one question at a time. However, the number of questions associated with each passage may vary.

As you move through the reading comprehension sample questions, try to determine a process that works best for you. You might begin by reading a passage carefully and thoroughly. Some test-takers prefer to skim the passages the first time through, or even to read the first question before reading the passage. You may want to reread any sentences that present complicated ideas or introduce terms that are new to you. Read each question and series of answers carefully. Make sure you understand exactly what the question is asking and what the answer choices are.

If you need to, you may go back to the passage and read any parts that are relevant to answering the question. Specific portions of the passages may be indicated in the related questions.

The following pages describe what reading comprehension questions are designed to measure, present the directions that will precede questions of this type, and describe the various question types. This chapter also provides test-taking strategies, sample questions, and detailed explanations of all the questions. The explanations further illustrate the ways in which reading comprehension questions evaluate basic reading skills.

7.1 What Is Measured

Reading comprehension questions measure your ability to understand, analyze, and apply information and concepts presented in written form. All questions are to be answered on the basis of what is stated or implied in the reading material, and no specific prior knowledge of the material is required.

The GMAT reading comprehension questions evaluate your ability to do the following:

- **Understand words and statements.**
  Although the questions do not test your vocabulary (they will not ask you to define terms), they do test your ability to interpret special meanings of terms as they are used in the reading passages. The questions will also test your understanding of the English language. These questions may ask about the overall meaning of a passage.

- **Understand logical relationships between points and concepts.**
  This type of question may ask you to determine the strong and weak points of an argument or evaluate the relative importance of arguments and ideas in a passage.

- **Draw inferences from facts and statements.**
  The inference questions will ask you to consider factual statements or information presented in a reading passage and reach conclusions on the basis of that information.

- **Understand and follow the development of quantitative concepts as they are presented in written material.**
  This may involve the interpretation of numerical data or the use of simple arithmetic to reach conclusions about material in a passage.

There are six kinds of reading comprehension questions, each of which tests a different skill. The reading comprehension questions ask about the following areas:

Main idea

Each passage is a unified whole—that is, the individual sentences and paragraphs support and develop one main idea or central point. Sometimes you will be told the central point in the passage itself, and sometimes it will be necessary for you to determine the central point from the overall organization or development of the passage. You may be asked in this kind of question to

- recognize a correct restatement, or paraphrasing, of the main idea of a passage
- identify the author's primary purpose or objective in writing the passage
- assign a title that summarizes, briefly and pointedly, the main idea developed in the passage

Supporting ideas

These questions measure your ability to comprehend the supporting ideas in a passage and differentiate them from the main idea. The questions also measure your ability to differentiate ideas that are *explicitly stated* in a passage from ideas that are *implied* by the author but are not explicitly stated. You may be asked about

- facts cited in a passage
- the specific content of arguments presented by the author in support of his or her views
- descriptive details used to support or elaborate on the main idea

Whereas questions about the main idea ask you to determine the meaning of a passage *as a whole*, questions about supporting ideas ask you to determine the meanings of individual sentences and paragraphs that *contribute* to the meaning of the passage as a whole. In other words, these questions ask for the main point of *one small part* of the passage.

Inferences

These questions ask about ideas that are not explicitly stated in a passage but are *implied* by the author. Unlike questions about supporting details, which ask about information that is directly stated in a passage, inference questions ask about ideas or meanings that must be inferred from information that is directly stated. Authors can make their points in indirect ways, suggesting ideas without actually stating them. Inference questions measure your ability to understand an author's intended meaning in parts of a passage where the meaning is only suggested. These questions do not ask about meanings or implications that are remote from the passage; rather, they ask about meanings that are developed indirectly or implications that are specifically suggested by the author.

To answer these questions, you may have to

- logically take statements made by the author one step beyond their literal meanings
- recognize an alternative interpretation of a statement made by the author
- identify the intended meaning of a word used figuratively in a passage

If a passage explicitly states an effect, for example, you may be asked to infer its cause. If the author compares two phenomena, you may be asked to infer the basis for the comparison. You may be asked to infer the characteristics of an old policy from an explicit description of a new one. When you read a passage, you should concentrate not only on the explicit meaning of the author's words, but also on the more subtle meaning implied by those words.

Applying information to a context outside the passage itself

These questions measure your ability to discern the relationships between situations or ideas presented by the author and other situations or ideas that might parallel those in the passage. In this kind of question, you may be asked to

- identify a hypothetical situation that is comparable to a situation presented in the passage
- select an example that is similar to an example provided in the passage
- apply ideas given in the passage to a situation not mentioned by the author
- recognize ideas that the author would probably agree or disagree with on the basis of statements made in the passage

Unlike inference questions, application questions use ideas or situations *not* taken from the passage. Ideas and situations given in a question are *like* those given in the passage, and they parallel ideas and situations in the passage; therefore, to answer the question, you must do more than recall what you read. You must recognize the essential attributes of ideas and situations presented in the passage when they appear in different words and in an entirely new context.

Logical structure

These questions require you to analyze and evaluate the organization and logic of a passage. They may ask you

- how a passage is constructed—for instance, does it define, compare or contrast, present a new idea, or refute an idea?
- how the author persuades readers to accept his or her assertions
- the reason behind the author's use of any particular supporting detail
- to identify assumptions that the author is making
- to assess the strengths and weaknesses of the author's arguments
- to recognize appropriate counterarguments

These questions measure your ability not only to comprehend a passage but also to evaluate it critically. However, it is important for you to realize that logical structure questions do not rely on any kind of formal logic, nor do they require you to be familiar with specific terms of logic or argumentation. You can answer these questions using only the information in the passage and careful reasoning.

About the style and tone

Style and tone questions ask about the expression of a passage and about the ideas in a passage that may be expressed through its diction—the author's choice of words. You may be asked to deduce the author's attitude to an idea, a fact, or a situation from the words that he or she uses to describe it. You may also be asked to select a word that accurately describes the tone of a passage—for instance, "critical," "questioning," "objective," or "enthusiastic."

To answer this type of question, you will have to consider the language of the passage as a whole. It takes more than one pointed, critical word to make the tone of an entire passage "critical." Sometimes, style and tone questions ask what audience the passage was probably intended for or what type of publication it probably appeared in. Style and tone questions may apply to one small part of the passage or to the passage as a whole. To answer them, you must ask yourself what meanings are contained in the words of a passage beyond the literal meanings. Did the author use certain words because of their emotional content, or because a particular audience would expect to hear them? Remember, these questions measure your ability to discern meaning expressed by the author through his or her choice of words.

7.2 Test-Taking Strategies

1. **Do not expect to be completely familiar with any of the material presented in reading comprehension passages.**
   You may find some passages easier to understand than others, but all passages are designed to present a challenge. If you have some familiarity with the material presented in a passage, do not let this knowledge influence your choice of answers to the questions. Answer all questions on the basis of what is *stated or implied* in the passage itself.

2. **Analyze each passage carefully, because the questions require you to have a specific and detailed understanding of the material.**
   You may find it easier to do the analysis first before moving to the questions. You may find that you prefer to skim the passage the first time and read more carefully once you understand what a question asks. You may even want to read the question before reading the passage. You should choose the method most suitable for you.

3. **Focus on key words and phrases, and make every effort to avoid losing the sense of what is discussed in the passage.**
   Keep the following in mind:
   - Note how each fact relates to an idea or an argument.
   - Note where the passage moves from one idea to the next.
   - Separate main ideas from supporting ideas.
   - Determine what conclusions are reached and why.

4. **Read the questions carefully, making certain that you understand what is asked.**
   An answer choice that accurately restates information in the passage may be incorrect if it does not answer the question. If you need to, refer back to the passage for clarification.

5. **Read all the choices carefully.**
   Never assume that you have selected the best answer without first reading all the choices.

6. **Select the choice that answers the question best in terms of the information given in the passage.**
   Do not rely on outside knowledge of the material to help you answer the questions.

7. **Remember that comprehension—not speed—is the critical success factor when it comes to reading comprehension questions.**

7.3 The Directions

These are the directions that you will see for reading comprehension questions when you take the GMAT exam. If you read them carefully and understand them clearly before going to sit for the test, you will not need to spend too much time reviewing them once you are at the test center and the test is under way.

The questions in this group are based on the content of a passage. After reading the passage, choose the best answer to each question. Answer all questions following the passage on the basis of what is *stated or implied in the passage.*

7.4 Practice Questions

Each of the reading comprehension questions is based on the content of a passage. After reading the passage answer all questions pertaining to it on the basis of what is stated or implied in the passage. For each question, select the best answer of the choices given.

Line Biologists have advanced two theories to explain why schooling of fish occurs in so many fish species. Because schooling is particularly widespread among species of small fish, both theories assume that schooling offers the advantage of some protection from predators.

Proponents of theory A dispute the assumption that a school of thousands of fish is highly visible. Experiments have shown that any fish can be seen, even in very clear water, only within a sphere of 200 meters in diameter. When fish are in a compact group, the spheres of visibility overlap. Thus the chance of a predator finding the school is only slightly greater than the chance of the predator finding a single fish swimming alone. Schooling is advantageous to the individual fish because a predator's chance of finding any particular fish swimming in the school is much smaller than its chance of finding at least one of the same group of fish if the fish were dispersed throughout an area.

However, critics of theory A point out that some fish form schools even in areas where predators are abundant and thus little possibility of escaping detection exists. They argue that the school continues to be of value to its members even after detection. They advocate theory B, the "confusion effect," which can be explained in two different ways.

Sometimes, proponents argue, predators simply cannot decide which fish to attack. This indecision supposedly results from a predator's preference for striking prey that is distinct from the rest of the school in appearance. In many schools the fish are almost identical in appearance, making it difficult for a predator to select one. The second explanation for the "confusion effect" has to do with the sensory confusion caused by a large number of prey moving around the predator. Even if the predator makes the decision to attack a particular fish, the movement of other prey in the school can be distracting. The predator's difficulty can be compared to that of a tennis player trying to hit a tennis ball when two are approaching simultaneously.

Questions 405–408 refer to the passage.

405. According to the passage, theory B states that which of the following is a factor that enables a schooling fish to escape predators?

(A) The tendency of fish to form compact groups
(B) The movement of other fish within the school
(C) The inability of predators to detect schools
(D) The ability of fish to hide behind one another in a school
(E) The great speed with which a school can disperse

406. According to the passage, both theory A and theory B have been developed to explain how

(A) fish hide from predators by forming schools
(B) forming schools functions to protect fish from predators
(C) schooling among fish differs from other protective behaviors
(D) small fish are able to make rapid decisions
(E) small fish are able to survive in an environment densely populated by large predators

407. According to one explanation of the "confusion effect," a fish that swims in a school will have greater advantages for survival if it

(A) tends to be visible for no more than 200 meters
(B) stays near either the front or the rear of a school
(C) is part of a small school rather than a large school
(D) is very similar in appearance to the other fish in the school
(E) is medium-sized

408. The author is primarily concerned with

(A) discussing different theories
(B) analyzing different techniques
(C) defending two hypotheses
(D) refuting established beliefs
(E) revealing new evidence

Scientists long believed that two nerve clusters in the human hypothalamus, called suprachiasmatic nuclei (SCNs), were what controlled our circadian rhythms. Those rhythms are the biological cycles that recur approximately every 24 hours in synchronization with the cycle of sunlight and darkness caused by Earth's rotation. Studies have demonstrated that in some animals, the SCNs control daily fluctuations in blood pressure, body temperature, activity level, and alertness, as well as the nighttime release of the sleep-promoting agent melatonin. Furthermore, cells in the human retina dedicated to transmitting information about light levels to the SCNs have recently been discovered.

Four critical genes governing circadian cycles have been found to be active in every tissue, however, not just the SCNs, of flies, mice, and humans. In addition, when laboratory rats that usually ate at will were fed only once a day, peak activity of a clock gene in their livers shifted by 12 hours, whereas the same clock gene in the SCNs remained synchronized with light cycles. While scientists do not dispute the role of the SCNs in controlling core functions such as the regulation of body temperature and blood pressure,. scientists now believe that circadian clocks in other organs and tissues may respond to external cues other than light—including temperature changes—that recur regularly every 24 hours.

Questions 409–411 refer to the passage.

409. The primary purpose of the passage is to

(A) challenge recent findings that appear to contradict earlier findings

(B) present two sides of an ongoing scientific debate

(C) report answers to several questions that have long puzzled researchers

(D) discuss evidence that has caused a long-standing belief to be revised

(E) attempt to explain a commonly misunderstood biological phenomenon

410. The passage mentions each of the following as a function regulated by the SCNs in some animals EXCEPT

(A) activity level

(B) blood pressure

(C) alertness

(D) vision

(E) temperature

411. The author of the passage would probably agree with which of the following statements about the SCNs?

(A) The SCNs are found in other organs and tissues of the body besides the hypothalamus.

(B) The SCNs play a critical but not exclusive role in regulating circadian rhythms.

(C) The SCNs control clock genes in a number of tissues and organs throughout the body.

(D) The SCNs are a less significant factor in regulating blood pressure than scientists once believed.

(E) The SCNs are less strongly affected by changes in light levels than they are by other external cues.

In their study of whether offering a guarantee of service quality will encourage customers to visit a particular restaurant, Tucci and Talaga have found that the effect of such guarantees is mixed. For higher-priced restaurants, there is some evidence that offering a guarantee increases the likelihood of customer selection, probably reflecting the greater financial commitment involved in choosing an expensive restaurant. For lower-priced restaurants, where one expects less assiduous service, Tucci and Talaga found that a guarantee could actually have a negative effect: a potential customer might think that a restaurant offering a guarantee is worried about its service. Moreover, since customers understand a restaurant's product and know what to anticipate in terms of service, they are empowered to question its quality. This is not generally true in the case of skilled activities such as electrical work, where, consequently, a guarantee might have greater customer appeal.

For restaurants generally, the main benefit of a service guarantee probably lies not so much in customer appeal as in managing and motivating staff. Staff members would know what service standards are expected of them and also know that the success of the business relies on their adhering to those standards. Additionally, guarantees provide some basis for defining the skills needed for successful service in areas traditionally regarded as unskilled, such as waiting tables.

Questions 412–414 refer to the passage.

412. The primary purpose of the passage is to

(A) question the results of a study that examined the effect of service-quality guarantees in the restaurant industry

(B) discuss potential advantages and disadvantages of service-quality guarantees in the restaurant industry

(C) examine the conventional wisdom regarding the effect of service-quality guarantees in the restaurant industry

(D) argue that only certain restaurants would benefit from the implementation of service-quality guarantees

(E) consider the impact that service-quality guarantees can have on the service provided by a restaurant

413. It can be inferred that the author of the passage would agree with which of the following statements about the appeal of service guarantees to customers?

(A) Such guarantees are likely to be somewhat more appealing to customers of restaurants than to customers of other businesses.

(B) Such guarantees are likely to be more appealing to customers who know what to anticipate in terms of service.

(C) Such guarantees are likely to have less appeal in situations where customers are knowledgeable about a business's product or service.

(D) In situations where a high level of financial commitment is involved, a service guarantee is not likely to be very appealing.

(E) In situations where customers expect a high level of customer service, a service guarantee is likely to make customers think that a business is worried about its service.

414. According to the passage, Tucci and Talaga found that service guarantees, when offered by lower-priced restaurants, can have which of the following effects?

(A) Customers' developing unreasonably high expectations regarding service

(B) Customers' avoiding such restaurants because they fear that the service guarantee may not be fully honored

(C) Customers' interpreting the service guarantee as a sign that management is not confident about the quality of its service

(D) A restaurant's becoming concerned that its service will not be assiduous enough to satisfy customers

(E) A restaurant's becoming concerned that customers will be more emboldened to question the quality of the service they receive

The argument for "monetizing"—or putting a monetary value on—ecosystem functions may be stated thus: Concern about the depletion of natural resources is widespread, but this concern, in the absence of an economic argument for conservation, has not translated into significant conservational progress. Some critics blame this impasse on environmentalists, whom they believe fail to address the economic issues of environmental degradation. Conservation can appear unprofitable when compared with the economic returns derived from converting natural assets (pristine coastlines, for example) into explicitly commercial ones (such as resort hotels). But according to David Pearce, that illusion stems from the fact that "services" provided by ecological systems are not traded on the commodities market, and thus have no readily *quantifiable* value. To remedy this, says Pearce, one has to show that all ecosystems have economic value—indeed, that all ecological services are economic services. Tourists visiting wildlife preserves, for example, create jobs and generate income for national economies; undisturbed forests and wetlands regulate water runoff and act as water-purifying systems, saving millions of dollars worth of damage to property and to marine ecosystems. In Gretchen Daily's view, monetization, while unpopular with many environmentalists, reflects the dominant role that economic considerations play in human behavior, and the expression of economic value in a common currency helps inform environmental decision-making processes.

Questions 415–418 refer to the passage.

415. Information in the passage suggests that David Pearce would most readily endorse which of the following statements concerning monetization?

(A) Monetization represents a strategy that is attractive to both environmentalists and their critics.

(B) Monetization is an untested strategy, but it is increasingly being embraced by environmentalists.

(C) Monetization should at present be restricted to ecological services and should only gradually be extended to such commercial endeavors as tourism and recreation.

(D) Monetization can serve as a means of representing persuasively the value of environmental conservation.

(E) Monetization should inform environmental decision-making processes only if it is accepted by environmentalist groups.

416. Which of the following most clearly represents an example of an "ecological service" as that term is used in line 20 ?

(A) A resort hotel located in an area noted for its natural beauty

(B) A water-purifying plant that supplements natural processes with nontoxic chemicals

(C) A wildlife preserve that draws many international travelers

(D) A nonprofit firm that specializes in restoring previously damaged ecosystems

(E) A newsletter that keeps readers informed of ecological victories and setbacks

417. According to the passage, Daily sees monetization as an indication of which of the following?

(A) The centrality of economic interests to people's actions
(B) The reluctance of the critics of environmentalism to acknowledge the importance of conservation
(C) The inability of financial interests and ecological interests to reach a common ideological ground
(D) The inevitability of environmental degradation
(E) The inevitability of the growth of ecological services in the future

418. Which of the following can be inferred from the passage concerning the environmentalists mentioned in line 8 ?

(A) They are organized in opposition to the generation of income produced by the sale of ecological services.
(B) They are fewer in number but better organized and better connected to the media than their opponents.
(C) They have sometimes been charged with failing to use a particular strategy in their pursuit of conservational goals.
(D) They have been in the forefront of publicizing the extent of worldwide environmental degradation.
(E) They define environmental progress differently and more conservatively than do other organized groups of environmentalists.

Much research has been devoted to investigating what motivates consumers to try new products. Previous consumer research suggests that both the price of a new product and the way it is advertised affect consumers' perceptions of the product's performance risk (the possibility that the product will not function as consumers expect and/or will not provide the desired benefits). Some of this research has concluded that a relatively high price will reduce a consumer's perception of the performance risk associated with purchasing a particular product, while other studies have reported that price has little or no effect on perceived performance risk. These conflicting findings may simply be due to the nature of product advertisements: a recent study indicates that the presentation of an advertised message has a marked effect on the relationship between price and perceived performance risk.

Researchers have identified consumers' perception of the credibility of the source of an advertised message—i.e., the manufacturer—as another factor affecting perceived performance risk: one study found that the greater the source credibility, the lower the consumer's perception of the risk of purchasing an advertised new product. However, past research suggests that the relationship between source credibility and perceived performance risk may be more complex: source credibility may interact with price in a subtle way to affect consumers' judgments of the performance risk associated with an advertised product.

Questions 419–422 refer to the passage.

419. According to the passage, the studies referred to in line 12 reported which of the following about the effect of price on consumers' perception of the performance risk associated with a new product?

(A) Although most consumers regard price as an important factor, their perception of the performance risk associated with a new product is ultimately determined by the manufacturer's reputation.

(B) Price interacts with the presentation of an advertised message to affect perceived performance risk.

(C) Price does not significantly affect consumers' perception of the performance risk associated with a new product.

(D) Consumers tend to regard price as more important than the manufacturer's credibility when they are buying from that manufacturer for the first time.

(E) Consumers are generally less concerned about a new product's performance risk when that product is relatively expensive.

420. The "past research" mentioned in line 25 suggests which of the following about perceived performance risk?

(A) The more expensive a new product is, the more likely consumers may be to credit advertised claims about that product.

(B) The more familiar consumers are with a particular manufacturer, the more willing they may be to assume some risk in the purchase of a new product being advertised by that manufacturer.

(C) Consumers' perception of the performance risk associated with a new product being advertised may be influenced by an interplay between the product's price and the manufacturer's credibility.

(D) Consumers may be more likely to believe that a product will function as it is advertised to do when they have bought products from a particular manufacturer before.

(E) The price of a particular advertised product may have less impact than the manufacturer's credibility on consumers' assessment of the performance risk associated with that product.

421. The passage is primarily concerned with

(A) challenging the implications of previous research into why consumers try new products
(B) suggesting new marketing strategies for attracting consumers to new products
(C) reconciling two different views about the effect of price on consumers' willingness to try new products
(D) describing a new approach to researching why consumers try new products
(E) discussing certain findings regarding why consumers try new products

422. Which of the following, if true, would most tend to weaken the conclusions drawn from "some of this research" (line 8)?

(A) In a subsequent study, consumers who were asked to evaluate new products with relatively low prices had the same perception of the products' performance risk as did consumers who were shown the same products priced more expensively.
(B) In a subsequent study, the quality of the advertising for the products that consumers perceived as having a lower performance risk was relatively high, while the quality of the advertising for the products that consumers perceived as having a higher performance risk was relatively poor.
(C) In a subsequent study, the products that consumers perceived as having a lower performance risk were priced higher than the highest priced products in the previous research.
(D) None of the consumers involved in this research had ever before bought products from the manufacturers involved in the research.
(E) Researchers found that the higher the source credibility for a product, the more consumers were willing to pay for it.

Historians remain divided over the role of banks in facilitating economic growth in the United States in the late eighteenth and early nineteenth centuries. Some scholars contend that banks played a minor role in the nation's growing economy. Financial institutions, they argue, appeared only after the economy had begun to develop, and once organized, followed conservative lending practices, providing aid to established commercial enterprises but shunning those, such as manufacturing and transportation projects, that were more uncertain and capital-intensive (i.e., requiring greater expenditures in the form of capital than in labor).

A growing number of historians argue, in contrast, that banks were crucial in transforming the early national economy. When state legislatures began granting more bank charters in the 1790s and early 1800s, the supply of credit rose accordingly. Unlike the earliest banks, which had primarily provided short-term loans to well-connected merchants, the banks of the early nineteenth century issued credit widely. As Paul Gilje asserts, the expansion and democratization of credit in the early nineteenth century became the driving force of the American economy, as banks began furnishing large amounts of capital to transportation and industrial enterprises. The exception, such historians argue, was in the South; here, the overwhelmingly agrarian nature of the economy generated outright opposition to banks, which were seen as monopolistic institutions controlled by an elite group of planters.

Questions 423–427 refer to the passage.

423. The primary purpose of the passage is to

(A) compare the economic role played by southern banks with the economic role played by banks in the rest of the United States during the late eighteenth and early nineteenth centuries

(B) reevaluate a conventional interpretation of the role played by banks in the American economy during the late eighteenth and early nineteenth centuries

(C) present different interpretations of the role played by banks in the American economy during the late eighteenth and early nineteenth centuries

(D) analyze how the increasing number of banks in the late eighteenth and early nineteenth centuries affected the American economy

(E) examine how scholarly opinion regarding the role played by banks in the American economy during the late eighteenth and early nineteenth centuries has changed over time

424. The passage suggests that the scholars mentioned in line 4 would argue that the reason banks tended not to fund manufacturing and transportation projects in the late eighteenth and early nineteenth centuries was that

(A) these projects, being well established and well capitalized, did not need substantial long-term financing from banks

(B) these projects entailed a level of risk that was too great for banks' conservative lending practices

(C) banks preferred to invest in other, more speculative projects that offered the potential for higher returns

(D) bank managers believed that these projects would be unlikely to contribute significantly to economic growth in the new country

(E) bank managers believed funding these projects would result in credit being extended to too many borrowers

425. The passage suggests that Paul Gilje would be most likely to agree with which of the following claims about the lending practices of the "earliest banks" (see line 21)?

(A) These lending practices were unlikely to generate substantial profits for banks.
(B) These lending practices only benefited a narrow sector of the economy.
(C) The restrictive nature of these lending practices generated significant opposition outside of the South.
(D) The restrictive nature of these lending practices forced state legislatures to begin granting more bank charters by the early nineteenth century.
(E) These lending practices were likely to be criticized by economic elites as being overly restrictive.

426. The passage suggests that the opposition to banks in the South in the early nineteenth century stemmed in part from the perception that banks

(A) did not benefit more than a small minority of the people
(B) did not support the interests of elite planters
(C) were too closely tied to transportation and industrial interests
(D) were unwilling to issue the long-term loans required by agrarian interests
(E) were too willing to lend credit widely

427. Which of the following statements best describes the function of the last sentence of the passage?

(A) It provides evidence tending to undermine the viewpoint of the scholars mentioned in line 5.
(B) It resolves a conflict over the role of banks summarized in the first paragraph.
(C) It clarifies some of the reasons state legislatures began granting more bank charters.
(D) It qualifies a claim made earlier in the passage about the impact of banks on the American economy in the early nineteenth century.
(E) It supports a claim made earlier in the passage about how the expansion of credit affected the economy.

Io and Europa, the inner two of Jupiter's four largest moons, are about the size of Earth's moon and are composed mostly or entirely of rock and metal. Ganymede and Callisto are larger and roughly half ice. Thus, these four moons are somewhat analogous to the planets of the solar system, in which the rock- and metal-rich inner planets are distinct from the much larger gas- and ice-rich outer planets. Jupiter's moons are, however, more "systematic": many of their properties vary continuously with distance from Jupiter. For example, Io is ice-free, Europa has a surface shell of ice, and while Ganymede and Callisto are both ice-rich, outermost Callisto has more.

This compositional gradient has geological parallels. Io is extremely geologically active, Europa seems to be active on a more modest scale, and Ganymede has undergone bouts of activity in its geological past. Only Callisto reveals no geological activity. In similar fashion, Callisto's surface is very heavily cratered from the impact of comets and asteroids; Ganymede, like Earth's moon, is heavily cratered in parts; Europa is very lightly cratered; and no craters have been detected on Io, even though Jupiter's gravity attracts comets and asteroids passing near it, substantially increasing the bombardment rate of the inner moons compared to that of the outer ones. But because of Io's high degree of geological activity, its surface undergoes more-or-less continuous volcanic resurfacing.

Questions 428–430 refer to the passage.

428. According to the passage, the difference in the amount of cratering on Callisto's and Io's respective surfaces can probably be explained by the difference between these two moons with respect to which of the following factors?

(A) Size

(B) Ice content

(C) The rate of bombardment by comets and asteroids

(D) The influence of Jupiter's other moons

(E) The level of geological activity

429. Which of the following best describes the purpose of the second paragraph of the passage?

(A) To provide further evidence of the systematic variation in the characteristics of Jupiter's four largest moons

(B) To present a comprehensive theory to explain the systematic variation in the characteristics of Jupiter's four largest moons

(C) To explain the significance of the systematic variation in the characteristics of Jupiter's four largest moons

(D) To introduce facts that contradict conventional assumptions about Jupiter's four largest moons

(E) To contrast the characteristics of Jupiter's four largest moons with the characteristics of the planets of the solar system

430. The author's reference to Jupiter's gravity in line 25 serves primarily to

(A) indicate why the absence of craters on Io's surface is surprising

(B) explain the presence of craters on the surface of Jupiter's four largest moons

(C) provide an explanation for the lack of geological activity on Callisto

(D) contrast Jupiter's characteristics with the characteristics of its four largest moons

(E) illustrate the similarity between Jupiter's four largest moons and the planets of the solar system

In an effort to explain why business acquisitions often fail, scholars have begun to focus on the role of top executives of acquired companies. Acquired companies that retain their top executives tend to have more successful outcomes than those that do not. Furthermore, existing research suggests that retaining the highest-level top executives, such as the CEO (chief executive officer) and COO (chief operating officer), is related more positively to postacquisition success than retaining lower-ranked top executives. However, this explanation, while insightful, suffers from two limitations. First, the focus on positional rank does not recognize the variation in length of service that may exist in top executive posts across companies, nor does it address which particular top executives (with respect to length of service) should be retained to achieve a successful acquisition outcome. Second, the relationship between retained top executives and acquisition outcomes offered by existing research is subject to opposing theoretical explanations related to length of service. The resource-based view (RBV) suggests that keeping acquired company top executives with longer organizational tenure would lead to more successful outcomes, as those executives have idiosyncratic and nontransferable knowledge of the acquired company that would be valuable for the effective implementation of the acquisition. The opposing position, offered by the upper echelons perspective (UEP), suggests that retaining top executives having short organizational tenure would lead to more successful outcomes, as they would have the adaptability to manage most effectively during the uncertainty of the acquisition process.

Responding to these limitations, Bergh conducted a study of executive retention and acquisition outcome that focused on the organizational tenure of retained company top executives in 104 acquisitions, followed over 5 years. Bergh considered the acquisition successful if the acquired company was retained and unsuccessful if it was divested. Bergh's findings support the RBV position. Apparently, the benefits of long organizational tenure lead to more successful outcomes than the benefits of short organizational tenure. While longer tenured top executives may have trouble adapting to change, it appears that their perspectives and knowledge bases offer unique value after the acquisition. Although from the UEP position it seems sensible to retain less tenured executives and allow more tenured ones to leave, such a strategy appears to lower the probability of acquisition success.

Questions 431–434 refer to the passage.

431. According to the passage, the research mentioned in line 6 suggests which of the following about lower-ranked top executives and postacquisition success?

(A) Given that these executives are unlikely to contribute to postacquisition success, little effort should be spent trying to retain them.

(B) The shorter their length of service, the less likely it is that these executives will play a significant role in postacquisition success.

(C) These executives are less important to postacquisition success than are more highly ranked top executives.

(D) If they have long tenures, these executives may prove to be as important to postacquisition success as are more highly ranked top executives.

(E) Postacquisition success is unlikely if these executives are retained.

432. The resource-based view, as described in the passage, is based on which of the following ideas?

(A) The managerial skills of top executives become strongest after the first five years of their tenure.

(B) Company-specific knowledge is an important factor in the success of an acquisition process.

(C) The amount of nontransferable knowledge possessed by long-tenured top executives tends to be underestimated.

(D) Effective implementation of an acquisition depends primarily on the ability of executives to adapt to change.

(E) Short-tenured executives are likely to impede the implementation of a successful acquisition strategy.

433. The passage suggests that Bergh and a proponent of the upper echelons perspective would be most likely to disagree over which of the following?

(A) Whether there is a positive correlation between short organizational tenure and managerial adaptability

(B) Whether there is a positive correlation between long organizational tenure and the acquisition of idiosyncratic and nontransferable knowledge

(C) Whether adaptability is a useful trait for an executive who is managing an acquisition process

(D) Whether retaining less-tenured top executives of an acquired company is an optimal strategy for achieving postacquisition success

(E) Whether retaining highest-level top executives of acquired companies is more important than retaining lower-ranked top executives

434. According to the passage, prior to Bergh's study, research on the role of top executives of acquired companies in business acquisition success was limited in which of the following ways?

(A) It did not address how the organizational tenure of top executives affects postacquisition success.

(B) It did not address why some companies have longer-tenured CEOs than others.

(C) It did not consider strategies for retaining long-tenured top executives of acquired companies.

(D) It failed to differentiate between the contribution of highest-level top executives to postacquisition success and that of lower-ranked top executives.

(E) It underestimated the potential contribution that lower-level top executives can make to postacquisition success.

Line When Jamaican-born social activist Marcus Garvey came to the United States in 1916, he arrived at precisely the right historical moment. What made the moment right was the return of African American soldiers from the First World War in 1918, which created an ideal constituency for someone with Garvey's message of unity, pride, and improved conditions for African American communities.

Hoping to participate in the traditional American ethos of individual success, many African American people entered the armed forces with enthusiasm, only to find themselves segregated from white troops and subjected to numerous indignities. They returned to a United States that was as segregated as it had been before the war. Considering similar experiences, anthropologist Anthony F. C. Wallace has argued that when a perceptible gap arises between a culture's expectations and the reality of that culture, the resulting tension can inspire a revitalization movement: an organized, conscious effort to construct a culture that fulfills long-standing expectations.

Some scholars have argued that Garvey created the consciousness from which he built, in the 1920s, the largest revitalization movement in African American history. But such an argument only tends to obscure the consciousness of identity, strength, and sense of history that already existed in the African American community. Garvey did not create this consciousness; rather, he gave this consciousness its political expression.

Questions 435–438 refer to the passage.

435. According to the passage, which of the following contributed to Marcus Garvey's success?

(A) He introduced cultural and historical consciousness to the African American community.

(B) He believed enthusiastically in the traditional American success ethos.

(C) His audience had already formed a consciousness that made it receptive to his message.

(D) His message appealed to critics of African American support for United States military involvement in the First World War.

(E) He supported the movement to protest segregation that had emerged prior to his arrival in the United States.

436. The passage suggests that many African American people responded to their experiences in the armed forces in which of the following ways?

(A) They maintained as civilians their enthusiastic allegiance to the armed forces.

(B) They questioned United States involvement in the First World War.

(C) They joined political organizations to protest the segregation of African American troops and the indignities they suffered in the military.

(D) They became aware of the gap between their expectations and the realities of American culture.

(E) They repudiated Garvey's message of pride and unity.

437. It can be inferred from the passage that the "scholars" mentioned in line 24 believe which of the following to be true?

(A) Revitalization resulted from the political activism of returning African American soldiers following the First World War.

(B) Marcus Garvey had to change a number of prevailing attitudes in order for his mass movement to find a foothold in the United States.

(C) The prevailing sensibility of the African American community provided the foundation of Marcus Garvey's political appeal.

(D) Marcus Garvey hoped to revitalize consciousness of cultural and historical identity in the African American community.

(E) The goal of the mass movement that Marcus Garvey helped bring into being was to build on the pride and unity among African Americans.

438. According to the passage, many African American people joined the armed forces during the First World War for which of the following reasons?

(A) They wished to escape worsening economic conditions in African American communities.

(B) They expected to fulfill ideals of personal attainment.

(C) They sought to express their loyalty to the United States.

(D) They hoped that joining the military would help advance the cause of desegregation.

(E) They saw military service as an opportunity to fulfill Marcus Garvey's political vision.

In the Sonoran Desert of northwestern Mexico and southern Arizona, the flowers of several species of columnar cacti—cardon, saguaro, and organ pipe—were once exclusively pollinated at night by nectar-feeding bats, as their close relatives in arid tropical regions of southern Mexico still are. In these tropical regions, diurnal (daytime) visitors to columnar cactus flowers are ineffective pollinators because, by sunrise, the flowers' stigmas become unreceptive or the flowers close. Yet the flowers of the Sonoran Desert cacti have evolved to remain open after sunrise, allowing pollination by such diurnal visitors as bees and birds. Why have these cacti expanded their range of pollinators by remaining open and receptive in daylight?

This development at the northernmost range of columnar cacti may be due to a yearly variation in the abundance—and hence the reliability—of migratory nectar-feeding bats. Pollinators can be unreliable for several reasons. They can be dietary generalists whose fidelity to a particular species depends on the availability of alternative food sources. Or, they can be dietary specialists, but their abundance may vary widely from year to year, resulting in variable pollination of their preferred food species. Finally, they may be dietary specialists, but their abundance may be chronically low relative to the availability of flowers.

Recent data reveals that during spring in the Sonoran Desert, the nectar-feeding bats are specialists feeding on cardon, saguaro, and organpipe flowers. However, whereas cactus-flower abundance tends to be high during spring, bat population densities tend to be low except near maternity roosts. Moreover, in spring, diurnal cactus-pollinating birds are significantly more abundant in this region than are the nocturnal bats. Thus, with bats being unreliable cactus-flower pollinators, and daytime pollinators more abundant and therefore more reliable, selection favors the cactus flowers with traits that increase their range of pollinators. While data suggest that population densities of nectar-feeding bats are also low in tropical areas of southern Mexico, where bats are the exclusive pollinators of many species of columnar cacti, cactus-flower density and bat population density appear to be much more evenly balanced there: compared with the Sonoran Desert's cardon and saguaro, columnar cacti in southern Mexico produce far fewer flowers per night. Accordingly, despite their low population density, bats are able to pollinate nearly 100 percent of the available flowers.

Questions 439–441 refer to the passage.

439. The primary purpose of the passage is to

(A) compare the adaptive responses of several species of columnar cacti in the Sonoran Desert with those in the arid tropical regions of southern Mexico
(B) discuss some of the possible causes of the relatively low abundance of migratory nectar-feeding bats in the Sonoran Desert
(C) provide a possible explanation for a particular evolutionary change in certain species of columnar cacti in the Sonoran Desert
(D) present recent findings that challenge a particular theory as to why several species of columnar cacti in the Sonoran Desert have expanded their range of pollinators
(E) compare the effectiveness of nocturnal and diurnal pollination for several different species of columnar cacti in the Sonoran Desert

440. According to the passage, which of the following types of nectar-feeding pollinators is likely to be an unreliable pollinator of a particular cactus flower?

(A) A dietary specialist whose abundance is typically high in relation to that of the flower
(B) A dietary specialist whose abundance is at times significantly lower than that of the flower
(C) A dietary generalist for whom that flower's nectar is not a preferred food but is the most consistently available food
(D) A dietary generalist for whom that flower's nectar is slightly preferred to other available foods
(E) A dietary generalist that evolved from a species of dietary specialists

441. According to the passage, present-day columnar cacti in the Sonoran Desert differ from their close relatives in southern Mexico in that the Sonoran cacti

(A) have flowers that remain open after sunset
(B) are pollinated primarily by dietary specialists
(C) can be pollinated by nectar-feeding bats
(D) have stigmas that are unreceptive to pollination at night
(E) are sometimes pollinated by diurnal pollinators

In terrestrial environments, gravity places special demands on the cardiovascular systems of animals. Gravitational pressure can cause blood to pool in the lower regions of the body, making it difficult to circulate blood to critical organs such as the brain. Terrestrial snakes, in particular, exhibit adaptations that aid in circulating blood against the force of gravity.

The problem confronting terrestrial snakes is best illustrated by what happens to sea snakes when removed from their supportive medium. Because the vertical pressure gradients within the blood vessels are counteracted by similar pressure gradients in the surrounding water, the distribution of blood throughout the body of sea snakes remains about the same regardless of their orientation in space, provided they remain in the ocean. When removed from the water and tilted at various angles with the head up, however, blood pressure at their midpoint drops significantly, and at brain level falls to zero. That many terrestrial snakes in similar spatial orientations do not experience this kind of circulatory failure suggests that certain adaptations enable them to regulate blood pressure more effectively in those orientations.

One such adaptation is the closer proximity of the terrestrial snake's heart to its head, which helps to ensure circulation to the brain, regardless of the snake's orientation in space. The heart of sea snakes can be located near the middle of the body, a position that minimizes the work entailed in circulating blood to both extremities. In arboreal snakes, however, which dwell in trees and often assume a vertical posture, the average distance from the heart to the head can be as little as 15 percent of overall body length. Such a location requires that blood circulated to the tail of the snake travel a greater distance back to the heart, a problem solved by another adaptation. When climbing, arboreal snakes often pause momentarily to wiggle their bodies, causing waves of muscle contraction that advance from the lower torso to the head. By compressing the veins and forcing blood forward, these contractions apparently improve the flow of venous blood returning to the heart.

Questions 442–449 refer to the passage.

442. The passage provides information in support of which of the following assertions?

(A) The disadvantages of an adaptation to a particular feature of an environment often outweigh the advantages of such an adaptation.

(B) An organism's reaction to being placed in an environment to which it is not well adapted can sometimes illustrate the problems that have been solved by the adaptations of organisms indigenous to that environment.

(C) The effectiveness of an organism's adaptation to a particular feature of its environment can only be evaluated by examining the effectiveness with which organisms of other species have adapted to a similar feature of a different environment.

(D) Organisms of the same species that inhabit strikingly different environments will often adapt in remarkably similar ways to the few features of those environments that are common.

(E) Different species of organisms living in the same environment will seldom adapt to features of that environment in the same way.

443. According to the passage, one reason that the distribution of blood in the sea snake changes little while the creature remains in the ocean is that

(A) the heart of the sea snake tends to be located near the center of its body

(B) pressure gradients in the water surrounding the sea snake counter the effects of vertical pressure gradients within its blood vessels

(C) the sea snake assumes a vertical posture less frequently than do the terrestrial and the arboreal snake

(D) the sea snake often relies on waves of muscle contractions to help move blood from the torso to the head

(E) the force of pressure gradients in the water surrounding the sea snake exceeds that of vertical pressure gradients within its circulatory system

444. It can be inferred from the passage that which of the following is true of species of terrestrial snakes that often need to assume a vertical posture?

(A) They are more likely to be susceptible to circulatory failure in vertical postures than are sea snakes.

(B) Their hearts are less likely to be located at the midpoint of their bodies than is the case with sea snakes.

(C) They cannot counteract the pooling of blood in lower regions of their bodies as effectively as sea snakes can.

(D) The blood pressure at their midpoint decreases significantly when they are tilted with their heads up.

(E) They are unable to rely on muscle contractions to move venous blood from the lower torso to the head.

445. The author describes the behavior of the circulatory system of sea snakes when they are removed from the ocean (see lines 17–20) primarily in order to

(A) illustrate what would occur in the circulatory system of terrestrial snakes without adaptations that enable them to regulate their blood pressure in vertical orientations
(B) explain why arboreal snakes in vertical orientations must rely on muscle contractions to restore blood pressure to the brain
(C) illustrate the effects of circulatory failure on the behavior of arboreal snakes
(D) illustrate the superiority of the circulatory system of the terrestrial snake to that of the sea snake
(E) explain how changes in spatial orientation can adversely affect the circulatory system of snakes with hearts located in relatively close proximity to their heads

446. It can be inferred from the passage that which of the following is a true statement about sea snakes?

(A) They frequently rely on waves of muscle contractions from the lower torso to the head to supplement the work of the heart.
(B) They cannot effectively regulate their blood pressure when placed in seawater and tilted at an angle with the head pointed downward.
(C) They are more likely to have a heart located in close proximity to their heads than are arboreal snakes.
(D) They become acutely vulnerable to the effects of gravitational pressure on their circulatory system when they are placed in a terrestrial environment.
(E) Their cardiovascular system is not as complicated as that of arboreal snakes.

447. The author suggests that which of the following is a disadvantage that results from the location of a snake's heart in close proximity to its head?

(A) A decrease in the efficiency with which the snake regulates the flow of blood to the brain
(B) A decrease in the number of orientations in space that a snake can assume without loss of blood flow to the brain
(C) A decrease in blood pressure at the snake's midpoint when it is tilted at various angles with its head up
(D) An increase in the tendency of blood to pool at the snake's head when the snake is tilted at various angles with its head down
(E) An increase in the amount of effort required to distribute blood to and from the snake's tail

448. The primary purpose of the third paragraph is to

(A) introduce a topic that is not discussed earlier in the passage
(B) describe a more efficient method of achieving an effect discussed in the previous paragraph
(C) draw a conclusion based on information elaborated in the previous paragraph
(D) discuss two specific examples of phenomena mentioned at the end of the previous paragraph
(E) introduce evidence that undermines a view reported earlier in the passage

449. In the passage, the author is primarily concerned with doing which of the following?

(A) Explaining adaptations that enable the terrestrial snake to cope with the effects of gravitational pressure on its circulatory system

(B) Comparing the circulatory system of the sea snake with that of the terrestrial snake

(C) Explaining why the circulatory system of the terrestrial snake is different from that of the sea snake

(D) Pointing out features of the terrestrial snake's cardiovascular system that make it superior to that of the sea snake

(E) Explaining how the sea snake is able to neutralize the effects of gravitational pressure on its circulatory system

Current feminist theory, in validating women's own stories of their experience, has encouraged scholars of women's history to view the use of women's oral narratives as the methodology, next to the use of women's written autobiography, that brings historians closest to the "reality" of women's lives. Such narratives, unlike most standard histories, represent experience from the perspective of women, affirm the importance of women's contributions, and furnish present-day women with historical continuity that is essential to their identity, individually and collectively.

Scholars of women's history should, however, be as cautious about accepting oral narratives at face value as they already are about written memories. Oral narratives are no more likely than are written narratives to provide a disinterested commentary on events or people. Moreover, the stories people tell to explain themselves are shaped by narrative devices and storytelling conventions, as well as by other cultural and historical factors, in ways that the storytellers may be unaware of. The political rhetoric of a particular era, for example, may influence women's interpretations of the significance of their experience. Thus a woman who views the Second World War as pivotal in increasing the social acceptance of women's paid work outside the home may reach that conclusion partly and unwittingly because of wartime rhetoric encouraging a positive view of women's participation in such work.

Questions 450–455 refer to the passage.

450. The passage is primarily concerned with

(A) contrasting the benefits of one methodology with the benefits of another
(B) describing the historical origins and inherent drawbacks of a particular methodology
(C) discussing the appeal of a particular methodology and some concerns about its use
(D) showing that some historians' adoption of a particular methodology has led to criticism of recent historical scholarship
(E) analyzing the influence of current feminist views on women's interpretations of their experience

451. According to the passage, which of the following shapes the oral narratives of women storytellers?

(A) The conventions for standard histories in the culture in which a woman storyteller lives
(B) The conventions of storytelling in the culture in which a woman storyteller lives
(C) A woman storyteller's experience with distinctive traditions of storytelling developed by the women in her family of origin
(D) The cultural expectations and experiences of those who listen to oral narratives
(E) A woman storyteller's familiarity with the stories that members of other groups in her culture tell to explain themselves

452. The author of the passage would be most likely to make which of the following recommendations to scholars of women's history?

(A) They should take into account their own life experiences when interpreting the oral accounts of women's historical experiences.

(B) They should assume that the observations made in women's oral narratives are believed by the intended audience of the story.

(C) They should treat skeptically observations reported in oral narratives unless the observations can be confirmed in standard histories.

(D) They should consider the cultural and historical context in which an oral narrative was created before arriving at an interpretation of such a narrative.

(E) They should rely on information gathered from oral narratives only when equivalent information is not available in standard histories.

453. Which of the following best describes the function of the last sentence of the passage?

(A) It describes an event that historians view as crucial in recent women's history.

(B) It provides an example of how political rhetoric may influence the interpretations of experience reported in women's oral narratives.

(C) It provides an example of an oral narrative that inaccurately describes women's experience during a particular historical period.

(D) It illustrates the point that some women are more aware than others of the social forces that shape their oral narratives.

(E) It identifies the historical conditions that led to the social acceptance of women's paid work outside the home.

454. According to the passage, scholars of women's history should refrain from doing which of the following?

(A) Relying on traditional historical sources when women's oral narratives are unavailable

(B) Focusing on the influence of political rhetoric on women's perceptions to the exclusion of other equally important factors

(C) Attempting to discover the cultural and historical factors that influence the stories women tell

(D) Assuming that the conventions of women's written autobiographies are similar to the conventions of women's oral narratives

(E) Accepting women's oral narratives less critically than they accept women's written histories

455. According to the passage, each of the following is a difference between women's oral narratives and most standard histories EXCEPT:

(A) Women's oral histories validate the significance of women's achievements.

(B) Women's oral histories depict experience from the point of view of women.

(C) Women's oral histories acknowledge the influence of well-known women.

(D) Women's oral histories present today's women with a sense of their historical relationship to women of the past.

(E) Women's oral histories are crucial to the collective identity of today's women.

Manufacturers have to do more than build large manufacturing plants to realize economies of scale. It is true that as the capacity of a manufacturing operation rises, costs per unit of output fall as plant size approaches "minimum efficient scale," where the cost per unit of output reaches a minimum, determined roughly by the state of existing technology and size of the potential market. However, minimum efficient scale cannot be fully realized unless a steady "throughput" (the flow of materials through a plant) is attained. The throughput needed to maintain the optimal scale of production requires careful coordination not only of the flow of goods through the production process, but also of the flow of input from suppliers and the flow of output to wholesalers and final consumers. If throughput falls below a critical point, unit costs rise sharply and profits disappear. A manufacturer's fixed costs and "sunk costs" (original capital investment in the physical plant) do not decrease when production declines due to inadequate supplies of raw materials, problems on the factory floor, or inefficient sales networks. Consequently, potential economies of scale are based on the physical and engineering characteristics of the production facilities—that is, on tangible capital—but realized economies of scale are operational and organizational, and depend on knowledge, skills, experience, and teamwork—that is, on organized human capabilities, or intangible capital.

The importance of investing in intangible capital becomes obvious when one looks at what happens in new capital-intensive manufacturing industries. Such industries are quickly dominated, not by the first firms to acquire technologically sophisticated plants of theoretically optimal size, but rather by the first to exploit the full potential of such plants. Once some firms achieve this, a market becomes extremely hard to enter. Challengers must construct comparable plants and do so after the first movers have already worked out problems with suppliers or with new production processes. Challengers must create distribution networks and marketing systems in markets where first movers have all the contacts and know-how. And challengers must recruit management teams to compete with those that have already mastered these functional and strategic activities.

Questions 456–460 refer to the passage.

456. The passage suggests that in order for a manufacturer in a capital-intensive industry to have a decisive advantage over competitors making similar products, the manufacturer must

(A) be the first in the industry to build production facilities of theoretically optimal size

(B) make every effort to keep fixed and sunk costs as low as possible

(C) be one of the first to operate its manufacturing plants at minimum efficient scale

(D) produce goods of higher quality than those produced by direct competitors

(E) stockpile raw materials at production sites in order to ensure a steady flow of such materials

457. The passage suggests that which of the following is true of a manufacturer's fixed and sunk costs?

(A) The extent to which they are determined by market conditions for the goods being manufactured is frequently underestimated.

(B) If they are kept as low as possible, the manufacturer is very likely to realize significant profits.

(C) They are the primary factor that determines whether a manufacturer will realize economies of scale.

(D) They should be on a par with the fixed and sunk costs of the manufacturer's competitors.

(E) They are not affected by fluctuations in a manufacturing plant's throughput.

458. In the context of the passage as a whole, the second paragraph serves primarily to

(A) provide an example to support the argument presented in the first paragraph

(B) evaluate various strategies discussed in the first paragraph

(C) introduce evidence that undermines the argument presented in the first paragraph

(D) anticipate possible objections to the argument presented in the first paragraph

(E) demonstrate the potential dangers of a commonly used strategy

459. The passage LEAST supports the inference that a manufacturer's throughput could be adversely affected by

(A) a mistake in judgment regarding the selection of a wholesaler
(B) a breakdown in the factory's machinery
(C) a labor dispute on the factory floor
(D) an increase in the cost per unit of output
(E) a drop in the efficiency of the sales network

460. The primary purpose of the passage is to

(A) point out the importance of intangible capital for realizing economies of scale in manufacturing
(B) show that manufacturers frequently gain a competitive advantage from investment in large manufacturing facilities
(C) argue that large manufacturing facilities often fail because of inadequate investment in both tangible and intangible capital
(D) suggest that most new industries are likely to be dominated by firms that build large manufacturing plants early
(E) explain why large manufacturing plants usually do not help manufacturers achieve economies of scale

A small number of the forest species of lepidoptera (moths and butterflies, which exist as caterpillars during most of their life cycle) exhibit regularly recurring patterns of population growth and decline—such fluctuations in population are known as population cycles. Although many different variables influence population levels, a regular pattern such as a population cycle seems to imply a dominant, driving force. Identification of that driving force, however, has proved surprisingly elusive despite considerable research. The common approach of studying causes of population cycles by measuring the mortality caused by different agents, such as predatory birds or parasites, has been unproductive in the case of lepidoptera. Moreover, population ecologists' attempts to alter cycles by changing the caterpillars' habitat and by reducing caterpillar populations have not succeeded. In short, the evidence implies that these insect populations, if not self-regulating, may at least be regulated by an agent more intimately connected with the insect than are predatory birds or parasites.

Recent work suggests that this agent may be a virus. For many years, viral disease had been reported in declining populations of caterpillars, but population ecologists had usually considered viral disease to have contributed to the decline once it was underway rather than to have initiated it. The recent work has been made possible by new techniques of molecular biology that allow viral DNA to be detected at low concentrations in the environment. Nuclear polyhedrosis viruses are hypothesized to be the driving force behind population cycles in lepidoptera in part because the viruses themselves follow an infectious cycle in which, if protected from direct sunlight, they may remain virulent for many years in the environment, embedded in durable crystals of polyhedrin protein. Once ingested by a caterpillar, the crystals dissolve, releasing the virus to infect the insect's cells. Late in the course of the infection, millions of new virus particles are formed and enclosed in polyhedrin crystals. These crystals reenter the environment after the insect dies and decomposes, thus becoming available to infect other caterpillars.

One of the attractions of this hypothesis is its broad applicability. Remarkably, despite significant differences in habitat and behavior, many species of lepidoptera have population cycles of similar length, between eight and eleven years. Nuclear polyhedrosis viral infection is one factor these disparate species share.

Questions 461–466 refer to the passage.

461. The primary purpose of the passage is to

(A) describe the development of new techniques that may help to determine the driving force behind population cycles in lepidoptera

(B) present evidence that refutes a particular theory about the driving force behind population cycles in lepidoptera

(C) present a hypothesis about the driving force behind population cycles in lepidoptera

(D) describe the fluctuating patterns of population cycles in lepidoptera

(E) question the idea that a single driving force is behind population cycles in lepidoptera

462. It can be inferred from the passage that the mortality caused by agents such as predatory birds or parasites was measured in an attempt to

(A) develop an explanation for the existence of lepidoptera population cycles

(B) identify behavioral factors in lepidoptera that affect survival rates

(C) identify possible methods for controlling lepidoptera population growth

(D) provide evidence that lepidoptera populations are self-regulating

(E) determine the life stages of lepidoptera at which mortality rates are highest

463. Which of the following, if true, would most weaken the author's conclusion in lines 18–22 ?

(A) New research reveals that the number of species of birds and parasites that prey on lepidoptera has dropped significantly in recent years.

(B) New experiments in which the habitats of lepidoptera are altered in previously untried ways result in the shortening of lepidoptera population cycles.

(C) Recent experiments have revealed that the nuclear polyhedrosis virus is present in a number of predators and parasites of lepidoptera.

(D) Differences among the habitats of lepidoptera species make it difficult to assess the effects of weather on lepidoptera population cycles.

(E) Viral disease is typically observed in a large proportion of the lepidoptera population.

464. According to the passage, before the discovery of new techniques for detecting viral DNA, population ecologists believed that viral diseases

(A) were not widely prevalent among insect populations generally

(B) affected only the caterpillar life stage of lepidoptera

(C) were the driving force behind lepidoptera population cycles

(D) attacked already declining caterpillar populations

(E) infected birds and parasites that prey on various species of lepidoptera

465. According to the passage, nuclear polyhedrosis viruses can remain virulent in the environment only when

(A) the polyhedrin protein crystals dissolve

(B) caterpillar populations are in decline

(C) they are present in large numbers

(D) their concentration in a particular area remains low

(E) they are sheltered from direct sunlight

466. It can be inferred from the passage that while inside its polyhedrin protein crystals, the nuclear polyhedrosis virus

(A) is exposed to direct sunlight

(B) is attractive to predators

(C) cannot infect caterpillars' cells

(D) cannot be ingested by caterpillars

(E) cannot be detected by new techniques of molecular biology

Resin is a plant secretion that hardens when exposed to air; fossilized resin is called amber. Although Pliny in the first century recognized that amber was produced from "marrow discharged by trees," amber has been widely misunderstood to be a semiprecious gem and has even been described in mineralogy textbooks. Confusion also persists surrounding the term "resin," which was defined before rigorous chemical analyses were available. Resin is often confused with gum, a substance produced in plants in response to bacterial infections, and with sap, an aqueous solution transported through certain plant tissues. Resin differs from both gum and sap in that scientists have not determined a physiological function for resin.

In the 1950s, entomologists posited that resin may function to repel or attract insects. Fraenkel conjectured that plants initially produced resin in nonspecific chemical responses to insect attack and that, over time, plants evolved that produced resin with specific repellent effects. But some insect species, he noted, might overcome the repellent effects, actually becoming attracted to the resin. This might induce the insects to feed on those plants or aid them in securing a breeding site. Later researchers suggested that resin mediates the complex interdependence, or "coevolution," of plants and insects over time. Such ideas led to the development of the specialized discipline of chemical ecology, which is concerned with the role of plant chemicals in interactions with other organisms and with the evolution and ecology of plant antiherbivore chemistry (plants' chemical defenses against attack by herbivores such as insects).

Questions 467–470 refer to the passage.

467. According to the passage, which of the following is true of plant antiherbivore chemistry?

(A) Changes in a plant's antiherbivore chemistry may affect insect feeding behavior.

(B) A plant's repellent effects often involve interactions between gum and resin.

(C) A plant's antiherbivore responses assist in combating bacterial infections.

(D) Plant antiherbivore chemistry plays only a minor role in the coevolution of plants and insects.

(E) Researchers first studied repellent effects in plants beginning in the 1950s.

468. Of the following topics, which would be most likely to be studied within the discipline of chemical ecology as it is described in the passage?

(A) Seeds that become attached to certain insects, which in turn carry away the seeds and aid in the reproductive cycle of the plant species in question

(B) An insect species that feeds on weeds detrimental to crop health and yield, and how these insects might aid in agricultural production

(C) The effects of deforestation on the life cycles of subtropical carnivorous plants and the insect species on which the plants feed

(D) The growth patterns of a particular species of plant that has proved remarkably resistant to herbicides

(E) Insects that develop a tolerance for feeding on a plant that had previously been toxic to them, and the resultant changes within that plant species

469. The author refers to "bacterial infections" (see line 11) most likely in order to

(A) describe the physiological function that gum performs in plants

(B) demonstrate that sap is not the only substance that is transported through a plant's tissues

(C) explain how modern chemical analysis has been used to clarify the function of resin

(D) show that gum cannot serve as an effective defense against herbivores

(E) give an example of how confusion has arisen with regard to the nature of resin

470. The author of the passage refers to Pliny most probably in order to

(A) give an example of how the nature of amber has been misunderstood in the past

(B) show that confusion about amber has long been more pervasive than confusion about resin

(C) make note of the first known reference to amber as a semiprecious gem

(D) point out an exception to a generalization about the history of people's understanding of amber

(E) demonstrate that Pliny believed amber to be a mineral

During the 1980s, many economic historians studying Latin America focused on the impact of the Great Depression of the 1930s. Most of these historians argued that although the Depression began earlier in Latin America than in the United States, it was less severe in Latin America and did not significantly impede industrial growth there. The historians' argument was grounded in national government records concerning tax revenues and exports and in government-sponsored industrial censuses, from which historians have drawn conclusions about total manufacturing output and profit levels across Latin America. However, economic statistics published by Latin American governments in the early twentieth century are neither reliable nor consistent; this is especially true of manufacturing data, which were gathered from factory owners for taxation purposes and which therefore may well be distorted. Moreover, one cannot assume a direct correlation between the output level and the profit level of a given industry as these variables often move in opposite directions. Finally, national and regional economies are composed of individual firms and industries, and relying on general, sweeping economic indicators may mask substantial variations among these different enterprises. For example, recent analyses of previously unexamined data on textile manufacturing in Brazil and Mexico suggest that the Great Depression had a more severe impact on this Latin American industry than scholars had recognized.

Questions 471–473 refer to the passage.

471. The primary purpose of the passage is to

(A) compare the impact of the Great Depression on Latin America with its impact on the United States

(B) criticize a school of economic historians for failing to analyze the Great Depression in Latin America within a global context

(C) illustrate the risks inherent in comparing different types of economic enterprises to explain economic phenomena

(D) call into question certain scholars' views concerning the severity of the Great Depression in Latin America

(E) demonstrate that the Great Depression had a more severe impact on industry in Latin America than in certain other regions

472. Which of the following conclusions about the Great Depression is best supported by the passage?

(A) It did not impede Latin American industrial growth as much as historians had previously thought.

(B) It had a more severe impact on the Brazilian and the Mexican textile industries than it had on Latin America as a region.

(C) It affected the Latin American textile industry more severely than it did any other industry in Latin America.

(D) The overall impact on Latin American industrial growth should be reevaluated by economic historians.

(E) Its impact on Latin America should not be compared with its impact on the United States.

473. Which of the following, if true, would most strengthen the author's assertion regarding economic indicators in lines 25–27 ?

(A) During an economic depression, European textile manufacturers' profits rise while their industrial output remains steady.

(B) During a national economic recession, United States microchips manufacturers' profits rise sharply while United States steel manufacturers' profits plunge.

(C) During the years following a severe economic depression, textile manufacturers' output levels and profit levels increase in Brazil and Mexico but not in the rest of Latin America.

(D) Although Japanese industry as a whole recovers after an economic recession, it does not regain its previously high levels of production.

(E) While European industrial output increases in the years following an economic depression, total output remains below that of Japan or the United States.

Among the myths taken as fact by the environmental managers of most corporations is the belief that environmental regulations affect all competitors in a given industry uniformly. In reality, regulatory costs—and therefore compliance—fall unevenly, economically disadvantaging some companies and benefiting others. For example, a plant situated near a number of larger noncompliant competitors is less likely to attract the attention of local regulators than is an isolated plant, and less attention means lower costs.

Additionally, large plants can spread compliance costs such as waste treatment across a larger revenue base; on the other hand, some smaller plants may not even be subject to certain provisions such as permit or reporting requirements by virtue of their size. Finally, older production technologies often continue to generate toxic wastes that were not regulated when the technology was first adopted. New regulations have imposed extensive compliance costs on companies still using older industrial coal-fired burners that generate high sulfur dioxide and nitrogen oxide outputs, for example, whereas new facilities generally avoid processes that would create such waste products. By realizing that they have discretion and that not all industries are affected equally by environmental regulation, environmental managers can help their companies to achieve a competitive edge by anticipating regulatory pressure and exploring all possibilities for addressing how changing regulations will affect their companies specifically.

Questions 474–477 refer to the passage.

474. It can be inferred from the passage that a large plant might have to spend more than a similar but smaller plant on environmental compliance because the larger plant is

(A) more likely to attract attention from local regulators

(B) less likely to be exempt from permit and reporting requirements

(C) less likely to have regulatory costs passed on to it by companies that supply its raw materials

(D) more likely to employ older production technologies

(E) more likely to generate wastes that are more environmentally damaging than those generated by smaller plants

475. According to the passage, which of the following statements about sulfur dioxide and nitrogen oxide outputs is true?

(A) Older production technologies cannot be adapted so as to reduce production of these outputs as waste products.

(B) Under the most recent environmental regulations, industrial plants are no longer permitted to produce these outputs.

(C) Although these outputs are environmentally hazardous, some plants still generate them as waste products despite the high compliance costs they impose.

(D) Many older plants have developed innovative technological processes that reduce the amounts of these outputs generated as waste products.

(E) Since the production processes that generate these outputs are less costly than alternative processes, these less expensive processes are sometimes adopted despite their acknowledged environmental hazards.

476. Which of the following best describes the relationship of the statement about large plants (lines 12–17) to the passage as a whole?

(A) It presents a hypothesis that is disproved later in the passage.
(B) It highlights an opposition between two ideas mentioned in the passage.
(C) It provides examples to support a claim made earlier in the passage.
(D) It exemplifies a misconception mentioned earlier in the passage.
(E) It draws an analogy between two situations described in the passage.

477. The primary purpose of the passage is to

(A) address a widespread environmental management problem and suggest possible solutions
(B) illustrate varying levels of compliance with environmental regulation among different corporations
(C) describe the various alternatives to traditional methods of environmental management
(D) advocate increased corporate compliance with environmental regulation
(E) correct a common misconception about the impact of environmental regulations

Milankovitch proposed in the early twentieth century that the ice ages were caused by variations in the Earth's orbit around the Sun. For some time this theory was considered untestable, largely because there was no sufficiently precise chronology of the ice ages with which the orbital variations could be matched.

To establish such a chronology it is necessary to determine the relative amounts of land ice that existed at various times in the Earth's past. A recent discovery makes such a determination possible: relative land-ice volume for a given period can be deduced from the ratio of two oxygen isotopes, 16 and 18, found in ocean sediments. Almost all the oxygen in water is oxygen 16, but a few molecules out of every thousand incorporate the heavier isotope 18. When an ice age begins, the continental ice sheets grow, steadily reducing the amount of water evaporated from the ocean that will eventually return to it. Because heavier isotopes tend to be left behind when water evaporates from the ocean surfaces, the remaining ocean water becomes progressively enriched in oxygen 18. The degree of enrichment can be determined by analyzing ocean sediments of the period, because these sediments are composed of calcium carbonate shells of marine organisms, shells that were constructed with oxygen atoms drawn from the surrounding ocean. The higher the ratio of oxygen 18 to oxygen 16 in a sedimentary specimen, the more land ice there was when the sediment was laid down.

As an indicator of shifts in the Earth's climate, the isotope record has two advantages. First, it is a global record: there is remarkably little variation in isotope ratios in sedimentary specimens taken from different continental locations. Second, it is a more continuous record than that taken from rocks on land. Because of these advantages, sedimentary evidence can be dated with sufficient accuracy by radiometric methods to establish a precise chronology of the ice ages. The dated isotope record shows that the fluctuations in global ice volume over the past several hundred thousand years have a pattern: an ice age occurs roughly once every 100,000 years. These data have established a strong connection between variations in the Earth's orbit and the periodicity of the ice ages.

However, it is important to note that other factors, such as volcanic particulates or variations in the amount of sunlight received by the Earth, could potentially have affected the climate. The advantage of the Milankovitch theory is that it is testable; changes in the Earth's orbit can be calculated and dated by applying Newton's laws of gravity to progressively earlier configurations of the bodies in the solar system. Yet the lack of information about other possible factors affecting global climate does not make them unimportant.

Questions 478–483 refer to the passage.

478. In the passage, the author is primarily interested in

(A) suggesting an alternative to an outdated research method

(B) introducing a new research method that calls an accepted theory into question

(C) emphasizing the instability of data gathered from the application of a new scientific method

(D) presenting a theory and describing a new method to test that theory

(E) initiating a debate about a widely accepted theory

479. The author of the passage would be most likely to agree with which of the following statements about the Milankovitch theory?

(A) It is the only possible explanation for the ice ages.

(B) It is too limited to provide a plausible explanation for the ice ages, despite recent research findings.

(C) It cannot be tested and confirmed until further research on volcanic activity is done.

(D) It is one plausible explanation, though not the only one, for the ice ages.

(E) It is not a plausible explanation for the ice ages, although it has opened up promising possibilities for future research.

480. It can be inferred from the passage that the isotope record taken from ocean sediments would be less useful to researchers if which of the following were true?

(A) It indicated that lighter isotopes of oxygen predominated at certain times.
(B) It had far more gaps in its sequence than the record taken from rocks on land.
(C) It indicated that climate shifts did not occur every 100,000 years.
(D) It indicated that the ratios of oxygen 16 and oxygen 18 in ocean water were not consistent with those found in fresh water.
(E) It stretched back for only a million years.

481. According to the passage, which of the following is true of the ratios of oxygen isotopes in ocean sediments?

(A) They indicate that sediments found during an ice age contain more calcium carbonate than sediments formed at other times.
(B) They are less reliable than the evidence from rocks on land in determining the volume of land ice.
(C) They can be used to deduce the relative volume of land ice that was present when the sediment was laid down.
(D) They are more unpredictable during an ice age than in other climatic conditions.
(E) They can be used to determine atmospheric conditions at various times in the past.

482. It can be inferred from the passage that precipitation formed from evaporated ocean water has

(A) the same isotopic ratio as ocean water
(B) less oxygen 18 than does ocean water
(C) less oxygen 18 than has the ice contained in continental ice sheets
(D) a different isotopic composition than has precipitation formed from water on land
(E) more oxygen 16 than has precipitation formed from fresh water

483. It can be inferred from the passage that calcium carbonate shells

(A) are not as susceptible to deterioration as rocks
(B) are less common in sediments formed during an ice age
(C) are found only in areas that were once covered by land ice
(D) contain radioactive material that can be used to determine a sediment's isotopic composition
(E) reflect the isotopic composition of the water at the time the shells were formed

Two works published in 1984 demonstrate contrasting approaches to writing the history of United States women. Buel and Buel's biography of Mary Fish (1736–1818) makes little effort to place her story in the context of recent historiography on women. Lebsock, meanwhile, attempts not only to write the history of women in one southern community, but also to redirect two decades of historiographical debate as to whether women gained or lost status in the nineteenth century as compared with the eighteenth century. Although both books offer the reader the opportunity to assess this controversy regarding women's status, only Lebsock's deals with it directly. She examines several different aspects of women's status, helping to refine and resolve the issues. She concludes that while women gained autonomy in some areas, especially in the private sphere, they lost it in many aspects of the economic sphere. More importantly, she shows that the debate itself depends on frame of reference: in many respects, women lost power in relation to men, for example, as certain jobs (delivering babies, supervising schools) were taken over by men. Yet women also gained power in comparison with their previous status, owning a higher proportion of real estate, for example. In contrast, Buel and Buel's biography provides ample raw material for questioning the myth, fostered by some historians, of a colonial golden age in the eighteenth century but does not give the reader much guidance in analyzing the controversy over women's status.

Questions 484–489 refer to the passage.

484. The primary purpose of the passage is to

(A) examine two sides of a historiographical debate

(B) call into question an author's approach to a historiographical debate

(C) examine one author's approach to a historiographical debate

(D) discuss two authors' works in relationship to a historiographical debate

(E) explain the prevalent perspective on a historiographical debate

485. The author of the passage mentions the supervision of schools primarily in order to

(A) remind readers of the role education played in the cultural changes of the nineteenth century in the United States

(B) suggest an area in which nineteenth-century American women were relatively free to exercise power

(C) provide an example of an occupation for which accurate data about women's participation are difficult to obtain

(D) speculate about which occupations were considered suitable for United States women of the nineteenth century

(E) illustrate how the answers to questions about women's status depend on particular contexts

486. With which of the following characterizations of Lebsock's contribution to the controversy concerning women's status in the nineteenth-century United States would the author of the passage be most likely to agree?

(A) Lebsock has studied women from a formerly neglected region and time period.

(B) Lebsock has demonstrated the importance of frame of reference in answering questions about women's status.

(C) Lebsock has addressed the controversy by using women's current status as a frame of reference.

(D) Lebsock has analyzed statistics about occupations and property that were previously ignored.

(E) Lebsock has applied recent historiographical methods to the biography of a nineteenth-century woman.

487. According to the passage, Lebsock's work differs from Buel and Buel's work in that Lebsock's work

(A) uses a large number of primary sources

(B) ignores issues of women's legal status

(C) refuses to take a position on women's status in the eighteenth century

(D) addresses larger historiographical issues

(E) fails to provide sufficient material to support its claims

488. The passage suggests that Lebsock believes that compared to nineteenth-century American women, eighteenth-century American women were

(A) in many respects less powerful in relation to men

(B) more likely to own real estate

(C) generally more economically independent

(D) more independent in conducting their private lives

(E) less likely to work as school superintendents

489. The passage suggests that Buel and Buel's biography of Mary Fish provides evidence for which of the following views of women's history?

(A) Women have lost power in relation to men since the colonial era.

(B) Women of the colonial era were not as likely to be concerned with their status as were women in the nineteenth century.

(C) The colonial era was not as favorable for women as some historians have believed.

(D) Women had more economic autonomy in the colonial era than in the nineteenth century.

(E) Women's occupations were generally more respected in the colonial era than in the nineteenth century.

Acting on the recommendation of a British government committee investigating the high incidence in white lead factories of illness among employees, most of whom were women, the Home Secretary proposed in 1895 that Parliament enact legislation that would prohibit women from holding most jobs in white lead factories. Although the Women's Industrial Defence Committee (WIDC), formed in 1892 in response to earlier legislative attempts to restrict women's labor, did not discount the white lead trade's potential health dangers, it opposed the proposal, viewing it as yet another instance of limiting women's work opportunities.

Also opposing the proposal was the Society for Promoting the Employment of Women (SPEW), which attempted to challenge it by investigating the causes of illness in white lead factories. SPEW contended, and WIDC concurred, that controllable conditions in such factories were responsible for the development of lead poisoning. SPEW provided convincing evidence that lead poisoning could be avoided if workers were careful and clean and if already extant workplace safety regulations were stringently enforced. However, the Women's Trade Union League (WTUL), which had ceased in the late 1880s to oppose restrictions on women's labor, supported the eventually enacted proposal, in part because safety regulations were generally not being enforced in white lead factories, where there were no unions (and little prospect of any) to pressure employers to comply with safety regulations.

Questions 490–492 refer to the passage.

490. The passage suggests that WIDC differed from WTUL in which of the following ways?

(A) WIDC believed that the existing safety regulations were adequate to protect women's health, whereas WTUL believed that such regulations needed to be strengthened.

(B) WIDC believed that unions could not succeed in pressuring employers to comply with such regulations, whereas WTUL believed that unions could succeed in doing so.

(C) WIDC believed that lead poisoning in white lead factories could be avoided by controlling conditions there, whereas WTUL believed that lead poisoning in such factories could not be avoided no matter how stringently safety regulations were enforced.

(D) At the time that the legislation concerning white lead factories was proposed, WIDC was primarily concerned with addressing health conditions in white lead factories, whereas WTUL was concerned with improving working conditions in all types of factories.

(E) At the time that WIDC was opposing legislative attempts to restrict women's labor, WTUL had already ceased to do so.

491. Which of the following, if true, would most clearly support the contention attributed to SPEW in lines 17–20?

(A) Those white lead factories that most strongly enforced regulations concerning worker safety and hygiene had the lowest incidences of lead poisoning among employees.

(B) The incidence of lead poisoning was much higher among women who worked in white lead factories than among women who worked in other types of factories.

(C) There were many household sources of lead that could have contributed to the incidence of lead poisoning among women who also worked outside the home in the late nineteenth century.

(D) White lead factories were more stringent than were certain other types of factories in their enforcement of workplace safety regulations.

(E) Even brief exposure to the conditions typically found in white lead factories could cause lead poisoning among factory workers.

492. The passage is primarily concerned with

(A) presenting various groups' views of the motives of those proposing certain legislation

(B) contrasting the reasoning of various groups concerning their positions on certain proposed legislation

(C) tracing the process whereby certain proposed legislation was eventually enacted

(D) assessing the success of tactics adopted by various groups with respect to certain proposed legislation

(E) evaluating the arguments of various groups concerning certain proposed legislation

It is an odd but indisputable fact that the seventeenth-century English women who are generally regarded as among the forerunners of modern feminism are almost all identified with the Royalist side in the conflict between Royalists and Parliamentarians known as the English Civil Wars. Since Royalist ideology is often associated with the radical patriarchalism of seventeenth-century political theorist Robert Filmer—a patriarchalism that equates family and kingdom and asserts the divinely ordained absolute power of the king and, by analogy, of the male head of the household—historians have been understandably puzzled by the fact that Royalist women wrote the earliest extended criticisms of the absolute subordination of women in marriage and the earliest systematic assertions of women's rational and moral equality with men. Some historians have questioned the facile equation of Royalist ideology with Filmerian patriarchalism; and indeed, there may have been no consistent differences between Royalists and Parliamentarians on issues of family organization and women's political rights, but in that case one would expect early feminists to be equally divided between the two sides.

Catherine Gallagher argues that Royalism engendered feminism because the ideology of absolute monarchy provided a transition to an ideology of the absolute self. She cites the example of the notoriously eccentric author Margaret Cavendish (1626–1673), duchess of Newcastle. Cavendish claimed to be as ambitious as any woman could be, but knowing that as a woman she was excluded from the pursuit of power in the real world, she resolved to be mistress of her own world, the "immaterial world" that any person can create within her own mind—and, as a writer, on paper. In proclaiming what she called her "singularity," Cavendish insisted that she was a self-sufficient being within her mental empire, the center of her own subjective universe rather than a satellite orbiting a dominant male planet. In justifying this absolute singularity, Cavendish repeatedly invoked the model of the absolute monarch, a figure that became a metaphor for the self-enclosed, autonomous nature of the individual person. Cavendish's successors among early feminists retained her notion of woman's sovereign self, but they also sought to break free from the complete political and social isolation that her absolute singularity entailed.

Questions 493–498 refer to the passage.

493. The author of the passage refers to Robert Filmer (see line 9) primarily in order to

(A) show that Royalist ideology was somewhat more radical than most historians appear to realize

(B) qualify the claim that patriarchalism formed the basis of Royalist ideology

(C) question the view that most early feminists were associated with the Royalist faction

(D) highlight an apparent tension between Royalist ideology and the ideas of early feminists

(E) argue that Royalists held conflicting opinions on issues of family organization and women's political rights

494. The passage suggests which of the following about the seventeenth-century English women mentioned in line 2 ?

(A) Their status as forerunners of modern feminism is not entirely justified.

(B) They did not openly challenge the radical patriarchalism of Royalist Filmerian ideology.

(C) Cavendish was the first among these women to criticize women's subordination in marriage and assert women's equality with men.

(D) Their views on family organization and women's political rights were diametrically opposed to those of both Royalist and Parliamentarian ideology.

(E) Historians would be less puzzled if more of them were identified with the Parliamentarian side in the English Civil Wars.

495. The passage suggests that Margaret Cavendish's decision to become an author was motivated, at least in part, by a desire to .

(A) justify her support for the Royalist cause

(B) encourage her readers to work toward eradicating Filmerian patriarchalism

(C) persuade other women to break free from their political and social isolation

(D) analyze the causes for women's exclusion from the pursuit of power

(E) create a world over which she could exercise total control

496. The phrase "a satellite orbiting a dominant male planet" (lines 41–42) refers most directly to

(A) Cavendish's concept that each woman is a sovereign self

(B) the complete political and social isolation of absolute singularity

(C) the immaterial world that a writer can create on paper

(D) the absolute subordination of women in a patriarchal society

(E) the metaphorical figure of the absolute monarch

497. The primary purpose of the passage is to

(A) trace the historical roots of a modern sociopolitical movement

(B) present one scholar's explanation for a puzzling historical phenomenon

(C) contrast two interpretations of the ideological origins of a political conflict

(D) establish a link between the ideology of an influential political theorist and that of a notoriously eccentric writer

(E) call attention to some points of agreement between opposing sides in an ideological debate

498. Which of the following, if true, would most clearly undermine Gallagher's explanation of the link between Royalism and feminism?

(A) Because of their privileged backgrounds, Royalist women were generally better educated than were their Parliamentarian counterparts.

(B) Filmer himself had read some of Cavendish's early writings and was highly critical of her ideas.

(C) Cavendish's views were highly individual and were not shared by the other Royalist women who wrote early feminist works.

(D) The Royalist and Parliamentarian ideologies were largely in agreement on issues of family organization and women's political rights.

(E) The Royalist side included a sizable minority faction that was opposed to the more radical tendencies of Filmerian patriarchalism.

Line Frazier and Mosteller assert that medical research could be improved by a move toward larger, simpler clinical trials of medical treatments. Currently, researchers collect far more background information on patients than is strictly required for their trials—substantially more than hospitals collect—thereby escalating costs of data collection, storage, and analysis. Although limiting information collection could increase the risk that researchers will overlook facts relevant to a study, Frazier and Mosteller contend that such risk, never entirely eliminable from research, would still be small in most studies. Only in research on entirely new treatments are new and unexpected variables likely to arise.

Frazier and Mosteller propose not only that researchers limit data collection on individual patients but also that researchers enroll more patients in clinical trials, thereby obtaining a more representative sample of the total population with the disease under study. Often researchers restrict study participation to patients who have no ailments besides those being studied. A treatment judged successful under these ideal conditions can then be evaluated under normal conditions. Broadening the range of trial participants, Frazier and Mosteller suggest, would enable researchers to evaluate a treatment's efficacy for diverse patients under various conditions and to evaluate its effectiveness for different patient subgroups. For example, the value of a treatment for a progressive disease may vary according to a patient's stage of disease. Patients' ages may also affect a treatment's efficacy.

Questions 499–503 refer to the passage.

499. The passage is primarily concerned with

(A) identifying two practices in medical research that may affect the accuracy of clinical trials

(B) describing aspects of medical research that tend to drive up costs

(C) evaluating an analysis of certain shortcomings of current medical research practices

(D) describing proposed changes to the ways in which clinical trials are conducted

(E) explaining how medical researchers have traditionally conducted clinical trials and how such trials are likely to change

500. Which of the following can be inferred from the passage about a study of the category of patients referred to in lines 20–22 ?

(A) Its findings might have limited applicability.

(B) It would be prohibitively expensive in its attempt to create ideal conditions.

(C) It would be the best way to sample the total population of potential patients.

(D) It would allow researchers to limit information collection without increasing the risk that important variables could be overlooked.

(E) Its findings would be more accurate if it concerned treatments for a progressive disease than if it concerned treatments for a nonprogressive disease.

501. It can be inferred from the passage that a study limited to patients like those mentioned in lines 20–22 would have which of the following advantages over the kind of study proposed by Frazier and Mosteller?

(A) It would yield more data and its findings would be more accurate.

(B) It would cost less in the long term, though it would be more expensive in its initial stages.

(C) It would limit the number of variables researchers would need to consider when evaluating the treatment under study.

(D) It would help researchers to identify subgroups of patients with secondary conditions that might also be treatable.

(E) It would enable researchers to assess the value of an experimental treatment for the average patient.

502. The author mentions patients' ages (line 32) primarily in order to

(A) identify the most critical variable differentiating subgroups of patients

(B) cast doubt on the advisability of implementing Frazier and Mosteller's proposals about medical research

(C) indicate why progressive diseases may require different treatments at different stages

(D) illustrate a point about the value of enrolling a wide range of patients in clinical trials

(E) substantiate an argument about the problems inherent in enrolling large numbers of patients in clinical trials

503. According to the passage, which of the following describes a result of the way in which researchers generally conduct clinical trials?

(A) They expend resources on the storage of information likely to be irrelevant to the study they are conducting.

(B) They sometimes compromise the accuracy of their findings by collecting and analyzing more information than is strictly required for their trials.

(C) They avoid the risk of overlooking variables that might affect their findings, even though doing so raises their research costs.

(D) Because they attempt to analyze too much information, they overlook facts that could emerge as relevant to their studies.

(E) In order to approximate the conditions typical of medical treatment, they base their methods of information collection on those used by hospitals.

There are recent reports of apparently drastic declines in amphibian populations and of extinctions of a number of the world's endangered amphibian species. These declines, if real, may be signs of a general trend toward extinction, and many environmentalists have claimed that immediate environmental action is necessary to remedy this "amphibian crisis," which, in their view, is an indicator of general and catastrophic environmental degradation due to human activity.

To evaluate these claims, it is useful to make a preliminary distinction that is far too often ignored. A declining population should not be confused with an endangered one. An endangered population is always rare, almost always small, and, by definition, under constant threat of extinction even without a proximate cause in human activities. Its disappearance, however unfortunate, should come as no great surprise. Moreover, chance events—which may indicate nothing about the direction of trends in population size—may lead to its extinction. The probability of extinction due to such random factors depends on the population size and is independent of the prevailing direction of change in that size.

For biologists, population declines are potentially more worrisome than extinctions. Persistent declines, especially in large populations, indicate a changed ecological context. Even here, distinctions must again be made among declines that are only apparent (in the sense that they are part of habitual cycles or of normal fluctuations), declines that take a population to some lower but still acceptable level, and those that threaten extinction (e.g., by taking the number of individuals below the minimum viable population). Anecdotal reports of population decreases cannot distinguish among these possibilities, and some amphibian populations have shown strong fluctuations in the past.

It is indisputably true that there is simply not enough long-term scientific data on amphibian populations to enable researchers to identify real declines in amphibian populations. Many fairly common amphibian species declared all but extinct after severe declines in the 1950s and 1960s have subsequently recovered, and so might the apparently declining populations that have generated the current appearance of an amphibian crisis. Unfortunately, long-term data will not soon be forthcoming, and postponing environmental action while we wait for it may doom species and whole ecosystems to extinction.

Questions 504–509 refer to the passage.

504. The primary purpose of the passage is to

(A) assess the validity of a certain view
(B) distinguish between two phenomena
(C) identify the causes of a problem
(D) describe a disturbing trend
(E) allay concern about a particular phenomenon

505. It can be inferred from the passage that the author believes which of the following to be true of the environmentalists mentioned in lines 5–6 ?

(A) They have wrongly chosen to focus on anecdotal reports rather than on the long-term data that are currently available concerning amphibians.
(B) Their recommendations are flawed because their research focuses too narrowly on a single category of animal species.
(C) Their certainty that population declines in general are caused by environmental degradation is not warranted.
(D) They have drawn premature conclusions concerning a crisis in amphibian populations from recent reports of declines.
(E) They have overestimated the effects of chance events on trends in amphibian populations.

506. It can be inferred from the passage that the author believes which of the following to be true of the amphibian extinctions that have recently been reported?

(A) They have resulted primarily from human activities causing environmental degradation.
(B) They could probably have been prevented if timely action had been taken to protect the habitats of amphibian species.
(C) They should not come as a surprise, because amphibian populations generally have been declining for a number of years.
(D) They have probably been caused by a combination of chance events.
(E) They do not clearly constitute evidence of general environmental degradation.

507. According to the passage, each of the following is true of endangered amphibian species EXCEPT:

(A) They are among the rarest kinds of amphibians.
(B) They generally have populations that are small in size.
(C) They are in constant danger of extinction.
(D) Those with decreasing populations are the most likely candidates for immediate extinction.
(E) They are in danger of extinction due to events that sometimes have nothing to do with human activities.

508. Which of the following most accurately describes the organization of the passage?

(A) A question is raised, a distinction regarding it is made, and the question is answered.
(B) An interpretation is presented, its soundness is examined, and a warning is given.
(C) A situation is described, its consequences are analyzed, and a prediction is made.
(D) Two interpretations of a phenomenon are described, and one of them is rejected as invalid.
(E) Two methods for analyzing a phenomenon are compared, and further study of the phenomenon is recommended.

509. Which of the following best describes the function of the sentence in lines 35–38 ?

(A) To give an example of a particular kind of study
(B) To cast doubt on an assertion made in the previous sentence
(C) To raise an objection to a view presented in the first paragraph
(D) To provide support for a view presented in the first paragraph
(E) To introduce an idea that will be countered in the following paragraph

While the most abundant and dominant species within a particular ecosystem is often crucial in perpetuating the ecosystem, a "keystone" species, here defined as one whose effects are much larger than would be predicted from its abundance, can also play a vital role. But because complex species interactions may be involved, identifying a keystone species by removing the species and observing changes in the ecosystem is problematic. It might seem that certain traits would clearly define a species as a keystone species; for example, *Pisaster ochraceus* is often a keystone predator because it consumes and suppresses mussel populations, which in the absence of this starfish can be a dominant species. But such predation on a dominant or potentially dominant species occurs in systems that do as well as in systems that do not have species that play keystone roles. Moreover, whereas *P. ochraceus* occupies an unambiguous keystone role on wave-exposed rocky headlands, in more wave-sheltered habitats the impact of *P. ochraceus* predation is weak or nonexistent, and at certain sites sand burial is responsible for eliminating mussels. Keystone status appears to depend on context, whether of particular geography or of such factors as community diversity (for example, a reduction in species diversity may thrust more of the remaining species into keystone roles) and length of species interaction (since newly arrived species in particular may dramatically affect ecosystems).

Questions 510–513 refer to the passage.

510. The passage mentions which of the following as a factor that affects the role of *P. ochraceus* as a keystone species within different habitats?

(A) The degree to which the habitat is sheltered from waves
(B) The degree to which other animals within a habitat prey on mussels
(C) The fact that mussel populations are often not dominant within some habitats occupied by *P. ochraceus*
(D) The size of the *P. ochraceus* population within the habitat
(E) The fact that there is great species diversity within some habitats occupied by *P. ochraceus*

511. Which of the following hypothetical experiments most clearly exemplifies the method of identifying species' roles that the author considers problematic?

(A) A population of seals in an Arctic habitat is counted in order to determine whether it is the dominant species in that ecosystem.
(B) A species of fish that is a keystone species in one marine ecosystem is introduced into another marine ecosystem to see whether the species will come to occupy a keystone role.
(C) In order to determine whether a species of monkey is a keystone species within a particular ecosystem, the monkeys are removed from that ecosystem and the ecosystem is then studied.
(D) Different mountain ecosystems are compared to determine how geography affects a particular species' ability to dominate its ecosystem.
(E) In a grassland experiencing a changing climate, patterns of species extinction are traced in order to evaluate the effect of climate changes on keystone species in that grassland.

512. Which of the following, if true, would most clearly support the argument about keystone status advanced in the last sentence of the passage (lines 24–31)?

(A) A species of bat is primarily responsible for keeping insect populations within an ecosystem low, and the size of the insect population in turn affects bird species within that ecosystem.

(B) A species of iguana occupies a keystone role on certain tropical islands, but does not play that role on adjacent tropical islands that are inhabited by a greater number of animal species.

(C) Close observation of a savannah ecosystem reveals that more species occupy keystone roles within that ecosystem than biologists had previously believed.

(D) As a keystone species of bee becomes more abundant, it has a larger effect on the ecosystem it inhabits.

(E) A species of moth that occupies a keystone role in a prairie habitat develops coloration patterns that camouflage it from potential predators.

513. The passage suggests which of the following about the identification of a species as a keystone species?

(A) Such an identification depends primarily on the species' relationship to the dominant species.

(B) Such an identification can best be made by removing the species from a particular ecosystem and observing changes that occur in the ecosystem.

(C) Such an identification is likely to be less reliable as an ecosystem becomes less diverse.

(D) Such an identification seems to depend on various factors within the ecosystem.

(E) Such an identification can best be made by observing predation behavior.

Conodonts, the spiky phosphatic remains (bones and teeth composed of calcium phosphate) of tiny marine animals that probably appeared about 520 million years ago, were once among the most controversial of fossils. Both the nature of the organism to which the remains belonged and the function of the remains were unknown. However, since the 1981 discovery of fossils preserving not just the phosphatic elements but also other remains of the tiny soft-bodied animals (also called conodonts) that bore them, scientists' reconstructions of the animals' anatomy have had important implications for hypotheses concerning the development of the vertebrate skeleton.

The vertebrate skeleton had traditionally been regarded as a defensive development, champions of this view postulating that it was only with the much later evolution of jaws that vertebrates became predators. The first vertebrates, which were soft-bodied, would have been easy prey for numerous invertebrate carnivores, especially if these early vertebrates were sedentary suspension feeders. Thus, traditionalists argued, these animals developed coverings of bony scales or plates, and teeth were secondary features, adapted from the protective bony scales. Indeed, external skeletons of this type are common among the well-known fossils of ostracoderms, jawless vertebrates that existed from approximately 500 to 400 million years ago.

However, other paleontologists argued that many of the definitive characteristics of vertebrates, such as paired eyes and muscular and skeletal adaptations for active life, would not have evolved unless the first vertebrates were predatory. Teeth were more primitive than external armor according to this view, and the earliest vertebrates were predators.

The stiffening notochord along the back of the body, V-shaped muscle blocks along the sides, and posterior tail fins help to identify conodonts as among the most primitive of vertebrates. The lack of any mineralized structures apart from the elements in the mouth indicates that conodonts were more primitive than the armored jawless fishes such as the ostracoderms. It now appears that the hard parts that first evolved in the mouth of an animal improved its efficiency as a predator, and that aggression rather than protection was the driving force behind the origin of the vertebrate skeleton.

Questions 514–516 refer to the passage.

514. According to the passage, the anatomical evidence provided by the preserved soft bodies of conodonts led scientists to conclude that

(A) conodonts had actually been invertebrate carnivores

(B) conodonts' teeth were adapted from protective bony scales

(C) conodonts were primitive vertebrate suspension feeders

(D) primitive vertebrates with teeth appeared earlier than armored vertebrates

(E) scientists' original observations concerning the phosphatic remains of conodonts were essentially correct

515. The second paragraph in the passage serves primarily to

(A) outline the significance of the 1981 discovery of conodont remains to the debate concerning the development of the vertebrate skeleton

(B) contrast the traditional view of the development of the vertebrate skeleton with a view derived from the 1981 discovery of conodont remains

(C) contrast the characteristics of the ostracoderms with the characteristics of earlier soft-bodied vertebrates

(D) explain the importance of the development of teeth among the earliest vertebrate predators

(E) present the two sides of the debate concerning the development of the vertebrate skeleton

516. It can be inferred that on the basis of the 1981 discovery of conodont remains, paleontologists could draw which of the following conclusions?

(A) The earliest vertebrates were sedentary suspension feeders.

(B) Ostracoderms were not the earliest vertebrates.

(C) Defensive armor preceded jaws among vertebrates.

(D) Paired eyes and adaptations for activity are definitive characteristics of vertebrates.

(E) Conodonts were unlikely to have been predators.

Jon Clark's study of the effect of the modernization of a telephone exchange on exchange maintenance work and workers is a solid contribution to a debate that encompasses two lively issues in the history and sociology of technology: technological determinism and social constructivism.

Clark makes the point that the characteristics of a technology have a decisive influence on job skills and work organization. Put more strongly, technology can be a primary determinant of social and managerial organization. Clark believes this possibility has been obscured by the recent sociological fashion, exemplified by Braverman's analysis, that emphasizes the way machinery reflects social choices. For Braverman, the shape of a technological system is subordinate to the manager's desire to wrest control of the labor process from the workers. Technological change is construed as the outcome of negotiations among interested parties who seek to incorporate their own interests into the design and configuration of the machinery. This position represents the new mainstream called social constructivism.

The constructivists gain acceptance by misrepresenting technological determinism: technological determinists are supposed to believe, for example, that machinery imposes appropriate forms of order on society. The alternative to constructivism, in other words, is to view technology as existing outside society, capable of directly influencing skills and work organization.

Clark refutes the extremes of the constructivists by both theoretical and empirical arguments. Theoretically he defines "technology" in terms of relationships between social and technical variables. Attempts to reduce the meaning of technology to cold, hard metal are bound to fail, for machinery is just scrap unless it is organized functionally and supported by appropriate systems of operation and maintenance. At the empirical level Clark shows how a change at the telephone exchange from maintenance-intensive electromechanical switches to semielectronic switching systems altered work tasks, skills, training opportunities, administration, and organization of workers. Some changes Clark attributes to the particular way management and labor unions negotiated the introduction of the technology, whereas others are seen as arising from the capabilities and nature of the technology itself. Thus Clark helps answer the question: "When is social choice decisive and when are the concrete characteristics of technology more important?"

Questions 517–524 refer to the passage.

517. The primary purpose of the passage is to

(A) advocate a more positive attitude toward technological change

(B) discuss the implications for employees of the modernization of a telephone exchange

(C) consider a successful challenge to the constructivist view of technological change

(D) challenge the position of advocates of technological determinism

(E) suggest that the social causes of technological change should be studied in real situations

518. Which of the following statements about the modernization of the telephone exchange is supported by information in the passage?

(A) The new technology reduced the role of managers in labor negotiations.

(B) The modernization was implemented without the consent of the employees directly affected by it.

(C) The modernization had an impact that went significantly beyond maintenance routines.

(D) Some of the maintenance workers felt victimized by the new technology.

(E) The modernization gave credence to the view of advocates of social constructivism.

519. Which of the following most accurately describes Clark's opinion of Braverman's position?

(A) He respects its wide-ranging popularity.

(B) He disapproves of its misplaced emphasis on the influence of managers.

(C) He admires the consideration it gives to the attitudes of the workers affected.

(D) He is concerned about its potential to impede the implementation of new technologies.

(E) He is sympathetic to its concern about the impact of modern technology on workers.

520. The information in the passage suggests that which of the following statements from hypothetical sociological studies of change in industry most clearly exemplifies the social constructivists' version of technological determinism?

(A) It is the available technology that determines workers' skills, rather than workers' skills influencing the application of technology.

(B) All progress in industrial technology grows out of a continuing negotiation between technological possibility and human need.

(C) Some organizational change is caused by people; some is caused by computer chips.

(D) Most major technological advances in industry have been generated through research and development.

(E) Some industrial technology eliminates jobs, but educated workers can create whole new skills areas by the adaptation of the technology.

521. The information in the passage suggests that Clark believes that which of the following would be true if social constructivism had not gained widespread acceptance?

(A) Businesses would be more likely to modernize without considering the social consequences of their actions.

(B) There would be greater understanding of the role played by technology in producing social change.

(C) Businesses would be less likely to understand the attitudes of employees affected by modernization.

(D) Modernization would have occurred at a slower rate.

(E) Technology would have played a greater part in determining the role of business in society.

522. According to the passage, constructivists employed which of the following to promote their argument?

(A) Empirical studies of business situations involving technological change

(B) Citation of managers supportive of their position

(C) Construction of hypothetical situations that support their view

(D) Contrasts of their view with a misstatement of an opposing view

(E) Descriptions of the breadth of impact of technological change

523. The author of the passage uses the expression "are supposed to" in line 25 primarily in order to

(A) suggest that a contention made by constructivists regarding determinists is inaccurate

(B) define the generally accepted position of determinists regarding the implementation of technology

(C) engage in speculation about the motivation of determinists

(D) lend support to a comment critical of the position of determinists

(E) contrast the historical position of determinists with their position regarding the exchange modernization

524. Which of the following statements about Clark's study of the telephone exchange can be inferred from information in the passage?

(A) Clark's reason for undertaking the study was to undermine Braverman's analysis of the function of technology.

(B) Clark's study suggests that the implementation of technology should be discussed in the context of conflict between labor and management.

(C) Clark examined the impact of changes in the technology of switching at the exchange in terms of overall operations and organization.

(D) Clark concluded that the implementation of new switching technology was equally beneficial to management and labor.

(E) Clark's analysis of the change in switching systems applies only narrowly to the situation at the particular exchange that he studied.

Because the framers of the United States Constitution (written in 1787) believed that protecting property rights relating to inventions would encourage the new nation's economic growth, they gave Congress—the national legislature—a constitutional mandate to grant patents for inventions. The resulting patent system has served as a model for those in other nations. Recently, however, scholars have questioned whether the American system helped achieve the framers' goals. These scholars have contended that from 1794 to roughly 1830, American inventors were unable to enforce property rights because judges were "antipatent" and routinely invalidated patents for arbitrary reasons. This argument is based partly on examination of court decisions in cases where patent holders ("patentees") brought suit alleging infringement of their patent rights. In the 1820s, for instance, 75 percent of verdicts were decided against the patentee. The proportion of verdicts for the patentee began to increase in the 1830s, suggesting to these scholars that judicial attitudes toward patent rights began shifting then.

Not all patent disputes in the early nineteenth century were litigated, however, and litigated cases were not drawn randomly from the population of disputes. Therefore the rate of verdicts in favor of patentees cannot be used by itself to gauge changes in judicial attitudes or enforceability of patent rights. If early judicial decisions were prejudiced against patentees, one might expect that subsequent courts—allegedly more supportive of patent rights—would reject the former legal precedents. But pre-1830 cases have been cited as frequently as later decisions, and they continue to be cited today, suggesting that the early decisions, many of which clearly declared that patent rights were a just recompense for inventive ingenuity, provided a lasting foundation for patent law. The proportion of judicial decisions in favor of patentees began to increase during the 1830s because of a change in the underlying population of cases brought to trial. This change was partly due to an 1836 revision to the patent system: an examination procedure, still in use today, was instituted in which each application is scrutinized for its adherence to patent law. Previously, patents were automatically granted upon payment of a $30 fee.

Questions 525–529 refer to the passage.

525. The passage implies that which of the following was a reason that the proportion of verdicts in favor of patentees began to increase in the 1830s ?

(A) Patent applications approved after 1836 were more likely to adhere closely to patent law.

(B) Patent laws enacted during the 1830s better defined patent rights.

(C) Judges became less prejudiced against patentees during the 1830s.

(D) After 1836, litigated cases became less representative of the population of patent disputes.

(E) The proportion of patent disputes brought to trial began to increase after 1836.

526. The passage implies that the scholars mentioned in line 8 would agree with which of the following criticisms of the American patent system before 1830 ?

(A) Its definition of property rights relating to inventions was too vague to be useful.

(B) Its criteria for the granting of patents were not clear.

(C) It made it excessively difficult for inventors to receive patents.

(D) It led to excessive numbers of patent-infringement suits.

(E) It failed to encourage national economic growth.

527. It can be inferred from the passage that the frequency with which pre-1830 cases have been cited in court decisions is an indication that

(A) judicial support for patent rights was strongest in the period before 1830

(B) judicial support for patent rights did not increase after 1830

(C) courts have returned to judicial standards that prevailed before 1830

(D) verdicts favoring patentees in patent-infringement suits did not increase after 1830

(E) judicial bias against patentees persisted after 1830

528. It can be inferred from the passage that the author and the scholars referred to in line 21 disagree about which of the following aspects of the patents defended in patent-infringement suits before 1830 ?

(A) Whether the patents were granted for inventions that were genuinely useful

(B) Whether the patents were actually relevant to the growth of the United States economy

(C) Whether the patents were particularly likely to be annulled by judges

(D) Whether the patents were routinely invalidated for reasons that were arbitrary

(E) Whether the patents were vindicated at a significantly lower rate than patents in later suits

529. The author of the passage cites which of the following as evidence challenging the argument referred to in lines 14–15 ?

(A) The proportion of cases that were decided against patentees in the 1820s

(B) The total number of patent disputes that were litigated from 1794 to 1830

(C) The fact that later courts drew upon the legal precedents set in pre-1830 patent cases

(D) The fact that the proportion of judicial decisions in favor of patentees began to increase during the 1830s

(E) The constitutional rationale for the 1836 revision of the patent system

Jacob Burckhardt's view that Renaissance European women "stood on a footing of perfect equality" with Renaissance men has been repeatedly cited by feminist scholars as a prelude to their presentation of rich historical evidence of women's inequality. In striking contrast to Burckhardt, Joan Kelly in her famous 1977 essay, "Did Women Have a Renaissance?" argued that the Renaissance was a period of economic and social decline for women relative both to Renaissance men and to medieval women. Recently, however, a significant trend among feminist scholars has entailed a rejection of both Kelly's dark vision of the Renaissance and Burckhardt's rosy one. Many recent works by these scholars stress the ways in which differences among Renaissance women—especially in terms of social status and religion—work to complicate the kinds of generalizations both Burckhardt and Kelly made on the basis of their observations about upper-class Italian women.

The trend is also evident, however, in works focusing on those middle- and upper-class European women whose ability to write gives them disproportionate representation in the historical record. Such women were, simply by virtue of their literacy, members of a tiny minority of the population, so it is risky to take their descriptions of their experiences as typical of "female experience" in any general sense. Tina Krontiris, for example, in her fascinating study of six Renaissance women writers, does tend at times to conflate "women" and "women writers," assuming that women's gender, irrespective of other social differences, including literacy, allows us to view women as a homogeneous social group and make that group an object of analysis. Nonetheless, Krontiris makes a significant contribution to the field and is representative of those authors who offer what might be called a cautiously optimistic assessment of Renaissance women's achievements, although she also stresses the social obstacles Renaissance women faced when they sought to raise their "oppositional voices." Krontiris is concerned to show women intentionally negotiating some power for themselves (at least in the realm of public discourse) against potentially constraining ideologies, but in her sober and thoughtful concluding remarks, she suggests that such verbal opposition to cultural stereotypes was highly circumscribed; women seldom attacked the basic assumptions in the ideologies that oppressed them.

Questions 530–536 refer to the passage.

530. The author of the passage discusses Krontiris primarily to provide an example of a writer who

(A) is highly critical of the writings of certain Renaissance women

(B) supports Kelly's view of women's status during the Renaissance

(C) has misinterpreted the works of certain Renaissance women

(D) has rejected the views of both Burckhardt and Kelly

(E) has studied Renaissance women in a wide variety of social and religious contexts

531. According to the passage, Krontiris's work differs from that of the scholars mentioned in line 12 in which of the following ways?

(A) Krontiris's work stresses the achievements of Renaissance women rather than the obstacles to their success.

(B) Krontiris's work is based on a reinterpretation of the work of earlier scholars.

(C) Krontiris's views are at odds with those of both Kelly and Burkhardt.

(D) Krontiris's work focuses on the place of women in Renaissance society.

(E) Krontiris's views are based exclusively on the study of a privileged group of women.

532. According to the passage, feminist scholars cite Burckhardt's view of Renaissance women primarily for which of the following reasons?

(A) Burckhardt's view forms the basis for most arguments refuting Kelly's point of view.
(B) Burckhardt's view has been discredited by Kelly.
(C) Burckhardt's view is one that many feminist scholars wish to refute.
(D) Burckhardt's work provides rich historical evidence of inequality between Renaissance women and men.
(E) Burckhardt's work includes historical research supporting the arguments of the feminist scholars.

533. It can be inferred that both Burckhardt and Kelly have been criticized by the scholars mentioned in line 12 for which of the following?

(A) Assuming that women writers of the Renaissance are representative of Renaissance women in general
(B) Drawing conclusions that are based on the study of an atypical group of women
(C) Failing to describe clearly the relationship between social status and literacy among Renaissance women
(D) Failing to acknowledge the role played by Renaissance women in opposing cultural stereotypes
(E) Failing to acknowledge the ways in which social status affected the creative activities of Renaissance women

534. The author of the passage suggests that Krontiris incorrectly assumes that

(A) social differences among Renaissance women are less important than the fact that they were women
(B) literacy among Renaissance women was more prevalent than most scholars today acknowledge
(C) during the Renaissance, women were able to successfully oppose cultural stereotypes relating to gender
(D) Renaissance women did not face many difficult social obstacles relating to their gender
(E) in order to attain power, Renaissance women attacked basic assumptions in the ideologies that oppressed them

535. The last sentence in the passage serves primarily to

(A) suggest that Krontiris's work is not representative of recent trends among feminist scholars
(B) undermine the argument that literate women of the Renaissance sought to oppose social constraints imposed on them
(C) show a way in which Krontiris's work illustrates a "cautiously optimistic" assessment of Renaissance women's achievements
(D) summarize Krontiris's view of the effect of literacy on the lives of upper- and middle-class Renaissance women
(E) illustrate the way in which Krontiris's study differs from the studies done by Burckhardt and Kelly

536. The author of the passage implies that the women studied by Krontiris are unusual in which of the following ways?

(A) They faced obstacles less formidable than those faced by other Renaissance women.
(B) They have been seen by historians as more interesting than other Renaissance women.
(C) They were more concerned about recording history accurately than were other Renaissance women.
(D) Their perceptions are more likely to be accessible to historians than are those of most other Renaissance women.
(E) Their concerns are likely to be of greater interest to feminist scholars than are the ideas of most other Renaissance women.

Line When asteroids collide, some collisions cause an asteroid to spin faster; others slow it down. If asteroids are all monoliths—single rocks—undergoing random collisions, a graph of their rotation rates should show a bell-shaped distribution with statistical "tails" of very fast and very slow rotators. If asteroids are rubble piles, however, the tail representing the very fast rotators would be missing, because any loose aggregate spinning faster than once every few hours (depending on the asteroid's bulk density) would fly apart. Researchers have discovered that all but five observed asteroids obey a strict limit on rate of rotation. The exceptions are all smaller than 200 meters in diameter, with an abrupt cutoff for asteroids larger than that.

The evident conclusion—that asteroids larger than 200 meters across are multicomponent structures or rubble piles—agrees with recent computer modeling of collisions, which also finds a transition at that diameter. A collision can blast a large asteroid to bits, but after the collision those bits will usually move slower than their mutual escape velocity. Over several hours, gravity will reassemble all but the fastest pieces into a rubble pile. Because collisions among asteroids are relatively frequent, most large bodies have already suffered this fate. Conversely, most small asteroids should be monolithic, because impact fragments easily escape their feeble gravity.

Questions 537–540 refer to the passage.

537. The passage implies which of the following about the five asteroids mentioned in line 12 ?

(A) Their rotation rates are approximately the same.

(B) They have undergone approximately the same number of collisions.

(C) They are monoliths.

(D) They are composed of fragments that have escaped the gravity of larger asteroids.

(E) They were detected only recently.

538. The discovery of which of the following would call into question the conclusion mentioned in line 16 ?

(A) An asteroid 100 meters in diameter rotating at a rate of once per week

(B) An asteroid 150 meters in diameter rotating at a rate of 20 times per hour

(C) An asteroid 250 meters in diameter rotating at a rate of once per week

(D) An asteroid 500 meters in diameter rotating at a rate of once per hour

(E) An asteroid 1,000 meters in diameter rotating at a rate of once every 24 hours

539. According to the passage, which of the following is a prediction that is based on the strength of the gravitational attraction of small asteroids?
    (A) Small asteroids will be few in number.
    (B) Small asteroids will be monoliths.
    (C) Small asteroids will collide with other asteroids very rarely.
    (D) Most small asteroids will have very fast rotation rates.
    (E) Almost no small asteroids will have very slow rotation rates.

540. The author of the passage mentions "escape velocity" (see line 22) in order to help explain which of the following?
    (A) The tendency for asteroids to become smaller rather than larger over time
    (B) The speed with which impact fragments reassemble when they do not escape an asteroid's gravitational attraction after a collision
    (C) The frequency with which collisions among asteroids occur
    (D) The rotation rates of asteroids smaller than 200 meters in diameter
    (E) The tendency for large asteroids to persist after collisions

Most attempts by physicists to send particles faster than the speed of light involve a remarkable phenomenon called quantum tunneling, in which particles travel through solid barriers that appear to be impenetrable. If you throw a ball at a wall, you expect it to bounce back, not to pass straight through it. Yet subatomic particles perform the equivalent feat. Quantum theory says that there is a distinct, albeit small, probability that such a particle will tunnel its way through a barrier; the probability declines exponentially as the thickness of the barrier increases. Though the extreme rapidity of quantum tunneling was noted as early as 1932, not until 1955 was it hypothesized—by Wigner and Eisenbud—that tunneling particles sometimes travel faster than light. Their grounds were calculations that suggested that the time it takes a particle to tunnel through a barrier increases with the thickness of the barrier until tunneling time reaches a maximum; beyond that maximum, tunneling time stays the same regardless of barrier thickness. This would imply that once maximum tunneling time is reached, tunneling speed will increase without limit as barrier thickness increases. Several recent experiments have supported this hypothesis that tunneling particles sometimes reach superluminal speed. According to measurements performed by Raymond Chiao and colleagues, for example, photons can pass through an optical filter at 1.7 times the speed of light.

Questions 541–543 refer to the passage.

541. The author of the passage mentions calculations about tunneling time and barrier thickness in order to

(A) suggest that tunneling time is unrelated to barrier thickness

(B) explain the evidence by which Wigner and Eisenbud discovered the phenomenon of tunneling

(C) describe data recently challenged by Raymond Chiao and colleagues

(D) question why particles engaged in quantum tunneling rarely achieve extremely high speeds

(E) explain the basis for Wigner and Eisenbud's hypothesis

542. The passage implies that if tunneling time reached no maximum in increasing with barrier thickness, then

(A) tunneling speed would increase with barrier thickness

(B) tunneling speed would decline with barrier thickness

(C) tunneling speed would vary with barrier thickness

(D) tunneling speed would not be expected to increase without limit

(E) successful tunneling would occur even less frequently than it does

543. Which of the following statements about the earliest scientific investigators of quantum tunneling can be inferred from the passage?

(A) They found it difficult to increase barrier thickness continually.

(B) They anticipated the later results of Chiao and his colleagues.

(C) They did not suppose that tunneling particles could travel faster than light.

(D) They were unable to observe instances of successful tunneling.

(E) They made use of photons to study the phenomenon of tunneling.

7.5 Answer Key

405. B
406. B
407. D
408. A
409. D
410. D
411. B
412. B
413. C
414. C
415. D
416. C
417. A
418. C
419. C
420. C
421. E
422. A
423. C
424. B
425. B
426. A
427. D
428. E
429. A
430. A
431. C
432. B
433. D
434. A
435. C
436. D
437. B
438. B
439. C
440. B
441. E
442. B
443. B
444. B
445. A
446. D
447. E
448. D
449. A
450. C
451. B
452. D
453. B
454. E
455. C
456. C
457. E
458. A
459. D
460. A
461. C
462. A
463. B
464. D
465. E
466. C
467. A
468. E
469. A
470. D
471. D
472. D
473. B
474. B
475. C
476. C
477. E
478. D
479. D
480. B
481. C
482. B
483. E
484. D
485. E
486. B
487. D
488. C
489. C
490. E
491. A
492. B
493. D
494. E
495. E
496. D
497. B
498. C
499. D
500. A
501. C
502. D
503. A
504. A
505. D
506. E
507. D
508. B
509. C
510. A
511. C
512. B
513. D
514. D
515. E
516. B
517. C
518. C
519. B
520. A
521. B
522. D
523. A
524. C
525. A
526. E
527. B
528. D
528. C
530. D
531. E
532. C
533. B
534. A
535. C
536. D
537. C
538. D
539. B
540. E
541. E
542. D
543. C

7.6 Answer Explanations

The following discussion of reading comprehension is intended to familiarize you with the most efficient and effective approaches to the kinds of problems common to reading comprehension. The particular questions in this chapter are generally representative of the kinds of reading comprehension questions you will encounter on the GMAT exam. Remember that it is the problem solving strategy that is important, not the specific details of a particular question.

Questions 405–408 refer to the passage on page 362.

405. According to the passage, theory B states that which of the following is a factor that enables a schooling fish to escape predators?

(A) The tendency of fish to form compact groups
(B) The movement of other fish within the school
(C) The inability of predators to detect schools
(D) The ability of fish to hide behind one another in a school
(E) The great speed with which a school can disperse

Supporting idea

This question depends on understanding what the passage states about theory B, the "confusion effect." One element of theory B is that predators may experience sensory confusion created by large numbers of moving fish in a school.

A The compactness of groups of schooling fish is an element of theory A, not theory B.
B Correct. It is the movement of schooling fish around a predator that creates sensory confusion in the predator; this movement may distract the predator and help protect individual fish in the school.
C According to the passage's description of theory A, predators are actually slightly more likely to detect schools than they are to detect individual fish.
D Theory B does not involve fish hiding behind one another but rather moving around the predator.
E The passage does not discuss the speed of dispersal of schools of fish.

The correct answer is B.

406. According to the passage, both theory A and theory B have been developed to explain how

(A) fish hide from predators by forming schools
(B) forming schools functions to protect fish from predators
(C) schooling among fish differs from other protective behaviors
(D) small fish are able to make rapid decisions
(E) small fish are able to survive in an environment densely populated by large predators

Supporting idea

The passage states in its first paragraph that two theories were developed to explain why schooling occurs in so many fish species and that they both assume that schooling helps protect fish from predators.

A While theory A involves an explanation of how schooling makes an individual fish less likely to be found by predators, theory B explains how schooling protects fish even when they are detected by predators.
B Correct. Both theory A and theory B begin with the assumption that schooling provides protection from predators, and each theory offers a different explanation for how that protection occurs.
C The passage does not discuss protective behaviors other than schooling.
D The decision-making ability of predators, not schooling fish, is discussed in the passage; schooling is presented as an instinctive behavior.
E The passage suggests that only theory B helps explain schooling behavior in environments where many predators, large or otherwise, are found, and that theory A explains schooling in areas where predators are not as abundant.

The correct answer is B.

407. According to one explanation of the "confusion effect," a fish that swims in a school will have greater advantages for survival if it

(A) tends to be visible for no more than 200 meters
(B) stays near either the front or the rear of a school
(C) is part of a small school rather than a large school
(D) is very similar in appearance to the other fish in the school
(E) is medium-sized

Inference

The "confusion effect" is discussed in the third and fourth paragraphs. The first explanation of the "confusion effect" proposes that because predators prefer to select distinctive prey, they find it difficult to select one fish from among many that look the same.

A The 200-meter visibility of fish is part of the explanation for theory A, not theory B (the "confusion effect").
B The location of an individual fish within a school is not discussed in the passage as being important to the "confusion effect."
C The size of a school of fish is not discussed as an element of the "confusion effect."
D Correct. Because predators, according to the "confusion effect," prefer to select prey that is distinct from the rest of the school, a fish that is similar in appearance to the other fish in its school would most likely enjoy a survival advantage.
E The size of a fish relative to the other fish in its school would most likely contribute to its ability to survive: that is, if it resembled other fish in size, it would be safer, based on what the passage says about the "confusion effect." Furthermore, the passage gives no reason to think that merely being medium-sized would confer any advantage (unless the other fish were medium-sized as well).

The correct answer is D.

408. The author is primarily concerned with

(A) discussing different theories
(B) analyzing different techniques
(C) defending two hypotheses
(D) refuting established beliefs
(E) revealing new evidence

Main idea

Determining the author's primary concern depends on understanding the focus of the passage as a whole. The author presents two theories that purport to account for why fish, particularly small fish, tend to school and explains the arguments of proponents of each theory.

A Correct. The author discusses two theories—identified as theory A and theory B—that account for the tendency of fish to school.
B The author is not concerned with different techniques in the passage.
C The two theories of why fish school could be referred to as hypotheses, but the author is not primarily concerned with defending them; rather, the passage explains how each attempts to account for the phenomenon in question.
D The author presents, rather than refutes, beliefs about why fish tend to school.
E The author reveals no evidence, new or otherwise, in the passage. The passage is a general discussion of scientific opinions based on existing evidence.

The correct answer is A.

Questions 409–411 refer to the passage on page 364.

409. The primary purpose of the passage is to

(A) challenge recent findings that appear to contradict earlier findings

(B) present two sides of an ongoing scientific debate

(C) report answers to several questions that have long puzzled researchers

(D) discuss evidence that has caused a long-standing belief to be revised

(E) attempt to explain a commonly misunderstood biological phenomenon

Main idea

This question depends on understanding the passage as a whole. The passage begins by describing a long-held belief regarding humans' circadian rhythms: that the SCNs control them. It then goes on to explain that new findings have led scientists to believe that other organs and tissues may be involved in regulating the body's circadian rhythms as well.

A The passage does not challenge the more-recent findings. Furthermore, the recent findings that the passage recounts do not contradict earlier findings; rather, when placed alongside those earlier findings, they have led scientists to reach additional conclusions.

B The passage does not discuss a two-sided debate; no findings or conclusions are disputed by any figures in the passages.

C There is only one question at issue in the passage: whether the SCN alone control human circadian rhythms. Furthermore, nothing in the passage suggests that researchers have been puzzled for a long time about this.

D **Correct.** The new evidence regarding circadian rhythm–related gene activity in all the body's tissue has led scientists to revise their long-standing belief that the SCN alone control circadian rhythms.

E The biological phenomenon of circadian rhythms is not, at least as far as the passage is concerned, misunderstood. Its causes are being investigated and refined.

The correct answer is D.

410. The passage mentions each of the following as a function regulated by the SCNs in some animals EXCEPT

(A) activity level

(B) blood pressure

(C) alertness

(D) vision

(E) temperature

Supporting idea

This question asks about what is NOT specifically mentioned in the passage with regard to functions regulated by the SCN. Those functions, as identified in the passage, are blood pressure, body temperature, activity level, alertness, and the release of melatonin.

A The passage includes activity level in its list of functions regulated by the SCN.

B The passage includes blood pressure in its list of functions regulated by the SCN.

C The passage includes alertness in its list of functions regulated by the SCN.

D **Correct.** While the passage does say that cells in the human retina transmit information to the SCN, there is no suggestion that the SCN reciprocally control vision.

E The passage includes temperature in its list of functions regulated by the SCN.

The correct answer is D.

411. The author of the passage would probably agree with which of the following statements about the SCNs?

(A) The SCNs are found in other organs and tissues of the body besides the hypothalamus.

(B) The SCNs play a critical but not exclusive role in regulating circadian rhythms.

(C) The SCNs control clock genes in a number of tissues and organs throughout the body.

(D) The SCNs are a less significant factor in regulating blood pressure than scientists once believed.

(E) The SCNs are less strongly affected by changes in light levels than they are by other external cues.

Main idea

The author of the passage discusses the SCN in the passage in order to explain that they are most likely not, as long believed, solely responsible for the control of our circadian rhythms.

A The author states that the SCN are nerve clusters in the hypothalamus, and nothing in the passage contradicts or undermines the supposition that they are only in the hypothalamus.

B Correct. The author points out in the second paragraph that the SCN control core circadian function, but that circadian clocks found elsewhere in the body have an effect as well.

C The evidence offered in the second paragraph about the activity of the clock gene in rat livers suggests that these clock genes are not under the SCN's control. The passage does not suggest that the SCN control any of the non-SCN controllers of circadian rhythms.

D The author states in the second paragraph that scientists do not dispute the idea that the SCN regulate blood pressure.

E The first paragraph indicates that the SCN respond to light levels; clock genes in other tissues are the ones that may respond to other external cues.

The correct answer is B.

Questions 412–414 refer to the passage on page 366.

412. The primary purpose of the passage is to

(A) question the results of a study that examined the effect of service-quality guarantees in the restaurant industry

(B) discuss potential advantages and disadvantages of service-quality guarantees in the restaurant industry

(C) examine the conventional wisdom regarding the effect of service-quality guarantees in the restaurant industry

(D) argue that only certain restaurants would benefit from the implementation of service-quality guarantees

(E) consider the impact that service-quality guarantees can have on the service provided by a restaurant

Main idea

This question depends on understanding the passage as a whole. The first paragraph describes Tucci and Talaga's findings regarding the effect of service-quality guarantees: that they have different, more positive results for higher-priced restaurants than for lower-priced ones, which could be affected negatively. The second paragraph explains that a particular benefit from service guarantees could accrue to restaurants generally.

A The passage does not question the results of Tucci and Talaga's study; rather, the passage appears to accept the results of the study as accurate.

B Correct. The potential advantages involve the management and motivation of service staff, as well as, for higher-priced restaurants, a greater likelihood of being selected by customers over other restaurants. Potential disadvantages for lower-priced restaurants include the possibility that potential customers may believe that such restaurants are concerned about the quality of their service.

C The passage does not indicate whether there is any conventional wisdom regarding service-quality guarantees in the restaurant industry.

D The second paragraph of the passage suggests that restaurants in general could potentially enjoy some benefits from the implementation of service-quality guarantees. For lower-priced restaurants, these benefits could offset the possible negative effects of service-quality guarantees described in the first paragraph.

E The second paragraph of the passage indicates an effect that service-quality guarantees could have on a restaurant's staff and the service that the staff provides, but this is only one of the subsidiary points contributing to the focus of the passage as a whole. The first is more concerned with the question of what effect these guarantees would have on whether customers choose to patronize that restaurant.

The correct answer is B.

413. It can be inferred that the author of the passage would agree with which of the following statements about the appeal of service guarantees to customers?

(A) Such guarantees are likely to be somewhat more appealing to customers of restaurants than to customers of other businesses.

(B) Such guarantees are likely to be more appealing to customers who know what to anticipate in terms of service.

(C) Such guarantees are likely to have less appeal in situations where customers are knowledgeable about a business's product or service.

(D) In situations where a high level of financial commitment is involved, a service guarantee is not likely to be very appealing.

(E) In situations where customers expect a high level of customer service, a service guarantee is likely to make customers think that a business is worried about its service.

Inference

This question asks for an inference from the passage about the author's view of why and how service guarantees would appeal to customers. The question does not ask specifically about service guarantees in the context of restaurants, but rather service guarantees in general. The end of the first paragraph addresses this general question: a service guarantee may appeal most to customers in the case of activities whose quality they are less likely to know how to question.

A The author states that a service guarantee might have greater appeal in the case of skilled activities than it would for restaurant customers.

B According to the author, customers who know what to expect in terms of service—a group that includes restaurant customers—would likely find service guarantees less appealing.

C **Correct.** The author makes clear that service guarantees would be less appealing to restaurant customers when they know what to expect in terms of the quality of service.

D The passage provides some evidence that where a high level of financial commitment is involved, a service guarantee may be more rather than less appealing than in other situations. In discussing higher-priced restaurants, which require a relatively high level of financial commitment, the author states that Tucci and Talaga found evidence that a service guarantee would likely appeal to customers.

E The author implies that customers of higher-priced restaurants expect a high level of service, certainly a level higher than that expected by customers of lower-priced restaurants. But it is at lower-priced restaurants that Tucci and Talaga found that a service guarantee makes customers think a given restaurant is concerned about its service.

The correct answer is C.

414. According to the passage, Tucci and Talaga found that service guarantees, when offered by lower-priced restaurants, can have which of the following effects?

(A) Customers' developing unreasonably high expectations regarding service
(B) Customers' avoiding such restaurants because they fear that the service guarantee may not be fully honored
(C) Customers' interpreting the service guarantee as a sign that management is not confident about the quality of its service
(D) A restaurant's becoming concerned that its service will not be assiduous enough to satisfy customers
(E) A restaurant's becoming concerned that customers will be more emboldened to question the quality of the service they receive

Supporting ideas

This question requires identifying Tucci and Talaga's findings regarding service guarantees offered by lower-priced restaurants. The passage states directly that these researchers found in these situations that a guarantee could lead potential customers to think that the restaurant has concerns about its service.

A The passage does not report that Tucci and Talaga found that service guarantees create unreasonably high expectations regarding service.

B The passage does not report that Tucci and Talaga found that customers doubted that service guarantees would be honored.

C **Correct.** The passage explicitly indicates that Tucci and Talaga found that potential customers of lower-priced restaurants could interpret service guarantees as indicating worries about the quality of service.

D The passage indicates that Tucci and Talaga found that customers might think that lower-priced restaurants are offering service guarantees because they are concerned that the quality of their service is too low, but the passage does not indicate that service guarantees lead such restaurants to have concerns about the quality of their service, and in fact it may be that such guarantees could lead to improvements in service.

E The passage indicates that service guarantees offered at lower-priced restaurants may empower customers to question the quality of service, but it does not indicate that service guarantees lead restaurants to have concerns about this.

The correct answer is C.

Questions 415–418 refer to the passage on page 368.

415. Information in the passage suggests that David Pearce would most readily endorse which of the following statements concerning monetization?

(A) Monetization represents a strategy that is attractive to both environmentalists and their critics.
(B) Monetization is an untested strategy, but it is increasingly being embraced by environmentalists.
(C) Monetization should at present be restricted to ecological services and should only gradually be extended to such commercial endeavors as tourism and recreation.
(D) Monetization can serve as a means of representing persuasively the value of environmental conservation.
(E) Monetization should inform environmental decision-making processes only if it is accepted by environmentalist groups.

Inference

This question requires an understanding of David Pearce's view of monetization. According to the passage, Pearce finds the idea that conservation is unprofitable to be an illusion. He argues for showing the economic value of ecosystems in order to make progress in conserving those ecosystems.

A The passage attributes to Gretchen Daily the view that monetization is unpopular with environmentalists. The passage gives no reason to believe that Pearce would endorse the idea that environmentalists currently find monetization attractive.

B The passage gives no indication that monetization is increasingly being embraced by environmentalists, even if Pearce thinks it should be.

C The passage indicates Pearce's belief that some types of tourism are also types of ecological services that have economic value and that they should be monetized.

D **Correct.** Pearce believes that monetization quantifies the value of the services provided by ecological systems—and if that value is quantified, people are more likely to be persuaded to conserve those systems.

E Pearce is arguing, against some environmentalists, that monetization should inform the decision-making process with regard to preserving ecosystems.

The correct answer is D.

416. Which of the following most clearly represents an example of an "ecological service" as that term is used in line 20 ?

(A) A resort hotel located in an area noted for its natural beauty

(B) A water-purifying plant that supplements natural processes with nontoxic chemicals

(C) A wildlife preserve that draws many international travelers

(D) A nonprofit firm that specializes in restoring previously damaged ecosystems

(E) A newsletter that keeps readers informed of ecological victories and setbacks

Application

Based on the passage, *ecological services* are services provided by natural assets that have not been converted into commercial assets. Thus any example of such an ecological service requires that the area providing it is natural.

A The passage mentions resort hotels as an example of explicitly commercial assets. Although some hotels might be situated in ecologically valuable natural environments, any ecological services in such cases would be contributed by the natural environments, not by the hotels themselves.

B Water purifying is *an ecological* service if it is supplied by *undisturbed forests and wetlands*. The word *plant* here must mean a technological installation, not a botanical organism, because it is said to supplement—not to be part of—the natural processes. Thus it is not a natural asset and therefore does not provide an ecological service as described in the passage.

C **Correct.** The passage states that a wildlife preserve that creates jobs and generates income would be providing an ecological service.

D A nonprofit firm that restores damaged ecosystems would be performing a valuable ecology-related service, but it would not itself be an example of a natural asset providing an ecological service.

E Environmentalists and others would most likely find such a newsletter informative, but it would not be an ecological service, because it is not a service provided by a natural asset.

The correct answer is C.

417. According to the passage, Daily sees monetization as an indication of which of the following?

(A) The centrality of economic interests to people's actions

(B) The reluctance of the critics of environmentalism to acknowledge the importance of conservation

(C) The inability of financial interests and ecological interests to reach a common ideological ground

(D) The inevitability of environmental degradation

(E) The inevitability of the growth of ecological services in the future

Supporting ideas

This question asks about Daily's view of monetization, and according to the passage, she sees monetization as a practice that *reflects the dominant role that economic decisions play in human behavior.*

A **Correct.** According to the passage, Daily believes that economic interests are central to people's actions, and monetization of ecological services would take that central role realistically into account.

B Monetization, as Daily sees it, is a way of assigning value to conservation and thus acknowledging its importance. Many environmentalists, rather than their critics, are reluctant to embrace monetization, according to Daily.

C For Daily, monetization represents a way for financial interests and ecological interests to reach a common ground; by using this *common currency*, both sides can make good decisions about the environment.

D Monetization, on Daily's view, would help to prevent environmental degradation; the passage does not suggest that she regards such degradation as at all inevitable.

E Daily does not see monetization as inevitably spurring the growth of ecological services but as more likely preventing their decline by leaving those *services* undisturbed.

The correct answer is A.

418. Which of the following can be inferred from the passage concerning the environmentalists mentioned in line 8 ?

(A) They are organized in opposition to the generation of income produced by the sale of ecological services.

(B) They are fewer in number but better organized and better connected to the media than their opponents.

(C) They have sometimes been charged with failing to use a particular strategy in their pursuit of conservational goals.

(D) They have been in the forefront of publicizing the extent of worldwide environmental degradation.

(E) They define environmental progress differently and more conservatively than do other organized groups of environmentalists.

Inference

The sentence in question states that critics blame environmentalists for their failure *to address the economic issues of environmental degradation.*

A The passage states that in the absence of monetization, conservation can appear unprofitable. But this does not mean that the environmentalists in question are opposed to conservation generating income.

B The passage does not address the issue of the number of environmentalists in question, the number of those opposed to them, or whether either group is better connected to the media.

C **Correct.** The passage indicates that critics of the environmentalists in question believe environmentalists are to blame for not using an effective economics-based strategy to promote conservation.

D Although it may be the case that the environmentalists in question have been prominent in publicizing worldwide environmental degradation, the passage does not provide grounds for inferring that they have been.

E The passage suggests that certain critics consider environmentalists in general to be at fault for failing to address economic issues. In this respect, the passage makes no distinctions among different environmentalist groups, organized or otherwise.

The correct answer is C.

Questions 419–422 refer to the passage on page 370.

419. According to the passage, the studies referred to in line 12 reported which of the following about the effect of price on consumers' perception of the performance risk associated with a new product?

(A) Although most consumers regard price as an important factor, their perception of the performance risk associated with a new product is ultimately determined by the manufacturer's reputation.

(B) Price interacts with the presentation of an advertised message to affect perceived performance risk.

(C) Price does not significantly affect consumers' perception of the performance risk associated with a new product.

(D) Consumers tend to regard price as more important than the manufacturer's credibility when they are buying from that manufacturer for the first time.

(E) Consumers are generally less concerned about a new product's performance risk when that product is relatively expensive.

Supporting ideas

The question asks about information explicitly provided in the passage. The first paragraph explains that there are *conflicting findings* in the research about how the price of a product affects a consumer's perception of the performance risk of that product. Some studies have found that higher priced products reduce the perception of performance risk. The *other studies* referred to in line 12, however, have found little or no connection between price and perceived performance risk.

A The passage does not mention that these studies consider the manufacturer's reputation.

B The passage does not mention that these studies consider advertising messages.

C **Correct.** The passage indicates that these studies have found little or no connection between relative price and consumers' perception of performance risk.

D The passage does not mention that these studies consider the manufacturer's credibility.

E Although some studies have found that a relatively high price reduces the perception of performance risk, the passage explains that the studies referred to in line 12 have not confirmed that finding.

The correct answer is C.

420. The "past research" mentioned in line 25 suggests which of the following about perceived performance risk?

(A) The more expensive a new product is, the more likely consumers may be to credit advertised claims about that product.

(B) The more familiar consumers are with a particular manufacturer, the more willing they may be to assume some risk in the purchase of a new product being advertised by that manufacturer.

(C) Consumers' perception of the performance risk associated with a new product being advertised may be influenced by an interplay between the product's price and the manufacturer's credibility.

(D) Consumers may be more likely to believe that a product will function as it is advertised to do when they have bought products from a particular manufacturer before.

(E) The price of a particular advertised product may have less impact than the manufacturer's credibility on consumers' assessment of the performance risk associated with that product.

Supporting ideas

The question asks about information explicitly provided in the passage. The second paragraph explains that, according to some research, consumers perceive a product as having less performance risk when they trust the source of advertising about that product. *Past research*, however, suggests that performance risk is affected not merely by the credibility of the source, but by an interaction between source credibility and the price of the product.

A The passage does not indicate that the past research addressed the question of how the price of a product affects consumers' perception of advertised claims. It only says that the research suggests that the two factors *interact*.

B Although the passage discusses consumers' perception of how risky a purchase might be, it does not address the relationship between familiarity and willingness to assume risk.

C **Correct.** The *past research* suggests that performance risk is affected by an interaction between the price of the product and the credibility of the source of the advertising about the product—in other words, the manufacturer.

D The *past research* suggests that consumers' beliefs about a product's performance are affected not merely by their perception of the manufacturer, but by an interplay between source credibility and product price. The passage does not mention any possible role of prior experience in this interplay.

E The passage does not discuss whether price or the manufacturer's credibility has more of an effect on perceived performance risk.

The correct answer is C.

421. The passage is primarily concerned with

(A) challenging the implications of previous research into why consumers try new products
(B) suggesting new marketing strategies for attracting consumers to new products
(C) reconciling two different views about the effect of price on consumers' willingness to try new products
(D) describing a new approach to researching why consumers try new products
(E) discussing certain findings regarding why consumers try new products

Main idea

The question depends on understanding the passage as a whole. The passage begins with a statement explaining that much research has investigated *what motivates consumers to try new products*. It then defines one such motivating factor—perception of performance risk. The remainder of the passage summarizes research into how price and a manufacturer's advertising affect consumers' perception of performance risk.

A The passage summarizes research findings that conflict with one another but does not support some findings over others.

B The passage does not suggest any new marketing strategies.

C The first paragraph mentions a study that could reconcile two conflicting findings, but this is only a supporting point in the passage's larger purpose of summarizing research.

D The passage does not describe new research approaches.

E **Correct**. The passage discusses studies about performance risk, which is a factor that motivates consumers to try new products.

The correct answer is E.

422. Which of the following, if true, would most tend to weaken the conclusions drawn from "some of this research" (see line 8)?

(A) In a subsequent study, consumers who were asked to evaluate new products with relatively low prices had the same perception of the products' performance risk as did consumers who were shown the same products priced more expensively.
(B) In a subsequent study, the quality of the advertising for the products that consumers perceived as having a lower performance risk was relatively high, while the quality of the advertising for the products that consumers perceived as having a higher performance risk was relatively poor.
(C) In a subsequent study, the products that consumers perceived as having a lower performance risk were priced higher than the highest priced products in the previous research.

(D) None of the consumers involved in this research had ever before bought products from the manufacturers involved in the research.

(E) Researchers found that the higher the source credibility for a product, the more consumers were willing to pay for it.

Evaluation

The question depends on evaluating the reasoning behind the conclusions of some research and deciding which evidence would weaken them. The research concludes that higher prices reduce consumers' perception of performance risk associated with a particular product. This conclusion involves a claim of cause and effect, so evidence showing that higher prices do not cause that effect would weaken the argument.

A **Correct.** If lowering prices has no effect on consumers' perception of performance risk, the conclusions of the research are called into question.

B A correlation between quality of advertising and perceived performance risk is not clearly relevant to the research conclusions about the effects of price.

C This answer choice provides no basis for comparison among prices within the subsequent study. For all we can tell, the prices that correlated with higher perceived performance risk in the subsequent study may have been lower than those that correlated with lower perceived risk. In that case, the subsequent study would tend to strengthen, not weaken, the conclusions drawn from the earlier research.

D Consumers' lack of familiarity with other products from the manufacturers is not clearly relevant to the studies' conclusions about the effects of price.

E Credibility of the source of advertisements is discussed as a separate issue in the second paragraph and is not clearly relevant to these studies' conclusions about the effects of price. To the extent that it may be obliquely relevant, it tends to strengthen, rather than to weaken, the conclusions.

The correct answer is A.

Questions 423–427 refer to the passage on page 372.

423. The primary purpose of the passage is to

(A) compare the economic role played by southern banks with the economic role played by banks in the rest of the United States during the late eighteenth and early nineteenth centuries

(B) reevaluate a conventional interpretation of the role played by banks in the American economy during the late eighteenth and early nineteenth centuries

(C) present different interpretations of the role played by banks in the American economy during the late eighteenth and early nineteenth centuries

(D) analyze how the increasing number of banks in the late eighteenth and early nineteenth centuries affected the American economy

(E) examine how scholarly opinion regarding the role played by banks in the American economy during the late eighteenth and early nineteenth centuries has changed over time

Main idea

The question depends on understanding the passage as a whole. The passage describes two contrasting views about the role banks played in the economic growth of the United States around the turn of the nineteenth century. The first paragraph describes the view that banks played only a small role. The second paragraph describes the contrasting view that banks played a critical role.

A The mention of banks in the South is a small part of a larger discussion about the role of banks in the country as a whole.

B The passage describes two major views held by historians; it does not reevaluate either of those views.

C **Correct.** The passage describes two different views about the role that banks played in America's growing economy.

D The passage does not analyze any aspect of the relationship between the increasing number of banks and the economy. It alludes to the increase in numbers only within a broader description of two contrasting views about how banks affected the economy.

E The passage suggests that at the time when it was written, the two views it describes were both still held among historians.

The correct answer is C.

424. The passage suggests that the scholars mentioned in line 4 would argue that the reason banks tended not to fund manufacturing and transportation projects in the late eighteenth and early nineteenth centuries was that

(A) these projects, being well established and well capitalized, did not need substantial long-term financing from banks
(B) these projects entailed a level of risk that was too great for banks' conservative lending practices
(C) banks preferred to invest in other, more speculative projects that offered the potential for higher returns
(D) bank managers believed that these projects would be unlikely to contribute significantly to economic growth in the new country
(E) bank managers believed funding these projects would result in credit being extended to too many borrowers

Inference

The question asks about information implied by the passage. According to the scholars' view described in the first paragraph, banks followed conservative lending practices: they shunned projects that were uncertain and that required substantial investments in capital. It follows that, according to those scholars, the reason banks chose not to fund certain projects was that they entailed too great a risk.

A The passage indicates that manufacturing and transportation projects were less well established than those the banks preferred to fund, not more so.
B Correct. Because the projects were *uncertain* and required a great deal of capital, banks considered them too risky.
C The passage indicates that banks followed conservative lending practices and avoided investments that were uncertain.
D The passage does not mention banks' beliefs about economic growth, and it does not provide any basis for inferring that the scholars in question held any particular views regarding such beliefs.
E The passage does not mention, or provide a basis for inferences about, bank managers' concerns about numbers of borrowers.

The correct answer is B.

425. The passage suggests that Paul Gilje would be most likely to agree with which of the following claims about the lending practices of the "earliest banks" (see line 21) ?

(A) These lending practices were unlikely to generate substantial profits for banks.
(B) These lending practices only benefited a narrow sector of the economy.
(C) The restrictive nature of these lending practices generated significant opposition outside of the South.
(D) The restrictive nature of these lending practices forced state legislatures to begin granting more bank charters by the early nineteenth century.
(E) These lending practices were likely to be criticized by economic elites as being overly restrictive.

Inference

This question asks about conclusions that can be logically inferred from information provided in the passage. According to the second paragraph, Paul Gilje believes that a driving force in American economic growth in the early nineteenth century was banks' lending to a larger and more diverse group of borrowers. The question asks what this would imply about Gilje's view toward earlier banks—which, the passage explains, offered credit only to *well-connected merchants*.

A The profitability of banks' lending practices is not at issue in the discussion.
B Correct. The passage says that the earliest banks had primarily made loans only to a narrow sector—well-connected merchants—and that they began lending more broadly in the early nineteenth century. It then cites Gilje's view to corroborate and explicate this claim. This strongly suggests that Gilje agrees with the claim.
C Opposition to the earliest banks is not mentioned or alluded to in the discussion.
D The passage provides no basis for inferring that Gilje held any particular view as to why legislatures began granting more bank charters.

E The passage does not mention or provide a basis for inference about the views of economic elites regarding the lending practices of the earliest banks in the United States. It thus provides no basis for inferring that Gilje would have any particular opinion on this topic.

The correct answer is B.

426. The passage suggests that the opposition to banks in the South in the early nineteenth century stemmed in part from the perception that banks

(A) did not benefit more than a small minority of the people
(B) did not support the interests of elite planters
(C) were too closely tied to transportation and industrial interests
(D) were unwilling to issue the long-term loans required by agrarian interests
(E) were too willing to lend credit widely

Inference

The question asks about statements that can be inferred from information provided in the passage. The second paragraph explains that people who opposed banks in the South saw them as monopolies controlled by elite planters. This would imply that those who opposed banks believed that most people in the South did not benefit from them.

A **Correct.** Since people opposed the banks on the grounds that they were monopolies controlled by an elite group of planters, they likely thought banks did not benefit most of the population.

B The passage implies that people believed the banks did serve the interests of elite planters.

C The passage indicates that people believed banks in the South were tied to planters, not to transportation and industrial interests.

D Southern banks' willingness to provide long-term loans is not discussed or alluded to in the passage.

E The passage does not imply that anyone believed banks in the South were willing to lend credit widely. Since people believed the banks were controlled by the elite, they more likely thought banks were unwilling to lend credit widely.

The correct answer is A.

427. Which of the following statements best describes the function of the last sentence of the passage?

(A) It provides evidence tending to undermine the viewpoint of the scholars mentioned in line 5.
(B) It resolves a conflict over the role of banks summarized in the first paragraph.
(C) It clarifies some of the reasons state legislatures began granting more bank charters.
(D) It qualifies a claim made earlier in the passage about the impact of banks on the American economy in the early nineteenth century.
(E) It supports a claim made earlier in the passage about how the expansion of credit affected the economy.

Evaluation

This question asks about the function of the last sentence in relation to the rest of the passage. The first paragraph describes the view of one set of historians. The second paragraph describes the contrasting view of a second set of historians. The last sentence of the passage points out an exception mentioned by the second set of historians.

A The last sentence pertains to the view of historians described in the second paragraph, not those described in the first paragraph.

B The conflict between the two differing views is not resolved by the passage.

C The passage does not explain why legislatures began granting more bank charters.

D **Correct.** The second set of historians claim banks spurred American economic growth at the turn of the nineteenth century, but the last sentence adds an exception to that claim.

E The last sentence does not support the claim made by the second set of historians, but rather serves as an exception to that claim.

The correct answer is D.

Questions 428–430 refer to the passage on page 374.

428. According to the passage, the difference in the amount of cratering on Callisto's and Io's respective surfaces can probably be explained by the difference between these two moons with respect to which of the following factors?

(A) Size
(B) Ice content
(C) The rate of bombardment by comets and asteroids
(D) The influence of Jupiter's other moons
(E) The level of geological activity

Supporting idea

Cratering is discussed in the second paragraph. The passage states that Callisto is heavily cratered, while Io has no detectable craters. Io is the moon closest to Jupiter, and Callisto is the farthest away. Their relative positions are accompanied by a corresponding difference in geological activity: Io is very geologically active, while Callisto is not active at all. Io's geological activity means that it is being regularly resurfaced, so it is unlikely to retain any evidence of cratering—unlike Callisto, which experiences no resurfacing, leaving its craters intact.

A While the passage makes clear that Callisto is larger than Io, it does not address whether their relative size explains the difference in their respective amounts of cratering.

B According to the passage, Callisto and Io differ in terms of their ice content, but nothing in the passage indicates that that content affects the cratering on their surfaces.

C The passage states that Io experiences a higher rate of bombardment than Callisto does, but while that bombardment most likely causes cratering on Io, its surface does not retain those craters. Thus, the rate of bombardment does not, in itself, explain the difference in cratering on the surface of the two moons.

D The only other moons of Jupiter discussed in the passage are Ganymede and Europa, and the passage does not consider their effect on the cratering of Callisto and Io.

E **Correct.** Because Io experiences a high degree of geological activity, its surface is continuously resurfaced, which means that the surface shows no craters. Callisto, on the other hand, is not geologically active and thus is not resurfaced regularly, which explains why its surface is heavily cratered.

The correct answer is E.

429. Which of the following best describes the purpose of the second paragraph of the passage?

(A) To provide further evidence of the systematic variation in the characteristics of Jupiter's four largest moons
(B) To present a comprehensive theory to explain the systematic variation in the characteristics of Jupiter's four largest moons
(C) To explain the significance of the systematic variation in the characteristics of Jupiter's four largest moons
(D) To introduce facts that contradict conventional assumptions about Jupiter's four largest moons
(E) To contrast the characteristics of Jupiter's four largest moons with the characteristics of the planets of the solar system

Evaluation

This question depends on understanding how the second paragraph functions in the context of the passage as a whole. The first paragraph discusses the way in which the composition of Jupiter's four largest moons varies with distance from Jupiter, and the second paragraph extends the idea of distance-based variation to geological activity and surface appearance.

A **Correct.** The second paragraph presents evidence related to the amount of geological activity and surface cratering in order to extend the first paragraph's suggestion that the characteristics of Jupiter's four largest moons vary systematically based on their distance from Jupiter.

B The passage does not offer a theory to account for the systematic variation in the characteristics of Jupiter's largest moons; it merely describes several instances of that variation.

C The second paragraph provides more examples of the systematic variation in the characteristics of Jupiter's largest moons rather than explaining that variation's significance.

D The passage describes Jupiter's moons but does not identify any conventional assumptions about those moons that are contradicted by facts introduced in the passage.

E The first paragraph suggests that Jupiter's moons exhibit differences in characteristics that are more "systematic" than are those of the planets in the solar system, but the characteristics are not themselves contrasted; in fact, the first paragraph suggests that they are similar. The second paragraph does not discuss the planets of the solar system at all.

The correct answer is A.

430. The author's reference to Jupiter's gravity in line 25 serves primarily to

(A) indicate why the absence of craters on Io's surface is surprising

(B) explain the presence of craters on the surface of Jupiter's four largest moons

(C) provide an explanation for the lack of geological activity on Callisto

(D) contrast Jupiter's characteristics with the characteristics of its four largest moons

(E) illustrate the similarity between Jupiter's four largest moons and the planets of the solar system

Evaluation

The reference to Jupiter's gravity is part of the author's discussion of cratering on Jupiter's moons; Jupiter's gravity is strong enough to attract comets and asteroids that then bombard its inner moons. A high bombardment rate would seem to indicate that a great deal of cratering would occur on those inner moons, and yet the passage reports that, unexpectedly, on the innermost moon, Io, no craters have been detected.

A **Correct.** Jupiter's gravity attracts comets and asteroids, which increases the bombardment rate of its inner moons, including Io. This bombardment makes it surprising that Io's surface shows no cratering.

B The passage discusses the likely effect of Jupiter's gravity on its inner moons but not its outer moons; two of the large moons the passage discusses are outer moons.

C According to the passage, Callisto, an outer moon, lacks geological activity because of its distance from Jupiter; Jupiter's gravity is not offered as a contributing factor to this inactivity.

D The passage does not contrast Jupiter with its moons; rather, it compares the moons to one another.

E The first paragraph of the passage suggests that Jupiter's moons vary in a way similar to that of the planets of the solar system, but the author does not refer to Jupiter's gravity to illustrate the similarity in this variation.

The correct answer is A.

Questions 431–434 refer to the passage on page 376.

431. According to the passage, the research mentioned in line 6 suggests which of the following about lower-ranked top executives and postacquisition success?

(A) Given that these executives are unlikely to contribute to postacquisition success, little effort should be spent trying to retain them.

(B) The shorter their length of service, the less likely it is that these executives will play a significant role in postacquisition success.

(C) These executives are less important to postacquisition success than are more highly ranked top executives.

(D) If they have long tenures, these executives may prove to be as important to postacquisition success as are more highly ranked top executives.

(E) Postacquisition success is unlikely if these executives are retained.

Supporting idea

The question asks about information provided by the passage. According to the third sentence, research suggests that retaining the highest-level top executives in an acquisition is more strongly associated with success than retaining lower-ranked top executives—which suggests, in turn, that lower-ranked top executives are less important than top-level executives to postacquisition success, though it does not suggest that they are unimportant to such success.

A The research indicates that lower-ranked top executives are less strongly associated with success than are higher-ranked executives but does not provide advice about retention efforts.

B The research mentioned in the third sentence does not consider length of service.

C **Correct.** The research indicates that lower-ranked top executives are less strongly associated with postacquisition success than are the highest-ranked executives.

D The research mentioned in the third sentence does not consider length of service.

E The research suggests that lower-ranked top executives are less strongly associated with postacquisition success but does not suggest that they decrease the likelihood of success.

The correct answer is C.

432. The resource-based view, as described in the passage, is based on which of the following ideas?

(A) The managerial skills of top executives become strongest after the first five years of their tenure.

(B) Company-specific knowledge is an important factor in the success of an acquisition process.

(C) The amount of nontransferable knowledge possessed by long-tenured top executives tends to be underestimated.

(D) Effective implementation of an acquisition depends primarily on the ability of executives to adapt to change.

(E) Short-tenured executives are likely to impede the implementation of a successful acquisition strategy.

Evaluation

This question requires analysis of the reasoning underlying one of the two explanations described in the passage. The resource-based view (RBV) holds that retaining high-level executives with long tenure will contribute to success because those people have important company-specific knowledge. This view rests on the assumption that company-specific knowledge is valuable to postacquisition success.

A In RBV, executives with long tenure are valuable not specifically for their managerial skills but for their knowledge about the acquired company. The passage does not restrict to five years the period in which this knowledge is gained.

B **Correct.** RBV values executives' knowledge of the acquired company and is based on the belief that company-specific knowledge is valuable for postacquisition success.

C The passage does not indicate that RBV claims that executives' company-specific knowledge is generally undervalued. But the passage does indicate that RBV regards such knowledge as valuable to postacquisition success.

D In RBV, executives with long tenure are valuable not for their ability to adapt to change, but for their knowledge about the acquired company.

E RBV does not suggest that short-tenured executives impede postacquisition success, only that they are less important to success than the highest-ranked executives.

The correct answer is B.

433. The passage suggests that Bergh and a proponent of the upper echelons perspective would be most likely to disagree over which of the following?

(A) Whether there is a positive correlation between short organizational tenure and managerial adaptability

(B) Whether there is a positive correlation between long organizational tenure and the acquisition of idiosyncratic and nontransferable knowledge

(C) Whether adaptability is a useful trait for an executive who is managing an acquisition process

(D) Whether retaining less-tenured top executives of an acquired company is an optimal strategy for achieving postacquisition success

(E) Whether retaining highest-level top executives of acquired companies is more important than retaining lower-ranked top executives

Inference

The question asks about conclusions that can reasonably be drawn from the information provided in the passage. Bergh's study supports the resource-based view (RBV), which suggests that top executives with long tenure are more valuable to postacquisition success than other executives. The upper echelons perspective (UEP), in contrast, suggests that top executives with shorter tenure are more valuable to postacquisition success. Thus, Bergh and a proponent of UEP would likely disagree about whether long or short tenure top executives are more valuable to a positive outcome in a postacquisition situation.

A The passage does not provide sufficiently specific information about statistical relationships to determine whether Bergh and proponents of UEP would agree or disagree about whether there is such a positive correlation.

B There is a weak suggestion in the passage that Bergh believes such a positive correlation exists, but there is no indication that a proponent of UEP would question such a correlation.

C The passage does not indicate that Bergh would disagree with proponents of UEP that adaptability is a valuable trait in an executive who is managing an acquisition.

D Correct. The passage suggests that proponents of UEP believe that retaining less-tenured top executives during and after an acquisition is a better strategy, while Bergh believes that retaining longer-tenured top executives is better.

E The passage suggests that Bergh and proponents of UEP agree that retaining the highest-level top executives is more important to postacquisition success than is retaining lower-ranked top executives.

The correct answer is D.

434. According to the passage, prior to Bergh's study, research on the role of top executives of acquired companies in business acquisition success was limited in which of the following ways?

(A) It did not address how the organizational tenure of top executives affects postacquisition success.

(B) It did not address why some companies have longer-tenured CEOs than others.

(C) It did not consider strategies for retaining long-tenured top executives of acquired companies.

(D) It failed to differentiate between the contribution of highest-level top executives to postacquisition success and that of lower-ranked top executives.

(E) It underestimated the potential contribution that lower-level top executives can make to postacquisition success.

Supporting idea

This question asks about information explicitly provided in the passage. The first paragraph summarizes research indicating that retaining highest-level top executives during and after an acquisition is more strongly associated with successful outcomes than retaining lower-ranking top executives. The paragraph then states that this research has limitations, including failing to take into account how long the highest-ranking executives have worked for the company. The second paragraph explains that Bergh's study responds to those limitations by analyzing the role of tenure (length of service in the organization).

A **Correct.** The passage indicates that the research about the role of highest-level executives in acquisitions is limited by its failure to consider tenure.

B The passage does not portray the failure of the research to address this as a limitation of the research in question.

C The passage does not portray the failure of the research to consider this as a limitation of the research in question.

D The passage indicates that the research does, in fact, differentiate between the respective contributions of these two groups of top executives.

E Undervaluing the contributions of lower-level top executives is not one of the limitations mentioned in the passage.

The correct answer is A.

Questions 435–438 refer to the passage on page 378.

435. According to the passage, which of the following contributed to Marcus Garvey's success?

(A) He introduced cultural and historical consciousness to the African American community.

(B) He believed enthusiastically in the traditional American success ethos.

(C) His audience had already formed a consciousness that made it receptive to his message.

(D) His message appealed to critics of African American support for United States military involvement in the First World War.

(E) He supported the movement to protest segregation that had emerged prior to his arrival in the United States.

Supporting idea

To answer this question, find what the passage states explicitly about how Marcus Garvey achieved his success. The passage begins by stating that Garvey arrived at the right time: that returning African American soldiers were primed to receive what he had to say about the African American community. These soldiers already held strong beliefs about their rights to opportunities for success; the passage concludes that the divide between the soldiers' expectations and their experiences led to Garvey's success.

A The passage states that African American people were in possession of a strong cultural and historical consciousness prior to Garvey's arrival in the United States.

B The passage attributes belief in the traditional American success ethos to African American people who joined the armed forces; it does not mention Garvey's beliefs on this subject.

C **Correct.** African American soldiers who had experienced segregation during the First World War were ready to hear what Garvey had to say.

D Critics of African American support for United States involvement in the First World War are not mentioned in the passage.

E While Garvey most likely would have supported a movement to protest segregation, such a movement is not discussed in the passage.

The correct answer is C.

436. The passage suggests that many African American people responded to their experiences in the armed forces in which of the following ways?

(A) They maintained as civilians their enthusiastic allegiance to the armed forces.

(B) They questioned United States involvement in the First World War.

(C) They joined political organizations to protest the segregation of African American troops and the indignities they suffered in the military.

(D) They became aware of the gap between their expectations and the realities of American culture.

(E) They repudiated Garvey's message of pride and unity.

Inference

According to the passage, African Americans enthusiastically joined the armed services but were confronted with continued segregation, both in the military and when they returned home. The passage does not explicitly state their response to these experiences, but a response can be inferred. The second paragraph refers to anthropologist Anthony F. C. Wallace, who argued that a revitalization movement may be brought about by the perception of a gap between expectations and reality, and such a revitalization did occur in African American communities following the First World War; thus, many African American people may have become aware of a gap such as Wallace described.

A The passage states that African American troops experienced segregation and other indignities while in the military; these experiences could reasonably be inferred to have dampened their enthusiasm for the armed forces. Regardless, the passage does not suggest an enthusiastic allegiance.

B The passage describes African American people's enthusiasm about joining the military. Although they experienced segregation and other indignities while in the military, the passage does not suggest that their opinion about involvement in the war changed.

C While African American troops may have joined political organizations, the passage does not provide any actual evidence of this having occurred.

D Correct. The fact that, as the passage states, a revitalization movement occurred in the African American community following the First World War suggests that the returning soldiers did become aware of the gap between their expectations of an improved situation with regard to segregation and the reality of continued segregation in the United States.

E The passage does not suggest that African American troops repudiated Garvey's message. On the contrary, it states that Garvey built *the largest revitalization movement in African American history*. This suggests that the members of the African American community, including the returning soldiers, were extremely receptive to Garvey's message.

The correct answer is D.

437. It can be inferred from the passage that the "scholars" mentioned in line 24 believe which of the following to be true?

(A) Revitalization resulted from the political activism of returning African American soldiers following the First World War.

(B) Marcus Garvey had to change a number of prevailing attitudes in order for his mass movement to find a foothold in the United States.

(C) The prevailing sensibility of the African American community provided the foundation of Marcus Garvey's political appeal.

(D) Marcus Garvey hoped to revitalize consciousness of cultural and historical identity in the African American community.

(E) The goal of the mass movement that Marcus Garvey helped bring into being was to build on the pride and unity among African Americans.

Inference

To determine what it is logical to infer regarding the scholars discussed in the third paragraph, look at the context in which they are mentioned. According to the passage, these scholars argue that Garvey was responsible for creating a particular consciousness within the African American community, a consciousness that the passage identifies as *identity, strength, and* [a] *sense of history*. Unlike the passage author, these scholars believe strongly in Garvey's responsibility for this consciousness, so they would most likely reject any suggestion that it existed prior to his arrival and activism.

A According to the passage, the scholars believe that Garvey was responsible for the creation of the consciousness that led to revitalization, which suggests that revitalization resulted from Garvey's activism, not soldiers' activism.

B Correct. According to the passage, the scholars believe that Garvey created the consciousness that led to his revitalization movement. This suggests that he had to change prevailing attitudes in order to foster this new consciousness.

C According to the passage, the scholars believe that Garvey created a new consciousness in the African American community; thus, the prevailing sensibility could not have provided a foundation for his appeal.

D According to the passage, the scholars believe that Garvey built his revitalization movement on a new consciousness of cultural and historical identity, not a previously existing one.

E According to the passage, the scholars' position is that Garvey's movement was built on a new sense of pride and unity that he provided, and that that sense did not precede Garvey's work.

The correct answer is B.

438. According to the passage, many African American people joined the armed forces during the First World War for which of the following reasons?

(A) They wished to escape worsening economic conditions in African American communities.
(B) They expected to fulfill ideals of personal attainment.
(C) They sought to express their loyalty to the United States.
(D) They hoped that joining the military would help advance the cause of desegregation.
(E) They saw military service as an opportunity to fulfill Marcus Garvey's political vision.

Supporting idea

This question depends on identifying what the passage states directly about African American people's reasons for joining the armed forces. The reason offered by the passage is that the African American people who entered the armed forces did so because they were *hoping to participate in the traditional American ethos of individual success.*

A Although this is a plausible reason for entering the armed forces, the passage does not discuss economic conditions.

B **Correct.** The passage states that African American people who joined the armed forces during the First World War wanted to achieve individual success.

C The passage does not discuss African American people's loyalty to the United States.

D The passage states that African American troops experienced segregation, but it does not suggest that they had hoped their joining the military would promote desegregation.

E The passage suggests that African American troops did not become aware of Marcus Garvey's political vision until after they returned from the First World War.

The correct answer is B.

Questions 439–441 refer to the passage on page 380.

439. The primary purpose of the passage is to

(A) compare the adaptive responses of several species of columnar cacti in the Sonoran Desert with those in the arid tropical regions of southern Mexico
(B) discuss some of the possible causes of the relatively low abundance of migratory nectar-feeding bats in the Sonoran Desert
(C) provide a possible explanation for a particular evolutionary change in certain species of columnar cacti in the Sonoran Desert
(D) present recent findings that challenge a particular theory as to why several species of columnar cacti in the Sonoran Desert have expanded their range of pollinators
(E) compare the effectiveness of nocturnal and diurnal pollination for several different species of columnar cacti in the Sonoran Desert

Main idea

This question depends on understanding the passage as a whole. The first paragraph discusses an evolutionary change undergone by columnar cacti in the Sonoran Desert with regard to pollination. The second paragraph offers a possible reason for this change—migratory nectar-feeding bats are unreliable pollinators—and the third paragraph goes on to provide evidence that supports the reason given in the second paragraph.

A The passage does compare the adaptations of cacti in the Sonoran Desert with those of cacti in southern Mexico, but it does so in support of a larger point about the Sonoran Desert cacti.

B The relatively low abundance of migratory nectar-feeding bats in the Sonoran Desert is important to the passage in that it provides a reason why the columnar cacti in that region have made certain adaptations. But the passage does not explain why the bats are not particularly abundant.

C **Correct.** The flowers of the columnar cacti in the Sonoran Desert have evolved to remain open after sunrise, and the passage is primarily concerned with explaining why this change may have taken place.

D The passage presents recent findings that support, rather than challenge, a theory as to why the columnar cacti of the Sonoran Desert have expanded their range of pollinators. The passage does not allude to any competing theory that may be challenged by the findings.

E Any comparison of the effectiveness of nocturnal and diurnal pollination for columnar cacti in the Sonoran Desert is made in support of the passage's primary concern: explaining why these cacti have come to remain open and receptive to pollination in daylight.

The correct answer is C.

440. According to the passage, which of the following types of nectar-feeding pollinators is likely to be an unreliable pollinator of a particular cactus flower?

(A) A dietary specialist whose abundance is typically high in relation to that of the flower
(B) A dietary specialist whose abundance is at times significantly lower than that of the flower
(C) A dietary generalist for whom that flower's nectar is not a preferred food but is the most consistently available food
(D) A dietary generalist for whom that flower's nectar is slightly preferred to other available foods
(E) A dietary generalist that evolved from a species of dietary specialists

Supporting idea

This question depends on recognizing the qualities of an unreliable pollinator, as described in the passage. The second paragraph addresses this issue: it explains that the unreliability of pollinators can arise in any of three ways: they may be dietary generalists with alternative sources of food; they may be dietary specialists whose own abundance varies; or they may be dietary specialists whose abundance is chronically low in relation to the flowers.

A A dietary specialist whose abundance is high in relation to the flowers on which it feeds would likely be a reliable pollinator.

B **Correct.** A dietary specialist whose abundance is at times significantly lower than that of the flower it pollinates would be, according to the passage, unreliable.

C A dietary generalist who finds the flower of a particular species more consistently available than other suitable food sources would most likely be a reliable pollinator of that flower.

D A dietary generalist who prefers the flower's nectar would likely be a reliable pollinator of that flower compared to other flowers.

E The passage provides no reason to believe that the evolution of a pollinator's dietary preference has any bearing on its reliability as a pollinator.

The correct answer is B.

441. According to the passage, present-day columnar cacti in the Sonoran Desert differ from their close relatives in southern Mexico in that the Sonoran cacti

(A) have flowers that remain open after sunset
(B) are pollinated primarily by dietary specialists
(C) can be pollinated by nectar-feeding bats
(D) have stigmas that are unreceptive to pollination at night
(E) are sometimes pollinated by diurnal pollinators

Supporting idea

This question depends on identifying a difference noted in the passage between columnar cacti in the Sonoran Desert and their relatives in southern Mexico. The first paragraph states that in southern Mexico, columnar cactus flowers are not receptive to pollination by diurnal pollinators, whereas in the Sonoran Desert, the flowers have evolved to allow diurnal pollination.

A The cacti in both the Sonoran Desert and southern Mexico have flowers that remain open after sunset, because cacti in both locations can be pollinated nocturnally.

B Sonoran Desert cacti are pollinated, at least partially, by nectar-feeding bats, which are dietary specialists. But the cacti in southern Mexico are pollinated by these specialists, too.

C Sonoran Desert cacti can be pollinated by nectar-feeding bats—but so can cacti in southern Mexico.

D Cacti in the Sonoran Desert have stigmas that have evolved to be receptive to pollination both at night and during the day.

E **Correct.** The distinction between cacti in the Sonoran Desert and those in southern Mexico is that Sonoran Desert cacti have evolved to allow pollination during the day—that is, pollination by diurnal pollinators.

The correct answer is E.

Questions 442–449 refer to the passage on page 382.

442. The passage provides information in support of which of the following assertions?

(A) The disadvantages of an adaptation to a particular feature of an environment often outweigh the advantages of such an adaptation.

(B) An organism's reaction to being placed in an environment to which it is not well adapted can sometimes illustrate the problems that have been solved by the adaptations of organisms indigenous to that environment.

(C) The effectiveness of an organism's adaptation to a particular feature of its environment can only be evaluated by examining the effectiveness with which organisms of other species have adapted to a similar feature of a different environment.

(D) Organisms of the same species that inhabit strikingly different environments will often adapt in remarkably similar ways to the few features of those environments that are common.

(E) Different species of organisms living in the same environment will seldom adapt to features of that environment in the same way.

Application

This question requires recognizing a principle underlying the passage's overall discussion. The passage makes a general claim about terrestrial animals' need to overcome the effect of gravity on their blood circulation systems, and it then uses the specific example of terrestrial snakes to illustrate this claim. To help identify the adaptations used by terrestrial snakes, the passage describes what happens to sea snakes, which are aquatic and less affected by gravity's influence, when they are subjected to a terrestrial environment. The specific problems faced by these snakes strongly suggest that terrestrial snakes have developed ways to overcome these problems. The passage then identifies specific physiological differences between sea snakes and terrestrial snakes that demonstrate how terrestrial snakes overcome gravity's influence.

A The passage discusses how species have successfully adapted to their specific environments and does not mention that these adaptations create disadvantages in that environment.

B **Correct.** The passage discusses the problems faced by sea snakes when they are subjected to a terrestrial environment and then examines terrestrial snakes to illustrate how certain adaptations solved these problems.

C The passage is not concerned with evaluating the effectiveness of species' adaptations to their environments; it takes for granted that these adaptations are effective.

D The passage is concerned with how species adapt differently to different environments and not with how adaptations to different environments are similar.

E The passage discusses how different environments affect how species have adapted, not how different species adapt to a similar environment.

The correct answer is B.

443. According to the passage, one reason that the distribution of blood in the sea snake changes little while the creature remains in the ocean is that

(A) the heart of the sea snake tends to be located near the center of its body

(B) pressure gradients in the water surrounding the sea snake counter the effects of vertical pressure gradients within its blood vessels

(C) the sea snake assumes a vertical posture less frequently than do the terrestrial and the arboreal snake

(D) the sea snake often relies on waves of muscle contractions to help move blood from the torso to the head

(E) the force of pressure gradients in the water surrounding the sea snake exceeds that of vertical pressure gradients within its circulatory system

Supporting ideas

This question asks for an identification of factual information in the passage. Given that the contrast between sea snakes and terrestrial snakes is being used to identify adaptations used by terrestrial animals to overcome the effect of gravity on their circulation systems, the passage needs initially to illustrate why it is that sea snakes are not confronted with the same problems that gravity causes for terrestrial snakes. This information therefore needs to come fairly early in the passage.

A The passage identifies the location of a sea snake's heart as a factor that minimizes the effort required to pump blood to both extremities but not as a cause of the even distribution of blood in sea snakes.

B Correct. The passage states explicitly in lines 11–17 that while sea snakes are in the ocean, the vertical pressure gradients in their blood vessels are counteracted by the pressure gradients in the water.

C The passage does not discuss the frequency with which any snakes assume certain postures.

D The passage discusses muscle contractions only in relation to arboreal snakes.

E The passage states that the vertical pressures within sea snakes' blood vessels are *counteracted* (line 13) by the water's pressure, which suggests that the pressures are equalized, not that one force exceeds the other.

The correct answer is B.

444. It can be inferred from the passage that which of the following is true of species of terrestrial snakes that often need to assume a vertical posture?

(A) They are more likely to be susceptible to circulatory failure in vertical postures than are sea snakes.

(B) Their hearts are less likely to be located at the midpoint of their bodies than is the case with sea snakes.

(C) They cannot counteract the pooling of blood in lower regions of their bodies as effectively as sea snakes can.

(D) The blood pressure at their midpoint decreases significantly when they are tilted with their heads up.

(E) They are unable to rely on muscle contractions to move venous blood from the lower torso to the head.

Inference

This question requires using information given about how arboreal snakes, which are frequently in vertical postures, have adapted to gravity's influence to make an assumption that other terrestrial snakes that are frequently in these postures are likely to have similar adaptations. The passage implies that sea snakes have hearts at the midpoint of their bodies because the water's pressure gradients help distribute blood evenly. It then illustrates that arboreal snakes have hearts closer to their heads to help keep blood flowing to their brains when they are in vertical postures.

A The passage does not suggest that any of the snakes mentioned are ill-adapted to their particular environments.

B Correct. The passage states that arboreal snakes have hearts close to their heads and not at the midpoints of their bodies, so it is reasonable to conclude that any terrestrial snake that frequently assumes vertical postures would be unlikely to have hearts at their bodies' midpoint.

C As with answer choice (A), the passage does not suggest that any species of snake is ill-adapted to its environment.

D The passage states that sea snakes lose pressure at their midpoints when they are tilted on land with heads up but that terrestrial snakes do not have this problem.

E Because arboreal snakes use muscle contractions to circulate blood when they are vertical, it is likely that most terrestrial snakes that frequently assume vertical postures also have this capability.

The correct answer is B.

445. The author describes the behavior of the circulatory system of sea snakes when they are removed from the ocean (see lines 17–20) primarily in order to

(A) illustrate what would occur in the circulatory system of terrestrial snakes without adaptations that enable them to regulate their blood pressure in vertical orientations

(B) explain why arboreal snakes in vertical orientations must rely on muscle contractions to restore blood pressure to the brain

(C) illustrate the effects of circulatory failure on the behavior of arboreal snakes

(D) illustrate the superiority of the circulatory system of the terrestrial snake to that of the sea snake

(E) explain how changes in spatial orientation can adversely affect the circulatory system of snakes with hearts located in relatively close proximity to their heads

Evaluation

Answering this question requires understanding why sea snakes have been brought into the passage's overall discussion about how terrestrial animals have overcome the influence of gravity on their blood circulation. The passage uses the effects that gravity has on sea snakes when they are taken out of water to identify problems that terrestrial snakes must have adapted to in order to survive.

A Correct. The passage uses the problems sea snakes have when taken out of water to illustrate that without certain adaptations, terrestrial snakes would likely have similar problems.

B The passage discusses sea snakes to illustrate problems faced by terrestrial snakes, not to explain how terrestrial snakes have adapted to gravity's influence.

C The passage does not discuss the effects of circulatory failure on arboreal snakes.

D The passage does not compare or contrast the effectiveness of the various adaptations used by different snakes.

E The passage does not imply that snakes with hearts close to their heads are adversely affected by spatial positions.

The correct answer is A.

446. It can be inferred from the passage that which of the following is a true statement about sea snakes?

(A) They frequently rely on waves of muscle contractions from the lower torso to the head to supplement the work of the heart.

(B) They cannot effectively regulate their blood pressure when placed in seawater and tilted at an angle with the head pointed downward.

(C) They are more likely to have a heart located in close proximity to their heads than are arboreal snakes.

(D) They become acutely vulnerable to the effects of gravitational pressure on their circulatory system when they are placed in a terrestrial environment.

(E) Their cardiovascular system is not as complicated as that of arboreal snakes.

Inference

Answering this question requires understanding why sea snakes are discussed in the passage and what happens to them when they are taken out of water and subjected to the force of gravity. The second paragraph implies strongly that sea snakes will not survive certain terrestrial situations for which they are not adapted.

A The passage associates muscle contractions to circulate blood with arboreal snakes only.

B According to the passage, sea snakes' inability to regulate blood pressure occurs only when they are taken out of water.

C The passage states clearly that arboreal snakes have hearts closer to their heads than do sea snakes.

D Correct. The passage states that in certain postures, sea snakes placed in a terrestrial environment will lose all blood pressure at their brains, which is an acute vulnerability.

E The passage does not provide the information needed to compare the complexity of the various snakes discussed.

The correct answer is D.

447. The author suggests that which of the following is a disadvantage that results from the location of a snake's heart in close proximity to its head?

(A) A decrease in the efficiency with which the snake regulates the flow of blood to the brain

(B) A decrease in the number of orientations in space that a snake can assume without loss of blood flow to the brain

(C) A decrease in blood pressure at the snake's midpoint when it is tilted at various angles with its head up

(D) An increase in the tendency of blood to pool at the snake's head when the snake is tilted at various angles with its head down

(E) An increase in the amount of effort required to distribute blood to and from the snake's tail

Inference

This question asks for an inference about the location of a snake's heart being closer to the brain than to the midpoint of its body. In the third paragraph, the passage states that in terrestrial snakes, which must fight the influence of gravity, the closer proximity of the heart to the head ensures blood circulation to the brain. The passage notes, however, that this makes it more difficult for such snakes to maintain blood circulation to the tail.

A The passage states that snakes have hearts closer to their heads to more efficiently circulate blood to the brain.

B The passage suggests that having the heart close to the head increases the spatial orientations a snake can assume without losing blood flow to the brain, rather than decreases the number of orientations.

C The passage indicates that this is true only of sea snakes with hearts near their body's midpoint.

D The passage mentions blood pooling in the lower portions of a terrestrial organism's body but does not imply that blood can pool at a snake's head.

E Correct. Because, as the passage states, it is more difficult for a snake with its heart close to its head to circulate blood to the tail, and therefore its body is likely to put more effort into circulating blood to the tail.

The correct answer is E.

448. The primary purpose of the third paragraph is to

(A) introduce a topic that is not discussed earlier in the passage

(B) describe a more efficient method of achieving an effect discussed in the previous paragraph

(C) draw a conclusion based on information elaborated in the previous paragraph

(D) discuss two specific examples of phenomena mentioned at the end of the previous paragraph

(E) introduce evidence that undermines a view reported earlier in the passage

Evaluation

Answering this question requires recognizing how the passage develops its main point. The first paragraph sets up a general claim about gravity's influence on terrestrial organisms. The second paragraph then describes the ill effects that gravity has on sea snakes to identify problems that terrestrial snakes have had to adapt to. The third paragraph then uses examples to illustrate how terrestrial snakes have adapted to gravity's influence.

A The topic of the third paragraph is the adaptations developed by terrestrial snakes to survive gravity's influence, which is part of the discussion in both the first and second paragraphs.

B There is no comparison in the passage of the efficiency of the different methods used by snakes to adapt to gravity's influence.

C The third paragraph is concerned with illustrating certain adaptations used by snakes and offers no conclusions about the problems terrestrial snakes have had to adapt to, which is the topic of the second paragraph.

D **Correct.** The end of the second paragraph refers to *certain adaptations* (line 23) that the third paragraph then goes on to identify and discuss.

E The third paragraph supports the main idea of the passage and is not used to counter any claim made earlier.

The correct answer is D.

449. In the passage, the author is primarily concerned with doing which of the following?

(A) Explaining adaptations that enable the terrestrial snake to cope with the effects of gravitational pressure on its circulatory system

(B) Comparing the circulatory system of the sea snake with that of the terrestrial snake

(C) Explaining why the circulatory system of the terrestrial snake is different from that of the sea snake

(D) Pointing out features of the terrestrial snake's cardiovascular system that make it superior to that of the sea snake

(E) Explaining how the sea snake is able to neutralize the effects of gravitational pressure on its circulatory system

Main idea

Answering this question involves assessing what the passage as a whole is attempting to do. While the passage begins by making a general claim about gravity's influence on the cardiovascular systems of terrestrial animals, it immediately points to terrestrial snakes as a good example supporting this claim. The rest of the passage is then devoted to illustrating, using the observations involving sea snakes, how gravity's influence has shaped the cardiovascular systems of terrestrial snakes.

A **Correct.** The entire passage is devoted to an explanation of how terrestrial snakes have adapted to gravity's influence.

B While the passage does compare the systems of the two snakes, it does so for the larger purpose of demonstrating gravity's influence on terrestrial snakes.

C The passage is more concerned with *how* the systems of the two snakes are different, rather than *why*, in order to identify how terrestrial snakes have adapted to gravity's influence.

D There is no judgment in the passage as to the superiority of one snake's system over the other.

E While the passage does explain how sea snakes do this, it does so only for the larger purpose of identifying how terrestrial snakes have adapted to gravity's influence.

The correct answer is A.

Questions 450–455 refer to the passage on page 386.

450. The passage is primarily concerned with

(A) contrasting the benefits of one methodology with the benefits of another

(B) describing the historical origins and inherent drawbacks of a particular methodology

(C) discussing the appeal of a particular methodology and some concerns about its use

(D) showing that some historians' adoption of a particular methodology has led to criticism of recent historical scholarship

(E) analyzing the influence of current feminist views on women's interpretations of their experience

Main idea

This question asks for an abstract view of what the passage as a whole is primarily doing. The passage introduces a particular methodology that scholars of women's history have been encouraged to employ, explaining why the use of the methodology is supported. The passage then goes on to raise some concerns about the use of the methodology and cites one example in which caution is needed.

A The passage is primarily concerned with only one methodology.

B The passage mentions why the methodology had been encouraged but does not give the history of its origins; while it cautions historians to employ the methodology carefully, it is not concerned with drawbacks of its proper use.

C **Correct.** The passage discusses why the use of a methodology is being encouraged and then offers some concerns about its use.

D The passage does not discuss any criticism of recent scholarship in women's history.

E There is no mention in the passage that feminist theory is influencing how women in general think about their experiences.

The correct answer is C.

451. According to the passage, which of the following shapes the oral narratives of women storytellers?

(A) The conventions for standard histories in the culture in which a woman storyteller lives

(B) The conventions of storytelling in the culture in which a woman storyteller lives

(C) A woman storyteller's experience with distinctive traditions of storytelling developed by the women in her family of origin

(D) The cultural expectations and experiences of those who listen to oral narratives

(E) A woman storyteller's familiarity with the stories that members of other groups in her culture tell to explain themselves

Supporting ideas

This question asks for an identification of specific information provided by the passage. In the second paragraph, the passage describes certain concerns about using oral narratives. One of these concerns is that *the stories people tell to explain themselves are shaped by . . . storytelling conventions* (lines 17–19) and other influences tied to the teller's cultural and historical context.

A The passage uses *standard histories* (line 7) to refer to the usual work of scholars and not to something that influences oral narratives.

B **Correct.** The passage raises as a concern that oral narratives may be influenced by storytelling conventions present in the culture of the speaker.

C The passage does not mention the family of origin of women storytellers.

D The passage does not mention the expectations of the listeners of oral narratives.

E The passage does not discuss women storytellers' familiarity with the oral narratives belonging to other groups of women.

The correct answer is B.

452. The author of the passage would be most likely to make which of the following recommendations to scholars of women's history?

(A) They should take into account their own life experiences when interpreting the oral accounts of women's historical experiences.

(B) They should assume that the observations made in women's oral narratives are believed by the intended audience of the story.

(C) They should treat skeptically observations reported in oral narratives unless the observations can be confirmed in standard histories.

(D) They should consider the cultural and historical context in which an oral narrative was created before arriving at an interpretation of such a narrative.

(E) They should rely on information gathered from oral narratives only when equivalent information is not available in standard histories.

Application

Answering this question involves recognizing what the author believes about oral narratives and then applying this belief to a hypothetical situation in which the author makes recommendations to scholars of women's history. While acknowledging the appeal of oral narratives to these scholars, in the second paragraph the author urges caution when using these narratives as sources of *disinterested commentary* (line 16). The passage then states that people's oral narratives are shaped by *cultural and historical factors* (line 20), which presumably relate to the cultural and historical context within which the narratives are spoken.

A The passage does not mention the personal life experiences of scholars.

B The passage does not mention the intended audiences of oral narratives.

C The passage mentions *standard histories* (line 7) only as a reference to scholarly works that often have shortcomings.

D Correct. The passage cautions that oral narratives may be biased due to cultural and historical factors, and it is therefore reasonable to suppose that the author would recommend that scholars consider this when using such information.

E The passage does not refer to oral narratives as being valuable only for filling a gap in the available historical record.

The correct answer is D.

453. Which of the following best describes the function of the last sentence of the passage?

(A) It describes an event that historians view as crucial in recent women's history.

(B) It provides an example of how political rhetoric may influence the interpretations of experience reported in women's oral narratives.

(C) It provides an example of an oral narrative that inaccurately describes women's experience during a particular historical period.

(D) It illustrates the point that some women are more aware than others of the social forces that shape their oral narratives.

(E) It identifies the historical conditions that led to the social acceptance of women's paid work outside the home.

Evaluation

This question requires recognizing how a particular part of the passage is related to the overall reasoning in the passage. The first paragraph introduces a methodology and describes the methodology's appeal. The second paragraph then raises concerns about the use of the methodology, drawing attention to the cultural and historical bias that may be present in oral narratives. In line 21, the passage refers specifically to the influence *political rhetoric* may have on a woman's understanding of her experience. In the final sentence, the passage provides a specific hypothetical example of a woman at the time of the Second World War to illustrate this concern.

A The last sentence employs a hypothetical example and does not describe a particular event as being important to historians.

B Correct. After contending that political rhetoric may influence oral narratives, the passage uses the example of the Second World War in the final sentence to support this claim.

C The last sentence does not provide a particular example of an oral narrative.

D The passage does not claim that some women are more aware than others of the social forces that may bear on them.

E The passage does not claim that social conditions during the Second World War led to acceptance of women in the workplace.

The correct answer is B.

454. According to the passage, scholars of women's history should refrain from doing which of the following?

(A) Relying on traditional historical sources when women's oral narratives are unavailable
(B) Focusing on the influence of political rhetoric on women's perceptions to the exclusion of other equally important factors
(C) Attempting to discover the cultural and historical factors that influence the stories women tell
(D) Assuming that the conventions of women's written autobiographies are similar to the conventions of women's oral narratives
(E) Accepting women's oral narratives less critically than they accept women's written histories

Inference

Answering this question requires recognizing which option is directly inferable from information in the passage. After describing in the first paragraph why oral narratives are appealing to historians, the passage begins the second paragraph by imploring scholars of women's history to *be as cautious about accepting oral narratives … as … written memories* (lines 12–14). The passage then goes on to describe potential bias in oral narratives, suggesting that scholars should be as critical of them as they are of written sources.

A The passage does not claim that traditional historical sources should be avoided by scholars.
B The passage mentions the influence of political rhetoric merely as one example of potential bias.
C The passage suggests that scholars *should* attempt to be aware of cultural and historical factors.
D The passage does not discuss the conventions of women's written autobiographies.
E **Correct.** The passage implies that written histories and oral narratives should receive the same level of critical scrutiny by scholars.

The correct answer is E.

455. According to the passage, each of the following is a difference between women's oral narratives and most standard histories EXCEPT:

(A) Women's oral histories validate the significance of women's achievements.
(B) Women's oral histories depict experience from the point of view of women.
(C) Women's oral histories acknowledge the influence of well-known women.
(D) Women's oral histories present today's women with a sense of their historical relationship to women of the past.
(E) Women's oral histories are crucial to the collective identity of today's women.

Supporting ideas

This question asks for information that is stated in the passage, and it requires a process of elimination. In line 7, oral narratives are presented as being *unlike most standard histories*, and the passage then goes on in lines 7–11 to list characteristics of oral histories that most standard histories do not have. The answer to this question will therefore contain a characteristic of women's oral histories that is not described in lines 7–11.

A The passage states that, unlike most standard histories, women's oral histories *affirm the importance of women's contributions* (lines 8–9).
B The passage states that, unlike most standard histories, women's oral histories *represent experience from the perspective of women* (lines 7–8).
C **Correct.** The passage does not mention the influence of well-known women on women's oral histories.
D The passage states that, unlike most standard histories, women's oral histories *furnish present-day women with historical continuity* (lines 9–10).
E The passage states that, unlike most standard histories, women's oral histories furnish a historical sense that is *essential to their identity, individually and collectively* (line 11).

The correct answer is C.

Questions 456–460 refer to the passage on page 388.

456. The passage suggests that in order for a manufacturer in a capital-intensive industry to have a decisive advantage over competitors making similar products, the manufacturer must

(A) be the first in the industry to build production facilities of theoretically optimal size
(B) make every effort to keep fixed and sunk costs as low as possible
(C) be one of the first to operate its manufacturing plants at minimum efficient scale
(D) produce goods of higher quality than those produced by direct competitors
(E) stockpile raw materials at production sites in order to ensure a steady flow of such materials

Inference

This question asks for an inference about what a manufacturer in a capital-intensive industry must do to have an advantage over competitors making similar products. The passage addresses this question by stating that advantage accrues to those firms that are the first to exploit the full potential of optimally sized, technologically sophisticated plants. In this context, exploiting the full potential of such plants means operating them at *minimum efficient scale.* Based on the definition in the first paragraph, this means that the plant must have an output of such a size that the cost per unit of output is at a minimum.

A The passage says that for new capital-intensive firms to dominate the market, it is not enough for them to have optimally sized plants; the plants must also be operated in a way that fully exploits their potential.

B While keeping fixed and sunk costs low would obviously help keep overall costs low, the passage does not suggest that this is decisive in enabling a firm to have an advantage over competitors.

C **Correct.** Being among the first manufacturers to operate plants at minimum efficient scale means that those plants are being exploited to their full potential. This strategy would most likely give such manufacturers a decisive advantage over new firms hoping to compete effectively.

D The passage does not discuss the quality of goods made by manufacturers.

E The passage does not suggest that stockpiling raw materials is the most efficient way to ensure a steady flow of raw materials into the manufacturing process, though the passage states that such a steady flow is a factor in achieving minimum efficient scale.

The correct answer is C.

457. The passage suggests that which of the following is true of a manufacturer's fixed and sunk costs?

(A) The extent to which they are determined by market conditions for the goods being manufactured is frequently underestimated.
(B) If they are kept as low as possible, the manufacturer is very likely to realize significant profits.
(C) They are the primary factor that determines whether a manufacturer will realize economies of scale.
(D) They should be on a par with the fixed and sunk costs of the manufacturer's competitors.
(E) They are not affected by fluctuations in a manufacturing plant's throughput.

Inference

This question asks about what the passage implies about fixed and sunk costs. The passage states that when production declines due to certain factors, such costs remain at the same level (which may be high), and the cost per unit produced (*unit costs*) rises sharply.

A The passage discusses the impact of market conditions on determining what the optimal size of a manufacturing plant is (which affects fixed and sunk costs). But it makes no claim about the frequency with which such an impact is "underestimated."

B The passage emphasizes that failing to keep throughput at an efficiently high level reduces profitability because that failure results in increased cost per unit (to which, of course, the plant's fixed and sunk costs contribute). But the passage does not claim that keeping aggregate fixed and sunk costs very low is necessary in order to have the most competitive production operation.

C The passage emphasizes that the crucial factor in achieving economies of scale is efficient operation of the production facilities, not the size of the firm's fixed and sunk costs (even though such costs are clearly in part determined by the size and design of the production facilities).

D While a manufacturer's fixed and sunk costs may be on a par with those of the manufacturer's competitors, the passage provides no grounds for inferring that there is any need for them to be (for example, physical plants that employ different technologies may have different price tags).

E **Correct.** According to the passage, "throughput" refers to the flow of materials through a plant. This flow can vary as a result of various factors, but fixed and sunk costs—financial resources already committed—remain the same regardless of such variation.

The correct answer is E.

458. In the context of the passage as a whole, the second paragraph serves primarily to

(A) provide an example to support the argument presented in the first paragraph

(B) evaluate various strategies discussed in the first paragraph

(C) introduce evidence that undermines the argument presented in the first paragraph

(D) anticipate possible objections to the argument presented in the first paragraph

(E) demonstrate the potential dangers of a commonly used strategy

Evaluation

This question asks about the rhetorical function of the second paragraph. While the first paragraph argues that a crucial factor in achieving economies of scale is intangible capital, or organized human capabilities, the second paragraph uses the example of new capital-intensive manufacturing industries to help show that this is indeed the case.

A **Correct.** The second paragraph provides an example that illustrates the claims made in the first paragraph. It discusses the way in which intangible capital—e.g., distribution networks, marketing systems, smooth production processes, and qualified management teams—enables manufacturers in new capital-intensive manufacturing industries to realize economies of scale and achieve market dominance.

B The second paragraph does, in a sense, "evaluate" investment in intangible capital: it suggests that such investment is necessary. However, investment in intangible capital is the only strategy it discusses.

C The second paragraph supports rather than undermines the first paragraph's argument.

D Nothing in the second paragraph suggests that there are, or could be, any objections to the first paragraph's argument.

E The second paragraph discusses the potential positive outcomes of investing in intangible capital. It suggests that there might be negative consequences to not making such investments, but it does not indicate that avoiding such investments is a commonly used strategy.

The correct answer is A.

459. The passage LEAST supports the inference that a manufacturer's throughput could be adversely affected by

(A) a mistake in judgment regarding the selection of a wholesaler

(B) a breakdown in the factory's machinery

(C) a labor dispute on the factory floor

(D) an increase in the cost per unit of output

(E) a drop in the efficiency of the sales network

Application

This question may be best approached by using an elimination strategy—first finding the four choices that can reasonably be inferred from the passage, and then checking to make sure that the remaining choice cannot reasonably be inferred. This requires understanding the information the passage gives about throughput, then making inferences about what can cause throughput to drop. The passage defines throughput generally as *the flow of materials through a plant* and goes on to explain that it involves coordination of the production process itself, as well as obtaining materials from suppliers and marketing and distributing the manufactured products. Anything that damages this flow of materials and products would be said to have an adverse effect on throughput.

A Making a poor judgment about a wholesaler would most likely have an adverse effect on throughput, in that it could affect *the flow of output to wholesalers and final consumers*.

B A breakdown in machinery would likely fall into the category of *problems on the factory floor* mentioned in the passage and would likely prove damaging to throughput because of its effect on the production process itself.

C A labor dispute would also likely fall into the category of *problems on the factory floor* mentioned in the passage and would probably cause a decline in production and thus adversely affect throughput.

D **Correct.** The passage emphasizes that changes in throughput can cause increases or decreases in costs per unit. But the passage is not committed to any claims about how changes in costs per unit might affect throughput.

E The passage suggests that inefficient sales networks could cause a decline in production. Thus a decrease in sales efficiency would most likely adversely affect a manufacturer's ability to provide goods to consumers, and thus would create problems with throughput.

The correct answer is D.

460. The primary purpose of the passage is to

(A) point out the importance of intangible capital for realizing economies of scale in manufacturing
(B) show that manufacturers frequently gain a competitive advantage from investment in large manufacturing facilities
(C) argue that large manufacturing facilities often fail because of inadequate investment in both tangible and intangible capital
(D) suggest that most new industries are likely to be dominated by firms that build large manufacturing plants early
(E) explain why large manufacturing plants usually do not help manufacturers achieve economies of scale

Main idea

This question depends on understanding the passage as a whole. In general, it makes an argument for investing in intangible capital as a way for manufacturers to realize economies of scale, and it supports its argument with an example.

A **Correct.** The passage focuses on intangible capital as a crucial factor in realizing economies of scale.

B According to the passage, manufacturers gain competitive advantage by building plants of optimal size that they then fully exploit; nothing in the passage suggests that large plants are frequently optimal.

C The passage assumes that manufacturers invest appropriately in tangible capital and argues that it is important for them to invest in intangible capital as well.

D The passage states that new capital-intensive manufacturing industries are dominated not by firms that are the first to build large plants, but by firms that exploit the full potential of their plants.

E The passage indicates that economies of scale can be achieved in plants of optimal size. The passage does not suggest that large plants cannot be optimal.

The correct answer is A.

Questions 461–466 refer to the passage on page 390.

461. The primary purpose of the passage is to

(A) describe the development of new techniques that may help to determine the driving force behind population cycles in lepidoptera

(B) present evidence that refutes a particular theory about the driving force behind population cycles in lepidoptera

(C) present a hypothesis about the driving force behind population cycles in lepidoptera

(D) describe the fluctuating patterns of population cycles in lepidoptera

(E) question the idea that a single driving force is behind population cycles in lepidoptera

Main idea

This question depends on understanding the passage as a whole in order to identify its purpose. The first paragraph defines population cycles of lepidoptera and discusses some ways those cycles have been studied. It suggests that a particular agent may regulate these cycles. The second paragraph describes a candidate for this agent: nuclear polyhedrosis viruses. The third paragraph explains why this hypothesis is compelling.

A The passage mentions new techniques in molecular biology, but it does so in order to explain why a particular candidate for the agent behind population cycles has come to light.

B The theory the passage presents is that there is a driving force behind lepidoptera population cycles. It does not refute this theory; rather, it offers a convincing case for nuclear polyhedrosis viruses as that force. It also discusses some previous approaches to seeking plausible hypotheses but does not focus on refuting any particular hypothesis.

C **Correct.** The passage is primarily concerned with presenting the hypothesis that nuclear polyhedrosis viruses are the driving force behind lepidoptera population cycles.

D The first paragraph describes the fluctuating patterns of lepidoptera population cycles, but it does so to explain what population cycles are, so that it can then go on to attempt to account for those cycles.

E The passage is concerned with making a case for nuclear polyhedrosis viruses as the driving force behind at least some lepidoptera population cycles, not with questioning the idea that there is a driving force.

The correct answer is C.

462. It can be inferred from the passage that the mortality caused by agents such as predatory birds or parasites was measured in an attempt to

(A) develop an explanation for the existence of lepidoptera population cycles

(B) identify behavioral factors in lepidoptera that affect survival rates

(C) identify possible methods for controlling lepidoptera population growth

(D) provide evidence that lepidoptera populations are self-regulating

(E) determine the life stages of lepidoptera at which mortality rates are highest

Inference

The passage states that mortality caused by various agents, birds and parasites among them, was measured because this was the common approach to studying causes of population cycles. This in turn suggests that those scientists engaged in such measuring in the case of lepidoptera were attempting to come up with a definitive explanation for why those lepidoptera population cycles occurred.

A **Correct.** Measuring mortality caused by various agents was part of the attempt to determine the driving force behind lepidoptera population cycles.

B The passage does not indicate that behavioral factors in lepidoptera are related to their mortality as caused by agents such as predatory birds or parasites.

C The passage is concerned not with controlling lepidoptera population growth, but rather with determining why population cycles occur.

D According to the information in the passage, scientists sought to measure mortality caused by particular agents in order to determine the driving force behind lepidoptera population cycles. In suggesting that mortality caused by these agents is not that force, the measurements may have indicated that the cycles could be self-regulating, but they were not undertaken in order to provide such evidence.

E The passage discusses mortality primarily in the caterpillar stage and does not suggest that any research was directed toward comparing caterpillar mortality rates with mortality rates in other life stages of the insects.

The correct answer is A.

463. Which of the following, if true, would most weaken the author's conclusion in lines 18–22 ?

(A) New research reveals that the number of species of birds and parasites that prey on lepidoptera has dropped significantly in recent years.

(B) New experiments in which the habitats of lepidoptera are altered in previously untried ways result in the shortening of lepidoptera population cycles.

(C) Recent experiments have revealed that the nuclear polyhedrosis virus is present in a number of predators and parasites of lepidoptera.

(D) Differences among the habitats of lepidoptera species make it difficult to assess the effects of weather on lepidoptera population cycles.

(E) Viral disease is typically observed in a large proportion of the lepidoptera population.

Evaluation

The sentence in question presents the author's conclusion that lepidoptera populations may be self-regulating or regulated by something more closely connected to the insects than predatory birds or parasites are. To weaken that conclusion requires weakening its support, namely, that mortality caused by predators and parasites seems not to affect population cycles, and that changing habitats and reducing populations has not altered population cycles either.

A A drop in birds and parasites preying on lepidoptera would not weaken the author's conclusion; mortality caused by these predators has not affected population cycles.

B Correct. New experiments involving changes in habitat that did succeed in altering population cycles would suggest that the populations are not in fact self-regulating, and that the search for another cycle-altering agent may be unnecessary.

C This finding would support the idea that the nuclear polyhedrosis virus is responsible for population cycles—that is, that the virus is the closely connected agent the author concludes is responsible.

D The suggestion that the effects of weather may not have been adequately assessed is remotely relevant to the author's conclusion, but the mere difficulty of assessing the effects provides no positive reason to suppose that weather may be the cause of the cycles. On the other hand, answer choice B does offer evidence for an alternative explanation.

E Viral disease is what the author ultimately suggests is the agent that drives the lepidoptera population cycles in question. The wide presence of viruses in lepidoptera could help support the author's conclusion.

The correct answer is B.

464. According to the passage, before the discovery of new techniques for detecting viral DNA, population ecologists believed that viral diseases

(A) were not widely prevalent among insect populations generally

(B) affected only the caterpillar life stage of lepidoptera

(C) were the driving force behind lepidoptera population cycles

(D) attacked already declining caterpillar populations

(E) infected birds and parasites that prey on various species of lepidoptera

Supporting Idea

This question addresses what the passage states directly about population ecologists' beliefs regarding viral diseases prior to the discovery of new viral DNA–detection techniques. The second paragraph of the passage states that these ecologists believed viral disease contributed to population decline that was already underway rather than initiating it.

A The second paragraph states that viral disease had been reported; thus, population ecologists were aware of its existence in insect populations. The passage is consistent with ecologists having believed that it was prevalent.

B The passage focuses mainly on the caterpillar life stage of lepidoptera, but there is nothing to suggest that scientists held particular beliefs regarding viral diseases' restriction to that life stage.

C It is after, not before, the discovery of new techniques for detecting viral DNA when populations ecologists came to believe that such diseases were the driving force behind the population cycles.

D Correct. As stated in the passage, population ecologists believed that viral diseases contributed to already occurring population decline.

E The passage does not discuss whether viral diseases may infect any lepidoptera predators.

The correct answer is D.

465. According to the passage, nuclear polyhedrosis viruses can remain virulent in the environment only when

(A) the polyhedrin protein crystals dissolve

(B) caterpillar populations are in decline

(C) they are present in large numbers

(D) their concentration in a particular area remains low

(E) they are sheltered from direct sunlight

Supporting Idea

The passage states in the second paragraph that these viruses remain virulent for many years if they are protected from direct sunlight. They are embedded in crystals of polyhedrin protein.

A The viruses remain virulent partially because of their being contained in polyhedrin protein crystals. They would most likely not remain virulent if those crystals dissolved.

B The viruses remain virulent even when caterpillar populations are not in decline; that is how the viruses initiate new population declines.

C According to the passage, viral DNA has been detected in the environment at low concentrations, yet the viruses are still virulent. Thus, they need not be present in large numbers.

D Nothing in the passage indicates that the concentration of these viruses must be low for them to be virulent.

E Correct. The passage says that if the viruses are protected from direct sunlight, they remain virulent for many years. The context strongly suggests that if they are not so protected, they do not remain virulent.

The correct answer is E.

466. It can be inferred from the passage that while inside its polyhedrin protein crystals, the nuclear polyhedrosis virus

(A) is exposed to direct sunlight

(B) is attractive to predators

(C) cannot infect caterpillars' cells

(D) cannot be ingested by caterpillars

(E) cannot be detected by new techniques of molecular biology

Inference

The passage indicates that the polyhedrin protein crystals protect the nuclear polyhedrosis virus when it is in the environment. When a caterpillar ingests those crystals, they dissolve. That releases the virus, whereupon it infects the caterpillar's cells. Thus it is reasonable to infer that the virus must be released from the crystals before it can infect the caterpillar.

A The passage states that nuclear polyhedrosis viruses remain embedded in polyhedrin protein crystals if protected from direct sunlight, not that the virus is exposed to light when it is in the protein crystals.

B Nothing in the passage indicates that any organism preys on the virus itself or that it attracts predators to caterpillars that it infects.

C **Correct.** The virus must be released from the crystals before it can infect caterpillars' cells.

D The passage states that caterpillars ingest the polyhedrin protein crystals.

E According to the passage, new techniques of molecular biology enable the detection of viral DNA in the environment. The nuclear polyhedrosis virus persists in the environment inside protein crystals. The passage suggests that the new techniques are able to detect the virus inside its crystals but does not provide any evidence about whether they detect it directly or infer its presence indirectly.

The correct answer is C.

Questions 467–470 refer to the passage on page 392.

467. According to the passage, which of the following is true of plant antiherbivore chemistry?

(A) Changes in a plant's antiherbivore chemistry may affect insect feeding behavior.

(B) A plant's repellent effects often involve interactions between gum and resin.

(C) A plant's antiherbivore responses assist in combating bacterial infections.

(D) Plant antiherbivore chemistry plays only a minor role in the coevolution of plants and insects.

(E) Researchers first studied repellent effects in plants beginning in the 1950s.

Supporting ideas

This question addresses what the information in the passage indicates about plant antiherbivore chemistry—that is, plants' chemical defenses against herbivore attacks. The second paragraph of the passage cites the views of various scientists regarding the possible role of resin in antiherbivore chemistry; plants could have evolved resin specifically to repel insects.

A **Correct.** According to the second paragraph, various scientists have suggested that a change in antiherbivore chemistry, here specifically involving resin, could repel insects; alternatively, some insects could have been attracted to resin, feeding more heavily on plants that produced it. Other researchers have suggested that even if resin does not directly repel or attract insects, it may indirectly affect insect-feeding behavior by mediating changes in plants' antiherbivore chemistry.

B The first paragraph states that plants produce gum in response to bacterial infections. Although this does not rule out the hypothesis that gum also contributes to plants' antiherbivore chemistry, the passage provides no evidence that it does so.

C According to the passage, a plant's antiherbivore responses have developed to combat predators, such as insects, that eat plants. The passage provides no evidence that such responses also combat bacterial infections.

D The second paragraph indicates that plant antiherbivore chemistry plays a major role in the discipline of chemical ecology, and chemical ecology concerns itself with coevolution of plants and insects.

E According to the passage, it was in the 1950s that entomologists began discussing resin's possible role in repelling and attracting insects. The passage does not suggest that this marked the beginning of their study of repellent effects more generally.

The correct answer is A.

468. Of the following topics, which would be most likely to be studied within the discipline of chemical ecology as it is described in the passage?

(A) Seeds that become attached to certain insects, which in turn carry away the seeds and aid in the reproductive cycle of the plant species in question

(B) An insect species that feeds on weeds detrimental to crop health and yield, and how these insects might aid in agricultural production

(C) The effects of deforestation on the life cycles of subtropical carnivorous plants and the insect species on which the plants feed

(D) The growth patterns of a particular species of plant that has proved remarkably resistant to herbicides

(E) Insects that develop a tolerance for feeding on a plant that had previously been toxic to them, and the resultant changes within that plant species

Application

The discipline of chemical ecology, as it is described in the passage, deals with how plants use chemicals to interact with other organisms—in particular, how they defend against attack—and how those interactions have evolved. To be studied within that discipline, a specific topic would need to address some aspect of that chemical interaction.

A The passage provides no reason to suppose that the topic of seeds and how they travel would be studied within chemical ecology, given that it does not discuss how chemicals might be involved in the reproductive cycle.

B The passage provides no indication that chemical ecology would be concerned with how weed-destroying insects would aid agricultural production.

C The passage provides no indication that deforestation would involve plant chemicals or that its effects would be studied in chemical ecology.

D The passage provides no indication that a plant's resistance to herbicides would be studied in chemical ecology, but the passage does suggest that the focus of chemical ecology is on how plants chemically interact with other organisms.

E **Correct.** Chemical ecology developed to deal with the interdependence between plants and insects. Insects' developing a tolerance for feeding on a once-toxic plant, and the plants' resultant changes, is a situation of just such interdependence: plants and insects coevolving.

The correct answer is E.

469. The author refers to "bacterial infections" (see line 11) most likely in order to

(A) describe the physiological function that gum performs in plants

(B) demonstrate that sap is not the only substance that is transported through a plant's tissues

(C) explain how modern chemical analysis has been used to clarify the function of resin

(D) show that gum cannot serve as an effective defense against herbivores

(E) give an example of how confusion has arisen with regard to the nature of resin

Evaluation

The author mentions *bacterial infections* in the first paragraph as the reason why plants produce the substance known as gum.

A **Correct.** The author states directly that plants produce gum in response to bacterial infections.

B The author states directly that sap is transported through plant tissues. The passage does not address the question of whether bacterial infections or anything related to them are similarly transported.

C The passage indicates that rigorous chemical analysis is now available, but scientists still do not know resin's function. The reference to bacterial infections is related to gum, not resin.

D The reference to bacterial infections indicates the actual purpose served by gum; it does not function to show ways in which gum is inadequate.

E Gum itself serves as an example of the confusion surrounding the nature of resin; bacterial infections, to which gum production is a response, do not serve as that example.

The correct answer is A.

470. The author of the passage refers to Pliny most probably in order to

(A) give an example of how the nature of amber has been misunderstood in the past
(B) show that confusion about amber has long been more pervasive than confusion about resin
(C) make note of the first known reference to amber as a semiprecious gem
(D) point out an exception to a generalization about the history of people's understanding of amber
(E) demonstrate that Pliny believed amber to be a mineral

Evaluation

The passage states generally that *amber has been widely misunderstood* but cites Pliny as noting correctly, in the first century, that amber resulted from a substance discharged by trees.

A Pliny's observation was, according to the author, accurate and not a misunderstanding.

B The author equates confusion about amber with confusion about resin; the reference to Pliny does not indicate which of the two, amber or resin, has been more widely misunderstood.

C The author indicates that others, not Pliny, mischaracterized amber as a semiprecious gem—and when that mischaracterization first occurred is not identified.

D Correct. Pliny's recognition that amber came from a substance discharged by trees stands, in the author's account, as an exception to the widespread incorrect identifications of the substance.

E Others held the belief that amber was a mineral. The passage indicates that Pliny recognized that amber came from trees but provides no evidence that he also considered it a mineral.

The correct answer is D.

Questions 471–473 refer to the passage on page 394.

471. The primary purpose of the passage is to

(A) compare the impact of the Great Depression on Latin America with its impact on the United States
(B) criticize a school of economic historians for failing to analyze the Great Depression in Latin America within a global context
(C) illustrate the risks inherent in comparing different types of economic enterprises to explain economic phenomena
(D) call into question certain scholars' views concerning the severity of the Great Depression in Latin America
(E) demonstrate that the Great Depression had a more severe impact on industry in Latin American than in certain other regions

Main idea

This question depends on understanding the passage as a whole. The passage first describes the view of many economic historians of the 1980s. It next describes the evidence on which that view is based. The remainder of the passage raises issues about the rationale for that view.

A The comparison between Latin America and the United States is only a small part of a larger argument analyzing studies of the Great Depression in Latin America.

B The passage does not discuss a global context for the Great Depression.

C The passage does not primarily aim to illustrate risks that may be generally inherent in explaining economic phenomena.

D Correct. The passage claims that certain scholars underestimate the severity of the Great Depression in Latin America.

E The passage does not claim that the impact of the Great Depression on Latin American industry was generally more severe than its impact on industry elsewhere.

The correct answer is D.

472. Which of the following conclusions about the Great Depression is best supported by the passage?

(A) It did not impede Latin American industrial growth as much as historians had previously thought.

(B) It had a more severe impact on the Brazilian and the Mexican textile industries than it had on Latin America as a region.

(C) It affected the Latin American textile industry more severely than it did any other industry in Latin America.

(D) The overall impact on Latin American industrial growth should be reevaluated by economic historians.

(E) Its impact on Latin America should not be compared with its impact on the United States.

Inference

This question asks which conclusion is most strongly supported by the passage. The passage presents the rationale of some historians for their conclusion that the Great Depression did not significantly interfere with economic growth in Latin America. It then critiques that rationale and conclusion. By questioning the historians' claims, the passage suggests that a reevaluation of the Great Depression's effect on Latin America is needed.

A The passage does not significantly support this. The passage indicates that, in fact, the Great Depression impeded Latin American economic development more than some historians had thought.

B The passage does not significantly support this. The passage does not compare the impact on the Brazilian and Mexican textile industries to the impact on the Latin American region.

C The passage does not significantly support this. The passage does not compare the effect of the Great Depression on the textile industry to its effect on other industries.

D **Correct.** As presented in the passage, the passage author's critique of the historians' rationale for their claims provides significant support for the conclusion that their claims should be reevaluated.

E The passage does not significantly support the claim that the comparison in question should not be made.

The correct answer is D.

473. Which of the following, if true, would most strengthen the author's assertion regarding economic indicators in lines 25–27 ?

(A) During an economic depression, European textile manufacturers' profits rise while their industrial output remains steady.

(B) During a national economic recession, United States microchips manufacturers' profits rise sharply while United States steel manufacturers' profits plunge.

(C) During the years following a severe economic depression, textile manufacturers' output levels and profit levels increase in Brazil and Mexico but not in the rest of Latin America.

(D) Although Japanese industry as a whole recovers after an economic recession, it does not regain its previously high levels of production.

(E) While European industrial output increases in the years following an economic depression, total output remains below that of Japan or the United States.

Application

The question involves applying information from outside the passage to a claim made by the author. The text in lines 25–27 asserts that broad economic indicators pertaining to a nation or region can obscure differences between individual firms or industries within that nation or region. The question asks which evidence would most strengthen the support for that conclusion.

A This refers only to the relationship between a single industry's profits and its output, not to general economic indicators.

B **Correct.** The phrase *a national recession* refers to a general economic indicator. Suppose that in a situation described as a national recession, one industry (microchip manufacturing) prospers while another industry (steel manufacturing) does not. This would provide some additional support, over and above that given in the passage, for the assertion that broad economic indicators may mask differences between industries.

C Economic differences between countries do not strengthen the support for the author's assertion regarding variations among different firms and industries in one country or region.

D This has no obvious bearing on how sweeping economic indicators can mask differences between industries or enterprises in a single country or region.

E A comparison of different countries does not pertain to the assertion regarding variation among firms and industries in the same country.

The correct answer is B.

Questions 474–477 refer to the passage on page 396.

474. It can be inferred from the passage that a large plant might have to spend more than a similar but smaller plant on environmental compliance because the larger plant is

(A) more likely to attract attention from local regulators

(B) less likely to be exempt from permit and reporting requirements

(C) less likely to have regulatory costs passed on to it by companies that supply its raw materials

(D) more likely to employ older production technologies

(E) more likely to generate wastes that are more environmentally damaging than those generated by smaller plants

Inference

This item depends on understanding the implications of the passage's discussion of differences between large and small plants. It asks what might be true of a larger plant that would compel it to spend more than a smaller plant on environmental compliance. The passage addresses this issue by stating that smaller plants are often not subject to the same permit or reporting requirements that larger plants are.

A The likelihood of attracting regulatory attention is discussed only in the context of comparing plants that are *isolated* with small plants that are near large noncompliant ones. The passage does not suggest that size is generally the crucial determining factor in attracting regulatory attention.

B **Correct.** According to the passage, certain permit or reporting requirements may not apply to smaller plants; this suggests that larger plants are less likely than smaller plants to be exempt from these requirements, and thus that the larger plants would have to spend more to comply.

C The passage does not discuss the passing on of regulatory costs from suppliers to plants.

D The passage does not suggest that larger plants are any more likely than smaller plants to employ older production technologies.

E The passage does not distinguish between the types of wastes emitted by larger plants and those emitted by smaller plants.

The correct answer is B.

475. According to the passage, which of the following statements about sulfur dioxide and nitrogen oxide outputs is true?

(A) Older production technologies cannot be adapted so as to reduce production of these outputs as waste products.

(B) Under the most recent environmental regulations, industrial plants are no longer permitted to produce these outputs.

(C) Although these outputs are environmentally hazardous, some plants still generate them as waste products despite the high compliance costs they impose.

(D) Many older plants have developed innovative technological processes that reduce the amounts of these outputs generated as waste products.

(E) Since the production processes that generate these outputs are less costly than alternative processes, these less expensive processes are sometimes adopted despite their acknowledged environmental hazards.

Supporting idea

This item depends on identifying what the passage states explicitly about outputs of sulfur dioxide and nitrogen oxide. The passage says that plants that produce these outputs are those that use older industrial coal-fired burners, and that such plants are subject to extensive compliance costs imposed by new regulations.

A The passage does not address the question of whether older production technologies might be adapted to reduce outputs of sulfur dioxide and nitrogen oxide.

B The passage states that new regulations have imposed high compliance costs on companies that produce sulfur dioxide and nitrogen oxide outputs, not that these outputs are prohibited.

C **Correct.** The passage states that some companies are still using the older kinds of burners that generate sulfur dioxide and nitrogen oxide outputs, and that new regulations have imposed high compliance costs on these companies.

D The passage does not address the question of whether older plants have developed new processes to reduce the amounts of sulfur dioxide and nitrogen oxide they produce.

E Sulfur dioxide and nitrogen oxide outputs, the passage suggests, are produced only by older industrial coal-fired burners; newer facilities (using alternative processes) do not employ this technology, the expense of which is not mentioned in the passage.

The correct answer is C.

476. Which of the following best describes the relationship of the statement about large plants (lines 12–17) to the passage as a whole?

(A) It presents a hypothesis that is disproved later in the passage.

(B) It highlights an opposition between two ideas mentioned in the passage.

(C) It provides examples to support a claim made earlier in the passage.

(D) It exemplifies a misconception mentioned earlier in the passage.

(E) It draws an analogy between two situations described in the passage.

Evaluation

This question asks about the role played in the passage by the following statement: *Additionally, large plants can spread compliance costs such as waste treatment across a larger revenue base; on the other hand, some smaller plants may not even be subject to certain provisions such as permit or reporting requirements by virtue of their size.* This statement describes situations in which compliance costs for plants of different sizes may differ, which serve as evidence in support of the passage's main claim: that environmental regulations do *not* affect all competitors in a given industry uniformly.

A The statement in question is not a hypothesis; rather, it reports factors that are known to affect the varying impact of environmental regulations.

B This is too vague to be a good description of the kind of relationship the question asks about. The statement in question does present a contrast—it suggests that larger plants' compliance costs are lower under some circumstances, while smaller plants' compliance costs are lower under other circumstances. But this purports to state two facts rather than mere *ideas*; they are contrasting facts but not in any meaningful sense *opposed*, since they can easily coexist.

C **Correct.** The statement provides examples to support the initial claim made in the passage that regulatory costs fall unevenly on competitors in an industry: large plants can spread compliance costs around, and smaller plants may not even have to pay certain costs.

D This statement helps to dispel, not exemplify, a misconception mentioned earlier in the passage—i.e., the myth that environmental regulations affect all companies in an industry the same way.

E The statement does not suggest that the situation of larger and smaller plants is similar (or analogous) to any other situation mentioned in the passage.

The correct answer is C.

477. The primary purpose of the passage is to

(A) address a widespread environmental management problem and suggest possible solutions

(B) illustrate varying levels of compliance with environmental regulation among different corporations

(C) describe the various alternatives to traditional methods of environmental management

(D) advocate increased corporate compliance with environmental regulation

(E) correct a common misconception about the impact of environmental regulations

Main idea

This question depends on understanding the passage as a whole. Its first sentence indicates its main purpose: to dispel a myth about environmental regulations that is often taken as fact.

A The passage is not about the management of any environmental problem, which would be a problem about how to prevent or undo damage to the environment. The passage primarily aims to dispel a belief that the passage says is widely held by environmental managers.

B The passage refers to variations in firms' levels of compliance with environmental regulations, but its primary purpose is not to illustrate those varying levels, nor does it do so.

C The passage suggests that most environmental managers are mistaken about a key concept; its primary purpose is not to describe traditional methods of environmental management or alternatives to those traditional methods, nor does it do so.

D The passage takes no position on whether companies should increase their compliance with environmental regulation.

E **Correct.** The passage primarily aims to dispel the belief that environmental regulations affect all companies in an industry uniformly.

The correct answer is E.

Questions 478–483 refer to the passage on page 398.

478. In the passage, the author is primarily interested in

(A) suggesting an alternative to an outdated research method

(B) introducing a new research method that calls an accepted theory into question

(C) emphasizing the instability of data gathered from the application of a new scientific method

(D) presenting a theory and describing a new method to test that theory

(E) initiating a debate about a widely accepted theory

Main idea

This question concerns the main point of the passage. A careful examination of the overall structure of the passage will reveal the main point. In the first paragraph, the author briefly presents Milankovitch's theory and explains why it could not be tested early on. In the second and third paragraphs, the author describes how a new method allows testing of the theory and shows how evidence from the testing supports the theory. While the final paragraph acknowledges that other factors should be considered, the author's primary interest in this passage is in presenting Milankovitch's theory and the recently discovered method for testing it.

A A new research method is described, but no previous method is discussed.

B As described in the passage, the new method tests and confirms the theory; there is no mention that the theory is accepted or that the method casts doubt on it.

C Nothing in the passage suggests that "instability of data" is an issue.

D Correct. The author presents Milankovitch's theory and describes the oxygen isotope method of testing it.

E The theory is nowhere said to be "widely accepted" and the author does not debate the theory.

The correct answer is D.

479. The author of the passage would be most likely to agree with which of the following statements about the Milankovitch theory?

(A) It is the only possible explanation for the ice ages.

(B) It is too limited to provide a plausible explanation for the ice ages, despite recent research findings.

(C) It cannot be tested and confirmed until further research on volcanic activity is done.

(D) It is one plausible explanation, though not the only one, for the ice ages.

(E) It is not a plausible explanation for the ice ages, although it has opened up promising possibilities for future research.

Application

The author's reaction to the statements about the Milankovitch theory must be based on how the author treats the theory in the passage. The first, second, and third paragraphs describe the theory and the use of a new research method to test the theory. The passage states that data from these tests *have established a strong connection between variations in the Earth's orbit and the periodicity of the ice ages*, suggesting that the author of the passage believes the theory is plausible. In the final paragraph, the author points to other factors that might be involved, suggesting that the theory might not provide a complete explanation.

A In the last paragraph, the author suggests that because there are still other untested factors that may have effects on climate, other explanations are possible.

B Though in the last paragraph the author points to other factors that may be involved, these are not presented by the author as indicating limitations that diminish the plausibility of the theory—they are acknowledged merely as possibilities that are not now understood—and nothing else in the passage suggests that the theory is "too limited."

C The author shows how the theory has been tested; volcanic activity is not part of this theory.

D Correct. The author's presentation of the theory and the tests of the theory show that the author finds the theory plausible; the mention of other factors shows the author does not think that all other explanations have been ruled out, even if they are as yet untested.

E The theory was a plausible explanation from its beginning, but it was not testable until recently; scientists would be unlikely to try to devise means to test a theory that did not strike them as antecedently plausible.

The correct answer is D.

480. It can be inferred from the passage that the isotope record taken from ocean sediments would be less useful to researchers if which of the following were true?

(A) It indicated that lighter isotopes of oxygen predominated at certain times.

(B) It had far more gaps in its sequence than the record taken from rocks on land.

(C) It indicated that climate shifts did not occur every 100,000 years.

(D) It indicated that the ratios of oxygen 16 and oxygen 18 in ocean water were not consistent with those found in fresh water.

(E) It stretched back for only a million years.

Inference

To make an inference about the isotope record from ocean sediments, examine what the passage says about that record. The third paragraph discusses that record and lists its two advantages. First, it is a global record with *remarkably little variation* in samples from varied locations. Second, it is *more continuous* than the record from rocks. If either of these advantages were not true, then it is logical to infer that the record would be less useful.

A According to lines 14–16, the lighter isotope does predominate; this is part of the record and does not affect its usefulness.

B Correct. In lines 37–42, the author states that an advantage of the ocean record is that it is *a more continuous record than that taken from rocks on land.* If this were not true, the ocean record would be less useful.

C If the record were to show that the shifts did not occur every 100,000 years, Milankovitch's theory would be weakened. This impact on the theory does not make the isotope record less useful to researchers. The record is useful precisely because it can offer evidence to confirm or refute such theories.

D This inconsistency would not affect the usefulness of the ocean-water record. Researchers would simply need to accommodate the fresh-water inconsistency.

E The record would still be useful. Lines 42–46 attest to the establishment of a pattern based on data from *the past several hundred thousand years.*

The correct answer is B.

481. According to the passage, which of the following is true of the ratios of oxygen isotopes in ocean sediments?

(A) They indicate that sediments found during an ice age contain more calcium carbonate than sediments formed at other times.

(B) They are less reliable than the evidence from rocks on land in determining the volume of land ice.

(C) They can be used to deduce the relative volume of land ice that was present when the sediment was laid down.

(D) They are more unpredictable during an ice age than in other climatic conditions.

(E) They can be used to determine atmospheric conditions at various times in the past.

Supporting ideas

The phrase *according to the passage* suggests that the answer to the question is most likely stated in the passage. Lines 12–14 state that the relative volume of land ice can be deduced from the ratio of oxygen 18 to oxygen 16 in ocean sediments.

A There is no evidence in the passage about this point.

B The ocean record is described in lines 38–39 as *more continuous*, so it is unlikely to be less reliable. In any case, reliability is not discussed.

C Correct. Lines 12–14 explain that *the land-ice volume for a given period can be deduced from the ratio of two oxygen isotopes.*

D There is no evidence in the passage to support this statement.

E The passage does not discuss the use of this record in determining past atmospheric conditions.

The correct answer is C.

482. It can be inferred from the passage that precipitation formed from evaporated ocean water has

(A) the same isotopic ratio as ocean water

(B) less oxygen 18 than does ocean water

(C) less oxygen 18 than has the ice contained in continental ice sheets

(D) a different isotopic composition than has precipitation formed from water on land

(E) more oxygen 16 than has precipitation formed from fresh water

Inference

Any inference about precipitation from evaporated ocean water needs to be based on what the passage says. Lines 20–22 show that *heavier isotopes tend to be left behind when water evaporates from the ocean surfaces*. Therefore, the evaporated water would contain less oxygen 18 and the remaining ocean water would contain more. It is logical to infer that precipitation formed from this evaporated water would also contain less oxygen 18.

A Lines 20–24 explain that the water remaining in the ocean after evaporation has more oxygen 18.

B **Correct.** Since *the heavier isotopes tend to be left behind*, there will be less oxygen 18 in the evaporated water and in the precipitation that forms from it.

C The passage suggests that the ocean water evaporates and through subsequent precipitation helps form the ice sheets, so the amount of oxygen 18 in the ice sheets should be similar to the amount in the precipitation formed from the evaporated water.

D The passage does not discuss precipitation formed from water on land.

E The passage does not discuss precipitation formed from fresh water.

The correct answer is B.

483. It can be inferred from the passage that calcium carbonate shells

(A) are not as susceptible to deterioration as rocks

(B) are less common in sediments formed during an ice age

(C) are found only in areas that were once covered by land ice

(D) contain radioactive material that can be used to determine a sediment's isotopic composition

(E) reflect the isotopic composition of the water at the time the shells were formed

Inference

Any inference about calcium carbonate shells needs to be based on what the passage says about these shells. Lines 24–32 explain the role of these shells in forming sediments and establishing a chronology for ice ages. The shells *were constructed with oxygen atoms drawn from the surrounding ocean*. Lines 29–32 make it clear that if the sediments reveal a higher ratio of oxygen 18, it is because more oxygen 18 had been left behind when the ocean water evaporated and contributed to the growth of continental ice sheets. It can thus be inferred that the shells that make up those sediments must reflect the proportion of oxygen 18 found in the ocean water at the time they were formed.

A The only mention of rocks in the passage is a comparison of "gappiness" of the rock and sedimentary specimen records in lines 38–39; this information does not allow any firm inference to be made with respect to relative susceptibility to deterioration, though a more continuous record might be the result of less susceptibility to deterioration.

B The passage does not make any reference to the relative abundance of these shells during ice ages; no such inference can be drawn.

C The only information in the passage that might support this statement is found in lines 29–32, but that information, about the correlation between oxygen ratios in sediment specimens and land ice, describes a relation that implies nothing about distributions of such specimens.

D Though the passage does indirectly indicate that the shells contained radioactive material, nothing in the passage suggests that radioactive material is used to determine isotopic composition.

E **Correct.** The passage explains that oxygen atoms in the surrounding water are one of the building blocks of calcium carbonate shells. The isotopic composition of the surrounding water changes during the ice age cycles, so it is logical that the isotopic composition of the shells will change depending on when they were formed.

The correct answer is E.

Questions 484–489 refer to the passage on page 400.

484. The primary purpose of the passage is to

(A) examine two sides of a historiographical debate

(B) call into question an author's approach to a historiographical debate

(C) examine one author's approach to a historiographical debate

(D) discuss two authors' works in relationship to a historiographical debate

(E) explain the prevalent perspective on a historiographical debate

Main idea

This question requires understanding what the passage as a whole is attempting to do. The passage opens by introducing two books published in 1984 that both concern the history of women in the United States. The passage then makes it clear that one book deals *directly* (line 15) with the issue of women's status, while the other does not. The passage then goes on to discuss the perspective that each book takes and what each book has to offer for an assessment of women's status in the eighteenth and nineteenth centuries.

A The two books discussed in the passage do not take different sides on a particular debate but rather are described as being more or less useful to the debate itself.

B The passage focuses on how two different books contain information useful to a particular historiographical debate but does not call into question the approach of either book.

C The passage focuses on two authors' works, not one.

D Correct. The passage discusses what two different books have to offer in relation to a particular historiographical debate.

E The passage does not describe any perspective on a particular historiographical debate as being more prevalent than any other.

The correct answer is D.

485. The author of the passage mentions the supervision of schools primarily in order to

(A) remind readers of the role education played in the cultural changes of the nineteenth century in the United States

(B) suggest an area in which nineteenth-century American women were relatively free to exercise power

(C) provide an example of an occupation for which accurate data about women's participation are difficult to obtain

(D) speculate about which occupations were considered suitable for United States women of the nineteenth century

(E) illustrate how the answers to questions about women's status depend on particular contexts

Evaluation

Answering this question depends on understanding what role a particular piece of information plays in the passage as a whole. The author implicitly supports Lebsock's contention (beginning at line 20) that different frames of reference can produce different perspectives on the debate about women's status in the eighteenth and nineteenth centuries. The author then summarizes different contexts cited by Lebsock to support the contention about frames of reference. As part of this summary, the author refers to *supervising schools* (lines 24–25) as an example of a job that apparently showed women losing power.

A The passage does not discuss the role of education in the nineteenth century.

B The passage does mention some ways in which, according to Lebsock, *women … gained power* (lines 25–26) in the nineteenth century, but *supervising schools* is not among them.

C The passage does not discuss the difficulty of obtaining data about particular occupations.

D The passage makes no judgments about the suitability for women of any jobs in the nineteenth century.

E Correct. The passage mentions supervising schools as part of an illustration of Lebsock's claim that the debate about women's status depends on the context being examined.

The correct answer is E.

486. With which of the following characterizations of Lebsock's contribution to the controversy concerning women's status in the nineteenth-century United States would the author of the passage be most likely to agree?

(A) Lebsock has studied women from a formerly neglected region and time period.

(B) Lebsock has demonstrated the importance of frame of reference in answering questions about women's status.

(C) Lebsock has addressed the controversy by using women's current status as a frame of reference.

(D) Lebsock has analyzed statistics about occupations and property that were previously ignored.

(E) Lebsock has applied recent historiographical methods to the biography of a nineteenth-century woman.

Supporting ideas

Answering this question requires recognizing information explicitly given in the passage. The passage introduces the work of Lebsock in line 6 and then goes on to describe several characteristics of Lebsock's book. In lines 20–22, the author introduces Lebsock's claim that the historiographical debate about women's status is dependent on frame of reference and calls that claim important; the passage then gives an example showing how frame of reference affects views of women's status. In so doing, the author displays an implicit agreement with Lebsock's discussion on this point.

A The author of the passage portrays neither the place nor time period that Lebsock focuses on as having been neglected by historians.

B Correct. The author describes as important Lebsock's idea that frame of reference informs the debate about women's status.

C According to the passage, Lebsock's book deals with women's status in the eighteenth and nineteenth centuries, not the present status of women.

D The passage does not mention or imply that Lebsock analyzed statistics in writing her book.

E Although the passage does describe Lebsock's book as pertaining to an ongoing historiographical debate, it identifies the book's topic as *women in one southern community* (lines 7–8), not the life of a single woman.

The correct answer is B.

487. According to the passage, Lebsock's work differs from Buel and Buel's work in that Lebsock's work

(A) uses a large number of primary sources

(B) ignores issues of women's legal status

(C) refuses to take a position on women's status in the eighteenth century

(D) addresses larger historiographical issues

(E) fails to provide sufficient material to support its claims

Supporting ideas

This question asks for recognition of information contained in the passage. In the first sentence, the passage states that Buel and Buel's work and Lebsock's work have *contrasting approaches*. The passage then proceeds, using descriptions of each work's approach, to illustrate how the works differ. The passage notes that Buel and Buel's work *makes little effort* to place its biographical subject *in the context of recent historiography on women* (lines 5–6), whereas Lebsock's work attempts *to redirect two decades of historiographical debate* about women's status.

A Primary sources are not mentioned in the passage in relation to either work discussed.

B The legal status of women is not mentioned in the passage.

C Lebsock's work is described in the passage as attempting to redirect the debate about women's status in the eighteenth and nineteenth centuries.

D Correct. The passage suggests that by not placing its subject's story in the context of historiography, Buel and Buel's work does not therefore address larger historiographical issues, as Lebsock's does.

E The passage tends to support Lebsock's views and does not refer to any lack of support for the claims made in Lebsock's work.

The correct answer is D.

488. The passage suggests that Lebsock believes that compared to nineteenth-century American women, eighteenth-century American women were

(A) in many respects less powerful in relation to men

(B) more likely to own real estate

(C) generally more economically independent

(D) more independent in conducting their private lives

(E) less likely to work as school superintendents

Inference

This question requires making an inference based on information given in the passage. As part of the passage's description of Lebsock's contribution to the historiographical debate about women's status in the eighteenth and nineteenth centuries, Lebsock's conclusions about women's autonomy are described. As part of this description, the passage cites Lebsock's conclusion that nineteenth-century women lost economic autonomy when compared to eighteenth-century women (lines 17–20).

A The passage states that in many ways women in the nineteenth century *lost power in relation to men* (line 23), which would imply that in those respects eighteenth-century women had more power in relation to men, not less. The only increase mentioned in nineteenth-century women's power is associated with owning more real estate.

B The passage states that more nineteenth-century women owned real estate.

C **Correct.** As the passage states, Lebsock concluded that nineteenth-century women lost economic autonomy compared to eighteenth-century women.

D The passage states that nineteenth-century women gained more independence in their private lives.

E The passage cites school superintendents as an example of an occupation more likely to be held by eighteenth-century women.

The correct answer is C.

489. The passage suggests that Buel and Buel's biography of Mary Fish provides evidence for which of the following views of women's history?

(A) Women have lost power in relation to men since the colonial era.

(B) Women of the colonial era were not as likely to be concerned with their status as were women in the nineteenth century.

(C) The colonial era was not as favorable for women as some historians have believed.

(D) Women had more economic autonomy in the colonial era than in the nineteenth century.

(E) Women's occupations were generally more respected in the colonial era than in the nineteenth century.

Inference

This question requires understanding what the passage implies. The approach that Buel and Buel's work takes is specifically described in lines 3–6 and again in lines 28–34. In lines 29–32, the passage states that Buel and Buel's work *provides ample raw material for questioning the myth … of a colonial golden age in the eighteenth century*, referring to a myth about women's status. In describing this golden age as a myth fostered by some historians, the passage suggests that this era was not as favorable to women as these historians suggest.

A The passage describes Lebsock's work as providing such evidence, not Buel and Buel's work.

B The passage does not pertain to the level of concern women had for their status.

C **Correct.** The final paragraph of the passage describes Buel and Buel's work as providing material that calls into question claims that the eighteenth century was especially favorable to women.

D The passage refers to the economic autonomy of women in relation to Lebsock's work, not Buel and Buel's work.

E The passage does not refer to whether any particular occupations held by women were more respected at one time or another.

The correct answer is C.

Questions 490–492 refer to the passage on page 402.

490. The passage suggests that WIDC differed from WTUL in which of the following ways?

(A) WIDC believed that the existing safety regulations were adequate to protect women's health, whereas WTUL believed that such regulations needed to be strengthened.

(B) WIDC believed that unions could not succeed in pressuring employers to comply with such regulations, whereas WTUL believed that unions could succeed in doing so.

(C) WIDC believed that lead poisoning in white lead factories could be avoided by controlling conditions there, whereas WTUL believed that lead poisoning in such factories could not be avoided no matter how stringently safety regulations were enforced.

(D) At the time that the legislation concerning white lead factories was proposed, WIDC was primarily concerned with addressing health conditions in white lead factories, whereas WTUL was concerned with improving working conditions in all types of factories.

(E) At the time that WIDC was opposing legislative attempts to restrict women's labor, WTUL had already ceased to do so.

Inference

To answer this question you need to understand the differences between WIDC and WTUL as they are described in the passage. The only information about WTUL in the passage is that it had stopped opposing restrictions on women's labor in the late 1880s, and that, because existing safety regulations were not being enforced, it supported the proposal to prohibit women from working in white lead factories. WIDC, on the other hand, was formed in 1892 specifically to oppose restrictions on women's labor, and it opposed the proposal.

A According to the passage, WIDC did believe that existing safety regulations, if enforced, could prevent lead poisoning. WTUL may or may not have believed that the safety regulations needed to be strengthened; all the passage states is that WTUL did not believe that the safety regulations were likely to be enforced.

B The passage states that WTUL believed that because there were no unions to pressure employers, the employers would not comply with safety regulations. The passage does not present any information on which to base a conclusion about WIDC's beliefs regarding union pressure on employers.

C Based on information in the passage, both WIDC and SPEW believed that enforcing safety regulations could protect women against lead poisoning. WIDC supported SPEW's position on the matter. WTUL believed that safety regulations were unlikely to be enforced because of the lack of unions.

D The passage states that WIDC viewed the proposal to restrict women's employment in white lead factories as an instance of legislation designed to limit women's work opportunities—precisely the legislation that WIDC was formed to oppose. Thus, WIDC was not primarily concerned with the factories' health conditions.

E **Correct.** WIDC began opposing legislative attempts to restrict women's labor in 1892 and continued to do so through at least 1895, when the Home Secretary proposed prohibiting women from working in white lead factories. WTUL stopped opposing restrictions on women's labor in the late 1880s, before WIDC was even founded. Thus, the passage suggests that WTUL had stopped opposing restrictions on women's labor well before WIDC worked to oppose such legislation.

The correct answer is E.

491. Which of the following, if true, would most clearly support the contention attributed to SPEW in lines 17–20 ?

(A) Those white lead factories that most strongly enforced regulations concerning worker safety and hygiene had the lowest incidences of lead poisoning among employees.

(B) The incidence of lead poisoning was much higher among women who worked in white lead factories than among women who worked in other types of factories.

(C) There were many household sources of lead that could have contributed to the incidence of lead poisoning among women who also worked outside the home in the late nineteenth century.

(D) White lead factories were more stringent than were certain other types of factories in their enforcement of workplace safety regulations.

(E) Even brief exposure to the conditions typically found in white lead factories could cause lead poisoning among factory workers.

Evaluation

This question requires the reader to find a statement that would provide additional support for the contention made in the following statement: *SPEW contended, and WIDC concurred, that controllable conditions in such factories were responsible for the development of lead poisoning.* Information suggesting that when conditions were controlled, lead poisoning was less likely to develop would provide support for SPEW's contention.

A **Correct.** If incidences of lead poisoning were low in those factories that enforced hygiene and safety regulations, that would suggest that lead poisoning was not an inevitable result of working in a white lead factory—but rather that lead poisoning was the result of poor hygiene and safety practices.

B It would not be particularly surprising for the incidence of lead poisoning to be higher among women working in white lead factories than among women working in other kinds of factories—but such a finding would say nothing about whether controllable conditions had any effect on the development of lead poisoning.

C The existence of household sources of lead that might contribute to lead poisoning would weaken, not support, SPEW's contention that controllable factory conditions were responsible for the development of lead poisoning.

D If white lead factories enforced workplace safety regulations more stringently than did some other types of factories, it might be the case that SPEW's contention was incorrect: that even controlled conditions could not prevent a high incidence of lead poisoning.

E If the conditions typically found in white lead factories were particularly bad with regard to safety and hygiene, it could conceivably be the case that SPEW's contention was true—that is, that the conditions that caused lead poisoning were controllable. But it might also be the case that an uncontrollable aspect of those conditions caused lead poisoning. Thus, this neither supports nor undermines SPEW's contention clearly.

The correct answer is A.

492. The passage is primarily concerned with

(A) presenting various groups' views of the motives of those proposing certain legislation

(B) contrasting the reasoning of various groups concerning their positions on certain proposed legislation

(C) tracing the process whereby certain proposed legislation was eventually enacted

(D) assessing the success of tactics adopted by various groups with respect to certain proposed legislation

(E) evaluating the arguments of various groups concerning certain proposed legislation

Main idea

Answering this question depends on identifying the overall point of the passage. The passage is mainly concerned with explaining the reasons behind the positions taken by WIDC and SPEW, which opposed the proposal to enact legislation prohibiting women from holding most white lead factory jobs, and the reasoning of WTUL, which supported the proposal.

A The passage explains how WIDC viewed the proposal, but it does not indicate what any of the groups believed about the motivations of the Home Secretary, who made the proposal.

B **Correct.** The passage contrasts the reasoning of the WIDC and SPEW, both of which believed that enforcing safety regulations would make the proposed legislation unnecessary, with the reasoning of WTUL, which thought that safety regulations were unlikely to be enforced and thus supported the proposal.

C The passage simply states that the proposal was eventually enacted; it does not trace the process by which this occurred.

D The passage implies that WIDC and SPEW were unsuccessful in their opposition to the proposed legislation, but it identifies only one tactic used in opposition to it: SPEW's attempt to challenge it by investigating the causes of lead poisoning.

E The passage does not evaluate the groups' arguments concerning the proposed legislation; rather, it presents those arguments without comment on their quality or value.

The correct answer is B.

Questions 493–498 refer to the passage on page 404.

493. The author of the passage refers to Robert Filmer (see line 9) primarily in order to

(A) show that Royalist ideology was somewhat more radical than most historians appear to realize

(B) qualify the claim that patriarchalism formed the basis of Royalist ideology

(C) question the view that most early feminists were associated with the Royalist faction

(D) highlight an apparent tension between Royalist ideology and the ideas of early feminists

(E) argue that Royalists held conflicting opinions on issues of family organization and women's political rights

Evaluation

This question asks about the role of Filmer in the passage. The author states that Filmer's radical patriarchalism is associated with Royalist ideology and then goes on to define radical patriarchalism as an ideology that asserts the power of the king and the male head of the household. Early feminists, however, questioned the subordination of women in marriage. Thus, there seems to be a conflict between these two sets of ideas.

A Although the passage refers to Filmer's view as *radical patriarchalism*, it provides no evidence regarding any differences in the degrees to which historians consider that view, or Royalism in general, to be radical.

B Filmer's work supports the claim that patriarchalism was the basis of Royalist ideology; it does not qualify such a claim.

C That Filmer's approach was one of radical patriarchalism makes it surprising that early feminists were associated with the Royalist faction, but it does not provide any grounds for questioning whether they were so associated.

D **Correct.** There is apparent tension between Filmer's radical patriarchalism, if that is indeed essential to Royalist ideology, and the ideas of early feminists, who questioned such patriarchalism.

E The author refers to Filmer in order to suggest, initially, a uniformity among Royalists regarding family and women; it is only later in the passage that this view becomes more complicated.

The correct answer is D.

494. The passage suggests which of the following about the seventeenth-century English women mentioned in line 2?

(A) Their status as forerunners of modern feminism is not entirely justified.

(B) They did not openly challenge the radical patriarchalism of Royalist Filmerian ideology.

(C) Cavendish was the first among these women to criticize women's subordination in marriage and assert women's equality with men.

(D) Their views on family organization and women's political rights were diametrically opposed to those of both Royalist and Parliamentarian ideology.

(E) Historians would be less puzzled if more of them were identified with the Parliamentarian side in the English Civil Wars.

Inference

The first sentence of the passage refers to women who are both regarded as forerunners of modern feminism and identified as Royalists. The passage goes on to suggest that, given Royalist ideology's association with Filmer's radical patriarchalism (equating absolute power of the king with absolute power of the male head of household), it is surprising that feminism would find any footing within such an ideology.

A Nothing in the passage disputes the idea that the seventeenth-century English women in question should be considered the forerunners of modern feminism.

B Gallagher provides the example of Margaret Cavendish as a writer who did openly challenge radical patriarchalism—albeit only in her writings.

C The passage states that Cavendish had successors among early feminists, but it does not indicate whether she herself was the first seventeenth-century English woman to assert women's equality.

D The passage does not indicate what the Parliamentarian view of family organization and women's political rights was, so there is no way to determine whether the Royalist forerunners of modern feminism were opposed to that view.

E **Correct.** The basic puzzle the passage sets out to solve is why the forerunners of modern feminism would have been associated with the Royalist side, which seems to have been based on radical patriarchalism. Historians would most likely have been less surprised if these women had been identified with the Parliamentarian side, which presumably did not embrace radical patriarchalism.

The correct answer is E.

495. The passage suggests that Margaret Cavendish's decision to become an author was motivated, at least in part, by a desire to

(A) justify her support for the Royalist cause
(B) encourage her readers to work toward eradicating Filmerian patriarchalism
(C) persuade other women to break free from their political and social isolation
(D) analyze the causes for women's exclusion from the pursuit of power
(E) create a world over which she could exercise total control

Inference

This question asks about Margaret Cavendish's reasons for becoming an author. The second paragraph describes her as someone who *insisted that she was a self-sufficient being*; she understood that, given the real-world strictures in place, she could achieve this self-sufficiency in her own mind and on paper as a writer. So her decision to become a writer can be inferred to be motivated by her desire to exercise power and control.

A The passage states that Cavendish justified her being the center of her own universe by invoking the Royalist figure of the absolute monarch; there is no suggestion in the passage that Cavendish felt the need to justify any support for the actual Royalist cause.

B The passage gives no direct indication that Cavendish was even aware of Filmerian patriarchalism.

C The second paragraph states that Cavendish's idea of absolute singularity carried with it the idea of social and political isolation; Cavendish was most likely not motivated by a desire to persuade other women to break free from such isolation.

D Cavendish took the exclusion of women from the pursuit of power for granted; the passage does not suggest that she was concerned with its causes.

E **Correct.** According to the passage, Cavendish considered herself a self-sufficient being who was at the center of her own universe; in her writing, she wanted to create a world in which this was also true.

The correct answer is E.

496. The phrase "a satellite orbiting a dominant male planet" (lines 41–42) refers most directly to

(A) Cavendish's concept that each woman is a sovereign self
(B) the complete political and social isolation of absolute singularity
(C) the immaterial world that a writer can create on paper
(D) the absolute subordination of women in a patriarchal society
(E) the metaphorical figure of the absolute monarch

Evaluation

The phrase in question is *a satellite orbiting a dominant male planet*. The passage states that this was the idea that Cavendish was reacting against; she preferred instead the idea that she was the center of her own universe, her own sovereign, subject to no one.

A The idea of a satellite orbiting a dominant male planet refers not to Cavendish's idea that each woman is a sovereign self, but rather to the idea directly opposed to that: each woman must submit to a dominant male.

B A *satellite orbiting a dominant male planet* is by definition not isolated, nor is it singular.

C According to the passage, Cavendish wished to create her own world as a writer so that she did not have to be a *satellite.*

D **Correct.** The phrase refers to the idea that in a patriarchal society, women are as satellites to men, who are the dominant planets.

E While radical patriarchy does equate the monarch with the male head of the household, the in question phrase is most directly about the relationship, under patriarchy, between women and men.

The correct answer is D.

497. The primary purpose of the passage is to

(A) trace the historical roots of a modern sociopolitical movement

(B) present one scholar's explanation for a puzzling historical phenomenon

(C) contrast two interpretations of the ideological origins of a political conflict

(D) establish a link between the ideology of an influential political theorist and that of a notoriously eccentric writer

(E) call attention to some points of agreement between opposing sides in an ideological debate

Main idea

This question asks about the passage as a whole. The passage is mainly concerned with outlining Catherine Gallagher's attempt to explain why, given Royalist ideology's apparent association with radical patriarchalism, Royalist women offered feminist critiques of women's subordination in marriage and asserted their equality with men.

A The passage makes no connection between early feminism and its modern form.

B **Correct.** The passage presents a puzzling historical phenomenon, that Royalist women critiqued patriarchalism, in the first paragraph, and then presents Catherine Gallagher's explanation for that phenomenon in the second paragraph.

C While the passage discusses the political conflict between the Royalists and Parliamentarians in the English Civil Wars in the first paragraph, neither this conflict, nor its ideological origins are the focus of the passage. Furthermore, the passage does not offer any interpretations of the origins of the conflict.

D The passage attempts to unlink the ideology of political theorist Robert Filmer and the eccentric author Margaret Cavendish by suggesting that Filmer's radical patriarchalism was not the only way of understanding Royalist ideology. Cavendish provided a different understanding entirely.

E While both sides of the ideological debate did agree on the absolute monarchy, the passage as a whole does not focus on this agreement, but rather on the disagreement about where, theoretically, the idea of absolute monarchy leads.

The correct answer is B.

498. Which of the following, if true, would most clearly undermine Gallagher's explanation of the link between Royalism and feminism?

(A) Because of their privileged backgrounds, Royalist women were generally better educated than were their Parliamentarian counterparts.

(B) Filmer himself had read some of Cavendish's early writings and was highly critical of her ideas.

(C) Cavendish's views were highly individual and were not shared by the other Royalist women who wrote early feminist works.

(D) The Royalist and Parliamentarian ideologies were largely in agreement on issues of family organization and women's political rights.

(E) The Royalist side included a sizable minority faction that was opposed to the more radical tendencies of Filmerian patriarchalism.

Inference

This question asks about how to undermine the way in which Gallagher connects Royalism and feminism. According to Gallagher, Cavendish's work exemplifies the connection between these ideas, because Cavendish took the idea of absolute monarchy and extended that to the idea of absolute self, an idea that should, Cavendish believed, apply to women as well as men.

A Gallagher's explanation of the link between Royalism and feminism does not depend on the education level of Royalist women relative to Parliamentarian women.

B Filmer most likely would have been critical of Cavendish's ideas, had he encountered them, but the passage does not indicate that Gallagher's argument had anything to do with whether Filmer read Cavendish's writings.

C **Correct.** Gallagher uses Cavendish's work to explain how Royalism gave rise to feminism, but if Cavendish's views were completely atypical of other Royalist women, then those views cannot explain the link as Gallagher suggests they do.

D The passage states in the first paragraph that if the Royalists and Parliamentarians were in agreement *on issues of family organization and women's political rights*, then feminists should have been divided between the two sides—but they were not. So this idea, if true, would undermine that statement, but not Gallagher's argument about the link between Royalists and feminists.

E If more Royalists were opposed to Filmer's radical patriarchalism, then Cavendish's writings would seem to be more representative of tendencies in Royalist ideology, thus making Gallagher's case stronger, not weaker.

The correct answer is C.

Questions 499–503 refer to the passage on page 406.

499. The passage is primarily concerned with

(A) identifying two practices in medical research that may affect the accuracy of clinical trials
(B) describing aspects of medical research that tend to drive up costs
(C) evaluating an analysis of certain shortcomings of current medical research practices
(D) describing proposed changes to the ways in which clinical trials are conducted
(E) explaining how medical researchers have traditionally conducted clinical trials and how such trials are likely to change

Main idea

This question requires an understanding of what the passage as a whole is doing. The passage introduces Frazier and Mosteller as proposing changes to the ways clinical trials in medical research are currently conducted. The rest of the passage then describes these proposed changes together with the support Frazier and Mosteller provide for adopting these changes.

A The passage identifies practices in medical research to help illustrate the basis for Frazier and Mosteller's proposed changes.

B The passage mentions medical research costs as one example within the larger description of Frazier and Mosteller's proposed changes.

C The passage is not concerned with evaluating Frazier and Mosteller's proposed changes.

D **Correct.** The passage describes the changes proposed by Frazier and Mosteller to the way clinical trials are conducted.

E The passage is not concerned with establishing the likelihood of any changes to the way medical research is conducted.

The correct answer is D.

500. Which of the following can be inferred from the passage about a study of the category of patients referred to in lines 20–22 ?

(A) Its findings might have limited applicability.
(B) It would be prohibitively expensive in its attempt to create ideal conditions.
(C) It would be the best way to sample the total population of potential patients.
(D) It would allow researchers to limit information collection without increasing the risk that important variables could be overlooked.
(E) Its findings would be more accurate if it concerned treatments for a progressive disease than if it concerned treatments for a nonprogressive disease.

Inference

This question requires drawing an inference from information given in the passage. In describing the proposals put forth by Frazier and Mosteller, the passage states in lines 15–20 that they propose using more patients in clinical trials than are currently being used, and that the trials would thereby obtain *a more representative sample of the total population with the disease under study*. The passage then states that researchers often *restrict* (lines 20–22) their trials to certain types of patients, therefore limiting the applicability of their findings.

A **Correct.** The passage states that the researchers preferred to restrict the types of patients used in their studies, thereby using a less representative sample than if they used a more inclusive group of patients.

B The passage mentions the added expense of clinical trials only in relation to data storage, collection, and analysis.

C The passage describes the category of patients referred to as restricted and therefore unrepresentative of the total population.

D While the passage does mention the amount of data collected about an individual patient, that topic is not connected to the category of patients referred to in lines 20–22.

E The passage does not suggest that a study using the category of patients referred to would be more effective in investigating progressive diseases.

The correct answer is A.

501. It can be inferred from the passage that a study limited to patients like those mentioned in lines 20–22 would have which of the following advantages over the kind of study proposed by Frazier and Mosteller?

(A) It would yield more data and its findings would be more accurate.
(B) It would cost less in the long term, though it would be more expensive in its initial stages.
(C) It would limit the number of variables researchers would need to consider when evaluating the treatment under study.
(D) It would help researchers to identify subgroups of patients with secondary conditions that might also be treatable.
(E) It would enable researchers to assess the value of an experimental treatment for the average patient.

Inference

This question requires understanding what the information in the passage implies. The passage explains that Frazier and Mosteller's proposal involves enrolling more patients in clinical trials (lines 18–19) than is the case with the category of patients referred to. The passage then explains that broadening the range of trial participants would allow an evaluation of particular treatments *under various conditions* and *for different patient subgroups* (line 29). This strongly suggests that limiting the patients used to those described in the referred text would limit the number of variables researchers would need to consider.

A The passage suggests that not limiting the patients used in clinical trials will yield more data than restricting them will.

B The passage refers to the costs of clinical trials only as they concern the collection, storage, and analysis of data collected from participants.

C **Correct.** By limiting the patients used to those having the ailment under study, the passage suggests that researchers need to consider fewer variables in their assessment of a treatment.

D The passage suggests that ***not*** limiting the types of patients used in clinical trials will better allow researchers to evaluate subgroups.

E The passage suggests that limiting the types of patients available for clinical trials results in data for specific, rather than average, populations.

The correct answer is C.

502. The author mentions patients' ages (line 32) primarily in order to

(A) identify the most critical variable differentiating subgroups of patients
(B) cast doubt on the advisability of implementing Frazier and Mosteller's proposals about medical research
(C) indicate why progressive diseases may require different treatments at different stages
(D) illustrate a point about the value of enrolling a wide range of patients in clinical trials
(E) substantiate an argument about the problems inherent in enrolling large numbers of patients in clinical trials

Evaluation

Answering this question requires understanding how a particular piece of information functions in the passage as a whole. The passage is concerned with describing the proposals of Frazier and Mosteller. One of these proposals, described in the second paragraph, involves broadening the range of participants used in clinical trials. The passage states that in following this proposal, Frazier and Mosteller suggest that the effectiveness of treatments can be assessed for different patient subgroups. To affirm the value of broadening the range of participants, the passage then cites two examples of criteria by which relevant subgroups might be identified: disease stages and patients' ages.

A The passage makes no judgment as to the value of the subgroups it refers to in relation to broadened participation in clinical trials.
B The passage does not call into question the potential effectiveness of Frazier and Mosteller's proposals.
C The passage's example of patients' ages is not intended to be causally connected to its previous example regarding progressive diseases.
D **Correct.** Patients' ages are referred to in the passage to identify subgroups that could be evaluated if the range of participants in clinical trials were broadened.
E The passage refers to patients' ages in support of Frazier and Mosteller's proposal that more patients be used in clinical trials.

The correct answer is D.

503. According to the passage, which of the following describes a result of the way in which researchers generally conduct clinical trials?

(A) They expend resources on the storage of information likely to be irrelevant to the study they are conducting.
(B) They sometimes compromise the accuracy of their findings by collecting and analyzing more information than is strictly required for their trials.
(C) They avoid the risk of overlooking variables that might affect their findings, even though doing so raises their research costs.
(D) Because they attempt to analyze too much information, they overlook facts that could emerge as relevant to their studies.
(E) In order to approximate the conditions typical of medical treatment, they base their methods of information collection on those used by hospitals.

Supporting ideas

This question asks for an identification of specific information given in the passage. The passage describes the proposals of Frazier and Mosteller as attempting to improve the way clinical trials have generally been conducted. In describing how current trials are generally conducted, the passage states that researchers *collect far more background information on patients than is strictly required for their trials* (lines 4–6) and that they therefore escalate the costs of the trials.

A **Correct.** The passage states that researchers generally collect more information than they need to perform their clinical trials, which drives up the costs of the trials.
B The passage makes no judgment about the accuracy of the information collected by researchers who currently hold clinical trials.
C The passage states that the risk of overlooking relevant information in clinical trials is *never entirely eliminable* (line 11).
D The passage states that researchers generally collect more information than is relevant, not that they overlook relevant information.
E The passage states that, in general, researchers currently collect more information than hospitals do (line 6).

The correct answer is A.

Questions 504–509 refer to the passage on page 408.

504. The primary purpose of the passage is to

(A) assess the validity of a certain view
(B) distinguish between two phenomena
(C) identify the causes of a problem
(D) describe a disturbing trend
(E) allay concern about a particular phenomenon

Main idea

This question requires understanding, in general terms, the purpose of the passage as a whole. The first paragraph identifies an area of concern: declines in amphibian populations may constitute a crisis, one that indicates humans' catastrophic effects on the environment. The rest of the passage then goes on to evaluate, as the second paragraph states, whether claims of crisis-level extinctions as a result of human activity are valid. In making this evaluation, the passage discusses the possible causes of extinctions, biologists' prioritization of population declines over extinctions, and the fact that we lack extensive long-term data on amphibian populations.

A **Correct.** The passage's main purpose is to assess whether the view that humans are causing crisis-level declines in amphibian populations is valid.
B The passage takes care, particularly in the third paragraph, to distinguish between population declines and extinctions, but this is not its primary purpose.
C The passage makes clear that it is difficult to identify the real extent of the problem facing amphibian populations, much less identify its causes.
D The first paragraph notes what may seem to be a disturbing trend—the decline in amphibian populations—but the rest of the passage is concerned not with describing that trend in greater detail, but rather with determining whether it is in fact occurring.
E While the passage provides possible grounds for concluding that concern about declining amphibian populations is overblown, it concludes by suggesting that we might, because we lack data, doom species and ecosystems to extinction. Thus, the overall purpose is not to allay concern.

The correct answer is A.

505. It can be inferred from the passage that the author believes which of the following to be true of the environmentalists mentioned in lines 5–6 ?

(A) They have wrongly chosen to focus on anecdotal reports rather than on the long-term data that are currently available concerning amphibians.
(B) Their recommendations are flawed because their research focuses too narrowly on a single category of animal species.
(C) Their certainty that population declines in general are caused by environmental degradation is not warranted.
(D) They have drawn premature conclusions concerning a crisis in amphibian populations from recent reports of declines.
(E) They have overestimated the effects of chance events on trends in amphibian populations.

Inference

This question asks about the author's view of the environmentalists mentioned in the first paragraph. These environmentalists have claimed, based on amphibian population declines, that the situation is a crisis and that immediate action must be taken. The author, however, states that the declines are only *apparently* drastic and questions whether they are real, thus suggesting that the environmentalists are drawing conclusions in the absence of a complete consideration of the situation.

A The passage indicates that anecdotal reports are insufficient, but so too are other resources. The fourth paragraph of the passage makes clear that there is not enough long-term data available on which to base conclusions about amphibian populations.
B The passage does not indicate that the environmentalists under discussion have conducted research on any animal species.

C The passage does not indicate that the environmentalists in question hold, with certainty, any particular view regarding population declines in general.

D Correct. The author argues that the recent declines may have several different causes, and that environmentalists have jumped to a conclusion about the cause of the declines as well as their significance.

E The environmentalists, in attributing population declines to intentional human activity, have more likely underestimated than overestimated the effects of chance events on amphibian populations.

The correct answer is D.

506. It can be inferred from the passage that the author believes which of the following to be true of the amphibian extinctions that have recently been reported?

(A) They have resulted primarily from human activities causing environmental degradation.
(B) They could probably have been prevented if timely action had been taken to protect the habitats of amphibian species.
(C) They should not come as a surprise, because amphibian populations generally have been declining for a number of years.
(D) They have probably been caused by a combination of chance events.
(E) They do not clearly constitute evidence of general environmental degradation.

Inference

The author suggests throughout the passage that recently reported amphibian extinctions may have several different causes: they may be due to any number of chance events, for example, or may simply be the result of a small population that finds itself unable to continue under difficult conditions, whatever causes those conditions.

A The author states in the second paragraph that extinctions may occur without a proximate cause in human activities and does not make a commitment to any particular explanation of the amphibian extinctions.

B That chance events can cause extinctions suggests that even if habitats had been protected, extinctions still might have occurred.

C In the second paragraph, the author says that extinctions *should come as no great surprise*, but this option is imprecise. The amphibian populations have not generally *been declining for a number of years*. The author says in the third paragraph that amphibian populations show strong fluctuations; further, in the fourth paragraph, the author says that there is insufficient long-term data to conclude that amphibian populations have been, or are, in decline.

D The author suggests that the extinctions may have been caused by chance events, but there is not enough data to know whether or not this is probable.

E Correct. The reported extinctions could have resulted from several different causes; thus, they are not clear evidence of general environmental degradation.

The correct answer is E.

507. According to the passage, each of the following is true of endangered amphibian species EXCEPT:

(A) They are among the rarest kinds of amphibians.
(B) They generally have populations that are small in size.
(C) They are in constant danger of extinction.
(D) Those with decreasing populations are the most likely candidates for immediate extinction.
(E) They are in danger of extinction due to events that sometimes have nothing to do with human activities.

Application

This question asks what the passage does not say is true of endangered amphibian species. The second paragraph discusses endangered species, stating that they are *always rare, almost always small, and, by definition, under constant threat of extinction*, which may be caused by chance events. The possibility of their extinction, the passage states, depends only on the population size, and not whether that population is increasing or decreasing.

A The second paragraph mentions rarity as a characteristic of endangered amphibian species.

B According to the second paragraph, endangered amphibian species are generally those of small populations.

C The second paragraph states that an endangered population is under constant threat of extinction.

D Correct. The last sentence of the second paragraph states that the probability of extinction due to chance events is independent of how a population changes in size. Immediate extinction would more likely come from such events, whereas population decline is gradual, even if fairly rapid.

E Endangered species, according to the second paragraph, may become extinct due to chance events—that is, events that have nothing to do with human activities.

The correct answer is D.

508. Which of the following most accurately describes the organization of the passage?

(A) A question is raised, a distinction regarding it is made, and the question is answered.

(B) An interpretation is presented, its soundness is examined, and a warning is given.

(C) A situation is described, its consequences are analyzed, and a prediction is made.

(D) Two interpretations of a phenomenon are described, and one of them is rejected as invalid.

(E) Two methods for analyzing a phenomenon are compared, and further study of the phenomenon is recommended.

Evaluation

This question asks about the organization of the passage as a whole. In the first paragraph, the author tells about a situation that has been interpreted in a particular way by environmentalists. The passage then proceeds to consider whether that interpretation is valid, and while it does not come to a definitive conclusion on that point, the final paragraph warns about the possible consequences of not taking the action recommended by the environmentalists.

A The passage does initially raise a question regarding whether the environmentalists' interpretation of events is valid, but it does not answer that question, for the appropriate long-term data are not available.

B Correct. The passage presents environmentalists' interpretation of recent news regarding amphibians, then examines the soundness of that interpretation. Finally, the author warns that postponing environmental action may have disastrous consequences.

C The first paragraph describes a situation of possibly drastic declines in amphibian populations but does not follow this description with an analysis of its consequences.

D The passage suggests that apparent declines in amphibian populations may or may not constitute a crisis, but it does not reject either idea.

E While the passage does imply, in its final paragraph, that long-term data on amphibian populations should be collected, the passage does not compare two methods for analyzing amphibian populations or population declines in those populations.

The correct answer is B.

509. Which of the following best describes the function of the sentence in lines 35–38 ?

(A) To give an example of a particular kind of study

(B) To cast doubt on an assertion made in the previous sentence

(C) To raise an objection to a view presented in the first paragraph

(D) To provide support for a view presented in the first paragraph

(E) To introduce an idea that will be countered in the following paragraph

Evaluation

The sentence in question discusses the way in which anecdotal reports of population decreases cannot help biologists determine whether those decreases are normal fluctuations, take populations to lower levels that are not actually worrisome, or actually threaten extinctions. This indicates that the view mentioned in the first paragraph—reports of declines indicate a catastrophic crisis—may be mistaken.

A The sentence does not address a particular kind of study; it objects to the use of anecdotal reports in place of actual study.

B The previous sentence describes the possibilities referred to in the sentence in question. The sentence does not cast doubt on any of those possibilities.

C **Correct.** The view that reports of amphibian population declines indicate a crisis, as presented in the first paragraph, is countered by the objection here that there are several possible causes for population declines, and anecdotal reports cannot distinguish among those possibilities.

D The first paragraph is concerned with articulating the view that amphibian population declines constitute a crisis. This sentence does not support that view; instead, it offers reason to question it.

E The sentence introduces the idea that amphibian populations have fluctuated in the past, and the following paragraph supports this idea by stating that several amphibian species that appeared almost extinct in the 1950s and 1960s have recovered. Thus, the paragraph does not counter the sentence.

The correct answer is C.

Questions 510–513 refer to the passage on page 410.

510. The passage mentions which of the following as a factor that affects the role of *P. ochraceus* as a keystone species within different habitats?

(A) The degree to which the habitat is sheltered from waves

(B) The degree to which other animals within a habitat prey on mussels

(C) The fact that mussel populations are often not dominant within some habitats occupied by *P. ochraceus*

(D) The size of the *P. ochraceus* population within the habitat

(E) The fact that there is great species diversity within some habitats occupied by *P. ochraceus*

Supporting idea

This question depends on recognizing what the passage states about the factors affecting *P. ochraceus*'s role as a keystone species, which is different in different habitats. According to the passage, *P. ochraceus* consumes and suppresses mussel populations in some habitats—specifically, those that are wave-exposed—making it a keystone predator in those habitats. But in wave-sheltered habitats, *P. ochraceus* does not play the same role in suppressing mussel populations.

A **Correct.** The passage clearly states that *P. ochraceus*'s role in wave-exposed habitats differs from its role in wave-sheltered habitats.

B The passage says that the impact of *P. ochraceus* predation on mussels is not strong in wave-sheltered habitats, but this is not—at least not at all sites—because other animals are preying on the mussels; rather, at least at some sites, it is because mussels are controlled by sand burial.

C The passage does not suggest that mussel populations are dominant in any habitats occupied by *P. ochraceus*.

D The size of the *P. ochraceus* population affects the size of the mussel population within wave-exposed habitats, but the passage does not suggest that *P. ochraceus*'s role as a keystone species depends on the size of its population within those habitats.

E The only other species the passage mentions in conjunction with *P. ochraceus* habitats is the mussel; the passage does not address species diversity in these habitats.

The correct answer is A.

511. Which of the following hypothetical experiments most clearly exemplifies the method of identifying species' roles that the author considers problematic?

(A) A population of seals in an Arctic habitat is counted in order to determine whether it is the dominant species in that ecosystem.

(B) A species of fish that is a keystone species in one marine ecosystem is introduced into another marine ecosystem to see whether the species will come to occupy a keystone role.

(C) In order to determine whether a species of monkey is a keystone species within a particular ecosystem, the monkeys are removed from that ecosystem and the ecosystem is then studied.

(D) Different mountain ecosystems are compared to determine how geography affects a particular species' ability to dominate its ecosystem.

(E) In a grassland experiencing a changing climate, patterns of species extinction are traced in order to evaluate the effect of climate changes on keystone species in that grassland.

Application

Answering this question depends on recognizing what the author says about identifying species' roles in habitats and then extending that to another situation. The author considers a particular method of studying keystone species problematic: removing a suspected keystone species from its habitat and observing what happens to the ecosystem. The author finds this problematic because interactions among species are complex.

A The author does not discuss counting the members of a population as a problematic way of determining whether that population is a dominant species.

B The method that the author finds problematic has to do with observing what happens to an ecosystem when a keystone species is removed from it, not with observing what happens to a different ecosystem when the species is introduced into it.

C **Correct.** The author states explicitly that removing a species from a habitat in order to determine its keystone status is problematic. Removing the monkeys from their habitat is a clear example of this problematic practice.

D Comparison of habitats in order to determine geography's effect on a particular species' dominance would most likely find favor with the author, for this is the approach the author seems to advocate in investigating *P. ochraceus*'s keystone status.

E The author does not discuss tracing patterns of extinction or changing climates in the passage.

The correct answer is C.

512. Which of the following, if true, would most clearly support the argument about keystone status advanced in the last sentence of the passage (lines 24–31)?

(A) A species of bat is primarily responsible for keeping insect populations within an ecosystem low, and the size of the insect population in turn affects bird species within that ecosystem.

(B) A species of iguana occupies a keystone role on certain tropical islands, but does not play that role on adjacent tropical islands that are inhabited by a greater number of animal species.

(C) Close observation of a savannah ecosystem reveals that more species occupy keystone roles within that ecosystem than biologists had previously believed.

(D) As a keystone species of bee becomes more abundant, it has a larger effect on the ecosystem it inhabits.

(E) A species of moth that occupies a keystone role in a prairie habitat develops coloration patterns that camouflage it from potential predators.

Evaluation

To answer this question, focus on the argument advanced in the last sentence of the passage and identify what information would support that argument. In the last sentence of the passage, the author claims that keystone status depends on context. The author then offers three contextual factors that may affect a species' keystone status: geography, community diversity (i.e., the number of species in a given habitat), and length of species interaction. Evidence supporting this argument would show that context is important to a species' keystone status.

A This scenario does not indicate anything about keystone status; this is simply a description of how species populations in a single ecosystem affect one another.

B Correct. That the iguana is a keystone species in a location that has limited species diversity but not a keystone species in a location that has greater species diversity suggests that keystone status does indeed depend on context. Thus, this example supports the author's argument in the last sentence of the passage.

C That biologists were mistaken about keystone species in a particular ecosystem does not have a bearing on whether keystone status is context dependent.

D It is not surprising that an increase in a species' population would lead to that species having a larger effect on its ecosystem—but this does not speak directly to the question of whether keystone status itself depends on context.

E A keystone species enhancing its ability to survive in a single ecosystem does not lend any support to the idea that keystone status depends on context. The moth's keystone status would have to undergo some change for this to have a bearing on the question of context.

The correct answer is B.

513. The passage suggests which of the following about the identification of a species as a keystone species?

(A) Such an identification depends primarily on the species' relationship to the dominant species.

(B) Such an identification can best be made by removing the species from a particular ecosystem and observing changes that occur in the ecosystem.

(C) Such an identification is likely to be less reliable as an ecosystem becomes less diverse.

(D) Such an identification seems to depend on various factors within the ecosystem.

(E) Such an identification can best be made by observing predation behavior.

Inference

Answering this question requires identifying how the passage suggests that keystone species should be identified. The passage identifies a particular way in which keystone status should *not* be determined: removing a species and observing what happens to the ecosystem. The passage also argues that keystone status depends strongly on context: that is, an ecosystem's characteristics, including its geography and inhabitants, determine its keystone species.

A While the passage uses an example of a keystone species, *P. ochraceus*, which preys on a species that would, in the keystone species' absence, be dominant, there is nothing to suggest that a keystone species *must* have a particular relationship with the dominant, or potentially dominant, species in an ecosystem.

B The passage explicitly states that this method of identification would be problematic.

C A reduction in an ecosystem's diversity might alter which species occupy keystone roles in that ecosystem, the passage suggests, but there is no indication that identifying such species would become more difficult.

D **Correct.** If, as the passage suggests, keystone status for any given species depends on the context of the ecosystem in which it lives, then it is likely that identifying keystone species depends strongly on understanding what factors of the ecosystem contribute to creating keystone status. The passage lists such factors as geography, community diversity, and species interaction.

E While the passage uses a predator, *P. ochraceus*, as its example of a keystone species, there is no indication that predation is an essential component of the actual definition of keystone species (*one whose effects are much larger than would be predicted from its abundance*).

The correct answer is D.

Questions 514–516 refer to the passage on page 412.

514. According to the passage, the anatomical evidence provided by the preserved soft bodies of conodonts led scientists to conclude that

(A) conodonts had actually been invertebrate carnivores

(B) conodonts' teeth were adapted from protective bony scales

(C) conodonts were primitive vertebrate suspension feeders

(D) primitive vertebrates with teeth appeared earlier than armored vertebrates

(E) scientists' original observations concerning the phosphatic remains of conodonts were essentially correct

Supporting ideas

This question depends on understanding how a particular type of evidence—the preserved soft bodies of conodonts—supports a particular conclusion stated in the passage. The third paragraph makes this relationship explicit, explaining that certain features of conodonts show them to be more primitive than other vertebrates. Further, those features indicate that they came before ostracoderms and other armored jawless fishes. These remains support the conclusion stated in the second paragraph regarding teeth being more primitive than external armor.

A The passage states explicitly that conodonts were not invertebrates but rather vertebrates.

B This view is attributed to certain traditionalists but is contradicted by other paleontological evidence presented in the second and third paragraphs. According to the third paragraph, the evidence provided by the preserved soft bodies of conodonts undermines this traditional view.

C The final sentence of the passage indicates that the evidence in question supports the conclusion that conodonts were predators rather than suspension feeders.

D **Correct.** The third paragraph explains how conodonts' remains support the conclusion that teeth were more primitive than external armor.

E The second paragraph explains that originally, scientists thought that early vertebrates were not predators—but the remainder of the passage indicates that this idea is inconsistent with more recent evidence described in the passage.

The correct answer is D.

515. The second paragraph in the passage serves primarily to

(A) outline the significance of the 1981 discovery of conodont remains to the debate concerning the development of the vertebrate skeleton
(B) contrast the traditional view of the development of the vertebrate skeleton with a view derived from the 1981 discovery of conodont remains
(C) contrast the characteristics of the ostracoderms with the characteristics of earlier soft-bodied vertebrates
(D) explain the importance of the development of teeth among the earliest vertebrate predators
(E) present the two sides of the debate concerning the development of the vertebrate skeleton

Evaluation

This question depends on understanding the second paragraph in the context of the passage as a whole. The second paragraph begins by noting the traditional view of the vertebrate skeleton—that it was a defense against predators—and then goes on to explain that other paleontologists argued against this idea, claiming instead that vertebrates began as predators and that teeth were a more primary feature than external armor.

A The second paragraph focuses on describing the debate rather than on the distinctive contribution of the 1981 discovery to that debate.

B The second paragraph does not explicitly indicate whether the opposition to the traditional view originally rested on the 1981 discovery of conodont remains. In fact, the surrounding discussion, in the first and third paragraphs, suggests that the discovery in 1981 turned out to support the opposing view, which some paleontologists already held at that time.

C The mention of ostracoderms in the second paragraph merely serves to indicate how the traditionalists' arguments might have seemed plausible. The paragraph as a whole is not devoted to contrasting the ostracoderms with earlier soft-bodied vertebrates.

D The development of teeth figures in the second paragraph, but this development is mentioned first as a feature that some believed to have been adapted from protective scales; only the final sentence of the paragraph connects teeth to early vertebrate predators.

E **Correct.** According to the passage, the debate concerning the development of the vertebrate skeleton hinges on whether vertebrates began as predators, with teeth, or whether skeletal defenses such as external armor evolved first. The primary purpose of the second paragraph is to distinguish these two sides.

The correct answer is E.

516. It can be inferred that on the basis of the 1981 discovery of conodont remains, paleontologists could draw which of the following conclusions?

(A) The earliest vertebrates were sedentary suspension feeders.
(B) Ostracoderms were not the earliest vertebrates.
(C) Defensive armor preceded jaws among vertebrates.
(D) Paired eyes and adaptations for activity are definitive characteristics of vertebrates.
(E) Conodonts were unlikely to have been predators.

Inference

What could paleontologists conclude, based on the 1981 discovery of conodont remains? That discovery, according to the passage, supported the view of certain paleontologists that the earliest vertebrates were predators with teeth—unlike the ostracoderms, which had no jaws.

A According to the second paragraph, traditionalists believed that early vertebrates were sedentary suspension feeders. But the 1981 discovery supported instead the hypothesis that early vertebrates were predators instead.

B **Correct.** According to the third paragraph, the conodonts' body structures indicated that they were more primitive than the ostracoderms, so the ostracoderms must not have been the earliest vertebrates.

C Traditionalists argued that teeth were adapted from bony scales that provided defensive armor, but the 1981 discovery suggested that teeth preceded such scales.

D Paleontologists knew prior to the 1981 discovery that paired eyes and other adaptations are characteristics of vertebrates. They used this knowledge to help them interpret the 1981 discovery.

E The third paragraph indicates that conodonts, given their teeth, were most likely predators.

The correct answer is B.

Questions 517–528 refer to the passage on page 414.

517. The primary purpose of the passage is to

(A) advocate a more positive attitude toward technological change

(B) discuss the implications for employees of the modernization of a telephone exchange

(C) consider a successful challenge to the constructivist view of technological change

(D) challenge the position of advocates of technological determinism

(E) suggest that the social causes of technological change should be studied in real situations

Main idea

This question asks for an assessment of what the passage as a whole is doing. The passage introduces Clark's study as a *solid contribution* (line 3) to the debate between technological determinists and social constructivists. In the second paragraph, Braverman is introduced as holding a position of social constructivism, a position that Clark takes issue with. In the final paragraph, the passage holds that *Clark refutes the extremes of the constructivists* (line 31), and Clark's arguments challenging social constructivism are then described.

A The passage takes no position on the merits of technological change but is concerned only with the role of such change in society.

B The passage mentions telephone exchange workers as an example that helps illustrate the more central debate between determinists and constructivists.

C **Correct.** The passage is mainly concerned with portraying Clark's view as a successful challenge to constructivism.

D The passage describes Clark's view as a successful challenge to social constructivism, not technological determinism.

E The passage is concerned with describing a challenge to social constructivism and not with suggesting the context in which technological change ought to be studied.

The correct answer is C.

518. Which of the following statements about the modernization of the telephone exchange is supported by information in the passage?

(A) The new technology reduced the role of managers in labor negotiations.

(B) The modernization was implemented without the consent of the employees directly affected by it.

(C) The modernization had an impact that went significantly beyond maintenance routines.

(D) Some of the maintenance workers felt victimized by the new technology.

(E) The modernization gave credence to the view of advocates of social constructivism.

Supporting ideas

This question requires recognizing information contained in the passage. The passage states in the first paragraph that Clark's study focused on the modernization of a telephone exchange and the effect this had on maintenance work and workers. After describing Braverman's analysis in the second paragraph as being at odds with Clark's views, the passage discusses Clark's views in more detail in the final paragraph. As part of this discussion, the passage notes that Clark shows how a change from *maintenance-intensive electromechanical switches to semielectronic switching systems* at the telephone exchange *altered work tasks, skills, training opportunities, administration, and organization of workers* (lines 42–44). Thus, the passage shows that the modernization of the telephone exchange affected much more than maintenance routines.

A The passage does not discuss whether new technology reduces the role of managers in labor negotiations.

B The passage does not discuss the role of employee consent in the modernization of the telephone exchange.

C Correct. The passage states that the modernization of the telephone exchange affected tasks, skills, training, administration, and the organization of workers.

D The passage does not suggest that maintenance workers felt victimized by the modernization of the telephone exchange.

E The passage describes modernization as a fact viewable from a perspective of social constructivism or technological determinism, but that does not in itself support either view.

The correct answer is C.

519. Which of the following most accurately describes Clark's opinion of Braverman's position?

(A) He respects its wide-ranging popularity.

(B) He disapproves of its misplaced emphasis on the influence of managers.

(C) He admires the consideration it gives to the attitudes of the workers affected.

(D) He is concerned about its potential to impede the implementation of new technologies.

(E) He is sympathetic to its concern about the impact of modern technology on workers.

Inference

Answering this question requires inferring what the passage's author likely believes. The passage describes Braverman's position as one of mainstream social constructivism (lines 23–24), a position that Clark takes issue with. Although it describes Braverman's position, the rest of the passage is devoted to showing how Clark's position takes issue with Braverman's.

In the second paragraph, the passage describes Clark as holding that *technology can be a primary determinant of social and managerial organization* (lines 9–11), which suggests that managers are sometimes subordinate to technological change. In lines 15–17, however, Braverman is described as holding that *the shape of a technological system is subordinate to the manager's desire to wrest control of the labor process from the workers*, which shows that Clark and Braverman are at odds on this point.

A Since the passage says that Clark believes an important insight *has been obscured by the recent sociological fashion* that Braverman's views exemplify (lines 11–14), one cannot infer that Clark respects the popularity of Braverman's views.

B Correct. The passage shows that Clark believes managers to have less influence over how technology affects an organization than Braverman claims that they have.

C The passage does not indicate that Clark admires any aspect of Braverman's position.

D The passage does not indicate that Clark considers impediments to modernization.

E The passage does not indicate that Clark is sympathetic to any concerns attributed to Braverman.

The correct answer is B.

520. The information in the passage suggests that which of the following statements from hypothetical sociological studies of change in industry most clearly exemplifies the social constructivists' version of technological determinism?

(A) It is the available technology that determines workers' skills, rather than workers' skills influencing the application of technology.

(B) All progress in industrial technology grows out of a continuing negotiation between technological possibility and human need.

(C) Some organizational change is caused by people; some is caused by computer chips.

(D) Most major technological advances in industry have been generated through research and development.

(E) Some industrial technology eliminates jobs, but educated workers can create whole new skills areas by the adaptation of the technology.

Application

This question requires understanding different points of view discussed in the passage. In the first paragraph, the passage mentions the debate involving technological determinism and social constructivism. In the second and third paragraphs, the passage uses Braverman's analysis to illustrate the social constructivists' position and in the third paragraph suggests that the constructivists are *misrepresenting technological determinism* (line 24). In lines 29–30, the constructivists are reported to hold that technological determinism views technology as *existing outside society, capable of directly influencing skills and work organization.*

A **Correct.** This statement is consistent with the constructivists' view that technological determinism sees technology as outside of society, influencing workers' skills.

B The passage states that the constructivists hold that *technological determinists are supposed to believe . . . that machinery imposes appropriate forms of order on society* (lines 25–27), suggesting that no negotiation is present.

C According to the description of them in the passage, constructivists portray technological determinists as believing that technology, not people, drives organizational change.

D The passage does not portray either constructivists or determinists as being concerned with technological research and development.

E The passage does not portray either constructivists or determinists as being concerned with technology-driven job elimination or creation.

The correct answer is A.

521. The information in the passage suggests that Clark believes that which of the following would be true if social constructivism had not gained widespread acceptance?

(A) Businesses would be more likely to modernize without considering the social consequences of their actions.

(B) There would be greater understanding of the role played by technology in producing social change.

(C) Businesses would be less likely to understand the attitudes of employees affected by modernization.

(D) Modernization would have occurred at a slower rate.

(E) Technology would have played a greater part in determining the role of business in society.

Inference

Answering this question involves understanding a point of view as it is described in the passage. The passage aligns Clark's study closely with the technological determinists, summarizing his view in lines 9–11: *technology can be a primary determinant of social and managerial organization*. In the following sentence, the passage states that Clark believes that *this possibility is obscured by the recent sociological fashion, exemplified by Braverman's analysis* (lines 11–13). After illustrating Braverman's analysis, the passage then states that it represents *social constructivism*.

A According to the passage, Clark holds that constructivists obscure how modernization might have social consequences.

B **Correct.** According to the passage, Clark sees constructivism as obscuring the possibility that technology plays a primary role in social change.

C The passage does not discuss how the attitudes of employees are perceived by their employers.

D The passage describes a debate about the history and sociology of technology; it does not suggest that sociological analyses affect the pace of modernization.

E The passage describes a debate about the history and sociology of technology; it does not suggest that sociological analyses affect the role that technology plays in business.

The correct answer is B.

522. According to the passage, constructivists employed which of the following to promote their argument?

(A) Empirical studies of business situations involving technological change
(B) Citation of managers supportive of their position
(C) Construction of hypothetical situations that support their view
(D) Contrasts of their view with a misstatement of an opposing view
(E) Descriptions of the breadth of impact of technological change

Supporting ideas

Answering this question involves recognizing information given in the passage. The passage indicates that a debate exists between technological determinists and social constructivists, suggesting that these views are in opposition. The passage goes on to state that *constructivists gain acceptance by misrepresenting technological determinism* (lines 23–24). This misrepresentation is presented as the *alternative to constructivism* (lines 27–28), suggesting that constructivists promoted their own view by contrasting it with a misrepresentation of determinists' views.

A The passage mentions empirical studies in relation to Clark's study but not Braverman's analysis.
B The passage does not mention that managers were supportive of any particular point of view within the sociology of technology.
C The passage does not mention any hypothetical situations as being used by the constructivists in support of their view.
D **Correct.** The passage indicates that the constructivists have come into fashion by contrasting their own views with a misrepresentation of the views of technological determinists.
E The passage does not describe the constructivists as making determinations regarding the degree of impact that technological change has on social or managerial organization.

The correct answer is D.

523. The author of the passage uses the expression "are supposed to" in line 25 primarily in order to

(A) suggest that a contention made by constructivists regarding determinists is inaccurate
(B) define the generally accepted position of determinists regarding the implementation of technology
(C) engage in speculation about the motivation of determinists
(D) lend support to a comment critical of the position of determinists
(E) contrast the historical position of determinists with their position regarding the exchange modernization

Evaluation

This question requires understanding how a particular phrase functions in the passage as a whole. In the third paragraph the passage states that *constructivists gain acceptance by misrepresenting technological determinism* (lines 23–24) and follows this claim with an example of this misrepresentation, stating that *technological determinists are supposed to believe, for example* (lines 25–26). This line implies that the constructivist view of the determinists is inaccurate.

A **Correct.** The passage uses the expression in part to provide an example of the constructivists' misrepresentation of the determinists.
B The passage indicates that the view attributed to the determinists is a misrepresentation, not one that is generally accepted by determinists.
C The expression in the passage is part of a discussion about the motivation of constructivists, not determinists.
D The expression in the passage is part of a discussion that is critical of the constructivists, not the determinists.
E The passage does not describe either the historical position of determinists or their position on the exchange modernization.

The correct answer is A.

524. Which of the following statements about Clark's study of the telephone exchange can be inferred from information in the passage?

(A) Clark's reason for undertaking the study was to undermine Braverman's analysis of the function of technology.

(B) Clark's study suggests that the implementation of technology should be discussed in the context of conflict between labor and management.

(C) Clark examined the impact of changes in the technology of switching at the exchange in terms of overall operations and organization.

(D) Clark concluded that the implementation of new switching technology was equally beneficial to management and labor.

(E) Clark's analysis of the change in switching systems applies only narrowly to the situation at the particular exchange that he studied.

Inference

This question requires understanding what the passage implies in its discussion of a point of view. The details of Clark's views are discussed primarily in the final paragraph. The passage states that on an empirical level, Clark demonstrates that technological change regarding switches at the telephone exchange *altered work tasks, skills, training opportunities, administration, and organization of workers* (lines 42–44). The passage goes on to state Clark's contention that these changes even influenced negotiations between management and labor unions.

A The passage indicates that Clark's study addressed the extremes of both technological determinism and social constructivism. It cites Braverman as a proponent of social constructivism but provides no evidence that Clark's motivation in beginning his study was specifically to target an analysis offered by Braverman.

B The passage indicates that Clark attributed some organizational change to the way labor and management negotiated the introduction of technology but does not mention conflict between them.

C **Correct.** According to the passage, Clark concludes that changes to the technology of switches had an influence on several aspects of the overall operations and organization of the telephone exchange.

D The passage does not indicate that Clark assesses the benefits of technological change to either labor or management.

E The passage indicates that Clark believes the change in switching technology influenced many aspects of the overall operations of the telephone exchange.

The correct answer is C.

Questions 525–529 refer to the passage on page 416.

525. The passage implies that which of the following was a reason that the proportion of verdicts in favor of patentees began to increase in the 1830s ?

(A) Patent applications approved after 1836 were more likely to adhere closely to patent law.

(B) Patent laws enacted during the 1830s better defined patent rights.

(C) Judges became less prejudiced against patentees during the 1830s.

(D) After 1836, litigated cases became less representative of the population of patent disputes.

(E) The proportion of patent disputes brought to trial began to increase after 1836.

Inference

The question asks which statement can be reasonably inferred, from information provided in the passage, to be a reason for the increase in proportion of verdicts favoring patentees, starting in the 1830s. The second paragraph argues that what changed in that decade was not judges' attitudes toward patent law, but the types of patent cases that were litigated. It explains that a law passed in 1836 required that, for the first time in U.S. history, applications for patents had to be examined for their adherence to patent law before a patent would be issued. This information implies that patents granted after 1836 were more likely to adhere to patent law and were thus more likely to be upheld in court.

A **Correct**. The passage implies that patents granted after the 1836 law went into effect were more likely to adhere to patent law.

B The passage does not indicate that any law mentioned made changes to the definition of patent rights; rather, the passage indicates that the patent system was revised to require that patent applications be reviewed for adherence to existing law.

C The passage rejects the explanation that judges' attitudes toward patent rights became more favorable.

D The passage indicates that the population of disputes that were litigated changed after 1836, but it does not suggest that the population of litigated disputes differed from that of patent disputes as a whole.

E The passage does not indicate any change in the proportion of patent disputes brought to trial.

The correct answer is A.

526. The passage implies that the scholars mentioned in line 8 would agree with which of the following criticisms of the American patent system before 1830?

(A) Its definition of property rights relating to inventions was too vague to be useful.

(B) Its criteria for the granting of patents were not clear.

(C) It made it excessively difficult for inventors to receive patents.

(D) It led to excessive numbers of patent-infringement suits.

(E) It failed to encourage national economic growth.

Inference

This question asks about a statement implied by the passage. The scholars mentioned in line 8 question whether U.S. patent law achieved its goal. That goal is described in the first sentence of the passage: to encourage America's economic growth. Thus, it is reasonable to conclude that the scholars would criticize the pre-1830 patent system for failing to encourage economic growth.

A The scholars contend that judges rejected patents for arbitrary reasons, not because the definition of property rights was vague.

B The passage does not indicate that the scholars were critical of the criteria for granting patents.

C The scholars are concerned with inventors' attempts to protect their patents, not the difficulty of acquiring a patent in the first place.

D The passage does not imply that the scholars in question believed that too many patent-infringement suits were brought to court, but rather that too few succeeded.

E **Correct.** The scholars doubt that patent law helped to achieve its goal, which was to encourage economic growth.

The correct answer is E.

527. It can be inferred from the passage that the frequency with which pre-1830 cases have been cited in court decisions is an indication that

(A) judicial support for patent rights was strongest in the period before 1830

(B) judicial support for patent rights did not increase after 1830

(C) courts have returned to judicial standards that prevailed before 1830

(D) verdicts favoring patentees in patent-infringement suits did not increase after 1830

(E) judicial bias against patentees persisted after 1830

Inference

The question asks what is indicated by the frequency with which pre-1830 cases have been cited in court decisions. The second paragraph rejects some scholars' claims that judges prior to the 1830s were *antipatent*, while judges after that time were more accepting of patent rights. The passage supports its critique by pointing out that decisions made by judges before the 1830s have been cited as precedents by later judges just as frequently as post-1830s decisions have been. This implies that later judges' attitudes toward patent rights were similar to those of pre-1830s judges. Thus, there is no reason to believe judges' attitudes toward patent rights changed at that time.

A The passage argues that judicial support for patents did not change in the 1830s.
B **Correct**. Pre-1830s court decisions have been cited as frequently as later decisions, suggesting no change in judges' attitudes.
C The passage does not indicate that judicial standards changed from, and then returned to, those that prevailed before 1830.
D Although actual numbers of favorable verdicts are not mentioned, the passage indicates that the proportion of verdicts decided in favor of patentees did, in fact, increase beginning in the 1830s.
E The passage rejects the notion that judges were biased against patentees either before or after 1830.

The correct answer is B.

528. It can be inferred from the passage that the author and the scholars referred to in line 21 disagree about which of the following aspects of the patents defended in patent-infringement suits before 1830?

(A) Whether the patents were granted for inventions that were genuinely useful
(B) Whether the patents were actually relevant to the growth of the United States economy
(C) Whether the patents were particularly likely to be annulled by judges
(D) Whether the patents were routinely invalidated for reasons that were arbitrary
(E) Whether the patents were vindicated at a significantly lower rate than patents in later suits

Inference

The question depends on recognizing differences between two explanations—one favored by the scholars mentioned in line 21, the other favored by the author—for the frequency with which patents were invalidated in U.S. courts prior to 1830. The first paragraph describes the scholars' view that judges before 1830 were *antipatent* and rejected patentees' claims for *arbitrary reasons*. The author of the passage rejects that view. As an alternate explanation, the author in the second paragraph implies that earlier patents often violated copyright law; this view is supported with reference to an 1836 revision to the patent system which instituted a procedure by which patent applications were inspected to ensure adherence to patent law.

A The author and the scholars are both focused on protecting inventors' property rights, not with their inventions' utility.
B Although the passage suggests that the scholars thought America's patent system did not help encourage economic growth, there is no suggestion that either the scholars or the author believes actual patents defended in court were irrelevant to economic growth.
C Both the scholars and the author believe that patents defended in court prior to 1830 were more likely to be invalidated than were patents in later legal disputes.
D **Correct.** The scholars claim that judges before 1830 decided against patentees for arbitrary reasons, but the passage suggests that the patents may have been invalidated because they failed to adhere to patent law.
E Both the scholars and the author accept that patents were upheld in court less often before 1830 than after.

The correct answer is D.

529. The author of the passage cites which of the following as evidence challenging the argument referred to in lines 14–15 ?

(A) The proportion of cases that were decided against patentees in the 1820s
(B) The total number of patent disputes that were litigated from 1794 to 1830
(C) The fact that later courts drew upon the legal precedents set in pre-1830 patent cases
(D) The fact that the proportion of judicial decisions in favor of patentees began to increase during the 1830s
(E) The constitutional rationale for the 1836 revision of the patent system

Supporting idea

The question asks what evidence the author brings to bear against the argument referred to in lines 14–15. In the first paragraph, the author summarizes scholars' arguments to the conclusion that judges' attitudes toward patent rights shifted in the 1830s, based on the fact that judges earlier had routinely ruled against patentees in lawsuits whereas judges after that time provided more protection for patent rights. In the second paragraph the author challenges the claim that judges' attitudes shifted. The author provides evidence that judges after the 1830s cited legal precedents set in pre-1830s cases, suggesting that their views had not changed.

A The proportion of cases decided against patentees in the 1920s is cited as evidence that supports the scholars' argument in the first paragraph, not as evidence challenging their views.

B The total number of disputes litigated is not mentioned in the passage.

C Correct. The fact that judges after 1830 cited earlier cases as precedents is used as evidence to challenge scholars' claims that judges' attitudes shifted around 1830.

D The change in the proportion of decisions in favor of patentees is a fact that both the scholars and the author of the passage attempt to explain.

E No constitutional rationale for the 1836 law is mentioned in the passage.

The correct answer is C.

Questions 530–536 refer to the passage on page 418.

530. The author of the passage discusses Krontiris primarily to provide an example of a writer who

(A) is highly critical of the writings of certain Renaissance women
(B) supports Kelly's view of women's status during the Renaissance
(C) has misinterpreted the works of certain Renaissance women
(D) has rejected the views of both Burckhardt and Kelly
(E) has studied Renaissance women in a wide variety of social and religious contexts

Evaluation

This question focuses on the author's reason for mentioning Krontiris's work. The passage states that Krontiris, in her discussion of six Renaissance women writers, is an example of scholars who are optimistic about women's achievements but also suggest that these women faced significant obstacles. She is a writer who, in other words, agrees with neither Kelly's negative views nor Burckhardt's positive approach.

A The passage indicates that Krontiris uses the Renaissance women writers' works as historical evidence, not that she offered any criticism of the works themselves.

B Krontiris's work, according to the author, is cautiously optimistic about women's achievements during the Renaissance. This contradicts Kelly's view that the status of women declined during this time.

C The author suggests that Krontiris may have erred in taking her six subjects as representative of all women during the Renaissance, not that she made any misinterpretations of their actual writing.

D Correct. The author uses Krontiris as an example of those feminist scholars who have rejected the overgeneralized approaches of both Kelly and Burckhardt.

E The author makes clear that Krontiris's study focuses on literate Renaissance women, who constituted a small minority.

The correct answer is D.

531. According to the passage, Krontiris's work differs from that of the scholars mentioned in line 12 in which of the following ways?

(A) Krontiris's work stresses the achievements of Renaissance women rather than the obstacles to their success.
(B) Krontiris's work is based on a reinterpretation of the work of earlier scholars.
(C) Krontiris's views are at odds with those of both Kelly and Burkhardt.
(D) Krontiris's work focuses on the place of women in Renaissance society.
(E) Krontiris's views are based exclusively on the study of a privileged group of women.

Supporting idea

This question asks what the passage directly states about the difference between Krontiris's work and the feminist scholars mentioned in the first paragraph. The feminist scholars mentioned in the first paragraph explore differences among Renaissance women, particularly their social status and religion, and thus complicate Burckhardt's and Kelly's generalizations. Krontiris's work, on the other hand, focuses on Renaissance women writers, who are a distinctly privileged and small social group.

A The second paragraph makes clear that Krontiris addresses the obstacles faced by Renaissance women.
B The passage does not suggest that Krontiris is reinterpreting or drawing on reinterpretations of the work of earlier scholars.
C The second paragraph shows that Krontiris's work does complicate both Burckhardt's and Kelly's views, but in this, she is in agreement with the feminist scholars mentioned in the first paragraph.
D Both Krontiris and the feminist scholars mentioned in the first paragraph are concerned with the place of women in Renaissance society.
E **Correct.** The feminist scholars mentioned in the first paragraph are concerned with women of different social classes and religions, whereas Krontiris's work focuses on a limited social group.

The correct answer is E.

532. According to the passage, feminist scholars cite Burckhardt's view of Renaissance women primarily for which of the following reasons?

(A) Burckhardt's view forms the basis for most arguments refuting Kelly's point of view.
(B) Burckhardt's view has been discredited by Kelly.
(C) Burckhardt's view is one that many feminist scholars wish to refute.
(D) Burckhardt's work provides rich historical evidence of inequality between Renaissance women and men.
(E) Burckhardt's work includes historical research supporting the arguments of the feminist scholars.

Supporting idea

This question asks what the passage says explicitly about why feminist scholars reference Burckhardt's view of Renaissance women. The first paragraph states that Burckhardt's view is that Renaissance women enjoyed *perfect equality* with men, and then follows that by noting how feminist scholars have *repeatedly cited* this view to contrast it with extensive evidence of women's inequality during the Renaissance.

A The passage does not indicate that any feminist scholars cite Burckhardt to refute Kelly's view. It uses Krontiris as an example of scholars who refute Kelly's point of view to a certain degree, but Krontiris does not use Burckhardt's view as her basis for doing so; Krontiris argues against Burckhardt as well.
B According to the first paragraph, Kelly's work was in certain ways inconsistent with Burckhardt's view, but that is not a reason why Burckhardt's view is cited by feminist scholars. Rather, according to the passage, they cite it in order to argue against it.
C **Correct.** Many feminist scholars wish to refute Burckhardt's view that Renaissance women and men were equal.
D As the first paragraph makes clear, Burckhardt's work emphasizes equality, not inequality, between Renaissance women and men.
E The passage does not discuss the historical research on which Burckhardt based his work.

The correct answer is C.

533. It can be inferred that both Burckhardt and Kelly have been criticized by the scholars mentioned in line 12 for which of the following?

(A) Assuming that women writers of the Renaissance are representative of Renaissance women in general
(B) Drawing conclusions that are based on the study of an atypical group of women
(C) Failing to describe clearly the relationship between social status and literacy among Renaissance women
(D) Failing to acknowledge the role played by Renaissance women in opposing cultural stereotypes
(E) Failing to acknowledge the ways in which social status affected the creative activities of Renaissance women

Inference

Line 12 refers to feminist scholars who have rejected both Kelly's and Burckhardt's views of the status of Renaissance women. The next sentence states that the feminist scholars use class and religious differences among Renaissance women to argue against Kelly's and Burckhardt's generalizations, which were based on upper-class Italian women.

A The second paragraph suggests that Krontiris at times conflates Renaissance women writers and women in general, but the passage does not indicate that the feminist scholars believe this of Kelly or Burckhardt.

B **Correct.** The feminist scholars mentioned study different types of Renaissance women and so reject Kelly's and Burckhardt's conclusions that were based on a group that was not in fact typical.

C Krontiris, not Kelly and Burckhardt, is the scholar who, according to the passage, fails to address the relationship between literacy and social status.

D The passage provides no grounds for determining whether Kelly, Burckhardt, or the feminist scholars mentioned in the first paragraph dealt with Renaissance women's opposition to cultural stereotypes; Krontiris's work is concerned with this question.

E The first paragraph suggests that feminist scholars criticized Kelly and Burckhardt for failing to acknowledge the ways in which social status complicates any generalizations that can be made about Renaissance women's lives, not their creative activities specifically.

The correct answer is B.

534. The author of the passage suggests that Krontiris incorrectly assumes that

(A) social differences among Renaissance women are less important than the fact that they were women

(B) literacy among Renaissance women was more prevalent than most scholars today acknowledge

(C) during the Renaissance, women were able to successfully oppose cultural stereotypes relating to gender

(D) Renaissance women did not face many difficult social obstacles relating to their gender

(E) in order to attain power, Renaissance women attacked basic assumptions in the ideologies that oppressed them

Inference

The first statement the author makes about Krontiris, in the second paragraph, concerns what the author characterizes as a problem with Krontiris's work. Krontiris takes the Renaissance women writers she studies as representative of all Renaissance women; the author says that designating *women* as the most important grouping fails to consider whether other social differences might make for differences in experience.

A **Correct.** The author indicates that Krontiris's error lies in assuming that women's identity as women trumps social and other differences.

B The author does not suggest that Krontiris assumes inappropriate literacy levels among Renaissance women, but rather that Krontiris does not give sufficient consideration to the idea that women who could read and write most likely led lives very different from those of women who could not read and write.

C The author says that Krontiris suggests that there were many cultural stereotypes that women were not able to oppose effectively.

D Krontiris, according to the author, acknowledges the many social obstacles faced by women on the basis of their gender.

E According to the author, Krontiris's concluding remarks suggest that Renaissance women *seldom attacked the basic assumptions in the ideologies that oppressed them.*

The correct answer is A.

535. The last sentence in the passage serves primarily to

(A) suggest that Krontiris's work is not representative of recent trends among feminist scholars

(B) undermine the argument that literate women of the Renaissance sought to oppose social constraints imposed on them

(C) show a way in which Krontiris's work illustrates a "cautiously optimistic" assessment of Renaissance women's achievements

(D) summarize Krontiris's view of the effect of literacy on the lives of upper- and middle-class Renaissance women

(E) illustrate the way in which Krontiris's study differs from the studies done by Burckhardt and Kelly

Evaluation

The function of the final sentence of the passage is to indicate how Krontiris's work takes neither a completely positive nor completely negative view of Renaissance women's experiences—i.e., how her work is representative of those authors who are cautiously optimistic about the achievements of Renaissance women.

A The passage discusses Krontiris's work as an example of the trend described in the latter part of the first paragraph and mentioned in the first line of the second paragraph. The last sentence in the passage shows that Krontiris's work is in fact representative of recent trends among feminist scholars.

B The last sentence in the passage states that Renaissance women's opposition to cultural stereotypes was circumscribed, but it also suggests that these women did gain some power for themselves. Thus, the sentence does not serve primarily to undermine the argument that the women sought to oppose social constraints.

C **Correct.** Krontiris's work illustrates the "cautiously optimistic" view by embracing both the idea that Renaissance women could gain a certain amount of power and the idea that the extent of their opposition was limited.

D The last sentence in the passage summarizes Krontiris's view, but that view does not, according to the passage, take into account the effect of literacy on the members of a particular social class.

E The main function of the final sentence of the passage is to take up the idea of the *cautiously optimistic* assessment offered in the penultimate sentence. This does mark a significant departure from both Burckhardt and Kelly, but the distinction between their work and that of other feminist scholars is marked more clearly earlier in the passage.

The correct answer is C.

536. The author of the passage implies that the women studied by Krontiris are unusual in which of the following ways?

(A) They faced obstacles less formidable than those faced by other Renaissance women.

(B) They have been seen by historians as more interesting than other Renaissance women.

(C) They were more concerned about recording history accurately than were other Renaissance women.

(D) Their perceptions are more likely to be accessible to historians than are those of most other Renaissance women.

(E) Their concerns are likely to be of greater interest to feminist scholars than are the ideas of most other Renaissance women.

Inference

The women Krontiris studied are unusual, the author suggests, because they were literate, thus putting them among the minority of Renaissance women. That they could write, however, means that their written reflections are part of the historical record, whereas the direct impressions of experiences had by Renaissance women who could not write about their lives are lost to history.

A The author implies that the obstacles faced by Krontiris's subjects may have been different from those faced by other women, not that they were less formidable.

B The author does not imply that the women studied by Krontiris are seen as more interesting; rather, the author indicates that their work is that which is available for study.

C The women Krontiris studies were able to record their own history because they, unlike most other Renaissance women, were literate. This does not imply that they were more concerned with recording history accurately.

D Correct. Because Krontiris's subjects were literate, they were able to write down, and thus preserve for historians, their perceptions in a way that most other Renaissance women were not.

E The author does not suggest that feminist scholars in general are more interested in the concerns of middle- and upper-class literate women than they are with women of other classes.

The correct answer is D.

Questions 537–540 refer to the passage on page 420.

537. The passage implies which of the following about the five asteroids mentioned in line 12 ?

(A) Their rotation rates are approximately the same.
(B) They have undergone approximately the same number of collisions.
(C) They are monoliths.
(D) They are composed of fragments that have escaped the gravity of larger asteroids.
(E) They were detected only recently.

Inference

In line 12, *five observed asteroids*, refers to the five asteroids whose rotation rates are exceptions to the strict limit on the rate of rotation found in all other observed asteroids. These five asteroids all have diameters smaller than 200 meters. The passage indicates that if asteroids were all monoliths—that is, single rocks—then their rotation rates would form a bell curve when graphed, but if asteroids were piles of rubble, the tail of the bell curve indicating very fast rotation rates would be missing. Among asteroids larger than 200 meters, this tail is missing, and only the five asteroids described as exceptions have rotation rates falling at the very high end of the bell curve.

A All that the passage states about the rotation rates of these five asteroids is that they do not obey a strict limit. The passage does not rule out that their rates of rotation are significantly different from one another.

B According to the passage, frequent collisions occur among asteroids. But the passage does not suggest that asteroids that are of similar sizes, or that have particularly high rotation rates, will be similar in terms of the number of collisions that they have undergone to reach those distinctive states.

C Correct. The second paragraph states that *most small asteroids* should be monolithic, and the five observed asteroids are all smaller than 200 meters in diameter.

D The five asteroids are most likely not composed of fragments because, as the passage states, small asteroids should be monoliths.

E The passage notes that researchers have observed these five asteroids, along with others, but it does not indicate when these asteroids were originally detected.

The correct answer is C.

538. The discovery of which of the following would call into question the conclusion mentioned in line 16 ?

(A) An asteroid 100 meters in diameter rotating at a rate of once per week
(B) An asteroid 150 meters in diameter rotating at a rate of 20 times per hour
(C) An asteroid 250 meters in diameter rotating at a rate of once per week
(D) An asteroid 500 meters in diameter rotating at a rate of once per hour
(E) An asteroid 1,000 meters in diameter rotating at a rate of once every 24 hours

Application

The conclusion that the text in line 16 points to is that asteroids with diameters greater than 200 meters are *multicomponent structures or rubble piles*. To call that conclusion into question, an observation would have to suggest that asteroids larger than 200 meters across are not such multicomponent structures. According to the first paragraph, rubble piles cannot be fast rotators: spinning faster than once every few hours would make them fly apart.

A Nothing in the passage suggests that the behavior of an asteroid 100 meters in diameter is relevant to a conclusion about the behavior of asteroids greater than 200 meters in diameter.

B Nothing in the passage suggests that the behavior of an asteroid 150 meters in diameter would have any effect on a conclusion about the constitution of asteroids with diameters greater than 200 meters.

C An asteroid 250 meters in diameter rotating at a rate of once per week would be rotating at a slow enough rate to hold together a pile of rubble. Thus, this observation would be entirely consistent with the conclusion about asteroids larger than 200 meters in diameter.

D **Correct.** Assuming that an asteroid composed of a pile of rubble is of a great enough density, a rotation rate greater than one revolution every few hours would make it fly apart. So a 500-meter asteroid rotating at a rate of once per hour—that is, faster than the crucial speed—would fly apart if it were not a monolith. The conclusion states that all asteroids larger than 200 meters are multicomponent structures (that is, are not monoliths), so the discovery of a 500-meter asteroid rotating at a rate of once an hour would call into question that conclusion.

E An asteroid rotating at a rate of once every 24 hours would, regardless of size, be rotating much more slowly than the *once every few hours* that the passage claims would make a pile of rubble of a sufficient density fly apart. So an asteroid with a diameter of 1,000 meters that rotated once per day could be a pile of rubble and not conflict with the conclusion.

The correct answer is D.

539. According to the passage, which of the following is a prediction that is based on the strength of the gravitational attraction of small asteroids?

(A) Small asteroids will be few in number.
(B) Small asteroids will be monoliths.
(C) Small asteroids will collide with other asteroids very rarely.
(D) Most small asteroids will have very fast rotation rates.
(E) Almost no small asteroids will have very slow rotation rates.

Supporting ideas

Regarding small asteroids, the second paragraph states that they have feeble gravity. Any fragments from impacts would escape that gravity, and thus, the passage states, the small asteroids *should be monolithic*.

A Small asteroids could be few in number, but the passage does not offer such a prediction.

B **Correct.** This prediction is offered in the second paragraph, based on the fact that small asteroids do not have strong gravitational attraction. Any impact fragments will easily escape the weak gravitational attraction of the small asteroids.

C The passage discusses large asteroids collisions in more detail than small-asteroid collisions, but it provides no basis for predicting how often large and small asteroids will, comparatively, be involved in such collisions.

D The first paragraph indicates that the rotation rates of small asteroids can exceed the upper limit on the rotation rates of large asteroids, but it does not indicate that most small asteroids have rotation rates that exceed this upper limit.

E The passage only indicates that there are few observed exceptions to the upper limit on rotation rates of large asteroids, and these exceptions are all smaller than 200 meters in diameter; the passage does not indicate that there are few small asteroids that have very slow rotation rates.

The correct answer is B.

540. The author of the passage mentions "escape velocity" (see line 22) in order to help explain which of the following?

(A) The tendency for asteroids to become smaller rather than larger over time
(B) The speed with which impact fragments reassemble when they do not escape an asteroid's gravitational attraction after a collision
(C) The frequency with which collisions among asteroids occur
(D) The rotation rates of asteroids smaller than 200 meters in diameter
(E) The tendency for large asteroids to persist after collisions

Evaluation

This question asks about the purpose of the author's use of the phrase *escape velocity* in the second paragraph. The author is discussing what occurs after an asteroid collision, in which a large asteroid might be blasted to bits. The bits, according to the author, will move slower than their *mutual escape velocity*—that is, the speed at which they would have to move to get away from each other and not reassemble, under the influence of gravity, into a rubble pile.

A The author is emphasizing the asteroid bits that do not escape rather than those that do. Asteroids may become smaller over time, but the fact that most bits move slower than their escape velocity would not help to explain this shrinkage.

B That the bits of asteroid move slower than their escape velocity helps explain why the fragments reassemble, but it does not help explain the speed with which they reassemble.

C According to the author, asteroid collisions occur frequently, but the escape velocity of the resulting fragments does not help to explain that frequency.

D The concept of escape velocity may help explain why small asteroids are monoliths, but it has no relevance, at least as far as the passage indicates, to those asteroids' rotation rates.

E **Correct.** After a collision, it is the asteroid fragments' failure to reach escape velocity that allows the fragments' gravitational pull to reassemble them into a rubble pile.

The correct answer is E.

Questions 541–543 refer to the passage on page 422.

541. The author of the passage mentions calculations about tunneling time and barrier thickness in order to

(A) suggest that tunneling time is unrelated to barrier thickness
(B) explain the evidence by which Wigner and Eisenbud discovered the phenomenon of tunneling
(C) describe data recently challenged by Raymond Chiao and colleagues
(D) question why particles engaged in quantum tunneling rarely achieve extremely high speeds
(E) explain the basis for Wigner and Eisenbud's hypothesis

Evaluation

This question asks why the author discusses calculations about tunneling time and barrier thickness. According to the passage, these calculations provided the grounds for Wigner and Eisenbud's hypothesis that tunneling particles may travel faster than light.

A The passage states that tunneling time is related to barrier thickness, up to the point at which tunneling time reaches a maximum.

B The passage indicates that the phenomenon of tunneling was noted at least as early as 1932. It provides no evidence that Wigner and Eisenbud discovered it.

C The passage uses Chiao's work to support the idea that tunneling particles may move faster than light, not challenge it.

D The author describes calculations about tunneling time and barrier thickness in order to explain that particles engaged in quantum tunneling may in fact achieve extremely high speeds, not to explain the rarity of the phenomenon.

E **Correct.** The calculations about tunneling time and barrier thickness supported Wigner and Eisenbud's hypothesis that quantum tunneling could occur at speeds faster than that of light.

The correct answer is E.

542. The passage implies that if tunneling time reached no maximum in increasing with barrier thickness, then

(A) tunneling speed would increase with barrier thickness
(B) tunneling speed would decline with barrier thickness
(C) tunneling speed would vary with barrier thickness
(D) tunneling speed would not be expected to increase without limit
(E) successful tunneling would occur even less frequently than it does

Inference

The passage states that because tunneling time reaches a maximum, then tunneling speed must increase as barrier thickness increases. But if tunneling time did not reach such a maximum, then speed need not increase without limit; the particle could have as low a speed in thicker barriers as in thinner ones and take longer to tunnel through a barrier.

A If tunneling time could not reach a maximum, then speed might increase, decrease, or remain the same as barrier thickness increases.

B If tunneling time could not reach a maximum, then speed might increase, decrease, or remain the same as barrier thickness increases.

C Tunneling speed could vary with barrier thickness if tunneling time could not reach a maximum, but there is no basis in the passage on which to conclude that this is definitely so.

D **Correct.** The tunneling particle could have as low a speed in thicker barriers as in thinner ones and simply take longer to make its way through a thicker barrier.

E The passage states that the probability of successful tunneling declines as the thickness of the barrier increases. However, it does not address the issue of whether the differences in probability of successful tunneling are due to the greater time required to go through thicker barriers.

The correct answer is D.

543. Which of the following statements about the earliest scientific investigators of quantum tunneling can be inferred from the passage?

(A) They found it difficult to increase barrier thickness continually.
(B) They anticipated the later results of Chiao and his colleagues.
(C) They did not suppose that tunneling particles could travel faster than light.
(D) They were unable to observe instances of successful tunneling.
(E) They made use of photons to study the phenomenon of tunneling.

Inference

This question asks about the earliest investigators of quantum tunneling. The passage notes that quantum tunneling's *extreme rapidity* was observed in 1932; thus, the earliest investigators of this phenomenon knew of its existence at that time. Not until 1955 did Wigner and Eisenbud hypothesize that the particles traveled faster than light. Thus, it is logical to infer that the earliest investigators did not imagine such a speed.

A There is nothing in the passage to suggest that the earliest investigators of quantum tunneling had difficulty manipulating barrier thickness.

B The passage states that Chiao and his colleagues measured photons moving at 1.7 times the speed of light—but the passage does not provide evidence that the earliest investigators anticipated such speeds.

C **Correct.** The passage suggests that prior to 1955, investigators of quantum tunneling had not hypothesized that the particles could travel faster than the speed of light.

D The passage indicates that by 1932, investigators had noted the rapidity of quantum tunneling; although this does not entail that they observed the phenomenon, it is consistent with their having been able to do so.

E The passage indicates that Chiao's work involves photons, but it does not indicate the type of particles used or observed by the earliest investigators of the phenomenon.

The correct answer is C.

8.0 Critical Reasoning

8.0 Critical Reasoning

Critical reasoning questions appear in the Verbal section of the GMAT® exam. The Verbal section uses multiple-choice questions to measure your ability to read and comprehend written material, to reason and to evaluate arguments, and to correct written material to conform to standard written English. Because the Verbal section includes content from a variety of topics, you may be generally familiar with some of the material; however, neither the passages nor the questions assume knowledge of the topics discussed. Critical reasoning questions are intermingled with reading comprehension and sentence correction questions throughout the Verbal section of the test.

You will have 75 minutes to complete the Verbal section, or about 1¾ minutes to answer each question. Although critical reasoning questions are based on written passages, these passages are shorter than reading comprehension passages. They tend to be less than 100 words in length and generally are followed by one or two questions. For these questions, you will see a split computer screen. The written passage will remain visible at the top of the screen. In turn, each associated question will appear either below or above the relevant passage. You will see only one question at a time.

Critical reasoning questions are designed to test the reasoning skills involved in (1) making arguments, (2) evaluating arguments, and (3) formulating or evaluating a plan of action. The materials on which questions are based are drawn from a variety of sources. The GMAT exam does not expect any familiarity with the subject matter of those materials.

In these questions, you are to analyze the situation on which each question is based, and then select the answer choice that most appropriately answers the question. Begin by reading the passages carefully, then reading the five answer choices. If the correct answer is not immediately obvious to you, see whether you can eliminate some of the wrong answers. Reading the passage a second time may be helpful in illuminating subtleties that were not immediately evident.

Answering critical reasoning questions requires no specialized knowledge of any particular field; you don't have to have knowledge of the terminology and conventions of formal logic. The sample critical reasoning questions in this chapter illustrate the variety of topics the test may cover, the kinds of questions it may ask, and the level of analysis it requires.

The following pages describe what critical reasoning questions are designed to measure and present the directions that will precede questions of this type. Sample questions and explanations of the correct answers follow.

8.1 What Is Measured

Critical reasoning questions are designed to provide one measure of your ability to reason effectively in the following areas:

- **Argument construction**
  Questions in this category may ask you to recognize such things as the basic structure of an argument, properly drawn conclusions, underlying assumptions, well-supported explanatory hypotheses, and parallels between structurally similar arguments.

- **Argument evaluation**
  These questions may ask you to analyze a given argument and to recognize such things as factors that would strengthen or weaken the given argument; reasoning errors committed in making that argument; and aspects of the method by which the argument proceeds.
- **Formulating and evaluating a plan of action**
  This type of question may ask you to recognize such things as the relative appropriateness, effectiveness, or efficiency of different plans of action, factors that would strengthen or weaken the prospects of success of a proposed plan of action, and assumptions underlying a proposed plan of action.

8.2 Test-Taking Strategies

1. **Read very carefully the set of statements on which a question is based.**
   Pay close attention to
   - what is put forward as factual information
   - what is not said but necessarily follows from what is said
   - what is claimed to follow from facts that have been put forward
   - how well substantiated are any claims that a particular conclusion follows from the facts that have been put forward

   In reading the arguments, it is important to pay attention to the logical reasoning used; the actual truth of statements portrayed as fact is not important.

2. **Identify the conclusion.**
   The conclusion does not necessarily come at the end of the text; it may come somewhere in the middle or even at the beginning. Be alert to clues in the text that an argument follows logically from another statement or statements in the text.

3. **Determine exactly what each question asks.**
   You might find it helpful to read the question first, before reading the material on which it is based; don't assume that you know what you will be asked about an argument. An argument may have obvious flaws, and one question may ask you to detect them. But another question may direct you to select the one answer choice that does NOT describe a flaw in the argument.

4. **Read all the answer choices carefully.**
   Do not assume that a given answer is the best without first reading all the choices.

8.3 The Directions

These are the directions you will see for critical reasoning questions when you take the GMAT exam. If you read them carefully and understand them clearly before going to sit for the test, you will not need to spend too much time reviewing them when you are at the test center and the test is under way.

For these questions, select the best of the answer choices given.

8.4 Practice Questions

Each of the critical reasoning questions is based on a short argument, a set of statements, or a plan of action. For each question, select the best answer of the choices given.

544. Neuroscientist: Memory evolved to help animals react appropriately to situations they encounter by drawing on the past experience of similar situations. But this does not require that animals perfectly recall every detail of all their experiences. Instead, to function well, memory should generalize from past experiences that are similar to the current one.

The neuroscientist's statements, if true, most strongly support which of the following conclusions?

(A) At least some animals perfectly recall every detail of at least some past experiences.

(B) Perfectly recalling every detail of all their past experiences could help at least some animals react more appropriately than they otherwise would to new situations they encounter.

(C) Generalizing from past experiences requires clear memories of most if not all the details of those experiences.

(D) Recalling every detail of all past experiences would be incompatible with any ability to generalize from those experiences.

(E) Animals can often react more appropriately than they otherwise would to situations they encounter if they draw on generalizations from past experiences of similar situations.

545. Astronomer: Most stars are born in groups of thousands, each star in a group forming from the same parent cloud of gas. Each cloud has a unique, homogeneous chemical composition. Therefore, whenever two stars have the same chemical composition as each other, they must have originated from the same cloud of gas.

Which of the following, if true, would most strengthen the astronomer's argument?

(A) In some groups of stars, not every star originated from the same parent cloud of gas.

(B) Clouds of gas of similar or identical chemical composition may be remote from each other.

(C) Whenever a star forms, it inherits the chemical composition of its parent cloud of gas.

(D) Many stars in vastly different parts of the universe are quite similar in their chemical compositions.

(E) Astronomers can at least sometimes precisely determine whether a star has the same chemical composition as its parent cloud of gas.

546. With employer-paid training, workers have the potential to become more productive not only in their present employment but also in any number of jobs with different employers. To increase the productivity of their workforce, many firms are planning to maintain or even increase their investments in worker training. But some training experts object that if a trained worker is hired away by another firm, the employer that paid for the training has merely subsidized a competitor. They note that such hiring has been on the rise in recent years.

Which of the following would, if true, contribute most to defeating the training experts' objection to the firms' strategy?

(A) Firms that promise opportunities for advancement to their employees get, on average, somewhat larger numbers of job applications from untrained workers than do firms that make no such promise.

(B) In many industries, employees who take continuing-education courses are more competitive in the job market.

(C) More and more educational and training institutions are offering reduced tuition fees to firms that subsidize worker training.

(D) Research shows that workers whose training is wholly or partially subsidized by their employer tend to get at least as much training as do workers who pay for all their own training.

(E) For most firms that invest in training their employees, the value added by that investment in employees who stay exceeds the value lost through other employees' leaving to work for other companies.

547. Candle Corporation's television stations are likely to have more income from advertisers than previously. This is because advertisers prefer to reach people in the 18- to 49-year-old age group and the number of people in that group watching Candle television is increasing. Furthermore, among Candle viewers, the percentage of viewers 18 to 49 years old is increasing.

Which of the following, if true, would most strengthen the argument that Candle Corporation will receive more income from advertisers?

(A) Advertisers carefully monitor the demographic characteristics of television audiences and purchase advertising time to reach the audiences they prefer to reach.

(B) Among people over 49 years old, fewer viewers of Candle stations buy products advertised on television than do viewers of other stations.

(C) There will be increasingly more advertisements on television that are directed at viewers who are over 49 years old.

(D) Candle stations plan to show reruns of television shows during hours when other stations run shows for the first time.

(E) People 18 to 49 years old generally have less disposable income to spend than do people over 49 years old.

548. A provincial government plans to raise the gasoline tax to give people an incentive to drive less, reducing traffic congestion in the long term. However, skeptics point out that most people in the province live in areas where cars are the only viable transportation to jobs and stores and therefore cannot greatly change their driving habits in response to higher gasoline prices.

In light of the skeptics' objection, which of the following, if true, would most logically support the prediction that the government's plan will achieve its goal of reducing traffic congestion?

(A) The revenue from the tax will be used to make public transportation a viable means of transportation to jobs and stores for far more people.

(B) The tax will encourage many residents to switch to more fuel-efficient cars, reducing air pollution and other problems.

(C) Because gasoline has been underpriced for decades, the province has many neighborhoods where cars are the only viable means of transportation.

(D) Most residents who cannot greatly change their driving habits could compensate for high gasoline prices by reducing other expenses.

(E) Traffic congestion is an especially serious problem for people for whom cars are the only viable means of transportation.

549. Editorial: The roof of Northtown's municipal equipment-storage building collapsed under the weight of last week's heavy snowfall. The building was constructed recently and met local building-safety codes in every particular, except that the nails used for attaching roof supports to the building's columns were of a smaller size than the codes specify for this purpose. Clearly, this collapse exemplifies how even a single, apparently insignificant departure from safety standards can have severe consequences.

Which of the following, if true, most seriously weakens the editorial's argument?

(A) The only other buildings to suffer roof collapses from the weight of the snowfall were older buildings constructed according to less exacting standards than those in the codes.

(B) The amount of snow that accumulated on the roof of the equipment-storage building was greater than the predicted maximum that was used in drawing up the safety codes.

(C) Because the equipment-storage building was not intended for human occupation, some safety-code provisions that would have applied to an office building did not apply to it.

(D) The municipality of Northtown itself has the responsibility for ensuring that buildings constructed within its boundaries meet the provisions of the building-safety codes.

(E) Because the equipment-storage building was used for storing snow-removal equipment, the building was almost completely empty when the roof collapsed.

550. Political theorist: Even with the best spies, area experts, and satellite surveillance, foreign policy assessments can still lack important information. In such circumstances intuitive judgment is vital. A national leader with such judgment can make good decisions about foreign policy even when current information is incomplete, since __________.

Which of the following, if true, most logically completes the argument?

(A) the central reason for failure in foreign policy decision making is the absence of critical information

(B) those leaders whose foreign policy decisions have been highly ranked have also been found to have good intuitive judgment

(C) both intuitive judgment and good information are required for sound decision making

(D) good foreign policy decisions often lead to improved methods of gathering information

(E) intuitive judgment can produce good decisions based on past experience, even when there are important gaps in current information

551. During the earliest period of industrialization in Britain, steam engines were more expensive to build and operate than either windmills or water mills, the other practicable sources of power for factories. Yet despite their significant cost disadvantage, steam-powered factories were built in large numbers well before technical improvements brought their cost down. Furthermore, they were built even in regions where geographical conditions permitted the construction of wind- and water-powered factories close to major markets.

Which of the following, if true, most helps to explain the proliferation of steam-powered factories during the earliest period of industrialization in Britain?

(A) In many areas of Britain, there were fewer steam-powered factories than wind- or water-powered factories in the earliest period of industrialization.

(B) Unlike wind- or water-powered factories, steam-powered factories were fueled with coal, which sometimes had to be transported significant distances from the mine to the site of the factory.

(C) It was both difficult and expensive to convert a factory from wind power or water power to steam power.

(D) In the early period of industrialization, many goods sold in towns and cities could not be mass-produced in factories.

(E) In Britain, the number of sites where a wind- or water-powered factory could be built was insufficient to provide for all of the demand for factory-produced goods at the time.

552. Snowmaking machines work by spraying a mist that freezes immediately on contact with cold air. Because the sudden freezing kills bacteria, QuickFreeze is planning to market a wastewater purification system

that works on the same principle. The process works only when temperatures are cold, however, so municipalities using it will still need to maintain a conventional system.

Which of the following, if true, provides the strongest grounds for a prediction that municipalities will buy QuickFreeze's purification system despite the need to maintain a conventional purification system as well?

(A) Bacteria are not the only impurities that must be removed from wastewater.

(B) Many municipalities have old wastewater purification systems that need to be replaced.

(C) Conventional wastewater purification systems have not been fully successful in killing bacteria at cold temperatures.

(D) During times of warm weather, when it is not in use, QuickFreeze's purification system requires relatively little maintenance.

(E) Places where the winters are cold rarely have a problem of water shortage.

553. Suncorp, a new corporation with limited funds, has been clearing large sections of the tropical Amazon forest for cattle ranching. This practice continues even though greater profits can be made from rubber tapping, which does not destroy the forest, than from cattle ranching, which does destroy the forest.

Which of the following, if true, most helps to explain why Suncorp has been pursuing the less profitable of the two economic activities mentioned above?

(A) The soil of the Amazon forest is very rich in nutrients that are important in the development of grazing lands.

(B) Cattle-ranching operations that are located in tropical climates are more profitable than cattle-ranching operations that are located in cold-weather climates.

(C) In certain districts, profits made from cattle ranching are more heavily taxed than profits made from any other industry.

(D) Some of the cattle that are raised on land cleared in the Amazon are killed by wildcats.

(E) The amount of money required to begin a rubber-tapping operation is twice as high as the amount needed to begin a cattle ranch.

554. Archaeologists use technology to analyze ancient sites. It is likely that this technology will advance considerably in the near future, allowing archaeologists to gather more information than is currently possible. If they study certain sites now, they risk contaminating or compromising them for future studies. Therefore, in order to maximize the potential for gathering knowledge in the long run, a team of archaeologists plans to delay the examination of a newly excavated site.

Which of the following would be most useful to investigate for the purpose of evaluating the plan's prospects for achieving its goal?

(A) Whether any of the contents of the site will significantly deteriorate before the anticipated technology is available

(B) Whether there will continue to be improvements on the relevant technology

(C) Whether the team can study a site other than the newly excavated site for the time being

(D) Whether the site was inhabited by a very ancient culture

(E) Whether the anticipated technology will damage objects under study

555. A newly discovered painting seems to be the work of one of two seventeenth-century artists, either the northern German Johannes Drechen or the Frenchman Louis Birelle, who sometimes painted in the same style as Drechen. Analysis of the carved picture frame, which has been identified as the painting's original seventeenth-century frame, showed that it is made of wood found widely in northern Germany at the time, but rare in the part of France where Birelle lived. This shows that the painting is most likely the work of Drechen.

Which of the following is an assumption that the argument requires?

(A) The frame was made from wood local to the region where the picture was painted.

(B) Drechen is unlikely to have ever visited the home region of Birelle in France.

(C) Sometimes a painting so resembles others of its era that no expert is able to confidently decide who painted it.

(D) The painter of the picture chose the frame for the picture.

(E) The carving style of the picture frame is not typical of any specific region of Europe.

556. Beginning in 1966 all new cars sold in Morodia were required to have safety belts and power steering. Previously, most cars in Morodia were without these features. Safety belts help to prevent injuries in collisions, and power steering helps to avoid collisions in the first place. But even though in 1966 one-seventh of the cars in Morodia were replaced with new cars, the number of car collisions and collision-related injuries did not decline.

Which of the following, if true about Morodia, most helps to explain why the number of collisions and collision-related injuries in Morodia failed to decline in 1966?

(A) Because of a driver-education campaign, most drivers and passengers in cars that did have safety belts used them in 1966.

(B) Most of the new cars bought in 1966 were bought in the months of January and February.

(C) In 1965, substantially more than one-seventh of the cars in Morodia were replaced with new cars.

(D) An excessive reliance on the new safety features led many owners of new cars to drive less cautiously in 1966 than before.

(E) The seat belts and power steering put into new cars sold in 1966 had to undergo strict quality-control inspections by manufacturers, whether the cars were manufactured in Morodia or not.

557. In order to reduce the number of items damaged while in transit to customers, packaging consultants recommended that the TrueSave mail-order company increase the amount of packing material so as to fill any empty spaces in its cartons. Accordingly, TrueSave officials instructed the company's packers to use more packing material than before, and the packers zealously acted on these instructions and used as much as they could. Nevertheless, customer reports of damaged items rose somewhat.

Which of the following, if true, most helps to explain why acting on the consultants' recommendation failed to achieve its goal?

(A) The change in packing policy led to an increase in expenditure on packing material and labor.

(B) When packing material is compressed too densely, it loses some of its capacity to absorb shock.

(C) The amount of packing material used in a carton does not significantly influence the ease with which a customer can unpack the package.

(D) Most of the goods that TrueSave ships are electronic products that are highly vulnerable to being damaged in transit.

(E) TrueSave has lost some of its regular customers as a result of the high number of damaged items they received.

558. Parland's alligator population has been declining in recent years, primarily because of hunting. Alligators prey heavily on a species of freshwater fish that is highly valued as food by Parlanders, who had hoped that the decline in the alligator population would lead to an increase in the numbers of these fish available for human consumption. Yet the population of this fish species has also declined, even though the annual number caught for human consumption has not increased.

Which of the following, if true, most helps to explain the decline in the population of the fish species?

(A) The decline in the alligator population has meant that fishers can work in some parts of lakes and rivers that were formerly too dangerous.

(B) Over the last few years, Parland's commercial fishing enterprises have increased the number of fishing boats they use.

(C) The main predator of these fish is another species of fish on which alligators also prey.

(D) Many Parlanders who hunt alligators do so because of the high market price of alligator skins, not because of the threat alligators pose to the fish population.

(E) In several neighboring countries through which Parland's rivers also flow, alligators are at risk of extinction as a result of extensive hunting.

559. A certain automaker aims to increase its market share by deeply discounting its vehicles' prices for the next several months. The discounts will cut into profits, but because they will be heavily advertised the manufacturer hopes that they will attract buyers away from rival manufacturers' cars. In the longer term, the automaker envisions that customers initially attracted by the discounts may become loyal customers.

In assessing the plan's chances of achieving its aim, it would be most useful to know which of the following?

(A) Whether the automaker's competitors are likely to respond by offering deep discounts on their own products

(B) Whether the advertisements will be created by the manufacturer's current advertising agency

(C) Whether some of the automaker's models will be more deeply discounted than others

(D) Whether the automaker will be able to cut costs sufficiently to maintain profit margins even when the discounts are in effect

(E) Whether an alternative strategy might enable the automaker to enhance its profitability while holding a constant or diminishing share of the market

560. In virtually any industry, technological improvements increase labor productivity, which is the output of goods and services per person-hour worked. In Parland's industries, labor productivity is significantly higher than it is in Vergia's industries. Clearly, therefore, Parland's industries must, on the whole, be further advanced technologically than Vergia's are.

The argument is most vulnerable to which of the following criticisms?

(A) It offers a conclusion that is no more than a paraphrase of one of the pieces of information provided in its support.

(B) It presents as evidence in support of a claim information that is inconsistent with other evidence presented in support of the same claim.

(C) It takes one possible cause of a condition to be the actual cause of that condition without considering any other possible causes.

(D) It takes a condition to be the effect of something that happened only after the condition already existed.

(E) It makes a distinction that presupposes the truth of the conclusion that is to be established.

561. Chaco Canyon, a settlement of the ancient Anasazi culture in North America, had massive buildings. **It must have been a major Anasazi center**. Analysis of wood samples shows that some of the timber for the buildings came from the Chuska and San Mateo mountains, 50 miles from Chaco Canyon. **Only a major cultural center would have the organizational power to import timber from 50 miles away**.

In the argument given, the two portions in boldface play which of the following roles?

(A) The first is a premise used to support the argument's main conclusion; the second is the argument's main conclusion.

(B) The first is the argument's main conclusion; the second is a premise used to support that conclusion.

(C) The first is one of two premises used to support the argument's main conclusion; the second is the other of those two premises.

(D) The first is a premise used to support the argument's main conclusion; the second is a premise used to support another conclusion drawn in the argument.

(E) The first is inferred from another statement in the argument; the second is inferred from the first.

562. The Maxilux car company's design for its new luxury model, the Max 100, included a special design for the tires that was intended to complement the model's image. The winning bid for supplying these tires was submitted by Rubco. Analysts concluded that the bid would only just cover Rubco's costs on the tires, but Rubco executives claim that winning the bid will actually make a profit for the company.

Which of the following, if true, most strongly justifies the claim made by Rubco's executives?

(A) In any Maxilux model, the spare tire is exactly the same make and model as the tires that are mounted on the wheels.

(B) Rubco holds exclusive contracts to supply Maxilux with the tires for a number of other models made by Maxilux.

(C) The production facilities for the Max 100 and those for the tires to be supplied by Rubco are located very near each other.

(D) When people who have purchased a carefully designed luxury automobile need to replace a worn part of it, they almost invariably replace it with a part of exactly the same make and type.

(E) When Maxilux awarded the tire contract to Rubco, the only criterion on which Rubco's bid was clearly ahead of its competitors' bids was price.

563. Which of the following most logically completes the passage?

Most bicycle helmets provide good protection for the top and back of the head, but little or no protection for the temple regions on the sides of the head. A study of head injuries resulting from bicycle accidents showed that a large proportion were caused by blows to the temple area. Therefore, if bicycle helmets protected this area, the risk of serious head injury in bicycle accidents would be greatly reduced, especially since _______.

(A) among the bicyclists included in the study's sample of head injuries, only a very small proportion had been wearing a helmet at the time of their accident

(B) even those bicyclists who regularly wear helmets have a poor understanding of the degree and kind of protection that helmets afford

(C) a helmet that included protection for the temples would have to be somewhat larger and heavier than current helmets

(D) the bone in the temple area is relatively thin and impacts in that area are thus very likely to cause brain injury

(E) bicyclists generally land on their arm or shoulder when they fall to the side, which reduces the likelihood of severe impacts on the side of the head

564. Which of the following most logically completes the argument?

In a typical year, Innovair's airplanes are involved in 35 collisions while parked or being towed in airports, with a resulting yearly cost of $1,000,000 for repairs. To reduce the frequency of ground collisions, Innovair will begin giving its ground crews additional training, at an annual cost of $500,000. Although this will cut the number of ground collisions by about half at best, the drop in repair costs can be expected to be much greater, since _______.

(A) most ground collisions happen when ground crews are rushing to minimize the time a delayed airplane spends on the ground

(B) a ground collision typically occurs when there are no passengers on the airplane

(C) the additional training will focus on helping ground crews avoid those kinds of ground collisions that cause the most costly damage

(D) the $500,000 cost figure for the additional training of ground crews includes the wages that those crews will earn during the time spent in actual training

(E) most ground collisions have been caused by the least experienced ground-crew members

565. Hunter: **Many people blame hunters alone for the decline in Greenrock National Forest's deer population over the past ten years.** Yet clearly, black bears have also played an important role in this decline. In the past ten years, the forest's protected black bear population has risen sharply, and examination of black bears found dead in the forest during the deer hunting season showed that a number of them had recently fed on deer.

In the hunter's argument, the portion in boldface plays which of the following roles?

(A) It is the main conclusion of the argument.

(B) It is a finding that the argument seeks to explain.

(C) It is an explanation that the argument concludes is correct.

(D) It provides evidence in support of the main conclusion of the argument.

(E) It introduces a judgment that the argument opposes.

566. Many agriculturally intensive areas of the world are beginning to encounter water scarcity problems. As a result, many farmers in these areas are likely to reduce their output as the water supply they need in order to maintain production shrinks. However, one group of farmers in such a region plans to increase their production by implementing techniques for water conservation.

Which of the following, if true, would most strongly support the prediction that the group's plan will succeed?

(A) Farmers that can gain a larger share of the food market in their regions will be better positioned to control more water resources.

(B) Most agricultural practices in areas with water shortages are water-intensive.

(C) Other regions of the world not facing water shortages are likely to make up for the reduction in agricultural output.

(D) Demand for agricultural products in the group's region is not expected to decline.

(E) More than half the water used for agriculture in the farmers' region is lost to evaporation or leakage from irrigation channels.

567. Physician: The hormone melatonin has shown promise as a medication for sleep disorders when taken in synthesized form. Because the long-term side effects of synthetic melatonin are unknown, however, I cannot recommend its use at this time.

Patient: Your position is inconsistent with your usual practice. You prescribe many medications that you know have serious side effects, so concern about side effects cannot be the real reason you will not prescribe melatonin.

The patient's argument is flawed because it fails to consider that

(A) the side effects of synthetic melatonin might be different from those of naturally produced melatonin

(B) it is possible that the physician does not believe that melatonin has been conclusively shown to be effective

(C) sleep disorders, if left untreated, might lead to serious medical complications

(D) the side effects of a medication can take some time to manifest themselves

(E) known risks can be weighed against known benefits, but unknown risks cannot

568. Hollywood restaurant is replacing some of its standard tables with tall tables and stools. The restaurant already fills every available seat during its operating hours, and the change in seating arrangements will not result in an increase in the restaurant's seating capacity. Nonetheless, the restaurant's management expects revenue to increase as a result of the seating change without any concurrent change in menu, prices, or operating hours.

Which of the following, if true, provides the best reason for the expectation?

(A) One of the taller tables takes up less floor space than one of the standard tables.

(B) Diners seated on stools typically do not linger over dinner as long as diners seated at standard tables.

(C) Since the restaurant will replace only some of its standard tables, it can continue to accommodate customers who do not care for the taller tables.

(D) Few diners are likely to avoid the restaurant because of the new seating arrangement.

(E) The standard tables being replaced by tall tables would otherwise have to be replaced with new standard tables at a greater expense.

569. A major network news organization experienced a drop in viewership in the week following the airing of a controversial report on the economy. The network also received a very large number of complaints regarding the report. The network, however, maintains that negative reactions to the report had nothing to do with its loss of viewers.

Which of the following, if true, most strongly supports the network's position?

(A) The other major network news organizations reported similar reductions in viewership during the same week.

(B) The viewers who registered complaints with the network were regular viewers of the news organization's programs.

(C) Major network news organizations publicly attribute drops in viewership to their own reports only when they receive complaints about those reports.

(D) This was not the first time that this network news organization has aired a controversial report on the economy that has inspired viewers to complain to the network.

(E) Most network news viewers rely on network news broadcasts as their primary source of information regarding the economy.

570. Only a reduction of 10 percent in the number of scheduled flights using Greentown's airport will allow the delays that are so common there to be avoided. Hevelia airstrip, 40 miles away, would, if upgraded and expanded, be an attractive alternative for fully 20 percent of the passengers using Greentown airport. Nevertheless, experts reject the claim that turning Hevelia into a full-service airport would end the chronic delays at Greentown.

Which of the following, if true, most helps to justify the experts' position?

(A) Turning Hevelia into a full-service airport would require not only substantial construction at the airport itself, but also the construction of new access highways.
(B) A second largely undeveloped airstrip close to Greentown airport would be a more attractive alternative than Hevelia for many passengers who now use Greentown.
(C) Hevelia airstrip lies in a relatively undeveloped area but would, if it became a full-service airport, be a magnet for commercial and residential development.
(D) If an airplane has to wait to land, the extra jet fuel required adds significantly to the airline's costs.
(E) Several airlines use Greentown as a regional hub, so that most flights landing at Greentown have many passengers who then take different flights to reach their final destinations.

571. For similar cars and comparable drivers, automobile insurance for collision damage has always cost more in Greatport than in Fairmont. Police studies, however, show that cars owned by Greatport residents are, on average, slightly less likely to be involved in a collision than cars in Fairmont. Clearly, therefore, insurance companies are making a greater profit on collision-damage insurance in Greatport than in Fairmont.

In evaluating the argument, it would be most useful to compare

(A) the level of traffic congestion in Greatport with the level of traffic congestion in Fairmont
(B) the cost of repairing collision damage in Greatport with the cost of repairing collision damage in Fairmont
(C) the rates Greatport residents pay for other forms of insurance with the rates paid for similar insurance by residents of Fairmont
(D) the condition of Greatport's roads and streets with the condition of Fairmont's roads and streets
(E) the cost of collision-damage insurance in Greatport and Fairmont with that in other cities

572. The air quality board recently informed Coffee Roast, a small coffee roasting firm, of a complaint regarding the smoke from its roaster. Recently enacted air quality regulations require machines roasting more than 10 pounds of coffee to be equipped with expensive smoke-dissipating afterburners. The firm, however, roasts only 8 pounds of coffee at a time. Nevertheless, the company has decided to purchase and install an afterburner.

Which of the following, if true, most strongly supports the firm's decision?

(A) Until settling on the new air quality regulations, the board had debated whether to require afterburners for machines roasting more than 5 pounds of coffee at a time.
(B) Coffee roasted in a machine equipped with an afterburner has its flavor subtly altered.
(C) The cost to the firm of an afterburner is less than the cost of replacing its roaster with a smaller one.
(D) Fewer complaints are reported in areas that maintain strict rules regarding afterburners.
(E) The firm has reason to fear that negative publicity regarding the complaints could result in lost sales.

573. The tulu, a popular ornamental plant, does not reproduce naturally, and is only bred and sold by specialized horticultural companies. Unfortunately, the tulu is easily devastated by a contagious fungal rot. The government ministry plans to reassure worried gardeners by requiring all tulu plants to be tested for fungal rot before being sold. However, infected plants less than 30 weeks old have generally not built up enough fungal rot in their systems to be detected reliably. And many tulu plants are sold before they are 24 weeks old.

Which of the following, if performed by the government ministry, could logically be expected to overcome the problem with their plan to test for the fungal rot?

(A) Releasing a general announcement that tulu plants less than 30 weeks old cannot be effectively tested for fungal rot

(B) Requiring all tulu plants less than 30 weeks old to be labeled as such

(C) Researching possible ways to test tulu plants less than 24 weeks old for fungal rot

(D) Ensuring that tulu plants not be sold before they are 30 weeks old

(E) Quarantining all tulu plants from horticultural companies at which any case of fungal rot has been detected until those tulu plants can be tested for fungal rot

574. People who do regular volunteer work tend to live longer, on average, than people who do not. It has been found that "doing good," a category that certainly includes volunteer work, releases endorphins, the brain's natural opiates, which induce in people a feeling of well-being. Clearly, there is a connection: Regular releases of endorphins must in some way help to extend people's lives.

14 Feb

Which of the following, if true, most seriously undermines the force of the evidence given as support for the hypothesis that endorphins promote longevity?

(A) People who do regular volunteer work are only somewhat more likely than others to characterize the work they do for a living as "doing good."

(B) Although extremely high levels of endorphins could be harmful to health, such levels are never reached as a result of the natural release of endorphins.

(C) There are many people who have done some volunteer work but who do not do such work regularly.

(D) People tend not to become involved in regular volunteer work unless they are healthy and energetic to begin with.

(E) Releases of endorphins are responsible for the sense of well-being experienced by many long-distance runners while running.

575. In Mernia commercial fossil hunters often sell important fossils they have found, not to universities or museums, but to individual collectors, who pay much better but generally do not allow researchers access to their collections. To increase the number of fossils available for research, some legislators propose requiring all fossils that are found in Mernia to be sold only to universities or museums.

Which of the following, if true, most strongly indicates that the legislators' proposal will fail to achieve its goal?

(A) Some fossil hunters in Mernia are not commercial fossil hunters, but rather are amateurs who keep the fossils that they find.

(B) Most fossils found in Mernia are common types that have little scientific interest.

(C) Commercial fossil hunters in Mernia currently sell some of the fossils they find to universities and museums.

(D) Many universities in Mernia do not engage in fossil research.

(E) Most fossils are found by commercial fossil hunters, and they would give up looking for fossils if they were no longer allowed to sell to individual collectors.

576. The Eurasian ruffe, a fish species inadvertently introduced into North America's Great Lakes in recent years, feeds on the eggs of lake whitefish, a native species, thus threatening the lakes' natural ecosystem. To help track the ruffe's spread, government agencies have produced wallet-sized cards about the ruffe. The cards contain pictures of the ruffe and explain the danger they pose; the cards also request anglers to report any ruffe they catch.

Which of the following, if true, would provide most support for the prediction that the agencies' action will have its intended effect?

(A) The ruffe has spiny fins that make it unattractive as prey.

(B) Ruffe generally feed at night, but most recreational fishing on the Great Lakes is done during daytime hours.

(C) Most people who fish recreationally on the Great Lakes are interested in the preservation of the lake whitefish because it is a highly prized game fish.

(D) The ruffe is one of several nonnative species in the Great Lakes whose existence threatens the survival of lake whitefish populations there.

(E) The bait that most people use when fishing for whitefish on the Great Lakes is not attractive to ruffe.

577. Which of the following most logically completes the argument below?

Although the number of large artificial satellites orbiting the Earth is small compared to the number of small pieces of debris in orbit, the large satellites interfere more seriously with telescope observations because of the strong reflections they produce. Because many of those large satellites have ceased to function, the proposal has recently been made to eliminate interference from nonfunctioning satellites by exploding them in space. This proposal, however, is ill conceived, since ________.

(A) many nonfunctioning satellites remain in orbit for years

(B) for satellites that have ceased to function, repairing them while they are in orbit would be prohibitively expensive

(C) there are no known previous instances of satellites' having been exploded on purpose

(D) the only way to make telescope observations without any interference from debris in orbit is to use telescopes launched into extremely high orbits around the Earth

(E) a greatly increased number of small particles in Earth's orbit would result in a blanket of reflections that would make certain valuable telescope observations impossible

578. Thyrian lawmaker: Thyria's Cheese Importation Board inspects all cheese shipments to Thyria and rejects shipments not meeting specified standards. Yet only 1 percent is ever rejected. Therefore, since the health consequences and associated economic costs of not rejecting that 1 percent are negligible, whereas the board's operating costs are considerable, for economic reasons alone the board should be disbanded.

Consultant: I disagree. The threat of having their shipments rejected deters many cheese exporters from shipping substandard product.

The consultant responds to the lawmaker's argument by

(A) rejecting the lawmaker's argument while proposing that the standards according to which the board inspects imported cheese should be raised

(B) providing evidence that the lawmaker's argument has significantly overestimated the cost of maintaining the board

(C) objecting to the lawmaker's introducing into the discussion factors that are not strictly economic

(D) pointing out a benefit of maintaining the board, which the lawmaker's argument has failed to consider

(E) shifting the discussion from the argument at hand to an attack on the integrity of the cheese inspectors

579. The growing popularity of computer-based activities was widely expected to result in a decline in television viewing, since it had been assumed that people lack sufficient free time to maintain current television viewing levels while spending increasing amounts of free time on the computer. That assumption, however, is evidently false: In a recent mail survey concerning media use, a very large majority of respondents who report increasing time spent per week using computers report no change in time spent watching television.

Which of the following would it be most useful to determine in order to evaluate the argument?

(A) Whether a large majority of the survey respondents reported watching television regularly

(B) Whether the amount of time spent watching television is declining among people who report that they rarely or never use computers

(C) Whether the type of television programs a person watches tends to change as the amount of time spent per week using computers increases

(D) Whether a large majority of the computer owners in the survey reported spending increasing amounts of time per week using computers

(E) Whether the survey respondents' reports of time spent using computers included time spent using computers at work

580. Although the school would receive financial benefits if it had soft drink vending machines in the cafeteria, we should not allow them. Allowing soft drink machines there would not be in our students' interest. If our students start drinking more soft drinks, they will be less healthy.

The argument depends on which of the following?

(A) If the soft drink vending machines were placed in the cafeteria, students would consume more soft drinks as a result.

(B) The amount of soft drinks that most students at the school currently drink is not detrimental to their health.

(C) Students are apt to be healthier if they do not drink soft drinks at all than if they just drink small amounts occasionally.
(D) Students will not simply bring soft drinks from home if the soft drink vending machines are not placed in the cafeteria.
(E) The school's primary concern should be to promote good health among its students.

581. Many athletes inhale pure oxygen after exercise in an attempt to increase muscular reabsorption of oxygen. Measured continuously after exercise, however, the blood lactate levels of athletes who inhale pure oxygen are practically identical, on average, to those of athletes who breathe normal air. The lower the blood lactate level is, the higher the muscular reabsorption of oxygen is.

If the statements above are all true, they most strongly support which of the following conclusions?

(A) Athletes' muscular reabsorption of oxygen is not increased when they inhale pure oxygen instead of normal air.
(B) High blood lactate levels cannot be reduced.
(C) Blood lactate levels are a poor measure of oxygen reabsorption by muscles.
(D) The amount of oxygen reabsorbed by an athlete's muscles always remains constant.
(E) The inhaling of pure oxygen has no legitimate role in athletics.

582. Which of the following most logically completes the argument?

Sviatovin is a medieval Moringian text whose author and exact date of composition are unknown. However, the events in the life of Prince Sviatov that the text describes occurred in 1165, and in the diagram of Sviatov's family that accompanies the text his father, who died in 1167, is identified as still living. Thus *Sviatovin* must have been written between 1165 and 1167, assuming that _____.

(A) the life of Prince Sviatov is not the subject of any other medieval Moringian texts
(B) the author of *Sviatovin* intended it to provide as accurate a report about Prince Sviatov's exploits as possible
(C) the diagram accurately represents the composition of Sviatov's family at the time *Sviatovin* was written
(D) *Sviatovin* is the earliest Moringian text whose composition can be dated to within a few years
(E) *Sviatovin* was not written by Sviatov's father himself

583. A study of ticket sales at a summer theater festival found that people who bought tickets to individual plays had a no-show rate of less than 1 percent, while those who paid in advance for all ten plays being performed that summer had a no-show rate of nearly 30 percent. This may be at least in part because the greater the awareness customers retain about the cost of an item, the more likely they are to use it.

Which of the following would, if true, best serve as an alternative explanation of the results of the study?

(A) The price per ticket was slightly cheaper for those who bought all ten tickets in advance.
(B) Many people who attended the theater festival believed strongly that they should support it financially.
(C) Those who attended all ten plays became eligible for a partial refund.
(D) Usually, people who bought tickets to individual plays did so immediately prior to each performance that they attended.
(E) People who arrived just before the performance began could not be assured of obtaining seats in a preferred location.

584. Although there is no record of poet Edmund Spenser's parentage, we do know that as a youth Spenser attended the Merchant Tailors' School in London for a period between 1560 and 1570. Records from this time indicate that the Merchant Tailors' Guild then had only three members named Spenser: Robert Spenser, listed as a gentleman; Nicholas Spenser, elected the Guild's Warden in 1568; and John Spenser, listed as a "journeyman cloth-maker." Of these, the last was likely the least affluent of the three—and most likely Edmund's father, since school accounting records list Edmund as a scholar who attended the school at a reduced fee.

Which of the following is an assumption on which the argument depends?

(A) Anybody in sixteenth-century London who made clothing professionally would have had to be a member of the Merchant Tailors' Guild.

(B) The fact that Edmund Spenser attended the Merchant Tailors' School did not necessarily mean that he planned to become a tailor.

(C) No member of the Guild could become Guild warden in sixteenth-century London unless he was a gentleman.

(D) Most of those whose fathers were members of the Merchant Tailors' Guild were students at the Merchant Tailors' School.

(E) The Merchant Tailors' School did not reduce its fees for the children of the more affluent Guild members.

585. Trancorp currently transports all its goods to Burland Island by truck. The only bridge over the channel separating Burland from the mainland is congested, and trucks typically spend hours in traffic. Trains can reach the channel more quickly than trucks, and freight cars can be transported to Burland by barges that typically cross the channel in an hour. Therefore, to reduce shipping time, Trancorp plans to switch to trains and barges to transport goods to Burland.

Which of the following would be most important to know in determining whether Trancorp's plan, if implemented, is likely to achieve its goal?

(A) Whether transportation by train and barge would be substantially less expensive than transportation by truck

(B) Whether there are boats that can make the trip between the mainland and Burland faster than barges can

(C) Whether loading the freight cars onto barges is very time consuming

(D) Whether the average number of vehicles traveling over the bridge into Burland has been relatively constant in recent years

(E) Whether most trucks transporting goods into Burland return to the mainland empty

586. Rainwater contains hydrogen of a heavy form called deuterium. The deuterium content of wood reflects the deuterium content of rainwater available to trees during their growth. Wood from trees that grew between 16,000 and 24,000 years ago in North America contains significantly more deuterium than wood from trees growing today. But water trapped in several North American caves that formed during that same early period contains significantly less deuterium than rainwater in North America contains today.

Which of the following, if true, most helps to reconcile the two findings?

(A) There is little deuterium in the North American caves other than the deuterium in the water trapped there.

(B) Exposure to water after a tree has died does not change the deuterium content of the wood.

(C) Industrialization in North America over the past 100 years has altered the deuterium content of rain.

(D) Trees draw on shallow groundwater from rain that falls during their growth, whereas water trapped in caves may have fallen as rainwater thousands of years before the caves formed.

(E) Wood with a high deuterium content is no more likely to remain preserved for long periods than is wood with a low deuterium content.

587. Which of the choices most logically completes the following argument?

NowNews, although still the most popular magazine covering cultural events in Kalopolis, has recently suffered a significant drop in advertising revenue because of falling circulation. Many readers have begun buying a competing magazine that, at 50 cents per copy, costs less than *NowNews* at $1.50 per copy. In order to boost circulation and thus increase advertising revenue, *NowNews*'s publisher has proposed making it available at no charge. However, this proposal has a serious drawback, since ______.

(A) those Kalopolis residents with the greatest interest in cultural events are regular readers of both magazines.

(B) one reason *NowNews's* circulation fell was that its competitor's reporting on cultural events was superior.

(C) the newsstands and stores that currently sell *NowNews* will no longer carry it if it is being given away for free.

(D) at present, 10 percent of the total number of copies of each issue of *NowNews* are distributed free to students on college campuses in the Kalopolis area.

(E) *NowNews's* competitor would begin to lose large amounts of money if it were forced to lower its cover price.

588. Archaeologist: Researchers excavating a burial site in Cyprus found a feline skeleton lying near a human skeleton. Both skeletons were in the same sediment at the same depth and equally well-preserved, suggesting that the feline and human were buried together about 9,500 years ago. This shows that felines were domesticated around the time farming began, when they would have been useful in protecting stores of grain from mice.

Which of the following, if true, would most seriously weaken the archaeologist's argument?

(A) Archaeologists have not found any remains of stores of grain in the immediate vicinity of the burial site.

(B) The burial site in Cyprus is substantially older than any other known burial site in which a feline skeleton and a human skeleton appear to have been buried together.

(C) Paintings found near the burial site seem to show people keeping felines as domestic companions, but do not show felines hunting mice.

(D) In Cyprus, there are many burial sites dating from around 9,500 years ago in which the remains of wild animals appear to have been buried alongside human remains.

(E) Before felines were domesticated, early farmers had no effective way to protect stores of grain from mice.

589. The heavy traffic in Masana is a growing drain on the city's economy—the clogging of the streets of the central business district alone cost the economy more than $1.2 billion over the past year. In order to address this problem, officials plan to introduce congestion pricing, by which drivers would pay to enter the city's most heavily trafficked areas during the busiest times of the day.

Which of the following, if true, would most strongly indicate that the plan will be a success?

(A) Approximately one-fifth of the vehicles in the central business district are in transit from one side of the city to the other.

(B) Planners expect that, without congestion pricing, traffic in Masana is likely to grow by 6 percent in the next five years.

(C) In other urban areas, congestion pricing has strongly encouraged carpooling (sharing of rides by private commuters).

(D) Several studies have shown that a reduction in traffic of 15 percent in Masana could result in 5,500 or more new jobs.

(E) Over 30 percent of the vehicles in the city's center are occupied by more than one person.

590. Economist: The most economically efficient way to reduce emissions of air pollutants is to tax them in proportion to the damage they are likely to cause. But in Country Y, many serious pollutants are untaxed and unregulated, and policy makers strongly oppose new taxes. Therefore, the best way to achieve a reduction in air pollutant emissions in Country Y would be to institute fixed upper limits on them.

Which of the following is an assumption of the economist's argument?

(A) Policy makers in Country Y oppose all new taxes equally strongly, regardless of any benefits they may provide.

(B) Country Y's air pollutant emissions would not fall significantly if they were taxed in proportion to the damage they are likely to cause.

(C) Policy makers in Country Y strongly favor reductions in air pollutant emissions.

(D) Country Y's policy makers believe that air pollutant emissions should be reduced with maximum economic efficiency.

(E) Policy makers in Country Y do not oppose setting fixed upper limits on air pollutant emissions as strongly as they oppose new taxes.

591. Humans get Lyme disease from infected ticks. Ticks get infected by feeding on animals with Lyme disease, but the ease of transmission from host animal to tick varies. With most species of host animal, transmission of Lyme disease to ticks is extremely rare, but white-footed mice are an exception, readily passing Lyme disease to ticks. And white-footed mouse populations greatly expand, becoming the main food source for ticks, in areas where biodiversity is in decline.

The information in the passage most strongly supports which of the following?

(A) In areas where many humans are infected with Lyme disease, the proportion of ticks infected with Lyme disease is especially high.

(B) Very few animals that live in areas where there are no white-footed mice are infected with Lyme disease.

(C) Humans are less at risk of contracting Lyme disease in areas where biodiversity is high.

(D) Ticks feed on white-footed mice only when other host species are not available to them.

(E) The greater the biodiversity of an area, the more likely any given host animal in that area is to pass Lyme disease to ticks.

592. Many industrialized nations are trying to reduce atmospheric concentrations of carbon dioxide, a gas released by the burning of fossil fuels. One proposal is to replace conventional cement, which is made with calcium carbonate, by a new "eco-cement." This new cement, made with magnesium carbonate, absorbs large amounts of carbon dioxide when exposed to the atmosphere. Therefore, using eco-cement for new concrete building projects will significantly help reduce atmospheric concentrations of carbon dioxide.

Which of the following, if true, most strengthens the argument?

(A) The cost of magnesium carbonate, currently greater than the cost of calcium carbonate, probably will fall as more magnesium carbonate is used in cement manufacture.

(B) Eco-cement is strengthened when absorbed carbon dioxide reacts with the cement.

(C) Before the development of eco-cement, magnesium-based cement was considered too susceptible to water erosion to be of practical use.

(D) The manufacture of eco-cement uses considerably less fossil fuel per unit of cement than the manufacture of conventional cement does.

(E) Most building-industry groups are unaware of the development or availability of eco-cement.

593. Which of the following most logically completes the argument below?

Davison River farmers are currently deciding between planting winter wheat this fall or spring wheat next spring. Winter wheat and spring wheat are usually about equally profitable. Because of new government restrictions on the use of Davison River water for irrigation, per acre yields for winter wheat, though not for spring wheat, would be much lower than average. Therefore, planting spring wheat will be more profitable than planting winter wheat, since ________.

(A) the smaller-than-average size of a winter wheat harvest this year would not be compensated for by higher winter wheat prices

(B) new crops of spring wheat must be planted earlier than the time at which standing crops of winter wheat are ready to be harvested

(C) the spring wheat that farmers in the Davison River region plant is well adapted to the soil of the region

(D) spring wheat has uses that are different from those of winter wheat

(E) planting spring wheat is more profitable than planting certain other crops, such as rye

594. Advertisement: When your car's engine is running at its normal operating temperature, any major brand of motor oil will protect it about as well as Tuff does. When the engine is cold, it is a different story: Tuff motor oil flows better at lower temperatures than its major competitors do. So, if you want your car's engine to have maximum protection, you should use Tuff.

Which of the following, if true, most strengthens the argument in the advertisement?

(A) Tuff motor oil provides above-average protection for engines that happen to overheat.

(B) Tuff motor oil is periodically supplied free of charge to automobile manufacturers to use in factory-new cars.

(C) Tuff motor oil's share of the engine oil market peaked three years ago.

(D) Tuff motor oil, like any motor oil, is thicker and flows less freely at cold temperatures than at hot temperatures.

(E) Tuff motor oil is manufactured at only one refinery and shipped from there to all markets.

595. *The Testament of William Thorpe* was published around 1530 as an appendix to Thorpe's longer *Examination*. Many scholars, however, doubt the attribution of the *Testament* to Thorpe because, whereas the *Examination* is dated 1406, the *Testament* is dated 1460. One scholar has recently argued that the 1460 date be amended to 1409, based on the observation that when these numbers are expressed as Roman numerals, MCCCCLX and MCCCCIX, it becomes easy to see how the dates might have become confused through scribal error.

Which of the following, if true, would most support the scholar's hypothesis concerning the date of the *Testament*?

(A) The sole evidence that historians have had that William Thorpe died no earlier than 1460 was the presumed date of publication of the *Testament*.

(B) In the preface to the 1530 publication, the editor attributes both works to William Thorpe.

(C) Few writers in fifteenth-century England marked dates in their works using only Roman numerals.

(D) The *Testament* alludes to a date, "Friday, September 20," as apparently contemporaneous with the writing of the *Testament*, and September 20 fell on a Friday in 1409 but not in 1460.

(E) The *Testament* contains few references to historical events that occurred later than 1406.

596. To reduce productivity losses from employees calling in sick, Corporation X implemented a new policy requiring employees to come into work unless they were so sick that they had to go to a doctor. But a year after the policy was implemented, a study found that Corporation X's overall productivity losses due to reported employee illnesses had increased.

Which of the following, if true, would best explain why the policy produced the reverse of its intended effect?

(A) After the policy was implemented, employees more frequently went to the doctor when they felt sick.

(B) Before the policy was implemented, employees who were not sick at all often called in sick.

(C) Employees coming into work when sick often infect many of their coworkers.

(D) Unusually few employees became genuinely sick during the year after the policy was implemented.

(E) There are many other factors besides employee illness that can adversely affect productivity.

597. Advertising by mail has become much less effective, with fewer consumers responding. Because consumers are increasingly overwhelmed by the sheer amount of junk mail they receive, most discard almost all offers without considering them. Thus, an effective way for corporations to improve response rates would be to more carefully target the individuals to whom they mail advertising, thereby cutting down on the amount of junk mail each consumer receives.

Which of the following, if true, would most support the recommendation above?

(A) There are cost-effective means by which corporations that currently advertise by mail could improve response rates.

(B) Many successful corporations are already carefully targeting the individuals to whom they mail advertising.

(C) Any consumer who, immediately after receiving an advertisement by mail, merely glances at it, is very likely to discard it.

(D) Improvements in the quality of the advertising materials used in mail that is carefully targeted to individuals can improve the response rate for such mail.

(E) Response rates to carefully targeted advertisements by mail are considerably higher, on average, than response rates to most other forms of advertising.

598. Petrochemical industry officials have said that the extreme pressure exerted on plant managers during the last five years to improve profits by cutting costs has done nothing to impair the industry's ability to operate safely. However, environmentalists contend that the recent rash of serious oil spills and accidents at petrochemical plants is traceable to cost-cutting measures.

Which of the following, if true, would provide the strongest support for the position held by industry officials?

(A) The petrochemical industry benefits if accidents do not occur, since accidents involve risk of employee injury as well as loss of equipment and product.

(B) Petrochemical industry unions recently demanded that additional money be spent on safety and environmental protection measures, but the unions readily abandoned those demands in exchange for job security.

(C) Despite major cutbacks in most other areas of operation, the petrochemical industry has devoted more of its resources to environmental and safety measures in the last five years than in the preceding five years.

(D) There is evidence that the most damaging of the recent oil spills would have been prevented had cost-cutting measures not been instituted.

(E) Both the large fines and the adverse publicity generated by the most recent oil spill have prompted the petrochemical industry to increase the resources devoted to oil-spill prevention.

599. Economist: The price of tap water in our region should be raised drastically. **Supplies in local freshwater reservoirs have been declining for years** because water is being used faster than it can be replenished. Since the price of tap water has been low, **few users have bothered to adopt even easy conservation measures**.

The two sections in boldface play which of the following roles in the economist's argument?

(A) The first is a conclusion for which support is provided, and which in turn supports the main conclusion; the second is the main conclusion.

(B) The first is an observation for which the second provides an explanation; the second is the main conclusion but not the only conclusion.

(C) The first is a premise supporting the argument's main conclusion; so is the second.

(D) The first is the only conclusion; the second provides an explanation for the first.

(E) The first is the main conclusion; the second is a conclusion for which support is provided, and which in turn supports the first.

600. Politician: Hybrid cars use significantly less fuel per kilometer than nonhybrids. And fuel produces air pollution, which contributes to a number of environmental problems. Motorists can save money by driving cars that are more fuel efficient, and they will be encouraged to drive hybrid cars if we make them aware of that fact. Therefore, we can help reduce the total amount of pollution emitted by cars in this country by highlighting this advantage of hybrid cars.

Which of the following, if true, would most indicate a vulnerability of the politician's argument?

(A) People with more fuel-efficient cars typically drive more than do those with less fuel-efficient cars.
(B) Not all air pollution originates from automobiles.
(C) Hybrid cars have already begun to gain popularity.
(D) Fuel-efficient alternatives to hybrid cars will likely become available in the future.
(E) The future cost of gasoline and other fuel cannot be predicted with absolute precision or certainty.

601. Which of the following most logically completes the passage?

A recent government study links the high rates of respiratory ailments in Groverston to airborne pollutants released by the Woodco plywood manufacturing plant there. To address the problem, the government imposed strict regulations on emissions which will go into effect in four years.

Although Woodco plans to cut its emissions in half two years ahead of schedule, it is unlikely that the rate of respiratory ailments will decline before the regulations go into effect, since ________.

(A) the number of facilities capable of treating respiratory ailments is not likely to increase
(B) reducing emissions even further than planned would necessitate decreasing production at Woodco
(C) it is difficult to make accurate, long-term predictions about emissions
(D) not all respiratory ailments are caused by airborne pollutants
(E) three new plywood manufacturing plants are about to go into production in Groverston

602. One summer, floods covered low-lying garlic fields situated in a region with a large mosquito population. Since mosquitoes lay their eggs in standing water, flooded fields would normally attract mosquitoes, yet no mosquitoes were found in the fields. Diallyl sulfide, a major component of garlic, is known to repel several species of insects, including mosquitoes, so it is likely that diallyl sulfide from the garlic repelled the mosquitoes.

Which of the following, if true, most strengthens the argument?

(A) Diallyl sulfide is also found in onions but at concentrations lower than in garlic.
(B) The mosquito population of the region as a whole was significantly smaller during the year in which the flooding took place than it had been in previous years.
(C) By the end of the summer, most of the garlic plants in the flooded fields had been killed by waterborne fungi.
(D) Many insect species not repelled by diallyl sulfide were found in the flooded garlic fields throughout the summer.
(E) Mosquitoes are known to be susceptible to toxins in plants other than garlic, such as marigolds.

603. Which of the following most logically completes the passage?

Pecan growers get a high price for their crop when pecans are comparatively scarce, but the price drops sharply when pecans are abundant. Thus, in high-yield years, growers often hold back part of their crop in refrigerated warehouses for one or two years, hoping for higher prices in the future. This year's pecan crop was the smallest in five years. It is nonetheless quite possible that a portion of this year's crop will be held back, since ________.

(A) each of the last two years produced recordbreaking pecan yields
(B) the quality of this year's pecan crop is no worse than the quality of the pecan crops of the previous five years
(C) pecan prices have not been subject to sharp fluctuations in recent years
(D) for some pecan growers, this year's crop was no smaller than last year's
(E) the practice of holding back part of one year's crop had not yet become widespread the last time the pecan crop was as small as it was this year

604. Coffee shop owner: A large number of customers will pay at least the fair market value for a cup of coffee, even if there is no formal charge. Some will pay more than this out of appreciation of the trust that is placed in them. And our total number of customers is likely to increase. We could therefore improve our net cash flow by implementing an honor system in which customers pay what they wish for coffee by depositing money in a can.

Manager: We're likely to lose money on this plan. Many customers would cheat the system, paying a very small sum or nothing at all.

Which of the following, if true, would best support the owner's plan, in light of the manager's concern?

(A) The new system, if implemented, would increase the number of customers.

(B) By roasting its own coffee, the shop has managed to reduce the difficulties (and cost) of maintaining an inventory of freshly roasted coffee.

(C) Many customers stay in the cafe for long stretches of time.

(D) The shop makes a substantial profit from pastries and other food bought by the coffee drinkers.

(E) No other coffee shop in the area has such a system.

605. Which of the following most logically completes the argument?

By competing with rodents for seeds, black ants help control rodent populations that pose a public health risk. However, a very aggressive species of black ant, the Loma ant, which has recently invaded a certain region, has a venomous sting that is often fatal to humans. Therefore, the planned introduction into that region of ant flies, which prey on Loma ants, would benefit public health, since ________.

(A) ant flies do not attack black ants other than Loma ants

(B) Loma ants are less effective than many bird species in competing with rodents for seeds

(C) certain other species of black ants are more effective than Loma ants in competing with rodents for seeds

(D) the sting of Loma ants can also be fatal to rodents

(E) some pesticides that could be used to control Loma ants are harmful to the environment

606. Journalist: In physics journals, the number of articles reporting the results of experiments involving particle accelerators was lower last year than it had been in previous years. Several of the particle accelerators at major research institutions were out of service the year before last for repairs, so it is likely that the low number of articles was due to the decline in availability of particle accelerators.

Which of the following, if true, most seriously undermines the journalist's argument?

(A) Every article based on experiments with particle accelerators that was submitted for publication last year actually was published.

(B) The average time scientists must wait for access to a particle accelerator has declined over the last several years.

(C) The number of physics journals was the same last year as in previous years.

(D) Particle accelerators can be used for more than one group of experiments in any given year.

(E) Recent changes in the editorial policies of several physics journals have decreased the likelihood that articles concerning particle-accelerator research will be accepted for publication.

607. Birds have been said to be descended from certain birdlike dinosaur species with which they share distinctive structural features. The fossil record, however, shows that this cannot be so, since there are bird fossils that are much older than the earliest birdlike dinosaur fossils that have been found.

Which of the following is an assumption on which the argument relies?

(A) The birdlike dinosaurs have no living descendants.

(B) There are no flightless dinosaur species that have the distinctive structural features shared by birds and birdlike dinosaurs.

(C) There are no birdlike dinosaur fossils that are older than the bird fossils but have not yet been unearthed.

(D) It could not have been the case that some birds were descended from one of the birdlike dinosaur species and other birds from another.

(E) Birds cannot have been descended from dinosaur species with which the birds do not share the distinctive structural features.

608. City council member: Demand for electricity has been increasing by 1.5 percent a year, and there simply is no more space to build additional power plants to meet future demand increases. We must therefore begin to curtail usage, which is why I propose passing ordinances requiring energy-conservation measures in all city departments.

The city council member's proposal assumes which of the following?

(A) Existing power plants do not have the capacity to handle all of the projected increase in demand for electricity.

(B) No city departments have implemented energy-conservation measures voluntarily.

(C) Passing ordinances designed to curtail electricity usage will not have negative economic consequences for the city.

(D) Residential consumers are not responsible for the recent increases in demand for electricity.

(E) City departments that successfully conserve energy will set a good example for residential and industrial consumers of electricity.

609. Which of the following most logically completes the argument below?

Using broad-spectrum weed killers on weeds that are competing with crops for sunlight, water, and nutrients presents a difficulty: how to keep the crop from being killed along with the weeds. For at least some food crops, specially treated seed that produces plants resistant to weed killers is under development. This resistance wears off as the plants mature. Therefore, the special seed treatment will be especially useful for plants that ______.

(A) produce their crop over an extended period of time, as summer squash does

(B) produce large seeds that are easy to treat individually, as corn and beans do

(C) provide, as they approach maturity, shade dense enough to keep weeds from growing

(D) are typically grown in large tracts devoted to a single crop

(E) are cultivated specifically for the seed they produce rather than for their leaves or roots

610. Previously, Autoco designed all of its cars itself and then contracted with specialized parts suppliers to build parts according to its specifications. Now it plans to include its suppliers in designing the parts they are to build. Since many parts suppliers have more designers with specialized experience than Autoco has, Autoco expects this shift to reduce the overall time and cost of the design of its next new car.

Which of the following, if true, most strongly supports Autoco's expectation?

(A) When suppliers provide their own designs, Autoco often needs to modify its overall design.

(B) In order to provide designs for Autoco, several of the parts suppliers will have to add to their existing staffs of designers.

(C) Parts and services provided by outside suppliers account for more than 50 percent of Autoco's total costs.

(D) When suppliers built parts according to specifications provided by Autoco, the suppliers competed to win contracts.

(E) Most of Autoco's suppliers have on hand a wide range of previously prepared parts designs that can readily be modified for a new car.

611. In Stenland, many workers have been complaining that they cannot survive on minimum wage, the lowest wage an employer is permitted to pay. The government is proposing to raise the minimum wage. Many employers who pay their workers the current minimum wage argue that if it is raised, unemployment will increase because they will no longer be able to afford to employ as many workers.

Which of the following, if true in Stenland, most strongly supports the claim that raising the minimum wage there will not have the effects that the employers predict?

(A) For any position with wages below a living wage, the difficulty of finding and retaining employees adds as much to employment costs as would raising wages.

(B) Raising the minimum wage does not also increase the amount employers have to contribute in employee benefits.

(C) When inflation is taken into account, the proposed new minimum wage is not as high as the current one was when it was introduced.

(D) Many employees currently being paid wages at the level of the proposed new minimum wage will demand significant wage increases.

(E) Many employers who pay some workers only the minimum wage also pay other workers wages that are much higher than the minimum.

612. Which of the following most logically completes the argument?

The attribution of the choral work *Lacrimae* to the composer Pescard (1400–1474) has been regarded as tentative, since it was based on a single treatise from the early 1500s that named Pescard as the composer. Recently, several musical treatises from the late 1500s have come to light, all of which name Pescard as the composer of *Lacrimae*. Unfortunately, these newly discovered treatises lend no support to the attribution of *Lacrimae* to Pescard, since ________.

(A) the treatise from the early 1500s misidentifies the composers of some of the musical works it considers

(B) the author of the treatise from the early 1500s had no very strong evidence on which to base the identification of Pescard as the composer of *Lacrimae*

(C) there are works that can conclusively be attributed to Pescard that are not even mentioned in the treatise from the early 1500s

(D) the later treatises probably had no source for their attribution other than the earlier treatise

(E) no known treatises from the 1600s identify Pescard as the composer of *Lacrimae*

613. When trying to identify new technologies that promise to transform the marketplace, market researchers survey the managers of those companies that are developing new technologies. Such managers have an enormous stake in succeeding, so they invariably overstate the potential of their new technologies. Surprisingly, however, market researchers typically do not survey a new technology's potential buyers, even though it is the buyers—not the producers—who will ultimately determine a technology's commercial success.

Which of the following, if true, best accounts for the typical survey practices among market researchers?

(A) If a new technology succeeds, the commercial benefits accrue largely to the producers, not to the buyers, of that technology.

(B) People who promote the virtues of a new technology typically fail to consider that the old technology that is currently in use continues to be improved, often substantially.

(C) Investors are unlikely to invest substantial amounts of capital in a company whose own managers are skeptical about the commercial prospects of a new technology they are developing.

(D) The potential buyers for not-yet-available technologies can seldom be reliably identified.

(E) The developers of a new technology are generally no better positioned than its potential buyers to gauge how rapidly the new technology can be efficiently mass-produced.

614. Infotek, a computer manufacturer in Katrovia, has just introduced a new personal computer model that sells for significantly less than any other model. Market research shows, however, that very few Katrovian households without personal computers would buy a computer, regardless of its price. Therefore, introducing the new model is unlikely to increase the number of computers in Katrovian homes.

Which of the following is an assumption on which the argument depends?

(A) Infotek achieved the lower price of the new model by using components of lower quality than those used by other manufacturers.

(B) The main reason cited by consumers in Katrovia for replacing a personal computer is the desire to have an improved model.

(C) Katrovians in households that already have computers are unlikely to purchase the new Infotek model as an additional computer for home use.

(D) The price of other personal computers in Katrovia is unlikely to drop below the price of Infotek's new model in the near future.

(E) Most personal computers purchased in Katrovia are intended for home use.

615. Fast-food restaurants make up 45 percent of all restaurants in Canatria. Customers at these restaurants tend to be young; in fact, studies have shown that the older people get, the less likely they are to eat in fast-food restaurants. Since the average age of the Canatrian population is gradually rising and will continue to do so, the number of fast-food restaurants is likely to decrease.

Which of the following, if true, most seriously weakens the argument?

(A) Fast-food restaurants in Canatria are getting bigger, so each one can serve more customers.

(B) Some older people eat at fast-food restaurants more frequently than the average young person.

(C) Many people who rarely eat in fast-food restaurants nevertheless eat regularly in restaurants.

(D) The overall population of Canatria is growing steadily.

(E) As the population of Canatria gets older, more people are eating at home.

616. In order to withstand tidal currents, juvenile horseshoe crabs frequently burrow in the sand. Such burrowing discourages barnacles from clinging to their shells. When fully grown, however, the crabs can readily withstand tidal currents without burrowing, and thus they acquire substantial populations of barnacles. Surprisingly, in areas where tidal currents are very weak, juvenile horseshoe crabs are found not to have significant barnacle populations, even though they seldom burrow.

Which of the following, if true, most helps to explain the surprising finding?

(A) Tidal currents do not themselves dislodge barnacles from the shells of horseshoe crabs.

(B) Barnacles most readily attach themselves to horseshoe crabs in areas where tidal currents are weakest.

(C) The strength of the tidal currents in a given location varies widely over the course of a day.

(D) A very large barnacle population can significantly decrease the ability of a horseshoe crab to find food.

(E) Until they are fully grown, horseshoe crabs shed their shells and grow new ones several times a year.

617. Last year a chain of fast-food restaurants, whose menu had always centered on hamburgers, added its first vegetarian sandwich, much lower in fat than the chain's other offerings. Despite heavy marketing, the new sandwich accounts for a very small proportion of the chain's sales. The sandwich's sales would have to quadruple to cover the costs associated with including it on the menu. Since such an increase is unlikely, the chain would be more profitable if it dropped the sandwich.

Which of the following, if true, most seriously weakens the argument?

(A) Although many of the chain's customers have never tried the vegetarian sandwich, in a market research survey most of those who had tried it reported that they were very satisfied with it.

(B) Many of the people who eat at the chain's restaurants also eat at the restaurants of competing chains and report no strong preference among the competitors.

(C) Among fast-food chains in general, there has been little or no growth in hamburger sales over the past several years as the range of competing offerings at other restaurants has grown.

(D) When even one member of a group of diners is a vegetarian or has a preference for low-fat food, the group tends to avoid restaurants that lack vegetarian or low-fat menu options.

(E) An attempt by the chain to introduce a lower-fat hamburger failed several years ago, since it attracted few new customers and most of the chain's regular customers greatly preferred the taste of the regular hamburgers.

618. Transportation expenses accounted for a large portion of the total dollar amount spent on trips for pleasure by residents of the United States in 1997, and about half of the total dollar amount spent on transportation was for airfare. However, the large majority of United States residents who took trips for pleasure in 1997 did not travel by airplane but used other means of transportation.

If the statements above are true, which of the following must also be true about United States residents who took trips for pleasure in 1997?

(A) Most of those who traveled by airplane did so because the airfare to their destination was lower than the cost of other available means of transportation.

(B) Most of those who traveled by airplane did so because other means of transportation to their destination were unavailable.

(C) Per mile traveled, those who traveled by airplane tended to spend more on transportation to their destination than did those who used other means of transportation.

(D) Overall, people who did not travel by airplane had lower average transportation expenses than people who did.

(E) Those who traveled by airplane spent about as much, on average, on other means of transportation as they did on airfare.

619. Voters commonly condemn politicians for being insincere, but politicians often must disguise their true feelings when they make public statements. If they expressed their honest views—about, say, their party's policies—then achieving politically necessary compromises would be much more difficult. Clearly, the very insincerity that people decry shows that our government is functioning well.

Which of the following, if true, most seriously undermines this reasoning?

(A) Achieving political compromises is not all that is necessary for the proper functioning of a government.

(B) Some political compromises are not in the best long-term interest of the government.

(C) Voters often judge politicians by criteria other than the sincerity with which they express their views.

(D) A political party's policies could turn out to be detrimental to the functioning of a government.

(E) Some of the public statements made by politicians about their party's policies could in fact be sincere.

620. To reduce waste of raw materials, the government of Sperland is considering requiring household appliances to be broken down for salvage when discarded. To cover the cost of salvage, the government is planning to charge a fee, which would be imposed when the appliance is first sold. Imposing the fee at the time of salvage would reduce waste more effectively, however, because consumers tend to keep old appliances longer if they are faced with a fee for discarding them.

Which of the following, if true, most seriously weakens the argument?

(A) Increasing the cost of disposing of an appliance properly increases the incentive to dispose of it improperly.

(B) The fee provides manufacturers with no incentive to produce appliances that are more durable.

(C) For people who have bought new appliances recently, the salvage fee would not need to be paid for a number of years.

(D) People who sell their used, working appliances to others would not need to pay the salvage fee.

(E) Many nonfunctioning appliances that are currently discarded could be repaired at relatively little expense.

621. When there is less rainfall than normal, the water level of Australian rivers falls and the rivers flow more slowly. Because algae whose habitat is river water grow best in slow-moving water, the amount of algae per unit of water generally increases when there has been little rain. By contrast, however, following a period of extreme drought, algae levels are low even in very slow-moving river water.

Which of the following, if true, does most to explain the contrast described above?

(A) During periods of extreme drought, the populations of some of the species that feed on algae tend to fall.

(B) The more slowly water moves, the more conducive its temperature is to the growth of algae.

(C) When algae populations reach very high levels, conditions within the river can become toxic for some of the other species that normally live there.

(D) Australian rivers dry up completely for short intervals in periods of extreme drought.

(E) Except during periods of extreme drought, algae levels tend to be higher in rivers in which the flow has been controlled by damming than in rivers that flow freely.

622. Increased use of incineration is sometimes advocated as a safe way to dispose of chemical waste. But opponents of incineration point to the 40 incidents involving unexpected releases of dangerous chemical agents that were reported just last year at two existing incinerators commissioned to destroy a quantity of chemical waste material. Since designs for proposed new incinerators include no additional means of preventing such releases, leaks will only become more prevalent if use of incineration increases.

Which of the following, if true, most seriously weakens the argument?

(A) At the two incinerators at which leaks were reported, staff had had only cursory training on the proper procedures for incinerating chemical waste.

(B) Other means of disposing of chemical waste, such as chemical neutralization processes, have not been proven safer than incineration.

(C) The capacity of existing incinerators is sufficient to allow for increased incineration of chemical waste without any need for new incinerators.

(D) The frequency of reports of unexpected releases of chemical agents at newly built incinerators is about the same as the frequency at older incinerators.

(E) In only three of the reported incidents of unexpected chemical leaks did the releases extend outside the property on which the incinerators were located.

623. Public health expert: **Increasing the urgency of a public health message may be counterproductive.** In addition to irritating the majority who already behave responsibly, **it may undermine all government pronouncements on health by convincing people that such messages are overly cautious.** And there is no reason to believe that those who ignore measured voices will listen to shouting.

The two sections in boldface play which of the following roles in the public health expert's argument?

(A) The first is a conclusion for which support is provided, but is not the argument's main conclusion; the second is an unsupported premise supporting the argument's main conclusion.

(B) The first is a premise supporting the only explicit conclusion; so is the second.

(C) The first is the argument's main conclusion; the second supports that conclusion and is itself a conclusion for which support is provided.

(D) The first is a premise supporting the argument's only conclusion; the second is that conclusion.

(E) The first is the argument's only explicit conclusion; the second is a premise supporting that conclusion.

624. Several industries have recently switched at least partly from older technologies powered by fossil fuels to new technologies powered by electricity. It is thus evident that less fossil fuel is being used as a result of the operations of these industries than would have been used if these industries had retained their older technologies.

Which of the following, if true, most strengthens the argument above?

(A) Many of the industries that have switched at least partly to the new technologies have increased their output.

(B) Less fossil fuel was used to manufacture the machinery employed in the new technologies than was originally used to manufacture the machinery employed in the older technologies.

(C) More electricity is used by those industries that have switched at least partly to the new technologies than by those industries that have not switched.

(D) Some of the industries that have switched at least partly to the new technologies still use primarily technologies that are powered by fossil fuels.

(E) The amount of fossil fuel used to generate the electricity needed to power the new technologies is less than the amount that would have been used to power the older technologies.

625. The difference in average annual income in favor of employees who have college degrees, compared with those who do not have such degrees, doubled between 1980 and 1990. Some analysts have hypothesized that increased competition between employers for employees with college degrees drove up income for such employees.

Which of the following, if true, most seriously undermines the explanation described above?

(A) During the 1980s a growing percentage of college graduates, unable to find jobs requiring a college degree, took unskilled jobs.

(B) The average age of all employees increased slightly during the 1980s.

(C) The unemployment rate changed very little throughout most of the 1980s.

(D) From 1980 to 1990 the difference in average income between employees with advanced degrees and those with bachelor's degrees also increased.

(E) During the 1980s there were some employees with no college degree who earned incomes comparable to the top incomes earned by employees with a college degree.

626. Which of the following most logically completes the passage?

According to the last pre-election poll in Whippleton, most voters believe that the three problems government needs to address, in order of importance, are pollution, crime, and unemployment. Yet in the election, candidates from parties perceived as strongly against pollution were defeated, while those elected were all from parties with a history of opposing legislation designed to reduce pollution. These results should not be taken to indicate that the poll was inaccurate, however, since __________.

(A) some voters in Whippleton do not believe that pollution needs to be reduced

(B) every candidate who was defeated had a strong antipollution record

(C) there were no issues other than crime, unemployment, and pollution on which the candidates had significant differences of opinion

(D) all the candidates who were elected were perceived as being stronger against both crime and unemployment than the candidates who were defeated

(E) many of the people who voted in the election refused to participate in the poll

627. Manufacturing plants in Arundia have recently been acquired in substantial numbers by investors from abroad. Arundian politicians are proposing legislative action to stop such investment, justifying the proposal by arguing that foreign investors, opportunistically exploiting a recent fall in the value of the Arundian currency, were able to buy Arundian assets at less than their true value.

Which of the following, if true, casts the most serious doubt on the adequacy of the Arundian politicians' justification for the proposed legislation?

(A) The Arundian government originally welcomed the fall in the value of the Arundian currency because the fall made Arundian exports more competitive on international markets.

(B) Foreign investors who acquired Arundian manufacturing plants generally did so with no intention of keeping and running those plants over the long term.

(C) Without the recent fall in the value of the Arundian currency, many of the Arundian assets bought by foreign investors would have been beyond the financial reach of those investors.

(D) In Concordia, a country broadly similar to Arundia, the share of manufacturing assets that is foreign-controlled is 60 percent higher than it is in Arundia.

(E) The true value of an investment is determined by the value of the profits from it, and the low value of the Arundian currency has depressed the value of any profits earned by foreign investors from Arundian assets.

628. Proposed new safety rules for Beach City airport would lengthen considerably the minimum time between takeoffs from the airport. In consequence, the airport would be able to accommodate 10 percent fewer flights than currently use the airport daily. The city's operating budget depends heavily on taxes generated

by tourist spending, and most of the tourists come by plane. Therefore, the proposed new safety rules, if adopted, will reduce the revenue available for the operating budget.

The argument depends on assuming which of the following?

(A) There are no periods of the day during which the interval between flights taking off from the airport is significantly greater than the currently allowed minimum.

(B) Few, if any, of the tourists who use Beach City airport do so when their main destination is a neighboring community and not Beach City itself.

(C) If the proposed safety rules are adopted, the reduction in tourist numbers will not result mainly from a reduction in the number of tourists who spend relatively little in Beach City.

(D) Increasing the minimum time between takeoffs is the only way to achieve necessary safety improvements without a large expenditure by the city government on airport enhancements.

(E) The response to the adoption of the new safety rules would not include a large increase in the number of passengers per flight.

629. The introduction of new drugs into the market is frequently prevented by a shortage of human subjects for the clinical trials needed to show that the drugs are safe and effective. Since the lives and health of people in future generations may depend on treatments that are currently experimental, practicing physicians are morally in the wrong when, in the absence of any treatment proven to be effective, they fail to encourage suitable patients to volunteer for clinical trials.

Which of the following, if true, casts most doubt on the conclusion of the argument?

(A) Many drugs undergoing clinical trials are intended for the treatment of conditions for which there is currently no effective treatment.

(B) Patients do not share the physician's professional concern for public health, but everyone has a moral obligation to alleviate suffering when able to do so.

(C) Usually, half the patients in a clinical trial serve as a control group and receive a nonactive drug in place of the drug being tested.

(D) An experimental drug cannot legally be made available to patients unless those patients are subjects in clinical trials of the drug.

(E) Physicians have an overriding moral and legal duty to care for the health and safety of their current patients.

630. As a construction material, bamboo is as strong as steel and sturdier than concrete. Moreover, in tropical areas bamboo is a much less expensive construction material than either steel or concrete and is always readily available. In tropical areas, therefore, building with bamboo makes better economic sense than building with steel or concrete, except where land values are high.

Which of the following, if true, most helps to explain the exception noted above?

(A) Buildings constructed of bamboo are less likely to suffer earthquake damage than are steel and concrete buildings.

(B) Bamboo is unsuitable as a building material for multistory buildings.

(C) In order to protect it from being damaged by termites and beetles, bamboo must be soaked, at some expense, in a preservative.

(D) In some tropical areas, bamboo is used to make the scaffolding that is used during large construction projects.

(E) Bamboo growing in an area where land values are increasing is often cleared to make way for construction.

631. Newspaper editors should not allow reporters to write the headlines for their own stories. The reason for this is that, while the headlines that reporters themselves write are often clever, what typically makes them clever is that they allude to little-known information that is familiar to the reporter but that never appears explicitly in the story itself.

Which of the following, if true, most strengthens the argument?

(A) The reporter who writes a story is usually better placed than the reporter's editor is to judge what the story's most newsworthy features are.

(B) To write a headline that is clever, a person must have sufficient understanding of the story that the headline accompanies.

(C) Most reporters rarely bother to find out how other reporters have written stories and headlines about the same events that they themselves have covered.

(D) For virtually any story that a reporter writes, there are at least a few people who know more about the story's subject matter than does the reporter.

(E) The kind of headlines that newspaper editors want are those that anyone who has read a reporter's story in its entirety will recognize as clever.

632. Scientists have modified feed corn genetically, increasing its resistance to insect pests. Farmers who tried out the genetically modified corn last season applied less insecticide to their corn fields and still got yields comparable to those they would have gotten with ordinary corn. Ordinary corn seed, however, costs less, and what these farmers saved on insecticide rarely exceeded their extra costs for seed. Therefore, for most feed-corn farmers, switching to genetically modified seed would be unlikely to increase profits.

Which of the following would it be most useful to know in order to evaluate the argument?

(A) Whether there are insect pests that sometimes reduce feed-corn yields, but against which commonly used insecticides and the genetic modification are equally ineffective

(B) Whether the price that farmers receive for feed corn has remained steady over the past few years

(C) Whether the insecticides typically used on feed corn tend to be more expensive than insecticides typically used on other crops

(D) Whether most of the farmers who tried the genetically modified corn last season applied more insecticide than was actually necessary

(E) Whether, for most farmers who plant feed corn, it is their most profitable crop

633. Debater: The average amount of overtime per month worked by an employee in the manufacturing division of the Haglut Corporation is 14 hours. Most employees of the Haglut Corporation work in the manufacturing division. Furthermore, the average amount of overtime per month worked by any employee in the company generally does not fluctuate much from month to month. Therefore, each month, most employees of the Haglut Corporation almost certainly work at least some overtime.

The debater's argument is most vulnerable to criticism on which of these grounds?

(A) It takes for granted that the manufacturing division is a typical division of the corporation with regard to the average amount of overtime its employees work each month.

(B) It takes for granted that if a certain average amount of overtime is worked each month by each employee of the Haglut Corporation, then approximately the same amount of overtime must be worked each month by each employee of the manufacturing division.

(C) It confuses a claim from which the argument's conclusion about the Haglut Corporation would necessarily follow with a claim that would follow from the argument's conclusion only with a high degree of probability.

(D) It overlooks the possibility that even if, on average, a certain amount of overtime is worked by the members of some group, many members of that group may work no overtime at all.

(E) It overlooks the possibility that even if most employees of the corporation work some overtime each month, any one corporate employee may, in some months, work no overtime.

634. Proponents of the recently introduced tax on sales of new luxury boats had argued that a tax of this sort would be an equitable way to increase government revenue because the admittedly heavy tax burden would fall only on wealthy people and neither they nor anyone else would suffer any economic hardship. In fact, however, 20 percent of the workers employed by manufacturers of luxury boats have lost their jobs as a direct result of this tax.

The information given, if true, most strongly supports which of the following?

(A) The market for luxury boats would have collapsed even if the new tax on luxury boats had been lower.

(B) The new tax would produce a net gain in tax revenue for the government only if the yearly total revenue that it generates exceeds the total of any yearly tax-revenue decrease resulting from the workers' loss of jobs.

(C) Because many people never buy luxury items, imposing a sales tax on luxury items is the kind of legislative action that does not cost incumbent legislators much popular support.

(D) Before the tax was instituted, luxury boats were largely bought by people who were not wealthy.

(E) Taxes can be equitable only if their burden is evenly distributed over the entire population.

635. In Wareland last year, 16 percent of licensed drivers under 21 and 11 percent of drivers ages 21–24 were in serious accidents. By contrast, only 3 percent of licensed drivers 65 and older were involved in serious accidents. These figures clearly show that the greater experience and developed habits of caution possessed by drivers in the 65-and-older group make them far safer behind the wheel than the younger drivers are.

Which of the following is an assumption on which the argument depends?

(A) Drivers 65 and older do not, on average, drive very many fewer miles per year than drivers 24 and younger.

(B) Drivers 65 and older do not constitute a significantly larger percentage of licensed drivers in Wareland than drivers ages 18–24 do.

(C) Drivers 65 and older are less likely than are drivers 24 and younger to drive during weather conditions that greatly increase the risk of accidents.

(D) The difference between the accident rate of drivers under 21 and of those ages 21–24 is attributable to the greater driving experience of those in the older group.

(E) There is no age bracket for which the accident rate is lower than it is for licensed drivers 65 and older.

636. In the past the country of Malvernia has relied heavily on imported oil. Malvernia recently implemented a program to convert heating systems from oil to natural gas. Malvernia currently produces more natural gas each year than it uses, and oil production in Malvernian oil fields is increasing at a steady pace. If these trends in fuel production and usage continue, therefore, Malvernian reliance on foreign sources for fuel is likely to decline soon.

Which of the following would it be most useful to establish in evaluating the argument?

(A) When, if ever, will production of oil in Malvernia outstrip production of natural gas?

(B) Is Malvernia among the countries that rely most on imported oil?

(C) What proportion of Malvernia's total energy needs is met by hydroelectric, solar, and nuclear power?

(D) Is the amount of oil used each year in Malvernia for generating electricity and fuel for transportation increasing?

(E) Have any existing oil-burning heating systems in Malvernia already been converted to natural-gas-burning heating systems?

637. Exposure to certain chemicals commonly used in elementary schools as cleaners or pesticides causes allergic reactions in some children. Elementary school nurses in Renston report that the proportion of schoolchildren sent to them for treatment of allergic reactions to those chemicals has increased significantly over the past ten years. Therefore, either Renston's schoolchildren have been exposed to greater quantities of the chemicals, or they are more sensitive to them than schoolchildren were ten years ago.

Which of the following is an assumption on which the argument depends?

(A) The number of school nurses employed by Renston's elementary schools has not decreased over the past ten years.

(B) Children who are allergic to the chemicals are no more likely than other children to have allergies to other substances.

(C) Children who have allergic reactions to the chemicals are not more likely to be sent to a school nurse now than they were ten years ago.

(D) The chemicals are not commonly used as cleaners or pesticides in houses and apartment buildings in Renston.

(E) Children attending elementary school do not make up a larger proportion of Renston's population now than they did ten years ago.

638. Normally, the pineal gland governs a person's sleep-wake cycle by secreting melatonin in response to the daily cycle of light and darkness as detected by the eye. Nonetheless, many people who are totally blind due to lesions in the visual cortex of the brain easily maintain a 24-hour sleep-wake cycle. So the neural pathway by which the pineal gland receives information from the eye probably does not pass through the visual cortex.

For purposes of evaluating the argument it would be most useful to establish which of the following?

(A) Whether melatonin supplements help people who have difficulty maintaining a 24-hour sleep cycle to establish such a pattern

(B) Whether the melatonin levels of most totally blind people who successfully maintain a 24-hour sleep-wake cycle change in response to changes in exposure to light and darkness

(C) Whether melatonin is the only substance secreted by the pineal gland

(D) Whether most people who do not have a 24-hour sleep-wake cycle nevertheless have a cycle of consistent duration

(E) Whether there are any people with normal vision whose melatonin levels respond abnormally to periods of light and darkness

639. **In countries where automobile insurance includes compensation for whiplash injuries sustained in automobile accidents, reports of having suffered such injuries are twice as frequent as they are in countries where whiplash is not covered.** Presently, no objective test for whiplash exists, so it is true that spurious reports of whiplash injuries cannot be readily identified. Nevertheless, these facts do not warrant the conclusion drawn by some commentators that in the countries with the higher rates of reported whiplash injuries, half of the reported cases are spurious. Clearly, **in countries where automobile insurance does not include compensation for whiplash, people often have little incentive to report whiplash injuries that they actually have suffered.**

In the argument given, the two boldfaced portions play which of the following roles?

(A) The first is a claim that the argument disputes; the second is a conclusion that has been based on that claim.

(B) The first is a claim that has been used to support a conclusion that the argument accepts; the second is that conclusion.

(C) The first is evidence that has been used to support a conclusion for which the argument provides further evidence; the second is the main conclusion of the argument.

(D) The first is a finding whose implications are at issue in the argument; the second is a claim presented in order to argue against deriving certain implications from that finding.

(E) The first is a finding whose accuracy is evaluated in the argument; the second is evidence presented to establish that the finding is accurate.

640. Last year Comfort Airlines had twice as many delayed flights as the year before, but the number of complaints from passengers about delayed flights went up three times. It is unlikely that this disproportionate increase in complaints was rooted in an increase in overall dissatisfaction with the service Comfort Airlines provides, since the airline made a special effort to improve other aspects of its service last year.

Which of the following, if true, most helps to explain the disproportionate increase in customer complaints?

(A) Comfort Airlines had more flights last year than the year before.

(B) Last year a single period of unusually bad weather caused a large number of flights to be delayed.

(C) Some of the improvements that Comfort Airlines made in its service were required by new government regulations.

(D) The average length of a flight delay was greater last year than it was the year before.

(E) The average number of passengers per flight was no higher last year than the year before.

641. Last year a global disturbance of weather patterns disrupted harvests in many of the world's important agricultural areas. Worldwide production of soybeans, an important source of protein for people and livestock alike, was not adversely affected, however. Indeed, last year's soybean crop was actually slightly larger than average. Nevertheless, the weather phenomenon is probably responsible for a recent increase in the world price of soybeans.

Which of the following, if true, provides the strongest justification for the attribution of the increase in soybean prices to the weather phenomenon?

(A) Last year's harvest of anchovies, which provide an important protein source for livestock, was disrupted by the effects of the weather phenomenon.

(B) Most countries that produce soybeans for export had above-average harvests of a number of food crops other than soybeans last year.

(C) The world price of soybeans also rose several years ago, immediately after an earlier occurrence of a similar global weather disturbance.

(D) Heavy rains attributable to the weather phenomenon improved grazing pastures last year, allowing farmers in many parts of the world to reduce their dependence on supplemental feed.

(E) Prior to last year, soybean prices had been falling for several years.

642. Most of the year, the hermit thrush, a North American songbird, eats a diet consisting mainly of insects, but in autumn, as the thrushes migrate to their Central and South American wintering grounds, they feed almost exclusively on wild berries. Wild berries, however, are not as rich in calories as insects, yet thrushes need to consume plenty of calories in order to complete their migration. One possible explanation is that berries contain other nutrients that thrushes need for migration and that insects lack.

Which of the following, if true, most seriously calls into question the explanation given for the thrush's diet during migration?

(A) Hermit thrushes, if undernourished, are unable to complete their autumn migration before the onset of winter.

(B) Insect species contain certain nutrients that are not found in wild berries.

(C) For songbirds, catching insects requires the expenditure of significantly more calories than eating wild berries does.

(D) Along the hermit thrushes' migration routes, insects are abundant throughout the migration season.

(E) There are some species of wild berries that hermit thrushes generally do not eat, even though these berry species are exceptionally rich in calories.

643. The kinds of hand and wrist injuries that result from extended use of a computer while maintaining an incorrect posture are common among schoolchildren in Harnville. Computers are important to the school curriculum there, so instead of reducing the amount their students use computers, teachers plan to bring about a sharp reduction in the number of these injuries by carefully monitoring their students' posture when using computers in the classroom.

Which of the following would it be most useful to know in order to assess the likelihood that the teachers' plan will be successful?

(A) Whether extended use of a computer while maintaining incorrect posture can cause injuries other than hand and wrist injuries
(B) Whether hand and wrist injuries not caused by computer use are common among schoolchildren in Harnville
(C) What proportion of schoolchildren in Harnville with hand and wrist injuries use computers extensively outside the classroom
(D) Whether changes in the curriculum could reduce the schools' dependence on computers
(E) What proportion of schoolchildren in Harnville already use correct posture while using a computer

644. A certain cultivated herb is one of a group of closely related plants that thrive in soil with high concentrations of metals that are toxic to most other plants. Agronomists studying the growth of this herb have discovered that it produces large amounts of histidine, an amino acid that, in test-tube solutions, renders these metals chemically inert. Hence, the herb's high histidine production must be the key feature that allows it to grow in metal-rich soils.

In evaluating the argument, it would be most important to determine which of the following?

(A) Whether the herb can thrive in soil that does not have high concentrations of the toxic metals
(B) Whether others of the closely related group of plants also produce histidine in large quantities
(C) Whether the herb's high level of histidine production is associated with an unusually low level of production of some other amino acid
(D) Whether growing the herb in soil with high concentrations of the metals will, over time, reduce their concentrations in the soil
(E) Whether the concentration of histidine in the growing herb declines as the plant approaches maturity

645. Many people suffer an allergic reaction to certain sulfites, including those that are commonly added to wine as preservatives. However, since there are several winemakers who add sulfites to none of the wines they produce, people who would like to drink wine but are allergic to sulfites can drink wines produced by these winemakers without risking an allergic reaction to sulfites.

Which of the following is an assumption on which the argument depends?

(A) These winemakers have been able to duplicate the preservative effect produced by adding sulfites by means that do not involve adding any potentially allergenic substances to their wine.
(B) Not all forms of sulfite are equally likely to produce the allergic reaction.
(C) Wine is the only beverage to which sulfites are commonly added.
(D) Apart from sulfites, there are no substances commonly present in wine that give rise to an allergic reaction.
(E) Sulfites are not naturally present in the wines produced by these winemakers in amounts large enough to produce an allergic reaction in someone who drinks these wines.

646. A new law gives ownership of patents—documents providing exclusive right to make and sell an invention—to universities, not the government, when those patents result from government-sponsored university research. Administrators at Logos University plan to sell any patents they acquire to corporations in order to fund programs to improve undergraduate teaching.

Which of the following, if true, would cast the most doubt on the viability of the college administrators' plan described above?

(A) Profit-making corporations interested in developing products based on patents held by universities are likely to try to serve as exclusive sponsors of ongoing university research projects.

(B) Corporate sponsors of research in university facilities are entitled to tax credits under new federal tax-code guidelines.

(C) Research scientists at Logos University have few or no teaching responsibilities and participate little if at all in the undergraduate programs in their field.

(D) Government-sponsored research conducted at Logos University for the most part duplicates research already completed by several profitmaking corporations.

(E) Logos University is unlikely to attract corporate sponsorship of its scientific research.

647. Since it has become known that **several of a bank's top executives have been buying shares in their own bank,** the bank's depositors, who had been worried by rumors that the bank faced impending financial collapse, have been greatly relieved. They reason that, since top executives evidently have faith in the bank's financial soundness, those worrisome rumors must be false. Such reasoning might well be overoptimistic, however, since **corporate executives have been known to buy shares in their own company in a calculated attempt to dispel negative rumors about the company's health.**

In the argument given, the two boldfaced portions play which of the following roles?

(A) The first describes evidence that has been taken as supporting a conclusion; the second gives a reason for questioning that support.

(B) The first describes evidence that has been taken as supporting a conclusion; the second states a contrary conclusion that is the main conclusion of the argument.

(C) The first provides evidence in support of the main conclusion of the argument; the second states that conclusion.

(D) The first describes the circumstance that the argument as a whole seeks to explain; the second gives the explanation that the argument seeks to establish.

(E) The first describes the circumstance that the argument as a whole seeks to explain; the second provides evidence in support of the explanation that the argument seeks to establish.

648. Between 1980 and 2000 the sea otter population of the Aleutian Islands declined precipitously. There were no signs of disease or malnutrition, so there was probably an increase in the number of otters being eaten by predators. Orcas will eat otters when seals, their normal prey, are unavailable, and the Aleutian Islands seal population declined dramatically in the 1980s. Therefore, orcas were most likely the immediate cause of the otter population decline.

Which of the following, if true, most strengthens the argument?

(A) The population of sea urchins, the main food of sea otters, has increased since the sea otter population declined.

(B) Seals do not eat sea otters, nor do they compete with sea otters for food.

(C) Most of the surviving sea otters live in a bay that is inaccessible to orcas.

(D) The population of orcas in the Aleutian Islands has declined since the 1980s.

(E) An increase in commercial fishing near the Aleutian Islands in the 1980s caused a slight decline in the population of the fish that seals use for food.

649. Studies in restaurants show that the tips left by customers who pay their bill in cash tend to be larger when the bill is presented on a tray that bears a credit-card logo. Consumer psychologists hypothesize that simply seeing a credit-card logo makes many credit-card holders willing to spend more because it reminds them that their spending power exceeds the cash they have immediately available.

Which of the following, if true, most strongly supports the psychologists' interpretation of the studies?

(A) The effect noted in the studies is not limited to patrons who have credit cards.

(B) Patrons who are under financial pressure from their credit-card obligations tend to tip less when presented with a restaurant bill on a tray with a credit-card logo than when the tray has no logo.

(C) In virtually all of the cases in the studies, the patrons who paid bills in cash did not possess credit cards.

(D) In general, restaurant patrons who pay their bills in cash leave larger tips than do those who pay by credit card.

(E) The percentage of restaurant bills paid with a given brand of credit card increases when that credit card's logo is displayed on the tray with which the bill is presented.

650. In an experiment, each volunteer was allowed to choose between an easy task and a hard task and was told that another volunteer would do the other task. Each volunteer could also choose to have a computer assign the two tasks randomly. Most volunteers chose the easy task for themselves and under questioning later said they had acted fairly. But when the scenario was described to another group of volunteers, almost all said choosing the easy task would be unfair. This shows that most people apply weaker moral standards to themselves than to others.

Which of the following is an assumption required by this argument?

(A) At least some volunteers who said they had acted fairly in choosing the easy task would have said that it was unfair for someone else to do so.

(B) The most moral choice for the volunteers would have been to have the computer assign the two tasks randomly.

(C) There were at least some volunteers who were assigned to do the hard task and felt that the assignment was unfair.

(D) On average, the volunteers to whom the scenario was described were more accurate in their moral judgments than the other volunteers were.

(E) At least some volunteers given the choice between assigning the tasks themselves and having the computer assign them felt that they had made the only fair choice available to them.

651. Country X's recent stock-trading scandal should not diminish investors' confidence in the country's stock market. For one thing, **the discovery of the scandal confirms that Country X has a strong regulatory system**, as the following considerations show. In any stock market, some fraudulent activity is inevitable. If a stock market is well regulated, any significant stock-trading fraud in it will very likely be discovered. This deters potential perpetrators and facilitates improvement in regulatory processes.

In the argument, the portion in boldface plays which of the following roles?

(A) It is the argument's only conclusion.

(B) It is a conclusion for which the argument provides support and which itself is used to support the argument's main conclusion.

(C) It is the argument's main conclusion and is supported by another explicitly stated conclusion for which further support is provided.

(D) It is an assumption for which no explicit support is provided and is used to support the argument's only conclusion.

(E) It is a compound statement containing both the argument's main conclusion and an assumption used to support that conclusion.

652. **Delta Products Inc. has recently switched at least partly from older technologies using fossil fuels to new technologies powered by electricity.** The question has been raised whether it can be concluded that **for a given level of output Delta's operation now causes less fossil fuel to be consumed than it did formerly.** The answer, clearly, is yes, since the amount of fossil fuel used to generate the electricity needed to power the new technologies is less than the amount needed to power the older technologies, provided level of output is held constant.

In the argument given, the two boldfaced portions play which of the following roles?

(A) The first identifies the content of the conclusion of the argument; the second provides support for that conclusion.
(B) The first provides support for the conclusion of the argument; the second identifies the content of that conclusion.
(C) The first states the conclusion of the argument; the second calls that conclusion into question.
(D) The first provides support for the conclusion of the argument; the second calls that conclusion into question.
(E) Each provides support for the conclusion of the argument.

• 653. Theater Critic: The play *La Finestrina*, now at Central Theater, was written in Italy in the eighteenth century. The director claims that this production is as similar to the original production as is possible in a modern theater. Although the actor who plays Harlequin the clown gives a performance very reminiscent of the twentieth-century American comedian Groucho Marx, Marx's comic style was very much within the comic acting tradition that had begun in sixteenth-century Italy.

The considerations given best serve as part of an argument that

(A) modern audiences would find it hard to tolerate certain characteristics of a historically accurate performance of an eighteenth-century play
(B) Groucho Marx once performed the part of the character Harlequin in *La Finestrina*
(C) in the United States the training of actors in the twentieth century is based on principles that do not differ radically from those that underlay the training of actors in eighteenth-century Italy
(D) the performance of the actor who plays Harlequin in *La Finestrina* does not serve as evidence against the director's claim
(E) the director of *La Finestrina* must have advised the actor who plays Harlequin to model his performance on comic performances of Groucho Marx

654. Although the discount stores in Goreville's central shopping district are expected to close within five years as a result of competition from a SpendLess discount department store that just opened, those locations will not stay vacant for long. In the five years since the opening of Colson's, a nondiscount department store, a new store has opened at the location of every store in the shopping district that closed because it could not compete with Colson's.

Which of the following, if true, most seriously weakens the argument?

(A) Many customers of Colson's are expected to do less shopping there than they did before the SpendLess store opened.
(B) Increasingly, the stores that have opened in the central shopping district since Colson's opened have been discount stores.
(C) At present, the central shopping district has as many stores operating in it as it ever had.
(D) Over the course of the next five years, it is expected that Goreville's population will grow at a faster rate than it has for the past several decades.
(E) Many stores in the central shopping district sell types of merchandise that are not available at either SpendLess or Colson's.

655. Last year all refuse collected by Shelbyville city services was incinerated. This incineration generated a large quantity of residual ash. In order to reduce the amount of residual ash Shelbyville generates this year to half of last year's total, the city has revamped its collection program. This year city services will separate for recycling enough refuse to reduce the number of truckloads of refuse to be incinerated to half of last year's number.

Which of the following is required for the revamped collection program to achieve its aim?

(A) This year, no materials that city services could separate for recycling will be incinerated.
(B) Separating recyclable materials from materials to be incinerated will cost Shelbyville less than half what it cost last year to dispose of the residual ash.
(C) Refuse collected by city services will contain a larger proportion of recyclable materials this year than it did last year.
(D) The refuse incinerated this year will generate no more residual ash per truckload incinerated than did the refuse incinerated last year.
(E) The total quantity of refuse collected by Shelbyville city services this year will be no greater than that collected last year.

656. Veterinarians generally derive some of their income from selling several manufacturers' lines of pet-care products. Knowing that pet owners rarely throw away mail from their pet's veterinarian unread, one manufacturer of pet-care products offered free promotional materials on its products to veterinarians for mailing to their clients. Very few veterinarians accepted the offer, however, even though the manufacturer's products are of high quality.

Which of the following, if true, most helps to explain the veterinarians' reaction to the manufacturer's promotional scheme?

(A) Most of the veterinarians to whom the free promotional materials were offered were already selling the manufacturer's pet-care products to their clients.

(B) The special promotional materials were intended as a supplement to the manufacturer's usual promotional activities rather than as a replacement for them.

(C) The manufacturer's products, unlike most equally good competing products sold by veterinarians, are also available in pet stores and in supermarkets.

(D) Many pet owners have begun demanding quality in products they buy for their pets that is as high as that in products they buy for themselves.

(E) Veterinarians sometimes recommend that pet owners use products formulated for people when no suitable product specially formulated for animals is available.

657. The average hourly wage of television assemblers in Vernland has long been significantly lower than that in neighboring Borodia. Since Borodia dropped all tariffs on Vernlandian televisions three years ago, the number of televisions sold annually in Borodia has not changed. However, recent statistics show a drop in the number of television assemblers in Borodia. Therefore, updated trade statistics will probably indicate that the number of televisions Borodia imports annually from Vernland has increased.

Which of the following is an assumption on which the argument depends?

(A) The number of television assemblers in Vernland has increased by at least as much as the number of television assemblers in Borodia has decreased.

(B) Televisions assembled in Vernland have features that televisions assembled in Borodia do not have.

(C) The average number of hours it takes a Borodian television assembler to assemble a television has not decreased significantly during the past three years.

(D) The number of televisions assembled annually in Vernland has increased significantly during the past three years.

(E) The difference between the hourly wage of television assemblers in Vernland and the hourly wage of television assemblers in Borodia is likely to decrease in the next few years.

658. Guidebook writer: I have visited hotels throughout the country and have noticed that in those built before 1930 the quality of the original carpentry work is generally superior to that in hotels built afterward. Clearly carpenters working on hotels before 1930 typically worked with more skill, care, and effort than carpenters who have worked on hotels built subsequently.

Which of the following, if true, most seriously weakens the guidebook writer's argument?

(A) The quality of original carpentry in hotels is generally far superior to the quality of original carpentry in other structures, such as houses and stores.

(B) Hotels built since 1930 can generally accommodate more guests than those built before 1930.

(C) The materials available to carpenters working before 1930 were not significantly different in quality from the materials available to carpenters working after 1930.

(D) The better the quality of original carpentry in a building, the less likely that building is to fall into disuse and be demolished.

(E) The average length of apprenticeship for carpenters has declined significantly since 1930.

659. Scientists typically do their most creative work before the age of forty. It is commonly thought that this happens because aging by itself brings about a loss of creative capacity. However, studies show that **of scientists who produce highly creative work beyond the age of forty, a disproportionately large number entered their field at an older age than is usual**. Since by the age of forty the large majority of scientists have been working in their field for at least fifteen years, the studies' finding strongly suggests that the real reason why scientists over forty rarely produce highly creative work is not that they have aged but rather that **scientists over forty have generally spent too long in their field**.

In the argument given, the two portions in boldface play which of the following roles?

(A) The first is a claim, the accuracy of which is at issue in the argument; the second is a conclusion drawn on the basis of that claim.

(B) The first is an objection that has been raised against a position defended in the argument; the second is that position.

(C) The first is evidence that has been used to support an explanation that the argument challenges; the second is that explanation.

(D) The first is evidence that has been used to support an explanation that the argument challenges; the second is a competing explanation that the argument favors.

(E) The first provides evidence to support an explanation that the argument favors; the second is that explanation.

660. NorthAir charges low fares for its economy-class seats, but it provides very cramped seating and few amenities. Market research shows that economy passengers would willingly pay more for wider seating and better service, and additional revenue provided by these higher ticket prices would more than cover the additional cost of providing these amenities. Even though NorthAir is searching for ways to improve its profitability, it has decided not to make these improvements.

Which of the following, if true, would most help to explain NorthAir's decision in light of its objectives?

(A) None of NorthAir's competitors offers significantly better seating and service to economy-class passengers than NorthAir does.

(B) On many of the routes that NorthAir flies, it is the only airline to offer direct flights.

(C) A few of NorthAir's economy-class passengers are satisfied with the service they receive, given the low price they pay.

(D) Very few people avoid flying on NorthAir because of the cramped seating and poor service offered in economy class.

(E) The number of people who would be willing to pay the high fares NorthAir charges for its business-class seats would decrease if its economy-class seating were more acceptable.

661. Which of the following most logically completes the argument given?

Asthma, a chronic breathing disorder, is significantly more common today among adult competitive swimmers than it is among competitive athletes who specialize in other sports. Although chlorine is now known to be a lung irritant and swimming pool water is generally chlorinated, it would be rash to assume that frequent exposure to chlorine is the explanation of the high incidence of asthma among these swimmers, since __________.

(A) young people who have asthma are no more likely to become competitive athletes than are young people who do not have asthma

(B) competitive athletes who specialize in sports other than swimming are rarely exposed to chlorine

(C) competitive athletes as a group have a significantly lower incidence of asthma than do people who do not participate in competitive athletics

(D) until a few years ago, physicians routinely recommended competitive swimming to children with asthma, in the belief that this form of exercise could alleviate asthma symptoms

(E) many people have asthma without knowing they have it and thus are not diagnosed with the condition until they begin engaging in very strenuous activities, such as competitive athletics

662. In the country of Marut, the Foreign Trade Agency's records were reviewed in 1994 in light of information then newly available about neighboring Goro. The review revealed that in every year since 1963, the agency's projection of what Goro's gross national product (GNP) would be five years later was a serious underestimate. The review also revealed that in every year since 1963, the agency estimated Goro's GNP for the previous year—a Goro state secret—very accurately.

Of the following claims, which is most strongly supported by the statements given?

(A) Goro's GNP fluctuated greatly between 1963 and 1994.
(B) Prior to 1995, Goro had not released data intended to mislead the agency in making its five-year projections.
(C) The amount by which the agency underestimated the GNP it projected for Goro tended to increase over time.
(D) Even before the new information came to light, the agency had reason to think that at least some of the five-year projections it had made were inaccurate.
(E) The agency's five-year projections of Goro's GNP had no impact on economic planning in Marut.

663. Vargonia has just introduced a legal requirement that student-teacher ratios in government-funded schools not exceed a certain limit. All Vargonian children are entitled to education, free of charge, in these schools. When a recession occurs and average incomes fall, the number of children enrolled in government-funded schools tends to increase. Therefore, though most employment opportunities contract in economic recessions, getting a teaching job in Vargonia's government-funded schools will not be made more difficult by a recession.

Which of the following would be most important to determine in order to evaluate the argument?

(A) Whether in Vargonia there are any schools not funded by the government that offer children an education free of charge
(B) Whether the number of qualified applicants for teaching positions in government-funded schools increases significantly during economic recessions
(C) What the current student-teacher ratio in Vargonia's government-funded schools is
(D) What proportion of Vargonia's workers currently hold jobs as teachers in government-funded schools
(E) Whether in the past a number of government-funded schools in Vargonia have had student-teacher ratios well in excess of the new limit

664. In Colorado subalpine meadows, nonnative dandelions co-occur with a native flower, the larkspur. Bumblebees visit both species, creating the potential for interactions between the two species with respect to pollination. In a recent study, researchers selected 16 plots containing both species; all dandelions were removed from eight plots; the remaining eight control plots were left undisturbed. The control plots yielded significantly more larkspur seeds than the dandelion-free plots, leading the researchers to conclude that the presence of dandelions facilitates pollination (and hence seed production) in the native species by attracting more pollinators to the mixed plots.

Which of the following, if true, most seriously undermines the researchers' reasoning?

(A) Bumblebees preferentially visit dandelions over larkspurs in mixed plots.
(B) In mixed plots, pollinators can transfer pollen from one species to another to augment seed production.
(C) If left unchecked, nonnative species like dandelions quickly crowd out native species.
(D) Seed germination is a more reliable measure of a species' fitness than seed production.
(E) Soil disturbances can result in fewer blooms, and hence lower seed production.

665. An experiment was done in which human subjects recognize a pattern within a matrix of abstract designs and then select another design that completes that pattern. The results of the experiment were surprising. The lowest expenditure of energy in neurons in the brain was found in those subjects who performed most successfully in the experiments.

Which of the following hypotheses best accounts for the findings of the experiment?

(A) The neurons of the brain react less when a subject is trying to recognize patterns than when the subject is doing other kinds of reasoning.

(B) Those who performed best in the experiment experienced more satisfaction when working with abstract patterns than did those who performed less well.

(C) People who are better at abstract pattern recognition have more energy-efficient neural connections.

(D) The energy expenditure of the subjects' brains increases when a design that completes the initially recognized pattern is determined.

(E) The task of completing a given design is more capably performed by athletes, whose energy expenditure is lower when they are at rest.

666. With seventeen casinos, Moneyland operates the most casinos in a certain state. Although intent on expanding, it was outmaneuvered by Apex Casinos in negotiations to acquire the Eldorado chain. To complete its acquisition of Eldorado, Apex must sell five casinos to comply with a state law forbidding any owner to operate more than one casino per county. Since Apex will still be left operating twenty casinos in the state, it will then have the most casinos in the state.

Which of the following, if true, most seriously undermines the prediction?

(A) Apex, Eldorado, and Moneyland are the only organizations licensed to operate casinos in the state.

(B) The majority of Eldorado's casinos in the state will need extensive renovations if they are to continue to operate profitably.

(C) Some of the state's counties do not permit casinos.

(D) Moneyland already operates casinos in the majority of the state's counties.

(E) Apex will use funds it obtains from the sale of the five casinos to help fund its acquisition of the Eldorado chain.

667. It is widely assumed that people need to engage in intellectual activities such as solving crossword puzzles or mathematics problems in order to maintain mental sharpness as they age. In fact, however, simply talking to other people—that is, participating in social interaction, which engages many mental and perceptual skills—suffices. Evidence to this effect comes from a study showing that the more social contact people report, the better their mental skills.

Which of the following, if true, most seriously weakens the force of the evidence cited?

(A) As people grow older, they are often advised to keep exercising their physical and mental capacities in order to maintain or improve them.

(B) Many medical conditions and treatments that adversely affect a person's mental sharpness also tend to increase that person's social isolation.

(C) Many people are proficient both in social interactions and in solving mathematical problems.

(D) The study did not itself collect data but analyzed data bearing on the issue from prior studies.

(E) The tasks evaluating mental sharpness for which data were compiled by the study were more akin to mathematics problems than to conversation.

8.5 Answer Key

544. E
545. C
546. E
547. A
548. A
549. B
550. E
551. E
552. C
553. E
554. A
555. A
556. D
557. B
558. C
559. A
560. C
561. B
562. D
563. D
564. C
565. E
566. E
567. E
568. B
569. A
570. E
571. B
572. E
573. D
574. D
575. E
576. C
577. E
578. D
579. E
580. A
581. A
582. C
583. D
584. E
585. C
586. D
587. C
588. D
589. C
590. E
591. C
592. D
593. A
594. A
595. D
596. C
597. E
598. C
599. C
600. A
601. E
602. D
603. A
604. D
605. A
606. E
607. C
608. A
609. C
610. E
611. A
612. D
613. D
614. C
615. D
616. E
617. D
618. D
619. A
620. A
621. D
622. A
623. E
624. E
625. A
626. D
627. E
628. E
629. E
630. B
631. E
632. D
633. D
634. B
635. A
636. D
637. C
638. B
639. D
640. D
641. A
642. C
643. C
644. B
645. E
646. D
647. A
648. C
649. B
650. A
651. B
652. B
653. D
654. B
655. D
656. C
657. C
658. D
659. E
660. E
661. D
662. D
663. B
664. E
665. C
666. A
667. B

8.6 Answer Explanations

The following discussion is intended to familiarize you with the most efficient and effective approaches to critical reasoning questions. The particular questions in this chapter are generally representative of the kinds of critical reasoning questions you will encounter on the GMAT exam. Remember that it is the problem solving strategy that is important, not the specific details of a particular question.

544. Neuroscientist: Memory evolved to help animals react appropriately to situations they encounter by drawing on the past experience of similar situations. But this does not require that animals perfectly recall every detail of all their experiences. Instead, to function well, memory should generalize from past experiences that are similar to the current one.

The neuroscientist's statements, if true, most strongly support which of the following conclusions?

(A) At least some animals perfectly recall every detail of at least some past experiences.

(B) Perfectly recalling every detail of all their past experiences could help at least some animals react more appropriately than they otherwise would to new situations they encounter.

(C) Generalizing from past experiences requires clear memories of most if not all the details of those experiences.

(D) Recalling every detail of all past experiences would be incompatible with any ability to generalize from those experiences.

(E) Animals can often react more appropriately than they otherwise would to situations they encounter if they draw on generalizations from past experiences of similar situations.

Argument Construction

Situation A neuroscientist claims that memory evolved to help animals learn how to react appropriately by generalizing from past experiences but that this does not require animals to remember all details of those experiences.

Reasoning *What conclusion would the neuroscientist's theory about memory most strongly support?* The neuroscientist asserts that the evolutionary function of memory is to help animals learn to react appropriately by drawing on generalizations from similar experiences they have had. If memory is to serve this function, drawing on generalizations must actually help animals learn to react more appropriately than they otherwise would, even when they do not remember all the details of past experiences.

A Even if no animal ever recalls all the details of any past experience, animals could still learn through generalizations, as the neuroscientist claims.

B This statement could be false even if all of what the neuroscientist says is true. Even if it were never helpful for any animal to recall every detail of all its past experiences, animals could still benefit by learning through generalizations.

C Generalizations from experiences might be made while the experiences are occurring, so that only the generalizations and not the details need to be remembered.

D The neuroscientist only claims that remembering perfect details is not required for memory to serve its function, not that such perfect recall is incompatible with memory serving its function.

E **Correct.** If the evolutionary function of memory is to help animals react more appropriately by drawing on generalizations from past experiences, it follows that animal memories can often successfully serve this function in this manner.

The correct answer is E.

545. Astronomer: Most stars are born in groups of thousands, each star in a group forming from the same parent cloud of gas. Each cloud has a unique, homogeneous chemical composition. Therefore, whenever two stars have the same chemical composition as each other, they must have originated from the same cloud of gas.

Which of the following, if true, would most strengthen the astronomer's argument?

(A) In some groups of stars, not every star originated from the same parent cloud of gas.

(B) Clouds of gas of similar or identical chemical composition may be remote from each other.

(C) Whenever a star forms, it inherits the chemical composition of its parent cloud of gas.

(D) Many stars in vastly different parts of the universe are quite similar in their chemical compositions.

(E) Astronomers can at least sometimes precisely determine whether a star has the same chemical composition as its parent cloud of gas.

Argument Evaluation

Situation Most stars are born in groups, any one of which forms from a parent gas cloud with a unique, homogenous chemical composition.

Reasoning What would be additional evidence that any two stars with the same chemical composition originated from the same gas cloud? The implicit reasoning is that since the chemical composition of each gas cloud is unique and homogenous, any two stars that formed from gas with the same chemical composition must have originated from the same cloud. The astronomer then infers that if two stars have the same composition now, they must have originated from the same cloud. This inference requires the assumption that the composition each star has now depends only on the composition of the cloud in which it originated. Any evidence that supports this assumption will strengthen the argument.

A Whether or not stars born in different clouds of gas are ever in the same "group" is not clearly relevant to whether or not they ever have the same chemical composition.

B How remote clouds of similar compositions are from each other is not clearly relevant to whether stars that have the same chemical composition may have formed from different clouds of gas. Also, the suggestion that different gas clouds may have identical compositions conflicts with the astronomer's premise that the composition of each cloud from which stars form is unique.

C **Correct.** If each star's composition is identical to that of its parent cloud, and each cloud's composition is unique, then any two stars identical in composition must have formed from the same parent cloud.

D If anything, this would suggest that stars with the same composition might have formed from different clouds, so it would weaken rather than strengthen the argument.

E If astronomers could do this, they might be able to obtain additional evidence for or against the position taken in the argument, but this, in itself, provides no reason to suppose that the evidence would support, rather than weaken, that position. They might find that the stars' compositions do not precisely correlate with the compositions of the stars' parent gas clouds.

The correct answer is C.

546. With employer-paid training, workers have the potential to become more productive not only in their present employment but also in any number of jobs with different employers. To increase the productivity of their workforce, many firms are planning to maintain or even increase their investments in worker training. But some training experts object that if a trained worker is hired away by another firm, the employer that paid for the training has merely subsidized a competitor. They note that such hiring has been on the rise in recent years.

Which of the following would, if true, contribute most to defeating the training experts' objection to the firms' strategy?

(A) Firms that promise opportunities for advancement to their employees get, on average, somewhat larger numbers of job applications from untrained workers than do firms that make no such promise.

(B) In many industries, employees that take continuing-education courses are more competitive in the job market.

(C) More and more educational and training institutions are offering reduced tuition fees to firms that subsidize worker training.

(D) Research shows that workers whose training is wholly or partially subsidized by their employer tend to get at least as much training as do workers who pay for all their own training.

(E) For most firms that invest in training their employees, the value added by that investment in employees who stay exceeds the value lost through other employees' leaving to work for other companies.

Evaluation of a Plan

Situation Many firms pay to train their workers in order to increase their workforces' productivity. But in recent years firms have been increasingly hiring away from each other workers who have had such training.

Reasoning *What would most help address the concern that firms that pay to train workers are thereby subsidizing competitors that hire away those workers?* In order for the employer-paid training to be worthwhile for a given firm despite the risk of subsidizing competitors that may hire away the trained workers, that firm has to gain more benefits from the training than it loses by subsidizing such competitors. Any evidence that this is true for most firms would help to address the experts' concern.

A A typical firm does not necessarily want larger numbers of applications from unqualified workers. And if hired, those workers can still be hired away by competitors after the firm has paid to train them, just as the experts warned.

B This suggests that in many industries, companies, rather than investing in employee training, prefer to hire employees who already have specifically relevant training (perhaps funded by other companies). If anything, this slightly supports, rather than defeats, the training experts' view. No firm has an interest in making its own employees more competitive in the job market unless the firm is likely to benefit from their being so.

C Even firms that pay reduced tuition fees for worker training may lose the money they pay for those fees and effectively subsidize competitors that hire the trained employees away. So this does not defeat the training experts' objection.

D The more highly trained workers—regardless of whether their training was company subsidized or not—would presumably be prime targets for recruitment by competing firms, just as the experts warned. The research finding in question does not help defeat the experts' objection.

E **Correct.** This explicitly indicates that most firms gain more than they lose from the general practice of firms paying to train their workers.

The correct answer is E.

547. Candle Corporation's television stations are likely to have more income from advertisers than previously. This is because advertisers prefer to reach people in the 18- to 49-year-old age group and the number of people in that group watching Candle television is increasing. Furthermore, among Candle viewers, the percentage of viewers 18 to 49 years old is increasing.

Which of the following, if true, would most strengthen the argument that Candle Corporation will receive more income from advertisers?

(A) Advertisers carefully monitor the demographic characteristics of television audiences and purchase advertising time to reach the audiences they prefer to reach.

(B) Among people over 49 years old, fewer viewers of Candle stations buy products advertised on television than do viewers of other stations.

(C) There will be increasingly more advertisements on television that are directed at viewers who are over 49 years old.

(D) Candle stations plan to show reruns of television shows during hours when other stations run shows for the first time.

(E) People 18 to 49 years old generally have less disposable income to spend than do people over 49 years old.

Argument Evaluation

Situation Both the number and the percentage of Candle television viewers who are 18 to 49 years old are increasing. Advertisers prefer to reach people in this age group.

Reasoning *What evidence, when combined with the cited facts, would most support the prediction that Candle will receive more income from advertisers?* The argument assumes that the increasing number and percentage of Candle viewers in the age group that advertisers prefer to reach will probably encourage advertisers to spend more on advertising with Candle. This assumption could be supported by evidence that the advertisers realize that Candle is getting more viewers in that preferred age range or by evidence that this awareness will influence the advertisers' purchase of advertising time.

A **Correct.** Advertisers monitoring demographics will probably realize that Candle has increasing numbers of viewers in their preferred age range. If they purchase advertising to reach viewers in that age range, then they will probably purchase more advertising time with Candle.

B This gives advertisers less reason to advertise on Candle to reach viewers over 49 years old. Other things being equal, that makes Candle likely to receive less income from advertisers, not more income.

C Since the percentage of Candle viewers 18 to 49 years old is growing, the percentage over 49 years old is probably shrinking. This could make advertisers seeking to reach older viewers less inclined to advertise on Candle even as they increase their overall television advertising.

D Advertisers are not necessarily inclined to purchase more advertising during showings of reruns than during original airings of television shows and may even be inclined to purchase less advertising during such showings.

E This gives advertisers less incentive to try to reach audiences between 18 and 49 years old and hence less reason to purchase advertising on Candle.

The correct answer is A.

548. A provincial government plans to raise the gasoline tax to give people an incentive to drive less, reducing traffic congestion in the long term. However, skeptics point out that most people in the province live in areas where cars are the only viable transportation to jobs and stores and therefore cannot greatly change their driving habits in response to higher gasoline prices.

In light of the skeptics' objection, which of the following, if true, would most logically support the prediction that the government's plan will achieve its goal of reducing traffic congestion?

(A) The revenue from the tax will be used to make public transportation a viable means of transportation to jobs and stores for far more people.

(B) The tax will encourage many residents to switch to more fuel-efficient cars, reducing air pollution and other problems.

(C) Because gasoline has been underpriced for decades, the province has many neighborhoods where cars are the only viable means of transportation.

(D) Most residents who cannot greatly change their driving habits could compensate for high gasoline prices by reducing other expenses.

(E) Traffic congestion is an especially serious problem for people for whom cars are the only viable means of transportation.

Evaluation of a Plan

Situation A provincial government plans to raise the gasoline tax in order to reduce traffic congestion by discouraging people from driving. But skeptics point out that most people in the province have no viable form of transportation other than driving.

Reasoning *What would suggest that raising the gasoline tax will reduce traffic congestion even though most people in the province have no viable form of transportation other than driving?* The skeptics point out that since most people in the province have no way to reach jobs or stores except by car, they will not be able to reduce their driving much even if the gasoline tax increases. Any evidence that raising the gasoline tax would reduce traffic congestion despite this obstacle would help to support the plan in light of the skeptics' objection.

A **Correct.** If the tax will fund these public transit improvements, then far more people will have a viable means of transportation other than driving, undermining the basis of the skeptics' objection.

B People switching to fuel-efficient cars would not reduce traffic congestion.

C This essentially only tends to support the skeptics' objection. Unless the plan somehow helps to alleviate the necessity of driving (by, for example, making alternative transportation available), the information provided gives no reason to suppose that the higher costs would significantly reduce traffic congestion.

D If residents cannot greatly change their driving habits, then the tax will not reduce traffic congestion.

E This suggests that many residents in the province could benefit if the plan did reduce traffic congestion, but it does not provide a reason to believe the plan will have that effect.

The correct answer is A.

549. Editorial: The roof of Northtown's municipal equipment-storage building collapsed under the weight of last week's heavy snowfall. The building was constructed recently and met local building-safety codes in every particular, except that the nails used for attaching roof supports to the building's columns were of a smaller size than the codes specify for this purpose. Clearly, this collapse exemplifies how even a single, apparently insignificant departure from safety standards can have severe consequences.

Which of the following, if true, most seriously weakens the editorial's argument?

(A) The only other buildings to suffer roof collapses from the weight of the snowfall were older buildings constructed according to less exacting standards than those in the codes.

(B) The amount of snow that accumulated on the roof of the equipment-storage building was greater than the predicted maximum that was used in drawing up the safety codes.

(C) Because the equipment-storage building was not intended for human occupation, some safety-code provisions that would have applied to an office building did not apply to it.

(D) The municipality of Northtown itself has the responsibility for ensuring that buildings constructed within its boundaries meet the provisions of the building-safety codes.

(E) Because the equipment-storage building was used for storing snow-removal equipment, the building was almost completely empty when the roof collapsed.

Argument Evaluation

Situation The roof of a recently constructed building collapsed under heavy snowfall. The only way the building did not meet safety standards was that some nails for the roof supports were smaller than prescribed by the building codes.

Reasoning *What would make it less likely that the building's collapse resulted from a single, apparently minor departure from safety standards?* The building met safety standards except for the size of the nails. So if the collapse exemplifies how a departure from safety standards can have severe consequences, as the conclusion claims, then the size of the nails had to be responsible for the collapse. Thus, evidence that a factor other than the size of the nails could fully account for the collapse would weaken the argument.

A This suggests that the snow would not have been heavy enough to collapse the roof if the construction had completely met the safety standards, so it strengthens, rather than weakens, the argument.

B **Correct.** This suggests that the snow could have collapsed the roof even if the nails had met the safety standards, thus casting doubt on the assumption that the nails' inadequacy was responsible for the collapse.

C The claim that the safety requirements for this building were weaker than some others tends slightly to strengthen, rather than weaken, the hypothesis that the bad consequences resulted partly from a failure to comply. Even if safety-code provisions for an equipment-storage building differ from those for an office building, they may still be adequate to ensure the roof's stability.

D The question of who was responsible for ensuring compliance with the safety codes is irrelevant to whether a failure to comply was responsible for the roof's collapse.

E This suggests that the alleged consequences of failing to meet safety standards were less severe than they could have been, but it is irrelevant to determining the cause of the collapse.

The correct answer is B.

550. Political theorist: Even with the best spies, area experts, and satellite surveillance, foreign policy assessments can still lack important information. In such circumstances intuitive judgment is vital. A national leader with such judgment can make good decisions about foreign policy even when current information is incomplete, since ______.

Which of the following, if true, most logically completes the argument?

(A) the central reason for failure in foreign policy decision making is the absence of critical information
(B) those leaders whose foreign policy decisions have been highly ranked have also been found to have good intuitive judgment
(C) both intuitive judgment and good information are required for sound decision making
(D) good foreign policy decisions often lead to improved methods of gathering information
(E) intuitive judgment can produce good decisions based on past experience, even when there are important gaps in current information

Argument Construction

Situation National leaders sometimes must make foreign policy decisions while lacking important information.

Reasoning *What would most help support the claim that a national leader with intuitive judgment can make good foreign policy decisions without complete information?* The word *since* preceding the blank indicates that the blank should be filled with a premise supporting the statement immediately before the blank. So an observation that supports the claim that a national leader with intuitive judgment can make good foreign policy decisions without complete information would logically complete the argument.

A This gives us no reason to suppose that intuitive judgment helps national leaders avoid such failures.

B This does not specify who ranked the foreign policy decisions, nor how they determined the rankings, so it gives us no reason to accept those rankings. For all we know, the anonymous rankers may have used the dubious rankings they created as the sole evidence for their so-called findings about which leaders have good intuitive judgment.

C This implies that intuitive judgment alone is inadequate without good information, so it undermines rather than supports the claim that national leaders can make good foreign policy decisions with intuitive judgment while lacking complete information.

D This gives us no reason to suppose that good foreign policy decisions can be made in the first place by leaders lacking important information.

E **Correct.** This suggests that national leaders can make good foreign policy decisions using intuitive judgment based on their past foreign policy experience, even without complete information about the current situations they're facing.

The correct answer is E.

551. During the earliest period of industrialization in Britain, steam engines were more expensive to build and operate than either windmills or water mills, the other practicable sources of power for factories. Yet despite their significant cost disadvantage, steam-powered factories were built in large numbers well before technical improvements brought their cost down. Furthermore, they were built even in regions where geographical conditions permitted the construction of wind- and water-powered factories close to major markets.

Which of the following, if true, most helps to explain the proliferation of steam-powered factories during the earliest period of industrialization in Britain?

(A) In many areas of Britain, there were fewer steam-powered factories than wind- or water-powered factories in the earliest period of industrialization.

(B) Unlike wind- or water-powered factories, steam-powered factories were fueled with coal, which sometimes had to be transported significant distances from the mine to the site of the factory.

(C) It was both difficult and expensive to convert a factory from wind power or water power to steam power.

(D) In the early period of industrialization, many goods sold in towns and cities could not be mass-produced in factories.

(E) In Britain, the number of sites where a wind- or water-powered factory could be built was insufficient to provide for all of the demand for factory-produced goods at the time.

Argument Construction

Situation Although steam engines were more expensive than windmills and water mills in early industrial Britain, many steam-powered factories were built even in regions where the construction of wind- and water-powered factories was geographically feasible.

Reasoning *Why might steam-powered factories have proliferated despite their cost disadvantage?* Early industrialists would have needed some positive reason to choose steam over less expensive power sources for their factories. For example, steam engines might have operated faster or more effectively than windmills or water mills. Or steam engines might have received government subsidies. Or conditions restricting the number or locations of windmills and water mills might have forced industrialists to use steam power instead.

A This suggests that the steam-powered factories did not initially proliferate as widely as they might have, but it does not explain why they proliferated to the extent that they did.

B The inconvenience of transporting coal for steam-powered factories would have made those factories less likely to proliferate, not more likely.

C The difficulty of converting factories to steam power would have made steam-powered factories less likely to proliferate, not more likely.

D The technological inability to mass-produce popular products in factories would have made factories in general less likely to proliferate, including steam-powered factories.

E **Correct.** The inadequate number of sites for wind- and water-powered factories might have encouraged early industrialists to build steam-powered factories instead, since the high demand for factory-produced goods could have made these factories profitable despite their cost disadvantage.

The correct answer is E.

552. Snowmaking machines work by spraying a mist that freezes immediately on contact with cold air. Because the sudden freezing kills bacteria, QuickFreeze is planning to market a wastewater purification system that works on the same principle. The process works only when temperatures are cold, however, so municipalities using it will still need to maintain a conventional system.

Which of the following, if true, provides the strongest grounds for a prediction that municipalities will buy QuickFreeze's purification system despite the need to maintain a conventional purification system as well?

(A) Bacteria are not the only impurities that must be removed from wastewater.

(B) Many municipalities have old wastewater purification systems that need to be replaced.

(C) Conventional wastewater purification systems have not been fully successful in killing bacteria at cold temperatures.

(D) During times of warm weather, when it is not in use, QuickFreeze's purification system requires relatively little maintenance.

(E) Places where the winters are cold rarely have a problem of water shortage.

Evaluation of a Plan

Situation QuickFreeze is planning to market wastewater purification systems that work by spraying a mist that freezes on contact with cold air. The sudden freezing kills bacteria. Because the system works only at cold temperatures, municipalities using it will still need to maintain a conventional system.

Reasoning *Which statement provides the strongest grounds for thinking that at least some municipalities will buy the purification system despite the need to maintain a conventional purification system as well?* The passage tells us why a municipality using a QuickFreeze wastewater purification system would still need a conventional system. But why would a municipality want the QuickFreeze system *in addition* to a conventional system? If conventional systems are not fully effective at cold temperatures, the QuickFreeze system would allow municipalities that sometimes experience cold temperatures to purify their wastewater more effectively.

A There is no basis in the passage for determining whether the QuickFreeze system will help remove impurities other than bacteria from wastewater. If it does not, this answer choice implies that the QuickFreeze system would not be sufficient for purifying wastewater. This would actually undermine the prediction.

B The passage states that municipalities using the QuickFreeze system would still need a conventional system. Thus, the old conventional wastewater systems would still need to be replaced with new conventional systems. This answer choice provides no reason to think municipalities would buy the QuickFreeze system.

C **Correct.** This statement, if true, would strengthen the prediction, because it provides a valid reason why the QuickFreeze system could be needed alongside conventional ones: it is more effective in cold weather.

D Although this claim does undercut one reason for thinking municipalities might *not* be likely to purchase the QuickFreeze system, it provides little reason to think that they will purchase such a system. Perhaps in times of cold weather, the QuickFreeze system is very expensive to maintain.

E The issue of whether or not there are water shortages in places where winters are cold is not directly relevant. If conventional wastewater systems are sufficient to purify water in such places, municipalities would not need the QuickFreeze system (as they would still need to maintain a conventional purification system).

The correct answer is C.

553. Suncorp, a new corporation with limited funds, has been clearing large sections of the tropical Amazon forest for cattle ranching. This practice continues even though greater profits can be made from rubber tapping, which does not destroy the forest, than from cattle ranching, which does destroy the forest.

Which of the following, if true, most helps to explain why Suncorp has been pursuing the less profitable of the two economic activities mentioned above?

(A) The soil of the Amazon forest is very rich in nutrients that are important in the development of grazing lands.

(B) Cattle-ranching operations that are located in tropical climates are more profitable than cattle-ranching operations that are located in cold-weather climates.

(C) In certain districts, profits made from cattle ranching are more heavily taxed than profits made from any other industry.

(D) Some of the cattle that are raised on land cleared in the Amazon are killed by wildcats.

(E) The amount of money required to begin a rubber-tapping operation is twice as high as the amount needed to begin a cattle ranch.

Argument Construction

Situation Suncorp is a new corporation with limited funds. It has been clearing large sections of the tropical Amazon forest for ranching, even though rubber-tapping would be more profitable.

Reasoning *What would explain why Suncorp is clearing sections of the rain forest for ranching, even though rubber tapping would be more profitable?* Because Suncorp has limited funds, if rubber tapping has much higher start-up costs, Suncorp might not have enough money to start rubber-tapping operations. If cattle ranching has much lower start-up costs than rubber tapping, Suncorp might be able to afford such an operation.

A This statement gives a reason why cattle ranching in the Amazon might be more profitable than one might otherwise think it would be. However, we already know from the passage that rubber tapping would be more profitable than cattle ranching. So, this answer choice does not help explain why cattle ranching might be preferable to rubber tapping.

B The comparison between the profitableness of cattle ranching in tropical climates and in cold-weather climates is irrelevant. The passage only covers cattle ranching in the tropical Amazon forest. This answer choice would at most explain why Suncorp is undertaking cattle ranching in the Amazon rather than in some cold-weather location.

C This statement makes what needs to be explained harder to understand, for it indicates that cattle ranching in the Amazon might be less profitable than one would otherwise think.

D Like answer choice (C), this statement indicates a disadvantage of cattle ranching in the Amazon. So, it does not explain why cattle ranching would be preferred to some other economic activity.

E **Correct.** Because it costs less to begin cattle ranching than it does to begin rubber tapping, Suncorp—which has limited funds—would have a reason to pursue cattle ranching over a potentially more profitable activity.

The correct answer is E.

554. Archaeologists use technology to analyze ancient sites. It is likely that this technology will advance considerably in the near future, allowing archaeologists to gather more information than is currently possible. If they study certain sites now, they risk contaminating or compromising them for future studies. Therefore, in order to maximize the potential for gathering knowledge in the long run, a team of archaeologists plans to delay the examination of a newly excavated site.

Which of the following would be most useful to investigate for the purpose of evaluating the plan's prospects for achieving its goal?

(A) Whether any of the contents of the site will significantly deteriorate before the anticipated technology is available
(B) Whether there will continue to be improvements on the relevant technology
(C) Whether the team can study a site other than the newly excavated site for the time being
(D) Whether the site was inhabited by a very ancient culture
(E) Whether the anticipated technology will damage objects under study

Evaluation of a Plan

Situation To avoid prematurely compromising a newly excavated site, an archaeological team plans to postpone examining it until more advanced technology is developed that will let them gather more information from it. Their goal is to maximize the potential for gathering knowledge.

Reasoning *What would be most helpful to investigate in order to assess how likely it is that delaying examination of the site will maximize the potential for gathering knowledge from it?* In order to maximize (or even increase) the potential for gathering knowledge from the site by delaying its examination, the risk of compromising the site by examining it now has to be greater than the risk that the site will be compromised as much or more by delaying the examination. The delay might also increase the risk that the site will never be examined at all—for example, the team might lose its funding while it delays, or changes in local political conditions might prevent the site's future examination. Investigating any of these risks could be helpful in assessing the likelihood that the team's plan will achieve its goal.

A **Correct.** If any of the site's contents will significantly deteriorate before the technology becomes available, that could reduce the ability to gather future information from the site even more than examining and compromising the site now would.

B The passage already tells us that it is likely the technology *will advance considerably in the near future*. Given this information, further inquiry into whether there will be any ongoing (perhaps minor) improvements is somewhat redundant and probably of minimal value with respect to evaluating the plan's likelihood of success.

C Even if the team can study a second site in the meanwhile, they might maximize the overall potential for gathering knowledge by delaying the examination of either site, both sites, or neither site until more advanced technology is available.

D The age of the culture that inhabited the site is irrelevant to assessing the risks of delaying the site's examination until more advanced technology is available.

E Even if the anticipated technology will damage or destroy the objects under study, it might still maximize the amount of knowledge that can be gathered from those objects. Without any comparison between the damage risk that would be incurred by proceeding with the current technology and the damage risk that would be incurred by waiting, the mere fact that some damage would occur is irrelevant.

The correct answer is A.

555. A newly discovered painting seems to be the work of one of two seventeenth-century artists, either the northern German Johannes Drechen or the Frenchman Louis Birelle, who sometimes painted in the same style as Drechen. Analysis of the carved picture frame, which has been identified as the painting's original seventeenth-century frame, showed that it is made of wood found widely in northern Germany at the time, but rare in the part of France where Birelle lived. This shows that the painting is most likely the work of Drechen.

Which of the following is an assumption that the argument requires?

(A) The frame was made from wood local to the region where the picture was painted.

(B) Drechen is unlikely to have ever visited the home region of Birelle in France.

(C) Sometimes a painting so resembles others of its era that no expert is able to confidently decide who painted it.

(D) The painter of the picture chose the frame for the picture.

(E) The carving style of the picture frame is not typical of any specific region of Europe.

Argument Construction

Situation The original frame of a seventeenth-century painting that seems to be by either the northern German Johannes Drechen or the Frenchman Louis Birelle is made of a type of wood much more common in northern Germany than in France, suggesting that Drechen was the painter.

Reasoning *What must be true in order for the facts presented to support the conclusion that the painting is by Drechen?* The argument is that in the seventeenth century, the type of wood in the frame was more common in northern Germany where Drechen was from than in France where Birelle was from, so probably Drechen painted the picture. In order for this inference to be plausible, the argument must implicitly assume that the frame's wood was from the same region the painter was from. And in order to justify this assumed connection between the wood and the region the painter was from, the argument must also assume that the painter painted the picture in that region.

A **Correct.** If the frame were not made of wood local to the region where the picture was painted, or if that region in turn were not where the painter was from, then the cited fact about where the wood was more common would be irrelevant to the conclusion about who painted the picture.

B The argument is compatible with the plausible hypothesis that Drechen visited France at some point during his lifetime but did not frame this or any painting with French wood.

C Even if experts always felt confident in deciding who painted any picture, examining the wood in the picture frame might help them decide correctly.

D The argument is compatible with the plausible hypothesis that the picture was sold to a local customer who then chose a frame of local wood.

E The argument would be even stronger if this were false and the carving style of the frame were typical of northern Germany specifically.

The correct answer is A.

556. Beginning in 1966 all new cars sold in Morodia were required to have safety belts and power steering. Previously, most cars in Morodia were without these features. Safety belts help to prevent injuries in collisions, and power steering helps to avoid collisions in the first place. But even though in 1966 one-seventh of the cars in Morodia were replaced with new cars, the number of car collisions and collision-related injuries did not decline.

Which of the following, if true about Morodia, most helps to explain why the number of collisions and collision-related injuries in Morodia failed to decline in 1966?

(A) Because of a driver-education campaign, most drivers and passengers in cars that did have safety belts used them in 1966.

(B) Most of the new cars bought in 1966 were bought in the months of January and February.

(C) In 1965, substantially more than one-seventh of the cars in Morodia were replaced with new cars.

(D) An excessive reliance on the new safety features led many owners of new cars to drive less cautiously in 1966 than before.

(E) The seat belts and power steering put into new cars sold in 1966 had to undergo strict quality-control inspections by manufacturers, whether the cars were manufactured in Morodia or not.

Argument Construction

Situation Starting in 1966, new cars sold in Morodia were required to have safety belts and power steering. But the numbers of car collisions and collision-related injuries did not decline that year.

Reasoning *What could explain why the newly required safety features did not reduce the numbers of collisions and collision-related injuries in 1966?* The passage says that power steering helps to prevent collisions and that safety belts help to prevent collision-related injuries. Since most Morodian cars previously lacked these features, and one-seventh of them were replaced with new cars in 1966, the proportion of cars with these features must have increased that year. This should have reduced the numbers of collisions and collision-related injuries unless some other factor counteracted the reductions. Evidence of any such countervailing factor would help to explain why the numbers did not decrease.

A Increased usage of safety belts should have reduced the number of collision-related injuries, so it would not help explain why this number did not decrease.

B If the new cars bought in 1966 were mostly purchased early in the year, the increased proportion of cars with the newly required safety features should have started more significantly reducing the numbers of collisions and collision-related injuries early in the year, producing greater reductions for the year as a whole.

C However, many cars were replaced in the year before the safety features were required, in 1966 the replacement of one-seventh of all Morodian cars should still have increased the overall proportion of Morodian cars with the safety features and thus reduced the numbers of collisions and collision-related injuries.

D **Correct.** If many owners of the cars with the new safety features drove less cautiously, their recklessness could have increased the overall numbers of collisions and collision-related injuries despite any benefits from the safety features.

E Strict quality-control inspections should have made the safety features more reliable, further reducing the numbers of collisions and collision-related injuries.

The correct answer is D.

557. In order to reduce the number of items damaged while in transit to customers, packaging consultants recommended that the TrueSave mail-order company increase the amount of packing material so as to fill any empty spaces in its cartons. Accordingly, TrueSave officials instructed the company's packers to use more packing material than before, and the packers zealously acted on these instructions and used as much as they could. Nevertheless, customer reports of damaged items rose somewhat.

Which of the following, if true, most helps to explain why acting on the consultants' recommendation failed to achieve its goal?

(A) The change in packing policy led to an increase in expenditure on packing material and labor.

(B) When packing material is compressed too densely, it loses some of its capacity to absorb shock.

(C) The amount of packing material used in a carton does not significantly influence the ease with which a customer can unpack the package.

(D) Most of the goods that TrueSave ships are electronic products that are highly vulnerable to being damaged in transit.

(E) TrueSave has lost some of its regular customers as a result of the high number of damaged items they received.

Evaluation of a Plan

Situation Mail-order company TrueSave wants to reduce the number of items damaged while in transit to customers. Packaging consultants recommended that to achieve this goal, the company should use more packing material to fill empty spaces in its cartons. The company's packers began using as much packing material as they could, yet reports of damaged items rose rather than fell.

Reasoning *What would help explain why the company's acting on the recommendation did not achieve its goal?* The recommendation involved increasing the amount of packing material, so there must have been something about that increase that led to more damage. More damage would be likely to result if stuffing more packing material into shipping boxes made the packaging less effective.

A An increase in expenditure on packing material and labor might affect the company's profitability, but it would have no effect on whether items were damaged in transit.

B **Correct.** This statement adequately explains why more items, rather than fewer, were damaged in transit.

C If customers were able to remove their items just as easily from boxes filled with more packing material as from boxes using less packing material, the items would be unaffected by an increase in the amount of packing material used.

D The kind of goods TrueSave ships most frequently is not relevant to the question of why increasing the amount of packing material failed to reduce the number of items damaged in transit, since they most likely shipped this same kind of goods both before and after making the recommended change.

E The loss of regular customers helps explain why TrueSave turned to the packaging consultants for help, but it does not help explain why those consultants' recommendation failed to reduce the number of items damaged in transit.

The correct answer is B.

558. Parland's alligator population has been declining in recent years, primarily because of hunting. Alligators prey heavily on a species of freshwater fish that is highly valued as food by Parlanders, who had hoped that the decline in the alligator population would lead to an increase in the numbers of these fish available for human consumption. Yet the population of this fish species has also declined, even though the annual number caught for human consumption has not increased.

Which of the following, if true, most helps to explain the decline in the population of the fish species?

(A) The decline in the alligator population has meant that fishers can work in some parts of lakes and rivers that were formerly too dangerous.

(B) Over the last few years, Parland's commercial fishing enterprises have increased the number of fishing boats they use.

(C) The main predator of these fish is another species of fish on which alligators also prey.

(D) Many Parlanders who hunt alligators do so because of the high market price of alligator skins, not because of the threat alligators pose to the fish population.

(E) In several neighboring countries through which Parland's rivers also flow, alligators are at risk of extinction as a result of extensive hunting.

Argument Construction

Situation Due to hunting, Parland's alligator population has been declining. Parlanders had hoped that the population of a certain prized species of freshwater fish that alligators prey on would have increased as a result, but the population of this freshwater fish has actually declined.

Reasoning *What would explain why the population of the freshwater species has declined?* Suppose alligators prey not only on the prized freshwater fish but also on another species of fish that is the main predator of those fish. If there are fewer alligators to prey on the predator fish, there may well be more of the predator fish. An increase in the population of the predator fish could help explain why the population of the prized freshwater fish has declined: there are now more of the predator fish around to prey on them.

A Though this statement suggests that the population of the prized fish species may have declined due to their being caught in greater numbers by fishers, the passage tells us that the number of these fish caught for human consumption has not increased. Therefore, this statement cannot explain the species' decline in population.

B The passage tells us that the number of fish caught for human consumption has not increased. This answer choice does not provide any explanation for why the population of these fish has declined.

C **Correct.** Since alligators prey on the predator fish, a decline in the alligator population could result in an increase in the population of the predator fish, which could lead to an increase in nonhuman consumption of the prized freshwater fish.

D We already know from the passage that hunting has led to a decline in the population of alligators. It is irrelevant what motivated the hunting of alligators.

E The fact that alligators are at risk of extinction due to hunting in neighboring countries does not help explain why the prized freshwater fish species is declining in population. If it is puzzling why the fish population is declining despite the reduction in Parland's alligator population, it would be just as puzzling if the alligator population elsewhere was declining.

The correct answer is C.

559. A certain automaker aims to increase its market share by deeply discounting its vehicles' prices for the next several months. The discounts will cut into profits, but because they will be heavily advertised the manufacturer hopes that they will attract buyers away from rival manufacturers' cars. In the longer term, the automaker envisions that customers initially attracted by the discounts may become loyal customers.

In assessing the plan's chances of achieving its aim, it would be most useful to know which of the following?

(A) Whether the automaker's competitors are likely to respond by offering deep discounts on their own products
(B) Whether the advertisements will be created by the manufacturer's current advertising agency
(C) Whether some of the automaker's models will be more deeply discounted than others
(D) Whether the automaker will be able to cut costs sufficiently to maintain profit margins even when the discounts are in effect
(E) Whether an alternative strategy might enable the automaker to enhance its profitability while holding a constant or diminishing share of the market

Evaluation of a Plan

Situation An automaker is planning to offer deep discounts on its vehicles' prices in order to increase its market share. The automaker's profit margins will be reduced by this action. By advertising the discounts, the automaker hopes to attract customers who might otherwise be inclined to buy rival manufacturers' cars. These customers would ideally then develop loyalty to the automaker's cars.

Reasoning *What would it be most useful to know in assessing whether offering deep discounts will enable the automaker to increase its market share?* To achieve an increase in market share, the automaker would have to take customers away from other automakers. Under what circumstances would other automakers be able to retain their customers, if those customers are more likely to purchase cars from automakers that offer deep discounts (and then remain loyal to those automakers)? The other automakers might try to retain their customers by matching the discounts. Thus it would be useful to know whether the other automakers would indeed offer such discounts.

A **Correct.** If the answer to this question were yes, the plan would probably not achieve its aim of increasing market share. If the answer were no, the plan would have a good chance of succeeding.

B Since there is no information about the effectiveness of the automaker's current advertising, it would not be useful to know whether the same advertising agency will produce the ads publicizing the discount.

C Knowing whether some models will be more deeply discounted than others might help in assessing which of the automaker's models will sell best, but it would not help in assessing the overall chance of the automaker increasing its market share.

D The discounts the automaker plans to offer will cut into profits, according to the information given, so the question of whether the automaker can maintain profit margins while the discounts are in effect has already been answered.

E While it might be useful to the automaker to know about alternative strategies, such knowledge does not help in assessing the likelihood that the plan under discussion will achieve its aim.

The correct answer is A.

560. In virtually any industry, technological improvements increase labor productivity, which is the output of goods and services per person-hour worked. In Parland's industries, labor productivity is significantly higher than it is in Vergia's industries. Clearly, therefore, Parland's industries must, on the whole, be further advanced technologically than Vergia's are.

The argument is most vulnerable to which of the following criticisms?

(A) It offers a conclusion that is no more than a paraphrase of one of the pieces of information provided in its support.
(B) It presents as evidence in support of a claim information that is inconsistent with other evidence presented in support of the same claim.
(C) It takes one possible cause of a condition to be the actual cause of that condition without considering any other possible causes.
(D) It takes a condition to be the effect of something that happened only after the condition already existed.
(E) It makes a distinction that presupposes the truth of the conclusion that is to be established.

Argument Evaluation

Situation Technological improvements in nearly every industry increase labor productivity, which is the output of goods and services per person-hour worked. Because labor productivity is significantly higher in Parland than Vergia, Parland's industries are, in general, more technologically advanced than Vergia's.

Reasoning *To which criticism is the argument most vulnerable?* Though one factor, such as technological advancements, may lead to greater labor productivity, it may not be the only such factor, or even a necessary factor, leading to great labor productivity. Therefore, the mere fact that one region's labor is more productive than another's is not sufficient to establish that the former region is more technologically advanced than the latter region is.

A The conclusion is not merely a paraphrase of the pieces of information provided in its support. Indeed, the problem with the argument is that the conclusion goes too far beyond what the premises merit.

B The premises of the argument are not inconsistent with one another.

C **Correct.** This accurately describes the flaw in the argument because the reasons given in the argument for its conclusion would be good reasons only if there were no other plausible explanations for Parland's greater labor productivity.

D The argument does not mention how long Parland has had more productive labor, or when technological improvements would have occurred.

E Neither of the premises contains anything that presupposes the conclusion to be true.

The correct answer is C.

561. Chaco Canyon, a settlement of the ancient Anasazi culture in North America, had massive buildings. **It must have been a major Anasazi center**. Analysis of wood samples shows that some of the timber for the buildings came from the Chuska and San Mateo mountains, 50 miles from Chaco Canyon. **Only a major cultural center would have the organizational power to import timber from 50 miles away**.

In the argument given, the two portions in boldface play which of the following roles?

(A) The first is a premise used to support the argument's main conclusion; the second is the argument's main conclusion.

(B) The first is the argument's main conclusion; the second is a premise used to support that conclusion.

(C) The first is one of two premises used to support the argument's main conclusion; the second is the other of those two premises.

(D) The first is a premise used to support the argument's main conclusion; the second is a premise used to support another conclusion drawn in the argument.

(E) The first is inferred from another statement in the argument; the second is inferred from the first.

Argument Construction

Situation The ancient Anasazi settlement at Chaco Canyon had massive buildings, for which some of the timber came from mountains 50 miles away.

Reasoning *What roles do the statement that Chaco Canyon must have been a major Anasazi center and the statement that only a major center would have the organizational power to import timber from 50 miles away play in the argument?* The first and third sentences in the passage are both factual observations. Since no further support is provided for either of them, neither can be a conclusion in the argument. The fourth sentence is a speculative generalization about major cultural centers. None of the other statements gives us any reason to think this generalization is true, so it cannot be a conclusion in the argument, either. However, the third and fourth sentences together imply that Chaco Canyon was a major cultural center, and the first sentence indicates that it was Anasazi. So together, the first, third, and fourth sentences all support the claim that Chaco Canyon was a major Anasazi cultural center and thus more generally a major Anasazi center, as the second sentence asserts. Therefore, the first, third, and fourth sentences are all premises that jointly support the second sentence as a conclusion.

A As explained above, the first boldface sentence is a conclusion supported by the latter, not the other way around.

B **Correct.** As explained above, the first boldface sentence is the argument's only stated conclusion, and in that sense its main conclusion, while all the other sentences are premises used to support it.

C As explained above, the first boldface sentence is the argument's conclusion, not a premise used to support the conclusion.

D As explained above, the first boldface sentence is the argument's only stated conclusion, and there is no reason to suppose that the argument is intended to lead to any other tacit conclusion that the second boldface sentence is intended to support.

E As explained above, the first boldface sentence is inferred from the three other statements in the argument together, not from any one of them alone. The second boldface sentence is a speculative generalization that cannot be, and is not meant to be, inferred from the former or from any other statement in the argument.

The correct answer is B.

562. The Maxilux car company's design for its new luxury model, the Max 100, included a special design for the tires that was intended to complement the model's image. The winning bid for supplying these tires was submitted by Rubco. Analysts concluded that the bid would only just cover Rubco's costs on the tires, but Rubco executives claim that winning the bid will actually make a profit for the company.

Which of the following, if true, most strongly justifies the claim made by Rubco's executives?

(A) In any Maxilux model, the spare tire is exactly the same make and model as the tires that are mounted on the wheels.

(B) Rubco holds exclusive contracts to supply Maxilux with the tires for a number of other models made by Maxilux.

(C) The production facilities for the Max 100 and those for the tires to be supplied by Rubco are located very near each other.

(D) When people who have purchased a carefully designed luxury automobile need to replace a worn part of it, they almost invariably replace it with a part of exactly the same make and type.

(E) When Maxilux awarded the tire contract to Rubco, the only criterion on which Rubco's bid was clearly ahead of its competitors' bids was price.

Argument Construction

Situation Rubco won a bid for supplying tires for the Max 100, a new luxury model by Maxilux. The bid would barely cover the cost of the tires, but Rubco executives claim that winning the bid will be profitable.

Reasoning *What would support the executives' claim?* Rubco is not expected to make a profit from supplying the tires for the new cars, so we must look for some other way that Rubco could derive a profit as a result of winning the bid. If by winning the bid Rubco created an inevitable market for itself in replacement tires—on which Rubco could earn a profit—then the executives' claim may be justified.

A We have already been told that the bid is expected to barely cover the costs of supplying the tires on the new cars, so the analysts mentioned in the passage have presumably already taken into account that there is a spare tire supplied for the Max 100.

B If winning the bid led Rubco to win more exclusive contracts with the Maxilux, that might help support the executives' claim. But this statement indicates only that Rubco already has several exclusive contracts to supply Maxilux with tires, not that winning the bid has led to, or will lead to, more such contracts, which is what would be needed.

C As in answer choice (A), this is relevant to the costs of supplying the tires for the Max 100, but presumably this was taken into account by the analysts when they concluded that the bid would barely cover Rubco's costs on the tires.

D **Correct.** This indicates that by winning the bid Rubco has created a way to profit from the contract with Maxilux, specifically, by creating a market for replacement tires.

E This is likely one of the reasons that Rubco's bid only just covers Rubco's costs on the tires; it does nothing to justify the executives' claims that the bid will lead to a profit for Rubco.

The correct answer is D.

563. Which of the following most logically completes the passage?

Most bicycle helmets provide good protection for the top and back of the head, but little or no protection for the temple regions on the sides of the head. A study of head injuries resulting from bicycle accidents showed that a large proportion were caused by blows to the temple area. Therefore, if bicycle helmets protected this area, the risk of serious head injury in bicycle accidents would be greatly reduced, especially since ________.

(A) among the bicyclists included in the study's sample of head injuries, only a very small proportion had been wearing a helmet at the time of their accident

(B) even those bicyclists who regularly wear helmets have a poor understanding of the degree and kind of protection that helmets afford

(C) a helmet that included protection for the temples would have to be somewhat larger and heavier than current helmets

(D) the bone in the temple area is relatively thin and impacts in that area are thus very likely to cause brain injury

(E) bicyclists generally land on their arm or shoulder when they fall to the side, which reduces the likelihood of severe impacts on the side of the head

Argument Construction

Situation Bicycle helmets protect the top and back of the head, but not the sides or temples. A study found that a large proportion of head injuries caused by biking accidents were caused by blows to the temple area.

Reasoning *Why would the risk of serious head injury in bicycle accidents be greatly reduced if bicycle helmets protected the temple regions?* If for some reason a serious head injury is particularly likely when there is impact to the temple area, then bicycle helmets that protect that area would be apt to reduce the number of serious head injuries from bicycle accidents. One such reason is that the bone in the temple area is relatively thin.

A This point is irrelevant because it gives us no information about the seriousness or the likelihood of injuries due to impact to the temple area.

B Whether bicyclists who regularly wear helmets have a good understanding of what protection their helmets afford is not relevant as to whether serious head injuries are particularly likely to occur from impact to the temple area.

C This point is relevant only to what a helmet that protected the temple area would be like, not to the seriousness of injuries resulting from impact to that area. If anything, this point counts as a reason *against* the conclusion, not *for* it. If such helmets are heavier and larger, they may be used less than they otherwise would be. If fewer helmets are used, then improvements to helmet design will have less of an effect in reducing serious head injuries.

D **Correct.** This statement provides a reason why the temple area of the rider's head needs protection: impacts to this area are very likely to cause brain injuries.

E This is largely irrelevant. Even if it suggests that head injuries do not generally result from bicyclists falling to the side, it does not indicate that such injuries are rare or that there is not great risk of serious injury in those cases in which there is impact to the temple area.

The correct answer is D.

564. Which of the following most logically completes the argument?

In a typical year, Innovair's airplanes are involved in 35 collisions while parked or being towed in airports, with a resulting yearly cost of $1,000,000 for repairs.

To reduce the frequency of ground collisions, Innovair will begin giving its ground crews additional training, at an annual cost of $500,000. Although this will cut the number of ground collisions by about half at best, the drop in repair costs can be expected to be much greater, since ________.

(A) most ground collisions happen when ground crews are rushing to minimize the time a delayed airplane spends on the ground
(B) a ground collision typically occurs when there are no passengers on the airplane
(C) the additional training will focus on helping ground crews avoid those kinds of ground collisions that cause the most costly damage
(D) the $500,000 cost figure for the additional training of ground crews includes the wages that those crews will earn during the time spent in actual training
(E) most ground collisions have been caused by the least experienced ground-crew members

Evaluation of a Plan

Situation An airline will give its ground crews additional training to reduce the frequency of the collisions its airplanes are involved in while parked or being towed in airports.

Reasoning *What premise would most logically support the conclusion that the additional training will reduce repair costs from ground collisions much more than it reduces the number of such collisions?* The key word *since* before the blank shows that the argument should be completed with a premise that supports the preceding claim that the *drop in repair costs can be expected to be much greater*. A suitable premise might provide evidence that the training will disproportionately help to prevent the ground collisions that result in the higher repair costs as opposed to the less serious collisions that result in lower repair costs.

A We are given no reason to believe that the additional training would affect how much ground crews rush to minimize delays.

B The number of passengers is not clearly relevant to the repair costs resulting from a ground collision and in any case would not be affected by additional ground crew training.

C **Correct.** If the training especially helps the ground crews avoid those kinds of collisions that cause the most costly damage, then it will probably reduce repair costs even more than it reduces the number of collisions.

D Whether the cited expense for training includes wages is irrelevant to whether the training will reduce repair costs more than it reduces the number of collisions.

E This suggests that the additional training may help reduce the number of collisions, not that it will reduce repair costs more than it reduces the number of collisions.

The correct answer is C.

565. Hunter: **Many people blame hunters alone for the decline in Greenrock National Forest's deer population over the past ten years.** Yet clearly, black bears have also played an important role in this decline. In the past ten years, the forest's protected black bear population has risen sharply, and examination of black bears found dead in the forest during the deer hunting season showed that a number of them had recently fed on deer.

In the hunter's argument, the portion in boldface plays which of the following roles?

(A) It is the main conclusion of the argument.

(B) It is a finding that the argument seeks to explain.

(C) It is an explanation that the argument concludes is correct.

(D) It provides evidence in support of the main conclusion of the argument.

(E) It introduces a judgment that the argument opposes.

Argument Construction

Situation The hunter claims that hunters have been identified by many people as the sole cause of the decline in Greenrock National Forest's deer population. But the hunter argues that black bears have also contributed to the deer population decline. Black bears are protected and have increased in number, and they have been found to have fed recently on deer.

Reasoning *What role in the argument is played by the hunter's statement that many people blame hunters alone for the decline in the national forest's deer population?* In this statement, the hunter claims that many people have judged hunters responsible for the decline. The hunter then goes on to offer evidence supporting a different judgment: that hunters are not solely responsible, but that black bears are also to blame.

A The hunter's main conclusion is that black bears have also contributed to the decline in the deer population.

B The argument seeks to offer a reason for the finding that the deer population has declined, not the finding that people blame hunters for that decline.

C The hunter does not conclude that blaming hunters for the decline in the deer population is correct; rather, the hunter suggests that black bears should also be blamed.

D The hunter believes that hunters are *not* solely responsible for the decline in the deer population, so people's suggestion that they *are* responsible does not support the hunter's main conclusion.

E **Correct.** The boldfaced statement cites a judgment that the hunter attributes to many people, and that the hunter argues is incorrect. The hunter opposes the judgment that hunters alone are responsible for the decline in the deer population.

The correct answer is E.

566. Many agriculturally intensive areas of the world are beginning to encounter water scarcity problems. As a result, many farmers in these areas are likely to reduce their output as the water supply they need in order to maintain production shrinks. However, one group of farmers in such a region plans to increase their production by implementing techniques for water conservation.

Which of the following, if true, would most strongly support the prediction that the group's plan will succeed?

(A) Farmers who can gain a larger share of the food market in their regions will be better positioned to control more water resources.

(B) Most agricultural practices in areas with water shortages are water-intensive.

(C) Other regions of the world not facing water shortages are likely to make up for the reduction in agricultural output.

(D) Demand for agricultural products in the group's region is not expected to decline.

(E) More than half the water used for agriculture in the farmers' region is lost to evaporation or leakage from irrigation channels.

Evaluation of a Plan

Situation Farmers in many agriculturally intensive regions will probably reduce their output because the regions' water supplies are dwindling, but one group of farmers in such a region plans to use water conservation techniques to increase their output.

Reasoning *What would provide evidence that water conservation techniques will help the farmers increase production despite their region's dwindling water supplies?* In order for the water conservation techniques to be effective, they must result in significantly more water becoming available for the farmers to use. Because overall supplies are shrinking, rather than growing, that can only happen if the farmers are currently losing or wasting a great deal of water in ways that could be prevented with water conservation techniques.

A This suggests an advantage the farmers will gain if their water conservation plan enables them to increase production, but it provides no evidence that the plan actually will enable them to increase production.

B This suggests that the plan would have to yield quite a lot of conserved water in order for the farmers to increase production, but it offers no evidence that the plan will do so. Thus, it provides some reason to question whether the plan will succeed.

C Whether regions without water shortages will increase production is not directly relevant to the question of whether a particular measure would lead to increased production in one region that does have a water shortage.

D This has some slight, indirect relevance to the question of whether the farmers' plan will succeed: it suggests that if the farmers do manage to increase production, they will continue to have a market for what they produce. However, it does not address the issue of whether they will be able to increase production. Furthermore, even if demand for agricultural products in the group's region were expected to decline, it could still remain high enough to support the farmers' increased output from their water conservation plan.

E **Correct.** This suggests that the farmers are losing a lot of water in ways that the water conservation techniques might prevent, so it provides evidence that employing some such techniques could enable the farmers to save enough water to increase their output.

The correct answer is E.

567. Physician: The hormone melatonin has shown promise as a medication for sleep disorders when taken in synthesized form. Because the long-term side effects of synthetic melatonin are unknown, however, I cannot recommend its use at this time.

Patient: Your position is inconsistent with your usual practice. You prescribe many medications that you know have serious side effects, so concern about side effects cannot be the real reason you will not prescribe melatonin.

The patient's argument is flawed because it fails to consider that

(A) the side effects of synthetic melatonin might be different from those of naturally produced melatonin

(B) it is possible that the physician does not believe that melatonin has been conclusively shown to be effective

(C) sleep disorders, if left untreated, might lead to serious medical complications

(D) the side effects of a medication can take some time to manifest themselves

(E) known risks can be weighed against known benefits, but unknown risks cannot

Argument Evaluation

Situation The physician refuses to prescribe synthetic melatonin to treat sleep disorders despite this medication's promise. The reason the physician offers for this refusal is that the long-term side effects of synthetic melatonin are unknown. The patient responds that because the physician prescribes other medications that are known to have serious side effects, it cannot be a concern for synthetic melatonin's side effects that is prompting the physician's refusal to prescribe that medication.

Reasoning *What does the patient's argument fail to consider?* The patient says that the inconsistency in the physician's position lies in the physician's unwillingness to prescribe synthetic melatonin coupled with a willingness to prescribe other medications that are known to have serious side effects. But notice that the physician does not say that synthetic melatonin has *serious* side effects; rather, the physician points out that the long-term side effects of synthetic melatonin are unknown. The physician most likely prescribes medications that have serious side effects because the medications' benefits outweigh the risks posed by their side effects. In the case of synthetic melatonin, however, this kind of decision cannot be made.

A The patient's argument has to do with whether the physician's refusal to prescribe synthetic melatonin is consistent with the physician's usual prescription practices. The question of whether naturally produced melatonin has different side effects than synthetic melatonin has no bearing on that argument.

B It is quite reasonable for the patient's argument not to mention this possibility, especially since the physician expresses a belief that synthetic melatonin may be effective—but expresses no belief about whether or not it has been conclusively shown to be effective.

C Awareness that sleep disorders can lead to serious medical complications most likely prompts the patient's desire for treatment—but the patient's not mentioning this possible consequence of sleep disorders does not indicate a flaw in the argument.

D The patient makes clear that the physician prescribes medications that have serious side effects; the time those side effects take to manifest themselves is not relevant to the argument.

E **Correct.** The patient's argument is flawed in failing to consider this key difference between known risks and unknown risks. If the patient had considered this key difference, the patient would have realized that the physician's position is not at all inconsistent, and that the physician's refusal to prescribe is genuinely based on a concern about an unknown risk.

The correct answer is E.

568. Hollywood restaurant is replacing some of its standard tables with tall tables and stools. The restaurant already fills every available seat during its operating hours, and the change in seating arrangements will not result in an increase in the restaurant's seating capacity. Nonetheless, the restaurant's management expects revenue to increase as a result of the seating change without any concurrent change in menu, prices, or operating hours.

Which of the following, if true, provides the best reason for the expectation?

(A) One of the taller tables takes up less floor space than one of the standard tables.

(B) Diners seated on stools typically do not linger over dinner as long as diners seated at standard tables.

(C) Since the restaurant will replace only some of its standard tables, it can continue to accommodate customers who do not care for the taller tables.

(D) Few diners are likely to avoid the restaurant because of the new seating arrangement.

(E) The standard tables being replaced by tall tables would otherwise have to be replaced with new standard tables at a greater expense.

Argument Construction

Situation Hollywood restaurant is replacing some of its tables with taller tables and stools, and the management expects this will increase revenue, despite the fact that the restaurant already fills all of its available seats and that this change will not increase seating capacity. Furthermore, there will not be any change in menu, prices, or operating hours.

Reasoning *What would strongly support the management's expectation?* Since the new seating will not increase the restaurant's seating capacity, the management's expectations must be based on a belief that the change to taller tables and stools will somehow change diners' behavior, perhaps by leading them to order more food, or to stay at their tables for a shorter time, thereby allowing the restaurant to serve more diners during its operating hours without increasing seating capacity. If diners seated at tall tables and on tall stools spend less time lingering over their dinners, then they will leave sooner, opening up the tables for more diners. Because the restaurant, before the change, already fills every available seat during its operating hours, it is reasonable to think that it will be able to serve more diners than it currently does, thereby selling more food and thus increasing revenue.

A This would be relevant if we could infer from it that seating capacity will increase. However, the passage indicates that the new seating arrangement will not result in greater capacity.

B Correct. Because the restaurant will be able to serve more meals during its operating hours, the restaurant's revenue can be expected to increase.

C This may indicate that the restaurant is less likely to alienate customers who do not care for tall tables and stools, but that only supports the claim that the restaurant will not lose customers and therefore lose revenue; it does not indicate that the restaurant will see revenue increase.

D Again, this merely indicates that there will not be a loss—or much loss—of revenue, not that there will be an increase in revenue.

E Less expensive tables will decrease the restaurant's costs, but it will not increase the restaurant's revenue.

The correct answer is B.

569. A major network news organization experienced a drop in viewership in the week following the airing of a controversial report on the economy. The network also received a very large number of complaints regarding the report. The network, however, maintains that negative reactions to the report had nothing to do with its loss of viewers.

Which of the following, if true, most strongly supports the network's position?

(A) The other major network news organizations reported similar reductions in viewership during the same week.

(B) The viewers who registered complaints with the network were regular viewers of the news organization's programs.

(C) Major network news organizations publicly attribute drops in viewership to their own reports only when they receive complaints about those reports.

(D) This was not the first time that this network news organization has aired a controversial report on the economy that has inspired viewers to complain to the network.

(E) Most network news viewers rely on network news broadcasts as their primary source of information regarding the economy.

Argument Construction

Situation A major network news organization aired a controversial report on the economy, and the following week the network's viewership declined. The network claims that the loss of viewers was not connected with negative reactions to the report.

Reasoning *Which statement most strongly supports the network's position?* If other major news network organizations had similar drops in viewership, it is implausible to think that the controversial report accounted for the other organizations' drops in viewership. On the other hand, it is not implausible to suppose that whatever did cause the drop in the viewership experienced by other network news organizations—e.g., holidays, weather, popular non-news programming—also had that effect on the organization that ran the controversial report. This would give some reason to believe that it was not the report that accounts for the organization's drop in viewership.

A **Correct.** This statement indicates that something other than the airing of the report could account for the subsequent drop in the organization's viewership.

B If anything, this statement tends to undermine the network's claim, because it suggests that the report offended people who otherwise might have continued to watch the organization's programming.

C Since the network did in fact receive complaints about the report, this statement is irrelevant.

D The fact that the network has received complaints before about controversial reports on the economy that the network's news organization has aired tells us nothing about whether this recent report caused a subsequent drop in viewership.

E The fact that viewers turn to network news broadcasts as their primary source of information about the economy tells us nothing about whether viewers might stop watching a particular network news organization's programs as a result of its airing a controversial report on the economy.

The correct answer is A.

570. Only a reduction of 10 percent in the number of scheduled flights using Greentown's airport will allow the delays that are so common there to be avoided. Hevelia airstrip, 40 miles away, would, if upgraded and expanded, be an attractive alternative for fully 20 percent of the passengers using Greentown airport. Nevertheless, experts reject the claim that turning Hevelia into a full-service airport would end the chronic delays at Greentown.

Which of the following, if true, most helps to justify the experts' position?

(A) Turning Hevelia into a full-service airport would require not only substantial construction at the airport itself, but also the construction of new access highways.

(B) A second largely undeveloped airstrip close to Greentown airport would be a more attractive alternative than Hevelia for many passengers who now use Greentown.

(C) Hevelia airstrip lies in a relatively undeveloped area but would, if it became a full-service airport, be a magnet for commercial and residential development.

(D) If an airplane has to wait to land, the extra jet fuel required adds significantly to the airline's costs.

(E) Several airlines use Greentown as a regional hub, so that most flights landing at Greentown have many passengers who then take different flights to reach their final destinations.

Evaluation of a Plan

Situation To avoid the delays now common at Greentown's airport, the number of scheduled flights there would need to be reduced by 10 percent. If the nearby Hevelia airstrip were expanded and upgraded, it would be an attractive alternative for 20 percent of Greentown airport's passengers. Still, experts do not believe that the delays at Greentown would end even if Hevelia were turned into a full-service airport.

Reasoning *Which statement most supports the experts' position?* If the number of flights at Greentown's airport did not drop by at least 10 percent, despite the fact that 20 percent of the passengers who currently use Greentown's airport would find nearby Hevelia airstrip an attractive alternative, then the delays would not be avoided. Airlines generally use certain airports as regional hubs—an airport through which an airline routes most of its traffic—so, even if many passengers would be willing to use Hevelia airstrip, the number of flights at Greentown may not decline significantly, or at all.

A The experts' position concerns what would happen to the flight delays at Greentown airport if the Hevelia airstrip were converted into a full-service airport. So the fact that there are great costs involved in making such a conversion—possibly making such a conversion unlikely—has no bearing on the effects such a conversion would have on flight delays at Greentown if the conversion were to be carried out.

B This statement indicates that the undeveloped airstrip near Greentown might be a better way to alleviate flight delays at Greentown, but it tells us nothing about the effects that converting the Hevelia airstrip to a full-service airport would have were it to be carried out.

C This in no way explains why converting the Hevelia airstrip into a full-service airport would not alleviate the problem with flight delays at Greentown.

D This provides a reason to think that reducing the number of flights at Greentown might make the airport more efficient. But that has no bearing on the effect that converting the Hevelia airstrip to a full-service airport might have on flight delays at Greentown.

E **Correct.** This statement provides support for the experts' position because it gives a reason for thinking that the number of scheduled flights at Greentown would not be reduced, even if Hevelia airstrip became an attractive alternative for some 20 percent of Greentown's passengers.

The correct answer is E.

571. For similar cars and comparable drivers, automobile insurance for collision damage has always cost more in Greatport than in Fairmont. Police studies, however, show that cars owned by Greatport residents are, on average, slightly less likely to be involved in a collision than cars in Fairmont. Clearly, therefore, insurance companies are making a greater profit on collision-damage insurance in Greatport than in Fairmont.

In evaluating the argument, it would be most useful to compare

(A) the level of traffic congestion in Greatport with the level of traffic congestion in Fairmont
(B) the cost of repairing collision damage in Greatport with the cost of repairing collision damage in Fairmont
(C) the rates Greatport residents pay for other forms of insurance with the rates paid for similar insurance by residents of Fairmont
(D) the condition of Greatport's roads and streets with the condition of Fairmont's roads and streets
(E) the cost of collision-damage insurance in Greatport and Fairmont with that in other cities

Argument Evaluation

Situation A particular kind of insurance, that for collision damage, costs more in Greatport than in Fairmont. The cars of Greatport residents are, however, less likely to be involved in collisions than are cars of Fairmont residents. So insurance companies must be making a greater profit on collision-damage insurance in Greatport than in Fairmont.

Reasoning *What would it help to consider in evaluating the argument?* Insurance companies would make greater profits on collision-damage insurance in Greatport than they make in Fairmont if they pay out less money in response to Greatport residents' claims than they do in response to Fairmont's residents' claims. That Greatport residents' cars are involved in fewer collisions than are Fairmont's residents' cars supports this—if there are fewer collisions overall, then the insurance companies might pay out less money overall. But the number of collisions is only one factor contributing to how much money an insurance company pays out in response to claims; another factor is the amount of damage inflicted on the cars involved in collisions and how much it costs to repair that damage. These costs would need to be considered before concluding that insurance companies' profits on collision-damage insurance are greater in Greatport than in Fairmont.

A The level of traffic congestion probably contributes to the frequency of collisions in each town. The information given, however, includes the statement that Greatport cars are less likely to be involved in collisions than are Fairmont cars. Why this occurs—whether, for example, traffic congestion is a contributory factor—is not relevant.

B Correct. This is clearly a factor that would affect the profitability of insurance in the two towns—and is therefore highly relevant to evaluating the argument, especially its conclusion.

C The argument's conclusion is about insurance companies' profits on collision-damage insurance alone, so other types of insurance, and the rates paid for them, are not relevant.

D The condition of the roads and streets in each town probably contributes to the frequency of collisions in each town. The information given, however, includes the statement that Greatport cars are less likely to be involved in collisions than are Fairmont cars. Why this is so—whether, for example, the condition of the roads is a contributory cause—is not relevant.

E Since the argument is concerned solely with collision-insurance costs and profits in Greatport and Fairmont, comparing the cost of insurance in those towns with the cost of insurance elsewhere would provide no useful insight.

The correct answer is B.

572. The air quality board recently informed Coffee Roast, a small coffee roasting firm, of a complaint regarding the smoke from its roaster. Recently enacted air quality regulations require machines roasting more than 10 pounds of coffee to be equipped with expensive smoke-dissipating afterburners. The firm, however, roasts only 8 pounds of coffee at a time. Nevertheless, the company has decided to purchase and install an afterburner.

Which of the following, if true, most strongly supports the firm's decision?

(A) Until settling on the new air quality regulations, the board had debated whether to require afterburners for machines roasting more than 5 pounds of coffee at a time.

(B) Coffee roasted in a machine equipped with an afterburner has its flavor subtly altered.

(C) The cost to the firm of an afterburner is less than the cost of replacing its roaster with a smaller one.

(D) Fewer complaints are reported in areas that maintain strict rules regarding afterburners.

(E) The firm has reason to fear that negative publicity regarding the complaints could result in lost sales.

Evaluation of a Plan

Situation After being informed of a complaint about smoke from its coffee roaster, a firm decided to purchase and install an afterburner to reduce or eliminate emissions of smoke, even though the roaster roasts too little coffee at a time for an afterburner to be legally required.

Reasoning *What would have been a good reason for the firm to buy and install the afterburner?* The only factors mentioned that might give the firm reason to buy an afterburner are the complaint about smoke and the regulations requiring an afterburner. Since the regulations do not apply in this case, the complaint is more likely to have motivated the firm's decision. Any serious potential consequences the firm might have faced from failure to address the complaint could have provided a good reason to buy and install the afterburner.

A If this debate had still been ongoing when the firm made its decision, uncertainty about the pending regulations might have justified the decision. But the debate had already been settled before the firm decided to purchase the afterburner, and the regulations clearly did not require one.

B An unspecified alteration in flavor is not clearly a good reason to use an afterburner—the afterburner might worsen the flavor.

C The firm's roaster was already small enough that the regulations did not require it to be replaced, even without an afterburner.

D This reason relates only to rules regarding afterburners, not to Coffee Roast's purchase of an afterburner, which was not mandated by regulations. Furthermore, it could be that the air quality regulations recently enacted are among the strictest in any region, which could result in fewer complaints regardless of whether Coffee Roast installs an afterburner.

E **Correct.** Since installing an afterburner is a plausible way to address the complaint and prevent future complaints, the firm has plausible reasons to believe this strategy will help it avoid the negative publicity and lost sales it fears. These considerations could have reasonably justified its decision.

The correct answer is E.

573. The tulu, a popular ornamental plant, does not reproduce naturally, and is only bred and sold by specialized horticultural companies. Unfortunately, the tulu is easily devastated by a contagious fungal rot. The government ministry plans to reassure worried gardeners by requiring all tulu plants to be tested for fungal rot before being sold. However, infected plants less than 30 weeks old have generally not built up enough fungal rot in their systems to be detected reliably. And many tulu plants are sold before they are 24 weeks old.

Which of the following, if performed by the government ministry, could logically be expected to overcome the problem with their plan to test for the fungal rot?

(A) Releasing a general announcement that tulu plants less than 30 weeks old cannot be effectively tested for fungal rot
(B) Requiring all tulu plants less than 30 weeks old to be labeled as such
(C) Researching possible ways to test tulu plants less than 24 weeks old for fungal rot
(D) Ensuring that tulu plants not be sold before they are 30 weeks old
(E) Quarantining all tulu plants from horticultural companies at which any case of fungal rot has been detected until those tulu plants can be tested for fungal rot

Evaluation of a Plan

Situation There is a contagious fungal rot that devastates the tulu, a popular ornamental plant. To reassure worried gardeners, the government ministry plans to require that tulu plants be tested for the rot before being sold. However, many tulu plants are sold before they are 24 weeks old, yet fungal rot in plants less than 30 weeks old generally cannot be detected reliably.

Reasoning *What could the government ministry do to overcome the problem?* The problem arises from the fact that tulu plants are frequently sold before they are 24 weeks old, which is too soon for any fungal rot that is present to have built up enough in their root systems to be detected. Since the goal of the testing is to ensure that infected tulu plants not be sold, an obvious solution would be to make sure that no plants are sold before they are old enough for fungal rot to have built up to a detectable level. Thus, tulu plants should not be sold before they are 30 weeks old.

A Releasing such an announcement would help overcome the problem if it guaranteed that no one would buy or sell tulu plants before the plants were 30 weeks old, but it is far from certain that such an announcement would guarantee this.

B Since some people may not be aware of the significance of such labeling, such labeling might have very little effect.

C There is no guarantee that such research will be successful at reducing the age at which tulu plants can be reliably tested.

D **Correct.** If the government ensures that no tulu plants less than 30 weeks of age are sold, then the specific problem mentioned in the passage would be overcome.

E This will not help overcome the problem. Such a quarantine program might lead horticultural companies to start selling tulu plants only if they are less than 24 weeks old, thereby minimizing the chance of quarantine by minimizing the chance of detection.

The correct answer is D.

574. People who do regular volunteer work tend to live longer, on average, than people who do not. It has been found that "doing good," a category that certainly includes volunteer work, releases endorphins, the brain's natural opiates, which induce in people a feeling of well-being. Clearly, there is a connection: Regular releases of endorphins must in some way help to extend people's lives.

Which of the following, if true, most seriously undermines the force of the evidence given as support for the hypothesis that endorphins promote longevity?

(A) People who do regular volunteer work are only somewhat more likely than others to characterize the work they do for a living as "doing good."

(B) Although extremely high levels of endorphins could be harmful to health, such levels are never reached as a result of the natural release of endorphins.

(C) There are many people who have done some volunteer work but who do not do such work regularly.

(D) People tend not to become involved in regular volunteer work unless they are healthy and energetic to begin with.

(E) Releases of endorphins are responsible for the sense of well-being experienced by many long-distance runners while running.

Argument Evaluation

Situation People who volunteer regularly live longer on average than people who do not. Doing good work, including volunteer work, releases endorphins, which induce a feeling of well-being.

Reasoning *What additional findings would suggest that the cited evidence does not indicate that endorphins increase longevity?* The argument implicitly assumes that the reason regular volunteers tend to live longer is that volunteering lengthens their lives. It further assumes that no factor that is correlated with volunteering, other than the endorphin release, would plausibly explain how volunteering could have this effect. Findings that cast doubt on either of these assumptions would undermine the connection between the cited evidence and the conclusion that endorphins promote longevity.

A Volunteering might greatly boost volunteers' endorphin levels even if the work the volunteers do for a living is no different from other people's work.

B Even if unnaturally high endorphin levels could harm health, the levels attainable through volunteer work may promote health.

C The argument is about an observed correlation in a certain group of people (those who regularly do volunteer work). How many people are outside that group (i.e., do not regularly do volunteer work) is independent of the question of what causes the observed correlation. Even if some people volunteer only occasionally, volunteering regularly may promote longevity by causing regular releases of endorphins.

D **Correct.** This suggests that the initially better health of people who choose to volunteer could fully explain the cited correlation between volunteering and longevity.

E Unless we are also given evidence that long-distance runners tend not to live longer than other people, this does not undermine the purported evidence in the argument. Endorphins might promote longevity in both regular volunteers and long-distance runners.

The correct answer is D.

575. In Mernia commercial fossil hunters often sell important fossils they have found, not to universities or museums, but to individual collectors, who pay much better but generally do not allow researchers access to their collections. To increase the number of fossils available for research, some legislators propose requiring all fossils that are found in Mernia to be sold only to universities or museums.

Which of the following, if true, most strongly indicates that the legislators' proposal will fail to achieve its goal?

(A) Some fossil hunters in Mernia are not commercial fossil hunters, but rather are amateurs who keep the fossils that they find.

(B) Most fossils found in Mernia are common types that have little scientific interest.

(C) Commercial fossil hunters in Mernia currently sell some of the fossils they find to universities and museums.

(D) Many universities in Mernia do not engage in fossil research.

(E) Most fossils are found by commercial fossil hunters, and they would give up looking for fossils if they were no longer allowed to sell to individual collectors.

Evaluation of a Plan

Situation Fossil hunters in Mernia often sell important fossils to collectors who do not make them accessible to researchers. To increase the number of fossils available for research, some legislators propose requiring all fossils found in Mernia to be sold only to universities or museums.

Reasoning *What would most strongly suggest that requiring all fossils found in Mernia to be sold only to universities or museums would not increase the number of fossils available for research?* To increase the number of fossils available for research, the proposed requirement will have to be implemented and effectively enforced. It will presumably have to increase the total number of fossils sold to universities and museums. And those institutions will have to make more of the fossils in their collections available to researchers than the private collectors do. Evidence that any of those conditions will not be fulfilled would suggest that the legislators' proposal will fail to achieve its goal.

A Even if the legislation does not affect fossils kept by amateurs, it might still result in many more fossils being sold to universities or museums rather than to private collectors, and thus might still increase the number of fossils available for research.

B Even if few Mernian fossils are interesting to researchers, the legislation could still achieve its goal of making more fossils available for research.

C Even if commercial fossil hunters already sell a few fossils to universities and museums, the legislation could encourage them to sell many more fossils.

D The universities that do not engage in fossil research presumably will not be interested in buying fossils even if the legislation passes. But the fossil hunters can just sell their fossils to other universities and museums that do engage in fossil research.

E **Correct.** This suggests that if the legislation passes, fossils will simply be left in the ground rather than sold to private collectors. That would not increase the total number of fossils available for research.

The correct answer is E.

576. The Eurasian ruffe, a fish species inadvertently introduced into North America's Great Lakes in recent years, feeds on the eggs of lake whitefish, a native species, thus threatening the lakes' natural ecosystem. To help track the ruffe's spread, government agencies have produced wallet-sized cards about the ruffe. The cards contain pictures of the ruffe and explain the danger they pose; the cards also request anglers to report any ruffe they catch.

Which of the following, if true, would provide most support for the prediction that the agencies' action will have its intended effect?

(A) The ruffe has spiny fins that make it unattractive as prey.

(B) Ruffe generally feed at night, but most recreational fishing on the Great Lakes is done during daytime hours.

(C) Most people who fish recreationally on the Great Lakes are interested in the preservation of the lake whitefish because it is a highly prized game fish.

(D) The ruffe is one of several nonnative species in the Great Lakes whose existence threatens the survival of lake whitefish populations there.

(E) The bait that most people use when fishing for whitefish on the Great Lakes is not attractive to ruffe.

Evaluation of a Plan

Situation The Eurasian ruffe, a species not native to the Great Lakes, is threatening the native lake whitefish. Government agencies hope that wallet-sized cards identifying the ruffe, explaining the danger they pose, and asking anglers to report their ruffe catches will help them track the ruffe's spread.

Reasoning *What point would support the idea that the agencies' action will have its intended effect?* The cards are intended to help government agencies track the ruffe's spread. They will be useful for this purpose only if anglers actually report the ruffe they catch. Thus anything that increases the odds of anglers' doing such reporting would make it more likely that the cards will have their intended effect.

A If ruffe are unattractive as prey, they will probably spread more quickly in the Great Lakes. This will most likely have little effect on whether the wallet-sized cards will help government agencies track the ruffe.

B If ruffe feed at night, while fishing is done in the daytime, it is unlikely that anglers would catch ruffe. Thus few catches would be reported to government agencies, making it more difficult for those agencies to track the spread of ruffe.

C **Correct.** This statement properly identifies a point that supports the prediction that the agencies' action will have its intended effect—that is, those who are interested in preserving the lake whitefish will be likely to report catches of ruffe, which threaten whitefish, thus enabling the agencies' tracking of the spread of ruffe.

D That the ruffe is one of several nonnative species threatening the Great Lakes lessens the odds that the whitefish will survive, but this has no effect on the question of whether the wallet-sized cards will help government agencies track the ruffe's spread.

E This would make it likely that anglers would catch few ruffe. If anglers do not catch many ruffe, there will not be many to report to government agencies, which would in turn make it more difficult for those agencies to track the ruffe's spread.

The correct answer is C.

577. Which of the following most logically completes the argument below?

Although the number of large artificial satellites orbiting the Earth is small compared to the number of small pieces of debris in orbit, the large satellites interfere more seriously with telescope observations because of the strong reflections they produce. Because many of those large satellites have ceased to function, the proposal has recently been made to eliminate interference from nonfunctioning satellites by exploding them in space. This proposal, however, is ill conceived, since ______.

(A) many nonfunctioning satellites remain in orbit for years

(B) for satellites that have ceased to function, repairing them while they are in orbit would be prohibitively expensive

(C) there are no known previous instances of satellites' having been exploded on purpose

(D) the only way to make telescope observations without any interference from debris in orbit is to use telescopes launched into extremely high orbits around the Earth

(E) a greatly increased number of small particles in Earth's orbit would result in a blanket of reflections that would make certain valuable telescope observations impossible

Evaluation of a Plan

Situation Many large artificial satellites orbiting Earth no longer function. Reflections from these satellites interfere with telescope observations. A proposal has been made to eliminate this interference by exploding these satellites in space.

Reasoning *Why is the proposal ill conceived?* If exploding the large artificial satellites—thereby creating a large amount of debris—would result in an increase in interference with telescope observation, the proposal would be self-defeating, and therefore would be ill conceived.

A The fact that many nonfunctioning satellites remain in orbit for years would seem to make the proposal *more* attractive. If large nonfunctioning artificial satellites generally do not remain in orbit for years—e.g., if they fall out of orbit—then there might be no need to explode the satellites. Therefore this statement is not correct.

B This statement, too, makes the proposal more attractive—the opposite of what is called for. If nonfunctioning satellites cannot be repaired, then that eliminates one possible reason for not blowing them up.

C The fact that there are no known instances of intentional explosions of satellites does not show that the plan is ill conceived. At most this might suggest that the consequences of such an explosion are not well understood, but even that is not very strongly suggested. For instance, if large artificial satellites have accidentally blown up, scientists may have studied the results and have good reason to believe that no ill effects will result from exploding the satellites.

D This is not a cogent reason for thinking the proposal to be ill conceived. Even if the proposal would not eliminate *all interference* with ground based telescopes, it might still greatly reduce interference.

E **Correct.** If exploding large nonfunctioning satellites would lead to more interference, then we have a reason to think that the proposal is ill conceived.

The correct answer is E.

578. Thyrian lawmaker: Thyria's Cheese Importation Board inspects all cheese shipments to Thyria and rejects shipments not meeting specified standards. Yet only 1 percent is ever rejected. Therefore, since the health consequences and associated economic costs of not rejecting that 1 percent are negligible, whereas the board's operating costs are considerable, for economic reasons alone the board should be disbanded.

Consultant: I disagree. The threat of having their shipments rejected deters many cheese exporters from shipping substandard product.

The consultant responds to the lawmaker's argument by

(A) rejecting the lawmaker's argument while proposing that the standards according to which the board inspects imported cheese should be raised

(B) providing evidence that the lawmaker's argument has significantly overestimated the cost of maintaining the board

(C) objecting to the lawmaker's introducing into the discussion factors that are not strictly economic

(D) pointing out a benefit of maintaining the board, which the lawmaker's argument has failed to consider

(E) shifting the discussion from the argument at hand to an attack on the integrity of the cheese inspectors

Argument Construction

Situation The Thyrian lawmaker argues that the Cheese Importation Board should be disbanded, because its operating costs are high and it rejects only a small percentage of the cheese it inspects. The consultant disagrees, pointing out that the board's inspections deter those who export cheese to Thyria from shipping substandard cheese.

Reasoning *What strategy does the consultant use in the counterargument?* The consultant indicates to the lawmaker that there is a reason to retain the board that the lawmaker has not considered. The benefit the board provides is not that it identifies a great deal of substandard cheese and rejects it (thus keeping the public healthy), but that the possibility that their cheese could be found substandard is what keeps exporters from attempting to export low-quality cheese to Thyria.

A The consultant does reject the lawmaker's argument, but the consultant does not propose higher standards. Indeed, in suggesting that the board should be retained, the consultant implies that the board's standards are appropriate.

B The consultant does not provide any evidence related to the board's cost.

C The only point the lawmaker raises that is not strictly economic is about the health consequences of disbanding the board, but the consultant does not address this point at all.

D **Correct.** This statement properly identifies the strategy the consultant employs in his or her counterargument. The consultant points out that the board provides a significant benefit that the lawmaker did not consider.

E The consultant does not attack the integrity of the cheese inspectors; to the contrary, the consultant says that their inspections deter the cheese exporters from shipping substandard cheese.

The correct answer is D.

579. The growing popularity of computer-based activities was widely expected to result in a decline in television viewing, since it had been assumed that people lack sufficient free time to maintain current television-viewing levels while spending increasing amounts of free time on the computer. That assumption, however, is evidently false: In a recent mail survey concerning media use, a very large majority of respondents who report increasing time spent per week using computers report no change in time spent watching television.

Which of the following would it be most useful to determine in order to evaluate the argument?

(A) Whether a large majority of the survey respondents reported watching television regularly

(B) Whether the amount of time spent watching television is declining among people who report that they rarely or never use computers

(C) Whether the type of television programs a person watches tends to change as the amount of time spent per week using computers increases

(D) Whether a large majority of the computer owners in the survey reported spending increasing amounts of time per week using computers

(E) Whether the survey respondents' reports of time spent using computers included time spent using computers at work

Argument Evaluation

Situation The argument is intended to debunk the assumption that people lack sufficient free time to maintain television-viewing levels while spending increasing amounts of free time on the computer. To do so, it cites a survey of media use in which a large majority of respondents who spend increasing amounts of time using computers also claim to have not altered the amount of time they spend watching television.

Reasoning *What would it be most useful to know in order to evaluate the argument?* The argument uses the survey results to claim that people have enough free time to both maintain their television viewing levels and spend increasing amounts of free time on the computer. But the survey, as reported here, did not address whether people are spending their *free time* on the computer; the respondents reported increasing *time* spent per week using computers. Since the argument is about free time, it is important to know whether this is actually what the respondents were reporting.

A The argument is concerned with the *change* in the amount of television watched by those whose computer use increased, so whether the survey's respondents reported watching television regularly is irrelevant.

B The argument is concerned with the change in the amount of television watched by those whose computer use has increased, so it does not matter whether the amount of time spent watching television among people who do not use computers is declining, remaining the same, or increasing.

C The argument is concerned with the *amount* of television watched by those whose computer use has increased, not the type of television programs such a person does or does not watch.

D The argument here is concerned with people who report spending increasing amounts of time on the computer; what computer owners do is a separate question.

E **Correct.** This statement properly identifies something that would be useful to know in evaluating the argument: whether the survey data included time spent using computers at work—if it did, this would make the data misleading as evidence for the argument's conclusion.

The correct answer is E.

580. Although the school would receive financial benefits if it had soft drink vending machines in the cafeteria, we should not allow them. Allowing soft drink machines there would not be in our students' interest. If our students start drinking more soft drinks, they will be less healthy.

The argument depends on which of the following?

(A) If the soft drink vending machines were placed in the cafeteria, students would consume more soft drinks as a result.
(B) The amount of soft drinks that most students at the school currently drink is not detrimental to their health.
(C) Students are apt to be healthier if they do not drink soft drinks at all than if they just drink small amounts occasionally.
(D) Students will not simply bring soft drinks from home if the soft drink vending machines are not placed in the cafeteria.
(E) The school's primary concern should be to promote good health among its students.

Argument Construction

Situation Allowing soft drink vending machines in a school cafeteria would financially benefit the school, but students who drink more soft drinks would become less healthy.

Reasoning *What must be true in order for the claim that students drinking more soft drinks would cause them to become less healthy to justify the conclusion that soft drink vending machines should not be allowed in the cafeteria?* The argument is that because drinking more soft drinks would be unhealthy for the students, allowing the vending machines would not be in the students' interest, so the vending machines should not be allowed. This reasoning depends on the implicit factual assumption that allowing the vending machines would result in the students drinking more soft drinks. It also depends on the implicit value judgment that receiving financial benefits should be less important to the school than preventing a situation that would make the students less healthy.

A **Correct.** If the cafeteria vending machines would not result in students consuming more soft drinks, then allowing the machines would not harm the students' health in the way the argument assumes.

B Even if the amount of soft drinks the students currently drink were unhealthy, enabling the students to drink more could make them even less healthy.

C Even if drinking small amounts of soft drinks occasionally would not harm the students, vending machines in the cafeteria could lead the students to drink excessive amounts.

D Even if students who cannot buy soft drinks in the cafeteria sometimes bring them from home instead, adding vending machines in the cafeteria could increase the students' overall soft drink consumption.

E A concern does not have to be the primary one in order to be valid and important. It could be held that promoting students' good health should not be the schools' primary concern but should still be a more important concern than the financial benefits from the vending machines.

The correct answer is A.

581. Many athletes inhale pure oxygen after exercise in an attempt to increase muscular reabsorption of oxygen. Measured continuously after exercise, however, the blood lactate levels of athletes who inhale pure oxygen are practically identical, on average, to those of athletes who breathe normal air. The lower the blood lactate level is, the higher the muscular reabsorption of oxygen is.

If the statements above are all true, they most strongly support which of the following conclusions?

(A) Athletes' muscular reabsorption of oxygen is not increased when they inhale pure oxygen instead of normal air.
(B) High blood lactate levels cannot be reduced.
(C) Blood lactate levels are a poor measure of oxygen reabsorption by muscles.
(D) The amount of oxygen reabsorbed by an athlete's muscles always remains constant.
(E) The inhaling of pure oxygen has no legitimate role in athletics.

Argument Construction

Situation Blood lactate levels after exercise are practically identical in athletes who breathe normal air and in those who inhale pure oxygen after exercise. The lower the blood lactate level, the higher the muscular reabsorption of oxygen.

Reasoning *What conclusion do the stated facts most strongly support?* We are told that lower blood lactate levels correspond consistently to higher muscular reabsorption of oxygen. Since athletes who breathe pure oxygen after exercise have blood lactate levels practically identical to those in athletes who breathe normal air, probably muscular reabsorption of oxygen does not differ significantly between athletes who breathe pure oxygen and those who breathe pure air.

A **Correct.** As explained above, the stated facts suggest that muscular reabsorption of oxygen does not differ significantly between athletes who breathe pure oxygen and those who breathe pure air. So breathing pure oxygen instead of normal air after exercise probably does not increase athletes' muscular reabsorption of oxygen.

B None of the statements indicates that blood lactate levels cannot be reduced by means other than inhaling pure oxygen.

C We are told that blood lactate levels are negatively correlated with muscular reabsorption of oxygen. This negative correlation might allow muscular reabsorption of oxygen to be precisely determined by measuring blood lactate levels.

D Muscular reabsorption of oxygen might vary for reasons unrelated to whether an athlete has been inhaling pure oxygen.

E Inhaling pure oxygen might have some legitimate role unrelated to muscular reabsorption of oxygen.

The correct answer is A.

582. Which of the following most logically completes the argument?

Sviatovin is a medieval Moringian text whose author and exact date of composition are unknown. However, the events in the life of Prince Sviatov that the text describes occurred in 1165, and in the diagram of Sviatov's family that accompanies the text his father, who died in 1167, is identified as still living. Thus *Sviatovin* must have been written between 1165 and 1167, assuming that ______.

(A) the life of Prince Sviatov is not the subject of any other medieval Moringian texts

(B) the author of *Sviatovin* intended it to provide as accurate a report about Prince Sviatov's exploits as possible

(C) the diagram accurately represents the composition of Sviatov's family at the time Sviatovin was written

(D) *Sviatovin* is the earliest Moringian text whose composition can be dated to within a few years

(E) *Sviatovin* was not written by Sviatov's father himself

Argument Construction

Situation A medieval Moringian text was written about Prince Sviatov. It is not known exactly when the text was written, but the events described in it occurred in 1165 and a diagram in the text indicates that Sviatov's father—who died in 1167—was alive at the time it was composed.

Reasoning *What completion of the blank would provide the best reason for believing the argument's conclusion?* The argument's conclusion is that the book *Sviatovin* was written between 1165 and 1167. The reasoning given is this: It could not have been written before 1165 because it includes events that took place in that year. It could not have been written after 1167 because Sviatov's father died in that year. A diagram in the book suggests he was alive when the book was written. Was the diagram correct in that suggestion? The argument depends on assuming that it was.

A The argument focuses on one text and its date of composition. The argument does not need to make any assumptions about other texts.

B The argument does not assume this. Issues about the accurate reporting of Sviatov's exploits (or about the author's intention to report them accurately) are irrelevant to the argument, which hinges on the accuracy of the diagram that accompanies the text. The diagram does not report Sviatov's exploits.

C Correct. The reasoning in the argument assumes that the diagram was correct in representing the Prince's father as still living when the text was composed. If his father was not living when the text was written, then the information that his father actually died in 1167 is no guarantee that the text was composed by then.

D See the explanation for answer choice (A) above. The degree of precision with which scholars have succeeded in dating other Moringian texts is entirely irrelevant.

E The conclusion concerns when *Sviatovin* was written and not by whom it was written. If, contrary to answer choice (E), it were known that the author was Sviatov's father, this would actually provide strong support for the argument's conclusion. Thus answer choice (E) does not provide a good reason for the argument's conclusion.

The correct answer is C.

583. A study of ticket sales at a summer theater festival found that people who bought tickets to individual plays had a no-show rate of less than 1 percent, while those who paid in advance for all ten plays being performed that summer had a no-show rate of nearly 30 percent. This may be at least in part because the greater the awareness customers retain about the cost of an item, the more likely they are to use it.

Which of the following would, if true, best serve as an alternative explanation of the results of the study?

(A) The price per ticket was slightly cheaper for those who bought all ten tickets in advance.

(B) Many people who attended the theater festival believed strongly that they should support it financially.

(C) Those who attended all ten plays became eligible for a partial refund.

(D) Usually, people who bought tickets to individual plays did so immediately prior to each performance that they attended.

(E) People who arrived just before the performance began could not be assured of obtaining seats in a preferred location.

Argument Construction

Situation People who bought tickets to individual plays at a theater festival had a much lower no-show rate than did people who paid in advance for all ten plays.

Reasoning *What factor other than greater awareness of the ticket costs could explain why people who bought tickets individually were more likely to attend the plays?* The passage suggests that people who bought tickets individually were more likely to attend the plays because they were more vividly aware of what they had paid for each ticket. But there are other possible explanations—perhaps the people who bought the tickets individually were more eager to attend each play for its own sake, or had other characteristics or incentives that made them more likely to attend the plays.

A A slight price difference would not plausibly explain why the no-show rate was thirty times greater among those who bought all the tickets in advance than among those who bought them individually.

B This could be true of many people who bought their tickets individually as well as many who bought them in advance.

C This would provide an added incentive for those who bought tickets in advance to attend all the plays.

D **Correct.** If people who bought individual tickets usually did so right before each performance, they would have much less time after buying the tickets to change their minds about whether to attend than would people who bought all the tickets in advance.

E If anything, this might present an additional difficulty for those who bought individual tickets without advance planning, so it would not help to explain the lower no-show rate among buyers of individual tickets.

The correct answer is D.

584. Although there is no record of poet Edmund Spenser's parentage, we do know that as a youth Spenser attended the Merchant Tailors' School in London for a period between 1560 and 1570. Records from this time indicate that the Merchant Tailors' Guild then had only three members named Spenser: Robert Spenser, listed as a gentleman; Nicholas Spenser, elected the Guild's Warden in 1568; and John Spenser, listed as a "journeyman cloth-maker." Of these, the last was likely the least affluent of the three—and most likely Edmund's father, since school accounting records list Edmund as a scholar who attended the school at a reduced fee.

Which of the following is an assumption on which the argument depends?

(A) Anybody in sixteenth century London who made clothing professionally would have had to be a member of the Merchant Tailors' Guild.

(B) The fact that Edmund Spenser attended the Merchant Tailors' School did not necessarily mean that he planned to become a tailor.

(C) No member of the Guild could become Guild warden in sixteenth century London unless he was a gentleman.

(D) Most of those whose fathers were members of the Merchant Tailors' Guild were students at the Merchant Tailors' School.

(E) The Merchant Tailors' School did not reduce its fees for the children of the more affluent Guild members.

Argument Construction

Situation Records indicate that the poet Edmund Spenser attended the Merchant Tailors' School for a reduced fee as a youth. There is no record of his parentage, but at the time the Merchant Tailors' Guild had only three members named Spenser, of whom the least affluent was probably John Spenser.

Reasoning *What must be true in order for the cited facts to support the conclusion that John Spenser was probably Edmund Spenser's father?* The implicit reasoning is that since Edmund Spenser attended the Merchant Tailors' School at a reduced fee, his father must have been poor. And since John Spenser was probably the poorest of the three men named Spenser in the Merchant Tailors' Guild, he was probably Edmund Spenser's father. This reasoning assumes that only the children of poor parents had reduced fees at the Merchant Tailors' School, that the children at the school generally had fathers in the Merchant Tailors' Guild, that children in that time and place generally shared their fathers' surnames, and that the two other Spensers in the Merchant Tailors' Guild were not poor enough for their children to qualify for reduced fees.

A John Spenser, as a tailor and member of the guild, could have been Edmund Spenser's father even if some other professional tailors did not belong to the guild and did not have children at the school.

B Although Edmund Spenser became a poet as an adult, he and all his classmates might have attended the school as children because they planned to become tailors.

C The argument assumes that a Guild's Warden probably would have been wealthier than a journeyman cloth-maker, but that might have been probable even if the Guild's Warden were not a "gentleman."

D Even if most children of fathers in the guild did not attend the school, all the children who did attend the school might have had fathers in the guild.

E **Correct.** If the school reduced its fees for children of wealthier guild members, then the fact that Edmund Spenser's fees were reduced would not provide evidence that his father was the poorest of the three Spensers in the guild, as the argument requires.

The correct answer is E.

585. Trancorp currently transports all its goods to Burland Island by truck. The only bridge over the channel separating Burland from the mainland is congested, and trucks typically spend hours in traffic. Trains can reach the channel more quickly than trucks, and freight cars can be transported to Burland by barges that typically cross the channel in an hour. Therefore, to reduce shipping time, Trancorp plans to switch to trains and barges to transport goods to Burland.

Which of the following would be most important to know in determining whether Trancorp's plan, if implemented, is likely to achieve its goal?

(A) Whether transportation by train and barge would be substantially less expensive than transportation by truck

(B) Whether there are boats that can make the trip between the mainland and Burland faster than barges can

(C) Whether loading the freight cars onto barges is very time consuming

(D) Whether the average number of vehicles traveling over the bridge into Burland has been relatively constant in recent years

(E) Whether most trucks transporting goods into Burland return to the mainland empty

Evaluation of a Plan

Situation Transporting goods to Burland Island by truck takes many hours, because the trucks must take the congested single bridge that reaches the island. Trains can get goods to the channel separating Burland from the mainland more quickly than trucks can, and the freight cars can then be loaded onto barges that can cross the channel in an hour. Trancorp plans to reduce shipping time by switching from trucks to trains and barges.

Reasoning *What would it be most important to know in determining whether Trancorp will achieve its goal of reducing shipping time?* Trancorp's plan could fail to reduce shipping time if there were some aspect of the new shipping process, involving the trains and the barges, that took more time than anticipated.

A The goal of Trancorp's plan is to reduce shipping time. This might lower costs—but whether or not it does so is not directly relevant to whether or not the plan's goal is achieved.

B Trancorp's plan involves the use of barges. If some boats can make the trip between the mainland and Burland faster than barges can, that might be something to consider for the future, but it has nothing to do with whether the current plan will reduce shipping time.

C **Correct.** This statement properly identifies something that would be important in determining whether Trancorp's plan for reducing shipping time will achieve its goal—that is, whether loading the freight cars onto the barges will use up all the time saved by not using trucks.

D Regardless of variation in traffic, the bridge, according to the information provided in the passage, is congested and typically causes trucking delays. Given this information, the degree of variation is not helpful in evaluating Transcorp's plan.

E The state of the trucks returning to the mainland has nothing to do with whether Trancorp's plan for reducing shipping time will achieve its goal.

The correct answer is C.

586. Rainwater contains hydrogen of a heavy form called deuterium. The deuterium content of wood reflects the deuterium content of rainwater available to trees during their growth. Wood from trees that grew between 16,000 and 24,000 years ago in North America contains significantly more deuterium than wood from trees growing today. But water trapped in several North American caves that formed during that same early period contains significantly less deuterium than rainwater in North America contains today.

Which of the following, if true, most helps to reconcile the two findings?

(A) There is little deuterium in the North American caves other than the deuterium in the water trapped there.

(B) Exposure to water after a tree has died does not change the deuterium content of the wood.

(C) Industrialization in North America over the past 100 years has altered the deuterium content of rain.

(D) Trees draw on shallow groundwater from rain that falls during their growth, whereas water trapped in caves may have fallen as rainwater thousands of years before the caves formed.

(E) Wood with a high deuterium content is no more likely to remain preserved for long periods than is wood with a low deuterium content.

Argument Construction

Situation In North America, wood from trees that grew 16,000 to 24,000 years ago contains more deuterium than wood from trees growing today. But water in caves that formed during that same period contains less deuterium than rainwater contains today.

Reasoning *What could explain the puzzling discrepancy between the observed deuterium levels in wood and in caves?* Since the deuterium content of wood from trees reflects the deuterium content of rainwater available to the trees while they grew, the deuterium levels observed in wood suggests that North American rainwater contained more deuterium 16,000 to 24,000 years ago than it contains today. But this conclusion seems at odds with the low deuterium levels in water in caves that formed 16,000 to 24,000 years ago. Several factors might explain the discrepancy: the water in those caves might not be rainwater from the period when the caves formed; or some natural process might have altered the deuterium levels in the cave water or the wood; or the wood or caves in which deuterium levels were measured might be statistically abnormal somehow.

A If the caves had absorbed deuterium out of the rainwater trapped in them, there would probably be deuterium in the cave walls. So the observation that there is little deuterium in the caves apart from that in the water eliminates one possible explanation for the oddly low deuterium levels in the cave water.

B This suggests that the deuterium levels in the wood accurately reflect higher deuterium levels in rainwater that fell 16,000 to 24,000 years ago, but it does not explain why the deuterium levels are so low in water in the caves that formed then.

C This could explain why deuterium levels in rainwater have changed, but it does not help explain the discrepancy between the high deuterium levels in the wood and the low deuterium levels in the cave water.

D **Correct.** If the water in the caves fell as rainwater thousands of years before the caves formed, it may date from a period when rainwater contained much less deuterium than during the period 16,000 to 24,000 years ago, and much less than today.

E If wood with high deuterium content were more likely to be preserved, then wood from 16,000 to 24,000 years ago might have a high deuterium content even if the rainwater then had a low deuterium content. So the observation that wood with more deuterium is not more likely to be preserved eliminates one possible explanation for the discrepancy.

The correct answer is D.

587. Which of the following most logically completes the argument below?

NowNews, although still the most popular magazine covering cultural events in Kalopolis, has recently suffered a significant drop in advertising revenue because of falling circulation. Many readers have begun buying a competing magazine that, at 50 cents per copy, costs less than *NowNews* at $1.50 per copy. In order to boost circulation and thus increase advertising revenue, *NowNews's* publisher has proposed making it available at no charge, but this proposal has a serious drawback, since ______.

(A) Those Kalopolis residents with the greatest interest in cultural events are regular readers of both magazines.

(B) One reason *NowNews's* circulation fell was that its competitor's reporting on cultural events was superior.

(C) The newsstands and stores that currently sell NowNews will no longer carry it if it is being given away for free.

(D) At present, 10 percent of the total number of copies of each issue of *NowNews* are distributed free to students on college campuses in the Kalopolis area.

(E) *NowNews's* competitor would begin to lose large amounts of money if it were forced to lower its cover price.

Argument Construction

Situation *NowNews* is suffering declines in circulation and advertising revenue due to competition from a lower-priced magazine. The publisher proposes offering *NowNews* for free to reverse these declines.

Reasoning *What would suggest that the publisher's proposal will fail to increase circulation and advertising revenue?* The proposal's intended effect is simply to increase advertising revenue by increasing circulation. Any evidence that offering the magazine for free will not result in more copies being circulated or will not attract advertisers would therefore be evidence of a drawback in the proposal. So a statement offering such evidence would logically complete the argument.

A The fact that certain highly motivated Kalopolis residents still read *NowNews* even at a cost of $1.50 per issue leaves open the possibility that providing the magazine free might still boost readership.

B This suggests that improving its cultural reporting might help *NowNews* increase its circulation, not that the publisher's proposal will fail to do so.

C **Correct.** If the proposal leads newsstands and stores to stop carrying *NowNews*, circulation and advertising revenue would probably decline as a result.

D Even if 10 percent of the copies of *NowNews* are already distributed for free, distributing the remaining 90 percent for free could still increase circulation and advertising revenue as the publisher intends.

E Forcing a competing magazine to lower its cover price and lose lots of money would be an advantage rather than a drawback of the proposal, as far as the publisher of *NowNews* was concerned.

The correct answer is C.

588. Archaeologist: Researchers excavating a burial site in Cyprus found a feline skeleton lying near a human skeleton. Both skeletons were in the same sediment at the same depth and equally well-preserved, suggesting that the feline and human were buried together about 9,500 years ago. This shows that felines were domesticated around the time farming began, when they would have been useful in protecting stores of grain from mice.

Which of the following, if true, would most seriously weaken the archaeologist's argument?

(A) Archaeologists have not found any remains of stores of grain in the immediate vicinity of the burial site.

(B) The burial site in Cyprus is substantially older than any other known burial site in which a feline skeleton and a human skeleton appear to have been buried together.

(C) Paintings found near the burial site seem to show people keeping felines as domestic companions, but do not show felines hunting mice.

(D) In Cyprus, there are many burial sites dating from around 9,500 years ago in which the remains of wild animals appear to have been buried alongside human remains.

(E) Before felines were domesticated, early farmers had no effective way to protect stores of grain from mice.

Argument Evaluation

Situation A human skeleton and a feline skeleton were apparently buried together in Cyprus about 9,500 years ago.

Reasoning *What would most strongly suggest that the skeletons do not show that felines were domesticated around the time farming began?* The argument implicitly assumes that farming in Cyprus began around 9,500 years ago, so evidence against that assumption would weaken the argument. The argument could also be weakened by evidence that felines were domesticated much earlier, that the feline skeleton was not from a domesticated cat, or that the two skeletons were not actually buried together around 9,500 years ago.

A Even if archaeologists searched for evidence of a grain store, the fact that no such evidence was found near the burial site is at best only weak evidence that no grain store existed there or slightly farther away.

B The lack of corroborating evidence from other burial sites would weaken the argument slightly but would still be compatible with the hypothesis that this site revealed one of the very first burials of a domesticated cat.

C This would cast doubt on the hypothesis that cats were domesticated mainly to protect stores of grain, but not on the argument's conclusion that cats were domesticated around the time farming began.

D **Correct.** If many wild animals were buried alongside humans in Cyprus around 9,500 years ago, then the feline skeleton is just as likely to be that of a wild animal than that of a domesticated cat.

E Since this would provide an additional reason why early farmers might have domesticated the local cats, it would strengthen rather than weaken the argument.

The correct answer is D.

589. The heavy traffic in Masana is a growing drain on the city's economy—the clogging of the streets of the central business district alone cost the economy more than $1.2 billion over the past year. In order to address this problem, officials plan to introduce congestion pricing, by which drivers would pay to enter the city's most heavily trafficked areas during the busiest times of the day.

Which of the following, if true, would most strongly indicate that the plan will be a success?

(A) Approximately one-fifth of the vehicles in the central business district are in transit from one side of the city to the other.
(B) Planners expect that, without congestion pricing, traffic in Masana is likely to grow by 6 percent in the next five years.
(C) In other urban areas, congestion pricing has strongly encouraged carpooling (sharing of rides by private commuters).
(D) Several studies have shown that a reduction in traffic of 15 percent in Masana could result in 5,500 or more new jobs.
(E) Over 30 percent of the vehicles in the city's center are occupied by more than one person.

Evaluation of a Plan

Situation Traffic congestion in Masana has been harming the city's economy. To address the problem, officials plan to make drivers pay to enter the city's most heavily trafficked areas during the busiest times of day.

Reasoning *What would most strongly suggest that the plan will reduce the harm to Masana's economy from traffic congestion?* In order to succeed, the plan will have to be implemented and effectively enforced. Furthermore, the prices drivers pay will have to be high enough to significantly change their behavior in ways that reduce the amount of traffic congestion in the city. Finally, the economic benefits from the reduced traffic congestion will have to substantially outweigh any economically damaging side effects of the congestion pricing. Any evidence that any of these conditions will hold would provide at least some support for the prediction that the plan will succeed.

A This provides no evidence that the congestion pricing would affect the behavior of either the one-fifth of drivers whose vehicles traverse the city or of the other four-fifths of drivers, nor does it give any evidence that the plan would produce overriding economic benefits.

B This indicates that the traffic problem will grow worse if the plan is not implemented, but it does not provide any evidence that the plan will help address the problem.

C **Correct.** This indicates that similar plans have successfully changed drivers' behavior in other cities in a way likely to reduce the number of cars on the road in heavily trafficked areas at busy times of day without producing harmful economic side effects. Thus, it provides evidence that the strategy could also be successful in Masana.

D Although this suggests that reducing traffic congestion would be economically beneficial, it doesn't provide any evidence that the plan will succeed in reducing traffic congestion.

E This suggests that many drivers in the city center are already carpooling, which, if anything, indicates that the plan will be less able to further affect those drivers' behavior and thus could be less effective than it might otherwise be.

The correct answer is C.

590. Economist: The most economically efficient way to reduce emissions of air pollutants is to tax them in proportion to the damage they are likely to cause. But in Country Y, many serious pollutants are untaxed and unregulated, and policy makers strongly oppose new taxes. Therefore, the best way to achieve a reduction in air pollutant emissions in Country Y would be to institute fixed upper limits on them.

Which of the following is an assumption of the economist's argument?

(A) Policy makers in Country Y oppose all new taxes equally strongly, regardless of any benefits they may provide.
(B) Country Y's air pollutant emissions would not fall significantly if they were taxed in proportion to the damage they are likely to cause.
(C) Policy makers in Country Y strongly favor reductions in air pollutant emissions.
(D) Country Y's policy makers believe that air pollutant emissions should be reduced with maximum economic efficiency.
(E) Policy makers in Country Y do not oppose setting fixed upper limits on air pollutant emissions as strongly as they oppose new taxes.

Argument Construction

Situation Although taxing air pollution emissions in proportion to the damage they cause is the most economically efficient way to reduce those emissions, many serious pollutants in Nation Y are untaxed and unregulated, and the nation's policy makers strongly oppose new taxes. Therefore, fixed upper limits on such emissions would more effectively reach this goal.

Reasoning *What must be true in order for the factors the economist cites to support the claim that fixing upper limits on air pollutant emissions in Nation Y would be the best way to reduce those emissions?* Political opposition to taxation in Nation Y is the only factor the economist cites to support the argument's conclusion that it would be best to institute fixed upper limits on air pollutants. In order for the premise to support the conclusion, there must be less political opposition in Nation Y to instituting such limits than there would be to the proportional taxation approach the economist prefers.

A Even if the policy makers oppose some new taxes less than others, they could still oppose the proportional taxation approach strongly enough for it to be utterly infeasible.

B Even if the proportional taxation scheme would significantly reduce emissions, it still might not be the best approach for Nation Y if it would generate too much political opposition to be viable there.

C Even if policy makers in Nation Y do not strongly favor reducing emissions, fixing upper limits on emissions might still be a better and more politically feasible way to reduce emissions than any alternative is.

D Since fixing upper emissions limits would be no more economically efficient than the proportional taxation scheme, the policy makers' support for economic efficiency would not make the former approach any more politically feasible than the latter.

E **Correct.** If the policy makers opposed fixing upper emissions limits as strongly as they oppose new taxes, then their opposition to new taxes would no longer support the conclusion that fixing the emissions limits is a better way to reduce emissions.

The correct answer is E.

591. Humans get Lyme disease from infected ticks. Ticks get infected by feeding on animals with Lyme disease, but the ease of transmission from host animal to tick varies. With most species of host animal, transmission of Lyme disease to ticks is extremely rare, but white-footed mice are an exception, readily passing Lyme disease to ticks. And white-footed mouse populations greatly expand, becoming the main food source for ticks, in areas where biodiversity is in decline.

The information in the passage most strongly supports which of the following?

(A) In areas where many humans are infected with Lyme disease, the proportion of ticks infected with Lyme disease is especially high.
(B) Very few animals that live in areas where there are no white-footed mice are infected with Lyme disease.
(C) Humans are less at risk of contracting Lyme disease in areas where biodiversity is high.
(D) Ticks feed on white-footed mice only when other host species are not available to them.
(E) The greater the biodiversity of an area, the more likely any given host animal in that area is to pass Lyme disease to ticks.

Argument Construction

Situation White-footed mice readily pass Lyme disease to ticks, which pass it to humans. White-footed mouse populations expand where biodiversity is declining.

Reasoning *What conclusion do the stated facts support?* Since declining biodiversity causes white-footed mouse populations to increase, and white-footed mice are especially likely to pass Lyme disease to ticks, and ticks pass it to humans, declining biodiversity could reasonably be expected to increase the incidence of Lyme disease in both ticks and humans.

A In areas where many humans are infected with Lyme disease, the total number of ticks may be unusually high, so even if the number of infected ticks is unusually high, the proportion of infected ticks may not be unusually high

B Most animals with Lyme disease may get it from sources other than ticks that have fed on infected mice.

C **Correct.** If biodiversity is high, then any biodiversity decline that has already begun has likely not yet reached a point where white-footed mouse populations have greatly expanded, so the risk of people contracting Lyme disease is still relatively less than in areas where biodiversity is low and where significant decline in biodiversity has likely already occurred.

D Even if ticks feed on white-footed mice when few other species are available for them to feed on, they may also sometimes feed on white-footed mice when there are many other species for them to feed on.

E The passage suggests that the overall incidence of Lyme disease is probably lower in more biodiverse areas, so any given host animal in those areas would probably be less likely to pass Lyme disease to a tick.

The correct answer is C.

592. Many industrialized nations are trying to reduce atmospheric concentrations of carbon dioxide, a gas released by the burning of fossil fuels. One proposal is to replace conventional cement, which is made with calcium carbonate, by a new "eco-cement." This new cement, made with magnesium carbonate, absorbs large amounts of carbon dioxide when exposed to the atmosphere. Therefore, using eco-cement for new concrete building projects will significantly help reduce atmospheric concentrations of carbon dioxide.

Which of the following, if true, most strengthens the argument?

(A) The cost of magnesium carbonate, currently greater than the cost of calcium carbonate, probably will fall as more magnesium carbonate is used in cement manufacture.

(B) Eco-cement is strengthened when absorbed carbon dioxide reacts with the cement.

(C) Before the development of eco-cement, magnesium-based cement was considered too susceptible to water erosion to be of practical use.

(D) The manufacture of eco-cement uses considerably less fossil fuel per unit of cement than the manufacture of conventional cement does.

(E) Most building-industry groups are unaware of the development or availability of eco-cement.

Argument Evaluation

Situation Many nations are trying to reduce atmospheric concentrations of carbon dioxide. One proposed method is to use a new type of "eco-cement" that absorbs carbon dioxide from air.

Reasoning *What evidence, combined with the cited facts, would most support the prediction that using eco-cement will significantly help reduce atmospheric concentrations of carbon dioxide?* The prediction assumes that the use of eco-cement would be an effective way to reduce carbon dioxide levels. Any evidence supporting this assumption will support the prediction.

A Since eco-cement uses magnesium carbonate, the prediction that magnesium carbonate prices will fall suggests that a potential financial barrier to widespread eco-cement use will diminish. However, those prices may not fall enough to make eco-cement cost-competitive with regular cement.

B Even if absorbed carbon dioxide strengthens eco-cement, the strengthened eco-cement might still be much weaker than regular cement and thus might never become widely used, in which case it will not significantly help reduce atmospheric concentrations of carbon dioxide.

C Even if eco-cement is less susceptible to water erosion than earlier forms of magnesium-based cement were, it might still be much more susceptible to water erosion than regular cement is, and thus might never become widely used.

D **Correct.** This suggests that manufacturing eco-cement produces much less carbon dioxide than manufacturing regular cement does, so it supports the claim that widespread use of eco-cement would be an effective way to reduce carbon dioxide levels.

E If anything, this lack of awareness makes it less likely that eco-cement will become widely used, which in turn makes it less likely that eco-cement will significantly help reduce atmospheric concentrations of carbon dioxide.

The correct answer is D.

593. Which of the following most logically completes the argument below?

Davison River farmers are currently deciding between planting winter wheat this fall or spring wheat next spring. Winter wheat and spring wheat are usually about equally profitable. Because of new government restrictions on the use of Davison River water for irrigation, per acre yields for winter wheat, though not for spring wheat, would be much lower than average. Therefore, planting spring wheat will be more profitable than planting winter wheat, since ________.

(A) the smaller-than-average size of a winter wheat harvest this year would not be compensated for by higher winter wheat prices

(B) new crops of spring wheat must be planted earlier than the time at which standing crops of winter wheat are ready to be harvested

(C) the spring wheat that farmers in the Davison River region plant is well adapted to the soil of the region

(D) spring wheat has uses that are different from those of winter wheat

(E) planting spring wheat is more profitable than planting certain other crops, such as rye

Argument Construction

Situation Farmers in the Davison River region must choose between planting winter wheat in the fall and planting spring wheat next spring. The crops tend to be equally profitable. This year's winter wheat crop yield is likely to be lower than average. The spring wheat yield should not be lower than average. Thus, for these reasons (plus one that the argument omits), spring wheat will be more profitable than winter wheat.

Reasoning *Which point would logically complete the argument?* What would ensure spring wheat's profitability over winter wheat? Since the yield per acre of winter wheat is likely to be lower than usual, there will most likely be less winter wheat to sell. Winter wheat could match its usual profitability if the price farmers receive for it were to rise. If its price does not rise, however, it is unlikely to match its usual profitability. It would thus be unlikely to match spring wheat's profitability.

A **Correct.** If this is true, it would mean that smaller-than-average winter wheat yields would translate into lower-than-usual profits on winter wheat (while spring wheat would be as profitable as winter wheat would normally be). This would justify the conclusion that spring wheat will be more profitable than winter wheat.

B This provides support for the idea that farmers must choose between planting winter wheat and planting spring wheat, but it does not help determine which would be more profitable to plant.

C This does not help explain why spring wheat is likely to be more profitable than winter wheat, because it gives no information about how well winter wheat is adapted to the soil of the region.

D That spring wheat and winter wheat have different uses is not helpful in supporting a conclusion about which kind of wheat will be more profitable. It might help to know which of their uses are more profitable than others.

E Since the question is whether it will be more profitable to plant winter wheat or to plant spring wheat, the fact that spring wheat is more profitable than nonwheat crops is not relevant.

The correct answer is A.

594. Advertisement: When your car's engine is running at its normal operating temperature, any major brand of motor oil will protect it about as well as Tuff does. When the engine is cold, it is a different story: Tuff motor oil flows better at lower temperatures than its major competitors do. So, if you want your car's engine to have maximum protection, you should use Tuff.

Which of the following, if true, most strengthens the argument in the advertisement?

(A) Tuff motor oil provides above-average protection for engines that happen to overheat.

(B) Tuff motor oil is periodically supplied free of charge to automobile manufacturers to use in factory-new cars.

(C) Tuff motor oil's share of the engine oil market peaked three years ago.

(D) Tuff motor oil, like any motor oil, is thicker and flows less freely at cold temperatures than at hot temperatures.

(E) Tuff motor oil is manufactured at only one refinery and shipped from there to all markets.

Argument Evaluation

Situation An advertisement argues that since Tuff motor oil flows better than its major competitors at low temperatures and works about as well as they do at normal temperatures, it provides *maximum protection* for car engines.

Reasoning *What additional evidence would suggest that Tuff motor oil provides the best available protection for car engines?* The argument requires the assumptions that no type of motor oil other than the "major brands" provides superior protection, that flowing better at lower temperatures ensures superior protection at those temperatures, and that Tuff protects car engines at least as well as its competitors do at above-normal temperatures. Any evidence supporting any of these assumptions would strengthen the argument.

A **Correct.** If Tuff provides above-average protection when engines overheat, in addition to the solid protection it provides at normal and low temperatures, it may well provide the best available protection overall.

B The company that makes Tuff might give automobile manufacturers free motor oil as a promotional gimmick even if Tuff is an inferior product.

C Tuff's sales might have declined over the past three years because consumers have realized that Tuff is an inferior product.

D The similar responses of Tuff and other motor oils to temperature changes do not suggest that Tuff provides better protection overall than those other motor oils do.

E Even if Tuff is manufactured at only one refinery, it may still be an inferior product.

The correct answer is A.

595. *The Testament of William Thorpe* was published around 1530 as an appendix to Thorpe's longer Examination. Many scholars, however, doubt the attribution of the *Testament* to Thorpe because, whereas the *Examination* is dated 1406, the *Testament* is dated 1460. One scholar has recently argued that the 1460 date be amended to 1409, based on the observation that when these numbers are expressed as Roman numerals, MCCCCLX and MCCCCIX, it becomes easy to see how the dates might have become confused through scribal error.

Which of the following, if true, would most support the scholar's hypothesis concerning the date of the *Testament*?

(A) The sole evidence that historians have had that William Thorpe died no earlier than 1460 was the presumed date of publication of the *Testament*.

(B) In the preface to the 1530 publication, the editor attributes both works to William Thorpe.

(C) Few writers in fifteenth-century England marked dates in their works using only Roman numerals.

(D) The *Testament* alludes to a date, "Friday, September 20," as apparently contemporaneous with the writing of the *Testament*, and September 20 fell on a Friday in 1409 but not in 1460.

(E) The *Testament* contains few references to historical events that occurred later than 1406.

Argument Construction

Situation *The Testament of William Thorpe*, dated 1460, was published around 1530 as an appendix to Thorpe's *Examination*, dated 1406. But when expressed in Roman numerals, 1460 could easily be confused with 1409.

Reasoning *Given the facts cited, what would provide additional evidence that Thorpe's* Testament *dates from 1409 rather than 1460?* The scholar's hypothesis that the work dates from 1409 is based on the observation that in Roman numerals, 1409 might easily have been improperly transcribed as 1460. This hypothesis could be supported by evidence that the manuscripts were dated in Roman numerals, or by any independent evidence that 1409 is a more likely date for the *Testament* than 1460.

A This suggests that scholars have no biographical evidence that the *Testament* was published in 1460, but they could still have abundant evidence of other types to support that date, such as the text's cultural allusions or references to other works.

B The editor of the 1530 publication could easily have been mistaken about the authorship of one or both works. And even if the editor were correct, Thorpe might have lived long enough to write one work in 1406 and the other in 1460.

C This would cast doubt on the scholar's argument by providing evidence that the original manuscripts were not dated only in Roman numerals.

D **Correct.** This provides strong evidence directly supporting the hypothesis that the *Testament* dates from 1409 specifically.

E Even if the *Testament* contained only one reference to a historical event that occurred later than 1406 (for example, one event in 1459), that reference alone could provide strong evidence that the work dates from 1460 rather than 1409.

The correct answer is D.

596. To reduce productivity losses from employees calling in sick, Corporation X implemented a new policy requiring employees to come into work unless they were so sick that they had to go to a doctor. But a year after the policy was implemented, a study found that Corporation X's overall productivity losses due to reported employee illnesses had increased.

Which of the following, if true, would best explain why the policy produced the reverse of its intended effect?

(A) After the policy was implemented, employees more frequently went to the doctor when they felt sick.

(B) Before the policy was implemented, employees who were not sick at all often called in sick.

(C) Employees coming into work when sick often infect many of their coworkers.

(D) Unusually few employees became genuinely sick during the year after the policy was implemented.

(E) There are many other factors besides employee illness that can adversely affect productivity.

Evaluation of a Plan

Situation After a company started requiring employees to come to work unless they were sick enough to have to go to a doctor, the company's productivity losses from reported employee illness increased.

Reasoning *What would explain why the policy increased productivity losses from reported employee illness?* Any factors that could have plausibly caused the policy to increase employee absenteeism from reported illness or to reduce the employees' productivity at work as a result of reported illness could explain why the policy increased productivity losses from reported illness.

A Even though the policy required sick employees to consult a doctor, there is no reason to think that employees' doing so would have made them less productive than they would otherwise have been when absent from work.

B This suggests that the policy made it more difficult for employees to falsely claim illness as an excuse for a work absence. Reduction in absences should result in productivity gains rather than losses.

C **Correct.** This could have been a result of the policy and would have led to productivity losses possibly greater than those seen before the policy was introduced.

D This would help to explain lower productivity losses from reported illness after the policy was implemented, not higher productivity losses.

E The question is what could explain how the policy increased productivity losses from reported employee illness specifically, not productivity losses from any other factors.

The correct answer is C.

597. Advertising by mail has become much less effective, with fewer consumers responding. Because consumers are increasingly overwhelmed by the sheer amount of junk mail they receive, most discard almost all offers without considering them. Thus, an effective way for corporations to improve response rates would be to more carefully target the individuals to whom they mail advertising, thereby cutting down on the amount of junk mail each consumer receives.

Which of the following, if true, would most support the recommendation above?

(A) There are cost-effective means by which corporations that currently advertise by mail could improve response rates.

(B) Many successful corporations are already carefully targeting the individuals to whom they mail advertising.

(C) Any consumer who, immediately after receiving an advertisement by mail, merely glances at it is very likely to discard it.

(D) Improvements in the quality of the advertising materials used in mail that is carefully targeted to individuals can improve the response rate for such mail.

(E) Response rates to carefully targeted advertisements by mail are considerably higher, on average, than response rates to most other forms of advertising.

Evaluation of a Plan

Situation Advertising by mail has become less effective because consumers overwhelmed with the amount of junk mail they receive discard almost all of it without considering it.

Reasoning *What would most help to support the claim that making mail advertising more carefully targeted would improve response rates?* The passage recommends targeted advertising, reasoning that since targeted advertising would reduce the total amount of junk mail consumers receive, it would generate higher response rates. Any additional evidence for the claim that carefully targeted advertising would improve response rates would support this recommendation.

A Even if targeted advertising and every other means of improving response rates were too expensive to be cost-effective, targeted advertising could still be effective for any corporation willing to pay the expense.

B If many corporations already mail targeted advertising, and mail advertising is nonetheless yielding declining response rates, that suggests that targeted mail is an ineffective way to increase response rates.

C This could be equally true for targeted and untargeted mail advertising, so it does not suggest that the former is more effective.

D The question under consideration is whether more carefully targeted mail advertising would in itself increase response rates, not whether higher quality advertising would do so.

E **Correct.** This provides some evidence that carefully targeted mail advertising is associated with higher response rates than untargeted mail advertising is, and therefore that targeting mail advertising more carefully would improve response rates.

The correct answer is E.

598. Petrochemical industry officials have said that the extreme pressure exerted on plant managers during the last five years to improve profits by cutting costs has done nothing to impair the industry's ability to operate safely. However, environmentalists contend that the recent rash of serious oil spills and accidents at petrochemical plants is traceable to cost-cutting measures.

Which of the following, if true, would provide the strongest support for the position held by industry officials?

(A) The petrochemical industry benefits if accidents do not occur, since accidents involve risk of employee injury as well as loss of equipment and product.

(B) Petrochemical industry unions recently demanded that additional money be spent on safety and environmental protection measures, but the unions readily abandoned those demands in exchange for job security.

(C) Despite major cutbacks in most other areas of operation, the petrochemical industry has devoted more of its resources to environmental and safety measures in the last five years than in the preceding five years.

(D) There is evidence that the most damaging of the recent oil spills would have been prevented had cost-cutting measures not been instituted.

(E) Both the large fines and the adverse publicity generated by the most recent oil spill have prompted the petrochemical industry to increase the resources devoted to oil-spill prevention.

Argument Evaluation

Situation Petrochemical industry officials claim that pressure on plant managers to cut costs over the past five years has not made the industry's operations any less safe. Environmentalists claim that recent oil spills and accidents show otherwise.

Reasoning *What evidence would most strongly suggest that the cost-cutting pressure was not responsible for the recent rash of oil spills and accidents?* Evidence that the plant managers did not cut costs in any specific ways likely to have increased the likelihood of oil spills and accidents would support the industry officials' position that the cost-cutting pressure has not made petrochemical operations any less safe.

A Even if the petrochemical industry has good reasons to try to prevent accidents, the recent rash of serious accidents suggests that it is failing to do so and that the cost-cutting pressure might be responsible.

B This suggests that the unions, whose members could directly observe the cost-cutting pressure's effects, share the environmentalists' belief that this pressure contributed to the oil spills and accidents. Because the unions abandoned their demands, their concerns probably have not been addressed.

C **Correct.** This suggests that, as the industry officials claim, the cost-cutting pressure has not in itself reduced the industry's effectiveness at preventing oil spills and accidents. Thus, it suggests that other factors are probably responsible for the recent problems.

D This clearly suggests that the cost-cutting measures have indeed caused the industry to operate less safely, as the environmentalists claim.

E Although this suggests that the industry is now trying to address the recent problems, the cost-cutting measures might nonetheless have caused all those problems.

The correct answer is C.

599. Economist: The price of tap water in our region should be raised drastically. **Supplies in local freshwater reservoirs have been declining for years** because water is being used faster than it can be replenished. Since the price of tap water has been low, **few users have bothered to adopt even easy conservation measures.**

The two sections in boldface play which of the following roles in the economist's argument?

(A) The first is a conclusion for which support is provided, and which in turn supports the main conclusion; the second is the main conclusion.

(B) The first is an observation for which the second provides an explanation; the second is the main conclusion but not the only conclusion.

(C) The first is a premise supporting the argument's main conclusion; so is the second.

(D) The first is the only conclusion; the second provides an explanation for the first.

(E) The first is the main conclusion; the second is a conclusion for which support is provided, and which in turn supports the first.

Argument Construction

Situation Local water supplies have been declining for years because of excessive water use and low prices. Few users have adopted even easy conservation measures.

Reasoning *What roles do the two boldface statements play in the argument?* Both are factual observations. Since no further evidence or support is provided for either, neither can be a conclusion in the argument. However, interconnected causal explanations, signaled by *because* and *since,* are provided for both. The observation in the first boldface statement is causally explained by the further observation that water is being used faster than it can be replenished, which in turn is causally explained by the entire final sentence. The observation in the second boldface statement is causally explained by the observation that the price of tap water has been low. The only remaining portion of the argument is the initial sentence, a recommendation supported by these four observations together, and by the causal claims in which they are embedded. Thus, the four observations (including the two boldface statements) and the causal claims containing them are all premises, and the initial statement is the argument's only conclusion.

A As explained above, the two boldface statements are premises of the argument. Although causal explanations are provided for both, no support or evidence is provided for either.

B As explained above, the second boldface statement does provide part of the causal explanation for the observation in the first boldface statement. But no support is provided for either statement, so neither is a conclusion.

C **Correct.** As explained above, each of the statements is a premise that serves along with other claims to support the recommendation in the initial sentence, which is the argument's only conclusion, and in that sense its main conclusion.

D As explained above, the second boldface statement does provide part of the causal explanation for the observation in the first boldface statement. But no support is provided for either statement, so neither is a conclusion in the argument.

E As explained above, the two boldface statements are premises of the argument. Although causal explanations are provided for both, no support or evidence is provided for either.

The correct answer is C.

600. Politician: Hybrid cars use significantly less fuel per kilometer than nonhybrids. And fuel produces air pollution, which contributes to a number of environmental problems. Motorists can save money by driving cars that are more fuel efficient, and they will be encouraged to drive hybrid cars if we make them aware of that fact. Therefore, we can help reduce the total amount of pollution emitted by cars in this country by highlighting this advantage of hybrid cars.

Which of the following, if true, would most indicate a vulnerability of the politician's argument?

(A) People with more fuel-efficient cars typically drive more than do those with less fuel-efficient cars.

(B) Not all air pollution originates from automobiles.

(C) Hybrid cars have already begun to gain popularity.

(D) Fuel-efficient alternatives to hybrid cars will likely become available in the future.

(E) The future cost of gasoline and other fuel cannot be predicted with absolute precision or certainty.

Argument Evaluation

Situation According to a politician, hybrid cars use less fuel per kilometer than nonhybrids, and fuel produces air pollution. Motorists can save money by driving fuel-efficient cars, and will be encouraged to do so if made aware of the fact. The politician concludes that highlighting this fact will result in a reduction in air pollution.

Reasoning *What would suggest that telling motorists they can save money by driving fuel-efficient cars would not reduce automotive air pollution, despite the facts cited by the politician?* The politician's implicit reasoning is that since hybrid cars use less fuel per kilometer, and fuel produces air pollution, motorists who drive hybrid cars must produce less air pollution than those who drive nonhybrids. The politician concludes that encouraging motorists to drive hybrid cars by telling them they would save money on fuel will therefore reduce automotive air pollution. Evidence that motorists who drive hybrid cars produce just as much automotive air pollution as those who drive nonhybrids would undermine this argument.

A **Correct.** If drivers of hybrid cars tend to drive more kilometers than drivers of nonhybrids, then they may consume just as much fuel and produce just as much air pollution as the nonhybrid car drivers do, despite their lower fuel use per kilometer.

B The politician's argument is only about air pollution from cars specifically, not air pollution from all sources.

C Even if hybrid cars are beginning to gain popularity, informing motorists of the cost savings from fuel efficiency could help these cars become more popular than they would otherwise be.

D Encouraging motorists to switch to hybrid cars now could reduce fuel use and automotive air pollution in the near future even if other, more fuel-efficient vehicles will become available further in the future.

E Even if the future cost of fuel cannot be predicted accurately, encouraging motorists to switch to hybrid cars could reduce air pollution as the politician argues.

The correct answer is A.

601. Which of the following most logically completes the passage?

A recent government study links the high rates of respiratory ailments in Groverston to airborne pollutants released by the Woodco plywood manufacturing plant there. To address the problem, the government imposed strict regulations on emissions which will go into effect in four years. Although Woodco plans to cut its emissions in half two years ahead of schedule, it is unlikely that the rate of respiratory ailments will decline before the regulations go into effect, since _______.

(A) the number of facilities capable of treating respiratory ailments is not likely to increase

(B) reducing emissions even further than planned would necessitate decreasing production at Woodco

(C) it is difficult to make accurate, long-term predictions about emissions

(D) not all respiratory ailments are caused by airborne pollutants

(E) three new plywood manufacturing plants are about to go into production in Groverston

Argument Construction

Situation A government study linked high rates of respiratory illness in Groverston to air pollutants released by a plywood manufacturing plant. A government-imposed restriction on emissions will go into effect in four years. But the Woodco manufacturing plant plans to cut its emissions in half two years ahead of schedule.

Reasoning *Which of the possible completions of the passage will provide the most support for the argument's conclusion?* The argument's conclusion is that the rate of respiratory illness is unlikely to decline before the regulations go into effect four years from now. That is a surprising claim, given that the existing plywood factory is going to *halve* its emissions two years from now—so this claim requires additional support (to be provided by completing the blank). Such additional support is provided by the information that three new plywood manufacturing plants will soon be starting production in Groverston. This suggests that even if Groverston reduces its emissions by half over the next two years—and even if each of the three new plants have only, let's say, *one quarter* of the emissions of the existing plant as currently operated—the *total amount* of airborne pollutants from plywood manufacture in the Groverston area will not decline. Since the total airborne pollution from the plants will not decline, we should not expect that the rate of respiratory illnesses from such pollution would decline either.

A The argument focuses on the incidence of respiratory ailments in Groverston, not on the availability of treatment facilities for such ailments once they occur. So this statement is largely irrelevant to the argument.

B This information provides no support for the argument's conclusion. It merely indicates a practical difficulty Woodco would have in making more than a 50 percent reduction in its emissions. However, even with the 50 percent emissions reduction that Woodco plans to implement in two years, the rate of respiratory ailments should decline.

C First, it is not clear that a prediction about levels of emissions in Groverston three or four years from now is a *long-term prediction*. More to the point, if it would be very difficult to predict the emissions even two years from now, that would not support a conclusion that rates of respiratory ailments are unlikely to decline. Rather, it would support the conclusion that we do not know whether rates will decline.

D This information raises the possibility that within the next four years, an increase in the occurrence of factors *other than* airborne pollutants might make a decline in respiratory ailments unlikely. However, the passage provides no information whatsoever that implies an increase in the occurrence of such "other" factors.

E **Correct.** This helps to support the conclusion that rates of respiratory ailments in Groverston are unlikely to decline before the new government regulations go into effect.

The correct answer is E.

602. One summer, floods covered low-lying garlic fields situated in a region with a large mosquito population. Since mosquitoes lay their eggs in standing water, flooded fields would normally attract mosquitoes, yet no mosquitoes were found in the fields. Diallyl sulfide, a major component of garlic, is known to repel several species of insects, including mosquitoes, so it is likely that diallyl sulfide from the garlic repelled the mosquitoes.

Which of the following, if true, most strengthens the argument?

(A) Diallyl sulfide is also found in onions but at concentrations lower than in garlic.

(B) The mosquito population of the region as a whole was significantly smaller during the year in which the flooding took place than it had been in previous years.

(C) By the end of the summer, most of the garlic plants in the flooded fields had been killed by waterborne fungi.

(D) Many insect species not repelled by diallyl sulfide were found in the flooded garlic fields throughout the summer.

(E) Mosquitoes are known to be susceptible to toxins in plants other than garlic, such as marigolds.

Argument Evaluation

Situation When summer floods covered garlic fields in an area with many mosquitoes, no mosquitoes were found in the fields, even though flooded fields would normally attract mosquitoes to lay their eggs in the water. Diallyl sulfide, which is found in garlic, repels mosquitoes and some other insect species, and likely accounts for the lack of mosquitoes in the area.

Reasoning *Given the facts cited, what would provide additional evidence that diallyl sulfide from the garlic made mosquitoes avoid the flooded fields?* The argument would be strengthened by any independent evidence suggesting that diallyl sulfide pervaded the flooded fields or excluding other factors that might explain the absence of mosquitoes in the fields.

A This could strengthen the argument if mosquitoes also avoid flooded onion fields, but we do not know whether they do.

B This would weaken the argument by suggesting that the general mosquito population decline, rather than the diallyl sulfide, could explain the absence of mosquitoes from the fields.

C It is not clear how this would affect the amount of diallyl sulfide in the flooded fields, so this does not provide evidence that the diallyl sulfide repelled the mosquitoes.

D **Correct.** This provides evidence that there was no factor other than diallyl sulfide that reduced insect populations in the flooded garlic fields.

E If anything, this would weaken the argument, since it is at least possible that some of these toxins were present in the flooded fields.

The correct answer is D.

603. Which of the following most logically completes the passage?

Pecan growers get a high price for their crop when pecans are comparatively scarce, but the price drops sharply when pecans are abundant. Thus, in high-yield years, growers often hold back part of their crop in refrigerated warehouses for one or two years, hoping for higher prices in the future. This year's pecan crop was the smallest in five years. It is nonetheless quite possible that a portion of this year's crop will be held back, since ______.

(A) each of the last two years produced record-breaking pecan yields
(B) the quality of this year's pecan crop is no worse than the quality of the pecan crops of the previous five years
(C) pecan prices have not been subject to sharp fluctuations in recent years
(D) for some pecan growers, this year's crop was no smaller than last year's
(E) the practice of holding back part of one year's crop had not yet become widespread the last time the pecan crop was as small as it was this year

Argument Construction

Situation The price of pecans tends to drop sharply in years when pecans are abundant. So in high-yield years, growers often hold back part of the harvest in refrigerated warehouses. This year's harvest was the smallest in five years.

Reasoning *What would provide the best completion of the argument?* The argument's conclusion is that some of this year's crop might be held back. The blank to be completed should provide a reason in support of that conclusion. What would lead us to believe that some of this year's crop might go into cold storage even though the crop was unusually small? Only in high-yield years does this usually happen. But suppose there is *already* a large quantity of pecans in cold storage from previous harvests. Given this information, it would make perfect sense to expect that the pecans already in cold storage would be marketed first, while some of the latest crop would be stored. This would avoid the market oversupply and lower producer prices that might result if both all of this year's crop and all of the already stored pecans were marketed this year.

A **Correct.** This answer choice provides information that makes it more probable that the conclusion is true.

B The argument provides no information whatsoever that would suggest the decision to store or not to store pecans is based on evaluation of the crop's quality.

C This information is of little or no relevance. It is reasonable to think that predictions about pecan prices this year would affect the decision to store or not to store. But the information in this answer choice sheds little or no light on what this year's pecan prices might be, given that, as the passage tells us, this year's crop is exceptionally small.

D It is not surprising that some growers had crops this year that were as big as their crops the year before. But what matters, what affects the price of pecans, is the overall size of total pecan production and the abundance or scarcity of pecans at the time.

E This piece of history about marketing and storage practices explains why pecans were not placed in storage in previous small-yield years, but it provides no reason to believe that some of the new pecan crop will be stored this year.

The correct answer is A.

604. Coffee shop owner: A large number of customers will pay at least the fair market value for a cup of coffee, even if there is no formal charge. Some will pay more than this out of appreciation of the trust that is placed in them. And our total number of customers is likely to increase. We could therefore improve our net cash flow by implementing an honor system in which customers pay what they wish for coffee by depositing money in a can.

Manager: We're likely to lose money on this plan. Many customers would cheat the system, paying a very small sum or nothing at all.

Which of the following, if true, would best support the owner's plan, in light of the manager's concern?

(A) The new system, if implemented, would increase the number of customers.

(B) By roasting its own coffee, the shop has managed to reduce the difficulties (and cost) of maintaining an inventory of freshly roasted coffee.

(C) Many customers stay in the cafe for long stretches of time.

(D) The shop makes a substantial profit from pastries and other food bought by the coffee drinkers.

(E) No other coffee shop in the area has such a system.

Evaluation of a Plan

Situation The owner and the manager of a coffee shop disagree about whether allowing customers to pay for coffee on an honor system would increase or decrease profits.

Reasoning *What would be the best evidence that the honor-system plan would increase profits even if many customers cheated the system?* The owner argues that profits would increase because many customers will choose to pay as much or more than before and the total number of customers will likely increase. But the manager points out that many customers would also choose to pay little or nothing. Assuming that the manager is correct about that, what further support could the owner present for the claim that the plan would still be profitable?

A Since the owner has already basically asserted this, asserting it again would not provide any significant additional support for the plan.

B This suggests that the shop is already profitable, not that the honor-system plan would make it more profitable.

C Customers who stay in the cafe for long stretches would not necessarily pay any more per cup on the honor-system plan than other customers would.

D **Correct.** If the customer base increases (as both the owner and the manager seem to agree), more customers will likely purchase highly profitable pastries and other foods, thus boosting profits.

E The reason no other coffee shop in the area has an honor system may be that their owners and managers have determined that it would not be profitable.

The correct answer is D.

605. Which of the following most logically completes the argument?

By competing with rodents for seeds, black ants help control rodent populations that pose a public health risk. However, a very aggressive species of black ant, the Loma ant, which has recently invaded a certain region, has a venomous sting that is often fatal to humans. Therefore, the planned introduction into that region of ant flies, which prey on Loma ants, would benefit public health, since ________.

(A) ant flies do not attack black ants other than Loma ants

(B) Loma ants are less effective than many bird species in competing with rodents for seeds

(C) certain other species of black ants are more effective than Loma ants in competing with rodents for seeds

(D) the sting of Loma ants can also be fatal to rodents

(E) some pesticides that could be used to control Loma ants are harmful to the environment

Argument Construction

Situation Black ants help to control populations of rodents by competing with them for seeds. But a very aggressive species of black ant, the Loma ant, has a sting that can be fatal to humans. Ant flies prey on Loma ants and their presence can thereby benefit public health.

Reasoning *Which of the possible completions of the passage provides the most support for the conclusion?* The argument's conclusion is that introducing ant flies into the region where Loma ants have recently invaded would benefit public health. We know from the passage that black ants, generally, benefit public health by keeping down rodent populations. However, the sting of Loma ants, a species of black ant, can be fatal to humans. Ant flies prey on Loma ants. To that extent their introduction in the region would tend to benefit public health by making fatal Loma stinging of humans less likely. But if these ant flies also prey on black ants other than the Loma ants, then to that extent they would undermine another public health benefit associated with controlling rodents. Thus, the information that ant flies do not prey on black ants other than Loma ants would provide strong logical support for the conclusion.

A **Correct.** This most logically completes the argument because it addresses a potential downside of introducing the ant flies into the region. The potential downside is that it might reduce the desirable effect that other species of black ants have in keeping down the rodent populations.

B We have no idea whether the bird species that are more effective than Loma ants at competing with rodents for seeds are even present in the region in question.

C This does not help the conclusion very much because we do not know *from the passage* whether ant flies prey on other species of black ants besides Loma ants.

D If anything, this is a reason *not to introduce ant flies* into the region. This answer choice at least suggests that Loma ants might have some positive effect on public health because they might keep down rodent populations by reducing their survival chances.

E This provides very little support for the conclusion. It does not exclude the possibility that there are pesticides—perhaps several—that would control Loma ants effectively without harming the environment. So it is not a strong reason for introducing ant flies.

The correct answer is A.

606. Journalist: In physics journals, the number of articles reporting the results of experiments involving particle accelerators was lower last year than it had been in previous years. Several of the particle accelerators at major research institutions were out of service the year before last for repairs, so it is likely that the low number of articles was due to the decline in availability of particle accelerators.

Which of the following, if true, most seriously undermines the journalist's argument?

(A) Every article based on experiments with particle accelerators that was submitted for publication last year actually was published.

(B) The average time scientists must wait for access to a particle accelerator has declined over the last several years.

(C) The number of physics journals was the same last year as in previous years.

(D) Particle accelerators can be used for more than one group of experiments in any given year.

(E) Recent changes in the editorial policies of several physics journals have decreased the likelihood that articles concerning particle-accelerator research will be accepted for publication.

Argument Evaluation

Situation A journalist attributes the low number of articles about particle accelerators in physics journals to the fact that several accelerators at major research institutions had been out of service the previous year.

Reasoning *What point undermines the journalist's argument?* The journalist assumes that the researchers' lack of access to the accelerators is responsible for the decline in the number of articles. What else could explain fewer articles? What if the decline is due, not to the availability of the accelerators for experiments, but to policies regarding publishing articles related to such experiments? An alternate explanation is that changes in the editorial policies of physics journals, rather than the effect of the out-of-service accelerators, could well be responsible for the lower number of published articles about particle-accelerator research.

A This statement rules out the possibility that submitted articles were not published, and eliminating this alternate explanation tends to support the argument.

B A decline in waiting time would seem to promote more articles about accelerator research being written and published, not fewer.

C While the decline in articles could be explained by a decline in the number of journals, this statement eliminates that alternate explanation.

D If the accelerators can be used for multiple experiments, then it is reasonable to expect more articles related to them, not fewer.

E **Correct.** This statement properly identifies a point that undermines the journalist's reasoning.

The correct answer is E.

607. Birds have been said to be descended from certain birdlike dinosaur species with which they share distinctive structural features. The fossil record, however, shows that this cannot be so, since there are bird fossils that are much older than the earliest birdlike dinosaur fossils that have been found.

Which of the following is an assumption on which the argument relies?

(A) The birdlike dinosaurs have no living descendants.

(B) There are no flightless dinosaur species that have the distinctive structural features shared by birds and birdlike dinosaurs.

(C) There are no birdlike dinosaur fossils that are older than the bird fossils but have not yet been unearthed.

(D) It could not have been the case that some birds were descended from one of the birdlike dinosaur species and other birds from another.

(E) Birds cannot have been descended from dinosaur species with which the birds do not share the distinctive structural features.

Argument Construction

Situation Although birds have been said to be descended from birdlike dinosaurs, some bird fossils predate the earliest known birdlike dinosaur fossils.

Reasoning *What must be true in order for the premise that some bird fossils predate the earliest known birdlike dinosaur fossils to support the conclusion that birds are not descended from birdlike dinosaurs?* The argument implicitly reasons that since the cited bird fossils predate the earliest known birdlike dinosaur fossils, they must be from birds that lived before the earliest birdlike dinosaurs, and which therefore could not have been descended from birdlike dinosaurs. This reasoning assumes that any birdlike dinosaurs that lived before the first birds would have left fossils that still exist. It also assumes that no undiscovered birdlike dinosaur fossils predate the cited bird fossils.

A The argument is only about whether birds are descended from birdlike dinosaurs. Whether birdlike dinosaurs have any living descendants other than birds is irrelevant.

B The argument is only about birds and birdlike dinosaurs. It is not about other types of dinosaurs that were not birdlike.

C **Correct.** If any undiscovered birdlike dinosaur fossils predate the cited bird fossils, then the latter fossils' age does not support the conclusion that birds are not descended from birdlike dinosaurs.

D The argument purports to establish that the relative ages of bird fossils and birdlike dinosaur fossils show that birds cannot be descended from any of the known birdlike dinosaur species. In doing this, it acknowledges multiple birdlike dinosaur species and leaves open the question of whether some birds may be descended from one such species and other birds from another such species.

E The argument does not claim that the known fossil record shows that birds cannot be descended from dinosaurs. It only claims that the record shows that they cannot be descended from the birdlike dinosaurs that shared their distinctive structural features.

The correct answer is C.

608. City council member: Demand for electricity has been increasing by 1.5 percent a year, and there simply is no more space to build additional power plants to meet future demand increases. We must therefore begin to curtail usage, which is why I propose passing ordinances requiring energy-conservation measures in all city departments.

The city council member's proposal assumes which of the following?

(A) Existing power plants do not have the capacity to handle all of the projected increase in demand for electricity.

(B) No city departments have implemented energy-conservation measures voluntarily.

(C) Passing ordinances designed to curtail electricity usage will not have negative economic consequences for the city.

(D) Residential consumers are not responsible for the recent increases in demand for electricity.

(E) City departments that successfully conserve energy will set a good example for residential and industrial consumers of electricity.

Argument Construction

Situation A city council member proposes energy-conservation measures for all city government departments because there is no room to build new power plants to meet future increases in the demand for electricity.

Reasoning *What must be true in order for the factors the city council member cites to help justify the proposal?* The city council member says electricity usage must be curtailed on account of an increasing demand for electricity and a lack of space for new power plants that could meet future demand increases. In order for this reasoning to help justify the proposal, the cited factors must actually establish a need to curtail electricity usage.

A **Correct.** If current power plants could satisfy the projected increased demand for electricity, then the increasing demand and the lack of room to build new plants would not establish a need to curtail electricity usage.

B The proposed ordinances could still be necessary even if one city department had voluntarily implemented energy-conservation measures.

C Passing the ordinances could still be necessary even if they would have some negative economic effects.

D No matter who is responsible for the recent increases in demand, curtailing the city government's electricity usage could still help to reduce demand.

E Ordinances to curtail the city government's energy usage could be economically necessary regardless of whether or not departments that obey the ordinances set a good example.

The correct answer is A.

609. Which of the following most logically completes the argument below?

Using broad-spectrum weed killers on weeds that are competing with crops for sunlight, water, and nutrients presents a difficulty: how to keep the crop from being killed along with the weeds. For at least some food crops, specially treated seed that produces plants resistant to weed killers is under development. This resistance wears off as the plants mature. Therefore, the special seed treatment will be especially useful for plants that ______.

(A) produce their crop over an extended period of time, as summer squash does
(B) produce large seeds that are easy to treat individually, as corn and beans do
(C) provide, as they approach maturity, shade dense enough to keep weeds from growing
(D) are typically grown in large tracts devoted to a single crop
(E) are cultivated specifically for the seed they produce rather than for their leaves or roots

Argument Construction

Situation A difficulty in using broad-spectrum weed killers is keeping them from killing the food crops along with the weeds. Specially treated seed is being developed that will protect certain food crop plants in their earlier stages of growth.

Reasoning *Which is the best completion for the conclusion?* The conclusion is incompletely stated as "Therefore, the special seed treatment will be especially useful for plants that ______." The question is what sorts of plants does the passage suggest the seed treatment would be especially useful for. We have been told that this treatment makes the plants resistant to weed killer, but that this resistance wears off when the plant matures. So the treatment will be most useful with plants that are not harmed by weed killer and that suffer no significant disadvantage when the resistance wears off as the plant matures. Choice (C) is the correct answer choice because it describes a sort of plant that can combat weeds and requires no weed killer once the plant matures.

A Given that the seed treatment wears off as the plant matures, it would not be especially useful for plants that produce their crops over an extended period.

B We have not been told whether small seeds are more difficult to treat, and so we have no basis to conclude that the special seed treatment would be *especially useful* for plants that have large seeds that are easy to treat individually. We have also been given no reason to think that it is better to treat seeds individually.

C **Correct.** Plants that, as they approach maturity, produce shade dense enough to keep weeds from growing, would benefit from resistance to weed killer when young and would not need weed killer when they have matured and lost their resistance.

D We have been given no reason to think that the seed treatment would be especially useful for plants grown in a large tract devoted to a single crop. For example, why would it be less useful for small tracts with a variety of crops?

E A plant harvested for its roots, fruits, or leaves, rather than for its seeds, would derive no less an advantage from resistance to weed killers in earlier stages of growth.

The correct answer is C.

610. Previously, Autoco designed all of its cars itself and then contracted with specialized parts suppliers to build parts according to its specifications. Now it plans to include its suppliers in designing the parts they are to build. Since many parts suppliers have more designers with specialized experience than Autoco has, Autoco expects this shift to reduce the overall time and cost of the design of its next new car.

Which of the following, if true, most strongly supports Autoco's expectation?

(A) When suppliers provide their own designs, Autoco often needs to modify its overall design.

(B) In order to provide designs for Autoco, several of the parts suppliers will have to add to their existing staffs of designers.

(C) Parts and services provided by outside suppliers account for more than 50 percent of Autoco's total costs.

(D) When suppliers built parts according to specifications provided by Autoco, the suppliers competed to win contracts.

(E) Most of Autoco's suppliers have on hand a wide range of previously prepared parts designs that can readily be modified for a new car.

Evaluation of a Plan

Situation A car manufacturer plans to have its parts suppliers start helping to design the parts they build for the manufacturer. Many parts suppliers have more designers with specialized experience than the manufacturer has.

Reasoning *What would make it more likely that having the parts suppliers help design the parts will reduce the time and cost of designing the manufacturer's next new car?* In order for the change to reduce the time and cost, the parts suppliers involved in designing the next car will probably have to do their portion of the design process faster and cheaper than the manufacturer would have, and the design collaboration process will have to avoid producing substantial new inefficiencies.

A The additional need to modify the overall design would probably make the design process slower and more expensive, not faster and cheaper.

B The additional need to hire more designers would probably increase design costs, not reduce them.

C Although this suggests that the change is likely to substantially affect the design's expense, it does not indicate whether the expense will increase or decrease.

D If anything, this competition probably made Autoco's previous design process cheaper. It does not suggest that the new design process, which may involve less competition, will be faster or cheaper than the previous one.

E **Correct.** Modifying the previously prepared parts designs will probably be faster and cheaper than creating new designs from scratch.

The correct answer is E.

611. In Stenland, many workers have been complaining that they cannot survive on minimum wage, the lowest wage an employer is permitted to pay. The government is proposing to raise the minimum wage. Many employers who pay their workers the current minimum wage argue that if it is raised, unemployment will increase because they will no longer be able to afford to employ as many workers.

Which of the following, if true in Stenland, most strongly supports the claim that raising the minimum wage there will not have the effects that the employers predict?

(A) For any position with wages below a living wage, the difficulty of finding and retaining employees adds as much to employment costs as would raising wages.

(B) Raising the minimum wage does not also increase the amount employers have to contribute in employee benefits.

(C) When inflation is taken into account, the proposed new minimum wage is not as high as the current one was when it was introduced.

(D) Many employees currently being paid wages at the level of the proposed new minimum wage will demand significant wage increases.

(E) Many employers who pay some workers only the minimum wage also pay other workers wages that are much higher than the minimum.

Argument Evaluation

Situation Stenland's government proposes to raise the minimum wage because many workers have complained they cannot survive on it. But many employers claim that raising the minimum wage will increase unemployment.

Reasoning *What evidence would most strongly suggest that raising the minimum wage will not increase unemployment?* The employers with minimum-wage workers implicitly reason that because raising the minimum wage will increase the wages they have to pay each worker, it will reduce the number of workers they can afford to employ, and thus will increase unemployment. Evidence that the increased wage would not actually increase the employers' expenses per employee would cast doubt on their prediction, as would evidence that reducing the number of minimum-wage workers would not increase the nation's overall unemployment rate.

A **Correct.** This suggests that raising the minimum wage would make it easier for employers to find and retain minimum-wage employees, and that the savings would fully offset the cost of paying the higher wages. If there were such offsetting savings, the employers should still be able to afford to employ as many workers as they currently do.

B Even if raising the minimum wage does not increase employers' costs for employee benefits, paying the higher wage might still in itself substantially increase employers' overall costs per employee.

C For all we know, the current minimum wage might have substantially increased unemployment when it was introduced.

D These additional demands would probably raise employers' overall costs per employee, making it more likely that increasing the minimum wage would increase overall unemployment.

E Even if some workers receive more than the minimum wage, raising that wage could still raise employers' expenses for employing low-wage workers, making it too expensive for the employers to employ as many workers overall.

The correct answer is A.

612. Which of the following most logically completes the argument?

The attribution of the choral work *Lacrimae* to the composer Pescard (1400–1474) has been regarded as tentative, since it was based on a single treatise from the early 1500s that named Pescard as the composer. Recently, several musical treatises from the late 1500s have come to light, all of which name Pescard as the composer of *Lacrimae*. Unfortunately, these newly discovered treatises lend no support to the attribution of *Lacrimae* to Pescard, since ________.

(A) the treatise from the early 1500s misidentifies the composers of some of the musical works it considers

(B) the author of the treatise from the early 1500s had no very strong evidence on which to base the identification of Pescard as the composer of *Lacrimae*

(C) there are works that can conclusively be attributed to Pescard that are not even mentioned in the treatise from the early 1500s

(D) the later treatises probably had no source for their attribution other than the earlier treatise

(E) no known treatises from the 1600s identify Pescard as the composer of *Lacrimae*

Argument Construction

Situation A choral work has been tentatively attributed to Pescard based on a single treatise from the early 1500s. But several treatises from the late 1500s have recently been discovered, and all of them attribute the work to Pescard.

Reasoning *Which of the answer choices provides the strongest reason for the conclusion?* The argument's conclusion is that the newly discovered late-1500 treatises lend no support to the attribution of *Lacrimae* to Pescard. It is worth noting that prior to the conclusion the passage provides information which suggests that these newly discovered treatises *do* lend support to the attribution. So the question is: Why don't they? A good reason for thinking they do not is that the newly discovered treatises probably derive solely from the attribution given in the earlier text. Thus the attributions in the later treatises are only as reliable as the attribution in the earlier treatise—and the argument suggests that that reliability has not been conclusively established.

A This makes the treatise from the early 1500s less reliable, but it does not explain why the newly discovered treatises are unreliable.

B Like answer choice (A), this is irrelevant. The question is not why the treatise from the early 1500s fails to lend support to the attribution but why the treatises from the late 1500s fail to do so.

C This is irrelevant because it does not refer to the newly discovered treatises whose attribution of *Lacrimae* is at issue.

D **Correct.** The question is whether these newly discovered treatises lend *additional* support. *Lacrimae* has already been tentatively attributed to Pescard based on the text from the early 1500s. So, if the later treatises base their attribution solely on the earlier treatise, then they provide no additional support beyond that already provided by the earlier treatise.

E This leaves open the possibility that there was no treatise at all in the 1600s that discussed Pescard or *Lacrimae*. Also, it fails to provide significant evidence either for or against Pescard's having composed *Lacrimae*. But even if it did provide such evidence, it would be irrelevant because the issue is why the late-1500 treatises fail to provide significant support for the attribution of *Lacrimae* to Pescard, not whether Pescard composed the work.

The correct answer is D.

613. When trying to identify new technologies that promise to transform the marketplace, market researchers survey the managers of those companies that are developing new technologies. Such managers have an enormous stake in succeeding, so they invariably overstate the potential of their new technologies. Surprisingly, however, market researchers typically do not survey a new technology's potential buyers, even though it is the buyers—not the producers—who will ultimately determine a technology's commercial success.

Which of the following, if true, best accounts for the typical survey practices among market researchers?

(A) If a new technology succeeds, the commercial benefits accrue largely to the producers, not to the buyers, of that technology.

(B) People who promote the virtues of a new technology typically fail to consider that the old technology that is currently in use continues to be improved, often substantially.

(C) Investors are unlikely to invest substantial amounts of capital in a company whose own managers are skeptical about the commercial prospects of a new technology they are developing.

(D) The potential buyers for not-yet-available technologies can seldom be reliably identified.

(E) The developers of a new technology are generally no better positioned than its potential buyers to gauge how rapidly the new technology can be efficiently mass-produced.

Argument Construction

Situation Market researchers seeking to identify new technologies that have the potential to transform the marketplace survey managers of companies developing new technologies, but typically not the potential buyers of new technologies, even though managers tend to overstate the potential of their new technologies and it is the buyers who determine the products' commercial success.

Reasoning *What best explains why it is managers, not buyers, that the market researchers survey?* Why, despite the information in the passage, are managers of technology companies surveyed while potential buyers are typically not? A partial explanation would be that it is difficult to reliably determine who the potential buyers of new technologies will be. If market researchers cannot identify who the potential buyers of as-yet unavailable technologies will be, that explains why they are not typically surveyed—and why the next best alternative may be to survey managers.

A This answer choice tells us who would benefit from commercial success of new technologies. But it says nothing about whose opinion would be most valuable in predicting the commercial success of new technologies.

B At most, this could help explain why managers overstate the potential of their new technologies. But it does not explain the motives of market researchers in relying on the managers' rather than buyers' opinions about new technologies.

C Given that managers of technology companies will want to attract investors, this helps to explain why the managers would tend to overstate the potential of their new technologies. But it does not help to explain the survey practices.

D **Correct.** This accounts for why potential buyers of new technologies are not typically sought out in surveys by market researchers: It is difficult to determine in advance who they are.

E This, like answer choice (C), tends to make the practices of market researchers more difficult rather than easier to understand. If developers of new technologies are no better at gauging how rapidly a new technology can be mass-produced (a factor affecting commercial success), then all the more reason to survey potential buyers rather than the managers.

The correct answer is D.

614. Infotek, a computer manufacturer in Katrovia, has just introduced a new personal computer model that sells for significantly less than any other model. Market research shows, however, that very few Katrovian households without personal computers would buy a computer, regardless of its price. Therefore, introducing the new model is unlikely to increase the number of computers in Katrovian homes.

Which of the following is an assumption on which the argument depends?

(A) Infotek achieved the lower price of the new model by using components of lower quality than those used by other manufacturers.

(B) The main reason cited by consumers in Katrovia for replacing a personal computer is the desire to have an improved model.

(C) Katrovians in households that already have computers are unlikely to purchase the new Infotek model as an additional computer for home use.

(D) The price of other personal computers in Katrovia is unlikely to drop below the price of Infotek's new model in the near future.

(E) Most personal computers purchased in Katrovia are intended for home use.

Argument Construction

Situation In Katrovia, a new personal computer model costs less than any other model. But market research shows that very few Katrovian households without personal computers would buy even cheap ones.

Reasoning *What must be true in order for the stated facts to support the conclusion that introducing the new computer model is unlikely to increase the overall number of computers in Katrovian homes?* The market research supports the conclusion that no new computer model is likely to significantly increase the number of computers in Katrovian homes that currently lack computers. But the overall number of computers in Katrovian homes will still increase if Katrovian homes that already have computers buy additional computers while keeping their existing ones. So the argument has to assume that the new computer model will not increase the number of additional computers purchased for Katrovian homes that already have computers.

A Even if Infotek used high-quality components in the new computer model, Katrovians might still refuse to buy it.

B Replacing a personal computer does not change the overall number of personal computers in homes, so Katrovians' motives for replacing their computers are irrelevant to the argument.

C Correct. As explained above, unless computers of the new model are purchased as additional computers for Katrovian homes that already have computers, the new model's introduction is unlikely to increase the overall number of computers in Katrovian homes.

D The assumption that other personal computer prices would stay relatively high does not help establish the link between its premises and its conclusion. If answer choice D were false, the argument would be no weaker than it is without any consideration of other computers' potential prices.

E If most personal computers purchased in Katrovia were not intended for home use, then the new model's introduction would be even less likely to increase the number of personal computers in Katrovian homes. So the argument does not depend on assuming that most of the computers purchased are for home use.

The correct answer is C.

615. Fast-food restaurants make up 45 percent of all restaurants in Canatria. Customers at these restaurants tend to be young; in fact, studies have shown that the older people get, the less likely they are to eat in fast-food restaurants. Since the average age of the Canatrian population is gradually rising and will continue to do so, the number of fast-food restaurants is likely to decrease.

Which of the following, if true, most seriously weakens the argument?

(A) Fast-food restaurants in Canatria are getting bigger, so each one can serve more customers.
(B) Some older people eat at fast-food restaurants more frequently than the average young person.
(C) Many people who rarely eat in fast-food restaurants nevertheless eat regularly in restaurants.
(D) The overall population of Canatria is growing steadily.
(E) As the population of Canatria gets older, more people are eating at home.

Argument Evaluation

Situation In Canatria, the older people get, the less likely they are to eat in fast-food restaurants. The average age of Canatrians is increasing.

Reasoning *What evidence would most weaken the support provided by the cited facts for the prediction that the number of fast-food restaurants in Canatria is likely to decrease?* The argument implicitly reasons that since studies have shown that Canatrians tend to eat in fast-food restaurants less as they get older, and since Canatrians are getting older on average, the proportion of Canatrians eating in fast-food restaurants will decline. The argument assumes that this means the overall number of fast-food restaurant customers will decline and that demand will decrease enough to reduce the number of fast-food restaurants that can sustain profitability. Consequently, fewer new fast-food restaurants will open or more old ones will close, or both. Thus, the number of fast-food restaurants in Canatria will fall. Any evidence casting doubt on any inference in this chain of implicit reasoning will weaken the argument.

A This strengthens the argument by providing additional evidence that the total number of fast-food restaurants will decrease. If the average number of customers per fast-food restaurant is increasing, then fewer fast-food restaurants will be needed to serve the same—or a lesser—number of customers.

B Even if a few individuals do not follow the general trends described, those trends could still reduce the overall demand for and number of fast-food restaurants.

C The argument is only about fast-food restaurants, not restaurants of other types.

D **Correct.** This suggests that even if the proportion of Canatrians eating at fast-food restaurants declines, the total number doing so may not decline. Thus, the total demand for and profitability of fast-food restaurants may not decline either, so the total number of fast-food restaurants in Canatria may not decrease.

E If anything, this strengthens the argument by pointing out an additional trend likely to reduce the demand for, and thus the number of, fast-food restaurants in Canatria.

The correct answer is D.

616. In order to withstand tidal currents, juvenile horseshoe crabs frequently burrow in the sand. Such burrowing discourages barnacles from clinging to their shells. When fully grown, however, the crabs can readily withstand tidal currents without burrowing, and thus they acquire substantial populations of barnacles. Surprisingly, in areas where tidal currents are very weak, juvenile horseshoe crabs are found not to have significant barnacle populations, even though they seldom burrow.

Which of the following, if true, most helps to explain the surprising finding?

(A) Tidal currents do not themselves dislodge barnacles from the shells of horseshoe crabs.
(B) Barnacles most readily attach themselves to horseshoe crabs in areas where tidal currents are weakest.
(C) The strength of the tidal currents in a given location varies widely over the course of a day.
(D) A very large barnacle population can significantly decrease the ability of a horseshoe crab to find food.
(E) Until they are fully grown, horseshoe crabs shed their shells and grow new ones several times a year.

Argument Construction

Situation Juvenile horseshoe crabs withstand tidal currents by burrowing in the sand. This action makes barnacles less likely to cling to their shells. Adult horseshoe crabs can withstand currents, so they do not burrow, and barnacles become more likely to cling to their shells. Surprisingly, however, juvenile horseshoe crabs that do not burrow, because tidal currents do not threaten them, do not have significant numbers of barnacles clinging to their shells.

Reasoning *What would most help explain the finding that nonburrowing juvenile horseshoe crabs do not have significant barnacle populations?* The finding suggests that there is some way in which nonburrowing juvenile horseshoe crabs either discourage barnacles from clinging to their shells, or get rid of the barnacles that do cling to their shells. Identifying how this is accomplished will explain the finding.

A This gives a reason why juvenile horseshoe crabs that do not burrow *would* have significant barnacle populations.

B If barnacles in areas of weak tidal currents readily attach themselves to horseshoe crabs, then it would be more likely for juvenile horseshoe crabs in such areas to have significant barnacle populations.

C The areas under discussion are those where tidal currents are very weak. The strength of currents may vary widely there, but presumably they are still weak compared to other areas.

D The surprising finding under discussion is why certain juvenile horseshoe crabs do not have significant barnacle populations, despite failing to engage in behavior that dislodges barnacles. That a very large barnacle population can hurt a horseshoe crab does not help explain such a finding.

E **Correct.** This statement properly identifies something that helps explain the surprising finding: If juvenile horseshoe crabs regularly shed their shells, they also regularly shed the barnacles that cling to those shells. Thus juvenile horseshoe crabs would most likely be found not to have significant barnacle populations.

The correct answer is E.

617. Last year a chain of fast-food restaurants, whose menu had always centered on hamburgers, added its first vegetarian sandwich, much lower in fat than the chain's other offerings. Despite heavy marketing, the new sandwich accounts for a very small proportion of the chain's sales. The sandwich's sales would have to quadruple to cover the costs associated with including it on the menu. Since such an increase is unlikely, the chain would be more profitable if it dropped the sandwich.

Which of the following, if true, most seriously weakens the argument?

(A) Although many of the chain's customers have never tried the vegetarian sandwich, in a market research survey most of those who had tried it reported that they were very satisfied with it.

(B) Many of the people who eat at the chain's restaurants also eat at the restaurants of competing chains and report no strong preference among the competitors.

(C) Among fast-food chains in general, there has been little or no growth in hamburger sales over the past several years as the range of competing offerings at other restaurants has grown.

(D) When even one member of a group of diners is a vegetarian or has a preference for low-fat food, the group tends to avoid restaurants that lack vegetarian or low-fat menu options.

(E) An attempt by the chain to introduce a lower-fat hamburger failed several years ago, since it attracted few new customers and most of the chain's regular customers greatly preferred the taste of the regular hamburgers.

Argument Evaluation

Situation Last year a fast-food restaurant chain specializing in hamburgers started offering a low-fat vegetarian sandwich and marketed it heavily. The new sandwich's sales are far too low to cover the costs associated with including it on the menu.

Reasoning *What evidence would most weaken the support provided by the cited facts for the prediction that it would be more profitable for the chain to drop the sandwich?* The implicit argument is that since the new sandwich's sales are too low to cover the costs associated with including it on the menu, offering the sandwich diminishes the chain's profitability and will continue to do so if the sandwich continues to be offered. This reasoning assumes that the sandwich provides the chain no substantial indirect financial benefits except through its direct sales. It also assumes that the sandwich's sales will not increase sufficiently to make the sandwich a viable product. Any evidence casting doubt on either of these assumptions will weaken the argument.

A This gives information only about the respondents to the survey who had tried the sandwich (possibly very few), who were probably already more open to liking a vegetarian sandwich than any of the chain's other customers. So their responses are probably unrepresentative of the chain's customers in general and do not suggest that the sandwich has enough market potential.

B Although the issue of competition with other restaurants is not raised in the information provided, this new information, if anything, strengthens the argument, by suggesting that the introduction of the new sandwich has not significantly enhanced customer preference for eating at the restaurants that offer the new sandwich.

C This suggests that the cause of stagnation in fast-food restaurants' hamburger sales has been competition from non-fast-food restaurants, but not that the non-fast-food restaurants competed by offering vegetarian options.

D **Correct.** This suggests that even if the sandwich's sales are low, it may indirectly increase the chain's overall profits by encouraging large groups to eat at the chain.

E This strengthens the argument by suggesting that the chain's customers are generally not interested in low-fat menu options such as the new sandwich.

The correct answer is D.

618. Transportation expenses accounted for a large portion of the total dollar amount spent on trips for pleasure by residents of the United States in 1997, and about half of the total dollar amount spent on transportation was for airfare. However, the large majority of United States residents who took trips for pleasure in 1997 did not travel by airplane but used other means of transportation.

If the statements above are true, which of the following must also be true about United States residents who took trips for pleasure in 1997?

(A) Most of those who traveled by airplane did so because the airfare to their destination was lower than the cost of other available means of transportation.

(B) Most of those who traveled by airplane did so because other means of transportation to their destination were unavailable.

(C) Per mile traveled, those who traveled by airplane tended to spend more on transportation to their destination than did those who used other means of transportation.

(D) Overall, people who did not travel by airplane had lower average transportation expenses than people who did.

(E) Those who traveled by airplane spent about as much, on average, on other means of transportation as they did on airfare.

Argument Construction

Situation In 1997, about half of total transportation spending by U.S. residents taking trips for pleasure was for airfare. But the large majority of U.S. residents who took trips for pleasure in 1997 did not travel by airplane.

Reasoning *What can be deduced from the stated facts?* The information provided indicates that among U.S. residents who took trips for pleasure in 1997, those who traveled by airplane were a small minority. Yet this small minority's spending for airfare accounted for half of all transportation spending among residents taking trips for pleasure. It follows that on average, those who traveled by airplane must have spent far more per person on transportation than those who did not travel by airplane.

A This does not follow logically from the information given. Most of those who traveled by airplane may have done so even if flying was more expensive than other modes of transportation—for example, because flying was faster or more comfortable.

B This does not follow from the information given. Most of those who traveled by airplane may have done so even if many other modes of transportation were available—the other modes may all have been less desirable.

C This does not follow from the information given. Those who traveled by airplane may have traveled much farther on average than those who used other means of transportation, so their transportation spending per mile traveled need not have been greater.

D **Correct.** As explained above, those who traveled by airplane must have spent more per person on transportation than those who did not travel by airplane, on average. In other words, those who did not travel by airplane must have had lower average transportation expenses than those who did.

E This does not follow from the information given. Although half the total dollar spending on transportation was for airfare, much of the transportation spending that was not for airfare was by the large majority of U.S. residents who did not travel by airplane.

The correct answer is D.

619. Voters commonly condemn politicians for being insincere, but politicians often must disguise their true feelings when they make public statements. If they expressed their honest views—about, say, their party's policies—then achieving politically necessary compromises would be much more difficult. Clearly, the very insincerity that people decry shows that our government is functioning well.

Which of the following, if true, most seriously undermines this reasoning?

(A) Achieving political compromises is not all that is necessary for the proper functioning of a government.
(B) Some political compromises are not in the best long-term interest of the government.
(C) Voters often judge politicians by criteria other than the sincerity with which they express their views.
(D) A political party's policies could turn out to be detrimental to the functioning of a government.
(E) Some of the public statements made by politicians about their party's policies could in fact be sincere.

Argument Evaluation

Situation Politicians must often make insincere public statements because expressing their true feelings would make it harder for them to achieve politically necessary compromises.

Reasoning *What would suggest that the argument's premises do not establish that politicians' insincerity shows our government is functioning well?* The implicit reasoning is that insincerity helps politicians achieve politically necessary compromises, and these compromises help our government to function well, so insincerity must show that our government is functioning well. Evidence that these necessary compromises do not ensure that our government functions well would undermine the argument's reasoning, as would evidence that politicians' insincerity has other substantial effects that hinder the government's functioning.

A **Correct.** If governments may function poorly even when insincerity allows necessary political compromises to be made, then the argument's premises do not establish that politicians' insincerity shows our government is functioning well.

B The argument does not require that all political compromises help government to function well, only that politically necessary compromises do.

C Even if voters often judge politicians by criteria other than their sincerity, they may also often decry politicians' insincerity, not realizing or caring that such insincerity helps the government function well.

D Even if a political party's policies impair the government's functioning, politically necessary compromises by politicians in that party could improve the government's functioning.

E Even if politicians sometimes speak sincerely about their party's policies, their general willingness to be insincere as needed to achieve politically necessary compromises could be a sign that the government is functioning well.

The correct answer is A.

620. To reduce waste of raw materials, the government of Sperland is considering requiring household appliances to be broken down for salvage when discarded. To cover the cost of salvage, the government is planning to charge a fee, which would be imposed when the appliance is first sold. Imposing the fee at the time of salvage would reduce waste more effectively, however, because consumers tend to keep old appliances longer if they are faced with a fee for discarding them.

Which of the following, if true, most seriously weakens the argument?

(A) Increasing the cost of disposing of an appliance properly increases the incentive to dispose of it improperly.

(B) The fee provides manufacturers with no incentive to produce appliances that are more durable.

(C) For people who have bought new appliances recently, the salvage fee would not need to be paid for a number of years.

(D) People who sell their used, working appliances to others would not need to pay the salvage fee.

(E) Many nonfunctioning appliances that are currently discarded could be repaired at relatively little expense.

Evaluation of a Plan

Situation A government is considering requiring household appliances to be broken down for salvage when discarded. To cover the salvage costs, the government plans to charge a fee on appliance sales.

Reasoning *What would suggest that charging the fee at the time of salvage would less effectively reduce waste than charging the fee at the time of sale would?* The argument is that charging the fee at the time of salvage would reduce waste of raw materials because it would encourage consumers to keep their appliances longer before salvaging them. This argument could be weakened by pointing out other factors that might increase waste if the fee is charged at the time of salvage or reduce waste if the fee is charged at the time of sale.

A **Correct.** This suggests that charging the fee at the time of salvage rather than the time of sale would encourage consumers to discard their appliances illegally, thereby increasing waste of raw materials by reducing the proportion of discarded appliances that are salvaged.

B This factor would remain the same regardless of whether the fee was charged at the time of sale or the time of salvage.

C This might be a reason for consumers to prefer the fee be charged at the time of salvage rather than the time of sale, but it does not suggest that charging the fee at the time of salvage would reduce waste less effectively.

D This provides an additional reason to expect that charging the fee at the time of salvage would help reduce waste, so it strengthens rather than weakens the argument.

E This would give consumers an additional reason to keep using their old appliances and postpone paying a fee at the time of salvage, so it strengthens rather than weakens the argument.

The correct answer is A.

621. When there is less rainfall than normal, the water level of Australian rivers falls and the rivers flow more slowly. Because algae whose habitat is river water grow best in slow-moving water, the amount of algae per unit of water generally increases when there has been little rain. By contrast, however, following a period of extreme drought, algae levels are low even in very slow-moving river water.

Which of the following, if true, does most to explain the contrast described above?

(A) During periods of extreme drought, the populations of some of the species that feed on algae tend to fall.

(B) The more slowly water moves, the more conducive its temperature is to the growth of algae.

(C) When algae populations reach very high levels, conditions within the river can become toxic for some of the other species that normally live there.

(D) Australian rivers dry up completely for short intervals in periods of extreme drought.

(E) Except during periods of extreme drought, algae levels tend to be higher in rivers in which the flow has been controlled by damming than in rivers that flow freely.

Argument Construction

Situation When Australian rivers flow slowly due to little rain, algae populations in those rivers increase. But after periods of extreme drought, algae levels are low even in water moving at speeds that would normally show population increases.

Reasoning *What would explain the contrast between algae levels in slow-moving water resulting from little rain and slow-moving water after a drought?* There must be some difference between what happens during periods in which there is simply less rainfall than normal and periods in which there is extreme drought, a difference that affects the algae population.

A This indicates one of the consequences of drought, and slightly suggests that this might be due to a lower algae level. But it does nothing to explain why algae levels might be lower after a drought.

B This could explain why some rivers that are slow-moving and have little water might have a high algae level—but not why the algae level is low in such rivers after a period of drought.

C This explains why levels of other species might be low when algae populations are high, not why algae populations are high when there is little rain, but low following a period of extreme drought.

D **Correct.** This statement properly identifies something that helps explain the contrast. According to the information given, the habitat of the algae under discussion is river water. If the river dries up, the algae will probably not survive. Then after the drought, algae population levels would likely take a while to rise again.

E This emphasizes that there is a contrast between what happens to algae during periods of extreme drought and what happens to them at other times, but it does not help explain that contrast.

The correct answer is D.

622. Increased use of incineration is sometimes advocated as a safe way to dispose of chemical waste. But opponents of incineration point to the 40 incidents involving unexpected releases of dangerous chemical agents that were reported just last year at two existing incinerators commissioned to destroy a quantity of chemical waste material. Since designs for proposed new incinerators include no additional means of preventing such releases, leaks will only become more prevalent if use of incineration increases.

Which of the following, if true, most seriously weakens the argument?

(A) At the two incinerators at which leaks were reported, staff had had only cursory training on the proper procedures for incinerating chemical waste.

(B) Other means of disposing of chemical waste, such as chemical neutralization processes, have not been proven safer than incineration.

(C) The capacity of existing incinerators is sufficient to allow for increased incineration of chemical waste without any need for new incinerators.

(D) The frequency of reports of unexpected releases of chemical agents at newly built incinerators is about the same as the frequency at older incinerators.

(E) In only three of the reported incidents of unexpected chemical leaks did the releases extend outside the property on which the incinerators were located.

Argument Evaluation

Situation Last year, at two chemical waste incinerators, there were forty reported incidents involving unexpected releases of dangerous chemicals. Designs for proposed new incinerators include no additional safeguards against such releases. Therefore, increased use of incineration will likely make such releases more prevalent.

Reasoning *What would undermine the support provided for the conclusion that leaks will become more prevalent if more chemical waste is disposed of through incineration?* The argument draws a general conclusion about chemical waste incineration from evidence about only two particular incinerators. This reasoning would be undermined by any evidence that the leaks at those two incinerators were the result of something other than insufficient safeguards against such releases.

A **Correct.** If the staff training at the two incinerators was cursory, then the leaks may have been the results of staff not knowing how to use safeguards with which the incinerators are equipped that, if properly used, would have prevented the release of dangerous chemicals. Therefore, if staff at newer incinerators will be better trained, leaks might not become more prevalent even if chemical waste incineration becomes more common.

B Other chemical waste disposal methods may be safer than incineration even if no one has proven so; and even if they're not safer overall, they may involve fewer leaks.

C Continuing to use existing incinerators might well produce just as many leaks as switching to new incinerators would.

D This suggests that new incinerators produce as many leaks as older incinerators do, a finding that provides additional evidence that increased incineration even with proposed new incinerators would lead to more leaks.

E The argument is not about how far the releases from leaks extend, only about how many of them are likely to occur.

The correct answer is A.

623. Public health expert: **Increasing the urgency of a public health message may be counterproductive**. In addition to irritating the majority who already behave responsibly, **it may undermine all government pronouncements on health by convincing people that such messages are overly cautious**. And there is no reason to believe that those who ignore measured voices will listen to shouting.

The two sections in boldface play which of the following roles in the public health expert's argument?

(A) The first is a conclusion for which support is provided, but is not the argument's main conclusion; the second is an unsupported premise supporting the argument's main conclusion.

(B) The first is a premise supporting the only explicit conclusion; so is the second.

(C) The first is the argument's main conclusion; the second supports that conclusion and is itself a conclusion for which support is provided.

(D) The first is a premise supporting the argument's only conclusion; the second is that conclusion.

(E) The first is the argument's only explicit conclusion; the second is a premise supporting that conclusion.

Argument Construction

Situation A public health expert argues against increasing the urgency of public health messages by pointing out negative effects that may arise from such an increase, as well as by questioning its efficacy.

Reasoning *What roles are played in the argument by the two claims in boldface?* The first claim in boldface states that increasing the urgency of public health messages may be counterproductive. After making this claim, the public health expert mentions two specific reasons this could be so: it could irritate people who already behave responsibly, and it could convince people that all public health messages are too cautious. (The latter reason in the second claim in boldface). The phrase [*i*]*n addition to* indicates that neither claim in the second sentence is intended to support or explain the other. However, since each claim in the second sentence gives a reason to believe the claim in the first sentence, each independently supports the first sentence as a conclusion. The word [*a*]*nd* beginning the third sentence reveals that its intended role in the argument is the same as that of the two claims in the second sentence.

A Everything stated after the first sentence is intended to help support it, so the first sentence is the argument's main conclusion.

B Everything stated after the first sentence is intended to help support it, so the first sentence is a conclusion, not a premise.

C Each of the three claims in the second and third sentences is presented as an independent reason to accept the general claim in the first sentence. Therefore, nothing in the passage is intended to support the second statement in boldface as a conclusion.

D Everything stated after the first sentence is intended to help support it, so the first sentence is a conclusion, not a premise.

E **Correct.** Each of the three claims in the second and third sentences is presented as an independent reason to accept the general claim in the first sentence. Thus, each of those claims is a premise supporting the claim in the first sentence as the argument's only conclusion.

The correct answer is E.

624. Several industries have recently switched at least partly from older technologies powered by fossil fuels to new technologies powered by electricity. It is thus evident that less fossil fuel is being used as a result of the operations of these industries than would have been used if these industries had retained their older technologies.

Which of the following, if true, most strengthens the argument above?

(A) Many of the industries that have switched at least partly to the new technologies have increased their output.

(B) Less fossil fuel was used to manufacture the machinery employed in the new technologies than was originally used to manufacture the machinery employed in the older technologies.

(C) More electricity is used by those industries that have switched at least partly to the new technologies than by those industries that have not switched.

(D) Some of the industries that have switched at least partly to the new technologies still use primarily technologies that are powered by fossil fuels.

(E) The amount of fossil fuel used to generate the electricity needed to power the new technologies is less than the amount that would have been used to power the older technologies.

Argument Evaluation

Situation Several industries have now switched, at least partly, to technologies using electricity rather than fossil fuels. Thus, less fossil fuel will be consumed as a result of the operation of these industries than otherwise would have been.

Reasoning *Which option most strengthens the argument?* One way to strengthen an argument is to eliminate or minimize one of its flaws or weaknesses. Because the conclusion is stated in terms of "fossil fuel consumed *as a result* of the operation of these industries," the claim would encompass even any fossil fuel that might be used to generate the electricity that the newer technologies use. Yet the premise of the argument does not address this issue. So the argument is strengthened if it turns out that less fossil fuel was used to produce the electricity than would have been used to power the older technologies.

A In an indirect way, this option slightly weakens rather than strengthens the argument. For *if* fossil fuels are used to produce the electricity now used by the industries and *if* it is because of these newer technologies that output has increased, the argument's conclusion is *less* likely.

B It does not matter how much fossil fuel was used to manufacture the older technologies *originally*. That has no bearing on whether more fossil fuel would have been expended as a result of the *continued operation* of the industries if the partial switch to newer technologies had not occurred.

C This is what we would expect, but it in no way strengthens the argument.

D This may seem to weaken the argument by indicating that the switch from older technologies will have less of an impact on fossil fuel consumption by these industries than we might have assumed. But since the conclusion makes no claim about how much consumption has been reduced, it is not clear that this option has any bearing on the strength of the argument one way or the other.

E **Correct.** This is the option that most strengthens the argument.

The correct answer is E.

625. The difference in average annual income in favor of employees who have college degrees, compared with those who do not have such degrees, doubled between 1980 and 1990. Some analysts have hypothesized that increased competition between employers for employees with college degrees drove up income for such employees.

Which of the following, if true, most seriously undermines the explanation described above?

(A) During the 1980s a growing percentage of college graduates, unable to find jobs requiring a college degree, took unskilled jobs.

(B) The average age of all employees increased slightly during the 1980s.

(C) The unemployment rate changed very little throughout most of the 1980s.

(D) From 1980 to 1990 the difference in average income between employees with advanced degrees and those with bachelor's degrees also increased.

(E) During the 1980s there were some employees with no college degree who earned incomes comparable to the top incomes earned by employees with a college degree.

Argument Evaluation

Situation The amount by which average annual income for employees with college degrees exceeds that for employees without such degrees doubled between 1980 and 1990.

Reasoning *What evidence would most strongly suggest that increased competition among employers for employees with college degrees does not explain the relative increase in those employees' incomes?* Such increased competition could not explain the relative increase in income for employees with college degrees if the competition did not actually increase, or if such competition occurred but did not result in employers paying higher wages or salaries, or if the increase in competition to hire employees without college degrees was even greater. So evidence that any of those conditions existed would undermine the analysts' explanation.

A **Correct.** This suggests that the supply of college graduates grew relative to employers' demand for them, and hence that employers' competition for college-educated employees did not actually increase.

B The average age might have increased equally for employees with college degrees and for those without them, so the increase is not clearly relevant to explaining why the difference between these two groups' average incomes grew.

C Even if the overall unemployment rate did not change, competition for college-educated employees could have increased while competition for other employees decreased.

D This statement gives information comparing income trends among two groups of those with college degrees, and is irrelevant to the comparison of income trends for those with college degrees and those without college degrees.

E Even if there was strong competition and high pay for certain unusual types of employees without college degrees, increasing competition for employees with college degrees might have explained the overall growing difference in average pay between employees with college degrees and those without.

The correct answer is A.

626. Which of the following most logically completes the passage?

According to the last pre-election poll in Whippleton, most voters believe that the three problems government needs to address, in order of importance, are pollution, crime, and unemployment. Yet in the election, candidates from parties perceived as strongly against pollution were defeated, while those elected were all from parties with a history of opposing legislation designed to reduce pollution. These results should not be taken to indicate that the poll was inaccurate, however, since ______.

(A) some voters in Whippleton do not believe that pollution needs to be reduced

(B) every candidate who was defeated had a strong antipollution record

(C) there were no issues other than crime, unemployment, and pollution on which the candidates had significant differences of opinion

(D) all the candidates who were elected were perceived as being stronger against both crime and unemployment than the candidates who were defeated

(E) many of the people who voted in the election refused to participate in the poll

Argument Construction

Situation A pre-election poll indicated that most voters believed the three problems government needs to address, in order of importance, are pollution, crime, and unemployment. But in the election, candidates from parties with a history of opposing anti-pollution legislation beat candidates from parties perceived as more strongly against pollution.

Reasoning *What would most help explain how the poll might have been accurate despite the election results?* Since the poll indicated that voters were most concerned about pollution, it suggested that candidates from anti-pollution parties would be more likely to be elected, other things being equal—and yet those candidates were not elected. There are many possible explanations for this outcome that are compatible with the poll having been accurate. For example, voters might have been swayed by the candidates' personalities, qualifications, or advertising more than by their positions on the issues. Or some candidates might have convinced voters that their personal positions on the issues were different from those of their parties. Or voters might have chosen candidates based on their positions on crime and unemployment, considering those issues together more important than pollution alone. Any statement suggesting that any such factors explained the election results would logically complete the passage by providing a reason to believe that the poll could have been accurate despite those results.

A If the number of voters who did not believe that pollution needed to be reduced was large enough to explain the election results, then the poll was probably inaccurate. So this does not explain how the poll might have been accurate despite those results.

B This eliminates the possibility that candidates were defeated for having weak antipollution records conflicting with their parties' antipollution stances, so it eliminates one explanation of how the poll might have been accurate despite the election results. Thus, it slightly weakens the conclusion of the argument instead of providing a premise to support it.

C This eliminates the possibility that differences of opinion among the candidates on these other issues might explain the election results, but it does not explain how the poll could have been accurate despite the election results.

D Correct. The poll indicated that voters believed that the government needs to address crime and unemployment as well as pollution. So if the poll was accurate, the election outcome might have resulted from voters considering candidates' positions on crime and unemployment to be jointly more important than their positions on pollution.

E If anything, this provides a reason to doubt that the poll accurately reflected voters' opinions. It does not explain how the poll might have accurately reflected those opinions despite the election results.

The correct answer is D.

627. Manufacturing plants in Arundia have recently been acquired in substantial numbers by investors from abroad. Arundian politicians are proposing legislative action to stop such investment, justifying the proposal by arguing that foreign investors, opportunistically exploiting a recent fall in the value of the Arundian currency, were able to buy Arundian assets at less than their true value.

Which of the following, if true, casts the most serious doubt on the adequacy of the Arundian politicians' justification for the proposed legislation?

(A) The Arundian government originally welcomed the fall in the value of the Arundian currency because the fall made Arundian exports more competitive on international markets.

(B) Foreign investors who acquired Arundian manufacturing plants generally did so with no intention of keeping and running those plants over the long term.

(C) Without the recent fall in the value of the Arundian currency, many of the Arundian assets bought by foreign investors would have been beyond the financial reach of those investors.

(D) In Concordia, a country broadly similar to Arundia, the share of manufacturing assets that is foreign-controlled is 60 percent higher than it is in Arundia.

(E) The true value of an investment is determined by the value of the profits from it, and the low value of the Arundian currency has depressed the value of any profits earned by foreign investors from Arundian assets.

Argument Evaluation

Situation After a recent fall in the value of Arundian currency, foreign investors have been acquiring many Arundian manufacturing plants. Arundian politicians are proposing legislation to stop such investment.

Reasoning *What would most undermine the Arundian politicians' justification for the proposed legislation?* The politicians are justifying their proposal by claiming that foreign investors have been exploiting the fall in the currency's value by buying Arundian assets at less than their *true value* (whatever that means). Any evidence that their claim is false or meaningless would undermine their justification for the proposal, as would any evidence that the claim, even if true, does not provide a good reason to stop the foreign investments.

A This suggests that the foreign investors got a good deal on the manufacturing plants, since it provides evidence that those plants will now be more competitive and profitable. So, if anything, it supports the politicians' justification for their proposal rather than undermining it.

B This suggests that the foreign investors generally believe the manufacturing plants are undervalued, and intend to sell them at a profit as soon as the currency rises enough. So it supports the politicians' justification for their proposal rather than undermining it.

C This suggests that the recent fall in the currency's value made Arundian assets cost less than usual for foreign investors, thus arguably allowing the investors to buy the assets at less than their *true value*. So, if anything, it supports the politicians' justification for their proposal rather than undermining it.

D The Arundian politicians might consider the example of Concordia to be a warning of the disaster that could befall Arundia unless the legislation is enacted. So the situation in Concordia might be cited as support for the politicians' justification of their proposal.

E **Correct**. This implies that the fall in the Arundian currency's value has reduced the *true value* of Arundian manufacturing plants and any profits they may make, so it undermines the politicians' claim that the foreign investors exploited the fall in the currency's value to acquire the plants for less than their *true value*.

The correct answer is E.

628. Proposed new safety rules for the Beach City airport would lengthen considerably the minimum time between takeoffs from the airport. In consequence, the airport would be able to accommodate 10 percent fewer flights than currently use the airport daily. The city's operating budget depends heavily on taxes generated by tourist spending, and most of the tourists come by plane. Therefore, the proposed new safety rules, if adopted, will reduce the revenue available for the operating budget.

The argument depends on assuming which of the following?

(A) There are no periods of the day during which the interval between flights taking off from the airport is significantly greater than the currently allowed minimum.

(B) Few, if any, of the tourists who use the Beach City airport do so when their main destination is a neighboring community and not Beach City itself.

(C) If the proposed safety rules are adopted, the reduction in tourist numbers will not result mainly from a reduction in the number of tourists who spend relatively little in Beach City.

(D) Increasing the minimum time between takeoffs is the only way to achieve necessary safety improvements without a large expenditure by the city government on airport enhancements.

(E) The response to the adoption of the new safety rules would not include an increase in the number of passengers per flight.

Argument Construction

Situation Proposed safety rules for a city airport would reduce the number of daily flights the airport can accommodate. The city's operating budget depends heavily on taxes generated by tourists, who mostly come by plane. Therefore, adopting the safety rules will result in lower revenue available for the operating budget.

Reasoning *What must be true in order for the cited facts to support the conclusion that the proposed rules would reduce the revenue for the operating budget?* The implicit reasoning is that since the rules would reduce the number of flights that can be accommodated, they would thereby reduce the number of tourists arriving by plane, which in turn would reduce the tax revenue that tourist spending generates for the operating budget. This assumes that the actual number of daily flights would fall along with the number that the airport can accommodate; that fewer daily flights would mean fewer people flying into the airport; that fewer people flying into the airport would mean fewer tourists flying into the airport; that fewer tourists flying into the airport would mean fewer tourists visiting the city; that fewer tourists visiting the city would mean less taxable spending by tourists; and that less taxable spending by tourists would mean less revenue overall for the operating budget.

A Even if flights depart the airport less frequently during some periods of the day, increasing the minimum time between flights at busy times of day could reduce the total number of daily flights from the airport.

B Even if half the tourists flying into the airport were bound for other nearby towns, the other half could still spend enough in town to generate lots of revenue for the operating budget.

C It is possible that most tourists spend relatively little in the city, but a few spend a lot. In that case, even if a reduction in tourist numbers resulted mainly from a declining number of tourists who spend relatively little, it could also greatly reduce the already small number of tourists who spend a lot.

D This suggests that the proposed rules might be financially better for the city than any alternative way to improve safety, whereas the argument's conclusion is that the proposed rules are financially disadvantageous.

E **Correct.** If adopting the proposed rules would result in a large increase in the number of passengers per flight, fewer daily flights would not necessarily mean fewer passengers or fewer tourists overall.

The correct answer is E.

629. The introduction of new drugs into the market is frequently prevented by a shortage of human subjects for the clinical trials needed to show that the drugs are safe and effective. Since the lives and health of people in future generations may depend on treatments that are currently experimental, practicing physicians are morally in the wrong when, in the absence of any treatment proven to be effective, they fail to encourage suitable patients to volunteer for clinical trials.

Which of the following, if true, casts most doubt on the conclusion of the argument?

(A) Many drugs undergoing clinical trials are intended for the treatment of conditions for which there is currently no effective treatment.

(B) Patients do not share the physician's professional concern for public health, but everyone has a moral obligation to alleviate suffering when able to do so.

(C) Usually, half the patients in a clinical trial serve as a control group and receive a nonactive drug in place of the drug being tested.

(D) An experimental drug cannot legally be made available to patients unless those patients are subjects in clinical trials of the drug.

(E) Physicians have an overriding moral and legal duty to care for the health and safety of their current patients.

Argument Evaluation

Situation A shortage of human subjects for clinical trials needed to show that new drugs are safe and effective often prevents those drugs from being introduced into the market. The lives and health of future generations may depend on treatments that are now experimental.

Reasoning *What would cast doubt on the judgment that doctors are morally obligated to encourage their patients to volunteer for clinical trials?* Note that the argument's conclusion, unlike its premises, is a moral judgment. This judgment could be cast into doubt by a moral principle that would be likely to conflict with it under the conditions described. For example, a principle suggesting that it is sometimes morally unacceptable for doctors to encourage their patients to volunteer for clinical trials would also suggest that they are not morally obligated to encourage their patients to volunteer for clinical trials, since anything morally obligatory must also be morally acceptable.

A If anything, this highlights how important it is to ensure that these drugs undergo clinical trials to benefit future generations, so it supports rather than casts doubt on the argument's conclusion.

B This suggests that patients are morally obligated to volunteer for clinical trials to help prevent suffering in future generations. If anything, this supports the claim that doctors are morally obligated to encourage their patients to volunteer.

C The clinical trial will probably not harm any patients in the control group, yet their participation will benefit future generations. So, if anything, this supports the claim that doctors should encourage their patients to volunteer.

D This legal barrier makes it even more essential for the drugs to undergo clinical trials in order to benefit patients, so it supports rather than casts doubt on the argument's conclusion.

E **Correct.** Since the experimental drugs' safety is being tested during the trials, the drugs may prove unsafe for subjects in the trials. If doctors have an overriding moral duty to keep their current patients safe, then it may be morally unacceptable for them to encourage those patients to volunteer for the trials.

The correct answer is E.

630. As a construction material, bamboo is as strong as steel and sturdier than concrete. Moreover, in tropical areas bamboo is a much less expensive construction material than either steel or concrete and is always readily available. In tropical areas, therefore, building with bamboo makes better economic sense than building with steel or concrete, except where land values are high.

Which of the following, if true, most helps to explain the exception noted above?

(A) Buildings constructed of bamboo are less likely to suffer earthquake damage than are steel and concrete buildings.

(B) Bamboo is unsuitable as a building material for multistory buildings.

(C) In order to protect it from being damaged by termites and beetles, bamboo must be soaked, at some expense, in a preservative.

(D) In some tropical areas, bamboo is used to make the scaffolding that is used during large construction projects.

(E) Bamboo growing in an area where land values are increasing is often cleared to make way for construction.

Argument Construction

Situation Bamboo is as strong as steel and sturdier than concrete when used as a construction material. In tropical areas, bamboo is much less expensive and is always readily available.

Reasoning *What explains the exception specified in the conclusion?* The argument's conclusion is that in tropical areas bamboo is a more economical building material than steel or concrete, *except where land values are high.* The information in the passage makes clear why bamboo is a more economical building material in tropical areas than are concrete or steel. So the question is: Why must an exception be made for areas where land values are high? Multistory buildings are particularly desirable in areas where land values are high, but bamboo may not be suitable for such buildings.

A This explains why bamboo would be preferable to steel or concrete in tropical areas especially prone to earthquakes. However, there is no clear connection to be made between areas where land values are high and areas especially prone to earthquakes.

B **Correct.** Multistory buildings provide a greater area of floor space for a given site area, and in that sense are more economical. A single-story building with the same floor space will occupy a much bigger site, so the higher the land values, the more likely it is that a multistory building will be built on that land. Thus, given this information, bamboo is less suitable for areas where land values are high.

C This undermines, to some extent, the claim that bamboo is an economical building material. But it does nothing to explain why it would be less economical specifically in areas where land values are high.

D This is irrelevant. Bamboo is used to build scaffolding for construction projects and as a building material for permanent structures. There is no way to infer from this that bamboo is less economical specifically in areas where land values are high.

E The fact that bamboo is cleared from an area to make room for construction in no way implies that bamboo would not be a suitable and economical building material for the area once it has been cleared.

The correct answer is B.

631. Newspaper editors should not allow reporters to write the headlines for their own stories. The reason for this is that, while the headlines that reporters themselves write are often clever, what typically makes them clever is that they allude to little-known information that is familiar to the reporter but that never appears explicitly in the story itself.

Which of the following, if true, most strengthens the argument?

(A) The reporter who writes a story is usually better placed than the reporter's editor is to judge what the story's most newsworthy features are.

(B) To write a headline that is clever, a person must have sufficient understanding of the story that the headline accompanies.

(C) Most reporters rarely bother to find out how other reporters have written stories and headlines about the same events that they themselves have covered.

(D) For virtually any story that a reporter writes, there are at least a few people who know more about the story's subject matter than does the reporter.

(E) The kind of headlines that newspaper editors want are those that anyone who has read a reporter's story in its entirety will recognize as clever.

Argument Evaluation

Situation The headlines newspaper reporters write for their own stories are often clever only because they allude to little-known information that never appears explicitly in the stories themselves.

Reasoning *What would most help the argument support the conclusion that newspaper editors should not allow reporters to write headlines for their own stories?* The argument's only explicit premise is that the headlines newspaper reporters write for their own stories are often clever only because they allude to little-known information that never appears explicitly in the stories themselves. In order for this premise to support the conclusion that newspaper editors should not allow reporters to write their own headlines, it would be helpful to be given a reason why editors should avoid headlines alluding to such little-known information.

A This suggests that reporters are likely to write better headlines for their stories than editors are, so it weakens the argument that editors should not allow reporters to write their own headlines.

B Since a reporter who wrote a story is likely to understand that story well, this does not provide a reason why editors should not allow reporters to write their own headlines.

C If most reporters did what is suggested, they could perhaps hone their headline-writing skills—unless almost all reporters are weak in such skills, as suggested in the given information. The fact that they do not bother to do so may help explain why reporters' headline-writing skills are weak. An explanation of why this is so does not provide additional support for the argument's conclusion.

D The people who know more about a story's subject matter than the reporter writing the story might be just as likely to see the cleverness of allusions to little-known information as the reporters are. So, to the extent that this is relevant at all, it slightly weakens the argument by suggesting that obscurely clever headlines sometimes function as intended.

E **Correct.** The argument's explicit premise suggests that typically a reporter's headline for his or her own story cannot be recognized as clever by a reader who has read the whole story. So if editors want headlines that anyone who has read the accompanying stories would recognize as clever, they have a reason not to let reporters write the headlines.

The correct answer is E.

632. Scientists have modified feed corn genetically, increasing its resistance to insect pests. Farmers who tried out the genetically modified corn last season applied less insecticide to their corn fields and still got yields comparable to those they would have gotten with ordinary corn. Ordinary corn seed, however, costs less, and what these farmers saved on insecticide rarely exceeded their extra costs for seed. Therefore, for most feed-corn farmers, switching to genetically modified seed would be unlikely to increase profits.

Which of the following would it be most useful to know in order to evaluate the argument?

(A) Whether there are insect pests that sometimes reduce feed-corn yields, but against which commonly used insecticides and the genetic modification are equally ineffective
(B) Whether the price that farmers receive for feed corn has remained steady over the past few years
(C) Whether the insecticides typically used on feed corn tend to be more expensive than insecticides typically used on other crops
(D) Whether most of the farmers who tried the genetically modified corn last season applied more insecticide than was actually necessary
(E) Whether, for most farmers who plant feed corn, it is their most profitable crop

Argument Evaluation

Situation Farmers who grew feed corn genetically engineered to be pest resistant got yields comparable to those of farmers growing ordinary feed corn, but did so while using less pesticide. Since the amount saved on pesticide was rarely in excess of the extra costs for the genetically modified corn, most farmers will probably not increase profits by choosing the genetically engineered variety.

Reasoning *Which would be most useful to know in evaluating the argument?* To answer a question such as this, one should look for information that would strengthen or weaken the argument. If one had information that the farmers growing the genetically modified corn could have increased their yields last year at lower cost, this would be helpful in evaluating the argument, because this would show that the argument is weak.

A It does not matter to the argument whether there are pests against which pesticides and genetic resistance are equally ineffective, because that is compatible with there being pests against which they are not equally effective.

B Whether prices of feed corn go up or down affects the comparison groups equally.

C The relative cost of insecticides for other crops has no bearing on the argument because the argument is concerned with only feed corn.

D **Correct.** This option provides the information that it would be most useful to know in evaluating the argument. It shows that farmers growing genetically modified corn last year could have attained higher profits than they in fact did.

E The argument concerns only the relative profitability of growing one variety of feed corn versus another.

The correct answer is D.

633. Debater: The average amount of overtime per month worked by an employee in the manufacturing division of the Haglut Corporation is 14 hours. Most employees of the Haglut Corporation work in the manufacturing division. Furthermore, the average amount of overtime per month worked by any employee in the company generally does not fluctuate much from month to month. Therefore, each month, most employees of the Haglut Corporation almost certainly work at least some overtime.

The debater's argument is most vulnerable to criticism on which of these grounds?

(A) It takes for granted that the manufacturing division is a typical division of the corporation with regard to the average amount of overtime its employees work each month.

(B) It takes for granted that if a certain average amount of overtime is worked each month by each employee of the Haglut Corporation, then approximately the same amount of overtime must be worked each month by each employee of the manufacturing division.

(C) It confuses a claim from which the argument's conclusion about the Haglut Corporation would necessarily follow with a claim that would follow from the argument's conclusion only with a high degree of probability.

(D) It overlooks the possibility that even if, on average, a certain amount of overtime is worked by the members of some group, many members of that group may work no overtime at all.

(E) It overlooks the possibility that even if most employees of the corporation work some overtime each month, any one corporate employee may, in some months, work no overtime.

Argument Evaluation

Situation Most of the employees of the Haglut Corporation work in the manufacturing division, where employees average 14 hours per month in overtime. The average amount of overtime per month for employees at Haglut does not fluctuate much from month to month.

Reasoning *What is the argument's greatest weakness?* The argument's conclusion is that almost certainly each month most of the employees of Haglut work at least some overtime. Answer choice (D) identifies the argument's greatest weakness because it points out how the conclusion of the argument could be false even if all of the supporting information were true. For example, it could be that less than half of the employees work any overtime at all, but those that do work overtime work much more than 14 hours per month.

A The argument leaves open the possibility that in some divisions of the corporation, the average monthly overtime of its employees is quite different from 14 hours, even if (as the argument states) that average does not change much from month to month.

B The argument does not assume that there is a monthly amount of overtime worked by each employee of the manufacturing division equivalent to the company-wide average monthly overtime per employee.

C This does not identify a weakness that can be detected in the argument. Since the claims mentioned here are not specified, the passage provides no evidence that clearly indicates that this type of confusion is playing a role in the argument.

D **Correct.** The argument ignores the possibility that most of the employees of Haglut work no overtime at all in a particular month—which is quite consistent with the argument's assertion that the average number of monthly overtime hours per employee within the manufacturing division is 14.

E The possibility described by this is not overlooked by the argument, because this possibility is consistent with the conclusion. It could easily be that most employees of the corporation work some overtime each month—as the conclusion envisions—but that there are always some employees who do not work any overtime.

The correct answer is D.

634. Proponents of the recently introduced tax on sales of new luxury boats had argued that a tax of this sort would be an equitable way to increase government revenue because the admittedly heavy tax burden would fall only on wealthy people and neither they nor anyone else would suffer any economic hardship. In fact, however, 20 percent of the workers employed by manufacturers of luxury boats have lost their jobs as a direct result of this tax.

The information given, if true, most strongly supports which of the following?

(A) The market for luxury boats would have collapsed even if the new tax on luxury boats had been lower.

(B) The new tax would produce a net gain in tax revenue for the government only if the yearly total revenue that it generates exceeds the total of any yearly tax-revenue decrease resulting from the workers' loss of jobs.

(C) Because many people never buy luxury items, imposing a sales tax on luxury items is the kind of legislative action that does not cost incumbent legislators much popular support.

(D) Before the tax was instituted, luxury boats were largely bought by people who were not wealthy.

(E) Taxes can be equitable only if their burden is evenly distributed over the entire population.

Argument Construction

Situation Proponents of a recently introduced tax on sales of new luxury boats argued that it would be an equitable way to increase government revenue because the tax would fall only on the wealthy and cause no economic hardship. But because of the tax, 20 percent of luxury-boat manufacturing workers have lost their jobs.

Reasoning *What conclusion do the statements about the proponents' argument and the tax's effects support?* Since the tax caused many workers to lose their jobs, apparently the proponents were incorrect in asserting that it would cause no one to suffer any economic hardship. Thus, their justification for concluding that the tax is an equitable way to increase government revenue is factually inaccurate, casting doubt on that conclusion.

A The passage indicates that the tax directly caused a significant decrease (though not necessarily a collapse) in the market for luxury boats. But the passage contains no evidence about whether such a decrease might not have occurred if the new tax had been somewhat lower.

B Correct. Since the tax caused the workers to lose their jobs, it might have made the government lose revenue from payroll taxes that the laid-off workers would have paid if they had kept their jobs. So if the yearly total revenue generated directly and indirectly by the tax were less than those total yearly payroll taxes and any other tax revenue that was lost as a result of the tax, the tax would have caused a net loss in tax revenue.

C The passage contains no information about what types of legislative actions cost, or do not cost, incumbent legislators popular support.

D Although the passage suggests that some of the tax proponents' assumptions were wrong, it contains no information suggesting that those proponents were wrong in thinking that luxury boats are purchased mainly by wealthy people.

E The passage does not provide any basis for determining what makes a tax equitable or about whether the luxury boat tax is equitable. The tax's proponents evidently felt that a tax whose burden falls only on the wealthy rather than evenly on the entire population can be equitable.

The correct answer is B.

635. In Wareland last year, 16 percent of licensed drivers under 21 and 11 percent of drivers ages 21–24 were in serious accidents. By contrast, only 3 percent of licensed drivers 65 and older were involved in serious accidents. These figures clearly show that the greater experience and developed habits of caution possessed by drivers in the 65-and-older group make them far safer behind the wheel than the younger drivers are.

Which of the following is an assumption on which the argument depends?

(A) Drivers 65 and older do not, on average, drive very many fewer miles per year than drivers 24 and younger.

(B) Drivers 65 and older do not constitute a significantly larger percentage of licensed drivers in Wareland than drivers ages 18–24 do.

(C) Drivers 65 and older are less likely than are drivers 24 and younger to drive during weather conditions that greatly increase the risk of accidents.

(D) The difference between the accident rate of drivers under 21 and of those ages 21–24 is attributable to the greater driving experience of those in the older group.

(E) There is no age bracket for which the accident rate is lower than it is for licensed drivers 65 and older.

Argument Evaluation

Situation Last year in Wareland, a much higher percentage of drivers 24 and under than of drivers 65 and older were in serious accidents.

Reasoning *What must be true for the observation about the accident rates to support the conclusion that the greater experience and caution of drivers 65 and older make them safer behind the wheel than the younger drivers?* Several factors other than greater experience and caution could explain the lower accident rate among the older drivers. For example, the older drivers might simply drive much less than the younger ones, but still get in just as many accidents per mile driven. Or perhaps because the older drivers are more often retired, their schedules less often lead them to drive at times of day when accident rates are greater for everyone. Or they might be more likely to live in rural areas with less traffic and lower accident rates. The argument depends on assuming that none of these factors fully explains the difference in accident rates.

A **Correct.** Although we are given no information about the possible extent of any difference in average miles driven, the (somewhat vague) information that drivers 65 and older drive *very many fewer miles per year*, on average, than drivers 24 and younger would cast serious doubt on the statistical argument given. The argument assumes that the difference in miles driven is not sufficiently substantial to undermine the argument.

B The argument is only about the discrepancy between the percentages of the drivers in two specific age groups who were in serious accidents last year. The percentages of licensed drivers who fall in these age groups are irrelevant.

C Even if drivers 65 and older are just as likely as younger drivers to drive in inclement weather, they may do so far more carefully than the younger drivers, so the older drivers' greater experience and caution could still explain their lower accident rates.

D Even if greater experience does not explain the difference between the accident rates of the two younger groups of drivers, it might still explain the differences between the accident rate of those two younger groups taken together and that of drivers aged 65 and older.

E The accident rate could be lower for drivers in late middle age than for those 65 and older because drivers in late middle age are also cautious and experienced, but their reflexes and vision tend to be less impaired. Even if that were true, the experience and caution of the drivers 65 and older might still make them safer than drivers 24 and under.

The correct answer is A.

636. In the past the country of Malvernia has relied heavily on imported oil. Malvernia recently implemented a program to convert heating systems from oil to natural gas. Malvernia currently produces more natural gas each year than it uses, and oil production in Malvernian oil fields is increasing at a steady pace. If these trends in fuel production and usage continue, therefore, Malvernian reliance on foreign sources for fuel is likely to decline soon.

Which of the following would it be most useful to establish in evaluating the argument?

(A) When, if ever, will production of oil in Malvernia outstrip production of natural gas?
(B) Is Malvernia among the countries that rely most on imported oil?
(C) What proportion of Malvernia's total energy needs is met by hydroelectric, solar, and nuclear power?
(D) Is the amount of oil used each year in Malvernia for generating electricity and fuel for transportation increasing?
(E) Have any existing oil-burning heating systems in Malvernia already been converted to natural-gas-burning heating systems?

Argument Evaluation

Situation Malvernia has relied heavily on imported oil, but recently began a program to convert heating systems from oil to natural gas. Malvernia produces more natural gas than it uses, so it will probably reduce its reliance on imported oils if these trends continue.

Reasoning *Which option provides the information that it would be most useful to know in evaluating the argument?* In other words, we are looking for the option which—depending on whether it was answered yes or no—would either most weaken or most strengthen the argument. The argument indicates that Malvernia will be using less oil for heating and will be producing more oil domestically. But the conclusion that Malvernia's reliance on foreign oil will decline, assuming the current trends mentioned continue, would be seriously undermined if there was something in the works that was bound to offset these trends, for instance, if it turned out that the country's need for oil was going to rise drastically in the coming years.

A Since both counteract the need for imported oil, it makes little difference to the argument whether domestic oil production exceeds domestic natural gas.

B Whether there are many countries that rely more on foreign oil than Malvernia would have little impact on whether Malvernia's need for foreign oil can be expected to decline.

C Since there is no information in the argument about whether Malvernia can expect an increase or decrease from these other energy sources, it does not matter how much they now provide.

D **Correct.** This option provides the information that it would be most useful to know in evaluating the argument.

E The argument tells us that a program has begun *recently* to convert heating systems from oil to gas. So, even if no such conversions have been completed, the argument still indicates that they can be expected to occur.

The correct answer is D.

637. Exposure to certain chemicals commonly used in elementary schools as cleaners or pesticides causes allergic reactions in some children. Elementary school nurses in Renston report that the proportion of schoolchildren sent to them for treatment of allergic reactions to those chemicals has increased significantly over the past ten years. Therefore, either Renston's schoolchildren have been exposed to greater quantities of the chemicals, or they are more sensitive to them than schoolchildren were ten years ago.

Which of the following is an assumption on which the argument depends?

(A) The number of school nurses employed by Renston's elementary schools has not decreased over the past ten years.

(B) Children who are allergic to the chemicals are no more likely than other children to have allergies to other substances.

(C) Children who have allergic reactions to the chemicals are not more likely to be sent to a school nurse now than they were ten years ago.

(D) The chemicals are not commonly used as cleaners or pesticides in houses and apartment buildings in Renston.

(E) Children attending elementary school do not make up a larger proportion of Renston's population now than they did ten years ago.

Argument Construction

Situation Some children have allergic reactions to some of the chemicals commonly used in elementary schools as cleaners and pesticides. The number of children sent to elementary school nurses in Renston for allergic reactions to such chemicals has risen significantly over the past ten years.

Reasoning *What must the argument assume?* The argument's conclusion presents just two alternatives: either the children are exposed to more of the chemicals than children in earlier years *or* they are more sensitive. But there is a third possible explanation for the significant increase in school-nurse visits that the school nurses have reported: that children are just more inclined to go to the school nurse when they experience an allergic reaction than were children several years ago. For the conclusion to follow from its premises, the argument must assume that this is not the correct explanation.

A If the number of elementary school nurses in Renston elementary schools had decreased over the past ten years, that would in no way explain the rise in the proportion of children reporting to school nurses for allergic reactions.

B Only school-nurse visits for allergic reactions to the cleaners and pesticides used in elementary schools are in question in the argument. Of course there could be school-nurse visits for allergic reactions to other things, but that issue does not arise in the argument.

C **Correct.** This can be seen by considering whether the argument would work if we assume that this were false, i.e., that a school-nurse visit *is* more likely in such cases. As noted above, this provides an alternative to the two explanations that the conclusion claims are the sole possibilities.

D This does not need to be assumed by the argument. The argument's conclusion suggests that children may in recent years have had greater exposure to the chemicals, not that this exposure has occurred exclusively in the schools. The argument does not rely on this latter assumption.

E The argument does not need to make this assumption. The argument is framed in terms of proportions of children having school-nurse visits for certain allergic reactions. *How many* children there are or what proportion such children are of Renston's total population is not directly relevant to the argument.

The correct answer is C.

638. Normally, the pineal gland governs a person's sleep-wake cycle by secreting melatonin in response to the daily cycle of light and darkness as detected by the eye. Nonetheless, many people who are totally blind due to lesions in the visual cortex of the brain easily maintain a 24-hour sleep-wake cycle. So the neural pathway by which the pineal gland receives information from the eye probably does not pass through the visual cortex.

For purposes of evaluating the argument it would be most useful to establish which of the following?

(A) Whether melatonin supplements help people who have difficulty maintaining a 24-hour sleep cycle to establish such a pattern

(B) Whether the melatonin levels of most totally blind people who successfully maintain a 24-hour sleep-wake cycle change in response to changes in exposure to light and darkness

(C) Whether melatonin is the only substance secreted by the pineal gland

(D) Whether most people who do not have a 24-hour sleep-wake cycle nevertheless have a cycle of consistent duration

(E) Whether there are any people with normal vision whose melatonin levels respond abnormally to periods of light and darkness

Argument Evaluation

Situation Normally, a person's sleep-wake cycle is governed by the pineal gland secreting melatonin in response to the daily cycle of light and darkness as detected by the eye. Yet many people who are totally blind due to lesions of the visual cortex easily maintain a 24-hour sleep-wake cycle.

Reasoning *What additional information would be most helpful in evaluating the argument?* The argument's conclusion is that the neural pathway by which the pineal gland receives information probably does not pass through the visual cortex. This is suggested by the fact that people without a well-functioning visual cortex (e.g., people with a certain type of blindness) can nonetheless maintain a 24-hour sleep-wake cycle. Is it by the pineal gland's secretion of melatonin that they do so? The argument tells us that *normally* (i.e., in sighted people), this is the mechanism for sleep regulation. But the argument depends on assuming that a similar mechanism is operating in people who are blind but have well-regulated sleep cycles. The best choice will be the one that helps us decide whether that assumption is correct.

A This question would not give us an answer that would help in evaluating the argument. A "no" answer would not clarify whether the pineal gland-melatonin mechanism operates in people who are blind. A "yes" answer would do no better. The question refers only to people who have sleep dysfunctions (which the argument does not address).

B **Correct.** Answering this question would provide the most useful information for evaluating the argument. A "yes" answer would help confirm a key assumption of the argument: that blind people rely on the pineal gland-melatonin mechanism for sleep regulation. A "no" answer would help disconfirm that assumption.

C Whether or not there are other substances secreted by the pineal gland makes no difference to the reasoning. The argument relies on the premise that the pineal gland governs the sleep cycle *by secreting melatonin*. For example, if the pineal gland sometimes secreted adrenaline, that would still have no bearing on the argument.

D The consistency or inconsistency of the duration of some people's sleep patterns has no relevance to the reasoning. Their sleep patterns could be due to any of a number of factors.

E This does not help, for there could be sighted people whose melatonin levels respond abnormally simply because of a pineal-gland abnormality.

The correct answer is B.

639. **In countries where automobile insurance includes compensation for whiplash injuries sustained in automobile accidents, reports of having suffered such injuries are twice as frequent as they are in countries where whiplash is not covered.** Presently, no objective test for whiplash exists, so it is true that spurious reports of whiplash injuries cannot be readily identified. Nevertheless, these facts do not warrant the conclusion drawn by some commentators that in the countries with the higher rates of reported whiplash injuries, half of the reported cases are spurious. Clearly, **in countries where automobile insurance does not include compensation for whiplash, people often have little incentive to report whiplash injuries that they actually have suffered.**

In the argument given, the two boldfaced portions play which of the following roles?

(A) The first is a claim that the argument disputes; the second is a conclusion that has been based on that claim.

(B) The first is a claim that has been used to support a conclusion that the argument accepts; the second is that conclusion.

(C) The first is evidence that has been used to support a conclusion for which the argument provides further evidence; the second is the main conclusion of the argument.

(D) The first is a finding whose implications are at issue in the argument; the second is a claim presented in order to argue against deriving certain implications from that finding.

(E) The first is a finding whose accuracy is evaluated in the argument; the second is evidence presented to establish that the finding is accurate.

Argument Evaluation

Situation Reported whiplash injuries are twice as common in countries where car insurance companies pay compensation for such injuries as they are in countries where insurance companies do not. Although there is no objective test for whiplash, this does not mean, as some suggest, that half of the reports of such injuries are fake. It could simply be that where insurance will not pay for such injuries, people are less inclined to report them.

Reasoning *What roles do the two boldfaced portions play in the argument?* The first portion tells us about the correlation between reported cases of whiplash in countries and the willingness of insurance companies in those countries to compensate for whiplash injuries. The argument next states that whiplash is difficult to objectively verify. The argument then asserts that *although* this last fact, taken together with the first boldfaced portion, has led some to infer that over half of the reported cases in countries with the highest whiplash rates are spurious, such an inference is unwarranted. The second boldfaced portion then helps to explain why such an inference is not necessarily warranted by offering an alternative explanation.

A The claim made in the first boldfaced portion is never disputed in the argument; at dispute is how to account for the fact that this claim is true. The second is not the argument's conclusion.

B In a manner of speaking, perhaps, the argument uses the first portion to support its conclusion; but there is no indication that it has been used elsewhere to do so. In any case, the second boldfaced portion is not the argument's conclusion.

C The first has been used to support a conclusion that the argument *rejects*; the second boldfaced portion is not the argument's conclusion.

D **Correct.** This option correctly identifies the roles played in the argument by the boldfaced portions.

E The accuracy of the first boldfaced portion is never questioned in the argument; nor is the second intended to somehow help show that the first is accurate. Rather, the argument assumes that the first portion is accurate.

The correct answer is D.

640. Last year Comfort Airlines had twice as many delayed flights as the year before, but the number of complaints from passengers about delayed flights went up three times. It is unlikely that this disproportionate increase in complaints was rooted in an increase in overall dissatisfaction with the service Comfort Airlines provides, since the airline made a special effort to improve other aspects of its service last year.

Which of the following, if true, most helps to explain the disproportionate increase in customer complaints?

(A) Comfort Airlines had more flights last year than the year before.
(B) Last year a single period of unusually bad weather caused a large number of flights to be delayed.
(C) Some of the improvements that Comfort Airlines made in its service were required by new government regulations.
(D) The average length of a flight delay was greater last year than it was the year before.
(E) The average number of passengers per flight was no higher last year than the year before.

Argument Construction

Situation Last year Comfort Airlines had twice as many delayed flights as it did the year before, but three times as many passenger complaints about delayed flights. The airline made a special effort to improve other aspects of its service last year.

Reasoning *What could explain why the number of complaints about delayed flights increased disproportionately to the number of delayed flights last year?* In other words, why did the average number of passenger complaints per delayed flight go up last year? One obvious possibility is that the average number of passengers per delayed flight was greater last year than it had been the year before. Another is that the flight delays tended to cause worse problems for passengers last year than they had the year before, so that on average each delay was more upsetting for the passengers.

A This helps explain why the airline had more delayed flights last year, but not why the increase in complaints about delayed flights was disproportionate to the increase in delayed flights.

B This helps explain why the airline had more delayed flights last year. But, if anything, the situation should have reduced the number of passenger complaints per delayed flight, since many passengers should have realized that the unusually bad weather was not the airline's fault.

C If any of the improvements concerned handling of flight delays, for example, and passengers were aware that government regulations addressed this, then passengers might have complained more than previously. But the information we are given here is too general and too vague to explain the disproportionate increase in complaints.

D **Correct.** Longer flight delays would have more severely inconvenienced passengers and thus would probably have generated more passenger complaints per delay.

E This rules out the possibility that an increased number of passengers per delayed flight could have caused the disproportionate increase in the number of complaints about delayed flights. But no alternative explanation is offered.

The correct answer is D

641. Last year a global disturbance of weather patterns disrupted harvests in many of the world's important agricultural areas. Worldwide production of soybeans, an important source of protein for people and livestock alike, was not adversely affected, however. Indeed, last year's soybean crop was actually slightly larger than average. Nevertheless, the weather phenomenon is probably responsible for a recent increase in the world price of soybeans.

Which of the following, if true, provides the strongest justification for the attribution of the increase in soybean prices to the weather phenomenon?

(A) Last year's harvest of anchovies, which provide an important protein source for livestock, was disrupted by the effects of the weather phenomenon.

(B) Most countries that produce soybeans for export had above-average harvests of a number of food crops other than soybeans last year.

(C) The world price of soybeans also rose several years ago, immediately after an earlier occurrence of a similar global weather disturbance.

(D) Heavy rains attributable to the weather phenomenon improved grazing pastures last year, allowing farmers in many parts of the world to reduce their dependence on supplemental feed.

(E) Prior to last year, soybean prices had been falling for several years.

Argument Construction

Situation A weather disturbance last year disrupted harvests worldwide but did not reduce production of soybeans, a protein source for both people and livestock. Soybean prices increased nonetheless, likely a result of the weather.

Reasoning *What evidence would suggest that the weather disturbance caused the increase in soybean prices even though it did not reduce soybean production?* Prices tend to increase when the supply of a product falls relative to the demand for the product. But the production of soybeans did not fall. Evidence that the weather disturbance either hindered the global distribution of soybeans or increased global demand for soybeans could support the claim that the weather disturbance caused the increase in soybean prices.

A **Correct.** If the weather disturbance reduced the anchovy harvest, and anchovies provide protein for livestock just as soybeans do, then more soybeans for livestock feed would be needed to compensate for the lack of anchovies. The resulting increase in demand for soybeans could thus have increased global soybean prices.

B This is not surprising, given that the weather disturbance did not severely affect the soybean-producing countries, but it does not explain how the weather disturbance could have caused soybean prices to increase.

C The rise in soybean prices after the earlier weather disturbance could easily have been a coincidence. Or, unlike last year's disturbance, the earlier disturbance could have reduced soybean production.

D This suggests that demand for soybeans should have fallen as a result of the weather disturbance, so it does not explain why soybean prices rose.

E If soybean prices were unusually low for some temporary reason when the weather disturbance occurred, they might have been likely to rise back to normal levels even without the weather disturbance.

The correct answer is A.

642. Most of the year, the hermit thrush, a North American songbird, eats a diet consisting mainly of insects, but in autumn, as the thrushes migrate to their Central and South American wintering grounds, they feed almost exclusively on wild berries. Wild berries, however, are not as rich in calories as insects, yet thrushes need to consume plenty of calories in order to complete their migration. One possible explanation is that berries contain other nutrients that thrushes need for migration and that insects lack.

Which of the following, if true, most seriously calls into question the explanation given for the thrush's diet during migration?

(A) Hermit thrushes, if undernourished, are unable to complete their autumn migration before the onset of winter.

(B) Insect species contain certain nutrients that are not found in wild berries.

(C) For songbirds, catching insects requires the expenditure of significantly more calories than eating wild berries does.

(D) Along the hermit thrushes' migration routes, insects are abundant throughout the migration season.

(E) There are some species of wild berries that hermit thrushes generally do not eat, even though these berry species are exceptionally rich in calories.

Argument Evaluation

Situation Hermit thrushes are songbirds that usually eat insects but switch to eating berries when migrating. The thrushes need lots of calories to migrate, but berries contain fewer calories than insects do. Perhaps the berries contain nutrients that insects do not provide.

Reasoning *What would cast doubt on the claim that the thrushes switch to berries because berries contain nutrients that insects lack and that the thrushes need for their migration?* Evidence that berries do not contain such nutrients or that thrushes do not decrease their net calorie consumption by eating berries would cast doubt on the proposed explanation. So would any evidence that supported an alternative explanation for the diet change during migration—for example, seasonal or regional differences in the amount or quality of berries or insects available for the thrushes to consume.

A Even if thrushes need to be well-nourished to finish migrating before winter, extra nutrients found in berries but not insects might help provide the nourishment they need.

B Even if insects contain *certain nutrients* not found in wild berries, those specific nutrients may not be the ones the thrushes need for their migration.

C **Correct.** This suggests that the thrushes might gain more net calories from eating berries than from eating insects, which could explain why they switch to eating berries even if the berries contain no extra nutrients.

D By ruling out a lack of insects to eat while migrating as an alternative explanation for why the thrushes switch to eating berries, this would support the proposed explanation.

E The calorie-rich species of berries the thrushes do not eat might be poisonous or indigestible for them, even if the species of berries the thrushes do eat contain nutrients they need to migrate.

The correct answer is C.

643. The kinds of hand and wrist injuries that result from extended use of a computer while maintaining an incorrect posture are common among schoolchildren in Harnville. Computers are important to the school curriculum there, so instead of reducing the amount their students use computers, teachers plan to bring about a sharp reduction in the number of these injuries by carefully monitoring their students' posture when using computers in the classroom.

Which of the following would it be most useful to know in order to assess the likelihood that the teachers' plan will be successful?

(A) Whether extended use of a computer while maintaining incorrect posture can cause injuries other than hand and wrist injuries
(B) Whether hand and wrist injuries not caused by computer use are common among schoolchildren in Harnville
(C) What proportion of schoolchildren in Harnville with hand and wrist injuries use computers extensively outside the classroom
(D) Whether changes in the curriculum could reduce the schools' dependence on computers
(E) What proportion of schoolchildren in Harnville already use correct posture while using a computer

Evaluation of a Plan

Situation Hand and wrist injuries from using computers while maintaining poor posture are common among schoolchildren in Harnville. Teachers plan to greatly reduce the number of such injuries by monitoring their students' posture while the students use computers in the classroom.

Reasoning *What would be most helpful to know to determine the likelihood that the teachers' plan will succeed?* The primary concern is the *posture* students adopt while using computers. To succeed, the teachers' plan must reduce the time students spend with poor posture while using computers and reduce it enough to greatly reduce the number of injuries. To know how likely this is, it would help to know how effectively the teachers will be able to monitor and improve their students' posture inside the classroom. But how many of the students use computers *outside of school* while maintaining poor posture and how often do they do so? If many students do so quite often, they may develop hand and wrist injuries regardless of what happens in school.

A The teachers do not plan to reduce any injuries other than hand and wrist injuries, so whether computer use with poor posture causes any such other injuries is irrelevant to the likelihood that their plan will produce its intended effect.

B The plan being discussed concerns only the reduction of hand and wrist injuries caused specifically by computer use with poor posture, so the frequency of hand and wrist injuries from other causes is irrelevant to the likelihood that the plan will produce its intended effect.

C **Correct.** If the students' school use of computers is a large part of their overall computer use, any retraining that accompanies the monitoring might have some effect on their posture and related injury rates overall. However, the greater the proportion of children with hand and wrist injuries who use computers extensively outside the classroom, the more children are likely to keep developing the injuries regardless of any monitoring at school, so the less effective the teachers' plan involving only computer use at school is likely to be.

D Knowing whether this is the case might help in developing a potential alternative to the teachers' plan, but if it did, this would not help significantly toward assessing the likelihood that the actual plan will succeed. The teachers' actual plan involves monitoring computer use in school without reducing such use. Other possible means of achieving the plan's goal are not part of the plan and are therefore irrelevant to the likelihood that the teachers' actual plan will succeed.

E The passage indicates that the proportion of the schoolchildren maintaining poor posture while using computers is high enough for many to develop hand and wrist injuries as a result. Whatever the exact proportion is, the teachers' plan may or may not succeed in reducing it.

The correct answer is C.

644. A certain cultivated herb is one of a group of closely related plants that thrive in soil with high concentrations of metals that are toxic to most other plants. Agronomists studying the growth of this herb have discovered that it produces large amounts of histidine, an amino acid that, in test-tube solutions, renders these metals chemically inert. Hence, the herb's high histidine production must be the key feature that allows it to grow in metal-rich soils.

In evaluating the argument, it would be most important to determine which of the following?

(A) Whether the herb can thrive in soil that does not have high concentrations of the toxic metals

(B) Whether others of the closely related group of plants also produce histidine in large quantities

(C) Whether the herb's high level of histidine production is associated with an unusually low level of production of some other amino acid

(D) Whether growing the herb in soil with high concentrations of the metals will, over time, reduce their concentrations in the soil

(E) Whether the concentration of histidine in the growing herb declines as the plant approaches maturity

Argument Evaluation

Situation A certain herb and closely related species thrive in soil full of metals toxic to most plants. The herb produces much histidine, which makes those metals chemically inert. Histidine production, therefore, is largely what accounts for the herb's thriving in metal-rich soils.

Reasoning *What evidence would help determine whether the herb's histidine production is what enables it to thrive in metal-rich soils?* The argument is that since the herb's histidine chemically neutralizes the metals that are toxic to most plants, it must explain why the herb can thrive in metal-rich soils. To evaluate this argument, it would be helpful to know about the relationship between other closely related plant species' histidine production and the ability to thrive in metal-rich soils. It would also be helpful to know about any other factors that might plausibly explain why the herb can thrive in those soils.

A Whether or not the herb thrives in metal-free soils, histidine production could enable it to thrive in soils that contain toxic metals.

B Correct. If the closely related plants do not produce much histidine, whatever other factor allows them to thrive in metal-rich soils would likely account for why the herb thrives in those soils as well.

C The given information suggests no particular reason to suppose that a low level of some unspecified amino acid would enable a plant to thrive in metal-rich soils.

D The herb might absorb metals from any metal-rich soil it grows in, regardless of why it thrives in that soil.

E Whether or not histidine concentrations in the herb decline as it approaches maturity, there could still be enough histidine in the growing herb to neutralize the metals and explain why it can grow in metal-rich soil.

The correct answer is B.

645. Many people suffer an allergic reaction to certain sulfites, including those that are commonly added to wine as preservatives. However, since there are several winemakers who add sulfites to none of the wines they produce, people who would like to drink wine but are allergic to sulfites can drink wines produced by these winemakers without risking an allergic reaction to sulfites.

Which of the following is an assumption on which the argument depends?

(A) These winemakers have been able to duplicate the preservative effect produced by adding sulfites by means that do not involve adding any potentially allergenic substances to their wine.

(B) Not all forms of sulfite are equally likely to produce the allergic reaction.

(C) Wine is the only beverage to which sulfites are commonly added.

(D) Apart from sulfites, there are no substances commonly present in wine that give rise to an allergic reaction.

(E) Sulfites are not naturally present in the wines produced by these winemakers in amounts large enough to produce an allergic reaction in someone who drinks these wines.

Argument Construction

Situation People who are allergic to certain sulfites can avoid risking an allergic reaction by drinking wine from one of the several producers that does not add sulfites.

Reasoning *On what assumption does the argument depend?* Drinking wine to which no sulfites have been *added* will not prevent exposure to sulfites if, for instance, sulfites occur naturally in wines. In particular, if the wines that do not have sulfites added have sulfites present naturally in quantities sufficient to produce an allergic reaction, drinking these wines will not prevent an allergic reaction. The argument therefore depends on assuming that this is not the case.

A The argument does not require this because the conclusion does not address allergic reactions to substances other than sulfites.

B The argument specifically refers to "certain sulfites" producing allergic reactions. It is entirely compatible with certain other forms of sulfites not producing allergic reactions in anyone.

C This is irrelevant. The argument does not claim that one can avoid having an allergic reaction to sulfites *from any source* just by restricting one's wine consumption to those varieties to which no sulfites have been added.

D Once again, the argument's conclusion does not address allergic reactions to substances other than sulfites in wine.

E **Correct.** The argument relies on this assumption.

The correct answer is E.

646. A new law gives ownership of patents—documents providing exclusive right to make and sell an invention—to universities, not the government, when those patents result from government-sponsored university research. Administrators at Logos University plan to sell any patents they acquire to corporations in order to fund programs to improve undergraduate teaching.

Which of the following, if true, would cast the most doubt on the viability of the college administrators' plan described above?

(A) Profit-making corporations interested in developing products based on patents held by universities are likely to try to serve as exclusive sponsors of ongoing university research projects.

(B) Corporate sponsors of research in university facilities are entitled to tax credits under new federal tax-code guidelines.

(C) Research scientists at Logos University have few or no teaching responsibilities and participate little if at all in the undergraduate programs in their field.

(D) Government-sponsored research conducted at Logos University for the most part duplicates research already completed by several profit-making corporations.

(E) Logos University is unlikely to attract corporate sponsorship of its scientific research.

Evaluation of a Plan

Situation Universities own the patents resulting from government-sponsored research at their institutions. One university plans to sell its patents to corporations to fund a program to improve teaching.

Reasoning *Which point casts doubt on the university's plan?* The university's plan assumes there will be a market for its patents, and that the corporations will want to buy them. What might make this untrue? If some of the corporations have already done the same or similar research, they will not be prospective buyers of the university's patents.

A This point is irrelevant to the plan to sell patents in order to fund a program.

B The university plans to sell the patents to the corporations, not to invite the corporations to sponsor research.

C This point is irrelevant to the university's plan to sell off patents since the plan does not specify that the research scientists will be involved in the programs to improve undergraduate teaching.

D **Correct.** This statement properly identifies a factor that casts doubt on the university's plan to sell its patents to corporations.

E The plan concerns selling patents resulting from government-sponsored research, not attracting corporate sponsorship for research.

The correct answer is D.

647. Since it has become known that **several of a bank's top executives have been buying shares in their own bank**, the bank's depositors, who had been worried by rumors that the bank faced impending financial collapse, have been greatly relieved. They reason that, since top executives evidently have faith in the bank's financial soundness, those worrisome rumors must be false. Such reasoning might well be overoptimistic, however, since **corporate executives have been known to buy shares in their own company in a calculated attempt to dispel negative rumors about the company's health.**

In the argument given, the two boldfaced portions play which of the following roles?

(A) The first describes evidence that has been taken as supporting a conclusion; the second gives a reason for questioning that support.

(B) The first describes evidence that has been taken as supporting a conclusion; the second states a contrary conclusion that is the main conclusion of the argument.

(C) The first provides evidence in support of the main conclusion of the argument; the second states that conclusion.

(D) The first describes the circumstance that the argument as a whole seeks to explain; the second gives the explanation that the argument seeks to establish.

(E) The first describes the circumstance that the argument as a whole seeks to explain; the second provides evidence in support of the explanation that the argument seeks to establish.

Argument Evaluation

Situation Top executives at a bank that has been rumored to be in financial trouble have been buying shares in the bank. Bank depositors see this as a good sign, because they believe that it indicates that the executives have faith in the bank. However, corporate executives sometimes do this just to dispel rumors about a company's health.

Reasoning *What is the role that the two boldfaced portions play in the argument?* The first boldfaced portion states that bank executives are buying bank shares, which the passage indicates is taken by bank depositors to be evidence of the executives' faith in the bank. The passage then tells us what some have inferred from this, and finally offers in the second boldfaced statement evidence that undermines this inference.

A **Correct.** This option correctly identifies the roles played by the boldfaced portions.

B This correctly describes the first statement's role, but the second statement is not offered as a conclusion—no evidence is given for it; rather it is evidence for something else.

C The second statement is not offered as a conclusion; no evidence is given for it.

D The second statement is not itself offered as an explanation of why these bank executives are investing in the bank; if it were, that would mean that the bank executives are doing so *because* corporate executives are known to do such things in a calculated effort to dispel worries. Furthermore the argument does not conclude that this other explanation (which the boldfaced portion points to) is correct, only that the one inferred by depositors may not be.

E The argument is not so much seeking to establish an explanation of its own as it is trying to undermine that inferred by the depositors.

The correct answer is A.

648. Between 1980 and 2000 the sea otter population of the Aleutian Islands declined precipitously. There were no signs of disease or malnutrition, so there was probably an increase in the number of otters being eaten by predators. Orcas will eat otters when seals, their normal prey, are unavailable, and the Aleutian Islands seal population declined dramatically in the 1980s. Therefore, orcas were most likely the immediate cause of the otter population decline.

Which of the following, if true, most strengthens the argument?

(A) The population of sea urchins, the main food of sea otters, has increased since the sea otter population declined.

(B) Seals do not eat sea otters, nor do they compete with sea otters for food.

(C) Most of the surviving sea otters live in a bay that is inaccessible to orcas.

(D) The population of orcas in the Aleutian Islands has declined since the 1980s.

(E) An increase in commercial fishing near the Aleutian Islands in the 1980s caused a slight decline in the population of the fish that seals use for food.

Argument Evaluation

Situation A sea otter population declined even though there were no signs of disease or malnutrition. The local seal population also declined. Orcas eat otters when seals are unavailable, and thus are probably the cause of the decline in the otter population.

Reasoning *What would be evidence that predation by orcas reduced the sea otter population?* Disease and malnutrition are ruled out as alternative explanations of the decline in the sea otter population. The argument could be further strengthened by casting doubt on other possible explanations, such as predation by other animals, or by presenting observations that predation of otters by orcas would help to explain.

A Regardless of whether or not orcas ate the sea otters, the sea urchin population would most likely have increased when the population of sea otters preying on them decreased.

B Because the seal population declined during the initial years of the otter population decline, predation by and competition with seals were already implausible explanations of the otter population decline.

C Correct. Orcas eating most of the accessible otters could plausibly explain this observation, which therefore provides additional evidence that orca predation reduced the sea otter population.

D If the orca population declined at the same time as the sea otter population, it would be less likely that increasing predation by orcas reduced the otter population.

E Since the sea otters showed no signs of malnutrition, they were probably getting enough fish. But if they were not, commercial fishing rather than orcas might have caused the otter population decline.

The correct answer is C.

649. Studies in restaurants show that the tips left by customers who pay their bill in cash tend to be larger when the bill is presented on a tray that bears a credit-card logo. Consumer psychologists hypothesize that simply seeing a credit-card logo makes many credit-card holders willing to spend more because it reminds them that their spending power exceeds the cash they have immediately available.

Which of the following, if true, most strongly supports the psychologists' interpretation of the studies?

(A) The effect noted in the studies is not limited to patrons who have credit cards.

(B) Patrons who are under financial pressure from their credit-card obligations tend to tip less when presented with a restaurant bill on a tray with a credit-card logo than when the tray has no logo.

(C) In virtually all of the cases in the studies, the patrons who paid bills in cash did not possess credit cards.

(D) In general, restaurant patrons who pay their bills in cash leave larger tips than do those who pay by credit card.

(E) The percentage of restaurant bills paid with a given brand of credit card increases when that credit card's logo is displayed on the tray with which the bill is presented.

Argument Evaluation

Situation Studies have found that restaurant customers give more generous tips when their bills are brought on trays bearing a credit-card logo. Psychologists speculate that this is because the logo reminds customers of their ability to spend more money than they have.

Reasoning *Which of the options most helps to support the psychologists' explanation of the studies?* The psychologists' hypothesis is that the credit-card logos on the trays bring to the minds of those who tip more the fact that they have more purchasing power than merely the cash that they have at hand. This explanation would not be valid even if those people who are *not* reminded of their own excess purchasing power—if in fact they have any such power—when they see such a logo nonetheless tip more in such trays. Thus, if restaurant patrons who are under financial pressure from their credit-card obligations do not tip more when their bills are presented on trays bearing credit-card logos, then the psychologists' interpretation of the studies is supported.

A This undermines the psychologists' interpretation, for it shows that the same phenomenon occurs even when the alleged cause has been removed.

B **Correct.** This option identifies the result that would most strengthen the psychologists' interpretation.

C This undermines the psychologists' interpretation by showing that the same phenomenon occurs even when the alleged cause has been removed; patrons cannot be reminded of something that is not there.

D To the extent that this bears on the interpretation of the study, it weakens it. Patrons *using* credit cards are surely aware that they have credit, and yet they spend *less* generously.

E This does not support the idea that being reminded that one has a credit card induces one to be *more generous*, only that it induces one to *use* that credit card.

The correct answer is B.

650. In an experiment, each volunteer was allowed to choose between an easy task and a hard task and was told that another volunteer would do the other task. Each volunteer could also choose to have a computer assign the two tasks randomly. Most volunteers chose the easy task for themselves and under questioning later said they had acted fairly. But when the scenario was described to another group of volunteers, almost all said choosing the easy task would be unfair. This shows that most people apply weaker moral standards to themselves than to others.

Which of the following is an assumption required by this argument?

(A) At least some volunteers who said they had acted fairly in choosing the easy task would have said that it was unfair for someone else to do so.

(B) The most moral choice for the volunteers would have been to have the computer assign the two tasks randomly.

(C) There were at least some volunteers who were assigned to do the hard task and felt that the assignment was unfair.

(D) On average, the volunteers to whom the scenario was described were more accurate in their moral judgments than the other volunteers were.

(E) At least some volunteers given the choice between assigning the tasks themselves and having the computer assign them felt that they had made the only fair choice available to them.

Argument Construction

Situation In an experiment, most volunteers chose to do an easy task themselves and leave a hard task for someone else. They later said they had acted fairly, but almost all volunteers in another group to which the scenario was described said choosing the easy task would be unfair, indicating that most people apply weaker moral standards to themselves.

Reasoning *What must be true in order for the facts presented to support the conclusion that most people apply weaker moral standards to themselves than to others?* One set of volunteers said they had acted fairly in taking the easy task, whereas different volunteers said that doing so would be unfair. In neither case did any of the volunteers actually judge their own behavior differently from how they judged anyone else's. So the argument implicitly infers from the experimental results that most of the volunteers would judge their own behavior differently from someone else's if given the chance. This inference assumes that the volunteers in the second group would have applied the same moral standards that those in the first group did if they had been in the first group's position, and vice versa.

A **Correct.** If none of the volunteers who said their own behavior was fair would have judged someone else's similar behavior as unfair, then their relaxed moral judgment of themselves would not suggest that they applied weaker moral standards to themselves than to others.

B Even if this is so, the experimental results could still suggest that the volunteers would apply weaker moral standards to themselves than to others.

C The argument would be equally strong even if volunteers who were assigned the hard task did not know that someone else had gotten an easier task—or even if no volunteers were actually assigned the hard task at all.

D Even if the moral standards applied by the volunteers who judged themselves were as accurate as those applied by the volunteers to whom the scenario was described, the former standards were still weaker.

E Even if all the volunteers in the first group had felt that all the choices available to them would have been fair for them to make personally, they might have applied stricter moral standards to someone else in the same position.

The correct answer is A.

651. Country X's recent stock-trading scandal should not diminish investors' confidence in the country's stock market. For one thing, **the discovery of the scandal confirms that Country X has a strong regulatory system**, as the following considerations show. In any stock market, some fraudulent activity is inevitable. If a stock market is well regulated, any significant stock-trading fraud in it will very likely be discovered. This deters potential perpetrators and facilitates improvement in regulatory processes.

In the argument, the portion in boldface plays which of the following roles?

(A) It is the argument's only conclusion.

(B) It is a conclusion for which the argument provides support and which itself is used to support the argument's main conclusion.

(C) It is the argument's main conclusion and is supported by another explicitly stated conclusion for which further support is provided.

(D) It is an assumption for which no explicit support is provided and is used to support the argument's only conclusion.

(E) It is a compound statement containing both the argument's main conclusion and an assumption used to support that conclusion.

Argument Construction

Situation Country X recently had a stock-trading scandal.

Reasoning *What role does the statement that the scandal's discovery confirms that Country X has a strong regulatory system play in the argument?* In the sentence containing the boldface statement, the phrase *For one thing* indicates that the statement is being used to justify the claim in the preceding sentence. Thus, the boldface statement must support that preceding sentence as a conclusion. Directly after the boldface statement, the phrase as *the following considerations show* indicates that the subsequent sentences are being used to support the boldface statement. Thus, the boldface statement is a conclusion supported by the sentences following it, and this statement itself supports the sentence preceding it, which must be the argument's main conclusion.

A As explained above, the boldface statement supports the claim in the preceding sentence, so it cannot be the argument's only conclusion.

B **Correct.** As explained above, the boldface statement is supported by the statements following it and in turn is used to support the argument's main conclusion in the statement preceding it.

C As explained above, the boldface statement cannot be the argument's main conclusion, because it supports a further conclusion presented in the sentence preceding it.

D As explained above, the sentences following the boldface statement are the explicit support provided for it.

E As explained above, the argument's main conclusion is stated only in the first sentence, which precedes the boldface statement. It is not repeated anywhere in the boldface statement.

The correct answer is B.

652. **Delta Products Inc. has recently switched at least partly from older technologies using fossil fuels to new technologies powered by electricity.** The question has been raised whether it can be concluded that **for a given level of output Delta's operation now causes less fossil fuel to be consumed than it did formerly.** The answer, clearly, is yes, since the amount of fossil fuel used to generate the electricity needed to power the new technologies is less than the amount needed to power the older technologies, provided level of output is held constant.

In the argument given, the two boldfaced portions play which of the following roles?

(A) The first identifies the content of the conclusion of the argument; the second provides support for that conclusion.

(B) The first provides support for the conclusion of the argument; the second identifies the content of that conclusion.

(C) The first states the conclusion of the argument; the second calls that conclusion into question.

(D) The first provides support for the conclusion of the argument; the second calls that conclusion into question.

(E) Each provides support for the conclusion of the argument.

Argument Evaluation

Situation Delta switched from technologies using fossil fuels to ones using electricity. It has been asked whether this results in less fossil fuel used per level of output. The answer is that it does.

Reasoning *What roles do the two boldfaced portions play in the argument?* The first boldfaced statement is simply asserted by the passage. But the second boldfaced statement, when it is first introduced, is not asserted to be true, but rather is identified as something that might be inferred from the first statement. By the end of the passage the argument concludes that the second statement is true.

A This option simply reverses the roles that the statements play in the argument.

B **Correct.** This option identifies the roles the boldfaced portions play.

C Nothing in the passage is intended to support the first statement; and the second statement is not supposed to call the first into question.

D This correctly identifies the role of the first statement, but the second boldfaced portion does not call the argument's conclusion into question—it is part of a sentence that refers to the question whether that conclusion can be drawn from the first statement.

E Again, this is only half right. The second boldfaced portion is not offered as support for the conclusion; if it were offered as such support, the argument would be guilty of circular reasoning, since the second boldfaced portion states exactly what the argument concludes.

The correct answer is B.

653. Theater Critic: The play *La Finestrina*, now at Central Theater, was written in Italy in the eighteenth century. The director claims that this production is as similar to the original production as is possible in a modern theater. Although the actor who plays Harlequin the clown gives a performance very reminiscent of the twentieth-century American comedian Groucho Marx, Marx's comic style was very much within the comic acting tradition that had begun in sixteenth-century Italy.

The considerations given best serve as part of an argument that

(A) modern audiences would find it hard to tolerate certain characteristics of a historically accurate performance of an eighteenth-century play

(B) Groucho Marx once performed the part of the character Harlequin in *La Finestrina*

(C) in the United States the training of actors in the twentieth century is based on principles that do not differ radically from those that underlay the training of actors in eighteenth-century Italy

(D) the performance of the actor who plays Harlequin in *La Finestrina* does not serve as evidence against the director's claim

(E) the director of *La Finestrina* must have advised the actor who plays Harlequin to model his performance on comic performances of Groucho Marx

Argument Construction

Situation The director of the local production of *La Finestrina* says it is as similar to the original production as is possible in a modern theater. The actor playing Harlequin gives a performance reminiscent of Groucho Marx, whose comic style falls within an acting tradition which began in sixteenth-century Italy.

Reasoning *For which of the options would the consideration given best serve as an argument?* The actor's performance was reminiscent of someone who fell within a tradition going back to sixteenth-century Italy. The play was written, and therefore was likely first performed, in eighteenth-century Italy. All of this suggests that there could be a similarity between the performances of Harlequin in the local production and in the original production. While the two performances *might* have been quite dissimilar, there is nothing *here* that supports that.

A Regardless of how plausible this option might be on its own merits, the passage provides no support for it because the passage provides no information about the characteristics of a historically accurate performance of an eighteenth-century play.

B The passage neither says this nor implies it.

C The passage says nothing about the training of actors, so this option would be supported by the passage only in a very roundabout, indirect way.

D **Correct.** This is the option that the considerations most support.

E That the performance reminded the theater critic of Groucho Marx hardly shows that the similarity was intentional, let alone that it was at the director's instruction.

The correct answer is D.

654. Although the discount stores in Goreville's central shopping district are expected to close within five years as a result of competition from a SpendLess discount department store that just opened, those locations will not stay vacant for long. In the five years since the opening of Colson's, a nondiscount department store, a new store has opened at the location of every store in the shopping district that closed because it could not compete with Colson's.

Which of the following, if true, most seriously weakens the argument?

(A) Many customers of Colson's are expected to do less shopping there than they did before the SpendLess store opened.
(B) Increasingly, the stores that have opened in the central shopping district since Colson's opened have been discount stores.
(C) At present, the central shopping district has as many stores operating in it as it ever had.
(D) Over the course of the next five years, it is expected that Goreville's population will grow at a faster rate than it has for the past several decades.
(E) Many stores in the central shopping district sell types of merchandise that are not available at either SpendLess or Colson's.

Argument Evaluation

Situation Due to competition from a recently opened SpendLess discount department store, discount stores in Goreville's central shopping district are expected to close within five years. But those locations will not be vacant long, for new stores have replaced all those that closed because of the opening five years ago of a Colson's nondiscount department store.

Reasoning *The question is which option would most weaken the argument?* The arguer infers that stores that leave because of the SpendLess will be replaced in their locations by other stores because that is what happened after the Colson's department store came in. Since the reasoning relies on a presumed similarity between the two cases, any information that brings to light a relevant dissimilarity would weaken the argument. If the stores that were driven out by Colson's were replaced mostly by discount stores, that suggests that the stores were replaced because of a need that no longer exists after the opening of SpendLess.

A The fact that Colson's may be seeing fewer customers does not mean that the discount stores that close will not be replaced; they might be replaced by stores that in no way compete with Colson's or SpendLess.

B **Correct.** This option most seriously weakens the argument.

C If anything, this strengthens the argument by indicating that Goreville's central shopping district is thriving.

D This, too, strengthens the argument because one is more likely to open a new store in an area with a growing population.

E Because this statement does not indicate whether any of these stores that offer goods not sold at SpendLess or Colson's will be among those that are closing, it is not possible to determine what effect it has on the strength of the argument.

The correct answer is B.

655. Last year all refuse collected by Shelbyville city services was incinerated. This incineration generated a large quantity of residual ash. In order to reduce the amount of residual ash Shelbyville generates this year to half of last year's total, the city has revamped its collection program. This year city services will separate for recycling enough refuse to reduce the number of truckloads of refuse to be incinerated to half of last year's number.

Which of the following is required for the revamped collection program to achieve its aim?

(A) This year, no materials that city services could separate for recycling will be incinerated.

(B) Separating recyclable materials from materials to be incinerated will cost Shelbyville less than half what it cost last year to dispose of the residual ash.

(C) Refuse collected by city services will contain a larger proportion of recyclable materials this year than it did last year.

(D) The refuse incinerated this year will generate no more residual ash per truckload incinerated than did the refuse incinerated last year.

(E) The total quantity of refuse collected by Shelbyville city services this year will be no greater than that collected last year.

Argument Construction

Situation To cut in half the residual ash produced at its incinerator, the city will separate for recycling enough refuse to cut in half the number of truckloads of refuse going to the incinerator.

Reasoning *Which option is required if the city's revamped collection program is to achieve its aim?* Cutting the number of truckloads of refuse in half must reduce the amount of residual ash to half last year's level. But if removal of the recycled refuse does not proportionately reduce the amount of ash, this will not happen. So if the amount of residual ash produced per truckload increases after recycling, then the amount of ash produced will not be cut in half by cutting in half the number of truckloads.

A This merely indicates that no further reduction of ash through recycling could be achieved this year; it indicates nothing about how much the ash will be reduced.

B This suggests a further benefit from recycling, but does not bear on the amount of ash that will be produced.

C Since no information is provided about how much, if any, recyclable materials were removed from the refuse last year, this does not affect the reasoning.

D **Correct.** This states a requirement for the collection program to achieve its aim.

E This is not a requirement because even if the city collects more refuse this year, it could still cut in half the amount of residual ash by cutting in half the number of truckloads going to the incinerator.

The correct answer is D.

656. Veterinarians generally derive some of their income from selling several manufacturers' lines of pet-care products. Knowing that pet owners rarely throw away mail from their pet's veterinarian unread, one manufacturer of pet-care products offered free promotional materials on its products to veterinarians for mailing to their clients. Very few veterinarians accepted the offer, however, even though the manufacturer's products are of high quality.

Which of the following, if true, most helps to explain the veterinarians' reaction to the manufacturer's promotional scheme?

(A) Most of the veterinarians to whom the free promotional materials were offered were already selling the manufacturer's pet-care products to their clients.

(B) The special promotional materials were intended as a supplement to the manufacturer's usual promotional activities rather than as a replacement for them.

(C) The manufacturer's products, unlike most equally good competing products sold by veterinarians, are also available in pet stores and in supermarkets.

(D) Many pet owners have begun demanding quality in products they buy for their pets that is as high as that in products they buy for themselves.

(E) Veterinarians sometimes recommend that pet owners use products formulated for people when no suitable product specially formulated for animals is available.

Evaluation of a Plan

Situation Veterinarians generally derive some income from selling various manufacturers' pet-care products, but very few veterinarians accepted free promotional materials from one such manufacturer to mail to their clients.

Reasoning *What would most help explain why so few veterinarians accepted the free promotional materials to mail to their clients?* The passage says that veterinarians generally derive income from selling pet-care products, which suggests that it should have been in many veterinarians' financial interest to accept and mail out the free promotional materials to increase sales. Any evidence that mailing out these specific promotional materials from this manufacturer would not actually have been in many veterinarians' financial interest could help explain why so few veterinarians accepted the materials.

A This suggests that most of the veterinarians should have had a financial interest in accepting and mailing out the promotional materials in order to increase their sales of the manufacturer's products.

B Even if the promotional materials supplemented the manufacturer's usual promotional activities, they could still have increased the veterinarians' sales of the manufacturer's products and thus generated more income for the veterinarians.

C **Correct.** If this manufacturer's products are available in pet stores and supermarkets but most other products sold by veterinarians are not, then distributing the manufacturer's promotional materials could have encouraged customers to buy this manufacturer's products from pet stores and supermarkets rather than to buy competing products from the veterinarians. Thus, the veterinarians may have been concerned that the promotions would reduce their profits.

D The passage says the manufacturer's products are of high quality, so we have no reason to suppose that clients' demand for quality products would discourage veterinarians from accepting the manufacturer's promotional materials.

E Presumably the manufacturer's products are specially formulated for pets, so any products veterinarians recommend only when no specially formulated pet-care products are available would not reduce the veterinarians' interest in promoting the manufacturer's products.

The correct answer is C.

657. The average hourly wage of television assemblers in Vernland has long been significantly lower than that in neighboring Borodia. Since Borodia dropped all tariffs on Vernlandian televisions three years ago, the number of televisions sold annually in Borodia has not changed. However, recent statistics show a drop in the number of television assemblers in Borodia. Therefore, updated trade statistics will probably indicate that the number of televisions Borodia imports annually from Vernland has increased.

Which of the following is an assumption on which the argument depends?

(A) The number of television assemblers in Vernland has increased by at least as much as the number of television assemblers in Borodia has decreased.

(B) Televisions assembled in Vernland have features that televisions assembled in Borodia do not have.

(C) The average number of hours it takes a Borodian television assembler to assemble a television has not decreased significantly during the past three years.

(D) The number of televisions assembled annually in Vernland has increased significantly during the past three years.

(E) The difference between the hourly wage of television assemblers in Vernland and the hourly wage of television assemblers in Borodia is likely to decrease in the next few years.

Argument Construction

Situation Television assemblers in Vernland are paid less than those in neighboring Borodia. The number of televisions sold in Borodia has not dropped since its tariffs on Vernlandian TVs were lowered three years ago, but the number of TV assemblers in Borodia has. So TV imports from Vernland have likely increased.

Reasoning *What assumption does the argument depend on?* The fact that fewer individuals in Borodia are working as TV assemblers is offered as evidence that TV imports from Vernland into Borodia have likely increased. That piece of evidence is relevant *only* as an indication that the number of TVs being produced within Borodia has decreased. But a drop in the number of TV assemblers does not indicate a drop in the number of TVs being assembled *if* the number of TVs an average assembler puts together has increased. Thus, the argument must be assuming that the average time it takes an assembler to put together a TV has not significantly decreased.

A The argument does not rely on any information about the number of television assemblers in Vernland nor for that matter on the number of TVs assembled in Vernland.

B The argument need not assume there is any difference in the features of the TVs produced in the two countries. Increased sales of Vernlandian TVs in Borodia could be due to any number of other reasons, such as price or quality.

C **Correct.** This option states an assumption on which the argument depends.

D The argument does not depend upon this being so: Vernland's domestic TV sales (or perhaps its exports to countries other than Borodia) may have decreased by more than its imports into Borodia have increased.

E The argument's conclusion addresses what *has* happened; the argument in no way relies on any assumptions about what may or may not happen in the coming years.

The correct answer is C.

658. Guidebook writer: I have visited hotels throughout the country and have noticed that in those built before 1930 the quality of the original carpentry work is generally superior to that in hotels built afterward. Clearly carpenters working on hotels before 1930 typically worked with more skill, care, and effort than carpenters who have worked on hotels built subsequently.

Which of the following, if true, most seriously weakens the guidebook writer's argument?

(A) The quality of original carpentry in hotels is generally far superior to the quality of original carpentry in other structures, such as houses and stores.

(B) Hotels built since 1930 can generally accommodate more guests than those built before 1930.

(C) The materials available to carpenters working before 1930 were not significantly different in quality from the materials available to carpenters working after 1930.

(D) The better the quality of original carpentry in a building, the less likely that building is to fall into disuse and be demolished.

(E) The average length of apprenticeship for carpenters has declined significantly since 1930.

Argument Evaluation

Situation The original carpentry in hotels built before 1930 shows superior care, skill, and effort to that in hotels built after 1930. This leads to the conclusion that carpenters working on hotels before 1930 were superior in skill, care, and effort to those that came after.

Reasoning *Which option most seriously weakens the argument?* The argument draws an inference from a comparison between carpentry in hotels of different eras to a judgment about the carpenters working on hotels in those eras. One way to weaken this inference is by finding some way in which the carpentry in the hotels may be unrepresentative of the skill, care, and effort of the carpenters working in the eras. The comparison is between the carpentry evident in hotels of the two eras *that still exist*. Thus, if there is some reason to think that hotels with good carpentry survive longer than those with bad carpentry, then still-existing hotels from the older era will have disproportionately more good carpentry, even assuming no difference between the skill, care, and effort of the carpenters from the two eras.

A This option applies equally to both eras, so it has no bearing on the argument.

B It is not clear whether carpenters working on larger hotels would exercise more, less, or the same skill and care as those working on smaller hotels; thus this option does not weaken the argument.

C The argument does not rely, even implicitly, on there being any difference in the quality of materials used in the two eras, so it does not weaken the argument to point out that no such difference exists.

D **Correct.** This weakens the reasoning in the argument by showing a respect in which the comparison between *existing* hotels is unrepresentative.

E The longer a carpenter works as an apprentice, the more skill he or she is apt to have upon becoming a full-fledged carpenter. So this option would tend to slightly strengthen rather than weaken the argument.

The correct answer is D.

659. Scientists typically do their most creative work before the age of forty. It is commonly thought that this happens because aging by itself brings about a loss of creative capacity. However, studies show that **of scientists who produce highly creative work beyond the age of forty, a disproportionately large number entered their field at an older age than is usual.** Since by the age of forty the large majority of scientists have been working in their field for at least fifteen years, the studies' finding strongly suggests that the real reason why scientists over forty rarely produce highly creative work is not that they have aged but rather that **scientists over forty have generally spent too long in their field.**

In the argument given, the two portions in boldface play which of the following roles?

(A) The first is a claim, the accuracy of which is at issue in the argument; the second is a conclusion drawn on the basis of that claim.

(B) The first is an objection that has been raised against a position defended in the argument; the second is that position.

(C) The first is evidence that has been used to support an explanation that the argument challenges; the second is that explanation.

(D) The first is evidence that has been used to support an explanation that the argument challenges; the second is a competing explanation that the argument favors.

(E) The first provides evidence to support an explanation that the argument favors; the second is that explanation.

Argument Evaluation

Situation It is generally thought that the reason scientists tend to do their most creative work before age forty is that creative capacity declines with age. Yet those scientists who do creative work after forty tend, disproportionately, to have started their careers in science later in life. So a better explanation is that many scientists over forty have just been at it too long.

Reasoning *What roles do the two portions of the argument that are in boldface play?* The argument describes a phenomenon and what is commonly thought to explain it. Then, the first boldfaced statement introduces evidence that suggests that there may be another explanation. After this evidence is further developed, the argument then concludes that there is indeed a better explanation for the phenomenon; that explanation is stated in the second boldfaced portion.

A The accuracy of the first statement is never called into question by the argument; rather, it is relied upon as the basis for the argument's conclusion.

B The first statement is not an objection against the position the argument defends; instead, it is a basis for that position.

C The first statement is not used to support a position the argument challenges, and the second statement is the explanation the argument supports, not the one it challenges.

D The second statement is indeed an explanation that the argument favors; but the first statement is not used to support a competing explanation that the argument challenges.

E **Correct.** This option correctly identifies the roles played by the boldfaced portions of the argument.

The correct answer is E.

660. NorthAir charges low fares for its economy-class seats, but it provides very cramped seating and few amenities. Market research shows that economy passengers would willingly pay more for wider seating and better service, and additional revenue provided by these higher ticket prices would more than cover the additional cost of providing these amenities. Even though NorthAir is searching for ways to improve its profitability, it has decided not to make these improvements.

Which of the following, if true, would most help to explain NorthAir's decision in light of its objectives?

(A) None of NorthAir's competitors offers significantly better seating and service to economy-class passengers than NorthAir does.

(B) On many of the routes that NorthAir flies, it is the only airline to offer direct flights.

(C) A few of NorthAir's economy-class passengers are satisfied with the service they receive, given the low price they pay.

(D) Very few people avoid flying on NorthAir because of the cramped seating and poor service offered in economy class.

(E) The number of people who would be willing to pay the high fares NorthAir charges for its business-class seats would decrease if its economy-class seating were more acceptable.

Evaluation of a Plan

Situation Market research shows that improving some amenities for economy-class passengers would allow NorthAir to raise its economy ticket prices more than enough to cover the additional cost of providing those amenities. But NorthAir has decided not to improve those amenities, even though it is looking for ways to improve its profitability.

Reasoning *What would most help explain why NorthAir decided not to improve the seating and other amenities, even though the resulting increase in economy-class ticket prices would more than cover the expense?* NorthAir is looking for ways to improve its profitability. Making improvements that would increase ticket prices enough to generate more revenue than they cost should improve profitability, other things being equal. But if improving the amenities would generate side effects that reduced profitability, those side effects would provide a good reason for NorthAir's decision not to improve the amenities and hence would help explain why NorthAir made that decision.

A The passage says that for NorthAir, the cost of providing better economy seating and other amenities would be more than met by the increased revenue from the higher ticket prices that passengers would be willing to pay. This could give NorthAir a competitive edge, with improved profitability.

B Even if NorthAir faces little or no competition on certain routes, offering extra amenities might increase passengers' interest in flying those routes. It might also lead passengers to choose NorthAir on other routes that competing airlines also serve. Both of these effects could improve NorthAir's profitability.

C Even if a few NorthAir economy passengers would not pay more for extra amenities, the market research indicates that most of them would, so offering the amenities could still improve NorthAir's profits attributable to economy-class seating.

D This suggests that improving the amenities would not increase the total number of NorthAir passengers. But improving the amenities might still enable the airline to increase its ticket prices per passenger enough to improve its profitability.

E **Correct**. This suggests that improving the economy-class amenities would reduce NorthAir's revenue from sales of business-class tickets, which are likely much more expensive than economy-class tickets. This reduction in revenue could be enough to reduce NorthAir's total profitability despite the increased revenue from economy-class ticket sales.

The correct answer is E.

661. Which of the following most logically completes the argument given?

Asthma, a chronic breathing disorder, is significantly more common today among adult competitive swimmers than it is among competitive athletes who specialize in other sports. Although chlorine is now known to be a lung irritant and swimming pool water is generally chlorinated, it would be rash to assume that frequent exposure to chlorine is the explanation of the high incidence of asthma among these swimmers, since ________.

(A) young people who have asthma are no more likely to become competitive athletes than are young people who do not have asthma

(B) competitive athletes who specialize in sports other than swimming are rarely exposed to chlorine

(C) competitive athletes as a group have a significantly lower incidence of asthma than do people who do not participate in competitive athletics

(D) until a few years ago, physicians routinely recommended competitive swimming to children with asthma, in the belief that this form of exercise could alleviate asthma symptoms

(E) many people have asthma without knowing they have it and thus are not diagnosed with the condition until they begin engaging in very strenuous activities, such as competitive athletics

Argument Construction

Situation Asthma is more common among competitive swimmers than among other competitive athletes. Chlorine is a lung irritant generally present in swimming pool water.

Reasoning *What would cast doubt on the hypothesis that exposure to chlorine in swimming pools accounts for the high incidence of asthma among adult competitive swimmers?* Evidence of any other factor that would provide an alternative explanation of why asthma is more common among adult competitive swimmers than among other competitive athletes would make it rash to assume that frequent exposure to chlorine explains the high incidence of asthma among these swimmers, so a statement providing such evidence would logically fill in the blank at the end of the passage to complete the argument.

A This might help explain why competitive athletes in general are not especially likely to have asthma, but it does not explain why adult competitive swimmers are more likely to have asthma than other competitive athletes are.

B This provides additional evidence that exposure to chlorine explains why adult competitive swimmers are more likely to have asthma than other competitive athletes are, so it does not cast doubt on that hypothesis.

C A lower incidence of asthma among competitive athletes than among nonathletes does not help explain the higher incidence of asthma among adult competitive swimmers than among other competitive athletes.

D **Correct.** Routinely encouraging children with asthma to take up competitive swimming would likely have made the proportion of adult competitive swimmers with asthma exceed the proportion of other competitive athletes with asthma, even if chlorine in swimming pool water never causes asthma in swimmers.

E This might help explain why people with asthma are just as likely as other people to become competitive athletes, but it does not help explain why adult competitive swimmers are more likely to have asthma than other competitive athletes are.

The correct answer is D.

662. In the country of Marut, the Foreign Trade Agency's records were reviewed in 1994 in light of information then newly available about neighboring Goro. The review revealed that in every year since 1963, the agency's projection of what Goro's gross national product (GNP) would be five years later was a serious underestimate. The review also revealed that in every year since 1963, the agency estimated Goro's GNP for the previous year—a Goro state secret—very accurately.

Of the following claims, which is most strongly supported by the statements given?

(A) Goro's GNP fluctuated greatly between 1963 and 1994.

(B) Prior to 1995, Goro had not released data intended to mislead the agency in making its five-year projections.

(C) The amount by which the agency underestimated the GNP it projected for Goro tended to increase over time.

(D) Even before the new information came to light, the agency had reason to think that at least some of the five-year projections it had made were inaccurate.

(E) The agency's five-year projections of Goro's GNP had no impact on economic planning in Marut.

Argument Construction

Situation A review in 1994 revealed that every year since 1963, Marut's Foreign Trade Agency had seriously underestimated what Goro's GNP would be five years later, but accurately estimated what Goro's GNP had been the previous year.

Reasoning *What conclusion do the stated facts most strongly support?* Goro's GNP in each year at least from 1969 through 1993 had been seriously underestimated by the agency five years in advance, yet was then accurately estimated by the agency one year after the fact. It follows that for each of these years, the agency's earlier projection of Goro's GNP must have been much lower than its later estimate.

A This is not supported by the information given. The fact that the agency consistently underestimated each year's GNP in its five-year projections and then correctly estimated it after the fact does not indicate that Goro's GNP fluctuated greatly.

B This is not supported by the information given. The reason the agency's five-year projections were inaccurate might well have been that Goro deliberately released data intended to mislead the agency in making those projections.

C This is not supported by the information given. The fact that the underestimates remained large throughout the years in question does not indicate that the underestimates increased over time.

D **Correct.** As explained above, for many years there were serious discrepancies between the agency's five-year projections of Goro's GNP and its retrospective estimates of each previous year's trade. In any year at least from 1970 through 1993, these discrepancies, if noticed, would have given the agency reason to doubt some of the five-year projections.

E This is not supported by the information given. Even though at least some of the five-year projections were eventually known to be serious underestimates, they could still have affected Marut's economic planning. The economic planners might have retained an unreasonable faith in the accuracy of the most recent projections.

The correct answer is D.

663. Vargonia has just introduced a legal requirement that student-teacher ratios in government-funded schools not exceed a certain limit. All Vargonian children are entitled to education, free of charge, in these schools. When a recession occurs and average incomes fall, the number of children enrolled in government-funded schools tends to increase. Therefore, though most employment opportunities contract in economic recessions, getting a teaching job in Vargonia's government-funded schools will not be made more difficult by a recession.

Which of the following would be most important to determine in order to evaluate the argument?

(A) Whether in Vargonia there are any schools not funded by the government that offer children an education free of charge

(B) Whether the number of qualified applicants for teaching positions in government-funded schools increases significantly during economic recessions

(C) What the current student-teacher ratio in Vargonia's government-funded schools is

(D) What proportion of Vargonia's workers currently hold jobs as teachers in government-funded schools

(E) Whether in the past a number of government-funded schools in Vargonia have had student-teacher ratios well in excess of the new limit

Argument Evaluation

Situation During a recession, the number of children in government-funded schools in Vargonia tends to increase. Vargonian children are entitled to a free education in these schools. A new law requires student-teacher ratios in these schools to remain below a certain limit.

Reasoning *Which of the five questions would provide us with the best information for evaluating the argument?* The argument's conclusion is that recessions do not make teaching jobs in Vargonia's government-funded schools harder to get. During recessions, the reasoning goes, more students will enroll in Vargonia's government-funded schools than in nonrecession times. Implicit in the argument is the thought that, because the new law sets an upper limit on the average number of students per teacher, schools that get an influx of new students would have to hire more teachers. During a recession, however, there might be much more competition in the labor market for teachers because many more qualified people are applying for teaching jobs.

A This information is not significant in the context of the argument, which does not need to assume that only government-funded schools provide free education.

B Correct. Getting an answer to this question would provide us with specific information useful in evaluating the argument. A "yes" answer to this question would suggest that competition for teaching jobs in Vargonian government-funded schools would be keener during recessions. A "no" answer would suggest that the level of competition would decrease during recessions.

C Discovering the current student-teacher ratio in Vargonia's schools would be of no value, by itself, in evaluating the argument. We do not know what the new upper limit on the student-teacher ratio is, and we do not know whether Vargonia is currently in a recession.

D Finding out whether the proportion this refers to is 1 percent, for example, or 4 percent, would tell us nothing about whether getting teaching jobs at government-funded schools in Vargonia becomes more difficult during a recession. Among other things, we do not know whether Vargonia is currently in a recession, and we do not know what proportion of Vargonia's workers would be qualified candidates for teaching jobs.

E This is of no relevance in evaluating the argument because, presumably, the new limit on student-teacher ratios will be complied with. Thus, even if student-teacher ratios in the past would have exceeded the new limit, the argument concerns whether, *in the future*, getting a teaching job in Vargonia's government-funded schools will be made more difficult by a recession.

The correct answer is B.

664. In Colorado subalpine meadows, nonnative dandelions co-occur with a native flower, the larkspur. Bumblebees visit both species, creating the potential for interactions between the two species with respect to pollination. In a recent study, researchers selected 16 plots containing both species; all dandelions were removed from eight plots; the remaining eight control plots were left undisturbed. The control plots yielded significantly more larkspur seeds than the dandelion-free plots, leading the researchers to conclude that the presence of dandelions facilitates pollination (and hence seed production) in the native species by attracting more pollinators to the mixed plots.

Which of the following, if true, most seriously undermines the researchers' reasoning?

(A) Bumblebees preferentially visit dandelions over larkspurs in mixed plots.

(B) In mixed plots, pollinators can transfer pollen from one species to another to augment seed production.

(C) If left unchecked, nonnative species like dandelions quickly crowd out native species.

(D) Seed germination is a more reliable measure of a species' fitness than seed production.

(E) Soil disturbances can result in fewer blooms, and hence lower seed production.

Argument Evaluation

Situation Bumblebees visit both larkspur and dandelions in certain meadows. A study found that more larkspur seeds were produced in meadow plots in which both larkspur and dandelions grew than in similar plots from which all dandelions had been removed. The researchers inferred that dandelions facilitate larkspur pollination.

Reasoning *What evidence would cast the most doubt on the inference from the study's findings to the conclusion that dandelions facilitate larkspur pollination by attracting more pollinators?* The argument assumes that the only relevant difference between the two types of plots was whether dandelions were present. Evidence that the plots differed in some other way that could provide a plausible alternative explanation of why more larkspur seeds were produced in the plots with dandelions would weaken the argument.

A This would suggest that the larkspur pollination should have been lower in the plots with dandelions, so it does not provide a plausible alternative explanation for the study's findings.

B This is fully compatible with the claim that the dandelions attracted more pollinators to the mixed plots, and it would also help to support the argument's conclusion that dandelions facilitated larkspur pollination in those plots.

C Although this suggests that the mixed plots won't remain mixed for long, it does not provide a plausible alternative explanation for the study's finding that larkspur seed production was higher in the mixed plots.

D The argument is not about how fit larkspurs are as a species, but about why they produced different numbers of seeds in the different plots.

E **Correct.** This provides a plausible alternative explanation for why larkspur seed production was lower in the plots from which dandelions had been removed, since digging them out would have disturbed the soil.

The correct answer is E.

665. An experiment was done in which human subjects recognize a pattern within a matrix of abstract designs and then select another design that completes that pattern. The results of the experiment were surprising. The lowest expenditure of energy in neurons in the brain was found in those subjects who performed most successfully in the experiments.

Which of the following hypotheses best accounts for the findings of the experiment?

(A) The neurons of the brain react less when a subject is trying to recognize patterns than when the subject is doing other kinds of reasoning.

(B) Those who performed best in the experiment experienced more satisfaction when working with abstract patterns than did those who performed less well.

(C) People who are better at abstract pattern recognition have more energy-efficient neural connections.

(D) The energy expenditure of the subjects' brains increases when a design that completes the initially recognized pattern is determined.

(E) The task of completing a given design is more capably performed by athletes, whose energy expenditure is lower when they are at rest.

Argument Construction

Situation Experimental subjects worked with pattern recognition and completion. The subjects who performed best showed the lowest expenditure of energy in neurons in the brain.

Reasoning *Which hypothesis best accounts for the findings?* In order to account for the findings, the hypothesis must suggest a plausible link between successful performance and the energy expenditure of neurons in the brain. Consider each answer choice, and evaluate its plausibility and logic. Where is there a reasonably direct relationship between the given factors and the conclusion that is drawn? Understand that hypotheses based on factors not included in the experiment cannot be used to account for the findings.

A The experiment did not compare types of reasoning so this hypothesis does not account for the results.

B No information is provided about subjects' satisfaction, so this hypothesis is not warranted.

C **Correct.** This statement properly identifies a hypothesis that connects subjects' performance with their energy expenditure and so could account for the experiment's results.

D The most successful subjects would presumably not have completed fewer patterns than average, so the posited increase in energy would likely lead to higher energy expenditures for them, not lower.

E No information is offered on the subjects, so no hypothesis about athletes is warranted.

The correct answer is C.

666. With seventeen casinos, Moneyland operates the most casinos in a certain state. Although intent on expanding, it was outmaneuvered by Apex Casinos in negotiations to acquire the Eldorado chain. To complete its acquisition of Eldorado, Apex must sell five casinos to comply with a state law forbidding any owner to operate more than one casino per county. Since Apex will still be left operating twenty casinos in the state, it will then have the most casinos in the state.

Which of the following, if true, most seriously undermines the prediction?

(A) Apex, Eldorado, and Moneyland are the only organizations licensed to operate casinos in the state.

(B) The majority of Eldorado's casinos in the state will need extensive renovations if they are to continue to operate profitably.

(C) Some of the state's counties do not permit casinos.

(D) Moneyland already operates casinos in the majority of the state's counties.

(E) Apex will use funds it obtains from the sale of the five casinos to help fund its acquisition of the Eldorado chain.

Argument Evaluation

Situation Moneyland operates seventeen casinos, the most in a certain state, and is intent on expanding. Another operator, Apex Casinos, is acquiring the Eldorado casino chain, but must sell five casinos to comply with a state law forbidding any owner to operate more than one casino per county. After these transactions, Apex will operate twenty casinos in the state.

Reasoning *What observation would cast the most doubt on the prediction that Apex will have the most casinos in the state after the transactions?* Apex will operate twenty casinos, whereas Moneyland now operates just seventeen, and no one else operates even that many. It follows that Apex will operate more casinos after its transactions than Moneyland or any other one owner now operates. However, if Moneyland also acquires three or more casinos during the transactions, then Apex will not have the most casinos in the state afterward. Thus, any observation suggesting that Moneyland is about to acquire several casinos would undermine the prediction.

A **Correct.** Since Apex is acquiring Eldorado, Moneyland and Apex will be the only remaining licensed casino operators in the state. Therefore, Moneyland is the only likely buyer for the five casinos Apex needs to sell. So Moneyland is likely to acquire the five casinos during the sale and end up with twenty-two casinos—more than Apex.

B This does not undermine the prediction. Even if the Eldorado casinos cannot operate profitably for long without extensive renovations, Apex will still have twenty casinos immediately after its transactions.

C This supports rather than undermines the prediction. If fewer counties permit casinos, there will be fewer opportunities for Moneyland or any other operator to acquire more casinos to surpass the twenty Apex will own.

D This supports rather than undermines the prediction. If Moneyland's seventeen casinos are in most of the state's counties already, then there are fewer counties in which Moneyland could acquire additional casinos to surpass the twenty Apex will own.

E This supports rather than undermines the prediction. Apex's use of the funds from selling the five casinos to acquire the Eldorado chain will not help anyone else to acquire more casinos to surpass the twenty Apex will own.

The correct answer is A.

667. It is widely assumed that people need to engage in intellectual activities such as solving crossword puzzles or mathematics problems in order to maintain mental sharpness as they age. In fact, however, simply talking to other people—that is, participating in social interaction, which engages many mental and perceptual skills—suffices. Evidence to this effect comes from a study showing that the more social contact people report, the better their mental skills.

Which of the following, if true, most seriously weakens the force of the evidence cited?

(A) As people grow older, they are often advised to keep exercising their physical and mental capacities in order to maintain or improve them.
(B) Many medical conditions and treatments that adversely affect a person's mental sharpness also tend to increase that person's social isolation.
(C) Many people are proficient both in social interactions and in solving mathematical problems.
(D) The study did not itself collect data but analyzed data bearing on the issue from prior studies.
(E) The tasks evaluating mental sharpness for which data were compiled by the study were more akin to mathematics problems than to conversation.

Argument Evaluation

Situation A study shows that the more social contact people report, the better their mental skills are, so engaging in social interaction is sufficient for maintaining mental sharpness.

Reasoning *What would suggest that the study does not establish the truth of the conclusion?* The study shows a correlation between mental sharpness and social interaction but does not indicate why this correlation exists. Evidence that mental sharpness contributes to social interaction or that some third factor affects both mental sharpness and social interaction, could provide an alternative explanation for the correlation and thus cast doubt on the explanation that social interaction contributes to mental sharpness.

A People are often wrongly advised to do things that are not actually beneficial. And even if exercising mental capacities does help to maintain them, the passage says that social interaction provides such exercise.

B **Correct.** This provides evidence that the correlation observed in the study results from mental sharpness facilitating social interaction, in which case the study results do not indicate that social interaction facilitates mental sharpness.

C This would be expected, given the argument's conclusion that social interaction helps to maintain better mental skills overall.

D A study that analyzes data from prior studies can provide evidence just as well as a study that collects its own data can.

E The argument's conclusion would be compatible with this observation, and would then suggest that social interaction contributes to the mental sharpness needed for tasks similar to math problems.

The correct answer is B.

To register for the GMAT exam go to www.mba.com

9.0 Sentence Correction

9.0 Sentence Correction

Sentence correction questions appear in the Verbal section of the GMAT® exam. The Verbal section uses multiple-choice questions to measure your ability to read and comprehend written material, to reason and evaluate arguments, and to correct written material to express ideas effectively in standard written English. Because the Verbal section includes passages from several different content areas, you may be generally familiar with some of the material; however, neither the passages nor the questions assume detailed knowledge of the topics discussed. Sentence correction questions are intermingled with critical reasoning and reading comprehension questions throughout the Verbal section of the test. You will have 75 minutes to complete the Verbal section or about 1¾ minutes to answer each question.

Sentence correction questions present a statement in which words are underlined. The questions ask you to select the best expression of the idea or relationship described in the underlined section from the answer options. The first answer choice always repeats the original phrasing, whereas the other four provide alternatives. In some cases, the original phrasing is the best choice. In other cases, the underlined section has obvious or subtle errors that require correction. These questions require you to be familiar with the stylistic conventions and grammatical rules of standard written English and to demonstrate your ability to improve incorrect or ineffective expressions. Sentence correction questions may include English-language idioms, which are standard constructions not derived from the most basic rules of grammar and vocabulary, but idioms are not intended to measure any specialized knowledge of colloquialisms or regionalisms.

You should begin these questions by reading the sentence carefully. Note whether there are any obvious grammatical errors as you read the underlined section. Then read the five answer choices carefully. If there was a subtle error you did not recognize the first time you read the sentence, it may become apparent after you have read the answer choices. If the error is still unclear, see whether you can eliminate some of the answers as being incorrect. Remember that in some cases, the original selection may be the best answer.

9.1 Basic English Grammar Rules

Sentence correction questions ask you to recognize and potentially correct at least one of the following grammar rules. However, these rules are not exhaustive. If you are interested in learning more about English grammar as a way to prepare for the GMAT exam, there are several resources available on the Internet.

Agreement

Standard English requires elements within a sentence to be consistent. There are two types of agreement: noun-verb and pronoun.

Noun-verb agreement: Singular subjects take singular verbs, whereas plural subjects take plural verbs.
Examples:
Correct: "I walk to the store." Incorrect: "I walks to the store."
Correct: "We go to school." Incorrect: "We goes to school."
Correct: "The number of residents has grown." Incorrect: "The number of residents have grown."
Correct: "The masses have spoken." Incorrect: "The masses has spoken."

Pronoun agreement: A pronoun must agree with the noun or pronoun it refers to in person, number, and gender.
Examples:
Correct: "When you dream, you are usually asleep." Incorrect: "When one dreams, you are usually asleep."
Correct: "When the kids went to sleep, they slept like logs." Incorrect: "When the kids went to sleep, he slept like a log."

Diction

Words should be chosen to reflect correctly and effectively the appropriate part of speech. There are several words that are commonly used incorrectly. When answering sentence correction questions, pay attention to the following conventions.

Among/between: Among is used to refer to relationships involving more than two objects. *Between* is used to refer to relationships involving only two objects.
Examples:
Correct: "We divided our winnings among the three of us." Incorrect: "We divided our winnings between the three of us."
Correct: "She and I divided the cake between us." Incorrect: "She and I divided the cake among us."

As/like: As can be a preposition meaning "in the capacity of," but more often is a conjunction of manner and is followed by a verb. *Like* is generally used as a preposition, and therefore is followed by a noun, an object pronoun, or a verb ending in *-ing*.
Examples:
Correct: "I work as a librarian." Incorrect: "I work like a librarian."
Correct: "Do as I say, not as I do." Incorrect: "Do like I say, not like I do."
Correct: "It felt like a dream." Incorrect: "It felt as a dream."
Correct: "People like you inspire me." Incorrect: "People as you inspire me."
Correct: "There's nothing like biking on a warm, autumn day." Incorrect: "There's nothing as biking on a warm, autumn day."

Mass and count words: Mass words are nouns quantified by an amount rather than by a number. *Count* nouns can be quantified by a number.
Examples:
Correct: "We bought a loaf of bread." Incorrect: "We bought one bread."
Correct: "He wished me much happiness." Incorrect: "He wished me many happinesses."
Correct: "We passed many buildings." Incorrect: "We passed much buildings."

Pronouns: Myself should not be used as a substitute for *I* or *me.*
Examples:
Correct: "Mom and I had to go to the store." Incorrect: "Mom and myself had to go to the store."
Correct: "He gave the present to Dad and me." Incorrect: "He gave the present to Dad and myself."

Grammatical Construction

Good grammar requires complete sentences. Be on the lookout for improperly formed constructions.

Fragments: Parts of a sentence that are disconnected from the main clause are called fragments.
Examples:
Correct: "We saw the doctor and his nurse at the party." Incorrect: "We saw the doctor at the party. And his nurse."

Run-on sentences: A run-on sentence is two or more independent clauses that run together without proper punctuation.
Examples:
Correct: "Jose Canseco is still a feared batter; most pitchers don't want to face him." Incorrect: "Jose Canseco is still a feared batter most pitchers don't want to face him."

Constructions: Avoid wordy, redundant constructions.
Examples:
Correct: "We could not come to the meeting because of a conflict." Incorrect: "The reason we could not come to the meeting is because of a conflict."

Idiom

It is important to avoid nonstandard expressions, although English idioms sometimes do not follow conventional grammatical rules. Be careful to use the correct idiom when using the constructions and parts of speech.

Prepositions: Specific prepositions have specific purposes.
Examples:
Correct: "She likes to jog in the morning." Incorrect: "She likes to jog on the morning."
Correct: "They ranged in age from 10 to 15." Incorrect: "They ranged in age from 10 up to 15."

Correlatives: Word combinations such as "not only … but also" should be followed by an element of the same grammatical type.
Examples:
Correct: "I have called not only to thank her but also to tell her about the next meeting." Incorrect: "I have called not only to thank her but also I told her about the next meeting."

Forms of comparison: Many forms follow precise constructions. *Fewer* refers to a specific number, whereas *less than* refers to a continuous quantity. *Between … and* is the correct form to designate a choice. *Farther* refers to distance, whereas *further* refers to degree.
Examples:
Correct: "There were fewer children in my class this year." Incorrect: "There were less children in my class this year."
Correct: "There was less devastation than I was told." Incorrect: "There was fewer devastation than I was told."
Correct: "We had to choose between chocolate and vanilla." Incorrect: "We had to choose between chocolate or vanilla." (It is also correct to say, "We had to choose chocolate or vanilla.")
Correct: "I ran farther than John, but he took his weight training further than I did."
Incorrect: "I ran further than John, but he took his weight training farther than I did."

Logical Predication

Watch out for phrases that detract from the logical argument.

Modification problems: Modifiers should be positioned so it is clear what word or words they are meant to modify. If modifiers are not positioned clearly, they can cause illogical references or comparisons, or distort the meaning of the statement.
Examples:
Correct: "I put the cake that I baked by the door." Incorrect: "I put the cake by the door that I baked."
Correct: "Reading my mind, she gave me the delicious cookie." Incorrect: "Reading my mind, the cookie she gave me was delicious."
Correct: "In the Middle Ages, the world was believed to be flat." Incorrect: "In the Middle Ages, the world was flat."

Parallelism

Constructing a sentence that is parallel in structure depends on making sure that the different elements in the sentence balance each other; this is a little bit like making sure that the two sides of a mathematical equation are balanced. To make sure that a sentence is grammatically correct, check to ensure that phrases, clauses, verbs, and other sentence elements parallel each other.

Examples:
Correct: "I took a bath, went to sleep, and woke up refreshed." Incorrect: "I took a bath, sleeping, and waking up refreshed."
Correct: "The only way to know is to take the plunge." Incorrect: "The only way to know is taking the plunge."

Rhetorical Construction

Good sentence structure avoids constructions that are awkward, wordy, redundant, imprecise, or unclear, even when they are free of grammatical errors.
Examples:
Correct: "Before we left on vacation, we watered the plants, checked to see that the stove was off, and set the burglar alarm." Incorrect: "Before we left to go on vacation, we watered, checked to be sure that the stove had been turned off, and set it."

Verb Form

In addition to watching for problems of agreement or parallelism, make sure that verbs are used in the correct tense. Be alert to whether a verb should reflect past, present, or future tense.
Examples:
Correct: "I went to school yesterday." "I go to school every weekday." "I will go to school tomorrow."

Each tense also has a perfect form (used with the past participle—e.g., walked, ran), a progressive form (used with the present participle—e.g., walking, running), and a perfect progressive form (also used with the present participle—e.g., walking, running).

Present perfect: Used with *has* or *have,* the present perfect tense describes an action that occurred at an indefinite time in the past or that began in the past and continues into the present.
Examples:
Correct: "I have traveled all over the world." (at an indefinite time)
Correct: "He has gone to school since he was five years old." (continues into the present)

Past perfect: This verb form is used with *had* to show the order of two events that took place in the past.
Example:
Correct: "By the time I left for school, the cake had been baked."

Future perfect: Used with *will have,* this verb form describes an event in the future that will precede another event.
Example:
Correct: "By the end of the day, I will have studied for all my tests."

Present progressive: Used with *am, is,* or *are,* this verb form describes an ongoing action that is happening now.
Examples:
Correct: "I am studying for exams." "The student is studying for exams." "We are studying for exams."

Past progressive: Used with *was* or *were,* this verb form describes something that was happening when another action occurred.
Examples:
Correct: "The student was studying when the fire alarm rang." "They were studying when the fire broke out."

Future progressive: Used with *will be* or *shall be,* this verb tense describes an ongoing action that will continue into the future.
Example:
Correct: "The students will be studying for exams throughout the month of December."

Present perfect progressive: Used with *have been* or *has been*, this verb tense describes something that began in the past, continues into the present, and may continue into the future.
Example:
Correct: "The student has been studying hard in the hope of acing the test."

Past perfect progressive: Used with *had been,* this verb form describes an action of some duration that was completed before another past action occurred.
Example:
Correct: "Before the fire alarm rang, the student had been studying."

Future perfect progressive: Used with *will have been*, this verb form describes a future, ongoing action that will occur before a specified time.
Example:
Correct: "By the end of next year, the students will have been studying math for five years."

9.2 Study Suggestions

There are two basic ways you can study for sentence correction questions:

- **Read material that reflects standard usage.**
  One way to gain familiarity with the basic conventions of standard written English is simply to read. Suitable material will usually be found in good magazines and nonfiction books, editorials in outstanding newspapers, and the collections of essays used by many college and university writing courses.
- **Review basic rules of grammar and practice with writing exercises.**
  Begin by reviewing the grammar rules laid out in this chapter. Then, if you have school assignments (such as essays and research papers) that have been carefully evaluated for grammatical errors, it may be helpful to review the comments and corrections.

9.3 What Is Measured

Sentence correction questions test three broad aspects of language proficiency:

- **Correct expression**
  A correct sentence is grammatically and structurally sound. It conforms to all the rules of standard written English, including noun-verb agreement, noun-pronoun agreement, pronoun consistency, pronoun case, and verb tense sequence. A correct sentence will not have dangling, misplaced, or improperly formed modifiers; unidiomatic or inconsistent expressions; or faults in parallel construction.
- **Effective expression**
  An effective sentence expresses an idea or relationship clearly and concisely as well as grammatically. This does not mean that the choice with the fewest and simplest words is necessarily the best answer. It means that there are no superfluous words or needlessly complicated expressions in the best choice.
- **Proper diction**
  An effective sentence also uses proper diction. (Diction refers to the standard dictionary meanings of words and the appropriateness of words in context.) In evaluating the diction of a sentence, you must be able to recognize whether the words are well chosen, accurate, and suitable for the context.

9.4 Test-Taking Strategies

1. **Read the entire sentence carefully.**
   Try to understand the specific idea or relationship that the sentence should express.

2. **Evaluate the underlined passage for errors and possible corrections before reading the answer choices.**
   This strategy will help you discriminate among the answer choices. Remember, in some cases the underlined passage is correct.

3. **Read each answer choice carefully.**
   The first answer choice always repeats the underlined portion of the original sentence. Choose this answer if you think that the sentence is best as originally written, but do so *only after* examining all the other choices.

4. **Try to determine how to correct what you consider to be wrong with the original sentence.**
Some of the answer choices may change things that are not wrong, whereas others may not change everything that is wrong.

5. **Make sure that you evaluate the sentence and the choices thoroughly.**
Pay attention to general clarity, grammatical and idiomatic usage, economy and precision of language, and appropriateness of diction.

6. **Read the whole sentence, substituting the choice that you prefer for the underlined passage.**
A choice may be wrong because it does not fit grammatically or structurally with the rest of the sentence. Remember that some sentences will require no correction. When the given sentence requires no correction, choose the first answer.

9.5 The Directions

These are the directions that you will see for sentence correction questions when you take the GMAT exam. If you read them carefully and understand them clearly before going to sit for the test, you will not need to spend too much time reviewing them once you are at the test center and the test is under way.

Sentence correction questions present a sentence, part or all of which is underlined. Beneath the sentence, you will find five ways of phrasing the underlined passage. The first answer choice repeats the original underlined passage; the other four are different. If you think the original phrasing is best, choose the first answer; otherwise, choose one of the others.

This type of question tests your ability to recognize the correctness and effectiveness of expression in standard written English. In choosing your answer, follow the requirements of standard written English; that is, pay attention to grammar, choice of words, and sentence construction. Choose the answer that produces the most effective sentence; this answer should be clear and exact, without awkwardness, ambiguity, redundancy, or grammatical error.

9.6 Practice Questions

Each of the sentence correction questions presents a sentence, part or all of which is underlined. Beneath the sentence you will find five ways of phrasing the underlined part. The first of these repeats the original; the other four are different. Follow the requirements of standard written English to choose your answer, paying attention to grammar, word choice, and sentence construction. Select the answer that produces the most effective sentence; your answer should make the sentence clear, exact, and free of grammatical error. It should also minimize awkwardness, ambiguity, and redundancy.

668. In a review of 2,000 studies of human behavior that date back to the 1940s, two Swiss psychologists, declaring that since most of the studies had failed to control for such variables as social class and family size, none could be taken seriously.

(A) psychologists, declaring that since most of the studies had failed to control for such variables as social class and family size,

(B) psychologists, declaring that most of the studies failed in not controlling for such variables like social class and family size, and

(C) psychologists declared that since most of the studies, having failed to control for such variables as social class and family size,

(D) psychologists declared that since most of the studies fail in controlling for such variables like social class and family size,

(E) psychologists declared that since most of the studies had failed to control for variables such as social class and family size,

669. In her presentation, the head of the Better Business Bureau emphasized that companies should think of the cost of conventions and other similar gatherings as not an expense, but as an investment in networking that will pay dividends.

(A) as not an expense, but as

(B) as not expense but

(C) not an expense, rather

(D) not as an expense, but as

(E) not in terms of expense, but

670. Recent interdisciplinary studies advance the argument that emotions, including those deemed personal or private is a social phenomenon, though one inseparable from bodily response.

(A) private is a social phenomenon, though one inseparable

(B) private, are social phenomena that are inseparable

(C) private are a social phenomenon but are not those separable

(D) private—are social phenomena but not separable

(E) also as private emotions, are social phenomena not inseparable

671. Manufacturers rate batteries in watt-hours; if they rate the watt-hour higher, the longer the battery can be expected to last.

(A) if they rate the watt-hour higher, the longer

(B) rating the watt-hour higher, it is that much longer

(C) the higher the watt-hour rating, the longer

(D) the higher the watt-hour rating, it is that much longer that

(E) when the watt-hour rating is higher, the longer it is

672. At the end of the 1930s, Duke Ellington was looking for a composer to assist him—someone not only who could arrange music for his successful big band, but mirroring his eccentric writing style as well in order to finish the many pieces he had started but never completed.

(A) someone not only who could arrange music for his successful big band, but mirroring his eccentric writing style as well in order to finish

(B) someone who could not only arrange music for his successful big band, but also mirror his eccentric writing style in order to finish

(C) someone who not only could arrange music for his successful big band, but also to mirror his eccentric writing style in finishing

(D) that being someone who could not only arrange music for his successful big band, but mirroring his eccentric writing style for finishing

(E) being someone not only who could arrange music for his successful big band, but mirror his eccentric writing style as well, finishing

673. While Noble Sissle may be best known for his collaboration with Eubie Blake, as both a vaudeville performer and as a lyricist for songs and Broadway musicals, also enjoying an independent career as a singer with such groups as Hahn's Jubilee Singers.

(A) and as a lyricist for songs and Broadway musicals, also enjoying

(B) and writing lyrics for songs and Broadway musicals, also enjoying

(C) and a lyricist for songs and Broadway musicals, he also enjoyed

(D) as well as writing lyrics for songs and Broadway musicals, he also enjoyed

(E) as well as a lyricist for songs and Broadway musicals, he had also enjoyed

674. Air traffic routes over the North Pole are currently used by only two or three planes a day, but it was found by a joint Canadian–Russian study to be both feasible as well as desirable if those routes are opened to thousands more commercial planes a year.

(A) Air traffic routes over the North Pole are currently used by only two or three planes a day, but it was found by a joint Canadian–Russian study to be both feasible as well as desirable if those routes are opened to thousands more commercial planes a year.

(B) Currently used by only two or three planes a day, a joint Canadian–Russian study has found that if air traffic routes over the North Pole are opened to thousands more commercial planes a year, it would be both feasible and desirable.

(C) A joint Canadian–Russian study, finding it to be both feasible as well as desirable to open air traffic routes over the North Pole, which are currently used by only two or three planes a day, to thousands more commercial planes a year.

(D) Although air traffic routes over the North Pole are currently used by only two or three planes a day, a joint Canadian–Russian study has found that opening those routes to thousands more commercial planes a year is both feasible and desirable.

(E) With air traffic routes over the North Pole currently used by only two or three planes a day, opening those routes to thousands more commercial planes a year has been found by a joint Canadian—Russian study as both feasible and desirable.

675. From an experiment using special extrasensory perception cards, each bearing one of a set of symbols, parapsychologist Joseph Banks Rhine claimed statistical proof for subjects who could use thought transference to identify a card in the dealer's hand.

(A) for subjects who could use thought transference to identify a card in the dealer's hand

(B) for a card in the dealer's hand to be identified by subjects with thought transference

(C) of subjects able to identify with thought transference a card in the dealer's hand

(D) that subjects could identify a card in the dealer's hand by using thought transference

(E) that subjects are capable to use thought transference for identifying a card in the dealer's hand

676. A long-term study of some 1,000 physicians indicates that the more coffee these doctors drank, the more they had a likelihood of coronary disease.

(A) more they had a likelihood of coronary disease

(B) more was their likelihood of having coronary disease

(C) more they would have a likelihood to have coronary disease

(D) greater was their likelihood of having coronary disease

(E) greater was coronary disease likely

677. The intricate structure of the compound insect eye, having hundreds of miniature eyes called ommatidia, help explain why scientists have assumed that it evolved independently of the vertebrate eye.

(A) having hundreds of miniature eyes called ommatidia, help explain why scientists have assumed that it

(B) having hundreds of miniature eyes that are called ommatidia, helps explain why scientists have assumed that they

(C) with its hundreds of miniature eyes that are called ommatidia, helps explain scientists' assuming that they

(D) with its hundreds of miniature eyes called ommatidia, help explain scientists' assuming that it

(E) with its hundreds of miniature eyes called ommatidia, helps explain why scientists have assumed that it

678. In 1979 lack of rain reduced India's rice production to about 41 million tons, nearly 25 percent less than those of the 1978 harvest.

(A) less than those of the 1978 harvest

(B) less than the 1978 harvest

(C) less than 1978

(D) fewer than 1978

(E) fewer than that of India's 1978 harvest

679. Hurricanes at first begin traveling from east to west, because that direction is the way the prevailing winds in the tropics blow, but they then veer off toward higher latitudes, in many cases changing direction toward the east before dissipating over the colder, more northerly waters or over land.

(A) Hurricanes at first begin traveling from east to west, because that direction is the way the prevailing winds in the tropics blow, but

(B) At first, hurricanes travel from east to west, because that is the direction of the prevailing winds in the tropics, but

(C) While hurricanes travel from east to west at first, the direction of the prevailing winds blowing in the tropics, and

(D) Because hurricanes at first travel from east to west, since it is the direction of the prevailing winds in the tropics,

(E) Hurricanes, beginning by traveling from east to west, because this is the direction of the prevailing winds in the tropics,

680. Unlike the virginal, whose single set of strings runs parallel to the front edge of the instrument, the harpsichord's several sets of strings are placed at right angles to its front edge.

(A) whose single set of strings runs parallel to the front edge of the instrument, the harpsichord's several sets of strings are

(B) with a single set of strings running parallel to the front edge of the instrument, the several sets of strings of the harpsichord are

(C) which has a single set of strings that runs parallel to the front edge of the instrument, in the case of the harpsichord, several sets of strings are

(D) which has a single set of strings that run parallel to the front edge of the instrument, the harpsichord has several sets of strings

(E) in which a single set of strings run parallel to the front edge of the instrument, the harpsichord's several sets of strings are

681. Although Alice Walker published a number of essays, poetry collections, and stories during the 1970s, her third novel, *The Color Purple*, which was published in 1982, brought her the widest acclaim in that it won both the National Book Award as well as the Pulitzer Prize.

(A) which was published in 1982, brought her the widest acclaim in that it won both the National Book Award as well as the Pulitzer Prize

(B) published in 1982, bringing her the widest acclaim by winning both the National Book Award and the Pulitzer Prize

(C) published in 1982, brought her the widest acclaim, winning both the National Book Award and the Pulitzer Prize

(D) was published in 1982 and which, winning both the National Book Award and the Pulitzer Prize, brought her the widest acclaim

(E) was published in 1982, winning both the National Book Award as well as the Pulitzer Prize, and bringing her the widest acclaim

682. Many experts regarded the large increase in credit card borrowing in March not as a sign that households were pressed for cash and forced to borrow, rather a sign of confidence by households that they could safely handle new debt.

(A) rather a sign of confidence by households that they could safely

(B) yet as a sign of households' confidence that it was safe for them to

(C) but a sign of confidence by households that they could safely

(D) but as a sign that households were confident they could safely

(E) but also as a sign that households were confident in their ability safely to

683. A pioneer journalist, Nellie Bly's exploits included circling the globe faster than Jules Verne's fictional Phileas Fogg.

(A) A pioneer journalist, Nellie Bly's exploits included

(B) The exploits of Nellie Bly, a pioneer journalist, included

(C) Nellie Bly was a pioneer journalist including in her exploits the

(D) Included in the pioneer journalist Nellie Bly's exploits are

(E) The pioneer journalist's exploits of Nellie Bly included

684. In 1913, the largely self-taught Indian mathematician Srinivasa Ramanujan mailed 120 of his theorems to three different British mathematicians; only one, G. H. Hardy, recognized the brilliance of these theorems, but thanks to Hardy's recognition, Ramanujan was eventually elected to the Royal Society of London.

(A) only one, G. H. Hardy, recognized the brilliance of these theorems, but

(B) they were brilliant, G. H. Hardy alone recognized, but

(C) these theorems were brilliant, but only one, G. H. Hardy recognized;

(D) but, only one, G. H. Hardy, recognizing their brilliance,

(E) only one G. H. Hardy recognized, but these theorems were brilliant

685. Cost cutting and restructuring has allowed the manufacturing company to lower its projected losses for the second quarter, and they are forecasting a profit before the end of the year.

(A) has allowed the manufacturing company to lower its projected losses for the second quarter, and they are forecasting

(B) has allowed for the manufacturing company to lower its projected losses in the second quarter and to forecast

(C) have allowed that the manufacturing company can lower the projected losses for the second quarter, and to forecast

(D) have allowed the manufacturing company to lower its projected second-quarter losses and to forecast

(E) have allowed for the manufacturing company to lower the projected losses in the second quarter, as well as forecasting

686. The Life and Casualty Company hopes that by increasing its environmental fund reserves to $1.2 billion, that it has set aside enough to pay for environmental claims and no longer has to use its profits and capital to pay those claims bit by bit, year by year.

(A) that it has set aside enough to pay for environmental claims and no longer has

(B) enough has been set aside with which environmental claims can be paid and it will have no longer

(C) it has set aside enough for payment of environmental claims and thus no longer having

(D) enough has been set aside to pay for environmental claims, thus no longer having

(E) it has set aside enough to pay for environmental claims and will no longer have

687. Like ancient Egyptian architectural materials that were recycled in the construction of ancient Greek Alexandria, so ancient Greek materials from the construction of that city were reused in subsequent centuries by Roman, Muslim, and modern builders.

(A) Like ancient Egyptian architectural materials that were recycled in the construction of
(B) Like recycling ancient Egyptian architectural materials to construct
(C) Just as ancient Egyptian architectural materials were recycled in the construction of
(D) Just as they recycled ancient Egyptian architectural materials in constructing
(E) Just like ancient Egyptian architectural materials that were recycled in constructing

688. Especially in the early years, new entrepreneurs may need to find resourceful ways, like renting temporary office space or using answering services, that make their company seem large and more firmly established than they may actually be.

(A) that make their company seem large
(B) to make their companies seem larger
(C) thus making their companies seem larger
(D) so that the companies seem larger
(E) of making their company seem large

689. Unlike the nests of leaf cutters and most other ants, situated underground or in pieces of wood, raider ants make a portable nest by entwining their long legs to form "curtains" of ants that hang from logs or boulders, providing protection for the queen and the colony larvae and pupae.

(A) the nests of leaf cutters and most other ants,
(B) the nests of leaf cutters and most other ants, which are
(C) leaf cutters and most other ants, whose nests are
(D) leaf cutters and most other ants in having nests
(E) those of leaf cutters and most other ants with nests

690. Turtles, like other reptiles, can endure long fasts, in their ability to survive on weekly or even monthly feedings; however, when food is readily available, they may eat frequently and grow very fat.

(A) fasts, in their ability to survive
(B) fasts, having their ability to survive
(C) fasts, due to having the ability of surviving
(D) fasts because they are able to survive
(E) fasts because of having the ability of surviving

691. Thai village crafts, as with other cultures, have developed through the principle that form follows function and incorporate readily available materials fashioned using traditional skills.

(A) as with
(B) as did those of
(C) as they have in
(D) like in
(E) like those of

692. Tropical bats play important roles in the rain forest ecosystem, aiding in the dispersal of cashew, date, and fig seeds; pollinating banana, breadfruit, and mango trees; and indirectly help produce tequila by pollinating agave plants.

(A) pollinating banana, breadfruit, and mango trees; and indirectly help produce
(B) pollinating banana, breadfruit, and mango trees; and indirectly helping to produce
(C) pollinating banana, breadfruit, and mango trees; and they indirectly help to produce
(D) they pollinate banana, breadfruit, and mango trees; and indirectly help producing
(E) they pollinate banana, breadfruit, and mango trees; indirectly helping the producing of

693. Discussion of greenhouse effects have usually had as a focus the possibility of Earth growing warmer and to what extent it might, but climatologists have indicated all along that precipitation, storminess, and temperature extremes are likely to have the greatest impact on people.

(A) Discussion of greenhouse effects have usually had as a focus the possibility of Earth growing warmer and to what extent it might,
(B) Discussion of greenhouse effects has usually had as its focus whether Earth would get warmer and what the extent would be,
(C) Discussion of greenhouse effects has usually focused on whether Earth would grow warmer and to what extent,

(D) The discussion of greenhouse effects have usually focused on the possibility of Earth getting warmer and to what extent it might,

(E) The discussion of greenhouse effects has usually focused on whether Earth would grow warmer and the extent that is,

694. In the seventh century B.C., the Roman alphabet was adapted from the Etruscan alphabet, which in turn had been adapted in the previous century from a western Greek alphabet, which itself had been adapted earlier in the same century from the Phoenician alphabet.

(A) which itself had been adapted earlier

(B) adapting itself earlier

(C) itself being adapted earlier

(D) having been earlier adapted itself

(E) earlier itself having been adapted

695. With corn, soybean, and wheat reserves being low enough so a poor harvest would send prices sky-rocketing, grain futures brokers and their clients are especially interested in weather that could affect crops.

(A) being low enough so

(B) so low such that

(C) so low that

(D) that are low enough so

(E) that are so low such that

696. By 1940, the pilot Jacqueline Cochran held seventeen official national and international speed records, and she earned them at a time when aviation was still so new for many of the planes she flew to be of dangerously experimental design.

(A) and she earned them at a time when aviation was still so new for many of the planes she flew to be

(B) earning them at a time that aviation was still so new for many of the planes she flew to be

(C) earning these at a time where aviation was still so new that many of the planes she flew were

(D) earned at a time in which aviation was still so new such that many of the planes she flew were

(E) earned at a time when aviation was still so new that many of the planes she flew were

697. The foundation works to strengthen local and regional agricultural markets and cooperating with governments, improving access for farmers for productive resources such as land and credit.

(A) cooperating with governments, improving access for farmers for

(B) cooperates with governments to improve access for farmers to

(C) cooperate with governments for improvements of access for farmers to

(D) cooperate with governments and improve accessibility for farmers for their

(E) in cooperation with governments to improve access for farmers for

698. A professor at the university has taken a sabbatical to research on James Baldwin's books that Baldwin wrote in France while he was living there.

(A) on James Baldwin's books that Baldwin wrote in France while he was living there

(B) about the books James Baldwin wrote in France

(C) into James Baldwin's books written while in France

(D) on the books of James Baldwin, written while he lived in France

(E) the books James Baldwin wrote while he lived in France

699. Researchers now regard interferon as not a single substance, but it is rather a biological family of complex molecules that play an important, though not entirely defined, role in the immune system.

(A) as not a single substance, but it is rather a biological family of complex molecules that play

(B) as not a single substance but as a biological family of complex molecules playing

(C) not as a single substance but as a biological family of complex molecules that play

(D) not to be a single substance but rather a biological family of complex molecules playing

(E) not as a single substance but instead as being a biological family of complex molecules that play

700. The remarkable similarity of Thule artifacts throughout a vast region can, in part, be explained as a very rapid movement of people from one end of North America to the other.

(A) The remarkable similarity of Thule artifacts throughout a vast region can, in part, be explained as
(B) Thule artifacts being remarkably similar throughout a vast region, one explanation is
(C) That Thule artifacts are remarkably similar throughout a vast region is, in part, explainable as
(D) One explanation for the remarkable similarity of Thule artifacts throughout a vast region is that there was
(E) Throughout a vast region Thule artifacts are remarkably similar, with one explanation for this being

701. The widely accepted big bang theory holds that the universe began in an explosive instant ten to twenty billion years ago and has been expanding ever since.

(A) that the universe began in an explosive instant ten to twenty billion years ago and has been expanding
(B) that the universe had begun in an explosive instant ten to twenty billion years ago and had been expanding
(C) that the beginning of the universe was an explosive instant ten to twenty billion years ago that has expanded
(D) the beginning of the universe to have been an explosive instant ten to twenty billion years ago that is expanding
(E) the universe to have begun in an explosive instant ten to twenty billion years ago and has been expanding

702. Between 14,000 and 8,000 B.C. the ice cap that covered northern Asia, Europe, and America began to melt, uncovering vast new areas that were to be occupied by migrating peoples moving northward.

(A) began to melt, uncovering vast new areas that were to be occupied
(B) began melting, to uncover vast new areas to be occupied
(C) began, by melting, to uncover vast new areas for occupation
(D) began, after melting, uncovering vast new areas which are to be occupied
(E) would begin to uncover, through melting, vast new areas for occupation

703. Bengal-born writer, philosopher, and educator Rabindranath Tagore had the greatest admiration for Mohandas K. Gandhi the person and also as a politician, but Tagore had been skeptical of Gandhi's form of nationalism and his conservative opinions about India's cultural traditions.

(A) for Mohandas K. Gandhi the person and also as a politician, but Tagore had been
(B) for Mohandas K. Gandhi as a person and as a politician, but Tagore was also
(C) for Mohandas K. Gandhi not only as a person and as a politician, but Tagore was also
(D) of Mohandas K. Gandhi as a person and as also a politician, but Tagore was
(E) of Mohandas K. Gandhi not only as a person and as a politician, but Tagore had also been

704. Traffic safety officials predict that drivers will be equally likely to exceed the proposed speed limit as the current one.

(A) equally likely to exceed the proposed speed limit as
(B) equally likely to exceed the proposed speed limit as they are
(C) equally likely that they will exceed the proposed speed limit as
(D) as likely that they will exceed the proposed speed limit as
(E) as likely to exceed the proposed speed limit as they are

705. Written early in the French Revolution, Mary Wollstonecraft's *A Vindication of the Rights of Man* (1790) and *A Vindication of the Rights of Woman* (1792) attributed Europe's social and political ills to be the result of the dominance of aristocratic values and patriarchal hereditary privilege.

(A) Mary Wollstonecraft's *A Vindication of the Rights of Man* (1790) and *A Vindication of the Rights of Woman* (1792) attributed Europe's social and political ills to be the result of

(B) Mary Wollstonecraft's *A Vindication of the Rights of Man* (1790) and *A Vindication of the Rights of Woman* (1792) attributed Europe's social and political ills to result from

(C) Mary Wollstonecraft's *A Vindication of the Rights of Man* (1790) and *A Vindication of the Rights of Woman* (1792) attributed Europe's social and political ills to

(D) in *A Vindication of the Rights of Man* (1790) and *A Vindication of the Rights of Woman* (1792), Mary Wollstonecraft attributed Europe's social and political ills to have been the result of

(E) Mary Wollstonecraft, in *A Vindication of the Rights of Man* (1790) and *A Vindication of the Rights of Woman* (1792), attributed Europe's social and political ills to

706. Using study groups managed by the principal popular organizations and political parties, the Swedish public was informed by the government about energy and nuclear power.

(A) the Swedish public was informed by the government about energy and nuclear power

(B) the government informed the Swedish public about energy and nuclear power

(C) energy and nuclear power information was given to the Swedish public by the government

(D) information about energy and nuclear power was given to the Swedish public by the government

(E) the public of Sweden was given energy and nuclear power information by the government

707. The use of the bar code, or Universal Product Code, which was created in part to enable supermarkets to process customers at a faster rate, has expanded beyond supermarkets to other retail outlets and have become readily accepted despite some initial opposition when it was first introduced in 1974.

(A) have become readily accepted despite some initial opposition when it was first introduced in 1974

(B) has become readily accepted despite some initial opposition when they were first introduced in 1974

(C) have become readily accepted despite some initial opposition when first introduced in 1974

(D) has become readily accepted despite some initial opposition when the bar code was first introduced in 1974

(E) bar codes have become readily accepted despite some initial opposition when it was first introduced in 1974

708. The Organization of Petroleum Exporting Countries (OPEC) had long been expected to announce a reduction in output to bolster sagging oil prices, but officials of the organization just recently announced that the group will pare daily production by 1.5 million barrels by the beginning of next year, but only if non-OPEC nations, including Norway, Mexico, and Russia, were to trim output by a total of 500,000 barrels a day.

(A) year, but only if non-OPEC nations, including Norway, Mexico, and Russia, were to trim output

(B) year, but only if the output of non-OPEC nations, which includes Norway, Mexico, and Russia, is trimmed

(C) year only if the output of non-OPEC nations, including Norway, Mexico, and Russia, would be trimmed

(D) year only if non-OPEC nations, which includes Norway, Mexico, and Russia, were trimming output

(E) year only if non-OPEC nations, including Norway, Mexico, and Russia, trim output

709. Not trusting themselves to choose wisely among the wide array of investment opportunities on the market, stockbrokers are helping many people who turn to them to buy stocks that could be easily bought directly.

(A) stockbrokers are helping many people who turn to them to buy stocks that could be easily

(B) stockbrokers are helping many people who are turning to them for help in buying stocks that they could easily have

(C) many people are turning to stockbrokers for help from them to buy stocks that could be easily

(D) many people are turning to stockbrokers for help to buy stocks that easily could have been

(E) many people are turning to stockbrokers for help in buying stocks that could be easily be

710. There are several ways to build solid walls using just mud or clay, but the most extensively used method has been <u>the forming of bricks out of mud or clay, and, after some preliminary air drying or sun drying, they are laid</u> in the wall in mud mortar.

(A) the forming of bricks out of mud or clay, and, after some preliminary air drying or sun drying, they are laid
(B) forming the mud or clay into bricks, and, after some preliminary air drying or sun drying, to lay them
(C) having bricks formed from mud or clay, and, after some preliminary air drying or sun drying, they were laid
(D) to form the mud or clay into bricks, and, after some preliminary air drying or sun drying, to lay them
(E) that bricks were formed from mud or clay, which, after some preliminary air drying or sun drying, were laid

711. A surge in new home sales and a drop in weekly unemployment <u>claims suggest that the economy might not be as weak as some analysts previously thought.</u>

(A) claims suggest that the economy might not be as weak as some analysts previously thought
(B) claims suggests that the economy might not be so weak as some analysts have previously thought
(C) claims suggest that the economy might not be as weak as have been previously thought by some analysts
(D) claims, suggesting about the economy that it might not be so weak as previously thought by some analysts
(E) claims, suggesting the economy might not be as weak as previously thought to be by some analysts

712. Retail sales rose 0.8 of 1 percent in August, intensifying expectations <u>that personal spending in the July–September quarter more than doubled that of</u> the 1.4 percent growth rate in personal spending for the previous quarter.

(A) that personal spending in the July–September quarter more than doubled that of
(B) that personal spending in the July–September quarter would more than double
(C) of personal spending in the July–September quarter, that it more than doubled
(D) of personal spending in the July–September quarter more than doubling that of
(E) of personal spending in the July–September quarter, that it would more than double that of

713. In the early part of the twentieth century, many vacationers found that driving automobiles and sleeping in tents allowed them to enjoy nature close at hand and tour at their own pace, <u>with none of the restrictions of passenger trains and railroad timetables or with the</u> formalities, expenses, and impersonality of hotels.

(A) with none of the restrictions of passenger trains and railroad timetables or with the
(B) with none of the restrictions of passenger trains, railroad timetables, nor
(C) without the restrictions of passenger trains and railroad timetables nor
(D) without the restrictions of passenger trains and railroad timetables or with the
(E) without the restrictions of passenger trains and railroad timetables or the

714. Over the next few years, increasing demands on the Chattahoochee River, which flows into the Apalachicola River, could alter the saline content of Apalachicola Bay, <u>which would rob the oysters there of their flavor, and to make them decrease in size,</u> less distinctive, and less in demand.

(A) which would rob the oysters there of their flavor, and to make them decrease in size,
(B) and it would rob the oysters there of their flavor, make them smaller,
(C) and rob the oysters there of their flavor, making them decrease in size,
(D) robbing the oysters there of their flavor and making them smaller,
(E) robbing the oysters there of their flavor, and making them decrease in size,

715. Elizabeth Barber, the author of both *Prehistoric Textiles*, a comprehensive work on cloth in the early cultures of the Mediterranean, and also of *Women's Work*, a more general account of early cloth manufacture, is an expert authority on textiles in ancient societies.

(A) also of *Women's Work*, a more general account of early cloth manufacture, is an expert authority on

(B) also *Women's Work*, a more general account of cloth manufacture, is an expert authority about

(C) of *Women's Work*, a more general account about early cloth manufacture, is an authority on

(D) of *Women's Work*, a more general account about early cloth manufacture, is an expert authority about

(E) *Women's Work*, a more general account of early cloth manufacture, is an authority on

716. Digging in sediments in northern China, evidence has been gathered by scientists suggesting that complex life-forms emerged much earlier than they had previously thought.

(A) evidence has been gathered by scientists suggesting that complex life-forms emerged much earlier than they had

(B) evidence gathered by scientists suggests a much earlier emergence of complex life-forms than had been

(C) scientists have gathered evidence suggesting that complex life-forms emerged much earlier than

(D) scientists have gathered evidence that suggests a much earlier emergence of complex life-forms than that which was

(E) scientists have gathered evidence which suggests a much earlier emergence of complex life-forms than that

717. Employing many different techniques throughout his career, Michelangelo produced a great variety of art works, including paintings, for example, in the Sistine Chapel, to sculpture, for example, the statue of David.

(A) including paintings, for example, in the Sistine Chapel, to sculpture, for example,

(B) including paintings, for example, in the Sistine Chapel, to sculpture, like

(C) including paintings, such as those in the Sistine Chapel, and sculpture, as

(D) ranging from paintings, such as those in the Sistine Chapel, to sculpture, such as

(E) ranging from paintings, such as in the Sistine Chapel, and sculpture, such as

718. Outlining his strategy for nursing the troubled conglomerate back to health, the chief executive's plans were announced on Wednesday for cutting the company's huge debt by selling nearly $12 billion in assets over the next 18 months.

(A) executive's plans were announced on Wednesday for cutting the company's huge debt by selling nearly $12 billion in assets over the next 18 months

(B) executive's plans, which are to cut the company's huge debt by selling nearly $12 billion in assets over the next 18 months, were announced on Wednesday

(C) executive's plans for cutting the company's huge debt by selling nearly $12 billion in assets over the next 18 months were announced on Wednesday

(D) executive announced plans Wednesday to cut the company's huge debt by selling nearly $12 billion in assets over the next 18 months

(E) executive announced plans Wednesday that are to cut the company's huge debt by selling nearly $12 billion in assets over the next 18 months

719. It is called a sea, but the landlocked Caspian is actually the largest lake on Earth, which covers more than four times the surface area of its closest rival in size, North America's Lake Superior.

(A) It is called a sea, but the landlocked Caspian is actually the largest lake on Earth, which covers

(B) Although it is called a sea, actually the landlocked Caspian is the largest lake on Earth, which covers

(C) Though called a sea, the landlocked Caspian is actually the largest lake on Earth, covering

(D) Though called a sea but it actually is the largest lake on Earth, the landlocked Caspian covers

(E) Despite being called a sea, the largest lake on Earth is actually the landlocked Caspian, covering

720. Neuroscientists, having amassed a wealth of knowledge over the past twenty years about the brain and its development from birth to adulthood, are now drawing solid conclusions about how the human brain grows and how babies acquire language.

(A) Neuroscientists, having amassed a wealth of knowledge over the past twenty years about the brain and its development from birth to adulthood, are
(B) Neuroscientists, having amassed a wealth of knowledge about the brain and its development from birth to adulthood over the past twenty years, and are
(C) Neuroscientists amassing a wealth of knowledge about the brain and its development from birth to adulthood over the past twenty years, and are
(D) Neuroscientists have amassed a wealth of knowledge over the past twenty years about the brain and its development from birth to adulthood,
(E) Neuroscientists have amassed, over the past twenty years, a wealth of knowledge about the brain and its development from birth to adulthood,

721. According to a recent study of consumer spending on prescription medications, increases in the sales of the 50 drugs that were advertised most heavily accounts for almost half of the $20.8 billion increase in drug spending last year, the remainder of which came from sales of the 9,850 prescription medicines that companies did not advertise or advertised very little.

(A) heavily accounts for almost half of the $20.8 billion increase in drug spending last year, the remainder of which came
(B) heavily were what accounted for almost half of the $20.8 billion increase in drug spending last year; the remainder of the increase coming
(C) heavily accounted for almost half of the $20.8 billion increase in drug spending last year, the remainder of the increase coming
(D) heavily, accounting for almost half of the $20.8 billion increase in drug spending last year, while the remainder of the increase came
(E) heavily, which accounted for almost half of the $20.8 billion increase in drug spending last year, with the remainder of it coming

722. Along the major rivers that traverse the deserts of northeast Africa, the Middle East, and northwest India, the combination of a reliable supply of water and good growing conditions both encouraged farming traditions that, in places, endure in at least 6,000 years.

(A) good growing conditions both encouraged farming traditions that, in places, endure in
(B) good growing conditions encouraged farming traditions that have, in places, endured for
(C) of good growing conditions have encouraged farming traditions that, in places, endured for
(D) of good growing conditions both encouraged farming traditions that have, in places, endured
(E) of good growing conditions encouraged farming traditions that have, in places, been enduring for

723. Despite its covering the entire planet, Earth has a crust that is not seamless or stationary, rather it is fragmented into mobile semirigid plates.

(A) Despite its covering the entire planet, Earth has a crust that is not seamless or stationary, rather it is
(B) Despite the fact that it covers the entire planet, Earth's crust is neither seamless nor is it stationary, but is
(C) Despite covering the entire planet, Earth's crust is neither seamless nor is it stationary, but rather
(D) Although it covers the entire planet, Earth's crust is neither seamless nor stationary, but rather
(E) Although covering the entire planet, Earth has a crust that is not seamless or stationary, but

724. Emily Dickinson's letters to Susan Huntington Dickinson were written over a period beginning a few years before Susan's marriage to Emily's brother and ending shortly before Emily's death in 1886, outnumbering her letters to anyone else.

(A) Dickinson were written over a period beginning a few years before Susan's marriage to Emily's brother and ending shortly before Emily's death in 1886, outnumbering

(B) Dickinson were written over a period that begins a few years before Susan's marriage to Emily's brother and ended shortly before Emily's death in 1886, outnumber

(C) Dickinson, written over a period beginning a few years before Susan's marriage to Emily's brother and that ends shortly before Emily's death in 1886 and outnumbering

(D) Dickinson, which were written over a period beginning a few years before Susan's marriage to Emily's brother, ending shortly before Emily's death in 1886, and outnumbering

(E) Dickinson, which were written over a period beginning a few years before Susan's marriage to Emily's brother and ending shortly before Emily's death in 1886, outnumber

725. At the end of 2001, motion picture industry representatives said that there were about a million copies of Hollywood movies available <u>online and expected piracy to increase with high-speed Internet connections that become more widely available</u>.

(A) online and expected piracy to increase with high-speed Internet connections that become more widely available

(B) online and expect the increase of piracy with the wider availability of high-speed Internet connections

(C) online, and they expect more piracy to increase with the wider availability of high-speed Internet connections

(D) online, and that they expected the increase of piracy as high-speed Internet connections would become more widely available

(E) online, and that they expected piracy to increase as high-speed Internet connections became more widely available

726. Making things even more difficult <u>has been general market inactivity lately, if not paralysis, which has provided</u> little in the way of pricing guidance.

(A) has been general market inactivity lately, if not paralysis, which has provided

(B) there is general market inactivity, if not paralysis, lately it has provided

(C) general market inactivity, if not paralysis, has lately provided

(D) lately, general market inactivity, if not paralysis, has provided

(E) is that lately general market inactivity, if not paralysis, which provides

727. <u>Unlike the conviction held by many of her colleagues that genes were</u> relatively simple and static, Barbara McClintock adhered to her own more complicated ideas about how genes might operate, and in 1983, at the age of 81, was awarded a Nobel Prize for her discovery that the genes in corn are capable of moving from one chromosomal site to another.

(A) Unlike the conviction held by many of her colleagues that genes were

(B) Although many of her colleagues were of the conviction of genes being

(C) Contrary to many of her colleagues being convinced that genes were

(D) Even though many of her colleagues were convinced that genes were

(E) Even with many of her colleagues convinced of genes being

728. Ryūnosuke Akutagawa's knowledge of the literatures of Europe, China, and <u>that of Japan were instrumental in his development as a writer, informing his literary style as much as</u> the content of his fiction.

(A) that of Japan were instrumental in his development as a writer, informing his literary style as much as

(B) that of Japan was instrumental in his development as a writer, and it informed both his literary style as well as

(C) Japan was instrumental in his development as a writer, informing both his literary style and

(D) Japan was instrumental in his development as a writer, as it informed his literary style as much as

(E) Japan were instrumental in his development as a writer, informing both his literary style in addition to

729. According to scientists who monitored its path, an expanding cloud of energized particles ejected from the Sun recently triggered a large storm in the magnetic field that surrounds Earth, which brightened the Northern Lights and also possibly knocking out a communications satellite.

(A) an expanding cloud of energized particles ejected from the Sun recently triggered a large storm in the magnetic field that surrounds Earth, which brightened the Northern Lights and also possibly knocking

(B) an expanding cloud of energized particles ejected from the Sun was what recently triggered a large storm in the magnetic field that surrounds Earth, and it brightened the Northern Lights and also possibly knocked

(C) an expanding cloud of energized particles ejected from the Sun recently triggered a large storm in the magnetic field that surrounds Earth, brightening the Northern Lights and possibly knocking

(D) a large storm in the magnetic field that surrounds Earth, recently triggered by an expanding cloud of energized particles, brightened the Northern Lights and it possibly knocked

(E) a large storm in the magnetic field surrounding Earth was recently triggered by an expanding cloud of energized particles, brightening the Northern Lights and it possibly knocked

730. In 1850, Lucretia Mott published her *Discourse on Women*, arguing in a treatise for women to have equal political and legal rights and for changes in the married women's property laws.

(A) arguing in a treatise for women to have equal political and legal rights

(B) arguing in a treatise for equal political and legal rights for women

(C) a treatise that advocates women's equal political and legal rights

(D) a treatise advocating women's equal political and legal rights

(E) a treatise that argued for equal political and legal rights for women

731. To develop more accurate population forecasts, demographers have to know a great deal more than now about the social and economic determinants of fertility.

(A) have to know a great deal more than now about the social and economic

(B) have to know a great deal more than they do now about the social and economical

(C) would have to know a great deal more than they do now about the social and economical

(D) would have to know a great deal more than they do now about the social and economic

(E) would have to know a great deal more than now about the social and economic

732. Laos has a land area about the same as Great Britain but only four million in population, where many are members of hill tribes ensconced in the virtually inaccessible mountain valleys of the north.

(A) about the same as Great Britain but only four million in population, where many

(B) of about the same size as Great Britain is, but in Laos there is a population of only four million, and many

(C) that is about the same size as Great Britain's land area, but in Laos with a population of only four million people, many of them

(D) comparable to the size of Great Britain, but only four million in population, and many

(E) comparable to that of Great Britain but a population of only four million people, many of whom

733. Having been named for a mythological nymph who cared for the infant Jupiter, the asteroid named Ida, in the middle of the belt of asteroids that orbit the Sun between Mars and Jupiter, was discovered in 1884.

(A) Having been named for a mythological nymph who cared for the infant Jupiter, the asteroid named Ida, in the middle of the belt of asteroids that orbit the Sun between Mars and Jupiter, was discovered in 1884.

(B) Discovered in 1884, the asteroid Ida, named for a mythological nymph who cared for the infant Jupiter, is in the middle of the belt of asteroids that orbit the Sun between Mars and Jupiter.

(C) In the middle of the belt of asteroids that orbit the Sun between Mars and Jupiter, the asteroid Ida, discovered in 1884 and named for a mythological nymph who cared for the infant Jupiter.

(D) The asteroid Ida, named for a mythological nymph who cared for the infant Jupiter and discovered in 1884, is in the middle of the belt of asteroids to orbit the Sun between Mars and Jupiter.

(E) Ida, an asteroid discovered in 1884 and which was named for a mythological nymph who cared for the infant Jupiter, is in the middle of the belt of asteroids to orbit the Sun between Mars and Jupiter.

734. In ancient Thailand, much of the local artisans' creative energy was expended for the creation of Buddha images and when they constructed and decorated the temples that enshrined them.

(A) much of the local artisans' creative energy was expended for the creation of Buddha images and when they constructed and decorated the temples that enshrined them

(B) much of the local artisans' creative energy was expended on the creation of Buddha images and on construction and decoration of the temples in which they were enshrined

(C) much of the local artisans' creative energy was expended on the creation of Buddha images as well as constructing and decoration of the temples in which they were enshrined

(D) creating images of Buddha accounted for much of the local artisans' creative energy, and also constructing and decorating the temples enshrining them

(E) the creation of Buddha images accounted for much of the local artisans' creative energy as well as construction and decoration of the temples that enshrined them

735. The English physician Edward Jenner found that if experimental subjects were deliberately infected with cowpox, which caused only a mild illness, they are immune from smallpox.

(A) which caused only a mild illness, they are immune from

(B) causing only a mild illness, they become immune from

(C) which causes only a mild illness, they are immune to

(D) causing only a mild illness, they became immune from

(E) which caused only a mild illness, they would become immune to

736. Covering 71 percent of Earth's surface, the oceans play an essential role in maintaining the conditions for human existence on land, moderating temperature by the absorption of heat and carbon dioxide, and giving pure water back to the atmosphere through evaporation.

(A) Covering 71 percent of Earth's surface, the oceans play an essential role in maintaining the conditions for human existence on land, moderating

(B) Covering 71 percent of Earth's surface and playing an essential role in maintaining the conditions for human existence on land, the oceans moderate

(C) The oceans cover 71 percent of Earth's surface and play an essential role in maintaining conditions for human existence on land, and by moderating

(D) The oceans cover 71 percent of Earth's surface, play an essential role in maintaining the conditions for human existence on land, and moderate

(E) The oceans cover 71 percent of Earth's surface, playing an essential role in maintaining the conditions for human existence on land, and they moderate

737. Some anthropologists believe that the genetic homogeneity evident in the world's people is the result of a "population bottleneck"—at some time in the past our ancestors suffered an event, greatly reducing their numbers and thus our genetic variation.

(A) at some time in the past our ancestors suffered an event, greatly reducing their numbers

(B) that at some time in the past our ancestors suffered an event that greatly reduced their numbers

(C) that some time in the past our ancestors suffered an event so that their numbers were greatly reduced,

(D) some time in the past our ancestors suffered an event from which their numbers were greatly reduced

(E) some time in the past, that our ancestors suffered an event so as to reduce their numbers greatly,

738. Foraging at all times of the day and night, but interspersing their feeding with periods of rest that last between one and eight hours, a sperm whale could eat so much as a ton of squid a day.

(A) between one and eight hours, a sperm whale could eat so

(B) between one and eight hours, sperm whales can eat as

(C) between one to eight hours, sperm whales could eat as

(D) from one to eight hours, sperm whales could eat so

(E) from one to eight hours, a sperm whale can eat so

739. In some types of pine tree, a thick layer of needles protects the buds from which new growth proceeds; consequently they are able to withstand forest fires relatively well.

(A) a thick layer of needles protects the buds from which new growth proceeds; consequently they are able to withstand forest fires relatively well

(B) a thick needle layer protects buds from where new growth proceeds, so that they can withstand forest fires relatively well

(C) a thick layer of needles protect the buds from which new growth proceeds; thus, they are able to withstand relatively well any forest fires

(D) since the buds from which new growth proceeds are protected by a thick needle layer, consequently they can therefore withstand forest fires relatively well

(E) because the buds where new growth happens are protected by a thick layer of needles, they are able to withstand forest fires relatively easily as a result

740. The tourism commission has conducted surveys of hotels in the most popular resorts, with the ultimate goal of reducing the guests who end up expressing overall dissatisfaction with the service in the hotels.

(A) with the ultimate goal of reducing the guests who end up expressing overall dissatisfaction with the service in the hotels

(B) with the goal to ultimately reduce the number of guests who end up expressing overall dissatisfaction with the hotels' service

(C) ultimately with the goal to reduce expressions of overall dissatisfaction by the guests with the hotel service

(D) in an ultimate attempt to reduce the number of guests that ends up expressing overall dissatisfaction with the hotels' service

(E) with the ultimate goal of reducing the number of guests who express overall dissatisfaction with the hotels' service

741. A new study suggests that the conversational pace of everyday life may be so brisk it hampers the ability of some children for distinguishing discrete sounds and words and, the result is, to make sense of speech.

(A) it hampers the ability of some children for distinguishing discrete sounds and words and, the result is, to make

(B) that it hampers the ability of some children to distinguish discrete sounds and words and, as a result, to make

(C) that it hampers the ability of some children to distinguish discrete sounds and words and, the result of this, they are unable to make

(D) that it hampers the ability of some children to distinguish discrete sounds and words, and results in not making

(E) as to hamper the ability of some children for distinguishing discrete sounds and words, resulting in being unable to make

742. The nineteenth-century chemist Humphry Davy presented the results of his early experiments in his "Essay on Heat and Light," a critique of all chemistry since Robert Boyle as well as a vision of a new chemistry that Davy hoped to found.

(A) a critique of all chemistry since Robert Boyle as well as a vision of a

(B) a critique of all chemistry following Robert Boyle and also his envisioning of a

(C) a critique of all chemistry after Robert Boyle and envisioning as well

(D) critiquing all chemistry from Robert Boyle forward and also a vision of

(E) critiquing all the chemistry done since Robert Boyle as well as his own envisioning of

743. To attract the most talented workers, some companies are offering a wider range of benefits, letting employees pick those most important to them.

(A) benefits, letting employees pick those most important to them

(B) benefits, letting employees pick the most important of them to themselves

(C) benefits and letting employees pick the most important to themselves

(D) benefits and let employees pick the most important to them

(E) benefits and let employees pick those that are most important to themselves

744. Many of the earliest known images of Hindu deities in India date from the time of the Kushan Empire, fashioned either from the spotted sandstone of Mathura or Gandharan grey schist.

(A) Empire, fashioned either from the spotted sandstone of Mathura or

(B) Empire, fashioned from either the spotted sandstone of Mathura or from

(C) Empire, either fashioned from the spotted sandstone of Mathura or

(D) Empire and either fashioned from the spotted sandstone of Mathura or from

(E) Empire and were fashioned either from the spotted sandstone of Mathura or from

745. Tides typically range from three to six feet, but while some places show no tides at all, some others, such as the Bay of Fundy, have tides of at least thirty feet and more.

(A) some others, such as the Bay of Fundy, have tides of at least thirty feet and more

(B) the others, such as the Bay of Fundy, that have tides of more than thirty feet

(C) others, such as the Bay of Fundy, have tides of more than thirty feet

(D) those at the Bay of Fundy, which has tides of more than thirty feet

(E) the ones at the Bay of Fundy have tides of at least thirty feet and more

746. A leading figure in the Scottish Enlightenment, Adam Smith's two major books are to democratic capitalism what Marx's *Das Kapital* is to socialism.

(A) Adam Smith's two major books are to democratic capitalism what

(B) Adam Smith's two major books are to democratic capitalism like

(C) Adam Smith's two major books are to democratic capitalism just as

(D) Adam Smith wrote two major books that are to democratic capitalism similar to

(E) Adam Smith wrote two major books that are to democratic capitalism what

747. Researchers studying the brain scans of volunteers who pondered ethical dilemmas have found that the basis for making tough moral judgments is emotion, not logic or analytical reasoning.

(A) the brain scans of volunteers who pondered ethical dilemmas have found that the basis for making tough moral judgments is

(B) the brain scans of volunteers who pondered ethical dilemmas and found the basis to make tough moral decisions to be

(C) the brain scans of volunteers pondering ethical dilemmas and found that the basis for making tough moral decisions is

(D) volunteers' brain scans while pondering ethical dilemmas have found the basis to make tough moral judgments to be

(E) volunteers' brain scans while they pondered ethical dilemmas have found that the basis for making tough moral judgments is

748. Rivaling the pyramids of Egypt or even the ancient cities of the Maya as an achievement, the army of terra-cotta warriors created to protect Qin Shi Huang, China's first emperor, in his afterlife is more than 2,000 years old and took 700,000 artisans more than 36 years to complete.

(A) the army of terra-cotta warriors created to protect Qin Shi Huang, China's first emperor, in his afterlife is more than 2,000 years old and took 700,000 artisans more than 36 years to complete

(B) Qin Shi Huang, China's first emperor, was protected in his afterlife by an army of terra-cotta warriors that was created more than 2,000 years ago by 700,000 artisans who took more than 36 years to complete it

(C) it took 700,000 artisans more than 36 years to create an army of terra-cotta warriors more than 2,000 years ago that would protect Qin Shi Huang, China's first emperor, in his afterlife

(D) more than 2,000 years ago, 700,000 artisans worked more than 36 years to create an army of terra-cotta warriors to protect Qin Shi Huang, China's first emperor, in his afterlife

(E) more than 36 years were needed to complete the army of terra-cotta warriors that 700,000 artisans created 2,000 years ago to protect Qin Shi Huang, China's first emperor, in his afterlife

749. In California, a lack of genetic variation in the Argentine ant has allowed the species to spread widely; due to their being so genetically similar to one another, the ants consider all their fellows to be a close relative and thus do not engage in the kind of fierce intercolony struggles that limits the spread of this species in its native Argentina.

(A) due to their being so genetically similar to one another, the ants consider all their fellows to be a close relative and thus do not engage in the kind of fierce intercolony struggles that limits

(B) due to its being so genetically similar, the ant considers all its fellows to be a close relative and thus does not engage in the kind of fierce intercolony struggles that limit

(C) because it is so genetically similar, the ant considers all its fellows to be close relatives and thus does not engage in the kind of fierce intercolony struggles that limits

(D) because they are so genetically similar to one another, the ants consider all their fellows to be close relatives and thus do not engage in the kind of fierce intercolony struggles that limit

(E) because of being so genetically similar to one another, the ants consider all their fellows to be a close relative and thus do not engage in the kind of fierce intercolony struggles that limits

750. Next month, state wildlife officials are scheduled to take over the job of increasing the wolf population in the federally designated recovery area, the number of which will however ultimately be dictated by the number of prey in the area.

(A) area, the number of which will however

(B) area; the size of the population, however, will

(C) area, however the number of wolves will

(D) area; the number of which will, however,

(E) area, when the size of the population will, however,

751. About 5 million acres in the United States have been invaded by leafy spurge, a herbaceous plant from Eurasia with milky sap that gives mouth sores to cattle, displacing grasses and other cattle food and rendering rangeland worthless.

(A) States have been invaded by leafy spurge, a herbaceous plant from Eurasia with milky sap that gives mouth sores to cattle, displacing grasses and other cattle food and rendering

(B) States have been invaded by leafy spurge, a herbaceous plant from Eurasia, with milky sap, that gives mouth sores to cattle and displaces grasses and other cattle food, rendering

(C) States have been invaded by leafy spurge, a herbaceous plant from Eurasia having milky sap that gives mouth sores to cattle and displacing grasses and other cattle food, rendering

(D) States, having been invaded by leafy spurge, a herbaceous plant from Eurasia with milky sap that gives mouth sores to cattle, displaces grasses and other cattle food, and renders

(E) States, having been invaded by leafy spurge, a herbaceous plant from Eurasia that has milky sap giving mouth sores to cattle and displacing grasses and other cattle food, rendering

752. <u>While it costs about the same to run nuclear plants as other types of power plants, it is the fixed costs that stem from building nuclear plants that makes it more expensive for them to generate electricity.</u>

(A) While it costs about the same to run nuclear plants as other types of power plants, it is the fixed costs that stem from building nuclear plants that makes it more expensive for them to generate electricity.

(B) While the cost of running nuclear plants is about the same as for other types of power plants, the fixed costs that stem from building nuclear plants make the electricity they generate more expensive.

(C) Even though it costs about the same to run nuclear plants as for other types of power plants, it is the fixed costs that stem from building nuclear plants that makes the electricity they generate more expensive.

(D) It costs about the same to run nuclear plants as for other types of power plants, whereas the electricity they generate is more expensive, stemming from the fixed costs of building nuclear plants.

(E) The cost of running nuclear plants is about the same as other types of power plants, but the electricity they generate is made more expensive because of the fixed costs stemming from building nuclear plants.

753. The 32 species that make up the dolphin family are closely related to whales and in fact <u>include the animal known as the killer whale, which can grow to be 30 feet long and is</u> famous for its aggressive hunting pods.

(A) include the animal known as the killer whale, which can grow to be 30 feet long and is

(B) include the animal known as the killer whale, growing as big as 30 feet long and

(C) include the animal known as the killer whale, growing up to 30 feet long and being

(D) includes the animal known as the killer whale, which can grow as big as 30 feet long and is

(E) includes the animal known as the killer whale, which can grow to be 30 feet long and it is

754. The first trenches <u>that were cut into a 500-acre site at Tell Hamoukar, Syria, have yielded strong evidence for centrally administered complex societies in northern regions of the Middle East that were arising simultaneously with but</u> independently of the more celebrated city-states of southern Mesopotamia, in what is now southern Iraq.

(A) that were cut into a 500-acre site at Tell Hamoukar, Syria, have yielded strong evidence for centrally administered complex societies in northern regions of the Middle East that were arising simultaneously with but

(B) that were cut into a 500-acre site at Tell Hamoukar, Syria, yields strong evidence that centrally administered complex societies in northern regions of the Middle East were arising simultaneously with but also

(C) having been cut into a 500-acre site at Tell Hamoukar, Syria, have yielded strong evidence that centrally administered complex societies in northern regions of the Middle East were arising simultaneously but

(D) cut into a 500-acre site at Tell Hamoukar, Syria, yields strong evidence of centrally administered complex societies in northern regions of the Middle East arising simultaneously but also

(E) cut into a 500-acre site at Tell Hamoukar, Syria, have yielded strong evidence that centrally administered complex societies in northern regions of the Middle East arose simultaneously with but

755. Companies are relying more and more on networked computers for such critical tasks as inventory management, electronic funds transfer, and electronic data interchange, in which standard business transactions are handled via computer rather than on paper.

(A) in which standard business transactions are handled via computer rather than on paper
(B) where computers handle standard business transactions rather than on paper
(C) in which computers handle standard business transactions instead of on paper
(D) where standard business transactions are handled, not with paper, but instead via computer
(E) in which standard business transactions are being handled via computer, in place of on paper

756. Combining enormous physical strength with higher intelligence, the Neanderthals appear as equipped for facing any obstacle the environment could put in their path, but their relatively sudden disappearance during the Paleolithic era indicates that an inability to adapt to some environmental change led to their extinction.

(A) appear as equipped for facing any obstacle the environment could put in their path,
(B) appear to have been equipped to face any obstacle the environment could put in their path,
(C) appear as equipped to face any obstacle the environment could put in their paths,
(D) appeared as equipped to face any obstacle the environment could put in their paths,
(E) appeared to have been equipped for facing any obstacle the environment could put in their path,

757. To map Earth's interior, geologists use a network of seismometers to chart seismic waves that originate in the earth's crust and ricochet around its interior, most rapidly traveling through cold, dense regions and slower through hotter rocks.

(A) interior, most rapidly traveling through cold, dense regions and slower
(B) interior, which travel most rapidly through cold, dense regions, and more slowly
(C) interior, traveling most rapidly through cold, dense regions and more slowly
(D) interior and most rapidly travel through cold, dense regions, and slower
(E) interior and that travel most rapidly through cold, dense regions and slower

758. Prices at the producer level are only 1.3 percent higher now than a year ago and are going down, even though floods in the Midwest and drought in the South are hurting crops and therefore raised corn and soybean prices.

(A) than a year ago and are going down, even though floods in the Midwest and drought in the South are hurting crops and therefore raised
(B) than those of a year ago and are going down, even though floods in the Midwest and drought in the South are hurting crops and therefore raising
(C) than a year ago and are going down, despite floods in the Midwest and drought in the South, and are hurting crops and therefore raising
(D) as those of a year ago and are going down, even though floods in the Midwest and drought in the South hurt crops and therefore raise
(E) as they were a year ago and are going down, despite floods in the Midwest and drought in the South, and are hurting crops and therefore raising

759. Fossils of the arm of a sloth found in Puerto Rico in 1991, and dated at 34 million years old, made it the earliest known mammal of the Greater Antilles Islands.

(A) sloth found in Puerto Rico in 1991, and dated at 34 million years old, made it the earliest known mammal of
(B) sloth, that they found in Puerto Rico in 1991, has been dated at 34 million years old, thus making it the earliest mammal known on
(C) sloth that was found in Puerto Rico in 1991, was dated at 34 million years old, making this the earliest known mammal of
(D) sloth, found in Puerto Rico in 1991, have been dated at 34 million years old, making the sloth the earliest known mammal on
(E) sloth which, found in Puerto Rico in 1991, was dated at 34 million years old, made the sloth the earliest known mammal of

760. Recently physicians have determined that stomach ulcers are not caused by stress, alcohol, or rich foods, but a bacterium that dwells in the mucous lining of the stomach.

(A) not caused by stress, alcohol, or rich foods, but
(B) not caused by stress, alcohol, or rich foods, but are by
(C) caused not by stress, alcohol, or rich foods, but by
(D) caused not by stress, alcohol, and rich foods, but
(E) caused not by stress, alcohol, and rich foods, but are by

761. The eyes of the elephant seal adapt to darkness more quickly than any other animal yet tested, thus allowing it to hunt efficiently under the gloomy conditions at its feeding depth of between 300 and 700 meters.

(A) The eyes of the elephant seal adapt to darkness more quickly than any other animal yet tested, thus allowing it
(B) The eyes of the elephant seal adapt to darkness more quickly than does any other animal yet tested, allowing them
(C) The eyes of the elephant seal adapt to darkness more quickly than do those of any other animal yet tested, allowing it
(D) Because they adapt to darkness more quickly than any other animal yet tested, the eyes of the elephant seal allow it
(E) Because the eyes of the elephant seal adapt to darkness more quickly than do those of any other animal yet tested, it allows them

762. A mutual fund having billions of dollars in assets will typically invest that money in hundreds of companies, rarely holding more than one percent of the shares of any particular corporation.

(A) companies, rarely holding more than one percent
(B) companies, and it is rare to hold at least one percent or more
(C) companies and rarely do they hold more than one percent
(D) companies, so that they rarely hold more than one percent
(E) companies; rarely do they hold one percent or more

763. Positing an enormous volcanic explosion at the end of the Permian period would explain the presence of a buried crater, account for the presence of the element iridium (originating deep within the earth), and the presence of quartz having been shattered by high-impact shock waves.

(A) account for the presence of the element iridium (originating deep within the earth), and the presence of quartz having been
(B) of the element iridium (originating deep within the earth), and of quartz
(C) the element iridium (originating deep within the earth), and explain the presence of quartz having been
(D) the presence of the element iridium (originating deep within the earth), and explain the presence of quartz
(E) explain the element iridium (originating deep within the earth), and the presence of quartz

764. The 19-year-old pianist and composer performed his most recent work all over Europe, Asia, and North America last year, winning prestigious awards in both London as well as Tokyo for his achievement at so young an age, and he is hoping to continue composing now that he has returned to Chicago.

(A) winning prestigious awards in both London as well as Tokyo for his achievement at so young an age, and he is hoping
(B) winning prestigious awards both in London and Tokyo for his achievement at such a young age, and hoping
(C) having won prestigious awards both in London and Tokyo for his achievement at so young an age, hoping
(D) winning prestigious awards in both London and Tokyo for his achievement at such a young age, and he hopes
(E) having won prestigious awards both in London as well as Tokyo for his achievement at so young an age, and he hopes

765. Starfish, with anywhere from five to eight arms, have a strong regenerative ability, and if one arm is lost it quickly replaces it, sometimes by the animal overcompensating and growing an extra one or two.

(A) one arm is lost it quickly replaces it, sometimes by the animal overcompensating and

(B) one arm is lost it is quickly replaced, with the animal sometimes overcompensating and

(C) they lose one arm they quickly replace it, sometimes by the animal overcompensating,

(D) they lose one arm they are quickly replaced, with the animal sometimes overcompensating,

(E) they lose one arm it is quickly replaced, sometimes with the animal overcompensating,

766. In 2000, a mere two dozen products accounted for half the increase in spending on prescription drugs, a phenomenon that is explained not just because of more expensive drugs but by the fact that doctors are writing many more prescriptions for higher-cost drugs.

(A) a phenomenon that is explained not just because of more expensive drugs but by the fact that doctors are writing

(B) a phenomenon that is explained not just by the fact that drugs are becoming more expensive but also by the fact that doctors are writing

(C) a phenomenon occurring not just because of drugs that are becoming more expensive but because of doctors having also written

(D) which occurred not just because drugs are becoming more expensive but doctors are also writing

(E) which occurred not just because of more expensive drugs but because doctors have also written

767. Similar to other early Mississippi Delta blues singers, the music of Robert Johnson arose from an oral tradition beginning with a mixture of chants, fiddle tunes, and religious music and only gradually evolved into the blues.

(A) Similar to other early Mississippi Delta blues singers, the music of Robert Johnson arose from an oral tradition beginning with

(B) Similar to that of other early Mississippi Delta blues singers, Robert Johnson made music that arose from an oral tradition that began with

(C) As with other early Mississippi Delta blues singers, Robert Johnson made music that arose from an oral tradition beginning as

(D) Like other early Mississippi Delta blues singers, Robert Johnson's music arose from an oral tradition beginning with

(E) Like the music of other early Mississippi Delta blues singers, the music of Robert Johnson arose from an oral tradition that began as

768. Thelonious Monk, who was a jazz pianist and composer, produced a body of work both rooted in the stride-piano tradition of Willie (The Lion) Smith and Duke Ellington, yet in many ways he stood apart from the mainstream jazz repertory.

(A) Thelonious Monk, who was a jazz pianist and composer, produced a body of work both rooted

(B) Thelonious Monk, the jazz pianist and composer, produced a body of work that was rooted both

(C) Jazz pianist and composer Thelonious Monk, who produced a body of work rooted

(D) Jazz pianist and composer Thelonious Monk produced a body of work that was rooted

(E) Jazz pianist and composer Thelonious Monk produced a body of work rooted both

769. Nobody knows exactly how many languages there are in the world, partly because of the difficulty of distinguishing between a language and the sublanguages or dialects within it, but those who have tried to count typically have found about five thousand.

(A) and the sublanguages or dialects within it, but those who have tried to count typically have found

(B) and the sublanguages or dialects within them, with those who have tried counting typically finding

(C) and the sublanguages or dialects within it, but those who have tried counting it typically find

(D) or the sublanguages or dialects within them, but those who tried to count them typically found

(E) or the sublanguages or dialects within them, with those who have tried to count typically finding

770. Although a number of excellent studies narrate the development of domestic technology and its impact on housewifery, these works do not discuss the contributions of the women employed by manufacturers and utility companies as product demonstrators and publicists, who initially promoted new and unfamiliar technology to female consumers.

(A) by manufacturers and utility companies as product demonstrators and publicists,
(B) to be product demonstrators and publicists by manufacturers and utility companies,
(C) to demonstrate and publicize their products by manufacturers and utility companies
(D) by manufacturers and utility companies to be demonstrators and publicists of their products
(E) by manufacturers and utility companies to demonstrate and publicize their products

771. The absence from business and financial records of the nineteenth century of statistics about women leave us with no record of the jobs that were performed by women and how they survived economically.

(A) from business and financial records of the nineteenth century of statistics about women leave us with no record of the jobs that were performed by women and
(B) from business and financial records of statistics about women from the nineteenth century leave us with no record of what jobs women performed or
(C) of statistics for women from business and financial records in the nineteenth century leaves us with no record of either the jobs that women were performing and of
(D) of statistics on women from business and financial records in the nineteenth century leave us with no record of the jobs that women performed or of
(E) of statistics about women from business and financial records of the nineteenth century leaves us with no record of either what jobs women performed or

772. Heating-oil prices are expected to be higher this year than last because refiners are paying about $5 a barrel more for crude oil than they were last year.

(A) Heating-oil prices are expected to be higher this year than last because refiners are paying about $5 a barrel more for crude oil than they were
(B) Heating-oil prices are expected to rise higher this year over last because refiners pay about $5 a barrel for crude oil more than they did
(C) Expectations are for heating-oil prices to be higher this year than last year's because refiners are paying about $5 a barrel for crude oil more than they did
(D) It is the expectation that heating-oil prices will be higher for this year over last because refiners are paying about $5 a barrel more for crude oil now than what they were
(E) It is expected that heating-oil prices will rise higher this year than last year's because refiners pay about $5 a barrel for crude oil more than they did

773. Even though Clovis points, spear points with longitudinal grooves chipped onto their faces, have been found all over North America, they are named for the New Mexico site where they were first discovered in 1932.

(A) Even though Clovis points, spear points with longitudinal grooves chipped onto their faces, have been found all over North America, they are named for the New Mexico site where they were first discovered in 1932.
(B) Although named for the New Mexico site where first discovered in 1932, Clovis points are spear points of longitudinal grooves chipped onto their faces and have been found all over North America.
(C) Named for the New Mexico site where they have been first discovered in 1932, Clovis points, spear points of longitudinal grooves chipped onto the faces, have been found all over North America.
(D) Spear points with longitudinal grooves that are chipped onto the faces, Clovis points, even though named for the New Mexico site where first discovered in 1932, but were found all over North America.
(E) While Clovis points are spear points whose faces have longitudinal grooves chipped into them, they have been found all over North America, and named for the New Mexico site where they have been first discovered in 1932.

774. Heavy commitment by an executive to a course of action, especially if it has worked well in the past, makes it likely to miss signs of incipient trouble or misinterpret them when they do appear.

(A) Heavy commitment by an executive to a course of action, especially if it has worked well in the past, makes it likely to miss signs of incipient trouble or misinterpret them when they do appear.

(B) An executive who is heavily committed to a course of action, especially one that worked well in the past, makes missing signs of incipient trouble or misinterpreting ones likely when they do appear.

(C) An executive who is heavily committed to a course of action is likely to miss or misinterpret signs of incipient trouble when they do appear, especially if it has worked well in the past.

(D) Executives' being heavily committed to a course of action, especially if it has worked well in the past, makes them likely to miss signs of incipient trouble or misinterpreting them when they do appear.

(E) Being heavily committed to a course of action, especially one that has worked well in the past, is likely to make an executive miss signs of incipient trouble or misinterpret them when they do appear.

775. According to recent studies comparing the nutritional value of meat from wild animals and meat from domesticated animals, wild animals have less total fat than do livestock fed on grain and more of a kind of fat they think is good for cardiac health.

(A) wild animals have less total fat than do livestock fed on grain and more of a kind of fat they think is

(B) wild animals have less total fat than livestock fed on grain and more of a kind of fat thought to be

(C) wild animals have less total fat than that of livestock fed on grain and have more fat of a kind thought to be

(D) total fat of wild animals is less than livestock fed on grain and they have more fat of a kind thought to be

(E) total fat is less in wild animals than that of livestock fed on grain and more of their fat is of a kind they think is

776. Yellow jackets number among the 900 or so species of the world's social wasps, wasps living in a highly cooperative and organized society where they consist almost entirely of females—the queen and her sterile female workers.

(A) wasps living in a highly cooperative and organized society where they consist almost entirely of

(B) wasps that live in a highly cooperative and organized society consisting almost entirely of

(C) which means they live in a highly cooperative and organized society, almost all

(D) which means that their society is highly cooperative, organized, and it is almost entirely

(E) living in a society that is highly cooperative, organized, and it consists of almost all

777. Before 1988, insurance companies in California were free to charge whatever rates the market would bear, needing no approval from regulators before raising rates.

(A) needing no approval from regulators before raising

(B) and it needed no approval by regulators before raising

(C) and needing no approval from regulators before they raised

(D) with approval not needed by regulators before they raised

(E) with no approval needed from regulators before the raising of

778. Marconi's conception of the radio was as a substitute for the telephone, a tool for private conversation; instead, it is precisely the opposite, a tool for communicating with a large, public audience.

(A) Marconi's conception of the radio was as a substitute for the telephone, a tool for private conversation; instead, it is

(B) Marconi conceived of the radio as a substitute for the telephone, a tool for private conversation, but which is

(C) Marconi conceived of the radio as a tool for private conversation that could substitute for the telephone; instead, it has become

(D) Marconi conceived of the radio to be a tool for private conversation, a substitute for the telephone, which has become

(E) Marconi conceived of the radio to be a substitute for the telephone, a tool for private conversation, other than what it is,

779. Because there are provisions of the new maritime code that provide that even tiny islets can be the basis for claims to the fisheries and oil fields of large sea areas, they have already stimulated international disputes over uninhabited islands.

(A) Because there are provisions of the new maritime code that provide that even tiny islets can be the basis for claims to the fisheries and oil fields of large sea areas, they have already stimulated

(B) Because the new maritime code provides that even tiny islets can be the basis for claims to the fisheries and oil fields of large sea areas, it has already stimulated

(C) Even tiny islets can be the basis for claims to the fisheries and oil fields of large sea areas under provisions of the new maritime code, already stimulating

(D) Because even tiny islets can be the basis for claims to the fisheries and oil fields of large sea areas under provisions of the new maritime code, this has already stimulated

(E) Because even tiny islets can be the basis for claims to the fisheries and oil fields of large sea areas under provisions of the new maritime code, which is already stimulating

780. Unlike the automobile company, whose research was based on crashes involving sport utility vehicles, the research conducted by the insurance company took into account such factors as a driver's age, sex, and previous driving record.

(A) company, whose research was based on

(B) company, which researched

(C) company, in its research of

(D) company's research, having been based on

(E) company's research on

781. Gusty westerly winds will continue to usher in a seasonably cool air mass into the region, as a broad area of high pressure will build and bring fair and dry weather for several days.

(A) to usher in a seasonably cool air mass into the region, as a broad area of high pressure will build and

(B) ushering in a seasonably cool air mass into the region and a broad area of high pressure will build that

(C) to usher in a seasonably cool air mass to the region, a broad area of high pressure building, and

(D) ushering a seasonably cool air mass in the region, with a broad area of high pressure building and

(E) to usher a seasonably cool air mass into the region while a broad area of high pressure builds, which will

782. With the patience of its customers and with its network strained to the breaking point, the on-line service company announced a series of new initiatives trying to relieve the congestion that has led to at least four class-action lawsuits and thousands of complaints from frustrated customers.

(A) the patience of its customers and with its network strained to the breaking point, the on-line service company announced a series of new initiatives trying to relieve

(B) the patience of its customers and its network strained to the breaking point, the on-line service company announced a series of new initiatives that try to relieve

(C) its network and the patience of its customers strained to the breaking point, the on-line service company announced a series of new initiatives to try to relieve

(D) its network and with the patience of its customers strained to the breaking point, the on-line service company announced a series of initiatives to try relieving

(E) its network and its customers' patience strained to the breaking point, the on-line service company announced a series of new initiatives to try relieving

783. November is traditionally the strongest month for sales of light trucks, but sales this past November, even when compared with sales in previous Novembers, accounted for a remarkably large share of total vehicle sales.

(A) but sales this past November, even when compared with sales in previous Novembers,

(B) but even when it is compared with previous Novembers, this past November's sales

(C) but even when they are compared with previous Novembers, sales of light trucks this past November

(D) so that compared with previous Novembers, sales of light trucks this past November

(E) so that this past November's sales, even compared with previous Novembers' sales,

784. Most of the country's biggest daily newspapers had lower circulation in the six months from October 1995 through March 1996 than a similar period a year earlier.

(A) a similar period

(B) a similar period's

(C) in a similar period

(D) that in a similar period

(E) that of a similar period

785. Mauritius was a British colony for almost 200 years, excepting for the domains of administration and teaching, the English language was never really spoken on the island.

(A) excepting for

(B) except in

(C) but except in

(D) but excepting for

(E) with the exception of

786. Although appearing less appetizing than most of their round and red supermarket cousins, heirloom tomatoes, grown from seeds saved during the previous year—they are often green and striped, or have plenty of bumps and bruises—heirlooms are more flavorful and thus in increasing demand.

(A) Although appearing less appetizing than most of their round and red supermarket cousins, heirloom tomatoes, grown from seeds saved during the previous year

(B) Although heirloom tomatoes, grown from seeds saved during the previous year, appear less appetizing than most of their round and red supermarket cousins

(C) Although they appear less appetizing than most of their round and red supermarket cousins, heirloom tomatoes, grown from seeds saved during the previous year

(D) Grown from seeds saved during the previous year, heirloom tomatoes appear less appetizing than most of their round and red supermarket cousins

(E) Heirloom tomatoes, grown from seeds saved during the previous year, although they appear less appetizing than most of their round and red supermarket cousins

787. The World Wildlife Fund has declared that global warming, a phenomenon most scientists agree to be caused by human beings in burning fossil fuels, will create havoc among migratory birds by altering the environment in ways harmful to their habitats.

(A) a phenomenon most scientists agree to be caused by human beings in burning fossil fuels,

(B) a phenomenon most scientists agree that is caused by fossil fuels burned by human beings,

(C) a phenomenon that most scientists agree is caused by human beings' burning of fossil fuels,

(D) which most scientists agree on as a phenomenon caused by human beings who burn fossil fuels,

(E) which most scientists agree to be a phenomenon caused by fossil fuels burned by human beings,

788. The largest of all the planets, not only is Jupiter three times so massive as Saturn, the next larger planet, but also possesses four of the largest satellites, or moons, in our solar system.

(A) not only is Jupiter three times so massive as Saturn, the next larger

(B) not only is Jupiter three times as massive as Saturn, the next largest

(C) Jupiter, not only three times as massive as Saturn, the next largest

(D) Jupiter not only is three times as massive as Saturn, the next largest

(E) Jupiter is not only three times so massive as Saturn, the next larger

789. While many of the dinosaur fossils found recently in northeast China seem to provide evidence of the kinship between dinosaurs and birds, the wealth of enigmatic fossils seem more likely at this stage that they will inflame debates over the origin of birds rather than settle them.

(A) seem more likely at this stage that they will inflame debates over the origin of birds rather than

(B) seem more likely that it will inflame debates over the origin of birds at this stage than

(C) seems more likely to inflame debates on the origin of birds at this stage rather than

(D) seems more likely at this stage to inflame debates over the origin of birds than to

(E) seems more likely that it will inflame debates on the origin of birds at this stage than to

790. Found only in the Western Hemisphere and surviving through extremes of climate, hummingbirds' range extends from Alaska to Tierra del Fuego, from sea-level rain forests to the edges of Andean snowfields and ice fields at altitudes of 15,000 feet.

(A) Found only in the Western Hemisphere and surviving through extremes of climate, hummingbirds' range extends

(B) Found only in the Western Hemisphere, hummingbirds survive through extremes of climate, their range extending

(C) Hummingbirds, found only in the Western Hemisphere and surviving through extremes of climate, with their range extending

(D) Hummingbirds, found only in the Western Hemisphere and surviving through extremes of climate, their range extends

(E) Hummingbirds are found only in the Western Hemisphere, survive through extremes of climate, and their range extends

791. She was less successful after she had emigrated to New York compared to her native Germany, photographer Lotte Jacobi nevertheless earned a small group of discerning admirers, and her photographs were eventually exhibited in prestigious galleries across the United States.

(A) She was less successful after she had emigrated to New York compared to

(B) Being less successful after she had emigrated to New York as compared to

(C) Less successful after she emigrated to New York than she had been in

(D) Although she was less successful after emigrating to New York when compared to

(E) She had been less successful after emigrating to New York than in

792. Scientists have recently found evidence that black holes—regions of space in which matter is so concentrated and the pull of gravity so powerful that nothing, not even light, can emerge from them—probably exist at the core of nearly all galaxies and the mass of each black hole is proportional to its host galaxy.

(A) exist at the core of nearly all galaxies and the mass of each black hole is proportional to

(B) exist at the core of nearly all galaxies and that the mass of each black hole is proportional to that of

(C) exist at the core of nearly all galaxies, and that the mass of each black hole is proportional to

(D) exists at the core of nearly all galaxies, and that the mass of each black hole is proportional to that of

(E) exists at the core of nearly all galaxies and the mass of each black hole is proportional to that of

793. The use of lie detectors is based on the assumption that lying produces emotional reactions in an individual that, in turn, create unconscious physiological responses.

(A) that, in turn, create unconscious physiological responses

(B) that creates unconscious physiological responses in turn

(C) creating, in turn, unconscious physiological responses

(D) to create, in turn, physiological responses that are unconscious

(E) who creates unconscious physiological responses in turn

794. Australian embryologists have found evidence that suggests that the elephant is descended from an aquatic animal, and its trunk originally evolving as a kind of snorkel.

(A) that suggests that the elephant is descended from an aquatic animal, and its trunk originally evolving

(B) that has suggested the elephant descended from an aquatic animal, its trunk originally evolving

(C) suggesting that the elephant had descended from an aquatic animal with its trunk originally evolved

(D) to suggest that the elephant had descended from an aquatic animal and its trunk originally evolved

(E) to suggest that the elephant is descended from an aquatic animal and that its trunk originally evolved

795. Most efforts to combat such mosquito-borne diseases like malaria and dengue have focused either on the vaccination of humans or on exterminating mosquitoes with pesticides.

(A) like malaria and dengue have focused either on the vaccination of humans or on exterminating

(B) like malaria and dengue have focused either on vaccinating of humans or on the extermination of

(C) as malaria and dengue have focused on either vaccinating humans or on exterminating

(D) as malaria and dengue have focused on either vaccinating of humans or on extermination of

(E) as malaria and dengue have focused on either vaccinating humans or exterminating

796. Among the Tsonga, a Bantu-speaking group of tribes in southeastern Africa, dance teams represent their own chief at the court of each other, providing entertainment in return for food, drink, and lodging.

(A) the court of each other, providing entertainment in return for

(B) the court of another and provide entertainment in return for

(C) the court of the other, so as to provide entertainment as a return on

(D) each other's court, entertainment being provided in return for

(E) another's court and provide entertainment as a return on

797. Almost like clones in their similarity to one another, the cheetah species' homogeneity makes them especially vulnerable to disease.

(A) the cheetah species' homogeneity makes them especially vulnerable to disease

(B) the cheetah species is especially vulnerable to disease because of its homogeneity

(C) the homogeneity of the cheetah species makes it especially vulnerable to disease

(D) homogeneity makes members of the cheetah species especially vulnerable to disease

(E) members of the cheetah species are especially vulnerable to disease because of their homogeneity

798. As sources of electrical power, windmills now account for only about 2,500 megawatts nationwide, but production is almost expected to double by the end of the year, which would provide enough electricity for 1.3 million households.

(A) almost expected to double by the end of the year, which would provide

(B) almost expected that it will double by the end of the year, thus providing

(C) expected that it will almost double by the end of the year to provide

(D) expected almost to double by the end of the year and thus to provide

(E) expected almost to double by the end of the year, which would thus be providing

799. While most of the earliest known ball courts in Mesoamerica date to 900–400 B.C., waterlogged latex balls found at El Manati and representations of ballplayers painted on ceramics found at San Lorenzo attest to the fact that the Mesoamerican ballgame was well established by the mid-thirteenth century B.C.

(A) waterlogged latex balls found at El Manati and representations of ballplayers painted on ceramics found at San Lorenzo attest

(B) waterlogged latex balls found at El Manati and the painting of representations of ballplayers on ceramics found at San Lorenzo attests

(C) waterlogged latex balls found at El Manati and ceramics painted with representations of ballplayers found at San Lorenzo attests

(D) the finding of waterlogged latex balls at El Manati and the painting of representations of ballplayers on ceramics found at San Lorenzo attests

(E) the finding of waterlogged latex balls at El Manati and of representations of ballplayers painted on ceramics at San Lorenzo attest

800. As criminal activity on the Internet becomes more and more sophisticated, not only are thieves able to divert cash from company bank accounts, they can also pilfer valuable information such as business development strategies, new product specifications, and contract bidding plans, and sell the data to competitors.

(A) they can also pilfer valuable information such as business development strategies, new product specifications, and contract bidding plans, and sell

(B) they can also pilfer valuable information that includes business development strategies, new product specifications, and contract bidding plans, and selling

(C) also pilfering valuable information including business development strategies, new product specifications, and contract bidding plans, selling

(D) but also pilfer valuable information such as business development strategies, new product specifications, and contract bidding plans to sell

(E) but also pilfering valuable information such as business development strategies, new product specifications, and contract bidding plans and selling

801. Last week local shrimpers held a news conference to take some credit for the resurgence of the rare Kemp's ridley turtle, saying that their compliance with laws requiring that turtle-excluder devices be on shrimp nets protect adult sea turtles.

(A) requiring that turtle-excluder devices be on shrimp nets protect

(B) requiring turtle-excluder devices on shrimp nets is protecting

(C) that require turtle-excluder devices on shrimp nets protect

(D) to require turtle-excluder devices on shrimp nets are protecting

(E) to require turtle-excluder devices on shrimp nets is protecting

802. A ruined structure found at Aqaba, Jordan, was probably a church, as indicated in its eastward orientation and by its overall plan, as well as artifacts, such as glass oil-lamp fragments, found at the site.

(A) A ruined structure found at Aqaba, Jordan, was probably a church, as indicated in its eastward orientation and by its overall plan, as well as

(B) A ruined structure found at Aqaba, Jordan, once probably being a church, was indicated by its eastward orientation, overall plan, and

(C) Indicating that a ruined structure found at Aqaba, Jordan, was probably a church were its eastward orientation and overall plan, but also the

(D) A ruined structure found at Aqaba, Jordan, was probably a church, as indicates its eastward orientation and overall plan, as well as the

(E) That a ruined structure found at Aqaba, Jordan, was probably a church is indicated by its eastward orientation and overall plan, as well as by the

803. In the major cities of industrialized countries at the end of the nineteenth century, important public places such as theaters, restaurants, shops, and banks had installed electric lighting, but electricity was in less than 1 percent of homes, where lighting was still provided mainly by candles or gas.

(A) electricity was in less than 1 percent of homes, where lighting was still

(B) electricity was in less than 1 percent of homes and lighting still

(C) there had been less than 1 percent of homes with electricity, where lighting was still being

(D) there was less than 1 percent of homes that had electricity, having lighting that was still

(E) less than 1 percent of homes had electricity, where lighting had still been

804. By 1999, astronomers had discovered 17 nearby stars that are orbited by planets about the size of Jupiter.

(A) had discovered 17 nearby stars that are orbited by planets

(B) had discovered 17 nearby stars with planets orbiting them that were

(C) had discovered that there were 17 nearby stars that were orbited by planets

(D) have discovered 17 nearby stars with planets orbiting them that are

(E) have discovered that 17 nearby stars are orbited by planets

805. Although she was considered among her contemporaries to be the better poet than her husband, later Elizabeth Barrett Browning was overshadowed by his success.

(A) Although she was considered among her contemporaries to be the better poet than her husband, later Elizabeth Barrett Browning was overshadowed by his success.

(B) Although Elizabeth Barrett Browning was considered among her contemporaries as a better poet than her husband, she was later overshadowed by his success.

(C) Later overshadowed by the success of her husband, Elizabeth Barrett Browning's poetry had been considered among her contemporaries to be better than that of her husband.

(D) Although Elizabeth Barrett Browning's success was later overshadowed by that of her husband, among her contemporaries she was considered the better poet.

(E) Elizabeth Barrett Browning's poetry was considered among her contemporaries as better than her husband, but her success was later overshadowed by his.

806. In no other historical sighting did Halley's Comet cause such a worldwide sensation as did its return in 1910–1911.

(A) did its return in 1910–1911

(B) had its 1910–1911 return

(C) in its return of 1910–1911

(D) its return of 1910–1911 did

(E) its return in 1910–1911

807. Rock samples taken from the remains of an asteroid about twice the size of the 6-mile-wide asteroid that eradicated the dinosaurs has been dated to be 3.47 billion years old and thus is evidence of the earliest known asteroid impact on Earth.

(A) has been dated to be 3.47 billion years old and thus is

(B) has been dated at 3.47 billion years old and thus

(C) have been dated to be 3.47 billion years old and thus are

(D) have been dated as being 3.47 billion years old and thus

(E) have been dated at 3.47 billion years old and thus are

9.7 Answer Key

668. E	703. B	738. B	773. A
669. D	704. E	739. A	774. E
670. B	705. C	740. E	775. B
671. C	706. B	741. B	776. B
672. B	707. D	742. A	777. A
673. C	708. E	743. A	778. C
674. D	709. E	744. E	779. B
675. D	710. D	745. C	780. E
676. D	711. A	746. E	781. E
677. E	712. B	747. A	782. C
678. B	713. E	748. A	783. A
679. B	714. D	749. D	784. C
680. D	715. E	750. B	785. C
681. C	716. C	751. B	786. B
682. D	717. D	752. B	787. C
683. B	718. D	753. A	788. D
684. A	719. C	754. E	789. D
685. D	720. A	755. A	790. B
686. E	721. C	756. B	791. C
687. C	722. B	757. C	792. B
688. B	723. D	758. B	793. A
689. C	724. E	759. D	794. E
690. D	725. E	760. C	795. E
691. E	726. D	761. C	796. B
692. B	727. D	762. A	797. E
693. C	728. C	763. B	798. D
694. A	729. C	764. D	799. A
695. C	730. E	765. B	800. A
696. E	731. D	766. B	801. B
697. B	732. E	767. E	802. E
698. E	733. B	768. D	803. A
699. C	734. B	769. A	804. A
700. D	735. E	770. A	805. D
701. A	736. A	771. E	806. C
702. A	737. B	772. A	807. E

9.8 Answer Explanations

The following discussion of sentence correction is intended to familiarize you with the most efficient and effective approaches to these kinds of questions. The particular questions in this chapter are generally representative of the kinds of sentence correction questions you will encounter on the GMAT exam.

668. In a review of 2,000 studies of human behavior that date back to the 1940s, two Swiss psychologists, declaring that since most of the studies had failed to control for such variables as social class and family size, none could be taken seriously.

(A) psychologists, declaring that since most of the studies had failed to control for such variables as social class and family size,

(B) psychologists, declaring that most of the studies failed in not controlling for such variables like social class and family size, and

(C) psychologists declared that since most of the studies, having failed to control for such variables as social class and family size,

(D) psychologists declared that since most of the studies fail in controlling for such variables like social class and family size,

(E) psychologists declared that since most of the studies had failed to control for variables such as social class and family size,

Verb form; Diction

The subject of the sentence, *two Swiss psychologists,* needs a main verb. The *-ing* verb form *declaring* cannot, on its own, be the main verb of a correct English sentence. Furthermore, the clause that addresses the reason for not taking the studies also seriously needs a subject (*most of the studies*) and a verb (*had failed*).

A The sentence needs a verb form that agrees in person and number with the subject *two Swiss psychologists* and that is in the appropriate tense.

B In addition to the problem with *declaring*, explained above, in this version of the sentence the phrase *failed in not controlling for* is awkward and does not mean the same thing as *failed to control for*. Also, the expression *such X like Y* is incorrect in English; the correct usage is *such X as Y*.

C The correct form for the sentence's main verb *declared* is used here, but *having failed* is a participial form and as such cannot be the main verb in the clause.

D English has a rule of sequence of tenses: once a verb form is marked for past tense, the following verb forms that describe the same object or event have to be in the past tense as well. Thus, *fail* is the wrong verb form. The expression *such X like Y* is incorrect in English; the correct usage is *such X as Y*.

E **Correct.** The subject *two Swiss psychologists* is followed by a verb in the past tense (*declared*); the dependent clause *since … family size* also has the correct verb form (*had failed*).

The correct answer is E.

669. In her presentation, the head of the Better Business Bureau emphasized that companies should think of the cost of conventions and other similar gatherings as not an expense, but as an investment in networking that will pay dividends.

(A) as not an expense, but as

(B) as not expense but

(C) not an expense, rather

(D) not as an expense, but as

(E) not in terms of expense, but

Parallelism; Idiom

This sentence is constructed around *not as X, but as Y*, which must start with the word *not* in accordance with this idiomatic pattern, and express both parts in a parallel way.

A This sentence improperly places *as* before *not.*

B This sentence improperly places *as* before *not.*

C This version lacks the required words *as* and *but*.

D Correct. The idiom has all of its parts and expresses the two opposed concepts in parallel terms.

E Although *in terms of* is an acceptable substitute for *as,* the construction is no longer parallel due to the lack of a second *in terms of* (or *as*) after *but*.

The correct answer is D.

670. Recent interdisciplinary studies advance the argument that emotions, including those deemed personal or private is a social phenomenon, though one inseparable from bodily response.

(A) private is a social phenomenon, though one inseparable

(B) private, are social phenomena that are inseparable

(C) private are a social phenomenon but are not those separable

(D) private—are social phenomena but not separable

(E) also as private emotions, are social phenomena not inseparable

Agreement; Rhetorical construction

The main problem is one of agreement: in the subordinate clause starting with *that*, the subject is the plural *emotions*, which demands the verb *are*, not *is*. Also, the phrase starting with *including* is a parenthetical expression that needs to be set off from the rest of the clause, with some punctuation to indicate a pause at its end (after *private*).

A The verb form *is* is incorrect, and should instead be *are*; the parenthetical expression is not separated at its end from the rest of the clause.

B Correct. *Are* is the correct agreeing verb form, and the comma after *private* correctly sets off the parenthetical expression.

C *Are* is correct, but nothing after *private* sets off the parenthetical expression from the subsequent material. In addition, *not those separable* is awkwardly phrased; it would be better as *not separable* or *inseparable* as in the correct answer choice B.

D The dash would be correct to set off the parenthetical expression only if *including* had been immediately preceded by a dash; otherwise a comma is needed. The phrase *not separable* is awkward; it would be better as *are not separable* or *are inseparable.*

E The phrase *also as private emotions* is wordy and unidiomatic. The phrase *social phenomena not inseparable* not only does not express the intended meaning, but is also awkward without a verb and a relative pronoun such as *that*: a better phrasing is *social phenomena that are not separable.*

The correct answer is B.

671. Manufacturers rate batteries in watt-hours; if they rate the watt-hour higher, the longer the battery can be expected to last.

(A) if they rate the watt-hour higher, the longer

(B) rating the watt-hour higher, it is that much longer

(C) the higher the watt-hour rating, the longer

(D) the higher the watt-hour rating, it is that much longer that

(E) when the watt-hour rating is higher, the longer it is

Logical predication; Grammatical construction; Parallelism

There is a cause-and-effect connection between the watt-hour rating and the battery life; therefore, the phrases describing the cause and effect have to be expressed in two parallel grammatical constructions using the two comparative forms of the modifiers *higher* and *longer*.

A Because of the way this version is constructed, the pronoun *they,* referring to *manufacturers,* illogically suggests that the manufacturers can make the batteries last longer simply by rating them higher. The cause and effect is also unparallel.

B *Rating the watt-hour higher* needs a subject; this faulty construction is known as a dangling modifier. It is possible to construe it as referring to *manufacturers,* which would be confusing. See explanation of (A) above.

C Correct. This version uses the correct logical and grammatical structure *the higher X, … the longer Y.*

D This version is unparallel and ungrammatical. The correct form is *the higher X, the longer Y.*

E This version is unparallel and ungrammatical. The correct form is *the higher X, the longer Y.*

The correct answer is C.

672. At the end of the 1930s, Duke Ellington was looking for a composer to assist him—<u>someone not only who could arrange music for his successful big band, but mirroring his eccentric writing style as well in order to finish</u> the many pieces he had started but never completed.

(A) someone not only who could arrange music for his successful big band, but mirroring his eccentric writing style as well in order to finish

(B) someone who could not only arrange music for his successful big band, but also mirror his eccentric writing style in order to finish

(C) someone who not only could arrange music for his successful big band, but also to mirror his eccentric writing style in finishing

(D) that being someone who could not only arrange music for his successful big band, but mirroring his eccentric writing style for finishing

(E) being someone not only who could arrange music for his successful big band, but mirror his eccentric writing style as well, finishing

Rhetorical construction; Parallelism

In describing the qualities Duke Ellington sought in a composer, the sentence uses the construction *not only … but also….* In this construction the clauses need to be parallel—for example, *not only subject verb, but also subject verb.*

A This version is wordy, awkward, and unparallel. Furthermore, the two verbs in the *not only … but also…* construction have to be in the same form, while here we have *arrange* and *mirroring.*

B **Correct.** This version exemplifies a truly parallel construction. Here, *not only* and *but also* are directly in front of the verbs they introduce. The verbs denoting the two qualities in the sought-after composer are the same form: *arrange, mirror.*

C This version is awkward and unparallel. The two verbs have to be in the same form, while here we have *arrange* and *to mirror.* Finally, the best way to express the causal relationship between the composer's qualities and finishing Ellington's pieces is to use the conjunction *in order to.*

D Instead of the shorter and clearer *someone who*, this version uses the longer phrase *that being someone who*, which is overly wordy. Furthermore, the verbs are not in the same form and so the construction is unparallel. Finally, the best way to express the causal relationship between the composer's qualities and finishing Ellington's pieces is to use the conjunction *in order to.*

E Placing *being* in front of *someone* is potentially misleading; it could illogically refer to Ellington himself. The *not only … but also …* construction is also unparallel. Finally, the best way to express the causal relationship between this composer's qualities and finishing Ellington's pieces is to use the conjunction *in order to.*

The correct answer is B.

673. While Noble Sissle may be best known for his collaboration with Eubie Blake, as both a vaudeville performer <u>and as a lyricist for songs and Broadway musicals, also enjoying</u> an independent career as a singer with such groups as Hahn's Jubilee Singers.

(A) and as a lyricist for songs and Broadway musicals, also enjoying

(B) and writing lyrics for songs and Broadway musicals, also enjoying

(C) and a lyricist for songs and Broadway musicals, he also enjoyed

(D) as well as writing lyrics for songs and Broadway musicals, he also enjoyed

(E) as well as a lyricist for songs and Broadway musicals, he had also enjoyed

Grammatical construction; Idiom; Parallelism

As worded, this sentence opens with a dependent clause (a clause that cannot stand on its own), which requires a main clause (also known as an independent clause) to complete the sentence;

however, there is no main clause. Also, given the placement of *as* before *both*, the *as* before *a lyricist* is incorrect. It would be acceptable to write *as both a vaudeville performer and a lyricist* or to write *both as a vaudeville performer and as a lyricist*; it is not acceptable to mix the two forms, as is done here.

A The dependent clause, *While . . . Broadway musicals*, is followed by a participial phrase rather than a main clause and is therefore ungrammatical. Furthermore, the word *as* before *a lyricist* violates the parallel structure required by the phrase *both . . . and*.

B The construction *as both a performer and writing lyrics* is incorrect. Also, like (A), this version of the sentence does not supply a main clause.

C **Correct.** Unlike (A) and (B), this version has a main clause. Also, unlike the other version, it correctly uses the *both x and y* form.

D Although this version does supply the main clause anticipated by *While . . .*, its use *as both a vaudeville performer as well as writing lyrics* is incorrect.

E This version's use of *both x as well as y* instead of *both x and y* is incorrect. It also introduces an inexplicable past perfect verb, *had . . . enjoyed*, in the main clause.

The correct answer is C.

674. Air traffic routes over the North Pole are currently used by only two or three planes a day, but it was found by a joint Canadian–Russian study to be both feasible as well as desirable if those routes are opened to thousands more commercial planes a year.

(A) Air traffic routes over the North Pole are currently used by only two or three planes a day, but it was found by a joint Canadian–Russian study to be both feasible as well as desirable if those routes are opened to thousands more commercial planes a year.

(B) Currently used by only two or three planes a day, a joint Canadian–Russian study has found that if air traffic routes over the North Pole are opened to thousands more commercial planes a year, it would be both feasible and desirable.

(C) A joint Canadian–Russian study, finding it to be both feasible as well as desirable to open air traffic routes over the North Pole, which are currently used by only two or three planes a day, to thousands more commercial planes a year.

(D) Although air traffic routes over the North Pole are currently used by only two or three planes a day, a joint Canadian–Russian study has found that opening those routes to thousands more commercial planes a year is both feasible and desirable.

(E) With air traffic routes over the North Pole currently used by only two or three planes a day, opening those routes to thousands more commercial planes a year has been found by a joint Canadian—Russian study as both feasible and desirable.

Rhetorical construction; Verb form; Logical predication

The point of the sentence is to share the results of a study about air routes over the North Pole, but the wording is confusing and verbose. The passive construction *it was found by a joint Canadian–Russian study to be* could be expressed more directly and clearly in active voice: *a joint Canadian–Russian study has found.*

A The passive construction *it was found by a joint Canadian–Russian study to be*, especially followed by the conditional *if*, is wordy, awkward, and unclear.

B *Used by only two or three planes* illogically modifies *a joint Canadian–Russian study*; the pronoun *it* has no clear antecedent.

C The subject *A joint Canadian–Russian study* has no verb; *to thousands more commercial planes* is located too far away from *to open*, which it is intended to modify.

D **Correct.** The sentence uses correctly placed modifiers and the active voice to explain clearly what a *joint Canadian–Russian study has found.*

E The passive construction *opening those routes . . . has been found by a joint Canadian–Russian study as both* is wordy and unidiomatic.

The correct answer is D.

675. From an experiment using special extrasensory perception cards, each bearing one of a set of symbols, parapsychologist Joseph Banks Rhine claimed statistical proof for subjects who could use thought transference to identify a card in the dealer's hand.

(A) for subjects who could use thought transference to identify a card in the dealer's hand
(B) for a card in the dealer's hand to be identified by subjects with thought transference
(C) of subjects able to identify with thought transference a card in the dealer's hand
(D) that subjects could identify a card in the dealer's hand by using thought transference
(E) that subjects are capable to use thought transference for identifying a card in the dealer's hand

Idiom; Rhetorical construction

This sentence is meant to indicate that Joseph Banks Rhine claimed that a certain experiment statistically proved that subjects could identify what symbol was on a card in a dealer's hand by using thought transference. The present version of the sentence does not convey the intended meaning well, however. What should follow *proof* is a statement of the assertion that Rhine claims the experiment has statistically proved, linked to the word *proof* by the word *that*. Instead *proof* is followed by a prepositional phrase *for subjects who. . . .*

A This version of the sentence inappropriately attempts to describe the claim by using a prepositional phrase, *for subjects who. . . .*

B Like (A), this version of the sentence inappropriately attempts to describe the claim by using a prepositional phrase, *for a card in. . . .*

C Like (A) and (B), this version of the sentence inappropriately attempts to describe the claim by using a prepositional phrase. While *proof* might reasonably be followed by *of*, the phrase that follows the preposition is ungrammatical, requiring a participle to modify *subjects*, such as *being able to. . . .*

D **Correct.** This version correctly uses the idiom *proof that* followed by an assertion.

E While this version of the sentence correctly follows *proof* with *that* followed by an assertion, it fails to use the appropriate idiom with *capable*; instead of *capable to use*, it should have *capable of using*.

The correct answer is D.

676. A long-term study of some 1,000 physicians indicates that the more coffee these doctors drank, the more they had a likelihood of coronary disease.

(A) more they had a likelihood of coronary disease
(B) more was their likelihood of having coronary disease
(C) more they would have a likelihood to have coronary disease
(D) greater was their likelihood of having coronary disease
(E) greater was coronary disease likely

Idiom; Rhetorical construction

This sentence describes the results of a study in which researchers found a correlation between the amounts of coffee that people drank and their likelihood of coronary disease. It most eloquently expresses this correlation as a comparison of parallel forms, using the idiom *the + comparative adjective phrase . . . the + comparative adjective phrase*. The two adjective phrases should have the same grammatical form.

A This version obscures the intended correlation between *coffee* and *likelihood*. The phrase *the more they had a likelihood* somewhat illogically indicates that the research subjects had likelihood to a greater degree rather than that their likelihood was greater.

B Although the adverb *more* is used to indicate a greater degree or extent in phrases such as *more likely*, the adjective *more* normally indicates greater quantity. Thus, the use of *more* as an adjective modifying *their likelihood* is nonstandard. Differences in a particular type of likelihood are normally thought of as matters of degree, not of quantity. *Greater* is the preferred adjective for indicating such differences.

C The conditional verb phrase *would have a likelihood to have* is redundant, wordy, and not comparable to the simple past tense *drank*.

D Correct. This version uses proper wording and is clear and concise.

E This completion of the comparison is not idiomatic; moreover, it is ungrammatical, attempting to use an adjective *greater* to describe an adverb, *likely*.

The correct answer is D.

677. The intricate structure of the compound insect eye, having hundreds of miniature eyes called ommatidia, help explain why scientists have assumed that it evolved independently of the vertebrate eye.

(A) having hundreds of miniature eyes called ommatidia, help explain why scientists have assumed that it

(B) having hundreds of miniature eyes that are called ommatidia, helps explain why scientists have assumed that they

(C) with its hundreds of miniature eyes that are called ommatidia, helps explain scientists' assuming that they

(D) with its hundreds of miniature eyes called ommatidia, help explain scientists' assuming that it

(E) with its hundreds of miniature eyes called ommatidia, helps explain why scientists have assumed that it

Agreement; Logical predication

This sentence addresses why scientists have decided that the vertebrate eye and the insect eye evolved independently of each other. The insect eye is much more intricate, with hundreds of miniature eyes. The sentence needs to be clear as to what has *hundreds of miniature eyes*. The *structure* or the *insect eye*? Furthermore, the singular subject *intricate structure* requires the singular verb *helps*.

A This wording misleadingly suggests that *the intricate structure* has *miniature eyes*, while the correct subject of the predicate *having* is *the compound insect eye*. Subject-verb agreement is violated.

B This wording misleads as in (A). Furthermore, the pronoun at the end of the underlined part of the sentence should refer back to *the compound insect eye*, so it cannot be plural.

C The phrase *helps explain scientists' assuming* correctly agrees with the subject *structure*. However, it is nonstandard and awkward; the use of *assuming* with the possessive is unwarranted. Finally, the pronoun at the end of the underlined part of the sentence should refer back to *the compound insect eye*, so it cannot be plural.

D The subject *structure* and the verb *help* do not agree in number. As in (C), *explain scientists' assuming* is verbose and awkward, and the use of the *assuming* with the possessive makes the construction unnecessarily complex.

E Correct. The phrase *with its hundreds* correctly refers back to *the compound insect eye*. The verb *helps* correctly agrees with the subject *structure*. Finally, the pronoun *it* correctly refers to the singular noun *the compound insect eye*.

The correct answer is E.

678. In 1979 lack of rain reduced India's rice production to about 41 million tons, nearly 25 percent less than those of the 1978 harvest.

(A) less than those of the 1978 harvest

(B) less than the 1978 harvest

(C) less than 1978

(D) fewer than 1978

(E) fewer than that of India's 1978 harvest

Logical predication; Diction

The crucial part of this sentence is the latter part, where India's 1979 production of 41 million tons of rice is compared to the production of the previous year. What was produced in 1979 was 25 percent less than what was produced in 1978. The grammatical means of comparison have to express correctly this relationship between the two harvests. It helps if you think of 41 million tons of rice as the collective equivalent of the 1979 harvest.

A This version exhibits redundant word choice. The pronoun *those* refers to the tons of the 1978 harvest. Both harvests are measured in tons, and it is clearer and simpler to compare with the harvest itself, not with the tons of the harvest.

B Correct. This version correctly compares the 1978 harvest with the 1979 harvest.

C This version is illogical. It compares rice production in tons with a year, 1978.

D In addition to the problem described in (C) above, this version uses the wrong comparative adjective. *Fewer* refers to countable nouns, while *less* refers to quantities. Since the comparative adjective should refer to rice production, *fewer* is not appropriate.

E Since the comparative adjective should refer to rice production, *fewer* is not appropriate. Furthermore, the pronoun *that* refers back to India's rice production [*fewer than the rice production of India's 1978 harvest*] and is redundant. The word *harvest* is sufficient here to express the comparison.

The correct answer is B.

679. Hurricanes at first begin traveling from east to west, because that direction is the way the prevailing winds in the tropics blow, but they then veer off toward higher latitudes, in many cases changing direction toward the east before dissipating over the colder, more northerly waters or over land.

(A) Hurricanes at first begin traveling from east to west, because that direction is the way the prevailing winds in the tropics blow, but

(B) At first, hurricanes travel from east to west, because that is the direction of the prevailing winds in the tropics, but

(C) While hurricanes travel from east to west at first, the direction of the prevailing winds blowing in the tropics, and

(D) Because hurricanes at first travel from east to west, since it is the direction of the prevailing winds in the tropics,

(E) Hurricanes, beginning by traveling from east to west, because this is the direction of the prevailing winds in the tropics,

Rhetorical construction; Grammatical construction

Hurricanes at first begin traveling is redundant. The sentence could start with *At first, hurricanes travel* or with *Hurricanes begin traveling*; there is no need to have both *at first* and *begin*. A concise version of the sentence would also avoid *that direction is the way the prevailing winds in the tropics blow*. The meaning of *way* here is already conveyed by *direction*.

A *At first* and *begin* are redundant. Also, *that direction is the way the prevailing winds blow* is unnecessarily wordy.

B Correct. This version of the sentence is grammatically correct and lacks redundancy.

C This sentence begins with a dependent clause (that is, a clause that cannot stand on its own), anticipating a main clause (also known as an independent clause) to complete the sentence; a main clause does follow, but it is connected to the initial dependent clause by the coordinating conjunction *and*, which would be appropriate here only if the initial clause was of the same grammatical type (that is, was also a main clause).

D The causal conjunction *Because* suggests that the direction in which hurricanes initially travel causes them later to veer off to the north, but this make little logical sense.

E This sentence opens with a main subject, *Hurricanes*, but this subject has no verb. The sentence's main verb, *veer*, has as a subject *they*.

The correct answer is B.

680. Unlike the virginal, whose single set of strings runs parallel to the front edge of the instrument, the harpsichord's several sets of strings are placed at right angles to its front edge.

(A) whose single set of strings runs parallel to the front edge of the instrument, the harpsichord's several sets of strings are

(B) with a single set of strings running parallel to the front edge of the instrument, the several sets of strings of the harpsichord are

(C) which has a single set of strings that runs parallel to the front edge of the instrument, in the case of the harpsichord, several sets of strings are

(D) which has a single set of strings that run parallel to the front edge of the instrument, the harpsichord has several sets of strings

(E) in which a single set of strings run parallel to the front edge of the instrument, the harpsichord's several sets of strings are

Parallelism; Agreement

The point of the sentence is to contrast two instruments, but the sentence has been written to contrast the *virginal* with the *sets of strings* on the harpsichord. The proper contrast is between the *virginal* and the *harpsichord.*

A The *virginal* is illogically contrasted with the *sets of strings* on the harpsichord. Note the possessive form *harpsichord's* in contrast to virginal.

B The *virginal* is illogically contrasted with the *sets of strings* on the harpsichord.

C *In the case of the harpsichord* is not parallel to the *virginal.*

D Correct. The contrast is properly drawn between *the virginal* and *the harpsichord.*

E The *virginal* is illogically contrasted with the *sets of strings* on the harpsichord; the verb *run* does not agree with the singular subject *set.*

The correct answer is D.

681. Although Alice Walker published a number of essays, poetry collections, and stories during the 1970s, her third novel, *The Color Purple*, which was published in 1982, brought her the widest acclaim in that it won both the National Book Award as well as the Pulitzer Prize.

(A) which was published in 1982, brought her the widest acclaim in that it won both the National Book Award as well as the Pulitzer Prize

(B) published in 1982, bringing her the widest acclaim by winning both the National Book Award and the Pulitzer Prize

(C) published in 1982, brought her the widest acclaim, winning both the National Book Award and the Pulitzer Prize

(D) was published in 1982 and which, winning both the National Book Award and the Pulitzer Prize, brought her the widest acclaim

(E) was published in 1982, winning both the National Book Award as well as the Pulitzer Prize, and bringing her the widest acclaim

Idiom; Grammatical construction

This sentence claims that the 1982 novel *The Color Purple* brought Alice Walker more acclaim than her many publications in the 1970s.

A The construction *both the American Book Award as well as the Pulitzer Prize* is unidiomatic; the correct idiomatic form is *both x and y.*

B Because this sentence uses only participial phrases in the clause following the initial, dependent clause, the sentence lacks a main verb and is therefore ungrammatical.

C Correct. This version correctly uses the form *both x and y* and is grammatically correct.

D The use of *which* is inappropriate here; although it would still be rhetorically inferior to the correct answer (C), this version would be acceptable if the word *which* were deleted.

E Like (A), this version of the sentence uses the unidiomatic form *both x as well as y.*

The correct answer is C.

682. Many experts regarded the large increase in credit card borrowing in March not as a sign that households were pressed for cash and forced to borrow, rather a sign of confidence by households that they could safely handle new debt.

(A) rather a sign of confidence by households that they could safely

(B) yet as a sign of households' confidence that it was safe for them to

(C) but a sign of confidence by households that they could safely

(D) but as a sign that households were confident they could safely

(E) but also as a sign that households were confident in their ability safely to

Idiom; Logical predication; Parallelism

The structure of this sentence expresses negation and affirmation: *Many experts regarded X not as a sign that Y, but as a sign of Z.* The idiomatic choice of words for this construction should involve two clauses introduced by *not as … but as….* It is also important to connect logically the adjective *confident* with the noun it describes, that is, *households.* If the adjective *confident* or its equivalent noun *confidence* is related to other words in the sentence, the message loses clarity and power.

A The idiomatic choice of words to express the negation of one clause and the affirmation of another is *not as … but as….* The affirmed clause is incorrectly introduced by *rather.* Furthermore, the preposition *by* does not express the idea that households are confident. The placement of the restrictive clause *that they could safely handle new debt* after *households* could also cause confusion.

B The idiomatic choice of words to express the negation of one clause and the affirmation of another is *not as … but as….* The affirmed clause is incorrectly introduced by *yet as.* The wording *it was safe for them [households] to handle new debt* changes the intended meaning, making the households less clearly an agent in the handling.

C The idiomatic choice of words to express the negation of one clause and the affirmation of another is *not as … but as….* The affirmed clause is incorrectly introduced by *but* without the *as*. Furthermore, the preposition *by* does not express the idea that households are confident.

D Correct. This version provides the correct logical structure. It also expresses the confidence of households using the most succinct and direct wording.

E The use of the word *also* is misleading here. If the first embedded clause is negated, the affirmed second clause cannot also be true. In addition, *in their ability*, while expressing the same idea as *could,* is redundant and *safely to handle* is awkward; the wording in (D) is superior.

The correct answer is D.

683. A pioneer journalist, Nellie Bly's exploits included circling the globe faster than Jules Verne's fictional Phileas Fogg.

(A) A pioneer journalist, Nellie Bly's exploits included
(B) The exploits of Nellie Bly, a pioneer journalist, included
(C) Nellie Bly was a pioneer journalist including in her exploits the
(D) Included in the pioneer journalist Nellie Bly's exploits are
(E) The pioneer journalist's exploits of Nellie Bly included

Logical predication; Modification

This sentence intends to discuss Nellie Bly, a pioneer journalist who counts among her exploits a very fast trip around the globe. The current construction is misleading because it suggests that Bly's exploits, not Bly herself, were a pioneer journalist.

A In this answer choice, *a pioneer journalist* incorrectly modifies *exploits*, rather than *Nellie Bly*.

B Correct. This version correctly attributes the modifier *a pioneer journalist* to *Nellie Bly.*

C The wording of this version is illogical because it makes *Nellie Bly* the subject of the verb *including.*

D Since this event clearly happened in the past, the tense of the verb *are* is wrong. Piling on too many descriptive words for the noun *exploits* (*the pioneer journalist Nellie Bly's exploits*) makes the phrase unwieldy and awkward.

E This version can be construed as entailing that the pioneer journalist and Nellie Bly are two different people, one exploiting the other.

The correct answer is B.

684. In 1913, the largely self-taught Indian mathematician Srinivasa Ramanujan mailed 120 of his theorems to three different British mathematicians; only one, G. H. Hardy, recognized the brilliance of these theorems, but thanks to Hardy's recognition, Ramanujan was eventually elected to the Royal Society of London.

(A) only one, G. H. Hardy, recognized the brilliance of these theorems, but

(B) they were brilliant, G. H. Hardy alone recognized, but

(C) these theorems were brilliant, but only one, G. H. Hardy recognized;

(D) but, only one, G. H. Hardy, recognizing their brilliance,

(E) only one G. H. Hardy recognized, but these theorems were brilliant

Logical predication; Grammatical construction

The point of the sentence is that only one of the British mathematicians with whom Srinivasa Ramanujan initially shared his theorems recognized their brilliance, but that recognition was sufficient to earn Ramanujan acclaim. The sentence has been correctly constructed, with the phrase *only one* referring clearly to *British mathematicians* and the noun *theorems* repeated to avoid confusion.

A **Correct.** The phrase *only one* refers clearly to *British mathematicians*, and the noun *theorems* is repeated to avoid confusion.

B *They* is intended to refer to *theorems* but instead refers to *mathematicians*, causing confusion.

C Structured in this way, the sentence does not make sense. *Only one* is intended to refer to *G. H. Hardy* but instead seems to refer to *theorems*, causing confusion. If *only one* is taken to refer to *G. H. Hardy*, the absence of a comma after the name and the absence of an object for *recognized* make the sentence ungrammatical.

D The sentence is ungrammatical because *G. H. Hardy* serves as the subject of a clause but is not paired with a verb.

E *Only one G. H. Hardy recognized* incorrectly implies (in an awkwardly inverted wording structure) that Hardy recognized only one theorem; *these theorems were brilliant thanks to Hardy's recognition* illogically suggests that Hardy's recognition is what made the theorems brilliant.

The correct answer is A.

685. Cost cutting and restructuring has allowed the manufacturing company to lower its projected losses for the second quarter, and they are forecasting a profit before the end of the year.

(A) has allowed the manufacturing company to lower its projected losses for the second quarter, and they are forecasting

(B) has allowed for the manufacturing company to lower its projected losses in the second quarter and to forecast

(C) have allowed that the manufacturing company can lower the projected losses for the second quarter, and to forecast

(D) have allowed the manufacturing company to lower its projected second-quarter losses and to forecast

(E) have allowed for the manufacturing company to lower the projected losses in the second quarter, as well as forecasting

Agreement; Idiom; Verb form

The point of the sentence is to explain the two main effects of the changes made by the company. However, the singular verb *has allowed* does not agree with the compound subject *cost cutting and restructuring*, which are far more plausibly understood as two actions rather than as two facets of a single action. In principle, *the manufacturing company* could be construed as plural (referring collectively to the decision makers and spokespeople who are projecting losses and forecasting a profit), but the plural pronoun *they* does not agree with the earlier *its*, which treats the antecedent as singular.

A The singular verb *has allowed* does not agree with the compound subject *cost cutting and restructuring*; the plural pronoun *they* does not agree with the intended singular antecedent *company.*

B The singular verb *has allowed* does not agree with the compound subject *cost cutting and restructuring*; *allowed for* is not the correct idiom.

C *Allowed that* is not the correct idiom; *can lower* and *to forecast* are not grammatically parallel.

D **Correct.** The sentence uses the correct subject–verb combination *cost cutting and restructuring have allowed*; the two occurrences of the pronoun *its* agree with each other in treating their antecedent *company* as singular; and the two effects *to lower* and *to forecast* are parallel and idiomatic.

E *Allowed for* is not the correct idiom; *to lower* and *as well as forecasting* are not parallel.

The correct answer is D.

686. The Life and Casualty Company hopes that by increasing its environmental fund reserves to $1.2 billion, that it has set aside enough to pay for environmental claims and no longer has to use its profits and capital to pay those claims bit by bit, year by year.

(A) that it has set aside enough to pay for environmental claims and no longer has
(B) enough has been set aside with which environmental claims can be paid and it will have no longer
(C) it has set aside enough for payment of environmental claims and thus no longer having
(D) enough has been set aside to pay for environmental claims, thus no longer having
(E) it has set aside enough to pay for environmental claims and will no longer have

Grammatical construction; Logical predication

All predicates need a proper logical subject. Here, the relevant predicates are the verbs *increase*, *set aside*, and *have.* With *it* as the subject for *set aside*—referring back to the Life and Casualty Company—all three verbs should have this as their understood subject. With a different subject for *set aside*, at least one of the other verbs lacks a proper logical subject. Also, this sentence uses the word *that* after *hope* to start the subordinate clause, but then incorrectly repeats the *that* after the initial adverbial phrase (*by increasing . . . billion*). Only the first *that* is grammatically correct.

A The additional *that* makes the sentence ungrammatical. Also, because in this context the hope is forward-looking (*bit by bit, year by year)*, it would be preferable to use the future tense, *will no longer have to*, instead of the present *no longer has to.*

B With *enough* as the subject of *set aside*, the next subject (*it*) is naturally interpreted as *enough*, but this is not a logical choice for the subject of *use.*

C The phrase *no longer having* is ungrammatical when connected to the rest of the sentence by *and*, which should connect two regular clauses; *no longer having . . .* is a mere phrase, not a clause, and *no longer has* would be correct.

D For *no longer having*, illogically, the implied subject is *enough*; the implied subject, instead, should be the company referred to at the beginning of the sentence.

E **Correct.** There is only one *that*, and *will no longer have to use* has its proper logical subject (*it*) from the clause preceding it.

The correct answer is E.

687. Like ancient Egyptian architectural materials that were recycled in the construction of ancient Greek Alexandria, so ancient Greek materials from the construction of that city were reused in subsequent centuries by Roman, Muslim, and modern builders.

(A) Like ancient Egyptian architectural materials that were recycled in the construction of
(B) Like recycling ancient Egyptian architectural materials to construct
(C) Just as ancient Egyptian architectural materials were recycled in the construction of
(D) Just as they recycled ancient Egyptian architectural materials in constructing
(E) Just like ancient Egyptian architectural materials that were recycled in constructing

Diction; Parallelism

When two situations are asserted to be similar, the proper way to express this is with the paired expressions *just as . . . so . . .*, not *like . . . so.* Moreover, the two compared situations should be expressed as clauses, not as noun phrases. Thus the clause *ancient Egyptian architectural materials were recycled* . . . is correct, as opposed to a noun phrase like *ancient Egyptian architectural materials that were recycled* . . .

A *Just as* and a following clause with a passive verb are preferred, but instead this option has *like* and a following noun phrase (*ancient Egyptian materials* . . .). It appears, somewhat implausibly, to say that the ancient Greek materials were similar to the earlier ancient Egyptian ones in that both were used by Roman, Muslim, and modern builders.

B *Just as* and a following clause with a passive verb are preferred, but instead this option has *like* and a following noun phrase (*recycling ancient Egyptian materials* . . .). It appears illogically to say that the action of recycling was similar to the ancient Greek materials in that both were reused in subsequent centuries.

C **Correct.** The expressions *just as* and *so* are paired to link the two clauses in parallel, and both clauses use the passive construction.

D *Just as* is used to connect two clauses, which is good, but the first clause employs the active construction rather than the preferred passive, so there is a failure of parallelism. Also, it is unclear what *they* refers to. The sentence appears to say illogically that some unidentified group's action of recycling was similar to the ancient Greek materials' being reused.

E *Just as* introducing a clause with a passive verb is preferable, but this sentence uses *like* and a following noun phrase (*ancient Egyptian materials* . . .). It appears, somewhat implausibly, to say that the ancient Greek materials were similar to the earlier ancient Egyptian ones in that both were used by Roman, Muslim, and modern builders.

The correct answer is C.

688. Especially in the early years, new entrepreneurs may need to find resourceful ways, like renting temporary office space or using answering services, <u>that make their company seem large</u> and more firmly established than they may actually be.

(A) that make their company seem large
(B) to make their companies seem larger
(C) thus making their companies seem larger
(D) so that the companies seem larger
(E) of making their company seem large

Grammatical construction; Diction

The clause beginning with *that* suggests that a company can be made to seem better than it actually is. The comparison signaled by *than* appears to be intended to apply to both the size of the company and the degree to which the company is firmly established. In that case, it is a mistake to use *large* instead of *larger*. If, on the other hand, *large* is not intended to be part of the comparison, it would be better to clarify this by separating the two topics in a construction such as *make their company seem large and also make it seem more firmly established*. . . . The phrase *resourceful ways* suggests purpose, so *ways* should connect with *to* or *of*, rather than a *that* clause to capture the intended meaning.

A *Large* is the incorrect form to express comparison; it should be *larger*; the *that* clause does not adequately capture the idea of purpose implicit in *ways*. The singular *company* does not agree with the plural pronoun *they*. Thus, the sentence either commits an agreement mistake or illogically says that entrepreneurs need to find ways to make themselves seem large and more firmly established.

B **Correct.** *Larger* is the correct form to express the comparative meaning, and *to* correctly follows *way*. *Companies* agrees with the plural *they*.

C The phrase beginning *thus making* does not capture the idea of purpose implicit in *ways*.

D Clauses beginning *so that* can express purpose, but do not fit with *ways* in the manner required here: *to* or *of* is needed after *ways*.

E *Large* is the incorrect form to express comparison; it should be *larger*. The singular *company* does not agree with the plural pronoun *they*. Thus, the sentence either commits an agreement mistake or illogically says that entrepreneurs need to find ways to make themselves seem large and more firmly established.

The correct answer is B.

689. Unlike the nests of leaf cutters and most other ants, situated underground or in pieces of wood, raider ants make a portable nest by entwining their long legs to form "curtains" of ants that hang from logs or boulders, providing protection for the queen and the colony larvae and pupae.

(A) the nests of leaf cutters and most other ants,

(B) the nests of leaf cutters and most other ants, which are

(C) leaf cutters and most other ants, whose nests are

(D) leaf cutters and most other ants in having nests

(E) those of leaf cutters and most other ants with nests

Logical predication

As worded, this sentence draws a contrast between raider ants and the nests of leaf cutters and most other ants. The appropriate contrast would be with leaf cutters and most other ants themselves, not their nests.

A As indicated above, the appropriate contrast is between raider ants and other kinds of ants (namely leaf cutters and most ants). As worded, this version of the sentence says something obviously true: of course the nests of leaf cutters and most other ants do not make portable nests.

B Like (A), this sentence compares nests with raider ants. Also, the referent of the relative pronoun *which* is ambiguous, possibly modifying *ants*, and possibly modifying *nests*.

C **Correct.** This version correctly draws the contrast between raider ants and other kinds of ants. Furthermore, unlike in (B) and (D), it is clear here that *situated underground or in pieces of wood* applies to the nests of leaf cutters and most other ants.

D This sentence correctly compares leaf cutters and other ants with raider ants, but the prepositional phrase *in having nests* suggests that it is raider ants, not leaf cutters and most other ants, that have nests situated underground or in pieces of wood; however, the rest of the sentence indicates that in fact raider ants' nests are not situated in such locations.

E The referent of *those* is unclear; presumably it refers to *nests*, but grammatically it has no clear antecedent. If it is taken to refer to nests, *those* creates an illogical comparison with *raider ants*.

The correct answer is C.

690. Turtles, like other reptiles, can endure long fasts, in their ability to survive on weekly or even monthly feedings; however, when food is readily available, they may eat frequently and grow very fat.

(A) fasts, in their ability to survive

(B) fasts, having their ability to survive

(C) fasts, due to having the ability of surviving

(D) fasts because they are able to survive

(E) fasts because of having the ability of surviving

Idiom; Diction

To express why turtles can endure long fasts—their ability to survive on only occasional feedings—it is clearer and more idiomatic to use *because* than to use *in* or *having*. Also, the noun *ability* here requires *to* introducing a noun phrase denoting the nature of the ability.

A *In* does not express the causal relationship clearly, whereas *because* does.

B *Having* does not express the causal relationship clearly.

C *Ability of* is incorrect; *ability* must be followed by *to* in order to express the intended meaning. *Due to having the ability* is awkward, nonstandard, and unnecessarily wordy.

D **Correct.** This option uses *because* to express the causal relation and uses *to* after *ability*.

E *Ability of* is incorrect; *ability* must be followed by *to* in order to express the intended meaning. *Because of having the ability* is awkward, nonstandard, and unnecessarily wordy.

The correct answer is D.

691. Thai village crafts, as with other cultures, have developed through the principle that form follows function and incorporate readily available materials fashioned using traditional skills.

(A) as with

(B) as did those of

(C) as they have in

(D) like in

(E) like those of

Logical predication; Diction; Verb form

The phrase *as with other cultures* is initially confusing given that no culture has been specifically mentioned; Thai village culture is indirectly referenced by the mention of *Thai village crafts*, so perhaps that is what is meant. But then, looking at the phrase in context, it becomes clear that the sentence is intended to indicate that the *crafts* of other cultures are similar in certain ways to Thai village crafts. Thus, the sentence should say *those of other cultures*. Furthermore, the use here of *as with* is questionable. To do the job it is supposed to do here (to indicate that the crafts of Thai villages are like the crafts of other cultures in a particular way), *as with* should be at the beginning of the sentence: *As with the crafts of other cultures, Thai village crafts have developed*. . . . Alternatively, *like* could be used here instead of *as with*.

A The appropriate comparison is between Thai village crafts and those (i.e., crafts) of other cultures, not the other cultures themselves. Additionally, *like* would be more appropriate here than *as with*.

B The verb form here is incorrect. [*D*]*id* is not parallel to *have* later in the sentence. The phrase *as have those of other cultures* would be parallel, but it is in the wrong position. To be correct, it would need to occur after the main verb is introduced: *Thai village crafts have developed, as have those of other cultures*, . . .

C The use of the pronoun *they* is inaccurate; the reader is likely to take its antecedent to be *Thai village crafts*, not *crafts*. Furthermore, even if the pronoun here were not problematic, if the construction *as they have in other cultures* is used, it should occur after the main verb (*have developed*) is introduced.

D The comparative term *like* compares two nouns or noun phrases, but in this version of the sentence, *like* compares a noun (*crafts*) with a prepositional phrase (*in other cultures*).

E **Correct.** [*T*]*hose of other cultures* clearly refers to the crafts of other cultures; *like* is appropriate for making a comparison between two sorts of things (*crafts*).

The correct answer is E.

692. Tropical bats play important roles in the rain forest ecosystem, aiding in the dispersal of cashew, date, and fig seeds; <u>pollinating banana, breadfruit, and mango trees; and indirectly help produce</u> tequila by pollinating agave plants.

(A) pollinating banana, breadfruit, and mango trees; and indirectly help produce

(B) pollinating banana, breadfruit, and mango trees; and indirectly helping to produce

(C) pollinating banana, breadfruit, and mango trees; and they indirectly help to produce

(D) they pollinate banana, breadfruit, and mango trees; and indirectly help producing

(E) they pollinate banana, breadfruit, and mango trees; indirectly helping the producing of

Logical predication; Parallelism

This sentence expresses a list of the roles tropical bats play in the rain forest ecosystem. Since these roles are enumerated in a list, and since the first member of the list is already provided, it is necessary to maintain the same structure for the rest of the members of the list in order to maintain parallelism and clarity. Note that semicolons separate the members of the list, leaving the commas to mark series of items within each member of the list.

A In this version, the third member of the list does not maintain the *-ing* verb form that the two previous members use.

B **Correct.** This version correctly maintains the parallel structure (*aiding in* . . .; *pollinating* . . .; *and helping* . . .).

C In this version, the third member of the list does not maintain the *-ing* verb form of the two previous members of the list. In addition, this member of the list includes a subject (*they*) while the other members do not, again violating parallelism.

D In order to maintain parallelism the verb that is the member of the list has to be in the *-ing* form, not its complement. Thus, the *-ing* has to be on the verb *help*, not on *produce*.

E Although this version maintains parallelism throughout, the phrase *helping the producing* is an incorrect construction in English.

The correct answer is B.

693. Discussion of greenhouse effects have usually had as a focus the possibility of Earth growing warmer and to what extent it might, but climatologists have indicated all along that precipitation, storminess, and temperature extremes are likely to have the greatest impact on people.

(A) Discussion of greenhouse effects have usually had as a focus the possibility of Earth growing warmer and to what extent it might,

(B) Discussion of greenhouse effects has usually had as its focus whether Earth would get warmer and what the extent would be,

(C) Discussion of greenhouse effects has usually focused on whether Earth would grow warmer and to what extent,

(D) The discussion of greenhouse effects have usually focused on the possibility of Earth getting warmer and to what extent it might,

(E) The discussion of greenhouse effects has usually focused on whether Earth would grow warmer and the extent that is,

Agreement; Parallelism

The sentence contrasts climatologists' views concerning greenhouse effects with other views that emphasize global warming. The main subject of the sentence is *discussion* . . ., which is singular, so the main verb should be singular. The two things that are said to be the focus of discussion should be in parallel form.

A The plural verb *have* . . . *had* does not agree with the singular subject *discussion*. The phrases *the possibility* . . . *warmer* and *to what* . . . *might* are not parallel.

B The verb form *has had as its focus* is unnecessarily wordy; the noun clauses are parallel in form, but it is not clear what *the extent* refers to.

C **Correct.** This has correct subject-verb agreement, eliminates the wordiness of the original sentence, and the phrases *whether* . . . *warmer* and *to what extent* are parallel.

D The singular subject *discussion* does not agree with the plural verb *have focused*. *The possibility of* . . . is not parallel with *to what extent*. . . .

E The two phrases following *on* are not in parallel form. What *that* refers to in *the extent that is* is unclear.

The correct answer is C.

694. In the seventh century B.C., the Roman alphabet was adapted from the Etruscan alphabet, which in turn had been adapted in the previous century from a western Greek alphabet, which itself had been adapted earlier in the same century from the Phoenician alphabet.

(A) which itself had been adapted earlier

(B) adapting itself earlier

(C) itself being adapted earlier

(D) having been earlier adapted itself

(E) earlier itself having been adapted

Rhetorical construction; Verb form; Logical predication

This sentence describes a string of adaptations of the alphabet, tracing back from the seventh century BC through two points in the eighth century BC. Because the latest of the three adaptations is temporally located in past tense, earlier adaptations should be located in the past perfect tense.

A **Correct.** This sentence is properly constructed and uses the appropriate verb forms for the relationships among the events that it describes.

B It is unclear what the participial phrase *adapting itself earlier* . . . refers to. The present participle could be used for an event that was simultaneous with, or part of, the event mentioned before the underlined portion. However, it is inappropriate for describing an event that took place even earlier than the seventh century BC, which has already been designated in the sentence as past tense. The reflexive form *adapting itself* is nonsensical in this sentence.

C The present tense of the reflexive participial phrase is inappropriate for describing an event prior to the seventh century BC, given that the seventh century BC has already been designated in the sentence as past tense.

D Without commas around *itself*, the pronoun appears to be reflexive. The combination of passive and reflexive then makes no sense. If *itself* is intended simply for emphasis, rather than as a reflexive pronoun, it would be preferable, in this context, to set it off with commas. But if it were intended in that way, it would seem to refer to the Roman alphabet, and the claim made in the sentence would be confusing and nearly nonsensical. This modifier is confusingly placed before the designation of time (*in the same century*) and source (*from the Phoenician alphabet*).

E The adverb *earlier* is misplaced before the pronoun *itself*; it should be immediately before the phrase *in the same century*.

The correct answer is A.

695. With corn, soybean, and wheat reserves being low enough so a poor harvest would send prices skyrocketing, grain futures brokers and their clients are especially interested in weather that could affect crops.

(A) being low enough so

(B) so low such that

(C) so low that

(D) that are low enough so

(E) that are so low such that

Idiom; Rhetorical construction

This sentence opens with a long participial phrase (*With . . . skyrocketing*) that describes conditions within which the action of the main clause (*grain futures brokers . . . crops*) occurs. The opening phrase compares one economic condition (grain reserve levels) with another (prices) using the idiomatic expression *so low that*. Some of the phrases used in expressing this kind of comparison are wordy and indirect (*being low enough so*). Thus, they are not standard in written English, even though they may be accepted in some informal speaking contexts.

A This phrase is wordy and unidiomatic.

B This phrase combines two idioms (*so . . . that* and *such that*) in a way that does not clearly make sense. It is wordy and redundant; both *so . . . that* and *such* signal comparison.

C **Correct.** This wording is standard, clear, and direct.

D The relative clause introduced by *that are* makes this phrase unnecessarily wordy and cumbersome; *enough* and *so* are redundant.

E This version of the phrase is the most redundant of all—piling comparative terms one upon the other (*that are so* and *such*). The repetition obscures instead of develops meaning.

The correct answer is C.

696. By 1940, the pilot Jacqueline Cochran held seventeen official national and international speed records, and she earned them at a time when aviation was still so new for many of the planes she flew to be of dangerously experimental design.

(A) and she earned them at a time when aviation was still so new for many of the planes she flew to be

(B) earning them at a time that aviation was still so new for many of the planes she flew to be

(C) earning these at a time where aviation was still so new that many of the planes she flew were

(D) earned at a time in which aviation was still so new such that many of the planes she flew were

(E) earned at a time when aviation was still so new that many of the planes she flew were

Rhetorical construction; Diction

Since this is a complex sentence with a lot of elements, its rhetorical construction is crucial in order to maintain effective communication. The underlined part emphasizes that on top of earning seventeen speed records, the pilot Jacqueline Cochran did so at a time when planes were of dangerous experimental design because aviation was still so new.

A This version is too wordy and does not contribute to clarity. Economical, clear expression connects *earned* directly with the noun *speed records*, which it modifies.

B Here, the word *earning* takes the pilot herself, not the *records*, as its subject. However, *earning* is close to *the records*, not to *Jacqueline Cochran*, making this sentence hard to process. In addition, the causal relationship between aviation being new and planes being of experimental design is more effectively communicated by the structure *so new that many X were Y*, not by the structure *so new for many X to be Y*.

C The word *earning* takes the pilot herself, not the records, as its subject. However, *earning* is close to *the records*, not to *Jacqueline Cochran*, making this sentence hard to understand. Furthermore, the use of *where* to modify *time* is wrong; *where* refers to place.

D The correct pronoun for *time* is *when*. The word *such* is redundant within *so new that many X were Y*.

E **Correct.** The word *earned* is close to the noun it modifies, *speed records*. This version uses the clearest expression of causal relationship: *so new that many X were Y*.

The correct answer is E.

697. The foundation works to strengthen local and regional agricultural markets and cooperating with governments, improving access for farmers for productive resources such as land and credit.

(A) cooperating with governments, improving access for farmers for

(B) cooperates with governments to improve access for farmers to

(C) cooperate with governments for improvements of access for farmers to

(D) cooperate with governments and improve accessibility for farmers for their

(E) in cooperation with governments to improve access for farmers for

Parallelism; Rhetorical construction

As written, this sentence does not clearly indicate whether *and* is intended to conjoin two things that the foundation does (working to strengthen markets and cooperating with governments) or two things that the foundation works to accomplish (strengthening markets and cooperating with governments). The latter is less plausible because of the redundancy of *works to cooperate*. In the former, the proper verb form, parallel with the present-tense *works*, would be *cooperates*. In the latter, the proper verb form, parallel with the infinitive *to strengthen*, would be *to cooperate* or simply *cooperate*. Only one of the answer choices resolves the uncertainty of meaning in a coherent and well-formed way.

A *Cooperating* is incorrect, since it is not in the same form as either *works* or *to strengthen*.

B **Correct.** This version correctly represents the foundation's two actions by putting the verbs *works* and *cooperates* in parallel form. *Cooperates . . . to improve* is the most concise phrasing to express the purpose of improving access.

C *Cooperate . . . for improvements of access for farmers* is awkwardly phrased and unnecessarily wordy.

D *Cooperate . . . and improving accessibility for farmers* is awkwardly phrased and unnecessarily wordy.

E *In cooperation* destroys the parallelism required by *works to*: there should be a verb following *works to*, not this prepositional phrase.

The correct answer is B.

698. A professor at the university has taken a sabbatical to research on James Baldwin's books that Baldwin wrote in France while he was living there.

(A) on James Baldwin's books that Baldwin wrote in France while he was living there

(B) about the books James Baldwin wrote in France

(C) into James Baldwin's books written while in France

(D) on the books of James Baldwin, written while he lived in France

(E) the books James Baldwin wrote while he lived in France

Diction; Rhetorical construction

The phrasing of this sentence is wordy and redundant: *books that Baldwin wrote in France while he was living there* could more concisely be expressed with *books James Baldwin wrote while he lived in France*. The verb *research* requires a direct object, not a preposition followed by its object.

A *On* incorrectly follows *to research*, and *books that Baldwin wrote in France while he was living there* includes redundant information.

B *About* incorrectly follows *to research.*

C *Into* incorrectly follows *to research*. Given this sentence structure, *while in France* seems to say, illogically, that the books were written while they were in France.

D *On* incorrectly follows *to research*; also, there is no need to make *written while he lived in France* into an independent phrase instead of a relative clause.

E **Correct.** *Research* takes a direct object, which describes the books directly without redundancy.

The correct answer is E.

699. Researchers now regard interferon as not a single substance, but it is rather a biological family of complex molecules that play an important, though not entirely defined, role in the immune system.

(A) as not a single substance, but it is rather a biological family of complex molecules that play

(B) as not a single substance but as a biological family of complex molecules playing

(C) not as a single substance but as a biological family of complex molecules that play

(D) not to be a single substance but rather a biological family of complex molecules playing

(E) not as a single substance but instead as being a biological family of complex molecules that play

Parallelism; Rhetorical construction

This sentence draws a contrast between how interferon is and is not regarded by researchers. However, the two parts of the contrast are not expressed in parallel form since the first is a prepositional phrase (*as not a single substance*), and the second is a clause (*it is rather a biological family*). Furthermore, the wording *regard interferon as not* is awkward and confusing. For clarity and proper parallelism, the contrast should be constructed using the expression *not as X but as Y*, where *X* and *Y* are both noun phrases.

A The contrast is not expressed using parallel grammatical structure, and *regard interferon as not* is awkward and confusing.

B The wording *regard interferon as not* is awkward and confusing and violates proper parallelism.

C **Correct.** The contrast is expressed using the parallel structure *not as a single substance but as a biological family.*

D The main defect here is that *regard interferon not to be a single substance* is unidiomatic; *regard ... as ...* is the correct form; and completing the parallelism correctly would require the repetition of *as*, in the phrase *but rather as ...*

E The contrast is not expressed using parallel grammatical structure since *a single substance* is a noun phrase, while *being a biological family* is a participial phrase; omitting the unnecessary words *being* and *instead* would improve the sentence.

The correct answer is C.

700. The remarkable similarity of Thule artifacts throughout a vast region can, in part, be explained as a very rapid movement of people from one end of North America to the other.

(A) The remarkable similarity of Thule artifacts throughout a vast region can, in part, be explained as

(B) Thule artifacts being remarkably similar throughout a vast region, one explanation is

(C) That Thule artifacts are remarkably similar throughout a vast region is, in part, explainable as

(D) One explanation for the remarkable similarity of Thule artifacts throughout a vast region is that there was

(E) Throughout a vast region Thule artifacts are remarkably similar, with one explanation for this being

Logical predication; Grammatical construction; Rhetorical construction

The intended meaning of the sentence is that the rapid movement of people across North America is one explanation of the *similarity of Thule artifacts throughout a vast region*. As worded, however, the sentence is illogical: The sentence indicates that the similarity in artifacts was a rapid movement of people, which makes no sense. Instead of equating similarity with movement, the sentence needs to identify this movement of people as a cause of similarity among artifacts.

A As worded, this version of the sentence makes the illogical statement that the similarity among artifacts is explainable *as a very rapid movement*. It should specify that the similarity of artifacts may be a consequence of the rapid population movement.

B This version of the sentence is syntactically awkward, and leaves unclear what the main subject, *one explanation*, is supposed to be an explanation of.

C Like (A), this version of the sentence equates the similarity of artifacts with the movement of people, when a causal connection is what is intended.

D Correct. This version adequately expresses the intended causal connection.

E This version is awkward, introducing the causal connection with the unnecessarily wordy and indirect string of prepositional phrases, *with one explanation for this*. . . .

The correct answer is D.

701. The widely accepted big bang theory holds that the universe began in an explosive instant ten to twenty billion years ago and has been expanding ever since.

(A) that the universe began in an explosive instant ten to twenty billion years ago and has been expanding

(B) that the universe had begun in an explosive instant ten to twenty billion years ago and had been expanding

(C) that the beginning of the universe was an explosive instant ten to twenty billion years ago that has expanded

(D) the beginning of the universe to have been an explosive instant ten to twenty billion years ago that is expanding

(E) the universe to have begun in an explosive instant ten to twenty billion years ago and has been expanding

Logical predication; Verb form

The sentence describes the central tenet of a theory about how the universe began. The focus of the second clause should be consistently on the subject *the universe*, and all verbs in the clause beginning with *that* must describe what the universe did at the initial explosive moment.

A Correct. Both verbs in the second clause correctly take *universe* as their subject.

B *Had begun* is the wrong tense because it describes action that occurred farther in the past than some other, specified past action.

C The relative clause *that has expanded* describes *instant*, which makes no sense.

D *The beginning of the universe to have been* ... is unnecessarily indirect and wordy; illogically suggests that *beginning* is expanding, not the universe.

E The verb phrases *to have begun* and *has been expanding* both reference the same subject of the clause, *universe*, and therefore need to be parallel.

The correct answer is A.

702. Between 14,000 and 8,000 B.C. the ice cap that covered northern Asia, Europe, and America began to melt, uncovering vast new areas that were to be occupied by migrating peoples moving northward.

(A) began to melt, uncovering vast new areas that were to be occupied

(B) began melting, to uncover vast new areas to be occupied

(C) began, by melting, to uncover vast new areas for occupation

(D) began, after melting, uncovering vast new areas which are to be occupied

(E) would begin to uncover, through melting, vast new areas for occupation

Verb form; Logical predication

The sentence explains what happened when an ice cap *began to melt*. The participial phrase *uncovering vast new areas* succinctly describes the immediate effects of the melting. The verb form *were to be occupied* is used to indicate that occupation would take place at a time in the future from the time of the melting.

A Correct. The sentence succinctly expresses immediate and future effects of the melting of an ice cap.

B The infinitive *to uncover* incorrectly implies that the ice cap melted for the purpose of uncovering new areas.

C Since *melting* is what caused new areas to be uncovered, that word should be part of the main verb, not placed in the nonrestrictive prepositional phrase *by melting.*

D It does not make sense to say that the ice cap *began . . . uncovering* new areas *after* it had melted—since the ice cap no longer existed in the areas where it had melted.

E Since *melting* is what caused new areas to be uncovered, that word should be part of the main verb, not placed in the nonrestrictive prepositional phrase *through melting.*

The correct answer is A.

703. Bengal-born writer, philosopher, and educator Rabindranath Tagore had the greatest admiration <u>for Mohandas K. Gandhi the person and also as a politician, but Tagore had been</u> skeptical of Gandhi's form of nationalism and his conservative opinions about India's cultural traditions.

(A) for Mohandas K. Gandhi the person and also as a politician, but Tagore had been

(B) for Mohandas K. Gandhi as a person and as a politician, but Tagore was also

(C) for Mohandas K. Gandhi not only as a person and as a politician, but Tagore was also

(D) of Mohandas K. Gandhi as a person and as also a politician, but Tagore was

(E) of Mohandas K. Gandhi not only as a person and as a politician, but Tagore had also been

Rhetorical construction; Parallelism

This sentence describes the writer and philosopher Tagore's two types of feelings for Gandhi. The underlined part of the sentence has to express correctly the time line of these two feelings (they happened simultaneously). The underlined part also has to express the correct relationship between the complements of admiration and skepticism.

A To maintain parallelism, it is important for two conjoined phrases to be of the same grammatical type. Thus, it is appropriate to conjoin *Gandhi the person and the politician,* or *Gandhi as a person and as a politician,* but it is nonstandard in English to mix and match. In addition, the use of the past perfect tense *had been* places the skepticism earlier on the time line than the admiration, which is misleading.

B Correct. This version correctly conjoins two parallel phrases, *Gandhi as a person and as a politician,* and, in using two simple past tenses to introduce the two emotions, marks them as holding at the same time.

C The phrase *not only X but also Y* matches the meaning of this sentence: Tagore had not only admiration but also skepticism. However *not only* has to precede *admiration* for this rhetorical construction to be parallel.

D The noun *admiration* as it is positioned in this sentence should take the preposition *for,* not *of,* since it refers to a person. The adverb *also* is redundant because it expresses the same meaning as the conjunction *and.*

E As in (D), the noun *admiration* should take the preposition *for.* As in (C), the rhetorical structure of *not only X but also Y* is violated. Finally, the use of the past perfect tense *had been* is misleading with respect to the time line.

The correct answer is B.

704. Traffic safety officials predict that drivers will be <u>equally likely to exceed the proposed speed limit as</u> the current one.

(A) equally likely to exceed the proposed speed limit as

(B) equally likely to exceed the proposed speed limit as they are

(C) equally likely that they will exceed the proposed speed limit as

(D) as likely that they will exceed the proposed speed limit as

(E) as likely to exceed the proposed speed limit as they are

Idiom; Parallelism

This sentence reports on a prediction that compares the likelihood of drivers exceeding a proposed new speed limit with the likelihood of drivers exceeding the current speed limit. The idiom *as x as y,* rather than the incorrect form *equally . . . as,* should be used to express the comparison.

A *Equally likely . . . as* is not an idiomatic form of comparison.

B This also offers a nonidiomatic form of comparison.

C The comparison is expressed nonidiomatically. Also, *the drivers will be equally likely* should be followed by *to exceed* rather than by *that they will exceed*. The resulting sentence is wordy and structurally flawed.

D The resulting sentence is wordy and structurally flawed. The idiomatic phrase *as x as y* is somewhat in use, but *as likely that they* is awkward, and the comparison is unclear and not parallel.

E **Correct.** The idiomatic phrase *as x as y* is properly used, and the comparison is clear and parallel.

The correct answer is E.

705. Written early in the French Revolution, Mary Wollstonecraft's *A Vindication of the Rights of Man* (1790) and *A Vindication of the Rights of Woman* (1792) attributed Europe's social and political ills to be the result of the dominance of aristocratic values and patriarchal hereditary privilege.

(A) Mary Wollstonecraft's *A Vindication of the Rights of Man* (1790) and *A Vindication of the Rights of Woman* (1792) attributed Europe's social and political ills to be the result of

(B) Mary Wollstonecraft's *A Vindication of the Rights of Man* (1790) and *A Vindication of the Rights of Woman* (1792) attributed Europe's social and political ills to result from

(C) Mary Wollstonecraft's *A Vindication of the Rights of Man* (1790) and *A Vindication of the Rights of Woman* (1792) attributed Europe's social and political ills to

(D) in *A Vindication of the Rights of Man* (1790) and *A Vindication of the Rights of Woman* (1792), Mary Wollstonecraft attributed Europe's social and political ills to have been the result of

(E) Mary Wollstonecraft, in *A Vindication of the Rights of Man* (1790) and *A Vindication of the Rights of Woman* (1792), attributed Europe's social and political ills to

Logical predication; Idiom

The phrase at the beginning needs a subject for *written*; most logically here it would be the books mentioned written by Mary Wollstonecraft; any other main-clause subject is therefore incorrect. The verb *attribute* idiomatically requires the preposition *to* followed by a noun phrase, not the infinitive marker *to* followed by a verb.

A The main subject is correctly predicated of *written*, but *attribute* is incorrectly followed by the infinitive *to* plus a verb (*be*).

B The main subject is correctly predicated of *written*, but *attribute* is incorrectly followed by the infinitive *to* plus a verb (*result*).

C **Correct.** The main subject is correctly predicated of *written*, and *attribute* is correctly followed by the preposition *to*.

D The subject of the main clause is *Mary Wollstonecraft*, and so this phrase is illogically forced to be taken as the subject of *written*. Also, *attribute* is incorrectly followed by *to* plus a verb (*have been*).

E The subject of the main clause is *Mary Wollstonecraft*, and so this phrase is illogically forced to be taken as the subject of *written*.

The correct answer is C.

706. Using study groups managed by the principal popular organizations and political parties, the Swedish public was informed by the government about energy and nuclear power.

(A) the Swedish public was informed by the government about energy and nuclear power

(B) the government informed the Swedish public about energy and nuclear power

(C) energy and nuclear power information was given to the Swedish public by the government

(D) information about energy and nuclear power was given to the Swedish public by the government

(E) the public of Sweden was given energy and nuclear power information by the government

Logical predication; Rhetorical construction

This sentence tries to describe a situation in which the government used study groups to inform the Swedish public. Therefore, it is incorrect to use *the Swedish public* as the subject of *inform* in this sentence, because doing so in this case illogically makes *the Swedish public* the subject of *using* as well. Additionally, *inform* is a more concise and direct way to express the idea in *give information*.

A Using *the Swedish public* as the subject of the main clause incorrectly makes it the subject of *using* as well.

B Correct. Using *the government* as the main subject correctly allows it to count as the subject of using; inform is a concise phrasing for the main action of the sentence.

C Energy and nuclear power information does not work as the subject of the main clause, since this also, illogically, makes it the subject of *using*. Also, this phrase delays the reader's understanding of the important noun *information* (a clearer phrasing is *information about energy and nuclear power*) and employs *give information* rather than the more concise *inform*.

D *Energy and nuclear power information* does not work as the main clause subject, since this also, illogically, makes it the subject of *using*. In addition, this version awkwardly uses *give information to* instead of the more concise *inform*.

E *The public of Sweden* is awkward compared to *the Swedish public*, and in any case is illogically taken as the subject of using; *given . . . information* could be phrased more concisely with *inform*.

The correct answer is B.

707. The use of the bar code, or Universal Product Code, which was created in part to enable supermarkets to process customers at a faster rate, has expanded beyond supermarkets to other retail outlets and <u>have become readily accepted despite some initial opposition when it was first introduced in 1974</u>.

(A) have become readily accepted despite some initial opposition when it was first introduced in 1974

(B) has become readily accepted despite some initial opposition when they were first introduced in 1974

(C) have become readily accepted despite some initial opposition when first introduced in 1974

(D) has become readily accepted despite some initial opposition when the bar code was first introduced in 1974

(E) bar codes have become readily accepted despite some initial opposition when it was first introduced in 1974

Agreement; Rhetorical construction

The subject of this sentence is *the use of the bar code*, the main noun of which is the singular *use*; thus, the corresponding main verb should be in the singular form *has*, not the plural *have*. The actual subject for this verb is merely understood, but when it is present, any pronoun that refers back to it must agree with it in number.

A The verb form *have* does not agree with the sentence's subject. The referent of *it* is potentially unclear.

B *Has* is correct; however, the rest of its clause is badly worded, because its subject *they* does not clearly refer back to the singular *Universal Product Code* (or *bar code*); a better choice is *it*.

C The plural *have* does not agree with the singular subject *use*.

D Correct. The verb is in the correct form *has*, and using *bar code* as the last clause's subject avoids an agreement problem.

E Restating the subject as the plural *bar codes* allows the following verb to be *have*, but it is then incorrect to use *it* later in the sentence, since *it* does not agree in number with *bar codes*.

The correct answer is D.

708. The Organization of Petroleum Exporting Countries (OPEC) had long been expected to announce a reduction in output to bolster sagging oil prices, but officials of the organization just recently announced that the group will pare daily production by 1.5 million barrels by the beginning of next <u>year, but only if non-OPEC nations, including Norway, Mexico, and Russia, were to trim output</u> by a total of 500,000 barrels a day.

(A) year, but only if non-OPEC nations, including Norway, Mexico, and Russia, were to trim output

(B) year, but only if the output of non-OPEC nations, which includes Norway, Mexico, and Russia, is trimmed

(C) year only if the output of non-OPEC nations, including Norway, Mexico, and Russia, would be trimmed

(D) year only if non-OPEC nations, which includes Norway, Mexico, and Russia, were trimming output

(E) year only if non-OPEC nations, including Norway, Mexico, and Russia, trim output

Rhetorical construction; Logical predication

The underlined part of this sentence deals with the conditions under which OPEC members will lower their own oil production by 1.5 million barrels by the beginning of next year. The important thing to notice here is the following logical relation: *X will do something only if Y does something else.*

A This version has redundant words, *were to* in front of *trim*, that do not add anything more in meaning. Furthermore, *were to trim* is not the proper verb form to accompany *will pare*. The addition of *but* before *only* is also redundant.

B This version uses the passive construction in the conditional clause *only if the output … is trimmed.* This use of the passive voice makes this sentence vague; it is now unclear who needs to trim the output of non-OPEC nations. Finally, the addition of *but* before *only* is redundant.

C As in (B), this version also introduces vagueness by using the passive construction. In addition, *would* in front of the passive verb *be trimmed* is redundant.

D This version uses an active verb, but in the past progressive form, *were trimming*. The progressive tense denotes actions in progress, so its use is not normally warranted in conditional sentences such as this one.

E **Correct.** This version uses the correct and most concise conditional structure, without redundancies.

The correct answer is E.

709. Not trusting themselves to choose wisely among the wide array of investment opportunities on the market, <u>stockbrokers are helping many people who turn to them to buy stocks that could be easily</u> bought directly.

(A) stockbrokers are helping many people who turn to them to buy stocks that could be easily

(B) stockbrokers are helping many people who are turning to them for help in buying stocks that they could easily have

(C) many people are turning to stockbrokers for help from them to buy stocks that could be easily

(D) many people are turning to stockbrokers for help to buy stocks that easily could have been

(E) many people are turning to stockbrokers for help in buying stocks that could easily be

Logical predication; Grammatical construction; Verb form

This sentence is intended to be about people who, because they do not trust themselves to make wise investment decisions, turn to stockbrokers for advice. As the sentence is worded, however, it is stockbrokers who do not trust themselves to choose wisely. The sentence is made even more incomprehensible by the peculiar placement of the adverbs in the phrase, *could be easily bought directly*.

A This version of the sentence incorrectly identifies the subject described by the opening modifier as *stockbrokers*; the adverb *easily* is misplaced in the phrase *could be easily bought*.

B As in (A), the opening clause illogically modifies *stockbrokers* rather than *many people*. The tense of the verb phrase *could easily have bought* does not match the tense of *are helping* earlier in the main clause.

C Although the opening modifier is correctly attached to *people* rather than *stockbrokers*, the sentence is unnecessarily wordy (*for help from them*).

D *To buy* is not idiomatic in this context—*in buying* would be correct—and the tense of the verb *could have been* does not match the tense of the verb earlier in the clause; the point is not that people are turning to stockbrokers for help in buying stocks that at some earlier time could have been bought directly, but rather that the stocks could be bought by the people directly at the very time they are seeking help from the stockbrokers.

E **Correct.** The opening clause correctly modifies *many people*, and the adverb is correctly placed.

The correct answer is E.

710. There are several ways to build solid walls using just mud or clay, but the most extensively used method has been the forming of bricks out of mud or clay, and, after some preliminary air drying or sun drying, they are laid in the wall in mud mortar.

(A) the forming of bricks out of mud or clay, and, after some preliminary air drying or sun drying, they are laid

(B) forming the mud or clay into bricks, and, after some preliminary air drying or sun drying, to lay them

(C) having bricks formed from mud or clay, and, after some preliminary air drying or sun drying, they were laid

(D) to form the mud or clay into bricks, and, after some preliminary air drying or sun drying, to lay them

(E) that bricks were formed from mud or clay, which, after some preliminary air drying or sun drying, were laid

Parallelism; Verb form

The purpose of the sentence is to describe the historically most popular method of building walls. The first clause announces this topic and the second clause describes the particular method. The clearest, most efficient way to accomplish these two pieces of business is to use a parallel structure. The *ways to build* in the first clause is narrowed to the single way *to form* and *to lay* in the second clause. There is no need to alternate the verb phrases between active and passive voice or to shift tenses.

A The active gerund phrase *the forming of bricks* does not fit with the passive verb phrase that follows (*they are laid*).

B The verb phrases *forming the mud* … and *to lay them* are not parallel.

C In addition to faulty parallelism between *having bricks formed* and *they were laid*, the tense in the second half of the sentence unaccountably shifts from present to past.

D **Correct.** The phrases *to form* and *to lay* in the second clause are parallel to *to build* in the first clause.

E The relative clause beginning with *which* apparently (but nonsensically) describes the closest nouns, *mud or clay*, rather than *bricks*.

The correct answer is D.

711. A surge in new home sales and a drop in weekly unemployment claims suggest that the economy might not be as weak as some analysts previously thought.

(A) claims suggest that the economy might not be as weak as some analysts previously thought

(B) claims suggests that the economy might not be so weak as some analysts have previously thought

(C) claims suggest that the economy might not be as weak as have been previously thought by some analysts

(D) claims, suggesting about the economy that it might not be so weak as previously thought by some analysts

(E) claims, suggesting the economy might not be as weak as previously thought to be by some analysts

Agreement; Grammatical construction

The plural subject of this sentence (*surge* and *drop*) requires a plural verb, *suggest*. The object of this verb, the clause beginning with *that*, should be presented in as clear and direct a manner as possible.

A **Correct.** The plural subject is matched with a plural verb.

B The singular verb *suggests* does not match the plural subject of the sentence.

C The sentence offers no plural subject to fit the passive verb *have been thought*.

D This construction is awkward, wordy, and imprecise; it also lacks a main verb; there is no reason to use passive voice, and *suggesting about the economy that it might* … introduces extra words that contribute nothing to the meaning of this sentence fragment.

E The passive construction makes this unnecessarily wordy; the lack of a main verb makes this a sentence fragment.

The correct answer is A.

712. Retail sales rose 0.8 of 1 percent in August, intensifying expectations that personal spending in the July–September quarter more than doubled that of the 1.4 percent growth rate in personal spending for the previous quarter.

(A) that personal spending in the July–September quarter more than doubled that of

(B) that personal spending in the July–September quarter would more than double

(C) of personal spending in the July–September quarter, that it more than doubled

(D) of personal spending in the July–September quarter more than doubling that of

(E) of personal spending in the July–September quarter, that it would more than double that of

Verb form; Logical predication

The sentence explains the expectations that resulted from a past retail sales trend. Since expectations look to the future but are not yet realized, the relative clause explaining these expectations should be conditional, employing the auxiliary verb *would.*

A The simple past-tense verb form does not express the forward-looking sense of *expectations.*

B Correct. By using the verb *would double,* this concise sentence indicates that the expectation has not yet been realized.

C This construction is awkward, announcing the topic (*personal spending*) and then elaborating in a relative clause that restates this topic as *it.*

D Although this option is not technically wrong, it is less clear and graceful than (B).

E Like (C), this sentence is awkward and unnecessarily wordy, announcing the topic and then using an additional clause to elaborate on it.

The correct answer is B.

713. In the early part of the twentieth century, many vacationers found that driving automobiles and sleeping in tents allowed them to enjoy nature close at hand and tour at their own pace, with none of the restrictions of passenger trains and railroad timetables or with the formalities, expenses, and impersonality of hotels.

(A) with none of the restrictions of passenger trains and railroad timetables or with the

(B) with none of the restrictions of passenger trains, railroad timetables, nor

(C) without the restrictions of passenger trains and railroad timetables nor

(D) without the restrictions of passenger trains and railroad timetables or with the

(E) without the restrictions of passenger trains and railroad timetables or the

Rhetorical construction; Diction

The sentence lays out some advantages that car travel and tent camping were perceived to offer over rail travel. The sentence attempts to describe these advantages in terms of the absence of any of a series of annoyances accompanying rail travel. But the sentence fails because of the mismatch between *with none of*... and *or with*... One way to successfully convey the intended meaning is to use the preposition *without* governing all the items in the series, expressed as nouns or noun phrases.

A By using *none of*... to introduce the first drawback of rail travel, and *or* to introduce the rest of them, this sentence suggests that the presence of drawbacks on the final list is an alternative to the absence of *restrictions.*

B *With none*... *nor*... is nonidiomatic (as opposed to *neither*... *nor*...).

C The structure *without*... *nor*... in the way used here is nonidiomatic. The negative *without* governs the whole list of drawbacks at the end of the sentence.

D The coupling of *without* and *or with* is confusing, suggesting, as in (A), that the drawbacks on the final list are an alternative to the absence of *restrictions.*

E Correct. The sentence is unambiguous and constructed in a way that *without* clearly distributes over all the items in the series.

The correct answer is E.

714. Over the next few years, increasing demands on the Chattahoochee River, which flows into the Apalachicola River, could alter the saline content of Apalachicola Bay, which would rob the oysters there of their flavor, and to make them decrease in size, less distinctive, and less in demand.

(A) which would rob the oysters there of their flavor, and to make them decrease in size,

(B) and it would rob the oysters there of their flavor, make them smaller,

(C) and rob the oysters there of their flavor, making them decrease in size,

(D) robbing the oysters there of their flavor and making them smaller,

(E) robbing the oysters there of their flavor, and making them decrease in size,

The sentence claims that demands for river water may change the saline content of the bay, possibly altering the flavor and size of oysters there and diminishing the oysters' marketability. The sentence is not parallel. It should read *which would rob the oysters . . . and make them decrease* to be parallel and grammatical. The series of three phrases after *make them* that describes what will happen to the oysters also needs to be parallel.

A The referent of the relative pronoun, *which*, is ambiguous; the two effects of altered saline content are not expressed in parallel form, with a relative clause expressing the first effect, and an infinitive phrase expressing the second.

B The referent of the pronoun *it* is ambiguous. Also, the effects of the bay's altered saline content are not expressed in parallel form—the first being an independent clause and the second a verb phrase.

C The comma before the conjunction *and* signals that an independent clause will follow *and*, but a verb phrase follows instead. The series of phrases following *making them* lacks appropriate parallelism.

D **Correct.** The potential effects on the oysters are expressed by two parallel participial phrases, the second of which lists three adjectives correctly in a series.

E The series of phrases following *making them* lacks appropriate parallelism.

The correct answer is D.

715. Elizabeth Barber, the author of both *Prehistoric Textiles*, a comprehensive work on cloth in the early cultures of the Mediterranean, and also of *Women's Work*, a more general account of early cloth manufacture, is an expert authority on textiles in ancient societies.

(A) also of *Women's Work*, a more general account of early cloth manufacture, is an expert authority on

(B) also *Women's Work*, a more general account of cloth manufacture, is an expert authority about

(C) of *Women's Work*, a more general account about early cloth manufacture, is an authority on

(D) of *Women's Work*, a more general account about early cloth manufacture, is an expert authority about

(E) *Women's Work*, a more general account of early cloth manufacture, is an authority on

Rhetorical construction; Idiom; Parallelism

Using a lot of parenthetical elements, this sentence communicates the main idea that Elizabeth Barber is an authority on textiles in ancient societies. It is the main rhetorical goal of the sentence to position the parenthetical elements so that they do not obscure the main idea. The parenthetical descriptions need to be streamlined enough to be informative, but not too long. In addition, several versions repeat *of* before the title *Women's Work* and doing so makes the sentence unparallel; the first *of* comes before *both* and so should distribute over both clauses.

A The use of *also of* before *Women's Work* is redundant and unparallel. It is sufficient to connect the two book titles like this: *both X and Y*. The meanings of the two nouns *expert* and *authority* largely overlap, so there is no need to modify one with the other.

B The use of *also* before *Women's Work* is redundant. It is sufficient to connect the two book titles like this: *both X and Y*. The meanings of the two nouns *expert* and *authority* largely overlap, so there is no need to modify one with the other. Finally, the noun *authority* takes the preposition *on*, not *about*.

C As in (A), repeating the preposition *of* before *Women's Work* makes the sentence unparallel. The noun *account* takes the preposition *of*, not *about*.

D As in (A) and (C), repeating the preposition *of* before *Women's Work* makes the sentence unparallel. The noun *account* takes the preposition *of*, not *about*. It is redundant to modify *authority* with *expert* because they express the same idea. Finally, the noun *authority* takes the preposition *on*, not *about*.

E **Correct.** This version is parallel, uses the most concise structure of the parenthetical descriptions, eschews the redundant modification of *authority*, and employs the correct prepositions.

The correct answer is E.

716. Digging in sediments in northern China, evidence has been gathered by scientists suggesting that complex life-forms emerged much earlier than they had previously thought.

(A) evidence has been gathered by scientists suggesting that complex life-forms emerged much earlier than they had

(B) evidence gathered by scientists suggests a much earlier emergence of complex life-forms than had been

(C) scientists have gathered evidence suggesting that complex life-forms emerged much earlier than

(D) scientists have gathered evidence that suggests a much earlier emergence of complex life-forms than that which was

(E) scientists have gathered evidence which suggests a much earlier emergence of complex life-forms than that

Logical predication; Modification

In principle, the relationship described in the first part of the underlined portion could be expressed with *scientists* as the subject (*scientists gathered evidence*) or with *evidence* as the subject (*evidence was gathered by scientists*). The latter construction could be effective in some contexts, but here its relationship to the rest of the sentence appears to commit the writer to the claim that the evidence was digging in China.

A This version has a dangling participle, *digging*. … *Digging in sediments in northern China* must modify *scientists*, not *evidence*. The passive structure of the main clause also creates an inadvisable distance between the words *evidence* and *suggesting*. Furthermore, the dependent clause starting with *suggesting* may be construed with either the evidence or the scientists, which makes this version unnecessarily ambiguous.

B This version has a dangling participle, *digging*. … *Digging in sediments in northern China* must modify *scientists*, not *evidence*.

C **Correct.** Choosing *scientists* as the subject of *gathered*, this version corrects the dangling participle. It also uses a parallel active form of the verb *emerge*, and does not use redundant material.

D In this context it would be preferable to use a verb (*emerged*). The phrasing used here (*suggests a much earlier emergence of*) sounds more stilted and is less clear and direct. In addition, inserting *that which* before *previously thought* is not only redundant but incorrect English.

E The problems described in (D) above are also in evidence here.

The correct answer is C.

717. Employing many different techniques throughout his career, Michelangelo produced a great variety of art works, including paintings, for example, in the Sistine Chapel, to sculpture, for example, the statue of David.

(A) including paintings, for example, in the Sistine Chapel, to sculpture, for example,

(B) including paintings, for example, in the Sistine Chapel, to sculpture, like

(C) including paintings, such as those in the Sistine Chapel, and sculpture, as

(D) ranging from paintings, such as those in the Sistine Chapel, to sculpture, such as

(E) ranging from paintings, such as in the Sistine Chapel, and sculpture, such as

Parallelism; Rhetorical construction

This sentence names painting and sculpture as two of the many kinds of art created by Michelangelo and provides examples of his work in those two art forms. Although the two sets of examples are expressed in parallel form, the position of the phrase *for example* that introduces them creates a choppy and awkward sentence since it must be surrounded by commas. A more concise way to construct parallel sets of examples is to express each using a phrase introduced by *such as*.

A The sentence is choppy and awkward due to the twofold use of the phrase *for example*, which must be surrounded by commas. The preposition *to*, in context, suggests a range, but it would then be needed to be preceded by *from*.

B The examples of art are not in parallel form since the first is introduced by *for example* followed by the prepositional phrase *in the Sistine Chapel,* and the second is introduced by the prepositional phrase *like. . .* The preposition *to* is unidiomatic and awkwardly used here.

C The examples of art are not in parallel form since the first is introduced by *such as,* and the second is introduced by *as.*

D **Correct.** The examples of art are in parallel form, each introduced with the words *such as.*

E Although the examples of art are both introduced by *such as*, the form is not parallel since the first is a prepositional phrase (*in the Sistine Chapel*) and the second is a noun phrase (*the statue of David*).

The correct answer is D.

718. Outlining his strategy for nursing the troubled conglomerate back to health, the chief executive's plans were announced on Wednesday for cutting the company's huge debt by selling nearly $12 billion in assets over the next 18 months.

(A) executive's plans were announced on Wednesday for cutting the company's huge debt by selling nearly $12 billion in assets over the next 18 months

(B) executive's plans, which are to cut the company's huge debt by selling nearly $12 billion in assets over the next 18 months, were announced on Wednesday

(C) executive's plans for cutting the company's huge debt by selling nearly $12 billion in assets over the next 18 months were announced on Wednesday

(D) executive announced plans Wednesday to cut the company's huge debt by selling nearly $12 billion in assets over the next 18 months

(E) executive announced plans Wednesday that are to cut the company's huge debt by selling nearly $12 billion in assets over the next 18 months

Logical predication; Verb form

In this sentence, the opening dependent clause beginning *Outlining his strategy* is a dangling modifier. Furthermore, the verb form for *announce* should make it clear that the chief executive is doing the announcing. In addition, *to cut* is a clearer phrase than *for cutting* in this sentence.

A The subject of the opening clause should be *executive*, not *plans*. The passive verb form *were announced* suggests that someone other than the chief executive is outlining the strategy. Putting the phrase *were announced* between *plans* and *for cutting* makes it somewhat unclear whether *for cutting* ... is intended to modify *announced* or *plans*.

B In addition to having a dangling modifier and the wrong form of the verb *announce*, this sentence is made less clear by separating the subject and verb with the long clause beginning with *which are*.

C This version has the same issues as in (A) and (B) and is made less clear by separating the subject and verb with the long clause beginning with *for cutting*.

D **Correct.** The opening clause properly modifies *chief executive* and the verb form *announced* makes it clear that the chief executive is doing the announcing.

E Although the opening clause correctly modifies *chief executive* in this version, the words *that are* are extraneous and also suggest that the plans themselves are doing the cutting and selling.

The correct answer is D.

719. It is called a sea, but the landlocked Caspian is actually the largest lake on Earth, which covers more than four times the surface area of its closest rival in size, North America's Lake Superior.

(A) It is called a sea, but the landlocked Caspian is actually the largest lake on Earth, which covers

(B) Although it is called a sea, actually the landlocked Caspian is the largest lake on Earth, which covers

(C) Though called a sea, the landlocked Caspian is actually the largest lake on Earth, covering

(D) Though called a sea but it actually is the largest lake on Earth, the landlocked Caspian covers

(E) Despite being called a sea, the largest lake on Earth is actually the landlocked Caspian, covering

Logical predication; Grammatical construction

The topic of this sentence is a single large body of water, the Caspian Sea. The wording needs to make it clear that being *the largest lake on Earth* and *covering more than four times the surface area of … Lake Superior* are both predicated of this one subject.

A The referent of *which* is unclear. Grammatically, its antecedent cannot be *the landlocked Caspian*, so it must be either *Earth* or *the largest lake on Earth*. The latter is a little odd, because the sentence has already said that the lake in question is the Caspian, so one would expect *and* instead of *which*. For these reasons and because *Earth* immediately precedes *which*, the sentence appears to say, illogically, that Earth covers more than four times the surface area of Lake Superior.

B As in (A), this appears to say, illogically, that Earth covers more than four times the surface area of Lake Superior.

C **Correct.** The wording is direct, unambiguous, and grammatically correct.

D The structure here is grammatically incoherent.

E *Despite being called a sea* indicates, somewhat illogically, that the largest lake being called a sea would lead one to expect it not to be the Caspian. This makes little sense, especially to those who are familiar with the name *Caspian Sea*.

The correct answer is C.

720. Neuroscientists, having amassed a wealth of knowledge over the past twenty years about the brain and its development from birth to adulthood, are now drawing solid conclusions about how the human brain grows and how babies acquire language.

(A) Neuroscientists, having amassed a wealth of knowledge over the past twenty years about the brain and its development from birth to adulthood, are

(B) Neuroscientists, having amassed a wealth of knowledge about the brain and its development from birth to adulthood over the past twenty years, and are

(C) Neuroscientists amassing a wealth of knowledge about the brain and its development from birth to adulthood over the past twenty years, and are

(D) Neuroscientists have amassed a wealth of knowledge over the past twenty years about the brain and its development from birth to adulthood,

(E) Neuroscientists have amassed, over the past twenty years, a wealth of knowledge about the brain and its development from birth to adulthood,

Grammatical construction; Logical predication

This sentence introduces the subject (*Neuroscientists*), pauses to explain what neuroscientists have accomplished in the past twenty years, and then concludes by explaining what neuroscientists are presently doing as a result of their past accomplishments. The second part of the sentence—the explanation—interrupts the flow of the sentence from the subject (*Neuroscientists*) to the predicate (*are now drawing solid conclusions …*); it should therefore be bracketed by commas. The sentence construction should provide a main verb for the subject *neuroscientists*.

A **Correct.** The explanatory phrase between the subject and predicate is set off by commas, and the main clause contains both a subject (*Neuroscientists*) and a corresponding verb (*are now drawing*).

B *And are* indicates that *are* follows a previous verb, but in fact the sentence has not yet provided a first main verb for the subject *Neuroscientists*; the sentence is therefore incomplete; *over the … years* appears to be modifying *adulthood*.

C *Amassing*, like *having amassed*, functions as an adjective, not a verb; the sentence therefore lacks the first main verb implied by the compound verb construction *and are now drawing. …*

D The final descriptor in present tense, *now drawing conclusions* ... does not fit the opening clause, which is in present-perfect tense (*have amassed a wealth* ...) and seems to modify *adulthood*.

E Like (D), this sentence attempts to attach a present-tense descriptor to a present-perfect clause.

The correct answer is A.

721. According to a recent study of consumer spending on prescription medications, increases in the sales of the 50 drugs that were advertised most heavily accounts for almost half of the $20.8 billion increase in drug spending last year, the remainder of which came from sales of the 9,850 prescription medicines that companies did not advertise or advertised very little.

(A) heavily accounts for almost half of the $20.8 billion increase in drug spending last year, the remainder of which came

(B) heavily were what accounted for almost half of the $20.8 billion increase in drug spending last year; the remainder of the increase coming

(C) heavily accounted for almost half of the $20.8 billion increase in drug spending last year, the remainder of the increase coming

(D) heavily, accounting for almost half of the $20.8 billion increase in drug spending last year, while the remainder of the increase came

(E) heavily, which accounted for almost half of the $20.8 billion increase in drug spending last year, with the remainder of it coming

Grammatical construction; Verb form

The sentence indicates that according to research, increases in sales of the relatively small number of the most heavily advertised drugs accounted for nearly half of last year's total increase in drug spending. The sentence is flawed because of subject-verb disagreement, and an ambiguity in the referent of *which*.

A The singular verb form *accounts* fails to agree in number with the plural subject *increases*. What the relative pronoun *which* refers to is unclear; to make clear sense, it should refer to *the . . . increase*.

B The phrase *were what accounted* is unnecessarily wordy; the semicolon before *the remainder* signals that a complete clause will follow, but what follows is not a complete clause.

C **Correct.** The sentence is clear and grammatically correct. The subject and verb agree.

D In the resulting sentence, no main verb follows the main subject *increases*.

E The resulting sentence lacks a main verb for the main subject *increases*.

The correct answer is C.

722. Along the major rivers that traverse the deserts of northeast Africa, the Middle East, and northwest India, the combination of a reliable supply of water and good growing conditions both encouraged farming traditions that, in places, endure in at least 6,000 years.

(A) good growing conditions both encouraged farming traditions that, in places, endure in

(B) good growing conditions encouraged farming traditions that have, in places, endured for

(C) of good growing conditions have encouraged farming traditions that, in places, endured for

(D) of good growing conditions both encouraged farming traditions that have, in places, endured

(E) of good growing conditions encouraged farming traditions that have, in places, been enduring for

Logical predication; Rhetorical construction

The time line of this sentence, captured by the use of verb tenses, is of utmost importance. A combination of factors (in the past) encouraged farming traditions that are still with us today. The conditions for the use of the present perfect tense *have endured* are in place.

A The word *both* repeats the meaning of *combination* and is thus redundant. The use of the present tense (*endure*) is not justified by the time line of the whole sentence. The correct preposition for this type of construction is *for* (an amount of time), not *in*.

B **Correct.** This version correctly employs the present perfect tense with the appropriate adverbial *for at least 6,000 years*.

C The repetition of the preposition *of* before *good growing conditions* makes no sense. It seems to indicate that there is both a combination of a reliable supply of water and a combination of good growing conditions.

D The preposition *of* should not be repeated in front of *good growing conditions*. The word *both* repeats the meaning of *combination* and is thus redundant.

E The preposition *of* should not be repeated in front of *good growing conditions*. The use of the present perfect progressive *have been enduring* is not grammatically incorrect, but it is rhetorically inappropriate and sounds exaggerated.

The correct answer is B.

723. Despite its covering the entire planet, Earth has a crust that is not seamless or stationary, rather it is fragmented into mobile semirigid plates.

(A) Despite its covering the entire planet, Earth has a crust that is not seamless or stationary, rather it is

(B) Despite the fact that it covers the entire planet, Earth's crust is neither seamless nor is it stationary, but is

(C) Despite covering the entire planet, Earth's crust is neither seamless nor is it stationary, but rather

(D) Although it covers the entire planet, Earth's crust is neither seamless nor stationary, but rather

(E) Although covering the entire planet, Earth has a crust that is not seamless or stationary, but

Idiom; Parallelism; Logical predication

A dangling modifier is an error in sentence structure whereby a participle is associated with a word other than the one intended or with no particular word at all. In this sentence, *Earth* is the closest word to the participial clause, and so the latter means that Earth is covering the entire planet (itself), which is a contradiction.

A This version has a dangling participle. The addition of *it is* before *fragmented* is unwarranted and makes the sentence ungrammatical. *Neither ... nor ... but rather* would make the intended relationship among *seamless*, *stationary*, and *fragmented* clearer and more precise than *not ... or ... rather*.

B Parallel structure is disrupted by the addition of *is it* after *nor* and by the addition of *is* after *but*.

C Parallel structure is disrupted by the addition of *is it* after *nor*.

D **Correct.** *Despite* and *although* are very close in meaning. However, *despite* is a preposition and needs to be followed by a noun or noun phrase, while *although* is a conjunction and should be followed by a finite clause. This version uses *although* correctly. The parallel structure is also clear and correct.

E *Although* is a conjunction and should be followed by a finite clause with a subject, not by a participle. In addition, the first clause represents a dangling modifier. Omitting *rather* from the parallel structure *neither X nor Y but rather Z* is possible, but not optimal.

The correct answer is D.

724. Emily Dickinson's letters to Susan Huntington Dickinson were written over a period beginning a few years before Susan's marriage to Emily's brother and ending shortly before Emily's death in 1886, outnumbering her letters to anyone else.

(A) Dickinson were written over a period beginning a few years before Susan's marriage to Emily's brother and ending shortly before Emily's death in 1886, outnumbering

(B) Dickinson were written over a period that begins a few years before Susan's marriage to Emily's brother and ended shortly before Emily's death in 1886, outnumber

(C) Dickinson, written over a period beginning a few years before Susan's marriage to Emily's brother and that ends shortly before Emily's death in 1886 and outnumbering

(D) Dickinson, which were written over a period beginning a few years before Susan's marriage to Emily's brother, ending shortly before Emily's death in 1886, and outnumbering

(E) Dickinson, which were written over a period beginning a few years before Susan's marriage to Emily's brother and ending shortly before Emily's death in 1886, outnumber

Parallelism; Grammatical construction

The main point of the sentence is that Dickinson's letters to her sister-in-law outnumber her letters to anyone else. To emphasize this point, *outnumber* should be the main verb, and the description introduced by the passive verb *were written* needs to be changed from a main clause to an adjectival phrase.

A The long, wordy opening clause gives too much emphasis to the period when Dickinson's letters were written; it is unclear what *outnumbering* refers to.

B The verbs describing the letter-writing period (*begins* and *ended*) are not parallel.

C The verbs describing the letter-writing period need to be in parallel form and agree in tense—e.g., *beginning* and *ending* or *that began* and *that ended*; this is a fragment because it lacks a main verb for *letters*.

D The lack of a main verb for the subject of the sentence, *letters*, makes this a fragment.

E Correct. The information about the period when Dickinson's letters were written is contained in an adjectival phrase set off by commas, and the main verb *outnumber* refers clearly to *letters*.

The correct answer is E.

725. At the end of 2001, motion picture industry representatives said that there were about a million copies of Hollywood movies available <u>online and expected piracy to increase with high-speed Internet connections that become more widely available</u>.

(A) online and expected piracy to increase with high-speed Internet connections that become more widely available

(B) online and expect the increase of piracy with the wider availability of high-speed Internet connections

(C) online, and they expect more piracy to increase with the wider availability of high-speed Internet connections

(D) online, and that they expected the increase of piracy as high-speed Internet connections would become more widely available

(E) online, and that they expected piracy to increase as high-speed Internet connections became more widely available

Rhetorical construction; Grammatical construction

Every clause needs a subject, either an overt subject or an understood subject (whose interpretation can come from a coordinated clause or some other nearby clause). In this sentence, the clause containing *expected* lacks a clear subject. The intended subject is *motion picture industry representatives*, but to clearly indicate that, the subject should either be repeated or be replaced with the pronoun *they*. Furthermore, *piracy to increase with high-speed Internet connections that become more widely available* is awkward, and it fails to clearly communicate the idea that piracy will increase as a result of high-speed Internet connections becoming available.

A The second clause is awkward and unclear; there is no clear subject for *expected*.

B There is no clear subject for *expect*.

C It is redundant to use both *more* and *increase*.

D This wording makes the meaning very unclear. *They expected the increase in piracy* appears to refer to a particular (past) increase, but this does not clearly make sense with the ensuing use of the conditional verb form *would become*, which is inappropriate here.

E Correct. In this version the verb *expect* has an overt subject, and the following phrasing clearly indicates that the expected increase in piracy is the result of high-speed Internet connections becoming more widely available.

The correct answer is E.

726. Making things even more difficult <u>has been general market inactivity lately, if not paralysis, which has provided</u> little in the way of pricing guidance.

(A) has been general market inactivity lately, if not paralysis, which has provided

(B) there is general market inactivity, if not paralysis, lately it has provided

(C) general market inactivity, if not paralysis, has lately provided

(D) lately, general market inactivity, if not paralysis, has provided

(E) is that lately general market inactivity, if not paralysis, which provides

Grammatical construction; Rhetorical construction

This sentence uses a special inverted structure, putting the predicate (*Making things even more difficult*) before the verb (*has been*) and the subject. In this construction, the subject (*general market inactivity*) can be directly compared with *paralysis*. Such contrasts are best made using phrases that are adjacent, not separated by other material (here, the adverb *lately*). If a more normal clause structure is used, *making things even more difficult* becomes a modifier, not the main predicate, so it should be clearly set off from the rest of the clause with a comma.

A This inverted structure makes *general market activity* the subject of *Making things even more difficult*. This would be legitimate by itself, but it requires *general market inactivity* to be next to both *if not paralysis* (for contrast) and *which* (marking a relative clause modifying *inactivity*). It cannot be next to both of these simultaneously.

B This is a run-on sentence, with two independent clauses (*Making things even more difficult there is general market inactivity, if not paralysis, and lately it has provided little in the way of pricing guidance*) conjoined merely by a comma, rather than by a coordinating conjunction, such as and. Also, the initial topic phrase (*Making things even more difficult*) is awkward without a following comma.

C The initial topic phrase (*Making things even more difficult*) should be followed by a comma.

D Correct. The topic phrase (*Making things even more difficult*) is properly separated from the subject by a comma, and *inactivity* and *if not paralysis* are adjacent for the clearest connection between them.

E This is a sentence fragment.

The correct answer is D.

727. Unlike the conviction held by many of her colleagues that genes were relatively simple and static, Barbara McClintock adhered to her own more complicated ideas about how genes might operate, and in 1983, at the age of 81, was awarded a Nobel Prize for her discovery that the genes in corn are capable of moving from one chromosomal site to another.

(A) Unlike the conviction held by many of her colleagues that genes were

(B) Although many of her colleagues were of the conviction of genes being

(C) Contrary to many of her colleagues being convinced that genes were

(D) Even though many of her colleagues were convinced that genes were

(E) Even with many of her colleagues convinced of genes being

Rhetorical construction; Idiom; Logical predication

The sentence compares a widely held conviction about genes with McClintock's adherence to her own ideas, then goes on to describe McClintock's accomplishments. The sentence must not compare widespread convictions with McClintock herself. The clearest and most efficient way to make the comparison is to introduce McClintock's colleagues' convictions in a dependent clause, followed by a main clause that introduces McClintock's different way of doing things and goes on to explain how successful she was.

A Incorrect comparison between *conviction* and *Barbara McClintock*.

B *Were of the conviction of genes being relatively simple* is wordy and awkward.

C *Contrary to many of her colleagues being convinced* is wordy and awkward.

D Correct. A dependent clause describing the beliefs of McClintock's colleagues is followed by the main clause presenting the contrasting beliefs of McClintock.

E *Even with many of her colleagues* … is wordy and indirect.

The correct answer is D.

728. Ryūnosuke Akutagawa's knowledge of the literatures of Europe, China, and that of Japan were instrumental in his development as a writer, informing his literary style as much as the content of his fiction.

(A) that of Japan were instrumental in his development as a writer, informing his literary style as much as

(B) that of Japan was instrumental in his development as a writer, and it informed both his literary style as well as

(C) Japan was instrumental in his development as a writer, informing both his literary style and

(D) Japan was instrumental in his development as a writer, as it informed his literary style as much as

(E) Japan were instrumental in his development as a writer, informing both his literary style in addition to

Logical predication; Agreement

When a verb follows a complex noun phrase made up of several parts, it agrees with the first noun in the phrase. In this case, *knowledge of the literatures of Europe, China, and Japan* is a singular noun and the correct verb form is *was*, not *were*. The various parts of an enumeration have to be alike: *the literatures of Europe, China, and Japan*. The logical relationship between the predicates is important.

A This version of the sentence violates the correct subject-verb agreement, and the correct structure of enumeration is disrupted by the addition of *that of* in front of *Japan*.

B The correct structure of enumeration is disrupted by the addition of *that of* in front of *Japan*. *Both … as well as …* is incorrect usage.

C Correct. The structure of the enumeration (*Europe, China, and Japan*) as well as the conjunction structure (*both X and Y*) are correct. The logical relationships among the parts of the sentence are clearly expressed.

D This phrasing makes it unclear what the writer is claiming. It appears to indicate that the effect of Akutagawa's knowledge on his development as a writer was due to the fact that both of the aspects of his writing were influenced to the same extent. However, it is implausible to suppose that this is what the writer intends. Furthermore, the comparison is ambiguous: did his knowledge inform his style as much as it informed the content, or did it inform his style as much as the content informed his style?

E The subject-verb agreement in this version is incorrect. *Both X in addition to Y* is incorrect usage.

The correct answer is C.

729. According to scientists who monitored its path, an expanding cloud of energized particles ejected from the Sun recently triggered a large storm in the magnetic field that surrounds Earth, which brightened the Northern Lights and also possibly knocking out a communications satellite.

(A) an expanding cloud of energized particles ejected from the Sun recently triggered a large storm in the magnetic field that surrounds Earth, which brightened the Northern Lights and also possibly knocking

(B) an expanding cloud of energized particles ejected from the Sun was what recently triggered a large storm in the magnetic field that surrounds Earth, and it brightened the Northern Lights and also possibly knocked

(C) an expanding cloud of energized particles ejected from the Sun recently triggered a large storm in the magnetic field that surrounds Earth, brightening the Northern Lights and possibly knocking

(D) a large storm in the magnetic field that surrounds Earth, recently triggered by an expanding cloud of energized particles, brightened the Northern Lights and it possibly knocked

(E) a large storm in the magnetic field surrounding Earth was recently triggered by an expanding cloud of energized particles, brightening the Northern Lights and it possibly knocked

Logical predication; Rhetorical construction; Verb form

The timing and logical relationships among the events described in this sentence are of utmost importance. The scientists monitored a cloud ejected from the Sun. The cloud triggered a large storm, whose consequences were the brightening of the Northern Lights and the possible knocking out of a satellite. The latter two events are in a conjunction, so they should be represented by similar verb forms.

A In this context, the shift in verb form from *which brightened* to *and also possibly knocking* is ungrammatical. The two verbs should be in the same verb form for parallel construction.

B *X was what triggered Y* is wordy and awkward, and its meaning is unclear in this context. Given the most plausible intended meaning of the sentence, the two conjunctions *and* … *and* … in the last clause are redundant. The comma after *Earth* turns the final part of the sentence into an independent clause, and it is unclear whether this is part of what the scientists claimed or a separate claim made by the writer.

C **Correct.** The conjoined elements are of parallel forms, and the logical relations between the events are clear and concisely communicated.

D The wording in this answer choice makes the intended meaning unclear. The information that the cloud particles were ejected from the Sun is lost. The sentence is ungrammatical; the second conjoined main verb, *knocked*, needs no pronoun subject *it* because its subject is *a large storm*.

E The wording in this answer choice makes the intended meaning unclear. The information that the cloud particles were ejected from the Sun is lost. The two conjoined verbs are of different form; the second conjoined verb includes an unnecessary pronoun subject.

The correct answer is C.

730. In 1850, Lucretia Mott published her *Discourse on Women*, arguing in a treatise for women to have equal political and legal rights and for changes in the married women's property laws.

(A) arguing in a treatise for women to have equal political and legal rights

(B) arguing in a treatise for equal political and legal rights for women

(C) a treatise that advocates women's equal political and legal rights

(D) a treatise advocating women's equal political and legal rights

(E) a treatise that argued for equal political and legal rights for women

Parallelism; Rhetorical construction

Mott's *Discourse* was a treatise, and it is redundant and confusing to present her as both publishing her *Discourse* and *arguing in a treatise,* as though they were two separate things. The verb *arguing* must be followed by a prepositional phrase beginning with *for*, but the verb *advocating* simply takes a direct object.

A After *published her Discourse* … *arguing in a treatise* is wordy and imprecise.

B *Arguing in a treatise* is redundant and awkward.

C The verb *advocates* does not work idiomatically with the prepositional phrase *for changes.* …

D The verbal *advocating* does not work idiomatically with the prepositional phrase *for changes.* …

E **Correct.** The title of Mott's publication is followed by a phrase describing the treatise, and *argued* is followed by *for.*

The correct answer is E.

731. To develop more accurate population forecasts, demographers have to know a great deal more than now about the social and economic determinants of fertility.

(A) have to know a great deal more than now about the social and economic

(B) have to know a great deal more than they do now about the social and economical

(C) would have to know a great deal more than they do now about the social and economical

(D) would have to know a great deal more than they do now about the social and economic

(E) would have to know a great deal more than now about the social and economic

Verb form; Logical predication

This sentence explains a hypothetical situation and therefore calls for a conditional—or contrary-to-fact—construction, because in order to more accurately predict population, demographers *would have to know* more than they presently know. A present-tense verb is required to describe the current state of demographers' knowledge, and the comparison made by the sentence must be between current and conditional knowledge, not between knowledge and time of knowing (*now*).

A Wrong comparison—between knowledge and time (*now*); conditional verb is needed.

B Conditional verb is needed; *economical* is the wrong adjective.

C *Economical* is the wrong adjective.

D Correct. Conditional knowledge, indicated by *would have to know*, is correctly compared to current knowledge.

E Wrong comparison—between what demographers need to know and *now*.

The correct answer is D.

732. Laos has a land area about the same as Great Britain but only four million in population, where many are members of hill tribes ensconced in the virtually inaccessible mountain valleys of the north.

(A) about the same as Great Britain but only four million in population, where many

(B) of about the same size as Great Britain is, but in Laos there is a population of only four million, and many

(C) that is about the same size as Great Britain's land area, but in Laos with a population of only four million people, many of them

(D) comparable to the size of Great Britain, but only four million in population, and many

(E) comparable to that of Great Britain but a population of only four million people, many of whom

Logical predication; Grammatical construction

The comparison in this sentence is between the land area of Laos and the land area of Great Britain, not between the land area of Laos and Great Britain. The phrase about the population of Laos is most clearly and efficiently expressed in an appositive using a relative pronoun to refer back to *people* rather than the more abstract *population*. Using this construction keeps the appropriate emphasis on the two main claims being made about Laos, one describing its land area and the other its sparse population.

A The comparison between land area and Great Britain is incorrect; *where* is an inappropriate referent to *population*, which does not designate a place.

B Inappropriate comparison between land area and Great Britain; the *there is* … construction is wordy and imprecise.

C The reference of *them* is unclear and the expression is generally awkward.

D The coordinating conjunction *and* gives undue emphasis to the claim that many of the people in Laos live in inaccessible places.

E Correct. The land area of Laos is correctly compared to *that of* Great Britain; *whom* refers appropriately to *people.*

The correct answer is E.

733. Having been named for a mythological nymph who cared for the infant Jupiter, the asteroid named Ida, in the middle of the belt of asteroids that orbit the Sun between Mars and Jupiter, was discovered in 1884.

(A) Having been named for a mythological nymph who cared for the infant Jupiter, the asteroid named Ida, in the middle of the belt of asteroids that orbit the Sun between Mars and Jupiter, was discovered in 1884.

(B) Discovered in 1884, the asteroid Ida, named for a mythological nymph who cared for the infant Jupiter, is in the middle of the belt of asteroids that orbit the Sun between Mars and Jupiter.

(C) In the middle of the belt of asteroids that orbit the Sun between Mars and Jupiter, the asteroid Ida, discovered in 1884 and named for a mythological nymph who cared for the infant Jupiter.

(D) The asteroid Ida, named for a mythological nymph who cared for the infant Jupiter and discovered in 1884, is in the middle of the belt of asteroids to orbit the Sun between Mars and Jupiter.

(E) Ida, an asteroid discovered in 1884 and which was named for a mythological nymph who cared for the infant Jupiter, is in the middle of the belt of asteroids to orbit the Sun between Mars and Jupiter

Rhetorical construction; Logical predication; Grammatical construction

This sentence describes a discovery that occurred in 1884 and provides some additional information about the object that was discovered. The most effectively worded answer choice opens with a past-participial phrase (*discovered* . . .) describing the subject of the sentence, *the asteroid Ida*. Ida's discovery is logically prior to its naming, described in a second past, following the subject (*named* . . .). The sentence is then completed with a present tense linking verb *is* + prepositional phrase to explain Ida's location.

A Opening with a past perfect passive verb, *Having been named,* this version of the sentence illogically suggests that being named for a mythological nymph preceded the discovery of Ida.

B **Correct.** This version is clear, logically coherent, and grammatically correct.

C This version of the sentence is ungrammatical; it has no main verb for the subject *the asteroid Ida*.

D The sequence of events is obscured by the placement of *named* before *discovered* in the compound participial phrases. The infinitive form *to orbit* is ungrammatical in place of the relative clause.

E This sentence awkwardly attempts to use a compound conjunction *and* to join the past participial phrase *discovered in 1884* with the relative clause *which was named*. . . . The infinitive form *to orbit* is ungrammatical in place of the relative clause.

The correct answer is B.

734. In ancient Thailand, <u>much of the local artisans' creative energy was expended for the creation of Buddha images and when they constructed and decorated the temples that enshrined them</u>.

(A) much of the local artisans' creative energy was expended for the creation of Buddha images and when they constructed and decorated the temples that enshrined them

(B) much of the local artisans' creative energy was expended on the creation of Buddha images and on construction and decoration of the temples in which they were enshrined

(C) much of the local artisans' creative energy was expended on the creation of Buddha images as well as constructing and decoration of the temples in which they were enshrined

(D) creating images of Buddha accounted for much of the local artisans' creative energy, and also constructing and decorating the temples enshrining them

(E) the creation of Buddha images accounted for much of the local artisans' creative energy as well as construction and decoration of the temples that enshrined them

Idiom; Parallelism; Rhetorical construction

The main point of the sentence is that artisans in ancient Thailand spent most of their creative energy on three tasks: creating Buddha images, and constructing and decorating temples to enshrine the Buddhas. These three tasks must be described in parallel forms. The verb *expended* should be followed by the preposition *on*, not *for*.

A *For* is the wrong preposition; the *and when* . . . clause introduces faulty parallelism; it is unclear what *they* refers to.

B **Correct.** The three activities are presented in parallel form: *creation of Buddha images* and *construction and decoration of the temples*.

C *Constructing* violates the parallelism otherwise maintained by *creation* and *decoration*.

D The *and also* phrase is awkwardly set apart from the main claim of the sentence—which is that all three tasks consumed much of the artisans' energy.

E This construction is awkward and unnecessarily wordy and says something different—that the images accounted for the construction and decoration of temples.

The correct answer is B.

735. The English physician Edward Jenner found that if experimental subjects were deliberately infected with cowpox, <u>which caused only a mild illness, they are immune from</u> smallpox.

(A) which caused only a mild illness, they are immune from

(B) causing only a mild illness, they become immune from

(C) which causes only a mild illness, they are immune to

(D) causing only a mild illness, they became immune from

(E) which caused only a mild illness, they would become immune to

Verb form

This sentence describes the result of infecting volunteers with cowpox. A conditional verb form is used to describe the cowpox infection: *if experimental subjects were deliberately infected.* The sentence then incorrectly uses simple present tense for the effects of that infection: *they are immune.* However, since the effects are dependent on an action that may or may not occur, the correct way to express those effects is by using another conditional verb form: *they would become immune.*

A The effects of a conditional situation are incorrectly expressed using the simple present tense verb *are.*

B The participle *causing* suggests that infecting the subjects with cowpox caused a mild illness only in some of the cases—but this does not seem to be the intended meaning. The effects of a conditional situation are incorrectly expressed using the simple present tense verb *become.* The preposition *from* is incorrect with *immune*; it should be *to.*

C The effects of a conditional situation are incorrectly expressed using the simple present tense verb *are.*

D See above the comment on *causing* in (B). The effects of a conditional situation are incorrectly expressed using the simple past tense verb *became.* The preposition with *immune* should be *to.*

E **Correct.** The effects of a conditional situation are correctly expressed using the conditional verb *would become.* The preposition *to* (rather than *from*) is correct with *immune.*

The correct answer is E.

736. Covering 71 percent of Earth's surface, the oceans play an essential role in maintaining the conditions for human existence on land, moderating temperature by the absorption of heat and carbon dioxide, and giving pure water back to the atmosphere through evaporation.

(A) Covering 71 percent of Earth's surface, the oceans play an essential role in maintaining the conditions for human existence on land, moderating

(B) Covering 71 percent of Earth's surface and playing an essential role in maintaining the conditions for human existence on land, the oceans moderate

(C) The oceans cover 71 percent of Earth's surface and play an essential role in maintaining conditions for human existence on land, and by moderating

(D) The oceans cover 71 percent of Earth's surface, play an essential role in maintaining the conditions for human existence on land, and moderate

(E) The oceans cover 71 percent of Earth's surface, playing an essential role in maintaining the conditions for human existence on land, and they moderate

Parallelism; Rhetorical construction; Grammatical construction

This sentence about the essential role oceans play in maintaining conditions for human existence on land begins with a participial phrase describing the vastness of the oceans, followed by the main clause (*oceans play an essential role . . .*). The object, *role*, is modified by a prepositional phrase that indicates what kind of role the oceans play (it plays a role *in maintaining the conditions for human existence on land*). This statement about the ocean's role in maintaining terrestrial conditions is elucidated by two parallel participial phrases that describe the oceans, explaining how they maintain conditions essential for human existence on land (*moderating . . . and giving . . .*).

A **Correct.** This version of the sentence effectively conveys the means by which the ocean plays an essential role in maintaining the conditions for human existence on land, using parallel verb forms.

B This version of the sentence is ungrammatical; *and giving . . .* suggests that this is part of a series of participial phrases, but it is not.

C The conjunction followed by a prepositional phrase *and by moderating . . .* anticipates a new subject—an agent that does something by moderating—but this subject never appears.

D This version of the sentence is structured as a series of verbs—*cover, play*, and *moderate*—all describing things the oceans do; the final participial phrase *giving . . . water . . .* violates the parallel structure set up in the sentence.

E This version of the sentence correctly makes *playing an essential role . . .* a function of the oceans' coverage of Earth's surface, but the introduction of a new main verb *moderate* fails to indicate that what follows (moderating temperature and returning pure water) identifies the role oceans play in maintaining conditions for human existence on land. Furthermore, the participial phrase *and giving pure water . . .* violates the parallel structure set up by the series of main verbs that appear earlier in this version of the sentence.

The correct answer is A.

737. Some anthropologists believe that the genetic homogeneity evident in the world's people is the result of a "population bottleneck"—<u>at some time in the past our ancestors suffered an event, greatly reducing their numbers</u> and thus our genetic variation.

(A) at some time in the past our ancestors suffered an event, greatly reducing their numbers

(B) that at some time in the past our ancestors suffered an event that greatly reduced their numbers

(C) that some time in the past our ancestors suffered an event so that their numbers were greatly reduced,

(D) some time in the past our ancestors suffered an event from which their numbers were greatly reduced

(E) some time in the past, that our ancestors suffered an event so as to reduce their numbers greatly,

Grammatical construction; Parallelism

The underlined part of this sentence is an explanatory rewording of the clause that follows *believe*. *Scientists believe that X*—[in other words,] *that Y*. In this construction, X and Y are parallel clauses.

A The omission of *that* after the dash makes the function of the final clause unclear. The structure makes that clause appear to be an awkward and rhetorically puzzling separate assertion that the writer has appended to the prior claim about what the anthropologists believe. The agent or cause of *reducing* is unclear.

B Correct. Repetition of *that* effectively signals the paraphrasing of the belief.

C The preposition *at* before *some time* is missing; without *at* the adverb *sometime* would be needed instead of this two-word noun phrase. The modifier of *event* is expressed with a wordy passive construction, which destroys the parallelism between it and what follows.

D Repetition of *that* signals the paraphrasing of the belief and is therefore needed. The preposition *at* before *some time* is missing. The modifier of *event* is expressed with a wordy passive construction, which destroys the parallelism between it and what follows.

E *That* is repeated in the paraphrase, but in the wrong place. A possible, and absurd, reading of this version is that our ancestors suffered an event in order to willfully reduce their own numbers and thus our genetic variation.

The correct answer is B.

738. Foraging at all times of the day and night, but interspersing their feeding with periods of rest that last <u>between one and eight hours, a sperm whale could eat so</u> much as a ton of squid a day.

(A) between one and eight hours, a sperm whale could eat so

(B) between one and eight hours, sperm whales can eat as

(C) between one to eight hours, sperm whales could eat as

(D) from one to eight hours, sperm whales could eat so

(E) from one to eight hours, a sperm whale can eat so

Agreement; Diction

Although this sentence, as presented, uses the conditional or past verb form *could*, it is more plausibly intended to make a general statement about the actual behavior of a species, a statement that holds in the present day. For that purpose, the present indicative *can* is preferable. *So much as* is not the correct wording to express the upper level of a variable amount; *as much as* should be used instead. Also, although the singular *a sperm whale* can be used to refer to sperm whales generally, the plural *their* needs to refer to the plural *sperm whales*.

A This sentence incorrectly uses *so*. Also, the plural *their* does not agree with the singular *sperm whale*.

B **Correct.** Both *can* and *as* are used; also, *sperm whales* agrees with the plural *their*.

C *To* is the wrong word to use with *between*. The proper construction would be *between . . . and* or *from . . . to*.

D This sentence incorrectly uses *so*.

E *So* is not the correct form; also the use of the singular *a sperm whale* does not agree with the plural *their*.

The correct answer is B.

739. In some types of pine tree, <u>a thick layer of needles protects the buds from which new growth proceeds; consequently they are able to withstand forest fires relatively well</u>.

(A) a thick layer of needles protects the buds from which new growth proceeds; consequently they are able to withstand forest fires relatively well

(B) a thick needle layer protects buds from where new growth proceeds, so that they can withstand forest fires relatively well

(C) a thick layer of needles protect the buds from which new growth proceeds; thus, they are able to withstand relatively well any forest fires

(D) since the buds from which new growth proceeds are protected by a thick needle layer, consequently they can therefore withstand forest fires relatively well

(E) because the buds where new growth happens are protected by a thick layer of needles, they are able to withstand forest fires relatively easily as a result

Grammatical construction; Rhetorical construction

This sentence is fine as written. It uses the correct *from which* to introduce the relative clause modifying *buds* and avoids redundant expressions of causation, such as *consequently . . . therefore*, or *because . . . as a result*.

A **Correct.** The relative clause starting with *from which* is in the correct form, and the causality is expressed efficiently and clearly with one word, *consequently*.

B In this context, *needle layer* is less precise than the more standard *layer of needles*, which makes it clear that the layer is composed of needles rather than being, for example, a layer of a needle. *From where* is not the correct form, because it is redundant in using two words that express the idea of location (*from* and *where*) instead of one.

C The short direct object *any forest fires* is separated from its verb *withstand* by an adverb phrase; this word order is awkward, and is acceptable only with very long direct objects and in some cases where there is no other reasonable way to eliminate ambiguity.

D This version is unnecessarily redundant in expressing causation, using all of *since*, *consequently*, and *therefore*. As in answer choice B, *layer of needles* would be more precise than *needle layer*.

E This version is unnecessarily redundant in expressing causation, using both *because* and *as a result*.

The correct answer is A.

740. The tourism commission has conducted surveys of hotels in the most popular resorts, <u>with the ultimate goal of reducing the guests who end up expressing overall dissatisfaction with the service in the hotels</u>.

(A) with the ultimate goal of reducing the guests who end up expressing overall dissatisfaction with the service in the hotels

(B) with the goal to ultimately reduce the number of guests who end up expressing overall dissatisfaction with the hotels' service

(C) ultimately with the goal to reduce expressions of overall dissatisfaction by the guests with the hotel service

(D) in an ultimate attempt to reduce the number of guests that ends up expressing overall dissatisfaction with the hotels' service

(E) with the ultimate goal of reducing the number of guests who express overall dissatisfaction with the hotels' service

Verb form; Rhetorical construction

This sentence seems to be saying something absurd: that the goal is to reduce the guests themselves, instead of to reduce the **number** of guests or the expressions of dissatisfaction. It is also awkward in introducing the superfluous *end up*; but at least, if it does so, the correct form to agree with the subject *guests* is *end up*, not *ends up*, which is used in answer choice D. In general, direct modifiers (such as *with the (hotel) service*) should not be separated from the word they modify (such as *dissatisfaction*) if possible.

A *Reducing the guests* is clearly not the intent of the sentence; it should be phrased as reducing the number of guests or the expressions of dissatisfaction.

B *With the goal to ultimately reduce* is awkward and unidiomatic.

C *With the hotel service* should be placed next to *dissatisfaction*; also, *ultimately with the goal* is awkward, better phrased as *with the ultimate goal.*

D The relative clause *that ends up* . . . modifies the plural *guests* (not, in this context, *number*), so the correct verb form is *end up.*

E **Correct.** The *with* phrase is concise, and it is the number of guests, not the guests themselves, that is to be reduced. *With the hotel's service* is adjacent to *dissatisfaction.* Also, in the relative clause starting with *who*, the implicit subject of *express* is *guests*, so this verb correctly agrees with its subject.

The correct answer is E.

741. A new study suggests that the conversational pace of everyday life may be so brisk it hampers the ability of some children for distinguishing discrete sounds and words and, the result is, to make sense of speech.

(A) it hampers the ability of some children for distinguishing discrete sounds and words and, the result is, to make

(B) that it hampers the ability of some children to distinguish discrete sounds and words and, as a result, to make

(C) that it hampers the ability of some children to distinguish discrete sounds and words and, the result of this, they are unable to make

(D) that it hampers the ability of some children to distinguish discrete sounds and words, and results in not making

(E) as to hamper the ability of some children for distinguishing discrete sounds and words, resulting in being unable to make

Rhetorical construction; Parallelism; Diction

The sentence describes a hypothesized causal series: The fast conversational pace impairs children's ability to distinguish individual sounds and words, and this, in turn, impairs their ability to make sense of speech. These two consequences, both impaired abilities, are most clearly and efficiently expressed in parallel infinitive phrases (*to distinguish* and *to make*). The explanatory phrase *as a result* before the second infinitive clarifies the sequence. The term *ability* should be followed by the preposition *to*, not *for.*

A *For* is the wrong preposition to follow *ability*; the phrase *and, the result is,* introduces a new clause which indicates that children's inability to distinguish sounds enables them to make sense of speech.

B **Correct.** The two abilities hampered by the fast pace of conversation are described with the parallel infinitive phrases *to distinguish* and *to make.*

C *The result of this* is a new subject that grammatically requires a new verb; the phrase is wordy and unclear.

D This version of the sentence nonsensically suggests that the pace of speech results in not making sense of speech, removing the children from the picture as the ones who are affected.

E The phrase is awkward, wordy, and unclear; *for* is the incorrect preposition to follow ability.

The correct answer is B.

742. The nineteenth-century chemist Humphry Davy presented the results of his early experiments in his "Essay on Heat and Light," a critique of all chemistry since Robert Boyle as well as a vision of a new chemistry that Davy hoped to found.

(A) a critique of all chemistry since Robert Boyle as well as a vision of a
(B) a critique of all chemistry following Robert Boyle and also his envisioning of a
(C) a critique of all chemistry after Robert Boyle and envisioning as well
(D) critiquing all chemistry from Robert Boyle forward and also a vision of
(E) critiquing all the chemistry done since Robert Boyle as well as his own envisioning of

Parallelism; Rhetorical construction

The main objective of the sentence is to describe "Essay on Heat and Light" as Davy's presentation of his own experiments and to further explain that the essay served as both a critique of previous chemistry and a vision of a new kind of chemistry. The clearest, most effective form for providing this explanation of the essay's function is to make *critique* and *vision* both appositives of "Essay on Heat and Light," and to present them in a parallel structure.

A **Correct.** The phrases describing the essay's function are presented in parallel form.

B *Critique* and *his envisioning* are not parallel; the phrase *and also his envisioning* is unnecessarily wordy; it is also unclear to whom *his* refers.

C The two descriptors are not parallel.

D The two descriptors are not parallel.

E The meaning is confused in the assertion that Davy critiqued his own vision of chemistry.

The correct answer is A.

743. To attract the most talented workers, some companies are offering a wider range of benefits, letting employees pick those most important to them.

(A) benefits, letting employees pick those most important to them
(B) benefits, letting employees pick the most important of them to themselves
(C) benefits and letting employees pick the most important to themselves
(D) benefits and let employees pick the most important to them
(E) benefits and let employees pick those that are most important to themselves

Diction; Parallelism; Verb form

The sentence describes the benefit options offered by some companies, which allow employees to *pick those most important to them. Letting* maintains the progressive sense of *are offering; those* refers clearly and concisely to *benefits*; and *them* is the correct pronoun to serve as the object of the preposition *to.*

A **Correct.** The sentence clearly and concisely explains benefit options that allow employees to *pick those most important to them.*

B *The most important of them to themselves* is wordy, and the function of *themselves* is unclear. Normally, *themselves* would be either reflexive or emphatic, but in this case it cannot reasonably be taken in either of those ways. This nonstandard use of the pronoun makes it unclear whether *to themselves* is supposed to modify *pick* or *most important of them.*

C The pronoun *themselves* is used incorrectly, and its intended function is unclear. Normally, *themselves* would be either reflexive or emphatic, but in this case it cannot reasonably be taken in either of those ways. This nonstandard use of the pronoun makes it unclear whether *to themselves* is supposed to modify *pick* or *most important of them.*

D The present tense verb *let* incorrectly shifts tense from the present progressive *are offering.*

E The present tense verb *let* incorrectly shifts tense from the present progressive *are offering*; the function of *themselves* is unclear. Normally, *themselves* would be either reflexive or emphatic, but in this case it cannot reasonably be taken in either of those ways. This nonstandard use of the pronoun makes it unclear whether *to themselves* is supposed to modify *pick* or *most important of them.*

The correct answer is A.

744. Many of the earliest known images of Hindu deities in India date from the time of the Kushan Empire, fashioned either from the spotted sandstone of Mathura or Gandharan grey schist.

(A) Empire, fashioned either from the spotted sandstone of Mathura or

(B) Empire, fashioned from either the spotted sandstone of Mathura or from

(C) Empire, either fashioned from the spotted sandstone of Mathura or

(D) Empire and either fashioned from the spotted sandstone of Mathura or from

(E) Empire and were fashioned either from the spotted sandstone of Mathura or from

Logical predication; Parallelism

The sentence makes two claims about the earliest known images of Hindu deities in India: They date from the Kushan Empire, and they are made from sandstone or schist. The clearest, most effective way to incorporate these two claims into a single sentence is to provide two parallel predicates for the single subject, *the earliest known images of Hindu deities in India.* The two options of media, presented as either/or choices, must also be given in parallel structure: *either from … or from …* or *from either … or. …*

A Placement of the modifier *fashioned …* suggests that the *Empire* (the closest noun), not the images of the deities, was fashioned out of these materials; to parallel *either from*, the preposition *from* should also follow *or.*

B Parallelism requires that *either* precede the first appearance of *from* or that the second appearance of *from* be eliminated.

C As in (A) and (B), the placement of the modifier after *Empire* is misleading; parallelism requires that the phrase *fashioned from*, or another comparable verb and preposition, follow *or.*

D Parallelism requires that a verb follow *or*, since a verb follows *either.*

E **Correct.** Two verbs, *date* and *were fashioned*, introduce parallel predicates for the subject, *earliest known images*; the choices of media are correctly presented with the structure *either from … or from.*

The correct answer is E.

745. Tides typically range from three to six feet, but while some places show no tides at all, some others, such as the Bay of Fundy, have tides of at least thirty feet and more.

(A) some others, such as the Bay of Fundy, have tides of at least thirty feet and more

(B) the others, such as the Bay of Fundy, that have tides of more than thirty feet

(C) others, such as the Bay of Fundy, have tides of more than thirty feet

(D) those at the Bay of Fundy, which has tides of more than thirty feet

(E) the ones at the Bay of Fundy have tides of at least thirty feet and more

Idiom; Grammatical construction

This sentence defines typical tides and then draws a contrast between locations with tides lower than that norm and locations with tides higher than the norm. The proper idiom for drawing this contrast is *some places* and *others*—not *some places* and *some others* as written. The height of tides in places such as the Bay of Fundy is expressed in a confusing manner since *at least thirty feet* sets a lower limit on the height. This wording is pointlessly redundant with the phrase *and more*, which follows it. *At least* would normally be used to indicate that the writer does not know, or prefers not to say, whether the tides are sometimes higher. *And more* rhetorically conflicts with this by signaling a definite commitment to the claim that they are (at least sometimes) higher. A charitable reading suggests that *tides of more than thirty feet* is the intended meaning.

A The sentence contains repetitive and redundant wording—*some places* and *some others*, and *at least thirty feet and more.*

B The final clause is incomplete because *that* introduces a subordinate clause, leaving the subject *others* with no main verb.

C **Correct.** A contrast is drawn between places with low tides and places with high tides using the expression *some places* and *others*, and the height of the high tides is expressed clearly and without redundancy.

D The pronoun *those*, which refers to *places*, does not make sense along with *at the Bay of Fundy*, which names a single place; the final clause is incomplete because *which* introduces a subordinate clause, leaving the subject *those* with no verb.

E The word *ones*, which refers to *places*, does not make sense along with *at the Bay of Fundy*, which names a single place; *at least thirty feet and more* is redundant and confusing.

The correct answer is C.

746. A leading figure in the Scottish Enlightenment, Adam Smith's two major books are to democratic capitalism what Marx's *Das Kapital* is to socialism.

(A) Adam Smith's two major books are to democratic capitalism what

(B) Adam Smith's two major books are to democratic capitalism like

(C) Adam Smith's two major books are to democratic capitalism just as

(D) Adam Smith wrote two major books that are to democratic capitalism similar to

(E) Adam Smith wrote two major books that are to democratic capitalism what

Idiom; Logical predication

A leading figure in the Scottish Enlightenment describes Adam Smith, not his two books, so the name of Adam Smith must immediately follow the opening phrase. The comparison between Smith's books and Marx's book is expressed as a ratio, so the correct idiomatic expression is *x is to y what a is to b.*

A The opening phrase is a dangling modifier because it describes Smith, not his books.

B The opening phrase is a dangling modifier; *like* is an incorrect word for making the comparison.

C The opening phrase is a dangling modifier; *just as* is an incorrect term for the comparison.

D *Similar to* is an incorrect conclusion to the comparison introduced by *are to.*

E **Correct.** The opening phrase is followed by the subject that it modifies, Adam Smith, and the comparison of the two men's work is presented idiomatically.

The correct answer is E.

747. Researchers studying the brain scans of volunteers who pondered ethical dilemmas have found that the basis for making tough moral judgments is emotion, not logic or analytical reasoning.

(A) the brain scans of volunteers who pondered ethical dilemmas have found that the basis for making tough moral judgments is

(B) the brain scans of volunteers who pondered ethical dilemmas and found the basis to make tough moral decisions to be

(C) the brain scans of volunteers pondering ethical dilemmas and found that the basis for making tough moral decisions is

(D) volunteers' brain scans while pondering ethical dilemmas have found the basis to make tough moral judgments to be

(E) volunteers' brain scans while they pondered ethical dilemmas have found that the basis for making tough moral judgments is

Logical predication; Grammatical construction

The sentence reports that researchers got volunteers to ponder ethical dilemmas and make moral judgments. Brain scans revealed that the volunteers' judgments were based on emotion rather than logical analysis. The main clause of this sentence is *Researchers . . . have found that . . .*; embedded within this sentence, the present participial phrase *studying . . .* describes the researchers, the relative clause *who pondered . . .* describes the volunteers, and the object of the main verb appears as a noun clause *that the basis . . . is. . . .*

A **Correct.** The sentence is coherent and grammatically correct.

B The use of the conjunction *and* immediately before *found* indicates that the past tense verbs *pondered* and *found* both have *volunteers* as subject, but this changes the original sentence, making it a long noun phrase rather than a complete sentence.

C The conjunction *and* leaves the verb *found* without a subject, and this changes the original sentence into a sequence of incoherently connected phrases rather than a complete sentence.

D The phrase *the basis to make* is unidiomatic, a sufficient reason for rejecting this option. The placement of the modifier *while pondering* appears in a form parallel to *studying* and means that the researchers, not the volunteers, were pondering ethical dilemmas. This does not make the sentence incoherent, but creates a sentence that fails to capture the meaning clearly intended in the original sentence.

E Because the word *volunteers'* is a possessive form, and functions adjectivally as a modifier of *brain scans*, *they* must refer back to *researchers* rather than to *volunteers'*. This is not incorrect in itself, but, as with (D), the resulting sentence fails to capture the intended meaning of the original sentence.

The correct answer is A.

748. Rivaling the pyramids of Egypt or even the ancient cities of the Maya as an achievement, <u>the army of terra-cotta warriors created to protect Qin Shi Huang, China's first emperor, in his afterlife is more than 2,000 years old and took 700,000 artisans more than 36 years to complete.</u>

(A) the army of terra-cotta warriors created to protect Qin Shi Huang, China's first emperor, in his afterlife is more than 2,000 years old and took 700,000 artisans more than 36 years to complete

(B) Qin Shi Huang, China's first emperor, was protected in his afterlife by an army of terra-cotta warriors that was created more than 2,000 years ago by 700,000 artisans who took more than 36 years to complete it

(C) it took 700,000 artisans more than 36 years to create an army of terra-cotta warriors more than 2,000 years ago that would protect Qin Shi Huang, China's first emperor, in his afterlife

(D) more than 2,000 years ago, 700,000 artisans worked more than 36 years to create an army of terra-cotta warriors to protect Qin Shi Huang, China's first emperor, in his afterlife

(E) more than 36 years were needed to complete the army of terra-cotta warriors that 700,000 artisans created 2,000 years ago to protect Qin Shi Huang, China's first emperor, in his afterlife

Logical predication; Rhetorical construction

The opening modifier, *Rivaling the pyramids* ... describes *the army of terra-cotta warriors*, which must immediately follow the modifier. The placement of the predicates that follow is important; they must clarify two things about the army of terra-cotta warriors: how old it is and how long it took to complete. The clearest and most effective way to express these two assertions is as parallel verb phrases, *is more than 2,000 years old* and *took ... more than 36 years to complete.*

A **Correct.** The opening phrase correctly modifies the subject, *the army of terra-cotta warriors*; the placement of modifiers and predicates in the main clause makes the meaning of the sentence clear.

B Opening phrase is a dangling modifier because it does not describe the subject *Qin Shi Huang*; in addition, the sentence is awkward and unclear.

C Opening phrase is a dangling modifier because it does not describe the subject *it*; the sequence of information presented is confusing and unclear.

D Opening phrase is a dangling modifier because it does not describe the subject *700,000 artisans.*

E Opening phrase is a dangling modifier because it does not describe the subject *more than 36 years.*

The correct answer is A.

749. In California, a lack of genetic variation in the Argentine ant has allowed the species to spread widely; due to their being so genetically similar to one another, the ants consider all their fellows to be a close relative and thus do not engage in the kind of fierce intercolony struggles that limits the spread of this species in its native Argentina.

(A) due to their being so genetically similar to one another, the ants consider all their fellows to be a close relative and thus do not engage in the kind of fierce intercolony struggles that limits
(B) due to its being so genetically similar, the ant considers all its fellows to be a close relative and thus does not engage in the kind of fierce intercolony struggles that limit
(C) because it is so genetically similar, the ant considers all its fellows to be close relatives and thus does not engage in the kind of fierce intercolony struggles that limits
(D) because they are so genetically similar to one another, the ants consider all their fellows to be close relatives and thus do not engage in the kind of fierce intercolony struggles that limit
(E) because of being so genetically similar to one another, the ants consider all their fellows to be a close relative and thus do not engage in the kind of fierce intercolony struggles that limits

Diction; Agreement

Words that express comparisons, such as *similar*, require either a plural object, with an optional expression of the entities being compared, or a singular object, in which case this explicit comparison is required. Thus *its being so genetically similar*, without this explicit comparison, is incorrect. Also, the two sides of the construction *consider . . . to be* must agree in number (*fellows . . . close relatives*, not *fellows . . . a close relative*).

A *Consider all their fellows to be a close relative* shows incorrect agreement, with plural *fellows* and singular *a close relative.*

B *Its being so genetically similar* is incorrect because there is no explicit statement of what the ant is similar to; also, the plural *fellows* and *singular a close relative* do not agree.

C *It is so genetically similar* is incorrect because there is no explicit statement of what the ant is similar to.

D **Correct.** The clause with *similar* uses the plural *they* and an explicit *to one another*, and agreement is respected between *ants* and *fellows.*

E The plural *fellows* and singular *a close relative* do not agree.

The correct answer is D.

750. Next month, state wildlife officials are scheduled to take over the job of increasing the wolf population in the federally designated recovery area, the number of which will however ultimately be dictated by the number of prey in the area.

(A) area, the number of which will however
(B) area; the size of the population, however, will
(C) area, however the number of wolves will
(D) area; the number of which will, however,
(E) area, when the size of the population will, however,

Grammatical construction; Diction

The point of the sentence is that the ultimate size of the wolf population will be determined according to the number of prey in the area. However, the phrase *the number of which* has no referent since it cannot logically refer to the noncount noun *population* or to the singular *wolf*, which is used adjectivally here to modify *population.* The idea can be expressed clearly by making *the size of the population* the subject of a new independent clause: *the size of the population* will *be dictated by the number of prey.*

A *The number of which* cannot logically refer to the noncount noun *population* or to the singular *wolf*, which is used adjectivally here to modify *population.*

B **Correct.** The idea is expressed clearly with an independent clause: *the size of the population* will *be dictated by the number of prey.*

C *However* is intended to serve as a conjunctive adverb between the two independent clauses, but the punctuation of the sentence creates confusion by suggesting that *however* is modifying *are scheduled.* A semicolon after *area* and a comma after *however* would make the intended function of *however* clear.

D *The number of which* cannot logically refer to the noncount noun *population*; the semicolon creates confusion since it is not followed by an independent clause.

E *When* illogically suggests that the size of the population will be determined at the moment wildlife officials take over the task. This conflicts with the ensuing claim that the determination will *ultimately* depend on a long-term condition (*the number of prey in the area*).

The correct answer is B.

751. About 5 million acres in the United States have been invaded by leafy spurge, a herbaceous plant from Eurasia with milky sap that gives mouth sores to cattle, displacing grasses and other cattle food and rendering rangeland worthless.

(A) States have been invaded by leafy spurge, a herbaceous plant from Eurasia with milky sap that gives mouth sores to cattle, displacing grasses and other cattle food and rendering

(B) States have been invaded by leafy spurge, *a herbaceous plant from Eurasia*, with milky sap, that gives mouth sores to cattle and displaces grasses and other cattle food, rendering

(C) States have been invaded by leafy spurge, a herbaceous plant from Eurasia having milky sap that gives mouth sores to cattle and displacing grasses and other cattle food, rendering

(D) States, having been invaded by leafy spurge, a herbaceous plant from Eurasia with milky sap that gives mouth sores to cattle, displaces grasses and other cattle food, and renders

(E) States, having been invaded by leafy spurge, a herbaceous plant from Eurasia that has milky sap giving mouth sores to cattle and displacing grasses and other cattle food, rendering

Logical predication; Grammatical construction

The sentence explains that leafy spurge causes mouth sores in cattle and also displaces other plants eaten by cattle. However, the structure of the sentence seems, illogically, to indicate that *displacing grasses* modifies either the immediately preceding phrase (*that gives mouth sores to cattle*) or the main subject of the sentence (*about 5 million acres in the United States*). A clearer way to express the effects of the leafy spurge invasion is with a compound predicate in the subordinate clause: *that gives mouth sores . . . and displaces grasses.*

A Displacing grasses appears illogically to modify either about 5 million acres in the United States or that gives mouth sores to cattle.

B **Correct.** The effects of the leafy spurge invasion are expressed clearly with a compound predicate in the subordinate clause: that gives mouth sores . . . and displaces grasses. The parenthetical commas around with milky sap make it clear that the entire phrase that gives . . . and displaces . . . rendering . . . is intended to modify a herbaceous plant from Eurasia. Although the sap may well be the means by which the plant gives mouth sores to cattle, the sentence can be well formed and meaningful without making a definite commitment to whether that is the case.

C *Having* and *displacing* should not be expressed in parallel form since the first is a permanent characteristic of leafy spurge and the second refers to an effect of the plant's invasion.

D The subject of the sentence, *5 million acres* is not clearly paired with a verb. The structure of the sentence suggests that *5 million acres* may be the intended subject of both *displaces* and *renders* but it is illogical to say that 5 million acres displaces grasses and renders rangeland worthless.

E The subject of the sentence, *5 million acres* is not clearly paired with a verb. The structure of the sentence suggests that *5 million acres* may be the intended subject of both *displaces* and *renders* but it is illogical to say that 5 million acres displaces grasses and renders rangeland worthless.

The correct answer is B.

752. While it costs about the same to run nuclear plants as other types of power plants, it is the fixed costs that stem from building nuclear plants that makes it more expensive for them to generate electricity.

(A) While it costs about the same to run nuclear plants as other types of power plants, it is the fixed costs that stem from building nuclear plants that makes it more expensive for them to generate electricity.

(B) While the cost of running nuclear plants is about the same as for other types of power plants, the fixed costs that stem from building nuclear plants make the electricity they generate more expensive.

(C) Even though it costs about the same to run nuclear plants as for other types of power plants, it is the fixed costs that stem from building nuclear plants that makes the electricity they generate more expensive.

(D) It costs about the same to run nuclear plants as for other types of power plants, whereas the electricity they generate is more expensive, stemming from the fixed costs of building nuclear plants.

(E) The cost of running nuclear plants is about the same as other types of power plants, but the electricity they generate is made more expensive because of the fixed costs stemming from building nuclear plants.

Agreement; Logical predication

The emphatic construction *it is X that does Y* (as in the phrase *it is Jane who knows the answer*) should be used only when there is a compelling reason to emphasize the doer of the action. In this sentence, the emphatic construction is used without good reason.

A This sentence uses the emphatic structure *it is ... that* without justification. The singular verb *makes* violates the agreement within the structure. The verb *makes* should agree with the notional subject (*the fixed costs*), not with the pronoun *it*.

B **Correct.** This answer choice clearly and succinctly compares the two types of costs.

C In addition to using the more cumbersome emphatic structure, this version violates the agreement within the structure. The verb should agree with the notional subject (*the fixed costs*), not with the pronoun *it*.

D The preposition *for* is redundant in comparing the two objects of *run*. Since it is not clear what *stemming* ... refers to, this is a dangling modifier.

E The passive construction *electricity ... is made more expensive because of* ... is wordy and cumbersome. The preposition *for* is necessary in the comparison of the costs.

The correct answer is B.

753. The 32 species that make up the dolphin family are closely related to whales and in fact include the animal known as the killer whale, which can grow to be 30 feet long and is famous for its aggressive hunting pods.

(A) include the animal known as the killer whale, which can grow to be 30 feet long and is

(B) include the animal known as the killer whale, growing as big as 30 feet long and

(C) include the animal known as the killer whale, growing up to 30 feet long and being

(D) includes the animal known as the killer whale, which can grow as big as 30 feet long and is

(E) includes the animal known as the killer whale, which can grow to be 30 feet long and it is

Rhetorical construction; Agreement

The subject of the sentence is *the 32 species that make up the dolphin family*, and the sentence makes two claims about them: They are closely related, and they include the killer whale. The relative pronoun *which* restates the object of the second verb, reintroducing *the animal known as the killer whale* as the subject of a relative clause followed by two parallel verbs: *can grow* and *is famous*.

A **Correct.** In this concise sentence, verbs agree in number with their subjects and the relative pronoun *which* indicates clearly that *the animal known as the killer whale* is the subject of the verbs in the dependent clause.

B Changing the verb to the participial *growing* introduces ambiguity, because it could refer back to the subject of the sentence (*32 species*).

C *The participial growing* might refer to *the 32 species*; the introduction of *being* is unnecessarily wordy and adds nothing in terms of meaning.

D *as big as* is an idiomatically incorrect expression of the comparison; the plural verb form *include* is needed to match the plural subject *the 32 species*.

E *It* simply restates the subject of the previous phrase, introducing more words but no additional meaning; the singular verb form *includes* should be the plural form *include*.

The correct answer is A.

754. The first trenches that were cut into a 500-acre site at Tell Hamoukar, Syria, have yielded strong evidence for centrally administered complex societies in northern regions of the Middle East that were arising simultaneously with but independently of the more celebrated city-states of southern Mesopotamia, in what is now southern Iraq.

(A) that were cut into a 500-acre site at Tell Hamoukar, Syria, have yielded strong evidence for centrally administered complex societies in northern regions of the Middle East that were arising simultaneously with but

(B) that were cut into a 500-acre site at Tell Hamoukar, Syria, yields strong evidence that centrally administered complex societies in northern regions of the Middle East were arising simultaneously with but also

(C) having been cut into a 500-acre site at Tell Hamoukar, Syria, have yielded strong evidence that centrally administered complex societies in northern regions of the Middle East were arising simultaneously but

(D) cut into a 500-acre site at Tell Hamoukar, Syria, yields strong evidence of centrally administered complex societies in northern regions of the Middle East arising simultaneously but also

(E) cut into a 500-acre site at Tell Hamoukar, Syria, have yielded strong evidence that centrally administered complex societies in northern regions of the Middle East arose simultaneously with but

Rhetorical construction; Agreement; Grammatical construction

This sentence, explaining interconnections among a number of events, needs to be streamlined as much as possible in order to become understandable. To this end, unnecessary words and structures should be eliminated. Prominent among these are the relative clauses beginning with *that*. Additionally, the subject of this sentence is the plural *trenches*, which requires a plural verb.

A *That were cut* … and *that were arising* … are unnecessarily wordy and create an unnecessarily complicated and confusing sentence structure.

B In addition to the unnecessarily wordy relative clauses, the singular verb *yields* does not agree with the plural subject *trenches*.

C *Having been cut* … is unnecessarily wordy; *arising simultaneously* must be followed by the preposition *with* in order to make sense.

D The singular verb *yields* does not agree with the plural subject *trenches*; *also* adds no meaning to the sentence.

E **Correct.** Unnecessary clauses and phrases are avoided, and the subject and verb of the main clause agree in number.

The correct answer is E.

755. Companies are relying more and more on networked computers for such critical tasks as inventory management, electronic funds transfer, and electronic data interchange, in which standard business transactions are handled via computer rather than on paper.

(A) in which standard business transactions are handled via computer rather than on paper

(B) where computers handle standard business transactions rather than on paper

(C) in which computers handle standard business transactions instead of on paper

(D) where standard business transactions are handled, not with paper, but instead via computer

(E) in which standard business transactions are being handled via computer, in place of on paper

Idiom; Logical predication; Rhetorical construction

The concluding comparison in this sentence uses the idiom *rather than*, which requires parallel structures. In this sentence the prepositional phrase *via computer* parallels *on paper*. Substituting *where* for *in which* creates a nonstandard idiom.

A **Correct.** This sentence uses standard idiomatic constructions and avoids the problems that are found in the other versions.

B *Where* is a nonstandard way to refer to a noun that does not name a location. If electronic data interchange were a location, this version would entail the odd claim that *on paper* is an alternative location at which computers would be expected to process information.

C The comparison of the clause *computers handle* . . . with the prepositional phrase *on paper* illogically treats a location (*on paper*) as an alternative to an activity (*computers handle*).

D As in (B), *where* is a nonstandard idiom. The commas around *not with paper* appear to make this phrase parenthetical; thus, it is somewhat unclear what *instead via computer* is contrasted with.

E The pile of prepositions in the phrase *in place of on paper* is unnecessarily confusing and wordy.

The correct answer is A.

756. Combining enormous physical strength with higher intelligence, the Neanderthals appear as equipped for facing any obstacle the environment could put in their path, but their relatively sudden disappearance during the Paleolithic era indicates that an inability to adapt to some environmental change led to their extinction.

(A) appear as equipped for facing any obstacle the environment could put in their path,

(B) appear to have been equipped to face any obstacle the environment could put in their path,

(C) appear as equipped to face any obstacle the environment could put in their paths,

(D) appeared as equipped to face any obstacle the environment could put in their paths,

(E) appeared to have been equipped for facing any obstacle the environment could put in their path,

Verb form; Diction

Because Neanderthals "disappeared," the verb describing their apparent abilities cannot be present tense, so *as equipped* must be changed to *to have been equipped*. The expression *equipped to face* is clearer and more direct than *equipped for facing*.

A *As equipped* indicates that Neanderthals still appear this way; *equipped* should be followed by an infinitive form instead of a prepositional phrase.

B **Correct.** The verb tense clearly indicates that the current evidence is about Neanderthals in the past.

C *As equipped* does not indicate that Neanderthals appeared this way in the past; while individual Neanderthals may well have followed different paths, this sentence is about the single evolutionary path taken by Neanderthals as a species.

D Present-tense *appear* is needed to parallel present-tense *indicates* and to reinforce that this is current evidence about Neanderthals in the past; as in (C), *paths* should be singular.

E *For facing* is an incorrect substitution of a prepositional phrase for an infinitive.

The correct answer is B.

757. To map Earth's interior, geologists use a network of seismometers to chart seismic waves that originate in the earth's crust and ricochet around its interior, most rapidly traveling through cold, dense regions and slower through hotter rocks.

(A) interior, most rapidly traveling through cold, dense regions and slower

(B) interior, which travel most rapidly through cold, dense regions, and more slowly

(C) interior, traveling most rapidly through cold, dense regions and more slowly

(D) interior and most rapidly travel through cold, dense regions, and slower

(E) interior and that travel most rapidly through cold, dense regions and slower

Grammatical construction; Parallelism

This sentence explains in detail an activity of geologists (using seismometers to chart waves), focusing primarily on the object, seismic waves. A description of these waves is developed in a relative clause (*that originate . . . hotter rocks*) that contains a compound verb phrase (*originate . . . ricochet . . .*). The action, *ricochet*, is further described in a participial phrase in which *traveling* . . . is then further described in a comparison of travel speeds in cold and hot regions of Earth's crust.

A The two expressions of comparison should be parallel. Because *most rapidly* is placed before the verb, it appears to modify the entire ensuing phrase, including *slower*. This and the contrast between the forms of *rapidly* and *slower* make the comparisons nonparallel. Some usage advisers consider *slower* to be only an adjective. Although *slower* is sometimes used as an adverb, that usage would be more appropriate with the parallel *faster*. The stark contrast between this typically adjectival form and the clearly adverbial *ly* form is somewhat jarring.

B The referent of the relative pronoun *which* is unclear.

C **Correct.** The modifiers are parallel and correctly positioned in relation to the verb.

D This version of the sentence offers *travel* as a compound verb parallel with *originate* and *ricochet* rather than as a description of how the waves ricochet. It has the same problems with parallelism as (A).

E Adding a relative clause *and that* . . . makes this sentence wordy and awkward.

The correct answer is C.

758. Prices at the producer level are only 1.3 percent higher now <u>than a year ago and are going down, even though floods in the Midwest and drought in the South are hurting crops and therefore raised</u> corn and soybean prices.

(A) than a year ago and are going down, even though floods in the Midwest and drought in the South are hurting crops and therefore raised

(B) than those of a year ago and are going down, even though floods in the Midwest and drought in the South are hurting crops and therefore raising

(C) than a year ago and are going down, despite floods in the Midwest and drought in the South, and are hurting crops and therefore raising

(D) as those of a year ago and are going down, even though floods in the Midwest and drought in the South hurt crops and therefore raise

(E) as they were a year ago and are going down, despite floods in the Midwest and drought in the South, and are hurting crops and therefore raising

Logical predication; Verb form

The sentence as written makes an illogical comparison between *prices at the producer level* and a time period (*a year ago*); surely the intended comparison is between such prices now and those of a year ago. The clause at the end of the sentence states that flooding and a drought *are hurting* crops, and as a result of this, they have *raised* prices of certain crops. *Are hurting* is in the present progressive tense, indicating an ongoing process; *raised* is in the simple past tense, indicating a completed action. It would be more appropriate to use the present progressive tense here as well, *[are] raising*.

A The first part of this version of the sentence illogically compares prices to a time; the second part of the sentence indicates that a completed action (*raised . . . prices*) results from an ongoing present condition (*floods . . . and drought . . . are hurting crops*).

B **Correct.** This version of the sentence makes an appropriate comparison (between prices now and those of a year ago), and uses tenses in an appropriate way.

C Like (A), this version of the sentence illogically compares prices to time past. Furthermore, in this version, *Prices* is the subject not only for the verb *are* but also for the verbs *are hurting* and *[are] raising*, which makes no sense.

D The comparative adjective *higher* requires the comparative term *than* instead of *as*; the tenses of the verbs in the latter half of the sentence, *hurt* (simple past) and *raise* (simple present), do not work together logically.

E Like (D), this version inappropriately uses *as* instead of *than* with *higher*. Furthermore, like (C), in this version *[p]rices* is the subject not only for the verb *are* but also for the verbs *are hurting* and *[are] raising*.

The correct answer is B.

759. Fossils of the arm of a sloth found in Puerto Rico in 1991, and dated at 34 million years old, made it the earliest known mammal of the Greater Antilles Islands.

(A) sloth found in Puerto Rico in 1991, and dated at 34 million years old, made it the earliest known mammal of

(B) sloth, that they found in Puerto Rico in 1991, has been dated at 34 million years old, thus making it the earliest mammal known on

(C) sloth that was found in Puerto Rico in 1991, was dated at 34 million years old, making this the earliest known mammal of

(D) sloth, found in Puerto Rico in 1991, have been dated at 34 million years old, making the sloth the earliest known mammal on

(E) sloth which, found in Puerto Rico in 1991, was dated at 34 million years old, made the sloth the earliest known mammal of

Agreement; Logical predication

The subject of the sentence is the plural *fossils*, not *sloth*, and therefore requires a plural verb. *It* therefore does not have a singular antecedent. To clarify the identification of the oldest known mammal, the noun *the sloth* must be explicitly identified.

A Because *sloth* is the object of a preposition and not the subject of the sentence, there is no reasonable antecedent for the pronoun *it*; in this construction, the subject of *made* is *fossils*, but it makes no sense to say that the *fossils* made it the earliest known mammal.

B The introduction of the mysterious *they*, a pronoun without a reference, adds confusion to this sentence; the singular verb does not agree with the plural subject.

C The relative clause *that was* … is wordy and awkward; the singular verb does not agree with the plural subject.

D **Correct.** The plural verb agrees with its plural subject, and *the sloth* is explicitly identified as *the earliest known mammal.*

E The singular verb does not agree with the plural subject.

The correct answer is D.

760. Recently physicians have determined that stomach ulcers are not caused by stress, alcohol, or rich foods, but a bacterium that dwells in the mucous lining of the stomach.

(A) not caused by stress, alcohol, or rich foods, but

(B) not caused by stress, alcohol, or rich foods, but are by

(C) caused not by stress, alcohol, or rich foods, but by

(D) caused not by stress, alcohol, and rich foods, but

(E) caused not by stress, alcohol, and rich foods, but are by

Parallelism; Diction

The formula used in this sentence *not this but that* requires parallel elements following *not* and *but.* This means that *not by stress, alcohol, or rich foods* must be balanced by *but by a bacterium.* … There is no need to repeat the verb *are caused*, or even the auxiliary verb *are*, because the verb precedes the *not by* … *but by* … formula. The substitution of the conjunction *and* for the conjunction *or* changes the meaning of the sentence: *Stress, alcohol and rich foods* identifies the combination of these three factors as a suggested cause of stomach ulcers, whereas *stress, alcohol, or rich foods* offers three individual possibilities. There is no way to tell which one of these is the intended meaning of the sentence.

A To preserve parallelism, *but* should be followed by *by*.

B There is no reason to repeat the auxiliary verb *are*.

C **Correct.** This sentence correctly uses the *not by* … *but by* … formula.

D To preserve parallelism, *but* should be followed by *by*.

E To preserve parallelism, *but* should be followed by *by*.

The correct answer is C.

761. The eyes of the elephant seal adapt to darkness more quickly than any other animal yet tested, thus allowing it to hunt efficiently under the gloomy conditions at its feeding depth of between 300 and 700 meters.

(A) The eyes of the elephant seal adapt to darkness more quickly than any other animal yet tested, thus allowing it

(B) The eyes of the elephant seal adapt to darkness more quickly than does any other animal yet tested, allowing them

(C) The eyes of the elephant seal adapt to darkness more quickly than do those of any other animal yet tested, allowing it

(D) Because they adapt to darkness more quickly than any other animal yet tested, the eyes of the elephant seal allow it

(E) Because the eyes of the elephant seal adapt to darkness more quickly than do those of any other animal yet tested, it allows them

Logical predication; Agreement

Logically, the eyes of the elephant seal should be contrasted with the eyes of other animals, not with the animals themselves. The sentence must make this comparison directly and precisely, with each subject interpretable as the subject of *adapt*. Given the correct subject (*those of any other animal yet tested*), which is plural, any reference to it must also be plural.

A *Any other animal yet tested* is incorrectly set up as the subject of *adapt*.

B *Any other animal yet tested* is incorrectly set up as the subject of *adapt*. The plural pronoun *them* seems to refer to eyes. Although there is a sense in which eyes can hunt, it is more reasonable to suppose that, in this context, the writer's intention is to mention how the eyes' quick adaptation allows the seal to hunt efficiently.

C **Correct.** The subject of the comparative phrase is correctly *those of any other animal yet tested*, the plural verb *do* correctly agrees with this subject (*those*), and the singular pronoun *it* correctly agrees with its antecedent (*elephant seal*).

D *Any other animal yet tested* is incorrectly set up as the subject of *adapt*.

E The subject is correct, but in the following clause *it* has no clear referent.

The correct answer is C.

762. A mutual fund having billions of dollars in assets will typically invest that money in hundreds of companies, rarely holding more than one percent of the shares of any particular corporation.

(A) companies, rarely holding more than one percent

(B) companies, and it is rare to hold at least one percent or more

(C) companies and rarely do they hold more than one percent

(D) companies, so that they rarely hold more than one percent

(E) companies; rarely do they hold one percent or more

Agreement; Logical predication

The participial phrase starting with *rarely holding* is predicated of the main subject *a mutual fund*. It elaborates on the effect of the main clause verb: since a mutual fund invests in hundreds of companies, it rarely holds more than one percent in any particular corporation.

A **Correct.** The participle *holding* in the embedded clause correctly refers to *a mutual fund*. It also correctly expresses the cause-and-effect relationship between investing in many companies and holding little in each company.

B The antecedent of *it is rare to hold* is not clear. The use of *it is rare* instead of *rarely* could be misleading.

C The use of *and* between the clauses makes them both main clauses. Thus, the cause-and-effect relationship between investing and holding is lost. The referent of *they* is unclear. It makes no sense to suppose that it refers to the hundreds of companies. Since it presumably refers to *a mutual fund*, it should be singular.

D The pronoun *they* refers to *a mutual fund* and thus should be singular.

E The pronoun *they* refers to *a mutual fund* and thus should be singular.

The correct answer is A.

763. Positing an enormous volcanic explosion at the end of the Permian period would explain the presence of a buried crater, account for the presence of the element iridium (originating deep within the earth), and the presence of quartz having been shattered by high-impact shock waves.

(A) account for the presence of the element iridium (originating deep within the earth), and the presence of quartz having been
(B) of the element iridium (originating deep within the earth), and of quartz
(C) the element iridium (originating deep within the earth), and explain the presence of quartz having been
(D) the presence of the element iridium (originating deep within the earth), and explain the presence of quartz
(E) explain the element iridium (originating deep within the earth), and the presence of quartz

Parallelism; Rhetorical construction

The sentence indicates that a volcanic explosion would explain the presence of three features, but those features are not expressed using parallel grammatical structures. The first two items in the list are verb phrases that involve needless repetition—*explain the presence of* and *account for the presence of*—while the third is an awkwardly worded noun phrase—*the presence of quartz having been shattered.* The three features can be identified more concisely with a list of prepositional phrases following *explain the presence*: *of a buried crater*, *of the element iridium*, and *of quartz.*

A The three features are not listed in parallel form; the sentence is wordy and awkward.

B **Correct.** The three features are identified with parallel prepositional phrases.

C The three features are not listed in parallel form since the first and third are verb phrases, while the second is a noun phrase; the wording is awkward and needlessly repetitive.

D The three features are not listed in parallel form since the first and third are verb phrases, while the second is a noun phrase; the wording is needlessly repetitive.

E The three features are not listed in parallel form since the first and second are verb phrases, while the third is a noun phrase; the sentence illogically states that an explosion would *explain the element iridium*, rather than explain the *presence* of the element.

The correct answer is B.

764. The 19-year-old pianist and composer performed his most recent work all over Europe, Asia, and North America last year, winning prestigious awards in both London as well as Tokyo for his achievement at so young an age, and he is hoping to continue composing now that he has returned to Chicago.

(A) winning prestigious awards in both London as well as Tokyo for his achievement at so young an age, and he is hoping
(B) winning prestigious awards both in London and Tokyo for his achievement at such a young age, and hoping
(C) having won prestigious awards both in London and Tokyo for his achievement at so young an age, hoping
(D) winning prestigious awards in both London and Tokyo for his achievement at such a young age, and he hopes
(E) having won prestigious awards both in London as well as Tokyo for his achievement at so young an age, and he hopes

Idiom; Grammatical construction

This sentence is about the past accomplishments and the future ambitions of a musician who recently won awards on a world tour. In some of the versions of the sentence, the phrase *as well as* is redundant with the word *both* before *London* and *Tokyo*. Idiomatically, the simple conjunction *and* completes the phrase beginning with *both.*

A The phrase *as well as* between *London* and *Tokyo* is not idiomatic (the idiomatic formula is *both X and Y*). The present progressive verb *is hoping* is unnecessarily wordy.

B Because *hoping* is parallel with *winning*, it suggests that the *hoping* and *winning* are contemporaneous, whereas in fact the musician won his awards last year but is now, in the present, upon his return, hoping to continue composing.

C The present-perfect participial phrase *having won* suggests that his winning took place before his performance tour. Furthermore, the use of *hoping* in this version of the sentence suggests that hoping is something the pianist did while on his performance tour *last year*, but the final phrase, *now that he has returned to Chicago*, indicates this is not so.

D **Correct.** This version of the sentence uses the correct idiomatic formula (*both X and Y*).

E The participial phrase *having won* . . . inaccurately states that the musician won his awards prior to his performance tour. Furthermore, *both in London as well as Tokyo* is unidiomatic, as indicated in the discussion of (A) above, and unparallel (*in* should either precede *both*, or else *in* should be added before *Tokyo*).

The correct answer is D.

765. Starfish, with anywhere from five to eight arms, have a strong regenerative ability, and if one arm is lost it quickly replaces it, sometimes by the animal overcompensating and growing an extra one or two.

(A) one arm is lost it quickly replaces it, sometimes by the animal overcompensating and

(B) one arm is lost it is quickly replaced, with the animal sometimes overcompensating and

(C) they lose one arm they quickly replace it, sometimes by the animal overcompensating,

(D) they lose one arm they are quickly replaced, with the animal sometimes overcompensating,

(E) they lose one arm it is quickly replaced, sometimes with the animal overcompensating,

Agreement; Idiom

In a conditional sentence *if X, (then) Y*, rhetorical flow is enhanced by the two clauses sharing the same structure. If one clause is passive, the other should be passive; if one clause is active, the other should be active, too.

A The conditional clause has a passive verb, while the result clause has an active verb. The pronoun *it* should be plural since it refers to *starfish*. We know that *starfish* is plural in this sentence because it agrees with *have* in the main clause.

B **Correct.** The conditional structure is clear and correct.

C This answer choice allows the unintended reading that the animal replaces the missing arm by overcompensating. The logical connection between *overcompensating* and *growing* is unclear.

D The conditional clause has an active verb, while the result clause has a passive verb. The second *they* should refer to *arm*, so the agreement is not correct. The logical connection between *overcompensating* and *growing* is unclear.

E The conditional clause has an active verb, while the result clause has a passive verb. The logical connection between *overcompensating* and *growing* is unclear.

The correct answer is B.

766. In 2000, a mere two dozen products accounted for half the increase in spending on prescription drugs, a phenomenon that is explained not just because of more expensive drugs but by the fact that doctors are writing many more prescriptions for higher-cost drugs.

(A) a phenomenon that is explained not just because of more expensive drugs but by the fact that doctors are writing

(B) a phenomenon that is explained not just by the fact that drugs are becoming more expensive but also by the fact that doctors are writing

(C) a phenomenon occurring not just because of drugs that are becoming more expensive but because of doctors having also written

(D) which occurred not just because drugs are becoming more expensive but doctors are also writing

(E) which occurred not just because of more expensive drugs but because doctors have also written

Rhetorical construction; Idiom

This sentence explains that a few high-cost products account for increased spending for two reasons—rising drug prices and more prescriptions for high-priced drugs. To present these two causes, the sentence employs a formula that requires parallel elements: *not just because of x, but because of y*, with *x* and *y* assuming the same grammatical form. One way to create this parallelism is to phrase both contributing causes as noun clauses beginning with *the fact that*. To streamline the sentence, unnecessary words and redundancies should be eliminated. One such redundancy is the repetition of meaning in *explained* and *because of*.

A It is redundant and confusing to say that the phenomenon in question is *explained* ... *because of*; the sentence structure is not parallel.

B **Correct.** This sentence correctly uses parallel structure.

C The phrasing *drugs that are becoming* and *doctors having also written* are awkward and confusing; the placement of *also* is incorrect.

D The structure of this sentence is not parallel.

E The placement of *also* is incorrect; the structure of the sentence is not parallel.

The correct answer is B.

767. Similar to other early Mississippi Delta blues singers, the music of Robert Johnson arose from an oral tradition beginning with a mixture of chants, fiddle tunes, and religious music and only gradually evolved into the blues.

(A) Similar to other early Mississippi Delta blues singers, the music of Robert Johnson arose from an oral tradition beginning with

(B) Similar to that of other early Mississippi Delta blues singers, Robert Johnson made music that arose from an oral tradition that began with

(C) As with other early Mississippi Delta blues singers, Robert Johnson made music that arose from an oral tradition beginning as

(D) Like other early Mississippi Delta blues singers, Robert Johnson's music arose from an oral tradition beginning with

(E) Like the music of other early Mississippi Delta blues singers, the music of Robert Johnson arose from an oral tradition that began as

Logical predication; Verb form

The sentence aims to compare the music of early Mississippi Delta Blues singers with the music of Robert Johnson. But what it does is illogically compare singers themselves with the music of Johnson. The second half of the sentence describes two stages of the oral tradition from which blues developed.

A *Similar to* is a wordy and imprecise form of comparison here. The second half of the sentence attempts to describe the stages of the oral tradition, but in a nonparallel form, presenting the first stage as a participial phrase and the second as a verb phrase.

B *Similar to* is wordy and imprecise. The pronoun *that* lacks a grammatical referent.

C The comparative phrase *as with* is an inappropriate form for comparing nouns and noun phrases. The second half of the sentence violates parallelism, attempting to express the first stage of the oral tradition as a present-participle phrase and the second as a past-tense verb phrase.

D This makes a sentence that illogically compares *singers* with *music*. It violates parallelism by coupling a participial phrase *beginning with* ... with a verb phrase *evolved into*. . . .

E **Correct.** The resulting sentence compares like with like. It uses a relative clause to describe the oral tradition from which blues developed, indicating the two stages of development with two verbs in parallel.

The correct answer is E.

768. Thelonious Monk, who was a jazz pianist and composer, produced a body of work both rooted in the stride-piano tradition of Willie (The Lion) Smith and Duke Ellington, yet in many ways he stood apart from the mainstream jazz repertory.

(A) Thelonious Monk, who was a jazz pianist and composer, produced a body of work both rooted

(B) Thelonious Monk, the jazz pianist and composer, produced a body of work that was rooted both

(C) Jazz pianist and composer Thelonious Monk, who produced a body of work rooted

(D) Jazz pianist and composer Thelonious Monk produced a body of work that was rooted

(E) Jazz pianist and composer Thelonious Monk produced a body of work rooted both

Grammatical construction; Rhetorical construction

The subject of the sentence is *Thelonious Monk*, and the sentence tells about two things that he did: *produced* and *stood apart*. The work he produced was rooted in the mainstream (*stride piano*) jazz tradition, yet at the same time, he deviated from this tradition. The use of a relative clause (*who was a jazz pianist* …) or an appositive (*the jazz pianist* …) introduces unnecessary wordiness and grammatical complexity. Since only one point is being made about Monk's body of work, the appearance of the word *both* in the clause presenting the claim about Monk's work is deceptive as well as grammatically incorrect.

A The relative clause introduces wordiness and confusion.

B The appositive introduces wordiness and unnecessary grammatical complexity.

C The sentence is a fragment because the main subject, *Thelonious Monk*, has no verb.

D Correct. The sentence concisely identifies Thelonious Monk and expresses the single point about his work without unnecessary or misleading words.

E The appearance of *both* is misleading, since only one point is being made about where Monk's musical roots are located.

The correct answer is D.

769. Nobody knows exactly how many languages there are in the world, partly because of the difficulty of distinguishing between a language <u>and the sublanguages or dialects within it, but those who have tried to count typically have found</u> about five thousand.

(A) and the sublanguages or dialects within it, but those who have tried to count typically have found

(B) and the sublanguages or dialects within them, with those who have tried counting typically finding

(C) and the sublanguages or dialects within it, but those who have tried counting it typically find

(D) or the sublanguages or dialects within them, but those who tried to count them typically found

(E) or the sublanguages or dialects within them, with those who have tried to count typically finding

Agreement; Idiom

This sentence first introduces a condition that makes it difficult to count languages and then, with the conjunction *but*, introduces the topic of those who defy these difficulties and try to count the world's languages anyway. Connecting these two parts of the sentence with *but* indicates that the second clause of the sentence is counter to expectation. The challenges of the task are explained using the example of a single language and its many sublanguages or dialects. When this example is referred to with a pronoun, the pronoun should be singular; when the languages being counted are referred to with a pronoun, this pronoun must be plural.

A Correct. The pronoun *it* agrees in number to its singular antecedent, and *but* indicates that the idea expressed in the final clause defies expectations.

B The plural pronoun *them* incorrectly refers to the singular antecedent *language*; connecting the two clauses with the preposition *with* loses the sense that counting languages despite the difficulties defies expectations.

C The second appearance of *it*, referring to world languages, is incorrect because it does not agree in number with *languages*.

D The conjunction *or* is incorrect—the idiomatic expression is *distinguishing between x and y*; the plural pronoun *them* does not agree with the singular antecedent *language*.

E The plural pronoun *them* incorrectly refers to the singular antecedent, *language; with* is an imprecise connector for the two clauses, losing the *counter-to-expectation* relationship between them.

The correct answer is A.

770. Although a number of excellent studies narrate the development of domestic technology and its impact on housewifery, these works do not discuss the contributions of the women employed <u>by manufacturers and utility companies as product demonstrators and publicists</u>, who initially promoted new and unfamiliar technology to female consumers.

(A) by manufacturers and utility companies as product demonstrators and publicists,

(B) to be product demonstrators and publicists by manufacturers and utility companies,

(C) to demonstrate and publicize their products by manufacturers and utility companies

(D) by manufacturers and utility companies to be demonstrators and publicists of their products

(E) by manufacturers and utility companies to demonstrate and publicize their products

Logical predication; Rhetorical construction

The point of the sentence is that studies do not include the contributions of women who promoted new domestic technology. The sentence indicates clearly that the women were *employed by manufacturers and utility companies*, worked as *product demonstrators and publicists*, and promoted new technology *to female consumers*.

A **Correct.** The sentence clearly describes the women's employment and contributions.

B This sentence structure appears to make *who initially promoted* refer to *manufacturers and utility companies* rather than to *the women*. This conflicts with the use of the word *who*, which would normally be expected to refer to persons rather than to abstract entities such as companies.

C *Their* refers to *the women*, incorrectly suggesting that the *products* belong to them. This sentence structure appears to make *who initially promoted* refer to *manufacturers and utility companies* rather than to *the women*. This conflicts with the word *who*, which would normally be expected to refer to persons rather than to abstract entities such as companies.

D *Who initially promoted* follows, and appears to refer to, *products*, which cannot logically be the referent.

E *Who initially promoted* follows, and appears to refer to, *products*, which cannot logically be the referent.

The correct answer is A.

771. The absence from business and financial records of the nineteenth century of statistics about women leave us with no record of the jobs that were performed by women and how they survived economically.

(A) from business and financial records of the nineteenth century of statistics about women leave us with no record of the jobs that were performed by women and

(B) from business and financial records of statistics about women from the nineteenth century leave us with no record of what jobs women performed or

(C) of statistics for women from business and financial records in the nineteenth century leaves us with no record of either the jobs that women were performing and of

(D) of statistics on women from business and financial records in the nineteenth century leave us with no record of the jobs that women performed or of

(E) of statistics about women from business and financial records of the nineteenth century leaves us with no record of either what jobs women performed or

Rhetorical construction; Agreement

This sentence is phrased awkwardly in two ways. The first relates to *absence of statistics*: it is best to place a noun modifier right next to the noun that it modifies, with no intervening material. Second, *jobs that were performed by women* is more complicated than necessary—*jobs women performed* is better, for example. Also, the singular noun *absence* requires the correct agreeing verb form *leaves*.

A *Absence* and *of statistics* are widely separated, and *leave* does not properly agree with its subject, *absence*.

B *Absence* and *of statistics* are widely separated, and *leave* does not properly agree with its subject, *absence*.

C *Jobs that women were performing* is unnecessarily long and complex. The *either* construction should be completed with *or*, not *and*.

D *Leave* does not properly agree with its subject, *absence*.

E **Correct.** *Leaves* agrees with *absence*. The phrase *of statistics* is next to the noun it modifies (*absence*), and *jobs women performed* is a nicely simple phrasing.

The correct answer is E.

772. Heating-oil prices are expected to be higher this year than last because refiners are paying about $5 a barrel more for crude oil than they were last year.

(A) Heating-oil prices are expected to be higher this year than last because refiners are paying about $5 a barrel more for crude oil than they were

(B) Heating-oil prices are expected to rise higher this year over last because refiners pay about $5 a barrel for crude oil more than they did

(C) Expectations are for heating-oil prices to be higher this year than last year's because refiners are paying about $5 a barrel for crude oil more than they did

(D) It is the expectation that heating-oil prices will be higher for this year over last because refiners are paying about $5 a barrel more for crude oil now than what they were

(E) It is expected that heating-oil prices will rise higher this year than last year's because refiners pay about $5 a barrel for crude oil more than they did

Rhetorical construction; Idiom

The sentence connects a comparison between this year's and last year's heating-oil prices with a comparison between this year's and last year's crude-oil prices. The most efficient, parallel expression of those comparisons is to use two comparative expressions, *higher than* and *more than.*

A **Correct.** This sentence expresses the comparison in succinct, parallel phrases.

B The comparative form, *higher*, anticipates the comparative term *than*, not *over*; in the second clause, the comparative terms *more than* should immediately follow *$5 a barrel.*

C *Expectations are for* … is an unnecessarily wordy and indirect expression; the possessive *year's* is not parallel with the adverbial phrase *this year.*

D *It is the expectation that* … is wordy and awkward; *for* and *what* are unnecessary.

E *It is expected that* … is wordy and awkward; the possessive *last year's* does not parallel the adverbial phrase *this year.*

The correct answer is A.

773. Even though Clovis points, spear points with longitudinal grooves chipped onto their faces, have been found all over North America, they are named for the New Mexico site where they were first discovered in 1932.

(A) Even though Clovis points, spear points with longitudinal grooves chipped onto their faces, have been found all over North America, they are named for the New Mexico site where they were first discovered in 1932.

(B) Although named for the New Mexico site where first discovered in 1932, Clovis points are spear points of longitudinal grooves chipped onto their faces and have been found all over North America.

(C) Named for the New Mexico site where they have been first discovered in 1932, Clovis points, spear points of longitudinal grooves chipped onto the faces, have been found all over North America.

(D) Spear points with longitudinal grooves that are chipped onto the faces, Clovis points, even though named for the New Mexico site where first discovered in 1932, but were found all over North America.

(E) While Clovis points are spear points whose faces have longitudinal grooves chipped into them, they have been found all over North America, and named for the New Mexico site where they have been first discovered in 1932.

Verb form; Rhetorical construction; Logical predication

Even though, *although*, and *while* introduce clauses that appear to be logically incompatible but in fact are not. In this sentence, the apparent incompatibility that must be clearly expressed is that although the spear points are named for a particular place in New Mexico, they are in fact found throughout North America. Because their discovery took place in 1932 and is not ongoing, the correct verb tense is simple past, not present perfect.

A **Correct.** The *even though* clause expresses clearly that the seeming incompatibility is between where the spear points have been found (*all over North America*) and the naming of the spear points for a single site in New Mexico.

B The sentence structure indicates that the expected incompatibility is between the geographically based name of the points and their physical properties, which makes no sense; *where discovered* is missing a subject—the correct form is *where they were first discovered*.

C *Have been first discovered* is the wrong tense, since the discovery is a discrete event completed in the past.

D The sequence of information in this sentence is confusing; *even though* and *but* both introduce information that is contrary to expectation, so to use them both to describe a single apparent contradiction is redundant and nonsensical.

E *While* introduces a description of Clovis points and suggests that this appears incompatible with their appearance all over North America, which makes no sense; *have been first discovered* is the wrong tense.

The correct answer is A.

774. Heavy commitment by an executive to a course of action, especially if it has worked well in the past, makes it likely to miss signs of incipient trouble or misinterpret them when they do appear.

(A) Heavy commitment by an executive to a course of action, especially if it has worked well in the past, makes it likely to miss signs of incipient trouble or misinterpret them when they do appear.

(B) An executive who is heavily committed to a course of action, especially one that worked well in the past, makes missing signs of incipient trouble or misinterpreting ones likely when they do appear.

(C) An executive who is heavily committed to a course of action is likely to miss or misinterpret signs of incipient trouble when they do appear, especially if it has worked well in the past.

(D) Executives' being heavily committed to a course of action, especially if it has worked well in the past, makes them likely to miss signs of incipient trouble or misinterpreting them when they do appear.

(E) Being heavily committed to a course of action, especially one that has worked well in the past, is likely to make an executive miss signs of incipient trouble or misinterpret them when they do appear.

Rhetorical construction; Logical predication

This sentence explains that an executive who is blindly committed to a proven course of action is likely to overlook or misinterpret indicators that the plan may no longer be working. The sentence needs to make clear *who* may misinterpret these indicators.

A The passive construction causes the sentence to be wordy and confusing; the reference for *it* is ambiguous, leaving the reader with questions about who or what is likely to miss these signs.

B The sentence structure indicates that the *executive*, not his or her strategy, causes signs to be overlooked; the modifier *when they do appear* is misplaced.

C The reference for the pronoun *it* is unclear because many nouns have intervened between the appearance of the logical referent (*course of action*) and *it*.

D *Misinterpreting* should be an infinitive verb form to parallel *miss*; the phrasing throughout the sentence is wordy and awkward.

E **Correct.** The grammatical structure of this sentence and the appropriate placement of modifiers expresses the meaning clearly and concisely.

The correct answer is E.

775. According to recent studies comparing the nutritional value of meat from wild animals and meat from domesticated animals, wild animals have less total fat than do livestock fed on grain and more of a kind of fat they think is good for cardiac health.

(A) wild animals have less total fat than do livestock fed on grain and more of a kind of fat they think is

(B) wild animals have less total fat than livestock fed on grain and more of a kind of fat thought to be

(C) wild animals have less total fat than that of livestock fed on grain and have more fat of a kind thought to be

(D) total fat of wild animals is less than livestock fed on grain and they have more fat of a kind thought to be

(E) total fat is less in wild animals than that of livestock fed on grain and more of their fat is of a kind they think is

Logical predication; Rhetorical construction

The sentence reports research findings on the comparison between the fat content of wild animals and that of domestic livestock. The most significant error in the sentence is in the phrase *they think*: the pronoun *they* either lacks a referent or is meant to refer back to *wild animals*, which would be nonsensical.

A The pronoun *they* fails to refer correctly.

B **Correct.** The phrase *thought to be* eliminates the most significant error in the original sentence. Note that while the phrase *less total fat than livestock* differs from the phrase *less total fat than do livestock* in the original, either would be correct here.

C The resulting sentence is unnecessarily wordy and confusing. The pronoun *that* is not only superfluous, but it fails to refer back to anything.

D The resulting sentence makes a nonsensical comparison between *total fat* and *livestock*.

E The resulting sentence is wordy and confusing. It lacks the required parallelism *in wild animals . . . in livestock*. The referent of the possessive pronoun *their* is ambiguous, as is the referent of the pronoun *they*.

The correct answer is B.

776. Yellow jackets number among the 900 or so species of the world's social wasps, wasps living in a highly cooperative and organized society where they consist almost entirely of females—the queen and her sterile female workers.

(A) wasps living in a highly cooperative and organized society where they consist almost entirely of

(B) wasps that live in a highly cooperative and organized society consisting almost entirely of

(C) which means they live in a highly cooperative and organized society, almost all

(D) which means that their society is highly cooperative, organized, and it is almost entirely

(E) living in a society that is highly cooperative, organized, and it consists of almost all

Idiom; Logical predication; Rhetorical construction

This sentence identifies yellow jackets as one of 900 types of social wasps and provides an explanation of the term *social wasps*. In this explanation, the society or population—not the individual wasps themselves—consists almost entirely of females. The three descriptors of social wasps (*cooperative, organized,* and *consisting almost entirely of females*) are most effectively expressed in parallel structures.

A *They*, referring to wasps, is an incorrect subject for *consist*.

B **Correct.** The three descriptors of the wasp society are in parallel form, and *consisting* properly modifies *society*.

C The sentence structure makes it unclear what *almost all females* describes.

D *And it is* ... violates the parallelism of the three descriptors of social wasps.

E *And it consists* ... violates the parallelism of the three descriptors.

The correct answer is B.

777. Before 1988, insurance companies in California were free to charge whatever rates the market would bear, needing no approval from regulators before raising rates.

(A) needing no approval from regulators before raising

(B) and it needed no approval by regulators before raising

(C) and needing no approval from regulators before they raised

(D) with approval not needed by regulators before they raised

(E) with no approval needed from regulators before the raising of

Logical predication; Rhetorical construction

The sentence explains that, prior to 1988, insurance companies in California could raise rates without regulators' approval. This idea is expressed concisely using a participial phrase and two prepositional phrases: *needing no approval from regulators before raising rates.* Unlike some of the answer choices that contain errors involving antecedents, this construction uses no pronouns and contains no such errors.

A **Correct.** The combination of a participial phrase and two prepositional phrases expresses the idea clearly with no errors involving pronouns or antecedents.

B The singular pronoun *it* has no clear antecedent. If *it* is taken to refer to the market (the only grammatically plausible antecedent), the sentence is illogical. *Whatever rates the market would bear* clearly indicates that *market* is being used in the sense of an abstract set of forces affecting prices. To say that the market, in that sense, raised taxes and that it needed no approval to do so is nonsensical.

C The construction *were ... and needing* is ungrammatical. The pronoun *they* is intended to refer to *companies* but could also seem, illogically, to refer to *regulators.*

D *By regulators* illogically indicates that regulators are the ones who did not need approval; the pronoun *they* is intended to refer to *companies* but could also seem, illogically, to refer to *regulators.*

E *Before the raising of* is wordy and awkward. Both that phrase and *with no approval needed* are strangely uninformative and rhetorically ineffective in that they appear to pointedly avoid telling who did not need the approval or who might have raised the rates.

The correct answer is A.

778. Marconi's conception of the radio was as a substitute for the telephone, a tool for private conversation; instead, it is precisely the opposite, a tool for communicating with a large, public audience.

(A) Marconi's conception of the radio was as a substitute for the telephone, a tool for private conversation; instead, it is

(B) Marconi conceived of the radio as a substitute for the telephone, a tool for private conversation, but which is

(C) Marconi conceived of the radio as a tool for private conversation that could substitute for the telephone; instead, it has become

(D) Marconi conceived of the radio to be a tool for private conversation, a substitute for the telephone, which has become

(E) Marconi conceived of the radio to be a substitute for the telephone, a tool for private conversation, other than what it is,

Rhetorical construction; Logical predication

The main point of this sentence is to explain that while Marconi felt the radio would substitute for the phone as an instrument of private communication, in fact it has become an instrument of mass communication. It is less wordy to use *Marconi* as the subject of the active verb *conceived* than to use the subject *conception* with the static verb *was.* The pronoun *it* positioned as the subject of the final verb *has become* refers back to *radio.* Versions of the sentence that use the relative pronoun *which* indicate that the telephone has become a mass medium.

A The nominalized subject, *conception,* leads to a wordy and awkward sentence.

B The reference for the relative pronoun *which* is ambiguous; the sentence as a whole is awkward.

C **Correct.** An active verb makes the first clause more concise; *it* in the second clause clearly refers to *the radio.*

D *Conceived of* ... should be followed by *as* rather than *to be.*

E *Conceived of* ... should be followed by *as* rather than *to be*; *other than what it is* is awkward, wordy, and redundant, overlapping the meaning of *precisely the opposite* ....

The correct answer is C.

779. Because there are provisions of the new maritime code that provide that even tiny islets can be the basis for claims to the fisheries and oil fields of large sea areas, they have already stimulated international disputes over uninhabited islands.

(A) Because there are provisions of the new maritime code that provide that even tiny islets can be the basis for claims to the fisheries and oil fields of large sea areas, they have already stimulated

(B) Because the new maritime code provides that even tiny islets can be the basis for claims to the fisheries and oil fields of large sea areas, it has already stimulated

(C) Even tiny islets can be the basis for claims to the fisheries and oil fields of large sea areas under provisions of the new maritime code, already stimulating

(D) Because even tiny islets can be the basis for claims to the fisheries and oil fields of large sea areas under provisions of the new maritime code, this has already stimulated

(E) Because even tiny islets can be the basis for claims to the fisheries and oil fields of large sea areas under provisions of the new maritime code, which is already stimulating

Logical predication; Grammatical construction

In this sentence, the *there are … that …* construction contributes nothing more than unnecessary words. The sentence needs to make clear whether *provisions* or *code* is the subject of the main verb *stimulated.*

A The *there are … that …* construction is unnecessarily wordy; in the predicate nominative instead of the subject position, *provisions* is not an obvious referent for the pronoun *they.*

B Correct. In this sentence, *the new maritime code* is clearly the antecedent of *it* in the main clause and thus the subject of *has already stimulated.*

C *Under provisions of the new maritime code* is a misplaced modifier, seeming to describe *sea areas*; the sentence does not make clear what is *stimulating … disputes.*

D The referent of *this* is unclear.

E The sentence is a fragment, opening with a dependent clause (*Because … code*) and concluding with a relative clause, but lacking a main, independent clause.

The correct answer is B.

780. Unlike the automobile company, whose research was based on crashes involving sport utility vehicles, the research conducted by the insurance company took into account such factors as a driver's age, sex, and previous driving record.

(A) company, whose research was based on

(B) company, which researched

(C) company, in its research of

(D) company's research, having been based on

(E) company's research on

Logical predication; Rhetorical construction

The point of the sentence is to contrast the research conducted by the automobile company and that conducted by the insurance company, but the sentence has been written in a way that contrasts *the automobile company* with *research.* The correct contrast is between *automobile company's research* and *research conducted by the insurance company.*

A *Automobile company* is incorrectly contrasted with *research.*

B *Automobile company* is incorrectly contrasted with *research.*

C *Automobile company* is incorrectly contrasted with *research.*

D *Having been based on* is wordy. This construction makes it unclear whether *having been based on crashes involving sport utility vehicles* is intended to modify *the automobile company's research* or *the research conducted by the insurance company.* The sentence structure slightly favors the latter interpretation, but it is somewhat implausible to suppose that this is the intended meaning.

E Correct. The sentence concisely contrasts the *automobile company's research* and *research conducted by the insurance company.*

The correct answer is E.

781. Gusty westerly winds will continue to usher in a seasonably cool air mass into the region, as a broad area of high pressure will build and bring fair and dry weather for several days.

(A) to usher in a seasonably cool air mass into the region, as a broad area of high pressure will build and

(B) ushering in a seasonably cool air mass into the region and a broad area of high pressure will build that

(C) to usher in a seasonably cool air mass to the region, a broad area of high pressure building, and

(D) ushering a seasonably cool air mass in the region, with a broad area of high pressure building and

(E) to usher a seasonably cool air mass into the region while a broad area of high pressure builds, which will

Verb form; Grammatical construction; Diction

The sentence offers a prediction that two concurrent weather events will bring a certain type of weather, but its use of the phrase *as . . . will build* causes confusion. The wording makes the sequence of events and the causal relationships among them unclear. Future tense is used to indicate that winds *will continue.* The relation of *as* to the rest of the sentence makes it unclear whether *as* is intended as a logical indicator (similar to *because*) or as a temporal indicator (equivalent to *while*). If *as* is intended in the former way, it would be preferable to resolve the ambiguity by using a word or phrase such as *because* or *given that.* If it is intended in the latter way, a present tense verb would be needed following *as* or *while* to show that the second event is concurrent with, or part of, the future situation: *while high pressure builds.* In addition, *usher in . . . into* is redundant and unidiomatic. A clear, concise way to express this idea is *will continue to usher a seasonably cool air mass into the region while a broad area of high pressure builds.*

A *Usher in … into* is redundant and unidiomatic. *As … will build* causes confusion.

B The absence of a comma after *region* makes this ungrammatical. *Ushering in . . . into* is redundant; *will build* is the wrong verb tense; the plural verb *bring* does not agree with *area*, the singular antecedent of *that.*

C The grammatical function of *a broad area of high pressure building* is unclear.

D *Ushering … in the region* is incorrect since *into* is needed to indicate movement from outside in; the subject of the verb *bring* is unclear.

E **Correct.** The idea is expressed with clear, correct combinations of verbs and subjects.

The correct answer is E.

782. With the patience of its customers and with its network strained to the breaking point, the on-line service company announced a series of new initiatives trying to relieve the congestion that has led to at least four class-action lawsuits and thousands of complaints from frustrated customers.

(A) the patience of its customers and with its network strained to the breaking point, the on-line service company announced a series of new initiatives trying to relieve

(B) the patience of its customers and its network strained to the breaking point, the on-line service company announced a series of new initiatives that try to relieve

(C) its network and the patience of its customers strained to the breaking point, the on-line service company announced a series of new initiatives to try to relieve

(D) its network and with the patience of its customers strained to the breaking point, the on-line service company announced a series of initiatives to try relieving

(E) its network and its customers' patience strained to the breaking point, the on-line service company announced a series of new initiatives to try relieving

Logical predication; Rhetorical construction

The sentence explains the online service provider's efforts to relieve congestion, but it has been written with confusing ambiguities. Because *the patience of its customers* is in a separate prepositional phrase from *its network*, it is not clear whether both or only the latter is *strained to the breaking point.* The phrase *trying to relieve* is probably meant to explain the purpose of the initiatives, but does not do so unambiguously (for example, *trying* could modify either *the company* or *initiatives*, and it is not clear which is intended). An unambiguous wording of the sentence would clarify that both *the patience of its customers* and *its network* are *strained to the breaking point* and that the purpose of the initiatives is *to try to relieve* the congestion.

A *The patience of its customers* is not clearly linked to *strained to the breaking point*; *trying to relieve* is an ambiguous and unidiomatic way of expressing the purpose of the initiatives.

B *That try to relieve* fails to express the purpose of the initiatives in a rhetorically acceptable way; moreover the present tense *try* is illogical here. The phrase *the patience of its customers and its network* is rhetorically flawed in that its structure makes it seem to be attributing *patience* to the *network.*

C **Correct.** The sentence indicates clearly that both *the patience of its customers* and *its network* are *strained to the breaking point* and that the company introduced initiatives aimed at relieving the congestion.

D *Its network* is not clearly linked to *strained to the breaking point*; with *to try*, the infinitive form *to relieve* is more rhetorically appropriate here than the verbal noun form *relieving*, in order to indicate the goal of the intervention.

E With *to try*, the infinitive form *to relieve* is more rhetorically appropriate here than the verbal noun form *relieving*, in order to indicate the goal of the intervention.

The correct answer is C.

783. November is traditionally the strongest month for sales of light trucks, <u>but sales this past November, even when compared with sales in previous Novembers,</u> accounted for a remarkably large share of total vehicle sales.

(A) but sales this past November, even when compared with sales in previous Novembers,

(B) but even when it is compared with previous Novembers, this past November's sales

(C) but even when they are compared with previous Novembers, sales of light trucks this past November

(D) so that compared with previous Novembers, sales of light trucks this past November

(E) so that this past November's sales, even compared with previous Novembers' sales,

Logical predication; Agreement

This sentence identifies November as traditionally being the month with the strongest sales of light trucks, and then goes on to indicate that even when compared to previous Novembers, this past November's sales accounted for a notably large portion of overall sales. It makes sense to make a comparison between sales in one November with sales in other Novembers. It does not make sense to compare sales to months, as in (C) and (D).

A **Correct.** This version makes the correct comparison between sales in one particular November and sales in previous Novembers.

B The antecedent of the word *it* is unclear. The sentence begins with the word *November*, which is used to refer not to a specific November, but to the month generally. If the antecedent of *it* is taken to be *November*, then the sentence compares November, taken generally, to previous Novembers. But previous to what? Since taking *November* to be the antecedent renders the sentence nonsensical, we may be inclined to look for the antecedent elsewhere; the only other possible candidate, however, is *this past November's sales*, which is ruled out because *it* is singular and *sales* is plural.

C The antecedent of the pronoun *they* is *sales*, making the comparison between *they* and *previous Novembers* illogical.

D The sentence illogically compares sales of light trucks with previous Novembers. The conjunction *so that* nonsensically introduces a causal relationship between November's typically strong sales and the aforementioned comparison.

E Like (D), this sentence introduces a nonsensical causal relationship, in this case between the fact that November typically has the strongest sales and the fact that this past November's sales accounted for a remarkably large share of total vehicle sales.

The correct answer is A.

784. Most of the country's biggest daily newspapers had lower circulation in the six months from October 1995 through March 1996 than <u>a similar</u> period a year earlier.

(A) a similar period

(B) a similar period's

(C) in a similar period

(D) that in a similar period

(E) that of a similar period

Logical Predication; Parallelism

The sentence compares newspaper circulation during two separate periods, but the comparison is not parallel because it has been drawn using a prepositional phrase, *in the six months*, and a noun phrase, *a similar period.* Both phrases compared by *than* should be prepositional phrases: *lower in the six months . . . than in a similar period.*

A *In the six months* and *a similar period* are not grammatically parallel. The sentence appears illogically to compare a period of time with an amount of circulation.

B *In the six months* and *a similar period's* are not grammatically parallel.

C **Correct.** *In the six months* and *in a similar period* are both prepositional phrases, making the comparison clear and properly idiomatic.

D *In the six months* and *that in a similar period* are not grammatically parallel; it is unclear what the antecedent of *that* is supposed to be.

E *In the six months* and *that of a similar period* are not grammatically parallel; it is unclear what the antecedent of *that* is supposed to be.

The correct answer is C.

785. Mauritius was a British colony for almost 200 years, <u>excepting for</u> the domains of administration and teaching, the English language was never really spoken on the island.

(A) excepting for
(B) except in
(C) but except in
(D) but excepting for
(E) with the exception of

Idiom; Grammatical construction

This two-clause sentence describes an apparent incompatibility: as a British colony, Mauritius might be expected to be English-speaking, but in fact it was not. To describe this apparent contradiction and to avoid a comma splice, the clauses should be joined by the conjunction *but.* *Domains* describes places *in* which English is spoken; *for* is the incorrect preposition. *Excepting* is not idiomatic English in this case.

A The lack of a conjunction causes a comma splice; *excepting for* is non-idiomatic.

B The lack of a conjunction causes a comma splice.

C **Correct.** The two independent clauses are separated by *but*, and *except in* is an appropriate idiom.

D *Excepting for* is non-idiomatic.

E The lack of a conjunction causes a comma splice.

The correct answer is C.

786. <u>Although appearing less appetizing than most of their round and red supermarket cousins, heirloom tomatoes, grown from seeds saved during the previous year</u>—they are often green and striped, or have plenty of bumps and bruises—heirlooms are more flavorful and thus in increasing demand.

(A) Although appearing less appetizing than most of their round and red supermarket cousins, heirloom tomatoes, grown from seeds saved during the previous year
(B) Although heirloom tomatoes, grown from seeds saved during the previous year, appear less appetizing than most of their round and red supermarket cousins
(C) Although they appear less appetizing than most of their round and red supermarket cousins, heirloom tomatoes, grown from seeds saved during the previous year
(D) Grown from seeds saved during the previous year, heirloom tomatoes appear less appetizing than most of their round and red supermarket cousins
(E) Heirloom tomatoes, grown from seeds saved during the previous year, although they appear less appetizing than most of their round and red supermarket cousins

Rhetorical construction; Grammatical construction

The intended meaning could be communicated more effectively by mentioning heirloom tomatoes as early as possible in the sentence, so that we know that the writer is comparing heirloom tomatoes with supermarket tomatoes. The placement of *heirloom tomatoes* and *heirlooms* makes the sentence ungrammatical.

A This is ungrammatical. If *heirloom tomatoes* is the subject of *are more flavorful* … then *heirlooms* has no predicate and is nonsensically superfluous. If *heirlooms* is the subject, *heirloom tomatoes* has no predicate.

B **Correct.** The noun *heirloom tomatoes* is mentioned early in the sentence, followed by a parenthetical definition, and is the subject of the verb *appear*, and *heirlooms* is the subject of *are*.

C The noun *heirloom tomatoes* appears too late in the sentence. Parsing is made harder by introducing the pronoun *they* and revealing its antecedent later in the sentence. The sentence is also ungrammatical. If *heirloom tomatoes* is the subject of *are more flavorful* … then *heirlooms* has no predicate and is nonsensically superfluous. If *heirlooms* is the subject, *heirloom tomatoes* has no predicate.

D Beginning the sentence with the explanatory clause *grown from seeds* … gives it too much importance. It could be construed as the reason why heirloom tomatoes appear less appetizing, which is contrary to the truth. The sentence is also ungrammatical.

E Rhetorical structure requires that *although* appear in the beginning of the clause to which it pertains. Placing it later necessitates the pronoun *they* with antecedent *heirloom tomatoes*, which is redundant. The sentence is also ungrammatical.

The correct answer is B.

787. The World Wildlife Fund has declared that global warming, <u>a phenomenon most scientists agree to be caused by human beings in burning fossil fuels,</u> will create havoc among migratory birds by altering the environment in ways harmful to their habitats.

(A) a phenomenon most scientists agree to be caused by human beings in burning fossil fuels,

(B) a phenomenon most scientists agree that is caused by fossil fuels burned by human beings,

(C) a phenomenon that most scientists agree is caused by human beings' burning of fossil fuels,

(D) which most scientists agree on as a phenomenon caused by human beings who burn fossil fuels,

(E) which most scientists agree to be a phenomenon caused by fossil fuels burned by human beings,

Logical predication; Rhetorical construction

The underlined portion of the sentence is an appositive defining *global warming* as a phenomenon caused by the burning of fossil fuels by humans. Because this appositive intervenes between the subject (*global warming*) and verb (*will create*) of a clause, it should be expressed as clearly and economically as possible so as not to confuse the meaning of the sentence as a whole.

A *To be caused* and *in burning* are wordy, awkward, and indirect.

B *That is* should immediately follow *phenomenon*, not *agree*.

C **Correct.** The phrase *human beings' burning* is more economical than constructions with prepositional phrases or relative clauses.

D The phrasing is wordy and indirect.

E The phrasing is wordy and the meaning is imprecise; it is not fossil fuels that cause global warming—it is the burning of fossil fuels by humans.

The correct answer is C.

788. The largest of all the planets, <u>not only is Jupiter three times so massive as Saturn, the next larger</u> planet, but also possesses four of the largest satellites, or moons, in our solar system.

(A) not only is Jupiter three times so massive as Saturn, the next larger

(B) not only is Jupiter three times as massive as Saturn, the next largest

(C) Jupiter, not only three times as massive as Saturn, the next largest

(D) Jupiter not only is three times as massive as Saturn, the next largest

(E) Jupiter is not only three times so massive as Saturn, the next larger

Diction; Idiom

This sentence begins with a phrase, [*t*]*he largest* …, describing the main subject *Jupiter*. The remainder of the sentence describes Jupiter's size and possession of moons, using the idiom *not only x but y* to introduce parallel adjective phrases.

A In this version of the sentence, *so massive as Saturn* violates the parallelism established by the idiom *as + adjective + as + noun*. For the sake of clarity, the noun described by the opening adjectival phrase should immediately follow that phrase. The phrase *next larger* is unidiomatic and unclear. The superlative (*largest*) is appropriate in this consideration of all the planets.

B As in (A), *Jupiter* should immediately follow the opening phrase.

C This version of the sentence violates the parallelism of the idiom *not only x but y*, following the first half of the template with an adjective phrase and the second half with a verb phrase.

D **Correct.** The placement of the subject in relation to the opening modifier, the properly constructed phrasing, and the proper use of comparison words make the meaning of the sentence clear.

E The phrase *so massive as* violates the idiom *as x as y*. Consideration of Jupiter's size among all the planets, including Saturn, requires the superlative form, *largest*.

The correct answer is D.

789. While many of the dinosaur fossils found recently in northeast China seem to provide evidence of the kinship between dinosaurs and birds, the wealth of enigmatic fossils <u>seem more likely at this stage that they will inflame debates over the origin of birds rather than</u> settle them.

(A) seem more likely at this stage that they will inflame debates over the origin of birds rather than

(B) seem more likely that it will inflame debates over the origin of birds at this stage than

(C) seems more likely to inflame debates on the origin of birds at this stage rather than

(D) seems more likely at this stage to inflame debates over the origin of birds than to

(E) seems more likely that it will inflame debates on the origin of birds at this stage than to

Agreement; Parallelism

This sentence states that whereas many dinosaur fossils from China suggest that there is a kinship between dinosaurs and birds, the *wealth* of fossils are more ambiguous about what they suggest about the ancestry of birds. The word *wealth* is a mass noun followed by a prepositional phrase; because *wealth* follows the article *the*, the emphasis is on it rather than on the noun in the prepositional phrase, *fossils*. The singular *wealth* requires a singular main verb (*seems*). The comparative expression *more likely* . . . must be followed by an infinitive verb (*to inflame*) so it will be parallel to the verb with which it is compared (*to settle*).

A The singular subject *wealth* does not agree with the plural verb *seem*; both items being compared should be in parallel form (*inflame* and *settle*); the relative clause *that they will inflame* violates the parallelism.

B Again, the relative clause violates the desired parallelism; the singular subject, *wealth*, requires a singular verb, *seems*.

C The subject and the verb agree with one another, but the placement of the modifier *at this stage* makes the modifier appear to describe *origin of the birds* rather than the verb *seems*.

D **Correct.** The verb *seems* agrees in number with the noun *wealth*; the infinitive *to inflame* is parallel with the verb to which it is compared, *to settle*.

E The clause *wealth . . . seems more likely that it will inflame* is not idiomatic, and *that it will inflame* is not parallel with the infinitive verb *to settle*.

The correct answer is D.

790. <u>Found only in the Western Hemisphere and surviving through extremes of climate, hummingbirds' range extends</u> from Alaska to Tierra del Fuego, from sea-level rain forests to the edges of Andean snowfields and ice fields at altitudes of 15,000 feet.

(A) Found only in the Western Hemisphere and surviving through extremes of climate, hummingbirds' range extends

(B) Found only in the Western Hemisphere, hummingbirds survive through extremes of climate, their range extending

(C) Hummingbirds, found only in the Western Hemisphere and surviving through extremes of climate, with their range extending
(D) Hummingbirds, found only in the Western Hemisphere and surviving through extremes of climate, their range extends
(E) Hummingbirds are found only in the Western Hemisphere, survive through extremes of climate, and their range extends

Logical predication; Grammatical construction

This sentence makes three points about hummingbirds: they live in the Western Hemisphere, they survive extreme climates, and their range is wide and varied. *Hummingbirds*, not *hummingbirds' range*, should be the subject of the sentence.

A The opening modifier, *found . . . and surviving . . .* should modify *hummingbirds*, not, as it does, *hummingbirds' range*.

B Correct. *Hummingbirds* is the subject of the sentence, and the use of the absolute phrase *their range extending* appropriately connects the final clause to the rest of the sentence.

C This version of the sentence has no main verb for the subject *Hummingbirds* and as a result is ungrammatical.

D Like (C), this version of the sentence has no main verb for the subject *Hummingbirds*.

E This version of the sentence begins with the subject *Hummingbirds* attached to a pair of verb phrases (*are found . . .* and *survive . . .*) followed by the conjunction *and*, which suggests that what follows should also be a verb phrase; instead, a new subject is introduced, *their range*. Replacing the comma before *survive* with *and* would render the sentence acceptable.

The correct answer is B.

791. <u>She was less successful after she had emigrated to New York compared to</u> her native Germany, photographer Lotte Jacobi nevertheless earned a small group of discerning admirers, and her photographs were eventually exhibited in prestigious galleries across the United States.

(A) She was less successful after she had emigrated to New York compared to
(B) Being less successful after she had emigrated to New York as compared to
(C) Less successful after she emigrated to New York than she had been in
(D) Although she was less successful after emigrating to New York when compared to
(E) She had been less successful after emigrating to New York than in

Idiom; Grammatical construction; Logical predication

This sentence compares the success Jacobi experienced after moving to New York to the success she had previously experienced in Germany. The phrase *less successful* anticipates the conclusion of the comparison with the phrase *than.* ... The main subject of the sentence is *photographer Lotte Jacobi*, and the main verb is *earned*. The opening clause *She was less successful* ... therefore creates a comma splice if the comma is not followed by a conjunction. The most efficient way to incorporate the information about Jacobi's comparative successes in Germany and in New York is to turn this clause into an adjectival phrase describing Jacobi.

A *Less successful* ... anticipates *than* rather than *compared to* ...; a comma is insufficient to join two independent clauses into a single sentence.

B *As compared to* is an incorrect way to complete the comparison introduced by *less*; *Being* ... is unnecessarily wordy and awkward.

C Correct. The idiomatic construction *less successful ... than* is incorporated into an introductory adjectival phrase modifying *Lotte Jacobi*.

D *When compared to* is an incorrect phrase to complete the comparison introduced by *less*.

E A comma is insufficient to join two independent clauses into a single sentence; past-perfect tense is misleading, since it refers to Jacobi's experience in New York, which in fact followed her experience in Germany.

The correct answer is C.

792. Scientists have recently found evidence that black holes—regions of space in which matter is so concentrated and the pull of gravity so powerful that nothing, not even light, can emerge from them—probably exist at the core of nearly all galaxies and the mass of each black hole is proportional to its host galaxy.

(A) exist at the core of nearly all galaxies and the mass of each black hole is proportional to

(B) exist at the core of nearly all galaxies and that the mass of each black hole is proportional to that of

(C) exist at the core of nearly all galaxies, and that the mass of each black hole is proportional to

(D) exists at the core of nearly all galaxies, and that the mass of each black hole is proportional to that of

(E) exists at the core of nearly all galaxies and the mass of each black hole is proportional to that of

Logical predication; Agreement

This sentence focuses attention on two hypotheses about black holes—one about their location and the other about their mass. These hypotheses appear as parallel relative clauses *that black holes . . . exist at . . .* and *that the mass . . . is proportional*. The subject of the first relative clause (*black holes*) is plural, so the clause must be completed with the plural form of *exist*.

A This version of the sentence does not provide the relative pronoun *that* to provide parallel structure for presenting the two things scientific evidence reveals about black holes. This leaves it somewhat unclear whether the final clause is intended to convey part of what the scientists discovered or to express a claim that the writer is making independently of the scientists' discovery. The sentence illogically compares *mass* to *galaxy*.

B **Correct.** The structure of the sentence makes the meaning clear, and the plural verb form agrees with the plural subject.

C The comma appears to signal that the final part of the sentence is intended as an independent clause expressing a separate claim rather than describing part of the scientists' discovery. But if it were intended in that way, it should be set off as a separate sentence, not conjoined with the preceding clause. Like (A), this version makes an illogical comparison between *mass* and *galaxy*.

D The singular verb *exists* does not agree with the plural subject *black holes*. As in (C), the comma is inappropriate because it does not introduce a new independent clause.

E The singular verb *exists* does not agree with the plural subject *black holes*. Like (A), this version lacks the relative pronoun *that*, which would clarify the relationship between the two clauses.

The correct answer is B.

793. The use of lie detectors is based on the assumption that lying produces emotional reactions in an individual that, in turn, create unconscious physiological responses.

(A) that, in turn, create unconscious physiological responses

(B) that creates unconscious physiological responses in turn

(C) creating, in turn, unconscious physiological responses

(D) to create, in turn, physiological responses that are unconscious

(E) who creates unconscious physiological responses in turn

Agreement; Rhetorical construction; Logical predication

This sentence describes a cause-and-effect sequence; in the underlined portion of the sentence, the relative pronoun *that* refers to the plural noun *reactions*. The verb in the relative clause must therefore be a plural verb. The causal sequence is most clearly expressed by a relative clause that turns the object *emotional reactions* (from the clause *lying causes emotional reactions in an individual*) into the subject (*that*) of a new clause (*that in turn create unconscious physiological responses*). *In turn* is best placed before the verb of the second relative clause, *create*, to clarify that a chain of events is being described.

A **Correct.** This construction clearly indicates the causal sequence.

B The singular verb *creates* does not agree with the subject referenced by the relative pronoun *that* (*reactions*).

C This construction is less successful at clarifying the chain of events because *creating* seems to refer back to *lying*; if used as a participial, *creating* would have to be preceded by a comma.

D This construction does not make clear the causal chain of events, because it is unclear which noun *to create* should attach to; the infinitive construction implies intent, which does not really make sense.

E Because *reactions* is not a person, *who* is the wrong relative pronoun to use.

The correct answer is A.

794. Australian embryologists have found evidence that suggests that the elephant is descended from an aquatic animal, and its trunk originally evolving as a kind of snorkel.

(A) that suggests that the elephant is descended from an aquatic animal, and its trunk originally evolving

(B) that has suggested the elephant descended from an aquatic animal, its trunk originally evolving

(C) suggesting that the elephant had descended from an aquatic animal with its trunk originally evolved

(D) to suggest that the elephant had descended from an aquatic animal and its trunk originally evolved

(E) to suggest that the elephant is descended from an aquatic animal and that its trunk originally evolved

Parallelism; Verb form

The clearest, most economical way of expressing the two things suggested by Australian embryologists' evidence is to format them as relative clauses serving as parallel direct objects of the verb *suggest.* It is awkward and confusing to string together relative clauses: *evidence that suggests that the elephant.* … A clearer way of making this connection is to turn the verb *suggests* into a participle modifying *evidence.* The word *descended* is a predicate adjective following the present-tense verb *is* and describing the present-day elephant. The verb *evolved* should be past tense because it describes how the trunk of the elephant *originally* evolved, not how it is evolving today.

A The string of relative phrases is awkward and confusing; the phrase following the conjunction *and* is not parallel with the relative clause *that the elephant is descended.* …

B The evidence *still* suggests these things about the evolution of the elephant and its trunk, so the present-perfect verb tense is inaccurate.

C *Had descended* is the wrong verb tense; *with* cannot be followed by an independent clause.

D *Had descended* is the wrong tense; the phrase following the conjunction *and* does not parallel the relative clause that precedes the conjunction.

E **Correct.** The two dependent clauses beginning with *that* are in parallel form and contain verbs in the correct tenses.

The correct answer is E.

795. Most efforts to combat such mosquito-borne diseases like malaria and dengue have focused either on the vaccination of humans or on exterminating mosquitoes with pesticides.

(A) like malaria and dengue have focused either on the vaccination of humans or on exterminating

(B) like malaria and dengue have focused either on vaccinating of humans or on the extermination of

(C) as malaria and dengue have focused on either vaccinating humans or on exterminating

(D) as malaria and dengue have focused on either vaccinating of humans or on extermination of

(E) as malaria and dengue have focused on either vaccinating humans or exterminating

Diction; Parallelism

The phrase *such … diseases like malaria and dengue* is not a correct way in English to indicate that the two diseases mentioned are examples of a larger category; the correct expression is *such … as.* …

A This use of *such … like …* is incorrect English; the correct expression is *such … as.…* It is better to keep the preposition *on* close to the verb it goes with, *focus*, so as not to repeat it.

B The correct expression is *such … as.…* It is better to keep the preposition *on* close to the verb it goes with, *focus*, so as not to repeat it. This use of the gerund *vaccinating* (followed by *of*) would normally be preceded by *the*, but this would make the phrase awkward. It would be preferable to use *vaccination*, which is parallel to *extermination*.

C This answer choice incorrectly repeats the preposition *on* before *exterminating*.

D This answer choice incorrectly repeats the preposition *on* before *extermination*. This use of the gerund *vaccinating* (followed by *of*) would normally be preceded by *the*, but this would make the phrase awkward. It would be preferable to use *vaccination*, which is parallel to *extermination*.

E **Correct.** This version uses *either … or …* correctly and appropriately uses the parallel forms *vaccinating* and *exterminating*.

The correct answer is E.

796. Among the Tsonga, a Bantu-speaking group of tribes in southeastern Africa, dance teams represent their own chief at the court of each other, providing entertainment in return for food, drink, and lodging.

(A) the court of each other, providing entertainment in return for

(B) the court of another and provide entertainment in return for

(C) the court of the other, so as to provide entertainment as a return on

(D) each other's court, entertainment being provided in return for

(E) another's court and provide entertainment as a return on

Diction; Idiom

The point of the sentence is that dancers representing one chief perform at the court of another chief *in return for* gifts. *The court of each other* is unidiomatic and unclear. It could be intended to indicate, somewhat implausibly, that each team has a court that the other teams visit, but *represent their own chief* strongly suggests that the court referred to is the court of another chief. The correct pronoun to refer to a different chief is *another*.

A *The court of each other* is unidiomatic and unclear. *Each other* seems to refer, somewhat illogically, to the dancers.

B **Correct.** The sentence clearly explains the idea, using the correct pronoun *another* and the correct idiom *in return for*.

C This could be confusing in that *the other* indicates that there is only one other chief, whereas *group of tribes* suggests that there may be a number of chiefs. *As a return on* is the incorrect idiom; *a return on* normally refers to a gain from an investment, not a direct exchange of one good for another.

D *Each other's court* somewhat illogically indicates that the dancers each have a court. *Entertainment being provided in return for* is awkward and indirect.

E *As a return on* is the incorrect idiom; *a return on* normally refers to a gain from an investment, not a direct exchange of one good for another.

The correct answer is B.

797. Almost like clones in their similarity to one another, the cheetah species' homogeneity makes them especially vulnerable to disease.

(A) the cheetah species' homogeneity makes them especially vulnerable to disease

(B) the cheetah species is especially vulnerable to disease because of its homogeneity

(C) the homogeneity of the cheetah species makes it especially vulnerable to disease

(D) homogeneity makes members of the cheetah species especially vulnerable to disease

(E) members of the cheetah species are especially vulnerable to disease because of their homogeneity

Agreement; Logical predication

Genetic homogeneity is presented as a cause of cheetahs' vulnerability to disease. The opening adjectival phrase refers to the fact that individual cheetahs are almost like clones of one another because of how genetically similar they are. This adjectival phrase should be followed by what it describes, individual cheetahs. But the structure of the sentence makes it seem that this adjectival phrase is meant—illogically—to describe *the cheetah species' homogeneity*. The sentence structure also fails to make clear that the intended reference is to just one (the only) cheetah species.

A The sentence nonsensically presents the opening phrase as describing *homogeneity*.

B The resulting sentence opens with a reference to a plurality of individuals (*to one another*), but confusingly identifies this with a single (collective) entity, a species.

C The resulting sentence nonsensically presents the opening phrase as describing *homogeneity*.

D The resulting sentence nonsensically presents the opening phrase as describing *homogeneity*.

E **Correct.** The sentence is clear and the opening phrase correctly modifies *members of the cheetah species*.

The correct answer is E.

798. As sources of electrical power, windmills now account for only about 2,500 megawatts nationwide, but production is almost expected to double by the end of the year, which would provide enough electricity for 1.3 million households.

(A) almost expected to double by the end of the year, which would provide

(B) almost expected that it will double by the end of the year, thus providing

(C) expected that it will almost double by the end of the year to provide

(D) expected almost double by the end of the year and thus to provide

(E) expected almost to double by the end of the year, which would thus be providing

Rhetorical construction; Idiom

The intended meaning of the sentence seems to be that the electricity production of windmills is expected to approximately double by year's end. But instead of saying *almost double*, we have *almost expected*, which is an unclear idea. Also unclear is what the relative pronoun *which* refers to.

A The placement of *almost* makes it nonsensically modify *is expected*. What the relative pronoun *which* refers to is ambiguous: for example, does it refer to the expectation, the possible doubling, or the year?

B The resulting sentence misplaces the adverb *almost*.

C The phrase *production is expected that it will*... makes no sense—as opposed to, for example, *it is expected that production will*....

D **Correct.** This sentence clearly conveys the expectations of production: *almost to double* and *thus to provide*. There is no ambiguity as to what will be providing *enough electricity*.

E The referent of the relative pronoun *which* is ambiguous, and the conditional verb form *would thus be providing* is unnecessarily wordy.

The correct answer is D.

799. While most of the earliest known ball courts in Mesoamerica date to 900–400 B.C., waterlogged latex balls found at El Manati and representations of ballplayers painted on ceramics found at San Lorenzo attest to the fact that the Mesoamerican ballgame was well established by the mid-thirteenth century B.C.

(A) waterlogged latex balls found at El Manati and representations of ballplayers painted on ceramics found at San Lorenzo attest

(B) waterlogged latex balls found at El Manati and the painting of representations of ballplayers on ceramics found at San Lorenzo attests

(C) waterlogged latex balls found at El Manati and ceramics painted with representations of ballplayers found at San Lorenzo attests

(D) the finding of waterlogged latex balls at El Manati and the painting of representations of ballplayers on ceramics found at San Lorenzo attests

(E) the finding of waterlogged latex balls at El Manati and of representations of ballplayers painted on ceramics at San Lorenzo attest

Logical predication; Agreement

The sentence points out two pieces of evidence that prove the early existence of ballgames in Mesoamerica: *waterlogged latex balls* and *representations of ballplayers.* The two noun phrases together serve as subjects for the verb *attest*, creating a sentence that logically and correctly expresses its main idea.

A **Correct.** *Waterlogged latex balls* and *representations of ballplayers* together serve as subjects for the verb *attest*.

B *Painting* could refer to something that has been painted, but on that interpretation the sentence does not make sense, because the painting is itself the representation and a single painting would not plausibly be on multiple ceramics. Alternatively, it could refer to an ongoing act of painting, which could not plausibly constitute the kind of evidence referred to. The singular verb *attests* does not agree with the compound subject *balls* and *painting*.

C The singular verb *attests* does not agree with the compound subject *balls* and *ceramics*.

D *Balls*, not *finding*, should be the subject of the verb since the balls are the evidence. *Painting* could refer to something that has been painted, but on that interpretation the sentence does not make sense, because the painting is itself the representation and a single painting would not plausibly be on multiple ceramics. Alternatively, it could refer to an ongoing act of painting, which could not plausibly constitute the kind of evidence referred to. The singular verb *attests* does not agree with the compound subject *finding* and *painting*.

E *Balls* and *representations* should be the subject of the verb *attest* since they are the evidence—not *finding*; the plural verb *attest* does not agree with the singular subject *finding*.

The correct answer is A.

800. As criminal activity on the Internet becomes more and more sophisticated, not only are thieves able to divert cash from company bank accounts, they can also pilfer valuable information such as business development strategies, new product specifications, and contract bidding plans, and sell the data to competitors.

(A) they can also pilfer valuable information such as business development strategies, new product specifications, and contract bidding plans, and sell

(B) they can also pilfer valuable information that includes business development strategies, new product specifications, and contract bidding plans, and selling

(C) also pilfering valuable information including business development strategies, new product specifications, and contract bidding plans, selling

(D) but also pilfer valuable information such as business development strategies, new product specifications, and contract bidding plans to sell

(E) but also pilfering valuable information such as business development strategies, new product specifications, and contract bidding plans and selling

Grammatical construction; Verb form

The two clauses in this *not only* . . . construction normally require subjects, which this sentence has. The second clause (beginning with *they can*) further divides into two clauses about pilfering and selling; here, the two verbs must have the same form, since each one is the main verb of its clause.

A **Correct.** *They* supplies the needed subject, and *pilfer* and *sell* are both in the bare verb form.

B *Selling* is the wrong form for the main verb of a finite clause; it should be *sell.*

C There is no subject for the *pilfer* clause, and *pilfering* would be the wrong form even if a subject were added.

D There is no subject for the *pilfer* clause.

E There is no subject for the *pilfer* clause, and both *selling* and *pilfering* have the wrong verb for the main verb of a finite clause; they should be *sell* and *pilfer*, respectively.

The correct answer is A.

801. Last week local shrimpers held a news conference to take some credit for the resurgence of the rare Kemp's ridley turtle, saying that their compliance with laws requiring that turtle-excluder devices be on shrimp nets protect adult sea turtles.

(A) requiring that turtle-excluder devices be on shrimp nets protect

(B) requiring turtle-excluder devices on shrimp nets is protecting

(C) that require turtle-excluder devices on shrimp nets protect

(D) to require turtle-excluder devices on shrimp nets are protecting

(E) to require turtle-excluder devices on shrimp nets is protecting

Rhetorical construction; Agreement

The subject of the clause introduced by *saying that* is the singular noun *compliance*. This subject requires the singular form of the verb *protect*. The clearest, most economical way to describe the laws in question is to follow the word *laws* with a present participle *requiring*. To use an infinitive, *to require*, seems to indicate that requiring these devices is the objective of the laws, when in fact the objective is to protect the sea turtles.

A The plural verb *protect* does not agree with the singular subject *compliance*.

B Correct. The singular verb *is protecting* agrees with the singular subject *compliance*, and the participial phrase beginning with *requiring* concisely and accurately describes the laws.

C The relative clause *that require* introduces unnecessary wordiness; the plural verb *protect* does not agree with the singular subject *compliance*.

D *To require* obscures the purpose of the laws; the plural verb phrase *are protecting* does not agree with the singular subject *compliance*.

E *To require* obscures the purpose of the laws.

The correct answer is B.

802. A ruined structure found at Aqaba, Jordan, was probably a church, as indicated in its eastward orientation and by its overall plan, as well as artifacts, such as glass oil-lamp fragments, found at the site.

(A) A ruined structure found at Aqaba, Jordan, was probably a church, as indicated in its eastward orientation and by its overall plan, as well as

(B) A ruined structure found at Aqaba, Jordan, once probably being a church, was indicated by its eastward orientation, overall plan, and

(C) Indicating that a ruined structure found at Aqaba, Jordan, was probably a church were its eastward orientation and overall plan, but also the

(D) A ruined structure found at Aqaba, Jordan, was probably a church, as indicates its eastward orientation and overall plan, as well as the

(E) That a ruined structure found at Aqaba, Jordan, was probably a church is indicated by its eastward orientation and overall plan, as well as by the

Logical predication; Parallelism

This sentence explains why a currently ruined structure probably used to be a church. In the best-worded answer choice, the abstract subject (the probability that a certain hypothesis is true) is explained abstractly in a relative clause (*That a ruined structure was probably . . .*) followed by a passive verb (*is indicated*), followed by the prepositional phrase (*by . . .*), which is completed by a parallel listing of forms of evidence, all presented as noun phrases in the expression, (*by*) (*its*) A + B, as well as (*by*) C.

A This version makes the relationship between *as well as* . . . and the rest of the sentence unclear. The most plausible hypothesis is that the artifacts are another of the types of evidence, parallel with the structure's orientation and its plan. The sentence violates the parallelism required in the list by failing to supply the preposition in the final item following *as well as*.

B The subject of this version of the sentence, *structure*, is completed by the verb *was indicated*, creating the illogical assertion that the structure itself, rather than its probable identity, was indicated by its orientation, plan, and attendant artifacts.

C Opening the sentence with the predicate adjective *indicating* leads to a confusing and awkward withholding of the subjects *orientation . . . plan . . . artifacts*.

D The only plausible subject for the singular verb *indicates* is the plural *orientation . . . plan, as well as the artifacts*. Very little about this sentence makes sense.

E **Correct.** The relationships among the parts of the sentence are clear and logical.

The correct answer is E.

803. In the major cities of industrialized countries at the end of the nineteenth century, important public places such as theaters, restaurants, shops, and banks had installed electric lighting, but electricity was in less than 1 percent of homes, where lighting was still provided mainly by candles or gas.

(A) electricity was in less than 1 percent of homes, where lighting was still

(B) electricity was in less than 1 percent of homes and lighting still

(C) there had been less than 1 percent of homes with electricity, where lighting was still being

(D) there was less than 1 percent of homes that had electricity, having lighting that was still

(E) less than 1 percent of homes had electricity, where lighting had still been

Rhetorical construction; Verb form

In this type of usage, a participle such as *provided* normally must be preceded by some form of the verb *be*. The best choice for this is the past tense *was*, since the main part of the clause describes the situation in the past tense (*electricity was . . .*). To link the ideas of lighting and electricity in homes, *where* is the most efficient and direct expression, superior to alternatives such as *and* or *having*.

A **Correct.** The participle is preceded by the appropriate form *was*, and the clauses are linked efficiently by *where*.

B There is no form of *be* in the second clause, and *and* does not clearly indicate the connection between the two clauses.

C *Had been* and *was being* represent inappropriate tenses, and the *there had been* construction is longer than necessary.

D Both *having lighting* and the *there was* construction are longer and more complicated than necessary. This sentence structure makes *there*, instead of *homes*, the subject of *having*.

E *Had been* is not the appropriate tense for this situation.

The correct answer is A.

804. By 1999, astronomers had discovered 17 nearby stars that are orbited by planets about the size of Jupiter.

(A) had discovered 17 nearby stars that are orbited by planets

(B) had discovered 17 nearby stars with planets orbiting them that were

(C) had discovered that there were 17 nearby stars that were orbited by planets

(D) have discovered 17 nearby stars with planets orbiting them that are

(E) have discovered that 17 nearby stars are orbited by planets

Verb form; Rhetorical construction

Opening with a past date (*1999*) describing the end point of a period of discovery, this sentence calls for a past perfect main verb to follow the subject *astronomers*. In order to economize on words and maximize clarity, the object of the main clause, *stars*, is modified by a passive relative clause *that are orbited by planets* followed by the adjective phrase *about the size of Jupiter*. This structure avoids an awkward and confusing string of relative clauses and prepositional phrases.

A **Correct.** This version is clear and uses the correct verb form *had discovered*.

B The use of a prepositional phrase *with planets* necessitates the introduction of a relative clause *that were . . .*, in which the referent of the relative pronoun *that* is somewhat uncertain (stars? or planets?). The past tense verb *were* suggests, improbably, that the size of the planets may have changed significantly since 1999.

C The string of relative clauses is awkward and wordy.

D If the sentence was written after 1999, the present perfect tense is illogical, because 1999 is in the past. If it was written in 1999, this way of referring to the then-present time is odd and misleading. The prepositional phrase is wordy and indirect.

E As in (D), the present perfect tense is illogical.

The correct answer is A.

805. Although she was considered among her contemporaries to be the better poet than her husband, later Elizabeth Barrett Browning was overshadowed by his success.

(A) Although she was considered among her contemporaries to be the better poet than her husband, later Elizabeth Barrett Browning was overshadowed by his success.
(B) Although Elizabeth Barrett Browning was considered among her contemporaries as a better poet than her husband, she was later overshadowed by his success.
(C) Later overshadowed by the success of her husband, Elizabeth Barrett Browning's poetry had been considered among her contemporaries to be better than that of her husband.
(D) Although Elizabeth Barrett Browning's success was later overshadowed by that of her husband, among her contemporaries she was considered the better poet.
(E) Elizabeth Barrett Browning's poetry was considered among her contemporaries as better than her husband, but her success was later overshadowed by his.

Idiom; Verb form; Logical predication

The sentence misuses the locution *the better poet*. It is acceptable to say *a better poet than* but not *the better poet than*. If you have already mentioned two poets *X* and *Y*, and you want to say that *X* is better than *Y*, you can either say *X is a better poet than Y*, or simply, *X is the better poet.*

A This version of the sentence misuses the idiom *the better poet*, most likely confusing it with the idiom *a better poet than*.

B [W]*as considered among her contemporaries as* is awkward and unnecessarily creates a potential misreading (she was considered to be among her contemporaries).

C The subject here is *Elizabeth Barrett Browning's poetry*, not *Elizabeth Barrett Browning*, so the antecedent of *her* in *her husband* could comically be taken to be *Elizabeth Barrett Browning's poetry*. Furthermore, the tense of *had been considered* pairs oddly with *Later overshadowed*. Each seems to be in reaction to some particular time *T*—later than *T* and earlier than *T*, but when *T* was or its significance is never indicated.

D **Correct.** This version avoids the problems of the other versions.

E This sentence comically compares Elizabeth Barrett Browning's poetry to her husband.

The correct answer is D.

806. In no other historical sighting did Halley's Comet cause such a worldwide sensation as did its return in 1910–1911.

(A) did its return in 1910–1911
(B) had its 1910–1911 return
(C) in its return of 1910–1911
(D) its return of 1910–1911 did
(E) its return in 1910–1911

Parallelism; Verb form; Logical predication

The single subject of this sentence is *Halley's Comet*, and its single verb phrase is *did cause.* The comparison presented by the sentence is between adverbial phrases describing times when the comet was seen. Grammatically, the items being compared are parallel prepositional phrases beginning with the preposition *in: in no other sighting* and *in its return in 1910–1911.* This is the clearest, most economical way of presenting the information. The options that introduce a second verb (*did* or *had*) violate the parallelism and introduce a comparison between the comet itself (subject of the verb *did cause*) and the comet's return (subject of the verb *did* or *had*).

A This sentence implies a comparison between the comet and its return.

B This sentence implies a comparison between the comet and its return; *had* is the wrong auxiliary verb form because it must be followed by *caused* instead of *cause.*

C **Correct.** The parallel prepositional phrases in this sentence correctly compare times when the comet was sighted.

D This sentence implies a comparison between the comet and its return.

E This sentence violates parallelism, implying a comparison between a prepositional phrase and a noun phrase.

The correct answer is C.

807. Rock samples taken from the remains of an asteroid about twice the size of the 6-mile-wide asteroid that eradicated the dinosaurs <u>has been dated to be 3.47 billion years old and thus is</u> evidence of the earliest known asteroid impact on Earth.

(A) has been dated to be 3.47 billion years old and thus is
(B) has been dated at 3.47 billion years old and thus
(C) have been dated to be 3.47 billion years old and thus are
(D) have been dated as being 3.47 billion years old and thus
(E) have been dated at 3.47 billion years old and thus are

Agreement; Idiom

The plural subject of this sentence, *Rock samples*, requires plural verb phrases—*have been dated* and *are* rather than *has been dated* and *is*. The idiomatic way of expressing estimation of age is with the phrase *dated at*.

A The subject and verbs do not agree; *dated to be* … is not idiomatic.

B The subject and verb do not agree; the conjunction *and thus* should be followed by a verb.

C *Dated to be* is not idiomatic.

D *As being* is not idiomatic; the conjunction *and thus* should be followed by a verb.

E **Correct.** The plural verbs match the plural subject, and the wording of the sentence is idiomatic.

The correct answer is E.

10.0 Integrated Reasoning

10.0 Integrated Reasoning

The Integrated Reasoning section measures your ability to understand and evaluate multiple sources and types of information—graphic, numeric, and verbal—as they relate to one another; use quantitative and verbal reasoning to solve complex problems; and solve multiple problems in relation to one another. This section includes text passages, tables, graphs, and other visual information from a variety of content areas; however, the materials and questions do not assume detailed knowledge of the topics discussed. The Integrated Reasoning section differs from the Quantitative and Verbal sections in two important ways: 1) It involves both mathematical and verbal reasoning, either separately or in combination, and 2) questions are answered using four different response formats rather than only traditional multiple-choice.

Four types of questions are used in the Integrated Reasoning section:

- Multi-Source Reasoning
- Table Analysis
- Graphics Interpretation
- Two-Part Analysis

Use your unique access code found in the back of this book to access 50 additional Integrated Reasoning practice questions with full answer explanations.

10.1 What Is Measured

Integrated Reasoning questions assess your ability to apply, evaluate, infer, recognize, and strategize.

Apply concepts presented in the information

Apply questions measure your ability to understand principles, rules, or other concepts in the information provided and apply them to a new context or predict consequences that would follow if new information were incorporated into the context provided. You may be asked to

- decide whether new examples would comply with or violate rules established in the information provided
- determine how a trend present in the information provided would be affected by new scenarios
- use principles established in the information provided to draw conclusions about new data

Evaluate information qualitatively

Evaluate questions measure your ability to make judgments about the quality of information. For example, you may be asked to

- decide whether a claim made in one source is supported or undermined by information provided in another source
- determine whether the information provided is sufficient to justify a course of action

- judge the strength of evidence offered in support of an argument or plan
- identify errors or gaps in the information provided

Draw inferences from the information

Infer questions ask about information or ideas that are not explicitly stated in the materials provided but can be derived from them. For example, you may be asked to

- calculate the probability of an outcome on the basis of given data
- indicate whether statements follow logically from the information provided
- determine the meaning of a term within the context in which it is used
- identify the rate of change in data gathered over time

Recognize parts or relationships in the information

Recognize questions measure your ability to identify information that is directly presented in the materials provided, including specific facts or details and relationships between pieces of information. For example, you may be asked to

- identify areas of agreement and disagreement between sources of information
- determine the strength of correlation between two variables
- indicate which element in a table has a given rank in a combination of categories
- identify facts provided as evidence in an argument

Make strategic decisions or judgments based on the information

Strategize questions ask about the means of achieving a goal within the context of particular needs or constraints. For example, you may be asked to

- choose a plan of action that minimizes risks and maximizes value
- identify tradeoffs required to reach a goal
- specify the mathematical formula that will yield a desired result
- determine which means of completing a task are consistent within given constraints

10.2 The Question Types

The four Integrated Reasoning question types are described in detail below.

Multi-Source Reasoning

Multi-Source Reasoning questions begin with two or three sources of information, each labeled with a tab, which appear on the left side of a split computer screen. One or more of the sources will contain a written passage. The other sources may be tables, graphs, diagrams, or other types of visual information. Only one source of information will be displayed at a time. To view a different source, select its tab from those that appear above the source which is currently displayed.

The sources of information are accompanied by questions that will ask you to synthesize, compare, interpret, or apply the information presented. As each question associated with the sources appears in turn on the right side of the screen, the initial source will appear again on the left side. You can click on the tabs to view any of the sources as many times as needed. However, you will see only one question at a time and cannot go back to earlier questions.

There are two question formats for Multi-Source Reasoning:

- Multiple-choice questions
- Multiple-dichotomous choice questions

For multiple-choice questions, select the best of the five answer choices given. Read each question and series of answer choices carefully. Make sure you understand exactly what the question is asking and what the answer choices are.

Multiple-dichotomous choice questions provide three phrases, statements, numerical values, or algebraic expressions that require an indication as to whether each meets a certain condition. For example, you may be asked whether

- each statement is true, according to the sources
- each statement or numerical value is consistent with the sources
- each statement or algebraic expression would solve a problem described in the sources
- the value of each algebraic expression can be determined on the basis of the sources

In answering both kinds of Multi-Source Reasoning questions, be aware of the information from each source provided and try to determine the process that works best for you. One strategy is to examine the sources carefully and thoroughly, another is to skim the sources the first time through, or to read the first question before examining the sources. Read each question carefully and make sure you understand *exactly* what the question is asking. If necessary, go back to the sources to review relevant information.

You will have 30 minutes to complete the Integrated Reasoning section, or an average of 2 minutes and 30 seconds to answer each multiple-choice or multiple-dichotomous choice question. Keep in mind that you will need time to examine the source materials that accompany the questions—and that this time must be factored into the per-question average.

Table Analysis

Table Analysis questions present a table similar to a spreadsheet. It can be sorted on any of its columns by selecting the column's title from a drop-down menu. There may be a brief text explaining the table or providing additional information. The question then presents three phrases, statements, numerical values, or algebraic expressions, and you must indicate for each one whether or not it meets a certain condition. For example, you may be asked whether

- each statement is true (yes or no), according to the information in the table
- each statement or numerical value is consistent or inconsistent with the information in the table
- each statement or numerical value can or cannot be determined on the basis of the information in the table

Read the question thoroughly to make sure you understand what is being asked. Then consider each phrase, statement, numerical value, or algebraic expression to learn what information in the table you need to make your decision. For example, in analyzing the table, you may need to,

- determine statistics such as mean, median, mode, or range
- determine ratios, proportions, or probabilities
- identify correlations between two sets of data
- compare an entry's rank in two or more of the table's categories

You will have 30 minutes to complete the Integrated Reasoning section, or an average of 2 minutes and 30 seconds to answer each question. Keep in mind that each Table Analysis question has three parts that all need to be answered in the time allowed.

Graphics Interpretation

Graphics Interpretation questions present a graph, diagram, or other visual representation of information, followed by one or more statements containing a total of two blanks. The blanks should be filled in with the option from each drop-down menu in order to create the most accurate statement or statements on the basis of the information provided.

Many of the graphs included in Graphics Interpretation questions involve two variables plotted on vertical and horizontal axes. Graphs of this type include *bar graphs, line graphs, scatterplots,* and *bubble graphs*. To read these graphs, determine what information is represented on each axis. Do this by carefully examining any information that may be provided, including labels on the axes, scales on the axes, the title of the graph, and accompanying text. To find the value of a data point on the graph, determine the corresponding values on the horizontal and vertical axes.

In the simple *bar graph* below, the first bar indicates that 7 units were sold on Monday of Week 1.

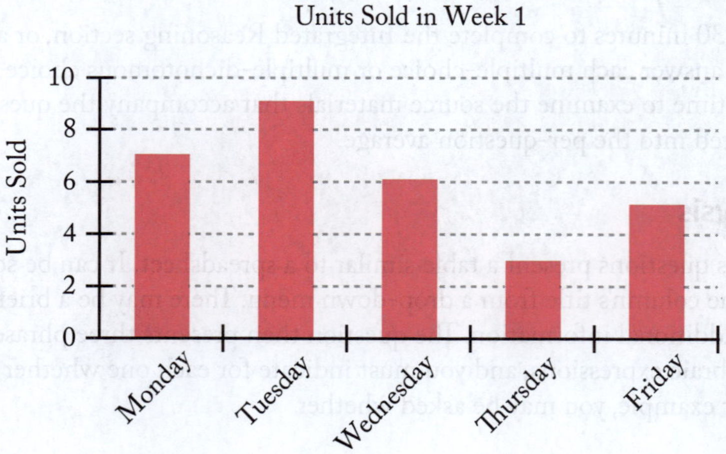

The same information is presented below as a line graph. Each point indicates the total number of units sold on a given day. The slope of the line connecting the points shows how the sales changed over time; a positive slope indicates that sales increased from the previous day, and a negative slope indicates that sales decreased.

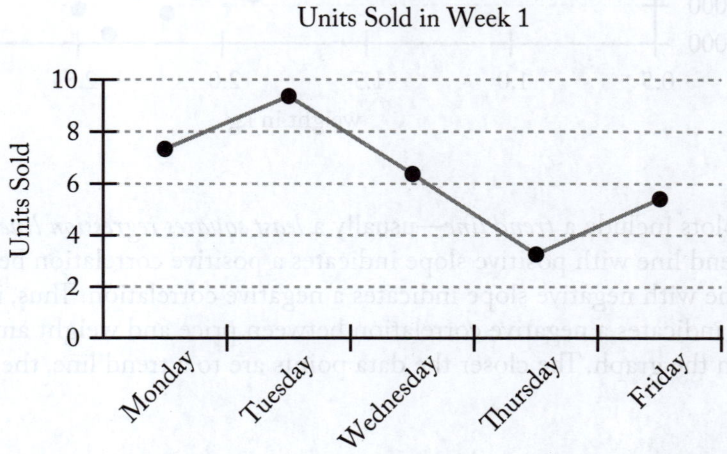

A third variable can be indicated with an additional vertical axis. In the following graph, the bars indicate the number of units sold on each day, which corresponds to the scale on the left axis. The line graph shows what percent of the total units were sold on each day. The scale for the percentages is shown on the right axis.

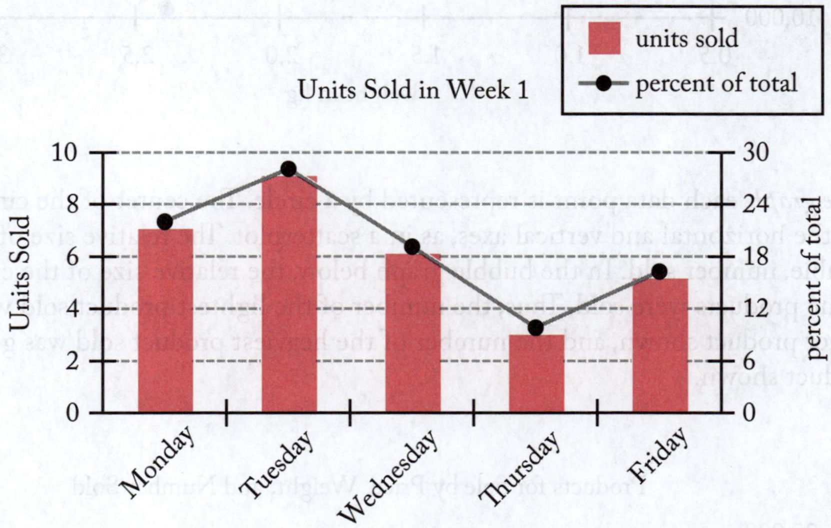

In a *scatterplot*, each dot is a single data point. In the scatterplot at the top of the next page, each dot represents a type of computer product available for purchase. A dot's position relative to the vertical axis indicates the product's price, and its position relative to the horizontal axis indicates its weight. Thus, the product that weighs 1.0 kg costs approximately 32,000 rupees.

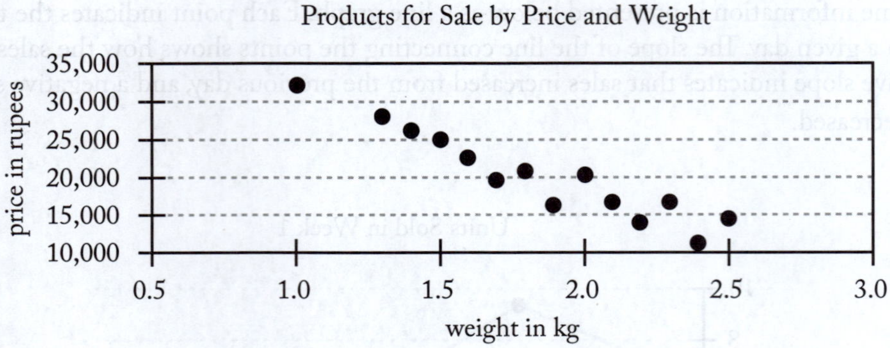

Some scatterplots include a *trend line*—usually a *least squares regression line*—that shows the trend of the data. A trend line with positive slope indicates a positive correlation between the two variables, and a trend line with negative slope indicates a negative correlation. Thus, in the scatterplot below, the trend line indicates a negative correlation between price and weight among the products represented on the graph. The closer the data points are to a trend line, the more strongly the data are correlated.

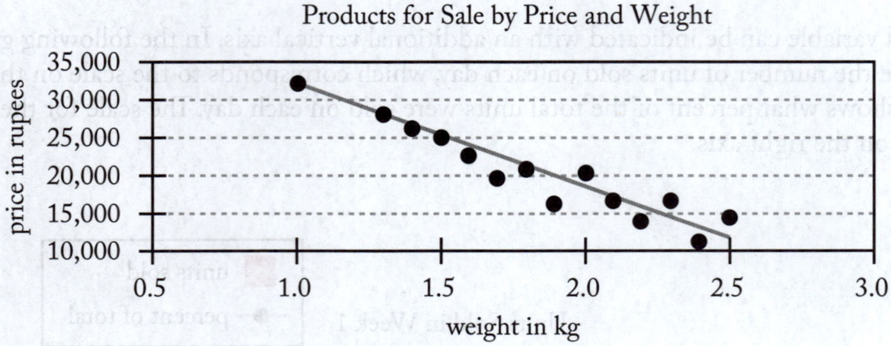

In a *bubble graph*, each data point is represented by a circle. The center of the circle indicates the values on the horizontal and vertical axes, as in a scatterplot. The relative size of a circle introduces a third variable, number sold. In the bubble graph below, the relative size of the circles indicates how many of the products were sold. Thus, the number of the lightest product sold was smaller than that of any other product shown, and the number of the heaviest product sold was greater than that of any other product shown.

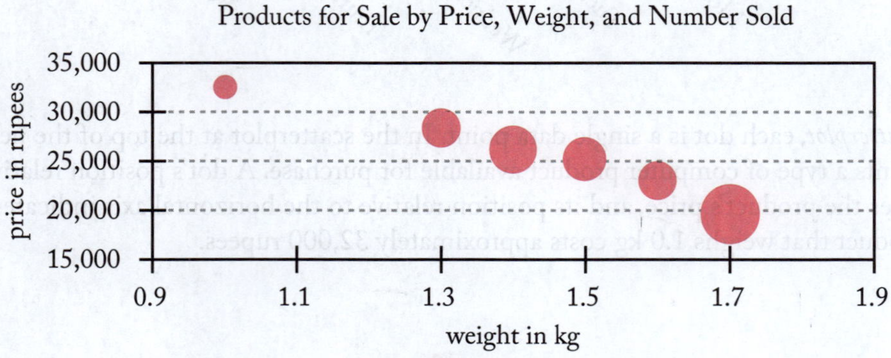

Other common kinds of graphics do not use vertical and horizontal axes. These include *pie charts, flow charts*, and *organization charts*.

A *pie chart* uses a circle divided into sectors to show what percent of the whole is represented by each component part. The circle represents the whole, and the relative size of each sector indicates its percent of the whole. Since the whole is 100%, the sum of the percentages of all the sectors is 100 (plus or minus a bit to account for rounding). Below is a pie chart created from the data used in the bar graph and line graph shown earlier. In this example, labels indicating the exact percents are not supplied, but it is still possible to gauge the size of the sectors relative to one another: the smallest percent of sales was on Thursday, and the largest was on Tuesday. In addition, the two radii that mark the boundaries of the Tuesday sector form an obtuse angle, which indicates that the sector is greater than one-fourth of the circle. Thus, Tuesday's sales comprised more than 25% of total sales.

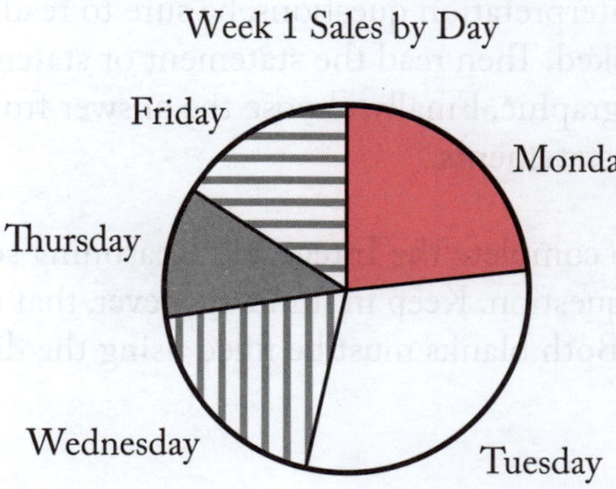

A *flow chart* is a diagram that shows the steps in a process. Often, the steps are represented by symbols, which are connected by arrows showing the flow of the process. Flow charts generally progress from top to bottom or from left to right. In the simple flow chart below, rectangles indicate steps to be completed. The diamond shape indicates a decision point: if the consultant is new, the process continues to the next step, *Append tax forms*. If the consultant is not new, that step is bypassed and the contract is mailed.

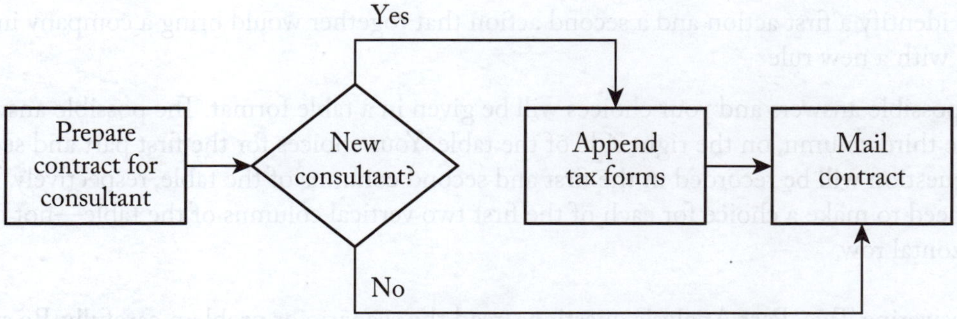

An *organization chart* represents the structure of an organization. Often, hierarchical relationships are shown with vertical lines and lateral relationships are shown with horizontal lines. In the organization chart at the top of the next page, each rectangle represents an employee or group of employees at a small restaurant. All the employees in the second row of rectangles report to the restaurant manager. In the third row, the food preparation staff and cleaning staff both report to the kitchen manager, and the serving staff report to the serving staff manager.

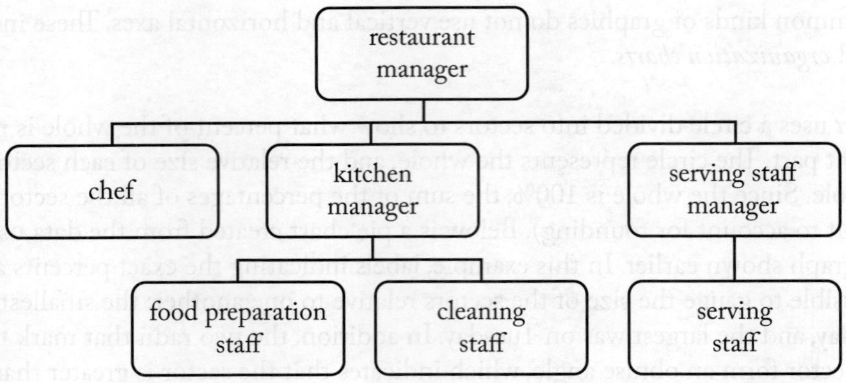

For all kinds of Graphics Interpretation questions, be sure to read the question carefully to be sure you understand what is being asked. Then read the statement or statements to determine what information you need to learn from the graphic. Finally, choose the answer from each drop-down menu that best completes the statement or statements.

You will have 30 minutes to complete the Integrated Reasoning section, or an average of 2 minutes and 30 seconds to answer each question. Keep in mind, however, that each Graphics Interpretation question has two blanks to be filled. Both blanks must be filled using the drop-down menus in the time allowed.

Two-Part Analysis

Two-Part Analysis questions present a brief written scenario or problem and ask you to make two choices related to that information. These choices are connected to each other in some way; for example, they might be two steps involved in solving a problem or two components required to successfully complete a task. In Two-Part Analysis questions you may be asked to, for example,

- calculate the proportions of two different components in a mixture
- determine something that would be lost and something that would be gained in a trade-off
- find the maximum number of two different products that could be purchased within a certain budget
- identify a first action and a second action that together would bring a company into compliance with a new rule

The possible answers and your choices will be given in a table format. The possible answers are listed in the third column, on the right side of the table. Your choices for the first part and second part of the question will be recorded in the first and second columns of the table, respectively. Remember that you need to make a choice for each of the first two vertical columns of the table—not one for each horizontal row.

In answering Two-Part Analysis questions, read the scenario or problem carefully. Be sure you understand what the question is asking. Read all the answer options to be sure that your choices are the best of those available, and be careful to mark your choices in the proper columns.

You will have 30 minutes to complete the Integrated Reasoning section, or an average of 2 minutes and 30 seconds to answer each question. Keep in mind that you must make the two choices for each Two-Part Analysis question within that average amount of time.

10.3 Test-Taking Strategies

Multi-Source Reasoning Questions

1. **Do not expect to be completely familiar with the material presented in Multi-Source Reasoning sets.**
   You may find some graphs, charts, tables, or verbal passages easier to understand than others. All of the material is designed to be challenging, but if you have familiarity with the subject matter, do not let this knowledge influence your answer choices. Answer all questions on the basis of what is given by the various sources of information.

2. **Analyze each source of information carefully, because the questions require a detailed understanding of the information presented.**
   Text passages often build ideas sequentially, so note as you read how each statement adds to the main idea of the passage as a whole. Some of the passages used with Multi-Source Reasoning items will be purely descriptive while others may contain strong opinions.

   Given that the graphic elements of Multi-Source Reasoning items come in various forms—such as tables, graphs, diagrams, or charts—briefly familiarize yourself with the information presented. If scales are provided, note the marked values and labels. Also note the major graphical elements of the information presented.

3. **Read the questions carefully, making sure you understand what is being asked.**
   Some of the questions will require you to recognize discrepancies among different sources of information, others will ask you to draw inferences using information from different sources, while others may require you to determine which one of the information sources is relevant. You can refer back to any of the sources at any time while you are answering the Multi-Source Reasoning questions.

4. **Select the answer choices that have the most support based on the information provided.**
   You may find it helpful to briefly familiarize yourself with the overall information given in the sources and then to focus more closely on the specific information needed to answer the question.

Table Analysis Questions

1. **Examine the table and accompanying text to determine the type of information provided.**
   Orienting yourself to the data at the outset will make it easier to locate the information necessary for completing the question.

2. **Read the question carefully.**
   The question will contain the condition that each phrase, statement, numerical value, or algebraic expression does or does not meet (for example, *is or is not consistent with the information provided*, or *can or cannot be inferred from the information provided*). Clearly understanding the condition will help you to clarify the choice to be made in each case.

3. **Read each phrase, statement, numerical value, or algebraic expression carefully to determine the data analysis required.**
Often, the phrase, statement, numerical value, or algebraic expression indicates a relationship that can be clarified by sorting the table on one or more of its columns. Careful reading can help you work more efficiently by using table sorts strategically to identify data of interest.

4. **Judge each phrase, statement, numerical value, or algebraic expression carefully on the basis of the condition specified.**
For each phrase, statement, numerical value, or algebraic expression, the two answer choices (such as *yes* or *no, true* or *false, consistent* or *inconsistent*) are mutually exclusive. Thus, you can focus your attention on whether or not the given condition has been met.

Graphics Interpretation Questions

1. **Read the graphic carefully.**
Quickly familiarize yourself with the information presented in the graphic. If scales are provided (such as on the axes) make note of the marked values. If there are labels, be sure to note any discrepancy between the units in the graph and the units discussed in the text.

2. **Read any accompanying text carefully.**
If there is accompanying text, it may clarify the meaning of the graphic. Text might also present information that is not contained in the graphic but that is necessary for answering the question.

3. **Scan the choices in the drop-down menu before you do any work.**
Some statements could be completed equally well with very general responses as with very specific responses. Checking the menu options gives you additional information about the task involved.

4. **Choose the option that best completes the statement.**
More than one option in a drop-down menu may seem plausible to you; in each menu, choose the one that makes the statement most accurate or logical. If the drop-down menu is preceded by a phrase such as "nearest to" or the "closest to," choose the option that is closest to the exact answer you compute. You may find that reading the entire statement again with your answer choice in place is a helpful way to check your work.

Two-Part Analysis Questions

1. **Read the information given carefully.**
All of the material presented is designed to be challenging, but if you have familiarity with the subject matter, do not let this knowledge influence your answer choices. Answer each question only on the basis of what is given.

2. **Determine exactly what the question is asking.**
Do not assume that the headings in the two response columns are complete descriptions of the tasks to be performed. Pay close attention to how the question describes the tasks. Often the headings in the two response columns are shorthand references to the tasks and may lack some details that could help you to better understand what you are supposed to do.

3. **Remember that only two choices are to be made.**
Select one answer in each of the first two columns of the response table. You do not need to make a choice for each *row* of the table. The third column contains possible answers for the two choices to be made.

4. **Do not choose an answer before reviewing all of the available answer choices.**
Do not assume that you have chosen the best answers in the two columns without reading all of the available options.

5. **Determine whether tasks are dependent or independent.**
Some Two-Part Analysis questions pose two independent tasks that can be carried out individually, and others pose one task with two dependent parts, each of which must be carried out correctly to create a single correct response. With questions of the dependent type, the question asked cannot be answered coherently without making both choices, so be sure to examine your answers in relation to one another.

6. **Keep in mind that one answer choice can be the correct response for both columns.**
If the tasks associated with the two response columns are not mutually exclusive, it is possible that one answer choice satisfies the conditions associated with both response columns.

10.4 The Directions

These directions are similar to the directions given for the four question types in the Integrated Reasoning section of the GMAT® exam. Understanding them clearly before taking the test will save you time during the test.

- **Multi-Source Reasoning**. Click on the tabs and examine all the relevant information from text, charts, and tables to answer the questions.
- **Table Analysis**. Analyze the table, sorting on columns as needed, to determine whether each of the options presented meets the given criterion or not.
- **Graphics Interpretation**. Interpret the graph or graphical image and select from each drop-down menu the option that creates the most accurate statement based on the information provided.
- **Two-Part Analysis**. Read the information provided, review the options presented in the table, and indicate which option meets the criterion presented in the first column and which option meets the criterion presented in the second column. Make only two selections, one in each column.

For the Integrated Reasoning section, an onscreen calculator is available. To access the calculator, click "Calculator" on the blue bar at the upper left of the screen. Note that the calculator can be dragged to any part of the screen.

You can view explanations of the format of the specific Integrated Reasoning questions anytime while working through this section by clicking on HELP.

11.0 Analytical Writing Assessment

11.0 Analytical Writing Assessment

The Analytical Writing Assessment (AWA) consists of one 30-minute writing task called the Analysis of an Argument. In this section, you must read a brief argument, analyze the reasoning behind it, and then write a critique of the argument. You are not asked to state your opinion but rather to analyze the one given. For example, you may, consider what questionable assumptions underlie the author's thinking, what alternative explanations or counterexamples might weaken the conclusion, or what sort of evidence could help strengthen or refute the argument.

For this task, you will use the computer keyboard to type your response. You will be able to use typical word-processing functions—that is, you can cut, copy, paste, undo, and redo. These functions can be accessed either by using the keyboard or by using the mouse to click on icons on the screen. You will be able to take notes when planning your response.

It is important that you plan carefully before you begin writing. Read the specific analytical writing task several times to make sure you understand exactly what is expected. Think about how you might present your analysis. You may want to sketch an outline to help you plan and organize. Keep in mind the 30-minute time limit as you plan your response—keep your analysis brief enough to allow for plenty of time to write a first draft, read it over carefully, and make any necessary corrections or revisions before you run out of time. As you write, try to keep your language clear, your sentences concise, and the flow of your ideas logical. State your premise clearly at the beginning, and make sure you present a strong conclusion at the end.

11.1 What Is Measured

The Analytical Writing Assessment is designed as a direct measure of your ability to think critically and communicate your ideas. More specifically, the Analysis of an Argument task tests your ability to formulate an appropriate and constructive critique of a prescribed conclusion based upon a specific line of thinking.

The argument that you will analyze may concern a topic of general interest, possibly related to business, or to a variety of other subjects. It is important to note, however, that no Analysis of an Argument question presupposes any specific knowledge of business or other specific content areas. Only your capacity to write analytically is assessed.

Professional essay raters, including college and university faculty members from various subject-matter areas, including but not limited to management education, will evaluate your essay. For information on how readers are qualified, visit mba.com. Readers are trained to be sensitive and fair in evaluating the responses of nonnative speakers of English. A computer scoring program will also evaluate your essays. Your responses will be scored on the basis of:

- the overall quality of your ideas
- your ability to organize, develop, and express those ideas
- how well you provide relevant supporting reasons and examples
- your ability to control the elements of standard written English

11.2 Test-Taking Strategies

1. **Read the question carefully.**
   Make sure you have taken all parts of a question into account before you begin to respond to it.

2. **Do not start to write immediately.**
   Take a few minutes to think about the question and plan a response before you begin writing. You may find it helpful to write a brief outline or jot down some ideas on the erasable notepad provided. Take care to organize your ideas and develop them fully, but leave time to reread your response and make any revisions that you think would improve it.

3. **Focus on the task of analyzing and critiquing a line of thinking or reasoning.**
   Get used to asking yourself questions such as the following: *What questionable assumptions might underlie the thinking? What alternative explanations might be given? What counterexamples might be raised? What additional evidence might prove useful in fully and fairly evaluating the reasoning?*

4. **Develop fully any examples you use.**
   Do not simply list your examples—explain how they illustrate your point.

5. **Discuss alternative explanations or counterexamples.**
   These techniques allow you to introduce illustrations and examples drawn from your observations, experiences, and reading.

6. **Make sure your response reads like a narrative.**
   Your response should not read like an outline. It should use full sentences, a coherent organizational scheme, logical transitions between points, and appropriately introduced and developed examples.

11.3 The Directions

These are the directions that you will see for the Analysis of an Argument essay. If you read them carefully and understand them clearly before going to sit for the test, you will not need to spend too much time reviewing them when you take the GMAT® exam. They read as follows:

ANALYSIS OF AN ARGUMENT

In this section, you will be asked to write a critique of the argument presented. *You are* not *asked to present your own views on the subject.*

Writing Your Response: Take a few minutes to evaluate the argument and plan a response before you begin writing. Be sure to leave enough time to reread your response and make any revisions that you think are necessary.

Evaluation of Your Response: Scores will reflect how well you:

- organize, develop, and express your ideas about the argument presented
- provide relevant supporting reasons and examples
- control the elements of standard written English

11.4 GMAT® Scoring Guide: Analysis of an Argument

6 Outstanding

A 6 paper presents a cogent, well-articulated critique of the argument and demonstrates mastery of the elements of effective writing.

A typical paper in this category exhibits the following characteristics:

- clearly identifies important features of the argument and analyzes them insightfully
- develops ideas cogently, organizes them logically, and connects them with clear transitions
- effectively supports the main points of the critique
- demonstrates control of language, including diction and syntactic variety
- demonstrates facility with the conventions of standard written English but may have minor flaws

5 Strong

A 5 paper presents a well-developed critique of the argument and demonstrates good control of the elements of effective writing.

A typical paper in this category exhibits the following characteristics:

- clearly identifies important features of the argument and analyzes them in a generally thoughtful way
- develops ideas clearly, organizes them logically, and connects them with appropriate transitions
- sensibly supports the main points of the critique
- demonstrates control of language, including diction and syntactic variety
- demonstrates facility with the conventions of standard written English but may have occasional flaws

4 Adequate

A 4 paper presents a competent critique of the argument and demonstrates adequate control of the elements of writing.

A typical paper in this category exhibits the following characteristics:

- identifies and analyzes important features of the argument
- develops and organizes ideas satisfactorily but may not connect them with transitions
- supports the main points of the critique
- demonstrates sufficient control of language to convey ideas with reasonable clarity
- generally follows the conventions of standard written English but may have some flaws

3 Limited

A 3 paper demonstrates some competence in analytical writing skills and in its control of the elements of writing but is plainly flawed.

A typical paper in this category exhibits one or more of the following characteristics:

- does not identify or analyze most of the important features of the argument, although some analysis of the argument is present
- mainly analyzes tangential or irrelevant matters, or reasons poorly
- is limited in the logical development and organization of ideas
- offers support of little relevance and value for points of the critique
- does not convey meaning clearly
- contains occasional major errors or frequent minor errors in grammar, usage, and mechanics

2 Seriously Flawed

A 2 paper demonstrates serious weaknesses in analytical writing skills.

A typical paper in this category exhibits one or more of the following characteristics:

- does not present a critique based on logical analysis, but may instead present the writer's own views on the subject
- does not develop ideas, or is disorganized and illogical
- provides little, if any, relevant or reasonable support
- has serious and frequent problems in the use of language and in sentence structure
- contains numerous errors in grammar, usage, and mechanics that interfere with meaning

1 Fundamentally Deficient

A 1 paper demonstrates fundamental deficiencies in analytical writing skills.

A typical paper in this category exhibits more than one of the following characteristics:

- provides little evidence of the ability to understand and analyze the argument
- provides little evidence of the ability to develop an organized response
- has severe and persistent errors in language and sentence structure
- contains a pervasive pattern of errors in grammar, usage, and mechanics that results in incoherence

0 No Score

A paper in this category is off topic, not written in English, is merely attempting to copy the topic, or consists only of keystroke characters.

NR Blank

11.5 Sample: Analysis of an Argument

Read the statement and the instructions that follow it, and then make any notes that will help you plan your response.

The following appeared as part of an article in a daily newspaper:

"The computerized on-board warning system that will be installed in commercial airliners will virtually solve the problem of midair plane collisions. One plane's warning system can receive signals from another's transponder—a radio set that signals a plane's course—in order to determine the likelihood of a collision and recommend evasive action."

Discuss how well reasoned you find this argument. In your discussion, be sure to analyze the line of reasoning and the use of evidence in the argument. For example, you may need to consider what questionable assumptions underlie the thinking and what alternative explanations or counterexamples might weaken the conclusion. You can also discuss what sort of evidence would strengthen or refute the argument, what changes in the argument would make it more logically sound, and what, if anything, would help you better evaluate its conclusion.

Sample Paper 6

The argument that this warning system will virtually solve the problem of midair plane collisions omits some important concerns that must be addressed to substantiate the argument. The statement that follows the description of what this warning system will do simply describes the system and how it operates. This alone does not constitute a logical argument in favor of the warning system, and it certainly does not provide support or proof of the main argument.

Most conspicuously, the argument does not address the cause of the problem of midair plane collisions, the use of the system by pilots and flight specialists, or who is involved in the midair plane collisions. First, the argument assumes that the cause of the problem is that the planes' courses, the likelihood of collisions, and actions to avoid collisions are unknown or inaccurate. In a weak attempt to support its claim, the argument describes a system that makes all of these things accurately known. But if the cause of the problem of midair plane collisions is that pilots are not paying attention to their computer systems or flight operations, the warning system will not solve the collision problem. Second, the argument never addresses the interface between individuals and the system and how this will affect the warning system's objective of obliterating the problem of collisions. If the pilot or flight specialist does not conform to what the warning system suggests, midair collisions will not be avoided. Finally, if planes other than commercial airliners are involved in the collisions, the problem of these collisions cannot be solved by a warning system that will not be installed on non-commercial airliners. The argument also does not address what would happen in the event that the warning system collapses, fails, or does not work properly.

Because the argument leaves out several key issues, it is not sound or persuasive. If it included the items discussed above instead of solely explaining what the system supposedly does, the argument would have been more thorough and convincing.

Explanation of Score 6

This response is, as the scoring guide requires of a 6, "cogent"and "well articulated": all the points made not only bear directly on the argument to be analyzed, but also contribute to a single, integrated development of the writer's critique. The writer begins by making the controlling point that a mere description of the warning system's mode of operation cannot serve as a true argument proving the system's effectiveness, since the description overlooks several major considerations. The writer then identifies these considerations—what causes midair collisions, how pilots will actually use the commercial airline warning system, what kinds of airplanes are typically involved in midair collisions—and, citing appropriate counterexamples (e.g., what if pilots do not pay attention to their instruments?), explains fully how each oversight undermines the conclusion that the warning system will virtually eliminate midair plane collisions.

Throughout, the writer complements the logically organized development of this critique with good, clear prose that demonstrates the ability not only to control language and vary sentence structure but also to express ideas forcibly (e.g., "the argument never addresses the interface between individuals and the system"). Of course, as in any response written under time constraints, occasional minor flaws can be found. For example, "the argument assumes that the cause of the problem is that the planes' courses, the likelihood of collisions, and actions to avoid collisions are unknown or inaccurate" is wordy and imprecise: how can a course, a likelihood, or actions be inaccurate? But flaws such as these, minor and infrequent, do not interfere with the overall clarity and forcefulness of this outstanding response.

Sample Paper 4

The argument is not logically convincing. It does not state whether all planes can receive signals from each other. It does not state whether planes constantly receive signals. If they only receive signals once every certain time interval, collisions will not definitely be prevented. Further if they receive a signal right before they are about to crash, they cannot avoid each other.

The main flaw in the argument is that it assumes that the two planes, upon receiving each other's signals, will know which evasive action to take. For example, the two planes could be going towards each other and then receive the signals. If one turns at an angle to the left and the other turns at an angle to the right, the two planes will still crash. Even if they receive an updated signal, they will not have time to avoid each other.

The following argument would be more sound and persuasive. The new warning system will solve the problem of midair plane collisions. Each plane will receive constant, continual signals from each other. If the two planes are headed in a direction where they will crash, the system will coordinate the signals, and tell one plane to go one way, and the other plane to go another way. The new system will ensure that the two planes will turn in different directions so they don't crash by trying to prevent the original crash. In addition, the two planes will be able to see themselves and the other on a computer screen, to aid in the evasive action.

Explanation of Score 4

This response competently cites a number of deficiencies in the argument presented: the information given about the nature of the signals sent and received and the evasive action recommended does not warrant the conclusion that the onboard warning system "will virtually solve the problem of midair plane collisions." However, in discussing these insufficiencies in the argument, the response reveals an unevenness in the quality of its reasoning. For example, while it is perfectly legitimate to point out that the argument assumes too much and says too little about the evasive action that will be recommended by the warning system, it is farfetched to suggest that the system might be so poorly designed as to route two approaching airplanes to the same spot. Likewise, while it is fair to question the effectiveness of a warning signal about which the argument says so little, it is not reasonable to assume that the system would be designed to space signals so far apart that they would prove useless. Rather than invent implausibly bad versions of the warning system to prove that it might be ineffective, a stronger response would analyze unexplored possibilities inherent in the information that is given—for example, the possibility that pilots might not be able to respond quickly and effectively to the radio signals the argument says they will receive when the new system is installed. The "more sound and persuasive argument" in the last paragraph, while an improvement on the original, continues to overlook this possibility and also assumes that other types of aircraft without transponders will pose no problems.

The organization of ideas, while generally sound, is sometimes weakened by needless repetition of the same points, as in sentences 4 and 5 of the last paragraph. The writing contains minor instances of awkwardness (e.g., "Each plane will receive constant, continual signals from each other" in paragraph 3), but is free of flaws that make understanding difficult. However, though the writing is generally clean and clear, the syntax does not show much variety. A few sentences begin with "if" clauses, but almost all the rest, even those that begin with a transitional phrase such as "for example" or "in addition," conform to a "subject, verb, complement" pattern. The first paragraph, in which the second and third sentences begin the same way ("It does not state"), is particularly repetitious.

Sample Paper 2

This argument has no information about air collisions. I think most cases happen in new airports because the air traffic I heavy. In this case sound airport control could solve the problem.

I think this argument is logically reasonable. Its assumption is that plane collisions are caused by planes that don't know each others positions. So pilots can do nothing, if they know each others position through the system it will solve the problem.

If it can provide evidence the problem is lack of knowledge of each others positions, it will be more sound and persuasive.

More information about air collisions is helpful, (the reason for air collisions).

Explanation of Score 2

This response is seriously flawed in several ways. First of all, it has very little substance. The writer appears to make only one point—that while it seems reasonable to assume that midair collisions would be less likely if pilots were sure of each other's positions, readers cannot adequately judge this assumption without more information about where, why, and how such collisions occur. This point, furthermore, is neither explained by a single reason beyond what is given in the topic nor supported by a single example. Legitimate though it is, it cannot, alone and undeveloped, serve as an adequate response to the argument.

Aside from being undeveloped, the response is confusing. At the outset, it seems to be critical of the argument. The writer begins by pointing to the inadequacy of the information given; then speculates, without evidence, that "most cases happen in new airports"; and then suggests that the problem should be addressed by improving "airport control," not (it is implied) by installing onboard warning systems. After criticizing the argument in the first paragraph, the writer confusingly seems to endorse it in the second. Then, in the remainder of the response, the writer returns to a critical stance.

The general lack of coherence is reflected in the serious and frequent writing problems that make meaning hard to determine—for example, the elliptical and ungrammatical "So pilots can do nothing, if they know each others position through the system it will solve the problem" (paragraph 2) or "If it can provide evidence the problem is lack of knowledge of each others positions, it will be more sound and persuasive" (paragraph 3). The prose suffers from a variety of basic errors in grammar, usage, and mechanics.

11.6 Analysis of an Argument Sample Topics

The following appeared as part of an annual report sent to stockholders by Olympic Foods, a processor of frozen foods:

"Over time, the costs of processing go down because as organizations learn how to do things better, they become more efficient. In color film processing, for example, the cost of a 3-by-5-inch print fell from 50 cents for five-day service in 1970 to 20 cents for one-day service in 1984. The same principle applies to the processing of food. And since Olympic Foods will soon celebrate its 25th birthday, we can expect that our long experience will enable us to minimize costs and thus maximize profits."

Discuss how well reasoned you find this argument. In your discussion be sure to analyze the line of reasoning and the use of evidence in the argument. For example, you may need to consider what questionable assumptions underlie the thinking and what alternative explanations or counterexamples might weaken the conclusion. You can also discuss what sort of evidence would strengthen or refute the argument, what changes in the argument would make it more logically sound, and what, if anything, would help you better evaluate its conclusion.

The following appeared in a memorandum from the business department of the Apogee Company:

"When the Apogee Company had all its operations in one location, it was more profitable than it is today. Therefore, the Apogee Company should close down its field offices and conduct all its operations from a single location. Such centralization would improve profitability by cutting costs and helping the company maintain better supervision of all employees."

Discuss how well reasoned ... etc.

The following appeared in a memorandum issued by a large city's council on the arts:

"In a recent citywide poll, 15 percent more residents said that they watch television programs about the visual arts than was the case in a poll conducted five years ago. During these past five years, the number of people visiting our city's art museums has increased by a similar percentage. Since the corporate funding that supports public television, where most of the visual arts programs appear, is now being threatened with severe cuts, we can expect that attendance at our city's art museums will also start to decrease. Thus some of the city's funds for supporting the arts should be reallocated to public television."

Discuss how well reasoned ... etc.

The following appeared in a report presented for discussion at a meeting of the directors of a company that manufactures parts for heavy machinery:

"The falling revenues that the company is experiencing coincide with delays in manufacturing. These delays, in turn, are due in large part to poor planning in purchasing metals. Consider further that the manager of the department that handles purchasing of raw materials has an excellent background in general business, psychology, and sociology, but knows little about the properties of metals. The company should, therefore, move the purchasing manager to the sales department and bring in a scientist from the research division to be manager of the purchasing department."

Discuss how well reasoned ... etc.

The following appeared in an announcement issued by the publisher of *The Mercury*, a weekly newspaper:

"Since a competing lower-priced newspaper, *The Bugle*, was started five years ago, *The Mercury's* circulation has declined by 10,000 readers. The best way to get more people to read *The Mercury* is to reduce its price below that of *The Bugle*, at least until circulation increases to former levels. The increased circulation of *The Mercury* will attract more businesses to buy advertising space in the paper."

Discuss how well reasoned ... etc.

The following appeared as part of an article in a magazine devoted to regional life:

"Corporations should look to the city of Helios when seeking new business opportunities or a new location. Even in the recent recession, Helios's unemployment rate was lower than the regional average. It is the industrial center of the region, and historically it has provided more than its share of the region's manufacturing jobs. In addition, Helios is attempting to expand its economic base by attracting companies that focus on research and development of innovative technologies."

Discuss how well reasoned ... etc.

The following appeared in the health section of a magazine on trends and lifestyles:

"People who use the artificial sweetener aspartame are better off consuming sugar, since aspartame can actually contribute to weight gain rather than weight loss. For example, high levels of aspartame have been shown to trigger a craving for food by depleting the brain of a chemical that registers satiety, or the sense of being full. Furthermore, studies suggest that sugars, if consumed after at least 45 minutes of continuous exercise, actually enhance the body's ability to burn fat. Consequently, those who drink aspartame-sweetened juices after exercise will also lose this calorie-burning benefit. Thus it appears that people consuming aspartame rather than sugar are unlikely to achieve their dietary goals."

Discuss how well reasoned ... etc.

The following appeared in the editorial section of a corporate newsletter:

"The common notion that workers are generally apathetic about management issues is false, or at least outdated: a recently published survey indicates that 79 percent of the nearly 1,200 workers who responded to survey questionnaires expressed a high level of interest in the topics of corporate restructuring and redesign of benefits programs."

Discuss how well reasoned ... etc.

The following appeared in the opinion column of a financial magazine:

"On average, middle-aged consumers devote 39 percent of their retail expenditure to department store products and services, while for younger consumers the average is only 25 percent. Since the number of middle-aged people will increase dramatically within the next decade, department stores can expect retail sales to increase significantly during that period. Furthermore, to take advantage of the trend, these stores should begin to replace some of those products intended to attract the younger consumer with products intended to attract the middle-aged consumer."

Discuss how well reasoned ... etc.

The following appeared in the editorial section of a local newspaper:

"This past winter, 200 students from Waymarsh State College traveled to the state capitol building to protest against proposed cuts in funding for various state college programs. The other 12,000 Waymarsh students evidently weren't so concerned about their education: they either stayed on campus or left for winter break. Since the group who did not protest is far more numerous, it is more representative of the state's college students than are the protesters. Therefore the state legislature need not heed the appeals of the protesting students."

Discuss how well reasoned ... etc.

The following appeared in the editorial section of a local newspaper:

"In the first four years that Montoya has served as mayor of the city of San Perdito, the population has decreased and the unemployment rate has increased. Two businesses have closed for each new business that has opened. Under Varro, who served as mayor for four years before Montoya, the unemployment rate decreased and the population increased. Clearly, the residents of San Perdito would be best served if they voted Montoya out of office and reelected Varro."

Discuss how well reasoned ... etc.

The following appeared as part of a promotional campaign to sell advertising space in the *Daily Gazette* to grocery stores in the Marston area:

"Advertising the reduced price of selected grocery items in the *Daily Gazette* will help you increase your sales. Consider the results of a study conducted last month. Thirty sale items from a store in downtown Marston were advertised in *The Gazette* for four days. Each time one or more of the 30 items was purchased, clerks asked whether the shopper had read the ad. Two-thirds of the 200 shoppers asked answered in the affirmative. Furthermore, more than half the customers who answered in the affirmative spent over $100 at the store."

Discuss how well reasoned ... etc.

The following appeared as part of a campaign to sell advertising time on a local radio station to local businesses:

"The Cumquat Café began advertising on our local radio station this year and was delighted to see its business increase by 10 percent over last year's totals. Their success shows you how you can use radio advertising to make your business more profitable."

Discuss how well reasoned ... etc.

The following appeared as part of a newspaper editorial:

"Two years ago Nova High School began to use interactive computer instruction in three academic subjects. The school dropout rate declined immediately, and last year's graduates have reported some impressive achievements in college. In future budgets the school board should use a greater portion of the available funds to buy more computers, and all schools in the district should adopt interactive computer instruction throughout the curriculum."

Discuss how well reasoned ... etc.

The following appeared as a part of an advertisement for Adams, who is seeking re-election as governor:

"Re-elect Adams, and you will be voting for proven leadership in improving the state's economy. Over the past year alone, 70 percent of the state's workers have had increases in their wages, 5,000 new jobs have been created, and six corporations have located their headquarters here. Most of the respondents in a recent poll said they believed that the economy is likely to continue to improve if Adams is re-elected. Adams's opponent, Zebulon, would lead our state in the wrong direction, because Zebulon disagrees with many of Adams's economic policies."

Discuss how well reasoned ... etc.

The following appeared as part of an article in the education section of a Waymarsh city newspaper:

"Throughout the last two decades, those who earned graduate degrees found it very difficult to get jobs teaching their academic specialties at the college level. Those with graduate degrees from Waymarsh University had an especially hard time finding such jobs. But better times are coming in the next decade for all academic job seekers, including those from Waymarsh. Demographic trends indicate that an increasing number of people will be reaching college age over the next 10 years; consequently, we can expect that the job market will improve dramatically for people seeking college-level teaching positions in their fields."

Discuss how well reasoned ... etc.

The following appeared in an article in a consumer-products magazine:

"Two of today's best-selling brands of full-strength prescription medication for the relief of excess stomach acid, Acid-Ease and Pepticaid, are now available in milder nonprescription forms. Doctors have written 76 million more prescriptions for full-strength Acid-Ease than for full-strength Pepticaid. So people who need an effective but milder nonprescription medication for the relief of excess stomach acid should choose Acid-Ease."

Discuss how well reasoned ... etc.

The following is an excerpt from a memo written by the head of a governmental department:

"Neither stronger ethics regulations nor stronger enforcement mechanisms are necessary to ensure ethical behavior by companies doing business with this department. We already have a code of ethics that companies doing business with this department are urged to abide by, and virtually all of these companies have agreed to follow it. We also know that the code is relevant to the current business environment because it was approved within the last year, and in direct response to specific violations committed by companies with which we were then working—not in abstract anticipation of potential violations, as so many such codes are."

Discuss how well reasoned ... etc.

The following appeared as part of an article in the travel section of a newspaper:

"Over the past decade, the restaurant industry in the country of Spiessa has experienced unprecedented growth. This surge can be expected to continue in the coming years, fueled by recent social changes: personal incomes are rising, more leisure time is available, single-person households are more common, and people have a greater interest in gourmet food, as evidenced by a proliferation of publications on the subject."

Discuss how well reasoned ... etc.

The following appeared in an article in a health and fitness magazine:

"Laboratory studies show that Saluda Natural Spring Water contains several of the minerals necessary for good health and that it is completely free of bacteria. Residents of Saluda, the small town where the water is bottled, are hospitalized less frequently than the national average. Even though Saluda Natural Spring Water may seem expensive, drinking it instead of tap water is a wise investment in good health."

Discuss how well reasoned ... etc.

The following appeared as part of an editorial in an industry newsletter:

"While trucking companies that deliver goods pay only a portion of highway maintenance costs and no property tax on the highways they use, railways spend billions per year maintaining and upgrading their facilities. The government should lower the railroad companies' property taxes, since sending goods by rail is clearly a more appropriate mode of ground transportation than highway shipping. For one thing, trains consume only a third of the fuel a truck would use to carry the same load, making them a more cost-effective and environmentally sound mode of transport. Furthermore, since rail lines already exist, increases in rail traffic would not require building new lines at the expense of taxpaying citizens."

Discuss how well reasoned ... etc.

The following appeared in the editorial section of a newspaper:

"As public concern over drug abuse has increased, authorities have become more vigilant in their efforts to prevent illegal drugs from entering the country. Many drug traffickers have consequently switched from marijuana, which is bulky, or heroin, which has a market too small to justify the risk of severe punishment, to cocaine. Thus enforcement efforts have ironically resulted in an observed increase in the illegal use of cocaine."

Discuss how well reasoned ... etc.

The following appeared in a speech delivered by a member of the city council:

"Twenty years ago, only half of the students who graduated from Einstein High School went on to attend a college or university. Today, two-thirds of the students who graduate from Einstein do so. Clearly, Einstein has improved its educational effectiveness over the past two decades. This improvement has occurred despite the fact that the school's funding, when adjusted for inflation, is about the same as it was 20 years ago. Therefore, we do not need to make any substantial increase in the school's funding at this time."

Discuss how well reasoned ... etc.

The following appeared in a memo from the customer service division to the manager of Mammon Savings and Loan:

"We believe that improved customer service is the best way for us to differentiate ourselves from competitors and attract new customers. We can offer our customers better service by reducing waiting time in teller lines from an average of six minutes to an average of three. By opening for business at 8:30 instead of 9:00, and by remaining open for an additional hour beyond our current closing time, we will be better able to accommodate the busy schedules of our customers. These changes will enhance our bank's image as the most customer-friendly bank in town and give us the edge over our competition."

Discuss how well reasoned ... etc.

The following appeared as part of an article in a magazine on lifestyles:

"Two years ago, City L was listed fourteenth in an annual survey that ranks cities according to the quality of life that can be enjoyed by those living in them. This information will enable people who are moving to the state in which City L is located to confidently identify one place, at least, where schools are good, housing is affordable, people are friendly, the environment is safe, and the arts flourish."

Discuss how well reasoned ... etc.

The following appeared in a memorandum from a member of a financial management and consulting firm:

"We have learned from an employee of Windfall, Ltd., that its accounting department, by checking about 10 percent of the last month's purchasing invoices for errors and inconsistencies, saved the company some $10,000 in overpayments. In order to help our clients increase their net gains, we should advise each of them to institute a policy of checking all purchasing invoices for errors. Such a recommendation could also help us get the Windfall account by demonstrating to Windfall the rigorousness of our methods."

Discuss how well reasoned ... etc.

The following appeared in a newspaper editorial:

"As violence in movies increases, so do crime rates in our cities. To combat this problem we must establish a board to censor certain movies, or we must limit admission to persons over 21 years of age. Apparently our legislators are not concerned about this issue since a bill calling for such actions recently failed to receive a majority vote."

Discuss how well reasoned ... etc.

The following appeared in the editorial section of a local newspaper:

"Commuter use of the new subway train is exceeding the transit company's projections. However, commuter use of the shuttle buses that transport people to the subway stations is below the projected volume. If the transit company expects commuters to ride the shuttle buses to the subway rather than drive there, it must either reduce the shuttle bus fares or increase the price of parking at the subway stations."

Discuss how well reasoned ... etc.

The following was excerpted from the speech of a spokesperson for Synthetic Farm Products, Inc.:

"Many farmers who invested in the equipment needed to make the switch from synthetic to organic fertilizers and pesticides feel that it would be too expensive to resume synthetic farming at this point. But studies of farmers who switched to organic farming last year indicate that their current crop yields are lower. Hence their purchase of organic farming equipment, a relatively minor investment compared to the losses that would result from continued lower crop yields, cannot justify persisting on an unwise course. And the choice to farm organically is financially unwise, given that it was motivated by environmental rather than economic concerns."

Discuss how well reasoned ... etc.

The following appeared in a newspaper story giving advice about investments:

"As overall life expectancy continues to rise, the population of our country is growing increasingly older. For example, more than 20 percent of the residents of one of our more populated regions are now at least 65 years old, and occupancy rates at resort hotels in that region declined significantly during the past six months. Because of these two related trends, a prudent investor would be well advised to sell interest in hotels and invest in hospitals and nursing homes instead."

Discuss how well reasoned ... etc.

The following appeared as part of the business plan of an investment and financial consulting firm:

"Studies suggest that an average coffee drinker's consumption of coffee increases with age, from age 10 through age 60. Even after age 60, coffee consumption remains high. The average cola drinker's consumption of cola, however, declines with increasing age. Both of these trends have remained stable for the past 40 years. Given that the number of older adults will significantly increase as the population ages over the next 20 years, it follows that the demand for coffee will increase and the demand for cola will decrease during this period. We should, therefore, consider transferring our investments from Cola Loca to Early Bird Coffee."

Discuss how well reasoned ... etc.

The following appeared in the editorial section of a West Cambria newspaper:

"A recent review of the West Cambria volunteer ambulance service revealed a longer average response time to accidents than was reported by a commercial ambulance squad located in East Cambria. In order to provide better patient care for accident victims and to raise revenue for our town by collecting service fees for ambulance use, we should disband our volunteer service and hire a commercial ambulance service."

Discuss how well reasoned ... etc.

The following is part of a business plan being discussed at a board meeting of the Perks Company:

"It is no longer cost-effective for the Perks Company to continue offering its employees a generous package of benefits and incentives year after year. In periods when national unemployment rates are low, Perks may need to offer such a package in order to attract and keep good employees, but since national unemployment rates are now high, Perks does not need to offer the same benefits and incentives. The money thus saved could be better used to replace the existing plant machinery with more technologically sophisticated equipment, or even to build an additional plant."

Discuss how well reasoned ... etc.

The following appeared as part of a plan proposed by an executive of the Easy Credit Company to the president:

"The Easy Credit Company would gain an advantage over competing credit card services if we were to donate a portion of the proceeds from the use of our cards to a well-known environmental organization in exchange for the use of its symbol or logo on our card. Since a recent poll shows that a large percentage of the public is concerned about environmental issues, this policy would attract new customers, increase use among existing customers, and enable us to charge interest rates that are higher than the lowest ones available."

Discuss how well reasoned ... etc.

The following appeared as part of a recommendation from the financial planning office to the administration of Fern Valley University:

"In the past few years, Fern Valley University has suffered from a decline in both enrollments and admissions applications. The reason can be discovered from our students, who most often cite poor teaching and inadequate library resources as their chief sources of dissatisfaction with Fern Valley. Therefore, in order to increase the number of students attending our university, and hence to regain our position as the most prestigious university in the greater Fern Valley metropolitan area, it is necessary to initiate a fund-raising campaign among the alumni that will enable us to expand the range of subjects we teach and to increase the size of our library facilities."

Discuss how well reasoned ... etc.

The following appeared in an article in a college departmental newsletter:

"Professor Taylor of Jones University is promoting a model of foreign language instruction in which students receive 10 weeks of intensive training, then go abroad to live with families for 10 weeks. The superiority of the model, Professor Taylor contends, is proved by the results of a study in which foreign language tests given to students at 25 other colleges show that first-year foreign language students at Jones speak more fluently after only 10 to 20 weeks in the program than do 9 out of 10 foreign language majors elsewhere at the time of their graduation."

Discuss how well reasoned ... etc.

The following appeared as part of an article in the business section of a local newspaper:

"Motorcycle X has been manufactured in the United States for more than 70 years. Although one foreign company has copied the motorcycle and is selling it for less, the company has failed to attract motorcycle X customers—some say because its product lacks the exceptionally loud noise made by motorcycle X. But there must be some other explanation. After all, foreign cars tend to be quieter than similar American-made cars, but they sell at least as well. Also, television advertisements for motorcycle X highlight its durability and sleek lines, not its noisiness, and the ads typically have voice-overs or rock music rather than engine-roar on the sound track."

Discuss how well reasoned ... etc.

The following appeared in the editorial section of a campus newspaper:

"Because occupancy rates for campus housing fell during the last academic year, so did housing revenues. To solve the problem, campus housing officials should reduce the number of available housing units, thereby increasing the occupancy rates. Also, to keep students from choosing to live off-campus, housing officials should lower the rents, thereby increasing demand."

Discuss how well reasoned ... etc.

The following appeared in an Avia Airlines departmental memorandum:

"On average, 9 out of every 1,000 passengers who traveled on Avia Airlines last year filed a complaint about our baggage-handling procedures. This means that although some 1 percent of our passengers were unhappy with those procedures, the overwhelming majority were quite satisfied with them; thus it would appear that a review of the procedures is not important to our goal of maintaining or increasing the number of Avia's passengers."

Discuss how well reasoned ... etc.

The following appeared as part of an article in a weekly newsmagazine:

"The country of Sacchar can best solve its current trade deficit problem by lowering the price of sugar, its primary export. Such an action would make Sacchar better able to compete for markets with other sugar-exporting countries. The sale of Sacchar's sugar abroad would increase, and this increase would substantially reduce Sacchar's trade deficit."

Discuss how well reasoned ... etc.

The following appeared as part of an article in a trade publication:

"Stronger laws are needed to protect new kinds of home-security systems from being copied and sold by imitators. With such protection, manufacturers will naturally invest in the development of new home-security products and production technologies. Without stronger laws, therefore, manufacturers will cut back on investment. From this will follow a corresponding decline not only in product quality and marketability, but also in production efficiency, and thus ultimately a loss of manufacturing jobs in the industry."

Discuss how well reasoned ... etc.

The following appeared in the opinion section of a national newsmagazine:

"To reverse the deterioration of the postal service, the government should raise the price of postage stamps. This solution will no doubt prove effective, since the price increase will generate larger revenues and will also reduce the volume of mail, thereby eliminating the strain on the existing system and contributing to improved morale."

Discuss how well reasoned ... etc.

The following appeared in an article in the health section of a newspaper:

"There is a common misconception that university hospitals are better than community or private hospitals. This notion is unfounded, however: the university hospitals in our region employ 15 percent fewer doctors, have a 20 percent lower success rate in treating patients, make far less overall profit, and pay their medical staff considerably less than do private hospitals. Furthermore, many doctors at university hospitals typically divide their time among teaching, conducting research, and treating patients. From this it seems clear that the quality of care at university hospitals is lower than that at other kinds of hospitals."

Discuss how well reasoned ... etc.

The following is part of a business plan created by the management of the Megamart grocery store:

"Our total sales have increased this year by 20 percent since we added a pharmacy section to our grocery store. Clearly, the customer's main concern is the convenience afforded by one-stop shopping. The surest way to increase our profits over the next couple of years, therefore, is to add a clothing department along with an automotive supplies and repair shop. We should also plan to continue adding new departments and services, such as a restaurant and a garden shop, in subsequent years. Being the only store in the area that offers such a range of services will give us a competitive advantage over other local stores."

Discuss how well reasoned ... etc.

The following appeared as part of a column in a popular entertainment magazine:

"The producers of the forthcoming movie *3003* will be most likely to maximize their profits if they are willing to pay Robin Good several million dollars to star in it—even though that amount is far more than any other person involved with the movie will make. After all, Robin has in the past been paid a similar amount to work in several films that were very financially successful."

Discuss how well reasoned ... etc.

The following appeared in a memorandum from the directors of a security and safety consulting service:

"Our research indicates that over the past six years no incidents of employee theft have been reported within ten of the companies that have been our clients. In analyzing the security practices of these ten companies, we have further learned that each of them requires its employees to wear photo identification badges while at work. In the future, therefore, we should recommend the use of such identification badges to all of our clients."

Discuss how well reasoned ... etc.

The following appeared as part of an article in the business section of a local newspaper:

"The owners of the Cumquat Cafe evidently made a good business decision in moving to a new location, as can be seen from the fact that the Cafe will soon celebrate its second anniversary there. Moreover, it appears that businesses are not likely to succeed at the old location: since the Cafe's move, three different businesses—a tanning salon, an antique emporium, and a pet-grooming shop—have occupied its former spot."

Discuss how well reasoned ... etc.

The following appeared in the editorial section of a local newspaper:

"The profitability of Croesus Company, recently restored to private ownership, is a clear indication that businesses fare better under private ownership than under public ownership."

Discuss how well reasoned ... etc.

The following appeared in the editorial section of a local newspaper:

"If the paper from every morning edition of the nation's largest newspaper were collected and rendered into paper pulp that the newspaper could reuse, about 5 million trees would be saved each year. This kind of recycling is unnecessary, however, since the newspaper maintains its own forests to ensure an uninterrupted supply of paper."

Discuss how well reasoned ... etc.

The following appeared as part of a business plan recommended by the new manager of a musical rock group called Zapped:

"To succeed financially, Zapped needs greater name recognition. It should therefore diversify its commercial enterprises. The rock group Zonked plays the same type of music that Zapped plays, but it is much better known than Zapped because, in addition to its concert tours and four albums, Zonked has a series of posters, a line of clothing and accessories, and a contract with a major advertising agency to endorse a number of different products."

Discuss how well reasoned ... etc.

The following appeared in a magazine article on trends and lifestyles:

"In general, people are not as concerned as they were a decade ago about regulating their intake of red meat and fatty cheeses. Walk into the Heart's Delight, a store that started selling organic fruits and vegetables and whole-grain flours in the 1960s, and you will also find a wide selection of cheeses made with high butterfat content. Next door, the owners of the Good Earth Cafe, an old vegetarian restaurant, are still making a modest living, but the owners of the new House of Beef across the street are millionaires."

Discuss how well reasoned ... etc.

The following editorial appeared in the Elm City paper:

"The construction last year of a shopping mall in downtown Oak City was a mistake. Since the mall has opened, a number of local businesses have closed, and the downtown area suffers from an acute parking shortage, and arrests for crime and vagrancy have increased in the nearby Oak City Park. Elm City should pay attention to the example of the Oak City mall and deny the application to build a shopping mall in Elm City."

Discuss how well reasoned ... etc.

The following appeared as part of an editorial in a weekly newsmagazine:

"Historically, most of this country's engineers have come from our universities; recently, however, our university-age population has begun to shrink, and decreasing enrollments in our high schools clearly show that this drop in numbers will continue throughout the remainder of the decade. Consequently, our nation will soon be facing a shortage of trained engineers. If we are to remain economically competitive in the world marketplace, then we must increase funding for education—and quickly."

Discuss how well reasoned ... etc.

The following appeared in an Excelsior Company memorandum:

"The Excelsior Company plans to introduce its own brand of coffee. Since coffee is an expensive food item, and since there are already many established brands of coffee, the best way to gain customers for the Excelsior brand is to do what Superior, the leading coffee company, did when it introduced the newest brand in its line of coffees: conduct a temporary sales promotion that offers free samples, price reductions, and discount coupons for the new brand."

Discuss how well reasoned ... etc.

The following appeared as part of an article in a health club trade publication:

"After experiencing a decline in usage by its members, Healthy Heart fitness center built an indoor pool. Since usage did not increase significantly, it appears that health club managers should adopt another approach—lowering membership fees rather than installing expensive new features."

Discuss how well reasoned ... etc.

The following appeared as part of an article in a popular arts-and-leisure magazine:

"The safety codes governing the construction of public buildings are becoming far too strict. The surest way for architects and builders to prove that they have met the minimum requirements established by these codes is to construct buildings by using the same materials and methods that are currently allowed. But doing so means that there will be very little significant technological innovation within the industry, and hence little evolution of architectural styles and design—merely because of the strictness of these safety codes."

Discuss how well reasoned ... etc.

The following is from a campaign by Big Boards Inc. to convince companies in River City that their sales will increase if they use Big Boards billboards for advertising their locally manufactured products:

"The potential of Big Boards to increase sales of your products can be seen from an experiment we conducted last year. We increased public awareness of the name of the current national women's marathon champion by publishing her picture and her name on billboards in River City for a period of three months. Before this time, although the champion had just won her title and was receiving extensive national publicity, only 5 percent of 15,000 randomly surveyed residents of River City could correctly name the champion when shown her picture; after the three-month advertising experiment, 35 percent of respondents from a second survey could supply her name."

Discuss how well reasoned ... etc.

The following appeared as part of an article on government funding of environmental regulatory agencies:

"When scientists finally learn how to create large amounts of copper from other chemical elements, the regulation of copper mining will become unnecessary. For one thing, since the amount of potentially available copper will no longer be limited by the quantity of actual copper deposits, the problem of over-mining will quickly be eliminated altogether. For another, manufacturers will not need to use synthetic copper substitutes, the production of which creates pollutants. Thus, since two problems will be settled—over-mining and pollution—it makes good sense to reduce funding for mining regulation and either save the money or reallocate it where it is needed more."

Discuss how well reasoned ... etc.

The following appeared as part of an article in a popular science magazine:

"Scientists must typically work 60 to 80 hours a week if they hope to further their careers; consequently, good and affordable all-day child care must be made available to both male and female scientists if they are to advance in their fields. Moreover, requirements for career advancement must be made more flexible so that preschool-age children can spend a significant portion of each day with a parent."

Discuss how well reasoned ... etc.

The following appeared as part of a recommendation by one of the directors of the Beta Company:

"The Alpha Company has just reduced its workforce by laying off 15 percent of its employees in all divisions and at all levels, and it is encouraging early retirement for other employees. As you know, the Beta Company manufactures some products similar to Alpha's, but our profits have fallen over the last few years. To improve Beta's competitive position, we should try to hire a significant number of Alpha's former workers, since these experienced workers can provide valuable information about Alpha's successful methods, will require little training, and will be particularly motivated to compete against Alpha."

Discuss how well reasoned ... etc.

The following appeared in the letters-to-the-editor section of a local newspaper:

"*Muscle Monthly*, a fitness magazine that regularly features pictures of bodybuilders using state-of-the-art exercise machines, frequently sells out, according to the owner of Skyview Newsstand. To help maximize fitness levels in our town's residents, we should, therefore, equip our new community fitness center with such machines."

Discuss how well reasoned ... etc.

The following appeared as part of an article in the business section of a local newspaper:

"The Cumquat Cafe made a mistake in moving to a new location. After one year at the new spot, it is doing about the same volume of business as before, but the owners of the RoboWrench plumbing supply wholesale outlet that took over its old location are apparently doing better: RoboWrench is planning to open a store in a neighboring city."

Discuss how well reasoned ... etc.

The following appeared in a memorandum from the director of human resources to the executive officers of Company X:

"Last year, we surveyed our employees on improvements needed at Company X by having them rank, in order of importance, the issues presented in a list of possible improvements. Improved communications between employees and management was consistently ranked as the issue of highest importance by the employees who responded to the survey. As you know, we have since instituted regular communications sessions conducted by high-level management, which the employees can attend on a voluntary basis. Therefore, it is likely that most employees at Company X now feel that the improvement most needed at the company has been made."

Discuss how well reasoned ... etc.

The following appeared in a memorandum from the vice president of Road Food, an international chain of fast-food restaurants:

"This past year, we spent almost as much on advertising as did our main competitor, Street Eats, which has fewer restaurants than we do. Although it appeared at first that our advertising agency had created a campaign along the lines we suggested, in fact our total profits were lower than those of Street Eats. In order to motivate our advertising agency to perform better, we should start basing the amount that we pay it on how much total profit we make each year."

Discuss how well reasoned ... etc.

The following appeared in the promotional literature for Cerberus dog food:

"Obesity is a great problem among pet dogs, just as it is among their human owners. Obesity in humans is typically caused by consuming more calories than the body needs. For humans, a proper diet for losing weight is a reduced-calorie diet that is high in fiber and carbohydrates but low in fat. Therefore, the best way for dog owners to help their dogs lose weight in a healthy way is to restrict the dog's diet to Cerberus reduced-calorie dog food, which is high in fiber and carbohydrates but low in fat."

Discuss how well reasoned ... etc.

The following appeared in an article in a travel magazine:

"After the airline industry began requiring airlines to report their on-time rates, Speedee Airlines achieved the number one on-time rate, with more than 89 percent of its flights arriving on time each month. And now Speedee is offering more flights to more destinations than ever before. Clearly, Speedee is the best choice for today's business traveler."

Discuss how well reasoned ... etc.

The following appeared in a memorandum to the planning department of an investment firm:

"Costs have begun dropping for several types of equipment currently used to convert solar energy into electricity. Moreover, some exciting new technologies for converting solar energy are now being researched and developed. Hence we can expect that solar energy will soon become more cost efficient and attractive than coal or oil as a source of electrical power. We should, therefore, encourage investment in Solario, a new manufacturer of solar-powered products. After all, Solario's chief executive was once on the financial planning team for Ready-to-Ware, a software engineering firm that has shown remarkable growth since its recent incorporation."

Discuss how well reasoned ... etc.

The following appeared in a memorandum from a company's marketing department:

"Since our company started manufacturing and marketing a deluxe air filter six months ago, sales of our economy filter—and company profits—have decreased significantly. The deluxe air filter sells for 50 percent more than the economy filter, but the economy filter lasts for only one month while the deluxe filter can be used for two months before it must be replaced. To increase repeat sales of our economy filter and maximize profits, we should discontinue the deluxe air filter and concentrate all our advertising efforts on the economy filter."

Discuss how well reasoned ... etc.

The following appeared in a memorandum from the president of a company that makes shampoo:

"A widely publicized study claims that HR2, a chemical compound in our shampoo, can contribute to hair loss after prolonged use. This study, however, involved only 500 subjects. Furthermore, we have received no complaints from our customers during the past year, and some of our competitors actually use more HR2 per bottle of shampoo than we do. Therefore, we do not need to consider replacing the HR2 in our shampoo with a more expensive alternative."

Discuss how well reasoned ... etc.

The following appeared in the editorial section of a local newspaper:

"The tragic crash of a medical helicopter last week points out a situation that needs to be addressed. The medical-helicopter industry supposedly has more stringent guidelines for training pilots and maintaining equipment than do most other airline industries, but these guidelines do not appear to be working: statistics reveal that the rate of medical-helicopter accidents is much higher than the rate of accidents for nonmedical helicopters or commercial airliners."

Discuss how well reasoned ... etc.

The following appeared as part of a recommendation from the business manager of a department store:

"Local clothing stores reported that their profits decreased, on average, for the three-month period between August 1 and October 31. Stores that sell products for the home reported that, on average, their profits increased during this same period. Clearly, consumers are choosing to buy products for their homes instead of clothing. To take advantage of this trend, we should reduce the size of our clothing departments and enlarge our home furnishings and household products departments."

Discuss how well reasoned ... etc.

The following appeared in a letter to the editor of a regional newspaper:

"In response to petitions from the many farmers and rural landowners throughout our region, the legislature has spent valuable time and effort enacting severe laws to deter motorists from picking fruit off the trees, trampling through the fields, and stealing samples of foliage. But how can our local lawmakers occupy themselves with such petty vandalism when crime and violence plague the nation's cities? The fate of apples and leaves is simply too trivial to merit their attention."

Discuss how well reasoned ... etc.

The following appeared as part of an editorial in a campus newspaper:

"With an increasing demand for highly skilled workers, this nation will soon face a serious labor shortage. New positions in technical and professional occupations are increasing rapidly, while at the same time the total labor force is growing slowly. Moreover, the government is proposing to cut funds for aid to education in the near future."

Discuss how well reasoned ... etc.

The following appeared as part of a memorandum from a government agency:

"Given the limited funding available for the building and repair of roads and bridges, the government should not spend any money this year on fixing the bridge that crosses the Styx River. This bridge is located near a city with a weakening economy, so it is not as important as other bridges; moreover, the city population is small and thus unlikely to contribute a significant enough tax revenue to justify the effort of fixing the bridge."

Discuss how well reasoned ... etc.

The following appeared as part of an article in an entertainment magazine:

"A series of books based on the characters from a popular movie are consistently best sellers in local bookstores. Seeking to capitalize on the books' success, Vista Studios is planning to produce a movie sequel based on the books. Due to the success of the books and the original movie, the sequel will undoubtedly be profitable."

Discuss how well reasoned … etc.

The following appeared in a letter to the editor of a popular science and technology magazine:

"It is a popular myth that consumers are really benefiting from advances in agricultural technology. Granted, consumers are, on the average, spending a decreasing proportion of their income on food. But consider that the demand for food does not rise in proportion with real income. As real income rises, therefore, consumers can be expected to spend a decreasing proportion of their income on food. Yet agricultural technology is credited with having made our lives better."

Discuss how well reasoned … etc.

The following appeared in the editorial section of a local newspaper:

"This city should be able to improve existing services and provide new ones without periodically raising the taxes of the residents. Instead, the city should require that the costs of services be paid for by developers who seek approval for their large new building projects. After all, these projects can be highly profitable to the developers, but they can also raise a city's expenses and increase the demand for its services."

Discuss how well reasoned … etc.

The following appeared in the editorial section of a local newspaper:

"In order to avoid the serious health threats associated with many landfills, our municipality should build a plant for burning trash. An incinerator could offer economic as well as ecological advantages over the typical old-fashioned type of landfill: incinerators can be adapted to generate moderate amounts of electricity, and ash residue from some types of trash can be used to condition garden soil."

Discuss how well reasoned … etc.

The following appeared in the editorial section of a monthly business newsmagazine:

"Most companies would agree that as the risk of physical injury occurring on the job increases, the wages paid to employees should also increase. Hence it makes financial sense for employers to make the workplace safer: they could thus reduce their payroll expenses and save money."

Discuss how well reasoned … etc.

The following appeared as part of a company memorandum:

"Adopting an official code of ethics regarding business practices may in the long run do our company more harm than good in the public eye. When one of our competitors received unfavorable publicity for violating its own code of ethics, it got more attention from the media than it would have if it had had no such code. Rather than adopt an official code of ethics, therefore, we should instead conduct a publicity campaign that stresses the importance of protecting the environment and assisting charitable organizations."

Discuss how well reasoned ... etc.

The following appeared in the editorial section of a daily newspaper:

"Although forecasts of presidential elections based on opinion polls measure current voter preference, many voters keep changing their minds about whom they prefer until the last few days before the balloting. Some do not even make a final decision until they enter the voting booth. Forecasts based on opinion polls are therefore little better at predicting election outcomes than a random guess would be."

Discuss how well reasoned ... etc.

The following appeared in the editorial section of a newspaper in the country of West Cambria:

"The practice of officially changing speed limits on the highways—whether by increasing or decreasing them—is a dangerous one. Consider what happened over the past decade whenever neighboring East Cambria changed its speed limits: an average of 3 percent more automobile accidents occurred during the week following the change than had occurred during the week preceding it—even when the speed limit was lowered. This statistic shows that the change in speed limit adversely affected the alertness of drivers."

Discuss how well reasoned ... etc.

The following appeared as part of a memorandum from the vice president of Nostrum, a large pharmaceutical corporation:

"The proposal to increase the health and retirement benefits that our employees receive should not be implemented at this time. An increase in these benefits is not only financially unjustified, since our last year's profits were lower than those of the preceding year, but also unnecessary, since our chief competitor, Panacea, offers its employees lower health and retirement benefits than we currently offer. We can assume that our employees are reasonably satisfied with the health and retirement benefits that they now have since a recent survey indicated that two-thirds of the respondents viewed them favorably."

Discuss how well reasoned ... etc.

The following appeared as part of an article on trends in television:

"A recent study of viewers' attitudes toward prime-time television programs shows that many of the programs that were judged by their viewers to be of high quality appeared on (noncommercial) television networks, and that, on commercial television, the most popular shows are typically sponsored by the bestselling products. Thus, it follows that businesses who use commercial television to promote their products will achieve the greatest advertising success by sponsoring only highly rated programs—and, ideally, programs resembling the highly rated noncommercial programs on public channels as much as possible."

Discuss how well reasoned ... etc.

The following appeared as part of an article in the business section of a daily newspaper:

"Company A has a large share of the international market in video-game hardware and software. Company B, the pioneer in these products, was once a $12 billion-a-year giant but collapsed when children became bored with its line of products. Thus Company A can also be expected to fail, especially given the fact that its games are now in so many American homes that the demand for them is nearly exhausted."

Discuss how well reasoned ... etc.

The following appeared as part of an article in a photography magazine:

"When choosing whether to work in color or in black-and-white, the photographer who wishes to be successful should keep in mind that because color photographs are more true to life, magazines use more color photographs than black-and-white ones, and many newspapers are also starting to use color photographs. The realism of color also accounts for the fact that most portrait studios use more color film than black-and-white film. Furthermore, there are more types of color film than black-and-white film available today. Clearly, photographers who work in color have an advantage over those who work in black-and-white."

Discuss how well reasoned ... etc.

The following appeared as part of a letter to the editor of a local newspaper:

"It makes no sense that in most places 15-year-olds are not eligible for their driver's license while people who are far older can retain all of their driving privileges by simply renewing their license. If older drivers can get these renewals, often without having to pass another driving test, then 15-year-olds should be eligible to get a license. Fifteen-year-olds typically have much better eyesight, especially at night; much better hand-eye coordination; and much quicker reflexes. They are also less likely to feel confused by unexpected developments or disoriented in unfamiliar surroundings, and they recover from injuries more quickly."

Discuss how well reasoned ... etc.

The following appeared in an ad for a book titled *How to Write a Screenplay for a Movie*:

"Writers who want to succeed should try to write film screenplays rather than books, since the average film tends to make greater profits than does even a best-selling book. It is true that some books are also made into films. However, our nation's film producers are more likely to produce movies based on original screenplays than to produce films based on books, because in recent years the films that have sold the most tickets have usually been based on original screenplays."

Discuss how well reasoned … etc.

The following appeared as part of an article in a daily newspaper:

"The computerized onboard warning system that will be installed in commercial airliners will virtually solve the problem of midair plane collisions. One plane's warning system can receive signals from another's transponder—a radio set that signals a plane's course—in order to determine the likelihood of a collision and recommend evasive action."

Discuss how well reasoned … etc.

The following appeared in a memorandum from the ElectroWares company's marketing department:

"Since our company started manufacturing and marketing a deluxe light bulb six months ago, sales of our economy light bulb—and company profits—have decreased significantly. Although the deluxe light bulb sells for 50 percent more than the economy bulb, it lasts twice as long. Therefore, to increase repeat sales and maximize profits, we should discontinue the deluxe light bulb."

Discuss how well reasoned … etc.

The following is taken from an editorial in a local newspaper:

"Over the past decade, the price per pound of citrus fruit has increased substantially. Eleven years ago, Megamart charged 15 cents a pound for lemons, but today it commonly charges over a dollar a pound. In only one of these last 11 years was the weather unfavorable for growing citrus crops. Evidently, then, citrus growers have been responsible for the excessive increase in the price of citrus fruit, and strict pricing regulations are needed to prevent them from continuing to inflate prices."

Discuss how well reasoned … etc.

The following appeared as part of an article in a local newspaper:

"Over the past three years the tartfish industry has changed markedly: fishing technology has improved significantly, and the demand for tartfish has grown in both domestic and foreign markets. As this trend continues, the tartfish industry on Shrimp Island can expect to experience the same overfishing problems that are already occurring with mainland fishing industries: without restrictions on fishing, fishers see no reason to limit their individual catches. As the catches get bigger, the tartfish population will be dangerously depleted while the surplus of tartfish will devalue the catch for fishers. Government regulation is the only answer: tartfish-fishing should be allowed only during the three-month summer season, when tartfish reproduce and thus are most numerous, rather than throughout the year."

Discuss how well reasoned … etc.

The following appeared in a proposal from the development office at Platonic University:

"Because Platonic University has had difficulty in meeting its expenses over the past three years, we need to find new ways to increase revenues. We should consider following the example of Greene University, which recently renamed itself after a donor who gave it $100 million. If Platonic University were to advertise to its alumni and other wealthy people that it will rename either individual buildings or the entire university itself after the donors who give the most money, the amount of donations would undoubtedly increase."

Discuss how well reasoned ... etc.

The following appeared as part of an article in the business section of a local newspaper:

"Hippocrene Plumbing Supply recently opened a wholesale outlet in the location once occupied by the Cumquat Café. Hippocrene has apparently been quite successful there because it is planning to open a large outlet in a nearby city. But the Cumquat Café, one year after moving to its new location, has seen its volume of business drop somewhat from the previous year's. Clearly, the former site was the better business location, and the Cumquat Café has made a mistake in moving to its new address."

Discuss how well reasoned ... etc.

The following appeared in the editorial section of a local paper:

"Applications for advertising spots on KMTV, our local cable television channel, decreased last year. Meanwhile a neighboring town's local channel, KOOP, changed its focus to farming issues and reported an increase in advertising applications for the year. To increase applications for its advertisement spots, KMTV should focus its programming on farming issues as well."

Discuss how well reasoned ... etc.

The following appeared as part of an article in a computer magazine:

"A year ago Apex Manufacturing bought its managers computers for their homes and paid for telephone connections so that they could access Apex computers and data files from home after normal business hours. Since last year, productivity at Apex has increased by 15 percent. Other companies can learn from the success at Apex: given home computers and access to company resources, employees will work additional hours at home and thereby increase company profits."

Discuss how well reasoned ... etc.

The following was excerpted from an article in a farming trade publication:

"Farmers who switched from synthetic to organic farming last year have seen their crop yields decline. Many of these farmers feel that it would be too expensive to resume synthetic farming at this point, given the money that they invested in organic farming supplies and equipment. But their investments will be relatively minor compared to the losses from continued lower crop yields. Organic farmers should switch to synthetic farming rather than persist in an unwise course. And the choice to farm organically is financially unwise, given that it was motivated by environmental rather than economic concerns."

Discuss how well reasoned ... etc.

The following appeared in a letter to prospective students from the admissions office at Plateau College:

"Every person who earned an advanced degree in science or engineering from Olympus University last year received numerous offers of excellent jobs. Typically, many graduates of Plateau College have gone on to pursue advanced degrees at Olympus. Therefore, enrolling as an undergraduate at Plateau College is a wise choice for students who wish to ensure success in their careers."

Discuss how well reasoned ... etc.

The following appeared in a memorandum sent by a vice-president of the Nadir Company to the company's human resources department:

"Nadir does not need to adopt the costly 'family-friendly' programs that have been proposed, such as part-time work, work at home, and jobsharing. When these programs were made available at the Summit Company, the leader in its industry, only a small percentage of employees participated in them. Rather than adversely affecting our profitability by offering these programs, we should concentrate on offering extensive training that will enable employees to increase their productivity."

Discuss how well reasoned ... etc.

The following appeared as part of an article in a trade magazine for breweries:

"Magic Hat Brewery recently released the results of a survey of visitors to its tasting room last year. Magic Hat reports that the majority of visitors asked to taste its low-calorie beers. To boost sales, other small breweries should brew low-calorie beers as well."

Discuss how well reasoned ... etc.

The following appeared in an editorial from a newspaper serving the town of Saluda:

"The Saluda Consolidated High School offers more than 200 different courses from which its students can choose. A much smaller private school down the street offers a basic curriculum of only 80 different courses, but it consistently sends a higher proportion of its graduating seniors on to college than Consolidated does. By eliminating at least half of the courses offered there and focusing on a basic curriculum, we could improve student performance at Consolidated and also save many tax dollars."

Discuss how well reasoned ... etc.

The following appeared as part of an article in the book section of a newspaper:

"Currently more and more books are becoming available in electronic form—either free-of-charge on the Internet or for a very low price-per-book on compact disc. Thus literary classics are likely to be read more widely than ever before. People who couldn't have purchased these works at bookstore prices will now be able to read them for little or no money; similarly, people who find it inconvenient to visit libraries and wait for books to be returned by other patrons will now have access to whatever classic they choose from their home or work computers. This increase in access to literary classics will radically affect the public taste in reading, creating a far more sophisticated and learned reading audience than has ever existed before."

Discuss how well reasoned ... etc.

The following appeared as an editorial in a magazine concerned with educational issues:

"In our country, the real earnings of men who have only a high-school degree have decreased significantly over the past 15 years, but those of male college graduates have remained about the same. Therefore, the key to improving the earnings of the next generation of workers is to send all students to college. Our country's most important educational goal, then, should be to establish enough colleges and universities to accommodate all high school graduates."

Discuss how well reasoned ... etc.

The following appeared as part of a business plan created by the management of the Take Heart Fitness Center:

"After opening the new swimming pool early last summer, Take Heart saw a 12 percent increase in the use of the center by its members. Therefore, in order to increase membership in Take Heart, we should continue to add new recreational facilities in subsequent years: for example, a multipurpose game room, a tennis court, and a miniature golf course. Being the only center in the area offering this range of activities would give us a competitive advantage in the health and recreation market."

Discuss how well reasoned ... etc.

The following appeared in a letter from a staff member in the office of admissions at Argent University:

"The most recent nationwide surveys show that undergraduates choose their major field primarily based on their perception of job prospects in that field. At our university, economics is now the most popular major, so students must perceive this field as having the best job prospects. Therefore, we can increase our enrollment if we focus our advertising and recruiting on publicizing the accomplishments of our best-known economics professors and the success of our economics graduates in finding employment."

Discuss how well reasoned ... etc.

The following appeared as part of a memorandum from the loan department of the Frostbite National Bank:

"We should not approve the business loan application of the local group that wants to open a franchise outlet for the Kool Kone chain of ice cream parlors. Frostbite is known for its cold winters, and cold weather can mean slow ice cream sales. For example, even though Frostbite is a town of 10,000 people, it has only one ice cream spot—the Frigid Cow. Despite the lack of competition, the Frigid Cow's net revenues fell by 10 percent last winter."

Discuss how well reasoned ... etc.

The following appeared as part of a letter to the editor of a local newspaper:

"Bayview High School is considering whether to require all of its students to wear uniforms while at school. Students attending Acorn Valley Academy, a private school in town, earn higher grades on average and are more likely to go on to college. Moreover, Acorn Valley reports few instances of tardiness, absenteeism, or discipline problems. Since Acorn Valley requires its students to wear uniforms, Bayview High School would do well to follow suit and require its students to wear uniforms as well."

Discuss how well reasoned ... etc.

The following appeared in a memo to the Saluda town council from the town's business manager:

"Research indicates that those who exercise regularly are hospitalized less than half as often as those who don't exercise. By providing a well-equipped gym for Saluda's municipal employees, we should be able to reduce the cost of our group health insurance coverage by approximately 50 percent and thereby achieve a balanced town budget."

Discuss how well reasoned ... etc.

The following appeared in a memorandum written by the assistant manager of a store that sells gourmet food items from various countries:

"A local wine store made an interesting discovery last month: it sold more French than Italian wine on days when it played recordings of French accordion music, but it sold more Italian than French wine on days when Italian songs were played. Therefore, I recommend that we put food specialties from one particular country on sale for a week at a time and play only music from that country while the sale is going on. By this means we will increase our profits in the same way that the wine store did, and we will be able to predict more precisely what items we should stock at any given time."

Discuss how well reasoned ... etc.

The following appeared in a memorandum from the director of research and development at Ready-to-Ware, a software engineering firm:

"The package of benefits and incentives that Ready-to-Ware offers to professional staff is too costly. Our quarterly profits have declined since the package was introduced two years ago, at the time of our incorporation. Moreover, the package had little positive effect, as we have had only marginal success in recruiting and training high-quality professional staff. To become more profitable again, Ready-to-Ware should, therefore, offer the reduced benefits package that was in place two years ago and use the savings to fund our current research and development initiatives."

Discuss how well reasoned … etc.

The following appeared as a memorandum from the vice-president of the Dolci candy company:

"Given the success of our premium and most expensive line of chocolate candies in a recent taste test and the consequent increase in sales, we should shift our business focus to producing additional lines of premium candy rather than our lower-priced, ordinary candies. When the current economic boom ends and consumers can no longer buy major luxury items, such as cars, they will still want to indulge in small luxuries, such as expensive candies."

Discuss how well reasoned … etc.

The following appeared in a memorandum from the business office of the Lovin' Cupful, a national restaurant chain:

"The Lovin' Cupful franchises in our northeast region have begun serving customers Almost, a brand new powdered instant tea, in place of brewed tea. Waiters report that only about 2 percent of the customers have complained, and that customers who want refills typically ask for 'more tea.' It appears, then, that 98 percent of the customers are perfectly happy with the switch, or else they cannot tell powdered instant from brewed tea. Therefore, in order to take advantage of the lower price per pound of Almost, all of our restaurants should begin substituting it for brewed tea."

Discuss how well reasoned … etc.

The following appeared in a memorandum from the director of marketing for a pharmaceutical company:

"According to a survey of 5,000 urban residents, the prevalence of stress headaches increases with educational level, so that stress headaches occur most often among people with graduate-school degrees. It is well established that, nationally, higher educational levels usually correspond with higher levels of income. Therefore, in marketing our new pain remedy, Omnilixir, we should send free samples primarily to graduate students and to people with graduate degrees, and we should concentrate on advertising in professional journals rather than in general interest magazines."

Discuss how well reasoned … etc.

The following appeared as part of an editorial in the Waymarsh city newspaper:

"Last year the parents of first graders in our school district expressed satisfaction with the reading skills their children developed but complained strongly about their children's math skills. To remedy this serious problem and improve our district's elementary education, everyone in the teacher-training program at Waymarsh University should be required to take more courses in mathematics."

Discuss how well reasoned ... etc.

The following appeared in a letter to the editor of a River City newspaper:

"The Clio Development Group should not be permitted to build a multilevel parking garage on Dock Street since most of the buildings on the block would have to be demolished. Because these buildings were erected decades ago, they have historic significance and must therefore be preserved as economic assets in the effort to revitalize a restored riverfront area. Recall how Lakesburg has benefited from business increases in its historic downtown center. Moreover, there is plenty of vacant land for a parking lot elsewhere in River City."

Discuss how well reasoned ... etc.

The following appeared in a corporate planning memorandum for a company that develops amusement parks:

"Because travel from our country to foreign countries has increased dramatically in recent years, our next project should be a 'World Tour' theme park with replicas of famous foreign buildings, rides that have international themes, and refreshment stands serving only foods from the country represented by the nearest ride. The best location would be near our capital city, which has large percentages of international residents and of children under the age of 16. Given the advantages of this site and the growing interest in foreign countries, the 'World Tour' theme park should be as successful as our space-travel theme park, where attendance has increased tenfold over the past decade."

Discuss how well reasoned ... etc.

The following appeared in a memorandum from the publisher to the staff of *The Clarion*, a large metropolitan newspaper:

"During the recent campaign for mayor, a clear majority of city readers who responded to our survey indicated a desire for more news about city government. To increase circulation, and thus our profits, we should therefore consistently devote a greater proportion of space in all editions of *The Clarion* to coverage of local news."

Discuss how well reasoned ... etc.

The following appeared in a memorandum from the assistant manager of Pageturner Books:

"Over the past two years, Pageturner's profits have decreased by 5 percent, even though we have added a popular café as well as a music section selling CDs and tapes. At the same time, we have experienced an increase in the theft of merchandise. We should therefore follow the example of Thoreau Books, which increased its profits after putting copies of its most frequently stolen books on a high shelf behind the payment counter. By doing likewise with copies of the titles that our staff reported stolen last year, we too can increase profitability."

Discuss how well reasoned ... etc.

The following appeared in a letter to the editor of a River City newspaper:

"The Clio Development Group's plan for a multilevel parking garage on Dock Street should be approved in order to strengthen the economy of the surrounding area. Although most of the buildings on the block would have to be demolished, they are among the oldest in the city and thus of little current economic value. Those who oppose the project should realize that historic preservation cannot be the only consideration: even Athens or Jerusalem will knock down old buildings to put up new ones that improve the local economy."

Discuss how well reasoned ... etc.

The following appeared in a memorandum from the owner of Carlo's Clothing to the staff:

"Since Disc Depot, the music store on the next block, began a new radio advertising campaign last year, its business has grown dramatically, as evidenced by the large increase in foot traffic into the store. While the Disc Depot's owners have apparently become wealthy enough to retire, profits at Carlo's Clothing have remained stagnant for the past three years. In order to boost our sales and profits, we should therefore switch from newspaper advertising to frequent radio advertisements like those for Disc Depot."

Discuss how well reasoned ... etc.

The following appeared as part of the business plan of the Capital Idea investment firm:

"Across town in the Park Hill district, the Thespian Theater, Pizzazz Pizza, and the Niblick Golf Club have all had business increases over the past two years. Capital Idea should therefore invest in the Roxy Playhouse, the Slice-o'-Pizza, and the Divot Golf Club, three new businesses in the Irongate district. As a condition, we should require them to participate in a special program: Any customer who patronizes two of the businesses will receive a substantial discount at the third. By motivating customers to patronize all three, we will thus contribute to the profitability of each and maximize our return."

Discuss how well reasoned ... etc.

The following appeared as part of an article in a newsletter for farmers:

"Users of Solacium, a medicinal herb now grown mainly in Asia, report that it relieves tension and promotes deep sleep. A recent study indicates that a large number of college students who took pills containing one of the ingredients in Solacium suffered less anxiety. To satisfy the anticipated demands for this very promising therapeutic herb and to reap the financial benefits, farmers in this country should begin growing it."

Discuss how well reasoned ... etc.

The following appeared in a memorandum from the president of Aurora, a company that sells organic milk (milk produced without the use of chemical additives):

"Sales of organic food products in this country have tripled over the past five years. If Aurora is to profit from this continuing trend, we must diversify and start selling products such as organic orange juice and organic eggs in addition to our regular product line. With the recent increase of articles in health magazines questioning the safety of milk and other food products, customers are even more likely to buy our line of organic products. And to help ensure our successful expansion, we should hire the founder of a chain of health-food stores to serve as our vice president of marketing."

Discuss how well reasoned ... etc.

The following appeared in a memorandum from the human resources department of Diversified Manufacturing:

"Managers at our central office report that their employees tend to be most productive in the days immediately preceding a vacation. To help counteract our declining market share, we could increase the productivity of our professional staff members, who currently receive four weeks paid vacation a year, by limiting them to a maximum of one week's continuous vacation time. They will thus take more vacation breaks during a year and give us more days of maximum productivity."

Discuss how well reasoned ... etc.

The following appeared in a memorandum from a regional supervisor of post office operations:

"During a two-week study of postal operations, the Presto City post office handled about twice as many items as the Lento City post office, even though the cities are about the same size. Moreover, customer satisfaction appears to be higher in Presto City, since the study found fewer complaints regarding the Presto City post office. Therefore, the postmasters at these two offices should exchange assignments: the Presto City postmaster will solve the problems of inefficiency and customer dissatisfaction at the Lento City office while the Lento City postmaster learns firsthand the superior methods of Presto City."

Discuss how well reasoned ... etc.

The following appeared in a memorandum written by the managing director of the Exeunt Theater Company:

"Now that we have moved to a larger theater, we can expect to increase our revenues from ticket sales. To further increase profits, we should start producing the plays that have been most successful when they were performed in our nation's largest cities. In addition, we should hire the Adlib Theater Company's director of fund-raising, since corporate contributions to Adlib have increased significantly over the three years that she has worked for Adlib."

Discuss how well reasoned … etc.

The following appeared in a memorandum from the human resources department of HomeStyle, a house remodeling business:

"This year, despite HomeStyle's move to new office space, we have seen a decline in both company morale and productivity, and a corresponding increase in administrative costs. To rectify these problems, we should begin using a newly developed software package for performance appraisal and feedback. Managers will save time by simply choosing comments from a preexisting list; then the software will automatically generate feedback for the employee. The human resources department at CounterBalance, the manufacturer of the countertops we install, reports satisfaction with the package."

Discuss how well reasoned … etc.

The following appeared as part of an article in a weekly newsmagazine:

"The country of Oleum can best solve the problem of its balance-of-trade deficit by further increasing the tax on its major import, crude oil. After Oleum increased the tax on imported crude oil four months ago, consumption of gasoline declined by 20 percent. Therefore, by imposing a second and significantly higher tax increase next year, Oleum will dramatically decrease its balance-of-trade deficit."

Discuss how well reasoned … etc.

The following appeared as part of a business plan by the Capital Idea investment firm:

"In recent years the worldwide demand for fish has grown, and improvements in fishing technology have made larger catches, and thus increased supply, possible: for example, last year's tuna catch was 9 percent greater than the previous year's. To capitalize on these trends, we should therefore invest in the new tartfish processing plant on Tartfish Island, where increasing revenues from tourism indicate a strong local economy."

Discuss how well reasoned … etc.

The following appeared in a speech by a stockholder of Consolidated Industries at the company's annual stockholders' meeting:

"In the computer hardware division last year, profits fell significantly below projections, the product line decreased from 20 to only 5 items, and expenditures for employee benefits increased by 15 percent. Nevertheless, Consolidated's board of directors has approved an annual salary of more than $1 million for our company's chief executive officer. The present board members should be replaced because they are unconcerned about the increasing costs of employee benefits and salaries, in spite of the company's problems generating income."

Discuss how well reasoned ... etc.

The following appeared in a memorandum from the business planning department of Avia Airlines:

"Of all the cities in their region, Beaumont and Fletcher are showing the fastest growth in the number of new businesses. Therefore, Avia should establish a commuter route between them as a means of countering recent losses on its main passenger routes. And to make the commuter route more profitable from the outset, Avia should offer a 1/3 discount on tickets purchased within two days of the flight. Unlike tickets bought earlier, discount tickets will be nonrefundable, and so gain from their sale will be greater."

Discuss how well reasoned ... etc.

The following appeared in a memorandum from the vice president of Gigantis, a development company that builds and leases retail store facilities:

"Nationwide over the past five years, sales have increased significantly at outlet stores that deal exclusively in reduced-price merchandise. Therefore, we should publicize the new mall that we are building at Pleasantville as a central location for outlet shopping and rent store space only to outlet companies. By taking advantage of the success of outlet stores, this plan should help ensure full occupancy of the mall and enable us to recover quickly the costs of building the mall."

Discuss how well reasoned ... etc.

The following appeared in a memorandum written by the chair of the music department to the president of Omega University:

"Mental health experts have observed that symptoms of mental illness are less pronounced in many patients after group music-therapy sessions, and job openings in the music-therapy field have increased during the past year. Consequently, graduates from our degree program for music therapists should have no trouble finding good positions. To help improve the financial status of Omega University, we should therefore expand our music-therapy degree program by increasing its enrollment targets."

Discuss how well reasoned ... etc.

The following appeared in a memorandum to the work-group supervisors of the GBS Company:

"The CoffeeCart beverage and food service located in the lobby of our main office building is not earning enough in sales to cover its costs, and so the cart may discontinue operating at GBS. Given the low staff morale, as evidenced by the increase in the number of employees leaving the company, the loss of this service could present a problem, especially since the staff morale questionnaire showed widespread dissatisfaction with the snack machines. Therefore, supervisors should remind the employees in their group to patronize the cart—after all, it was leased for their convenience so that they would not have to walk over to the cafeteria on breaks."

Discuss how well reasoned ... etc.

The following appeared as part of an article in a trade magazine:

"During a recent trial period in which government inspections at selected meat-processing plants were more frequent, the amount of bacteria in samples of processed chicken decreased by 50 percent on average from the previous year's level. If the government were to institute more frequent inspections, the incidence of stomach and intestinal infections throughout the country could thus be cut in half. In the meantime, consumers of Excel Meats should be safe from infection because Excel's main processing plant has shown more improvement in eliminating bacterial contamination than any other plant cited in the government report."

Discuss how well reasoned ... etc.

Appendix A Answer Sheets

Diagnostic Answer Sheet—Quantitative

1.	27.
2.	28.
3.	29.
4.	30.
5.	31.
6.	32.
7.	33.
8.	34.
9.	35.
10.	36.
11.	37.
12.	38.
13.	39.
14.	40.
15.	41.
16.	42.
17.	43.
18.	44.
19.	45.
20.	46.
21.	47.
22.	48.
23.	
24.	
25.	
26.	

Diagnostic Answer Sheet—Verbal

49.	75.
50.	76.
51.	77.
52.	78.
53.	79.
54.	80.
55.	81.
56.	82.
57.	83.
58.	84.
59.	85.
60.	86.
61.	87.
62.	88.
63.	89.
64.	90.
65.	91.
66.	92.
67.	93.
68.	94.
69.	95.
70.	96.
71.	97.
72.	98.
73.	99.
74.	100.

Problem Solving Answer Sheet

1.	32.	63.	94.	125.	156.	187.	218.
2.	33.	64.	95.	126.	157.	188.	219.
3.	34.	65.	96.	127.	158.	189.	220.
4.	35.	66.	97.	128.	159.	190.	221.
5.	36.	67.	98.	129.	160.	191.	222.
6.	37.	68.	99.	130.	161.	192.	223.
7.	38.	69.	100.	131.	162.	193.	224.
8.	39.	70.	101.	132.	163.	194.	225.
9.	40.	71.	102.	133.	164.	195.	226.
10.	41.	72.	103.	134.	165.	196.	227.
11.	42.	73.	104.	135.	166.	197.	228.
12.	43.	74.	105.	136.	167.	198.	229.
13.	44.	75.	106.	137.	168.	199.	230.
14.	45.	76.	107.	138.	169.	200.	
15.	46.	77.	108.	139.	170.	201.	
16.	47.	78.	109.	140.	171.	202.	
17.	48.	79.	110.	141.	172.	203.	
18.	49.	80.	111.	142.	173.	204.	
19.	50.	81.	112.	143.	174.	205.	
20.	51.	82.	113.	144.	175.	206.	
21.	52.	83.	114.	145.	176.	207.	
22.	53.	84.	115.	146.	177.	208.	
23.	54.	85.	116.	147.	178.	209.	
24.	55.	86.	117.	148.	179.	210.	
25.	56.	87.	118.	149.	180.	211.	
26.	57.	88.	119.	150.	181.	212.	
27.	58.	89.	120.	151.	182.	213.	
28.	59.	90.	121.	152.	183.	214.	
29.	60.	91.	122.	153.	184.	215.	
30.	61.	92.	123.	154.	185.	216.	
31.	62.	93.	124.	155.	186.	217.	

Data Sufficiency Answer Sheet

231.
232.
233.
234.
235.
236.
237.
238.
239.
240.
241.
242.
243.
244.
245.
246.
247.
248.
249.
250.
251.
252.
253.
254.
255.
256.
257.
258.
259.
260.
261.
262.
263.
264.
265.
266.
267.
268.
269.
270.
271.
272.
273.
274.
275.
276.
277.
278.
279.
280.
281.
282.
283.
284.
285.
286.
287.
288.
289.
290.
291.
292.
293.
294.
295.
296.
297.
298.
299.
300.
301.
302.
303.
304.
305.
306.
307.
308.
309.
310.
311.
312.
313.
314.
315.
316.
317.
318.
319.
320.
321.
322.
323.
324.
325.
326.
327.
328.
329.
330.
331.
332.
333.
334.
335.
336.
337.
338.
339.
340.
341.
342.
343.
344.
345.
346.
347.
348.
349.
350.
351.
352.
353.
354.
355.
356.
357.
358.
359.
360.
361.
362.
363.
364.
365.
366.
367.
368.
369.
370.
371.
372.
373.
374.
375.
376.
377.
378.
379.
380.
381.
382.
383.
384.
385.
386.
387.
388.
389.
390.
391.
392.
393.
394.
395.
396.
397.
398.
399.
400.
401.
402.
403.
404.

Reading Comprehension Answer Sheet

405.	433.	461.	489.	517.
406.	434.	462.	490.	518.
407.	435.	463.	491.	519.
408.	436.	464.	492.	520.
409.	437.	465.	493.	521.
410.	438.	466.	494.	522.
411.	439.	467.	495.	523.
412.	440.	468.	496.	524.
413.	441.	469.	497.	525.
414.	442.	470.	498.	526.
415.	443.	471.	499.	527.
416.	444.	472.	500.	528.
417.	445.	473.	501.	529.
418.	446.	474.	502.	530.
419.	447.	475.	503.	531.
420.	448.	476.	504.	532.
421.	449.	477.	505.	533.
422.	450.	478.	506.	534.
423.	451.	479.	507.	535.
424.	452.	480.	508.	536.
425.	453.	481.	509.	537.
426.	454.	482.	510.	538.
427.	455.	483.	511.	539.
428.	456.	484.	512.	540.
429.	457.	485.	513.	541.
430.	458.	486.	514.	542.
431.	459.	487.	515.	543.
432.	460.	488.	516.	

Critical Reasoning Answer Sheet

544.	569.	594.	619.	644.
545.	570.	595.	620.	645.
546.	571.	596.	621.	646.
547.	572.	597.	622.	647.
548.	573.	598.	623.	648.
549.	574.	599.	624.	649.
550.	575.	600.	625.	650.
551.	576.	601.	626.	651.
552.	577.	602.	627.	652.
553.	578.	603.	628.	653.
554.	579.	604.	629.	654.
555.	580.	605.	630.	655.
556.	581.	606.	631.	656.
557.	582.	607.	632.	657.
558.	583.	608.	633.	658.
559.	584.	609.	634.	659.
560.	585.	610.	635.	660.
561.	586.	611.	636.	661.
562.	587.	612.	637.	662.
563.	588.	613.	638.	663.
564.	589.	614.	639.	664.
565.	590.	615.	640.	665.
566.	591.	616.	641.	666.
567.	592.	617.	642.	667.
568.	593.	618.	643.	

Sentence Correction Answer Sheet

668.	696.	724.	752.	780.
669.	697.	725.	753.	781.
670.	698.	726.	754.	782.
671.	699.	727.	755.	783.
672.	700.	728.	756.	784.
673.	701.	729.	757.	785.
674.	702.	730.	758.	786.
675.	703.	731.	759.	787.
676.	704.	732.	760.	788.
677.	705.	733.	761.	789.
678.	706.	734.	762.	790.
679.	707.	735.	763.	791.
680.	708.	736.	764.	792.
681.	709.	737.	765.	793.
682.	710.	738.	766.	794.
683.	711.	739.	767.	795.
684.	712.	740.	768.	796.
685.	713.	741.	769.	797.
686.	714.	742.	770.	798.
687.	715.	743.	771.	799.
688.	716.	744.	772.	800.
689.	717.	745.	773.	801.
690.	718.	746.	774.	802.
691.	719.	747.	775.	803.
692.	720.	748.	776.	804.
693.	721.	749.	777.	805.
694.	722.	750.	778.	806.
695.	723.	751.	779.	807.

Graduate
Management
Admission
Council®

Caution!

The penalties for cheating on the GMAT® Exam are severe.

The following is considered cheating:

- Hiring someone to take the test
- Taking the test for someone else
- Memorizing test questions
- Sharing answers with others

The penalties for cheating are:

- Cancellation of your scores
- Ban on future testing
- School notification
- Possible legal prosecution

Has someone been trying to get you to cheat?

File a report via email: **pvtestsecurity@pearson.com**

Pearson
VUE

© 2017 Graduate Management Admission Council® (GMAC®). All rights reserved. GMAT® and Graduate Management Admission Council® are registered trademarks of the Graduate Management Admission Council in the United States and other countries. Pearson VUE is a trademark in the US and other countries of Pearson Education, Inc., or its affiliates.

Notes

Notes

Notes

Notes

Notes

Notes

Notes

Notes

Notes